Chronology of
the War at Sea
1939-1945

Volume Two: 1943-1945

▲

J. ROHWER AND
G. HÜMMELCHEN

Chronology of
the War at Sea
1939-1945

TRANSLATED FROM THE GERMAN BY
Derek Masters

Volume Two: 1943-1945

LONDON

IAN ALLAN

First published by Gerhard Stalling AG

English edition revised by the authors, edited by
A. J. Watts, and first published 1974

SBN 7110 0368 8

Published by Ian Allan Ltd, Shepperton, Surrey and printed in the United
Kingdom by The Press at Coombelands Ltd, Addlestone, Surrey

Translator's Note

For this English translation of the *Chronik des Seekrieges 1939-45* the authors have substantially amplified and revised the original German text so that the present book in effect represents a new edition of the work.

In the case of most navies—but not the Royal Navy and the US Navy—the authors use the expressions *Kapitänleutnant, Korvettenkapitän* and *Fregattenkapitän* to describe certain officer ranks: in agreement with the authors I have translated these Lieutenant-Commander, Commander and Commander* respectively (the asterisk denoting the senior of two Commander grades).

In dealing with Japanese units, I have used the normal British nomenclature i.e. battleship, cruiser and carrier *squadrons* and destroyer and submarine *flotillas*: but the reader should bear in mind that much of the literature on the subject today uses the American nomenclature i.e. battleship, cruiser and carrier *divisions* and destroyer and submarine *squadrons*.

Because of the difficulty in finding an English equivalent, I have left most German Air Force nomenclature in the original in the text but included the relevant formations in the Glossary.

Merchant ship and Auxiliary ship tonnage is normally GRT (Gross Register Tons).

D.R.M.

Abbreviations and Glossary

AA	Anti-Aircraft
AF	(*Artillerie-Fährprahm*) gun ferry barge
AK	Supply Transport (Auxiliary Kargo)
AKA	Attack Supply Transport (Auxiliary Kargo Attack)
AP	Troop Transport (Auxiliary Personnel)
APA	Attack Troop Transport (Auxiliary Personnel Attack)
APD	Fast Transport (Auxiliary Personnel Destroyer)
A/S	Anti-submarine
ASV-Radar	Anti-Surface-Vessel-Radar
ATF	Tug (Auxiliary Tug Fleet)
Batdiv	Battleship Division
BB	Battleship
BF	Base Force
BKA	Russian armoured cutter
BLT	Battalion Landing Team
Bn	Battalion
BO	Large Russian submarine chaser, patrol boat
Bord Fl Gr	(*Bordfliegergruppe*) Ship-borne wing, originally earmarked for uncompleted aircraft carrier
Capt 1st Class	Russian Captain
Capt 2nd Class	Russian Commander* (German *Fregatten-kapitän*)
Capt 3rd Class	Russian Commander (German *Korvetten-kapitän*)
*Cdr**	Fregattenkapitän (or corresponding rank) in the German, French, Italian, etc, navies
Cdr	Korvettenkapitän
DD	Destroyer
DE	Destroyer Escort
Desdiv	Destroyer Division (US)
Desron	Destroyer Squadron (US)
Div	Division
DM	(*Druckdosen*) Oyster Mines
EG	Escort Group
EMC	German Moored Mine (Last letter denotes Mark of mine)
ES	Escort Squadron
E-torpedo	Electric Drive Torpedo
F	F1-10 (*Flottenbegleiter*) Fleet Escort Vessel F100-1200 (*Fährprahm*) Landing Craft Tank
FAA	Fleet Air Arm
F.A.Gr	(*Fern Aufklärungs Gruppe*) Longrange reconnaissance wing
FAT	(*Flächen Absuchender* or *Feder Apparat Torpedo*) Pattern running torpedo

vii

FDS	Fighter Direction Ship
Fl Div	(*Fliegerdivision*) German Air Division. The *Fliegerdivision* was later renamed *Fliegerkorps* and could operate within, or independently of, a *Luftflotte* (Air Fleet)
Fl K	(*Fliegerkorps*) German Air Corps
Front	Russian Army Group
GB	Gunboat
Geschwader	German Air Group
Gruppe	German Air Wing
	(The *Geschwader* was the largest air formation with a nominal fixed strength. It usually comprised 90 aircraft in 3-4 *Gruppen,* with each *Gruppe* consisting of 3-4 *Staffeln* or squadrons)
HF/DF	High Frequency Direction Finding
Inf	Infantry
JG	(*Jagdgeschwader*) Fighter Group
K Fl Gr	(*Küstenfliegergruppe*) Coastal Air Wing
KFK	(*Kriegsfischkutter*) Naval fishing cutter
KG	(*Kampfgeschwader*) Bomber Group
LAT	(*Leichter Artillerieträger*) Light aux. gunboat
LCF	Landing Craft Flak
LCI	Landing Craft Infantry
LCI (*G*)	Landing Craft Infantry Gunboat
LCI (*M*)	Landing Craft Infantry Mortar
LCM	Landing Craft Mechanised
LCS	Landing Craft Support
LCT	Landing Craft Tank
LCVP	Landing Craft Vehicle Personnel
LG	(*Lehrgeschwader*) Air Trainer Group
LMBC	German Ground Mine (Laid by aircraft)
LSD	Landing Ship Dock
LSG	Landing Ship Gun
LSI	Landing Ship Infantry
LSM	Landing Ship Medium
LST	Landing Ship Tank
LSV	Landing Ship Vehicle
Luftwaffe	German Air Force
LUT	(*Lage unabhängiger torpedo*) pattern running torpedo
M	(*Minensucher*) Minesweeper
MAD	Magnetic Airborne Detector
MAS	Italian Motor Torpedo Boat, originally submarine-chaser
MFP	(*Marine Fährprahm*) Naval ferry barge
MGB	Motor Gun Boat
ML	Motor Launch
MMS	Motor Minesweeper
MO	Russian submarine-chaser (small)
MS	Italian motor torpedo boat
MS	Minesweeper

MTB	Motor Torpedo Boat
OKH	(*Oberkommando des Heeres*) Army High Command
OKM	(*Oberkommando der Marine*) Naval High Command
OKW	(*Oberkommando der Wehrmacht*) Armed Forces Command
PB-Flotilla	(*Vorposten*) Patrol Boat Flotilla
PC	Patrol Craft
PCE	Patrol Craft Escort
PT	Patrol Torpedo Boat
R	(*Räumboot*) Motor Minesweeper
RA	(*Räumboot Ausland*) Captured MMS in German Navy
RAAF	Royal Australian Air Force
RAN	Royal Australian Navy
RCAF	Royal Canadian Air Force
RCN	Royal Canadian Navy
RCT	Regimental Combat Team
Regt	Regiment
RIN	Royal Indian Navy
RN	Royal Navy
RNZN	Royal New Zealand Navy
RT	Trawler
S	(*Schnellboot*) Motor Torpedo Boat, E-boat
S.A.Gr	(*See Aufklärungs Gruppe*) Sea patrol wing
SAT	(*Schwerer Artillerieträger*) Heavy auxiliary gunboat
SC	Submarine-chaser
SF	(*Siebel Fähre*) Landing craft
SG	(*Schnelles Geleitboot*) Fast escort vessel
SG	Support group (Allied)
SGB	Steam gunboat
SKA	Russian patrol boat
SKL	(*Seekriegsleitung*) German Navy Staff
SKR	Russian patrol ship
SM	Submarine
SOE	Senior Officer Escort
Sqdn	Squadron
Stavka	Russian supreme headquarters
St G	(*Stukageschwader*) Dive Bomber Group
Supermarina	Italian Navy Staff
T	(*Torpedoboot*) Torpedo Boat
TA	(*Torpedoboot Ausland*) Captured foreign T-boat in German Navy
TB	Torpedo Boat
TF	Task Force
TG	Task Group
TKA	Russian motor torpedo boat
TMA, *TMB, TMC*	Ground Mine (torpedo-mine laid by U-boats)

Trägergruppe	Air Carrier Wing, originally earmarked for uncompleted aircraft carrier
TU	Task Unit
U	(*U-Boot*) U-boat
UDT	Underwater Demolition Team
UJ	(*Unterseebootjäger*) Submarine-chaser
UM	Submarine Mine
USAAF	US Army Air Force
USCG	US Coast Guard
USN–VP	US Navy Reconnaissance Squadron
USN–VPB	US Navy Patrol Bomber Squadron
V, Vs	(*Vorpostenboot*) Auxiliary patrol vessel, trawler, drifter, etc.
Wehrmacht	German Armed Forces
W/T	Wireless telegraphy
YMS	Yard Mine Sweeper
Z	(*Zerstörer*) Destroyer
ZG	(*Zerströrergeschwader*) Heavy Fighter Group
†	CO killed

1943

1 Jan Japan/Atlantic
The blockade-runner *Rhakotis* (6753 tons, Capt Jakobs), on the way from Japan, is located 200 nautical miles NW of Cape Finisterre by British air reconnaissance and is sunk by the cruiser *Scylla* which is directed to the scene.

1-5 Jan Arctic
The Soviet submarine *L-20* (Capt 3rd Class Tamman) sinks off Kongsfjord the steamer *Muansa* (5472 tons) proceeding in the company of *V5909*, lays a mine barrage (cleared) off Tanafjord and disembarks agents on the coast on 5 Feb. *L-22* (Capt 3rd Class Afonin) lays a mine barrage off Honningsvaag (cleared). The Soviet steamer *Krasnyj Partizan* (2418 tons), sailing on her own to England, is sunk in the Barents Sea by *U354* (Lt-Cdr Herbschleb).

1-19 Jan North Atlantic
In the central North Atlantic the 'Falke' group comprising the U-boats *U257*, *U404*, *U572*, *U71*, *U444*, *U384*, *U631*, *U333*, *U167*, *U706*, *U441*, *U525*, *U563*, *U632*, *U584*, *U607*, *U606*, *U226*, *U69*, *U201*, *U414* and *U403*, operates without success against the convoys ONS.158 (EG C.4), ON.159 (EG B.2) and ONS.160 (EG C.2). On 9 Jan and 10 Jan *U441* (Lt-Cdr Klaus Hartmann) sinks one unidentified ship; *U384* (Lt von Rosenberg-Gruszczynski) sinks a ship of 6155 tons and *U632* (Lt-Cdr Karpf) a ship of 6773 tons—all independents.

1-30 Jan Mediterranean
German and Italian attacks on Allied convoy traffic off the Algerian coast. On 1 Jan *U73* (Lt Deckert) sinks one ship of 7176 tons. In attacks by Ju 87s of St. G. 3 and by fighter bombers of J.G. 53 on the harbour of Bone two ships of 13181 tons sink; the cruiser *Ajax* is hit by a 500 kg bomb from a Ju 87 and three ships of 18973 tons are damaged. On 7 Jan *U371* (Lt-Cdr Mehl) sinks the A/S trawler *Jura* E of Algiers and torpedoes one ship of 7159 tons which is later sunk by bombs in Algiers. In a

sortie by the 3rd MTB Flotilla against the Algerian coast, *S58* (with the Flotilla Commander, Lt-Cdr Kemnade, on board) sinks the British A/S trawler *Horatio*. Torpedo aircraft of K.G. 26 sink two ships of 8677 tons off Bougie and damage one of 7191 tons. On 20 Jan *U453* (Lt-Cdr Frhr von Schlippenbach) sinks one ship of 5783 tons off Oran. Several attacks by the submarines *U83*, *Dandolo*, *Giada*, *Malachite* and *Mocenigo* are unsuccessful; on 30 Jan *Platino* (Lt-Cdr Patrelli-Campagnone) sinks the corvette *Samphire*. *U224*, *Avorio* and *Tritone* are sunk by escort vessels. In a torpedo attack by the German K.G. 26 on 29 Jan off Bougie the AA ship *Pozarica* (a total loss on 13 Feb) and the destroyer *Avon Vale* are torpedoed.

1-31 Jan Pacific
Of the American submarines arriving in their operational areas in January the following make sinkings off Japan: *Finback* (Lt-Cdr Hull) one ship of 271 tons; *Porpoise* (Lt-Cdr McKnight) one ship of 4999 tons and torpedoes one more ship; *Trigger* (Lt-Cdr Benson) one ship of 5188 tons and the destroyer *Okikaze*. In the Central Pacific *Whale* (Lt-Cdr Azer) sinks three ships of 18989 tons and *Wahoo* (Lt-Cdr Morton) three ships of 11348 tons and also torpedoes the destroyer *Harusame*. In the South Pacific *Guardfish* (Lt-Cdr Klakring) sinks the fast transport *No. 1* and the destroyer *Hakaze* and torpedoes one other ship; *Silversides* (Lt-Cdr Burlingame) sinks four ships of 27798 tons; *Gato* (Lt-Cdr Foley) sinks four ships of 12997 tons and torpedoes four ships; *Grampus* (Lt-Cdr Craig) torpedoes one ship; *Grayback* (Lt-Cdr Stephan) misses *I-18*; *Greenling* (Lt-Cdr Burton) sinks one ship of 3261 tons; *Growler* (Lt-Cdr Gilmore) sinks one ship of 5851 tons and torpedoes one other ship; *Swordfish* (Lt-Cdr Lewis) sinks one ship of 4122 tons. *Argonaut* does not return from an operation off Lae. In the South-West Pacific *Searaven*

(Lt Cassedy) sinks two ships of 5909 tons and torpedoes one ship; *Tautog* (Lt-Cdr Sieglaff) sinks two ships of 2873 tons; *Trout* (Lt-Cdr Ramage) sinks two ships of 4895 tons; *Gar* (Lt-Cdr Quirk) torpedoes the seaplane tender ship *Notoro*; and *Grayling* (Lt-Cdr Lee) torpedoes two ships.

1 Jan-3 Feb Western Atlantic
Of the U-boats operating E of the Caribbean *U105* (Lt-Cdr Nissen) sinks one sailing ship and one steamer of 5173 tons; *U217* (Lt-Cdr Reichenbach-Klinke) sinks one ship of 7957 tons; and *U124* (Lt-Cdr Mohr) sinks five ships of 28689 tons from the convoy TB.1 (12 ships), escorted by US corvettes and PC submarine-chasers on 9 Jan. *U109* and *U214* have no success.

1 Jan-9 Feb South Pacific
Final battle for Guadalcanal. In January Japanese destroyers continue the supply operations and from 1 Feb carry out the evacuation of Guadalcanal ordered on 4 Jan. Participating: the 2nd DD Flotilla (Rear-Adm Koyanagi) with the cruiser *Isuzu* and destroyers *Kuroshio*, *Oyashio*, *Kagero*, *Shiranui*, *Umikaze*, *Kawakaze*, *Suzukaze*, *Naganami* and *Makinami* and the 4th DD Flotilla (Rear-Adm Tanaka) with the cruiser *Agano* and destroyers *Arashi*, *Hagikaze*, *Nowake*, *Maikaze*, *Akigumo*, *Yugumo*, *Makigumo*, *Kazegumo*, *Hatsukaze*, *Yukikaze*, *Amatsukaze*, *Tokitsukaze*, *Urakaze*, *Isokaze*, *Tanikaze*, *Hamakaze* and *Akizuki*.
There are supply operations ('Tokyo Express') from Rabaul to Cape Esperance by night with air support from airfields at Munda and Vila on New Georgia.
1-2 Jan: Mission to Guadalcanal with 10 Japanese destroyers. Unsuccessful attacks by B-17 bombers; Navy SBD dive-bombers damage the *Suzukaze*. An attack by PT boats from Tulagi fails. Japanese destroyers throw supply containers overboard.
4-5 Jan: US TF 67 (Rear-Adm Ainsworth), comprising the cruisers *Nashville*, *St Louis* and *Helena* and the destroyers *Fletcher* and *O'Bannon*, shells Munda. Rear-Adm Tisdale with the cruisers *Honolulu*, *Achilles* (RNZN, damaged by bombs), *Columbia* and *Louisville* and the destroyers *Drayton*,

Lamson and *Nicholas*, forms a covering force SW of the Solomons. In the operation the *Helena* for the first time makes successful use of proximity fuses for AA fire.
On 10-11 Jan eight Japanese destroyers undertake a mission to Guadalcanal. Following reconnaissance reports the US PT boats *PT45*, *PT39*, *PT48*, *PT115*, *PT112*, *PT43*, *PT40*, *PT59*, *PT46* and *PT36* are deployed in several groups from Tulagi. In all, six boats are able to fire 21 torpedoes; the destroyer *Hatsukaze* is lightly damaged by one hit and *PT112* and *PT43* are lost in the Japanese defensive fire.
On 14-15 Jan nine Japanese destroyers undertake a mission to Guadalcanal. On the way USMC SBD dive-bombers from Henderson Field attack and slightly damage *Arashi*, *Urakaze*, *Tanikaze* and *Hamakaze* which, however, continue their journey. The PT boats *PT59*, *PT38*, *PT39*, *PT115*, *PT109*, *PT45*, *PT37*, *PT40*, *PT36*, *PT48*, *PT47*, *PT46* and *PT123* are deployed from Tulagi. Seven boats fire 17 torpedoes without success.
On 19 Jan the 'Cactus Striking Force' (Capt Briscoe), comprising the destroyers *Nicholas*, *O'Bannon*, *Radford* and *De Haven*, is transferred to Tulagi and using it as a base, repeatedly shells Japanese positions on Guadalcanal.
In the night 23-24 Jan Rear-Adm Ainsworth again shells Vila with the cruisers *Nashville* and *Helena* and the 'Cactus Striking Force.' Rear-Adm Tisdale with the *Honolulu*, *St Louis*, *Drayton*, *Lamson* and *Hughes* is available as a covering force. 59 aircraft from the carrier *Saratoga* provide air support from the S after breaking their flight at Henderson Field.
In a supply operation the Japanese submarine *I-1* is destroyed off Cape Esperance by the New Zealand corvettes *Kiwi* and *Moa* on 29 Jan.
On 30-31 Jan four and on 4-5 Feb five troop and supply transports bring reinforcements to Guadalcanal for the USMC forces. On 1 Feb the old destroyer *Stringham* and LCTs land one regiment on the West Coast of Guadalcanal, covered by the 'Cactus Striking Force' composed of the destroyers *Fletcher*, *Nicholas*, *Radford* and *De*

Haven. On 29-30 Jan US TF 18 (Rear-Adm Giffen), comprising the cruisers *Wichita, Chicago, Louisville, Montpelier Cleveland* and *Columbia* and the destroyers *La Vallette, Waller, Conway, Frazier, Chevalier, Edwards, Meade* and *Taylor*, as well as the escort carriers *Chenango* and *Suwanee* some way off, approaches from the S to cover the operation and to make a sortie into the Central Solomons. On the evening of 29 Jan the force is attacked near Rennell Island by Japanese torpedo aircraft which severely damage the *Chicago* and hit the *Wichita* and *Louisville* with duds. In a second attack the *Chicago* (Capt Davis) is sunk and the *La Valette* torpedoed on 30 Jan. 1049 survivors are rescued. The carrier forces, including the *Enterprise* (Rear-Adm Sherman) and *Saratoga* (Rear-Adm Ramsey), situated further to the S, and the battleship force (Rear-Adm Lee), comprising the *North Carolina, Indiana* and *Washington*, are not able to intervene.

Operation 'KE': Japanese evacuation of Guadalcanal. On 1-2 Feb 20 destroyers proceed from Rabaul to Cape Esperance. On the way 41 aircraft from Henderson Field attack and damage the *Makinami* which, however, continues her journey. The 'Cactus Striking Force' with *Nicholas, Fletcher, Radford* and *De Haven*, which is deployed from the W, is driven off by Japanese air attacks. The *De Haven* is lost by bomb hits and the *Nicholas* lightly damaged by near-misses. The US PT boats, *PT47, PT39, PT111, PT48, PT59, PT115, PT37, PT124, PT123, PT109* and *PT36*, are deployed from Tulagi. Five of them are able to fire 19 torpedoes. In taking avoiding action, the destroyer *Makigumo* runs on a mine barrage laid shortly before near the Japanese route by the US mine-laying destroyers *Preble, Montgomery* and *Tracy*, and sinks. The destroyer *Kawakaze* sinks *PT111* and two others, the *PT37* and *PT123*. 19 Japanese destroyers take troops and return to Rabaul.

On 4-5 Feb Rear-Adm Koyanagi with the cruiser *Isuzu* and 22 destroyers proceeds to Guadalcanal and evacuates the second group of the 17th Army. The force is attacked by 64 aircraft from Henderson Field: the destroyers *Mai-kaze* and *Shiranui* are badly, and the *Kuroshio* and *Hamakaze* lightly damaged, but are able to continue the operation. On 7-8 Feb 18 Japanese destroyers evacuate the remainder of the troops: in the process *Isokaze* and *Hamakaze* are badly damaged in attacks by 15 aircraft. In all, 11706 men are evacuated in the period 1-9 Feb. On 9 Feb the Guadalcanal operation is ended.

2 Jan   South West Pacific
Troops of I US Corps (Lt-Gen Eichelberger) capture Buna on New Guinea. By the end of January the Japanese bases at Goa and Sananda also fall. With that the threat to Port Moresby is removed.

3 Jan   South Atlantic
The German auxiliary cruiser *Schiff 28 Michel* (Capt von Ruckteschell) sinks the British freighter *Empire March* (7040 tons) in the South Atlantic.

3 Jan   Mediterranean
Attack by British small battle units on Palermo. 'Chariots' (human torpedoes) are launched from submarines *Thunderbolt* (Cdr Crouch) and *Trooper* (Lt Wraith): they penetrate the harbour and their attached charges severely damage the Italian cruiser *Ulpio Traiano* and the transport *Viminale*. The third submarine *P311* (Lt Cailey) was sunk by the Italian torpedo boat *Partenope* on 29 Dec 42.

3-12 Jan   Central Atlantic
U514 (Lt-Cdr Auffermann) reports E of Trinidad the tanker convoy TM.1 proceeding to the Mediterranean (9 tankers and EG B.5 (Cdr Boyle) with the destroyer *Havelock* and corvettes *Pimpernel, Saxifrage* and *Godetia*. She torpedoes the *British Vigilance* (8093 tons) the wreck of which is sunk on 24 Jan by *U105* (Lt Nissen). After a brief, but unsuccessful search for a GUF convoy reported by *U182*, the 'Delphin' group, which has been operating S of the Azores since 29 Dec and which comprises *U571, U620, U575, U381, U436* and *U442*, and *U134, U181, U522* and *U511*, which are in the area, are directed to TM.1 with which *U514* and *U125* try unsuccessfully to keep in contact. On 8 Jan *U381* (Lt-Cdr Count Pückler) sights the TM.1 and brings up three boats. *U436* (Cdr Seibicke) sinks the *Albert L. Ellsworth*

(8309 tons) and *Oltenia II* (6394 tons). *U571* (Lt-Cdr Möhlmann) is driven off by *Pimpernel*, and *Godetia* frustrates an attack by *U575* (Lt-Cdr Heydemann) with depth charges. On the morning of 9 Jan *U575* torpedoes the *Minister Wedel* (6833 tons) and *Norvik* (10034 tons) which *U522* (Lt-Cdr Schneider) later sinks. Soon after, *U442* (Cdr Hesse) sinks the *Empire Lytton* (9807 tons) and *U381* is attacked by *Havelock* with depth charges. On the evening of 9 Jan the *Vanja* avoids a salvo from *U134* (Lt-Cdr Schendel) which is damaged by depth charges from *Godetia*. *U511* (Lt-Cdr Schneewind) in the meantime sinks one independent of 5004 tons. On the evening of 10 Jan *U620* (Lt-Cdr Stein) misses the rump convoy and *U522* torpedoes the *British Dominion* (6983 tons), which *U620* later sinks. *U571* attacks the two remaining tankers, *Vanja* and *Cliona*, on 10 Jan and on 11 Jan in the evening. But they avoid these attacks and one by *U511* on the morning morning of 12 Jan.

The arrival of the air escort from Gibraltar and the reinforcement of the escort by the destroyer *Quiberon* and the corvettes *Pentstemon* and *Samphire* drive the U-boats off. The two tankers arrive in Gibraltar on 14 Jan.

4 Jan-19 Feb   Bay of Biscay
Of the US submarines deployed in the Bay of Biscay *Shad* (Lt-Cdr MacGregor) sinks the minesweeper *M4242* on 4 Jan and torpedoes the ore transport *Nordfels* (1214 tons) on 25 Jan. *Blackfish* (Lt-Cdr Davidson) sinks the patrol boat *V408* on 19 Feb. Further successes are prevented by torpedo failures.

6-23 Jan   Mediterranean
Last Italian convoys to and from Tripoli: a few large, but mostly smaller, ships and auxiliary warships, occasionally escorted by the destroyer *Saetta*, the torpedo boats *Orione*, *Animoso* and others as well as Italian ferry barges. Against them the British Force K is deployed from Malta: on 8-9 Jan the destroyers *Nubian* and *Kelvin* sink three schooners near Kuriat and in the night 15-16 Jan they attack S of Lampedusa the steamer *D'Annunzio* (4537 tons), escorted by the torpedo boat *Perseo*. The steamer sinks; the *Perseo* escapes. In the same night the destroyers *Paken-*

ham and *Javelin* sink one auxiliary ship. In the night 18-19 Jan *Pakenham*, *Nubian* and the Greek destroyer *Vasilissa Olga* sink the transport *Stromboli* (475 tons). Early on 20 Jan *Kelvin* and *Javelin* locate N of Tripoli a convoy consisting of 11 small Italian ships (minesweepers *R.D.31*, *R.D.36*, *R.D.37*, *R.D.39*, three auxiliary minesweepers and three small vessels) and destroy it. The Malta submarines make the following sinkings off the E Tunisian coast: *Umbra* (Cdr Maydon) sinks one ship of 1523 tons and two sailing ships and torpedoes one ship; *Unrivalled* (Lt Turner) sinks four sailing ships of 387 tons; *Unruffled* (Lt Stevens) four ships of 2295 tons; *Unseen* (Lt Crawford) three ships of 4137 tons, including one escorted by the torpedo boat *Calliope*; and *Unbroken* (Lt Mars) the *Edda* (6107 tons), escorted by the torpedo boat *San Martino*. The Italian submarines *Settimo*, *Narvalo*, *Otaria* and *Santarosa* transport ammunition and fuel to Tripoli. On the return *Narvalo* is sunk by the destroyers *Pakenham* and *Hursley* on 14 Jan and *Santarosa* by the British *MTB260* on 19 Jan. In the night 22-23 Jan Force K, comprising the cruisers *Cleopatra* and *Euryalus* and the destroyers *Jervis*, *Javelin*, *Nubian* and *Kelvin*, shells the withdrawal routes of the German-Italian Panzer armies near Zuara. Tripoli is evacuated by the rear guards on 23 Jan after the freighters *Marco Foscarini* (6342 tons), *Assiria* (2705 tons), *Marocchino* (1524 tons), *Tevere* (8289 tons) and *Guilia* (5921 tons), which are unable to put to sea, have been scuttled on 20 Jan.

6 Jan-7 Feb   Mediterranean
In 14 operations Italian destroyer forces consisting of three to five units bring back 15580 reserve troops to Tunis and Bizerta and evacuate wounded and prisoners. *Mitragliere* participates in 7 operations, *Gioberti* and *Camicia Nera* in five, *Da Noli*, *Granatiere*, *Premuda*, *Zeno* and *Corazziere* in four, *Ascari*, *Pigafetta* and *Malocello* in three, *Bombardiere* and *Legionario* in two and *Bersagliere* and *Carabiniere* in one. On the return *Bombardiere* is sunk off Marettimo on 17 Jan by the British submarine *United* (Lt Roxburgh). British mining operations against the

Italian convoy traffic of freighters and tankers are undertaken on the Italian routes inside the flanking mine barrages between the Gulf of Tunis and Sicily by the fast minelayers *Welshman* (7 Jan and 30 Jan) and *Abdiel* (9 Jan, 3 Feb and 7 Feb) and the minelaying submarine *Rorqual* (18 Jan). On the return from the second operation *Welshman* is sunk on 1 Feb by *U617* (Lt-Cdr Brandi). On 9 Jan a convoy runs on the mine barrage laid by *Abdiel*: the destroyer *Maestrale* is damaged and *Corsaro* sinks when she comes to her assistance. The destroyer *Saetta* and the torpedo boat *Uragano* sink on the same mine barrage on 3 Feb. The corvette *Procellaria* and the torpedo boat *Prestinari* sink on 31 Jan on the mine barrage just laid by *Welshman* and the German transport *Ankara* (4768 tons) sinks on *Rorqual's* barrage. Of the British submarines deployed near Marettimo and in the Tyrrhenian Sea, *Splendid* (Lt-Cdr McGeogh) sinks four ships of 10064 tons, including the *Emma* (7931 tons) on 16 Jan, which is escorted by the torpedo boats *Groppo, Uragano* and *Clio*; *Sahib* (Lt Bromage) sinks one ship of 1194 tons and *U304*; *Tribune* one ship of 6673 tons; *Turbulent* (Cdr Linton) three ships of 11234 tons; *Saracen* (Lt Lumby) one ship of 214 tons; and *Safari* (Cdr Bryant) four ships of 4137 tons. *Unbending* (Lt Stanley) torpedoes one ship. Torpedo aircraft from Malta sink three ships of 11929 tons from convoys and bombers two of 9016 tons. Apart from those named, the following Italian units take part in the escorting of the convoys; the destroyer *Lampo*, the torpedo boats *Fortunale, Orione, Ardito, Ardente, Animoso, Monsone, Ciclone, Cigno, Calliope, Partenope, Sirio, Pallade, Clio, Perseo, Castore, Lira, Libra, Climene, Dezza, Montanari, Cascino* and the corvettes *Antilope, Artemide, Gabbiano* and *Persefone*. Sorties by the British Force Q from Bone with the cruisers *Aurora, Penelope, Dido* and *Sirius*, are largely unsuccessful. The destroyers *Lightning* and *Loyal* sink one ship S of Sardinia on 18 Jan.

9-10 Jan   Indonesia
The Australian destroyer *Arunta* evacuates to Port Darwin 282 troops and 31 civilians from the Japanese-occupied island of Timor.

11 Jan   Norway
The German battleship *Scharnhorst* and the heavy cruiser *Prinz Eugen* with three destroyers are located by British air reconnaissance W of the Skagerrak when they are being transferred to Northern Norway and they return. The deployment of powerful forces of Coastal Command and of six submarines of the 9th SM Flotilla is unsuccessful.

12 Jan   North Pacific
Weak US Army forces (Brig-Gen Jones) occupy the Aleutian island of Amchitka in order to construct a fighter airfield. The operation is covered by TF 8 (Rear-Adm Kinkaid, who is relieved by Rear-Adm Theobald on 4 Jan). In the operations the destroyer *Worden* is lost when she goes aground.

12-19 Jan   North Atlantic
Stationed W of Ireland and S of the 'Falke' group, the 'Habicht' group, comprising *U383, U303, U624, U704, U438, U752, U613, U186* and *U268*, searches in vain for the convoy ONS.160 (EG C.2). On the way *U186* (Lt-Cdr Hesemann) sinks an independent of 7147 tons and on 17 Jan *U268* (Lt Heydemann) sinks the whale factory ship *Vestfold* (14547 tons), with three LCTs on board, belonging to the convoy HX.222 (EG C.1).

12-23 Jan   North Atlantic
The 'Jaguar' group operates in the area NE of Newfoundland against the convoys HX.222 (EG C.1) and SC.116 (EG B.6) with the U-boats *U96, U598, U266, U662, U123, U413, U594, U337* and *U706*. On 15 Jan *U337* is lost to a Fortress of No. 206 Sqdn RAF. On 22 Jan *U413* (Lt-Cdr Poel) sights the convoy SC.117 (EG B.3 Cdr Tait) comprising the new frigate *Swale*, the Polish destroyer *Garland*, the British corvettes *Narcissus* and *Orchis* and the French *Roselys, Lobélia* and *Aconit*). *U413* sinks a straggler of 3556 tons: W/T interference prevents a punctual deployment of the other boats. The 'Jaguar' group which is ordered to make a search does not find the convoy again.

14 Jan   Air War/Western Europe
RAF Bomber Command (Air Marshal Harris) receives orders to carry out heavy attacks on the U-boat bases at Lorient, St Nazaire, Brest and La Pallice. By the middle of February 1943

some 2000 bombers have been employed against Lorient alone. There are heavy attacks by RAF Bomber Command inter alia on 14-15 Jan and 29-30 Jan and by the 8th USAAF on 23 Jan.

14-25 Jan General Situation
Roosevelt and Churchill with the military staffs of the USA and Great Britain at the Casablanca Conference. Churchill and Roosevelt demand the 'Unconditional Surrender' of Germany. Agreement on further operations in the Mediterranean area: a landing on Sicily after the conquest of Tunisia. Victory over the German U-boats is given top priority in the Allied conduct of the war.

15 Jan-19 Feb Mediterranean
The British 'Inshore Squadron' supplies the British 8th Army as it advances through Tripolitania. In February alone 115137 tons of supplies are landed. Individual U-boats operate off Cyrenaica against this traffic: *U617* (Lt-Cdr Brandi) sinks four ships of 10800 tons from two convoys, apart from the fast minelayer *Welshman*. After the capture of Tripoli by the British 8th Army combined convoys proceed to Malta and Tripoli e.g. on 6-8 Feb MW.20 and XT.2 with an escort of 12 destroyers. Attacks by *U205* (Lt Bürgel) fail. On 17 Feb the boat is lost as a result of air attacks and depth charges from the destroyer *Paladin* when she attacks TX.1 and on 19 Feb *U562* is lost to an aircraft and the destroyers *Isis* and *Hursley* when attacking XT.3.

Off the Palestine coast *U431* (Lt Schöneboom) sinks four sailing ships in January; and *U81* (Lt Krieg) sinks five sailing ships in February and torpedoes one tanker of 6671 tons.

In British submarine operations in the Adriatic *Tigris* (Lt-Cdr Colvin) sinks one ship of 5413 tons on 20 Jan and *Thunderbolt* and *Trooper* sink several sailing ships in February. In the Aegean the Greek submarine *Papanicolis* sinks two sailing ships in January.

17 Jan-8 Feb Arctic
Convoy operation JW.52/RA.52. On 17 Jan JW.52 sets out with 14 ships (1 returns), escorted by an escort group comprising the destroyer *Onslaught* (Cdr Shelby), 7 others destroyers, two corvettes, one minesweeper and two trawlers. There is a covering force consisting of the cruisers *Kent*, *Glasgow* and *Bermuda* and a distant escort force (Adm Fraser) consisting of the battleships *Anson*, *Howe*, *King George V*, five cruisers and about 20 destroyers. British and Soviet submarines are in flanking formations off the Norwegian coast. The convoy is reported on 23 Jan by a BV 138 flying boat of K. Fl. Gr. 706. On 24 Jan four of five He 115 torpedo aircraft of 1/K. Fl. Gr. 406 deployed attack the convoy unsuccessfully losing two of their number. The U-boats ordered to the scene are out-manoeuvred by the escort group which makes skilful use of HF/DF; only *U622* (Lt-Cdr Queck) makes an unsuccessful attack on the convoy. *U625* (Lt Benker) misses the *Bermuda* and *Kent*. On 25 Jan the convoy is again located by air reconnaissance but not attacked. Five Soviet destroyers meet the convoy which enters the Kola Inlet on 27 Jan. The ice-breaker *Malygin* (1571 tons) is sunk by *U255* (Lt-Cdr Reche) and on 29 Jan the submarine sinks the Soviet steamer *Ufa* (1892 tons).

Convoy RA.52 sets out with 11 ships and the same escort from the Kola Inlet on 29 Jan. The five Soviet destroyers initially strengthen the escort. The convoy is reported on 1 Feb SW of Bear Island by *U625* and is unsuccessfully attacked. Air reconnaissance does not find it. On 3 Feb *U255* attacks the convoy and sinks the steamer *Greylock* (7460 tons).

The Allied submarines employed in the flanking formations attack German coastal traffic during and after the operation. The Norwegian submarine *Uredd* (Sub-Lt Rören) misses the MTB tender *Adolf Lüderitz* off Aalesund on 17 Jan. On 20 Jan the Soviet destroyers *Baku* and *Razumny* under Capt 1st Class Kolchin make a sortie against the Polar Coast and have a brief and indecisive engagement off Syltefjord with the minelayer *Skagerrak* which is on her way to lay a flanking mine barrage with the minesweepers *M322*, *M303* and the submarine-chasers *UJ 1104* and *UJ1105*.

After several misses by the Soviet submarines *Shch-404* (Capt 2nd Class Ivanov) off Svaerholt and by *M-172* and *Shch-402* (Capt 3rd Class Kautski) in Varangerfjord, *M-171* (Capt 3rd Class Starikov) torpedoes on 29 Jan the transport *Ilona Siemers* (3243 tons) escorted by *V5906* off Kongsfjord. On 1 Feb *Shch-403* (Capt 3rd Class Shuyski) sinks the patrol boat *V6115* off Makkaur, *M-172* (Capt 3rd Class Fisanovich) *V5909* off Kiberg and *L-20* (Capt 3rd Class Tamman) the transport *Othmarschen* (7007 tons) escorted by the submarine-chasers *UJ 1101* and *UJ1108* off Nordkyn.

17 Jan-14 Feb   Central Atlantic
After replenishing from *U463* (Cdr Wolfbauer) *U571, U620, U575, U381, U436, U442, U552, U511, U125* and *U514* form the 'Delphin' group S of the Azores to operate against US-Gibraltar convoys. From 24 Jan *U202, U558, U87, U264* and *U258* are added to the group. Only three stragglers from the convoy UGS.4 are sunk; the *City of Flint* (4963 tons) by *U575* (Lt-Cdr Heydemann) on 25 Jan and one Liberty Ship each by *U514* (Lt-Cdr Auffermann, 7177 tons) and *U442* (Cdr Hesse, 7176 tons) on 27 Jan. From 22 Jan *U218, U521, U43*, and later also *U66* and *U108*, form the 'Rochen' group in the area of the Canaries. After disembarking agents *U66* (Lt-Cdr Markworth) sinks one fishery vessel of 113 tons. On 7 Feb *U521* (Lt-Cdr Bargsten) sights the small coastal convoy Gibr.2 comprising three steamers and four A/S trawlers and having air escort; she sinks the trawler *Bredon*. The U-boats *U202 U558, U87, U264* and *U258* from the 'Delphin' group, which are ordered to the scene, do not arrive before the destroyer *Haydon* and the US submarine-chasers *PC471* and *PC474* join the convoy on 9 Feb. The remaining 'Delphin' boats operate W of Cape St Vincent where *U442* and *U620* are lost to the air escort in an operation against a KMS/OS convoy reported by air reconnaissance. The 'Rochen' group replenishes from *U118* from 10 Feb.

18-19 Jan   North Pacific
US TG 8.6 (Rear-Adm McMorris), consisting of the cruisers *Indianapolis* and *Richmond* and the destroyers *Bancroft, Caldwell, Coghlan* and *Gillespie*, bombards Attu.

18 Jan-1 Mar   South Pacific
In reconnaissance operations to Noumea, Auckland and into the Torres Strait the Japanese submarine *I-10* (Cdr T. Yamada) sinks one ship of 7176 tons and torpedoes one of 7141 tons. *I-8* (Capt Uchino) shells Canton Island on 23 Jan. Off the Australian coast *I-21* (Cdr* Matsumura) sinks five ships of 31437 tons. *I-18* (Cdr Muraoka) launches a midget submarine (no success) off Espiritu Santo on 25 Jan and is herself sunk on 11 Feb when she tries to attack a US force consisting of the cruiser *Helena* and the destroyers *Fletcher* and *O'Bannon*.
From Rabaul *Ro-100, Ro-101, Ro-102* and *Ro-103* operate in the area of the Solomons and off New Guinea.

19 Jan   Central Atlantic
The US carrier *Ranger*, acting as an aircraft transport, flies off a full complement of fighters to Accra to be transferred to the North African theatre of war.

19-24 Jan   Norway
The Norwegian 30th MTB flotilla, which is stationed in Lerwick (Shetlands), makes several raids with *MTB 618, MTB619, MTB620, MTB623, MTB 625, MTB626, MTB627* and *MTB630* on German naval communication posts in Sognefjord, on Stord and in Korsfjord. Attacks on steamers fail.

22 Jan-3 Feb   North Atlantic
The 'Landsknecht' group is formed from the former 'Falke' boats which are short of fuel supplies. It consists of the U-boats *U267, U465, U609, U402, U187, U262, U454, U553, U456, U614, U632, U257, U404, U584, U572, U71, U444, U384, U631* and *U333*. They operate without success W of Ireland. From 28 Jan most of the boats begin the return journey. *U553* is missing since then. On the way to a new formation *U456* (Lt-Cdr Teichert) sights on 1 Feb the convoy HX.224 (58 ships, EG C.4) (Lt-Cdr Piers) consisting of the destroyers HMCS *Restigouche*, HMS *Churchill*, the corvettes HMCS *Amherst, Collingwood, Brandon, Sherbrooke* and HMS *Celandine* and the rescue ship *Accrington*). Despite a heavy storm, *U456* keeps exemplary contact for three days and sinks two ships of 16633 tons. Of *U265, U614, U257* and *U632* (Lt-Cdr Karpf), stationed in the area, only the last sinks one straggler tanker

of 8190 tons whose survivors give valuable information about the following convoy, SC.118. *U265* is sunk on 3 Feb by a Fortress of No 220 Sqdn RAF flying as an escort.

22 Jan-15 Feb   North Atlantic

The 'Haudegen' group is formed SE of Greenland from the U-boats of the 'Falke' group which have adequate fuel supplies. It consists of *U414, U606, U607, U226, U403, U525, U69, U201, U383, U303, U624, U704, U438, U752, U613, U186, U268, U358, U707, U223,* and *U466.* On the way *U358* (Lt-Cdr Manke) attacks on 22 Jan the convoy UR.59 which is proceeding to Reykjavik and sinks one ship of 1456 tons. On 25 Jan *U624* (Lt-Cdr Count Soden-Fraunhofen) sinks one independent of 5112 tons. On 26 Jan *U266* and *U383* sight escorts of the convoy HX.223 which has been partly dispersed in a storm. *U466* listens to the convoy (24 ships, EG A.3 (Cdr Heineman) consisting of the US Coastguard cutters *Spencer, Campbell, Ingham* and corvettes HMCS *Dianthus, Chilliwack, Rosthern, Trillium* and *Dauphin*). *U358* sinks a straggler of 8221 tons and *U607* (Lt-Cdr Mengersen) the wreck of the tanker *Kjöllborg* (8259 tons) whose back was broken in the storm and which sinks before she is hit by *U594* trying to finish her off. On 2 Feb the most northerly boat of the 'Haudegen' group sights the Greenland supply convoy SG.19 consisting of three steamers escorted by the US Coastguard cutters *Tampa, Escabana* and *Comanche.* From *U186, U268, U358,* ▌*U707* and *U223* (Lt-Cdr Wächter), which are directed to it, the last sinks the US Army transport *Dorchester* (5649 tons)—they form the 'Nordsturm' group. The remaining 'Haudegen' boats proceed in loose formation NE of Newfoundland against the expected convoy SC.118, but they have no success.

24-25 Jan   North Sea

The German 2nd, 4th and 6th MTB Flotillas with 16 boats encounter the destroyers *Mendip* and *Windsor* in trying to attack a British convoy off Lowestoft and are driven off.

27 Jan   Air War/Germany

Fifty-five B17 bombers of the 8th USAAF carry out their first daylight attack on German territory without fighter protection. Target: Wilhelmshaven.

31 Jan   General Situation

Hitler appoints the Commander U-boats, Admiral Dönitz, C-in-C of the Navy in place of the retiring Grand-Admiral Raeder. Dönitz is promoted to the rank of Grand-Admiral.

1 Feb   Gibraltar

U118 (Cdr Czygan) lays a mine barrage in the Straits of Gibraltar on which the corvette *Weyburn* and three ships of 14064 tons are lost and the destroyer *Wivern* and two more ships of 11269 tons suffer severe damage.

1-28 Feb   Pacific

Of the US submarines which arrive in their operational area in February *Pickerel* (Lt-Cdr Alston) sinks two ships of 4174 tons off Japan; *Sawfish* (Lt-Cdr Sands) two ships of 7363 tons and torpedoes two more; *Tarpon* (Lt-Cdr Wogan) two ships of 27910 tons and *Tunny* (Lt-Cdr Scott) one ship of 5306 tons. In the Central Pacific *Flying Fish* (Lt-Cdr Donaho) sinks one ship of 994 tons, torpedoes two more and, together with *Snapper*, sinks one ship of 8358 tons. *Halibut* (Lt-Cdr Ross) sinks two ships of 10859 tons. In the South Pacific *Albacore* (Lt-Cdr Lake) sinks the Japanese destroyer *Oshio. Amberjack* does not return from an operation off Buka. In the South West Pacific *Thresher* (Lt-Cdr Millican) sinks two ships of 10956 tons.

2-9 Feb   North Atlantic

The Commander U-boats forms on 2 Feb the 'Pfeil' group consisting of *U594, U413, U267, U187, U465, U402, U609, U262, U454, U89, U135, U608* and *U266* to operate against convoy SC.118 which is expected in accordance with 'B' service reports and prisoners-of-war statements. On 4 Feb the convoy is reported by *U187* (Lt-Cdr Münnich), according to plan, in the middle of the patrol line. Apart from 'Pfeil', *U438, U624, U704, U613* and *U752* from the 'Haudegen' group and *U456* and *U614* from the HX.224 operation are directed to the scene. SC.118 consists of 61 ships with the EG B.2 (Lt-Cdr Proudfoot) comprising the destroyers *Vanessa, Vimy, Beverley* and the corvettes *Campanula, Mignon-*

ette, *Abelia* (British) and *Lobélia* (French), as well as the US Coastguard cutter *Bibb*. The *Bibb* and the rescue ship *Toward* locate with HF/DF the contact signal of *U187*, which is sunk by *Vimy* and *Beverely*. *U402*, *U608*, *U267*, *U609* and *U608* again, are also located on 4 Feb and in the night 4-5 Feb and are driven off by *Vimy*, *Beverley*, *Campanula*, *Bibb*, *Lobélia* and *Mignonette*. After a change of course *U609* establishes contact with a detached group but is attacked with depth charges from *Lobélia*, whilst *U262* (Lt Franke) sinks one ship of 2864 tons on the unprotected side but is shortly after heavily attacked with depth charges from *Vimy* and *Beverley*. *Vimy* forces the contact-keeper *U609*, which has closed up, to submerge again. From the stern *U413* (Lt-Cdr Poel) sinks one straggler of 5376 tons. On the evening of 5 Feb *U609* (Lt-Cdr Rodluff), which has come up again, is driven off by the escort, reinforced in the meantime by the US destroyers *Babbitt*, *Schenk* and the US Coastguard cutter *Ingham* from Iceland. On the morning of 6 Feb *U465* despatches a contact signal but is heavily bombed by a Fortress from No 220 Sqdn RAF directed to the D/F beam; the other boats are driven off. By the evening of 6 Feb *U609* again brings up *U438*, *U262*, *U456* and *U267*, but *Vimy* severely damages the last. Attempts by *U454*, *U438* and *U135* to attack are frustrated by *Lobélia*, *Abelia* and *Babbitt*. Only *U262* is able to fire, but torpedo failures prevent a success and depth charges from *Lobélia* damage the boat. After midnight *U402* (Lt-Cdr Frhr v. Forstner) gets through a gap in the convoy and during the night, in the course of two approaches, sinks six ships of 37075 tons, including the rescue ship *Toward*. A ship of 5740 tons, which has fallen somewhat behind, is sunk by *U614* (Lt-Cdr Sträter) whilst the *Lobélia* (Lt-Cdr De Morsier) sinks *U609*. On 7 Feb most of the boats are forced to the rear by the defence. Only *U402* keeps contact; she is temporarily driven off at mid-day by *Bibb* but returns with *U456*. Shortly after both boats are forced to submerge by *Bibb* and a Fortress of No 220 Sqdn RAF which also sinks *U624*. A new attempt by

U456 to attack is frustrated by *Beverley* thanks to HF/DF. Only *U402* sinks one more ship of 4265 tons in the night 7-8 Feb. An attack by *U608* on a disabled ship and the destroyer *Schenck* fails. In the morning aircraft drive off the last boats and damage *U135*. *U456* (Lt-Cdr Teichert) sinks on the return journey one ship of 700 tons W of the Bay of Biscay on 23 Feb.

4-5 Feb   Mediterranean
British bombing attack on naval base at La Spezia.

4-7 Feb   North Atlantic
The 'Hartherz' group is formed W of the Bay of Biscay with the U-boats *U183*, *U107*, *U519*, *U584*, *U572*, *U71*, *U621*, *U653*, *U628*, *U753* and *U332* to operate against the convoys located by the 'B' Service on the Gibraltar route. No targets are sighted. *U519* is sunk on 10 Feb by a Liberator of USAAF—A/S Sqdn 2.

4-9 Feb   Black Sea
Following the shelling of German positions in the Novorossisk area in the night 30-31 Jan by the Soviet cruiser *Voroshilov* and the destroyers *Besposhchadny*, *Boiki* and *Soobrazitelny*, Soviet landings are made W of Novorossisk early on 4 Feb. To divert the German defence the destroyer *Boiki* with four MO-IV patrol cutters shells Anapa in the night 3-4 Feb and four torpedo cutters cruise off Zhelezny Rog. The covering force (Vice-Adm Vladimirski), comprising the cruisers *Krasny Kavkaz*, *Krasny Krym*, the flotilla leader *Kharkov* and the destroyers *Besposhchadny* nad *Soobrazitelny*, shells the main landing area towards morning. The landing force (Rear-Adm Basisty), consisting of the gunboats *Krasny Adzharistan*, *Krasnaya Gruziya* and *Krasnaya Abkhaziya*, the destroyers *Nezamozhnik* and *Zheleznyakov*, the minesweepers *T-404/Shchit*, *T-411/Zashchitnik*, *T-412/Arseni Rasskin*, *T-407/Mina* and *T-403/Gruz*, as well as the 1st Patrol Cutter Div, loses the patrol cutters *SKA-051* and *SKA-0141* on a mine barrage. In the face of heavy defensive fire only parts of the 83rd and 255th Naval Brigades and the 165th Rifle Brigade are able to land and they are eliminated by 6 Feb. The other landing carried out by patrol cutters at Cape Myschako succeeds; the

bulk of the forces are brought up by gunboats from 5 Feb and by 9 Feb there are 17000 troops on shore. In operations by the German 1st MTB Flotilla (Lt-Cdr Christiansen) against supplies the *T-403/Gruz* and *Krasnaya Gruzya* are sunk by the end of February.

4-12 Feb Arctic
German mining operation against the roads of Kildin is carried out unnoticed in the night 5-6 Feb by the minelayer *Brummer* (Cdr Dr Brill) and the destroyers *Theodor Riedel* and *Z31*. On the way the Soviet submarine *L-20* misses the force off Nordkyn. At the same time two Soviet submarines try out for the first time direct tactical co-operation against a target off Kongsfjord. On the evening of 5 Feb *K-3* (Capt 3rd Class Malofeyev, with the Commander of the Submarine Brigade, Rear-Adm Vinogradov, on board) and *K-22* (Capt 3rd Class Kulbakin with the Commander of the 1st Div, Capt 2nd Class Kotelnikov, on board) attack the submarine-chasers *UJ1101* and *UJ1108* which are proceeding to the rendezvous with the mine-laying force. In Force 8 winds *K-3* sinks *UJ1108* but impedes *K-22*. Towards morning on 6 Feb *K-22*, and later also *L-20* miss the *Brummer* with salvoes. *K-22* sinks on a flanking mine barrage. On 12 Feb *K-3* torpedoes the transport *Fechenheim* (8116 tons) in a convoy.

4-27 Feb Indian Ocean
Convoy 'Pamphlet' with 30000 men of the 9th Australian Div proceeds from Suez to Sydney and Melbourne in the transports *Queen Mary, Aquitania, Ile de France, Nieuw Amsterdam* and *Queen of Bermuda*.
4 Feb: it leaves Suez with anti-submarine protection in the Red Sea and Gulf of Aden provided by the destroyers *Pakenham, Petard, Isis, Derwent, Hero* and *Vasilissa Olga* (Greek). Ocean escort: the cruiser *Devonshire* and from Socotra also the *Gambia*. Covering force in the Indian Ocean: Force A comprising the battleships *Resolution, Revenge* and *Warspite*, the cruiser *Mauritius* and six destroyers. Further E it is reinforced by the Dutch cruisers *Jacob van Heemskerck* and *Tromp* and two destroyers.
18 Feb: the convoy arrives in Fremantle. From there it continues with an escort

consisting of the cruisers *Adelaide, Heemskerck* and *Tromp* and the destroyer *Tjerk Hiddes* (Dutch). Covering force S of Australia: TF 44.3 consisting of the cruiser *Australia* and the US destroyers *Bagley, Henley* and *Helm*. From Melbourne the Dutch ships with the exception of *Heemskerck* are detached. In addition, the Free French destroyer *Le Triomphant*. The convoy arrives on 27 Feb without incident in Sydney.

4 Feb-6 June Bay of Biscay
First Bay offensive by No 19 Group RAF Coastal Command (Air-Vice Marshal Bromet) with 9 Liberators from No 224 Sqdn RAF, 16 Liberators from No 86 Sqdn (transferred to Iceland from March), 6 Catalinas from No 210 Sqdn, 16 Wellingtons each from No 304 Sqdn (Polish) and No 311 Sqdn (Czech), 16 Wellingtons from No 172 Sqdn, 9 Halifaxes from No 58 Sqdn, 9 Fortresses from No 59 Sqdn, 16 Whitleys from No 502 Sqdn, 6 Sunderlands each from No 10 Sqdn and 461 Sqdn RAAF, 12 Liberators (transferred to Morocco from March) from USAAF —A/S Sqdn 1 and 2. In addition, from Apl 6 Sunderlands from No 228 Sqdn RAF and 16 Wellingtons from No 407 Sqdn RCAF.
4-16 Feb: Operation 'Gondola'.—312 sorties, 19 sightings and 8 attacks. *U519* is sunk by USAAF-Sqdn 1. After 'Gondola' normal sorties until March: *U268* is sunk by No 172 Sqdn RAF and *U211, U508* and *U525* are damaged. In the first experimental deployment of a Wellington with 10 cm ASV-IV radar and 'Leigh Light' from No 172 Sqdn RAF, *U333* (Lt-Cdr Cremer) shoots down the aircraft. 21-28 Mar: Operation 'Enclose I'—182 sorties. There are few sightings by day because the U-boats submerged then and charge their batteries by night. On 22 Mar an ASV-IV/'Leigh Light' Wellington of No 172 Sqdn RAF sinks *U165*. *U338* (Lt-Cdr Kinzel) shoots down a Halifax of No 58 Sqdn RAF. Only one success in 27 sightings.
6-13 Mar: Operation 'Enclose II'. *U376* is lost to a ASV-IV/'Leigh Light' Wellington of No 172 Sqdn RAF. Increasing night attacks with radar locating that cannot be detected by 'Metox' and the shooting down of an

aircraft by *U438* lead to a change in German U-boat tactics: they now proceed submerged at night, charge their batteries by day and beat off aircraft with AA fire.

13 Apl-6 June: Operation 'Derange'. As a result of new German tactics, there is a marked increase in sightings by day with many attacks. In May there are 98 sightings and 64 attacks in which *U332*, *U465*, *U109*, *U663*, the U-tanker *U463*, *U440*, *U563* and *U418* are sunk. In Apl *U465*, *U566* and *U437* and in May *U415*, *U214*, *U591*, *U229*, *U523* and *U621* are damaged. On 24 May *U441* (Lt-Cdr G. von Hartmann) is used for the first time as an AA trap and in an engagement a Sunderland is shot down. But the boat suffers heavy loss and damage. In addition, *U666*, *U594*, *U648*, *U662* and *U459* each shoot down one aircraft.

The experience leads to the new German tactics of group sailings in the Bay of Biscay.

5 Feb-9 Mar   Mediterranean

In German and Italian operations against Allied supply traffic off the Algerian coast three torpedo aircraft on 6 Feb attack the convoy KMS.8 E of Oran and sink the Canadian corvette *Louisburg*. Attacks by the U-boats *U407* and *U596* on the convoy escorted by six British and eight Canadian corvettes fail. After the escort leaves off Algiers *U77* (Lt-Cdr O. Hartmann) sinks two ships of 13742 tons. On 5 Feb the Italian *Avorio* (Lt-Cdr Priggione) sinks the A/S trawler *Stronsay* off Philippeville but is herself sunk on 8 Feb by the Canadian corvette *Regina*. After a miss by *Platino*, *Acciaio* (Lt-Cdr Beltrami) sinks the A/S trawler *Tervani* on 7 Feb. In further attacks in February and March *U371* (Lt-Cdr Mehl) sinks one ship of 2089 tons and torpedoes one ship of 7176 tons; *U565* (Lt-Cdr W. Franken) torpedoes two ships of 17565 tons, one of which is destroyed by air torpedo; *U596* (Lt-Cdr Jahn) torpedoes two ships of 14180 tons. Other attacks by *Platino*, *U596*, *U371*, *U565*, *U458*, *U755* and *U602* fail. *Asteria* and *U443* fall victims on 17 Feb and 23 Feb to the British destroyers *Wheatland*, *Easton*, *Lamerton* and *Bicester*, and *U83* to aircraft on 4 Mar.

5 Feb-19 Apl   South Africa/Indian Ocean

After replenishing from *U459* (Cdr. v. Wilamowitz-Moellendorf) in the South Atlantic, the 'Seehund' group operates off South Africa. In individual attacks the boats make the following sinkings (inclusive of successes on the way to the area and on the return): *U506* (Lt-Cdr Würdemann) sinks two ships of 9980 tons; *U516* (Cdr Wiebe) four ships of 25586 tons, including the Dutch submarine depot ship *Colombia*; *U509* (Lt-Cdr W. Witte) two ships of 12066 tons; and *U160* (Lt-Cdr Lassen) three ships of 19353 tons. In addition, *U160* attacks on 3 Mar the convoy DN.21 (11 ships, escort: corvette *Nigella*, the A/S trawlers *Sondra*, *Norwich City* and *Viviana*) and in three approaches sinks four ships of 25852 tons and torpedoes two more of 15224 tons before the destroyers *Quiberon* and *Relentless* arrive. Five ships of 30071 tons fall victim to *U182* (Lt-Cdr N. Clausen) operating simultaneously off South Africa; but on the return the U-boat is sunk on 16 May W of Madeira by the US destroyer *Mackenzie*. The remaining boats return after replenishing from *U117*.

The Japanese submarine *I-27* (Lt-Cdr Fukumura), operating in March in the Gulf of Bombay, sinks one ship of 7132 tons.

9-19 Feb   North Atlantic

From 9 Feb to 15 Feb the 'Haudegen' group, comprising *U358*, *U186*, *U223*, *U69*, *U201*, *U403*, *U707*, *U606*, *U226*, *U525*, *U303*, *U607* and *U383*, is formed in a semi-circle NE of Newfoundland and waits in vain for the convoys HX.225 and SC.119. On 15 Feb the boats, except for *U358*, *U186*, *U223* and *U707* (the 'Taifun' group) start the journey to the supply boat, *U460*. In the process *U69* (Lt-Cdr U. Gräf) sights on 17 Feb the convoy ONS.165 (32 ships, EG B.6 (Cdr Heathcote) with destroyers *Fame*, *Viscount* and corvettes *Vervain*, *Kingcup* and Norwegian *Acanthus* and *Eglantine*). Directed to the contact signal located by HF/DF, *Viscount* sinks *U69* by ramming and *Fame* sinks *U201* (Lt Rosenberg) which is the second boat to come up. Of the former 'Haudegen' and 'Taifun' boats ordered to the scene, *U403* (Lt-Cdr Clausen) does not see the convoy again before the afternoon of 18 Feb but in two approaches sinks one ship of 5961 tons in the night 18-19 Feb. In the morning *U226* (Lt-Cdr Borchers) misses the convoy and contact is again lost. In the evening of 19 Feb *U525* (Lt-Cdr Drewitz) comes up for a short while and sinks one straggler of 3454 tons in the night 19-20 Feb. The operation is broken off because of the proximity to land.

9 Feb-22 Mar Mediterranean
Seven troop transport operations to Tunis and Bizerta for the German and Italian Panzer armies in Africa with the Italian destroyers *Malocello* (four trips), *Alpino* and *Pancaldo* (three trips each), *Pigafetta, Fuciliere, Premuda, Legionario* and *Ascari* (two trips each), *Da Noli, Zeno, Granatiere, Gioberti* and *Camicia Nera* (one trip each). Successive convoys with one to four freighters, escorted by one to five ships, including the destroyers *Lampo, Lubiana, Riboty*, the torpedo boats *Fortunale, Ciclone, Monsone, Groppo, Orione, Animoso, Tifone, Ardito, Calliope, Clio, Pallade, Sirio, Pegaso, Sagittario, Castore, Cigno, Libra, Antares, Cassiopea, Cascino* and the corvettes *Gabbiano, Persefone, Antilope, Artemide* and *Cicogna*, as well as the German 22nd SC Flotilla with *UJ2209, UJ2210* and *UJ2220*. Further troop and supply transports with many Italian and German naval ferry barges (the German 2nd Landing Flotilla). To counter this, the British lay mines within the German and Italian flanking barrages with the submarine *Rorqual* (24 Feb) and the fast minelayer *Abdiel* (27 Feb, 5 Mar and 8 Mar). On the two last barrages the torpedo boat *Ciclone* and one steamer of 1984 tons sink on 7 Mar and the destroyers *Malocello* and *Ascari* on 23 Mar. Torpedo aircraft from Malta sink six ships of 40048 tons and bombers four ships of 19434 tons. An attempted attack by the British *MTB61, MTB77* and *MTB82* on a convoy of four steamers and the torpedo boats *Monsone, Sirio* and the corvettes *Gabbiano* and *Antilope* S of Marettimo fails on 15-16 Feb. On 8 Mar the British destroyers *Pakenham* and *Paladin* in a sortie towards Pantelleria sink one ferry

barge. In a sortie by the destroyers of force Q stationed in Bone *S55* (Lt Weber), one of the German motor torpedo boats posted as flank protection W of her own minefields, fires at and sinks the British destroyer *Lightning*. On the route between Sicily and Tunisia and in the Tyrrhenian Sea the British submarine *Unison* (Lt Daniell) sinks three sailing ships; *Unbending* (Lt Stanley) three ships of 5535 tons; *Una* (Lt Norman) two ships of 7589 tons; *Unrivalled* (Lt Turner) one ship of 2216 tons; *Unruffled* (Lt Stevens) two ships of 5444 tons; *Unseen* (Lt Crawford) one ship of 2875 tons; *Sahib* (Lt Bromage) two sailing ships; *Splendid* (Lt-Cdr McGeogh) four ships of 14380 tons; *Saracen* (Lt Lumby) two tugs and torpedoes one ship; *Torbay* (Lt Clutterbuck) sinks four ships of 11552 tons and torpedoes one ship; *Taurus* (Lt-Cdr Wingfield) sinks two ships of 4893 tons and three small ships; *Trooper* (Lt Wraith) sinks two ships of 6993 tons and two sailing ships; *Sibyl* (Lt Turner) sinks one ship of 1593 tons; and the Dutch *Dolfijn* (Lt-Cdr v. Oostrom) sinks the Italian submarine *Malachite* and one ship of 1143 tons. In attacks on convoys the submarine *Tigris* is sunk on 27 Feb by the German submarine-chaser *UJ2210*; *Turbulent* (Cdr Linton, VC) is sunk on 12 Feb by Italian MAS boats; and *Thunderbolt* is sunk on 24 Mar by the corvette *Cicogna*.

9 Feb-16 Apl Western Atlantic
Of the U-boats operating in the area of the Brazilian Coast *U518* (Lt-Cdr F. W. Wissmann) sinks three independents of 15422 tons. Off Bahia she sights on 28 Feb the convoy BT.6 escorted by the Brazilian corvettes *Carioca* and *Caravelas* and the survey ship *Rio Branco*. In several approaches on 28 Feb and on 1 Mar she fires 14 torpedoes but, because of many failures, she is only able to sink one ship of 7176 tons. Convoy BT.6, which in the meantime is escorted by a US escort group consisting of the destroyer *Borie*, the corvettes *Courage* and *Tenacity* and the submarine-chasers *PC575* and *PC592* is attacked several times on 8-9 Mar off Cayenne by *U510* (Cdr Neitzel) which torpedoes eight ships of 54130 tons, three of which sink, totalling 18240

tons. Off the Brazilian coast the Italian *Barbarigo* (Lt-Cdr Rigoli) sinks three ships of 15584 tons but the *Cappellini*, *Bagnolini*, *Torelli* and *Archimede*, which follow, have no success. *Archimede* is sunk on 16 Apl by a Catalina of USN-VP. 83.

E of the Antilles a Catalina of USN-VP. 53 sinks *U156* (Cdr Hartenstein†) on 8 Mar. *U68* (Lt Lauzemis) sinks two ships of 10186 tons from the convoy GAT.49 in the Western Caribbean on 13 Mar. *U183* (Cdr Schäfer) sinks one ship of 2493 tons in the Yucatan Strait; *U185* (Lt-Cdr Maus) two ships in the area of the Windward Passage on 10 Mar from the convoy KG.123 and one ship on 6 Apl from a GK convoy totalling, in all, 20504 tons; and *U155* (Lt-Cdr Piening) two ships of 7973 tons in the Gulf of Mexico.

10-14 Feb   English Channel
In attempting to break through the Channel, escorted by the 8th MMS Flotilla (Lt-Cdr Muser), the auxiliary cruiser *Schiff 14* (Capt Thienemann) is attacked by Whirlibombers of Fighter Command and has to put in to Boulogne after being hit by bombs. After more air attacks which, however, do no more damage, the ship returns to Dunkirk on 14 Feb and there receives orders from the Navy Staff to return to the Baltic. Thus, the last attempt to bring an auxiliary cruiser into the Atlantic has failed.

10-25 Feb   Black Sea
In several operations the Soviet destroyers *Zheleznyakov*, *Nezamozhnik*, *Besposhchadny* and *Soobrazitelny* bring 8037 troops from Tuapse to Gelendzhik. There are further movements with steamers and small craft along the Caucasus Coast. Of the German U-boats *U24*, *U19*, and *U9*, deployed against these transports, *U19* (Lt Gaude) sinks the transport *Krasny Profintern* (4648 tons) on 14 Feb. In the night 21-22 Feb the Soviet flotilla leader *Kharkov* and the *Soobrazitelny* shell German positions off the Myschako bridgehead.

11-20 Feb   Air War/Germany
British air attacks on Wilhelmshaven on 11-12 Feb, 18-19 Feb and 19-20 Feb.

14-26 Feb   North Atlantic
The 'Ritter' group is formed in the Central North Atlantic from 14 Feb against the convoy HX.226 (EG C.3), expected according to 'B' Service reports. The group consists of *U529*, *U468*, *U377*, *U225*, *U653*, *U628*, *U623*, *U621*, *U753*, *U332*, *U454*, and *U603*, but the convoy is not located and Liberators of No 120 Sqdn RAF sent out to escort it sink *U529* and *U623* on 15 Feb. On 18 Feb and 19 Feb the 'B' Service reports the convoy ON.166 against which the 'Knappen' group with *U92*, *U604*, *U91* and *U600* is concentrated S of 'Ritter'. Towards mid-day on 20 Feb *U604* (Lt-Cdr Höltring) sights the ON.166 (40 ships, 9 stragglers (Commodore Magee), EG A.3 (Cdr Heineman) comprising the US Coastguard cutters *Spencer* and *Campbell*, the British corvette *Dianthus* and the Canadian corvettes *Chilliwack*, *Rosthern*, *Trillium* and *Dauphin*). In the night 20-21 Feb *U604* is located by *Spencer* with radar and attacked with depth charges before the groups directed to the scene arrive. On the morning of 21 Feb *U753* (Cdr v. Mannstein) makes contact with a straggler (5964 tons), which is later sunk by *U603* (Lt Bertelsmann) and *U332* (Lt Hüttemann). In the afternoon *U91* is bombed by one flying-boat which also drives off *U332*, *U454* and *U753* in co-operation with *Campbell*, *Dianthus* and *Dauphin*. In the night 21-22 Feb *U92* (Lt-Cdr Oelrich) comes up to the convoy and in two approaches torpedoes two ships of 9990 tons and 9348 tons respectively. The first is detached with *Dauphin* but later has to be sunk by her; the second is sunk by the Polish destroyer *Burza* (Cdr Pitułko) which joins the convoy after *U92* and *U753* have tried to finish her off with torpedo hits. By day on 22 Feb *U606*, *U603* and *U628* keep contact in turn and bring up *U92*, *U358*, *U223*, *U186* and *U753* by nightfall. Most of the boats are driven off. *U753*, which is attacked with depth charges from *Rosthern* and *Trillium*, and *U606* (Lt Döhler) attack almost simultaneously. *U606* torpedoes three ships of 17260 tons, two of which sink but the third ship of 4599 tons is only sunk when she is finished off by *U303* (Lt-Cdr Heine). Immediately after her own attack *U606* is assaulted with depth charges from *Chilliwack* and

Burza and is shortly after sunk by ramming from *Campbell*. The latter becomes unmanoeuvrable thanks to water pouring into the engine room and has to be taken in tow by *Burza*. In the night *U604* sinks the rescue ship *Stockport* (1683 tons) coming up from the rear. On the morning of 23 Feb *U628* (Lt Hasenschar) and *U186* (Lt-Cdr Hesemann) attack almost simultaneously. *U628* torpedoes two ships of 6907 tons and 6409 tons respectively which are later sunk by *U223* (Lt-Cdr Wächter) and *U603*. *U186* sinks two ships of 11608 tons. The attacks are facilitated because only *Spencer, Rosthern, Chilliwack* and *Dianthus* continue to escort the convoy, the last of which remains behind with the disabled ships. On 23 Feb *U628* and *U707* (Lt Gretschel) keep contact and by the evening bring up *U621, U358, U653, U468, U92* and *U600*. By a sharp change of course after dark the convoy which, initially, is escorted by only three ships, shakes the boats off and no attack takes place in the night 23-24 Feb. Only two stragglers of 7176 tons and 9382 tons respectively are sunk or torpedoed by *U707* and *U653* (Lt-Cdr Feiler). Not before the morning can *U600* (Lt-Cdr Zurmühlen) torpedo one ship of 4391 tons from the convoy which is now escorted by *Spencer, Chilliwack, Rosthern* and *Trillium*. The ship is later sunk by *U628*. On 24 Feb *U628* and *U603* keep contact and bring up *U621, U600* and *U604*, the last of which is damaged by depth charges. Air escort provided from Newfoundland drives the boats off. Only *U621* (Lt Kruschka) misses the *Spencer* in the evening. The escort is reinforced by the British destroyers *Mansfield* and *Witherington*. Towards morning on 25 Feb *U628, U92* and *U600* attack almost simultaneously: the first sinks one ship of 7264 tons but the two others miss the *Spencer*. On 25 Feb *U468* keeps contact but in the oncoming mist only *U600* and *U621* come up briefly. Contact is lost in the evening and the operation is broken off in the morning of 26 Feb.

15 Feb-14 Mar Arctic
The convoy JW.53 goes to sea on 15 Feb with 28 ships and a 'Through-Escort-Group' with the minesweepers *Jason*

(Cdr Lewis), *Halycon*, the 'Hunt' destroyers, *Pytchley, Middleton, Meynell* the corvettes *Dianella, Poppy, Bergamot* and the A/S trawlers *Lord Middleton* and *Lord Austin*. In the heavy storm six ships have to put in to Iceland and the escort carrier *Dasher* which was to provide the air escort and the cruiser *Sheffield* of the covering force return with considerable storm damage. Off Seidisfjord on 19 Feb the 'Fighting Escort Group', comprising the cruiser *Scylla* (Capt I. A. P. Macintyre) and the destroyers *Milne* (Capt Campbell), *Orkan* (Polish), *Orwell, Opportune, Obedient, Obdurate, Faulknor* (Capt Scott-Moncrieff), *Boadicea, Inglefield, Fury, Intrepid, Impulsive* and *Eclipse*, joins the convoy. Rear-Adm Burnett with the cruisers *Belfast* and *Cumberland* forms the covering force. Submarines of the British 9th SM Flotilla and Soviet submarines are stationed off the Norwegian coast. Of them *K-21* (Capt 2nd Class Lunin) lays a mine barrage near Arnöy on 18 Feb, disembarks agents and on 20 Feb fires six torpedoes into Bogen Bay. *M-122, Shch-422, M-119, M-172* and *M-171* make attacks in the area of Varangerfjord and on 19 Feb and on 20 Feb the Soviet Naval Air Force attacks the aircraft bases at Petsamo and Kirkenes.
German air reconnaissance reports the JW.53 on 23 Feb. In bad weather the convoy avoids the German U-boat concentrations by the use of HF/DF on on 24 Feb. Only *U622* misses two destroyers. On 25 Feb 10 Ju 88s of I/K.G. 30 attack and damage one ship of 7058 tons; an attack by some Ju 88s and *U255* on 26 Feb has no success. The convoy is met by four Soviet destroyers and arrives with 18 ships off the Kola Inlet on 26 Feb: six ships proceed with the destroyer *Uritski* and other ships into the White Sea.
On 27 Feb and 28 Feb Ju 87s of I/St. G. 5 make dive-bombing attacks on the ships of the convoy which has come into Murmansk. They badly damage three steamers of 11341 tons. In further attacks on 6 Mar and 13 Mar with the participation of Ju 88s of I/K.G. 30 one steamer of 7173 tons is destroyed and one of 6744 tons damaged. The convoy RA.53 with 30 ships, and escorted by the

same ships as JW.53, sets out from the Kola Inlet on 1 Mar. On 2 Mar it is first reported by *U255* (Lt-Cdr Reche) and shadowed, with short interruptions for several days. On 5 Mar *U255* sinks the steamer *Executive* (4978 tons) and torpedoes the *Richard Bland* (7191 tons) which continues on her way. An attack by 12 Ju 88s of I/K.G. 30 fails in the face of heavy AA fire. Contact is lost. On 9 March *U586* (Lt-Cdr v.d. Esch) sinks the straggler *Puerto Rican* (6076 tons) from the convoy scattered in the gale. One steamer founders in the gale and *U657* misses one ship. On 10 Mar *U255* sinks the *Richard Bland*. The radar of the battleship *King George V* of the distant escort does good work in collecting the scattered ships.

The German battleship *Scharnhorst* uses the stormy weather to proceed on 8 Mar from Gotenhafen to Bergen and on to Trondheim. From there she moves with the *Tirpitz*, destroyers and torpedo boats on 11 Mar to 12 Mar to Bogen Bay near Narvik, where the heavy cruiser *Lützow* already lies. This massing of the heavy German ships in Northern Norway and the demands made by the Battle of the Atlantic on the fleet destroyers of the Home Fleet (i.e. formation of Support Groups) compel the British Admiralty to stop the Murmansk convoys for the summer of 1943. The heavy German ships move to Altafjord from 22 Mar to 24 Mar.

16 Feb-13 Mar   Central Atlantic
From 16 Feb the 'Rochen' group, comprising *U504*, *U218*, *U521*, *U43*, *U66*, *U202*, *U558*, *U87*, *U264* and *U258*, searches for US-Gibraltar convoys S of the Azores and the 'Robbe' group, comprising *U437*, *U445*, *U410*, *U107*, *U103*, *U382*, *U569* and *U511*, N of the Azores. On 20 Feb *U264*, *U258* and *U437* are detached to accompany home the prize tanker *Hohenfriedberg/Herborg* (Capt Heidberg, 7892 tons), but the latter is located by USAAF Liberator 500 nautical miles SW of Cape Finisterre and is sunk by the British cruiser *Sussex*. The *Sussex* avoids a salvo of four torpedoes from *U264* (Lt Looks). On 22 Feb *U522* (Lt-Cdr Schneider) reports the tanker convoy UC.1 (33 ships, Escort Group comprising the British frigate *Ness*, the

sloops *Folkestone* and *Totland* and three corvettes and the Support Group comprising the US destroyer *Charles F. Hughes, Madison, Lansdowne* and *Hilary P. Jones*). The U-boats *U382*, *U569* and the 'Rochen' group are deployed. On the morning of 23 Feb *U522* sinks one tanker of 8882 tons and in the evening *U382* (Lt-Cdr Juli) torpedoes one tanker of 8252 tons with the acoustic homing torpedo 'Falke', used for the first time. *U202* (Lt-Cdr Poser) hits three tankers one of which (7989 tons) sinks. One tanker of 9811 tons is later sunk by *U558* (Lt-Cdr Krech) and one of 8482 tons continues her journey in the convoy. Further attacks by *U569*, *U558* and *U504* in the night 23-24 Feb and by *U521* and *U66* in the night 24-25 Feb fail. *U107* (Lt-Cdr Gelhaus) and *U66* (Lt-Cdr Markworth) each sink one independent of 7801 tons and 4312 tons respectively. From 28 Feb the 'Robbe' group operates with *U445*, *U410*, *U107*, *U103* and *U511* in the area W of Gibraltar. Three boats operate against the convoy KMS.10 located by air reconnaissance on 5 Mar W of Oporto; of them *U107* is driven off on 6 Mar, *U445* does not come up and *U410* (Lt Fenski) sinks one ship of 7133 tons and torpedoes one ship of 7134 tons. The same boats operate against the convoy OS.44 reported by air reconnaissance on 12 Mar, but only *U107* comes up and sinks four ships of 17376 tons. The 'Tümmler' group, replenished from *U461* from 27 Feb to 4 Mar and comprising *U504*, *U43*, *U66*, *U202* and *U558*, proceeds to the area of the Canaries. *U43* (Lt Schwantke) sinks the blockade-runner *Doggerbank* (Capt Schneidewind, 5154 tons) which turns up much earlier than expected. An operation by the 'Tümmler' group on a small south-bound convoy sighted by *U43* on 12-13 Mar fails because of the strong air escort.

17-18 Feb   North Sea
Seven motor torpedo boats of the 2nd and 4th MTB Flotillas under Lt-Cdr v. Mirbach and eight boats of the 6th MTB Flotilla (Lt-Cdr Obermaier) carry out a mining operation SE of Lowestoft and NE of Great Yarmouth respectively. The southern group, after dropping its barrage, is able to escape from the

corvette *Kittiwake*. Part of the northern group, in dropping their barrage, is involved in an engagement with the destroyers *Montrose* (Cdr Phipps) and *Garth* (Lt-Cdr Scartchard); *S71* is shelled to a standstill and sunk by *Garth* by gunfire and ramming.

18-19 Feb   North Pacific
US TG 8.6 (Rear-Adm McMorris), comprising the cruisers *Indianapolis* and *Raleigh* and the destroyers *Bancroft*, *Caldwell*, *Coghlan* and *Gillespie*, shells Holtz'Bay and Chicago Harbour on Attu.

18 Feb-3 Mar   North Atlantic
On 18 Feb the 'Neptun' group, consisting of *U759*, *U405*, *U448*, *U359*, *U135*, *U608*, *U376*, *U566* and *U659*, is formed SW of Iceland to operate against the expected convoy HX.226. When the convoy is not located, the group moves off on 20 Feb reinforced by *U89*, *U569* and *U377*, to the SW towards HX.227. The convoy is located on the morning of 27 Feb by the most northerly boat, *U759*. Radio interference prevents punctual deployment. *U759* is driven off by the escort of the 62 ship convoy, the EG B.6 (Cdr Heathcote) with the destroyers *Fame* and *Burza*, the corvettes *Vervain*, *Kingcup*, *Acanthus*, *Eglantine* and *Potentilla*. *U376*, *U377*, *U608*, *U448*, *U359* and *U135*, take up the pursuit but only *U405* (Cdr Hopmann) sinks a Liberty ship (7176 tons) which has fallen behind and which has on board the two MTBs *PT85* and *PT87*, destined for the Soviet Union. From 28 Feb *U709* and *U634* also take part. On 1 Mar *U759* shadows an independent which *U634* (Lt Dahlhaus) sinks (7176 tons). In the search *U608* reports in the afternoon the approaching convoy ON.168 against which *U405*, *U359*, *U569* and *U448* operate. Up to 3 Mar the convoys are not found again.

21 Feb   South Pacific
Operation 'Cleanslate': the US RCTs 103 and 169 of the 43rd Inf Div (Maj-Gen Hester) land from Guadalcanal on Russell Island without encountering resistance. They are supported by three Marine Ranger BLTs. By the end of February a total of 9000 men are landed by LCTs.

21-25 Feb   North Atlantic
The outward-bound *U664* (Lt A. Graef)

sights the convoy ONS.167, which is escorted by six warships of EG C.1, and sinks two ships of 13466 tons from it on the evening of 21 Feb. *U758*, *U591*, *U84* and *U432*, which are stationed in the area, are deployed as the 'Sturmbock' group and in the night 21-22 Feb and in the morning *U758* and *U664* get brief contact but are driven off. For 25 Feb a 'Sturmbock' patrol line is formed with the inclusion of boats returning from ON.166 and of boats replenished from *U460*; it consists of *U332*, *U432*, *U753*, *U226*, *U383*, *U758*, *U664*, *U84*, *U409* and *U591*. But on 26 Feb only destroyers are seen by *U664* and *U607*. On 25 Feb *U119* (Lt-Cdr Zech) lays a mine barrage off Reykjavik—with no known results.

23 Feb-30 May   Black Sea
German supply convoys 'Kleiner Bär 1-99' from Feodosia to Anapa to supply the Kuban bridgehead with at first two to three, then five to six MFP (naval ferry barges) of the 3rd Landing Flotilla (Cdr* Strempel) and from April sometimes also the 5th Landing Flotilla (Cdr Mehler). The torpedoes fired by the Soviet submarines (they include *M-117*, *M-111* and *L-4*) against convoys 8 (22 Mar), 41 (22 Apl), 88 (18 May) and 92 (21 May) run under the flat-bottomed MFPs. In air attacks on convoy 89 (19 May) *F308* and *F367* and on convoy 99 (30 May) *F332* sink. Soviet torpedo cutters do not attack.
Likewise, attempts by Soviet submarines to attack convoys below the South Crimean Coast are unsuccessful.
Soviet submarines and torpedo aircraft are deployed unsuccessfully W of the Crimea against German and Rumanian convoy traffic between Constanza and Sevastopol (Traffic Commander: Capt Kiderlen). From April patrol lines are formed with the submarines *S-33*, *Shch-209*, *M-35* and *M-112* in the open sea. On 20 Apl *S-33* (Capt 3rd Class Alexeyev) sinks largest Rumanian transport *Suceava* (6876 tons) escorted by the Rumanian destroyer *Regina Maria* and three German motor minesweepers.
The Rumanian mine-layer *Amiral Murgescu* and the German *Romania* lay several flanking barrages off Sulina and in the Bay of Odessa.

24 Feb Central Atlantic
The US carrier *Ranger* flies off a complement of fighter aircraft to Accra to be transferred to North Africa.

26-28 Feb English Channel
A group of the 5th MTB Flotilla, comprising *S65*, *S68*, *S81* and *S85*, attacks a British convoy in Lyme Bay and sinks from it the motor ship *Modavia* (4858 tons), *LCT381* (625 tons) as well as the trawlers *Harstad* and *Lord Hailsham*.
A southward-bound German convoy loses the patrol boat V*1318* on a mine off Ijmuiden on 27 Feb. In the night 27-28 Feb an attempted attack by the British *MGB77*, *MGB79*, *MGB81* and *MGB111* is frustrated by the defensive fire from the escorting vessels *M383*, *V1304*, *V1305*, *V1309*, *V1313*, *V1314* and *Fl.J.23*. *MGB79* is sunk.

26 Feb-11 Mar North Atlantic
On 26 Feb the 'Burggraf' group, comprising *U228*, *U527*, *U230*, *U523*, *U526*, *U616*, *U435*, *U615* and *U332*, is formed in the Central Atlantic and the 'Wildfang' group, comprising *U638*, *U89*, *U432*, *U758*, *U664*, *U84*, *U409* and *U591*, NE of Newfoundland to operate against convoys using the northern route. *U603*, *U91*, *U653*, *U621*, *U600* and *U468*, which have come after replenishing from *U462*, lengthen the 'Burggraf' group as it proceeds to the SW till 4 Mar and behind ,it *U634*, *U709*, *U566*, *U405*, *U359*, *U659* and *U448* take up waiting positions. On 6 Mar *U405* (Cdr Hopmann) sights the convoy SC.121 with 59 ships (Commodore Birnie†), from which, after heavy gales, many ships have become stragglers. Escort provided: EG A.3 (Cdr Heineman), comprising the US Coastguard cutter *Spencer*, the US destroyer *Greer*, the Canadian corvettes *Rosthern* and *Trillium*, the British corvette *Dianthus* and the rescue ship *Melrose Abbey*. The Commander U-boats deploys *U405*, *U409*, *U591*, *U230*, *U228*, *U566*, *U616*, *U448*, *U526*, *U634*, *U527*, *U659*, *U523*, *U709*, *U359*, *U332* and *U432* as the 'Westmark' group and forms the patrol line 'Ostmark' further to the E for 8 Mar from the 'Neuland' boats. It consists of *U229*, *U665*, *U641*, *U447*, *U190*, *U439*, *U530*, *U618* and

U642. After *U405* is driven off, *U566* and *U230* (Lt-Cdr Siegmann) get contact in the night 6-7 Mar. The latter, unnoticed by the escort, sinks one ship of 2868 tons. The freighter *Empire Impala* (6116 tons) which has stayed behind to recover survivors is sunk in the morning by *U591* (Lt-Cdr Zetzsche). On 7 Mar *U228*, *U230*, *U591*, *U409*, *U526* and *U634* keep contact in spite of Force 10 winds, snow and hail showers, but they are unable to attack. On the morning of 8 Mar the gale subsides and visibility is very variable: *U527* (Lt-Cdr Uhlig) misses the convoy; *U526* (?) (Lt-Cdr Möglich) sinks one ship of 3921 tons separated from the convoy. On the evening of 8 Mar *U527*, *U591*, *U190* (Lt-Cdr Wintermeyer) and *U642* (Lt-Cdr Brüning) each sink a straggler of 5242 tons, 5879 tons, 7015 tons and 2125 tons respectively. On 9 Mar the US Coastguard cutters *Bibb* and *Ingham* and the US destroyer *Babbitt* arrive as reinforcement for the escort from Iceland. Liberators of No 120 Sqdn RAF provide air escort and drive off the contact-keeper *U566*. Of the boats coming up by nightfall, including *U229*, *U409*, *U447*, *U641*, *U332*, *U230*, *U405* and *U605*, two are bombed from the air and four are attacked by depth charges from *Babbitt*, *Rosthern* and others. An attack by *U229* (Lt Schetelig) fails. On the evening of 9 Mar *U530* (Lt-Cdr K. Lange) sinks one straggler of 3058 tons. In the night *U409* (Lt Massmann) and *U405* attack almost simultaneously: they sink two ships and one ship respectively of 9826 tons and 4665 tons. A little later *U229* sinks one ship of 4946 tons and torpedoes one more of 3670 tons. In these attacks Commodore Birnie goes down with his ship. On 10 Mar it freshens up again to Force 10 winds and in snow and hail showers, apart from *U229* and *U616* (Lt Koitschka) whose salvoes miss, only *U523* and *U642* come briefly into contact with independents. In the afternoon the last contact-keeper, *U634*, is driven off. The partial non-functioning of the radar and W/T equipment, as a result of storm damage, greatly impedes the escort group which is further reinforced on 10 Mar by the British corvettes *Campion* and *Mallow*. Early on 11 Mar the operation is broken off.

27 Feb-1 Mar Air War/Western Europe

On 27 Feb the 8th USAAF makes a daylight attack on harbour installations in Brest. In the night 28 Feb-1 Mar 400 bombers of RAF Bomber Command attack the U-boat base at St Nazaire. In February 1000 tons of bombs, in all, are dropped on the U-boat pens without effect.

1-31 Mar Pacific

Of the US submarines which arrive in their operational areas in March, *Permit* (Lt-Cdr Chapple) sinks two ships of 5023 tons and torpedoes one more off Japan: *Scamp* (Lt-Cdr Ebert) torpedoes two ships; *Sunfish* (Lt-Cdr Peterson) sinks one ship of 3262 tons; and *Wahoo* (Cdr Morton) sinks nine ships of 19530 tons.

In the Central Pacific *Grayback* (Lt-Cdr Stephan) torpedoes one ship. *Trigger* (Lt-Cdr Benson) sinks one ship of 3103 tons; *Triton* (Lt-Cdr McKenzie) one ship of 3057 tons; *Tuna* (Lt-Cdr De Tar) one ship of 4697 tons; *Whale* (Lt-Cdr Burrows) one ship of 6486 tons; *Tunny* (Lt-Cdr Scott) two ships of 12400 tons and, together with *Finback* (Lt-Cdr Hull) and *Seadragon* (Lt-Cdr Rutter), one more ship of 10672 tons. *Triton* does not return.

Off Formosa and the Philippines *Kingfish* (Lt-Cdr Lowrance) sinks one ship of 8154 tons and *Gudgeon* (Lt-Cdr Port) two ships of 15437 tons and torpedoes one more.

2-4 Mar South West Pacific

A Japanese force (Rear-Adm Kimura), comprising eight transports and the destroyers *Shirayuki, Arashio, Asashio, Tokitsukaze, Yukikaze, Uranami, Shikinami* and *Asagumo*, sets out from Rabaul on 28 Feb to bring 6900 troops of the Japanese 51st Div (Lt-Gen Nakano) to Lae. Reported by a Liberator early on 2 Mar NE of Dampier Strait, it is attacked two hours later by 12 Fortresses which sink a transport and damage two. The destroyers *Yukikaze* and *Asagumo* go on ahead with 950 survivors. On 3 Mar the convoy is attacked in the Bismarck Sea by 355 American and Australian aircraft, some of them at very low level. The aircraft

of AAF South-West Pacific (Lt-Gen Kenney) sink all transports totalling 33730 tons and the destroyers *Shirayuki, Arashio, Asashio* and *Tokitsukaze*. Japanese destroyers and the submarines *I-17* and *I-26* save 2734 men. The remainder, who do not go down with the ships, are mown down in the water by guns of the US fighter bombers and by the depth charges and mg's of the MTBs *PT66, PT67, PT68, PT121, PT128, PT143* and *PT150* (Lt-Cdr Atkins) to prevent the Army round Lae being reinforced by survivors swimming to the shore.

2 Mar-11 Apl Mediterranean

Attempts by the submarines *Ascianghi* and *U593* to attack convoys near Tripoli and Alexandria fail on 2 Mar and 3 Mar. Aircraft attack the dual convoy MW.22 and XT.4 on 5 Mar and damage one ship of 6900 tons. In further attacks on convoys off the Cyrenaican coast *U593* (Lt-Cdr Kelbling) sinks four ships of 11581 tons on 18 Mar, 27 Mar and 11 Apl and off Palestine *U81* (Lt Krieg) sinks three ships of 454 tons.

On 19 Mar aircraft of K.G. 30, 54 and 77 attack Allied ships in the harbour of Tripoli and sink two ships of 8498 tons. The destroyer *Derwent* is damaged. First use of 'circling torpedoes'. In the Aegean the Greek submarine *Papanicolis* (Lt-Cdr Roussen) sinks three sailing ships.

3-4 Mar Air War/Germany

344 British bombers drop 800 tons of bombs on Hamburg.

4-8 Mar English Channel/North Sea

The German 2nd, 4th and 6th MTB Flotillas make a sortie into the area of Lowestoft and Great Yarmouth. On the way out *S70* is lost on a mine. They have engagements there with the British destroyers *Windsor* and *Southdown* and the corvette *Sheldrake*. On the return on the morning of 5 Mar they are attacked off Ijmuiden by Spitfire and Typhoon fighters which sink *S75*.

In an unsuccessful attack by German MTB's on a British convoy near Start Point there is an engagement with the Polish destroyer *Krakowiak*.

A further attack by German MTB's on 7-8 Mar near the Sunk Lightship is frustrated by the British destroyer

Mackay (Capt Jephson), *MGB20, MGB 17* and *MGB21*. In taking avoiding action, *S114* and *S119* collide. The latter is brought to a standstill and sunk by *MGB20* after the crew has been rescued by *S114*.

5 Mar North Atlantic
The outward-bound *U130* (Lt Keller) fires on the convoy XK.1 located by air reconnaissance W of Spain and sinks four ships of 16359 tons.

6-13 Mar North Atlantic
On 6 Mar the 'Neuland' group, comprising *U447, U229, U665, U633, U641, U190, U530, U642, U439, U618, U757, U406, U86, U373, U441* and *U440* is formed on the eastern side of the North Atlantic. On 7 Mar *U221* (Lt Trojer) sinks one independent of 3015 tons and *U633* is sunk by a Fortress of No 220 Sqdn RAF. After the northern boats have withdrawn, as the 'Ostmark' group, to SC.121 (see entry), the U-boats *U659, U448, U608, U757, U406, U86, U373, U441, U440, U221, U444, U336* and *U590* are concentrated as the 'Neuland' group against the convoy HX.228, located by the 'B' service on 8 Mar. At midday on 10 Mar *U336* (Lt-Cdr Hunger), stationed in the S, sights the HX.228 (60 ships, EG B.3 (Cdr Tait) consisting of the destroyers *Harvester, Escapade, Garland* (Polish), *Burza* (Polish), the corvettes *Narcissus, Orchis* and the French *Aconit, Roselys* and *Renoncule*). From 5 Mar to 14 Mar the American 6th SG (Capt Short), comprising the escort carrier *Bogue* and the destroyers *Belknap* and *Osmond-Ingram*, operates with the convoy for support. Apart from the 'Neuland' group, *U333, U432, U405, U566* and *U359* are deployed. After *U366* is driven off, *U444* (Lt Langfeld) takes over as second contact-keeper. Of the boats which come up in the night 10-11 Mar *U221* sinks two ships of 11977 tons; *U336, U86* and *U406* miss the convoy using, in part, FAT salvoes; and *U444* torpedoes one ship of 7197 tons, which is later sunk, together with another ship of 5001 tons by *U757* (Lt-Cdr Deetz). In the explosion *U757* is damaged. *U444* is sighted by *Harvester*; she submerges but has to surface after depth charge attacks and is rammed by the destroyer which for 10 minutes gets a propeller shaft stuck in the U-boat. *U444* tries, at slow speed and unable to submerge, to get away from the unmanoeuvrable destroyer but is located an hour later by the corvette *Aconit* (Lt-Cdr Levasseur) and sunk by ramming. After the repair of an engine, *Harvester* slowly follows the convoy while *Aconit* quickly closes up. In the morning, however, *Harvester's* second shaft breaks and the stationary ship is sunk towards midday by *U432* (Lt-Cdr Eckhardt). One hour later the returning *Aconit* locates the U-boat, compels her to surface with depth charges and sinks her with gunfire and by ramming. The lost contact with the convoy is re-established towards mid-day on 11 Mar by *U228* and *U406* but the boats are driven off by the strong escort, as are later *U359, U590* and *U405*. Attempts by *U440* and *U590* to attack in the night 11-12 Mar fail and towards morning *U590*, the last contact-keeper, is driven off. The deployment of the *Bogue* cannot be used to full advantage because the carrier sails in the middle of the convoy and has no freedom to manoeuvre.

6-16 Mar South Pacific
On 6 Mar the 'Cactus Striking Force' (Capt Briscoe), consisting of the destroyers *Fletcher, Nicholas, O'Bannon*, and *Radford* shells the Japanese airfield at Munda (New Georgia), using 1700 rounds without great success. TF 68 (Rear-Adm Merrill), comprising cruisers *Montpelier, Cleveland* and *Denver* and the destroyers *Conway, Cony* and *Waller* makes a sortie into Kula Gulf to shell the second Japanese airfield at Vila and encounters the two Japanese destroyers, *Murasame* and *Minegumo*, which have brought supplies. They are sunk by radar-directed gunfire and torpedo salvoes from the destroyer *Waller*. The US submarines *Grampus* (missing) and *Grayback* are stationed to support the operation.
On 16 Mar the destroyers (Cdr McInerney) *Nicholas, Radford, Strong* and *Taylor* again shell Vila.

7-10 Mar East Mediterranean
The Italian destroyer *Sella* lays three defensive barrages with 70 mines off Rhodes.

7-14 Mar   North Atlantic
The 'Raubgraf' group, comprising *U638, U89, U758, U664, U84, U615, U435, U603, U91, U653, U621, U600* and *U468*, is formed between Greenland and Newfoundland on 7 Mar on receipt of a 'B' Service report about the convoy ONS.169 (EG B.4). But the convoy is not located and the group is moved to another position for 12 Mar after decoding the route instructions for the convoy HX.229. On 11 Mar *U621* (Lt Kruschka) sinks a straggler from SC.121 of 5754 tons and on 12 Mar *U653* (Lt-Cdr Feiler) and *U468* (Lt Schamong) each sink a straggler of 3355 tons and 6537 tons respectively from the convoy ON.170 (EG B.2) which is also reported by *U603* on 13 Mar. But in the gale and driving snow only *U435, U468* and *U600* come up briefly. On 14 Mar the operation is broken off as hopeless and *U653* and *U89* begin the return journey.

9 March   Indian Ocean
The German merchant ships *Drachenfels* (6342 tons), *Ehrenfels* (7752 tons), and *Braunfels* (7847 tons), which are lying in Mormugao (Goa), scuttle themselves.

9-16 Mar   English Channel/North Sea
On 9 Mar the British *MTB624, MTB622* and *MTB617* attack three German minesweepers of the 21st MS Flotilla near Terschelling, but the torpedoes are out-manoeuvred. On 10-11 Mar the Free French *MTB94* and *MTB96* attack a German convoy off Morlaix and sink *M4620*. On 11-12 Mar the British *MTB38, MTB35* and *MTB24* attack a German convoy off Boulogne without success. On 15-16 Mar the Danish steamers *Maria Toft* (1922 tons) and *Agnete* (1458 tons) are sunk off Terschelling from a convoy escorted by the German 13th PB Flotilla by the British *MTB88* and *MTB93*. In the night 13-14 Mar *S92, S76, S29, S86* and *S89* drop 26 UMB mines in front of a convoy off Orfordness. The motor ship *Moravia* (306 tons) is lost on them.

10 Mar   South Atlantic
The German blockade-runner *Karin* (7322 tons) scuttles herself in the South Atlantic to avoid capture by the US cruiser *Savannah* and the destroyer *Eberle*.

12-19 Mar   Central Atlantic
Before the 'Unverzagt' group, com- prising *U130, U515, U172, U513, U106* and *U167*, and the 'Wohlgemut' group, comprising *U159, U109, U524, U67* and *U103*, take up their patrol lines in the area of the Azores to operate against the convoy located by the 'B' Service, *U130* (Lt Keller) sights the UGS.6 (45 ships, EG (Capt Wellborn) consisting of the US destroyers *Wainwright, Trippe, Champlin, Mayrant, Rowan, Rhind* and *Hobby*), but she is located by *Champlin* and sunk. In a calm sea the U-boats have difficulty in approaching the destroyers which are equipped with 10-cm radar but which, without HF/DF equipment, cannot locate the W/T signals of the U-boats. *U172* (Lt-Cdr Emmermann) sinks a straggler of 5565 tons on the evening of 13 Mar. The 'Tümmler' group, con- sisting of *U521, U504, U43, U66, U202* and *U558*, is also deployed. On 13 Mar *U513, U167* and *U172*, and on 14 Mar *U513, U167* and *U106*, are driven off and *U515* is damaged by depth charges. On 15 Mar *U159* and *U524* (Lt-Cdr v. Steinaecker) attempt underwater attacks by day in which *U524* sinks one ship of 8062 tons. On 16 Mar *U106* brings up 9 U-boats, but their attempted attacks are frustrated. Until evening *U524* and *U172* make simultaneous underwater attacks in which *Rhind* and several tankers are missed and one ship of 7191 tons is sunk. Towards the morning of 17 Mar *U558* misses the convoy. In the evening *U167* (Cdr Sturm) torpedoes one ship of 7200 tons, which is later sunk by *U521* (Lt-Cdr Bargsten). On 18 Mar strong air support is provided; *U524* still keeps contact but an attack is impossible and is therefore broken off by 19 Mar.

13-14 Mar   Norway
In a raid by the Norwegian *MTB619* and *MTB631* off Flörö one of three merchant ships (1249 tons) is sunk. *MTB631* goes aground and is lost.

14-20 Mar   North Atlantic
In order to avoid the 'Raubgraf' group which is shadowing the convoy ON.170, the convoys SC.122 and HX.229 are re-routed from the northern to the southern route. The W/T instructions are decoded by the German 'B' Service and the Commander U-boats therefore

concentrates *U435, U603, U615, U600, U758, U664, U84* and *U91* from ON. 170 into a narrow patrol line in front of the route of SC.122 for 15 Mar. It is designated as the 'Raubgraf' group. On the eastern side of the Atlantic, the 'Stürmer' group is formed to operate against SC.122: it consists of the boats coming from SC.121—*U305, U527, U666, U523, U229, U526, U642, U439, U338, U641, U665, U618, U190* and *U530*—and the new arrivals *U631, U598, U384*, and *U134* on 14 Mar. The 'Dränger' group is formed to operate against HX.229 with the boats coming from HX.228: *U373, U86, U336, U440, U590, U441, U406, U608, U333, U221* and *U610*. But in the prevailing gale SC.122 has passed the 'Raubgraf' patrol line before the U-boats get to their positions and HX. 229 goes round it to the S. *U91* sights escorts of the suspected convoy but, together with *U84, U664* and *U758* cannot find it. On the morning of 16 Mar *U653* (Lt-Cdr Feiler) sights HX.229 with 38 ships (Commodore Mayall). Of its EG B.4 only the destroyers *Volunteer* and *Beverley* and the corvettes *Anemone* and *Pennywort*, together with the destroyer *Mansfield* from the 'Western Local Escort Group' are with the convoy. *Mansfield* locates and drives off *U653* and then returns because of shortage of fuel. The Commander U-boats deploys the 'Raubgraf' group and two boats, *U228* and *U616*, just replenished from *U463*, and the 11 most southerly 'Stürmer' boats. The 'Raubgraf' boats establish contact on the afternoon of 16 Mar and in the night 16-17 Mar attack in quick succession the inadequately escorted HX.229. *U603* (Lt Bertelsmann) sinks one ship of 5214 tons; *U758* (Lt-Cdr Manseck) one ship of 6813 tons and torpedoes one more of 7176 tons, later sunk by *U91* (Lt-Cdr Walkerling); *U435* (Lt-Cdr Strelow) torpedoes one ship of 7196 tons which is also later sunk by *U91*; *U91*, attacking simultaneously with *U435*, sinks another ship of 6366 tons; *U616* (Lt Koitschka) misses the *Volunteer*; *U600* (Lt-Cdr Zurmühlen) hits three ships with a FAT salvo, of which the whaler *Southern Princess* (12156 tons) sinks, while the other two,

totalling 14839 tons, are later sunk by *U91*. *U228* (Lt Christophersen) misses an escort vessel. In the night 16-17 Mar the 'Stürmer' boats, coming from the N, establish contact with the convoy ahead, SC.122 (Commodore White), 51 ships, EG B.5 (Cdr Boyle) consisting of the destroyer *Havelock*, the frigate *Swale*, the corvettes *Godetia, Pimpernel, Buttercup, Lavender, Saxifrage* and the rescue ship *Zamalek*, as well as the destroyer *Leamington* from the 'Western Local Escort Group' and the US destroyer *Upshur* coming from ON.170). Thanks to HF/DF the escort is able to drive off 6 U-boats. Only *U338* (Lt-Cdr Kinzel) is able to fire. She sinks three ships of 17838 tons and torpedoes one more of 7134 tons which is later sunk by *U665* (Lt Haupt). When the Commander U-boats learns that two convoys are located, the remaining 'Stürmer' and 'Dränger' boats are deployed. By day on 17 Mar a Liberator from No 120 Sqdn RAF comes to SC.122 from Iceland and, together with *Swale, Upshur* and *Havelock*, drives off all contact-keeping boats. Only *U338* sinks one ship of 4071 tons in an underwater attack by day. In the case of HX.229 not all the escorts have closed up when at mid-day *U384* (Lt v. Rosenberg-Gruszczynski) and *U631* (Lt Krüger) attack almost simultaneously and each sink one ship of 7252 tons and 5158 tons respectively. In the afternoon a Liberator forces the contact-keeper *U600* underwater and by the morning of 18 Mar contact is lost, fortunately for the convoy, which is now only escorted by *Volunteer, Beverley, Anemone* and *Pennywort*. In the case of SC.122 the escort drives off most of the many 'Stürmer' and 'Dränger' boats as they come up from both sides: only *U305* (Lt-Cdr Bahr) sinks two ships of 13045 tons after dark on 17 Mar. On 18 Mar of 30 boats still operating 9 come into the area of the convoy, but they are forced underwater by the air escort; only *U221* (Lt-Cdr Trojer), led to the scene by *U610*, is able to sink two ships of 15484 tons from HX.229 in an underwater attack. On the evening of 18 Mar and in the night the leader of EG B.4, the destroyer *Highlander* (Cdr Day), and the US destroyer *Babbitt* reach convoy HX.229 and the USCG cutter *Ingham* SC.122. In the night 18-19 Mar the escorts drive off several U-boats. In the case of HX.229 a salvo from *U441* (Lt-Cdr K. Hartmann,) and a salvo from *U608* (Lt-Cdr Struckmeier) misses the *Highlander*: in the case of SC.122 *U666* (Lt Stengel), after a salvo miss, hits one ship of 5234 tons, which is later sunk by *U333* (Lt Schwaff). On the morning of 19 Mar the strong air escort drives off the U-boats from both convoys; only a straggler of 5848 tons is sunk by *U527* (Lt-Cdr Uhlig) and *U523* (Lt-Cdr Pietsch). In the afternoon of 19 Mar and in the night 19-20 Mar the corvette *Abelia* and the destroyer *Vimy* join the escort of HX.229 and the last contact-keepers, *U631* with HX.229 and *U642* with SC.122, are driven off in the morning. The air escort forces the boats underwater and *U384* is sunk by a Sunderland of No 201 Sqdn RAF. The Canadian corvette *Sherbrooke* joins HX.229. The Commander U-boats breaks off the operation early on 20 Mar. In all, 21 ships of 140842 tons are sunk in this biggest convoy battle of the Second World War. The losses sustained by the convoys SC.121, HX.228, SC.122 and HX.229 lead to fears in Britain that the convoy system will have to be abandoned.

15 Mar   South West Pacific
Formation of the 7th US Fleet (Adm Carpender): the former TF 44 becomes TF 74 comprising the cruisers *Australia*, *Hobart* and *Phoenix* and Desron 4 consisting of *Selfridge*, *Mugford*, *Patterson*, *Henley*, *Helm*, *Bagley* and *Ralph Talbot*.
In April *Phoenix* is relieved. Likewise in May Desron 4 is relieved by Desron 5 consisting of *Perkins*, *Conyngham*, *Mahan*, *Flusser*, *Drayton*, *Smith* and *Lamson* and the Australian *Arunta* and *Warramunga*.
In June 1943 the destroyers, with the exception of the last three, join TF 76 (Amphibious Force).

15 Mar-2 Apl   Mediterranean
On 15 Mar *U380* (Lt-Cdr Röther) sinks one ship of 7178 tons from an MKS convoy off the Algerian coast. On 16 Mar *U77* (Lt Hartmann) sinks another ship of 5222 tons and torpedoes one ship of 5229 tons. On 23 Mar torpedo air-

craft of K.G. 26 attack the convoy KMF.11 N of Cape Ténès and sink the British troop transport *Windsor Castle* (19141 tons). From 25 Mar to 27 Mar *U431*, *U77*, *U755* and *U596* attack, sometimes repeatedly, west and eastbound convoys off the Algerian coast, but only *U431* (Lt Schöneboom) is able to sink one ship of 6415 tons. On 27 Mar torpedo aircraft of K.G. 26 sink one transport of 9545 tons NW of Philippeville. *U77* is lost on 28 Mar to British escorting aircraft. On 30 Mar *U596* (Lt-Cdr Jahn) attacks the convoy ET.16 and sinks two ships of 16684 tons. *U755* (Lt-Cdr Göing) sinks two independents of 2075 tons and *U561* and *U375* have no success.

16 Mar-14 Apl   Arctic
In Soviet operations against the German supply traffic on the Norwegian Polar Coast the submarine *M-104* (Lt-Cdr Lukyanov) torpedoes in Varangerfjord the steamer *Johannisberger* (4533 tons), which is beached. *K-3* (Capt 3rd Class Malofeyev), after two abortive attacks off Nordkyn against convoys with *V5902* and *V5907* on 17 Mar and 21 Mar, is sunk by depth charges from the submarine-chaser group comprising *UJ 1102*, *UJ1106* and *UJ1111*. *M-174* is badly damaged on 24 Mar on a mine on a flanking barrage. On 28-29 Mar *S-102*, *S-55* and *S-101* attack successively off Laksfjord, Tanafjord and Korsfjord respectively a German eastern convoy with *V6109* and a western convoy with *M322*, but only *S-55* (Lt-Cdr Sushkin) sinks the steamer *Ajax* (2297 tons) out of the nine steamers and the nine escorts. Operations by the destroyers *Baku*, *Grozny*, and *Gromki* on 28 Mar and 31 Mar meet with no success. From the beginning to the middle of April *K-21* operates in Lopphavet, *S-56* off Tanafjord and *M-171* off Varangerfjord. Mines are laid several times in Varangerfjord by MO-IV's and torpedo-cutters, and the minelaying submarines *L-20* and *L-22* lay barrages off the Polar Coast.

17-31 Mar   Black Sea
The German U-boats *U19* (Lt Gaude) and *U24* (Lt-Cdr Petersen) operate against Soviet supply traffic on the Caucasus coast near Sukhumi and Gagry. *U19* damages one freighter and

U24 sinks the tanker *Sovietskaya Neft* (8228 tons) in Gagry Bay on 31 Mar. In sorties by the 1st MTB Flotilla (Cdr Christiansen) and the Italian IV MAS Flotilla as far as Tuapse and off the Myschako bridgehead *S26* and *S47* torpedo a medium-sized tanker on 17 Mar which is taken in tow to Tuapse and *S28* torpedoes a lighter wreck on 18 Mar. In the night 31-31 Mar *S72*, *S28*, *S47* and *S102* lay a mine barrage off Myschako. On 25 Mar the Soviet patrol cutter *SKA-065* (Lt Sivenko) beats off several attacks by German aircraft on a convoy and is damaged by aircraft fire.

18-23 Mar   Air War Germany/ Western Europe
On 18 Mar 97 B 17s and B 24s of the 8th USAAF attack the dockyards in Bremen-Vegesack. On 22 Mar 87 US bombers attack Wilhelmshaven; the tanker *Eurosee* (10327 tons) sinks.
In the night 22-23 Mar 282 bombers of RAF Bomber Command drop 500 tons of bombs on St Nazaire.

18 Mar-16 June   South Pacific
In operations off the Australian East Coast the Japanese submarine *I-26* (Cdr* Yokota) sinks two ships of 6857 tons; *I-177* (Lt-Cdr Nakagawa) one ship of 8724 tons from a convoy escorted inter alia, by the Australian minesweeper *Colac*, and the hospital ship *Centaur* (3222 tons); *I-178* (Cdr Utsuki) one ship of 7176 tons; *I-180* (Cdr Kusaka) two ships of 4376 tons and damages two more ships of 7713 tons; *I-174* (Lt-Cdr Nanbu), after several misses, one ship of 5551 tons from a convoy and torpedoes *LST469*. In operations off Samoa, Fiji and Noumea *I-25* (Cdr* M. Tagami) sinks one tanker of 10763 tons; *I-19* (Lt-Cdr Kinashi) two ships of 14357 tons and torpedoes one ship of 7181 tons; *I-17* (Lt-Cdr Harada) sinks one tanker of 10169 tons with the MTBs *PT165* and *PT173* on board. *I-178* does not return from her mission and *I-32* is bombed (16 Apl) as she sets out for Samoa.

21-30 Mar   North Atlantic
From 21 Mar the 'Seeteufel' group, consisting of *U306*, *U592*, *U188*, *U415*, *U663*, *U572*, *U564* and *U260*, is formed S of Iceland to operate against convoy ONS.1 located by the 'B' service.

In the following days *U610*, *U134*, *U526*, *U523*, *U598*, *U632*, *U706*, and later *U91*, join the group. On 24 Mar *U306* sights escorts of EG B.6 with ONS.1 N of the formation but the four northerly boats and *U168*, proceeding from the Denmark Strait, do not come up. From 25 March the 'Seewolf' group, comprising *U305*, *U591*, *U631*, *U86*, *U666*, *U618*, *U336*, *U333*, *U530*, *U527*, *U440*, *U373*, *U441*, *U590*, *U641*, *U642*, *U257*, *U84* and *U615*, is formed S of 'Seeteufel' to operate against SC.123 located by the 'B' Service. On the way to these formations *U469* and *U169* are sunk on 25 Mar and 27 Mar by Fortress bombers of No 206 Sqdn RAF. On the afternoon of 26 Mar *U564* (Lt Fiedler) sights the convoy SC.123 (EG B.2) and wrongly reports it as proceeding westwards. Of the 'Seeteufel' group directed to it *U663* and *U415* briefly establish contact with the convoy whose Ocean Escort Group is reinforced by the 6th SG (Capt Short), consisting of the US escort carrier *Bogue* and the destroyers *Belknap* and *George E. Badger*. Carrier aircraft force the boats under water. In 27 Mar *U305* (Lt-Cdr Bahr) sights the following convoy HX.230—45 ships, 9 escorts of EG B.1, reinforced by the 3rd SG (Capt McCoy), consisting of the destroyers *Offa*, *Obedient*, *Oribi*, *Orwell*, *Onslaught* and *Icarus*, making a total of 14 vessels. Of the 22 'Seewolf' and 'Seeteufel' boats deployed only *U305*, *U631*, *U591*, *U415* and *U610* (Lt-Cdr Frhr v. Freyberg) approach the convoy for a time: the last sinks one ship of 7176 tons. Impeded by a strong south-westerly gale and driven off by the strong air escort, which makes an appearance on 29 Mar, the boats are unable to register any successes. On 30 Mar *U631* is the last boat to lose contact. The operation is broken off.

21 Mar-22 Apl   East Mediterranean
Italian defensive mine barrages are laid out: on 21 Mar, 22 Mar, 23 Mar and 6 Apl four barrages with 191 mines off Corsica by the minelayer *Pelagosa*; on 11 Apl one barrage of 50 mines off Naples by the destroyer *Legionario*; and on 22 Apl one barrage of 122 mines off South-West Sardinia by the destroyer *Vivaldi* and the German

minelayers *Brandenburg* and *Pommern*.

22 Mar-9 Apl   Central Atlantic
After refuelling from returning boats, *U67*, *U159*, *U167*, *U513*, *U515*, *U123* and *U172* form the 'Seeräuber' group in the area of the Canaries to operate against the coastal convoy RS.3 (9 steamers and tugs and two corvettes) located by the 'B' Service. It is found on 27 Mar, and on 28 Mar *U167* (Cdr Sturm), *U159* (Lt-Cdr Witte) and *U172* (Lt-Cdr Emmermann) each sink one ship of 4621 tons, 5449 tons and 5319 tons respectively. Strong air support results in the loss of contact on 29 Mar. From 30 Mar the boats set out for individual operations in the area of Freetown, but they have no further success. *U167* is so badly damaged on 6 Apl by two aircraft of No 233 Sqdn RAF that she has to be abandoned after the crew has been taken off. The Italian submarine *Finzi* (Lt-Cdr Rossetto) sinks two independents of 9264 tons.

23 Mar-15 May   Baltic
Units of the Officer Commanding Minesweepers East (Rear-Adm Böhmer) and of the Finnish Fleet (Rear-Adm Rahola) lay mine and net barrages in the Gulf of Finland. From 24 Mar until the middle of April the German mine-layers *Kaiser* and *Roland* and 18-24 ferry barges of the 24th Landing Flotilla lay the barrages 'Nashorn I-X' containing 7293 mines between Naissaar and Porkkala and then until 9 May the naval ferry barges of the 24th Landing Flotilla lay the barrages 'Seeigel I-V' containing 1965 mines from Suursaari to the N of Narva Bay. They are guarded by pro-tection and explosive float barrages on the eastern side. From 22 Apl to 28 Apl the Finnish minelayer *Ruotsinsalmi* and VMV patrol boats lay the barrages 'Rukajärvi U, R, S' containing 686 mines and 750 barrage protection floats N of Suursaari. From 28 Mar to 15 May the German Net Barrage Force (Cdr Becker) lays a double submarine net ('Walross') W of 'Nashorn'. From 24 Apl German KM boats carry out offensive mining operations on the Leningrad Sea Canal ('Brutmaschine'); and from the beginning of May Finnish motor torpedo boats and German KM boats do the same in Kronstadt Bay ('Tiger') and off Lavansaari ('Salpa').

German Air Fleet 1, using 66 aircraft, drops ground mines in Kronstadt Bay on 21-22 Apl. On 30 Apl the outward-bound Soviet submarine *Shch-323* is lost (but later raised) on the 'Brut-maschine' barrage.

26 Mar   Pacific
Battle of the Komandorski Islands, the one daylight battle in the old style in the Pacific War. A US striking force (Rear-Adm McMorris), consisting of the heavy cruiser *Salt Lake City*, the light cruiser *Richmond* and the destroyers *Bailey*, *Coghlan*, *Dale* and *Monaghan*, is deployed against a strongly-escorted Japanese convoy for Attu. The superior Japanese force consists of the heavy cruisers *Nachi* (Vice-Adm Hosogaya) and *Maya*, the light cruisers *Abukuma* (Rear-Adm Mori) and *Tama*, the destroyers *Hatsushimo*, *Ikazuchi*, *Ina-zuma* and *Wakaba* and the transports *Asaka Maru* (7399 tons) and *Sakito Maru* (7126 tons). In a three and a half hour engagement *Nachi*, *Salt Lake City* and *Bailey* are damaged. Then Hoso-gaya breaks off the engagement in expectation of American bombers after the Japanese ships have expended most of their shells.

27 Mar   Great Britain
The British escort carrier *Dasher* is destroyed on the River Clyde as a result of a petrol explosion and fire.

27-30 Mar   North Atlantic
German air reconnaissance locates the convoy SL.126 with 37 ships and 6 escorts W of the Bay of Biscay. The outward-bound U-boats *U267*, *U571*, *U181*, *U404* and *U662* are deployed against it. *U404* establishes contact on 28 Mar and *U662* and *U404* on 29 Mar. In the night 29-30 Mar *U404* (Lt-Cdr v. Bülow) in two attacks sinks two ships of 15822 tons and *U662* (Lt-Cdr H. E. Müller) two ships of 13011 tons and torpedoes one ship of 7174 tons. After losing contact, the boats continue their outward journey.

27 Mar-28 Apl   Mediterranean
Supply transports for the German and Italian armies in Tunisia with freighters escorted by the Italian destroyers *Lubiana*, *Riboty*, *Lampo*, *Mitragliere*, the torpedo boats *Fortunale*, *Tifone*, *Orione*, *Ardimentoso*, *Groppo*, *Antares*, *Sagittario*, *Cigno*, *Cassiopea*, *Clio*,

Perseo, Pallade, Libra, Aretusa, Climene, Cosenz, Dezza, Bassini, the corvettes *Cicogna, Driade, Gabbiano, Euterpe* and the German submarine-chasers *UJ2202, UJ2207, UJ2205, UJ2208, UJ2203, UJ2210* and *UJ2204.* Also with Italian and German naval ferry barges, partly escorted by the 3rd German MTB Flotilla. Troop transports in three operations from 16 Apl to 18 Apl, 22 Apl to 24 Apl and 25 Apl to 28 Apl with the destroyers *Pigafetta, Pancaldo* and also the German destroyer *Hermes.* In April a total of 2800 troops, 18690 tons of supplies, 26 guns, 46 tanks, 268 vehicles and 13 motor cycles are brought to Tunisia.

Against them there are British mining operations with the submarine *Rorqual* (Lt-Cdr Napier) (22 Mar, 7 Apl, 21 Apl and 30 Apl) and the fast minelayer *Abdiel* (5 Apl and 7 Apl). In addition, there are air mining operations resulting in the sinking of one Italian ship of 1227 tons and the German KT13. Torpedo aircraft from Malta sink two ships of 6017 tons; bombers four ships of 21211 tons; and the torpedo boat *Aretusa* is damaged. The destroyer *Lubiana* and three ships are lost when they run on shoals.

On 27 Mar the destroyers HMS *Laforey* and the Polish *Blyskawica* shell Cape Serrat to simulate a landing.

On 1 Apl, of three steamers in a convoy escorted by the torpedo boats *Cigno, Cassiopea, Clio, Cosenz,* the corvette *Cicogna* and the German submarine-chasers *UJ2203, UJ2210* and *UJ2207,* one steamer is sunk by air torpedo and the two others, totalling 6912 tons, by the British *MTB266* and *MTB315.*

On 16 Apl the British destroyers *Pakenham* (Capt Stevens) and *Paladin* intercept an Italian convoy SW of Marsala but it escapes with the torpedo boats *Tifone* and *Climene,* while the torpedo boats *Cigno* and *Cassiopea* involve the destroyers in an engagement in which *Cigno* sinks, but not before the *Pakenham* is so severely hit that she has to be abandoned. *Cassiopea* is taken in tow by *Climene.*

On 28 Apl the British *MTB633, MTB637* and *MTB639* have no success against a convoy. The last is sunk by the escorting torpedo boat *Sagittario.*

In the night 28-29 Apl the British destroyers *Laforey* (Capt Hutton) and *Tartar* attack German motor torpedo boats near Marettimo.

On the route Sicily—Tunis/Bizerta and in the Tyrrhenian Sea, the British submarine *Unison* (Lt Daniell) sinks two ships of 8240 tons; *Sahib* (Lt Bromage) three ships of 4286 tons and five sailing ships; *Unseen* (Lt Crawford) torpedoes two ships; *Tribune* torpedoes one ship; *Unrivalled* (Lt Sprice) sinks two ships of 2446 tons; *Torbay* (Lt Clutterbuck) one ship of 3681 tons; *Unshaken* (Lt Whitton) one ship of 1227 tons; *Safari* (Cdr Bryant) three ships of 7411 tons; *Unbroken* (Lt Mars) two ships of 5017 tons and torpedoes one more ship; *Sibyl* (Lt Turner) one ship of 2940 tons; *Trident* (Lt Newstead) one ship of 520 tons; *Unruly* (Lt Fyfe) one ship of 1256 tons; *Ultor* (Lt Hunt) one ship of 2151 tons; *Taurus* (Lt-Cdr Wingfield) and *Saracen* (Lt Lumby) two ships of 13048 tons; *Sickel* (Lt Drummond) torpedoes one ship. *Unrivalled* also sinks the German submarine-chasers *UJ2201* and *UJ2202* in the Bay of Picarenzi on 29 Mar and *Unshaken* the torpedo boat *Climene* on 28 Apl. On 16 Apl the corvette *Gabbiano* (Cdr Ceccacci) sinks the submarine *Regent;* on 21 Apl the German destroyer *Hermes* (Cdr* Rechel) sinks the submarine *Splendid* near Capri; and on 24 Apl *Sahib* is attacked by *Giabbiano* near the Lipari Islands and is sunk by one Ju 88 of II/L.G. 1.

28-29 Mar   North Sea
Seven boats of the 2nd MTB Flotilla (Cdr Feldt) unsuccessfully attack the British convoy FS.1074 off Smith's Knoll and are driven off by *MGB321* and *MGB333* and the destroyers *Blencathra* and *Windsor.* After a collision *S29* has to be abandoned.

28 Mar-2 Apl   Bay of Biscay
On 28 Mar the Italian blockade-runner *Himalaya* (Capt Martinoli) sets out for Japan from the Gironde, escorted by the German torpedo boats *Falke, T2, T12, T18,* and *T23,* but, after the departure of the torpedo boats in the area of Cape Finisterre, she has to return when located by British air reconnaissance. Met by the torpedo boats *Kondor, T5, T9* and *T19,* the *Himalaya* returns to Bordeaux on 30

Mar. On the same day the 8th DD Flotilla (Capt Erdmenger), comprising *Z23*, *Z24*, *Z32*, and *Z37*, sets out, meets the Italian blockade-runner *Pietro Orseolo* (Lt-Cdr Tarchioni) on 1 Apl 140 nautical miles W of Vigo and beats off the attacks of the Beaufort and Torbeau torpedo aircraft directed to the scene by reconnaissance planes, shooting five down. US submarines *Shad* (Lt-Cdr MacGregor) obtains one torpedo hit on the *Orseolo* which is, however, towed into the Gironde on 2 Apl.

30 Mar   Japan/North Atlantic
The British light cruiser *Glasgow* meets the German blockade-runner *Regensburg* (8086 tons) in the Denmark Strait on her way from Eastern Asia. The German ship scuttles herself and the *Glasgow* rescues 6 survivors.

1-30 Apl   Pacific
Of the US submarines which arrive in their operational areas in April, *Flying Fish* (Lt-Cdr Donaho) sinks four ships of 8940 tons off Japan and *Scorpion* (Lt-Cdr Wylie) two ships of 8314 tons. *Pickerel* (Lt-Cdr Alston) does not return after sinking one minesweeper and torpedoing one minesweeper. In the Central Pacific *Drum* (Lt-Cdr McMahon) sinks two ships of 10189 tons; *Haddock* (Lt-Cdr Davenport) one ship of 7389 tons and torpedoes one more ship. *Pike* (Lt-Cdr McGregor) sinks one ship of 3802 tons; *Porpoise* (Lt-Cdr Bennett) one ship of 2032 tons; Seawolf (Lt-Cdr Gross) sinks one landing ship and torpedoes one other. In the South-West Pacific *Grayling* (Lt-Cdr Lee) sinks one ship of 4111 tons; *Tautog* (Lt-Cdr Sieglaff) one ship of 5214 tons and the destroyer *Isonami*; *Gudgeon* (Lt-Cdr Port) sinks one ship of 17526 tons and torpedoes one more ship. *Grenadier* does not return from an operation.

2 Apl-24 May   Western Atlantic
After meeting the returning blockade-runners *Regensburg*, *Pietro Orseolo* and *Irene* for the hand-over of radar search receiver equipment W of the Azores (23 Mar to 6 Apl) *U161* (Lt-Cdr Achilles) and *U174* proceed to the American East Coast, but only *U161* sinks one sailing ship of 255 tons. On 25 Apl both try to approach a convoy off Halifax but *U174* is sunk by a Ventura of USN-VP.125.

In the area of the Greater Antilles *U176* (Lt-Cdr Dierksen) sinks two ships of 4232 tons from a convoy on 13 May, escapes from the search made by the DE *Brennan*, eight submarine-chasers and one blimp, but is bombed on 15 May by a ship's aircraft and sunk by the Cuban submarine-chaser *CS.13*. *U129* (Cdr Witt) sinks three ships of 26950 tons but is driven off from an NG convoy on 21 Apl by the US destroyer *Swanson*.

2 Apl-15 June   Central Atlantic
From a wave of Type IX boats proceeding to the Freetown area, *U124* (Lt-Cdr J. Mohr) meets the convoy OS.45 on 2 Apl and, in a surprise attack, sinks two ships of 9547 tons. But she is herself sunk by ships of the 37th EG (the corvette *Stonecrop* and the sloop *Black Swan*). *U455* (Lt-Cdr Scheibe) and *U117* (Cdr Neumann) lay mine barrages off Casablanca on 10 Apl and 11 Apl on which one ship of 3777 tons sinks and two ships of 14269 tons are damaged. The remaining boats arrive in the Freetown area in the first ten days of April and by the middle of May they sink the following independents: *U515* (Lt-Cdr Henke), two ships of 6901 tons; *U123* (Lt v. Schröter), the British submarine *P615* and four ships of 24200 tons; *U105* (Lt-Cdr Nissen) one ship of 4669 tons; *U126* has, at first, no success. On 30 Apl *U515* encounters the convoy TS.37 (18 ships), escorted by one corvette and three A/S trawlers, and, in three approaches, sinks by 1 May seven ships of 43255 tons from it before a Support Group of three destroyers comes up. After being replenished from *U460*, *U515*, *U126* and *U105* continue the operation. Several convoys are sighted but only *U126* (Lt Kietz) torpedoes two ships of 13374 tons, of which one Liberty ship becomes a total loss. On 2 June *U105* is sunk by the French Potez flying-boat *Antarès* from Dakar. Off Dakar *U214* (Lt Count v. Treuberg) lays a mine barrage on which one ship of 6507 tons is damaged.

3-5 Apl   Air War
In the night 3-4 Apl 49 British bombers attack St Nazaire and 40 others Lorient. On the following night RAF Bomber Command drops 1300 tons of bombs on Kiel.
In the night 4-5 Apl 48 German bombers

drop mines in the Thames Estuary.

3-7 Apl   North Atlantic

The 'Löwenherz' group is formed SE of Greenland from the U-boats *U191*, *U168*, *U630*, *U635*, *U706*, *U260*, *U564*, *U592*, *U572*, *U563*, *U594*, *U584*, and *U632*, coming from HX.230 and from being replenished from *U463*. On 4 Apl the returning *U530* (Lt-Cdr K. Lange) sights the convoy HX.231 just W of the patrol line. It consists of 61 ships with the EG B.7 (Cdr Gretton) comprising the frigate *Tay*, the destroyer *Vidette* and the corvettes *Alisma*, *Pink*, *Snowflake* and *Loosestrife*. Apart from 'Löwenherz' *U229* and *U532* which are stationed in the area, are also deployed. *U530* brings up five boats before dusk and two more in the night. *U635* (Lt Eckelmann) and *U630* (Lt Wickler) each sink in the night one ship of 5529 tons and 9365 tons respectively and *U229* (Lt Schetelig) sinks one straggler of 3406 tons. *U572*, in trying to attack, is rammed and damaged. On 5 Apl strong air escort is provided by Liberators of No 86 Sqdn RAF which sink *U635* and force the contact-keeper *U260* underwater. *U563* (Lt-Cdr G. v. Hartmann) torpedoes one straggler of 9005 tons, which *U530* later sinks. In the afternoon *U706* (Lt-Cdr v. Zitzewitz) attacks the convoy and sinks one ship of 7124 tons. In the night 5-6 Apl *U632* (Lt-Cdr Karpf) sinks at first one straggler of 7065 tons and then, in an attack on the convoy, after missing the *Alisma*, is sunk by the *Tay*. Attacks by *U270* and *U134* fail. On 6 Apl the 4th SG, comprising the destroyers *Inglefield*, *Fury*, *Eclipse* and *Icarus*, reaches the convoy and, together with the air escort, drives off the contact-keeping U-boats *U270*, *U229*, *U564*, *U134* and *U563* and, on the morning of 7 Apl, *U260*.

5 Apl-20 Aug   South Africa/Indian Ocean

From 5 Apl to 20 Apl the German *U180* (Cdr Musenberg) operates off South Africa and sinks one ship of 8132 tons. On 26 Apl she transfers S of Mauritius the Indian nationalist leader, Subhas Chandra Bose, to the Japanese submarine *I-29* (Cdr* Izu) which brings him to Penang. On the return journey *U180* sinks one more ship of 5166 tons. The Italian submarine *Da Vinci* (Lt-Cdr Gazzana-Priaroggia), which on her way out has sunk in the South Atlantic the British troop transport *Empress of Canada* (21517 tons) and one other ship, sinks four ships off South Africa in April. After total sinkings of 58973 tons, she is sunk on the return journey near Cape Finisterre on 24 May by the British frigate *Ness* and the destroyer *Active*. From 26 Apl a wave of seven German Type IX-D U-boats arrive off South Africa and operate there until 10 June. *U198* sinks one ship on 17 May from the convoy LMD.17 (six steamers, two A/S trawlers); *U177* and *U178* sink two ships and one ship respectively on 28 May and 1 June from the CD.20 (Escort: four A/S trawlers). After being replenished from their tanker *Charlotte Schliemann* from 21 June to 26 June the boats continue their operations between Mauritius, East Africa and South Africa. *U198* sinks one ship on 1 Aug from the convoy BC.2 (four steamers, the corvettes *Freesia* and *Rockrose* and three trawlers) and *U196* one ship on 2 Aug from CB.21. *U177* repeatedly deploys the towing helicopter 'Bachstelze'. In all, the following sinkings are made up to 20 Aug: *U181* (Cdr Lüth) ten ships of 45332 tons; *U198* (Capt W. Hartmann) seven ships of 36778 tons; *U196* (Lt-Cdr Kentrat) two ships of 12285 tons; *U177* (Lt-Cdr Gysae) six ships of 38917 tons; *U178* (Cdr Dommes) six ships of 32683 tons; *U195* (Lt-Cdr Buchholz) two ships of 14391 tons and torpedoes one ship of 6797 tons; *U197* (Lt-Cdr Bartels) three ships of 21267 tons and torpedoes one ship of 7181 tons. As a result of radio traffic located by HF/DF, Catalina flying boats are deployed to sink *U197* on 20 Aug. At the end of June and at the beginning of July *U511* (Lt-Cdr Schneewind with the Japanese Vice-Adm Nomura on board) passes through the Indian Ocean on her way to Japan and sinks two ships of 14370 tons. *U178* goes to Penang in August; the remainder return to Bordeaux.

Operating from the Japanese naval base at Penang, the Japanese submarine *I-27* (Lt-Cdr Fukumura) sinks four ships of 18175 tons in the Gulf of Oman in May and June and torpedoes on 5 July one ship of 6797 tons from the convoy

PA.44; in June and July *I-29* (Cdr* Izu) sinks one ship of 5643 tons in the Gulf of Aden and *I-37* (Cdr Otani) two ships of 15254 tons off East Africa. *I-8* (Capt Uchino), after being replenished from *I-10* on 4 July, proceeds to France; *I-10* (Capt Tonozuka) sinks one ship of 7634 tons S of Chagos.

6 Apl   Mediterranean
US bombers sink the German freighter *San Diego* (6013 tons) off Bizerta and damage the Italian transport *Rovereto* (8564 tons) so badly that she has to be beached.

6 Apl-10 July   Bay of Biscay
Aircraft of RAF Bomber Command frequently drop bombs by night in the approaches and exit channels of the German U-boats in the Bay of Biscay. Units of the German Commander Naval Defence Forces West (Vice-Adm Ruge: acting in his absence, Capt Hagen) have protected the U-boats against mines with minimal losses to themselves from 1940 with the 4th Escort Div (Capt Lautenschlager) (the 2nd, 6th, 24th, 40th MS Flotillas, the 8th, 10th, 26th, 28th, 42nd, 44th MS Flotillas, the 4th and 6th PB Flotillas, the 2nd Mine Detonating Flotilla) and the 3rd Escort Div (Capt Breuning) (the 2nd, 7th PB Flotillas, the 6th Mine Detonating Flotilla and the 14th SC Flotilla). On 6 Apl *M4041*, on 16 Apl *U526*, on 14 June *Sperrbrecher 21* and on 10 July *M445* are lost on air mines.

7-12 Apl   North Atlantic
On 7 Apl the 'Adler' group is formed S of Greenland with *U188*, *U257*, *U84*, *U615*, *U267*, *U404*, *U662*, *U571*, *U613* and later *U71*. On the same day the expected convoy SC.125 passes with the EG B.6 to the W of the patrol line. *U257* sights the escort vessels but *U188*, *U257* and *U84* fail to come up and a patrol line further to the N on 8 Apl has no success. The group is, therefore, moved to the S to operate against the expected HX.232 (EG B.3). *U404* (Lt-Cdr v. Bülow) reports on the afternoon of 10 Apl the convoy ON.176 (46 ships, EG B.6 with the destroyers *Highlander*, *Beverley* and *Vimy* and five corvettes). Of the 'Adler' group boats deployed, *U188* (Lt-Cdr Lüdden) sinks the *Beverley* in a night attack on the convoy. *U571* (Lt-Cdr Möhlmann)

and *U84* (Lt-Cdr Uphoff) in shadowing, encounter the convoy ONS.2 (37 ships, EG C.1) which is sailing in the vicinity. *U571* sinks one ship of 3835 tons. On 11 Apl *U615* (Lt-Cdr Kapitzky) and *U613* (Lt-Cdr Köppe) each sink one straggler of 7177 tons and 1914 tons respectively. *U71*, *U662*, *U404*, and again *U71*, briefly keep contact with the convoy, but all boats are driven off by the strong air and sea escort. Only *U404* makes an unsuccessful attack in the night 11-12 Apl on ON.176. *U84*, *U662*, *U404*, *U613* and *U571* have to break off with damage and the operation is abandoned on 12 Apl.

7-18 Apl   South Pacific
Last Japanese air offensive (Operation 'I') in the Solomons under the personal command of Admiral of the Fleet Yamamoto. After the Japanese carriers *Zuikaku*, *Zuiho*, *Junyo* and *Hiyo* have brought 95 fighters, 65 dive-bombers and some torpedo aircraft to Rabaul and Buka to reinforce the 11th Air Fleet (86 fighters, 27 dive-bombers, 72 twin-engined torpedo bombers), 67 torpedo aircraft and dive-bombers with 110 fighters attack the US ships in the roads of Lunga/Guadalcanal and Tulagi on 7 Apl. They sink the US destroyer *Aaron Ward*, the tanker *Kanawha* and the New Zealand corvette *Moa*; one transport and one tanker are damaged. On 11 Apl, 22 aircraft with 72 fighters attack Oro Bay near Buna (New Guinea) and on 12 Apl, 43 bombers with 131 fighters Port Moresby. On 14 Apl a strong air force attacks Milne Bay where two transports are sunk. US W/T intelligence decodes Japanese W/T messages about a visit by Admiral Yamamoto to Buin Airfield (Bougainville). Sixteen Lightning long-distance fighters of the 339th Fighter Sqdn (Maj Mitchell) are deployed from Henderson Field (Guadalcanal). Losing one plane, they shoot down the two transport aircraft with Adm Yamamoto† and his Chief of Staff, Vice-Adm Ugaki (rescued), and three of the 9 escorting fighters. Adm Koga succeeds as C-in-C of the Combined Fleet.

9-10 Apl   Bay of Biscay
Another unsuccessful attempt by the Italian blockade-runner *Himalaya* to break out, in spite of the escort provided

by the German destroyers *Z23*, *Z24*, *Z32* and the torpedo boats *Kondor*, *T2*, *T5*, *T22* and *T23*. The ship is forced to return after heavy air attacks. Returning from the Mediterranean, the British fast minelayer *Adventure* (Capt Bowes-Lyon) encounters on 10 Apl 275 nautical miles W of Vigo the German blockade-runner *Irene/Silvaplana* (4793 tons, Capt Wendt) coming back from Eastern Asia. The ship scuttles herself.

10 Apl   Mediterranean
Eighty-four American B 24 Liberators attack the Italian naval base at La Maddalena (Sardinia): the heavy cruiser *Trieste* and the motor torpedo boats *MAS501* and *MAS503* are sunk and the heavy cruiser *Gorizia* is severely damaged (later towed to La Spezia).

10 Apl-28 May   Mediterranean
Whilst *U303* and *U414* come into the Mediterranean from the Atlantic, *U596* and *U617* attack British Naval forces unsuccessfully near Alboran (10 Apl) and the latter misses a KMF convoy (13 Apl). On 20 Apl *U565* (Lt-Cdr W. Franken) sinks two ships of 9986 tons from the convoy UGS.7 and an attack by *U453* fails. *U602* is lost off Algiers on 23 Apl from an unknown cause. *U371* (Lt Cdr Mehl) sinks one ship of 1162 tons on 27 Apl. Of the boats coming from the Atlantic, *U410* is damaged by aircraft and *U447* is sunk, E of Gibraltar. *U616* gets through but has no success. The same applies to *U375*, *U561* and *U407* operating off Algiers. *U414* (Lt Huth) sinks one ship of 5979 tons from a convoy on 18 May and torpedoes one ship of 7134 tons; but she is sunk by the British corvette *Vetch* on 25 May. On 21 May the Italian *Gorgo* is lost to the US destroyer *Nields* in an attack on a US convoy and *U303* is lost to the British submarine *Sickle* off Toulon. *U755* is destroyed by aircraft off Algiers on 28 May.

11-13 Apl   North Atlantic
The 'Lerche' group, comprising *U168*, *U532*, *U706*, *U563*, *U270*, *U630*, *U584*, *U260*, *U191* and *U203*, is formed to operate against the convoy HX.232 (EG B.3) expected on 11 Apl and the convoy, consisting of 47 ships, escorted by three destroyers and four corvettes, is located according to plan by *U584* (Lt-Cdr Deecke). In the night

11-12 Apl *U563* (Lt-Cdr v. Hartmann) sinks one ship of 7117 tons; *U168* (Lt-Cdr Pich) sinks one ship of 7261 tons and torpedoes one more ship of 2666 tons, which is later sunk by *U706* (Lt-Cdr v. Zitzewitz). On 12 Apl *U530*, which also takes part in the operations on her return journey, and the contact-keepers *U584*, *U203*, *U270* and *U168*, are driven off partly by the sea escort and partly by the air escort. On 13 Apl the operation is broken off and the boats proceed to *U462* for replenishment.

11-27 Apl   North Atlantic
From 11 Apl seven boats are stationed E of Newfoundland as the 'Meise' group and boats replenished from the tankers *U462* and *U463* join them and form a patrol line from 14 Apl to operate against the convoy SC.126 (38 ships, EG B.5 with *Havelock* (Cdr Boyle)). But the patrol line is avoided. The 'Meise' group, comprising *U134*, *U306*, *U631*, *U203*, *U552*, *U267*, *U706*, *U415*, *U413*, *U598*, *U191*, *U438*, *U613*, *U404*, *U571*, *U381*, *U108*, *U258*, *U610*, *U257* and *U84*, is moved as a result of 'B' Service reports on 18 Apl and 20 Apl to a position ahead of convoy HX.234 which tries to avoid the formation. On the way, *U108* (Lt-Cdr Wolfram) and *U732* (Lt Carlsen) each sink one so-far un-identified ammunition steamer from Iceland feeder convoys. On 21 Apl *U306* (Lt-Cdr v. Trotha) locates HX.234 (42 ships, EG B.4 with *Highlander* (Cdr Day) and seven other escorts) and sinks one ship of 10218 tons in the night. In closing up *U706* (Lt-Cdr v. Zitze-witz) encounters ONS.4 (EG B.2); *U203*, *U415*, *U191*, *U613* and *U438* (Lt-Cdr Heinsohn) take up the pursuit and the last also meets the following ON.178 (18 ships and 7 escorts of EG B.1) from which *U415* (Lt-Cdr Neide) sinks two ships of 8013 tons and *U191* (Lt-Cdr Fiehn) one ship of 5486 tons before contact is lost. On 22 Apl Catalinas of USN-VP.84 from Green-land and Iceland drive the 'Meise' group off HX.234; only *U306* maintains contact and sinks one ship of 7176 tons in an underwater attack by day on 23 Apl. *U954* (Lt-Cdr O. Loewe) torpedoes one more ship of 5313 tons before air escort is provided by Liberators from

No 210 Sqdn RAF, to which *U189* falls victim. In the search *U732* comes across the approaching ONS.4 (41 ships, EG B.2 with *Hesperus* (Cdr Macintyre) and six more escorts) to whose support the C-in-C Western Approaches, Adm Horton, has brought up the 5th SG with the escort carrier *Biter* (Capt Abel-Smith) and the destroyers *Pathfinder*, *Obdurate* and *Opportune*. Swordfishes from the *Biter* force *U732* to submerge; *U191*, which takes over as contact-keeper, is located with HF/DF by *Hesperus* and sunk with 'Hedgehog'. Of the shadowing boats *U954*, *U209*, *U648*, *U108*, *U404* and *U514*, only *U108* establishes contact with the convoy and *U404* (Cdr v. Bülow) with the Support Group. *U404* fires on the morning of 25 Apl a salvo against what is thought to be the carrier *Ranger*, which misses because of a premature fuse. On the same day a Swordfish from the *Biter* sights the returning *U203* which is sunk by the *Pathfinder*. The 11 'Meise' boats stationed near HX.234 are unable to fire in the night 23-24 Apl because of hail, rain and snow-storms and because of the skilful manoeuvring of the convoy; *U306* maintains contact on 24 Apl but the strong air escort for HX.234 and ONS.5, which is sailing in the vicinity, only allows *U610* to make an unsuccessful attack and *U710*, which is proceeding towards HX.234, is sunk by a Fortress of No 206 Sqdn RAF. After a miss by *U413* in the night, the remaining boats are driven off by the air escort and the reinforced sea escort with the 4th SG (destroyers *Faulknor*, *Eclipse*, *Fury* and *Icarus*).

12-21 Apl   North Sea/English Channel
In the night 12-13 Apl slight damage is done to both sides in an engagement between a German convoy and the British *MGB112*, *MGB111*, *MGB75* and *MGB74*. On 13-14 Apl the German 5th MTB Flotilla (Lt-Cdr Klug), comprising *S65*, *S81*, *S82*, *S90*, *S112*, *S116* and *S121*, attacks off the Lizard Head the British convoy PW.323 (six steamers, the Norwegian destroyers *Glaisdale* and *Eskdale*, two Norwegian and three British trawlers). *S90* (Lt Stohwasser) hits the *Eskdale* with two torpedoes; she is later sunk by *S112*

(Lt-Cdr Karl Müller) and *S65* (Lt Sobottka). *S121* (Lt Klocke) torpedoes the British freighter *Stanlake* (1742 tons) which is then finished off by *S90* and *S82* (Lt Dietrich). In the night 14-15 Apl the 2nd and 6th MTB Flotillas (Cdr Feldt) with *S94*, *S89*, *S92*, *S83*, *S86*, *S91*, *S114* and *S39* carry out a mining operation off Lowestoft. There are engagements with *MGB88* and *MGB91*, the destroyer *Westminster* and the corvette *Widgeon*, in which *S83* receives a light hit. The 4th MTB Flotilla (Lt-Cdr Lützow) with *S48*, *S63*, *S88*, *S120*, *S110*, *S87* and *S122* lays further barrages to the S. The trawler *Adonis* (1004 tons) is torpedoed and sunk. On 15 Apl there is an engagement off Cape de la Hogue between German patrol boats and submarine-chasers and the British *SGB6*, *MGB608* and *MGB615*. In an engagement off the Somme Estuary in the night 17-18 Apl the British *MGB 38* and *MGB39* sink the patrol boat *V1409*. In an attack on a German convoy early on 18 Apl off Scheveningen the British *MTB234*, *MTB241* and *MTB233* obtain shell hits, but attacks by Beaufighters off den Helder in the afternoon have no success. On 20-21 Apl four MTBs miss a German convoy of the Hook of Holland.

12 Apl-25 May   Mediterranean
The German 3rd MTB Flotilla lays defensive mine barrages off Sousse (12-13 Apl and 2 May), off Bizerta (14 Apl, 25 Apl and 6 May) and off Porto Empedocle (16-17 May, 23 May and 25 May): 385 mines in all.

13 Apl   South Atlantic
The blockade-runner *Portland* (7132 tons, Capt Tünemann) is found by the Free French light cruiser *Georges Leygues* on the Natal-Freetown route and scuttles herself.

15-18 Apl   North Atlantic
The outward-bound *U262* (Lt Franke) sights the convoy HX.233 sailing on the southern route (57 ships, EG A.3 (Cdr Heinemann) with the US Coastguard cutters *Spencer* and *Duane*, the Canadian corvettes *Wetaskiwin* and *Arvida* and the British *Dianthus*, *Bergamot* and *Bryony* and the Canadian destroyer *Skeena*, ordered up to give support). The outward-bound *U175*, *U628*, *U226*, *U358*, *U264*, *U382* and *U614* are

deployed against the convoy. On the morning of 16 Apl the contact-keeper *U262* is driven off and only in the night 16-17 Apl does *U175* (Lt Bruns) find the convoy again. Towards morning she brings up *U382* and *U628* (Lt-Cdr Hasenschar); the latter torpedoes one ship of 7134 tons which is later sunk by *U226* (Lt-Cdr Borchers). The contact-keeper *U175* is located by HF/DF and sunk by the *Spencer*. The 3rd SG (Capt McCoy), consisting of the destroyers *Offa*, *Oribi*, *Penn* and *Panther*, which comes up on 17 Apl to give support, forces *U264*, *U226* and *U382* to submerge in lengthy depth-charge pursuits. On the evening of 17 Apl *U614* is the last boat to lose contact and on 18 Apl the operation is broken off.

16-25 Apl   Air War
Bombers of the 8th USAAF attack Lorient and Brest by day on 16 Apl. In the night 24-25 Apl 39 German bombers drop mines in the Thames Estuary.

16 Apl-5 June   Arctic
On the Norwegian Polar Coast Soviet submarines try, partly on the basis of disembarked agents' reports and air reconnaissance, to attack German supply convoys. In Varangerfjord and off Vardö *M-172*, *M-105*, *M-171*, *M-172*, *M-104*, *M-122* (probably sunk on a flanking mine barrage), *M-106*, *M-105* and *M-106* are among those which operate in succession; but in spite of many attacks they and the occasional torpedo-cutters employed in small groups achieve no success. In the area between Syltefjord and Nordkyn *Shch-422*, *S-55*, *S-101*, *S-51*, *L-22* (which lays mines off Syltefjord on 6 May), *S-56*, *S-54* and *S-102* are among those operating. Further to the W *L-20* lays mines and *Shch-402* and *Shch-403* disembark agents on Arnöy. *Shch-422* (Capt 3rd Class Vidyaev) misses a convoy with *M361* on 19 Apl; and against the convoys, unsuccessfully attacked by *Shch-422* and *S-101* on 25 Apl and 1 May, DB-3 torpedo aircraft of the 24th Mine and Torpedo Air Regt are deployed with fighter protection from Airacobras of the 95th Fighter Regt, but they obtain no hits. On 29 Apl *S-55* (Capt 3rd Class Sushkin) sinks the steamer *Sturzsee* (708 tons) from a

convoy and on 17 May *S-56* (Capt 3rd Class Shchedrin) sinks the tanker *Eurostadt* (1118 tons) and hits the *Wartheland* (5096 tons) with a torpedo which does not explode. *S-51* makes several unsuccessful attacks. *Shch-422* is damaged on 31 May by depth charges from *UJ1206* and *M343*.

17 Apl-5 May   Black Sea
Operation 'Neptun': attack by the German V Army Corps on the Soviet Myschako bridgehead is halted on 25 Apl after initial successes. During the operation there are continual nightly sorties by the German 1st MTB Flotilla, the 3rd MMS Flotilla and the Italian IV MAS Flotilla against Soviet supply traffic: several small vessels and barges are sunk and pontoons destroyed by torpedoes from *S47*, *S51*, *S102*, *S72* and *S28*. The flotillas have frequent engagements with Soviet patrol cutters and torpedo cutters. Operations are continued after the halting of 'Neptun'. In the night 30 Apl-1 May the Soviet destroyers *Boiki* and *Besposhchadny*, which try in vain to attack *U19* on the way, shell Cape Meganon and Cape Chauda, and *Zheleznyakov* and the patrol ship *Shtorm* shell Anapa. The deployment of Soviet torpedo cutters against the harbour of Anapa is unsuccessful. On 5 May *U9* (Lt Schmidt-Weichert) torpedoes the Soviet tanker *Kreml* (7666 tons).

19-30 Apl   Central Pacific
Mining operations by US submarines: 19 Apl *Scorpion* off Kashima Nada; 20 Apl *Runner* off Hongkong; 21 Apl *Stingray* off Wenchow; and 30 Apl *Snook* off Saddle Island (China).

26 Apl   North Pacific
US TG 8.6 (Rear-Adm McMorris), comprising the cruisers *Detroit*, *Richmond* and *Santa Fe*, and six destroyers, shells Attu.

26 Apl-6 May   North Atlantic
The 'Amsel' group, comprising *U634*, *U223*, *U266*, *U377*, *U383*, *U525*, *U709*, *U448*, *U466* and *U186*, is formed on 26 Apl in the Central North Atlantic to operate against the convoy SC.127 expected in accordance with 'B' Service reports. The convoy consists of 55 ships and EG C.1 with *Itchen* (Lt-Cdr Bridgeman). But, unknown to it, the group is avoided by the convoy. After

an unsuccessful search for ONS.4 the patrol line 'Specht' is formed with *U438, U662, U630, U584, U168, U203, U706, U108, U514, U270, U260, U732, U92, U628, U707, U358, U264, U614, U226* and *U125* to operate against HX.235 (36 ships, EG C.4 with the destroyer *Churchill*). But this convoy passes between 'Specht' and 'Amsel'. It is heard by *U377* on 28 Apl, but the 6th SG, comprising the US escort carrier *Bogue* (Capt Short) and the destroyers *Belknap, Greene, Osmond-Ingram* and *Lea*, which is committed for support, drives off the five 'Amsel' boats deployed against it. On the way *U386* (Lt Kandler) sinks one ship of 1997 tons from a RU convoy on 24 Apl and *U107* (Lt-Cdr Gelhaus) one ship of 12411 tons on 1 May. On 28 Apl the 'Star' group, comprising *U650, U533, U386, U528, U231, U532, U378, U381, U192, U258, U552, U954, U648, U209, U531* and *U413*, takes up a patrol line S of Iceland against the convoy ONS.5 (42 ships, Commodore Capt Brook, EG B.7 consisting of the destroyers *Duncan* (Cdr Gretton), *Vidette*, the frigate *Tay*, the corvettes *Sunflower, Snowflake, Loosestrife, Pink*, and the trawlers *Northern Gem* and *Northern Spray*). The convoy is reported by *U650* (Lt v. Witzendorff). Forced by Catalina flying boats of USN-VP.84 to submerge several times, she brings up *U386* and *U378* by day. In the night 28-29 Apl *U386* is damaged by depth charges from *Sunflower*; *U650* and *U532* are attacked with depth charges after misses on the *Duncan* and *Snow-flake* and *U532* is again attacked by *Tay* during the day of 29 Apl. In an underwater attack by day, *U258* (Lt-Cdr v. Mässenhausen) sinks one ship of 6198 tons and *U528* is damaged by a Catalina of USN-VP.84. The C-in-C Western Approaches sends the destroyer *Oribi* from SC.127 to ONS.5 for support and the 3rd SG with the destroyers *Offa* (Capt McCoy), *Impulsive, Penn* and *Panther* from St John's. On 30 Apl and in the night 30 Apl-1 May the weather deteriorates and in very changeable visibility and with W/T interference, contact is lost after an unsuccessful attack by *U192* (Lt Happe) on 1 May by night. By day ONS.5 has to heave to

in a heavy gale and some of the ships are separated from the convoy. After the 'B' Service has located on 29 Apl the convoy SC.128 (33 ships, EG 40 with eight escorts) the 'Specht' and 'Amsel' groups are formed in a semi-circle on the convoy's course. On the evening of 1 May *U628* sights smoke clouds from the convoy, but the U-boats directed to the scene are diverted by escorts firing flares on the flank of SC.128 and the convoy avoids the U-boats by getting to the W of them. The 'Star' and 'Specht' boats coming from ONS.5 are concentrated in a new patrol line in front of SC.128 for 4 May. It consists of *U438, U630, U662, U584, U168, U514, U270, U260, U732, U628, U707, U358, U264, U226, U125, U378, U192, U648, U533, U531, U954, U413, U381, U231, U552, U209, U650* and *U614*. But the convoy passes to the W and in the process Canso flying boats of No 5 Sqdn RCAF sink *U630* and damage *U430*. In the evening ONS.5, coming from the N, sails into the middle of the 'Fink' group and is reported by *U620* (Lt-Cdr Hasenschar). 'Fink' and the groups stationed further S, 'Amsel 1', comprising *U638, U621, U402, U575, U504* and *U107*, and 'Amsel 2', comprising *U634, U223, U266, U383* and *U377* and two returning boats are at once deployed. As refuelling was impossible on 2 May, 3 May and 4 May because of the heavy sea, Cdr Gretton with *Duncan, Impulsive, Penn* and *Panther* is compelled to leave the convoy owing to fuel shortage. On 4 May *Tay* (Lt-Cdr Sherwood, SOE), *Vidette* (Lt Hart), *Sunflower* (Lt-Cdr Plomer), *Snow-flake* (Lt-Cdr Chesterman), *Loosestrife* (Lt-Cdr Stonehouse), *Offa* (Capt McCoy) and *Oribi* (Lt-Cdr Ingram) are with the convoy which still consists of 31 ships. *Pink* (Lt Atkinson) proceeds in the stern with five stragglers; and another five stragglers and *Northern Spray* try to catch up. *U125* (Lt-Cdr Folkers) sinks one of them (4635 tons) in the afternoon. By day on 4 May five boats, and in the night six boats, establish contact with the convoy itself; some are driven off by *Tay, Offa* and *Oribi* and *U270* is damaged by depth charges from *Vidette*. Of the attacking boats, *U628* sinks one ship of 5081 tons; *U264* (Lt-Cdr Looks) two ships of 10147 tons; and *U358* (Lt-Cdr Manke) two ships of 8076 tons. In addition, one straggler of 4737 tons falls victim to *U952* (Lt Curio). By day on 5 May *U192* encounters the *Pink* group but is located and sunk by 'Hedgehog'. A little later *U707* (Lt Gretschel) sinks one ship of 5565 tons from the group. In the course of the day 15 boats establish contact with the convoy itself; in underwater attacks *U584* (Lt-Cdr Deecke) and *U266* (Lt-Cdr v. Jessen) sink one ship and three ships respectively of 5507 tons and 12012 tons. Disaster seems likely to occur at night when two hours before dusk mist sets in with the result that the attacking U-boats proceed headlong on to the escorts which are able to see with their radar equipment. *Sunflower* locates four boats in succession, of which *U267* (Lt-Cdr Tinschert), after a miss, is damaged by gunfire. *Loosestrife* locates two boats one of which, *U638*, she surprises in an attempted attack and sinks with depth charges. *Vidette* drives three boats off. *Snowflake* locates almost simultaneously three boats of which *U531* (Lt-Cdr Neckel) misses the corvette, is covered with depth charges and forced to surface. Of the ships ordered up for support, *Oribi* comes across *U125* and rams her. But the boat is at first able to get away in a rain squall before she is found by *Snowflake* which, having expended all her depth charges, sinks her by gunfire. *Sunflower* locates and rams *U533* which escapes severely damaged. *Vidette* locates *U531*, which has submerged again, and sinks her with 'Hedgehog'. An attempt by *Offa* to ram a U-boat which she locates just misses and *Loosestrife* makes three more depth charge attacks. Towards morning the 1st SG (Capt Brewer), comprising the sloops *Pelican* and *Sennen* and the frigates *Jed*, *Wear* and *Spey*, arrive, having been sent by C-in-C Western Approaches from St John's for support. *Pelican* locates *U438* by radar, and together with *Jed*, sinks her. *Sennen*, on the way to the separated *Pink* group, encounters *U267* which, although damaged by gunfire, is able to escape. In the morning the operation is broken off by the Commander U-boats. This was the greatest success achieved by Type 271 M radar equipment in a convoy battle.

27-28 Apl   English Channel
The British destroyers *Goathland* and *Albrighton* attack a German convoy 60 nautical miles NNE of Ouessant and sink the submarine-chaser *UJ1402*.

27-29 Apl   Air War/Western Europe
Climax of the British air mining offensive. In the night of 27-28 Apl aircraft of RAF Bomber Command drop 459 mines in the Bay of Biscay and off the Dutch and North German coasts and in the night 28-29 Apl, using 226 aircraft, 568 mines in the same area but with the emphasis on the Baltic. Twenty-three aircraft are shot down. Inter alia, the German passenger ship *Gneisenau* (18160 tons) sinks on British mines in the Gjedser Narrows on 2-3 May.

29 Apl-13 May   Mediterranean
Final battle for Tunis and Bizerta. In last attempts to bring supplies to Africa, the destroyers *Pancaldo* (Cdr* Ferrieri-Caputi†) and *Hermes* (German, Cdr* Rechel), each with 300 men on board, and *Lampo* (Cdr Albanese) with ammunition are repeatedly attacked by Allied aircraft of Cape Bon on 30 Apl. *Pancaldo* and *Lampo* sink and *Hermes* is taken in tow when unable to move under her own steam. In rescue operations fighter bombers sink the Italian *MAS.552* and *Ms.25*. On 30 Apl the British destroyers *Nubian* and *Paladin* sink the transport *Fauna* (575 tons) off the Sicilian coast and on the night 3-4 May, in co-operation with the *Petard*, the transport *Campobasso* (3566 tons) and the torpedo boat *Perseo* (Cdr Marotta) off Kelibia. The transport *Belluno* reaches Tunis with the torpedo boat *Tifone* (Cdr Baccarini) on 4 May but both are bombed there. Liberator bombers sink the transport *Sant' Antonio* (6013 tons) on 4 May off Sicily; and the escorting torpedo boats *Groppo* and *Calliope* return. The last ships to arrive off Cape Bon are the German *KT5*, *KT9* and *KT21* on 7 May, but they are so badly hit by bombs and aircraft fire that they are abandoned and lost on 9 May. After the loss of Bizerta and Tunis on 7 May organised German and Italian resistance ceases on 9 May.

Some individual groups hold out until 13 May. In the Tunisian harbours the *Hermes*, the French destroyer *L'Audacieux*, the French submarines *Calypso*, *Nautilus*, *Turquoise* and *Circe*, 12 minesweepers, 25 freighters, 9 tugs and 23 smaller craft are sunk in some cases by air attacks and in others by scuttling as block ships. Small groups attempt to break through to Sicily and Sardinia in light craft but only a few boats, including several German and Italian motor torpedo boats and MAS boats and the largest ship, the German *KT22*, break through the blockade maintained from 7 May by the British destroyers from Force K in Malta (*Nubian*, *Paladin*, *Petard* and *Jervis*) and Force Q from Bone (*Laforey*, *Loyal*, *Tartar* and *Blyskawica*) and the 'Hunt' destroyers (*Zetland*, *Lamerton*, *Aldenham*, *Hursley*, *Kanaris* (Greek) *Dulverton*, *Lauderdale*, *Wilton* and others). They bring in some 700 prisoners.

29 Apl-27 May   South Atlantic
In operations off the Brazilian coast *U154* (Lt Kusch) hits one tanker of 8917 tons with an unexploded torpedo off Recife on 8 May. *U128* (Lt-Cdr Steinert) is located by land-based D/F when she transmits a W/T message. In the search which is ordered she is reported by US and Brazilian aircraft and damaged on 16 May by two Mariner flying boats of VP.72. She has to scuttle herself when the US destroyers *Moffett* and *Jouett* approach. After replenishing from *U460*, *U154* attacks the convoy BT.14 (12 steamers, escorts: the US destroyer *Borie*, the corvettes *Saucy*, *Tenacity* and *Courage* and the submarine-chaser *PC.592*) on 27 May. She sinks one ship of 8166 tons; and two ships of 15771 tons are torpedoed.

30 Apl-9 May   North Atlantic
The 'Drossel' group, comprising *U456*, *U230*, *U607*, *U436*, *U89*, *U600*, *U406*, *U659*, *U439*, *U447* and *U332*, operates W of Spain. *U332* is sunk by a Sunderland of No 461 Sqdn RAAF on 2 May. On 3 May air reconnaissance locates two convoys; one of them, an LST convoy, is briefly sighted by *U89*. *U659* and *U439*, in attempting to attack, collide and sink. On 5 May *U447* has a gun engagement with an LCT and shoots down a barrage balloon. *U456* fails to get up to a cruiser. On 6 May air reconnaissance sights the convoy SL.128 (48 ships, one sloop and four corvettes). On the morning of 7 May *U607* (Lt-Cdr Mengersen) misses the convoy; *U456* is attacked with depth charges and *U230*, as she keeps contact, twice with aircraft bombs. *U436* and *U89* (Lt-Cdr Lohmann) attack at midday: *U89* sinks one ship of 3803 tons before bad visibility results in loss of contact. From 9 May the group is deployed against HX.237.

1 May   Air War/Western Europe
Forty-eight B 17s of the 8th USAAF bombard St Nazaire.

1 May   North Sea
Naval engagement off Terschelling. Attack by the 31st MTB Flotilla (*MTB624*, *MTB632* and *MTB630*) and the 17th MGB Flotilla (*MGB605*, *MGB606*, *MGB610* and *MGB612*) on four boats of the 12th PB Flotilla (Cdr vom Hoff). *V1241* is sunk.

1-31 May   Pacific
Of the US submarines which arrive in their operational areas in May, *Pogy* (Lt-Cdr Wales) sinks two ships of 3423 tons; *S41* (Lt Hartman) one ship of 10036 tons; *Saury* (Lt-Cdr Dropp) four ships of 19934 tons; and *Sawfish* (Lt-Cdr Sands) one ship of 2921 tons off Japan and the Kuriles. In the Central Pacific *Finback* (Lt-Cdr Tyree) sinks three ships of 13044 tons; *Grayback* (Lt-Cdr Stephan) two ships of 12279 tons and also torpedoes the destroyer *Yugure*; *Permit* (Lt-Cdr Chapple) sinks one ship of 3156 tons and torpedoes one more ship. *Plunger* (Lt-Cdr Bear) sinks two ships of 15428 tons; *Pollack* (Lt-Cdr Llewellen) two ships of 8461 tons; *Scamp* (Lt-Cdr Ebert) one ship of 6853 tons; *Seal* (Lt-Cdr Dodge) one ship of 10215 tons; *Tambor* (Lt-Cdr Ambruster) one ship of 2486 tons; and *Whale* (Lt-Cdr Burrows) one ship of 3580 tons. In the South West Pacific *Gar* (Lt-Cdr Quick) sinks five ships of 8617 tons; *Grayling* (Lt-Cdr Lee) torpedoes one ship; *Grenadier* (Lt-Cdr Carr) sinks two ships of 3242 tons with mines; and *Trout* (Lt-Cdr Clark) sinks two ships of 5866 tons.

1 May-20 July   Mediterranean
Italian defensive mine barrages are laid out. On the Greek Western Coast the Italian minelayers *Barletta* and *Morosini* and the German minelayers *Drache* and *Bulgaria* lay 26 barrages and the Italian minelayers *Vieste* and *Buffoluto* a further one, making a total of 3156 mines. On the Sicilian coast the Italian ships *Vieste* and *Vallelunga* with the barges *G53*, *G56* and *G58* lay 12 barrages of 1036 mines. And on the coast of Sardinia the Italian ships *Durazzo*, *Volturno*, *Buccari*, *Mazara*, *Vieste* and *Buffoluto* and a force comprising the Italian destroyer *Vivaldi* (Capt Camicia) and the German minelayers *Pommern* and *Brandenburg* lay 24 barrages with 4248 mines. In the Aegean the German minelayer *Bulgaria* lays another three barrages with 140 mines and in the Adriatic the Italian *Fasana* one barrage with 137 mines.

2-12 May   North Sea
In the nights 2-3 May and 3-4 May 16 Do 217s of K.G.2 sow air mines in the Humber and Thames Estuaries and the convoy route between Dover and the Thames Estuary respectively. In the night 11-12 May 36 bombers drop mines on the convoy route Humber-Thames. Five aircraft are lost.

2 May-29 June   Mediterranean
In British submarine operations in the Western Mediterranean, sometimes in more than one mission, *Safari* (Cdr Bryant and Lt Lakin) sinks three ships of 2641 tons and one KT ship and also torpedoes one steamer of 3069 tons; *Sportsman* (Lt Gatehouse) sinks two ships of 5110 tons; *Tactician* (Lt-Cdr Collett) one ship of 385 tons; *Shakespeare* (Lt Ainslie) two ships of 241 tons; *Sickle* (Lt Drummond) the submarine-chaser *UJ2213* and *U303*; and *Trident* (Lt Newstead) torpedoes one ship of 11718 tons. In the Central Mediterranean and Southern Adriatic *Unrivalled* (Lt Sprice) sinks two ships of 986 tons; *Unbroken* (Lt Andrew) two ships of 5408 tons; *Unruly* (Lt Fyfe) one ship of 4485 tons and torpedoes one ship of 4000; *Unruffled* (Lt Stevens) one ship of 9895 tons; *United* (Lt Barlow) two ships of 8649 tons; *Ultor* (Lt Hunt) one ship of 137 tons; *Unison* (Lt Daniell) one ship of 2998 tons; *Unshaken* (Lt

Whitton) one ship of 1425 tons; and *Tactician* one ship of 8034 tons and one sailing ship. In the Aegean the British *Parthian* (Lt St John) sinks one sailing ship; the Greek *Katsonis* (Lt Laskos) two ships of 2908 tons and torpedoes one ship; and the British *Taurus* (Lt-Cdr Wingfield) and the Greek *Papanicolis* (Lt-Cdr Roussen) six and two caiques respectively.

4 May-2 June   North Pacific
Operation 'Landcrab': re-conquest of Attu by the 7th US Inf Div (Maj-Gen Brown, from 16 May Maj-Gen Landrum). Overall command: Rear-Adm Kinkaid, TF 16.
On 4 May the invasion fleet sets out from Cold Bay (Alaska). The landing plan for 8 May has to be deferred until 11 May because of the weather.
On 11 May TF 51 (Rear-Adm Rockwell) with four transports and one fast transport, escorted by the destroyers *Dewey*, *Dale*, *Monaghan* and *Aylwin*, two minelayers and four minesweepers, lands 3000 men of the reinforced 17th Inf Regt. They are followed by the other units in the next few days. Fire support is provided by TG 51.1 (Rear-Adm Kingman), comprising the battleships *Nevada*, *Pennsylvania* and *Idaho*, the escort carrier *Nassau* and the destroyers *Phelps*, *Farragut*, *Hull*, *MacDonough*, *Meade*, *Edwards*, *Abner Read* and *Ammen*. Southern covering force: TG 16.6 (Rear-Adm McMorris), consisting of the cruisers *Detroit*, *Raleigh*, *Richmond* and *Santa Fe* and the destroyers *Bancroft*, *Caldwell*, *Coghlan*, *Frazier* and *Gansevoort*. Northern covering force: Rear-Adm Giffen with the cruisers *Wichita*, *San Francisco* and *Louisville* and the destroyers *Balch*, *Hughes*, *Mustin* and *Morris*. *Narwhal* and *Nautilus* act as marker submarines. By 2 June a total of 12000 men are landed. By 30 May the resistance of the approximately 2600 Japanese defenders (Col Yamazaki) is broken. The Japanese plan to evacuate the defenders with the 5th Fleet is abandoned on 29 May. 2379 Japanese are killed and 28 taken prisoner. The remainder are evacuated by submarines. In support operations the Japanese submarine *I-31* twice narrowly misses the *Pennsylvania* and is afterwards

missing; *I-35* unsuccessfully attacks the *Santa Fe*. On the US side there are 600 dead and 1200 wounded.

5-8 May   English Channel

Three mining operations in the Channel by the German 2nd TB Flotilla (Cdr Erdmann) with *T23*, *T2*, *T5*, *T18* and *T22*. Six boats of the 5th MTB Flotilla lay 32 mines S of Selsey Bill.

6 May-8 June   Baltic

First attempt by Soviet submarines to break out with support from the Soviet Naval Air Force and strong forces of minesweepers and torpedo cutters. On 7 May *Shch-303* (Capt 3rd Class Travkin) sets out from Kronstadt and on 11 May from Lavansaari, breaks through the 'Seeigel' barrage and tries in vain from 18 May to 24 May to get through the net barrage. On the return the boat is sighted by an Ar 196 of S.A.Gr. 127 and is several times pursued by the naval ferry barges of the 24th Landing Flotilla ordered to search between the mine barrages. But she reaches Lavansaari again on 8 June through Narva Bay. Of the boats which set off on 19 May and 20 May *Shch-408* (Lt-Cdr Kuzmin) is damaged by six Finnish VMV boats and the minelayer *Riilahti* off the net barrage on 22 May, is again attacked on 23 May and 24 May by aircraft and by depth charges from the minelayer *Ruotsinsalmi*. She is destroyed on 26 May by KFKs of the German 31st MS Flotilla. *Shch-406* (Capt 3rd Class Osipov) is several times pursued on 27 May, 28 May and 29 May by the 24th Landing Flotilla and is sunk on 1 June near Steinskar by naval ferry barges of 24th Landing Flotilla after bombs have been dropped by an Ar 196.

7-13 May   South Pacific

US mining operations to prevent Japanese supplies reaching New Georgia. Whilst US TF 68 (Rear-Adm Ainsworth), consisting of the cruisers *Honolulu*, *Nashville* and *St Louis* and the destroyers *O'Bannon*, *Strong*, *Chevalier* and *Taylor*, makes a sortie into Vella Gulf to divert the Japanese, a minelaying force, comprising the destroyers *Radford*, *Preble*, *Gamble* and *Breese*, lays a barrage in Blackett Strait, on which a Japanese transport destroyer force runs on 8 May and loses *Oyashio*, *Kagero* and *Kuroshio*. Only *Michishio* escapes with heavy damage from air attacks after rescuing survivors. In a second operation in the night 12-13 May Rear-Adm Ainsworth shells Vila with the cruisers *Helena*, *Honolulu* and *Nashville* and the destroyers *O'Bannon*, *Strong*, *Chevalier*, *Taylor* and *Radford*; the cruiser *St Louis* with the destroyers *Jenkins* and *Fletcher* shells Munda; and *Preble*, *Gamble* and *Breese* lay a mine barrage off Kula Gulf which is cleared by the Japanese on the following day.

8-15 May   North Atlantic

From the 'Amsel 1 and 2' boats which did not participate in the ONS.5 operation the 'Rhein' group is formed to operate against HX.237, expected on the basis of a 'B' Service report. The group consists of *U709*, *U569*, *U525*, *U468*, *U448*, *U752*, *U466*, *U454*, *U359*, *U186*, *U403* and *U103*. The 'B' Service reports the convoy's evasive move to the S. At the Southern end of 'Rhein' *U359* (Lt Förster) locates HX. 237 on 9 May (46 ships, EG C.2 with the destroyer *Broadway* (Capt Chevasse), seven more escorts and one rescue tug), but she is immediately located by HF/DF and forced under water. A patrol line formed in front of the convoy is broken through after a Swordfish from the *Biter*, which reinforces EG C.2 with the 5th SG, has forced *U454*, which is barring the way, under water. *U403* again establishes contact on 10 May when shadowing the rescue tug which has fallen behind. She is able to drive off a Swordfish with AA fire but is forced to submerge by one of the three destroyers of the 5th SG. Because the boats can no longer get ahead, the operation is continued only with the boats of the 'Drossel' group coming from the E—*U456*, *U230*, *U607*, *U436*, *U89*, *U600*, *U221* and *U753*. The 'Rhein' group forms with the 'Elbe' group (made up of the ONS.5 boats) the groups 'Elbe 1' (*U634*, *U575*, *U584*, *U650*, *U752*, *U709*, *U569*, *U231*, *U525*, *U514*, *U468* and *U267*) and 'Elbe 2' (*U103*, *U621*, *U448*, *U466*, *U223*, *U454*, *U504*, *U402*, *U377*, *U359*, *U107*, *U383* and *U186*) to operate against the evasive move to the S made by SC.129 and likewise detected by the 'B' Service.

Thanks to a position decoded by the 'B' Service, *U436* (Cdr Seibicke) finds convoy HX.237 on evening of 11 May. *U403* (Lt-Cdr Clausen) and *U456* (Lt-Cdr Teichert) sink one straggler of 7138 tons and *U753* (Cdr v. Mannstein) misses the convoy. After dawn on 12 May the U-boats try to keep off the Swordfish aircraft from the *Biter* with their AA fire. *U230* (Lt-Cdr Siegmann) shoots one down but the U-boats are forced to submerge by the escorts summoned to the scene. *U89* is sunk by the *Broadway* directed by a Swordfish and the frigate *Lagan*. *U456*, after being badly damaged by a Liberator of No 120 Sqdn RAF, is sunk by the destroyer *Pathfinder* led to the spot by a Swordfish. *U628* (Lt-Cdr Hasenschar), a returning boat, keeps contact until the morning of 13 May while from the rear *U221* (Lt Trojer) and *U603* (Lt Baltz) each sink a straggler of 9432 tons and 4819 tons respectively. On the morning of 13 May Sunderland flying boats of No 423 Sqdn RCAF provide additional air escort and bring up the frigate *Lagan* and the corvette *Drumheller* to *U753*, which is sunk. With the convoy the corvettes *Chambly* and *Morden* drive off the other U-boats. The Commander U-boats has to break off the operation as hopeless. At the same time the C-in-C Western Approaches orders the 5th SG to proceed at full speed to the SC.129, which has been reported by *U504* (Lt Luis) in the evening of 11 May. While the escort drives off the contact-keeper located by HF/DF, *U402* (Cdr Frhr v. Forstner) attacks before dark the SC.129 (26 ships, EG B.2 with *Hesperus* (Cdr Macintyre) and eight other escorts) and sinks two ships of 7627 tons in an underwater attack. In the night 11-12 May *U383* and *U359* are driven off by the destroyer *Whitehall* and the corvette *Clematis*. *Hesperus* fights a dramatic duel with *U223* (Lt-Cdr Wächter) which is forced to surface by depth charges, misses the destroyer with five torpedoes but, in spite of depth charges designed to explode just beneath the surface, gunfire and a cautiously light ramming, does not sink and is able to escape. On the morning of 12 May *Hesperus* sinks the contact-keeper *U186*, located by HF/DF, but in the

course of the day 11 other boats establish contact and are located by HF/DF. By dusk they are all repulsed by *Hesperus*, *Whitehall* and the corvettes *Sweetbriar*, *Clematis* and *Heather* and thrown off by a sharp change of course. Early on 13 May air escort is provided by Swordfish aircraft from the *Biter* which has, come up meantime. In the afternoon Liberators from No 86 Sqdn RAF also arrive. On the following day they sink *U266* to the rear of the convoy. The operation is broken off. On the return journey *U607* (Lt-Cdr Mengersen) sinks a ship of 5589 tons.

11-23 May North Atlantic
On 11 May and 12 May the U-boat groups 'Isar' (*U304*, *U645*, *U952*, *U418*), 'Lech' (*U209*, *U202*, *U664*, *U91*) and 'Inn' (*U258*, *U381*, *U954*, *U92*) are formed SE of Cape Farewell. Of the boats proceeding to other proposed groups, *U640* (Lt Nagel) sights in the night 11-12 May the convoy ONS.7 (40 ships, EG B.5 with the frigate *Swale*, five other escorts and the rescue ship *Copeland*). Although repeatedly driven off, the boat relentlessly keeps contact until 13 May, so that *U760* *U636*, *U340*, *U731* and *U657* can be deployed as the 'Iller' group. Then *U640* is bombed by a Catalina of USN-VP.84 and is lost.
To restore the lost contact, the Commander U-boats forms from 15-16 May the groups 'Donau 1' (*U657*, *U760*, *U636*, *U340*, *U731*, *U304*, *U645*, *U952*, *U418*, *U258*, *U381*) and 'Donau 2' (*U954*, *U92*, *U209*, *U202*, *U664*, *U91*, *U707*, *U413*, *U952*, *U264*, *U378*, *U218*) from the above-named groups and from the 'Nahe' group setting out after replenishment. Convoy ONS.7 goes to the north-end of the formation. in the night 16-17 May: *U657* (Lt-Cdr Göllnitz) attacks and sinks one ship of 5196 tons but is then herself sunk by the *Swale*. On 17 May and 19 May the *U646* and *U273*, which are proceeding to their positions fall victims to reconnaissance Hudson bombers of No 269 Sqdn RAF S of Iceland. As a result of 'B' Service reports, on 17 May and 18 May the evasive movements of the convoys HX.238 and SC.130 are established and, in consequence, the formation is moved S and extended by the

newly-formed 'Oder' group in the S, consisting of *U221, U666, U558, U752, U336, U642, U603* and *U228*. But HX.238 (45 ships, EG C.3 with *Skeena*) passes the patrol line. The following convoy SC.130 (38 ships, Commodore Capt Forsythe, EG B.7 (Cdr Gretton) with the destroyers *Duncan, Vidette*, the frigate *Tay*, the corvettes *Snowflake, Sunflower, Pink, Loosestrife* and *Kitchener* (Canadian, attached until 19 May)), is reported in the night 18-19 May by *U304* (Lt Koch), which is able to bring up *U645* and *U952*. But contact is lost in the morning as the result of a sharp change in course. Air escort provided by Liberators of No 120 Sqdn RAF frustrates the efforts of the U-boats. Liberator T/120 sinks *U954* in its first approach and forces five other boats under water, of which *U952* is badly damaged by depth charges from the *Tay*. *U381* (Lt-Cdr Count von Pückler and Limburg), which is preparing an underwater attack, is located by *Snowflake* and sunk with the help of *Duncan* as the ships cover the area several times with depth charges. Two other boats escape from the *Pink* and *Sunflower* on the surface. At mid-day the 1st SG with the frigates *Wear, Jed, Spey* and the sloop *Sennen* comes up from the rear and sights two U-boats. One of them, *U209* (Lt-Cdr Brodda) fires torpedoes as she submerges but is sunk by *Sennen* and *Jed* with 'Hedgehogs'. *Duncan* frustrates an attack by *U707* which is damaged. The second Liberator, P/120, forces, partly in co-operation with *Vidette*, six boats under water and O/120 and Y/120 another four and two boats respectively, three of which are bombed. Before dusk *Jed* and *Spey* drive off the last contact-keeper: only *U92* (Lt-Cdr Oelrich) makes an unsuccessful attack. In the morning the operation is broken off and a Liberator sinks *U258*.

From the remaining boats *U552, U264, U378, U607, U221, U666, U752, U558, U336, U650, U642, U603, U228, U575, U621, U441, U305, U569, U468, U231* and *U218*, the Commander U-boats forms the 'Mosel' group on 19 May to operate against HX.239 located by the 'B'

Service (42 ships, EG B.3 (Cdr Evans) with the destroyers *Keppel* and *Escapade*, the frigate *Towy*, the corvettes *Orchis, Narcissus* and the French *Roselys, Lobélia* and *Renoncule*). Once again an evasive movement is ordered and is detected by the 'B' Service and the 'Mosel' group can be moved to the S. On the evening of 21 May ON.184 (39 ships, EG C.1 with the frigate *Itchen*) reaches the patrol line from the E. It is supported by the 6th SG (Capt Short) with the US escort carrier *Bogue* and the destroyers *Belknap, Greene, Osmond-Ingram* and *George E. Badger*. Avenger bombers from the *Bogue* damage *U231* and the destroyers *Osmond-Ingram* and *St Laurent* force two other boats under water. ON.184 passes through the gap. On 22 May *U468* (Lt Schamong) beats off an Avenger with AA fire. Only at midday does a report about the convoy come through from *U305* (Lt-Cdr Bahr). The southerly 'Mosel' boats are deployed but *U305* is bombed three times by Avengers and damaged. In the afternoon two Avengers sink *U569*. Simultaneously *U218* (Lt-Cdr Becker) hears the convoy HX.239 against which the remaining 'Mosel' boats and the 'Donau' boats coming from SC.130 are deployed. But this convoy, too, has been joined by a carrier force, the 4th SG with the *Archer* and the destroyers *Milne, Matchless, Eclipse* and *Fury* under Capt Scott-Moncrieff. A Swordfish from the *Archer* is beaten off by *U468* and the boat escapes, as does *U218*, from the destroyers sent to attack them. *U664* and *U413* report the convoy on 23 May but no boat attacks. *U752* (Lt-Cdr Schroeter) is hit, in submerging, by a Swordfish armed with rockets. This is the first successful use of rockets in this role. She is then able to hold off three Swordfish and one Martlet fighter with her 2 cm quadruple gun, but has to scuttle herself when approached by the destroyers *Keppel* and *Escapade*. Both convoys have passed the U-boat concentration without loss.

11 May-26 Aug Atlantic/Indian Ocean
Of the Italian submarines which set out as transports from Bordeaux *Tazzoli* and *Barbarigo* are lost in the Bay of Biscay. *Cappellini* (11 May-9 July),

Giuliani (16 May-17 June) and *Torelli* (18 June-26 Aug), which are met by the Italian colonial sloop *Eritrea*, reach Sabang and Singapore.

13 May   Mediterranean
107 US B 17 bombers drop 273 tons of bombs on the harbour installations at Cagliari.

13-14 May   English Channel
The German mine barrage 'S.W.12' (Operation 'Stemmbogen') is laid out in the Southern part of the North Sea, W of Hook of Holland, by the 1st and 7th MS Flotillas and the 9th MMS Flotilla. On the return the British *MTB234, MTB244, MTB241* and *MTB 232* attack the German force; in the engagement the leading German boat *M8* sinks after two torpedo hits.

13 May-8 June   Black Sea
In attacks on German traffic the Soviet torpedo cutters *TKA-115* and *TKA-125* fire torpedoes into the harbour of Anapa in the night 12-13 May. On the following night the harbour is shelled by the flotilla leader *Kharkov* and by *Boiki*. During this action there is an unsuccessful engagement with the German motor torpedo boats *S51, S26*, and *S49*. In the night 20-21 May *Kharkov* shells Feodosia and the destroyer *Besposhchadny* Alushta. Soviet aircraft lay, in an increasing scale, air mines of British make in the Kerch Strait, which cause losses.
In German attacks on Soviet supply traffic, *S72* and *S49* torpedo two small craft on 20 May off Sochi; *U49* and *U18* have no success off Sukhumi and Poti in face of strong defence. On 22 May Ju 87s of I Fl. K. attack several convoys off Gelendzhik. The patrol cutter *SKA-041* is sunk from a convoy escorted by the minesweepers *T-407/ Mina* and *T-409/Garpun*. The patrol ships *Shtorm* and *Shkval* take in tow the damaged transport *Internatsional*.

14-29 May   Air War Germany/ Western Europe
The 8th USAAF carries out daylight attacks on harbours: on 14 May with 108 Fortresses and 17 Liberators on Kiel (250 tons), in which the U-boats *U235, U236* and *U237*, being completed in the Germania yards, are sunk (later raised and repaired); on 15 May with 59 Fortresses on Emden; on 17 May with 119 Fortresses on the harbour installations of Lorient (250 tons) and with 35 Liberators on the docks of Bordeaux. (90 tons); on 19 May with a strong force on the dockyards at Kiel; on 21 May with many Fortresses on Wilhelmshaven (200 tons). On 29 May Fortresses and Liberators attack the U-boat bases at St Nazaire and La Pallice with 300 tons of bombs.

17 May   Spain
In a large fire in the Spanish naval base of El Ferrol the light cruisers *Miguel de Cervantes, Galicia* and *Mendes Nuñez* and the destroyers *Alsedo* and *Lazaga* are, in part, severely damaged.

20 May   Atlantic
Formation of the US 10th Fleet under direct command of the CNO, Adm King, to conduct and co-ordinate the battle against U-boats in the Atlantic.

23 May-12 June   English Channel
The German 2nd MTB Flotilla (Cdr Feldt), the 4th (Lt-Cdr Lützow), the 5th (Lt-Cdr Klug) and the 6th (Lt-Cdr Obermaier) with *S67, S83, S62, S94, S89, S98; S63, S110, S122, S117; S90, S65, S116, S82, S112, S81, S121; S79, S114, S76* and *S91* carry out mining operations off the British South Coast from Cherbourg and Peter Port: on 23-24 May between the Isle of Wight and Portland; on 28-29 May, on 30-31 May, on 5-6 June and on 11-12 June in Lyme Bay; and on 6-7 June off Start Point. In 77 sorties the boats lay 321 mines and 84 barrage protection floats.

24 May-5 June   North Atlantic
On 24 May the Commander U-boats decides, as a result of the heavy losses in the last convoy operations and the unsuccessful attacks made by the 'Donau' and 'Mosel' groups, to stop temporarily the battle against convoys in the North Atlantic until the situation has been clarified and new weapons become available. The boats with adequate fuel supplies are moved S to the USA/Gibraltar route and those with limited fuel supplies (*U264, U636, U731, U418, U645, U304, U664, U202, U91, U413, U378, U552, U650, U621* and *U575*) are distributed widely over the North Atlantic to simulate by their W/T traffic the presence of stronger groups.

D

Turning Point in the Battle of the Atlantic

The C-in-C Western Approaches deploys the 2nd SG (Capt Walker), comprising the sloops *Starling, Wren, Woodpecker, Cygnet, Wild Goose* and *Kite*, to make it possible for the convoys ONS.8 (52 ships, EG C.4 with the destroyer *Churchill*) from 22 May to 25 May and HX.240 (56 ships, EG C.5 with the destroyer *Ottawa*) from 27 May to 30 May to break through the U-boat groups suspected on the basis of the W/T picture. But no U-boat is found. Only the Liberator E/120 sinks *U304* near HX.240. *Starling* finds *U202* (Lt-Cdr Poser) on her third trip on 1 June and sinks her after a fifteen-hour hunt.

24 May-22 July   Western Atlantic

U190 has no success on the American East Coast. *U521* (Lt-Cdr Bargsten) is sunk on 2 June by the submarine-chaser *PC565* belonging to the escort of a NG convoy. Only *U66* (Lt-Cdr Markworth) sinks two tankers of 20368 tons and torpedoes a third of 10172 tons. One ship of 2937 tons sinks and one ship of 7176 tons is damaged on a mine barrage laid by *U119* (Cdr v. Kameke) off Halifax on 1 June.

25-28 May   Mediterranean

In attacks by American bombers on Messina on 25 May the Italian torpedo boat *Groppo* sinks. On 28 May the Italian torpedo boats *Angelo Bassini* and *Antares* and the corvette *F.R.52* sink in Livorno.

26 May-21 June   North Pacific

In up to three missions the Japanese submarines *I-7, I-2, I-5, I-6, I-9, I-21, I-24, I-35, I-168, I-169, I-171, I-155* and *I-157* evacuate, in all, 820 troops from Kiska to Paramushiro. In the course of the operations *I-24* is sunk on 10 June by the submarine-chaser *PC487*, *I-9* on 13 June by the destroyer *Frazier* and *I-7* on 22 June by the destroyer *Monaghan*. *I-2* and *I-157* are damaged when they go aground in the fog and *I-155* by heavy seas.

28-29 May   English Channel

In a mining operation by the British 50th and 52nd ML Flotillas and by *MTB219* and *MTB221* the covering force has an engagement near the West Dyck Bank with four patrol boats of the 13th and 14th PB Flotillas. *MGB110* sinks, *MGB108* and *MGB118* are damaged. Only *MGB116* is unhit. An attack by the British *MTB632, MTB 629, MTB628* and *MTB607* fails.

31 May   General Situation

Grand Admiral Dönitz transfers the responsibility for all naval armaments to the Armaments Minister, Speer.

31 May-13 June   Mediterranean

Operation 'Corkscrew': British attack on Pantelleria. The cruiser *Orion* (Capt Menzies), which carried out a shelling on 12-13 May, bombards the island on 31 May with the destroyers *Petard* and *Troubridge*. On 1 June the cruiser *Penelope* (Capt Belben) repeats the shelling with the destroyers *Paladin* and *Petard*, when *Penelope* is hit by the Italian coastal battery. In a sortie to the coast near Cape Spartivento the destroyers *Jervis* and *Vasilissa Olga* (Greek) sink two Italian steamers with the torpedo boat *Castore*. In the night 2-3 June *Orion, Paladin* and *Troubridge* shell Pantelleria and on 3 June the destroyers *Ilex* and *Isis*, followed on 5 June and 8 June by the cruiser *Newfoundland*. After the shellings and the dropping of 6200 tons of bombs by allied aircraft in 5285 sorties, a landing force (Rear-Adm McGrigor) with the 1st British Div on board appears off the island in the night 10-11 June with the headquarters ship *Largs*, the destroyers *Paladin* and *Petard* and the gunboat *Aphis*. Covering force: the British cruisers *Aurora* (Allied C-in-C Gen Eisenhower on board), *Newfoundland* (Rear-Adm Harcourt), *Orion, Penelope* and *Euryalus*, the destroyers *Laforey, Lookout, Loyal, Jervis, Tartar, Nubian, Troubridge* and *Whaddon* and eight MTBs. The Italian Rear-Adm Pavesi surrenders the island fortress of Pantelleria without further fighting on 11 June. On 12 June the island of Lampedusa also capitulates after a night shelling by *Orion, Penelope* and *Newfoundland*. Linosa surrenders to the destroyer *Nubian* on 13 June and Lampione on 14 June.

1-30 June   Pacific

Of the US submarines arriving in their operational areas in June, *Gunnell* (Lt-Cdr McCain) sinks two ships of 13397 tons; *Harder* (Lt-Cdr Dealy) two ships of 8378 tons; *Jack* (Lt-Cdr Dykers) three ships of 16551 tons; *Runner* (Lt-Cdr Bourland) two ships of 4969 tons; *S29* two ships of 5258 tons; *S30* (Lt-Cdr Stevenson) and *Sailfish* (Lt-Cdr Moore) two ships of 6908 tons; *Sculpin* (Lt-Cdr Chappell) two ships of 214 tons; *Sea Devil* (Lt-Cdr McGivern) one ship of 2211 tons; and *Seawolf* (Lt-Cdr Gross) one ship of 4739 tons; *Runner* is lost; and *Trigger* (Lt-Cdr Benson) sinks one ship of 2182 tons— all off the Kuriles and Japan. In the Central Pacific *Dace* (Lt-Cdr McMahon) sinks one ship of 5086 tons; *Greenling* (Lt-Cdr Grant) torpedoes one ship; *Growler* (Lt-Cdr Schade) sinks one ship of 5196 tons; *Guardfish* (Lt-Cdr Ward) one ship of 201 tons; *Sargo* (Lt-Cdr Carmick) one ship of 5226 tons; *Silversides* (Lt-Cdr Burlingame) one ship of 5256 tons; and *Tunny* one ship of 1964 tons. In the South West Pacific *Tautog* (Lt-Cdr Sieglaff) sinks one ship of 5447 tons.

1 June-15 July   Central Atlantic
The U-boats withdrawn from the North Atlantic, *U92*, *U558*, *U953*, *U951*, *U435*, *U666*, *U336*, *U232*, *U642*, *U221*, *U603*, *U228*, *U641*, *U569*, *U608*, *U211* and *U217*, are formed into the 'Trutz' group from 1 June SW of the Azores to operate against the convoy GUS.7A which set out from Gibraltar on 23 May. But the convoy locates the patrol line with HF/DF and avoids it by going S. On 4 June aircraft of the US Support Group (Capt Short), comprising the escort carrier *Bogue* and *Clemson, George E. Badger, Greene* and *Osmond-Ingram*, force *U228, U641* and *U603* to submerge. *U641* shoots down one aircraft. *U217* is sunk on 5 June by two aircraft from the *Bogue*. While *U488* (Lt Bartke) replenishes 14 boats of the 'Trutz' group without incident from 7 June to 13 June, the *Bogue* Group passes to the S with the convoy UGS.9 in an easterly direction. The outward-bound *U758* (Lt-Cdr Manseck) is able to hold off eight carrier aircraft with the 2 cm quadruple gun, used for the first time successfully, and to inflict considerable damage on some of them. But after meeting the U-tanker, *U118*, the latter is sunk on 12 June by eight aircraft from the *Bogue*. From 16 June

the replenished 'Trutz' boats form three overlapping patrol lines in the Central Atlantic: 1: (*U608, U228, U558, U642; 2: U641, U603, U666, U951, U953, U232, U336, U135;* and 3: *U221, U211, U435, U193* to operate against the expected convoy GUS.8 (Escort: TF 66 with the US Coastguard cutters *Bibb* and *Ingham*, the US destroyers *Doyle, Hamilton, Upshur, Greer,* the US minesweepers *Pioneer, Threat, Portent,* the French destroyer *Le Malin* and the sloops *La Gracieuse* and *Cdt Delage*; Support Group (Capt Isbell), comprising the escort carrier *Card*, the destroyers *Herbert, Du Pont* and *Dickerson*). The convoy avoids the patrol line, as does the UGS.10 coming from the W (70 ships, 7 destroyers, two minesweepers, Support Group (Capt Fick) comprising the escort carrier *Santee* and the destroyers *Overton, MacLeish* and *Bainbridge*). The outward-bound *U572* (Lt Kummetat) to the S is over-run and sinks the French naval tanker *Lot* (4220 tons). Whilst *U488* and *U530*, *U536, U170* and *U535*, which are used as temporary tankers, replenish ten medium boats and the 'Trutz' group searches further to the E, the convoy GUS.8A (43 ships, the US Coastguard cutters *Campbell, Spencer, Duane* and five destroyers) also passes to the S. From 29 June *U221* and *U558* go to Lisbon, *U193* and *U135* to the Canaries, the others form from 2 July the group 'Geier 1' (*U608, U633, U641* and *U228*), 'Geier 2' (*U211, U951, U953,* and *U435*) and 'Geier 3' (*U232, U642* and *U336*): they proceed slowly from the area S of the Azores in the direction of Portugal. As they do so, from 7 July to 9 July *U951* and *U232* are sunk by Liberators of USAAF—A/S-Sqdn 1 and 2 and *U435* by a Wellington of No 179 Sqdn RAF. *U193* is damaged by bombs near the Canaries. *U135* (Lt Luther) torpedoes on 15 July one ship of 4762 tons from the convoy OS.51 but is then sunk by the sloop *Rochester* and the corvettes *Balsam* and *Mignonette* of the 39th EG.

1 June-20 Sept   Black Sea
German supply convoys 'Hagen 1-91' with up to 13 naval ferry barges of the 1st, 3rd and 5th Landing Flotillas as well as tugs and lighters. From June there

are also 'Bansin' convoys from Feodosia to Anapa. There is also considerable ferry traffic in the Kerch Strait to supply the German 17th Army in the Kuban bridgehead. Frequent air attacks against these convoys do little damage. Submarine attacks on the flat-bottomed naval ferry barges made by *A-3*, *L-4*, *S-31*, *Shch-215*, *M-112*, *M-117*, *M-111* and other boats are unsuccessful. Only *M-111* (Capt 3rd Class Josseliani) sinks the tugs and lighters *Dunarea* (505 tons, 18 July) and *Hainburg* (28 Aug). Torpedo cutters have no success.

In operations with several boats against the Constanza-Sevastopol route *D-4* on 1 June misses the Italian tanker *Celeno* escorted by the Rumanian destroyer *Marasesti*, two German motor minesweepers and the submarine-chaser *Schiff 19*. On 7 July *S-33*, *Shch-201* and *Shch-203* operate against a convoy consisting of the steamers *Ardeal* and *Varna*, escorted by the Rumanian destroyers *Maresti* and *Marasesti* and the gunboats *Stihi* and *Ghigulescu*. *Shch-201* misses the convoy and *Marasesti* reports one submarine sunk by depth charges (*M-31*). W of the Crimea *D-4* (Lt-Cdr Gremyako) sinks on 11 Aug the steamer *Boj Feddersen* (6689 tons), damaged by aircraft, and on 20 Aug the steamer *Varna* (2141 tons). Of the Italian midget submarines deployed in hunting submarines, *CB.4* (Sub-Lt Sibille) reports one submarine (*Shch-207*) sunk here on 28 Aug.

Soviet submarine groups are deployed against German traffic from the Bosphorus on the basis of agents' reports. Thus, at the end of July and beginning of Aug, *L-4*, *Shch-216*, *M-117* and later *M-35* are deployed against the expected tanker *Firuz* (7327 tons). She is torpedoed on 6 Aug by *Shch-216* (Capt 3rd Class Karbovski) after being met by German motor minesweepers and the submarine-chaser *Xanten*. In addition, the small Turkish ships *Hudayi Bahri*, *Tayyari* and *Gurpinar* are sunk. At the end of Aug a new group operates off the Bosphorus and sinks the Turkish ships *Yilmaz* and *Verviske*. Likewise on 30 Aug *Shch-215* (Capt 3rd Class Greshilov) sinks the expected tanker *Thisbé* (1782 tons) after being met by

two Rumanian destroyers and two German submarine-chasers.

In the night 20-21 Aug the Soviet patrol patrol ships *Shtorm* and *Shkval* with four SKA patrol cutters shell Anapa airfield with rockets.

2-8 June   Mediterranean
The largest convoy of the war so far: on 2 June the convoys UGS.8A, consisting of 58 ships, and KMS.15, consisting of 71 ships, join up off Gibraltar and with 19 escort vessels proceeds via Oran and Algiers (where 86 ships are detached) to Malta and Tripoli.

4 June   Norway
The Norwegian *MTB620* and *MTB626* sink the steamer *Altenfels* (8132 tons) sailing in the company of *M468* in Korsfjord.

4-6 June   English Channel
Two mining operations by the German 5th TB Flotilla (Cdr Koppenhagen), comprising *T22*, *Möwe*, *Falke*, *Greif* and *Kondor*.

5 June   South Pacific
Air battle over Russell Island. The Japanese attack with 81 aircraft from Rabaul and lose 24 machines in engagements with 101 US aircraft. US losses: seven aircraft.

5 June-11 Aug   South Atlantic
In operations in Brazilian waters *U513* (Lt-Cdr Guggenberger) sinks four ships of 17151 tons and torpedoes one ship of 6003 tons; *U199* (Lt-Cdr Kraus) sinks one ship of 4161 tons and one sailing ship; *U172* (Lt-Cdr Emmermann) four ships of 22946 tons; *U185* (Lt-Cdr Maus) attacks on 7 July the convoy BT.18 (20 steamers, three Brazilian corvettes and one submarine-chaser) and sinks three ships of 21413 tons and torpedoes one ship of 6840 tons. Later she sinks two independents of 15368 tons. *U513* falls victim on 19 July, *U558* on 22-23 July, *U591* on 30 July and *U199* on 31 July to an air offensive by Mariners of VP.74, Liberators of VB.107 and Venturas of VB.127, as well as Brazilian aircraft. *U604* is bombed on 30 July by a Ventura of VB.129 and damaged by a Liberator on 3 Aug. On 11 Aug this aircraft is shot down by *U185* when taking over the crew of *U604*. *U604* is scuttled.

5 June-14 Aug   Western Atlantic
E of the Caribbean *U572* (Lt Kummetat)

sinks two sailing ships of 290 tons. *U590* (Lt Krüer) sinks one ship of 5228 tons. On 8 July *U510* (Lt Eick) attacks the convoy TJ.1 (20 ships, and the US destroyer *Somers*, four US and one Brazilian submarine-chasers) and sinks two ships of 17224 tons and later one more ship of 1641 tons. *U590* damages a Catalina of VP.94, deployed to escort TJ.1, with her AA fire, but is sunk by a second Catalina. On 21 July a Catalina with convoy TF.2 (18 steamers) sinks *U662*. On 23 July *U466* is bombed by a Liberator and on 3 Aug a Mariner of VP.205 sinks *U572*. *U67*, *U653*, *U415*, *U406* and *U466* return without successes. In operations in the Caribbean *U759* (Lt Friedrich) sinks two ships of 12764 tons and one sailing ship. In the area of the Windward Passage *U159* and *U759* are sunk on 15 July and 26 July by Mariner flying-boats of VP.32. *U134* (Lt-Cdr Brosin) shoots down the Blimp *K74* N of Cuba on 18 July. *U732* (Lt Carlsen) misses the convoy NG.376 and is attacked by depth charges from the corvette *Brisk*. *U615* (Lt-Cdr Kapitzky) sinks in the Caribbean one ship of 3177 tons and shoots down one Mariner flying boat from USN-VP.205. On 6 Aug the boat wards off six aircraft two of which are badly hit by AA fire; but, unable to dive, she has to scuttle herself on the approach of the US destroyer *Walker*. *U634* and *U359* are unsuccessful.

7 June-12 July   North Atlantic
U592, *U669*, *U341*, *U271*, *U334*, *U388*, *U420* and *U667* cruise in the North Atlantic to simulate stronger U-boat formations by transmitting W/T messages and brief signals. On 14 June *U334* is located by the 1st SG and sunk by the frigate *Jed* and the sloop *Pelican*. *U388* falls victim to a Catalina of USN-VP.84 from Iceland (the first use of the homing A/S torpedo 'Fido'). which also damages *U420*.

8 June   Japan
The Japanese battleship *Mutsu* sinks off Hiroshima after an internal explosion.

11-13 June   Air War/Germany
Bombers of the 8th USAAF carry out daylight attacks on harbour installations at Wilhelmshaven and Kiel on 11 June and 13 June respectively.

12 June-28 July   Arctic
In attacks by German FW 190 fighter bombers of J.G.5 on shipping targets in the Kola Inlet and off the Fisherman's Peninsula and, in particular, in attacks by Soviet DB-3, Hampden and Boston torpedo bombers of the 5th Mining and Torpedo Air Div on German convoys off the coasts of the Varanger Peninsula there are continual heavy air engagements between the escort fighters of the German J.G.5 and Soviet fighters and the objects of their protection. These lead to losses on both sides, but ship sinkings are rare exceptions. Off the Polar coast among the Soviet submarines to operate are *M-105*, *M-106*, *Shch-422*, *S-101*, *S-51*, *S-54*, *Shch-403*, *S-56*, *L-15* (mining operations), *L-22*, *S-55* and *K-21*. Of them *S-101* (Capt 2nd Class Egorov) makes five, *S-51* (Capt 2nd Class Kucherenko) and *M-105* (Lt-Cdr Khrulev) two each and *S-54* (Capt 3rd Class Bratishko) one, attack on convoys escorted by boats of the 61st PB Flotilla and the 12th SC Flotilla. *M-106* is sunk on 5 July near Vardö with depth charges and ramming by *UJ1206* and *UJ1217*. *Shch-422* is lost on one of the flanking mine barrages laid out by the German minelayers *Brummer*, *Ostmark*, *Roland* and *Kaiser*. *Shch-403* (Capt 3rd Class Shuiski) misses the *Brummer* laying out a mine barrage off Makkaur and *S-56* (Capt 3rd Class Shchedrin) sinks the minesweeper *M346* from a returning force off Gamvik and on 20 July the patrol boat *NKi09/Alane*.

12 June-2 Aug   Bay of Biscay
From the beginning of June the German U-boats pass through the Bay of Biscay in groups of two to five boats in order to be able to support each other in air attacks. Ju 88Cs of I/Z.G.1 (Capt Kunkel) provide fighter protection in the inner Bay but are far inferior to the British Beaufighters of No 248 Sqdn RAF and the Mosquitoes of No 10 Group Fighter Command. On 12 June British aircraft sight groups of three boats for the first time. On 13 June a Sunderland of No 228 Sqdn RAF attacks the group consisting of *U564*, *U185*, *U415*, *U634* and *U159*, damages *U564* but is itself shot down by AA fire. On 14 June a Whitley of No 10

OTU (Operational Training Unit) RAF sinks *U564*, accompanied by *U185*, but is also damaged by AA fire and shot down by a Ju 88. The German destroyers *Z24* and *Z32* set out to meet them, take off the survivors from *U185* and the boat sets out alone. From 14 June No 19 Group Coastal Command counters the new German tactics with the operations 'Musketry' and 'Seaslug': three times daily seven aircraft are deployed in parallel lines in the search area NW of Finisterre in order to be able to give quick support in case U-boats are sighted. There participate: Liberators of Nos 53, 86 and 224 Sqdns RAF and of USAAF—A.S. Sqdn 1, 4 and 19, Catalinas of No 210 Sqdn RAF and USN-VP.63 equipped with the magnetic locating equipment MAD, Sunderlands of Nos 226 and 228 Sqdns RAF and of Nos 10 and 461 Sqdns RAAF, Wellingtons of No 172 Sqdn RAF and of No 426 Sqdn RCAF with 'Leigh Lights' and of No 304 Polish Sqdn and No 311 Czech Sqdn, Fortresses of No 59 Sqdn RAF and Halifaxes of Nos 58 and 502 Sqdns RAF. In June the Italian *Barbarigo* is sunk; in July *U628*, *U126*, *U535*, *U514*, *U506*, *U607*, *U558*, *U459* (tanker), *U404* and *U614*. *U155*, *U68*, *U462*, *U650*, *U518*, *U462* (again), *U536*, *U170*, *U267*, *U441* (AA boat) and *U218* are brought in damaged. In defensive actions *U600*, *U462*, *U268*, *U43*, *U558*, *U459*, *U454* and *U383* all shoot down one aircraft each and fighters shoot down six more. U-tankers and damaged boats are escorted by two to four destroyers or torpedo boats: *Z24*, *Z23*, *Z32*, *T5*, *T19*, *T22*, *T24*, *T25*, *Falke*, *Greif*, *Möwe*, *Jaguar* and *Kondor* are deployed, sometimes more than once. On the British side support groups are deployed from 20 June W of the Bay with cruiser cover against German surface ships. In the first operation from 20 June to 28 June an aircraft leads the 2nd SG (Capt Walker) to the *U650*, *U119* and *U449* group: the sloop *Starling* sinks the tanker *U119* by ramming and *Wild Goose*, *Woodpecker*, *Kite* and *Wren* sink *U449*. Cover is provided by the cruiser *Scylla*. Relief is provided in five to eight day intervals by EG 40, EG B.5 (the destroyer *Havelock*), the 2nd SG (the sloop *Wild Goose*), the 5th SG (the frigate *Nene*), EG B.1 (the destroyer *Hurricane*), a destroyer group consisting of the Canadian *Iroquois*, *Athabaskan* and the Polish *Orkan*, EG B.5 (including the escort carrier *Archer*), with cover from the cruisers *Bermuda* and *Glasgow*. On 30 July an outward-bound group, consisting of the tankers *U461*, *U462* and the combat boat *U504*, is sighted by a Liberator of No 53 Sqdn RAF and reported to aircraft situated in the vicinity and the 2nd SG (Capt Walker). In repeated attacks by seven aircraft *U461* is sunk by the Sunderland U/461, *U462* by the Halifax S/502 and *U504* by the sloops *Kite*, *Woodpecker*, *Wren* and *Wild Goose*. On 1 Aug and 2 Aug *U454*, *U383*, *U106* and *U706* are also lost in air attacks. The torpedo boats *T22*, *T24* and *T25*, which answer *U383*'s distress signal, are able to rescue survivors from *U106*.

The losses compel the Commander U-boats to abandon the tactics of group sailings and to postpone further departures of the U-boats until they are equipped with the new Hagenuk search receiver to operate against 10cm radar. The losses of the tankers necessitate the breaking off of operations with the medium boats in distant areas.

15-17 June Indian Ocean

Schiff 28 Michel (Capt Gumprich), which put to sea from Batavia on 4 June on the last operation by a German auxiliary cruiser, sinks W of Australia the Norwegian motor ship *Hoegh Silverdawn* (7715 tons) and the Norwegian tanker *Ferncastle* (9940 tons).

15 June-23 July Black Sea

In operations against the Soviet supply traffic off the Caucasus coast *U24* (Lt-Cdr Petersen) sinks a minesweeper near Tuapse on 15 June, *U18* (Lt Fleige) the steamer *Leningrad* near Sukhumi on 23 June and the steamer *Voroshilov* (3908 tons) on 17 July from Soviet convoys. *U19*, *U23* and *U20* have no success.

In sorties by the 1st MTB Flotilla (Cdr Christiansen) with two to five boats there are engagements on 22-23 June and 25 June with Soviet patrol cutters. On 28-29 June mines are laid near Gelendzhik. On 6-7 July *S102* is lost on a mine S of Kerch as she returns.

On 19-20 July air attacks are out-manoeuvred and on 22-23 July two steamers are torpedoed.

15 June-17 July Central Atlantic
In operations in the area between the Canaries and Freetown *U508* (Lt-Cdr Staats) sinks three ships of 21112 tons; *U618* (Lt Baberg) one ship of 5225 tons; and *U757* (Lt-Cdr Deetz) one ship of 4116 tons. *U306* (Lt-Cdr v. Trotha) torpedoes one ship of 5882 tons from a convoy on 16 July in several approaches. *U333*, *U571*, *U358*, *U257*, *U600*, *U382*, *U340*, *U86* and *U445* return home without successes. *U468* and *U403* are sunk on 11 Aug and 17 Aug respectively by Liberators of No 200 Sqdn RAF, although *U468* shoots down the attacker.

16 June South Pacific
Ninety-four Japanese aircraft from Rabaul and New Georgia attack ships off Guadalcanal. *LST340* and the freighter *Celeno* are damaged; a convoy is unsuccessfully attacked. Fighter aircraft from Henderson Field and ships' AA fire have great successes in shooting down aircraft. Only one Japanese aircraft returns.

16 June-9 July Mediterranean
Preparatory movements by Allied convoys for the operation 'Husky' (Sicily). From 16 June to 1 July the convoys UGF.10A and UGF.10B, consisting of 28 transports with the 45th Inf Div on board, proceed from Norfolk to Oran and Algiers. Escort: the cruisers *Philadelphia* and *Brooklyn* respectively, each with 9 destroyers. From 17 June to 23 June the British Force H (Vice-Adm Willis), comprising the battleships *Nelson*, *Rodney*, *Valiant* and *Warspite*, the carrier *Indomitable* and the destroyers of the 4th, 8th and 24th Flotillas (14 British, two French, one Polish and one Greek), is transferred from Scapa Flow to Gibraltar and on to Oran. From there *Valiant* and *Warspite* together with the carrier *Formidable*, the cruisers *Aurora* and *Penelope* and six destroyers, proceed to Alexandria by 5 July. After the US battleships *Alabama* and *South Dakota* with five destroyers have arrived in Scapa Flow from Argentia at the end of June, the British battleships *Howe* and *King George V* are also moved to Gibraltar. There set out from the Clyde the convoys KMS.18A (20 June), KMS.18B (24 June), KMS.19 (25 June), KMF.18 (28 June) and KMF.19 (1 July), comprising, in all, 9 troop transports, 9 LSIs, 48 freighters, 17 LSTs, two LSGs, six tankers, one collier and one headquarters ship. On board are the 1st Canadian Inf Div, the 1st Canadian Armoured Brigade, the 40th and 41st Royal Marine Commandos and the 73rd British AA Brigade. On 4 July and 5 July KMS.18B loses three ships off the Algerian Coast as a result of attacks by the U-boats *U375* and *U593* (14396 and 6054 tons).

From Alexandria and Port Said there put to sea the convoys MWS.36 (3 July), MWF.36 (5 July), MWS.37 (6 July) and MWF.37 (9 July), consisting, in all, of one headquarters ship, 29 LSIs, 60 freighters, two LSGs and five tankers. On board are the British 5th and 50th Inf Divs, the 231st Infantry Brigade, the 4th Armoured Brigade and the 3rd Commando. On 6 July *U453* sinks one ship from MWS.36 off Derna (5757 tons). On 7 July a part of the covering force also sets out from Alexandria, comprising the *Warspite*, *Valiant*, *Formidable*, *Aurora* and *Penelope* and 9 destroyers. They are to join up on 9 July in the Gulf of Sirte with the *Nelson*, *Rodney*, *Indomitable*, the cruisers *Cleopatra* and *Euryalus* and eight destroyers coming from Oran. The support force, consisting of the cruisers *Newfoundland*, *Uganda*, *Mauritius* and *Orion* and six destroyers, follows from Alexandria.

From Algiers and Oran there set out the convoys NCS.1 (4 July), NCF.1 (5 July), NCS.2 (9 July) and NCF.2 (9 July) with one headquarters ship, 26 troop transports and 31 freighters. On board are the US 1st and 45th Inf Divs and elements of the 9th Inf Div which is in reserve.

The convoys TJF.1 (5 July), TJS.1 (8 July), and TJM.1 (8 July), consisting of 78 LSTs, 116 LCTs and 106 LSIs, follow from Bizerta. On board are the US 3rd Inf Div and the 2nd Armoured Div.

From Sfax there set out the convoys SBS.1 (7 July), SBM.1 (8 July) and SBF.1 (8 July), from Tripoli the MWS.36X (8 July) and from Malta the SBF.2 and SBF.3 (9 July), comprising, four landing ships, one headquarters ship, 42 LSTs, 77 LCTs and 43 LCIs. On board are the British 51st Inf Div and the British 23rd Armoured Brigade. With the convoy setting out from Algerian ports are the American cruisers, *Brooklyn*, *Birmingham*, *Savannah*, *Boise*, *Philadelphia*, the British monitor *Abercrombie* and 48 US destroyers. The British convoys are escorted inter alia, by 58 British and Allied destroyers, 36 escort vessels and 34 minesweepers.

To cover the operation, the submarines *Ultor*, *Unruly* and *Sokol* (Polish) are stationed N of the Straits of Messina and *Unshaken*, *United*, *Unbroken*, *Dzik* (Polish) and *Uproar* off Taranto.

17 June-5 July   Arctic
The Soviet ice-breakers are moved from the White Sea into the Kara Sea. On 17 June the ice-breakers *Mikoyan*, *Krassin* and the ice-breaker steamer *SKR-18/Fedor Litke* set out from Severodvinsk. They are under the orders of the Commander of the White Sea Flotilla, Rear-Adm Kucherov, on the destroyer *Uritski* with the destroyer *Kuibyshev*, the patrol ships *SKR-28*, *SKR-30* and the British minesweepers *Britomart* and *Jason*. From 18 June to 20 June cover is provided by the destroyers *Baku*, *Gremyashchi* and *Grozny*. The destroyers return on 20 June from the Kara Strait, the other escorts are on the edge of the ice in the Kara Sea and the ice-breakers reach Dikson on 22 June. A second convoy with the ice-breakers *Admiral Lazarev* and *Montcalm* escorted by Capt 1st Class Kolchin with *Baku*, *Gremyashchi*, *Gromki*, *Uritski*, *SKR.28*, *SKR.30* and *Britomart*, sails in the same way on 29 June to the Kara Strait in thick mist. The ice-breakers arrive in Dikson on 5 July.

20 June   Mediterranean
King George VI arrives in Malta on board the cruiser *Aurora*, escorted by the destroyers *Lookout*, *Jervis*, *Nubian* and *Eskimo*.

21-22 June   South Pacific
Preparatory landings for the operation 'Cartwheel' (see 29 June). On 21 June the fast transports *Dent* and *Waters* land elements of the 4th Marine Raider Bn near Segi Point (New Georgia). They are followed on the next day by two companies of the 43rd US Inf Div from the fast transports *Schley* and *Crosby*.

23-29 June   South West Pacific
The US VII Amphibious Force (Rear-Adm Barbey) with the fast transports *Brooks*, *Gilmer*, *Sands*, *Humphreys*, 17 LSTs and 20 LCTs, 20 LCIs and four YMSs lands the 112th US Cavalry Regt on Woodlark Island on 23-24 June and the 158th Inf Regt on Kiriwina E of New Guinea on 28-29 June. Cover and support for the operation is provided by the destroyers *Mugford*, *Helm*, *Bagley* and *Henley*.

23 June-4 July   South West Pacific
TF 74 (Vice-Adm Crutchley, RAN), consisting of the cruisers *Australia* and *Hobart* and the destroyers *Arunta*, *Warramunga* and *Lamson* (US), operates in the area of the Coral Sea and the eastern Arafura Sea to cover the operation 'Cartwheel' (see 29 June).

28 June   Air War
Bombers of the 8th USAAF drop 250 tons of bombs on St Nazaire. US bombers drop 230 tons of bombs on Livorno.

29 June-13 July   South Pacific
Beginning of the operation 'Cartwheel': US landings on New Georgia (Central Solomons). The Japanese submarine *Ro-103* (Lt Ichimura), which has sunk the transports *Aludra* and *Deimos*, each of 7440 tons, from a convoy returning from Guadalcanal near San Cristobal on 23 June, reports a US transport fleet on 29 June. It is, however, mistaken for a supply convoy for Guadalcanal. In the night 29-30 June US TF 36.2 (Rear-Adm Merrill), comprising the cruisers *Montpelier*, *Columbia*, *Cleveland* and *Denver* and the destroyers *Waller*, *Saufley*, *Philip*, *Renshaw* and *Pringle*, shells the Japanese base at Shortland (South Bougainville), while the minelayers *Preble*, *Gamble* and *Breese* lay a mine barrage undetected.

Early on 30 June US TF 31 (Rear-Adm Turner), consisting of the destroyer-minesweepers, *Talbot*, *Zane*, *Dent*, *Waters* and six transports, supported and escorted by the destroyers *Farenholt*, *Buchanan*, *McCalla*, *Ralph Talbot*, *Gwin*, *Woodworth*, *Radford* and *Jenkins*, lands the first battle group of the 43rd US Inf Div (Maj-Gen Hester) on Rendova. Air support is provided by the

Above: 1943: In the Far East American submarines continue sinking large numbers of unescorted Japanese merchant ships. The heavy losses cause serious shortages of war material in Japan. Escorted convoys are also subject to submarine attack, escorts as well as merchant ships being prime targets. The periscope photograph shows the American submarine *Wahoo* sinking the freighter *Buyo Maru* (5447 grt) on Jan 26, 1943 off New Guinea. *[Official USN*

Above: The increasing shipping losses force the Japanese to use a large proportion of their submarine fleet as supply vessels. The illustration shows the large submarine-cruiser *I-15* with two 'Daihatsu' tracked landing boats on board. *[BFZ/Fukui*

Below: In the Western hemisphere the tonnage-war is a race between Allied ship-building and sinkings by the Axis forces. More and more British War Emergency Ships and American 'Liberty' ships join the convoys, but these too are sunk in large numbers. The crisis in the Battle of the Atlantic is reached in March 1943. *[IWM*

The most successful U-boat hunters were the British sloops like the *Erne* (top). The *Erne* carried a type 272M radar aerial on the lattice mast aft, and an HF/DF antenna on top of the tripod foremast. These two devices were largely responsible for the successes of the Escort Groups which were usually composed of 1 or 2 destroyers or sloops, occasionally a new frigate and between 4 and 7 corvettes. The leaders of the groups were usually one of the sloops.

As they became available a number of the Escort Groups were reformed around an escort carrier. Such a group was the 4th, built around HMS *Biter* (*above*), the first of many American built British lend-lease escort carriers. These groups had four to six destroyers, lent from the Home Fleet to the Western Approaches Command, or a number of sloops such as the *Erne*. These groups formed roving missions in support of North Atlantic convoys facing a wolf-pack attack. Similar American 'Hunter-Killer' Groups with escort carriers and old flush-deck destroyers operated in the Middle Atlantic in support of US-Gibraltar convoys.   [IWM

Above: During the first months of 1943 the Axis supply convoys to Tunisia suffered heavy losses from attack by Allied submarines, aircraft and surface vessels. The picture shows a torpedo boat closing to rescue survivors from an Italian transport which it was escorting, and which has just been sunk. *[BFZ*

Below: Off the North African coast German aircraft of K.G.26 and K.Gr.100 and U-boats attacked the large Allied convoys and sank a few ships. In the Eastern Mediterranean U-boats operated off the Egyptian and Palestinian coasts. Here *U81* returns to Salamis after her twelfth patrol with 3 freighters and 3 sailing vessels sunk. *[BFZ*

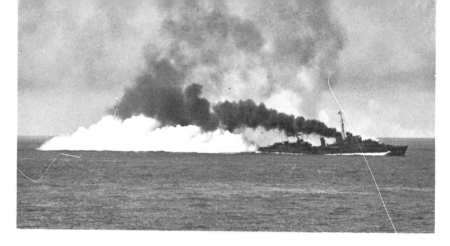

Above: At the beginning of June 1943, as a preparatory move to the landings on Sicily, British forces captured the island of Pantelleria. The destroyer *Nubian* is shown retiring under a smoke screen after carrying out a bombardment on June 8.   [*IWM*

Below: Operation 'Husky': Dive bombers attack the Allied landing forces unloading men and materials 4 miles south of Syracuse.   [*IWM*

Foot: Operation 'Husky': British troops of the Eighth Army going ashore from LCTs on July 10.   [*IWM*

Above: Aug 23, 1943: American forces land unopposed on Kiska, the Japanese having evacuated their forces unobserved by submarines and a cruiser-destroyer force which was screened by fog. The picture shows a captured Japanese midget submarine on Kiska. *[Official USN*

Below: Nov 1943: American forces take the island of Bougainville, the last of the islands to be captured in the Solomon chain. During the night of Nov 1 the 12th cruiser division shells the air base at Buka. *[IWM*

Above: Nov 1943: Tarawa, the main Japanese base in the Gilbert islands is the scene of an amphibious landing. Here the Americans gain the experience and techniques necessary to make their amphibious landings on the heavily defended islands of the Central Pacific. The illustration shows wreckage littering the beach at Betio island, Tarawa, after the assault. *[IWM*

Below: Jan 1944: Operation 'Shingle': During the Allied landings at Anzio—an attempt to outflank the German position in Italy—the landing forces come under heavy air attack, and radio controlled glider bombs score a number of successes. *[IWM*

Above: Operation 'Shingle': The cruiser *Spartan* is shown here bombarding German positions around Anzio. Some days later this vessel was sunk by *U410*. *[IWM*
Below: The Indian Ocean was a secondary theatre. In the first years of the war only Axis surface raiders and then U-boats attacked Allied shipping. The most successful of the U-boats was *U181* under Commander Luth, seen here returning to France from her second patrol on Oct 13, 1943. Her bunkers are empty and she has sunk 22 ships of 103712 grt in one year. *[BFZ*

Above: 1944: The British Eastern Fleet commences Operations against Japanese bases. During Operation 'Cockpit' in April 1944 a British-American carrier force attacks Sabang. The carriers are covered by Allied vessels including the battleship *Valiant* (left), the French battleship *Richelieu* (right) and escort carriers. *[IWM*

Above: Jan 1945: Operation 'Meridian': On Jan 24 carriers of the British Pacific Fleet raid two major oil refineries at Palembang on Sumatra. One oil refinery is almost completely destroyed and the other is forced to cease production for two months. *[IWM*
Below: The Battle of the Atlantic is by no means over even in 1944. In February U-boat packs attempt for the last time to attack a North Atlantic convoy in force, but are driven off by the escort and support groups. The most successful group is Captain Walker's 2nd Escort Group, which sinks 6 U-boats during this operation. The U-boats fight back: here a 'Gnat' fired by *U238* is countermined by depth charges from the sloop *Kite*. *[IWM*

land-based South Pacific Air Force (Vice-Adm Fitch). The landing also succeeds without resistance at several points in South New Georgia.
The following units are alerted to cover the operation against Japanese fleet attacks: TF 36.3 (Rear-Adm De Witt) with the carrier group (Rear-Adm Ramsey), consisting of the *Saratoga* and HMS *Victorious* with the AA cruisers *San Diego* and *San Juan* and the destroyers *Maury, Gridley, McCall, Craven, Fanning, Dunlap, Cummings,* and *Case*, and the battleship group (Rear-Adm Davis) consisting of the *Massachusetts, Indiana* and *North Carolina* and the destroyers *Selfridge, Stanly, Claxton, Dyson* and *Converse;* TF 36.4 (Rear-Adm Hill) comprising the old battleships *Maryland* and *Colorado;* and TF 36.5 (Rear-Adm McFall) comprising the escort carriers *Sangamon, Suwanee* and *Chenango* and the destroyers *Conway, Eaton, Lang, Stack, Sterett,* and *Wilson*. In addition, 11 submarines operate in the area of the Solomons and the Bismarck Archipelago. In a Japanese air attack on the invasion fleet on 30 June the transport *McCawley* receives a torpedo hit and has to be abandoned. On 1 July the second wave with three LSTs arrives off Rendova. The Japanese submarine *Ro-101* is damaged by *Radford*. In the night 2-3 July the Japanese cruiser *Yubari* and nine destroyers shell Rendova without much effect.
In the night 4-5 July the US fast transports *Dent, Talbot, McKean, Waters, Kilty, Crosby* and *Schley* land three battalions of the 37th Inf Div near Bairoko in Kula Gulf to prepare an attack on Munda. Cover for the operation is provided by TF 36.1 (Rear-Adm Ainsworth), comprising the cruisers *Honolulu* and *St Louis* and the destroyers *Nicholas, Strong, O'Bannon, Chevalier* and *Taylor*. Simultaneously, a Japanese destroyer force (Capt Orita), consisting of *Mochitsuki, Mikatsuki* and *Hamakaze* lands 1200 troops near Vila in Kula Gulf. They succeed in sinking the US destroyer *Strong* with 'long-lance' torpedoes at great range. The destroyer's detonating depth charges damage the *Chevalier*. 5-6 July: battle of Kula Gulf. The destroyer force of Capt Orita and

a second (Capt Yamashiro), consisting of *Amagiri, Hatsuyuki, Nagatsuki* and *Satsuki,* try to land another 2800 troops in Vila in the night, covered by Rear-Adm Akiyama with the destroyers *Niitsuki, Suzukaze* and *Tanikaze*. Adm Ainsworth with the *Honolulu, Helena* and *St Louis* and the destroyers *Nicholas, O'Bannon, Radford* and *Jenkins* are deployed against the Japanese force. In the engagement the Japanese covering force sinks the *Helena* with three torpedo hits but itself loses the *Niitsuki* in the radar-controlled fire of the US cruisers. Further attacks on both sides have no success. Of the Japanese second transport force the damaged *Nagatsuki* runs aground and is destroyed on 6 July by US dive bombers from Henderson Field. On 9 July four US destroyers shell Munda in the course of which attacks by some 100 Japanese aircraft are beaten off. In the night 11-12 July three cruisers and ten destroyers of US TG 36.2 (Rear-Adm Merrill) shell Munda with 3204 rounds of 6 inch shells and 5470 rounds of 5 inch shells. TF 36.1 covers the landing of supplies near Bairoko. On the way the *Taylor* sinks the Japanese submarine *Ro-107*.
12-13 July: battle of Kolombangara. In the night a new Japanese transport force, comprising the destroyers *Satsuki, Mikatsuki, Yunagi* and *Matsukaze* (with 1200 troops), covered by Rear-Adm Izaki† with the cruiser *Jintsu* and the destroyers *Mikatsuki, Yukikaze, Hamakaze, Kiyonami* and *Yugure,* proceeds to Kula Gulf. TF 36.1 (Rear-Adm Ainsworth), consisting of the cruisers *Honolulu, St Louis* and HMNZS *Leander* and the destroyers of Desron 21 (Capt McInerney), comprising *Nicholas, O'Bannon, Taylor, Jenkins* and *Radford,* and Desron 12 (Capt Ryan), comprising *Ralph Talbot, Buchanan, Maury, Woodworth* and *Gwin,* is deployed against this 'Tokyo Express'. In spite of radar on the American side the Japanese sight the US force first and the *Jintsu* fires her torpedoes before she is shelled to pieces by the radar-controlled fire of the US cruisers (2630 rounds fired). The *Leander* (Capt S. W. Roskill) drops out with a torpedo hit. The Japanese destroyers of the covering force fire their torpedoes

which, however, do not hit and they escape in a rain squall. In 18 minutes they reload their torpedo tubes and attack again. *Honolulu* and *St Louis* are badly damaged by torpedo hits from Capt Shimai's destroyers and the *Gwin* is sunk.

30 June Western Atlantic
The Vichy French warships interned in Martinique and Guadeloupe (Adm George Robert) are handed over to the Free French Navy: the aircraft carrier *Béarn*, the cruisers *Jeanne d'Arc* and *Emile Bertin* and some smaller vessels.

1-31 July Pacific
Of the US submarines which arrive in their operational areas in July the following make sinkings off Japan: *Plunger* (Lt-Cdr Bass) sinks one ship of 2482 tons and torpedoes one other ship; *Pompano* (Lt-Cdr Thomas) torpedoes one ship; *Scorpion* (Lt-Cdr Wylie) sinks two ships of 10002 tons; *Snook* (Lt-Cdr Triebel) two ships of 11155 tons; *Permit* (Cdr Chapple) two ships of 2999 tons; *Sawfish* (Lt-Cdr Sands) the mine-layer *Hirashima* and torpedoes one other ship. Off the Kuriles *S35* (Lt Monroe) sinks two ships of 5529 tons. Off Formosa *Flying Fish* (Capt Watkins) sinks two ships of 2863 tons. In the South West Pacific *Finback* (Lt-Cdr Tyree) sinks one submarine-chaser and two ships of 10789 tons; two more ships are torpedoed.

3-10 July English Channel
From 3 July to 7 July the German torpedo boats *T24* and *T25* move in several stages from the North Sea through the English Channel to the W. In the process they are unsuccessfully shelled by the Dover coastal batteries and attacked off Dunkirk on 5 July by the British *MTB240*, *MTB235* and *MTB202* and in Boulogne on 6 July by Typhoon fighter bombers. In the night 9-10 July they form a distant cover for a German convoy near Ouessant, which is screened by the 2nd MS Flotilla (Cdr Heydel), comprising *M9*, *M12*, *M10*, *M135* and *M84*. The convoy is attacked by the British destroyers *Melbreak*, *Wensleydale* and *Glaisdale* (Norwegian), which sink *M135*. In an engagement with the German torpedo boats, which then approach, *Melbreak* is badly damaged.

4 July Air War/Western Europe
US bombers attack the U-boat base at La Pallice.

4 July-8 Sept Mediterranean
In British submarine operations in the Western Mediterranean the following sinkings are made, sometimes in the course of several patrols: *Saracen* (Lt Lumby) sinks two ships of 2567 tons; *Safari* (Lt Lakin) the minelayer *Durazzo* and one small ship; *Torbay* (Lt Clutterbuck) one ship of 2609 tons; *Usurper* (Lt Mott) one ship of 2536 tons; *Somoon* (Lt Milner) the destroyer *Gioberti*; *Sickle* (Lt Drummond) the German escort vessel *SG7* (2526 tons); *Shakespeare* (Lt Ainslie) the Italian submarine *Velella*; *Sportsman* (Lt Gatehouse) and *Universal* (Lt Gordon) each one sailing ship; and the Dutch *Dolfijn* (Lt-Cdr v. Oostrom-Soede) one ship of 7890 tons and two ferry barges. In the Central Mediterranean and in the Adriatic *Rorqual* (Lt Napier) sinks one ship of 7020 tons; *Ultor* (Lt Hunt) one ship of 6200 tons and the torpedo boat *Lince*; *Unrivalled* (Lt Turner) two ships of 170 tons; *Uproar* (Lt Kershaw) one ship of 1977 tons; *Unshaken* (Lt Whitton) one ship of 6850 tons; *Unseen* (Lt Crawford) two ships of 1088 tons; and *Unsparing* (Lt Piper) one ship of 1162 tons. In the Aegean *Rorqual* (Cdr Napier) sinks one ship of 1798 tons; *Sickle* (Lt Drummond) three sailing ships of 204 tons; and *Torbay* (Lt Clutterbuck) one sailing ship of 591 tons.

6 July-15 Aug North Pacific
On 6 July a US TG (Rear-Adm Giffen), comprising the cruisers *Wichita*, *Portland*, *San Francisco* and *Santa Fe* and four destroyers, shells Kiska. The shelling is repeated by the destroyers *Aylwin* and *Monaghan* on five nights in the period from 8 July to 20 July.
A Japanese force, which sets out on 7 July from Paramushiro, is unable, because of the weather, to carry out the evacuation from Kiska and returns on 16 July.
On 15 July the submarine *Narwhal* shells Matsura.
On 22 July TG 16.21 (Rear-Adm Giffen), comprising the cruisers *Louisville*, *San Francisco*, *Wichita*, *Santa Fe* and the destroyers *Aylwin*, *Bache*, *Hughes*, *Mustin* and *Morris*, shells

Kiska and TG 16.22 (Rear-Adm Griffin) comprising the battleships *New Mexico* and *Mississippi*, the cruiser *Portland* and the destroyers *Monaghan, Abner Read, Farragut* and *Perry*, shells Little Kiska.

On 27 July a US TG, consisting of the battleships *Mississippi, Idaho*, the cruisers *Wichita, San Francisco, Portland* and destroyers, carries out 80 nautical miles W of Kiska a 'battle of the pips' with radar phantoms. The ships expend 518 rounds of 14 inch and 487 rounds of 8 inch shells.

A Japanese force (Rear-Adm Kimura), consisting of the cruisers *Tama, Abukuma, Kiso* and the destroyers *Ikazvchi, Inazuma, Wakaba, Hatsushimo, Asagumo, Hibiki, Yugumo, Kazegumo, Akigumo, Shimakaze, Naganami* and *Samidare* as well as the tanker *Nippon Maru* and the frigate *Kunajiri*, sets out from Paramushiro on 22 July and reaches Kiska on 28 July. *Kunajiri* and *Wakaba*, as a result of collisions on 26 July in bad weather with *Abukuma* and *Hatsushimo*, and *Tama*, because of engine trouble on 28 July have to return. In 55 minutes the 5183-strong garrison of Kiska is taken on board and evacuated unobserved by the enemy. They arrive in Paramushiro on 1 Aug.

In preparation for the landing on Kiska the US destroyers *Farragut* and *Hull* shell Kiska on 30 July. On 2 Aug TG 16.6 (Rear-Adm Baker), comprising the cruisers *Salt Lake City, Indianapolis, Raleigh, Detroit* and *Richmond* and the destroyers *Farragut, Meade, Frazier, Gansevoort* and *Edwards*, and TG 16.17 (Rear-Adm Kingman), comprising the battleships *Idaho* and *Tennessee* and the destroyers *Dale, Aylwin, Phelps* and *Anderson*, and on 12 Aug TG 16.6 again, shells Kiska. Aircraft drop 1310 tons of bombs in 1585 sorties.

Operation 'Cottage': on 15 Aug the assault force, which set out from Adak on 13 Aug, with 20 transports, 42 landing ships and boats and many auxiliary craft, lands 34426 men on the abandoned island of Kiska. Escort is provided by the destroyers *Farragut, Aylwin, Monaghan, Dewey, Hull, Dale, Bush, Daly, Mullany, Bancroft, Caldwell*, and *Coghlan*. Preparatory shelling is undertaken by Rear-Adm Kingman with the battle-

ships *Pennsylvania, Tennessee* and *Idaho*, the cruisers *Portland* and *Santa Fe* and the destroyers *Ammen, Abner Read* (damaged on a mine on 18 Aug), *Bache, Beale, Brownson, Hutchins* and *Phelps*. Air support is provided by 168 shore-based aircraft.

6 July-27 Aug Central Atlantic

From 6 July to 12 July *U487* (Lt Metz) replenishes *U195, U382, U598, U406, U591, U604, U662, U359* and *U466*, 600 nautical miles SW of the Azores. When the proposed tanker *U462* is no longer available, *U487* is given the task with the auxiliary tanker *U160* of replenishing the 'Monsun' group on 14 July on its way to the Indian Ocean. But from this group *U514* is sunk on 8 July by a 'Fido' homing torpedo from a Liberator of No 224 Sqdn RAF and *U506* on 12 July by USAAF-A/S Sqdn 1. After leaving convoy UGS.11 (61 ships, TF 62), the US Support Group (Capt Greer) with the carrier *Core* and the destroyers *Barker, Bulmer* and *Badger* encounters on the way to GUS.9 the tanker *U487* and sinks her with three aircraft. Detached from GUS.9, the Group with the carrier *Santee* (Capt Fick) and the destroyers *Bainbridge, Overton* and *MacLeish* encounters on 14 July and 15 July *U160* and the 'Monsun' *U509*, which are sunk by Avengers with 'Fido' torpedoes. On 16 July the returning *U67* falls victim to an Avenger from the *Core*. In supporting the convoy UGS.12 aircraft from the carrier *Bogue* (Capt, Dunn) sink on 23 July *U527* which has just been replenished from *U648*, while from the destroyers *Clemson, Osmond-Ingram* and *George E. Badger*, the last locates with Sonar *U613* which is on the way to a mining operation off Jacksonville and sinks her. On 24 July an aircraft of the *Santee* damages W of Madeira *U373* which is on the way to Port Lyautey with mines. On the return with GUS.10 an aircraft from the *Santee* sinks with 'Fido' *U43* which is in the process of replenishing *U403*. On 3 Aug the *Card* Group (Capt Isbell) with the destroyers *Barry, Goff*, and *Borie* arrives as support for UGS.13 in the area S of the Azores. An aircraft damages *U66* which is joined by *U117* on 7 Aug. Aircraft from the *Card* attack and sink *U117* with 'Fido'. On 8 Aug *U262* and *U664* shoot down two aircraft and *U664* (Lt Graef) misses the *Card* with a salvo but is sunk on 9 Aug by one of her aircraft. *Borie* outmanoeuvres an attack by *U262*. On 11 Aug *U525*, which is detached as an auxiliary tanker, is sunk by an aircraft from the *Card* with 'Fido' N of the Azores. *U760* and *U161*, which have handed over a search receiver to the Japanese *I-8*, escape from the *Croatan* (Capt Lyon) Group with the destroyers *Paul Jones*, *Parrott* and *Belknap*, which arrives with the convoy UGS.14 on 12 Aug. On 21 Aug *U134* also escapes from the Group.

From 12 Aug to 23 Aug *U129* and *U847*, which have helped as auxiliary tankers, succeed in replenishing four and seven boats respectively. On 23 Aug the *Core* Group again comes into the supply area with UGS.15. *U84*, which escapes from an attack on 23 Aug, and *U185* are sunk on 24 Aug with 'Fido' and the *Card*, which arrives to relieve, sinks the auxiliary tanker *U847* with 'Fido' on 27 Aug. *U508* avoids a 'Fido' attack. The heavy losses necessitate a reduction in the long-range operations. On the American East Coast *U566* (Lt-Cdr Hornkohl) sinks the US gunboat *Plymouth* on 5 Aug. *U107* (Lt Simmermacher) torpedoes one ship of 7176 tons.

8 July Norway

The British Fleet (Adm Fraser), comprising the battleships *Anson*, *Duke of York* and *Malaya*, the carrier *Furious*, two cruiser squadrons and three destroyer flotillas and a US TF (Rear-Adm Hustvedt), consisting of the battleships *Alabama* and *South Dakota*, the cruisers *Augusta* and *Tuscaloosa* and five destroyers, carry out a demonstration off Norway which, however, is not detected by the German air reconnaissance. The aim of diverting attention from the imminent landing in Sicily fails. When it is repeated at the end of July, some of the ships mentioned above and the British carriers *Illustrious* and *Unicorn* take part. Martlet fighters shoot down five German BV-138 reconnaissance aircraft.

10 July Mediterranean

Operation 'Husky': Allied landing in Sicily (C-in-C Gen Eisenhower; Deputy and C-in-C Land Forces, Gen Alexander; Naval Forces Adm Cunningham; Air Forces Air Chief Marshal Tedder; HQ in Malta). The British 8th Army (Gen Montgomery) is landed by the Eastern Naval Task Force (Adm Ramsay) between Syracuse and the Pachino Peninsula; the 7th US Army (Lt-Gen Patton) by the Western Naval Task Force (Vice-Adm Hewitt) near Scoglitti, Gela and Licata.

Force A (Rear-Adm Troubridge)—headquarters ship *Bulolo* with convoys MWS.36 and MWF.36 (see 16 June-9 July)—lands the British XIII Corps (Lt-Gen Dempsey) with the 3rd Royal Marine Commandos, the 5th Inf Div and the 50th Inf Div S of the Maddalena Peninsula in the sector 'Acid North' and S of Avola in the sector 'Acid South'. Beacon submarine: *Unruffled*.

Force N (Capt Lord Ashburn)—headquarters ship *Keren* with parts of the convoys MWS.36 and MWF.36—lands the British 231st Independent Brigade (Brigadier Urquhart) on the east coast of the Pachino Peninsula in the sector 'Bark East'. Beacon submarine: *Unseen*.

Force B (Rear-Adm McGrigor)—headquarters ship *Largs* with convoys SBS.1, SBM.1 and SBF.1—lands the British 51st Inf Div (Maj-Gen Wimberley) near Cape Passero. Beacon submarine: *Unison*.

Force V (Rear-Adm Vian)—headquarters ship *Hilary* with convoys KMS.18 and MKF.18—lands the 1st Canadian Div (Maj-Gen Simmonds) on the West Coast of the Pachino Peninsula. Beacon submarine: *Unrivalled*.

Troops of Forces N, B and V form XXX Corps (Lt-Gen Leese). The 1st airborne Div lands SW of Syracuse. Support Force East (Rear-Adm Harcourt) comprisees the cruisers *Newfoundland*, *Uganda*, *Mauritius*, *Orion*, the AA cruisers *Carlisle*, *Colombo* and *Delhi*, the AA ship *Palomares*, the monitors *Erebus*, and *Roberts*. In addition, there are the destroyers: *Inconstant*, *Eskimo*, *Laforey*, *Lookout*, *Loyal*, *Nubian*, *Tartar*, *Arrow*, *Venomous*, *Viceroy*, *Wallace*, *Wanderer*, *Wishart*, *Woolston*, *Wrestler*, *Aldenham*, *Blencathra*, *Clare*, *Eggesford*,

Hursley, Hurworth, Lauderdale, Ledbury, Rockwood, Wheatland, Wilton, Atherstone, Cleveland, Hambledon, Mendip, Quantock, Tynedale, Whaddon, Dulverton, Beaufort, Exmoor, Brocklesby, Tetcott, Blankney, Lamerton, Oakley, Liddesdale, Farndale, Calpe, Easton, Belvoir, Holcombe, Haydon, Brecon, Brissenden, Puckeridge, the Greek *Pindos, Adrias, Kanaris, Miaoulis, Themistokles,* and Polish *Krakowiak* and *Slazak*; the sloops *Shoreham, Chanticleer, Crane, Cygnet, Erne, Pheasant, Whimbrel,* and the Indian *Jumna* and *Sutlej*; the frigates *Bann, Dart, Plym, Test, Teviot* and *Trent*; the corvettes *Bluebell, Bryony, Camellia, Convolvulus, Delphinium, Dianella, Honeysuckle, Hyacinth, Hyderabad, Lotus, Oxlip, Pentstemon, Poppy, Primula, Rhododendron, Starwort, Vetch* and *Sakhtouris* (Greek); the cutters *Banff* and *Fishguard*; the minesweepers *Gawler, Lismore, Ipswich, Maryborough, Geraldton, Cairns, Cessnock, Wollongong* (all Australian) and 25 others. Also, the Dutch gunboats *Flores* and *Soemba*.

TF 85 (Rear-Adm Kirk)—headquarters ship *Ancon* with parts of the convoys NCF.1, TJF.1 and TJM.1—lands the 45th US Inf Div (Maj-Gen Middleton) with 25800 troops on both sides of Scoglitti in the sector 'Cent'. Beacon submarine: *Seraph*. Support group and escort: the cruiser *Philadelphia*, the British monitor *Abercrombie*, the destroyers *Earle, Cowie, Parker, Laub, Mackenzie, Kendrick, Doran, Boyle, Champlin, Nields, Davison, Mervine, Quick, Tillman* and *Beatty*. On board the *Ancon* is the General Commanding II US Corps, Lt-Gen Bradley.

TF 81 (Rear-Adm Hall)—headquarters ship *Samuel Chase* with parts of convoys NCF.1, TJF.1 and TJM.1—lands the 1st US Inf Div (Maj-Gen Allen) with 19250 troops near Gela in the sector 'Dime'. Beacon submarine: *Shakespeare*.

Support group and escort: the cruisers *Boise* and *Savannah*, the destroyers *Cole, Shubrick, Jeffers, Nelson, McLanahan, Murphy, Glennon, Maddox, Dallas, Gherardi, Butler, Herndon* and *Bernadou*.

TF 86 (Rear-Adm Conolly)—head-quarters ship *Biscayne* with the convoys TJF.1, TJM.1 and TJS.1—lands the 3rd US Inf Div (Maj-Gen Truscott) and parts of the 2nd US Armoured Div with 27650 troops both sides of Licata in the sector 'Joss'. Beacon submarine: *Safari*. Support group and escort: the cruisers *Brooklyn* and *Birmingham*, the destroyers *Bristol, Buck, Ludlow, Swanson, Roe, Edison, Woolsey, Wilkes,* and *Nicholson*.

TF 80 (Flagship and reserve force—Vice-Adm Hewitt)—headquarters ship *Monrovia* with the 18th RCT of the 1st US Inf Div and two RCTs of the 2nd Armoured Div on board transports and LSTs. Escort: the destroyers *Wainwright, Mayrant, Trippe, Rhind, Rowan, Plunkett, Niblack, Benson, Gleaves, Ordronaux*, Lt-Gen Patton is on board the *Monrovia*. The 82nd US Airborne Div is landed inland from Gela.

A covering force (Vice-Adm Willis, RN), comprising the battleships *Nelson, Rodney, Warspite* and *Valiant,* the carriers *Indomitable* and *Formidable,* the cruisers *Aurora, Penelope, Cleopatra,* and *Euryalus* and the destroyers *Quilliam, Queenborough, Quail, Isis, Faulknor, Echo, Intrepid, Raider, Eclipse, Fury, Inglefield, Ilex, Vasilissa Olga* (Greek), *Troubridge, Tyrian, Tumult, Offa* and *Piorun* (Polish), cruises in the Ionian Sea.

Reserve covering group: the battleships *King George V* and *Howe,* the cruisers *Dido* and *Sirius* and the destroyers *Jervis, Panther, Pathfinder, Penn, Paladin* and *Petard* S of Sardinia.

The RAF and US Air Force provide 3680 aircraft.

11 July Bay of Biscay
Three FW 200s of K.G.40, on reconnaissance flight, sight a British troop transport convoy W of Oporto. In spite of strong AA defence, they hit the transports *California* (16792 tons) and the *Duchess of York* (22021 tons) which catch fire and have to be abandoned. The third ship, *Port Fairy,* reaches Casablanca with one British destroyer. The destroyers HMCS *Iroquois,* HMS *Douglas* and the frigate HMS *Moyola* rescue all but 57 of the troops on the ships.

11-31 July Mediterranean
The Allied fleets support the operations

of the 7th US and 8th British Armies in Sicily. On 11 July the US cruisers *Savannah* and *Boise* with the US destroyers *Shubrick*, *Jeffers*, *Glennon*, *Butler* *Beatty*, *Laub*, *Cowie* and *Tillman* bring a German armoured counter-attack to a standstill near Gela. The British destroyers *Blankney* and *Brissenden* occupy Pozzallo with an improvised landing force. Within the British bridgehead the monitor *Erebus* and the cruisers *Orion*, *Uganda* and *Mauritius* support British units. As a diversionary move the British battleships *Howe* and *King George V* shell Favignana on the night 11-12 July and the cruisers *Dido* and *Sirius* Marsala on the W coast. An attempt by the British destroyers *Eskimo*, *Exmoor* and the Greek *Kanaris* to enter Augusta is beaten off by an Italian coastal battery under the personal command of the fortress commander, Rear-Adm Leonardi. Only on 12 July does Rear-Adm Troubridge, who has occupied Syracuse on 11 July, enter when the landing ship *Ulster Monarch* is able to disembark troops. On 12 July the US cruisers *Birmingham* and *Brooklyn* support the left flank of the 7th US Army. On 13 July the *Erebus* shells Catania and on 16 July the British monitor *Abercrombie* and the US cruisers *Birmingham* and *Philadelphia* shell Porto Empedocle. On 17 July the British battleship *Warspite* shells Catania again. As a result of German and Italian air attacks, the Allied invasion fleet loses the US destroyer *Maddox*, the US minesweeper *Sentinel* and eight transports of 54306 tons. The monitor *Erebus* and other ships are damaged by bombs. On 14 July Italian torpedo aircraft just miss the cruisers *Euryalus* and *Cleopatra* and on 16 July they hit the carrier *Indomitable*.

In the night 16-17 July in engagements between the German 7th MTB Flotilla (Cdr Trummer) and British MTBs, five German motor torpedo boats are, in part, severely damaged. The passing Italian cruiser *Scipione Africano* sinks *MTB305* and damages *MTB311*.

The proposed massive deployment of German and Italian submarines S of Sicily fails because the available German U-boats have been operating off the Algerian coast since 22 June. In these operations *U73* (Lt Deckert) sinks one ship of 1598 tons and torpedoes one tanker of 8299 tons; *U593* (Lt-Cdr Kelbling) sinks the US *LST333* and *LST387* as well as one ship of 6054 tons from the feeder convoy KMS.18B on 5 July. Shortly before, *U375* (Lt-Cdr J. Könenkamp) has sunk two ships of 14296 tons from this convoy. *U371* (Lt-Cdr Mehl) torpedoes two ships of 13376 tons from a western convoy on 10 July. Attacks by *U431* and *U617* fail. Off Cyrenaica *U453* (Lt-Cdr Frhr v. Schlippenbach) torpedoes one steamer of 6894 tons and on 6 July sinks one ship of 5454 tons from the feeder convoy MWS.36. *U81* operates in the Eastern Mediterranean where she sinks one steamer of 3742 tons and four sailing ships. As a result of this, from 11 July at first only Italian submarines make attacks and only *Dandolo* (Lt-Cdr Turcio) is able to torpedo the cruiser *Cleopatra* on 16 July. Attacks by *Argo*, *Nereide*, *Beilul*, *Diaspro*, *Alagi*, *Platino*, *Nichelio* and *Ambra* fail. The Italian *Flutto* and *U561* are sunk by the Allied MTBs in the Straits of Messina: the Italian *Acciaio*, *Remo* and *Micca* by the submarines *Unruly*, *United* and *Trooper*; *U409* by the destroyer *Inconstant*; *Nereide* by *Echo* and *Ilex*; *Ascianghi*, after an attack on a cruiser force, by *Laforey* and *Eclipse*; and the German *U375* by the US *PC624*. The Italian *Bronzo* surfaces on 12 July off Syracuse in the middle of a British force and is captured. When the German U-boats arrive, *U81* (Lt Krieg) fires torpedoes into the harbour of Syracuse on 21 July and torpedoes a steamer of 7472 tons on 22 July. On 23 July *U407* (Lt Brüller) torpedoes the cruiser *Newfoundland*.

15 July General Situation
General Morgan, Chief of the General Staff of the Supreme Commander of the Allied Expeditionary Forces, puts a draft plan before the Joint Chiefs of Staff for an invasion of France: 'Overlord' (North West France) and 'Anvil' (Southern France).

17 July-13 Aug South Pacific
TF 74, comprising the Australian cruisers *Australia* and *Hobart* and the US destroyers *Jenkins*, *O'Bannon*, *Radford* and *Nicholas*, is sent from Espiritu Santo to the NW on 16 July to make

good the losses in the fighting off New Georgia.

On 17 July 223 aircraft of the 'Air Force Solomons' (Rear-Adm Mitscher) attack Japanese ships off Buin (Bougainville) and sink the destroyer *Hatsuyuki*. Off Rendova the Japanese submarine *Ro-106* (Lt Nakamura) sinks on 18 July the landing ship *LST342*. At the end of July *Ro-103* is lost off New Georgia.

Of the Japanese submarines sent to reconnoitre for a new attempt to reinforce New Georgia, *I-11* (Cdr* M. Tagami) attacks TF 74, torpedoing the Australian cruiser *Hobart* on 20 July and also one ship of 7176 tons; *I-17* (Lt-Cdr Harada) is sunk off Espiritu Santo on 19 Aug by two US aircraft and the New Zealand corvette *Tui*; *I-19* (Cdr Kinashi) destroys one ship of 7176 tons off Fiji.

In the night 19-20 July three Japanese destroyers bring supplies to Vila, while Rear-Adm Nishimura cruises off Vella Gulf with three heavy and one light cruiser and six destroyers to provide cover against US cruiser sorties. On 20 July the force loses the destroyers *Yugure* and *Kiyonami* to US torpedo aircraft and bombers from Guadalcanal and the cruiser *Kumano* is damaged. On 22 July shore-based aircraft from New Georgia sink the Japanese seaplane tender *Nisshin* which is loaded with supplies and escorted by three destroyers On 28 July the Japanese destroyers *Ariake* and *Mikatsuki* are sunk in a supply operation off Rabaul. In the night 1-2 Aug five Japanese destroyers try to reach Kolombangara. 15 US PT boats are deployed against them, seven of which fire their 26 torpedoes without success. *PT109* (Lt John F. Kennedy) is rammed in the action by the destroyer *Amagiri* and sinks. Kennedy saves his crew with great difficulty.

On 24 July a force of US fast transports with a destroyer escort (Cdr Burke) supplies Bairoko Harbour. The destroyers shell Munda and Lailand on 25 July with little effect. The shelling is therefore repeated on 26 July to support the land operations which lead to the capture of Munda.

6-7 Aug: Battle in Vella Gulf. The US destroyer force (Cdr Moosbrugger) with *Dunlap, Craven, Maury, Lang, Sterett* and *Stack* intercepts the Japanese group (Capt Sugiura) comprising the *Hagikaze, Arashi, Kawakaze* and *Shigure*, which tries to reach Kolombangara with 900 men on board and 50 tons of supplies. Three of the Japanese destroyers sink as a result of torpedo hits by the US destroyers; only *Shigure* escapes. The survivors from the Japanese ships in the water refuse to be rescued.

19 July-4 Sept Mediterranean
Italian defensive mine barrages are laid out. The Italian minelayers *Vieste* and *Vallelunga* lay seven barrages with 500 mines in the Gulf of Naples; the Italian destroyer *Vivaldi* and the German minelayers *Pommern* and *Brandenburg* lay seven barrages with 1196 mines in the Gulf of Gaeta and the Gulf of Salerno; the Italian cruisers *Cadorna* and *Scipione Africano* with minelayers *Barletta* and *Morosini* lay 11 barrages with 1591 mines in the Gulf of Taranto. In the Aegean the German *Drache* and *Bulgaria* lay 15 barrages with 690 mines; in the Adriatic the Italian *Laurana* one barrage with 70 mines; the Italian *Buffoluto* and *Gasperi* two barrages with 280 mines off Acciaio (Corsica); and the German *Pommern* and *Brandenburg* three barrages of 410 mines in the Straits of Bonifacio.

20 July-10 Aug Arctic
German U-boats lay the following mine barrages from 20 July to 10 Aug to interfere with Soviet traffic in the Pechora Sea: *U625* (Lt-Cdr Benker) off the Yugor Strait; *U601* (Lt-Cdr Grau) off Belusha; *U629* (Lt Bugs) in the western entrance to Pechora Bay and off Russki Savorot; *U586* (Lt-Cdr v.d. Esch) E of Pechora Bay; *U212* (Lt-Cdr Vogler) and *U636* (Lt-Cdr Hildebrand) off Kolguev; and *U639* (Lt Wichmann) in the Pechora Sea. A convoy of 15 river ships setting out on 25 July from the Pechora Estuary for the Ob Estuary runs on these mine barrages. On 27 July it loses the minesweeper *T-58* off the Yugor Strait. On 30 July *U703* (Lt Brünner) sinks one patrol ship off Kostin Strait. The motor minesweepers *T-109* and *T-110*, delivered from Britain, are used to clear the ground mines. On 25 Aug the rescue ship *Shkval* is lost in the Yugor Strait.

22 July-14 Aug Mediterranean

On 22 July the 7th US Army captures Palermo. The US 8th Desron and the US 15th MTB Squadrons enter the port. In the next days the PTs carry out several attacks on small convoys and German MFPs. In a German air attack off Palermo the US destroyer *Mayrant* is damaged on 26 July. Severe damage is caused in attacks on Palermo on 31 July, 1 Aug and 4 Aug and the destroyer *Shubrick* is damaged. From 27 July US TF 88 (Rear-Adm Davidson) supports the US troops on the north coast of Sicily. The cruisers *Philadelphia* and *Savannah* and the destroyers *Gherardi*, *Nelson*, *Jeffers*, *Murphy*, *Trippe* and *Knight* participate.

Two Italian cruiser forces, consisting of *Montecuccoli* and *Eugenio di Savoia* and *Garibaldi* and *Duca d'Aosta* respectively which put in on 5-6 Aug and 7-8 Aug to carry out shelling, turn away prematurely as a result of uncertainty about enemy's position, and before TF 88 reaches the scene.

On 7-8 Aug the cruiser *Philadelphia* with three destroyers supports the landing of one BLT from two LSTs, one LCI and 7 LCTs on the north coast of Sicily behind the German lines. On 10-11 Aug the *Philadelphia* with six destroyers supports the landing of RCT 30. A further landing in regimental strength on 14-15 Aug encounters nothing because of the German withdrawal.

24 July Air War/Norway

208 Fortresses of the 8th USAAF bomb the harbour installations of Trondheim.

24-26 July English Channel

In moving from Boulogne to Ostend *S68* and *S77* are attacked N of Dunkirk by British MGBs and MTBs which sink *S77*. In the following night *S110*, *S136*, *S81* and *S88* are moved from the Hook of Holland to Boulogne, when *S88* is damaged on a mine but brought into Dunkirk.

24 July-3 Aug Air War/Germany

Heavy attacks on Hamburg. First use of 'Window' metal foils to interfere with German radar. RAF Bomber Command makes incendiary and HE bomb attacks on the residential areas which cause great damage and lead to heavy casualties among the civilian population in the nights 24-25 July (740 bombers, 2300 tons), 27-28 July (739 bombers, 2313 tons), 29-30 July (726 bombers, 2277 tons) and 2-3 Aug (partly unsuccessful owing to weather conditions—425 bombers, 939 tons). In all, 87 bombers are lost. The 8th USAAF makes daylight attacks on the yards in Hamburg and Kiel with 218 bombers on 25 July, on Hamburg, Wilhelmshaven and Hannover with 199 bombers on 26 July and on Kiel and Warnemünde on 29 July. Forty-four aircraft are lost in these operations. In the attacks on Hamburg many harbour craft and merchant ships, totalling about 170000 tons, are destroyed, including the passenger ship *General Artigas* (11524 tons and the new, uncompleted *Vaterland* (36000 tons). In the Stülcken yards, Hamburg, the new escort vessel *G1*, at Blohm and Voss the new U-boats *U996*, *U1011* and *U1102* and in Kiel *U395* and *U474* are destroyed before completion. In Hamburg delays are caused to the building programme.

25 July General Situation

King Victor Emmanuel III has Mussolini arrested and appoints Marshal Badoglio as the new head of government.

26 and 27 July North Atlantic

Bombers of Air Commander-Atlantic sink the British freighters *El Argentino* (9501 tons) and *Halizones* (5298 tons) in the Atlantic NW of Lisbon and badly damage two more freighters totalling 14399 tons.

27 July-16 Sept Baltic

New attempts by Soviet submarines to break out. With strong support from ground-attack aircraft of the Naval Air Force against the German-Finnish mine guards, Soviet minesweeper forces try to penetrate the 'Seeigel-Rukajärvi' mine barrages to facilitate the breakthrough by the submarines. There are numerous engagements. Soviet torpedo cutters try to divert the guards. Thanks to air attacks, the SAT *Ost* is lost on 4 Aug, the SAT *West* on 15 Sept and the Finnish escort vessel *Uisko* on 16 Sept. On 22 Aug a Finnish gunboat beats off a TKA attack and on 23 Aug the minelayer *Riilahti* is sunk by three Soviet TKAs. As a result of aircraft fire, there are casualties on board the boats of the 3rd and 25th MS Flotillas and the 3rd

PB Flotilla. Freedom of movement for German and Finnish ships is temporarily impeded by Soviet mining operations with torpedo cutters and aircraft. The Soviet submarines *S-12* (Capt 3rd Class Bashchenko) and *S-9* (Capt 3rd Class Mylnikov) are respectively lost on German and Finnish mine barrages and as a result of depth charges from German MFPs of the 24th Landing Flotilla, KFKs of the 31st MS Flotilla and Finnish escort vessels.

30 July-10 Sept   Black Sea
The German U-boats *U19*, *U24*, *U23*, *U18* and *U9* operate off the Caucasus coast against Soviet supply transports. *U24* (Lt-Cdr Petersen) sinks the tanker *Emba* (7886 tons) in Sukhumi on 30 July and one tug and two motor boats on 22 Aug; *U23* (Lt Wahlen) one motor minesweeper near Cape Kodor on 24 Aug; and *U18* (Lt Fleige) one submarine chaser (submarine trap) on 29 Aug.

1-31 Aug   Pacific
Of the American submarines which arrive in their operational areas in August *Paddle* (Lt-Cdr Rice) sinks one ship of 5248 tons and torpedoes one more ship; *Pollack* (Lt-Cdr Llewellen) two ships of 7042 tons; *Salmon* (Lt-Cdr Nicholas) one ship of 2460 tons; *Seawolf* (Lt-Cdr Gross) three ships of 12996 tons—all off Japan. In the Central Pacific *Pike* (Lt-Cdr McGregor) sinks one ship of 1911 tons and torpedoes one more ship; *Swordfish* (Lt-Cdr Parker) two ships of 6219 tons; *Tullibee* (Lt-Cdr Brindupke) one ship of 4164 tons; *Whale* (Lt-Cdr Burrows) one ship of 7149 tons; and *Plunger* (Lt-Cdr Bass) three ships of 13692 tons. Off Formosa *Sculpin* (Lt-Cdr Chappell) sinks one ship of 3185 tons and *Sunfish* (Lt-Cdr Petersen) two ships of 5479 tons. In the South West Pacific *Gar* (Lt-Cdr Lantrup) sinks one ship of 995 tons and *Grayling* (Lt-Cdr Brinker) one ship of 5480 tons. The boat is lost.

1 Aug-3 Oct   Arctic
Operation 'Wunderland II': German operations on the Siberian sea route. *U255* (Lt Harms), which on the way out has sunk on 27 July the Soviet survey ship *Akademik Shokalski* (300 tons), establishes a base on 1 Aug near Spory Navolok on the north-east coast of Novaya Zemlya. Here she refuels on

4 Aug a BV 138 flying-boat which on 5 Aug, 6 Aug, 7 Aug and 11 Aug reconnoitres as far as the Vilkitski Strait to prepare for operations against Soviet convoys by the 'Wiking' U-boat group, comprising *U302*, *U354*, *U711*, and by the cruiser *Lützow* standing ready in Altafjord. No convoys are sighted. When the flying-boat is no longer available, a second operation from 4 Sept to 6 Sept with support from *U255* and *U601* produces no result. On 21 Aug *U354* (Lt-Cdr Herbschleb) sights a convoy off Port Dikson and follows it eastwards. Only on 27 Aug and 28 Aug are *U354* and *U302* (Lt-Cdr Sickel), which have in the meantime made a sortie into the Vilkitski Strait, able to attack in the W Siberian Sea. They torpedo the steamer *Petrovski* (3771 tons) and sink the *Dikson* (2900 tons). From 13 Aug to 25 Sept the U-boats of the 'Dachs' group carry out mining operations in the Kara Sea: *U625* (Lt-Cdr Benker) E of the Yugor Strait; *U639* (Lt Wichmann) off the Ob Estuary (sunk on the return journey on 28 Aug NW of Novaya Zemlya by the Soviet submarine *S-101* (Lt-Cdr Trofimov, with the Div Cdr, Capt 2nd Class Egorov on board)); *U960* (Lt-Cdr Heinrich) E of the Matochkin Strait, where *U711* (Lt Lange) hunts a patrol ship in vain; *U636* (Lt-Cdr Hildebrand) off Dikson (on her mines the Soviet steamer *Tbilisi* (7179 tons) sinks); *U629* (Lt Bugs) off Amderma; *U601* (Lt-Cdr Grau) and *U960* off Dikson. *U711* explores Wardroper Island on 9 Sept and shells on 18 Sept and 24 Sept the W/T stations at Pravdy and Blagopoluchiya. At the end of September *U703* (Lt Brünner), *U601* and *U960* relieve the boats of the 'Wiking' group. On On 30 Sept they locate the Soviet convoy VA.18 coming from the E with the minelayer *Murman* (Capt 3rd Class Pokhmelnov), the minesweeper trawlers *T-31*, *T-63* and *T-42* and four steamers. On 30 Sept *U960* sinks the freighter *Arkhangelsk* (2480 tons) near the Sergeya-Kirova Islands and misses the *Mossovet*. On 1 Oct *U703* sinks the *Sergei Kirov* (4146 tons); *U601* misses the *Murman* and is shelled by her. *U960* sinks *T-42* and misses *A.Andreev*. As the 'Monsun' group, four to five

boats from *U269*, *U277*, *U387*, *U713*, *U307*, *U355*, *U360*, *U737* and *U956* take up positions between Spitzbergen and Bear Island.

3-4 Aug Gibraltar
An Italian small battle unit (Cdr Notari) attacks Allied ships in Gibraltar from the *Olterra* in Algeciras with three guided torpedoes and sinks the Norwegian tanker *Thorshøvdi* (9944 tons) and the American freighter *Harrison Gray Otis* (7176 tons). One freighter of 5975 tons is severely damaged.

3 Aug-17 Oct Pacific
The last German auxiliary cruiser *Schiff 28 Michel* (Capt Gumprich) sights the US troop transport *Hermitage* in the area of Pitcairn Island on 3 Aug and 7 Aug, but does not attack. On 29 Aug *Schiff 28* is able to escape from the US cruiser *Trenton* undetected W of the Chilean coast. In the night 10-11 Sept she sinks the Norwegian tanker *Indus* (9977 tons) in the middle of the Pacific halfway between the Panama Canal and Tahiti. On 22 Sept the auxiliary cruiser runs into a small convoy with the submarine-chasers *SC1042* and *SC1045* and two auxiliary vessels on the route Panama Canal-Australia. But because she over-estimates the strength of the enemy she does not attack the convoy. After a sortie to the USA-Hawaii route Gumprich begins the return journey to Japan on 7 Oct. On 17 Oct *Schiff 28* is sunk by three torpedoes from the US submarine *Tarpon* (Cdr Wogan) 90 nautical miles E of Yokohama. 116 men reach Japan in lifeboats.

4-5 Aug North Sea
Sorties by *S39*, *S74*, *S80*, *S94*, *S89*, *S86* and *S83* of the German 2nd and 6th MTB Flotillas (Cdr Feldt and Cdr Obermaier) into the area off Harwich. The British trawler *Red Gauntlet* is sunk there by *S86* (Lt Wrampe).

5 Aug-6 Sept Mediterranean
In submarine operations on the Sicilian East Coast *U453* and *Diaspro* and on the North Coast *U73* and *U431* miss Allied warship forces. *U380* (Lt-Cdr Roether) torpedoes one ship of 7191 tons off Palermo. S of Sicily *Argento* and *U458* are lost in attacks by the US destroyer *Buck* and the escort destroyers *Easton* and *Pindos* (Greek) respectively. Off Cyrenaica *U81* misses an eastern

convoy and on the Lebanese coast *U596* (Lt-Cdr Jahn) sinks four sailing ships and damages two unidentified small steamers. In attacks on convoys on the Algerian coast *U371* (Lt-Cdr Mehl) sinks one ship of 6004 tons and *U410* (Lt Fenski) sinks two ships of 14436 tons. *U616* misses warships. On 6 Sept *U617* (Lt-Cdr Brandi) sinks E of Gibraltar the escort destroyer *Puckeridge*. After air attacks and pursuit by three corvettes the boat has to be abandoned on the Moroccan coast on 12 Sept.

11 Aug English Channel
The 4th and 5th MTB Flotillas, which are transferred to L'Abervrach for a sortie into Plymouth Sound, are attacked in two waves by British fighter bombers: *S121* is sunk, *S117* badly damaged and four others slightly damaged. Only *S110* is undamaged.

12 Aug Baltic
In the Baltic the Swedish submarine *Illern* sinks after a collision with a freighter.

13 Aug Mediterranean
German He 111 torpedo bombers of K.G. 26 (Maj Klümper) are deployed following a reconnaissance report about the convoy UGS.13 (75 ships, escort: the destroyer *Blankney*, the corvettes *Convolvulus*, *Saxifrage*, *Godetia* and the Australian *Geraldton*, *Cairns*, *Cessnock* and *Wollongong*). But they attack near Alboran the convoy MKS.21 (40 ships, escort: the British sloops and minesweepers *Shoreham*, *Whitehaven*, *Hythe*, *Rye*, *Romney*, and the Australian corvettes *Gawler*, *Ipswich*, *Lismore* and *Maryborough*) which is proceeding in the opposite direction in the area to the N. The results are considerably exaggerated (170000 tons) by the pilots: in fact, only the British freighter *Empire Haven* (6852 tons) and the American freighter *Francis W. Pettygrove* (7176 tons) are damaged by torpedo hits.

13 Aug Indonesia
First attack by the 5th USAAF from Australia with 380 heavy B-24 bombers on the oilfields of Balikpapan (Borneo).

14-24 Aug General Situation
Conference between Roosevelt and Churchill in Quebec ('Quadrant'). The main item on the agenda, apart from the imminent surrender of Italy, is

operation 'Overlord', the invasion of France planned by the Joint Chiefs of Staff. The date: May 1, 1944. Churchill and the British delegation travel on the passenger ship *Queen Mary*, escorted by the carrier *Illustrious*, three cruisers and destroyers. The return journey is made on the battle cruiser *Renown*. In Quebec the First Sea Lord, Admiral of the Fleet Sir Dudley Pound, suffers a heart attack. His successor from 15 Oct is Adm Sir Andrew Cunningham.

15-25 Aug South Pacific
The US III Amphibious Force (Rear-Adm Wilkinson), comprising the fast transports *Stringham*, *Waters*, *Dent*, *Talbot*, *Kilty*, *Ward* and *McKean*, three LSTs and 11 LSIs, lands 4600 men from RCT 35 (25th US Div, Maj-Gen McClure) on Vella Lavella (Central Solomons). Cover and fire support is provided by the destroyers *Nicholas*, *O'Bannon*, *Taylor*, *Chevalier*, *Cony*, *Pringle*, *Waller*, *Saufley*, *Philip*, *Renshaw*, *Conway* and *Eaton*. On 17 Aug small Japanese craft land reinforcements on the north coast. Capt Ryan with the destroyers *Nicholas*, *O'Bannon*, *Taylor* and *Chevalier* are deployed against the covering force (Rear-Adm Ijuin), comprising the destroyers *Sazanami*, *Hamakaze*, *Shigure* and *Isokaze*. The American force avoids 31 Japanese torpedoes but in the pursuit engagement only slight damage is obtained on *Hamakaze* and *Isokaze*. The submarine-chasers *Ch5* and *Ch12* are sunk.
On 25 Aug the fighting by XIV US Corps (43rd, 37th and parts of 25th Inf Divs) on New Georgia ends with the capture of Bairoko.

15 Aug-29 Oct Arctic
In operations against German supply traffic off the Norwegian Polar Coast the Soviet submarines *L-15*, *S-54*, *S-102*, *L-22* and *Shch-402* have no success in August. *M-104* (Lt-Cdr Lukyanov) torpedoes the steamer *Rüdesheimer* (2036 tons) on 1 Sept. *L-20* (Capt 3rd Class Tamman) is damaged after laying out a mine barrage near Sletnes on 3 Sept by *UJ1209* when she attacks a convoy. On 3 Sept *S-51* (Capt 2nd Class Kucherenko) sinks the submarine-chaser *UJ1202* off Kongsfjord. On 11 Sept *M-107* (Lt-Cdr Kofanov) sinks *UJ1217* off Syltefjord.

On 14 Sept *Shch-404* (Lt-Cdr Makarenkov) misses a convoy off Vardö. On the receipt of his report torpedo aircraft of the 5th Mining and Torpedo Air Div are deployed with fighter protection but, thanks to J.G. 5, they suffer heavy losses without securing any hits. On 15 Sept the Soviet torpedo cutters *TKA-13* (Lt Shabalin) and *TKA-21* attack near Kiberg. In a repeat of this operation on 20-21 Sept *Shch-404* and the aircraft have no success, but *TKA-15* sinks the steamer *Antje Fritzen* (4330 tons). There is a similar operation on 12-13 Oct after *S-55* (Capt 3rd Class Sushkin) has sunk the mine detonating ship *Ammerland* (5381 tons) from a large German convoy in Porsangerfjord. Attacks on 13 Oct off Makkaur by *Shch-403* and off Vardö by *M-172* fail, as do air attacks off Kiberg. All three submarines are probably lost on the flanking mine barrages laid out in the summer and autumn months by the German minelayers *Brummer*, *Ostmark*, *Kaiser* and *Roland*. Likewise, *M-174* is also lost in October. The large submarine *K-1* is missing since September when she returned from the Kara Sea. After these losses the Soviet submarines are deployed much more cautiously.

17 Aug Atlantic
Portugal grants the Allies the use of bases in the Acores.

17 Aug Mediterranean
Withdrawal from Sicily (Operation 'Lehrgang') completed. The following are transported across the Straits of Messina (in command: Capt v. Liebenstein): 39569 German troops, including 4444 wounded; 9605 vehicles, 47 tanks 94 guns, over 2000 tons of ammunition and fuel about 15000 tons of other supplies; 62000 Italian troops, 227 vehicles and 41 guns. Because of the unusually strong AA defence of the crossing area, only a few small ferrying craft are lost in spite of continual Allied air attacks.

17-23 Aug South West Pacific
From 17 Aug to 22 Aug the 5th USAAF carries out an air offensive to neutralize the Japanese air bases in the Wewak area (New Guinea). On 22-23 Aug four destroyers of TF 74 under Capt Carter make a sortie from Milne Bay to Finschhafen to shell the area.

18 Aug   Mediterranean
The US cruisers *Philadelphia* and *Boise* and four destroyers shell Gioia-Taura and Palmi in Calabria.

22 Aug-1 Sept   South Pacific
Islands are occupied without fighting for the purpose of constructing air bases. On 22 Aug an advance party of the US 2nd Marine Airdrome Bn lands on Nukufetau in the Ellice Islands; on 27 Aug the remaining units and Seabees follow. On 28 Aug the 7th Marine Defence Bn occupies Nanomea.
In the Solomons area Arundel Island is occupied on 27 Aug by RCT 172 of the 43rd Inf Div to control Blackett Strait. On 1 Sept a TF (Rear-Adm Lee), comprising the LSD *Ashland* (the first use of such a ship) and the transport *Hercules*, lands army troops on Baker Island. Support is provided by the destroyers *Trathen*, *Spence*, *Boyd* and *Bradford*. Air cover is provided by the carriers *Princeton* and *Belleau Wood*.

23-28 Aug   Bay of Biscay
From 2 Aug the British air operation 'Derange' NW of Cape Finisterre is unsuccessful as a result of stopping outward-bound U-boats and the use of Spanish waters by homeward-bound submarines. The use of the long-range German aircraft He 177 of II/K.G. 40 leads to frequent air engagements in which a total of 17 A/S and six fighter aircraft of No 19 Group are lost. From 23 Aug there is a new operation 'Percussion' in the vicinity of the Spanish coast in co-operation with the 5th EG (the British frigates *Nene* and *Tweed*, the Canadian corvettes *Edmundston*, *Calgary* and *Snowberry*) and the 40th EG (the frigate *Exe* and five other sloops and corvettes) with the cruiser *Bermuda* for support. On the 25 Aug the German Hs 293 glider bombs are used for the first time against the British support groups. Fourteen Do 217s of II/K.G. 100 and seven Ju 88Cs attack both support groups when the sloop *Landguard* is damaged by four near-misses. On 28 Aug there is a second attack with 18 Do 217s against the 1st SG sent as relief and consisting of the sloop *Egret* and the frigates *Jed* and *Rother* with the destroyers HMCS *Athabaskan* and HMS *Grenville* for reinforcement. *Athabaskan* is hit and badly damaged; *Egret* blows up. The British Support Groups retire to the W and the inward and outward movements of the U-boats are facilitated.

23 Aug-11 Nov   South Pacific
A Japanese submarine group is deployed from Truk and Rabaul in the area of the New Hebrides. On 23 Aug *I-25* reconnoitres with her aircraft over Espiritu Santo but is sunk by the destroyer *Ellet* on 3 Sept when she tries to approach a US force. On 25 Aug *Ro-35* is lost when attacked with depth charges by the US destroyer *Patterson*. On 31 Aug *I-20* (Lt-Cdr Otsuka) torpedoes one tanker of 10872 tons but is sunk on 11 Sept by aircraft and the destroyer *Saufley*. On 11 Sept *I-39* (Cdr Tanaka) sinks the fleet tug *Navajo*. *I-26* reconnoitres in the area of the Fiji Islands. *I-182* is sunk by the US submarine *Trout* as she sets out S of Truk. A second wave of Japanese submarines operates from the middle of September to the beginning of November in the area of the New Hebrides. It comprises *I-171*, *I-39*, *I-181*, *I-32*, *I-21* and *Ro-36*, of which only *I-21* (Cdr Inada) sinks one ship of 6711 tons on 11 Nov. From the middle of November the submarines *Ro-104*, *Ro-105*, *Ro-100*, *Ro-109*, *I-38*, *I-16*, *I-6* and *I-171* are brought up chiefly for transport missions.

26 Aug   Air War/East Asia
American bombers attack the harbour of Hong Kong from bases in China.

29 Aug   Denmark
The German authorities declare a state of emergency when the Danish government rejects the German demand that it should declare a state of emergency and introduce summary courts and the death sentence for saboteurs. Beginning of strikes and sabotage: resignation of the Danish government. The Danish Army is disarmed by German troops. The Danish Fleet (Vice-Adm Vedel) is scuttled. The coastal defence ship *Peder Skram*, the submarines *Havhesten*, *Havkalen*, *Havfruen*, *Havmanden*, *Daphne*, *Dryaden*, *Rota*, *Flora* and *Bellona*, the tender *Henrik Gerner*, the minesweepers *Söbjörnen*, *Söulven* and *Söhunden*, the patrol (ex-torpedo) boats *Hvalrossen*, *Saelen*, *Nordkaperen*, *Makrelen* and *Narhvalen*, five small minesweepers and four minelayers sink

in Copenhagen. The coastal defence ship *Niels Juel* is beached in Isefjord. In Nyborg, Korsör and Kalundborg the crews of Danish ships are, in some cases, overwhelmed by force and the minesweepers *Sölöven*, *Söridderen* and *Söhesten* and the patrol boats *Springeren* and *Hajen* are among those seized. In Ulvsund the patrol boat *Havörnen* is blown up. Some of the ships are later raised, repaired and taken over by the German Navy. The patrol boat *Havkatten*, three motor minesweepers and nine small auxiliary craft escape to Sweden.

29 Aug   Indian Ocean
In operations in the Malacca Straits the British submarine *Trident* attacks the Japanese cruiser *Kashii* off Sabang with 8 torpedoes, all of which miss.

29-31 Aug   Bay of Biscay
T-24, *T-22* and *T-25* bring the Japanese submarine *I-8* (Capt Uchino) into Lorient.

31 Aug-1 Sept   Central Pacific
First carrier raid by the newly-formed US 'Fast Carrier Task Force'.
On 31 Aug-1 Sept TF 15 (Rear-Adm Pownall), comprising the carriers *Yorktown*, *Essex*, and *Independence*, attacks Marcus Island with cover from the battleship *Indiana*, the cruisers *Nashville* and *Mobile* and the destroyers *La Valette*, *Stevens*, *Ringgold*, *Schroeder*, *Sigsbee*, *Thatcher*, *Harrison*, *John Rodgers*, *McKee*, *Dashiell*, *Halford* and the tanker *Guadeloupe*. In 275 sorties in six attacks four aircraft are lost. Damage is done to shore installations. Japanese losses are slight.

31 Aug-3 Sept   Mediterranean
Operation 'Baytown': British landing in Calabria. On 31 Aug the battleships *Nelson* and *Rodney*, the cruiser *Orion* and the destroyers *Offa*, *Petard*, *Quail* *Queenborough*, *Quilliam*, *Tartar*, *Troubridge*, *Tyrian* and *Piorun* (Polish) carry out the preparatory shelling of the coast between Reggio Calabria and Pessaro. On 2 Sept the shelling is repeated by the battleships *Valiant* and *Warspite*, the cruisers *Orion* and *Mauritius*, some of the above-mentioned destroyers, the *Faulknor* and *Loyal*, the monitors *Erebus*, *Roberts* and *Abercrombie* as well as the gunboats *Aphis* and *Scarab*. On 3 Sept the British XIII Corps is

transported in 22 LSTs and 270 smaller landing craft across the Straits of Messina in face of little resistance and landed near Reggio and Villa San Giovanni. There is support from army artillery near Messina and from the guns of the monitors *Erebus*, *Roberts* and *Abercrombie*, the cruisers *Orion* and *Mauritius*, the gunboats *Aphis* and *Scarab* and six destroyers.

1-30 Sept   Pacific
Of the US submarines arriving in their operational areas in September *Harder* (Lt-Cdr Dealey) sinks five ships of 15354 tons and two sailing ships; *Pompano* (Lt-Cdr Thomas) two ships of 8558 tons and torpedoes one other ship; *Snook* (Lt-Cdr Triebel) sinks two ships of 10371 tons; *Trigger* (Lt-Cdr Donaho) sinks four ships of 27095 tons; and *Wahoo* (Cdr Morton) four ships of 13429 tons—all off Japan and in the Kuriles. *Cabrilla* (Lt-Cdr Hammond) torpedoes the escort carrier *Taiyo*; *Halibut* (Lt-Cdr Galantin) sinks three ships of 10394 tons and torpedoes the cruiser *Nachi* and one steamer; *Pargo* (Lt-Cdr Eddy), *S46* (Lt Glenn) and *Salmon* (Lt-Cdr Nicholas) each torpedo one ship; and *Pompano*, *S44* and *Wahoo* are lost in the above areas. In the Central Pacific *Bluefish* (Lt-Cdr Parker) sinks one ship of 3228 tons and the torpedo boat *Kasasagi*; *Drum* (Lt-Cdr McMahon) one ship of 1334 tons; *Gudgeon* (Lt-Cdr Post) one ship of 3158 tons and also torpedoes the destroyer *Oite* and two steamers. *Haddock* (Lt-Cdr Davenport) torpedoes the seaplane tender *Notoro* and one steamer; *Narwhal* (Lt-Cdr Latta) sinks one ship of 4211 tons; *Pogy* (Lt-Cdr Wales) one ship of 7005 tons; *Scamp* (Lt-Cdr Ebert) two ships of 10571 tons; *Snapper* (Lt-Cdr Clemenson) one ship of 860 tons; and *Trout* (Lt-Cdr Clark) two ships of 6912 tons. In the South West Pacific *Bonefish* (Lt-Cdr Hogan) sinks three ships of 24198 tons and one sailing ship; and *Bowfin* (Lt-Cdr Willingham) one ship of 8120 tons and two sailing ships. *Cisco* is lost.

1-9 Sept   South West Pacific
The US VII Amphibious Force (TF 76, Rear-Adm Barbey) sets out from Milne Bay on 1 Sept in order to land 8000 men of the Australian 9th Div (20th

and 26th Brigades on 3-4 Sept and 24th Brigade on 5-6 Sept)E of Lae (New Guinea). It comprises 39 LSTs, 20 LCIs, 9 LCTs, 14 transports, 12 submarine-chasers and three other vessels. The landing is supported by the US destroyers *Conyngham*, *Flusser*, *Perkins*, *Smith*, *Mahan*, *Lamson*, *Mugford*, *Drayton* and *Reid*. *Reid*, as radar picket destroyer, locates an approaching Japanese bomber force, early enough for it to be intercepted by US fighters. In further air attacks *LCI339* is sunk and *LST471*, *LST473* and *Conyngham* damaged. On 8 Sept the destroyers *Perkins*, *Flusser*, *Smith* and *Mahan*, and on 9 Sept the fast transports *Brooks*, *Gilmer*, *Humphreys* and *Sands*, bombard Lae in support of the operation.

2 Sept-19 Oct   Indonesia
Operation 'Jaywick': the Australian motor drifter *Krait* sets out with six canoes on board from Exmouth Gulf in Australia. On 9 Sept she goes through Lombok Strait and on 18 Sept the six canoes with six Limpet mines on board are launched off Singapore. *Krait* cruises for 14 days off South Borneo and the canoes carry out an attack on 21 Sept. Two ships of 7204 tons are destroyed. On 1 Oct and 3 Oct the canoes are met and, after passing through Lombok Strait on 10 Oct, the *Krait* arrives back in Exmouth Gulf on 19 Oct.

3-5 Sept   English Channel
The German 5th TB Flotilla (Cdr Koppenhagen), consisting of *T25*, *Möwe*, *Kondor*, *T19* and *T27*, carries out the mining operations 'Taube' and 'Rebhuhn' in the Channel.

3-9 Sept   Mediterranean
Preparatory movements for operation 'Avalanche' (see 9-16 Sept). The following convoys set out: from Tripoli on 3 Sept TSS.1, on 6 Sept TSM.1, TSF.1 and TSS.2, on 7 Sept TSS.3; from Palermo on 8 Sept TSF.1X; from Bizerta on 4 Sept FSS.1, on 6 Sept FSM.1, FSM.1X, on 7 Sept FSS.2, FSS.2X, FSX.3; from Termini on 8 Sept FSS.2Y; from Oran on 5 Sept NSF.1; and from Algiers on 6 Sept NSF.1X.
The convoys consist of a total of three headquarters ships, six attack transports, 15 infantry landing ships (LCIs), nine attack freighters, 94 LSTs, 131 LCIs, 66 LCTs, 21 LCSs, two fighter direction ships, three tankers, one petrol tanker, five tugs and two coastal motor boats. Three cruisers, two AA ships, two monitors, one gunboat, 31 destroyers, 21 motor torpedo boats, 36 PCs, 35 MLs, 37 minesweepers and 12 trawlers proceed with the convoys as escort. Force H (see 9 Sept) sets out from Malta on 7 Sept and, as a reserve covering force, Vice-Adm Power, sets out on 7 Sept from Algiers for Augusta with the British battleships *Howe* and *King George V*.
In the nights 6-7 Sept and 8-9 Sept German bomber units make attacks on Bizerta (convoy FSS.2) and units at sea. One LST is destroyed and one LCT is damaged.

6-9 Sept   Arctic
Operation 'Sizilien' (also 'Zitronella'): a German Task Force (Adm Kummetz), comprising the battleships *Tirpitz* (Capt Meyer) and *Scharnhorst* (Capt Hüffmeier) and the 4th (Capt Johannesson), the 5th (Capt Wolff) and the 6th (Capt Kothe) DD Flotillas, consisting of *Z27*, *Z29*, *Z30*, *Z31*, *Z33*, *Erich Steinbrinck*, *Karl Galster*, *Theodor Riedel* and *Hans Lody*, sets out to sea from Altafjord on the evening of 6 Sept to attack Allied bases on Spitzbergen. A battalion of the 349th Grenadier Regt is embarked on the destroyers. 8 Sept: at 0300 hrs Adm Kummetz detaches the *Scharnhorst* and the 5th and 6th DD Flotillas which then land their troops in Grönfjord and Advent Bay. The *Tirpitz* goes on with the 4th DD Flotilla to shell Barentsburg. Coastal batteries are destroyed, coal and supply dumps, water and electricity works are blown up. 9 Sept: the battle squadron returns to Altafjord.
On 19 Oct the US cruiser *Tuscaloosa* with one US and three British destroyers lands Norwegian troops in Spitzbergen to re-establish bases.

8-12 Sept   Mediterranean
On the afternoon of 8 Sept Gen Eisenhower announces in Algiers the conclusion of an armistice with Italy. At this point the planned German countermeasures ('Achse') come into force to disarm the main body of the Italian forces.

In accordance with the conditions of the armistice the Italian Fleet (Adm Bergamini†) sets out from La Spezia with the battleships *Roma*, *Vittorio Veneto* and *Italia* (9th Div), the cruisers *Eugenio di Savoia* (Div Adm Oliva), *Duca D'Aosta* and *Montecuccoli* (7th Div) and the destroyers *Mitragliere*, *Fuciliere*, *Carabiniere*, *Velite* (12th Flotilla), *Legionario*, *Oriani*, *Artigliere* and *Grecale* (14th Flotilla) and joins the cruisers *Duca degli Abruzzi*, *Garibaldi* and *Regolo* (8th Div) and the torpedo boat *Libra* coming from Genoa. The force is located by German air reconnaissance and is attacked W of the Straits of Bonifacio on the afternoon of 9 Sept by 11 Do 217s of III/K.G. 100, using FX 1400 wireless-controlled bombs, from Istres near Marseilles. Lt Schmetz obtains a direct hit on the *Roma* which sinks. The *Italia* is damaged by hits. The destroyers *Da Noli* and *Vivaldi*, coming from Castellamare, are shelled by German coastal batteries in the Straits of Bonifacio and are lost on mines and by gunfire respectively. Of the *Regolo*, *Mitragliere*, *Fuciliere* and *Carabiniere* left behind to rescue survivors and the torpedo boats *Libra*, *Orione*, *Orsa*, *Impetuoso* and *Pegaso* summoned to the scene, *Libra*, and *Orione* go to Bone, the others put into Port Mahon in the Balearics and are interned; *Pegaso* and *Impetuoso* sink after a collision just off the harbour. The rest of the Fleet proceeds to Malta under the command of Div Adm Oliva and is met on 10 Sept by the British battleships *Warspite* and *Valiant* with the destroyers *Faulknor*, *Fury*, *Echo*, *Intrepid*, *Raider*, *Vasilissa Olga* (Greek) and *Le Terrible* (French). On 9 Sept Adm Da Zara puts to sea from Taranto with the battleships *Andrea Doria* and *Caio Duilio* (5th Div), the cruisers *Cadorna* and *Pompeo Magno* and the destroyer *Da Recco* and arrives in Malta on 10 Sept escorted by the battleship *King George V*. In addition, the battleship *Giulio Cesare*, the aircraft depot ship *Miraglia*, the destroyer *Riboty* and the torpedo boat *Sagittario* arrive in Malta from Adriatic ports. The Italian submarines (33 in all), which are either concentrated in the area off Salerno in expectation of an Allied landing at the beginning of September or are in Italian harbours and fit for operations, assemble in Allied harbours. By 12 Sept 11 torpedo boats, eight corvettes and smaller craft reach Palermo from harbours in the Tyrrhenian Sea.

In the harbours occupied by German troops, the ships which are non-operational are scuttled by their crews e.g. the cruisers *Bolzano* and *Taranto*, the destroyers *Zeno*, *Corazziere* and *Maestrale*, the torpedo boats *Ghibli*, *Lira*, *Procione*, *Cascino*, *Montanari* and many small craft. Others are saved by German troops, including many ships buildings in the yards, some of which are finished for the German Navy.

9 Sept-3 Dec Indian Ocean
The Italian submarine *Cagni* (Cdr Rosselli-Lorenzini), which, while sailing in the South Atlantic, has torpedoed the British auxiliary cruiser *Asturias* (22048 tons) on 25 July, operates without success off South Africa until 9 Sept. After the Italian surrender she enters Durban on 20 Sept. The Colonial sloop *Eritrea*, sent to meet the Italian submarines, escapes from Sabang to Colombo.
Of the Japanese submarines operating from Penang *I-27* (Lt-Cdr Fukumura) sinks one ship of 5151 tons on the Indian West Coast and damages another of 7176 tons with an unexploded torpedo. *I-10* (Capt Tonozuka) sinks in September and October four ships of 22906 tons in the Gulf of Aden and torpedoes one tanker of 9057 tons on 5 Oct from the convoy AP.47. After refuelling from the tanker *Brake* from 9 Sept to 14 Sept the German U-boats of the 'Monsun' group operate on the Indian West Coast, in the Gulf of Oman, in the Gulf of Aden, on the East African Coast and round the Chagos Archipelago. By the end of October, *U532* (Cdr* Junker) sinks four ships of 24484 tons and torpedoes one ship of 5845 tons; *U188* (Lt-Cdr Lüdden) sinks one ship of 7176 tons and torpedoes one ship of 9977 tons; *U168* (Lt-Cdr Pich) sinks one ship of 2183 tons and six sailing ships. Further attacks by these boats and by *U183* (Cdr Schäfer) and *U533* (Lt-Cdr Henning) are partly impeded by torpedo failures. *U533* is sunk on 16 Oct by two aircraft in the Persian

Gulf. The other boats go to Penang. In October and November the Japanese submarine *I-37* (Cdr Otani) reconnoitres with her aircraft the Chagos Archipelago on 4 Oct, Diego Suarez on 10 Oct, Kilindini on 17 Nov and the Seychelles on 23 Nov. She sinks two ships of 13376 tons. Off the Indian South and West Coasts and the Chagos Archipelago the Japanese submarines *I-166*, *I-162* and *I-165* meet with no success in two operations in October and November. From November to the beginning of December *I-27* (Lt-Cdr Fukumura) sinks four ships of 23908 tons in the Gulf of Aden and torpedoes one ship of 7126 tons. The transport submarine *I-8*, coming from France, returns to Singapore on 28 Nov and reaches Japan. *I-34*, which sets out on a transport journey, is sunk off Penang by the British submarine *Taurus* on 12 Nov.

9-11 Sept   Mediterranean
In an improvised operation 'Slapstick' the British 12th Cruiser Sqdn (Commodore Agnew), comprising *Aurora*, *Penelope*, *Sirius*, *Dido*, the fast minelayer *Abdiel* and the US cruiser *Boise*, lands the 1st British Airborne Div in Taranto. The operation is covered by Vice-Adm Power with the battleships *Howe* and *King George V*, the latter of which meets the Italian ships coming from Taranto. During the operation the Italian corvette *Baionetta* goes with the cruiser *Scipione Africano* to Pescara to bring the Italian King and Government to Brindisi.
The German motor torpedo boats *S54* (Lt Klaus Degenhard-Schmidt) and *S61* (Petty Officer Blömker) leave Taranto on the evening of the Italian surrender having dropped a number of mines into the harbour undetected. The fast British minelayer *Abdiel* (2650 tons) sinks on one on 10 Sept with heavy losses among the 400 troops on board. On their way through the Adriatic the two motor torpedo boats sink the Italian gunboat *Aurora* (935 tons) off Ancona on 11 Sept and the Italian destroyer *Sella* S of Venice, and they capture the new troop transport *Leopardi* (4572 tons) with 700 troops on board. They reach Venice with their last drop of fuel and compel the local naval commander to surrender.

9-16 Sept   Mediterranean
Operation 'Avalanche': landing of the 5th US Army (Lt-Gen Clark) in the Bay of Salerno. Overall command of the amphibious operation: Adm Cunningham in Malta (with the destroyer *Hambledon*). 'Western Naval Task Force' (TF. 80) under Vice-Adm Hewitt on the headquarters ship *Ancon*. Attached: the AA ships *Ulster Queen* and *Palomares*. Beacon submarine: the British *Shakespeare*.
Southern Attack Force (TF 81, Rear-Adm Hall) with the headquarters ship *Samuel Chase*, 18 transports, three tank landing ships (*Boxer*, *Bruiser* and *Thruster*), 27 LSTs, 32 LCIs, six LCTs, four LCSs, eight PCs, nine AMs, 12 YMSs and 32 small vessels lands VI US Corps (Maj-Gen Dawley) with the 36th Inf Div (Maj-Gen Walker) and the 45th Inf Div (Maj-Gen Middleton) off Paestum. Support group and escort (Rear-Adm Davidson): US cruisers *Philadelphia*, *Savannah*, and *Brooklyn*, the British monitor *Abercrombie*, the Dutch gunboat *Flores* and the US destroyers *Wainwright*, *Trippe*, *Rhind*, *Rowan*, *Plunkett*, *Niblack*, *Benson*, *Gleaves*, *Mayo*, *Knight*, *Dallas*, *Bernadou*, *Cole*, *Woolsey*, *Ludlow*, *Bristol* and *Edison*.
Northern Attack Force: (TF 85, Commodore Oliver) with the headquarters ships *Hilary* and *Biscayne* (Rear-Adm Conolly), eight transports, four LSIs, 90 LSTs, 96 LCIs, 84 LCTs, 23 SCs and MLs, seven minesweepers and four tugs, lands the British X Corps (Lt-Gen McCreery) with the 46th Inf Div (Maj-Gen Freeman-Attwood), the 56th Inf Div (Maj-Gen Graham), the 7th Armoured Div (Maj-Gen Erskine), the 3rd US Ranger BLT and two British Commandos. Support group and escort (Rear-Adm Harcourt): the British cruisers *Mauritius*, *Uganda*, *Orion* and *Delhi*, the monitor *Roberts* and the destroyers (19th Flotilla) *Laforey*, *Lookout*, *Loyal*, *Nubian*, *Tartar* and (21st Flotilla) *Mendip*, *Dulverton*, *Tetcott*, *Belvoir*, *Brocklesby*, *Quantock*, *Blackmore*, *Brecon*, *Beaufort*, *Exmoor*, *Ledbury*, *Blankney* and *Pindos* (Greek).
Support Carrier Force (TF 88, Rear-Adm Vian): the cruisers *Euryalus*, *Scylla* and *Charybdis*, the light carrier

Unicorn, the escort carriers *Battler*, *Attacker*, *Hunter* and *Stalker* and the destroyers *Slazak* (Polish), *Krakowiak* (Polish), *Cleveland*, *Holcombe*, *Atherstone*, *Liddesdale*, *Farndale*, *Calpe* and *Haydon*.
Covering force: Force H (Vice-Adm Willis), consisting of the battleships *Nelson*, *Rodney*, (Rear-Adm Rivett-Carcac), *Warspite* (Rear-Adm La T. Bissett), *Valiant*, the carriers (Rear-Adm Moody) *Illustrious* and *Formidable* (Rear-Adm Talbot) and the destroyers (4th Flotilla) *Quilliam*, *Queenborough*, *Quail*, *Petard*, (24th Flotilla) *Troubridge*, *Tyrian*, *Tumult*, *Offa*, *Piorun* (Polish) and (8th Flotilla) *Faulknor*, *Intrepid*, *Eclipse*, *Inglefield*, *Fury*, *Ilex*, *Echo*, *Raider*, *Vasilissa Olga* (Greek) and the large French destroyers *Le Fantasque* and *Le Terrible*.
In an attack by German torpedo bombers in the night 8-9 Sept the *Warspite* and *Formidable* are narrowly missed.
The landing succeeds on 9 Sept against strong and increasing German resistance. But at first the disembarked troops fail to reach their target positions in spite of strong fire support from the cruisers and destroyers. The monitor *Abercrombie* is damaged by a mine and the destroyer *Laforey* by five shell hits. On 10 Sept and 11 Sept the landing troops make only slow progress. In the night 10-11 Sept three German motor torpedo boats of the 3rd MTB Flotilla attack a US convoy and sink the destroyer *Rowan*. On 11 Sept heavy German air attacks begin, in the course of which Do 127s of II and III/K.G. 100 drop FX 1400 wireless-controlled and Hs 293 glider bombs. On 11 Sept the *Savannah* is badly damaged by a direct hit and the *Philadelphia* is narrowly missed. On 13 Sept and 14 Sept three German divisions make a strong armoured attack which compresses the Allied bridgehead and creates a serious situation. For fire support the monitor *Roberts*, the cruisers *Maurituis*, *Uganda*, *Orion*, *Aurora*, *Philadelphia*, *Boise*, the destroyers *Loyal*, *Lookout*, *Tartar*, *Nubian*, *Brecon*, *Quantock* and *Eggesford* lie off the assault area. In air attacks with FX 1400s and Hs 293s the *Uganda* is seriously damaged by hits

and the *Philadelphia*, *Loyal* and *Nubian* slightly damaged by near-misses. The hospital ship *Newfoundland* sinks. On 14 Sept first the cruiser *Penelope* arrives and then *Euryalus*, *Scylla* and *Charybdis*. On 14 Sept and 15 Sept respectively a supply transport is heavily hit by bombs and lost. On 15 Sept the *Valiant* and *Warspite* intervene; the latter is hit and badly damaged on 16 Sept by two wireless-controlled bombs. On 16 Sept forward elements of the British 8th Army, coming up from the S, break through to the bridgehead near Salerno.

9-23 Sept   East Mediterranean
After the announcement of the Italian surrender there is fighting between the weaker German units and the stronger Italian garrison on Rhodes. The latter capitulates on 11 Sept. This prevents the British occupation of the island. From 10 Sept to 17 Sept small British battle groups and commando groups are brought by light British craft (MLs and MTBs) and Greek caiques to Casteloriso, Coo, Leros, Calino, Samos, Symi and Stampalia. On 12 Sept to 14 Sept the Indian sloop *Sutlej*, the Greek destroyer *Kondouriotis* and the French sloops *La Moqueuse* and *Commandant Dominé* bring British troops to Casteloriso but a repetition of the operation on 16 Sept has to be abandoned. The troops which have been brought there organize themselves for defence with the help of the Italian garrisons. On 16 Sept the British 8th DD Flotilla, comprising *Faulknor*, *Echo*, *Intrepid*, *Eclipse*, *Raider* and *Vasilissa Olga*, arrives in Alexandria as a reinforcement from the Central Mediterranean. The German Admiral commanding the Aegean, Rear-Adm Lange, tries to reinforce the Aegean Islands and to take off the Italian prisoners. In attacks on these convoys the Greek submarine *Katsonis* (Lt Laskos) is rammed and sunk by the German submarine-chaser *UJ2101* (Lt-Cdr Vollheim). On 17 Sept *Echo* and *Intrepid* sink the submarine-chaser *UJ2104* off Stampalia; on 18 Sept *Faulknor*, *Eclipse* and *Vasilissa Olga* attack a convoy and damage the ships *Pluto* and *Paula*. On 23 the *Eclipse* sinks S of Rhodes the German torpedo boat *TA10* and the steamer *Donizetti* with

1576 Italian prisoners on board, some of whom are rescued.

10-16 Sept   Black Sea

To start a major Soviet offensive against the German Kuban bridgehead, 8935 troops of the reinforced 255th Naval Inf Brigade are landed in the harbour of Novorossisk under the command of Rear-Adm Kholostyakov on 10 Sept in 129 small craft in two instalments, after 25 torpedo cutters under Capt 2nd Class Protsenko have opened the approach and eliminated the pockets of resistance. In the harbour area the Soviet units are engaged in heavy fighting with two German naval companies under Lt-Cdr Hossfeld and with reinforcements which are brought up. They are partly annihilated before the planned departures begin as part of the German withdrawal from the Kuban bridgehead. The Soviet torpedo cutters *TKA-124*, *TKA-125* and the patrol cutters *SKA-025*, *SKA-032* and *SKA-084* are lost as a result of action by the German defence.

10 Sept-5 Oct   East Mediterranean

In course of the German evacuation of Sardinia, which begins on 10 Sept, 25000 troops, 2300 vehicles and 5000 tons of supplies are brought across the Straits of Bonifacio to Corsica. After agreement with the Italian garrison the troops proceed to Bastia and are evacuated from there by air—21107 troops and 350 tons of supplies—or by sea to Livorno and Elba—6240 troops, 1200 prisoners and 5000 tons of supplies. 15 steamers and some 120 ferry barges and other small craft are employed under Capt v. Liebenstein. In a US air attack on 21 Sept five steamers are lost. The British submarine *Unseen* (Lt Crawford) sinks on 21 Sept the German minelayer *Brandenburg* and the night fighter direction ship *Kreta*; *Uproar* (Lt Herrick) sinks one ship of 731 tons and on 24 Sept, in conjunction with the Polish *Dzik* (Cdr Romanowski) and the British *Ultor* (Lt Hunt), the tanker *Champagne* (9946 tons); *Sibyl* (Lt Turner) sinks one ship of 2910 tons and the escort *Hummer*. The minelayer *Pommern* sinks on a mine on 5 Oct. From 11 Sept contingents of French troops are transported from Algiers to Ajaccio (Corsica): on 11-13

Sept 109 men by the French submarine *Casabianca* (Cdr* D'Herminier); on 13-14 Sept 500 men and 60 tons of supplies by the French destroyers *Le Fantasque* and *Le Terrible* (Capt Perzo); on 14-16 Sept 30 men and seven tons of supplies by the submarine *Perle*; on 16-17 Sept 550 men and 60 tons of supplies by the destroyers *Le Fantasque*, *Tempête* and *L'Alcyon*; on 16-18 Sept five tons by the submarine *Aréthuse*; on 17-18 Sept a US commando unit of 400 men and 20 tons of supplies by the Italian destroyers *Legionario* and *Oriani*; on 19-21 Sept 1200 men, 110 tons of supplies, six guns and six vehicles by the cruiser *Jeanne d'Arc* and the destroyers *Le Fantasque*, *Tempête*, *L'Alcyon*; on 22-23 Sept 1500 men and 200 tons by the cruiser *Montcalm* and destroyer *Le Fantasque*; on 23-25 Sept 350 men, 100 tons of supplies, 21 guns and 30 vehicles by the destroyers *Le Fortuné*, *L'Alcyon*, the landing ship *LST79* and the minesweepers *MMS1* and *MMS116*; on 25 Sept 850 men and 160 tons of supplies by the *Jeanne d'Arc*; on 26 Sept 750 men, 100 tons of supplies, 12 guns and 10 vehicles by the *Montcalm* and the British destroyer *Pathfinder*; on 28-30 Sept 200 men, four guns, 70 vehicles by *Le Fortuné* and *LST79* (both damaged in a German air attack); and on 30 Sept-1 Oct 700 men and 170 tons of supplies by *Jeanne d'Arc* and *L'Alcyon*.

10 Sept- 12 Nov   West and South Atlantic

In operations in distant waters *U161* (Lt-Cdt Achilles) and *U170* (Lt-Cdr Pfeffer) sink on the Brazilian coast three ships of 10770 tons and one ship of 4663 tons respectively. *U161* is sunk on 27 Sept by a flying boat of USN-VP.74. *U518* and *U123* have no success in the Gulf of Mexico and off the coast of Guiana. *U214* lays a mine barrage off Colon (Panama) on 9 Sept. *U220* (Lt Barber) lays a mine barrage off St John's on which two ships of 7199 tons are sunk. *U536* is not able to attack in the area S of Nova Scotia.

12 Sept-9 Oct   Black Sea

The German 17th Army (Gen Jaenecke), in a planned withdrawal through prepared defensive positions, evacuates the Kuban bridgehead (Operation 'Brunhild') and so prevents any breakthrough by the Soviet North Caucasus Front (Col-Gen Petrov) which simultaneously goes over to the attack. By using German naval ferry barges of the 1st, 3rd, 5th and 7th Landing Flotillas (Lt-Cdr Giele, Cdr* Strempel, Cdr Mehler and Cdr Stelter), Siebel ferries, engineer ferries and tugs, lighters and river tugs, 239669 troops, 16311 wounded, 27456 civilians, 115477 tons of supplies, 21230 vehicles, 27741 horse-driven vehicles, 1815 guns, 74 tanks, 74657 horses and 6255 head of cattle are transported across the Kerch Straits under the direction of the Admiral Commanding the Black Sea, Vice-Adm Kieseritzky† and the Naval Commandant Caucasus, Capt Grattenauer. Landings made by Soviet light craft on the south coast and by the Soviet Azov Flotilla (Rear-Adm Gorshkov) on the north coast are unable to prevent the German moves. The defence of the Kerch Straits against attacks by Soviet ships is undertaken by the 1st MTB Flotilla, the 3rd MMS Flotilla and gunboats. There are frequent engagements with light Soviet forces, e.g. on 17 Sept, 20 Sept and 24 Sept. In an attack by the 1st MTB Flotilla on Anapa on 26-27 Sept several steamers lying alongside the pier are hit.

On 30 Sept the Soviet destroyers *Sposobny*, *Boiki* and *Besposhchadny* make an unsuccessful sortie against the German evacuation transports on the south coast of the Crimea.

Off the Caucasus coast the German *U18* (Lt Fleige) sinks on 18 Sept a small ship near Tuapse; *U20* (Lt Schöler) lays on 20 Sept mines off Sochi and sinks a lighter off Anapa on 30 Sept.

S of Evpatoria the Soviet submarine *S-33* misses on 22 Sept the steamer *Santa Fé* escorted by the Rumanian destroyer *Regele Ferdinand*. On 28 Sept the submarine *M-113* runs on a mine W of the Crimea and reaches her base badly damaged.

12 Sept-20 Oct   Mediterranean
In U-boat operations against the Salerno bridgehead attacks by *U565*, *U616*, and again by *U565*, fail on 12 Sept, 15 Sept and 24 Sept. Only *U593* (Lt-Cdr Kelbling) sinks on 21 Sept and 25 Sept one ship of 7176 tons and the US minesweeper *Skill*. Off the Algerian

coast *U410* (Lt Fenski) sinks on 26 Sept and 30 Sept one ship from the convoy UGS.17 and two ships from a western convoy totalling 17031 tons. Off Cyrenaica *U596* (Lt Nonn) sinks one ship of 5542 tons.

From 2 Oct T-5 torpedoes are used for the first time in the Mediterranean. Off the Algerian coast *U223* (Lt-Cdr Wächter) sinks one ship of 4970 tons and *U371* (Lt-Cdr Mehl) from 11 Oct to 15 Oct the British minesweeper *Hythe*, the US destroyer *Bristol* and one ship of 7176 tons from GUS.18. Attacks by *U73* and *U431* are unsuccessful. Of the U-boats deployed against the Salerno bridgehead, *U616* (Lt Koitschka) sinks the US destroyer *Buck* and two attacks fail. Likewise, four attacks by *U380* and two by *U81* fail.

U73 (Lt Deckert) sinks one ship of 4531 tons off Bone.

17-19 Sept   Central Pacific
US air attacks on Tarawa.

On 17-18 Sept 25 Liberator bombers of the 11th Bomber Group of the 7th USAAF attack Tarawa (Gilbert Islands) from Canton and Funafuti.

On 18-19 Sept TF 15 (Rear-Adm Pownall), comprising the carriers *Lexington*, *Princeton* and *Belleau Wood*, covered by the cruisers *Santa Fé*, *Birmingham* and *Mobile* and the destroyers *Stevens*, *Caldwell*, *Ringgold*, *Coghlan*, *Schroeder*, *Hazelwood*, *Bradford*, *Harrison*, *John Rodgers*, *McKee*, *Bancroft*, *Dashiell* and the tanker *Guadeloupe*, carries out attacks on Tarawa. 190 sorties; four aircraft are lost.

On 19 Sept the Liberators repeat the attack. 12 Japanese aircraft and two motor torpedo boats are destroyed.

18-23 Sept   North Atlantic
Resumption of U-boat group operations in the North Atlantic after equipping the U-boats with eight 2-cm AA guns, search receiver equipment and acoustic torpedoes ('Zaunkönig'—T-5). The 'Leuthen' group, comprising *U584*, *U305*, *U731*, *U260*, *U641*, *U758*, *U378*, *U229*, *U386*, *U338*, *U645*, *U270*, *U275*, *U377*, *U666*, *U238*, *U422*, *U341*, *U952* and *U402*, is planned to operate on the eastern side of the North Atlantic against the convoys ON.202 and ONS.18 expected

from 20 Sept. Five of them are first replenished from *U460*, the others come through the Bay of Biscay without incident. On 19 Sept a Liberator of No 10 Sqdn RCAF sinks *U341* in the southern part of the patrol line in the morning. The British Admiralty reroutes the convoys to the NW. ON.202 has 38 ships and EG C.2, consisting of the destroyers HMCS *Gatineau* (Cdr Burnett) and HMS *Icarus*, the frigate HMS *Lagan*, the corvettes HMS *Polyanthus*, HMCS *Drumheller* and HMCS *Kamloops*. ONS.18 has 27 ships and EG B.3 consisting of the destroyers HMS *Keppel* (Cdr Evans), HMS *Escapade*, the frigate HMS *Towy*, the corvettes HMS *Orchis*, HMS *Narcissus*, FFS *Roselys*, FFS *Lobélia*, FFS *Renoncule* and the trawler *Northern Foam*. In the convoy there is also the 'merchant aircraft carrier' *Macalpine*. In the morning the Canadian 9th SG, comprising the frigate *Itchen*, the destroyers *St Croix* and *St Francis* and the corvettes *Chambly*, *Sackville* and *Morden*, receives orders to join the convoy ONS.18. On the evening of 19 Sept several U-boats, unknown to themselves, run into the escort of ONS.18: *Roselys* pursues a U-boat with depth charges and *Escapade* is badly damaged in a 'hedgehog' attack due to a premature fuse. Early on 20 Sept *U270* (Lt-Cdr Otto) reports ON.202 but is located by HF/DF and approached by the frigate *Lagan* (Lt-Cdr Bridgeman). *U270* hits the *Lagan* with a T-5 in the stern but *Gatineau* forces the U-boat to submerge. *Lagan* is taken in tow. The Commander U-boats deploys the 'Leuthen' group. The second contact-keeper, *U238* (Lt Hepp), is located by HF/DF and driven off by the *Polyanthus*. But she shadows the corvette and three hours later she is able to torpedo in an underwater attack two Liberty ships of 7176 tons: one sinks and the second is sunk later by *U645* (Lt-Cdr Ferro). T-5 torpedoes directed from *U645* and *U402* (Cdr Frhr v. Forstner) against the *Gatineau* and *Polyanthus*, which are escorting the rescue ship *Rathlin*, miss. On the morning of 20 Sept air escort is provided by Liberators of No 120 Sqdn RAF. Before sufficient U-boats are assembled in the area of the convoy, *U338* (Lt-Cdr Kinzel) gives the agreed signal 'Keep on the surface for defence' when the U-boats are meant to fight their way to the convoy with their AA fire against the air escort. The single U-boat is sunk by a Liberator with an acoustic homing A/S torpedo ('Fido'). Contact is, at first, lost when *U731* is driven off. The Admialty orders the convoys to join up under the SOE, Cdr Evans, and this is done by the evening. *U386* gains contact but is located by HF/DF and attacked with depth charges from *Keppel* and *Roselys*. A dusk attack by *U260* on steamers fails because the torpedoes do not explode. *St Croix* (Lt-Cdr Dobson), which is directed to a boat located by HF/DF, is hit by a T-5 from *U305* (Lt-Cdr Bahr) and finished off by her, while *Itchen*, which is sent for support, comes up and a T-5 explodes in her wash. In the night 20-21 Sept the U-boats try to shoot their way through to the steamers. *U229* (Lt Schetelig) misses the *Icarus* with a T-5; the latter, in avoiding the torpedo, collides slightly with *Drumheller*. *U260* (Lt-Cdr Purkhold) misses the *Narcissus*; and the *Polyanthus*, sent to support the *St Croix*, is sunk by *U952* (Lt Curio). More T-5 firings by *U229*, *U641* (Lt Rendtel), *U270*, *U377* (Lt Kluth) and *U584* (Lt-Cdr Deecke) fail or detonate in the wash of the escorts. Towards morning on 21 Sept mist sets in and *Renoncule* and *Roselys* drive off *U377* which is still keeping listening contact. When the mist lifts, the *Macalpine* flies off her Swordfish aircraft for air escort.

On the evening of 21 Sept *U584* comes up and leads seven other boats to the area. Two boats are driven off by *Renoncule* and one boat by *Roselys*. *U584* is damaged by gunfire from *Chambly* after a T-5 failure. *U952* is almost rammed by *Northern Foam*. Towards morning *Roselys*, *Lobélia* and *Renonucle* each drive off one more boat. *U229*, which is located by HF/DF, is sunk with gunfire and ramming by *Keppel*.

The mist lifts on the afternoon of 22 Sept and Swordfishes from the *Macalpine* and Liberators from No 10 Sqdn RCAF take over the air escort.

The U-boats attack with their AA guns and partly drive the aircraft off. *U377* and *U270* are damaged. *U420* wards off a bomber. *U260* is forced under water by *Itchen* after being located by HF/DF; *U952* misses the *Renoncule* with a T-5 and *U731* (Lt Techand) another corvette. In the dark *Morden* sights *U666* (Lt-Cdr Engel) in front of the convoy. The latter fires two T-5s, one of which explodes just to the stern of *Morden*, while the second hits and blows up the *Itchen*. In the resulting confusion, *U238* sinks three ships of 15872 tons with a FAT salvo. A T-5 from *U260* explodes in the wash of the *Chambly*. Towards morning mist sets in again. After dawn the U-boats have again to defend themselves against the Liberators of No 10 Sqdn RCAF, in the course of which *U422* is damaged. *U952* sinks one more ship of 6198 tons and hits a Liberty ship with an unexploded torpedo. *U758* (Lt-Cdr Manseck) finishes off one disabled ship and misses the *Rathlin* and *Lobélia* which have remained behind. On the morning of 23 Sept the operation has to be broken off.

The successes reported by the U-boats (12 escorts sunk with 24 T-5 firings and three more probables) result in the effectiveness of the new torpedo being greatly over-estimated.

21-22 Sept   Norway
Operation 'Source' with British midget submarines against the heavy German ships in Altafjord. Towed by the large submarines *Thrasher, Truculent, Stubborn, Syrtis, Sceptre* and *Seanymph*, the midget submarines *X5, X6, X7, X9, X10* and *X8* are to enter the fjord and attack the battleships *Tirpitz* and *Scharnhorst* and the cruiser *Lützow* with ground mines. *X9* and *X8* are lost on the way; *X5* probably sinks in a minefield in the entrance to the fjord; and *X10* has to return because of a breakdown. Only *X6* (Lt Cameron) and *X7* (Lt Plaice) succeed in getting inside the net defences of the *Tirpitz* and in laying the mines there. As a result of their detonation, *Tirpitz* is badly damaged and out of action until March 1944.
On 23 Sept *Lützow* sets out for the Baltic. She is located by British air

reconnaissance on 26 Sept and 27 Sept, but the Beaufighters and Tarpon torpedo bombers of No 832 Sqdn Fleet Air Arm sent out from Shetland pass by to the stern of the ship which reaches Gotenhafen on 1 Oct without experiencing any attack.

22 Sept-3 Oct   South West Pacific
The VII Amphibious Force (Rear-Adm Barbey) with the fast transport *Brooks*, LSTs and LSIs lands the 20th Australian Brigade on both sides of Finschhafen. Support is provided by the US destroyers *Lamson, Mugford, Drayton* and *Flusser*. The assault forces are escorted by the US destroyers *Conyngham, Perkins, Smith, Reid, Mahan* and *Henley*. On 25 Sept the Japanese submarines *I-177* and *I-176* try for the last time to supply Lae and Finschhafen. The Japanese submarines *Ro-100, Ro-104* and *Ro-108* are deployed against the American operation. The last of them sinks the *Henley* on 3 Oct. Finschhafen is captured on 2 Oct.

24-25 Sept   North Sea
Mining operation 'Probestück' by 29 German motor torpedo boats of the 2nd, 4th, 6th and 8th MTB Flotillas off Harwich and Orfordness. 120 mines are laid. In engagements *S96* sinks the trawler *Franctireur* and is herself rammed by *ML105* and has to be abandoned. Three British MLs are damaged.

25 Sept-7 Oct   South Pacific
From 25 Sept to 28 Oct the Japanese bring some 100 assault boats and other small craft to the northern beach of Kolombangara in order to evacuate the garrison (Maj-Gen Sasaki). Cover is provided by 11 destroyers and the submarines *Ro-105, Ro-106* and *Ro-109*, one of which misses the US cruiser *Columbia*. Then US destroyer forces are deployed to blockade Kolombangara: on 27-28 Sept Capt Gillan with *Charles Ausburne, Claxton, Dyson, Spence* and *Foote*; on 29-30 Sept Capt Walker with *Patterson, Foote, Ralph Talbot* and *McCalla*; on 1-2 Oct Capt Cooke with *Waller, Eaton* and *Cony* and Cdr Chandler with *Radford, Saufley* and *Grayson*; on 2-3 Oct Cdr Larson with *Ralph Talbot, Taylor* and *Perry*; and on 3-4 Oct the Chandler force. The Japanese (Rear-Adm Ijuin) are able to evacuate 9400 troops with des-

troyers, fast transports, assault boats, etc. About a third of the small craft and 1000 men fall victim to the US destroyers. After the conclusion of the Kolombangara withdrawal, Rear-Adm Ijuin tries on 6-7 Oct to evacuate Vella Lavella with the destroyers *Fumitsuki*, *Matsukaze*, *Yunagi* (transport force) and *Akigumo*, *Isokaze*, *Kazegumo*, *Yugumo*, *Shigure* and *Samidare*. Capt Walker with the US destroyers *Selfridge*, *Chevalier* and *O'Bannon* is sent from the N and Cdr Larson with *Ralph Talbot*, *Taylor* and *La Vallette* from the S to operate against the force which is located by air reconnaissance. Off the coast of Vella Lavella there is an engagement between the Walker force and the Japanese covering group. The three US destroyers fire 14 torpedoes, one of which hits the *Yugumo*. The latter's torpedo salvo, fired off first, hits the *Chevalier* which sinks after a collision with *O'Bannon*. *Selfridge* continues the engagement but is hit by one torpedo from the salvoes of *Samidare* and *Shigure*. But the Japanese turn away: Cdr Larson does not come up and is only able to sink the wreck of the *Yugumo*.

26-27 Sept   English Channel
British attack on a German convoy proceeding from Le Havre to Dunkirk. While the British *MGB108*, *MGB118* and *MGB117* try to engage the German escort vessels of the 15th PB Flotilla and the 2nd MMS Flotilla out at sea, the Dutch *MTB202*, *MTB204* and *MTB231* attack from the shore side off Fécamp and Bercq-sur-Mer and sink *V1501* and the freighters *Madali* (3019 tons) and *Jungingen* (800 tons).

26 Sept-12 Oct   East Mediterranean
German counter-attack in the Aegean. On 26 Sept Ju 88s of L.G.1 sink the destroyers HMS *Intrepid* and *Vasilissa Olga* (Greek) in the harbour of Leros and on 1 Oct the Italian *Euro*.
On 3 Oct German ships and emergency craft, escorted by the 21st SC Flotilla and supported by the Luftwaffe, carry out the operation 'Eisbär'. Troops are landed on Coo which overwhelm the garrison and take 1388 British and 3145 Italians prisoner. Owing to lack of fuel, the destroyers HMS *Aldenham*, *Pindos* and *Themistokles* (Greek) are unable to attack the invasion convoy which is located by British air reconnaissance.
On 5 Oct German bombers sink the Italian minelayer *Legnano* in Leros. On 7 Oct a convoy for Coo, reported by the British submarine *Unruly* and consisting of the freighter *Olympos* (5216 tons), seven naval ferry barges and the submarine-chaser *UJ2111*, is encountered by a British force consisting of the cruisers *Sirius* and *Penelope* and the destroyers *Faulknor* and *Fury* S of Levita and completely annihilated with the exception of one ferry barge. 1027 survivors are rescued by German ships and aircraft. The retiring British force is attacked in the Scarpanto Strait by Ju 87s of II/St. G. 3 and Ju 88s of L.G.1 and of II/K.G. 51 and *Penelope* is damaged by bomb hits. On 8 Oct the British submarine *Unruly* (Lt Fyfe) sinks the German minelayer *Bulgaria* (1108 tons) loaded with supplies for Cos and misses the minelayer *Drache*. On 9 Oct the British cruiser *Carlisle* makes a sortie into the sea S of Piraeus with the destroyers *Panther* and *Rockwood* in order to intercept further German convoys. In the Scarpanto Strait Ju 87s of II/St. G. 3 attack and sink the *Panther*. The *Carlisle* is severely damaged and taken in tow by *Rockwood* to Alexandria (she is not put in service again).

27 Sept-9 Oct   North Atlantic
On 27 Sept the U-boat group 'Rossbach' is formed in the Central North Atlantic to operate against the convoy ON.203 located by the German 'B' service. The group consists of *U389*, *U279*, *U643*, *U641*, *U731*, *U539*, *U666*, *U336*, *U758*, *U584*, *U419*, *U378*, *U952*, *U645*, *U260*, *U603*, *U275*, *U448*, *U305*, *U631* and *U402*. The convoy avoids the patrol line by passing to the N on 28-29 Sept. Escort is provided by EG C.4, comprising the British destroyers *Hotspur* and *Churchill* and the corvettes *Collingwood*, *Woodstock* (Canadian) and *Nasturtium*, *Orillia* and *Trillium* (British). In spite of a move to the N, the convoy ONS.19, reported by the 'B' Service, also passes N of the patrol line on 30 Sept when *U279* is attacked by a Hudson of No 269 Sqdn RAF. On 1 Oct convoy HX.258

passes to the S of the patrol line. *U631* is bombed; *U448* and *U402* beat off with AA fire Venturas from USN-VB.128. In operations to protect convoy ONS.204 *U610* and *U275* are attacked on 3 Oct by aircraft and *U336* and *U666* by escort vessels. *U666* is damaged by depth charges. On 4 Oct a Ventura of USN-VB.128 sinks *U336* and a Liberator of No 120 Sqdn RAF sinks *U279*; *U305*, *U731* and *U641* are damaged in air attacks; and on 5 Oct a Hudson of No 269 Sqdn RAF sinks *U389* with rockets. The convoy is not found.
From 6 Oct the 'Rossbach' group, comprising *U309*, *U762*, *U643*, *U641*, *U539*, *U448*, *U610*, *U419*, *U378*, *U645*, *U260*, *U603*, *U275*, *U631*, *U91*, *U731* and *U758*, is moved S to find the convoys HX.259 and SC.143 reported by the 'B' Service. On the evening of 7 Oct *U448* sights the 3rd SG (the destroyers *Musketeer*, *Oribi*, *Orwell* and *Orkan* (Polish)) detailed to support SC.143 (39 ships, one merchant aircraft carrier and nine escort vessels). In the course of the night eight boats establish contact with the escort vessels. *U378* is driven off by aircraft. *U758* (Lt-Cdr Manseck) is attacked by *Orkan* after a contact signal is located by the HF/DF of *Musketeer*. A T-5, fired in defence, detonates in the wash of the destroyer. *U610* misses a destroyer with a T-5. Towards morning on 8 Oct the *Orkan* (Cdr Hryniewiecki) is sunk by *U378* (Lt-Cdr Mäder) with a T-5. The air escort which arrives drives off the U-boats: Liberators from Nos 86 and 120 Sqdns RAF and a Sunderland of No 423 Sqdn RCAF sink *U419*, *U643* and *U610* and damage *U762*. A large German flying boat of the type BV 222, which is employed for the first time over the Atlantic, sights SC.143 but the U-boats do not receive its D/F bearings. Only *U91* misses a destroyer with a T-5 in the evening but is driven off by aircraft with 'Leigh Lights' which are used for the first time with a North Atlantic convoy at night. On the morning of 9 Oct the operation has to be broken off. *U645* (Lt-Cdr Ferro) comes across a scattered convoy group in bad visibility and sinks one ship of 5612 tons.

28 Sept-1 Nov   Central Atlantic
The U-tanker *U488* (Lt Bartke) replenishes on 28 Sept and 4 Oct the returning *U68*, *U155* and *U103* W of the Azores. *U460* (Lt-Cdr Schnoor), which replenished 8 North Atlantic boats in September, is sighted on 4 Oct when she is replenishing *U455*, *U264* and *U422* N of the Azores by an aircraft of the escort carrier *Card* (Capt Isbell). The supply boat submerges too late and with *U422* is sunk by 12 aircraft which attack in three waves. *U264* (Lt-Cdr Looks), which covers the diving operation, is badly damaged. The convoy UGS.19 passes by unmolested. On 11-12 Oct the supply group, comprising *U488* and *U402*, and *U584*, *U731* and *U378*, are repeatedly sighted by aircraft from the *Card*. The supply area is moved to the SE where the AA boats *U271* and *U256* take over the protection of the tanker. On 13 Oct aircraft sink *U402* and *U731* is damaged. In the new area it is possible to replenish *U758*, *U378*, *U641* and *U731* before the *Core* group arrives on 20 Oct with the destroyers *Greene*, *Belknap* and *Goldsborough*. They escort convoy UGS.20. Aircraft from the *Core* sink *U378* and damage *U271*. To support the tanker, *U220* arrives from a mining operation and refuels *U603* and *U256* before she is sunk on 28 Oct by an aircraft of the escort carrier *Block Island*. While *U488* goes further to the SW to replenish *U193*, *U103*, *U530* and *U129*, individual boats meet N of the Azores for mutual replenishment and support. On 30 Oct the *Card* Group with the destroyers *Borie*, *Goff* and *Barry*, which is escorting the convoy GUS.18, comes across one U-boat which escapes. On 31 Oct *U584* is sunk, but *U91* is able to submerge in time. On 1 Nov the *Borie* (Lt-Cdr Hutchins), which is sent to the engagement area, encounters *U405* (Cdr Hopmann†). In a one-hour duel involving torpedoes, gunfire and mutual rammings, as well as an attempt to board, *U405* sinks and *Borie* has to be abandoned.

29 Sept   Mediterranean
On board the British battleship *Nelson* in Malta Gen Eisenhower for the Allies and Marshal Badoglio for

Italy sign the Italian capitulation.

29-30 Sept English Channel

The German 5th TB Flotilla, comprising *T27*, *Kondor*, *Greif*, *T19* and *T26*, carries out the mining operation 'Talsohle' in the Channel.

30 Sept-8 Oct North Atlantic

In accordance with the Anglo-Portuguese agreement of 18 Aug Allied air bases are established on the Azores Islands of Fayal and Terceira: operation 'Alacrity'. To transport the installations and personnel for No 247 Group RAF (Air Vice-Marshal Bromet) three small convoys (Commodore Holt) proceed to the Azores, consisting of the transport *Franconia*, tankers, freighters and small craft for local defence. Escort is provided by the EG B.5, comprising the destroyers *Havelock*, *Volunteer*, *Warwick*, the corvettes *Buttercup*, *Lavender*, *Godetia*, the sloop *Lowestoft* and the 8th SG, consisting of the escort carrier *Fencer*, the destroyers *Inconstant*, *Garland* (Polish), *Burza* (Polish), *Viscount*, *Whitehall* and *Wrestler*. On 18 Oct the first Fortress bomber arrives and begins to be used operationally on 19 Oct.

1-31 Oct Pacific

Of the US submarines arriving in their operational area in October, *Grayback* (Lt-Cdr Moore) sinks three ships of 22423 tons, torpedoes one more ship and, in conjunction with *Shad*, sinks one ship of 9138 tons; *Lapon* (Lt-Cdr Stone) sinks two ships of 2339 tons; *S28* (Lt-Cdr Sislet) one ship of 1368 tons; *Tullibee* (Cdr Brindupke) one ship of 5866 tons; and *Salmon* (Lt-Cdr Nicholas) torpedoes one ship—all off the Kuriles and Japan. In the Central Pacific *Flying Fish* (Lt-Cdr Donaho) sinks one ship of 6550 tons and torpedoes one more ship; *Guardfish* (Lt-Cdr Ward) one ship of 5460 tons; *Peto* (Lt-Cdr Nelson) two ships of 9910 tons; *Rasher* (Cdr Hutchinson) four ships of 9143 tons; *Silversides* (Lt-Cdr Coye) four ships of 15397 tons; and *Tinosa* and *Steelhead* together one tanker of 8000 tons. In the South West Pacific *Gurnard* (Lt-Cdr Andrews) sinks two ships of 11468 tons; *Kingfish* (Lt-Cdr Stone) two ships of 2339 tons; *Puffer* (Lt-Cdr Jensen) torpedoes one ship; and *Seawolf* (Lt-

Cdr Gross) sinks two ships of 6399 tons.

2 Oct-27 Nov Baltic

There is a heavy increase in Soviet air attacks on shipping in the Baltic in which the Boston bombers (supplied under Lend Lease) of the Mining and Torpedo Div of the Naval Air Force are used with torpedoes. They also lay mines. The torpedo attacks are made especially in the area of the Irben Strait. There are many misses but on 1 Nov the steamer *Marienburg* (1322 tons) is sunk. Several German steamers are lost on mines; the Finnish ice-breaker *Sisu* is damaged. Ground-attack aircraft increasingly harass the mine guards in the Gulf of Finland. On 4 Nov the German minesweeper *M16* is severely, and *M18*, *M30*, *M459* and *M460* are slightly damaged.

3-4 Oct English Channel

There is an engagement between the German 4th TB Flotilla (Cdr Kohlauf), comprising *T23*, *T22*, *T25*, *T26* and *T27*, with five British destroyers off Les Sept Iles.

3 Oct-25 Dec Mediterranean

In Allied submarine operations in the Western Mediterranean the British *Ultimatum* (Lt Kett) sinks *U431* and *Ultor* (Lt Hunt) one ship of 3723 tons in October; *Uproar* (Lt Herrick) torpedoes one ship in November; *Untiring* (Lt Boyd) sinks one net tender; and *Universal* (Lt Gordon) one ship of 2497 tons. The French submarine *Orphée* (Lt-Cdr Dupont) sinks one tug; *Casabianca* (Lt Bellet) sinks the submarine-chaser *UJ6076* and torpedoes one ship. In October the Polish *Sokol* (Cdr Karnicki) sinks two small ships in the Adriatic. In the Aegean in November one ship is torpedoed by *Simoon* (Lt Milner) and one ship of 3160 tons by *Sickle* (Lt Drummond). One ship of 2609 tons and one dock are sunk by *Torbay* (Lt Clutterbuck). In December one ship of 5609 tons is sunk by *Sokol*; and one ship of 2719 tons and one ship of 3838 tons are sunk respectively by the British *Surf* (Lt Lambert) and *Sportsman* (Lt Gatehouse).

4 Oct Norway

Raid by the Home Fleet, reinforced by US units, on German shipping off

Bodö (Operation 'Leader'). Covered by the British battleships *Duke of York* and *Anson*, the US cruiser *Tuscaloosa*, three British cruisers and ten British and US destroyers, the US carrier *Ranger* flies off 30 Dauntless dive bombers and Avenger torpedo bombers and 12 fighters. They attack two German convoys and ships in the roads. They sink four steamers of 12697 tons and damage six other large ships and one ferry barge so badly that most of them have to be beached. Five aircraft are lost.

5-6 Oct Black Sea
Sortie by a Soviet destroyer force (Capt 2nd Class Negoda) on German evacuation transports off the Crimean coast. The flotilla leader *Kharkov* shells Yalta and Alushta in the night. The two destroyers *Besposhchadny* and *Sposobny* encounter on their way to Feodosia boats of the 1st MTB Flotilla and engage *S45*, *S28* and *S42*, and later *S51* and *S52*, without result on either side. Located in the morning by a German reconnaissance aircraft, the force, which has now joined up, is attacked by day in four sorties undertaken by a squadron of Ju 87s of St. G. 77. In the first attack *Kharkov* (Capt 2nd Class Shevchenko) is hit and taken in tow by *Sposobny* (Capt 3rd Class Gorshenin). In the second attack all three ships are hit: *Sposobny* tries in turn to tow the two other destroyers. In the third attack the *Besposhchadny* (Capt 3rd Class Parkhomenko) is sunk and, a little later, also the *Kharkov*. Finally, *Sposobny*, which tries to rescue the survivors, is sunk. After this loss, Stalin forbids the employment of surface ships from destroyer upwards without his permission.

5-6 Oct Central Pacific
US TF 14 (Rear-Adm Montgomery) makes attacks on Wake. It comprises the carriers *Essex*, *Yorktown*, *Lexington*, *Cowpens*, *Independence* and *Belleau Wood*, the cruisers *Nashville*, *Santa Fé*, *Birmingham*, *Mobile*, *New Orleans*, *Minneapolis* and *San Francisco* and the destroyers *Trathen*, *Hazelwood*, *Boyd*, *Bradford*, *Conner*, *Burns*, *Braine*, *Bullard*, *Kidd*, *Chauncey*, *Hull*, *Dale*, *Halford*, *Bancroft*, *Caldwell*, *Coghlan*, *Ringgold*, *Schroeder*, *Sigsbee*, *Harrison*, *John Rodgers*, *McKee*, *Murray* and *Dashiell*

and the tankers *Cimarron* and *Kaskaskia*. In 738 sorties 12 aircraft are lost due to enemy action and 14 due to accident. The cruisers carry out a brief shelling of the island.

7 Oct English Channel
Operation 'Gesellenprüfung'. Under the Commander of the 4th MTB Flotilla, Cdr Lützow, mines are sown in an extensive area S of Smith's Knoll by the 2nd, 4th, 6th and 8th MTB Flotillas with a total of 29 boats. *S62* and *S83* of the 2nd and *S93* and *S127* of the 8th Flotillas have to return because of engine trouble. The 2nd Flotilla drops 37, the 4th 44 and the 6th 40 mines (LMBs and UMBs).

8-10 Oct Black Sea
Operation 'Wiking': withdrawal of the 240 craft used to evacuate the Kuban bridgehead in four large convoys from the Kerch Strait to Sevastopol. An escort is provided by the 3rd and 30th MMS Flotillas and the 23rd SC Flotilla, with the 1st MTB Flotilla further out to the sea. The engineer assault boat *229* is sunk by air attack and the ferry barge *F474* by submarine.

9 Oct Air War/Germany
Bombers of the 8th USAAF attack Gotenhafen (Gdynia).

12 Oct South West Pacific
The 5th USAAF starts, with an attack by 349 aircraft, the air offensive against Rabaul to isolate the base. Four aircraft are lost.

12 Oct-7 Nov East Mediterranean
In British submarine operations against German supply traffic for Coo *Unruly* (Lt Fyfe) sinks the transport *Marguerite* (920 tons): 350 of the 900 prisoners on board are rescued. The submarine *Trooper* is sunk near Calino by the German submarine-trap *GA45* after sinking a sailing ship. On 15-16 Oct two attempts by the British destroyers *Belvoir* and *Beaufort* and the cruiser *Phoebe* and destroyers *Faulknor* and *Fury*, respectively, to locate a German convoy, fail owing to air attacks. On 16 Oct the submarine *Torbay* sinks one of the two steamers, the *Kari* (1925 tons). In the night 16-17 Oct the destroyers *Hursley* and *Miaoulis* (Greek) find the remaining ships and sink the submarine-chaser *UJ2109* (ex-British *Widnes*) and the

F

transport *Trapani* (1855 tons), the wreck of which is dispatched in the following night by the destroyers *Penn* and *Jervis*. In addition, the ferry barge *F338* and one sailing ship are set on fire. On 19 Oct and 20 Oct Mitchell bombers of the USAAF and Beaufighters of the RAF attack convoys N of Crete and sink, inter alia, the transport *Sinfra* (4470 tons) of whose 2664 prisoners (mostly Italian) 566 are rescued. Then the emphasis of British operations is shifted to supply transports to Leros and Samos. Up to 7 Nov 2230 troops and 470 tons of supplies are transported by surface ships and 17 men and 288 tons of supplies by the British submarines *Severn* and *Rorqual* and by the Italian *Zoea*, *Atropo*, *Corridoni* and *Menotti*. In the process, from 22 Oct to 24 Oct, the destroyers *Hurworth* and *Eclipse* are lost on a mine barrage laid by the German minelayer *Drache* E of Calino and the Greek destroyer *Adrias* loses her bows. In air attacks the cruiser *Sirius* and *Aurora* and the destroyer *Belvoir* are damaged. The Polish submarine *Sokol* (Cdr Karnicki) sinks five supply sailing ships; the British *Unsparing* (Lt Piper) the transport *Ingeborg* (1160 tons) and the customs sloop *Nioi*. In a sortie on 7 Nov the British destroyers *Penn* and *Pathfinder* sink the German submarine-trap *GA45*.

13 Oct   General situation
The Badoglio Government declares war on Germany.

15-18 Oct   North Atlantic
On the evening of 15 Oct *U844* (Lt G. Möller), on her way to the new 'Schlieffen' formation, reports the convoy ON.206 (65 ships, EG B.6 (Cdr Currie) with the British destroyers *Fame* and *Vanquisher* and the Norwegian corvettes *Rose* and *Potentilla*, as well as EG B.7 (Cdr Gretton) with the destroyers *Duncan* and *Vidette* and the corvettes *Sunflower*, *Loosestrife* and *Pink* operating as a support group). *U844* is driven off by *Vanquisher* and *Duncan*. Early on 16 Oct *U964* (Lt Hummerjohann) reports the convoy ONS.20 (52 ships, Escort: the 4th SG (Cdr Paramor) with the 'Lend-Lease' destroyer escorts, used for the first time, *Byard*, *Bentinck*, *Berry*,

Drury, *Bazely* and A/S trawlers). In order to bring the U-boats scattered round the two convoys up to the target the Commander U-boats orders the U-boats to fight their way through to the convoy with AA fire against the strong air escort provided in the morning by Liberators of Nos 59, 86 and 120 Sqdns RAF. In the process *U844*, *U964* and *U470* shoot down one Liberator and damage another, but they are themselves sunk one after the other. Only *U426* (Lt-Cdr Reich) comes up on the evening of 16 Oct to the convoy ONS.20 and sinks one ship of 6625 tons. EG B.7, from which *Duncan* and *Vidette* have frustrated four attempted attacks on ON.206, is detached to support the threatened ONS.20. On the way, *Sunflower* locates *U631* and sinks her with 'hedgehog'. In the night 16-17 Oct six U-boats in the vicinity of ONS.20 are driven off by *Bentinck*, *Duncan*, *Vidette*, *Barry*, *Drury* and *Bazely*. On the morning of 17 Oct *U309* again reports the ONS.20 but the 'Schlieffen' group (*U762*, *U231*, *U91*, *U448*, *U267*, *U413*, *U668*, *U841*, *U426*, *U540*, *U271*, and *U842*), which is deployed on the basis of her report and another from *U437*, is unable to make progress against the strong air escort. Nine U-boats are attacked: *U450* is sunk and *U448* and *U281* have casualties from aircraft fire. One Sunderland flying boat of No 423 Sqdn RCAF is shot down. *U608* is over-run towards evening by the convoy ONS.20 which has turned sharply to the SW and is attacked by depth charges. *U841* is sunk by *Byard*. The operation has to be broken off.

15 Oct-9 Nov   Black Sea
In operations on the Caucasus coast the German U-boat *U9* (Lt Klapdor) reports a hit on a tanker off Sochi on 29 Oct; *U23* (Lt Wahlen) from 15 Oct to 23 Oct the torpedoing of two freighters and the sinking of one fishing cutter; *U24* (Lt-Cdr Petersen) one motor minesweeper; and *U18* (Lt Fleige) one tanker.

Soviet submarines operate chiefly W of the Crimea. Near Cape Tarkhankut the submarine-chaser *Schiff 19* with three KFKs of the 23rd SC Flotilla sinks one submarine (*Shch-203?*) on 16 Oct. One attack by *Shch 201* on 19 Oct fails. On 25 Oct and 2 Nov *M-112* (Lt Khakhanov) and *M-35* (Lt-Cdr Prokofev) sink the lighters *Tyra 5* and *No 1293* respectively off Ak Mechet. On 4 Nov *Schiff 19* sinks the Soviet submarine *A-3* off the Tendra Peninsula.

20 Oct-12 Nov   South Pacific
Japanese operation 'Ro': the carrier aircraft of the Japanese 3rd fleet (1st Carrier Sqdn, comprising *Zuikaku*, *Shokaku* and *Zuiho*, and the 2nd Carrier Sqdn, comprising *Junyo*, *Hiyo* and *Ryuho*) are transferred from Truk to Rabaul to reinforce the latter and to carry out an air offensive from there against the Central Solomons. The carriers return to Japan and on the way the US submarine *Halibut* torpedoes the *Junyo* on 5 Nov.

The Japanese Combined Fleet (Adm Koga) is on the alert in Truk. It consists of the 1st Battle Sqdn with the battleships *Yamato* and *Musashi*; the 2nd Fleet (Vice-Adm Kurita) with the 4th Cruiser Sqdn consisting of *Atago*, *Takao*, *Maya* and *Chokai*, the 5th Cruiser Sqdn consisting of *Myoko* and *Haguro* (transferred to Rabaul), the 2nd DD Flotilla with the cruiser *Noshiro* and the destroyers (24th DD Div) *Umikaze*, *Suzukaze*, *Michishio*, (27th DD Div) *Harusame*, *Shiratsuyu*, *Shigure* and *Samidare* (transferred to Rabaul), (31st DD Div) *Naganami*, *Makinami* and *Onami*, (32nd DD Div) *Tamanami*, *Suzunami*, *Fujinami*, *Hayanami* and the attached *Shimakaze*. The 3rd Fleet (1st and 2nd Carrier Sqdns) consists of the 3rd Battle Sqdn, comprising *Kongo* and *Haruna*; the 7th Cruiser Sqdn comprising *Kumano*, *Suzuya* and *Mogami*; the 8th Cruiser Sqdn, comprising *Chikuma* and *Tone*; and the 10th DD Flotilla comprising the cruiser *Agano* (transferred to Rabaul) and destroyers (4th DD Div) *Nowake*, *Maikaze* and *Yamagumo*, (10th DD Div) *Akigumo*, *Kazegumo* and *Asagumo* (transferred to Rabaul), (16th DD Div) *Hatsukaze*, *Yukikaze* and *Amatsukaze*, (17th DD Div) *Urakaze*, *Isokaze*, *Tanikaze* and *Hamakaze* and (61st DD Div) *Akizuki*, *Sutsuki*, *Hatsutsuki* and *Wakatsuki* (transferred to Rabaul).

The carrier aircraft suffer heavy losses in the US carrier raids on Rabaul. They are withdrawn on 12 Nov.

20 Oct-20 Dec   West and South Atlantic
In operations in distant waters *U516* (Lt-Cdr Tillessen) sinks six ships of 24745 tons in the Caribbean and escapes from a week-long search. *U218* lays mines off Trinidad on 27 Oct and sinks one sailing ship. On the Brazilian coast *U155* (Lt-Cdr Piening) and *U848* (Cdr Rollmann) each sink one ship of 5393 tons and 4573 tons respectively. *U848* is sunk on 5 Nov by six aircraft from Ascension Island in a lengthy engagement. *U154* has no success. Off West Africa *U68* (Lt-Cdr Markworth) sinks the A/S trawler *Orfasay* and three ships of 17116 tons. *U103* lays mines off Takoradi (28 Oct).

22 Oct-18 Nov   Arctic
On 22 Oct the Soviet ice-breakers *Stalin* and *SKR-18/Fedor Litke* set out from Tiksi to return to the White Sea. On 26 Oct they are met in the Vilkitski Strait by the minelayer *Murman* and the ice-breaker steamer *SKR-19/Semen Dezhnev* and brought via Dikson to the Kara Strait. There they are met by a strong escort force (Rear-Adm Kucherov) comprising the destroyers *Baku*, *Grozny*, *Gromki*, *Kuibyshev*, *Razumny* and *Raz-yarenny* as well as the newly-arrived Lend-Lease minesweepers *T-112*, *T-113*, *T-114* and *T-115*. On the way from the Kara Strait (15 Nov) via Kolguev-North (16 Nov) into the Gorlo Strait (17 Nov) the escorts make many depth charge attacks on suspected U-boats and report two U-boats sunk and three more seriously damaged. In fact, no U-boat is in the vicinity of the convoy AB.55. *U636* (Lt-Cdr Hildebrand), the last boat, lays mines off the Yugor Straits on 14 Nov and then quickly returns. The other U-boats at sea, *U387*, *U354*, *U360*, *U307* and *U277*, are stationed in the passage between Spitzbergen and Bear Island as the 'Eisenbart' group. The convoy is continually located by the German 'B' Service and is sighted but not attacked by a Ju 88 carrying out armed reconnaissance north of Kolguev.

23 Oct   English Channel

The German 4th TB Flotilla (Cdr Kohlauf), comprising *T23*, *T22*, *T25*, *T26* and *T27*, while providing a distant escort for a small convoy, encounters off the North Brittany coast the British cruiser *Charybdis* (Capt Voelcker), the destroyers *Grenville* and *Rocket* and the 'Hunt' destroyers *Limbourne*, *Wensleydale*, *Talybont* and *Stevenstone*. They had set out from Plymouth on 22 Oct to intercept the blockade-runner *Münsterland*. *T23* (Lt-Cdr Weinlig) and *T27* (Cdr Verlohr) despatch the cruiser with several torpedo hits and *T22* (Lt-Cdr Blöse) sinks the escort destroyer *Limbourne*.

23 Oct-8 Nov   North Atlantic

On 23 Oct *U274*, which is on the way to the 'Siegfried' group, is sighted by a Liberator of No 224 Sqdn RAF which is providing air escort for the convoy ON.207 (EG C.1, 2nd SG). EG B.7 (Cdr Gretton), which is situated in the vicinity, is ordered to search for her and the destroyers *Duncan* and *Vidette* sink *U274* with 'hedgehogs'. From 24 Oct the 'Siegfried' group, comprising *U420*, *U405*, *U212*, *U91*, *U762*, *U231*, *U309*, *U608*, *U969*, *U267*, *U281*, *U413*, *U963*, *U437*, *U426*, *U842*, *U552*, *U592*, *U575*, *U226*, *U373*, *U709*, *U648* and *U967*, expects the convoy HX.262 to whose escort has been added from ON.207 the 2nd SG (Capt Walker) with the sloops *Starling*, *Kite*, *Woodcock*, *Wild Goose*, *Magpie* and the escort carrier *Tracker*. *U413* takes several bearings with an intermediate wave D/F on the talk of the escorts, but the boats do not come up on 25-26 Oct to the convoy which goes round to the S of the patrol line. *U608* and *U212* are bombed and a Sunderland of No 10 Sqdn RCAF from ON.207 sinks *U240*. The 'Siegfried' group is divided into three sections: *U967*, *U212*, *U405*, *U231*, *U608* and *U969* as section 1; *U267*, *U281*, *U413*, *U963*, *U437*, *U426*, *U552* and *U592* as section 2; and *U842*, *U575*, *U226*, *U373*, *U709* and *U648* as section 3. From 28 Oct they take up smaller patrol lines E of Newfoundland against the expected convoy SC.145 (32 ships, EG B.6, leading destroyer *Fame* (Cdr Currie), 8th SG with the escort carrier

Fencer, the destroyers *Inconstant* and the Polish *Garland* and *Burza*). *U714* transmits several wireless messages from the flank to make the convoy turn away into the formation. On 29 Oct *U405* and *U608* drive off Swordfishes from the *Fencer* with AA fire but the convoy passes by unnoticed. Further to the E the approaching *U282* is located with radar by the *Vidette*, which with EG B.7 has been ordered to support convoy ON.208. She is sunk by the corvette *Sunflower* with 'hedgehog'. The EG B.7 (leader *Duncan*) is detached from ON.208 to go to convoy HX.263. Against these convoys and ONS.21 about which there is only indirect information the Commander U-boats forms on 31 Oct E of Newfoundland the groups 'Körner' (*U714*, *U212*, *U969*, *U231*, *U267*, *U281*, *U413*, *U963*, *U843*, *U586* and *U280*) and 'Jahn' (*U437*, *U426*, *U552*, *U842*, *U575*, *U226*, *U379*, *U709*, *U648* and *U608*). But only *U714* sights one aircraft on 1 Nov to the extreme N. The convoys go round the formations. The boats are therefore divided into five sections 'Tirpitz 1-5', each of four-to five boats, in order to find convoy HX.264 expected from 5 Nov. Its escort is supported by the 2nd SG (Capt Walker). Aircraft from the *Tracker* force *U967* to submerge on 5 Nov. In the evening *Kite* (Lt-Cdr Rysegrave) sights *U226*. Capt Walker destroys the boat on the next morning with *Woodcock* (Lt-Cdr Winner) and *Starling*. In the afternoon *Wild Goose* (Cdr Wemyss) locates *U842* and with *Starling* sinks her. The convoy passes undetected. On 7 Nov the operation has to be broken off since to proceed by day on the surface has become impossible because of the strong air escort. On the evening of 8 Nov 2nd SG, which is returning to Argentia because of shortage of fuel, passes the patrol line 'Tirpitz 5' and *U648* (Lt Stahl) just misses the *Tracker* (Cdr McGrath) with a FAT salvo of three and a sloop with a T-5.

24-25 Oct   English Channel

Thirty-two German motor torpedo boats of the 2nd, 4th, 6th and 8th MTB Flotillas attack the British convoy FN.1160 off Cromer from Ijmuiden.

The convoy is escorted by the destroyers *Pytchley, Worcester, Eglinton, Campbell* and *Mackay* and by the MGBs *MGB609, MGB610, MGB607, MGB603, MGB315, MGB327* and the MLs *ML250* and *ML517*. The German motor torpedo boats are reported by returning British bombers and the convoy is warned. The motor torpedo boats which approach in several groups are driven off by *Pytchley, Worcester* and *Mackay*. Only *S74* (6th MTB Flotilla) is able to sink the trawler *William Stephen* which remains behind. *MGB607* and *MGB603* encounter boats of the withdrawing 4th MTB Flotilla and sink *S63* and *S88* (Cdr Lützow†). In engagements with *MTB439* and *MTB442*, which also come up, the first is damaged.

25 Oct-9 Nov   North Atlantic
Attempt at a single night's short operation with support from air reconnaissance by the Air Commander Atlantic, Lt-Gen Kessler. The convoy MKS.28, reported to have left Gibraltar on 23 Oct, is located by a FW200 of III/K.G.40 after it has joined SL.138 on 25 Oct. Then the 'Schill' group (*U306, U466, U262, U707, U333* and the AA U-boats *U211, U953* and *U441*) is formed by the Commander U-boats on what is thought to be the probable night route of the convoy on 29-30 Oct. The FW200s report the convoy on 27 Nov and 28 Nov: it has 56 ships and seven escorts. On the decisive 29 Oct the four FW 200s deployed fly past to the N and do not find the convoy. Not before mid-day on 30 Oct does a large BV 222 flying boat of the 1(F)/S.A.Gr. 129 locate the convoy which now consists of 60 ships with EG B.1. Towards morning on 31 Oct the convoy passes the patrol line. *U262* (Lt Franke) sinks in an underwater attack one ship of 2968 tons; *U333* (Lt-Cdr Cremer) misses an escort vessel with a T-5; *U441* is damaged; and *U306*, after being located by HF/DF, is sunk by the destroyer *Whitehall* and the corvette *Geranium*. Because of the strong air escort, the operation is broken off and the remaining boats are ordered to form a new patrol line. On 1 Nov *U953* sights an MKF convoy which is too fast for

an operation. The air reconnaissance provided on 2 Nov for the expected KMS.31 has no success. On 3 Nov *U333* sights a landing ship convoy and misses an escorting destroyer with a T-5. After unsuccessful air reconnaissance on 3 Nov, 4 Nov and 5 Nov, a FW 200 sights on 7 Nov the convoy MKS.29A, but it is not found again on 8 Nov. In the night 8-9 Nov it runs into the patrol line. *U262* transmits the first report; *U466* misses a destroyer with a T-5 and is damaged by depth charges; *U707* is sunk by a Fortress of No 220 Sqdn RAF from the Azores which is part of the air escort provided in the morning; *U262* and *U228* miss a destroyer and straggler respectively. Although the FW 200s report the convoy on two more occasions, *U211, U333* and *U358* do not come up.

27 Oct-6 Nov   South Pacific
As a diversion for the imminent operation against Bougainville 6300 men of the 8th New Zealand Brigade (Brig Row) are landed on the islands of Mono and Stirling in the Treasury Archipelago which are occupied until 6 Nov.
The 2nd US Marine Parachute Bn (Lt-Col Krulak) lands with 725 men from APDs on Choiseul, but is reembarked on 4 Nov after the failure of the diversionary exercise.
In an attack by Japanese aircraft, 12 out of 25 are shot down by the US fighter cover. The destroyer *Cony* is slightly damaged.

1-13 Nov   South Pacific
The US III Amphibious Force (TF 31, Rear-Adm Wilkinson) lands 14321 men of the 3rd Marine Div (Maj-Gen Turnage) at Cape Torokina from eight troop and four supply transports. Escort is provided by Desron 45 (Cdr Earle), comprising *Fullam, Guest, Bennett, Hudson, Anthony, Wadsworth, Terry, Braine, Conway, Sigourney* and *Renshaw*, together with four destroyer minesweepers, four large and four small minesweepers. The landing takes place without any resistance. The covering force (TF 39, Rear-Adm Merrill) with the 12th Cruiser Div, consisting of *Montpelier, Cleveland, Columbia* and *Denver*, and Desron 23 (Capt Burke), comprising *Charles F. Ausburne, Dyson,*

Stanly, Claxton, Spence, Thatcher, Converse and *Foote,* shells the Japanese air base at Buka on 1 Nov. Towards evening a force, consisting of the *Renshaw* and the minelayer destroyers, *Breeze, Gamble* and *Sicard,* lays a mine barrage to protect the landing area to the NW. After unsuccessful air attacks from Rabaul the Commander of the Japanese 8th Fleet (Adm Samejima) commits the available ships to attack the US invasion fleet on 1 Nov.

Battle of Empress Augusta Bay. In the night 1-2 Nov the Japanese 5th Cruiser Sqdn (Rear-Adm Omori) with the heavy cruisers *Myoko* and *Haguro,* the light cruiser *Sendai* (Rear-Adm Ijuin) with the destroyers *Shigure, Samidare* and *Shiratsuyu,* the cruiser *Agano* (Rear-Adm Osugi) with the destroyers *Naganami, Hatsukaze* and *Wakatsuki* encounter US TF 39. In avoiding a torpedo attack by US destroyers the *Samidare* and *Shiratsuyu* collide, but escape. The cruiser *Sendai* sinks in the radar-controlled fire of the US cruisers. The *Hatsukaze,* damaged in a collision with the *Myoko,* is later sunk by the US destroyers. On the American side the *Foote* is hit by a torpedo fired by the *Sendai* force but is taken in tow. *Denver* and *Spence* are hit by gunfire; *Thatcher* is damaged in a collision with *Spence.* The remaining Japanese cruisers suffer minor damage from gunfire. On the return the US force is attacked by Japanese carrier aircraft flown off from Rabaul, but only the *Montpelier* is hit by bombs. Rear-Adm Omori is relieved for failing to carry out his mission.

From the area W of the Solomons TF 38 (Rear-Adm Sherman) carries out carrier raids on the Japanese airfields at Buna and Buka on 1 Nov and 2 Nov with the carriers *Saratoga* and *Princeton,* the AA cruisers *San Diego* and *San Juan* and the destroyers *Farenholt, Lardner, Woodworth, Buchanan, Lansdowne, Grayson, Sterett, Stack, Wilson* and *Edwards.*

On 3 Nov the Japanese 2nd Fleet (Vice-Adm Kurita) and elements of the 3rd Fleet set out from Truk for Rabaul: the 4th Cruiser Sqdn, comprising the cruisers *Atago, Takao, Maya* and *Chokai* (returns on 4 Nov with two

destroyers as escort for damaged tanker); the 7th Cruiser Sqdn, comprising the cruisers *Suzuya, Kumano* and *Mogami;* the 8th Cruiser Sqdn, comprising the cruisers *Chikuma* and *Tone;* and eight to twelve destroyers of the 2nd and 10th DD Flotillas with the cruiser *Noshiro.* They are sighted on 4 Nov N of the Bismarck Archipelago by US Liberator bombers of the 5th USAAF. Against this force the *Saratoga* and *Princeton* fly off a group of 22 dive-bombers, 23 torpedo aircraft and 52 fighters after it comes into Rabaul. The Americans lose 10 aircraft but the heavy cruisers *Maya, Atago, Takao* and *Mogami* and the light cruisers *Agano, Noshiro* and the destroyer *Wakatsuki* are badly damaged. The destroyer *Fujinami* is hit by an unexploded air torpedo. After the carrier raid 27 Liberators, protected by 67 Lightnings of the USAAF, bomb the town and harbour of Rabaul. On the same evening the damaged Japanese cruisers *Atago, Chikuma, Kumano, Mogami, Suzuya* and *Tone* with five to six destroyers start the return to Truk where they arrive on 7 Nov.

In the night 6-7 Nov Japanese destroyers and one cruiser land a total of 1175 reinforcement troops near Cape Torokina and Buka. In the night of 8-9 Nov a US transport force arrives with the second wave (37th Inf Div) off Cape Torokina. Twenty-six dive-bombers and 71 fighters from the air groups of the Japanese carriers moved from Rabaul and two-engined torpedo aircraft of the 11th Air Fleet stationed there attack the transports on 8-9 Nov but only *President Jackson* is damaged. A second attack is directed against the covering force (Rear-Adm Du Bose), comprising the US cruisers *Santa Fé, Mobile* and *Birmingham* and four destroyers. The *Birmingham* is damaged by torpedo and bomb hits.

To knock out the Japanese sea and air forces in Rabaul, TF 38 (see above) carries out a further carrier raid on Rabaul on 11 Nov. But because of poor visibility this has little effect. A little later the aircraft of TG 50.3 (Rear-Adm Montgomery), comprising the carriers *Essex, Bunker Hill* and *Independence,* escorted by the destroyers *Sterett,*

Bullard, Murray, McKee, Stack, Wilson, Edwards, Kidd and *Chauncey,* attack from the E. They torpedo the *Agano* and the destroyer *Naganami* and sink the destroyer *Suzunami.* The light cruiser *Yubari* and the destroyers *Urakaze* and *Umikaze* are slightly damaged by near-misses. Sixty-seven fighters, 27 dive-bombers and 14 torpedo aircraft take off from Rabaul but these carrier aircraft are intercepted by the fighter escort of TG 50.3 and lose 33 of their number to the fighters and AA fire without registering a hit.

In the night 12-13 Nov the third wave (21st Marines and elements of the 37th Inf Div) of US transports arrives off Cape Torokina. Cover is provided by TF 39 which is attacked at first light by several two-engined aircraft. The cruiser *Denver* receives a torpedo hit.

On the Japanese side the successes of the four 'sea and air battles of Bougainville' are greatly exaggerated: the pilots report the sinking of five battleships, 10 carriers, 19 cruisers, 7 destroyers and 9 transports as well as the damaging of 24 more ships. But of the 173 Japanese carrier aircraft committed, 121 are lost, so that, for the time being, the Japanese carrier air force ceases to be operational.

1-30 Nov Pacific
Of the US submarines arriving in their operational areas in November, *Gudgeon* (Lt-Cdr Port) sinks one ship of 6783 tons and the frigate *Wakamiya*; *Halibut* (Lt-Cdr Galantin) one ship of 4653 tons and torpedoes the aircraft carrier *Junyo*; *Sargo* (Lt-Cdr Garnett) sinks two ships of 6419 tons; *Snapper* (Lt-Cdr Clemenson) one ship of 4575 tons; and *Trigger* (Lt-Cdr Dornin) four ships of 15124 tons—all off Japan. In the Central Pacific *Albacore* (Lt-Cdr Hagberg) sinks one ship of 4705 tons; *Drum* (Lt-Cdr MacMahon) one ship of 11621 tons; *Gato* (Lt-Cdr Foley) one ship of 5617 tons; *Harder* (Lt-Cdr Dealey) three ships of 15269 tons; *Raton* (Lt-Cdr Davis) four ships of 21611 tons; *Ray* (Lt-Cdr Harrell) one ship of 2562 tons; *Scamp* (Lt-Cdr Ebert) torpedoes the cruiser *Agano*; *Scorpion* (Lt-Cdr Wylie) torpedoes one ship; *Searaven* (Lt-Cdr Dry) sinks one ship

of 10032 tons; *Snook* (Lt-Cdr Triebel) two ships of 8440 tons; *Tautog* (Lt-Cdr Sieglaff) one submarine-chaser; *Thresher* (Lt-Cdr Hull) one ship of 4862 tons; and *Tinosa* four ships of 18907 tons. *Sculpin* is lost. In the South West Pacific *Bluefish* (Lt-Cdr Porter) sinks one ship of 10570 tons and the torpedo boat *Sanae* and torpedoes one more ship; *Bonefish* (Lt-Cdr Hogan) sinks two ships of 7366 tons; *Bowfin* (Lt-Cdr Griffith) five ships of 26589 tons; *Capelin* (Lt-Cdr Marshall) one ship of 3127 tons; and *Crevalle* (Lt-Cdr Munson) one ship of 6783 tons. *Capelin* is lost. In the Malacca Straits the British *Tally Ho* (Cdr Bennington) sinks one ship of 1914 tons.

1 Nov-4 Dec Black Sea
After an attempt to land near Cape Illy on 21 Oct has been repulsed, light forces of the Azov Flotilla (Rear-Adm Gorshkov) land elements of the 56th Soviet Army near Enikale on 1 Nov (which until 11 Nov advance to the edge of Kerch); and forces of the Novorossisk base (Rear-Adm Kholostyakov) land the 386th Naval Inf Bn near Eltigen. They are followed in the next few days by elements of the 18th Army. The bridgehead of Eltigen is blockaded by German motor minesweepers, naval ferry barges and motor torpedo boats under the Commander of the 3rd MMS Flotilla (Lt-Cdr Klassmann). Thirty-one naval ferry barges, six motor minesweepers and five motor torpedo boats take part in 355 operations over 29 days. *F419, F380, F594, F306, F341, F571, F574, F573, F360, F305* and *F369* are lost on mines and, principally, in air attacks. One motor torpedo boat, four motor minesweepers and 16 naval ferry barges are damaged. On the Soviet side in the landings and attempts to bring supplies 12 patrol cutters, including *SKA-0192, SKA-0135, SKA-0178, SKA-0158, SKA-0105, SKA-0114*, the motor minesweepers *KT-173, KT-411, KT-509*, the armoured cutter *BKA-132*, and approximately 150 assault boats and 40 other small craft are lost. From 4 Dec to 11 Dec the bridgehead is compressed; 2827 prisoners are taken and about 800 troops escape to the N. About 10000 dead are counted in the Eltigen area.

SKA-01012 and *TKA-101* are sunk by the 1st MTB Flotilla.

1 Nov-9 Dec   Arctic
Resumption of the Murmansk convoys. On 28 Oct an escort group (Capt Campbell) arrives in the Kola Inlet from Scapa Flow, consisting of the destroyer *Milne* and 7 more fleet destroyers, one escort destroyer, two minesweepers, (including *Harrier* with Capt Jay) and one corvette, as well as five Lend-Lease minesweepers (*T-111* to *T-115*) and six submarine-chasers (*Bo-201*, *Bo-204*, and *Bo-208* to *Bo-211*) for the Soviet Northern Fleet. The escort group sets out on 1 Nov with the convoy RA.54A (13 ships) from Archangel for Loch Ewe where it arrives on 14 Nov without having been located by German air reconnaissance. On 15 Nov the convoy JW.54A (18 ships, the Soviet minesweepers *T-116* and *T-117* and the submarine-chasers *Bo-206*, *Bo-207* and *Bo-212*, escorted by an escort group with eight British destroyers, one minesweeper and two corvettes) puts to sea from Loch Ewe and, only detected by the German 'B' Service, reaches the Kola Inlet, on 24 Nov, from where some of the ships proceed with Soviet escort to Archangel. A second convoy, JW.54B (14 ships, one rescue ship, an escort group of nine destroyers, three corvettes and one minesweeper), follows unobserved from 22 Nov to 2 Dec. Four Soviet destroyers meet it off the Kola coast. On 26 Nov RA.54B (nine ships and the escort group from JW.54A) leaves Archangel. Of the German U-boat group, 'Eisenbart', which has meanwhile reinforced (*U360*, *U713*, *U387*, *U354*, *U277*, *U307* and *U636*), only *U307* sights escort vessels briefly on 28 Nov. But she is immediately attacked with depth charges and damaged. The convoy reaches Loch Ewe on 9 Dec without loss.
To cover the operations, Vice-Adm Palliser cruises with the British cruisers *Kent*, *Jamaica* and *Bermuda* in the vicinity of the convoy in the Barents Sea. Vice-Adm Moore forms the distant covering force with the battleship *Anson*, the US cruiser *Tuscaloosa* and destroyers. Allied submarines of the British 9th SM Flotilla take up covering positions off North-West Norway. The Soviet mining submarines *L-15* and *L-20* lay mines in the German exit routes (cleared) and *L-15* attacks a German minelaying force and two submarines-chasers unsuccessfully on 22 Nov and 24 Nov. The Soviet submarines *M-119* and *M-200* operate off the Varanger Peninsula. Off Western Norway the Norwegian submarine *Ula* (Lt Sears) sinks two ships of 2579 tons.

2 Nov   Skagerrak
V1606 captures in the Skagerrak the fast motor boat *Master Slanfast* returning to Britain from Sweden.

2-3 Nov   English Channel
The German 5th MTB Flotilla (Cdr Klug), comprising *S143*, *S100*, *S112*, *S136*, *S138*, *S139*, *S140*, *S141* and *S142*, attacks the British convoy CW.221 off Hastings. This is the first torpedo attack since August 1941 in the eastern part of the Channel. *S146* sinks the freighter *Dona Isabel* (1179 tons), *S100* and *S138* the freighters *Foam Queen* (811 tons) and *Storaa* (1967 tons). There are engagements with the British destroyer *Whitshed* and *MGB41*, *MGB42*, *ML141*, *ML230*, *ML293* and *ML464*.

3 Nov   Air War/Germany
The 8th USAAF attacks Wilhelmshaven with about 400 B 17s and with strong fighter protection. Seven bombers are shot down.

4-5 Nov   English Channel/North Sea
The German 2nd (Cdr Feldt), 6th (Cdr Obermaier) and 8th (Cdr Zymalkowski) MTB Flotillas carry out with 18 boats— *S116* and *S114* have to return because of engine trouble—a mining operation off Smith's Knoll and in the Humber Estuary. The 2nd MTB Flotilla drops 48, the 6th 38 and the 8th 16 mines. The 4th MTB Flotilla (Lt-Cdr Causemann), which set out with four boats, breaks off the operation because of a leak on *S48*. The 1st group of the 2nd MTB Flotilla encounters the convoy FN.1170 E of Cromer and torpedoes two ships of 7422 tons from it. The 2nd group of the 6th MTB Flotilla is attacked on the return by British aircraft and has to abandon *S74* after severe damage. *S61* and *S116* are damaged but are able to get away. German fighter cover is not available.

5-15 Nov   South Pacific
TF 74, consisting of the Australian cruisers *Australia* and *Shropshire* and the destroyers *Ralph Talbot*, *Helm* (US), *Arunta* and *Warramunga* (Australian), is temporarily transferred from Milne Bay to the New Hebrides to reinforce the South Pacific Forces.

6 Nov   Mediterranean
Thirty-five torpedo aircraft of K.G.26 (Maj Klümper) attack the Allied convoy KMF.25A in the area E of Algiers and sink the US destroyer *Beatty* and the troop transports *Santa Elena* (9135 tons) and *Marnix van St Aldegonde* (19355 tons). The convoy is escorted by the British AA cruiser *Colombo*, 11 US destroyers (three of them radar pickets), three British and two Greek 'Hunt' destroyers.

10-19 Nov   Central Pacific
Preparations for the operation 'Galvanic'. The 'Northern Attack Force' (TF 52) sets out from Pearl Harbour on 10 Nov and the 'Southern Attack Force' (TF 53) from the New Hebrides on 13 Nov. On 15 Nov they replenish halfway between Baker and Canton and near Funafuti respectively and they join up on 17 Nov halfway between Baker and Nanomea to proceed together. From TF 50 (fast carriers) TG 50.1 and 50.2 set out from Pearl Harbour and TG 50.3 and 50.4 from Espiritu Santo.

10-24 Nov   East Mediterranean
Battle for Leros and Samos (Dodecanese). In the night 10-11 Nov the British destroyers *Petard*, *Rockwood* and *Krakowiak* (Polish) shell Calino and *Faulknor* Coo. On the morning of 11 Nov *Rockwood* is severely damaged by an Hs 293 glider bomb in an attack by 5/K.G. 100. On 12 Nov the German battle group 'Müller' (the 22nd Inf Div, Lt-Gen Müller) is landed on Leros (Operation 'Leopard'). It is transported on steamers, coastal craft and ferry barges. Escort is provided by the 9th TB Flotilla (Cdr Riede), comprising *TA15*, *TA14*, *TA17* and *TA19*, the motor torpedo boat *S55*, the 21st SC Flotilla (Cdr Dr Brandt) with five to six large and eight to ten small boats and the 12th MMS Flotilla (Lt-Cdr Mallmann and Lt Weissenborn) with ten to twelve motor minesweepers. Air

support is provided by X Fl. K. which uses 206 aircraft on the first day. In the nights 12-13 Nov and 13-14 Nov two British destroyer forces, consisting of *Faulknor*, *Beaufort* and *Pindos* (Greek) and *Dulverton*, *Echo* and *Belvoir* respectively, search unsuccessfully for the German transport ships. The *Faulknor* group shells targets on Leros twice. On 13 Nov Do 217s of 5/K.G. 100 attack the second group with Hs 293 glider bombs and sink the *Dulverton*. On 14 Nov *Echo* and *Belvoir* try to bring troop reinforcements from Samos to Leros. In the night 14-15 Nov a new British destroyer group, consisting of *Penn*, *Aldenham* and *Blencathra*, shells Leros. From 15 Nov to 16 Nov the German torpedo boats *TA15*, *TA14* and *TA16* bring troops from Piraeus to Calino. In the night 15-16 Nov the Allied destroyers *Fury*, *Exmoor* and *Krakowiak* shell Leros and in the night 16-17 Nov *Penn* and *Aldenham* shell Coo and *Exmoor* and *Krakowiak* Samos. After heavy fighting the British commander on Leros surrenders with 3200 British and 5350 Italian troops. On 17 Nov *TA15* arrives in Leros with supplies and on 19 Nov *TA15* comes again with *TA14* and *TA19*. While the larger British ships have to leave the Aegean, light German units occupy the islands of Lisso, Patmos, Furni and Ikera on 18 Nov. 310 Italian troops are taken prisoner.
On 22 Nov the garrison of Samos capitulates after the attack by Ju 87s of II/St. G. 3 on the town of Tigani. After a show of strength round the island the torpedo boats *TA15* and *TA19* with boats of the 21st SC Flotilla enter Vathi Bay on 23 Nov and land troops. 2500 Italian soldiers are disarmed. With that the reconquest of the Dodecanese Islands is completed.

11 Nov   Mediterranean
Sixteen Do 217s of II/K.G. 100, 23 He 111s of I/K.G. 26 and 17 Ju 88s of III/K.G. 26 are used against the Allied convoy KMS.31. Forty-eight aircraft attack NE of Oran and sink the transports *Birchbank* (5151 tons), *Indian Prince* (8587 tons) and *Carlier* (7217 tons). The French tanker *Nivôse* (4763 tons), which is also torpedoed, sinks after a collision. Seven aircraft are lost.

11-15 Nov North Atlantic
The boats of the 'Eisenbart' group which are loosely stationed in groups of three E of Newfoundland (*U538*, *U391*, *U542*, / *U843*, *U714*, *U424*, / *U764*, *U280*, *U969*, / *U212*, *U967*, *U575*, / *U709*, *U282*, *U963*, / *U552*, *U586*, / *U648*, *U274* and *U343*) wait in vain on 11 Nov for convoy HX.264 and on 14 Nov for SC.146. Only *U592* sights on the return a detached convoy group but her attack fails. On 15 Nov the boats are ordered to withdraw eastwards. On 16 Nov *U969* and *U542* sight convoy the convoy HX.265 and *U280* is sunk by a Liberator of No 86 Sqdn RAF belonging to the air escort. Convoy operations by the U-boats are broken off in the Western Atlantic. The remaining 'Eisenbart' boats try to operate against convoys on the eastern side of the Atlantic in brief operations by night and with support from air reconnaissance. This is because U-boats, on account of the enemy's air superiority, are no longer able to close up to a located convoy over great distances and only have a chance of firing their torpedoes if they are overrun by the convoy.

12 Nov General Situation
Churchill leaves Plymouth on board the battlecruiser *Renown* in order to attend the Cairo conference ('Sextant') with Roosevelt and Chiang Kai-shek.

12 Nov-27 Dec Black Sea
Of the German *U20*, *U18*, *U19* and *U9* deployed off the Caucasus coast, only *U18* (Lt Fleige) sinks one ship. The Soviet submarine *M-111* (Capt 3rd Class Josseliani) sinks the steamer *Theoderich* (3409 tons) near Burnas on 12 Nov; *M-117* (Lt-Cdr Kesaev) *F592* from a naval ferry barge convoy on 15 Nov; *D-4* (Lt-Cdr Trofimov) the steamer *Santa Fé* (4627 tons) which is escorted by the Rumanian mine-layer *Amiral Murgescu*, the destroyer *Marasesti* and the German motor minesweepers *R165*, *R197* and *R209*, on 23 Nov. W of the Crimea *L-6* (Lt-Cdr Gremyako) the tanker *Wolga-Don* (965 tons), which is escorted by the Rumanian gunboats *Stihi*, *Dumitrescu* and the German *UJ2301*, *UJ2309* and *R205*, on 25 Nov. After the sinking of *F566* from a naval ferry barge convoy on 2 Dec, *D-4* is sunk on 4 Dec by the German submarine-chasers *UJ103* and *UJ102* with depth charges. On the Rumanian coast *S-31* (Capt 3rd Class Belorukov) sinks *F580* on 9 Dec. One to two unsuccessful attacks on convoys are made in December by *Shch-201*, *Shch-216*, *S-33* and *M-117*. In the process some of them are attacked with depth charges by the submarine-chasers of the 1st and 23rd SC Flotillas and damaged.

13 Nov Mediterranean Adriatic
Units of the German 71st Inf Div, embarked on the transport *Ramb III*, three Siebel ferries and many small craft, land on the Adriatic islands of Krk, Cherso and Lussino. Escort is provided by the old cruiser *Niobe*, the torpedo boat *TA21*, the coastal defence boat *Najade* and seaplanes. Several coastal sailing ships are captured.

13-21 Nov North Atlantic
On 13 Nov agents report the departure of convoy MKS.30 from Gibraltar. It joins SL.139 on 14 Nov and then consists of 66 steamers and the 40th EG (Cdr Legassick) with the leader, the frigate *Exe*, and six other vessels. On 15 Nov a Ju 290 of F.A.Gr. 5 (Maj H. Fischer) transmits a precise report of the strength and course of the convoy which is found again early on 16 Nov by a BV 222 of 1 (F) S.A.Gr. 129. A patrol line 'Schill 1' comprising *U262*, *U228*, *U515*, *U358*, *U333*, *U211* and *U600*, is formed for the night 18-19 Nov in the area of Lisbon and then, after numerous reports from the Air Commander Atlantic on 17 Nov and 18 Nov, moved. On the afternoon of 18 Nov *U333* (Lt-Cdr Cremer) is attacked several times with depth charges by *Exe* and rammed, but she gets away. *U515* (Lt-Cdr Henke) is attacked by the sloops *Chanticleer* and *Crane* before she can send her contact report. She fires two T-5s; one of them hits the *Chanticleer* which is towed in a damaged state to the Azores. *U515* is shadowed by *Crane* for nearly 10 hours. In the evening the 7th SG (Capt Durnford-Slater, now S.O.E.) with the sloop *Pheasant* and four other escorts joins the convoy. In the night a Wellington of No 179 Sqdn RAF from Gibraltar, equipped with radar and

Leigh Light, locates *U211* and sinks the surprised AA U-boat. In the course of 19 Nov the 5th SG (Cdr Birch) with the British frigates *Nene* and *Tweed*, the Canadian corvettes *Calgary*, *Snowberry* and *Edmundston* and two more escorts, and a little later the British destroyers *Winchelsea* and *Watchman* from Gibraltar, join the convoy. FW 200s of III/K.G. 40 repeatedly keep contact and send bearings for the 'Schill 2' group (*U608*, *U709*, *U969*, *U343*, *U586*, *U648*, *U238*, *U86* and *U536*) formed for the night of 20 Nov. The bearings are received by five boats. At midnight *U238* (Lt Hepp) is overrun by the convoy and fires T-5s against one escort vessel; they explode in the wash of the ship. *Calgary* and *Snowberry* attack the boat with depth charges; two hours later, together with *Nene*, they force *U536* to surface and destroy her with gunfire. On 20 Nov the air reconnaissance fails, because Mosquitoes and Beaufighters of the RAF shoot down one FW 200 and one Ju 290 near Cape Ortegal and the radar sets of the other two machines do not work. Aircraft from Cornwall take over the air escorting of the convoy and they force the seven boats of the 'Schill 3' group, earmarked for the attack during the night 20-21 Nov, to submerge. *U618* (Lt-Cdr Baberg) and *U648* (Lt Stahl) shoot down a Sunderland of No 422 Sqdn RCAF and a Liberator of No 53 Sqdn RAF respectively. In the night 20-21 Nov the convoy passes the patrol line and early on 21 Nov the 4th SG with six frigates of the US Destroyer Escort type joins the convoy. The *Essington* attacks *U967* with depth charges; the *Foley* and the *Crane* of the Escort Group sink *U538*. The U-boats no longer come up. The Air Commander Atlantic (Lt-Gen Kessler) deploys II/K.G. 40 (Maj Mons) with a total of 25 long-range He 177 bombers over an area of 1400 Kms against the convoy, which is again located by air reconnaissance on 21 Nov. Twenty reach the target; three are shot down and two turn back. They drop 40 Hs 293 glider bombs which sink the freighter *Marsa* (4405 tons) and damage *Delius* (6055 tons). Greater successes are prevented by the AA fire of the strong escort, which is reinforced by the Canadian AA vessel *Prince Robert*.

14 Nov   Technology
The first Walter experimental U-boat *U794* (Type Wk 202) enters service in Kiel. On 16 Nov *U792* (Type Wa 201) follows in Hamburg. Speed underwater: 26 knots.

15 Nov   Air War/East Asia
US bombers attack harbour installations in Hong Kong.

15 Nov-27 Dec   Mediterranean
The British destroyer *Quail* and the minesweeper *Hebe* are lost on the mine barrages laid by *U453* (Lt-Cdr Frhr v. Schlippenbach) off Brindisi and Bari (25 Oct, 12 Nov and 28 Nov).
In attacks in the Gulf of Taranto *U81* (Lt Krieg) sinks one ship of 2887 tons on 18 Nov and *U596* (Lt Nonn) one ship of 8009 tons from the convoy HA.11 on 9 Nov. On 28 Nov *U407* (Lt Brüller) torpedoes the British cruiser *Birmingham* off Cyrenaica.
In operations against Allied convoys on the Algerian coast *U223*, *U73* and *U616* miss their targets on 4 Dec, 7 Dec, 8 Dec and 9 Dec; likewise *U380* on 23 Dec and 27 Dec. From the escort of convoy KMS.34 *U223* (Lt-Cdr Wächter) torpedoes the British frigate *Cuckmere* (she is not thought worth repairing) with a T-5 on 11 Dec. Early on the next day *U593* (Lt-Cdr Kelbling) sinks the British destroyer *Tynedale*. In the course of a 32-hour search by the US destroyers *Niblack*, *Wainwright*, *Benson* and the British *Calpe* and *Holcombe* she sinks the last and damages one bomber with AA fire before she herself is sunk. *U73* (Lt Deckert) is sunk in a similar search by the US destroyers *Niblack*, *Ludlow*, *Woolsey*, *Trippe* and *Edison* on 16 Dec after she has torpedoed a steamer of 7176 tons.

17-18 Nov   East Mediterranean
The German 11th MMS Flotilla (Lt-Cdr Freytag) with six motor minesweepers lays the mine barrage 'Notung' in the Ligurian Sea.

19-28 Nov   Central Pacific
Operation 'Galvanic': US landing (Adm Spruance) on the Gilbert Islands. To prepare and isolate the landing area, TF 50 (Rear-Adm Pownall) makes carrier raids on 19 Nov. TG 50.1 (Pownall) with the carriers *Yorktown*,

Lexington and *Cowpens*, the battleships *South Dakota* and *Washington*, the destroyers *Nicholas*, *Taylor*, *La Valette*, *Izard*, *Charrette* and *Conner* on Mili; TG 50.2 (Rear-Adm Radford) with the carriers *Enterprise*, *Belleau Wood* and *Monterey*, the battleships *Massachusetts*, *North Carolina* and *Indiana*, the destroyers *Boyd*, *Bradford*, *Brown*, *Fletcher*, *Radford* and *Jenkins* on Makin; TG 50.3 (Rear-Adm Montgomery) with the carriers *Essex*, *Bunker Hill* and *Independence*, the cruisers *Chester*, *Pensacola*, *Salt Lake City* and *Oakland*, the destroyers *Erben*, *Hale*, *Bullard*, *Kidd* and *Chauncey* on Tarawa; and TG 50.4 (Rear-Adm Sherman) with the carriers *Saratoga* and *Princeton*, the cruisers *San Diego* and *San Juan* and the destroyers *Stack*, *Sterett*, *Wilson* and *Edwards* on Nauru.

On 20 Nov TF 52 (Rear-Adm Turner) lands 6472 troops from the 27th US Inf Div (Maj-Gen R. Smith) on Makin from four troop transports, one supply transport and one dock ship. Escort: the destroyers *Mustin*, *Kimberly*, *Burns* and *Dale*. Fire support is provided by TG 52.2 (Rear-Adm Griffin) with the battleships *New Mexico*, *Pennsylvania*, *Idaho* and *Mississippi*, the cruisers *Minneapolis*, *San Francisco*, *New Orleans* and *Baltimore*, the destroyers *Dewey*, *Hull*, *Maury*, *Gridley*, *Phelps* and *MacDonough*. Air support is provided by TG 52.3 (Rear-Adm Mullinix†) with the escort carriers *Liscombe Bay*, *Coral Sea* and *Corregidor*, the destroyers *Morris*, *Franks*, *Hoel* and *Hughes*. The much inferior Japanese defenders hold up the still inexperienced infantry division and the small island of Makin is only taken on 23 Nov.

On 20 Nov TF 53 (Rear-Adm Hill) with 12 troop transports, three supply transports and one dock ship lands 18600 troops of the 2nd US Marine Div on Betio/Tarawa. Escort is provided by the destroyers *John Rodgers*, *Sigsbee*, *Heerman*, *Hazelwood*, *Harrison*, *McKee* and *Murray*; and fire support by TG 53.4 (Rear-Adm Kingman) with the battleships *Tennessee*, *Maryland* and *Colorado*, the cruisers *Portland*, *Indianapolis*, *Mobile* and *Santa Fé*, the destroyers *Bailey*, *Frazier*, *Gansevoort*, *Meade*, *Anderson*, *Russell*, *Ringgold*, *Dashiell* and *Schroeder*. Air support is provided by TG 53.6 (Rear-Adm Ragsdale) with the escort carriers *Suwanee*, *Chenango*, *Barnes* and *Nassau*, the destroyers *Aylwin*, *Farragut*, *Monaghan*, *Cotten*, *Cowell* and *Bancroft*. Led by the minesweepers *Pursuit* and *Requisite* and supported by the destroyers *Ringgold* and *Dashiell*, the first waves land on Betio from the lagoon. In calm waters they suffer heavy casualties at the hands of the Japanese defenders. On 23 Nov the approximately 4500 Japanese (Rear-Adm Shibasaki†) are overwhelmed. Only 17 Japanese and 129 Koreans are taken prisoner. US losses on Tarawa are 1009 dead and 2101 wounded. By 28 Nov the remaining islands of the Atoll and neighbouring Abemama are occupied.

There is Japanese counter-action from the outside in the form of air attacks in which the *Independence* receives a torpedo hit on 20 Nov. A Japanese submarine group is deployed. After unsuccessful attempts *I-36* has been able to reconnoitre over Pearl Harbour on 17 Oct with her aircraft. Then Capt Iwagami with *I-19*, *I-35*, *I-39*, *I-169* and *I-175* operates without success 300 nautical miles SW of Hawaii. On 20 Nov this group is deployed against the invasion fleet off Makin/Tarawa. In addition, *I-40*, *I-176* (Lt-Cdr Yamaguchi—she sinks the US submarine *Corvina* on 16 Nov) and *Ro-38* set out from Truk. Of these boats, *I-175* (Lt-Cdr Tabata) sinks the *Liscombe Bay* (644 dead) with three torpedoes on 23 Nov. The Japanese *I-35* is sunk on 23 Nov by the destroyers *Frazier* and *Meade*; *I-19* on 25 Nov by *Radford* when attempting to attack; and *I-40*, *Ro-38* and *I-21*, which is called up from the South Pacific, are lost from unknown causes.

Japanese cruisers reinforce bases in the Marshall Islands. On 19 Nov the *Isuzu* and *Nagara* set out from Truk for Mili where they arrive on 23 Nov. The *Nagara* comes straight back; the *Isuzu* goes on to Kwajalein and arrives there on 27 Nov. *Naka* goes to Kwajalein on 19 Nov, arriving there on 23 Nov and from there to Maloelap, but she breaks off the operation prematurely and returns to Truk. The operation is repeated by *Nagara* which sets out on 28 Nov, reaches Maloelap on 2-3 Dec and arrives in Kwajalein on 4 Dec.

On 24 Nov the cruisers *Chokai*, *Suzuya* and *Chikuma* and six to eight destroyers leave Truk for Kwajalein (they arrive on 26 Nov), go from there to Eniwetok on 27-28 Nov and return on 29-30 Nov. They return to Truk from Kwajalein from 4-5 Dec to 7 Dec together with the *Isuzu* and *Nagara*.

22 Nov-7 Dec   North Atlantic
The remaining 'Schill' boats (*U424*, *U843*, *U618*, *U600*, *U358*, *U542*, *U586*, *U262*, *U764*, *U86*, *U238*, *U648*, *U228*, *U969* and *U391*) are formed W of Spain as the 'Weddigen' group to operate against the expected combined convoy KMS.30/OS.59. In the night 22-23 Nov the 4th SG (Cdr Paramor) with the frigates (US DE type) *Byard*, *Bazely*, *Blackwood*, *Drury*, *Bentinck* and *Berry* passes the patrol line. *U648* is sunk; *U424* and *U714* are pursued with depth charges for up to 12 hours and forced under water. *U843* (Lt-Cdr Herwatz) misses one of the frigates with a T-5. The air escort deployed does not find the convoy on 23 Nov which passes further to the W. The support group remains in the area of the 'Weddigen' group. In the night 24-25 Nov night Wellingtons of No 179 Sqdn RAF from Gibraltar attack *U618* and *U542* and bring up the frigates which damage *U618*. *U586* has to start the return journey, having been damaged. Towards morning *Bazely* and *Blackwood* sink *U600*. At mid-day on 26 Nov German air reconnaissance locates the convoy MKS.31 with EG B.1 (Cdr Bayldon) comprising the leading destroyer *Hurricane* and six other vessels before it joins SL.140. In the night 26-27 Nov *U764* (Lt v. Bremen) misses a frigate of the 4th SG with a T-5 and is attacked with depth charges and later by a night aircraft. On 27 Nov the air reconnaissance again finds the now combined MKS.31/SL.140 with 68 ships and its escort reinforced by the 4th and 2nd SGs (Capt Walker) with the sloops *Starling*, *Kite*, *Wild Goose* and *Magpie*. The 'Weddigen' group is accordingly moved. In the

evening a BV 222 of 1 (F)/S.A.G. 129 is able to maintain contact with the convoy for five hours and to bring up six boats as a result of repeated D/F transmissions. The strong night air escort impedes the U-boats. *U391* is driven off; *U542* is sunk by a Leigh Light Wellington of No 179 Sqdn RAF; *U764* shoots down a Fortress of No 220 Sqdn RAF and *U262* shoots down another aircraft with AA fire. In the night *U764* and *U107* (Lt Simmermacher) unsuccessfully attack frigates of the 4th SG with two and one T-5s respectively. *U262* (Lt Franke) surfaces in the morning in the middle of the convoy and fires four torpedoes which, however, do not hit. *U238* (Lt Hepp) narrowly misses the corvette *Dahlia*. *U843* is driven off by the 2nd SG. On the morning of 29 Nov the US carrier group *Bogue* with the destroyers *George E. Badger*, *Osmond-Ingram*, *Clemson* and *Dupont* arrives in the operational area of the 'Weddigen' group, coming from the convoy UGS.24. *U764* and *U238* are attacked by several aircraft from the *Bogue* but are still able to submerge after sustaining casualties. *U86* is sunk. The Commander U-boats concentrates the remainder of the 'Weddigen' group (*U618*, *U238*, *U391*, *U107*, *U358*, *U228*, *U424* and *U843*) against the convoy KMS.34/OS.60 which, however, is neither located by the air reconnaissance deployed on 30 Nov and 1 Dec nor found by the U-boats. After an unsuccessful attempt to get the group to operate with the 'Coronel' group on 6 Dec against convoy ONS.24, 'Weddigen' is disbanded on 7 Dec.

22 Nov-6 Jan   West and South Atlantic
In operations in distant waters *U129* (Lt. v. Harpe) sinks one ship of 5441 tons and misses two destroyers with T-5s between Bermuda and Cape Hatteras. In the Gulf of Mexico *U193* (Cdr Pauckstadt) sinks one tanker of 10172 tons; in the Caribbean *U530* (Lt-Cdr K. Lange) torpedoes one tanker of 10193 tons. Off Freetown *U515* (Lt-Cdr Henke) sinks three ships of 20913 tons. In the South Atlantic *U849*, which is proceeding to the Indian Ocean, is sunk on 25 Nov by a

Liberator of USN-VP.107 from Ascension Island.
In the Central Atlantic the carrier group *Bogue* (Capt Dunn), while escorting the convoy GUS.23, encounters *U219* on 12 Dec which, having replenished three boats, is replenishing the outward-bound *U172*. The U-tanker gets away, but *U172* is sunk by aircraft and the destroyers *George E. Badger, Osmond-Ingram, Clemson* and *Du Pont*. On 20 Dec aircraft from the *Bogue* surprise *U850* on her way out to the Indian Ocean and sink her.

24 Nov   Mediterranean
US bombers attack Toulon and sink in the harbour the French light cruiser *Jean de Vienne*, the destroyer *Aigle*, the sloops *Chamois* and *L'Impétueuse* and the transport *Aude*.

24-27 Nov   Mediterranean
In the night 24-25 Nov 112 German bombers attack the harbour installations of La Maddalena (Sardinia) and Bastia (Corsica). In the night 26-27 Nov 76 German bombers attack Naples.

25 Nov   West Pacific
Bombers of the XIV USAAF attack Formosa for the first time from Chinese bases. Forty-two Japanese aircraft are destroyed on Shinchiku airfield.

25 Nov   South Pacific
Battle E of Cape St George (New Ireland). Desron 23 (Capt Burke), comprising *Charles Ausburne, Claxton, Dyson, Converse* and *Spence*, surprises a Japanese destroyer force (Capt Kagawa), consisting of *Amagiri, Yuguri* and *Uzuki*, which have troops on board for Buka (Northern Bougainville). It sinks the covering destroyers *Onami, Makinami* and *Yugiri* with gunfire and torpedoes. The Japanese submarine *I-177* later rescues 278 men from *Yugiri*.
On 30 Nov the destroyers under Capt Burke bombard Japanese positions near Cape Torokina.

26 Nov   English Channel
The German 5th MTB Flotilla, consisting of nine boats, drops 54 LMB mines near St Catherine's Point.

26 Nov   Mediterranean
He 177s of II/K.G. 40 (Maj R. Mons†) sink off Bougie the British troop transport *Rohna* (8602 tons) from the convoy KMF.26 with a Hs 293 glider bomb. There are over 1000 dead among the troops on board. Eight He 177s are shot down.

29 Nov   Air War/Germany
The 8th USAAF bombs Bremen.

29 Nov   South West Pacific
Destroyers of TG 74.2 (Capt Walker), comprising *Ralph Talbot, Helm, Arunta* and *Warramunga*, shell Japanese positions near Gasmata on the south coast of New Britain.

1-2 Dec   English Channel
The German 5th MTB Flotilla, consisting of nine boats, attacks from Cherbourg a strongly-escorted convoy, located by air reconnaissance off Beachy Head. *S142* sinks the British trawler *Aventurine*.

1-31 Dec   Pacific
Of the US submarines which arrive in their operational areas in December *Grayback* (Lt-Cdr Moore) sinks three ships of 8730 tons and the destroyer *Numakaze*; *Gunnel* (Lt-Cdr McCain) one ship of 4046 tons; *Gurnard* (Lt-Cdr Andrews) two ships of 7755 tons and torpedoes two more ships; *Herring* (Lt-Cdr Johnson) two ships of 10019 tons; *Sailfish* (Lt-Cdr Ward) two ships of 9562 tons—she also sinks the escort carrier *Chuyo* and torpedoes the light carrier *Ryuho*; *Sawfish* (Lt-Cdr Bannister) sinks one ship of 3266 tons—all off Japan.
In the Central Pacific *Apogon* (Lt-Cdr Schoeni) sinks one ship of 2962 tons; *Gato* (Lt-Cdr Foley) one ship of 2926 tons; *Greenling* (Lt-Cdr Grant) one ship of 1936 tons; *Pargo* (Lt-Cdr Eddy) two ships of 7807 tons; *Peto* (Lt-Cdr Nelson) one ship of 2345 tons; *Pogy* (Lt-Cdr Metcalf) two ships of 9910 tons; *Raton* (Lt-Cdr Davis) one ship of 5578 tons and torpedoes one more ship; *Ray* (Lt-Cdr Harrell) two ships of 8696 tons; *Silversides* (Lt-Cdr Coye) three ships of 7192 tons. In the South West Pacific *Cabrilla* (Lt-Cdr Hammond) sinks one ship of 2764 tons; *Flying Fish* (Lt-Cdr Risser) two ships of 18784 tons; *Narwhal* (Lt-Cdr Latta) one ship of 834 tons; *Puffer* (Lt-Cdr Selby) one ship of 6707 tons and the torpedo boat *Huyo*; *Bluefish* (Lt-Cdr Porter) one ship of 6046 tons; and *Tuna* (Lt-Cdr Hardin) one ship of 5484 tons.

2-3 Dec   Mediterranean
In the night 2-3 Dec 88 German bomb-

ers of Air Fleet 2 attack the harbour installations and ships in Bari. Thanks to bomb hits and an explosion on an ammunition ship, 18 transports totalling 71566 tons with 38000 tons of cargo are destroyed. Other ships and the harbour installations are badly damaged. There are more than 1000 dead and injured. The fire-fighting and rescue operations are impeded by a US freighter which is loaded with mustard gas shells and endangered by fires.

3 Dec   Skagerrak
The German minelayers *Ostmark*, *Brummer*, *Elsass* and the destroyers *Z31*, *Hans Lody* and *Theodor Riedel* carry out a mining operation in the Skagerrak.

3 Dec-15 Jan   Indian Ocean
The Japanese submarines *Ro-110* (Lt Ebato) and *Ro-111* (Lt-Cdr Nakamura) operate in the Bay of Bengal from Penang and each sink one ship of 4087 tons and 7934 tons respectively. In the Gulf of Oman *I-26* (Cdr Kusaka) sinks two ships of 14352 tons and torpedoes one ship of 8054 tons. *I-162* cruises in the area of Addu Atoll without success. The German *U178* (Lt-Cdr Spahr) sinks one ship of 7244 tons on the Indian West Coast and goes at the end of January to the area S of Mauritius to be replenished from the tanker *Charlotte Schliemann*.
On 16 Dec the Japanese *I-29* (Cdr Kinashi) puts to sea on a transport journey to France. From 25 Dec to 4 Jan she is replenished from the German supply ship *Bogota* and arrives in Lorient on 11 Mar.

4-5 Dec   East Mediterranean
The German 7th MTB Flotilla (Cdr Trummer) carries out the mining operation 'Ulan' with seven boats off the Italian West Coast.

4-8 Dec   Central Pacific
On 4 Dec the US 'Fast Carrier Task Force' makes a raid on Kwajalein. The following take part: TG 50.1 (Rear-Adm Pownall), comprising the carriers *Yorktown*, *Lexington* and *Cowpens*, the cruisers *Baltimore*, *San Francisco*, *New Orleans* and *Minneapolis*, the destroyers *Nicholas*, *Taylor*, *La Valette*, *Bullard*, *Kidd* and *Chauncey*; TG 50.3 (Rear-Adm Montgomery), comprising the carriers *Essex*, *Enterprise* and *Belleau Wood*, the cruisers *Portland*, *Mobile*,

Santa Fé, *San Juan* and *San Diego*, and the destroyers *Fletcher*, *Radford*, *Jenkins*, *Erben* and *Hale*. In several attacks by the 386 carrier-based aircraft six transport ships of 25316 tons are sunk; three ships of 17249 tons and the cruisers *Isuzu* and *Nagara* are damaged. Fifty-five Japanese aircraft are shot down and destroyed on the ground. Five US aircraft are lost.
In an attack by two-engined torpedo aircraft the *Lexington* receives a hit. The *Yorktown* carries out a diversionary raid on Wotje.
On 8 Dec US TG 50.8 (Rear-Adm Lee), comprising the battleships *South Dakota*, *Washington*, *Massachusetts*, *North Carolina* and *Indiana* and the destroyers *Lang*, *Boyd*, *Charette*, *Connor*, *Burns*, *Izard*, *Stack*, *Sterett*, *Wilson*, *Bradford*, *Brown* and *Cowell*, attacks Nauru and bombards the island with 810 rounds of 16-inch and 3400 rounds of 5-inch shells. A Japanese coastal battery damages *Boyd*. Air escort is provided by the carriers *Bunker Hill* and *Monterey*.

4-23 Dec   North Atlantic
An attempt with the 'Coronel' group (*U629*, *U761*, *U672*, *U544*, *U625*, *U421*, *U734*, *U541*, *U269*, *U962*, *U543*, *U92*, *U653*, *U801*, *U667* and *U415*) to locate the convoy ONS.24 in the eastern part of the North Atlantic in a short night operation fails because the air reconnaissance flown off (2 Ju 290s on 4 Dec and one Ju 290, one FW 200 and one BV 222 on 5 Dec) does not find the convoy which goes round to the N of the formation. In proceeding towards HX.268, expected according to 'B' Service reports on 8 Dec, *U269* sights a south-bound convoy against which the boats of the 'Weddigen' group also operate and from which *U421* briefly establishes contact. On 8 Dec HX.268 also passes to the N of the patrol line without air reconnaissance having been in contact. On 11 Dec, 12 Dec and 13 Dec the 'Coronel' boats, which are divided into three groups, search for convoy ON.214. Air reconnaissance carried out over three days with Ju 290s, FW 200s and BV 222s does not find it. The formation is known to the British command and the convoy avoids it by going to the S.

From 18 Dec until 23 Dec the boats *U364*, *U972*, *U981*, *U744*, *U741* and *U471* as the 'Sylt' group, *U960*, *U392*, *U302*, *U976*, *U311* and *U629* as the 'Amrum' group and *U92*, *U672*, *U544*, *U625*, *U653* and *U421* as the 'Föhr' group, are stationed in the Central North Atlantic in varying formations—without success. *U284* has to be sunk after suffering damage in rough seas and after the crew is taken off by *U629*.

5 Dec   Indian Ocean
Heavy Japanese air attacks on dock and harbour installations in Calcutta.

11-20 Dec   Air War/Germany
On 11 Dec bombers of the 8th USAAF attack Emden. On 13 Dec approximately 600 bombers of the 8th USAAF make a daylight attack on Kiel where the torpedo boat *T-15* and the motor minesweeper *R306* are among the vessels to sink. On 20 Dec the 8th USAAF attacks Bremen.

12-23 Dec   Bay of Biscay
Operation 'Stonewall': attempt to foil expected German blockade-runners. On 12 Dec the New Zealand cruiser *Gambia* and the British *Glasgow* set out from Plymouth and until about 23 Dec take turns cruising on a line 500 nautical miles NNW of the Azores. The cruisers put in to Horta (Azores) to refuel.

12 Dec-8 Jan   Arctic
Convoy operation in the Arctic. From 12 Dec to 22 Dec the convoy JW.55A (19 ships) makes its way to the Kola Inlet (20 Dec) and to the White Sea. Of the U-boats *U277*, *U387*, *U354* and *U636* stationed E of the Bear Island Passage, only the last locates escort vessels for a short time on 18 Dec, but does not get nearer the convoy. The distant covering force, consisting of the battleship *Duke of York* (Adm Fraser, C-in-C Home Fleet), the cruiser *Jamaica* and the destroyers *Savage, Saumarez, Stord* (Norwegian) and *Scorpion*, arrives in the Kola Inlet between 16 Dec and 18 Dec but then goes on to Akureyri (Iceland) to refuel and to meet JW.55B (19 ships) which sets out from Loch Ewe on 20 Dec. This convoy has with it an Escort Group (Capt McCoy), comprising the destroyers *Onslow, Onslaught, Orwell, Scourge, Impulsive* and the Canadians *Haida,*

Iroquois, Huron, as well as *Whitehall* and *Wrestler*, the minesweeper *Gleaner* and the corvettes *Honeysuckle* and *Oxlip*. The convoy is located by German air reconnaissance on 22 Dec, but an attack by some Ju 88s on 23 Dec does not penetrate the defence. On 23 Dec the convoy RA.55A (22 ships—one ship turned back—and the Escort Group (Capt Campbell), consisting of the destroyers *Milne, Meteor, Ashanti, Athabaskan* (Canadian), *Musketeer, Opportune, Virago, Matchless, Beagle* and *Westcott*, the minesweeper *Seagull* and the corvettes *Dianella, Poppy* and *Acanthus* (Norwegian), sets out from the Kola Inlet. A cruiser covering force (Vice-Adm Burnett) with *Belfast, Sheffield* and *Norfolk* operates in the Barents Sea.

On 24 Dec *U601* (Lt Hansen) from the U-boats of the 'Eisenbart' group (*U277, U387, U354, U601, U716, U957* and *U314*) is led to the scene by air reconnaissance and establishes contact with JW.55B but she, together with *U716* (Lt Dunkelberg), which fires a T-5 against a destroyer, is driven off. On 25 Dec a German Task Force (Rear-Adm Bey), consisting of the battleship *Scharnhorst* (Capt Hintze) and the 4th DD Flotilla (Capt Johannesson) with *Z29, Z30, Z33, Z34* and *Z38* is deployed against JW.55B. In the morning of 26 Dec Adm Bey forms a patrol line of destroyers to search in heavy seas for the convoy. Meanwhile, the British cruiser force comes up from the SE and locates the *Scharnhorst* by radar. Without calling her destroyers for support the *Scharnhorst* turns and has a short engagement with the cruisers from which the *Norfolk* obtains two hits. One puts the top radar of *Scharnhorst* out of action and she breaks off to search for the convoy to the N. Adm Burnett takes a position between the convoy and the enemy. At midday the *Scharnhorst* again meets the *Belfast, Sheffield* and *Norfolk* which are reinforced by the destroyers *Musketeer, Matchless, Opportune* and *Virago*. In bad visibility there is a short engagement during which *Norfolk* suffers two hits, but *Scharnhorst* mistakes the fountains of *Norfolk* for gunfire of battleships and turns away at high speed, trying to shake off the cruisers. Coming up at high speed from the SW, the *Duke of York* and *Jamaica* bar the *Scharnhorst's* way. In a pursuit engagement the British ships obtain some hits with their radar-controlled fire, but once again the *Scharnhorst* gets out of range until the destroyers *Savage* and *Saumarez* and the *Scorpion* and *Stord* get four torpedo hits in a skilful pincer attack and bring the ship to a halt. The *Scharnhorst* is battered by gunfire from the *Duke of York* and *Jamaica* and from the *Belfast* and *Norfolk*, which also arrive on the scene. She is also hit by another ten to eleven torpedoes from the destroyers *Musketeer*, *Opportune*, *Virago* and *Matchless*, as well as from the cruisers *Belfast* and *Jamaica*. She sinks in the evening of 26 Dec. Only 36 survivors are rescued by British destroyers, of which *Saumarez* is damaged.

The JW.55B arrives in the Kola Inlet without loss on 29 Dec. Soviet ships bring some steamers into the White Sea. The RA.55A arrives without loss on 1 Jan. On 31 Dec the RA.55B (eight ships, Escort Group Capt McCoy) puts to sea from the Kola Inlet and reaches Loch Ewe on 8 Jan without loss. An attack by *U957* with a T-5 fails.

Of the submarines of the British 9th SM Flotilla, concentrated as flanking cover, *Seadog* (Lt Pelly) sinks one ship of 8597 tons; the Dutch *O.15* misses a convoy on 26 Dec. Of the Soviet submarines *L-20*, *K-21* and *S-102* are deployed against the *Scharnhorst* on 26 Dec. In addition, during the journeys of these convoys, *L-15*, *L-22*, *S-15* and *S-103* operate off the Polar Coast and *M-105* and *M-201* in Varangerfjord where Soviet torpedo cutters repeatedly try to attack. They sink *V 6106* on 12 Dec.

13-14 Dec   South West Pacific
After an attack by the 5th USAAF, in which 433 tons of bombs are dropped, the VII Amphibious Force (TF 76, Rear-Adm Barbey), which has set out on 13 Dec from the Goodenough Islands with the Australian transport *Westralia*, the LSD *Carter Hall* and the fast transports *Humphreys* and *Sands*, lands 1600 men of the 112th US Cavalry

RCT (Brig-Gen Cunningham) on 14 Dec in Arawe (New Britain). The operation 'Director' is supported by the US destroyers *Reid*, *Smith*, *Lamson*, *Flusser* and *Mahan*. Escort: the destroyers *Conyngham*, *Shaw*, *Drayton*, *Mugford* and *Bagley*. Covering force: TF 74, comprising the Australian cruisers *Australia* and *Shropshire* and the destroyers *Arunta* and *Warramunga*.

**20-26 Dec   North Atlantic/
Bay of Biscay**
From 20 Dec the southern boats of the 'Coronel' formation (*U801*, *U107*, *U667*, *U618*, *U270*, *U541*, *U645*, *U962*, *U415*, *U305*, *U275*, *U382* and *U641*) are moved as the 'Borkum' group to the area SW of the Bay of Biscay to operate against the convoy MKS.33/SL.142. The deployment of five FW 200s by day and one BV 222 by night (20-21 Dec) and of other aircraft on 21 Dec produces no results. The Allied command deploys against the 'Borkum' group the US carrier group *Card* (Capt Isbell) with the destroyers *Leary*, *Schenck* and *Decatur* coming from convoy GUS.24. On 22 Dec and 23 Dec the carrier force is reported three times by German air reconnaissance. The Commander U-boats orders the 'Borkum' group to operate against it in order to cover the return of the blockade-runner *Osorno*, which is located on 23 Dec by a Wildcat from the *Card* in bad weather. In the night 23-24 Dec *U305* first sights the carrier force but is driven off by *Schenck* after being located by HF/DF. *U415* (Lt-Cdr Neide) misses the *Card* with a FAT salvo of three as she turns away and the *Decatur* with a T-5. The *Schenck* avoids a T-5 from *U645* and then sinks the boat with depth charges. *U275* (Lt Bork) gets a T-5 hit on the *Leary* which is detached to support her; and *U382* (Lt Zorn) finishes off the destroyer. In the evening of 24 Dec the convoy OS.62/KMS.36, coming from the N with the EG B.1 and the Support Group with the escort carrier *Striker*, runs into the 'Borkum' formation. The destroyer leader *Hurricane* is lost through a T-5 attack by *U305* (Lt-Cdr Bahr). At mid-day on 24 Dec the German 8th DD Flotilla (Capt Erdmenger), consisting of *Z27*, *Z23*,

G

Z24, Z32, Z37 and ZH1 with the 4th TB Flotilla (Cdr Kohlauf) under command and comprising T22, T23, T24, T25, T26 and T27, sets out from the Gironde Estuary to meet the Osorno (Capt Hellmann) (Operation 'Bernau'). Although from the dawn of 25 Dec Sunderland flying boats of No 201 Sqdn RAF, No 422 Sqdn RCAF and No 461 Sqdn RAAF are in contact, Capt Erdmenger is able to meet the Osorno at mid-day after she has shot down one flying boat. Attempted attacks by aircraft of No 19 Group Coastal Command are beaten off by Ju 88 long-range fighters of Air Commander Atlantic and by the AA fire of the ships. In coming into the Gironde Estuary on 26 Dec the Osorno damages her hull on the wreck of Sperrbrecher 21 and has to be beached to save the cargo.

21-22 Dec   Mediterranean/Adriatic
The British MTB226 and MTB228 sink the old German cruiser Niobe in the Adriatic NW of Zara.

22-23 Dec   East Mediterranean
The torpedo boats TA23 and TA24 and the minelayer Niedersachsen carry out the mining operation 'Attacke' off the northern extremity of Corsica.

23 Dec   English Channel
Unsuccessful probing sortie by the 5th MTB Flotilla, comprising S143, S136, S138, S139, S140, S141 and S142, against a British convoy. There are engagements with British escort forces.

23 Dec-8 Jan   North Atlantic
The U-boat groups 'Sylt', 'Amrum', and 'Föhr' are divided up in sections of three ('Rügen 1-6') W of Ireland: 1 (U364, U972, U981), 2 (U744, U545, U781), 3 (U471, U390, U546), 4 (U960, U392, U302, U976), 5 (U311, U92, U672) and 6 (U625, U653, U421). On 23 Dec U471 (Lt-Cdr Klövekorn) misses a troop transport of the convoy TU.5, of which the US battleship Arkansas forms part of the escort, and is then damaged by an aircraft of RAF Coastal Command. U653 (Lt Kandler) misses a frigate of a tanker convoy further to the S. An attack by U392 (Lt Schümann) on a small convoy on 26 Dec is also unsuccessful. On 30 Dec some boats establish contact with stragglers from the convoy ON.217: the Empire Hous-

man (7359 tons) is first missed by U744 (Lt Blischke), then torpedoed by U545 (Lt-Cdr Mannesmann) and later finished off by U744. U731 (Lt Count Keller) misses another ship. Individual boat formations from 5 Jan with U547, U545, U741, U762, U364, U972, U981, U390, U471, U392, U386, U302, U846, U311, U260, U92, U976, U757, U731, U309 and U666 also produce no success. On 8 Jan U757 is sunk by the convoy escorts Bayntun and Camrose.

24 Dec   Mediterranean
The large French destroyer Le Fantasque captures the German freighter Nicoline Maersk off the Spanish coast near Tortosa in the Western Mediterranean.

24-27 Dec   South West Pacific
Operation 'Dexterity'. The US VII Amphibious Force (TF 76, Rear-Adm Barbey) which sets out on 25 Dec, lands on the following day some 13000 troops of the US 1st Marine Div (Maj-Gen Rupertus) at Cape Gloucester. It consists of the transports Westralia and Etamin, the LSD Carter Hall, 24 LSTs, 15 LCIs, 12 LCTs, 14 LCMs, four PCs, seven SCs, three YMSs and other units. The first waves come with the fast transports Stringham, Crosby, Kilty, Dent, Ward, Brooks, Gilmer, Sands, Humphreys and Noa. Support and escort: the US destroyers Conyngham, Shaw, Drayton, Mugford, Bagley, Reid, Smith, Lamson, Flusser and Mahan. Fire support and cover: TG 74.1, consisting of the Australian cruisers (Rear-Adm Crutchley) Australia and Shropshire and the destroyers Arunta, Warramunga, Helm and Ralph Talbot; TG 74.2 (Rear-Adm Berkey) comprising the US cruisers Nashville, and Phoenix and the destroyers Bush, Ammen, Bache, Mullany, Hutchins, Beale, Daly and Brownson. The Brownson is sunk in an attack by 60 Japanese aircraft. Shaw is badly, and Drayton, Lamson, LST 66 and LST 202 more lightly, damaged.
On 24 Dec the cruisers Montpelier, Cleveland and Columbia with four destroyers shell Buka and Buin near Bougainville as a diversion. On 27 Dec Ainsworth's Task Force repeats the shelling near Kieta.

25 Dec-4 Jan   South West Pacific
Japanese troop transports from Truk to Rabaul and Kavieng. The proposed deployment of the battleship *Yamato* has to be abandoned after the torpedoing of the ship S of Truk by the US submarine *Skate* (Cdr McKinney). The operation is carried out by the cruisers *Kumano*, *Suzuya*, *Oyodo*, *Noshiro* and destroyers.
On 25 Dec US TG 50.2 (Rear-Adm Sherman), comprising the carriers *Bunker Hill* and *Monterey* and the destroyers *Bradford*, *Brown*, *Cowell*, *Bell*, *Charette* and *Conner*, carries out a raid on Kavieng (New Ireland). One steamer of 4861 tons is sunk and the minesweepers *W21* and *W22* and one steamer are damaged. On 1 Jan the carrier aircraft locate one of the returning Japanese cruiser forces and slightly damage the *Oyodo*, *Noshiro* and the destroyer *Yamagumo*. In a further raid on Kavieng on 4 Jan the Japanese destroyer *Fumitsuki* is damaged.

26-28 Dec   Bay of Biscay
Operation 'Trave': sortie by the 8th DD Flotilla and the 4th TB Flotilla (composition as in operation 'Bernau' with the exception of *ZH1*, which has to remain behind with condenser trouble) into the Bay of Biscay to bring the blockade-runner *Alsterufer* (Capt Piatek) into the Gironde.
Early on 27 Dec a Sunderland flying boat sights the *Alsterufer* 500 nautical miles NW of Cape Finisterre proceeding SE. The cruisers of operation 'Stonewall' (see 12 Dec) are then deployed: from E of the position the *Enterprise* (Capt Grant, RCN) and from 300 nautical miles W *Glasgow* (Capt Clarke) to a position 300 nautical miles NW of Finisterre. The *Gambia* (Capt William-Powlett in overall command) sets out from Fayal and *Penelope* and the fast minelayer *Ariadne* from Gibraltar. In addition, the large French destroyers *Le Fantasque* and *Le Malin* are deployed from the Azores. At 1615 hrs the *Alsterufer* (2729 tons) is hit by rockets from a Liberator bomber of No 311 Sqdn (Czech) and set on fire. The Halifax attack force which arrives at 1800 hrs sights the burning and sinking ship being abandoned by the crew. Four lifeboats with 74 men are picked up two days later by four Canadian corvettes.
Naval Group West only learns of the loss of the *Alsterufer* on the morning of 28 Dec and orders the destroyers to return. But before this the destroyers are located by Allied air reconnaissance with the result that *Glasgow* and *Enterprise* are able to find them at midday. Despite the gun superiority of the 11 destroyers and torpedo boats (25-15 cm and 24-10.5 cm guns against 19-6 inch and 13-4 inch guns), a pincer attack fails in the heavy sea which prevents the German ships from using their full speed. In the gun engagement *Z27* (Cdr Günther Schultz†) with the Commander of the 8th DD Flotilla on board (Capt Erdmenger†), *T25* (Cdr. v. Gartzen) and *T26* (Lt-Cdr Quedenfeldt) sink. Of the rest of the force *Z24*, *Z23*, *T24* and *T27* reach Brest and *Z32* and *Z37* the Gironde and *Z23* and *T22*, which retired to the S, St Jean de Luz. Sixty-two survivors are rescued by British ships, 164 by an Irish steamer and four by Spanish destroyers.
After the engagement *Glasgow*, *Enterprise* and *Ariadne* proceed to Plymouth where in spite of several German air attacks with glider bombs, they arrive on 29 Dec. *Penelope*, *Le Fantasque* and *Le Malin* return to Gibraltar. *Gambia*, and the newly-arrived cruiser *Mauritius*, continue the search until 1 Jan.

26 Dec-13 Jan   North Atlantic
The 'Borkum' group tries on 25 Dec and in the night 25-26 Dec to continue the operations against the convoy OS.62/KMS.36, but only *U305* and *U270* are able to fire T-5s unsuccessfully against the escorts of the Support Group which remain behind. On the way to a new concentration for 30 Dec against the expected convoy MKS.34/SL.143 the 'Borkum' group, comprising *U270*, *U801*, *U571*, *U305*, *U275*, *U382*, *U758*, *U641* and *U377* comes partly into contact on 29 Dec and 30 Dec with the 6th SG (British frigates and Canadian corvettes) which is trying to rescue the survivors of the engagement on 27 Dec. *U275* and *U270* are attacked by frigates and *U275* also by aircraft. The outward-bound *U629* (Lt Bugs) and *U541* (Lt-Cdr K. Petersen), which are also ordered to look for survivors, *U421* (Lt Kolbus) and *U543*

(Lt-Cdr Hellriegel) make, in some cases, several T-5 attacks on escort vessels, but they all fail. The convoy MKS.34/SL.143 with EG B.3, which is located by German air reconnaissance on 30 Dec and 31 Dec, passes the patrol line on 1-2 Jan. *U382* (Lt Zorn) *U275* (Lt Bork) and *U305* (Lt-Cdr Bahr) miss escort vessels with T-5s. An attempt to operate against a south-bound convoy on 2-3 Jan fails because no air reconnaissance is possible on account of shortages. Only *U270* (Lt-Cdr Otto), which has previously been bombed, misses a destroyer with a T-5. To make the locating of the patrol lines and their avoidance more difficult, the 'Borkum' boats are divided into three small sections: 1 (*U270, U305* and *U382*); 2 (*U758* and *U641*); and 3 *U377, U953* and *U231*). On 5 Jan, 6 Jan and 7 Jan the boats repeatedly come into contact with the 5th SG (frigates *Nene* and *Tweed* and the Canadian corvettes *Calgary, Snowberry, Edmundston* and *Camrose*) NW of Spain which is looking out for expected blockade-runners. On 5 Jan *U758* (Lt-Cdr Manseck) misses one corvette with a T-5. On 6 Jan *U270* shoots down one Fortress of No 220 Sqdn RAF and is herself damaged by it; and on 7 Jan *U305* sinks the *Tweed* with a T-5. On 8 Jan one Ju 290 of F.A.Gr.5, on 9 Jan three, and on 10 Jan and 11 Jan two, are deployed against the expected convoy MKS.35/SL.144. But only on 9 Jan does one aircraft sight the convoy W of Portugal. On the evening of 11 Jan *U305* gets sight of the convoy. The U-boats are able with their 3.7 cm AA guns to keep off the carrier aircraft of the US Support Group with the carrier *Block Island* (Capt Ramsey), but they are unable to press home their attack. In an attack on *U758*, rockets are used by carrier aircraft—without success. Only *U953* (Lt Marbach) misses the Canadian corvette *Lunenburg* of the Escort Group with a T-5. On 13 Jan the operation has to be broken off. A Wellington of No 172 Sqdn RAF, brought to the scene by an aircraft of the *Block Island*, sinks *U231*.

28 Dec English Channel
A British commando operation against the Channel Island of Sark fails.

**30 Dec-30 Jan Atlantic/
Indian Ocean**
The British 1st Battle Sqdn, comprising the battleships *Queen Elizabeth* and *Valiant*, and battlecruiser *Renown* sets out from Scapa Flow on 30 Dec for the Indian Ocean. The carriers *Illustrious* and *Unicorn* join them from the Clyde. They are escorted by seven destroyers. The force proceeds through the Mediterranean to Colombo where it arrives on 30 Jan.

1944

1-31 Jan Pacific
Of the US submarines which arrive in their operational areas in January *Batfish* (Lt-Cdr Merrill) sinks one ship of 5486 tons; *Finback* (Lt-Cdr Tyree) one ship of 10000 tons; *Seawolf* (Lt-Cdr Gross) four ships of 23361 tons and one ship in co-operation with *Whale*; *Snook* (Lt-Cdr Triebel) four ships of 16926 tons; *Steelhead* (Lt-Cdr Welchell) one ship of 6795 tons; *Sturgeon* (Lt-Cdr Murphy) two ships of 8603 tons; *Swordfish* (Lt-Cdr Hensel) three ships of 12243 tons; *Tambor* (Lt-Cdr Kefauver) four ships of 18484 tons; *Tautog* (Lt-Cdr Sieglaff) two ships of 6025 tons; *Whale* (Lt-Cdr Burrows) one ship of 5870 tons; and one ship of 4865 tons in co-operation with *Seawolf*—all off Japan. In the area of the Mandate Islands *Albacore* (Lt-Cdr Blanchard) sinks one ship of 2629 tons and the destroyer *Sazanami*; *Angler* (Lt-Cdr Olsen) one ship of 889 tons; *Balao* (Lt-Cdr Cole) torpedoes one ship; *Blackfish* (Lt-Cdr Davidson) sinks one ship of 2087 tons; *Gar* (Lt-Cdr Lantrup) two ships of 8994 tons; *Haddock* (Cdr Roach) torpedoes the carrier *Unyo*; *Hake* (Lt-Cdr Broach) sinks three ships of 19384 tons; *Scamp* (Lt-Cdr Ebert) sinks one ship of 9974 tons; *Seadragon* (Lt-Cdr Ashley) torpedoes one ship; *Seahorse* (Lt-Cdr Rutter) sinks five ships of 13716 tons; *Spearfish* (Lt-Cdr Williams) one ship of 3560 tons; *Trigger* (Lt-Cdr Dornis) two ships of 12376 tons; *Tullibee* (Cdr Brindupke) one ship of 549 tons. In the area of the Malayan Archipelago and the Philippines *Bowfin* (Lt-Cdr Griffith) sinks one ship of 4408 tons and torpedoes the seaplane tender *Kamoi*; *Crevalle* (Lt-Cdr Munson) sinks one ship of 2552 tons; *Flasher* (Lt-Cdr Whitaker) four ships of 10584 tons; *Kingfish* (Lt-Cdr Jukes) three ships of 14633 tons; *Rasher* (Lt-Cdr Laughon) one ship of 7251 tons; *Thresher* (Lt-Cdr McMillan) four ships of 14523 tons; and *Tinosa* (Lt-Cdr Weiss) four ships of 15484 tons.

2-5 Jan South Atlantic
From the middle of November 1943 US TF 41 (Rear-Adm Reid), comprising the cruisers *Omaha*, *Milwaukee*, *Cincinnati*, *Marblehead* and *Memphis* and the destroyers *Winslow*, *Moffett*, *Davis*, *Jouett* and *Somers*, operates in groups composed of one cruiser and one destroyer from Recife (Brazil) against the German blockade-runners coming from East Asia. Two groups made up of the French and Italian cruisers *Montcalm*, *Georges Leygues* and *Duca degli Abruzzi* and *Gloire*, *Suffren* and *Duca d'Aosta* respectively are deployed in turns from Freetown and Dakar. In addition, from the beginning of January the large French destroyers *Le Fantasque* and *Le Malin* are stationed in Horta (Azores). From Ascension Island, Natal and Freetown US, Brazilian, British and French air squadrons fly reconnaissance sorties. On 1 Jan a Liberator of VB.107 from Ascension Island sights the blockade-runner *Weserland* (Capt Krage). It is damaged by AA fire. On 2 Jan another is shot down and then in the night of 2-3 Jan the *Somers* sinks the blockade-runner with gunfire and rescues 133 survivors. On 4 Jan an aircraft from the *Omaha* sights the blockade-runner *Rio Grande* (Capt v. Allwörden, 6062 tons) which is sunk by the cruiser and the destroyer *Jouett* with gunfire. There is only one survivor. On 5 Jan the last German blockade-runner from East Asia, *Burgenland* (Capt Schütz, 7320 tons), is sighted by a US flying-boat from Natal and scuttles herself when *Omaha* and *Jouett* come within sight. The *Omaha*, *Jouett*, *Davis*, *Winslow*, the Brazilian corvette *Camorin* and the Brazilian steamer *Poti* recover over 2000 bales of rubber in the next few days.

2-23 Jan South West Pacific
The VII Amphibious Force (Rear-Adm Barbey) lands 2400 troops from the

126th RCT of the 32nd US Inf Div (Brig-Gen Martin) near Saidor (New Guinea) on 2 Jan from 9 APDs, two LSTs and several LCIs. The landing craft are escorted by the destroyers (Capt Carter) *Beale, Mahan, Flusser, Lamson, Drayton, Hutchins, Smith* and *Conyngham.* Covering force: Rear-Adm Crutchley RAN with the cruisers *Australia* and *Shropshire*, the destroyers *Arunta* and *Warramunga* (Australian) and the US destroyers *Helm, Ralph Talbot, Bush, Ammen, Bache* and *Mullany* with the cruisers *Nashville* and *Phoenix.* 12000 Japanese of the 18th Army (Lt-Gen Adachi) are cut off in Sio. On 7-8 Jan the Japanese submarine *I-177* evacuates Gen Adachi. The troops try to get to Madang via Gali but they suffer repeated losses from coastal shelling near Gali from US destroyers and on 26 Jan from Rear-Adm Berkey and his US cruisers *Nashville* and *Phoenix* and the destroyers *Bush, Ammen* and *Mullany* from Madang.

3-13 Jan   Mediterranean
Of the German U-boats employed against Allied supply traffic from Gibraltar along the Algerian coast to Naples *U642, U616* and *U380* attack convoys, sometimes repeatedly, without success. On 3-4 Jan *U952* and *U343* pass through the Straits of Gibraltar from the W; *U343* beats off heavy air attacks on 8 Jan with her AA guns and severely damages two aircraft.
On 10 Jan 30 torpedo aircraft of the 2nd Fl. Div. in Southern France sink the freighter *Ocean Hunter* (7178 tons) from the convoy KMS.37 N of Oran and torpedo the *Daniel Webster* (7176 tons) which is beached but regarded as a total loss.

5-6 Jan   Air War/Germany
On 5 Jan the 8th USAAF attacks Kiel. In the night 5-6 Jan 348 aircraft of RAF Bomber Command drop 1118 tons of bombs on Stettin.

5-6 Jan   English Channel
The German 5th MTB Flotilla (Lt-Cdr K. Müller) comprising *S141, S100, S142, S143, S138, S136* and *S84*, attacks the convoy WP.457 (SOE destroyer *Mackay*) off the British South West Coast. The boats fire a total of 23 torpedoes and sink the freighters *Polperro* (403 tons), *Under-wood* (1990 tons) and *Solstad* (1408 tons) as well as the trawler *Wallasea* (545 tons).

5 Jan-5 Mar   Black Sea
In January there operate against Soviet coastal traffic off the Caucasus the German U-boats *U19, U20,* (Lt Grafen), which torpedoes one tanker, and *U24.* In February *U18* (Lt Fleige), which sinks one steamer, *U19* (Lt Ohlenburg) and *U20*, which lays mines off Poti, operate off Batum and Poti. At the beginning of March *U20* and *U24* are deployed against Soviet traffic from Poti to Trapezunt. Soviet submarines are, in particular, employed against German convoy traffic between the now isolated Crimea and Constanza and Odessa, which the 10th Escort Div (Capt Weyher) escorts with the 1st, 3rd and 23rd SC Flotillas, the 3rd MS Flotilla and Rumanian forces. *L-23* (Capt 3rd Class Fartushny†, with the Commander of the Submarine Brigade, Capt 1st Class Krestovski† on board) attacks a convoy SW of Evpatoria on 5 Jan and is pursued by the submarine-chasers *Schiff 19, UJ303, UJ306, UJ316, UJ312* and *UJ2301.* After engagements with naval ferry barges on 1 Jan the boat is probably lost on 30 Jan when attacked by a BV 138 when she returns. *L-6* (Lt-Cdr Gremyako) lays a mine barrage; *Shch-216* (Capt 3rd Class Karbovski†) attacks convoys unsuccessfully on 9 Feb and 10 Feb and is sunk by depth charges from *UJ103* W of Evpatoria on 16 Feb. *M-112, M-35, Shch-209* and *Shch-205* have no success. During the Soviet offensive N of the lower Dnieper, Nikolaev has to be evacuated on 11 Mar after the blowing up of harbour and dockyard installations. Among the craft to be taken off are three uncompleted KT ships. From 6 Mar to 8 Mar the Soviet 2nd Torpedo Cutter Brigade (Capt 2nd Class Protsenko), comprising 10 TKAs, moves from Gelendzhik round the Crimea to Skadovsk. At the beginning of April six more TKAs follow.

7-29 Jan   North Atlantic
The U-boats of the 'Rügen' group (*U547, U545, U741, U981, U972* (missing from the beginning of January), *U364, U390, U762, U309, U731,*

U757, U666, U471, U392, U846, U311, U302 and *U976*) and, from the middle of January, the remaining 'Borkum' boats (*U305, U382, U377* and *U641*) and the newly-arrived *U571, U271, U212, U592, U231* and *U238*, operate W of Ireland singly and in varying concentrations. *U386* is deployed off the North Channel, *U260* off Reykjavik and, as weather boats, *U544, U763* and *U960* (Lt Heinrich) which sinks one ship of 7176 tons. On 8 Jan *U757* is sunk by the British DE *Bayntun* (4th SG) and the Canadian corvette *Camrose* (5th SG), which are part of the escort of the combined convoy OS.64/KMS.38. Various U-boats sight ships and search groups in the next few days but have no success. *U377* is lost on 15 Jan in such an encounter. On 17 Jan *U305* is sunk by the destroyer *Wanderer* and the landing ship *Glenearn*. US TG 21.12 (Capt Gallery), comprising the carrier *Guadalcanal*, the destroyer *Forrest* and the DEs *Pillsbury, Pope, Flaherty* and *Chatelain*, surprises a supply group, consisting of *U516, U539* and *U544* and aircraft sink *U544*. On the evening of 17 Jan an He 177 sights the convoy OS.65/KMS.39 (EG B.3, Commander Evans on the frigate *Towy*). But of the U-boats directed to the scene, only *U641* gets near on 19 Jan and is sunk by the corvette *Violet*. On 19 Jan *U390* misses a steamer further to the N. reconnaissance provided on 20 Jan, 21 Jan and 22 Jan cannot find the expected HX and SC convoys or the west-bound ON.220 (EG C.4). On 26 Jan and 27 Jan Ju 290s of FA.Gr.5 repeatedly report the combined convoy OS.66/KMS.40 and ON.221. Against them are concentrated the boats *U650, U231, U571, U281, U271, U212* and *U592* as the 'Hinein' group and *U989, U762, U547, U390, U984, U731, U545, U386, U309, U666, U406, U283* and *U985* as the 'Stürmer' group. No 15 Group Coastal Command reinforced by aircraft of No 19 Group, carries out massive operations against the U-boat formations in support of the convoys. *U571* and *U271* are sunk on 28 Jan and other boats are attacked. On 29 Jan the boats are summoned to France because of a false invasion alarm

and are then ordered to new positions.

8-28 Jan   Mediterranean/ Tyrrhenian Sea
In a British fighter bomber attack on 8 Jan the German escort vessel *SG20* (ex-torpedo boat *Papa*) is badly damaged by near-misses off Imperia and runs aground. In an air attack on Savona on 20 Jan the French destroyer *Valmy* receives two direct hits and *Le Hardi* slight damage as they lie in the harbour. In a fighter bomber attack on a German convoy near San Stefano on 28 Jan *R201* is sunk and *R199, R161* and *KT20* are damaged.

8 Jan-18 Mar   Mediterranean
An Allied air attack on Pola weakens the German U-boats employed in the Eastern Mediterranean. *U81* is destroyed and *U596* damaged. In February *U453* (Lt Lührs) sinks four sailing ships on the Syrian coast; *U407* (Lt Korndörfer) torpedoes one sailing ship and one ship of 6207 tons; *U596* (Lt Nonn) misses one Italian corvette off Brindisi on 23 Feb and on 7 Mar the Italian battleship *Giulio Cesare* S of the Gulf of Taranto; *U565* (Lt Henning) misses one corvette and a cruiser off Cyrenaica at the beginning of March. In another patrol S of Taranto *U453* attacks a convoy on 18 Mar but has no success.

10 Jan-12 Mar   South Pacific
Last Japanese submarine operations against bases in the South Pacific. The large submarine *I-11* (Cdr Izu) reports on 11 Jan the result of the periscope reconnaissance of Funafuti but is lost before carrying out the air reconnaissance missions over the Ellice Islands and Samoa. In the area of the New Hebrides *Ro-42* (Lt-Cdr Wada) sinks the harbour tanker *YO159* on 14 Jan and *Ro-37* is lost on 23 Jan after torpedoing the tanker *Cache* (12000 tons). *Ro-44* has no success. In February *Ro-106* aod *Ro-109* again operate from Rabaul without success in Huon Gulf. After the evacuation of Rabaul by the fleet (the army stays there until 1945) the last boats of the 7th SM Flotilla return to Truk. *Ro-39* and *Ro-40*, which are sent at the end of January and the beginning of February to operate against the US Fleets in the area of the Marshall Islands, do not return. In transport missions to Mille

and Wotje *I-175* is lost in February and *I-32* in March after a successful mission. Finally, *Ro-44* reconnoitres Majuro on 12 Mar and 13 Mar.

11 Jan-25 Feb   Indian Ocean
Reinforcement of the British Eastern Fleet (Vice-Adm Somerville), which at the end of 1943, consisted only of the battleship *Ramillies*, the escort carrier *Battler*, the 4th Cruiser Sqdn (Rear-Adm Read) with *Newcastle*, *Suffolk*, *Frobisher*, *Kenya*, *Ceylon* and the cruisers *Hawkins*, *Danae* and *Emerald* for convoy duties, the auxiliary cruisers *Alaunia* and *Chitral*, 11 destroyers, 13 frigates, sloops and corvettes and six submarines. In January the 1st Battle Sqdn (Vice-Adm Power) arrives with the *Queen Elizabeth*, *Valiant* and the battlecruiser *Renown*; the carriers (Rear-Adm Moody) *Illustrious* and *Unicorn*; the cruisers *Sussex* and *Tromp* (Dutch) with the Dutch destroyers *Van Galen* and *Tjerk Hiddes*. In addition to the 11th DD Flotilla (Capt De Winton), comprising *Rotherham*, *Racehorse*, *Raider*, *Rapid*, *Redoubt*, *Relentless*, *Rocket* and *Roebuck* and the 16th DD Div with *Paladin*, *Penn*, *Petard* and *Pathfinder*, the 4th DD Flotilla (Capt Onslow), comprising *Quilliam*, *Quadrant*, *Quality*, *Queenborough*, *Quiberon* and *Quickmatch*, is transferred at the beginning of March. From December 1943 the 4th SM Flotilla (Capt Ionides), consisting of *Trespasser*, *Taurus*, *Truculent*, *Tally Ho*, *Tantalus*, *Tantivy*, *Sea Rover*, *Stoic*, *Stonehenge* (missing from the end of February) and the Dutch *K-XIV* and *O.23*, are deployed against Japanese traffic in the Malacca Straits and on the West Coast of Siam as far as the Nicobar and Andaman Islands. In several operations there *Tally Ho* (Cdr Bennington) sinks two ships of 4876 tons and on 11 Jan the cruiser *Kuma* off Penang. *Templar* (Lt Beckley), torpedoes the cruiser *Kitakami* on 25 Feb.

11 Jan-2 May   Indian Ocean
The German U-boats of the 'Monsun' group operate in the Indian Ocean from Penang. *U532* (Cdr Junker) sinks two ships of 9457 tons and torpedoes one ship of 7283 tons SW of India; *U188* (Capt Lüdden) seven ships of 42549 tons, partly from convoys, and

seven dhows in the Gulf of Aden; *U168* (Lt-Cdr Pich) sinks two ships of 5875 tons and torpedoes one ship of 9804 tons off India; *U183* (Lt-Cdr Schneewind) sinks one ship of 5419 tons and torpedoes one tanker of 6993 tons in Addu Atoll. *U510* (Lt Eick), coming from France, sinks in the Gulf of Aden in February and March five ships of 31220 tons, some from convoys, and one dhow and also torpedoes one ship of 9970 tons. The operations are supported by German tankers including the *Charlotte Schliemann* which replenishes *U178* and *U510* on 27 Jan. The British cruiser *Newcastle* and the destroyer *Relentless* and seven Catalina flying boats are deployed from Mauritius on the basis of HF/DF bearings. One of the flying-boats reports the tanker and brings up the *Relentless* in the night of 11-12 Feb. When she comes into sight, the tanker scuttles herself. *U532* takes off the crew and refuels from *U178* on 27 Feb.

The British carrier *Illustrious* with the cruisers *Gambia* and *Sussex* and the destroyers *Rotherham* and *Tjerk Hiddes* (Dutch) carry out operation 'Sleuth' against suspected blockade-runners in the area SW of the Cocos Islands.

On 12 Mar *U188*, *U532* and *U168* are joined by the tanker *Brake* from Penang. But a British search group, consisting of the escort carrier *Battler*, the cruisers *Suffolk* and *Newcastle* and and destroyers *Roebuck* and *Quadrant*, are deployed against her. *Roebuck*, led to the scene by a carrier aircraft, forces the tanker to scuttle herself. *U168* takes off the crew. Of the transport U-boats *UIT23* is sunk by the British submarine *Tally Ho* (Cdr Bennington) on 14 Feb shortly after setting out in the Malacca Straits; *UIT24* has to give her fuel to *U532* on 18 Mar and return to Penang; and *UIT22* is sunk off South Africa by a Catalina flying boat on 11 Mar. The torpedo transport *U1062* reaches Penang, after refuelling from *U532* on 10 Apl. *U178* and *U188* return to Bordeaux, the other boats to Penang. Of the Japanese submarines, *I-27* (Lt-Cdr Fukumura) attacks a British convoy of five troop transports in the One and a Half Degree Channel

Above: Italian and German U-boats sustain heavy losses during attempts to attack the Allied landing forces around Sicily. The Italian submarine *Bronzo* (here) is captured on June 12 off Syracuse. The *Dandolo* and *U407*, however, register hits on the cruisers *Cleopatra* and *Newfoundland*.   *[IWM*

Below: Sept 1943: Operation 'Avalanche': Allied cruisers and destroyers support the VI US Corps and X British Corps landing to form a bridgehead at Salerno. Onloaded off the beaches by the large attack transports in the background, landing boats smash through waves toward the beach at Salerno on Sept 9.   *[Official USN*

Below: While German ground troops try to smash the Allied bridgehead at Salerno, squadrons of German Do 217 bombers equipped with radio controlled Hs.293 and FX.1400 bombs attack the Allied supporting ships. On July 11 the us *Savannah* is hit by a bomb near C turret.   *[Official USN*

Above: Sept 8, 1943: General Eisenhower announces the conclusion of an armistice with Italy. The Italian Fleet puts to sea from La Spezia to surrender, but is attacked on the way by German Do 217 bombers of L.Gr.100 armed with FX.1400 radio controlled bombs. The flagship *Roma*, newest of the Italian 35000-ton battleships is hit by one of the bombs and sunk.   [*BFZ*

Below: The Italian Fleet seen from the deck of the British battleship *King George V* arriving off Malta. Battleships *Italia* and *Vittorio Veneto* (left) with the cruisers *Garibaldi, Duca Degli Abruzzi, Eugenio di Savoia, Duca d'Aosta* and *Montecuccoli*.   [*IWM*

Above: In the Aegean Allied naval and air forces transport troops from Alexandria to the Dodecanese islands of Kos, Leros and Samsos. The islands were surrendered to the British by the Italian Badoglio forces. During October and November German naval forces, built around captured Italian torpedoboats, land troops on the islands which are recaptured. Here British, Indian and Italian prisoners await transport to the Greek mainland. The torpedoboat *TA15* (ex-*Francesco Crispi*) is moored in the background. [*BFZ*

Below: Dec 1943: Light German forces in the Kerch straits blockade the bridgehead of the Soviet 18th Army on the east coast of the Kerch peninsula from Dec 4-11. This allows German army forces to destroy the Eltigen bridgehead. [*BFZ*

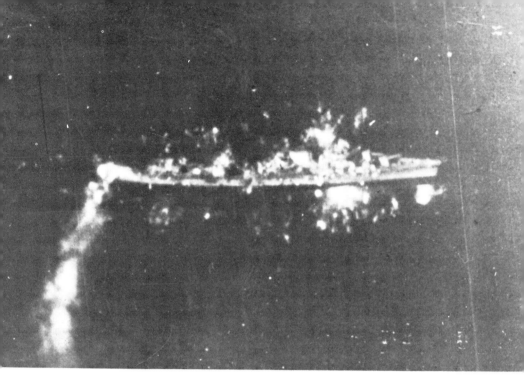

Above: Three Soviet destroyers fail to catch a large convoy of German light transport vessels coming from the Kerch straits and are attacked on their return southeast of the Crimean coast by German Ju 87 dive bombers. The destroyers (*Kharkov, Sposobny* and *Besposchadny* (photo) are sunk on Oct 6, 1943.   [*BFZ*

Below: Increasing attacks by Allied air forces on European ports force the Germans to build large concrete bunkers to keep their U-boats safe from air attack. Large bomb proof shelters are built at Brest, Lorient, St Nazaire and La Rochelle. Here *U515* is returning to Lorient from a successful patrol off West Africa where she attacked convoy TS.37 on Apr 30 and May 1, 1943.
                                                     [*BFZ*

Above: Autumn 1943: In an attempt to regain the lost initiative in the Atlantic the German U-boats are armed with the 'Gnat' acoustic torpedo, 'Naxos' radar search receiver and a heavy AA armament of one quadruple and two twin 20mm guns. It proves impossible to turn the tide against the RAF offensive in the Bay of Biscay. There is no effective counter to the 10cm radar, Leigh Light and new torpex bombs of the aircraft and the HF/DF, 10cm radar and hedgehogs of the escort vessels and the escort carriers. [BFZ

Below: In an attempt to beat the British blockade and bring vital raw imports to Germany a number of blockade runners leave the Far East. On March 30, 1943 the destroyers *Z24* (left) and *Z32* (right) of the 8th Destroyer Flotilla leave the Gironde to meet the Italian blockade runner *Pietro Orseolo* off Vigo and escort her to Bordeaux. [BFZ

Above: Aug 1943: The large Japanese submarine *I-8* from Penang is met in the Bay of Biscay by the torpedoboats *T24*, *T22* and *T25* and escorted to Lorient.   *[BFZ/Fukui*
Below: July 1943: To neutralise the danger which the German battleships *Tirpitz* and *Scharnhorst* pose for the passage of the Allied Russian convoys, the Home Fleet is temporarily augmented by an American task group of two modern battleships, the carrier *Ranger* and a number of cruisers. In July the C-in-C Home Fleet operates with British and American ships off Norway. Here the uss *South Dakota, Alabama* and HMS *Furious* are seen from the Flagship *Duke of York*.   *[IWM*

Above: Dec 1943: Each convoy to Murmansk is covered by a cruiser covering force and a heavy covering group against German surface attack. When the *Scharnhorst* and 5 destroyers sails to attack convoy JW.55B she is met by the cruisers *Belfast*, *Sheffield* and *Norfolk* in two short clashes and then shadowed to bring the battleship *Duke of York* and the cruiser *Jamaica* (photo) in contact when the *Scharnhorst* is finally sunk. [IWM

Below: Jan 1944: Ships of the Soviet Red Banner Baltic Fleet support the Leningrad Front during the breakthrough of the German encirclement from Jan 14-21. Here the destroyer *Opytny* fires her after 13cm guns from the Neva river. [BFZ

Above: The Germans try to close the Finnish Bay with minefields and large anti-submarine nets. To patrol these barrages against Russian attempts to sweep them the Type 35 minesweepers of the German 5th Flotilla are invaluable. Here *M16* is damaged by Russian air attacks. *[BFZ*

Below: May-Aug 1943: The Americans carry out operations to retake the islands in the Aleutian chain, captured by the Japanese in 1942. Kiska is subjected to many aerial and surface bombardments in softening up operations and with the lessons learnt when Attu was captured in May-June 1943, a large invasion fleet is assembled in Adak harbour on Aug 13 in preparation for the landing on Kiska. In the centre the battleships *Tennessee* and *Pensylvania* are anchored. In the foreground is the heavy cruiser *Portland* with some destroyers of Desron 1 to the right and many transports in the background. *[Official USN*

(Maldives) on 12 Feb. The convoy is escorted by the cruiser *Hawkins* and the destroyers *Petard* and *Paladin* and is on the way from Kilindini to Colombo. The submarine sinks the transport *Khedive Ismail* (7513 tons) with over 1000 British troops on board, but is herself sunk in a counter-attack by the two destroyers.

In the Bay of Bengal *Ro-110* (Lt Ebato), after torpedoing a steamer of 6274 tons from the convoy JC.36, is sunk on 11 Feb by the Indian sloop *Jumna* and the British minesweepers *Ipswich* and *Launceston* of the escort. *I-37* (Lt-Cdr Nakagawa) makes a sortie to the African coast and sinks three ships of 19312 tons, including the *British Chivalry* on 22 Feb. With her aircraft she reconnoitres Diego Suarez (Madagascar) on 4 Mar and Kilindini on 14 Mar. She escapes from a depth charge pursuit by the British sloop *Lulworth* on 16 Mar. In March *I-27* (Cdr Kusaka) sinks three ships of 23591 tons, including the *Richard Hovey* on 29 Mar, off the Indian West Coast and Bombay and lands agents on 25 Mar. In the Central Indian Ocean *I-166* misses one ship; *I-162* (Lt-Cdr Doi) and *I-165* (Lt-Cdr Shimizu) each sink one ship of 7127 tons and 3916 tons respectively; *I-8* (Cdr Ariizumi) sinks two ships of 12376 tons and one sailing ship, including the Dutch *Tjisalak* at the end of March. On 1 Mar the 7th Japanese Cruiser Sqdn (Rear-Adm Sakonju), comprising *Aoba*, *Chikuma* and *Tone*, sets out from the Sunda Strait to conduct mercantile warfare on the Australia-Aden route. In the area of the Sunda Strait it is escorted by the cruisers *Kinu* and *Oi* and the destroyers *Uranami*, *Shikinami* and *Amagiri*. On 9 Mar the *Tone* (Capt Mayuzumi) sinks the freighter *Behar* (6100 tons). Because the ship has sent off a distress signal. Rear-Adm Sakonju breaks off the operation and returns. As a result of orders from the Commander of the South West Area Fleet (Vice-Adm Takasu), the survivors are murdered when the *British Chivalry*, *Richard Hovey*, *Behar* and *Jean Nicolet* are sunk.

The only instance of firing on survivors by a German U-boat occurs on 13 Mar in the South Atlantic when *U852* (Lt-Cdr Eck), after dispatching the freighter *Peleus* (4695 tons), hits survivors as she tries to sink the wreckage of the ship. Another ship (5277 tons) is sunk off South Africa on 1 Apl. In April the boat operates off East Africa without success. As a result of HF/DF bearings on 30 Apl, a search is started with Wellingtons of Nos 621 and 8 Sqdns RAF which damage *U852* so badly on 2 May that she is beached on the Somali Coast and blown up.

12 Jan-11 Feb Arctic

Convoy operation JW.56/RA.56. On 12 Jan JW.56A sets out from Loch Ewe with 20 steamers but runs into a heavy storm on 16 Jan and has to put in to Akureyri (Iceland) where five ships stay behind with storm damage. On 21 Jan the convoy puts to sea again; 15 ships with an escort group (Capt Robson on *Hardy*) consisting of nine destoyers and two corvettes. Covering force: Vice-Adm Palliser with the cruisers *Kent*, *Norfolk* and *Belfast*. On 22 Jan the convoy JW.56B with 16 ships follows from Loch Ewe with an escort group (Capt Campbell on *Milne*), consisting of 13 destroyers and corvettes. As a result of agents' reports from Iceland, the Officer Commanding U-boats—Norway (Capt Peters) forms the 'Isegrim' group with ten boats in the Bear Island passage. Although the air reconnaissance provided produces no results, all the boats with the exception of the most northerly *U739* come up from mid-day on 25 Jan. and attack in the dark in the afternoon and night of 25-26 Jan. *U965* (Lt Ohling), *U601* (Lt Hansen), *U360* (Lt-Cdr Becker) (four times), *U425* (Lt Bentzien) (twice), *U737* (Lt-Cdr Brasack), *U278* (Lt Franze) and *U314* (Lt-Cdr Basse) fire T-5s against escort vessels, but only the destroyer *Obdurate* is damaged by a T-5 from *U360*. *U278*, *U360* and *U716* (Lt Dunkelberg) successively fire FAT salvoes at the convoy and hit the *Penelope Barker* (7177 tons), the flagship of the convoy Commodore, *Fort Bellingham* (7153 tons), and the *Andrew G. Curtin* (7200 tons) all of which sink. The *Fort Bellingham* is finished off by *U957* (Lt Schaar) which takes prisoners.

On 27 Jan the Soviet destroyers *Razyarenny*, *Razumny*, *Gremyashchi* and *Grozny* meet the convoy which sails into the Kola Inlet on 28 Jan. Capt Robson meets JW.56B with six destroyers to strengthen the A/S defence. After breaking off the operation against JW.56A, the Officer Commanding U-boats again forms the 'Werwolf' group, now reinforced by *U956*, *U472*, *U313*, *U973* and *U990*, in the Bear Island passage to operate against the next convoy. JW.56B is reported at mid-day on 29 Jan by *U956* (Lt Mohs) which, by midnight, has defended herself three times with T-5s against destroyers without securing any hits. By the morning of 30 Jan *U737*, *U601* (twice), *U957* (four times), *U278*, *U472* (Lt Frhr v. Forstner), *U425* (twice) and *U313* (Lt Schweiger) have fired T-5s against escort vessels, but only *U278* hits the *Hardy*, which has to be sunk by the *Venus*. *U737* and *U957* narrowly miss the *Milne* and the Norwegian *Stord*. *U314* is sunk by the destroyers *Whitehall* and *Meteor*. No boat reaches the merchant ships. Up to early on 31 Jan *U965*, *U425* (twice), *U737*, *U956* and *U990* (Lt-Cdr Nordheimer) fire T-5s without success against escorts. *U956* also fires T-5s on the return journey on 1 Feb, the day the 16 steamers arrive in the Kola Inlet.

The combined convoy RA.56 with 37 steamers and the combined escort of the two JW convoys, consisting of 23 destroyers and corvettes, which are further reinforced by three destroyers from Scapa Flow, avoids the concentration of the remaining boats of the 'Werwolf' group (*U425*, *U957*, *U713*, *U278*, *U973*, *U990*, *U313* and *U312*). It is located by German air reconnaissance on 6 Feb but is reported on the wrong course with the result that the U-boats search in the opposite direction. The convoy arrives in Loch Ewe on 11 Feb without loss.

14-21 Jan   Baltic
Break-out of the Soviet Leningrad Front (Gen of the Army Govorov) from the encirclement of the city. For this purpose the Baltic Fleet (Adm Tributs) has been transporting since 5 Nov 1943 under the command of Admiral Levchenko, the 2nd Assault Army in small

craft from Leningrad to the bridgehead around Oranienburg: 44000 troops, over 200 tanks, 600 guns, 30000 tons of supplies, 2400 vehicles and 6000 horses. The guns of the fleet are employed under the command of Vice-Adm Gren to support the offensive. The ships include: 1st Group (Kronstadt)—the still operational turrets of the beached battleship *Petropavlovsk* (ex-*Marat*); the destroyers *Strashny* and *Silny*; the gunboat *Volga*. 2nd Group (Leningrad, Vice-Adm Rall)—the battleship *Oktyabrskaya Revolutsiya*; the cruisers *Tallin* (ex-*Petropavlovsk*, ex-*Lützow*), *Maksim Gorki* and *Kirov*; the destroyers *Leningrad* and *Svirepy*. 3rd Group (Neva, Capt 1st Class Ivanov)—the destroyers *Optyny*, *Strogi*, *Stroiny* and *Grozyashchi*; the gunboats *Zeya*, *Sestroretsk* and *Oka*. In all, the ships' guns fire 24000 shells.

14 Jan-25 Feb   Norway
Intensification of the British submarine and air operations against German convoy traffic off the Norwegian coast. After unsuccessful submarine attacks by *Seadog* (Lt Pelly) at the beginning of January, there is an attack by British torpedo aircraft on two German convoys off Lister on 14 Jan: two ships of 9208 tons are sunk and *V5307* is damaged. On 20 Jan British torpedo aircraft attack a convoy near Stadlandet and damage the steamer *Emsland* (5180 tons) with the result that she has to be beached. The wreck is destroyed on 5 Feb by a torpedo from the submarine *Satyr* (Lt Weston) and by further air torpedo attacks on 11 Feb. On 20 Jan the German minelayer *Skagerrak* (1281 tons) is sunk by torpedo aircraft near Egersund. In attacks by British bombers on a convoy W of Stadlandet on 1 Feb *UJ1702* is sunk and the steamer *Valencia* (3096 tons) badly damaged and beached. From 7 Feb to 13 Feb the British submarine *Taku* (Lt Pitt) sinks three ships of 13246 tons from convoys in the area of Stavanger; *Stubborn* (Lt Duff) sinks two ships of 3960 tons on 11 Feb and misses a convoy off Foldafjord on 13 Feb. On 13 Feb the Norwegian *MTB627* and *MTB653* sink two coasters totalling 2026 tons near Kristiansand/North. The Norwegian submarine *Ula* (Lt

Sars) misses German convoys near Egersund on 20 Feb and 25 Feb.

15 Jan-5 Feb   Arctic

Soviet combined operation RV-1 against German convoy traffic on the Polar Coast with Adm Golovko in command. The air force of Northern Fleet (Lt-Gen Andreev) makes reconnaissance flights as far as Lopphavet. There the submarine *L-22* reconnoitres. N of the German flanking mine barrages from the North Cape to Kongsfjord the submarines *S-104*, *S-103*, *S-102*, *S-56*, *M-201* and *M-119* are alerted.

On 17 Jan a torpedo aircraft, when carrying out an armed reconnaissance, reports an east-bound convoy off Tanafjord and attacks unsuccessfully. Four torpedo cutters are deployed from Pummanki without result.

On 19 Jan *M-201* (Lt-Cdr Balin) misses a convoy off Tanafjord. On 20 Jan *S-56* (Capt 3rd Class Shchedrin) attacks the convoy off Sletnes and *S-102* (Capt 3rd Class Gorodnichi), which is deployed against the convoy when it is reported, also attacks it—without success. Similarly the deployment of the destroyers *Raz-yarenny*, *Razumny*, *Gremyashchi* and *Grozny* from 20 Jan to 22 Jan and of the reserve submarines *S-14*, *S-15* and *M-105* leads to no result. On 23 Jan *S-56* misses a convoy of three steamers, the submarine-chaser *UJ1206* and the harbour patrol vessel *NKi11*, which also drive off *S-102*.

On 28 Jan *S-56* sinks the *Henrietta Schulte* (5056 tons) from a west-bound convoy consisting of eight steamers. Escort: *K1*, *M273*, *V5912*, *V5914*, *V5913*, *V5916*, *V6111*, *UJ1208*, *UJ1206*, *UJ1209* and *UJ1212*.

15 Jan-12 Feb   Mediterranean/Adriatic

The German transportation of supplies by sea along the Dalmatian coast becomes increasingly difficult and costly because of the greater use of Allied fighter bombers from Italy. The British 24th DD Flotilla (T class) makes sorties in groups from Bari into the Central and Northern Adriatic. On 15-16 Jan *Blackmore* and *Ledbury* shell Durazzo; on 16-17 Jan *Troubridge* and *Tumult* Curzola; and on 18-19 Jan two destroyers Curzola again. On 1-2 Feb *Tumult* and *Tenacious* shell Recanati and Pedaso S of Ancona and on 4-5 Feb *Tumult* and *Teazer* Hvar and Curzola. On 12 Feb Curzola is shelled again.

16-21 Jan   English Channel

The German 5th MTB Flotilla (Cdr Klug), comprising *S143*, *S142*, *S141*, *S100*, *S138*, *S136* and *S84*, tries unsuccessfully to attack a west-bound convoy off Lizard Head in the night 16-17 Feb. After 11 torpedo misses the boats are driven off by the escort.

On 20-21 Jan the Flotilla (as above but with *S137* instead of *S136*) is attacked by Beaufighters of Coastal Command when making a sortie towards Start Point. It turns away with slight damage. The British destroyers, MGBs and MTBs, deployed to intercept the boats, find nothing.

The 4th MTB Flotilla (Lt-Cdr Fimmen), comprising *S87*, *S99*, *S117*, *S130* and *S150*, lays 23 LMB mines off Orfordness.

In the same night the German blockade-runner *Münsterland*, in trying to avoid shelling by British long-range batteries near Dover, goes ashore in fog W of Cap Blanc Nez and is destroyed by shelling. When they proceed through the channel *T28* and *T29* avoid the British MTBs deployed against them. *T28* springs a leak in the boiler room when attacked in the Straits of Dover by two Albacore aircraft of Coastal Command.

21-29 Jan   Mediterranean

Operation 'Shingle': landing by the VI US Corps (Maj-Gen Lucas) both sides of Anzio/Nettuno. On 21 Jan the ships set out from the Bay of Naples and early on 22 Jan the landing begins. TF 81 with Rear-Adm Lowry on the headquarters ship *Biscayne*. Southern Attack Force ('X-ray', Lowry), comprising five LSIs, 51 LSTs, four LCG/Fs, 60 LCIs, 32 LCTs, two LCT (R)s, 23 MLs and PC/SCs and 10 other craft and the beacon submarine *Uproar*, lands the 3rd US Inf Div (Maj-Gen Truscott). Support and escort Groups: the cruisers USS *Brooklyn* and HMS *Penelope*, the US destroyers *Plunkett*, *Gleaves*, *Niblack*, *Woolsey*, *Mayo*, *Trippe*, *Ludlow* and *Edison*, the British 'Hunt' destroyer *Croome*, the Greek

Themistokles and *Kriti*, the US DEs *Herbert C. Jones*, *Frederick C. Davis*, the Dutch gunboats *Flores* and *Zoemba*, the British AA ship *Palomares* and 23 US minesweepers.
Northern Attack Force ('Peter', Rear-Adm Troubridge) headquarters ship *Bulolo*—three LSIs, three large LSTs (*Boxer*, *Bruiser* and *Buster*), 30 LSTs, four LCG/Fs, 29 LCIs, 17 LCTs, one LCT(R), 17 PCs, SCs and MLs, 13 other craft and the beacon submarine *Ultor*, lands the 1st British Inf Div (Maj-Gen Penney). Support and Escort Groups: the cruisers *Orion* (Rear-Adm Mansfield) and *Spartan* (with the Soviet Rear-Adm Frolov on board), the AA ship *Ulster Queen*, the destroyers *Jervis*, *Janus*, *Laforey*, *Loyal*, *Inglefield*, *Tenacious*, *Urchin* and *Kempenfelt*, the 'Hunt' destroyers *Beaufort*, *Brecon*, *Wilton* and *Tetcott* and 16 mine-sweepers.
On 22 Jan 36034 troops and 3069 vehicles are landed. The minesweeper *Portent* is lost on a mine and *LCI20* as a result of a bomb hit. The AA ship *Palomares* is damaged on a mine. In an air attack on 23 Jan the destroyer *Janus* is sunk by air torpedo and the destroyer *Jervis* damaged by a Hs 293 glider bomb. When the supply convoy arrives on 24 Jan the hospital ship *St David* (2702 tons) is sunk in an air attack and the destroyer *Plunkett* damaged. The destroyer *Mayo* is damaged on a mine. On 26 Jan *LST422*, *LCI32* and *YMS30* are lost on mines and *LST336* is damaged by fighter bombers. On 29 Jan the cruiser *Spartan* and the transport *Samuel Huntington* (7181 tons) fall victims to air attacks with bombs and glider bombs. By 29 Jan 68886 troops, 508 guns and 237 tanks have been landed.

25 Jan–10 Mar   Mediterranean
From 30 Jan the cruisers *Dido*, *Delhi*, *Brooklyn* (US), *Phoebe*, *Orion*, *Penelope*, *Mauritius* and *Philadelphia* (US) and several destroyers listed in the entry 21-29 Jan are deployed, usually in pairs, to support the troops landed at Anzio. On 16 Feb the transport *Elihu Yale* (7176 tons) and *LCT35* are lost in bomb attacks and on 25 Feb the destroyer *Inglefield*. The DE *Herbert C. Jones* is damaged on 15 Feb.

Many attacks are made on ships of the landing fleet by the German submarines deployed against the invasion at Anzio. On 25 Jan *U223* (Lt Gerlach) attacks one corvette and *U230* (Lt-Cdr Siegmann) a group of destroyers with T-5s and salvoes—without success. On 29 Jan *U223* misses a destroyer with a T-5 and on the following day a landing boat and two LSTs with T-5s and salvoes. On 1 Feb *U371* (Lt-Cdr Mehl) misses two destroyers with T-5s and one LST on 3 Feb. On 15 Feb *U410* (Lt Fenski) sinks a Liberty ship (7154 tons) with a T-5 and on 16 Feb *U230* sinks the British *LST418* with a T-5 and misses one submarine-chaser. On 17 Feb *U410* misses a destroyer and a patrol ship and sinks the British cruiser *Penelope* with a T-5 and finishes her on 18 Feb. On the next day she misses another destroyer. On 20 Feb *U230* sinks the British *LST305* with a T-5 and *U410* the American *LST348* with a standard torpedo. On 24 Feb *U410* misses an LST and on 26 Feb *U952* (Lt Curio) a destroyer. *U616* (Lt Koitschka) misses a destroyer with a T-5 on both 2 Mar and 6 Mar. *U952* sinks a Liberty ship of 7176 tons on 10 Mar. The US destroyers *Plunkett*, *Frederick C. Davis* and *Herbert C. Jones* try to interfere with the long-range control of the glider bombs by jamming.

25 Jan–16 Apl   Atlantic
In operations in distant waters *U845* and *U539* cruise off Newfoundland until the beginning of March followed by *U802* and *U856*. From the middle of March *U170* and *U550* cruise between Bermuda, the Bahamas and the American east coast. In addition to some misses, *U845* (Cdr Weber) and *U802* (Lt-Cdr Schmoeckel) each sink one ship of 7039 tons and 1621 tons respectively. On 7 Apl the US Desdiv 32 (Cdr Melson), comprising *Boyle*, *Nields*, *Ordronaux*, *Champlin* and the DE *Huse*, is deployed against *U856* when she is found and the last two sink her. On 16 Apl *U550* (Lt-Cdr Hänert) sinks a tanker of 11017 tons but is herself sunk after a T-5 miss by the DEs *Gandy*, *Joyce* and *Peterson* which are deployed against her.
On the way to the Caribbean *U518* (Lt

Offermann) misses an escort carrier SW of the Azores on 13 Feb and sinks a ship of 3401 tons in the Caribbean on 7 Mar. *U154* misses a tanker and escapes on 15 Mar from the search made by the US submarine-chaser *PC.469* and, again, from the Columbian destroyer *Caldas* on 29-30 Mar. *U218* lays mines off Santa Lucia on 23 Mar and off San Juan on 1 Apl.

Off Freetown *U123* misses a convoy on 10 Mar; *U66* (Lt Seehausen) sinks four ships of 19754 tons in the Gulf of Guinea. *U214* lays mines off Casablanca on 3 Apl.

In the South Atlantic *U177* is sunk on her way to the Indian Ocean on 6 Feb by Liberators from Ascension Island. *UIT22* is damaged on 22 Feb and *U851* is missing from the middle of March.

In the middle of March US TG 21.16 (Capt Hughes), comprising the escort carrier *Block Island*, the destroyer *Corry* and the DEs *Thomas*, *Breeman*, *Bronstein* and *Bostwick*, operates SW of the Azores and, after a two-day hunt, sinks *U801* on 17 Mar and the torpedo transport *UI059* on her way to East Asia on 19 Mar. But the submarine shoots down one aircraft. The Group is relieved by the beginning of April by TG 21.11 (Capt Dunn), comprising the *Bogue*, the destroyer *Hobson* and the DEs *Haverfield*, *Janssen*, *Willis* and *Swenning*. It is followed by TG 21.12 (Capt Gallery), comprising *Guadalcanal*, the destroyer *Forrest* and the DEs *Pope*, *Pillsbury*, *Chatelain* and *Flaherty*. To it fall victim the hitherto very successful boats *U515* and *U68* on 9 Apl and 10 Apl on their way to West Africa after *U214* (Lt-Cdr Stock) has missed one of the DEs with a T-5 on 8 Apl.

26 Jan South West Pacific
TG 74.2 (Rear-Adm Berkey), comprising the cruisers *Phoenix* and *Boise* and the destroyers *Ammen*, *Mullany* and *Bush*, shell Madang and Alexishafen with 901 rounds of 6-inch and 2651 rounds of 5-inch shells.

26 Jan-24 Feb Mediterranean
On 26 Jan *U455* passes through the Straits of Gibraltar to the Mediterranean. On 1 Feb 40 torpedo aircraft of the 2nd Fl. Div attack the convoy UGS.30 N of Oran and sink the freighter *Edward Bates* (7176 tons). British Beaufighters, flown off from Sardinia, drive some of the torpedo aircraft away from the target. In a US air attack on Toulon on 4 Feb *U343*, *U380* and *U642* are damaged. On 5 Feb *U969* and on 17 Feb *U967* and *U586* pass through the Straits of Gibraltar. At first the boats operate off Algeria, where *U969* (Lt Dobbert) torpedoes two ships of 14352 tons from a west-bound convoy on 22 Feb. They are taken in tow but become total losses. To prevent further attempts to intrude, the US Catalina Sqdn VP.63, equipped with the MAD (Magnetic Airborne Detector) is employed from Morocco from the middle of February. It locates *U761* on 24 Feb which is sunk by the destroyers *Anthony* and *Wishart* once they are brought up.

29 Jan-6 Feb Central Pacific
TF 58 (Vice-Adm Mitscher) attacks Japanese bases in the Marshall Islands in support of operation 'Flintlock' (see 31 Jan).

TG 58.1 (Rear-Adm Reeves), consisting of the carriers *Enterprise*, *Yorktown* and *Belleau Wood*, the battleships *Massachusetts* (Rear-Adm Lee), *Indiana* (Rear-Adm Davis) and *Washington*, the cruiser *Oakland* and the destroyers *C. K. Bronson*, *Cotten*, *Dortch*, *Gatling*, *Healy*, *Cogswell*, *Caperton*, *Ingersoll* and *Knapp*, attacks Maloelap on 29 Jan and Kwajalein on 30 Jan and 31 Jan and up to 3 Feb. TG 58.2 (Rear-Adm Montgomery), consisting of the carriers *Essex*, *Intrepid* and *Cabot*, the battleships *South Dakota* (Rear-Adm Hanson), *Alabama* and *North Carolina*, the cruiser *San Diego* (Rear-Adm Wiltse) and the destroyers *Owen*, *Miller*, *The Sullivans*, *Stephen Potter*, *Hickox*, *Hunt*, *Lewis Hancock*, *Sterett* and *Stack*, attacks Roi from 29 Jan to 31 Jan and from 1 Feb to 3 Feb. TG 58.3 (Rear-Adm Sherman), consisting of the carriers *Bunker Hill*, *Monterey* and *Cowpens*, the battleships *Iowa* (Rear-Adm Hustvedt) and *New Jersey*, the cruiser *Wichita* and the destroyers *Izard*, *Charrette*, *Conner*, *Bell*, *Burns*, *Bradford*, *Brown*, *Cowell* and *Wilson*, attacks Eniwetok from 30 Jan to 2 Feb. TG 58.4 (Rear-Adm Ginder), consisting of the carriers *Saratoga, Princeton* and *Langley*, the cruisers *Boston* (Rear-Adm Thebaud), *Baltimore* and *San Juan* and the destroyers *Maury, Craven, Gridley, McCall, Dunlap, Fanning, Case* and *Cummings*, attacks Wotje on 29 Jan, Maloelap on 30-31 Jan and, after refuelling on 1 Feb, Eniwetok from 3 Feb to 6 Feb.

A total of 6232 sorties are flown. 22 aircraft are lost to the defences and 27 by accident.

In addition, there is the TG 50.15 (neutralization group) comprising the heavy cruisers *Chester, Pensacola* and *Salt Lake City* and the destroyers *Erben, Walker, Hale* and *Abbott*.

To cover operation 'Flintlock' US submarines are deployed around Truk: *Permit*; *Skipjack* (Lt-Cdr Molumphy), which sinks one ship of 6666 tons and the destroyer *Suzukaze*; and *Guardfish* (Lt-Cdr Ward), which sinks one ship of 10024 tons and the destroyer *Umikaze*. *Seal* is deployed off Ponape, *Sunfish* off Kusaie and *Searaven* off Eniwetok.

30-31 Jan   South West Pacific
The fast transports *Stringham, Talbot* and *Waters* land, with support from the US destroyers *Fullam* and *Guest*, 300 New Zealand and American troops to make an armed reconnaissance on the Green Islands and re-embark them on the following day.

31 Jan-5 Feb   English Channel
Six boats of the 5th MTB Flotilla sink the freighters *Emerald* (806 tons) and *Caleb Sprague* (1813 tons) from the convoy CW.243 and the trawler *Pine* (545 tons) SE of Beachy Head on 31 Jan.

On 5 Feb there is an engagement between *T29, M156* and *M206* and the British destroyers *Tanatside, Talybont, Brissenden* and *Wensleydale* off the North Brittany coast. *M156* is badly damaged: she arrives in L'Abervrach and is destroyed there in air attacks.

31 Jan-7 Feb   Central Pacific
After preparatory action by TF 58 (see 29 Jan), the 5th US Fleet (Vice-Adm Spruance) makes a landing on Kwajalein Atoll. Landing fleet (Rear-Adm Turner), Landing troops (Maj-Gen H.M. Smith, USMC). Operation: 'Flintlock'. Southern TF 52 (Rear-Adm Turner)

with two APDs, 12 APAs, three AKAs, three LSDs, 16 LSTs and 12 LSIs lands the 7th US Inf Div (Maj-Gen Corlett) on Kwajalein. Escort provided by destroyers *John Rodgers, Hazelwood, Haggard, Franks, Schroeder, Hailey*. Fire Support Group 52.8 (Rear-Adm Giffen) comprises the battleships *Idaho, Pennsylvania, New Mexico* and *Mississippi*, the cruisers *Minneapolis, New Orleans* and *San Francisco*, the destroyers *McKee, Stevens, Bailey, Frazier, Hall, Meade, Colahan, Murray, Harrison, Ringgold* and *Sigsbee*.

Air Support Group 52.9 (Rear-Adm Davison) comprises the escort carriers *Manila Bay, Coral Sea* and *Corregidor* and the destroyers *Bancroft, Coghlan, Caldwell* and *Halligan*.

Northern Attack Force 53 (Rear-Adm Connolly) with 12 APAs, three AKAs, two LSDs, 15 LSTs lands the 4th Marine Div (Maj-Gen Smith) on Roi. Escort provided by the destroyers *Remey, MacDonough, La Valette, Fletcher, Hughes, Ellet* and *Aylwin*. Fire Support Group 53.5 (Rear-Adm Oldendorf) comprises the battleships *Tennessee, Colorado* and *Maryland*, the cruisers *Louisville, Mobile, Santa Fé, Indianapolis* and *Biloxi*, the destroyers *Morris, Anderson, Mustin, Russell, Porterfield, Haraden, Hopewell, Johnston* and *Phelps*. Air Support Group 53.6 (Rear-Adm Ragsdale) comprises the escort carriers *Sangamon, Suwanee* and *Chenango* and the destroyers *Farragut, Monaghan* and *Dale*.

After bombardment by aircraft and, on 30 Jan, by battleships of TG 58.1, the landings are made on 31 Jan with fire support from TG 52.8 and TG 53.5. By 7 Feb 21342 troops have been landed in the S and 20104 in the N. Total losses: 372 dead and 1582 wounded. The resistance of the Japanese defenders (8675 men under Rear-Adm Akiyama) is broken by 7 Feb. There are only 265 prisoners.

On 31 Jan Task Group 51.2 (Rear-Adm Hill) with a battalion of the 27th US Inf Div on one APA, two APDs, one LST, escorted by the cruiser *Portland*, the escort carriers *Nassau* and *Natoma Bay* and the destroyers *Bullard, Black, Kidd* and *Chauncey*, occupies the undefended Majuro Atoll. It becomes an important base for the US Fleet. The first ships of TG 58 enter on 2 Feb.

31 Jan-20 Feb   North Atlantic
The British 2nd EG (Capt Walker), consisting of the sloops *Starling, Wild Goose, Kite, Magpie* and *Woodpecker* and the carriers *Nairana* and *Activity*, has been sent to support the convoys proceeding W of Ireland. It sinks *U592* on 31 Jan. From 3 Feb the U-boats W of Ireland are concentrated singly and in loose formation as 'Igel 1' (*U985, U714, U283, U989, U547, U984, U212, U545, U666, U386, U549, U441, U406* and *U746*) and 'Igel 2' group (*U281, U256, U650, U963, U731, U709, U91* and *U231*). Later they are joined by *U734* and *U546*, and *U618, U238, U424* and *U445* respectively. *U846, U260* and *U257* are detached as weather boats. In the N *U985* (Lt-Cdr Kessler) sinks one ship of 1735 tons from the convoy RA.56 proceeding from Iceland to Loch Ewe. The 'Igel' boats are deployed against the convoy SL.147/ MKS.38 which is reported by Ju 290s of F.A.Gr. 5 on 6 Feb N of the Azores, and again on 7 Feb and 8 Feb. With the convoy is EG B.3 (Cdr Evans) with the frigates *Towy, La Découverte* (French), the destroyer *Burza* (Polish), the corvettes *Orchis, Narcissus* and the French *Roselys, Aconit, Renoncule*, and the A/S trawler *Northern Spray*. The 2nd SG (Capt Walker) with sloops (see above) is deployed. On 8 Feb *Wild Goose* locates *U762*, which is sunk by *Starling* and *Woodpecker*. Early on 9 Feb *U734* (Lt Blauert) and *U238* (Lt Hess) just miss the *Wild Goose* and *Starling* and the *Kite* and *Magpie* with T-5s and are then sunk in the course of lengthy searches. During this operation the convoy UC.12 (US Escort Group) passes further to the N of the 'Igel' formation. On 10 Feb *U256* misses with T-5s escort vessels of HX.277 (EG B.1 and the 6th SG (six Canadian frigates)). On the evening of 10 Feb, and in the following night, aircraft of No 15 Group Coastal Command undertake massed sorties to cover HX.277 and the outward-bound ON.223 (EG B.7 (Cdr Gretton on *Duncan*), the 10th SG (four frigates) and the escort carriers *Fencer* and *Striker*). In the process *U545* and

U283 each shoot down, with the new 3.7 cm AA gun, one Leigh Light Wellington of No 612 Sqdn RAF and No 407 Sqdn RCAF, but they are themselves lost. *U714* rescues the crew of *U545*. In the evening of 10 Feb and in the night *U731, U413* and *U437* repeatedly attack, further to the S, the escorts of the convoy OS.67/KMS.41 (39th EG with the carrier *Pursuer*) unsuccessfully with T-5s and shake off the hunters with 'Aphrodite' balloons with anti-radar metal foil. On the evening of 12 Feb seven He 177s of II/K.G. 40, which try to attack the convoy, are driven off by the fighters from the *Pursuer*. They shoot down a He 177 and a contact-keeping FW 200. On 13 Feb air reconnaissance sights, W of the North Channel, one of the incoming HX.277 convoys, CU.13 (US Escort Group) or SL.147 which is supported by the carriers *Nairana* and *Activity*. Further to the W, *U445* misses a DE of the 3rd SG (Cdr Mills on *Duckworth*) with a T-5 and is damaged in a counterattack. On 14 Feb a Ju 290 and two Ju 88s locate, W of the North Channel, the convoys ONS.29 (EG B.6 (Cdr Curry on the destroyer *Fame*), the *Vanquisher* and *Vesper*, the frigate *Deveron* and the corvettes *Kingcup, Vervain, Eglantine, Rose* and *Acantus*—the last three Norwegian), ON.224 (EG C.1) and OS.68/KMS.42, one of which is found again on 15 Feb by the three Ju 290s sent out in search. On 16 Feb two Ju 290s are lost. Convoy HX.278 approaches from the SW on 16.2 with the EG B.2 (Cdr Macintyre on the destroyer *Hesperus*) and the Support and Escort Groups 2, B.7 and 10 (see above). *U546* and *U984* are able to beat off the night aircraft with their 3.7 cm AA guns but do not attack. After the U-boat formations are passed, the C-in-C Western Approaches (Adm Horton) sends on 17 Feb the 2nd SG and the EG B.7 to ON.224 and the 10th SG (Cdr Ormsby) with the frigates *Spey, Rother, Findhorn* and *Lossie* to ONS.29, which together with the carrier *Striker*, is reported in the afternoon by a Ju 290. The Commander U-boats assembles the boats *U441, U546, U549, U985, U989, U406, U764, U212, U256, U709, U424, U608, U91, U603, U386,*

U437, U264, U963, U281, U650 and *U231* as the 'Hai' group against the convoys. But it is recognized by the British who go round it to the S. The Commander U-boats tries to counter the evasive move, detected by the German 'B' Service, with massive air reconnaissance by 10 aircraft. Three aircraft find the convoy and one is shot down by fighters. In the night 18-19 Feb the convoys pass the U-boats. In the process the *Spey* sinks *U406*, among whose survivors are several German radar experts, and *U386*. *Woodpecker* and *Starling* sink the first U-boat fitted with schnorkel, *U264*. *U437* and *U256* miss escorts with T-5s. *U764* (Lt v. Bremen) torpedoes the sloop *Woodpecker*, which sinks in tow on 27 Feb. *U413* (Lt Poel), stationed on her own off the Scilly Isles, sinks the destroyer *Warwick* with a FAT on 20 Feb.

1-29 Feb Mediterranean/ Tyrrhenian Sea

In air attacks on Toulon on 4 Feb the French netlayer *Le Gladiateur* sinks and the escort vessel *SG16* (ex-sloop *Amiral Sénès*) is badly damaged. In attacks on Ercole and Livorno on 17 Feb and 18 Feb *R39* and *KT31* are sunk and *F770*, *R200* and the steamer *Ettore* (4270 tons) are beached after being heavily hit.

One sailing ship is sunk by the British submarine *Ultor* (Lt Hunt) and one ship damaged; the outward-bound minelayer *Niedersachsen* is sunk on 15 Feb by *Upstart* (Lt Chapman) and from 27 Feb to 29 Feb the ship *Cesteriane* (6664 tons), escorted by *SG15*, is torpedoed and the *Chieti* (3152 tons) is sunk by *Uproar* (Lt Herrick).

Mining operations by the German 10th TB Flotilla (Cdr v. Gartzen): 'Maulwurf' (1-2 Feb), 'Schlange' (3-4 Feb), 'Kobra' (16-17 Feb), 'Delphin' (25-26 Feb). There are engagements with enemy MTBs on 14-15 Feb and 18-19 Feb and the operation 'Nussknacker': shelling of Bastia (Corsica), in the course of which the torpedo boat *TA23* is in action three times, *TA24* five times, *TA25* once, *TA26* twice, *TA27* four times and *TA28* three times. *SG15* makes several sorties to Capreira.

1-29 Feb Pacific

Of the US submarines arriving in their operational areas in February, *Grayback* (Lt-Cdr Moore) sinks four ships of 21594 tons and torpedoes one ship; *Plunger* (Lt-Cdr Bass) sinks three ships of 9577 tons; and *Trout* (Lt-Cdr Clark) one ship of 7126 tons—all off Japan. In the area of the Mandate Islands *Balao* (Lt-Cdr Cole) sinks three ships of 15383 tons; *Bonefish* (Lt-Cdr Hogan) torpedoes one ship; *Cod* (Lt-Cdr Dempsey) sinks two ships of 9831 tons; *Hoe* (Lt-Cdr McCrea) one ship of 10526 tons and torpedoes one ship; *Pogy* (Lt-Cdr Metcalf) sinks two ships of 9204 tons and the destroyer *Minekaze* and torpedoes three ships; *Sargo* (Lt-Cdr Garnett) sinks two ships of 11808 tons. In the area of the Malayan Archipelago and the Philippines *Jack* (Lt-Cdr Dykers) sinks four ships of 20428 tons; *Puffer* (Lt-Cdr Selby) one ship of 15105 tons; *Rasher* (Lt-Cdr Laughon) four ships of 20221 tons; and *Ray* (Lt-Cdr Harrel) one ship of 1243 tons with a mine.

1 Feb-8 Mar Mediterranean/Aegean

In British air attacks in the Aegean area on 1 Feb the submarine-chaser *UJ2124* is sunk. On 2 Feb NE of Amorgos there is an attack on a convoy with three *TA* boats and the steamer *Leda* (4573 tons), which sinks. The torpedo boat *TA14* receives a bomb hit in the engine room. On 7 Feb the Swedish Red Cross steamer *Viril* (933 tons) is sunk in Chios. On 22 Feb the steamer *Lisa* (5343 tons), which is escorted by three TA boats, is sunk by air torpedo N of Heraklion and on 4 Mar the steamer *Sifnos* (387 tons) is sunk in Suda Bay.

The British submarine *Sportsman* (Lt Gatehouse) sinks the steamer *Petrella* (3209 tons) on 8 Feb and the Greek *Nereus* (Lt-Cdr Panaglotes) torpedoes the *Peter* (3754 tons) on 19 Feb. Further attacks fail. *Pipinos* and *Matrozos* have no success. On 8 Mar *TA15*, while proceeding with *TA19* from Heraklion to Piraeus, is sunk by British bombers.

3 Feb Air War/Germany

In an air attack by the 8th USAAF on Wilhelmshaven the accommodation ship *Monte Pasqual* (13870 tons) is burnt out and the minesweepers *M18* and *M29* are severely damaged.

4 Feb North Pacific

A US Task Group (Rear-Adm Baker),

comprising the cruisers *Detroit* and *Raleigh* and the destroyers *Meade, Frazier, Gansevoort* and *Edwards,* bombards Paramushiro (Kuriles).

10 Feb Arctic
A FW 200 of I/K.G. 40 sinks the British tanker *El Grillo* (7264 tons) off the East Coast of Iceland.

11-14 Feb Arctic
On 11-12 Feb 15 heavy Soviet bombers try to attack the *Tirpitz* with 1000 kg bombs. Only four aircraft find the target. A near-miss is obtained which causes slight damage.
In a Soviet air attack on Hammerfest on 14 Feb two Norwegian coasters totalling 652 tons are lost.

12-15 Feb English Channel/ North Sea
In the night 12-13 Feb the German 2nd MTB Flotilla (Cdr Feldt), comprising *S62, S98, S80, S92, S86, S67* and *S83,* carries out mining operations SE of Grimsby (26 LMB mines) and the 8th MTB Flotilla (Cdr Zymalkowski), comprising *S64, S65, S68, S85, S93, S99, S127, S129* and *S133,* SE of the Humber (36 LMB mines). *S99* and *S65* sink the trawler *Cap d'Antifer* with torpedoes.
In the night 13-14 Feb both flotillas repeat the mining operation E of Great Yarmouth. The 2nd Flotilla (composition as before) breaks off the operation prematurely; the 8th Flotilla with the mining boats *S85, S64, S127* and *S65* lays a barrage. The combat force comprises *S99, S93, S133, S129,* and *S127.* In the night 14-15 Feb the 2nd MTB Flotilla, comprising *S89, S98, S92, S80* and *S67,* lays 21 LMB mines SE of Great Yarmouth. When they retire they are pursued by the British corvettes *Mallard* and *Shearwater.* The deployment of the British *MTB455, MTB444, MTB443, MTB441* and *MTB439* is observed by German air reconnaissance and the returning 2nd Flotilla and the 8th Flotilla which set out as a combat group, comprising *S93, S64, S117, S127, S129, S85, S133, S99* and *S65,* are employed against them. In an engagement with three boats of the German 34th MS Flotilla *MTB455* and *MTB444* are damaged. *M3411* sinks after a collision when trying to avoid the enemy. In

ensuing engagements the other British MTBs and *S89* and *S133* are damaged. A sortie by 13 motor torpedo boats of the 5th and 9th Flotillas from Cherbourg against a convoy off Beachy Head is prematurely broken off when the force is located by British radar.

13 Feb Norway
Near Hustadvika in Central Norway the Norwegian *MTB627* and *MTB653* attack the Norwegian coasters *Irma* (1392 tons) and *Henry* (363 tons), which are in German service, and sink them.

15-19 Feb South Pacific
The III Amphibious Force (Rear-Adm Wilkinson) lands the 3rd New Zealand Div on Green Island (off New Ireland) on 15 Feb with nine APDs, escorted by the destroyers *Fullam, Guest, Bennett, Hudson* and *Halford,* 12 LCIs escorted by the destroyers *Waller, Pringle, Saufley, Philip, Renshaw* and *Sigourney* and seven LSTs escorted by the destroyers *Conway, Eaton, Anthony, Wadsworth, Terry* and *Braine.* Cover to the N and E is provided by TF 39 (Rear-Adm Merrill) with the cruisers *Montpelier* and *Columbia* and five destroyers and to the S by TF 38 (Rear-Adm Ainsworth) with the cruisers *Honolulu* and *St Louis* and five destroyers.
In the night 17-18 Feb Desron 12 (Capt Simpson) shells Kavieng with 3868 rounds of 5-inch shells from the destroyers *Farenholt, Buchanan, Lansdowne, Lardner* and *Woodworth* and Desron 23 (Capt Burke) shells Rabaul with 6681 rounds of 5-inch shells from *Charles Ausburne, Dyson, Stanly, Converse* and *Spence.* In the night 22-23 Feb Desron 23 shells Duke of York Island off Kavieng and on 23-24 Feb Desron 12 shells Kavieng again. On 24-25 Feb Desron 45 (Capt Earle) shells Rabaul with *Fullam, Bennett, Guest, Halford, Hudson, Anthony* and *Braine.* And on 29 Feb-1 Mar Desron 22 (Capt Petersen) shells it again with *Waller, Philip, Renshaw, Saufley, Conway, Eaton, Sigourney* and *Pringle.*

17-23 Feb Central Pacific
Operation 'Catchpole': TF 51.11 (Rear-Adm Hill) with two APDs, eight APAs, one AKA, one LSD, nine LSTs and six LCIs lands the reinforced 22nd Marine RCT and two

H

battalions of the 106th Regt of the 27th US Inf Div, totalling 8000 men, on Eniwetok. Escort: the destroyers *McCord*, *Trathen*, *Heerman*, *Hoel*, *Dewey*, *Hull*, *Hazelwood*, *Franks*, *Aylwin*, *Dale*, *Monaghan*, *Farragut*, *Haggard*, *Hailey* and *Johnston*. Fire Support Group (Rear-Adm Oldendorf) consists of the battleships *Pennsylvania*, *Colorado* and *Tennessee* and the cruisers *Indianapolis*, *Portland* and *Louisville*. Air Support Group (Rear-Adm Ragsdale) comprises the escort carriers *Sangamon*, *Suwanee* and *Chenango* and the destroyers *Morris*, *Hughes*, *Mustin* and *Ellet*. The landings are supported by TG 58.4 (see 29 Jan). On 17 Feb a landing takes place on Engebi and on 19 Feb on Eniwetok. By 23 Feb the resistance of the 3431 Japanese defenders (Maj-Gen Nishida) is overcome. There are only 64 prisoners. US losses: 195 dead and 521 wounded.

17-23 Feb   Central Pacific
On 12-13 Feb three groups of TF 58 (Vice-Adm Mitscher) set out from Majuro and replenish from five tankers on 15 Feb: Operation 'Hailstone'.
TG 58.1 (Rear-Adm Reeves) comprises the carriers *Enterprise*, *Yorktown* and *Belleau Wood*, the cruisers *Santa Fé*, *Mobile*, *Biloxi* and *Oakland* and destroyers as on 29 Jan.
TG 58.2 (Rear-Adm Montgomery) comprises the carriers *Essex*, *Intrepid* and *Cabot*, the cruisers *San Diego*, *San Francisco*, *Wichita* and *Baltimore* and destroyers as on 29 Jan, but with *Stembel* and without *Sterett*.
TG 58.3 (Rear-Adm Sherman) comprises the carriers *Bunker Hill*, *Monterey* and *Cowpens*, the battleships *North Carolina*, *Massachusetts*, *South Dakota* and *Alabama* and destroyers as on 29 Jan with the addition of *Sterett* and *Lang*. In addition, TG 50.9 comprises the battleships *Iowa* and *New Jersey* (Vice-Adm Spruance), the cruisers *Minneapolis* and *New Orleans*, the carrier *Cowpens* (see above) and the destroyers *Izard*, *Charrette*, *Burns* and *Bradford*.
Early on 17 Feb there is a fighter strike on the 365 Japanese aircraft at Truk with the aircraft from the five fleet carriers. The light carriers operate against shipping. Towards evening on

17 Feb the Japanese attack with seven Kates (torpedo bombers). A torpedo hit is scored on *Intrepid* which is brought into Majuro with *Cabot*, two cruisers and four destroyers. On 18 Feb the aircraft of the remaining fleet carriers attack shipping targets. 1250 sorties are made in all and 400 tons of bombs are dropped. The following ships are sunk: the cruiser *Naka*, the destroyers *Fumitsuki* and *Oite*, the auxiliary cruisers *Aikoku Maru* and *Kiyosumi Maru*, the submarine tenders *Rio de Janeiro Maru* and *Heian Maru* as well as six tankers and 17 freighters totalling 137019 tons. About 250 aircraft are destroyed. TG 50.9 steams round Truk and, in an engagement, the training cruiser *Katori* and the destroyers *Maikaze* and *Tachikaze* are sunk. They continue firing until the last moment. Only *Nowake* escapes the salvoes of the covering battleships fired from 35 km away.
During operation 'Hailstone' the US submarine *Seal* is stationed near Ponape and *Searaven* and *Darter* near Truk as lifeguard boats to rescue airmen forced into the water. *Skate* (Lt-Cdr Gruner), which sinks the cruiser *Agano* on 16 Feb, *Tang* (Lt-Cdr O'Kane), which sinks one ship of 7129 tons, *Sunfish*, *Aspro* (Cdr Stevenson), which sinks the submarine *I-43*, *Burrfish*, *Dace* and *Gato* (Cdr Foley), which sinks three ships of 6162 and three small craft, take up positions in the exit channels from Truk.
On 20 Feb aircraft of TG 58.1 attack Jaluit; on 23 Feb TG 58.3 bombards Tinian and Rota and TG 58.2 Saipan and Tinian. Japanese attempts to attack on 22 Feb. fail. Of the submarines *Searaven*, *Apogon*, *Skipjack*, *Tang* and *Sunfish* (Lt-Cdr Shelby) deployed, the latter two sink four ships of 14300 tons and two ships of 9437 tons respectively. 21300 tons of shipping sink as a result of carrier aircraft action.

20 Feb   Air War/Germany
The 1st Air Div of the USAAF attacks Hamburg with 432 B 17s.

20 Feb-10 Mar   Arctic
Convoy operations JW.57/RA.57. On 20 Feb convoy JW.57 sets out from Loch Ewe with 42 ships. Escort: Vice-Adm Glennie in the AA cruiser *Black*

Prince with the escort carrier *Chaser*, an Ocean Escort Group (Capt Campbell on the destroyer *Milne*), a Support Group (Cdr Tyson on the destroyer *Keppel*) with a total of 17 destroyers. Covering force: Vice-Adm Palliser with the cruisers *Kent*, *Norfolk* and *Berwick*. The convoy is located on 23 Feb by a Ju 88 of the Air Officer Commanding North (West) and for more than 10 hours a FW 200 maintains contact. The 'Werwolf' U-boat group (*U956*, *U674*, *U425*, *U601*, *U362*, *U739*, *U713*, *U313*, *U312* and *U990*) is deployed and, in addition, the 'Hartmut' group (*U472*, *U315*, *U673* and *U366*) sets out. On 24 Feb a FW 200 keeps contact in spite of attacks by Martlets from the *Chaser*, and brings up *U425*, *U601*, *U739* and *U713*. But the last is sunk by the *Keppel*. By the evening of 25 Feb the U-boats are driven off and a Catalina flying boat of No 210 Sqdn RAF sinks *U601*. In the evening *U990* (Lt-Cdr Nordheimer) sinks the destroyer *Mahratta* with a T-5: the destroyer *Impulsive* is able to rescue only a few of the crew. Although FW 200s and Ju 88s still keep contact on 26 Feb and 27 Feb, only *U956* (Lt Mohs), *U366* (Lt Langenburg) (four times), *U278* (Lt-Cdr Franze), *U312* (Lt-Cdr K. H. Nicolay) and *U362* (Lt Franz) are able to make unsuccessful T-5 attacks on escort vessels. On 28 Feb the convoy arrives in the Kola Inlet, observed by air reconnaissance. The remaining boats (*U739*, *U307*, *U315* and *U472*) are formed into the 'Boreas' group to operate against the expected west-bound convoy and the boats *U361*, *U959*, *U278*, *U973*, *U366*, *U673*, *U288* and *U354* join the formation in some cases, after brief replenishment.

During the passage of the convoy operation 'Bayleaf' is carried out. The carrier *Furious* makes a raid on the Norwegian coast on 24 Feb. The battleships *Anson* and *Richelieu* (French), two cruisers and seven destroyers belong to the force. Of them, the *Musketeer* and *Blyskawica* (Polish) are damaged in a collision.

On 2 Mar convoy RA.57 sets out again with 31 ships and the escort of JW.57. While Soviet destroyers, minesweepers and submarine-chasers look for submarines N of the Kola Estuary, the convoy makes a wide detour to the E, but it is located by air reconnaissance on 4 Mar. In the night *U739* (Lt Mangold) just misses the destroyer *Swift* and *U472* (Lt Frhr v. Forstner), after missing with a T-5, is damaged by an aircraft from the *Chaser* and has to scuttle herself under gunfire from the approaching destroyer *Onslaught*. By day *U703* (Lt Brünner) is able to sink the freighter *Empire Tourist* (7062 tons) from the convoy with a FAT salvo and just misses the *Milne* with a T-5. Air reconnaissance sends contact reports on 5 Mar, 6 Mar and 7 Mar, but on 5-6 Mar only *U278*, *U288* (Lt W. Meyer), *U959* (Lt Weitz) and *U673* (Lt Sauer) are able to make unsuccessful T-5 firings on destroyers. Because icing greatly impedes the operational use of the AA guns on the U-boats, the Swordfish aircraft, flown off from the *Chaser*, are able to sink *U366* and *U973*, in spite of the difficult weather conditions. The convoy arrives in Loch Ewe on 10 Mar.

20 Feb-1 Apl Arctic
From 20 Feb to 3 Mar the Soviet Northern Fleet organizes a new operation RV-2 against German convoy traffic off the Polar Coast. The submarine *L-20* puts a raiding party ashore near Makkaur on 20 Feb, the houses are searched and four Norwegians are taken prisoner. In addition, a mine barrage is laid in Porsangerfjord on 26 Feb. *K-21* reconnoitres in Lopphavet. The operational boats of the 'S' class take up waiting positions, and *M-104*, *M-105*, *M-119* and *M-201* are put on the alert, but no German convoys are found.

On 4 Mar *S-56* makes an underwater attack, for the first time, after establishing the enemy's position by listening, but she has no success.

On 17 Mar a German east-bound convoy with the gunboat *K-1* and four patrol boats is located by Soviet reconnaissance. *M-201* (Lt-Cdr Balin) misses the convoy off Syltefjord. Air attacks with some 50 bombers and torpedo aircraft fail against the German fighter defence of J.G. 5. The torpedo cutters do not reach the convoy.

On 19 Mar the submarine *M-105* (Lt-

Cdr Khrulev) misses one steamer and on 1 Apl *M-119* (Lt-Cdr Kolosov) a convoy.

Soviet torpedo aircraft sink the patrol boat *V6109* off Busse Sound on 23 Mar.

21-29 Feb English Channel

On 21 Feb 37 British Beaufighters of Coastal Command attack a German convoy near den Helder and sink *R131*. In the night 22-23 Feb the German 2nd MTB Flotilla (Cdr Feldt) comprising *S86*, *S67*, *S128*, *S94*, *S80*, *S92* and *S135*, and the 8th Flotilla (Cdr Zymalkowski), comprising *S93*, *S64*, *S117*, *S127*, *S129*, *S85*, *S99* and *S65*, try from Ijmuiden to attack a convoy near Smith's Knoll. They are driven off by the destroyers *Garth* and *Southdown* with *MTB609* and *MTB610*. In the action *S94* and *S128* collide and have to be abandoned.

In the night 24-25 Feb the 2nd Flotilla with *S80*, *S92*, *S135*, *S86* and *S67* and the 8th Flotilla with the eight boats listed above are deployed on a mining operation ESE of Great Yarmouth. In dropping the barrages the boats come into contact with the convoy FS.1371 which has been located by the 'B' Service. The destroyers *Vivien* and *Eglinton* drive the two groups off. The motor torpedo boats fire eight FAT and G 7A torpedoes. The freighter *Philipp M.* (2085 tons) is sunk.

In a sortie by the same boats of the 2nd and 8th Flotillas on 25-26 Feb against a convoy near Great Yarmouth the target is not found and the first group of the 8th MTB Flotilla is involved in an engagement with the destroyer *Meynell*, but escapes.

A sortie by the 9th and 5th Flotillas, comprising *S144*, *S145*, *S146*, *S130*, *S112*, *S143*, *S139*, *S142*, *S136* and *S84*, against a CW convoy on the British South Coast in the night 27-28 Feb misses the target. *S142* and *S136* are damaged in a collision.

In the night 28-29 Feb 14 boats of the 2nd and 8th Flotillas in a sortie against a south-bound convoy are reported by a British Swordfish aircraft and they break off the operation. Similarly, a sortie of eight boats of the 5th and 9th Flotillas in the Plymouth area is prematurely detected and therefore broken off.

21-29 Feb Mediterranean/Adriatic

On 21-22 Feb two British MGBs make a sortie towards Primosten. This is the first time that the base established on the island of Lissa is used for light naval forces. On 27 Feb the British destroyers *Tumult* and *Troubridge* shell Curzola.

On 28-29 Feb the large French destroyers (Capt Lancelot) *Le Terrible* and *Le Malin* make a sortie into the Northern Adriatic and find a German convoy near Isto sailing from Pola to Piraeus. It consists of the freighter *Kapitän Diederichsen* (ex-*Sabastiano Venier*, 6311 tons), the torpedo boats *TA36* and *TA37*, the submarine-chasers *UJ201* and *UJ205* and the motor minesweepers *R188*, *R190* and *R191*. *Le Terrible* sinks the freighter with gunfire and *Le Malin UJ201* by torpedo. The *TA37* receives a shell hit in the engine room and is taken in tow.

22 Feb-22 Mar North Atlantic

In changing individual positions *U441*, *U256*, *U985*, *U603*, *U963*, *U764*, *U281*, *U437*, *U212*, *U448*, *U91*, *U262*, *U709*, *U358*, *U608* and *U962* form the 'Preussen' group W of Ireland. *U413*, *U333* and *U621* are stationed S of Ireland, in the North Channel and in the North Minch, *U546* off Iceland, and *U549*, *U552* and *U550* as weather boats. The returning *U257* on 24 Feb runs into the escort of the convoy SC.153 (EG C.5, Commander Pullen on the destroyer *Ottawa*, the 3rd EG with the DEs *Duckworth*, *Essington*, *Rowley*, *Berry*, *Cooke* and *Domett* and the 6th EG with the frigates *Waskesiu*, *Outremont*, *Cape Breton*, *Grou* and *Nene*) and is sunk by *Waskesiu* and *Nene*. *U989* does not get to a group of the convoy stragglers. The 1st SG, employed to support the convoys W of Ireland and comprising the DEs *Affleck*, *Gore*, *Gould*, *Garlies*, *Balfour* and *Capel*, accounts for *U91* on 25 Feb and, after a 38-hour search, *U358* (Lt-Cdr Manke) on 29-30 Feb, following the latter's sinking of *Gould* with a T-5. The DEs of the US TG 21.16 (Capt Ramsey) with the escort carrier *Block Island* the destroyer *Corry* and the DEs *Thomas*, *Bronstein*, *Bostwick* and *Breeman* sink *U709* and *U603* 600 nautical miles N of the Azores on 1 Mar. W of the Bay of Biscay *U744* (Lt Blischke) sinks the landing ship *LST362* on 2 Mar. On 5 Mar the boat is found by the escort of the convoy HX.280, the EG C.2 (Lt-Cdr Davis) with the frigate *St Catherines*, the destroyers *Gatineau*, *Chaudière* and *Icarus* (British) and the corvettes *Chilliwack* and *Fennel* and is sunk after firing several unsuccessful T-5s in a 30-hour search with support from the British corvette *Kenilworth Castle*, which is ordered to the scene. In the following days *U741*, *U625*, *U653*, *U986*, *U267*, *U672* and the schnorkel boats *U415* and *U575* (Lt Boehmer) join the 'Preussen' group. The last-mentioned sinks with a T-5 the corvette *Asphodel* from the escort of the convoy SL.150/MKS.41 on 9 Feb. On the same day *U255* (Lt Harms) is located near the convoy CU.16 (Escort US TG 21.5 (Capt Kenner, USCG) with the DEs *Joyce*, *Poole*, *Harveson*, *Kirkpatrick*, *Leopold* and *Peterson*) by the DE *Leopold*; but she is able to sink the approaching *Leopold* with a T-5. The *Joyce* is narrowly missed. On 10 Mar *U845* (Cdr Weber) reports the convoy SC.154 (EG C.1) but, after a lengthy search, she is sunk by the destroyers *St Laurent*, *Forester* and the Canadian frigate *Swansea* and the corvette *Owensound*. T-5 attacks by *U653* and *U575* fail. The convoy HX.281 (EG B.6 with the destroyer *Fame*, the frigates *Deveron* and *Antigua*, the corvettes *Kingcup*, *Vervain*, *Eglantine*, *Rose* and *Acanthus*) passes the U-boat formations on 10.3 without any engagement. *U625* is sunk by a Sunderland flying boat of No 422 Sqdn RCAF; *U741* and *U256*, which are ordered to help, shoot down a Wellington of No 407 Sqdn RCAF. The convoy ON.227, which turns away to the S, is escorted on 12 Mar and 13 Mar by strong air formations from Cornwall and the Azores. Neverthless, *U311* shoots down one aircraft—a Fortress of No 206 Sqdn RAF. *U575* is attacked by Wellingtons of No 172 Sqdn RAF and No 206 Sqdn RAF and hunted by US TG 21.11 (Capt Dunn), comprising the escort carrier *Bogue*, the destroyers *Hobson* and the DEs *Haverfield*, *Jansen*, *Willis* and *Swenning* together with the Canadian frigate *Prince Rupert* of the Escort Group. She is sunk after

shooting down one of the carrier aircraft. On 14 Mar the sloops *Starling* and *Wild Goose* of the 2nd SG sink *U653* with help of Swordfish from the escort carrier *Vindex*. On 17 Mar *U415* is damaged by the escort of convoy CU.17 from which *U311* (Lt-Cdr Zander) sinks one tanker of 10342 tons on 19 Mar. As it is apparent that planned convoy operations are no longer possible in the North Atlantic with the available material, the Commander U-boats dissolves the 'Preussen' group, which still consists of *U255*, *U962*, *U986*, *U672*, *U267*, *U262*, *U92*, *U741*, *U302*, *U311*, *U667*, and *U437*. The boats continue to operate individually.

27 Feb   English Channel
In an engagement between escort vessels of a German convoy S of Jersey and the British *MTB415* and *MTB431*, *M4618* is hit but reaches Jersey.

29 Feb-9 Mar   South West Pacific
A destroyer force (Rear-Adm Fechteler) which sets out on 27 Feb with TG 76.3 (Capt Carter) comprising *Reid*, *Flusser*, *Mahan*, *Drayton*, *Smith*, *Bush*, *Welles*, *Stevenson* and *Stockton* and TG 76.2 with the APDs *Humphrey*, *Brooks* and *Sands*, lands on 29 Feb 1026 troops of the 5th Cavalry Regt (Brig-Gen Chase) in Hyäne Harbour on Los Negros (Admiralty Islands). Fire support is provided by TG. 74.2 (Rear-Adm Berkey) consisting of the cruisers *Phoenix* (on board Gen MacArthur and Vice-Adm Kinkaid, the Commander of the 7th Fleet) and *Nashville* and the destroyers *Daly*, *Hutchins*, *Bache* and *Beale*.
In the evening the ships withdraw. *Bush* and *Stockton* support the landed troops in the face of strong counter-attacks in the night 29 Feb-1 Mar. On 2 Mar the second wave of 1000 troops arrives in six LSTs and six LSMs, accompanied by Capt Dechaineux with the destroyers *Warramunga* (RAN), *Ammen* and *Mullany* and the minesweeper *Hamilton*. They are landed with support from the destroyers *Bush*, *Stockton* and *Welles* and the DMS *Long* which also come up. Because the destroyers are unable to silence the Japanese batteries in the N of Seeadler Harbour, TF 74 (Rear-

Adm Crutchley), comprising the cruisers *Shropshire* (RAN), *Phoenix* and *Nashville* and the destroyers *Daly*, *Hutchins*, *Bache* and *Beale*, shells the islands of Hauwei and Norilo on 4 Mar.

On 5 Mar the third wave of 1410 troops arrives with TG 76.1 (Capt Carter), consisting of the destroyers *Flusser*, *Drayton*, *Smith*, *Wilkes*, *Swanson*, *Nicholson*, *Stevenson*, *Thorn* and *Arunta* (RAN) and the APDs *Humphreys*, *Brooks* and *Sands*. On 6 Mar *Nicholson* is damaged by the still unsilenced batteries at the entrance of Seeadler Bay. For this reason the ships of TF 74 (see above) again shell the islands on 7 Mar. They fire 64 rounds of 8-inch, 1144 rounds of 6-inch and 5-inch and 92 rounds of 4-inch shells. On 9 Mar the new airfield is safe.

A fourth convoy arrives on 12 Mar, consisting of six LSTs and the destroyers *Warramunga*, *Flusser*, *Reid*, *Kalk*, *Gillespie* and *Hobby*. By 30 Mar the islands off Seeadler Harbour are occupied in the face of sometimes strong resistance by the Japanese defenders (Col Ezaki).

1-6 Mar   North Pacific
A sortie by a US Task Force (Rear-Adm Baker), comprising the cruiser *Richmond* and the destroyers *Picking*, *Wickes*, *Sproston*, *Young*, *W. D. Porter*, *Isherwood*, *Kimberly* and *Luce* into the Sea of Okhotsk to find a Japanese convoy, reported to have set out from Attu, has to be broken off because of the weather.

1-31 Mar   Pacific
Of the US submarines which arrive in their operational areas in March, *Barb* (Lt-Cdr Waterman) sinks one ship of 2219 tons; *Flying Fish* (Lt-Cdr Risser) three ships of 9828 tons; *Lapon* (Lt-Cdr Stones) three ships of 19947 tons; *Pollack* (Lt-Cdr Lewellen) two ships of 4141 tons and the submarine-chaser *Kusentai 54*; *Tautog* (Lt-Cdr Sieglaff) four ships of 11277 tons—all off Japan and Formosa. In the area of the Mandate Islands *Darter* (Lt-Cdr Stovall) sinks one ship of 2829 tons; *Nautilus* (Cdr Irvin) one ship of 6069 tons; *Picuda* (Lt-Cdr Rayborn) three ships of 12532 tons; *Stingray* (Lt-Cdr Loomis) one ship of 3943 tons. In the area of the Malayan Archipelago and the Philip-

pines *Bluefish* (Lt-Cdr Henderson) sinks one ship of 10536 tons; *Bowfin* (Lt-Cdr Griffith) three ships of 12744 tons; *Hake* (Lt-Cdr Broach) sinks one ship of 5154 tons and torpedoes one ship; *Peto* (Lt-Cdr Van Leunen) one ship of 4368 tons.

2-8 Mar   Mediterranean/Adriatic
The large French destroyers *Le Terrible* and *Le Fantasque* carry out a fruitless raid into the Northern Adriatic as far as the coast of Istria on 2-4 Mar. On 7-8 Mar they bombard Zante.

2 Mar-22 Apl   Norway
In submarine operations off the Norwegian coast the British *Venturer* (Lt Launders) sinks one ship of 2526 tons off Stadlandet on 2 Mar; *Sceptre* Lt-Cdr McIntosh) sinks one ship of 8340 tons in Foldafjord on 7 Mar; *Syrtis* (Lt Jupp) sinks one ship of 241 tons off Bodö, but is then sunk on a flanking mine barrage; *Satyr* sinks one ship of 340 tons off Stadlandet on 24 Mar; *Terrapin* (Lt-Cdr Martin) sinks one transport and the catapult ship *Schwabenland* totalling 14442 tons off Egersund on 24 Mar; the Norwegian *Ula* (Lt Sars) sinks two steamers of 6040 tons and *U974* and torpedoes one ship of 7603 tons on two patrols on 4-6 Apl and 19-22 Apl. *Unshaken* (Lt Whitton) sinks one ship of 3894 tons off Lister on 7 Apl. In an attack by the midget submarine *X24* (Lt Shean) in the harbour of Bergen two ships of 9492 tons are destroyed.

The submarine-chasers *UJ1703* and *UJ1704* and three Norwegian coasters are victims of British air attacks on the Norwegian south-west coast.

6-10 Mar   English Channel
In the night 6-7 Mar British MTB groups of the 53rd Flotilla make sorties against the German convoy routes off the Dutch coast. *MTB225*, *MTB241*, *MTB244* and *MTB234* have an engagement with the boats of the 34th MS Flotilla. One gun ferry and one patrol boat suffer damage. A sortie by *MGB617*, *MGB624*, *MGB629* and *MGB668* into the area of Terschelling on 9-10 Mar has no success.

7 Mar-1 May   Mediterranean/ Tyrrhenian Sea
In Allied air attacks the French cruiser *Marseillaise* and the destroyers *L'In-*

domptable and *Gerfaut* sink in Toulon on 7 Mar and *R161*, *RA256* and *UJ2209* in Livorno on 16-17 Mar. On 23 Mar four motor minesweepers of the 11th MMS Flotilla (Lt-Cdr Freytag) lay the mine barrage 'Hütte' on the East Coast of Corsica, while *TA28* and *TA29* make a sortie towards Capreira as a diversion. On 27 Mar a convoy with six naval ferry barges is destroyed off Vado by an Allied force (Cdr Allen, RN), comprising the British *MTB634*, *MGB662*, *MGB660*, *MGB659*, *LCG14*, *LCG19*, *LCG20* and the US *PT212*, *PT214*, *PT208* and *PT218*. On 30 Mar the German minelayer *Pommern* and three motor minesweepers carry out the mining operation 'Stachelschwein' NE of Capreira. From 2 Apl-26 Apl two boats of the 10th TB Flotilla (Cdr v. Gartzen), comprising *TA23*, *TA26*, *TA27*, *TA28* and *TA29*, carry out the mining operations 'Bumerang' and 'Aphrodite' (2-3 Apl and 3-4 Apl) near Portoferraio and S of Elba, 'Gatter' and 'Auster' (5-6 Apl and 8-9 Apl), 'Rappen' (12-13 Apl) NW of Elba, 'Stich' and 'Öse' (15 Apl and 18 Apl), 'Schimmel' (21-22 Apl) 'Karo Ass' (25-26 Apl) as well as the shelling of Bastia (22-23 Apl). From 3 Apl to 8 Apl the minelayer *Oldenburg* lays the barrages 'Herz Dame, König, Bube' SW of La Spezia. In the operation on 25-26 Apl *TA23* runs on a mine off Capreira and has to be abandoned. *TA26* and *TA29* have an engagement with a US PT force consisting of *PT218*, *PT202* and *PT213*.

The British submarine *Untiring* (Lt Boyd) sinks two ships of 3337 tons and the submarine-chaser *UJ6075* from 12 Apl to 1 May.

8-28 Mar Mediterranean
German attacks on Allied supply traffic proceeding from Gibraltar along the North African coast to Naples and Anzio.

On 8 Mar a formation of German torpedo aircraft is intercepted by Beaufighters from Sardinia before it reaches a troop convoy off Algiers.

On 17 Mar *U371* (Lt-Cdr Mehl) sinks the troop transport *Dempo* (17024 tons) and one freighter of 6165 tons from the convoy SNF.17 and escapes from the intensive U-boat search.

The attempts by German torpedo aircraft to attack by night the convoys KMS.44 on 19 Mar and KMS.45 on 29 Mar on the Algerian coast fail.

U-boat operations in the Western Mediterranean are very restricted as a result of losses. On 10 Mar the A/S trawler *Mull* sinks *U343* off Cagliari and the 'Hunt' destroyers *Exmoor*, *Blankney*, *Blencathra* and *Brecon U450* off Anzio. *U380* and *U410* fall victims to an air attack on Toulon on 11 Mar. On 16 Mar *U392* is located by two MAD Catalinas of USN-VP.63, when passing through the Straits of Gibraltar, and is sunk by the British destroyers *Affleck* and *Vanoc*. On 24-25 Mar *U466* and *U421* succeed in entering the Mediterranean, but *U618* has to return after several attempts. On 29 Mar *U223* (Lt Gerlach) is found by four British destroyers N of Sicily and is sunk after a long search by *Tumult*, *Hambledon* and *Blencathra*, the *Laforey* having been sunk first.

11 Mar-20 May Baltic
German and Finnish mine barrages are laid in the Gulf of Finland. From 5 Mar the German patrol vessels take up their positions after the thawing of the ice and are attacked by Soviet aircraft for the first time on 9 Mar.

On 12 Mar the destroyers *Z25*, *Z28* and *Z39* of the 6th DD Flotilla, recently moved into the Gulf of Finland, shell Soviet positions near Hungerburg. On 13 Mar the Net Defence Force begins to lay out the submarine net 'Walross' between Nargön and Porkkala. At the same time naval ferry barges of the 24th Landing Flotilla, minesweepers and motor minesweepers again lay parts of the 'Nashorn' mine barrages, while the minelayers *Linz*, *Roland* and *Brummer*, in eight operations, and the destroyers *Z25*, *Z28*, *Z35* and *Z39*, sometimes with *M3* and *M37*, in six operations, renew the 'Seeigel' barrages under Capt Kothe. On 21 Apl *Roland* is lost on one of her own barrages. By 26 Apl the destroyers, and by 20 May the minelayers and smaller craft, have laid 7599 mines and 2795 barrage protection devices. From 12 May to 20 May the Finnish minelayers *Ruotsinsalmi* and *Louhi* and smaller vessels lay out mine barrages N of Suursaari. In this period there are frequent attacks by Soviet ground attack aircraft.

13 Mar-15 May Aegean

In submarine operations in the Aegean in March the British *Ultor* (Lt Hunt) sinks one naval ferry barge; *Sportsman* (Lt Gatehouse) one small motor ship and four sailing ships and torpedoes one more ship; the Greek *Pipinos* (Lt-Cdr Palles) sinks one ship of 2290 tons. In April the British *Ultor* sinks six sailing ships; *Sportsman* the steamer *Lüneburg* (5809 tons); and *Rorqual* (Lt-Cdr Napier) the steamer *Wilhelmsburg* (4967 tons). The Dutch *Dolfijn* (Lt-Cdr v. Oostrom-Soede) sinks two sailing ships. In May the British *Ultimatum* (Lt Kett) sinks three sailing ships and destroys by gunfire five new constructions in Kalamata.

British aircraft sink *UJ2127* on 1 Apl and *UJ2141* on 15 Apl. British MTBs sink the auxiliary vessels *GR02* and *GR94* near Coo.

On 8-9 Apl the German minelayer *Drache* with the torpedo boats of the 9th TB Flotilla (Cdr* Dominik), *TA17* and *TA19*, carries out a mining operation in the Aegean and beats off air attacks.

14-31 Mar English Channel

In the night 14-15 Mar British MTBs attack two groups of the German 36th MS Flotilla (Cdr Grosse) off Gravelines and sink the leader, *M3630*, with a torpedo. *MTB417* sinks in the defensive fire. The withdrawing British force encounters boats of the 18th PB Flotilla (Cdr Boit) NE of Gris Nez.

In the night 15-16 Mar the 9th and 5th MTB Flotillas (Cdr v. Mirbach and Cdr Klug), comprising *S144*, *S145*, *S146*, *S150* and *S100*, *S143*, *S141*, *S139*, *S84* and *S140*, try to attack the British convoy WP.492 N of Land's End. The convoy is escorted by the corvettes *Azalea* and *Primrose*. The motor torpedo boats are detected on the way by British air reconnaissance. The cruiser *Bellona* out at sea with the destroyers *Ashanti* and *Tartar* takes up a covering position and the 'Hunt' destroyers *Melbreak* and *Brissenden*, two minesweepers and MTB groups are deployed to intercept. In the engagements *S143* receives a hit in the bows and the commander is killed.

Sorties by both flotillas on 16-17 Mar against Lizard Head and on 20-21 Mar against Weymouth are broken off because the approaching boats are prematurely located by British radar. *S84* and *S139* drop out after a collision.

On 20 Mar, after beating off attacks by the British *MTB202*, *MTB212*, *MTB206* and *MTB359* the convoy 'Hecht' with the tanker *Rekum* escorted by the 18th PB Flotilla runs into the fire of the British long-range guns at Dover. The tanker sinks. On 21 Mar the 10th MS Flotilla (Cdr Josephi) in escorting a convoy 'Bromberg' NE of Lezardieux, beats off attacks by British MTBs. The 4th and 5th TB Flotillas (Cdr Kohlauf and Cdr Hoffmann), comprising *T29*, *T27*, *Möwe*, *Kondor*, *Greif* and *Jaguar*, lay two barrages each of 180 EMC mines NW of Le Havre and N of Fécamp respectively on 21 Mar and 22 Mar. Escort is provided by the 5th and 9th MTB Flotillas. In the night 23-24 Mar the 2nd and 8th MTB Flotillas (Cdr Opdenhoff and Cdr Zymalkowski), comprising *S62*, *S67*, *S80*, *S83*, *S86* and *S92*, and *S64*, *S117*, *S85*, *S93*, *S99*, *S65*, *S133* and *S129*, make a sortie from Ijmuiden against the convoy route NE of Great Yarmouth. The 4th MTB Flotilla (Lt-Cdr Fimmen), consisting of *S159*, *S171* and *S187*, tries from the Hook of Holland to effect a diversion S of Lowestoft, but the operation is broken off because of early radar detection. When the operation is repeated on 25-26 Mar in the area of Hearty Knoll with the same units, there are engagements with British destroyers and MGBs in which *S67* and *S64* sustain slight damage.

In the nights 24-25 Mar and 25-26 Mar the 4th and 5th TB Flotillas (see above) each lay another 180 mines (barrage 'N 24'), in the course of which there are indecisive British MTB attacks off Barfleur.

In the same night Cdr Klug with *S145*, *S147*, *S150*, *S167*, *S140*, *S100*, *S143*, *S146*, *S144*, *S141* and *S138* makes a sortie in groups against a convoy near Falmouth. But the convoy escapes.

In an attack by 358 Marauder bombers on Ijmuiden on 26 Mar *S93* and *S129* are destroyed.

In the night 27-28 Mar the boats of the 4th and 5th TB Flotillas lay a five-row protective float barrage (360 floats) to protect the mine barrages laid out and then they move to Brest via Cherbourg on 29-30 Mar.

The 2nd, 8th and 4th MTB Flotillas try in the night 27-28 Mar to ambush British MGBs and MTBs. An attempted attack by three flotillas with 13 boats near Smith's Knoll fails in the night 29-30 Mar. In the following night the three flotillas, when they are returning from a sortie against a convoy, become involved off the Dutch coast in an engagement between German escort forces and the British *MTB350*, *MTB244*, *MTB245* and *MTB241*. The last boat sinks.

On Mar 29, in an attempt by *MGB40*, *MTB204*, *MGB613*, *MGB615*, *MGB611* and *MGB614* to attack a German force of three patrol boats, three gun ferries and 11 minesweeping cutters between Dieppe and Calais, *MGB611* and *MGB614* are damaged.

15-29 Mar   Mediterranean/Adriatic

On 15 Mar the German torpedo boat *TA20* carries out the mining operation 'Läufer' S of Ancona.

A raid by the large French destroyers *Le Terrible* and *Le Fantasque* on the Dalmatian coast on 15-16 Mar has no result. In setting out for a mining operation the German torpedo boat *TA36* runs on an old Italian mine barrage 15 nautical miles SSW of Fiume on 18 Mar and is lost. The remainder of the force, *TA20*, *TA21*, *UJ205* and the minelayer *Kiebitz*, lay a barrage E of San Giorgio in the night 18-19 Mar. In the same night the large French destroyers *Le Terrible* and *Le Fantasque* make a sortie from Bari to the area N of Navarino and attack a German convoy. The Siebel ferries *SF273* and *SF274* are sunk; *SF270* and the naval ferry barge *F124* are damaged and sunk on the next day by fighter bombers.

In air attacks on Sebenico on 27 Mar *UJ205* and *R191* are destroyed and *R188* and *R190* damaged. On 30 Mar the uncompleted corvettes *UJ206* and *UJ207* are destroyed in Venice.

On 29 Mar *TA20* with the Italian *Ms41* and *Ms75* lays the mine barrage 'Brücke' E of San Giorgio.

18 Mar   Central Pacific

US TG 50.10 (Rear-Adm Lee), comprising the carrier *Lexington*, the battleships *Iowa* and *New Jersey* and the destroyers *Dewey*, *Hull*, *MacDonough*, *Phelps*, *Bancroft*, *Meade* and *Edwards*, bombards Mille. Japanese coastal batteries get 15·2cm hits on the *Iowa*.

18-20 Mar   South West Pacific

In the night 18-19 Mar US TG 74.5, comprising the destroyers *Daly*, *Hutchins*, *Beale*, *Mullany* and *Ammen*, shells Wewak.

As a diversionary manoeuvre, the battleships *New Mexico*, *Tennessee*, *Idaho* and *Mississippi* (Rear-Adm Griffin) shell Kavieng on 20 Mar with more than 13000 rounds of 14-inch and 5-inch shells. Air cover for the force is provided by the escort carriers *Manila Bay* and *Natoma Bay*. There is a screen of 15 destroyers.

On the same day a US Amphibious Group (Commodore Reifsnider) consisting of 19 destroyers and landing craft lands four RCTs of the 4th Marine Div on Emirau (Bismarck Archipelago). Support is provided by a force comprising the cruisers *Santa Fé*, *Mobile*, *Biloxi*, *Oakland*, *Cleveland*, *Columbia* and *Montpelier*, the Fleet carriers *Enterprise* and *Belleau Wood* and the escort carriers *Coral Sea* and *Corregidor*. The landing encounters no resistance. An airfield and PT base are established.

On Bougainville the Japanese 6th Inf Div (Lt-Gen Hyakutake) with 12000 troops carries out an attack (Operation TA) on the US bridgehead near Cape Torokina of the reinforced 37th US Inf Div with some 27000 troops). The defence is supported from 9 Mar to 24 Mar by Desron 22 (Capt Petersen), comprising *Pringle*, *Conway*, *Sigourney*, *Eaton*, *Renshaw* and *Saufley*. The Japanese lose 5469 dead, the Americans 263.

21 Mar-2 Apl   Indian Ocean

Operation 'Diplomat'. On 21 Mar the British Eastern Fleet (Adm Somerville) sets out from Trincomalee and Colombo with the battleships *Queen Elizabeth* and *Valiant*, the battlecruiser *Renown*, the carrier *Illustrious*, the cruisers *London*, *Gambia* (RNZN), *Cey-*

Ion and *Cumberland* and the destroyers *Quilliam, Quality, Queenborough, Pathfinder, Van Galen* (Dutch), *Tjerk Hiddes* (Dutch), *Napier, Norman, Nepal* and *Quiberon* (the latter four Australian). The fleet replenishes on 24 Mar from three tankers, escorted by the Dutch cruiser *Tromp*, and at mid-day on 27 Mar meets SW of the Cocos Islands US TG 58.5, consisting of the carrier *Saratoga* and the destroyers *Cummings, Dunlap* and *Fanning*. On 2 Apl the ships return together to Trincomalee. On the same day, as reinforcement for the escort carrier *Battler*, the escort carriers *Atheling, Begum* and *Shah* arrive and, shortly afterwards, the French battleship *Richelieu*. From March the 8th SM Flotilla is formed with the boats *Sea Rover, Sirdar, Spiteful, Stoic, Storm, Stratagem* and *Surf*. In operations in the Straits of Malacca in March *Sea Rover* (Lt Angell) and *Truculent* (Lt Alexander) each sink one ship of 2002 tons and 1910 tons respectively. In April *Storm* (Lt Young) sinks the minesweeper *Sokaitei 7* and torpedoes two ships; *Taurus* (Lt-Cdr Wingfield) sinks one ship of 558 tons and lays a mine barrage off Penang, on which the Japanese submarine *I-37* is damaged.

22 Mar–6 May   North Atlantic
The U-boats *U267, U667* (schnorkel boats), *U262, U986, U741, U92, U962, U672, U311, U255, U302, U548, U385, U765, U342, U736* and *U473* operate individually in the North Atlantic between Ireland and Newfoundland as part of varying formations and also as weather boats. *U766, U821, U993, U970* and *U740*, which have also set out, are called back early to France to form the 'Landwirt' group. On 24 Mar and 27 Mar respectively *U302* and *U970* miss escort vessels with T-5s. *U302* (Lt-Cdr Sickel) sinks two ships of 9777 tons from the convoy SC.156 escorted by EG B.5, but is then sunk by the frigate *Swale*. On 8 Apl the sloops *Crane* and *Cygnet* of the 7th SG destroy *U962*. In the middle of April *U385* and *U667* repeatedly miss ships; *U667* and *U993* each shoot down one aircraft. *U448* (Lt Dauter), which is returning from Iceland, tries to attack the escort carrier *Biter* on 14 Apl but is located by the Canadian frigate *Swansea* (9th SG) and sunk with the help of the British sloop *Pelican* (7th SG). *U986* falls victim on 17 Apl to the escort of a small coastal convoy consisting of the US minesweeper *Swift* and the submarine-chaser *PC619*. *U311* and *U342* are lost in air attacks. On 3 May *U473* (Lt-Cdr Sternberg) misses a convoy escort with a T-5 and *U765* (Lt Wendt) torpedoes the US DE *Donnell* from a convoy. The 2nd SG (Capt Walker) with the sloops *Starling, Wild Goose, Wren, Magpie* and *Whimbrel* and the escort carrier *Tracker* and the 5th SG (Cdr Macintyre) with the DEs *Bickerton, Aylmer, Bligh, Kempthorne, Keats* and *Goodson* and the escort carrier *Vindex* are directed to the U-boats success report signals, located by HF/DF. After an 18-hour search *Starling, Wild Goose* and *Wren* compel *U473* to surface on 5 May and sink her in a 20-minutes gun and T-5 duel. *U765* is discovered by an aircraft from the *Vindex* and, likewise after a long hunt, is forced to surface by a carpet of depth charges from the *Bligh* and sunk by a second aircraft.

23 Mar–6 Apl   Central Pacific
Operation 'Desecrate': US TF 58 (Vice-Adm Mitscher, under the overall command of Adm Spruance) carries out carrier raids on Palau, Yap and Woleai. On 23 Mar TG 58.1 (Rear-Adm Reeves), consisting of the *Enterprise, Belleau Wood* and *Cowpens*, sets out from Espiritu Santo; and on 24 Mar TG 58.2 (Rear-Adm Montgomery), consisting of the *Bunker Hill, Hornet, Cabot* and *Monterey* and TG 58.3 (Rear-Adm Ginder), consisting of the *Yorktown, Lexington, Princeton* and *Langley*, set out from Majuro. Battleships, cruisers and destroyers as in the Hollandia operation (see 13 Apl). On 25 Mar the force is located by Japanese reconnaissance aircraft from Truk and again on 26 Mar when it joins up and replenishes SE of Truk. As a result, the Japanese Fleet leaves Palau in anticipation of an attack. The Carrier Fleet and the 2nd Fleet have already been transferred to Tawi-Tawi. The C-inC, Adm Koga, crashes (31 Mar) on a flight to Mindanao. His successor is Adm Toyoda.

The US submarines *Gar, Blackfish, Tang* and *Archerfish* are stationed to operate against the withdrawing ships and as lifeguards. *Tunny* (Lt-Cdr Scott) sinks on 23 Mar the Japanese submarine *I-42* and torpedoes on 29 Mar the *Musashi* from a departing naval force which also includes the cruiser *Oyodo* and two destroyers. *Tullibee* (Cdr Brindupke) is hit by her own torpedo in an attack on 26 Mar on a convoy and sinks. *Bashaw* (Lt-Cdr Nichols) torpedoes one steamer.

On the evening of 28 Mar Japanese aircraft try unsuccessfully to attack TF 58. On 30 Mar all three Task Groups attack Palau and on 31 Mar TG 58.2 and 58.3 make further attacks on Palau in which aircraft from *Lexington, Bunker Hill* and *Hornet* lay air mines. In all, the APD *No 31*, four submarine-chasers and 31 auxiliary warships and merchant ships of 129807 tons are sunk. Outside Palau the torpedo boat *Wakatake* and the repair ship *Akashi* sink. TG 58.1 attacks Yap on 31 Mar. On 1 Apl all three Task Groups attack Woleai, where the submarine *Harder*, acting as a life-guard, saves aircraft crews. Twenty-five aircraft are lost but 26 out of 44 pilots are rescued.

27 Mar-5 Apl   Arctic
Convoy operation JW.58/RA.58. On 27 Mar the convoy JW.58 with 49 ships (one returns to Iceland) sets out. With the convoy is the US cruiser *Milwaukee* on the way to be handed over to the Soviet Northern Fleet. Escort: Vice-Adm Dalrymple-Hamilton on the cruiser *Diadem* with the escort carriers *Tracker* and *Activity*, one close Escort Group and two Support Groups with a total of 20 destroyers, five sloops and five corvettes. On 29 Mar *U961*, which is on the way to the Atlantic, is located by the leader of the 2nd SG, *Starling* (Capt Walker)—the Group also includes the sloops *Wild Goose, Magpie, Wren* and *Whimbrel*—and sunk. On 30 Mar the C-in-C Home Fleet, Adm Fraser, puts out to sea from Scapa Flow as a covering force with the battleships *Anson* (Vice-Adm Moore) and *Duke of York*, the carriers *Furious* and *Victorious*, the escort carriers *Emperor, Searcher, Pursuer* and *Fencer*, the cruisers *Belfast, Royalist* (Rear-Adm

Bisset), *Sheffield* and *Jamaica* and 14 destroyers. On 30 Mar the convoy is found by German air reconnaissance, but the Martlet fighters of the *Tracker* and *Activity* shoot down one Ju 88 of 1/F.A.Gr 22 on 30 Mar, three FW 200s of 3/K.G. 40 on 31 Mar, one BV 138 of 1/S.A.Gr 130 on 1 Apl and one Ju 88 of 1/F.A.Gr 124 on 2 Apl. Of the three U-boat groups 'Thor' (*U278, U312, U313* and *U674*), 'Blitz' (*U277, U355, U711* and *U956*) and 'Hammer' (*U288, U315, U354* and *U968*) and the additional outward-bound boats *U716, U739, U360, U361* and *U990*, most of them get contact with the escort shortly after midnight on 1 Apl until the evening of 3 Apl and, in some cases, they make repeated T-5 attacks. But they are all unsuccessful: *U968* (Lt Westphalen) twice, *U674* (Lt Muhs) twice, *U278* (Lt-Cdr Franze) twice, *U313* (Lt Schweiger) once, *U711* (Lt Lange) twice, *U354* (Lt Sthamer) once, *U288* (Lt Meyer) once, *U990* (Lt-Cdr Nordheimer) once, *U739* (Lt Mangold) twice against the destroyer *Ashanti*, *U277* (Lt Lübsen) twice, *U315* (Lt Zoller) once and *U312* (Lt-Cdr K.-H. Nicolay) once. *U355* (Lt-Cdr La Baume) is damaged on 1 Apl by rockets from an Avenger of the *Tracker* and sunk by the destroyer *Beagle*. On 2 Apl *Keppel* sinks *U360* (Lt-Cdr Becker) with depth charges and on 3 Apl aircraft from the *Tracker* and *Activity* sink *U288* with rockets and depth charges, after the latter has shot down a Swordfish with AA fire. On 3 Apl Capt 1st Class Kolchin sets out from the Kola Inlet with the Soviet destroyers *Razyarenny, Gremyashchi, Razumny* and *Kuibishev*, four minesweepers and four submarine-chasers and escorts the convoy on 4-5 Apl to the Kola Inlet and, later, a group of nine steamers to the White Sea.

On 3 Apl Vice-Adm Moore makes a sortie (Operation 'Tungsten') with the *Anson*, the carriers, three cruisers and five destroyers of the covering force towards Northern Norway to attack the battleship *Tirpitz* in Altafjord. 41 Barracuda carrier bombers attack the *Tirpitz* (Capt Meyer) with fighter protection from 21 Corsairs and 20 Hellcats and obtain 14 hits for the loss of four aircraft. German losses: 122 dead and 316 wounded. The ship is out of action for three months. Forty Wildcat fighters provide fighter protection for the carrier force. The returning convoy RA.58 with 36 ships and the escort of JW.58 sets out from the Kola Inlet on 7 Apl. Because of heavy losses in operating against JW.58, the German Air Force can only fly night radar reconnaissance flights. The convoy is only found on 9 Apl. Of the U-boats formed in the two groups 'Donner' and 'Keil' (*U313, U636, U703, U277, U361, U362, U711, U716, U347* and *U990*) only *U361* (Lt-Cdr Seidel), *U362* (Lt Franz) (twice), *U703* (Lt Brüner) and *U313* make unsuccessful T-5 firings against destroyers on 10 Apl. The convoy is found again by air reconnaissance early on 11 Apl, but the operation has to be broken off because the U-boats are too far to the rear.

28 Mar-10 Apl   Black Sea
After the capture of Nikolaev on 28 Mar the Soviet 4th and the 3rd Ukrainian Fronts drive the German 6th and Rumanian 3rd Armies across the Lower Bug past Odessa to the Dniester. The attempt to encircle strong German and Rumanian forces in Odessa fails because 9300 wounded, 14845 troops and 54000 tons of mobile supplies can be evacuated from Odessa by sea. Eighteen sea-going ships in 26 missions, nine towing vessels in 27 missions, 15 tugs in 33 missions and 25 naval ferry barges in 76 missions are used. Many newly-built ships and lighters are taken away. The deployment of the Soviet submarines *L-6* (minelayer), *M-117, Shch-202, M-62* and others achieves no result. *S-31* attacks several convoys without success.

Of the German submarines, *U18* (Lt Fleige) and *U23* (Lt Wahlen) operate on the Caucasus coast and sink one towing convoy and one motor minesweeper respectively.

In March 45000 tons of supplies and the 111th Inf Div are brought to the German 17th Army on the Crimea by the sea route.

30 Mar-1 Apl   Mediterranean
On 30 Mar the convoy UGS.36 with 72 merchant ships and 18 LSTs passes through the Straits of Gibraltar. Escort:

TF64 (Capt Berdine, USN), consisting of the US destroyers *Decatur, Whipple, Alden, John D. Edwards,* the US DEs *Sellstrom, Ramsden, Mills, Rhodes, Savage, Tomich* and *Sloat* and the British 37th EG, comprising the AA cruiser *Colombo,* the Dutch frigate *Johan Maurits van Nassau,* the sloops *Black Swan, Amethyst* and *Deptford* and the Dutch *Friso,* the corvette *Campion* and the minesweeper *Speed* (JIG jamming transmitter for guided bombs). The U-boats deployed, *U421, U450* and *U969,* are not able to fire on 31 Jan; one is driven off by *Tomich* and *Black Swan.*

Before dawn on 1 Apl some 20 German torpedo aircraft attack and torpedo the US freighter *Jared Ingersoll* (7191 tons) W of Algiers.

1-30 Apl   Pacific
Of the US submarines arriving in their operational areas in April, the following make sinkings off Japan and Formosa: *Bang* (Lt-Cdr Gallaher) three ships of 10734 tons; *Guavina* (Lt-Cdr Teideman) one ship of 2331 tons and torpedoes one ship; *Haddock* (Lt-Cdr Davenport) one ship of 216 tons; *Halibut* (Lt-Cdr Galantin) two ships of 5085 tons and the minelayer *Kamome*; *Jack* (Lt-Cdr Dykers) one ship of 5425 tons and torpedoes one ship; *Pogy* (Lt-Cdr Metcalf) two ships of 7357 tons and the submarine *I-183*; *Sargo* (Lt-Cdr Garnett) one ship of 4851 tons; *Seadragon* (Lt-Cdr Ashley) one ship of 6886 tons and torpedoes one ship; *Whale* (Lt-Cdr Grady) one ship of 5401 tons. In the area of the Mandate Islands *Bluegill* (Lt-Cdr Gallaher) sinks two of 10667 tons; *Harder* (Lt-Cdr Dealey) one ship of 7061 tons and the destroyer *Ikazuchi*; *Seahorse* (Lt-Cdr Cutter) sinks two ships of 9744 tons and torpedoes two ships and also sinks the submarine *Ro-45*; *Silversides* (Lt-Cdr Coye) one ship of 1920 tons; *Trigger* (Lt-Cdr Harlfinger) one ship of 11739 tons. In the area of the Malayan Archipelago and the Philippines *Bonefish* (Lt-Cdr Edge) sinks one ship of 806 tons and torpedoes the destroyer *Inazuma* and one ship; *Crevalle* (Lt-Cdr Walker) sinks two ships of 17777 tons; *Flasher* (Lt-Cdr Whitaker) two ships of 6115 tons and a gunboat; *Haddo* (Lt-Cdr Nimitz)

torpedoes one ship; *Paddle* (Lt-Cdr Nowell) sinks two ships of 9732 tons; *Redfin* (Lt-Cdr Austin) sinks two ships of 6905 tons and the destroyer *Akigumo* and torpedoes one ship.

4 Apl-24 May   Atlantic
In operations in distant waters *U541* and *U548* cruise between Bermuda, the Bahamas and Nova Scotia. *U541* (Lt-Cdr Petersen) misses two convoys and on 26 May halts the Portuguese steamer *Serpa Pinto* (Jewish refugees among 200 passengers) and the Greek steamer *Thetis* sailing on Swiss charter. Both are released after reference back to Commander U-boats. *U548* (Lt Zimmermann) sinks on 7 May the frigate *Valleyfield* from the Canadian Escort Group of the convoy ONM.234 (three frigates and two corvettes).

E of the Brazilian coast *U129* (Lt Harpe) sinks two ships of 11965 tons in May. *U190*, *U155* and *U505* operate without success in the Gulf of Guinea and off Freetown.

SW of the Azores *U488* (Lt-Cdr Studt) replenishes four U-boats up to the end of April. On the way to the Indian Ocean the following boats pass through the Atlantic in turn: *U843* (Lt-Cdr Herwatz), which stops and releases one Portuguese and one Spanish steamer, sinks one ship of 7900 tons, is twice attacked by aircraft but escapes; *U196* (Lt-Cdr Kentrat); *U181* (Cdr* Freiwald), which sinks one ship of 5312 tons; *U537* (Lt-Cdr Schrewe); the Japanese *Ro-501* (Lt-Cdr Norita); *U198* (Lt Heusinger von Waldegg); *U859* (Lt-Cdr Jebsen) which sinks one straggler of 6254 tons from the convoy SC.157 in the North Atlantic; and the Japanese *I-29* (Cdr Kinashi).

In the Central Atlantic US Task Groups are employed successively against the refuelling areas and the passing U-boats. On 19 Apl the outward-bound *U543* evades a Task Group, comprising the escort carrier *Tripoli* (Capt Tucker) and four DEs. On 19-20 Apl TG 21.15 (Capt Vest), comprising *Croatan* and the DEs *Frost*, *Barber*, *Snowden*, *Huse* and *Inch*, is directed to *U66* by HF/DF when she is requesting replenishment. *U488* is found at the refuelling area on 25 Apl and sunk on 26-27 Apl by the DEs. The relieving

TG 21.11 (Capt Hughes), consisting of *Block Island* and the DEs *Ahrens*, *Eugene E. Elmore*, *Barr* and *Buckley*, searches for *U66*, which has again been located by HF/DF, from 1 May. On 5 May she surfaces in sight of the carrier, escapes, but is sunk on 6 May by *Buckley* in a surface attack involving gunfire, torpedoes and attempts by both ships to ram each other. The Japanese *Ro-501* falls victim to the next TG 22.2 (Capt Vosseler), consisting of *Bogue* and the DEs *Haverfield*, *Janssen*, *Willis*, *Francis M. Robinson* and *Wilhoite*, on 13 May. The Task Group employed in the South Atlantic from Recife (Capt Crist), consisting of the escort carrier *Solomons* and the DEs *Straub*, *Gustafson*, *Trumpeter* and *Herzog*, attacks *U196* on 23 Apl, but she escapes.

8-16 Apl   Black Sea
On 8 Apl the Soviet 2nd Guards Army goes over to the offensive in the Crimea against the German 50th Inf Div on the Perekop Isthmus and the Soviet 51st Army against the Rumanian 10th Div on the Sivash, whilst on 10 Apl, the Soviet Coastal Army attacks the German V Army Corps on the Kerch Peninsula. After the Soviet forces break through the Rumanian 10th Div and reach the Dzhankoy junction point, the German troops have to fall back quickly on Sevastopol. 10000 troops of the V Army Corps which has been partly driven off into the Yalta Mountains are evacuated from the eastern side to Balaklava and Sevastopol by naval ferry barges of the 1st Landing Flotilla (Lt-Cdr Giele). On 15-16 Apl the bulk of the German and Rumanian forces reach the fortress area. The evacuation of all superfluous troops (supply forces, etc.) and the Wehrmacht echelons from the Crimea to Constanza begins on 12 Apl. By 16 Apl 36000 German, 9600 Rumanian soldiers, 16000 Eastern Legionaries, 3800 prisoners-of-war and 1600 civilians are evacuated by sea on steamers and light craft, escorted by German and Rumanian warships under the Commander of the 10th Escort Div, Capt Weyher, and also, in part, by transport aircraft.

Deployed against the transport movements are the naval air forces of the Black Sea Fleet (Lt-Gen Ermachenkov)

with about 90 aircraft of the 9th and 11th Fighter Regts and the 23rd Ground Attack Regt in the Odessa area, 93 aircraft of the 2nd Guards Mining and Torpedo Air Div and the 40th Fighter Regt in the Skadovsk area, 86 aircraft of the 11th Ground Attack Div and the 30th Reconnaissance Regt from the area N of the Crimea and later from Evpatoria as well as 38 fighters of the 25th Fighter Regt from Kerch and later Feodosia. Up to 16 Apl they sink the motor minesweeper *R204*, the naval ferry barges *F565* and *F569* and damage *R205*, *F572* and the tug *Oituz*. An attack by the 2nd TKA Brigade from Skadovsk with the rocket-equipped *TKA-86* and the torpedo-cutters *TKA-14*, *TKA-85*, *TKA-94* and *TKA-104* is intercepted by the motor torpedo boats of the 1st MTB Flotilla which is stationed as flank protection. Attempted attacks by the submarines *S-31* (Capt 3rd Class Alexeev) (twice), *A-5* (Lt-Cdr Matveev) (twice), *Shch-215* (Capt 3rd Class Greshilov) and *L-6* (Lt-Cdr Gremyako) fail. Submarine-chasers of the 1st SC Flotilla attack several submarines with depth charges. A landing made on 13 Apl in Feodosia by light units of the Soviet Black Sea Fleet encounters no resistance: the harbour has already been abandoned.

10-16 Apl Mediterranean

On 10 Apl the convoy UGS.37 passes through the Straits of Gibraltar with 60 merchant ships and six LSTs. Escort: TF 65 (Cdr Headden, USN) comprising the US destroyers *Breckinridge*, *Blakeley*, *Biddle*, *Barney*, the US DEs *Stanton*, *Swasey*, *Price*, *Strickland*, *Forster*, *Stockdale*, *Hissem*, *Holder* and the British AA cruiser *Delhi*, the frigate *Nadder* and the US destroyer *Lansdale* and the British corvette *Jonquil* as JIG (radar jamming) ships. The deployment of the U-boats *U421*, *U969*, and *U471* (which reaches the Mediterranean on 6 Apl) meets with no success.

In the night 11-12 Apl there is an attack in the Cape Bengut area by some 20 torpedo aircraft of the German 2nd Fl. Div. *Holder* receives a hit and is brought in, but not repaired; *Stanton* and *Swasey* just avoid the attacks. Further on to Alexandria *U407* (Lt

Korndörfer) attacks the convoy off Cyrenaica and torpedoes two ships of 14386 tons, of which one sinks, and one is taken in tow to Alexandria but not repaired.

10-26 Apl Arctic

Soviet combined operation RV-3 against German convoy traffic off the Polar Coast.

On 10 Apl an attack by Ground Attack Regt 46 with three waves of 19 Il-2s, 16 Kittyhawks, 14 Airacobras and six YAK-1s on a German convoy fails. Torpedo-cutters sink the collier *Stör* (665 tons) off Kirkenes. *TKA-212* is lost. In Kirkenes two steamers are damaged by near-misses from low-flying aircraft. *S-104* and *M-105*, which are among the submarines, have no success. *S-54* is probably lost at this time on a flanking mine barrage.

In an attack by torpedo cutters, including *TKA-13* and *TKA-203*, on a German convoy off Petsamofjord on 22 Apl, the torpedoes are released too early with the result that the steamers are able to avoid them. In an air attack by Ground Attack Regt 46 on the convoy on 23 Apl the Commander of the formation, Capt Katunin, crashes into the sea just near a ship.

10 Apl-1 May English Channel

In the night 10-11 Apl the Norwegian *MTB715*, *MTB653*, *MTB623* and *MTB618* try to attack a German convoy off the Dutch coast but are driven off by the strong defensive fire.

A sortie by the 5th MTB Flotilla (Cdr Klug) with six boats from Cherbourg in a northerly direction on 12-13 Apl is detected early and leads to no result. Similarly, another operation with 13 boats from the 5th and 9th Flotillas against Lyme Bay on 13-14 Apl has no success.

A mining operation by the 4th and 8th Flotillas with 15 boats on 14-15 Apl is detected early from the VHF talk and broken off. From 17 Apl to 19 Apl the 5th TB Flotilla, comprising *Kondor*, *T27*, *T29*, *Möwe* and *Greif*, is transferred from Brest to Cherbourg as distant cover for a convoy.

On 18-19 Apl British fighter bombers sink the patrol boats *V1232*, *V1236* and *V1237* from a German force off the mouth of the Ems and Terschelling.

In the night 18-19 Apl the 8th Flotilla (Cdr Zymalkowski), consisting of *S87, S133, S127, S64, S83, S85* and *S67*, breaks off a mining operation because of the weather and after engagements with the British destroyer *Whitshed* and MGBs. *S64* and *S133* are damaged. In the same night the 5th Flotilla, consisting of *S112, S100, S141, S138, S140* and *S143*, lays EMC mines W of the Isle of Wight and has an engagement with the destroyer *Middleton* and MTBs, including *MTB 246*. E of the Isle of Wight the 9th Flotilla (Cdr v. Mirbach), consisting of *S146, S147, S144, S150, S130, S145* and *S167*, lays 30 EMC mines.

In the night 19-20 Apl the 8th Flotilla again breaks off a mining operation because of the weather. The 5th and 9th Flotillas (as above, but without *S140* and *S141*) make an unsuccessful sortie against a CW convoy and are driven off by the 'Hunt' destroyers *Berkeley, Middleton, Haldon* and *La Combattante* (French) and pursued. In the process *S144* goes aground near Calais.

In the night 21-22 Apl the 5th TB Flotilla, comprising *Kondor, Möwe* and *Greif*, lays a protection float barrage with 145 floats from Cherbourg. The 4th TB Flotilla, comprising *T29, T24* and *T27*, is transferred from Cherbourg to St Malo. From Cherbourg the 5th MTB Flotilla, consisting of *S100, S112, S143, S140* and *S138*, and the 9th MTB Flotilla, consisting of *S146, S150, S145, S130* and *S167*, make a sortie against a WP convoy near Dungeness and Hastings. In engagements with the destroyers *Volunteer* and *Middleton* and MGBs, including *MGB214* and *MGB617* and *MTB235, S167* and British boats are damaged.

In the night 23-24 Apl a sortie by the 4th and 8th MTB Flotillas with 11 boats towards the British south-east coast is unsuccessful. The 5th MTB Flotilla, consisting of *S100, S143, S138, S136, S140* and *S142*, attacks a CW convoy near Dungeness: Cdr v. Mirbach with *S100* sinks the tug *Roode Zee* (468 tons). The 9th MTB Flotilla, consisting of *S146, S147, S145, S167, S130* and *S150*, is involved in engagements near Hastings with the destroyers *Berkeley, Haldon, Stevenstone* and *Volunteer* and from St Malo to Brest, the torpedo

MGBs and MTBs. *MTB359* is damaged. The 5th TB Flotilla with *Kondor, Möwe* and *Greif* is deployed from Cherbourg against British MTBs near Cap Barfleur. Their attacks fail. *MTB671* is sunk.

On 25 Apl the 4th TB Flotilla (Cdr Kohlauf), consisting of *T29, T24* and *T27*, sets out from St. Malo and lays a mine barrage NW of Les Sept Iles. In the night 25-26 Apl there is an engagement with the British cruiser *Black Prince*, the British destroyer *Ashanti* and the Canadian destroyers *Athabaskan, Haida* and *Huron*. *T27* is hit at the beginning of the engagement and is sent back to Morlaix. *Haida* sinks *T29* (The Flotilla Commander, Lt-Cdr Grund and 135 men perish; 73 are rescued by a patrol vessel). *T24* reaches St. Malo in a damaged state.

In the same night six boats from the 5th and 9th MTB Flotillas are deployed against the concentrations located by air reconnaissance near Selsey Bill, Portsmouth and Southampton. They become involved in engagements with the destroyers *Berkeley, Rowley* (DE) and *La Combattante* (French) which sinks *S147*.

In the night 26-27 Apl the 5th TB Flotilla with *Kondor, Greif* and *Möwe* lays a barrage of 108 LMB mines N of Cherbourg. *T27* is transferred from Morlaix to St Malo.

In the night 27-28 Apl the 5th and 9th MTB Flotillas, comprising *S136, S138, S140, S142, S100, S143* and *S150, S130* and *S145*, attacks a force, consisting of eight US LSTs, escorted by the corvette *Azalea* and the destroyer *Saladin*, as it comes into Lyme Bay. *LST507* and *LST531* are sunk and *LST289* is torpedoed. When the British destroyer TF 27 (leader *Onslow*) is deployed, it misses the German motor torpedo boats. 197 sailors and 441 troops on board perish.

In the same night the 5th TB Flotilla lays another defensive barrage of 108 mines off Cherbourg. When avoiding a British fighter bomber attack, the force runs into a British minefield: the *Kondor* is damaged on a mine but brought in.

In the night 28-29 Apl, while moving from St Malo to Brest, the torpedo boats *T24* and *T27* encounter the Canadian destroyers *Athabaskan* and *Haida* off St Brieux. *T24* sinks *Athabaskan* with a torpedo salvo. *T27* has to be beached after an engagement with *Haida*. An attempt to get her away made by the 24th MS Flotilla fails, whereupon the minesweepers take off the crew. *T24* hits a ground mine in the morning, but is able to reach harbour. Eighty-five men are rescued from the *Athabaskan*. In the night 29-30 Apl four boats each from the 5th and 9th MTB Flotillas are deployed against targets located off Cherbourg, but they encounter nothing. When they later move to Le Havre *S138*, *S143*, and *S100* escape from the MGBs and the destroyers *Brilliant* and *Haldon* sent to find them. On 30 Apl the 5th TB Flotilla with *Möwe* and *Greif* carry out two, and on 1 May one, defensive mining operations when the barrages 'Blitz 38, 38A and 39' are laid with 260 LMB mines.

12 Apl-10 June   South West Pacific
The Australian destroyer *Vendetta*, the frigates *Gascoyne* and *Barcoo* and the corvettes *Ararat*, *Benalla*, *Bendigo*, *Bowen*, *Broome*, *Bunbury*, *Bundaberg*, *Castlemaine*, *Colac*, *Cowra*, *Deloraine*, *Geelong*, *Gladstone*, *Glenelg*, *Goulbourn*, *Gympie*, *Kapunda*, *Katoomba*, *Kiama*, *Lithgow*, *Rockhampton*, *Shepparton*, *Stawell*, *Strahan*, *Townsville*, *Wagga* and *Whyalla* are employed to escort convoys between Finschhafen and the Admiralty Islands, Madang and Hollandia. In these operations *Bundaberg*, *Stawell*, *Barcoo*, *Kapunda*, *Wagga* and *Lithgow* carry out, on different days, the shelling of Japanese positions between Madang and Hansa Bay and the outlying islands.

13 Apl-4 May   Central Pacific
Operation by US TF 58 (Vice-Adm Mitscher) to support the Hollandia landing. TF 58 sets out from Majuro on 13 Apl, is refuelled N of the Admiralty Islands on 19 Apl and begins its attacks on 21 Apl: TG 58.1 (Rear-Adm Clark), comprising *Hornet*, *Belleau Wood*, *Cowpens* and *Bataan*, makes fighter attacks on Wakde and Sarmi and shells them by night with the cruisers *Santa Fé*, *Mobile* and *Biloxi* and five destroyers of TG 58.1. On 22 Apl there is another carrier raid,

followed by other raids on 23 Apl and 24 Apl. TG 58.2 (Rear-Adm Montgomery), comprising *Bunker Hill*, *Yorktown*, *Monterey* and *Cabot*, carries out attacks on 21 Apl on Wakde and Hollandia and supports the landing in Humboldt Bay from 22 Apl to 24 Apl. TG 58.3 (Rear-Adm Reeves), comprising *Enterprise*, *Lexington*, *Princeton* and *Langley*, attacks Hollandia on 21 Apl and supports the landings near Tanahmerah Bay from 22 Apl to 24 Apl. There is very little resistance in the air after previous attacks by the 5th USAAF (Lt-Gen Kenney). Twenty-one carrier aircraft are lost. After refuelling on 27 Apl N of the Admiralty Islands, TF 58 makes a heavy attack on Truk on 29 Apl and 30 Apl. Of 104 Japanese aircraft available, 59 are destroyed in air fights and 34 on the ground. Twenty-six US aircraft are shot down and nine lost through accident. S of Truk the Japanese submarine *I-174* is sunk by TG 58.2 on 30 Apl. The US submarine *Tang* rescues 22 pilots who are shot down, some of them within the Truk lagoon.
On 30 Apl a cruiser-destroyer force (Rear-Adm Oldendorf), comprising the cruisers *Louisville*, *Portland*, *Wichita*, *Baltimore*, *Boston*, *Canberra*, *New Orleans*, *Minneapolis* and *San Francisco* and the destroyers *Bradford*, *Conner*, *Izard*, *Boyd*, *Brown*, *Cowell*, *Charrette* and *Burns*, shells the Satawan Islands group SE of Truk. On 1 May a battleship-destroyer force (Vice-Adm Lee) consisting of the battleships *Iowa*, *New Jersey*, *North Carolina*, *Indiana*, *Massachusetts*, *South Dakota* and *Alabama* and the destroyers *Miller*, *Owen*, *The Sullivans*, *Stephen Potter*, *Tingey*, *Converse*, *Thatcher*, *Pritchett*, *Cassin Young* and *Bell*, shells the island of Ponape. Air escort is provided by TG 58.1. This group enters Eniwetok on 4 May and TG 58.2 and TG 58.3 go to Majuro.

13 Apl-21 May   Mediterranean
In operations E of Sicily *U596* (Lt Nonn), the first boat to be fitted with schnorkel, misses an Italian corvette in the Strait of Otranto on 13 Apl and then operates without success off Taranto. *U565* cruises E of Sicily. They are relieved by *U453* (Lt Lührs) which

misses a west-bound convoy on 3 May. But on 18 May she attacks convoy HA.43, escorted by the Italian torpedo boats *Indomito, Libra, Fortunale, Monzambano* and the corvettes *Danaide* and *Urania* and sinks one ship of 7147 tons. This is the last U-boat success in the Mediterranean. The boat is then hunted by Italian ships and, subsequently, by British destroyers. *Termagant, Tenacious* and *Liddesdale* sink her on 21 May.

14 Apl   Indian Ocean
In Bombay the British freighter *Fort Stikine* (7142 tons), loaded with cotton and ammunition, catches fire and explodes. As a result of the explosion and the scattered burning cotton, harbour installations and many ships are set on fire. In addition to the Dutch freighters *Generaal v.d. Heyden* (1215 tons), *Generaal van Swieten* (1300 tons) and *Tinombo* (872 tons), which are destroyed, three Indian warships and another 14 merchants ships of 50500 tons suffer, in some cases, severe damage. 336 people are killed and over 1000 injured.

15 Apl-10 June   South West Pacific
Japanese operation 'Take-Ichi': convoy to reinforce troops on the Vogelkop Peninsula. It sets out with 20000 troops from Shanghai for Halmahera. On 26 Apl the transport *Yoshida Maru* (5425 tons) is sunk off Manila Bay by the US submarine *Jack*; on 6 May the transports *Tenshizan Maru* (6886 tons, *Taijima Maru* (6995 tons) and *Aden Maru* (5824 tons) are sunk by the US submarine *Gurnard*. Nearly half the troops embarked fail to reach Halmahera/Vogelkop.

16-24 Apl   Indian Ocean
Operation 'Cockpit': carrier raid on Sabang. On 16 Apl the British Eastern Fleet sets out in two groups from Trincomalee: TF 69 (Adm Somerville) with the battleships *Queen Elizabeth, Valiant, Richelieu*, the cruisers (Rear-Adm Reid) *Newcastle, Nigeria, Ceylon, Gambia* and *Tromp*, the destroyers *Rotherham, Racehorse, Penn, Petard*; *Quiberon, Napier, Nepal, Nizam* (RAN) and *Van Galen* (Dutch); and TF 70 (Vice-Adm Power) with the battlecruiser *Renown*, the carriers (Rear-Adm Moody), *Illustrious* and *Saratoga*, the

cruiser *London*, the destroyers *Quilliam, Quadrant, Queenborough, Cummings, Dunlap, Fanning* and the air/sea rescue submarine *Tactician*. On 18 Apl *Gambia* and *Ceylon* reinforce TF 70. On 19 Apl 46 bombers and 35 fighters fly off from the carriers to attack Sabang (North-West Sumatra) and surrounding airfields. One steamer is sunk and 24 aircraft are destroyed on the ground. One Allied fighter is lost but the pilot is rescued by the British submarine *Tactician*. When three Japanese torpedo aircraft try to attack, all the attackers are shot down by the fighter cover. The Fleet returns to Trincomalee.

17 Apl-4 May   Black Sea
The Soviet Naval Air Force (see 8 Apl), the 2nd TKA Brigade from Evpatoria and the 1st TKA Brigade from Yalta (from 19 Apl) and the Submarine Brigade (Rear-Adm Boltunov), which are jointly deployed on the basis of air reconnaissance, are used intensively against German and Rumanian transport traffic between the encircled fortress of Sevastopol (17th Army under Col-Gen Jaenecke) and Constanza.

Each day there are up to eight convoys, consisting of the steamers *Oituz, Ardeal, Alba Julia, Budapest, Danubius, Prodromos, Helga, Ossag, Geiserich, Kassa, Totila, Teja, Tisza* and *Durostor*, the KT ships *KT18, KT25* and *KT26*, many tugs and ferry barges of the 1st, 3rd and 7th Landing Flotillas (Lt-Cdr Giele, Lt-Cdr Kuppig and Cdr Stelter). The escort, under the overall command of the Admiral-Black Sea, Vice-Adm Brinkmann, is provided by the 10th Escort Div (Capt Weyher). The Rumanian naval forces are under Rear-Adm Marcellariu. The following ships are employed: the Rumanian destroyers *Regina Maria, Regele Ferdinand, Maresti, Marasesti*, the gunboats *Ghigulescu* and *Stihi*, the German 1st SC Flotilla (Cdr Gampert) comprising *UJ103, UJ104, UJ106, UJ115/Rosita* and *UJ116/Xanten*, the 3rd SC Flotilla (Lt Dr Teichmann) with the KFKs *UJ301* to *UJ307, UJ310, UJ313* to *UJ318*, the 23rd SC Flotilla (Cdr Wolters) with the KFKs *UJ2305, UJ2307, UJ2302, UJ2312, UJ2313* and *UJ2318* and the 3rd MMS Flotilla (Lt Klassmann)

I

consisting of *R35*, *R37*, *R164*, *R165*, *R166*, *R163*, *R196*, *R197*, *R203*, *R205*, *R206*, *R207*, *R216* and *RA54*. Flanking escort is provided by the 1st MTB Flotilla (Cdr Büchting) with 13 motor torpedo boats.

On 18 Apl the Soviet submarine *M-111* (Lt-Cdr Khomyakov) misses the steamer *Helga*. The *Alba Julia* (5700 tons) is set on fire by bombers and lost. In an attempt to attack the disabled steamer, the submarine *L-6* is destroyed by *UJ104* and *M-112* is driven off. On 22 Apl the submarines *M-62* (Lt-Cdr Malyshev) and *M-111* attack the *Ardeal* in turn without success. Bombers damage the *Ossag*, which sinks after being finished off by *M-35* (Lt-Cdr Prokofev), and *R207*. The submarine *Shch-201* (Capt 3rd Class Paramoshkin), attacks *UJ103* and is straddled with depth charges. From 26 Apl to 28 Apl *L-4*, *Shch-202*, *Shch-201* try, sometimes repeatedly, to attack convoys. In air attacks on 28 Apl *F406* and *R37* are damaged. Torpedo cutters attempt attacks on 16 Apl, 17 Apl, 18 Apl, 24 Apl, 26 Apl and 27 Apl. In the last, *UJ104* is torpedoed but brought into Sevastopol. In further attacks on 3-4 May the wreck of *UJ104*, *UJ2304*, the tug *Junak* and seven lighters are destroyed. The submarines *A-5* (Lt-Cdr Matveev), *M-62* and *M-111* attack three different convoys unsuccessfully. In addition to extensive supply missions, 13400 German and 29000 Rumanian troops are transported from Sevastopol in this period.

17 Apl-5 June   English Channel/ North Sea/Baltic
British mining offensive to block the German sea routes to the Channel in preparation for the operation 'Neptune'. Nos 1, 3, 4, 5 and 6 Groups RAF Bomber Command drop 4000 mines in this period, including, for the first time, acoustic ground mines for low frequencies and acoustic anchor mines.

The minelayers *Apollo* and *Plover* and the MTBs of the 9th, 13th, 14th, 21st and 64th MTB Flotillas and MLs of the 10th, 50th, 51st and 52nd ML Flotillas lay 3000 mines.
About 100 German ships, in all, run onto these mines.

19-20 Apl   Mediterranean
On 19 Apl convoy UGS.38 passes through the Straits of Gibraltar with 87 ships. Escort: TF 66 (Capt Duvall, USCG) with the USCG cutters *Taney*, *Duane*, the US DEs *Joseph E. Campbell*, *Laning*, *Fechteler*, *Fiske*, *Mosley*, *Pride*, *Falgout*, *Lowe*, *Menges*, *Newell*, *Chase* and *Fessenden*. In addition, there is the Dutch AA cruiser *Heemskerck* and, as JIG ships, the US destroyers *Lansdale*, the US minesweepers *Speed* and *Sustain*. An attack by *U969* on 20 Apl fails. On the evening of 20 Apl some 60 torpedo aircraft of III/K.G. 26 and of I and, III/K.G. 77 are deployed some of which in approaching locate a Corsica-Africa convoy and sink the French freighter *El Biar* (4678 tons) from it. The others attack in the radar gap from the African coast and sink the *Lansdale* and the freighters *Royal Star* (7900 tons) and *Paul Hamilton* (7177 tons) with torpedoes and damage the freighters *Samite* (7219 tons) and *Stephen Austin* (7176 tons). *Lowe*, *Taney* and *Heemskerck* narrowly avoid several torpedoes.

19-20 Apl   Mediterranean/Adriatic
The minelayer *Kiebitz* and the motor minesweeper *R185* carry out the mining operation 'Hermelin' from Pola.

20-21 Apl   Mediterranean/ Tyrrhenian Sea
One-man torpedoes ('*Neger*') are used against Allied ships off Anzio. Of 37 which enter the water, 14 get stuck on sandbanks and 23 attack. They obtain no successes. Only 13 *Neger* return.

21 Apl-6 May   Arctic
An escort force (Rear-Adm McGrigor), comprising the cruiser *Diadem*, the escort carriers *Activity* and *Fencer*, the 3rd DD Flotilla with *Milne*, *Meteor*, *Marne*, *Matchless*, *Musketeer*, *Verulam*, *Ulysses* and *Virago*, the 6th SG with the Canadian frigates *Waskesiu*, *Grou*, *Cape Breton* and *Outremont* and the 8th SG with the destroyers *Keppel*, *Walker*, *Beagle*, *Westcott*, *Whitehall*, *Wrestler*, *Inconstant*, *Boadicea* and the corvette *Lotus*, goes to the Kola Inlet to fetch convoy RA.59 where it arrives on 23 Apl. At the same time on 21 Apl Vice-Adm Moore proceeds with the battleship *Anson*, the carriers *Victorious*, *Furious*, *Searcher*, *Striker*, *Emperor* and

Pursuer and cruisers and destroyers to the northern Norwegian coast to carry out another raid on the *Tirpitz*. On 24 Apl and 25 Apl the weather prevents the aircraft from taking off. After refuelling the destroyers, the aircraft fly off on 26 Apl for an attack on shipping near Bodö. Here they find a south-bound convoy and sink three German ships of 15083 tons. Six aircraft are lost to the defenders fighters and AA fire.

After a feeder convoy of 16 steamers from the White Sea, accompanied by the Soviet destroyers *Gremyashchi* and *Gromki*, the minesweeper *T-119* and five patrol ships, arrives in the Kola Inlet on 27 Apl, convoy RA.59 puts to sea on the following day with the escort force. Initially, it is reinforced by the Soviet destroyers *Razyarenny*, *Grozny* and *Kuibyshev* the minesweepers *T-112*, *T-114*, *T-119* and the submarine-chasers *BO-201*, *BO-204*, *BO-205*, *BO-207*, *BO-209* and *BO-212*. The US crew of the cruiser *Milwaukee*/*Murmansk* are distributed among the ships, as are 2300 Soviet sailors who are to man the British units (one battleship, nine destroyers and four submarines) which are to be taken over as a share of the Italian war booty in Britain. Adm Levchenko is on board the *Fencer*. The convoy is located by German air reconnaissance towards midnight on 28-29 Apl. The U-boats, which are waiting for an east-bound convoy, are deployed against RA.59 from 30 Apl as the 'Donner' group (*U277*, *U636*, *U307*, *U278*) and the 'Keil' group (*U711*, *U739*, *U674*, *U354*, *U315*, *U959*, *U313*). After a FAT salvo miss from *U307* (Lt Herrle) on the convoy, *U387* (Lt-Cdr Büchler) and *U711* (Lt Lange) repeatedly attack destroyers and steamers with T-5s and FAT salvoes towards midnight on 30 Apl. *U711* sinks the *William S. Thayer* (7176 tons). In the course of 1 Apl *U278* (Lt-Cdr Franze), *U307* and *U959* (Lt Weitz) each miss destroyers twice with T-5s. Aircraft of the *Fencer* sink *U277* on 1 Apl and *U959* and *U674* on 2 May, while *U307* and *U711* again miss destroyers with T-5s. Early on 3 May *U278* is attacked by two Swordfish and one Martlet, but shoots down the latter and escapes.

22-28 Apl   South West Pacific
US landing operations 'Reckless' (Hollandia) and 'Persecution' (Aitape) under the overall command of Gen MacArthur and Vice-Adm Kinkaid (7th Fleet). Participating: I US Corps (Maj-Gen Eichelberger), TF 77 (Rear-Adm Barbey).
Aitape: TG 77.1 (Barbey) with the 163rd RCT (Brig-Gen Doe) of the 41st Inf Div on three APAs, one LSD, one AKA, 16 LCIs and seven LSTs. Escort: the destroyers *Hobby*, *Nicholson*, *Wilkes*, *Grayson*, *Gillespie*, *Kalk* and *Swanson*.
Tanahmerah Bay: TG 77.2 (Rear-Adm Fechteler) with the 24th Inf Div (Maj-Gen Irving) on one APA, one LSD, one AKA, five APDs, 16 LCIs and seven LSTs. Escort: the destroyers *Reid*, *Stevenson*, *Stockton*, *Thorn*, *Roe*, *Welles*, *Radford* and *Taylor*.
Humboldt Bay: TG 77.3 (Capt Noble) with the 41st Inf Div (Maj-Gen Fuller) on nine APDs, one LSD, one AKA and seven LSTs. Escort: the destroyers *La Valette*, *Nicholas*, *O'Bannon*, *Jenkins*, *Hopewell* and *Howorth*.
Air support: TG 78.1 (Rear-Adm Ragsdale), comprising the escort carriers *Sangamon*, *Suwanee*, *Chenango* and *Santee*, the destroyers *Morris*, *Anderson*, *Hughes*, *Mustin*, *Russell*, *Ellet*, *Landsdowne* and *Lardner*; and TG 78.2 (Rear-Adm Davison) comprising the escort carriers *Natoma Bay*, *Coral Sea*, *Corregidor* and *Manila Bay*, the destroyers *Erben*, *Walker*, *Hale*, *Abbot*, *Bullard*, *Kidd*, *Black*, *Chauncey* and *Stembel*.
Covering forces: TF 74 (Rear-Adm Crutchley) with the Australian cruisers *Australia* and *Shropshire*, the Australian destroyers *Arunta* and *Warramunga* and the US destroyers *Ammen* and *Mullany*; and TF 75 (Rear-Adm Berkey) with the cruisers *Phoenix*, *Boise* and *Nashville* (Gen MacArthur on board), the destroyers *Hutchins*, *Beale*, *Bache*, *Daly*, *Abner Read* and *Bush*.
The landings succeed against very slight resistance. The targets are reached by 28 Apl. Strong Japanese forces are cut off to the E.

1-31 May   Pacific
The US submarines arriving in their operational areas in May make the following sinkings: off Japan, Formosa and the Kuriles *Barb* (Lt-Cdr Fluckey)

sinks five ships of 15471 tons; *Burrfish* (Lt-Cdr Perkins) one ship of 5984 tons; *Flying Fish* (Lt-Cdr Risser) four ships of 12319 tons; *Guitarro* (Lt-Cdr Haskins) one ship of 2201 tons and the frigate *Awaji*; *Herring* (Lt-Cdr Zabriskie) three ships of 9080 tons and the frigate *Ishigaki*; *Picuda* (Lt-Cdr Rayborn) one ship of 3171 tons and the gunboat *Hashidate*; *Pollack* (Lt-Cdr Lewellen) the destroyer *Asanagi*; *Pompon* (Lt-Cdr Gimber) one ship of 742 tons; *Silversides* (Lt-Cdr Coye) six ships of 14152 tons; *Skate* (Lt-Cdr Gruner) one patrol ship; *Tautog* (Lt-Cdr Baskett) four ships of 16038 tons; *Tinosa* (Lt-Cdr Weiss) two ships of 12876 tons. In the area of the Mandate Islands *Angler* (Lt-Cdr Olsen) sinks one ship of 2105 tons; *Aspro* (Cdr Stevenson) two ships of 11107 tons; *Billfish* torpedoes one ship; *Bowfin* (Lt-Cdr Griffith) sinks one ship of 4667 tons; *Cero* (Lt-Cdr White) sinks one ship of 2825 tons and torpedoes one ship; *Hoe* (Lt-Cdr McCrea) sinks the frigate *Sado* and torpedoes one ship; *Sandlance* (Lt-Cdr Garrison) sinks five ships of 18328 tons; *Sturgeon* (Lt-Cdr Murphy) one ship of 1904 tons; *Tambor* (Lt-Cdr Kefauver) sinks one ship of 657 tons and torpedoes one ship; *Tuna* sinks one ship of 89 tons; and *Tunny* (Lt-Cdr Scott) one ship of 4955 tons. In the area of the Malayan Archipelago and the Philippines *Cabrilla* (Lt-Cdr Thompson) sinks one ship of 8360 tons; *Cod* (Lt-Cdr Dempsey) one ship of 7255 tons and the torpedo boat *Karukaya*; *Gurnard* (Lt-Cdr Andrews) four ships of 29794 tons; *Lapon* (Lt-Cdr Stone) two ships of 11253 tons; *Pargo* (Lt-Cdr Eddy) one ship of 758 tons; *Puffer* (Lt-Cdr Selby) three ships of 7847 tons; *Rasher* (Lt-Cdr Laughton) four ships of 10858 tons; *Raton* (Lt-Cdr Davis) one ship of 168 tons and torpedoes the frigate *Iki*, the corvette *Kaibokan 15* and the frigate *Matsuwa*. *Ray* (Lt-Cdr Harrel) sinks one ship of 6094 tons.

2-3 May   Mediterranean/Aegean
The British cruiser *Ajax* shells Rhodes and the large French destroyers *Le Fantasque* and *Le Malin* Coo.

3-5 May   Mediterranean
The convoy GUS.38 with 107 merchant ships approaches the Straits of Gibraltar

from the E. Escort: TF 66 (Capt Duval, USCG) with the USCG cutter *Taney*, 12 US DEs (see 19-20 Apl) and the British AA cruiser *Delhi*. On 3 May the DE *Menges* locates *U371* (Lt Fenski) with radar and approaches with a 'Foxer' astern, but she receives a T-5 hit. The DEs *Pride* and *Joseph E. Campbell* take up the pursuit and at mid-day the British 'Hunt' class destroyer *Blankney*, the US minesweeper *Sustain* and the French destroyers *L'Alcyon* and *Sénégalais* also come from Oran. *U371* withdraws and submerges in the night 3-4 May, but is located by *Sénégalais*. The U-boat fires T-5 torpedoes, one of which damages the approaching *Sénégalais*, and she then scuttles herself. In the meantime, the convoy proceeds and in the night 4-5 May *U967* (Lt-Cdr Brandi) is located by the DE *Laning*, but she is able to sink the DE *Fechteler* with a T-5 and retire. Two more T-5s from *U967* on escorts on 26 Apl and 8 May have no success.

4 May-3 June   Arctic/Norway
British carrier attacks on Northern Norway. On 6 May a British force, consisting of the carriers *Furious* and *Searcher*, the cruiser *Berwick*, the destroyers *Savage*, *Wizard*, *Wakeful*, *Algonquin* (Canadian) and *Piorun* and *Blyskawica* (Polish), makes a sortie towards the area Kristiansund/North. 18 Barracudas and 14 Seafires from *Furious* and 20 Wildcats from *Searcher* attack two German convoys and, with the loss of two aircraft, sink the ore steamer *Almora* (2522 tons) and the tanker *Saarburg* (7913 tons).
On 8 May a force, consisting of the escort carriers *Searcher*, *Striker* and *Emperor*, attacks a German convoy of five steamers and six escort vessels off Kristiansund/North. Heavy damage is caused on several steamers.
On 12 May Vice-Adm Moore sets out with the battleship *Anson*, the carriers *Victorious* and *Furious* and cruisers and destroyers to make a new attack on the *Tirpitz* in Altafjord. The 27 Barracudas, 28 Corsairs, four Seafires and four Wildcats flown off on 15 May have to return when off the Norwegian coast because of the weather (low clouds). A second group, consisting of the escort

carriers *Emperor* and *Striker*, the cruisers *Sheffield* and *Royalist* and the destroyers *Onslow*, *Obedient*, *Ursa*, *Wakeful*, *Piorun* and *Blyskawica*, makes sorties on 14 May and 15 May twice in the direction of Rörvik and Stadlandet and obtains many near-misses with carrier aircraft on German ships lying at anchor but no actual sinking. A third sortie by Vice-Adm Moore with the carriers *Victorious* and *Furious* to attack the *Tirpitz* on 28 May has to be abandoned because of the weather. The Barracudas attack a convoy off the Norwegian coast on 1 June and sink the ammunition steamer *Hans Leonhardt* (4170 tons) and set *Sperrbrecher 181* and the freighter *Florida* (5542 tons) on fire. A T-5 torpedo from *U957* on the carrier force on 30 May is not successful.

5-12 May   Black Sea
After Hitler, in spite of several requests, has rejected the idea of a timely withdrawal from Sevastopol, the Soviet 2nd Guards Army (Col-Gen Sakharov) in the northern sector on 5 May, followed in the next few days by the 51st Army (Lt-Gen Kreiser) and the Coastal Army (Gen Eremenko), attacks German and Rumanian positions of the 17th Army. Soviet troops having broken through to the Sapun Heights on 8 May, Hitler, in response to further appeals, gives the order to withdraw to the hardpressed remnants of the 17th Army (there are still 64700 troops on 3 May). The German and Rumanian warships and transports (see 17 Apl) are able, despite continual and very strong Soviet air attacks and the massive deployment of submarines, to evacuate 37500 men by 13 May, including 25677 troops and 6011 wounded in the last three days. As a result of attacks by Soviet air formations (see 8 Apl and the 8th Air Army (Lt-Gen Khryukin) and the 4th Air Army (Col-Gen Vershinin)), the transports *Totila* (2773 tons), *Teja* (3600 tons), *Helga* (2200 tons), *Danubius* (1489 tons), *Prodromos* (800 tons), the minelayer *Romania* (3152 tons), the submarine-chasers *UJ2313*, *UJ2314*, *UJ310*, three auxiliary vessels, five tugs, 11 lighters and other small craft are sunk. The transports *Durostor* (1309 tons) and *Geiserich* (712 tons), which

are damaged by bombs, are finished off by torpedoes from *A-5* (Lt-Cdr Matveev) and *Shch-201* (Capt 3rd Class Paramoshkin) respectively. Many attacks are made by the submarines deployed: *S-33*, *Shch-201*, *Shch-202*, *L-4*, *M-35*, *M-62*, *Shch-205* and *A-5*. But only *L-4* (Capt 3rd Class Polyakov) is able to torpedo the tanker *Friederike-Firuz* (7327 tons) from a convoy. In addition, *Shch-202* (Lt-Cdr Leonov) sinks the lighter *Elbe-5*, *M-35* (Lt-Cdr Prokofev) one barge and *S-33* (Capt 3rd Class Alexeev) one motor yacht. Of the troops embarked on the sunken transports, 8100 cannot be rescued. In all, 130000 German and Rumanian troops are evacuated by sea and 21457 by air between 12 Apl and 13 May. 78000 are left behind as prisoners or dead.

5 May-20 July   Black Sea
German and Rumanian submarines operate against Soviet coastal traffic on the Caucasus coast. In the Northern part *Requinul* has no success in April/May and June/July and *Marsouinul* in May. On 21 May the latter is damaged by depth charges. *U9* (Lt-Cdr Petersen) sinks a fishing cutter on 5 May and the minesweeper *T-411/Zashchitnik* on 11 May with a T-5 and torpedoes a tanker with one patrol vessel on 16 May. *U24* (Lt Landt-Hayen) sinks a patrol vessel on 12 May and perhaps another on 22 May. *U23* (Lt Wahlen) reports one steamer torpedoed, one tanker sunk as well as a fishing cutter and a motor gunboat. *U18* (Lt Arendt) sinks at the end of May/beginning of June a tug and a motor gunboat; *U19* (Lt Ohlenburg) sinks a tug and *U20* (Lt Grafen) the freighter *Pestel* (1850 tons) off Trapezunt on 19 June and four motor boats on 24 June.

6-27 May   Indian Ocean
Operation 'Transom': carrier raid on Soerabaya. On 6 May TF 65 (Adm Somerville) sets out from Trincomalee with the battleships *Queen Elizabeth*, *Valiant* and *Richelieu*, the cruisers *Newcastle*, *Nigeria* and *Tromp* and the destroyers *Rotherham*, *Racehorse*, *Penn*, *Van Galen*, *Napier*, *Nepal*, *Quiberon* and *Quickmatch*; and TF 66 (Vice-Adm Power) from Colombo with the battlecruiser *Renown* (transferred to TF 65 from 7 May), the carriers (Rear-Adm

Moody) *Illustrious* and *Saratoga*, the cruisers *Ceylon* and *Gambia* and the destroyers *Quilliam, Quadrant, Queenborough, Cummings, Dunlap* and *Fanning*. They replenish on 15 May in Exmouth Bay from TF 67, comprising six fleet tankers, one water tanker and, as escort, the cruisers *London* and *Suffolk*, which went on ahead from Trincomalee on 30 Apl. The cruisers join TF 66 from 14 May. Early on 17 May, S of Java, 45 Avenger and Dauntless dive-bombers, escorted by 40 Hellcat and Corsair fighters, fly off from both carriers to attack the harbour and oil refineries at Soerabaya. 12 aircraft are destroyed on the ground and one Allied plane is lost. The damage inflicted on the harbour installations and ships is greatly over-estimated; in fact, only one freighter of 993 tons is sunk. On 18 May *Saratoga* and the three US destroyers leave the force; the remainder return to Ceylon which they reach on 27 May.

In May in the Straits of Malacca the British submarines *Tantalus* (Lt-Cdr Mackenzie), *Sea Rover* (Lt Angell) and *Templar* (Lt Ridgeway) each sink one ship of 3165 tons, 1365 tons and 2658 tons respectively. One ship of 1400 tons sinks on mines laid by *Taurus* (Lt-Cdr Wingfield) and one other ship is damaged.

7 May-30 July   North Atlantic
Because of the build-up of the 'Landwirt' U-boat group in France, and 'Mitte' in Norway as a defence against invasion, only a few weather boats operate in the North Atlantic: until the end of May *U736, U955, U385*, then *U853, U534* and *U857* and, at the end of June/beginning of July, the experimental boat for the new AA turret VI, *U673*. In spite of the regular transmission of weather reports, no losses are sustained. *U853, U736* and *U385* make unsuccessful attacks on escorts. *U853* (Lt-Cdr Sommer) beats off attacks on 25 May by three Swordfish aircraft armed with rockets from the merchant aircraft carriers *Ancylus* and *MacKendrick*, but she is repeatedly located by HF/DF and attacked on 17 June by aircraft from the US Escort carrier *Croatan*. Nevertheless, she escapes.
From 20 May to 28 May the schnorkel

boats *U764, U441, U984, U953* and *U269* are formed into the 'Dragoner' group at the mouth of the Channel, N of Ouessant, as an exercise in repelling invasion. It has no success. From 15 June the schnorkel boat *U247* (Lt Matschulat), which sinks one trawler of 200 tons, operates in the Minches and *U719* in the North Channel. Both miss patrol vessels and *U247* misses a battleship with a salvo on 18 June. *U719* is sunk by the destroyer *Bulldog* on 26 June after a long search.

8-28 May   North Sea/English Channel
The French *MTB227, MTB91, MTB239* and *MTB92* attack a German supply convoy for the Channel Islands between Jersey and Guernsey and sink the small steamer *Bizon* (750 tons). *MTB227* is damaged by patrol boats of the 2nd PB Flotilla.
On 11 May British MTBs sink *V1311* off the Hook of Holland.
On 12-13 May the Norwegian *MTB715, MTB627, MTB653* and *MTB688* try unsuccessfully to attack a convoy off the Hook of Holland. The German 5th and 9th MTB Flotillas, comprising *S100, S112, S142, S136, S141* and *S140* and *S146, S145, S130* and *S150*, are involved in engagements when they try to attack off Selsey Bill. The destroyer *Haldon*, the frigate (DE) *Stayner*, the corvette *Gentian* and *MTB96, MTB227, MTB237* and *MTB 246* drive off the German motor torpedo boats. The French destroyer *La Combattante* (Cdr Patou) sinks *S141*; *S100* and *S142* are damaged.
On 16-17 May the 2nd MTB Flotilla, consisting of *S177, S178, S189, S180* and *S179*, lays 20 LMB mines near Hearty Knoll and is then pursued by the destroyer *Quorn*.
On 17-18 May all the German motor torpedo boat flotillas carry out mining operations: the 2nd Flotilla (Cdr Opdenhoff), consisting of *S177, S180, S179, S190, S189* and *S178*, S of Orfordness (20 LMB mines); the 8th Flotilla (Cdr Zymalkowski), consisting of *S64, S87, S127* and *S133* (mines), *S83, S117* and *S67* (torpedoes), near the Sunk Lightship (11 LMBs). The latter is pursued by the British corvette *Sheldrake* and MGBs, including *MGB321*, but arrives in

Ijmuiden without loss. The 4th Flotilla (Lt Fimmen), consisting of *S169, S171, S188, S174, S175, S172* and *S187*, carries out a mining operation against a CW convoy between Folkestone and Dungeness, lays 21 LMB and 14 M-1 mines, avoids on its return British destroyers and MGB groups deployed against it and then has a brief engagement with a German convoy comprising *Von der Gröben*, the 4th MMS Flotilla and KFKs without any damage being done. The 5th Flotilla (Cdr Klug) breaks off the operation with *S100, S112* and *S142* because of a destroyer engagement but with *S136, S138* and *S140* lays 12 LMC mines near Hope Nose (Lyme Bay). The 9th Flotilla (Cdr v. Mirbach), consisting of *S130, S168, S145, S146, S144* and *S150*, breaks through a destroyer group, lays 27 mines in Lyme Bay and, on the return, has another engagement with three destroyers and three MGB groups.

On 18-19 May the 9th Flotilla makes a reconnaissance sortie from Cherbourg to Le Havre and has a brief engagement with the SGBs *Grey Owl* and *Grey Wolf*. In the night 19-20 May the 5th Flotilla (see above) lays 10 BMC and 12 UMB mines near Start Point. On the return the flotilla is involved in a short engagement with the German patrol boats *V210* and *V208*, which are going to the help of *V205*. The latter is rescuing survivors from *V211*, sunk by *MTB90*, near Guernsey.

The 2nd Flotilla breaks off a mining operation near Smith's Knoll because of mist. The 8th Flotilla (see above) lays 12 UMB and 16 M-1 mines and six protective floats near Orfordness. The trawler *Wyoming* (302 tons) and the minesweeper *MMS227* sink on the barrages. On the return British Swordfish aircraft attack off Ostend; *S87* catches fire and sinks when being towed by *S83*.

The transfer of the torpedo boats *Jaguar* and *T24* from Brest to Cherbourg is abandoned when the latter hits a ground mine. *Jaguar* arrives in Cherbourg on 23 May and in the following night proceeds with *Kondor, Greif, Falke* and *Möwe* and the 6th MS Flotilla to Le Havre. On the way *Greif*

sinks after fighter bomber attacks and *Kondor* and *M84* are brought in badly damaged by ground mines. In the night 22-23 May the 5th MTB Flotilla with five boats (without *S136*) lays 20 UMB mines S of the Isle of Wight.

In the night 23-24 May the 9th MTB Flotilla breaks off a mining operation from Le Havre in the direction of the British South Coast because of the weather. The 5th Flotilla with five boats carries out a mining operation off Brighton but only drops eight UMB mines because of destroyer attacks. *S112* is hit by *Vanquisher* from the escort of convoy WP.526. In the night 27-28 May the 9th Flotilla with six boats lays 24 mines on the coastal route W of Beachy Head and the 5th Flotilla with five boats 20 UMB mines S of the Isle of Wight. Attacks by Beaufighter bombers and destroyers are unsuccessful.

9-11 May   Mediterranean

On 9 May the convoy UGS.40 with 65 ships passes through the Straits of Gibraltar. Escort: TF 60 (Cdr Sowell, USCG) with the USCG cutter *Campbell*, the US destroyers *Dallas, Bernadou, Ellis, Benson*, the US DEs *Evarts, Dobler, Decker, Smartt, Wyffels, Walter S. Scott, Brown* and *Wilhoite*. In addition, there are the British AA cruiser *Caledon*, the French DE *Tunisien*, the French PC submarine-chaser *Cimeterre* and the JIG ships, the US minesweepers *Sustain* and *Steady*. *U967* and *U616* do not get to the convoy. On the evening of 11 May 62 aircraft of I and III/K.G. 26 are deployed against the convoy. British Beaufighters flying from Sardinia intercept some of the attackers and lose two aircraft; the remainder attack in four waves in the area of Cape Bengut. The pilots believe that they have sunk a destroyer and seven freighters and damaged many others. In fact, no ship is hit and 19 aircraft are lost.

9 May-18 June   Mediterranean/ Tyrrhenian Sea

From 9 May to 17 May the French submarines *La Sultane* and *Curie* and the British *Ultor* make several attacks in which only some small ships are damaged. From the end of May/ beginning of June *Upstart* (Lt Chapman) sinks one ship of 2954 tons; *Universal* (Lt Gordon) *SG15*; *Untiring* (Lt Boyd) *UJ6078*; *Ultor* (Lt Hunt) *SG11* and five small craft; and the French *Casabianca* (Lt Bellet) a small submarine-chaser.

From 11 May to 28 May the German 10th TB Flotilla, consisting of *TA24*, *TA29* and *TA30*, carries out four mining operations ('Languste', 'Angel', 'Haken' and 'Widerhaken') and two reconnaissance sorties in the Ligurian Sea. On 24 May a US group, comprising *PT202*, *PT213* and *PT218*, attacks a German force and sinks *UJ2223*. *UJ2222* reaches Livorno badly damaged. On 27-28 May US PT boats sink *UJ2210*. In an engagement on the Ligurian Coast between *TA29* and *TA30* and *PT304*, *PT306* and *PT307* on 31 May both sides sustain light damage. From 2 June to 14 June two boats from *TA24*, *TA26*, *TA27* and *TA30* undertake, in turn, the mining operations 'Gemse', 'Brosche', 'Tor' and 'Weide'; in the process *TA27* is sunk by fighter bombers in Portoferraio on 9 June. The torpedo boats *TA26* and *TA30* sink on 15-16 June, in the mining operation 'Nadel', when they are attacked by *PT558*, *PT552* and *PT559*. On 17-18 June *TA29* and *TA24*, while laying the mine barrage 'Stein', are involved in an engagement with the US *PT207* and the British *MTB633*, *MTB640*, *MTB655* and *MGB658*. The German hospital ship *Erlangen*, which set out on 15 June to give aid, is set on fire by Allied aircraft and has to be beached near Sestri Levante.

U230 (Lt-Cdr Siegmann) sinks the US submarine-chaser *PC558* off Palermo.

11-29 May Arctic
Soviet combined operation RV-4 against German convoy traffic off the Polar Coast.

After a convoy is located by a Pe-2 reconnaissance plane off Svaerholt six Il-4 torpedo aircraft of the 9th Guards Mining & Torpedo Air Regt with five fighters attack on 11 May off Makkaur and a force of five Boston torpedo aircraft, six bombers and ten fighters off Kongsfjord and sink *V6113*.

On 13 May and 14 May Soviet air formations carry out ten attacks in 217 sorties on shipping targets in Kirkenes.

The steamers *Pernambuco* (4121 tons) and *Patagonia* (5898 tons) are set on fire, *UJ1210* is damaged and a minesweeper and a patrol boat are lightly hit. German Me 109s and AA guns shoot down at least six aircraft. On 25-26 May there is a combined attack on the German east-bound convoy with GB K-1. There are air torpedo and bomb attacks in ten waves with fighter cover in the course of which the steamer *Solviken* (3502 tons) is sunk by torpedo and *Herta Engeline Fritzen* (3672 tons) gets a bomb hit in the bow. The submarines *S-15*, *S-56*, *S-103*, and *M-201* are deployed. *M-201* (Lt-Cdr Balin) misses the convoy off Makkaur; shortly afterwards *S-15* (Lt-Cdr Vasilev) also misses. She survives a concentrated pursuit with depth charges from the submarine-chasers *UJ1209*, *UJ1212* and *UJ1219*.

On 29 May *S-103* (Capt 3rd Class Nechaev) attacks two German minesweepers off Laksfjord without success.

11 May-12 June Pacific
Japanese preparations for operation A-GO (defence of the Marianas line). On 11 May and 12 May elements of the 1st Mobile Fleet (Vice-Adm Ozawa) set out in two groups from Lingga Bay, where the 1st Carrier Sqdn has trained its pilots, for Tawi-Tawi. They arrive there on 15 May and join up on 16 May with the elements which set out from Japan on 12 May, the 2nd and 3rd Carrier Sqdns, the *Musashi* and other units.

Vice-Adm Ozawa then disposes of the 2nd Fleet with the 1st Battle Sqdn (Vice-Adm Ugaki) and the 3rd Battle Sqdn (Vice-Adm Suzuki), comprising the battleships *Yamato*, *Musashi*, *Nagato*, *Kongo*, *Haruna* and *Fuso*, the 4th (Vice-Adm Kurita), the 5th (Rear-Adm Hashimoto) and the 7th Cruiser Sqdns, consisting of the heavy cruisers *Atago*, *Takao*, *Maya*, *Chokai*, *Haguro*, *Myoko*, *Kumano*, *Suzuya*, *Tone*, *Chikuma* and *Mogami*, the 2nd DD Flotilla (Rear-Adm Hayakawa), consisting of the cruiser *Noshiro*, the 27th DD Div with the destroyers *Harusame*, *Shiratsuyu*, *Shigure* and *Samidare*, the 31st DD Div with *Okinami*, *Kishinami*, *Naganami* and *Asashimo* and the 32nd DD Div with *Tamanami*, *Hamanami*, *Fujinami* and

Hayanami and the attached *Shimakaze*. In addition, there is the 3rd Fleet with the 1st Carrier Sqdn (Ozawa), comprising *Taiho*, *Zuikaku* and *Shokaku*, the 2nd Carrier Sqdn (Rear-Adm Joshima), comprising *Junyo*, *Hiyo* and *Ryuho*, the 3rd Carrier Sqdn (Rear-Adm Obayashi), comprising *Chitose*, *Chiyoda* and *Zuiho* and the 10th DD Flotilla (Rear-Adm Kimura), consisting of the cruiser *Yahagi*, the 61st DD Div with the destroyers *Akizuki*, *Hatsuzuki*, *Wakatsuki* and *Shimotsuki*, the 4th DD Div with *Michishio*, *Nowake* and *Yamagumo*, the 10th DD Div with *Akigumo*, *Kazegumo* and *Asagumo* and the 17th DD Div with *Urakaze*, *Isokaze*, *Tanikaze*, *Hamakaze* and *Yukikaze*. There are also attached: *Minazuki*, *Hayashimo* and *Akishimo* (the latter joins later). The 1st and 2nd Supply Groups consist of nine tankers and the destroyers *Hibiki*, *Hatsushimo*, *Yunagi*, *Uzuki* and *Tsuga*.

Losses are sustained as a result of US submarine attacks when the ships exercise in the waters around Tawi-Tawi. On 22 May *Bonefish* reports the Fleet and hits the *Chitose* with two unexploded torpedoes. On 24 May *Gurnard* sinks the tanker *Tatekawa Maru*, on 3 June *Puffer* the tankers *Takasaki* and *Ashizuri* and on 6-7 June *Harder* (Cdr Dealey) the destroyers *Minazuki* and *Hayanami* and, on 8 June, also the *Tanikaze*. In the operations 'Kon' the *Kazegumo* is sunk on 3 June by the submarine *Hake* and *Harusame* on 8 June in an air attack.

16-31 May   Norway
Air offensive by No 18 Group RAF Coastal Command on the U-boats setting out for the Atlantic from Norway. Sunderlands of No 330 Sqdn (Norwegian) and No 4 OTU (Operational Training Unit) RAF, Catalinas of No 210 Sqdn RAF and Liberators of No 59 Sqdn RAF sight U-boats 22 times and make 13 attacks. They sink the outward-bound *U240*, *U241*, *U675* and *U292* and compel *U862* and *U958* to return. In addition, *U476*, which is proceeding to northern Norway, shoots down a Sunderland, but is herself so badly damaged that she has to be sunk by *U990* after the crew has been taken off. This boat, too, is sunk off Trond-

heim. *V5901* rescues 51 survivors from both boats. In this period only the mining U-boat *U233* and the schnorkel boats *U719*, *U767*, *U1191*, *U988*, *U671*, *U987* and *U247* get through to the Atlantic.

14-19 May   Mediterranean
U616 (Lt Koitschka) torpedoes two ships of 17854 tons from the convoy GUS.39 off Cape Tenes on 14 May. Whilst two British escorts keep the boat under water and aircraft of No 36 Sqdn RAF circle round the area, two US destroyer groups (Capt Converse), consisting of *Nields*, *Gleaves* and *Macomb* and *Ellyson*, *Hilary P. Jones*, *Hambleton*, *Rodman* and *Emmons*, set out from Oran. After a first depth charge attack from *Ellyson* in the night 14-15 May, contact is lost for the whole of 15 May; only in the following night does a Wellington locate the surfaced U-boat and bring the destroyers up which sink her in the morning.

In passing through the Straits of Gibraltar, *U731* is located on 15 May by two MAD Catalinas of USN-VP.63 and sunk by the submarine-chasers *Kilmarnock* and *Blackfly*. *U960* (Lt Heinrich), which has also broken through the Straits, attacks on 17 May the US destroyers returning from the search for *U616* and misses *Ellyson* with a salvo of three torpedoes. She is pursued by the newly-deployed US destroyer group, consisting of *Woolsey*, *Benson*, *Madison*, *Niblack* and *Ludlow*, and sunk with the co-operation of aircraft in the night 18-19 May.

15-27 May   Central Pacific
US TG 58.2 (Rear-Adm Montgomery), comprising the carriers *Essex*, *Wasp* and *San Jacinto*, the cruisers *Baltimore*, *Boston*, *Canberra*, *San Diego* and *Reno*, twelve destroyers, three escort destroyers and two tankers, sets out from Majuro on 14 May and carries out heavy carrier raids on Marcus Island on 19 May and 20 May and on Wake on 23 May.

17-18 May   South-west Pacific
On 17 May an amphibious group (Capt Noble), with 14 destroyers, six escort destroyers, two APAs, seven LSTs, 15 LCIs and five SCs, lands the 163rd RCT (Brig-Gen Doe, 7000 men) near Arara and, on the following day, on the outlying island of Wakde in order to

seize the airfield there. Support is provided by TF 74 (Rear-Adm Crutchley) and TF 75 (Rear-Adm Berkey) (for composition see 22 Apl under Hollandia operation, except *Trathen* instead of the destroyer *Bush*). US losses: 110 men. Japanese defenders: 759 men and one prisoner.

17-26 May   Central Pacific
Destroyers of the US 5th Fleet shell the island of Engebi in the Maloelap Atoll on 17 May, Wotje on 22 May and Mili in the Marshall Islands on 26 May.

17 May-3 Aug   Atlantic
In operations S of Nova Scotia *U1222* (Lt-Cdr Bielfeld) and *U107* (Lt-Cdr Simmermacher) make several unsuccessful attacks on convoys and escorts in May and June.

In the area of the Azores US Task Groups operate against suspected U-boat suppliers. *U549* (Lt-Cdr Krankenhagen), which is on the way to Brazil, is sighted on 28 May by an aircraft of TG 22.1 (Capt Hughes), consisting of *Block Island* and five DEs, but she is able to sink the carrier on 29 May with three torpedo hits, hit the DE *Barr* with a T-5 and just miss the DE *Eugene E. Elmore* with a T-5. While the DE *Ahrens* rescues survivors, *U549* is sunk by the DEs *Eugene E. Elmore* and *Robert I. Paine*. The relieving TG 22.3 (Capt Gallery), consisting of *Guadalcanal* and the DEs *Chatelain, Pillsbury, Pope, Flaherty* and *Jenks*, after obtaining an HF/DF bearing on 1 June, looks for the homeward-bound *U505*. The latter is forced to surface by depth charges from *Chatelain* on 4 June and, the crew having come off, she is taken over by a boarding party (Lt David) from the *Pillsbury*. The Group brings the boat to Bermuda on 19 June with her important booty of codes. Throughout June until the beginning of July the operation of the schnorkel U-boat *U543* (Lt-Cdr Hellriegel) off Freetown meets with no success. *U547* (Lt Niemeyer) sinks the A/S trawler *Birdlip* and a ship from a convoy off Liberia on 14 June and another ship on 2 July making a total of 8371 tons. From the beginning of June until the middle of July U-boats operate in the Caribbean: *U539* (Lt-Cdr Lauterbach-Emden) and *U516* (Lt-Cdr Tillessen) each sink one ship of 1517

tons and 9887 tons respectively and each torpedo one ship of 10195 tons and 4756 tons respectively. In addition, *U539* slightly damages two tankers with near-explosions and escapes from the *Card* and *Guadalcanal* Carrier Groups, sent to search for them in the Caribbean, both of which are sighted. The schnorkel boat *U530* has no success off Trinidad from the middle of June. TG 22.5 (Capt Vest), which relieves TG 22.3 in the area of the Azores and consists of *Croatan* and the DEs *Barber, Swasey, Snowden, Frost, Huse* and *Inch*, is directed to a HF/DF location on 10 June and the three last-named DEs sink the remaining U-tanker, *U490*, on 11 June before she is able to refuel a U-boat. The relieving TG 22.2 (Capt Vosseller), comprising *Bogue* and the DEs *Haverfield, Janssen, Willis, Francis M. Robinson* and *Wilhoite*, searches for *U530* from 15 June, which has reported by radio having handed over search receiver equipment to the Japanese transport submarine *I-52* (Cdr Uno). On 23-24 June *I-52* is sunk by two Avengers from the *Bogue* with the help of Sonobuoys.

On 2 July aircraft from TG 22.4 (Capt Tague), comprising *Wake Island* and the DEs *Douglas L. Howard, Fiske, Farquhar, J.R.Y. Blakely* and *Hill*, sink the homeward-bound *U543* E of the Azores in spite of strong AA fire. Further to the N the outward-bound *U154* falls victim to the DEs *Frost* and *Inch* of TG 22.5. The minelayer *U233* is sunk off Halifax on 5 July by the DEs *Baker* and *Thomas* of TG 22.10, comprising the *Card* and the other DEs *Bronstein, Breeman* and *Bostwick*.

On the way to East Asia *U860* (Cdr* Büchel) is sunk on 15 June by seven aircraft of US TG 41.6 (Capt Crist), including the escort carrier *Solomons*, after she has shot down two machines. *U861* (Cdr Oesten), which follows, proceeds to the Brazilian coast but does not sight the first contingent of the Brazilian Expeditionary Force leaving Rio de Janeiro for Italy on 2 July on the US troop transport *General William A. Mann* with the Brazilian destroyers *Marcilio Dias, Mariz e Barros* and *Greenhalgh*. On 20 July she sinks the Brazilian transport *Vital de Oliveira*

(1737 tons) and misses the submarine-chaser *Javari*. On 24 July she sinks a steamer of 7176 tons from the convoy JT.39 and escapes the search made by TG 41.6, comprising *Solomons* and the DEs *Trumpeter*, *Straub*, *Gustafson* and *Alger*, as well as *Greenhalgh* and *Mariz e Barros*. *U862* (Cdr Timm) sinks one ship of 6885 tons on 25 July.

17 May-23 Sept   Indian Ocean
In May the Japanese transport submarine *I-52* passes through the Indian Ocean on her way to Europe and at the beginning of June the damaged *U843* on her way to Penang. The Japanese *I-166* lands agents in Ceylon at the end of May and *I-165* cruises NW of Australia in June without success. *U183* (Lt-Cdr Schneewind), coming from Penang, sinks a ship of 5259 tons on 5 June NE of the Chagos Archipelago and replenishes *U537* (Lt-Cdr Schrewe) on her way from France on 25 June. The latter misses a tanker on 8 July and is hunted for several days by the destroyers *Racehorse* and *Raider*. The Japanese *I-8* (Capt Ariizumi) sinks two ships totalling 14118 tons near the Chagos Archipelago on 29 June and 2 July; in the process the survivors of the *Jean Nicolet* are murdered.
From the end of June German Type IX-D2 boats arrive in the Indian Ocean from the Atlantic. Of them, *U181* (Cdr* Freiwald) sinks three ships of 19557 tons in the Arabian Sea and is hunted in vain by aircraft and the Indian sloop *Sutlej* on 15 July. *U196* (Lt-Cdr Kentrat) sinks a ship of 7118 tons near the Laccadives. *U198* (Lt Heusinger v. Waldegg) sinks four ships of 22912 tons SE of Africa and Madagascar. From 4 July to 6 July she is hunted together with *U859* by South African aircraft, the British destroyer *Pathfinder* and a South African A/S trawler group. One Ventura aircraft is shot down. Following two sinkings on 6-7 Aug a submarine-hunting group, consisting of the escort carriers *Begum* and *Shah* and the frigates *Findhorn*, *Inver*, *Lossie* and *Parret*, is deployed. On 10 Aug an Avenger from the *Shah* attacks *U198*. On 12 Aug Catalina aircraft and aircraft from the *Shah* bring up the Indian sloop *Godavari* and the *Findhorn* and *Parret*, which sink *U198* with hedgehog. *U859*

(Lt-Cdr Jebsen), after being pursued on 22-23 Aug by aircraft, the sloop *Banff* and the frigate *Tay*, proceeds to the Gulf of Aden. There she sinks two ships of 14598 tons and evades the carrier submarine-hunter group on 2 Sept.
The homeward and outward-bound U-boats are frequently attacked by British submarines in the Straits of Malacca. On 20 June *Storm* and on 16 July *Templar* miss *U1062* which sets out twice to return to France. On 17 July *Tantalus* misses the outward-bound Japanese *I-166* which is shortly afterwards sunk by *Telemachus* (Cdr King). The Japanese transport submarine *I-29* arrives in Penang from France on 14 July, but when she continues her journey from Singapore she is sunk on 26 July by the US submarine *Sawfish* (Lt-Cdr Bannister). On 7 Aug *Stratagem* misses the returning *U181* and on 23 Sept *Trenchant* sinks *U859* as she arrives off Penang.
In the middle of August *U862* (Cdr Timm) and *U861* (Cdr Oesten) arrive in the area SE of South Africa and Madagascar. *U862* sinks four ships of 21134 tons and on 20 Aug shoots down a Catalina of No 265 Sqdn RAF. She evades the carrier submarine-hunter group. *U861* sinks one ship of 7464 tons and torpedoes one ship of 8139 tons on 20 Aug from the convoy DN.68, escorted by three A/S trawlers. She also sinks another ship of 5670 tons on 5 Sept.

19-31 May   Pacific
On a transport mission to Buin (Solomons) the Japanese submarine *I-16* is found on 19 May by a US destroyer escort group, consisting of *George*, *Raby* and *England*, which has just set out, and she is sunk by a hedgehog salvo. As it proceeds to the area NW of New Ireland the group encounters a concentration of Japanese submarines designed to operate against Allied naval operations on the coast of New Guinea. It consists of the submarine cruisers *I-44* and *I-53* and the submarines *Ro-106*, *Ro-104*, *Ro-105*, *Ro-116*, *Ro-109*, *Ro-112*, *Ro-108*, *Ro-113*, *Ro-117* and *Ro-111*. *England* (Lt-Cdr Pendleton) sinks with hedgehog salvoes *Ro-106* on 22 May, *Ro-104* on 23 May, *Ro-116* on 24 May, *Ro-108* on 26 May and

Ro-105 on 31 May. With six submarines sunk in 12 days this is the most successful submarine-hunting operation by a single ship in the Second World War.

25 May-13 June South West Pacific
On 25 May the VII Amphibious Force (TF 77, Rear-Adm Fechteler on the destroyer *Sampson*) sets out from Hollandia with eight LSTs, eight LCTs in tow, 63 LVTs and 25 DUKWs as well as 15 LCIs with the first four attack waves of the 41st US Inf Div (Maj-Gen Fuller). The plan is to land them on the South Coast of Biak on 27 May. Escort: eight destroyers. Cover and support are provided by TF 74 (TG 77.2, Rear-Adm Crutchley), comprising the Australian cruisers *Australia* and *Shropshire* and the destroyers *Arunta* and *Warramuga* and USS *Mullany* and *Ammen* and by TF 75 (TG 77.3, Rear-Adm Berkey) comprising the US cruisers *Phoenix*, *Boise* and *Nashville* and the destroyers *Hutchins*, *Daly*, *Beale*, *Bache*, *Trathen* and *Abner Read*. The approximately 10000 Japanese defenders (Col Kuzume) put up strong resistance. The Japanese attempt their reinforcement operation 'Kon'. Rear-Adm Sakonju, with the cruisers *Aoba* and *Kinu* and the destroyers *Shikinami*, *Uranami* and *Shigure*, takes 700 men on board in Zamboanga on 31 May and from Tawi-Tawi a covering force, consisting of the battleship *Fuso*, the cruisers *Myoko* and *Haguro* and five destroyers, proceeds to Davao. A third force, made up of the minelayers *Itsukushima* and *Tsugaru* and *LST127*, is to bring another 800 troops to Biak. On 2 June the forces put to sea but they are found by American reconnaissance planes and return on 3 June. The US submarine *Hake* sinks the destroyer *Kazegumo* off Davao. On 3 June Japanese aircraft of the 23rd Naval Air Flotilla (Rear-Adm Ito) try to attack US ships but the destroyers *Reid*, *Mustin* and *Russell* beat off the attackers. A second attempt to bring 600 troops to Biak is made by Adm Sakonju with the destroyers *Shikinami*, *Uranami*, and *Shigure*, escorted by the destroyers *Harusame*, *Shiratsuyu*, and *Samidare*. Cover is provided by the cruisers *Aoba* and *Kinu* near Vogelkop. US air reconnaissance finds the Japanese force,

whereupon Rear-Adm Crutchley with the cruisers *Australia*, *Phoenix*, *Boise*, the US Desdivs 42, 47 and 48, comprising *Fletcher*, *Jenkins*, *Radford*, *La Valette*, *Hutchins*, *Dale*, *Beale*, *Bache*, *Abner Read*, *Mullany*, *Trathen* and the Australian *Arunta* and *Warramunga*, are deployed against it. *Harusame* is sunk by US bombers. In an engagement in which the US destroyers try to catch the Japanese as they retire, *Shiratsuyu* is damaged but escapes. A third Japanese attempt to bring reinforcements to Biak is abandoned on the way because of the start of the US Marianas operation (12 June) and the ships are ordered to take part in the operation A-GO. This third attempt comprises two transport groups (A: Rear-Adm Sakonju with the cruisers *Aoba* and *Kinu* and the destroyers *Shikinami*, *Uranami*, *Yamagumo* and *Nowake*; and B: the minelayers *Itsukushima* and *Tsugaru*, one LST, freighters and submarine-chasers) with cover from a Task Force (Vice-Adm Ugaki), composed of the battleships *Yamato* and *Musashi*, the cruisers *Myoko*, *Haguro* and *Noshiro* and the destroyers *Shimakaze*, *Okinami* and *Asagumo*.

30-31 May Mediterranean
Aircraft of the 2nd Fl. Div, operating from Southern France, attack the Allied convoy UGS.42 in the Western Mediterranean and sink the British freighter *Nordeflinge* (2873 tons).

1-23 June Mediterranean/Aegean
On 1 June 17 Baltimores, 12 Marauders and 24 Beaufighters, escorted by 13 Spitfires and four Mustangs attack a German supply convoy of three freighters N of Crete proceeding to the island. The escort consists of the 9th TB Flotilla (Cdr* Dominik) with *TA16*, *TA17*, *TA14* and *TA19*, the 21st SC Flotilla (Cdr Dr Brandt) with four submarine-chasers and three motor minesweepers and air escort from one Ar 196 and six Ju 88s. The freighter *Sabine* (2252 tons), *UJ2101* and *UJ2105* sink after bomb hits; the freighter *Gertrud* (1960 tons), *R211* and *TA16* reach Heraklion damaged and there on 2 June the torpedo boat is destroyed by an explosion on the *Gertrud*. On the return, the third steamer, *Tanais* (1545 tons), is sunk on 9 June by the British

submarine *Vivid* (Lt Varley). After this disaster contact with Crete is only maintained by small craft sailing individually.

The British submarine *Unsparing* (Lt Piper) sinks *UJ2106* and the ferry *SF284*, and the *Vampire* (Lt Taylor) three sailing ships. Three more sailing ships are damaged.

1-30 June   Pacific
The following sinkings are made by US submarines arriving in their operational areas in June: off Japan, Formosa and the Kuriles *Archerfish* (Lt-Cdr Wright) sinks the corvette *Kaibokan 24*; *Bang* (Lt-Cdr Gallaher) torpedoes two ships; *Batfish* (Lt-Cdr Fyfe) sinks three ships of 1251 tons; *Flier* (Lt-Cdr Crowley) sinks one ship of 10330 tons and torpedoes one ship; *Grouper* (Lt-Cdr Walling) sinks one ship of 2857 tons; *Growler* (Lt-Cdr Schade) one ship of 1923 tons; *Pintado* (Lt-Cdr Clarey) three ships of 13193 tons; *Plaice* (Lt-Cdr Stevens) two ships of 1843 tons; *Seahorse* (Lt-Cdr Cutter) sinks five ships of 17556 tons and torpedoes one ship; *Sealion* (Lt-Cdr Reich) sinks four ships of 7759 tons; *Spearfish* (Lt-Cdr Williams) sinks one ship of 2510 tons and torpedoes one ship; *Swordfish* (Lt-Cdr Montross) sinks one ship of 4804 tons and the destroyer *Hatsukaze*; *Sturgeon* (Lt-Cdr Murphy) two ships of 13951 tons; *Tang* (Lt-Cdr O'Kane) ten ships of 39159 tons; *Whale* (Lt-Cdr Grady) torpedoes one ship. In the area of the Mandate Islands *Bream* (Lt-Cdr Chapple) sinks one ship of 5704 tons and torpedoes one ship; *Shark* (Lt-Cdr Blakely) sinks four ships 21672 tons. In the area of the Malayan Archipelago and the Philippines *Bashaw* (Lt-Cdr Nichols) torpedoes one ship; *Bluefish* (Lt-Cdr Henderson) sinks two ships of 4734 tons; *Darter* (Lt-Cdr Stovall) the fast minelayer *Tsugaru*; *Flasher* (Lt-Cdr Whitaker) four ships of 23582 tons and the cruiser *Oi* and torpedoes two more ships; *Flounder* (Lt-Cdr Stevens) one ship of 2681 tons; *Jack* (Lt-Cdr Krapf) three ships of 15745 tons; *Pargo* (Lt-Cdr Eddy) one ship of 5236 tons and the corvette *Kaibokan 10*; and *Redfin* (Lt-Cdr Austin) two ships of 8169 tons.

1 June-31 Dec   North Sea/Baltic
Air-mining offensive by the RAF against German shipping routes in the North Sea, the Skagerrak, the Kattegat and in the western and southern parts of the Baltic. In a total of 1900 sorties, 1778 mines are laid in June, 708 in July, 1586 in August, 748 in September, 1133 in October, 750 in November and 1160 in December. Thirty-six aircraft are lost. In all, 124 ships totalling 74545 tons sink on the mines and 66 totalling 100915 tons are damaged.

3 June   Arctic/Greenland
A German transport aircraft of the type Ju 290 brings back the 'Bassgeiger' weather station (26 men) operating in Greenland since August 1943.

3 June-18 July   Norway
Continuation of the air offensive by No 18 Group RAF Coastal Command against U-boats off Norway, using Cansos of No 162 Sqdn RCAF, Catalinas of No 210 Sqdn RAF, Liberators of No 86 Sqdn RAF, Fortresses of No 206 Sqdn RAF and Beaufighters of No 333 Sqdn (Norwegian). On 3 June No 162 Sqdn RCAF sinks the schnorkel boat *U477*.

On 6 June the outward-bound non-schnorkel boats, *U294*, *U290*, *U958*, *U980* and *U1000*, are stopped. On 8 June and 10 June the boats of the 'Mitte' group (*U276*, *U397*, *U975*, *U242*, *U999*, *U677*, *U1001*, *U998*, *U1007*, *U982*, *U987*, *U745* and *U1156*) set out to form a defensive concentration off Norway. On 20-21 June there come as reliefs *U396*, *U994*, *U771*, *U317* and *U1192* and on 5 July *U319*, *U286* and *U299*. Aircraft sink the schnorkel boats *U715*, *U423*, *U1225* and *U478* which are proceeding to the Atlantic and damage *U804* and *U865*. Of the Norway boats, *U980*, *U317*, *U347*, *U361* and *U742* are sunk and *U998*, *U396*, *U299*, *U994* and *U286* are damaged. The British submarine *Satyr* (Lt Weston) sinks *U987*. On 16 July the last boats, *U1163* and *U295*, are recalled.

6 June   English Channel
Operation 'Neptune' (amphibious phase of the operation 'Overlord'): the major Allied landing in Normandy. Overall command: Supreme Commander SHAEF, Gen Eisenhower; land forces 21st Army Group, Gen Montgomery;

Naval Forces Adm Ramsay; co-ordination of air forces, Air-Chief Marshal Tedder.

After heavy air attacks (3467 heavy bombers, 1645 medium, light and torpedo bombers, 5409 fighters—and 2316 transport aircraft are deployed) the 82nd and 101st US Airborne Divs land on the southern part of the Cotentin Peninsula and the British 6th Airborne Div SE of Caen by parachute. In the morning, supported by strong naval forces, there follow by sea the 4th US Inf Div on the East Coast of the Cotentin Peninsula ('Utah'), the 1st US Inf Div near Vierville ('Omaha') the 50th British Inf Div near Arromanches ('Gold'), the 3rd Canadian Inf Div near Courseulles ('Juno') and the 3rd British Div near Lyon-sur-Mer ('Sword'). Forces deployed: 'Western Naval Task Force' (Rear-Adm Kirk on the US cruiser *Augusta*) with the 1st US Army (Lt-Gen Bradley). First, 102 US, British and Allied minesweepers clear the approaches with 16 buoy-layers. In the night Force U (Rear-Adm Moon on the headquarters ship *Bayfield*, VII US Corps, Lt-Gen Collins) with the 4th US Inf Div (Maj-Gen Barton) on the convoys U.2A, U.2B, U.1, U.3, U.3C, U.4, U.5A and U.5B and Force O (Rear-Adm Hall on the headquarters ship *Ancon*, V US Corps, Lt-Gen Gerow) with the 29th Inf Div (Maj-Gen Huebner) on the convoys O.2A, O.2B, O.1, O.3, O.3C, O.4A, O.4B and O.5 approach. The convoys for 'Utah' and 'Omaha' consist of 16 attack transports, one LSD, 106 LSTs, one LSR, 15 LCCs, 93 LCIs, 350 LCTs, 34 LCSs, 94 LCAs, 189 LCVPs, 38 LCS(S)s, 54 LCPs and, for fire support, nine LCGs, 11 LCFs, 14 LCT(R)s, two LCS(M)s and 36 LCS(S)s.

Support Force for 'Utah': Force A (Rear-Adm Deyo), comprising the US battleship *Nevada*, the British monitor *Erebus*, the US cruisers *Tuscaloosa* and *Quincy*, the British cruisers *Hawkins*, *Black Prince* and *Enterprise*, the Dutch gunboat *Soemba*, the US destroyers *Hobson*, *Fitch*, *Forrest*, *Corry* (Desdiv 20), *Butler Shubrick*, *Herndon*, *Gherardi* (Desdiv 34) and the DEs *Bates* and *Rich*. Support force for 'Omaha': Force C (Rear-Adm Bryant), comprising the US

battleships *Texas* and *Arkansas*, the British cruiser *Glasgow*, the French cruisers *Montcalm* and *Georges Leygues*, the US destroyers *McCook*, *Carmick*, *Doyle*, *Baldwin*, *Harding*, *Satterlee*, *Thompson* (Desron 18) *Emmons* and the British 'Hunt' destroyers *Melbreak*, *Tanatside* and *Talybont*.

As escorts for the approaching 'U and O' convoys, the US destroyers *Jeffers*, *Glennon* (Desron 17), *Barton*, *O'Brien*, *Walke*, *Laffey*, *Meredith* (Desron 60) and the French corvettes *Aconit* and *Renoncule*; and the US destroyers *Frankford*, *Nelson*, *Murphy*, *Plunkett* (Desron 33), the British destroyers *Vesper* and *Vidette*, the US DEs *Borum*, *Amesbury* and *Blessman* and the French frigates *L'Aventure* and *L'Escarmouche* are respectively deployed.

The British battleship *Nelson*, the British cruiser *Bellona*, the US destroyers *Somers*, *Davis* and *Jouett* (Desdiv 18) and the French frigates *La Surprise* and *La Découverte* are available as a reserve for the 'Western Task Force'.

On 6 June 23250 troops are landed in the 'Utah' and 34250 troops in the 'Omaha' sectors.

'Eastern Naval Task Force' (Rear-Adm Vian on the British cruiser *Scylla*) with the 2nd British Army (Lt-Gen Dempsey). First, 102 British and Canadian minesweepers with 27 buoy-layers clear the approaches. In the night Force G (Commodore Douglas-Pennant on the headquarters ship *Bulolo*), XXX British Corps (Lt-Gen Bucknall) with the 50th British Div on the convoys G.1 to G.13; Force J (Commodore Oliver on the headquarters ship *Hilary*) with the 3rd Canadian Div on the convoys J.1 to J.13; and Force S (Rear-Adm Talbot on the headquarters ship *Largs*), British I Corps (Lt-Gen Crocker) with the British 3rd Inf Div on the convoys S.1 to S.8 approach. The convoys for 'Gold', 'Juno' and 'Sword' consist of 37 LSIs, 130 LSTs, two LSRs, one LSD, 11 LCCs, 116 LCIs, 39 LCI(S)s, 487 LCTs, 66 LCSs, 408 LCAs, 73 LCS(S)s, 90 LCPs and 10 LCP(S)s. In addition, for fire support: 16 LCG(L)s, 22 LCT(R)s, 14 LCS(L)s, 24 LCS(M)s, 18 LCFs, 45 LCA(H)s and 103 LCTs with armament.

Support force for 'Gold': Force K (Capt

Longley-Cook), comprising the British cruisers *Argonaut*, *Orion*, *Ajax* and *Emerald*, the Dutch gunboat *Flores*, the British destroyers (25th Flotilla) *Grenville*, *Ulster*, *Ulysses*, *Undaunted*, *Undine*, *Urania*, *Urchin*, *Ursa* and *Jervis* and the British 'Hunt' destroyers *Cattistock*, *Cottesmore*, *Pytchley* and *Krakowiak* (Polish).

Support force for 'Juno': Force E (Rear-Adm Dalrymple-Hamilton) comprising the British cruisers *Belfast* and *Diadem* and the British destroyers *Faulknor* (8th Flotilla), *Fury* and *Kempenfelt* (27th Flotilla), *Venus*, *Vigilant*, *Algonquin* (Canadian), *Sioux* (Canadian) and the 'Hunt' destroyers *Stevenstone*, *Bleasdale*, *Glaisdale* (Norwegian) and *La Combattante* (French).

Support force for 'Sword': Force D (Rear-Adm Patterson), comprising the British battleships *Warspite* and *Ramillies*, the monitor *Roberts*, the cruisers *Mauritius*, *Arethusa*, *Frobisher*, *Danae* and *Dragon* (Polish) and the destroyers *Saumarez* (23rd Flotilla), *Scorpion*, *Scourge*, *Serapis*, *Swift*, *Stord* (Norwegian), *Svenner* (Norwegian), *Verulam*, *Virago*, *Kelvin*, and the 'Hunt' destroyers *Slazak* (Polish), *Middleton* and *Eglinton*.

Six destroyers, four sloops, eight frigates, 17 corvettes and 21 trawlers are deployed (British, Canadian, French and Norwegian) to escort the G, J and S convoys.

The British battleship *Rodney* and the cruiser *Sirius* are among the ships which form the reserve for the 'Eastern Task Force'.

On 6 June 24970 troops are landed in the 'Gold' sector, 21400 troops in the 'Juno' and 28845 troops in the 'Sword'. To escort the first follow-up wave Force B (Commodore Edgar), consisting of the US destroyers *Rodman*, *Ellyson* and *Hambleton*, the British destroyers *Boadicea*, *Volunteer* and *Vimy*, the 'Hunt' destroyers *Brissenden* and *Wensleydale*, and the corvettes *Azalea*, *Bluebell* and *Kitchener* (Canadian), is deployed in the W; and in the E Force L (Rear-Adm Parry) comprising the 'Hunt' class destroyer *Cotswold*, the escort destroyer *Vivacious*, the frigates *Chelmer* and *Halsted*, the corvettes *Clematis*, *Godetia*, *Mignonette*, *Narcissus*

and *Oxlip* and three A/S trawlers, 49 LSTs, 19 LCI(L)s and 53 LCT(3)s.

The British 10th DD Flotilla consisting of *Tartar*, *Ashanti*, *Haida* (Canadian), *Huron* (Canadian), *Blyskawica* (Polish), *Piorun* (Polish), *Eskimo* and *Javelin*, a group of frigates and eight groups of coastal forces with MTBs and MGBs, form the covering force against attacks by surface craft in the western entrance to the Channel. In the E the same role is undertaken by the 17th DD Flotilla, consisting of *Onslow*, *Onslaught*, *Offa*, *Oribi*, *Obedient*, *Orwell*, *Isis* and *Impulsive* and seven groups of coastal forces. In addition, the following belong to the escort forces:

Cruisers: *Despatch*, *Ceres* and *Capetown*.

Destroyers: *Kimberley*, *Opportune*, *Pathfinder*, *Beagle*, *Bulldog*, *Icarus*, *Campbell*, *Mackay*, *Montrose*, *Walpole*, *Windsor*, *Whitshed*, *Vanquisher*, *Versatile*, *Wanderer*, *Walker*, *Westcott*, *Wrestler*, *Caldwell*, *Leeds*, *Lincoln*, *Ramsey*, *Skate*, *Saladin* and *Sardonyx*.

'Hunt' destroyers: *Cattistock* *Eglinton*, *Garth*, *Holderness*, *Meynell*, *Avon Vale*, *Belvoir*, *Goathland* and *Haldon*.

Sloops: *Scarborough*, *Rochester*, *Hart*, *Kite*, *Lapwing*, *Lark*, *Magpie* and *Pheasant*.

Frigates: *Deveron* and *Nene*.

Frigates (ex-US DEs): *Cubitt*, *Dakins*, *Ekins*, *Holmes*, *Lawford*, *Retalick*, *Stayner* and *Thornborough*.

Corvettes: *Puffin*; British 'Flower': *Armeria*, *Balsam*, *Burdock*, *Buttercup*, *Campanula*, *Celandine*, *Dianthus*, *Gentian*, *Heather*, *Honeysuckle*, *Lavender*, *Nasturtium*, *Pennywort*, *Primrose*, *Starwort*, *Sunflower*, *Wallflower*, the French *Cdt Estienne D'Orves*, the Norwegian *Acanthus*, *Eglantine*, *Potentilla*, *Rose*, the Canadian *Alberni*, *Baddeck*, *Battleford*, *Calgary*, *Camrose*, *Drumheller*, *Lindsay*, *Louisburg*, *Lunenburg*, *Mimico*, *Moosejaw*, *Port Arthur*, *Prescott*, *Regina*, *Rimouski*, *Summerside*, *Trentonian* and *Woodstock*.

In all, seven battleships, two monitors, 23 cruisers, three gunboats, 105 destroyers and 1073 smaller naval vessels are employed. On 6 June the German Navy has in the Channel area five torpedo boats, 34 motor torpedo boats (five others are non-operational)

163 minesweepers and motor mine-sweepers, 57 patrol boats and 42 gun carriers. On the Atlantic coast from Brest to Bayonne there are available: five destroyers, one torpedo boat, 146 minesweepers and motor minesweepers and 59 patrol boats.

6-13 June   English Channel
German surface vessels attempt to attack the invasion fleet. In the night 5-6 June *V1509* sinks in a reconnaissance sortie from Le Havre to the W in an engagement with British covering forces. In the night of 6 June the 5th TB Flotilla (Cdr Hoffmann) with *T28*, *Möwe*, *Jaguar* and *Falke* attacks ships of Force S belonging to the British Eastern Task Force off 'Sword' beach and sinks the Norwegian destroyer *Svenner*. Other torpedoes run between the battleships *Warspite* and *Ramillies* and miss the headquarters ship *Largs*.
In the night 6-7 June *T28*, *Möwe* and *Jaguar* attack unsuccessfully from Le Havre. The 5th MTB Flotilla (Cdr Klug), comprising *S136*, *S138*, *S140*, *S142*, *S100* and *S139* (*S84* returns because of engine trouble), and the 9th MTB Flotilla (Cdr v. Mirbach), comprising *S130*, *S144*, *S145*, *S146*, *S150*, *S167* and *S168*, set out from Cherbourg. On the way out, off Cap Barfleur, *S139* and, later, *S140*, are lost on mine barrages laid earlier by the British 64th MTB Flotilla (Lt-Cdr Wilkie). *S142*, *S100*, *S150* and *S168* break through the defences of the coastal forces and sink *LST715* and one LCT off St Vaast. The other boats are driven off by the frigate *Stayner* (Lt-Cdr Hall) and *MTB448* and *MTB478*.
Off Le Havre the 4th MMS Flotilla (Lt-Cdr Anhalt) becomes involved in an engagement with the British 55th MTB Flotilla (Lt-Cdr Bradford) and the Canadian 29th MTB Flotilla (Lt-Cdr Law). While laying the barrage 'Blitz 25' *R49* is badly damaged, as are *MTB624* and *MTB682*. The 4th MTB Flotilla (Lt-Cdr Fimmen), comprising *S169*, *S171*, *S172*, *S174*, *S173*, *S175*, *S187* and *S188*, sets out from Boulogne, but finds no targets. Only *S172* misses a destroyer with torpedoes.
The 2nd Flotilla (Cdr Opdenhoff), comprising *S177*, *S178*, *S179*, *S181* and *S189*, and the 8th Flotilla (Cdr Zymalkowski), comprising *S83*, *S117*, *S127* and *S133*, proceed from Ostend into the southern part of the North Sea on a fruitless reconnaissance sortie.
In the night 7-8 June the 2nd Flotilla is transferred from Ostend to Boulogne.
The 4th Flotilla with eight boats attacks a convoy escorted by the destroyer *Beagle*; *S174*, *S175*, *S187* and *S172* report hits on landing craft. *LST376* and *LST314* are sunk. The destroyers *Saumarez*, *Stord*, *Virago* and *Isis*, which are deployed, do not come up. The 5th Flotilla, comprising *S100*, *S138*, *S84*, *S136* and *S142* attacks from Cherbourg but is driven off in engagements with the frigates *Stayner* and *Retalick* (Lt-Cdr Brownrigg). *S84*, *S138* and *S142* are hit. The 9th Flotilla with six boats attacks a landing force, which is escorted by the British *ML903*, and sinks *LCI105* and *LCT875*. In engagements *S168* and *S145* are damaged.
In the night 8-9 June the 8th DD Flotilla (Capt. v. Bechtolsheim) tries to make a sortie from Brest into the invasion area with *Z32*, *Z24*, *ZH1* and *T24*, but is intercepted NW of the Ile de Bas by the British 10th DD Flotilla (Capt Jones), consisting of *Tartar*, *Ashanti*, *Haida* (Canadian) and *Huron* (Canadian), as well as *Blyskawica* (Polish), *Piorun* (Polish), *Eskimo* and *Javelin*. In the engagement *ZH1* is sunk by torpedoes from the *Ashanti*, *Z32* after a duel with *Haida* and *Huron* is beached near the Ile de Bas and blown up. *Tartar* is severely damaged.
In the same night the 5th MTB Flotilla with five boats and the 9th Flotilla with three boats set out from Cherbourg on a mining operation. They are driven off by the US destroyers *Frankford*, *Baldwin* and *Hambleton*, belonging to the 'Dixie' Patrol (Capt Saunders, USN), but they drop their mines. The 4th Flotilla sets out with seven boats and the 2nd with four, but the boats do not reach the mining area and return. The 5th TB Flotilla, comprising *T28*, *Möwe* and *Jaguar*, becomes involved in an engagement with the British 55th MTB Flotilla.
In the night 9-10 June the 5th MTB Flotilla, comprising *S84*, *S100*, *S136*, *S138* and *S142*, and the 9th MTB Flotilla, comprising *S130*, *S144*, *S146*,

S150 and *S167*, are again driven off by the US destroyers of the 'Dixie' Patrol. An attack by the torpedo boats *T28*, *Möwe* and *Jaguar*, setting out from Le Havre, on a destroyer patrol, consisting of *Glaisdale* (Norwegian), *Ursa* and *Krakowiak* (Polish), is out-manoeuvred by the latter. The 4th MTB Flotilla with *S188*, *S169*, *S173*, *S172*, *S187* and *S175* goes to sea on a mining operation and lays 24 mines; on the way out and on the return there are engagements with destroyers. *S188* reports a hit on a LST, *S172* and *S187* each a hit on a steamer of 2000 tons. The 2nd Flotilla with four boats from Boulogne attacks a supply convoy. *S177*, *S178*, *S179* and *S189* fire FAT torpedoes and each claim to have sunk a steamer of 900 tons and 1500 tons. They put into Le Havre. The 8th Flotilla, which is being transferred from Flushing to Boulogne, returns when *S180* and *S190* hit mines. In the night 10-11 June the 5th MTB Flotilla (Lt-Cdr Johannsen), comprising *S84*, *S100*, *S112*, *S136*, *S138* and *S142*, and the 9th MTB Flotilla, comprising *S130*, *S144*, *S146*, *S150* and *S167*, set out from Cherbourg. The 5th Flotilla becomes involved in an engagement with the British 35th MTB Flotilla (Lt-Cdr Cowen) and the frigate *Stayner*. *MTB448* and *S136* are lost. The frigate *Halstead* is hit in the bow by a torpedo salvo. The 9th Flotilla breaks through the defence after a short engagement with the SGBs *Grey Wolf* and *Grey Goose* and sinks the US tug *Partridge* and *LST496* and torpedoes *LST538*. Off Cherbourg *S130* is badly damaged in a fighter bomber attack. The 4th MTB Flotilla, comprising *S169*, *S171*, *S173*, *S187*, *S188* and *S172* lays a barrage of 24 UMB mines W of Le Havre and escapes from an attempt at interception by the destroyers *Sioux* (Canadian) and *Krakowiak* (Polish), and by the 55th MTB Flotilla with the frigate *Duff*. The 2nd MTB Flotilla with *S177*, *S179*, *S189* and *S178* outmanoeuvres a destroyer patrol, consisting of *Stord* (Norwegian), *Scorpion*, *Scourge* and *Kelvin*, and attacks a supply convoy S of the Isle of Wight. The freighters *Brackenfield* (657 tons) *Ashanti* (534 tons) and *Dungrange*

(621 tons) from the convoy are sunk by *S177* and *S178* (which sinks two of them). The destroyers pursue the motor torpedo boats to Boulogne. In the night 11-12 June *S84* and *S100* and *S146* and *S144* from the 5th and 9th Flotillas respectively are transferred from Cherbourg to Le Havre when they have several engagements with the destroyers of the 'Dixie' Patrol. *S150* and *S167* and *S138* and *S142* attack a destroyer force consisting of *Somers*, *Laffey* and *Nelson*, and in the action Cdr v. Mirbach torpedoes the *Nelson* with *S138*. The 2nd Flotilla becomes involved in an engagement with *MTB 461*, *MTB463* and *MTB464* of the Canadian 29th MTB Flotilla and its frigate leader off Le Havre. *S181* and *S179* suffer damage from acoustic mine detonations as they come in. The 4th Flotilla with *S169*, *S187*, *S173*, *S188*, *S171* and *S172* sets out from Boulogne and is involved in an engagement with a destroyer patrol consisting of *Onslow*, *Onslaught*, *Offa* and *Oribi*. The second group is engaged by MGBs from which *MGB17* is sunk by *S171* with gunfire. In the night 12-13 June the motor torpedo boats *S150*, *S167*, *S138* and *S142* from Cherbourg, with support from the coastal batteries at Cap Barfleur, break through the destroyer defence of the 'Dixie' Patrol and, off Le Havre, encounter a destroyer patrol consisting of *Glaisdale* (Norwegian), *Stevenstone* and *Isis* which damage *S138*. *S100*, *S84* and *S143* (5th Flotilla) and *S169*, *S173*, *S188*, *S171* and *S172* (4th Flotilla) set out from Le Havre and become involved in fighter bomber attacks and engagements with escort forces including the Canadian corvettes *Camrose*, *Baddeck* and *Louisburg*. *S169* returns after hitting a mine. The 2nd Flotilla sets out with four boats from Le Havre to Boulogne, escapes from the Canadian 29th MTB Flotilla, but is attacked before coming in by Beaufighters of Nos 143 and 236 Sqdns RAF which successively sink *S178*, *S189* and *S179* and *R97* (which comes to their assistance) and damage *S181*, *M402* and *R99*. *T28* and *Möwe* attack the destroyers *Stord* and *Scorpion* unsuccessfully off Le Havre.

K

6-30 June   English Channel

Allied warship losses off the Normandy coast: as a result of German air attacks, the US destroyer *Meredith II* and the British destroyer *Boadicea*; as a result of mines, the US destroyers *Corry*, *Glennon* and *Rich* and the British destroyers *Wrestler*, *Fury* and *Swift*; as a result of coastal artillery the French destroyer *Mistral*. In addition, a number of smaller ships and transports sink as a result of mines and coastal artillery.

6-30 June   English Channel/ Bay of Biscay

The following forces are deployed against the U-boat danger for the invasion: the reinforced No 19 Group RAF Coastal Command; and, under the C-in-C Western Approaches, the escort carriers *Tracker*, *Activity* and *Vindex* with SG 1 (the DEs *Affleck*, *Balfour*, *Bentley*, *Capel*, *Garlies* and *Gore*), SG 2 (the sloops *Starling*, *Wild Goose* and *Wren*, the frigates *Loch Killin*, *Loch Fada*, *Dominica* and *Lochy*), SG 3 (the DEs *Duckworth*, *Essington*, *Rowley*, *Berry*, *Cooke* and *Domett*), SG 4 (the DEs *Bentinck*, *Byard*, *Calder*, *Bazely*, *Blackwood*, and *Drury*) SG 5 (the DEs *Bickerton*, *Aylmer*, *Bligh*, *Kempthorne*, *Keats* and *Goodson*), SG 6 (the Canadian frigates *Waskesiu*, *Outremont*, *Cape Breton*, *Grou* and *Teme*) and SG 9 (the Canadian frigates *Matane*, *Swansea*, *Stormont*, *Port Colborne*, *St John* and *Meon*); and under the C-in-C Plymouth the destroyers of SG 11 (the Canadian *Ottawa*, *Kootenay*, *Chaudière*, *St Laurent* and *Gatineau*), SG 12 (the Canadian *Qu'Appelle*, *Saskatchewan*, *Skeena* and *Restigouche*) and SG 14 (the British *Hesperus*, *Havelock*, *Fame* and *Inconstant*). Four to six Groups of the C-in-C Western Approaches operate in the operational areas 'CA' W of the Channel and the Bay of Biscay and two groups of destroyers in the entrance to the Channel.

On 6 June 17 U-boats set out from Brest, 14 from St Nazaire, four from La Pallice and one from Lorient from the 'Landwirt' group. On 7 June aircraft of No 19 Group sink the homeward-bound *U955* and *U970* in the Bay of Biscay. The Brest boats, *U963*, *U989*, *U256* and *U415*, have to return damaged; on 8 June a Liberator of No

224 Sqdn RAF (F/O Moore) sinks *U629* and *U373* in turn and others damage *U413*; and on 9 June *U740* is sunk. It proves impossible to enter the Channel with the non-schnorkel boats. *U766* from the Brest boats, *U228*, *U255*, *U260*, *U270*, *U281*, *U382*, *U437*, *U445*, *U608*, *U650*, *U714*, *U758*, *U985* and *U993* from the St Nazaire boats, *U262* and *U333* from La Pallice and *U981* from Lorient are stationed in the Bay of Biscay until 15 June. Of the nine schnorkel boats *U212* has to return twice; the others try to enter the invasion area, followed by *U767*, *U1191*, *U988*, *U671* and *U971* which come from Norway. On 7 June and 8 June *U984* (Lt Sieder) fires four, *U621* (Lt Struckmann) two and *U953* (Lt Marbach) four T-5s against the four destroyers of the 12th SG. But they all detonate prematurely or in the ships' wash. Early on 9 June *U764* (Lt v. Bremen) fires four T-5s during a destroyer engagement without securing a hit. Up to 11 June *U621*, *U269* (Lt Uhl) and *U275* (Lt Bork) attack destroyer groups unsuccessfully in the western entrance to the Channel. *U821* (Lt Knackfuss) is lost in an air attack. From 14 June the first U-boats reach the shipping routes simultaneously with the Support Groups some of which are moved to the Channel. On 14 June *U984* misses a search group and on 15 June *U621* sinks the landing ship *LST280*, *U767* (Lt Dankleff) the frigate *Mourne* operating with the 5th SG, and *U764* the DE *Blackwood* of the 4th SG (taken in tow but a total loss). On 18 June *U621* misses two US battleships with a salvo. *U767* is sunk by the 14th SG and *U441* (Lt-Cdr Hartmann) by a Wellington of No 304 Sqdn (Polish). Of the schnorkel U-boats arriving in the second half of June, *U763* (Lt-Cdr Cordes) misses a search group with two T-5s in the night 22-23 June; *U971* (Lt Zeplin) is sunk in the western Channel by the destroyers *Eskimo* and *Haida* after an attempted attack fails because of faulty firing. On 25 June the DEs *Affleck* and *Balfour* sink *U1191*, the *Bickerton* (Cdr Macintyre) *U269*, while *U984* from the same group torpedoes the *Goodson* and misses a DE. On 27-29 June *U988* (Lt Dobberstein)

torpedoes the corvette *Pink* (total loss) and sinks two ships of 9444 tons before she is sunk on 29 June by the 3rd SG.
On 29 June *U984* attacks the convoy EMC.17 and hits four ships of 28790 tons of which only one ship is beached and can be salvaged, the other three becoming total losses. *U671* (Lt-Cdr Hegewald) misses a destroyer from a search group on 30 June. After another unsuccessful attack on a search group on 2 July, the boat is damaged by depth charges and has to put in to Boulogne. The schnorkel mining U-boats *U214* and *U218* lay mines off Plymouth on 26 June and off Land's End on 1 July. One ship of 7177 tons is damaged on 6 July on the latter barrage.
By 30 June 570 Liberty ships, 788 coastal motor boats, 905 LSTs, 1442 LCTs, 180 troop transports and 372 LCIs reach the assault area in supply convoys. The convoys are chiefly escorted by British and Canadian corvettes.

7 June-2 July   English Channel
Operation 'Neptune'. In the days after the first landing the following units are put ashore in Normandy from the follow-up convoys:
In the 'Utah' sector: the 90th US Inf Div 7-9 June; the 9th US Inf Div 10-13 June.
In the 'Omaha' sector: the 2nd US Inf Div 7-8 June; the 2nd US Armoured Div 10-13 June.
In the 'Gold' sector: the 7th British Armoured Div 8-10 June; the 49th Inf Div 11-12 June.
In the 'Juno' and 'Sword' sectors, the 51st British Inf Div 9-11 June.
By 12 June 326000 troops, 104000 tons of supplies and 54000 vehicles are landed By 2 July the figure is increased to four Corps of the 1st US Army with two Armoured and 11 Inf Divs and four Corps of the 2nd British Army with three Armoured and four Inf Divs, totalling 929000 troops, 177000 vehicles and 586000 tons of supplies.
On 7 June Gen Eisenhower and Adm Ramsay visit the assault area on board the fast minelayer *Apollo*. On 12 June *PT71* brings Generals Marshall, Eisenhower, Arnold, Bradley and Hodges and Admirals King, Stark, Kirk, Moon and Wilkes to Normandy.

10-11 June   English Channel
The British 58th MTB Flotilla, comprising *MTB687*, *MTB681*, *MTB683*, *MTB666*, *MTB723* and *MTB684*, attacks the German convoy 1253 off den Helder and sinks the patrol boats *V1314*, *V2020* and *V2021* for the loss of *MTB681*.
In the following night (10-11 June) the Norwegian 54th MTB Flotilla (Lt-Cdr Monsen), comprising *MTB712*, *MTB 715*, *MTB618*, *MTB623* and *MTB688*, attacks off the Hook of Holland the German 11th MS Flotilla (Cdr Seifert), which is being transferred from Borkum and which includes *M348*, *M307*, *M347* *M264* and *M131*. *MTB712* is damaged.

10-22 June   Indian Ocean
From 10 June to 13 June the British carrier *Illustrious* and the escort carrier *Atheling*, with covering forces, carry out a diversionary raid on Sabang for the US operation 'Forager' (Marianas) to tie down parts of the Japanese Fleet.
On 19 June Vice-Adm Power carries out operation 'Pedal', a carrier raid on Port Blair (Nicobars) with the carrier *Illustrious*, the battlecruiser *Renown* and the French battleship *Richelieu*, as well as light forces. Eight Corsairs and 15 Barracudas attack the airfield and harbour. Two aircraft are lost.
In June in the Straits of Malacca and to the N of it the British submarine *Stoic* (Lt Marriott) sinks two ships of 4141 tons and six small craft; *Tantalus* (Lt-Cdr Mackenzie) one ship of 536 tons; *Truculent* (Lt Alexander) one ship of 3040 tons; *Spiteful* (Lt Sherwood) one small ship; and the Dutch *K-XIV* (Lt-Cdr v. Hooff) torpedoes a Japanese minelayer.

10-28 June   Arctic
Soviet combined operation (RV-5) against German convoy traffic off the Polar Coast. The submarine *L-20* lays mines near Rolvsöy and reconnoitres; *S-14*, *S-104*, *M-200* and *M-201* are in waiting positions. On 15 June the first German summer convoy from Kirkenes to Petsamo, which has a strong escort and is helped by smoke screens, is brought through without loss, in spite of attacks by Soviet torpedo cutters and aircraft. On 15 June a Soviet reconnaissance aircraft sights a German convoy of 10 steamers near Hammerfest. Escort:

M31, M35, M154, M202, M252 (the 5th MS Flotilla, Cdr Klünder), *R202, R160, R223, V6102, V6107, V6110, V6722, V6111, V6725, UJ1220, UJ 1209, UJ1219, UJ1211* and *UJ1212.* It is reported on the evening of 16 June by reconnaissance aircraft in Svaerholthavet. On 17 June the German *M35, UJ1220* and *UJ1209* drive off the submarine *M-200* (Lt-Cdr Gladkov). In attacks by Il-2s of Ground Attack Regt 46, the steamer *Florianopolis* (7419 tons) is hit. Il-4 torpedo aircraft sink the steamer *Dixie* (1610 tons) S of Vardö with parachute torpedoes. The mines laid by Soviet torpedo cutters on the convoy's route off Kirkenes are cleared by motor minesweepers. Soviet bombers make attacks on the incoming convoy when the steamer *Marga Cords* (1112 tons) is damaged.

A return convoy, consisting of five steamers, six patrol boats, five submarine-chasers and two motor minesweepers, which sets out from Kirkenes on 19 June, is located by Soviet air reconnaissance S of Vardö shortly after midnight (daylight) on 20 June. The submarine *M-201* (Lt-Cdr Balin), which is shortly afterwards seen by a He 115 as she fires, is forced underwater by *UJ1209, UJ1219, UJ1220* and *UJ1222* and attacked many times with depth charges; but she escapes. An attempted attack by *M-200* or *S-14* off Syltefjord is frustrated by a BV 138. After some steamers have left, the Soviet submarine *S-104* (Capt 2nd Class Turaev) attacks the rest of the convoy, consisting of *L.M. Russ* and *R159, R173, V6107, V6111, NKi08, NKi12, UJ1211* and *UJ1209,* off Tanafjord and sinks *UJ1209.* On 22 June Soviet Il-2s, Airacobras and Kittyhawks attack a small convoy near Vardö and damage the gun ferry *AF39.* On June 27 and 28 June Soviet bomber formations with fighter protection carry out attacks on shipping in Kirkenes, in which the small steamer *Herta* (717 tons) and the *Florianopolis* are burnt out.

In a Kirkenes-Petsamo convoy on 28 June out of six steamers (escort: the 7th and 21st MMS Flotillas) the *Vulkan* (989 tons) is lost by action from coastal batteries and the *Nerissa* (992 tons) is sunk by torpedo cutter.

10 June-Beginning of July 1944
Central Pacific
On receipt of a report from the reconnaissance aircraft flown off from *I-10* that the anchorage at Majuro is empty, the Japanese Navy deploys its available submarines in the area E of the chain of the Marianas towards which it is thought the US Fleet is proceeding. The submarines involved are *I-5, I-6, I-10, I-38, I-41, I-44, I-53, I-184, I-185, Ro-36, Ro-44, Ro-48, Ro-109, Ro-112, Ro-113, Ro-114, Ro-115* and *I-117.* But only *Ro-114* (Lt Ata) makes an unsuccessful attack on a battleship of the *Iowa* class (16 June), *Ro-115* (Lt Koreeda) on a tanker (19 June) and *I-6* (Lt-Cdr Fumon) on a carrier (30 June), because the main body of the American forces operates W of the Marianas. On the other hand the following boats fall victim to the American submarine hunt: *Ro-36* (13 June), *Ro-44* (15 June), *Ro-114* (17 June), *Ro-117* (17 June), *I-184* (19 June), *I-185* (22 June), *I-6* (30 June) and *I-10* (4 July).

11 June   Black Sea
American air attack on Constanza.

11-17 June   Central Pacific
US TF 58 (Vice-Adm Mitscher) makes carrier raids on the Marianas and Vulcan Islands in support of operation 'Forager'.

TG 58.1 (Rear-Adm Clark): the carriers *Hornet, Yorktown, Belleau Wood* and *Bataan,* the cruisers *Boston, Baltimore, Canberra* and *Oakland,* the destroyers *Izard, Charrette, Conner, Bell, Burns, Boyd, Bradford, Brown* and *Cowell.*

TG 58.2 (Rear-Adm Montgomery): the carriers *Bunker Hill, Wasp, Monterey* and *Cabot,* the cruisers *Santa Fé, Mobile, Biloxi* and *San Juan,* the destroyers *Owen, Miller, The Sullivans, Stephen Potter, Tingey, Hickox, Hunt, Lewis Hancock* and *Marshall.*

TG 58.3 (Rear-Adm Reeves): the carriers *Enterprise, Lexington, San Jacinto* and *Princeton,* the cruisers *Indianapolis* (Adm Spruance), *Reno, Montpelier, Cleveland* and *Birmingham,* the destroyers *C.K. Bronson, Cotten, Dortch, Gatling, Healy, Cogswell, Caperton, Ingersoll, Knapp, Anthony, Wadsworth, Terry* and *Braine.*

TG 58.4 (Rear-Adm Harrill): the carriers *Essex, Langley* and *Cowpens,* the cruisers *San Diego, Vincennes, Houston* and *Miami,* the destroyers *Lansdowne, Lardner, McCalla, Lang, Sterett, Wilson, Case, Ellet, Charles Ausburne, Stanly, Dyson, Converse, Spence* and *Thatcher.*
Battle Line TG 58.7 (Vice-Adm Lee), at first distributed among the other four groups: the battleships *Washington, North Carolina, Iowa, New Jersey, Indiana, South Dakota* and *Alabama,* the cruisers *Wichita, Minneapolis, New Orleans* and *San Francisco,* the destroyers *Mugford, Conyngham, Patterson, Bagley, Selfridge, Halford, Guest, Bennett, Fullam, Hudson, Yarnall, Twining, Stockham* and *Monssen.* The Task Group shells Saipan on 13 June.
On 11 June all four groups first carry out a fighter strike on all the Mariana Islands, in which 36 Japanese aircraft are destroyed. TG 58.4 attacks a convoy which has just set out from Saipan and sinks the torpedo boat *Ootori,* three submarine-chasers and 10 ships of 30000 tons. On 12 June and 13 June the TG 58.2, 58.3 and 58.4 attack Saipan and Tinian and TG 58.1 Guam. On 14 June and 15 June there are only individual sorties over the Marianas while TGs 58.2 and 58.3 replenish. Rear-Adm Clark with TGs 58.1 and 58.4 to the N attacks Iwojima, Chichijima and Hahajima on the afternoon of 15 June and on 16 June. On the way to the rendezvous of TF 58, TG 58.4 attacks the island of Pagan again on 17 June.

13 June   English Channel
Between St Malo and Jersey the destroyers *Piorun* and *Ashanti* attack a German convoy and sink *M343.* On the German side *M412, M422, M432, M442* and *M452* are damaged and on the Allied side *Piorun.* In trying to help the minesweeping flotilla *V203* and *M4615* are damaged by fighter bombers.
13 June   North Pacific
A US Task Group (Rear-Adm Small), consisting of two heavy and two light cruisers and nine destroyers, shells Matsuwa in the Kuriles.
13 June   Philippines
The US submarine *Narwhal* shells oil tanks near Bula on Ceram.

14-15 June   English Channel
In the night 14-15 June 325 Lancaster bombers of RAF Bomber Command attack Le Havre. The following boats are destroyed or sunk: the torpedo boats *Falke, Jaguar, Möwe* of the 5th TB Flotilla; the motor torpedo boats *S169, S171, S172, S173, S187* and *S188* of the 4th, *S84, S100, S138, S142* and *S143* of the 5th and *S144, S146* and *S150* of the 9th Flotillas (the Commander of the 5th Flotilla, Lt-Cdr Johannsen†); the escort vessels *PA1* and *PA2*; the motor minesweeper *R182*; the minesweepers *M3801, M3802, M3822, M3855, M3873, M3874* and *M4627*; the patrol boats *V207, V1505, V1506, V1511, V1537, V1540, V1541* and *V1805*; and many smaller auxiliary naval craft and harbour vessels.
On the following night 300 Lancasters attack Boulogne. The following vessels are sunk: the motor minesweeper tenders *Von der Gröben, Brommy, Von der Lippe,* the motor minesweepers *R81, R92, R93, R125, R129, R130, R232,* the minesweepers *M402, M3815,* the patrol boats *V1814, V1815,* three tugs and five harbour defence vessels. In addition, the motor minesweepers *R96, R100* and *R117* are badly damaged.
14 June-9 July   Central Pacific
Operation 'Forager': TF 52 (Vice-Adm Turner) lands the V Amphibious Corps (Lt-Gen H. M. Smith) on Saipan. On 14 June the Fire Support Groups begin with their preparatory shelling and support the troops on 15 June: TG 52.17 (Rear-Adm Oldendorf), comprising the battleships *Tennessee, California, Maryland* and *Colorado,* the cruisers *Indianapolis* (TF 58 until 14 June), *Louisville, Birmingham, Montpelier* and *Cleveland,* the destroyers *Remey, Wadleigh, Norman Scott, Mertz, Robinson, Bayley, Albert W. Grant, Halsey Powell, Coghlan, Monssen, McDermut, McGowan, Melvin, McNair, Yarnall, Twining* and *Stockham.*
TG 52.10 (Rear-Adm Ainsworth), comprising the battleships *Pennsylvania, Idaho* and *New Mexico,* the cruisers *Honolulu, Minneapolis, San Francisco, Wichita, New Orleans* and *St Louis,* the destroyers *Anthony, Wadsworth, Hudson*

Halford, Terry, Braine, Guest, Bennett and *Fullam*. In addition, two APDs, two DMSs and one AVD. Air support is provided by TG 52.14 (Rear-Adm Bogan), comprising the escort carriers *Fanshaw Bay, Midway, White Plains* and *Kalinin Bay*, the destroyers *Cassin Young, Irwin, Ross, Porterfield, Callaghan* and *Longshaw*.
TG 52.11 (Rear-Adm Sallada), comprising the escort carriers *Kitkun Bay, Gambier Bay, Corregidor* and *Coral Sea*, the destroyers *Laws, Morrison, Benham, Bullard, Kidd* and *Chauncey*.
On 15 June the transport group TG 52.3 (Capt Knowles) with 13 APAs, five AKs and one LSD lands the 2nd Marine Div (Maj-Gen Watson) and the transport group TG 52.4 (Capt Loomis) with 13 APAs, three AKAs and three LSDs lands the 4th Marine Div (Maj-Gen Schmidt). An escort is provided by the destroyers *Newcomb, Bennion, Heywood L. Edwards, Bryant, Prichett, Philip, Cony, Mugford, Selfridge, Ralph Talbot, Patterson, Bagley, Phelps, Shaw* and *Renshaw*.
Further waves arrive on landing ships and boats; in all, TF 52 consists of 551 ships. A total of 67451 men are landed. After heavy fighting with the Japanese defenders (Lt-Gen Saito with the reinforced 43rd Inf Div and naval units under Vice-Adm Nagumo) the island is captured on 9 July. Japanese losses: 23811 dead, 1780 prisoners. US losses: 3426 dead and 13099 wounded.

15 June   North Sea
Beaufighter torpedo bombers of Coastal Command sink the transport *Coburg* (7900 tons) from a German convoy, the motor torpedo boat tender *Gustav Nachtigal* and the minesweeper *M103* N of the island of Schiermonnikoog.

15-21 June   Baltic
Soviet attack on the offshore islands of the Karelian Isthmus. On 15 June the Finnish IV Corps has to withdraw under pressure from the 59th and 21st Soviet Armies from the Mannerheim position to Viborg. At the outset there is fire support from the battleship *Oktyabrskaya Revolutsiya*. To cover the seaward flank, the Finns use light naval forces and two submarines and call for German support. *T30* and *T31* the 3rd MS Flotilla, the 1st MMS Flotilla and an

AF Group of the 24th Landing Flotilla are employed in Viborg Bay and in Koivisto Sound. In an attack by Soviet torpedo cutters under Capt 2nd Class Osipov *T31* is lost and in air attacks on 20-21 June *AF32* and the mine transport *Otter* sink and the motor minesweeper tender *Nettelbeck, M29, R119* and *R120* are damaged. Soviet landings on Koivisto are delayed but not prevented. By 23 June the islands are evacuated and occupied by the Russians who are supported, inter alia, by the gunboats *Volga, Zeya, Kama* and *Oka*.

16-17 June   Mediterranean/Adriatic
The large French destroyers *Le Fantasque* and *Le Terrible* make a sortie into the Gulf of Quarnaro and sink the small tanker *Giuliana* (350 tons) in the company of the German motor minesweepers *R4, R8, R14* and *R15*, which get away.

16-29 June   English Channel
In the nights 15-16 June, 16-17 June and 17-18 June the last three motor torpedo boats, *S130, S145* and *S168*, set out from Cherbourg, but they are driven off by destroyer patrols and the British SGB Flotilla (Lt-Cdr Baker). The Boulogne group, comprising *S177, S181, S174* and *S175*, does not find any targets on 16 June and is attacked by fighter bombers. In the following night, the group, reinforced by *S180* and *S190*, turns back after fighter bomber attacks. The *S83, S127* and *S133*, coming from Ostend, find no targets on 16 June and become involved in several air attacks on 17 June in which *S133* and *S83* are damaged.
In the night 16-17 June the Canadian 65th MTB Flotilla (Lt-Cdr Kirkpatrick), comprising *MTB748, MTB745, MTB 726* and *MTB727*, attacks a German convoy W of the Cotentin Peninsula: *MTB748* torpedoes the minesweeper *M133* which is towed into harbour.
In the night 18-19 June the German 2nd MTB Flotilla with six boats is transferred from Boulogne to Le Havre. In the storm, which reaches its climax during the night and lasts until 22 June, operations by light craft on both sides are impossible. The artificial harbour, 'Mulberry A', off the Omaha beachhead, is made unusable because of the storm and many landing craft are driven onto the

beach and destroyed. The landing of supplies is severely disrupted.

In the night 22-23 June the Canadian 65th MTB Flotilla, consisting of *MTB 748, MTB727, MTB745* and *MTB743* and four British MTBs, attacks a German convoy near St Helier (Jersey) and sinks the supply ship *Hydra*. The 9th MTB Flotilla, which on 19 June went with three boats from Cherbourg to St Malo on a transport mission, returns to Cherbourg. The 2nd Flotilla, consisting of *S177, S181, S180, S190, S174, S175* and *S167*, lays mines in Seine Bay. In engagements with British destroyer patrols *S190* is hit and has to be abandoned. *S83, S127* and *S133* are transferred from Ostend to Boulogne.

In the night 23-24 June Cherbourg is evacuated. *S130, S145* and *S168* proceed to St Malo. Off Cap de la Hogue a convoy, in spite of covering fire from the naval coastal battery 'Yorck', is attacked by two groups each of three MTBs of the British 14th MTB Flotilla (Lt Shaw) and three boats of the 35th MTB Flotilla (Lt-Cdr McCowen) and loses *AF66* and three coastal motor ships and, later, two tugs in the company of the 6th Gun Carrier Flotilla near the Channel Islands. The 2nd Flotilla (Cdr Opdenhoff) with three boats lays another barrage of 12 DM-1 mines, while three boats, forming the torpedo group, have engagements with destroyers, including the *Stord* and *Venus*, and MTBs. *S175* is badly, and *S181*, lightly damaged.

In the night 24-25 June the motor torpedo boats go from St Malo to Alderney. The 2nd Flotilla with five boats has to abandon a mining operation after fighter bomber attacks. The three boats from Boulogne are transferred to Le Havre. On 25-26 June the new 6th MTB Flotilla (*S76, S90, S91, S97, S114, S132, S39* and *S135*) is transferred from Cuxhaven to Ijmuiden. In the night 25-26 June the three boats *S130, S168* and *S145* try to break through from Alderney to Dieppe. S of Selsey Bill they are involved in an engagement with the Canadian destroyers *Gatineau* and *Chaudière* which out-manoeuvre the torpedoes and force *S145* to return after being hit. The boat goes to St Malo on 27 June.

In an attack by four British MTBs off St Helier in the night 26-27 June *M4620* is lost. In the following night the converted trawler *M4611* sinks off Jersey after an engagement at very short range with the destroyers *Eskimo* and *Huron*. After *V213* obtains hits on the destroyers, the boat escapes to Jersey. A sortie from Le Havre by the 2nd and 8th MTB Flotillas in the night 27-28 June has no success. The next night *S174, S177, S180* and *S181* lay 16 DM-1 mines and *S83, S167, S127* and *S133* cover the operation.

17-19 June Mediterranean/ Tyrrhenian Sea
Allied 'Coastal Forces', including 37 US PT boats, land Senegalese riflemen of the French 9th Colonial Div on Elba, who occupy the island in two days after the initial resistance has been broken. Larger ships are not used because of the many German mine barrages.

18-22 June Central Pacific
Battle of the Philippine Sea.
To support the Marianas operation, the US submarines (TF 17, Vice-Adm Lockwood) are disposed from 12 June as follows: *Plunger, Gar, Archerfish, Plaice* and *Swordfish* in the area of Bonin Island; *Pintado, Pilotfish* and *Tunny* SE of Formosa; *Albacore, Seawolf, Bang, Finback* and *Stingray* in the area of the Marianas; *Flying Fish, Muskallunge, Seahorse, Pipefish* and *Cavalla* E of the Philippines; and *Growler* off Surigao Strait. And from the submarines of the 7th Fleet (Rear-Adm Christie) *Hake, Bashaw* and *Paddle* SE of Mindanao; *Harder, Haddo, Redfin* and *Bluefish* off Tawi-Tawi; and *Jack* and *Flier* off Luzon. During the Japanese preparatory movements for the operation A-GO *Harder* (Cdr Dealey) sinks the destroyers *Minatsuki, Hayanami* and *Tanikaze* off Tawi-Tawi and torpedoes the *Urakaze*. The Fleet, which sets out from Tawi-Tawi on 13 June, is reported by *Redfin* (Lt-Cdr Austin), the passing of the carriers through the San Bernardino Strait by *Flying Fish* (Lt-Cdr Risser) on 15 June and the presence of the battleship squadron E of Mindanao by *Seahorse* (Lt-Cdr Cutter). On 16-17 June the Japanese forces, after joining up and while they refuel from

two tanker groups, are twice reported by *Cavalla* (Lt-Cdr Kossler). In this way Adm Spruance receives timely warnings and can assemble (18 June) TF 58 (see 11 June) W of the Marianas to cover the operation 'Forager'. The Japanese Fleet (Vice-Adm Ozawa) consists of the Van (Vice-Adm Kurita), comprising the light carriers *Chitose*, *Chiyoda* and *Zuiho*, the battleships *Yamato*, *Musashi*, *Haruna* and *Kongo*, the cruisers *Atago*, *Takao*, *Maya* and *Chokai* and the destroyers *Naganami*, *Asashimo*, *Kishinami*, *Okinami*, *Tamanami*, *Hamakaze*, *Fujinami* and *Shimakaze* with the cruiser *Noshiro*; Carrier Group A (Vice-Adm Ozawa), comprising the carriers *Taiho*, *Shokaku* and *Zuikaku*, the cruisers *Myoko* and *Haguro* and the destroyers *Asagumo*, *Isokaze*, *Hatsutsuki*, *Wakatsuki*, *Akitsuki* and *Shimotsuki* with the cruiser *Yahagi*; and Carrier Group B (Rear-Adm Joshima) comprising the carriers *Junyo*, *Hiyo* and *Ryuho*, the battleship *Nagato*, the cruiser *Mogami* and the destroyers *Michishio*, *Nowake*, *Yamagumo*, *Shigure*, *Samidare*, *Hayashimo*, *Akashimo* (sunk en route after a collision on 15 June) and *Shiratsuyu*. The tanker groups consist of four tankers with the destroyers *Hibiki*, *Hatsushimo*, *Yunagi* and *Tsuga* and two tankers and the destroyers *Yukikaze* and *Uzuki* respectively. Ozawa's intention is to fly off the carrier aircraft outside the range of TF 58, to touch down on Guam after the attack and then to fly back making a second attack. The Japanese reconnaissance aircraft locate parts of TF 58 on the evening of 18 June and early on 19 June. From 0800 to 1100 hours the Japanese carriers fly off 372 aircraft in four waves, but they are located with radar by the US ships at a range of up to 150 kms and intercepted by fighters (300 sorties) which are at once flown off. They are, in part, supported by the ships' AA fire and shoot down 242 aircraft ('Turkey Shoot'). Only a few aircraft break through and obtain one bomb hit on the *South Dakota* and near-misses on *Indiana* and *Bunker Hill*. No more than 29 US fighters are lost. In the landing operation on Guam US fighters attack and shoot down 30 aircraft and the 19 which land are badly damaged. Shortly

after the Japanese aircraft fly off, the US submarine *Albacore* (Cdr Blanchard) attacks Group A and hits the *Taiho*, which sinks after explosions. *Cavalla* sinks the *Shokaku* with three torpedoes. While Ozawa refuels from the tankers on 20 June, Mitscher approaches and in the afternoon flies off 216 aircraft at great range. They encounter only 35 fighters over the Japanese ships. The carrier *Hiyo* and two tankers are sunk; the *Zuikaku*, *Chiyoda*, *Haruna* and *Maya* are damaged. Twenty US aircraft are lost. In spite of lighting up the flight decks, 72 machines are lost in crash landings or coming down in the sea. Of 209 flying personnel from these aircraft 160 are rescued. In the night 20-21 June the C-in-C of the Combined Fleet in Tokyo, Adm Toyoda, gives the order to withdraw. Adm Spruance rejects Mitscher's proposal to continue the pursuit with the fast battleships. The Japanese fleet, therefore, escapes.
After refuelling on 22-23 June three groups of TF 58 go to Eniwetok. Rear-Adm Clark makes a sortie to the N with the carriers *Hornet*, *Yorktown*, *Bataan* and *Belleau Wood* and on 24 June carries out a raid on Iwojima and Chichijima in which another 66 Japanese aircraft are destroyed. A Japanese attack is intercepted.

20 June-14 Aug   Mediterranean/ Tyrrhenian Sea
On 20-21 June the German torpedo boats *TA25* and *TA29* carry out a mining operation 'Messer' in the Ligurian Sea. In an engagement with US PT boats *TA25* sinks.
The Italian destroyer *Grecale* and the motor torpedo boat *Ms74* bring British and Italian small battle units to La Spezia, which penetrate the harbour and destroy the heavy cruiser *Bolzano* which is being repaired.
At the end of June and the beginning of July, the British submarine *Universal* (Lt Gordon) sinks the harbour patrol boat *FM06* and two blockships totalling 8752 tons; *Ultor* (Lt Hunt) sinks one naval ferry barge and two blockships totalling 8575 tons; *Vampire* (Lt Taylor) one sailing ship; and *Universal* one small submarine-chaser. At the end of July and the beginning of August, *Ultor* sinks the submarine-chaser *UJ*

Above: Aug 1944: Allied troops land in Southern France. Here troops probe the beach for mines while the infantry advance along the edge of the shore. *[Official USN]*
Below: The *Tirpitz* forms the greatest danger to the Russian convoys. After the damage suffered in the midget submarine raid of September 1943 is repaired the Fleet Air Arm again attempts to put the battleship out of action. In Operation 'Tungsten' a carrier force with (background left to right) *Furious, Victorious, Anson* and *Belfast*, seen here from one of the escort carriers, damages the vessel with four bombs.

[IWM]

Above: Aug 1944: A new cycle of convoys to Murmansk is begun. During the first operation a carrier force unsuccessfully attacks the *Tirpitz*. The carrier *Nabob* is torpedoed by *U354* which also hits the frigate *Bickerton* with an acoustic torpedo. Here the Canadian destroyer *Algonquin* assists the damaged *Nabob*.   [IWM

Below: After many only partially successful attacks the famous RAF bomber squadrons 9 and 617 (of dambuster fame) hit the *Tirpitz* with a number of the large 5.4-ton blockbuster bombs. The *Tirpitz* capsizes.
                                                    [IWM

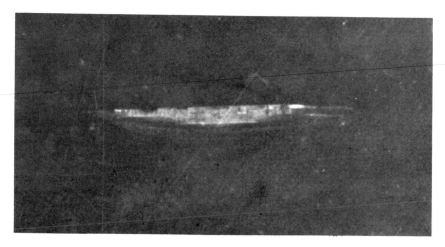

Above: From August 1944 to May 1945 the Allies continue to run convoys to Murmansk, escorted by British destroyer groups. Here the destroyer *Scorpion* runs down the side of convoy RA.64 during February 1945. The convoy lost one freighter and two escorts to U-boats and was the last convoy to be attacked by German aircraft, which sank one straggler.

[IWM

Below: In 1944 the Soviet Northern Fleet attempts to attack German shipping off the Norwegian Polar Coast in combined operations by aircraft, submarines, surface vessels and MTBs. In the Kola fiord a patrol vessel (left) is passed by a returning submarine of the S class, while a destroyer of the *Gremyashci* type is going astern to leave the harbour.

[BFZ

Above: April-May 1944: German and Romanian vessels and merchant ships evacuate 130000 men of the 17th Army from Sevastopol to Constanza. A further 215000 men are evacuated by aircraft. During the final days of the evacuation (May 5-13) 8100 men are lost through Soviet air, MTB and submarine attacks. Here one of the 64 MFPs involved in the evacuation, *F336*, is seen arriving at Constanza from Sevastopol, overcrowded with troops.   [*BFZ*

Below: Heavy air raids by RAF Bomber Command and the 8th USAAF disrupt the German programme of building new fast U-boats. Here the capsized pocket-battleship *Admiral Scheer* is seen at the Deutsche Werke yard at Kiel with two bow sections of new Type XXI U-boats in the foreground.   [*IWM*

Above: In the last carrier operation of the European war the British escort carriers *Queen*, *Searcher* and *Trumpeter* attack the German U-boat base at Harstad—Norway on May 4, where their aircraft sink the depot ship *Black Watch* and *U711*, the most successful U-boat in the north, which has just returned from the last convoy battle of the war. In the foreground the A A cruiser *Nymphe* (the former Norwegian coast defence ship *Tordenskjöld*)   [IWM

Below: U-boats continue fighting until the last day of the war sinking ships off the North Cape, the Firth of Forth, off Reykjavik, off New York and in the English Channel. Here *U516*, coming from a transport run to the beleaguered fortress of St Nazaire, flying her black flag of surrender, is met by the destroyer *Cavendish* and escorted to Loch Foyle.   [IWM

Above: In the Baltic the largest evacuation operation ever undertaken begins to rescue nearly 2m people from the advancing Red Army. All remaining German surface ships are called in to support the defending army units with gunfire. Here the destroyer *Z34* fires her 5.9-inch battery against Russian armoured columns off Oxoeft on April 3. A week later this ship was torpedoed by two Russian MTBs, but was towed back to Swinemunde.   *[BFZ*

Above: Off the Kurische Nehrung German MFPs rescue civilian refugees coming over the ice from the shore and ferry them to the large evacuation ships off Hela.   *[BFZ*

Below: On Oct 20, 1944 the US Sixth Army lands on Leyte Gulf in the Philippines. Some days later LSTs and LCTs are unloading tanks, trucks and supplies on beach 'White' near Tacloban peninsula. *[BFZ*

Top: On Oct 21, 1944 the Japanese Centre Force departs from its anchorage in Brunei Bay to attack the American landing forces at Leyte. From left to right are: battleship *Fuso*, cruiser *Mogami* with the battleship *Musashi* behind, battleship *Yamashiro*, cruiser *Chokai*, battleship *Yamato* and cruiser *Maya*.   *[BFZ/Fukui*

Above: During the Battle of Samar on Oct 25, 1944 the Japanese cruiser *Suzuya* is hit by a Helldiver from the American carrier *Hancock* with a 1000lb armour piercing bomb. The cruiser was hit earlier in the day by aircraft of the escort carriers before opening fire on Sprague's group.
[Official USN

Above: In the north a Japanese decoy force of carriers (without any aircraft) attempted to lure the American carrier forces away from Leyte Gulf where they were covering the landing forces. The Japanese almost succeeded. Here the hybrid battleship-carrier *Hyuga* comes under air attack from American carrier aircraft.   [*IWM*

Below: Feb 19, 1945: LVTs of the first five assault waves loaded with Leathernecks of the 5th US Marine Div race for beaches 'Green' and 'Red', during the landing on Iwo Jima. The smoke of the pre-landing bombardment by ships like the old battle-ship *Tennessee* (right) is clearing above airfield No 1 and Mount Suribachi.
                    [*Official USN*

2211; *Ultimatum* one small submarine-chaser and two naval ferry barges including *F811*; *Upstart* (Lt Chapman) one small ship; *Universal* one sailing ship; and the French *Curie* (Lt Chailley) torpedoes a steamer.

From 6 July to 26 July *TA24*, *TA28* and *TA29* from the 10th TB Flotilla put to sea practically every night on mining operations (five), reconnaissance sorties (ten) and coastal shelling (one). On 28-29 June, on 15-16 July, on 19-20 July and on 25-26 July there are engagements with Allied PTs and MTBs. On 12-13 Aug *TA24* and *TA29* carry out another reconnaissance sortie.

20 June-18 Aug   Baltic
In continual attacks by Soviet ground attack aircraft and fighter bombers of the Baltic Fleet's Air Force (Lt-Gen Samokhin) on German patrol vessels in Narva Bay and the operational harbours in Estonia and Finland the destroyer *Z39*, the minesweepers *M15*, *M29* and *M3112*, the ferry barge *F194* and the AA escort *FJ26* are damaged in June. There are 68 dead and 144 wounded. In July *M20*, *M143*, *F237*, *F498*, *V1707* and the AA cruiser *Niobe* are sunk and *M3*, *M14*, *M15*, *M19*, *M29*, *M30*, *M453*, *M460*, *M3114*, *V1705* and *F259* are damaged. There are 148 dead and 269 wounded.
In August the attacks slacken off somewhat. *M14*, *M443*, *M3109*, *M3128*, *M3137*, *F258*, *AF21* and *R67* are damaged. Throughout the period the mine barrages are repeatedly reinforced by naval ferry barges of the 24th Landing Flotilla.
In an attempt to reinforce the 'Seeigel' barrage the 6th TB Flotilla (Cdr Koppenhagen) runs into its own mine barrage on 17-18 Aug and loses *T22*, *T30* and *T32* with 393 men some of whom are taken prisoner. Only *T23* returns.

22-28 June   Baltic
A German-Finnish Commando operation (Steinhäger) is launched against the island of Narvi occupied by the Russians on 22 June with light craft. With support from the German 2nd TB Flotilla (Cdr Kassbaum) with *T30*, *T8* and *T10*, the 3rd MS Flotilla (Cdr Kieffer) with *M18*, *M19*, *M22*, *M15* and *M30* and the 1st MMS Flotilla (Lt-Cdr W. E. Schneider)

with *R67*, *R68*, *R76* and *R249*, Finnish units are to be landed by the 2nd Finnish Patrol Flotilla (Lt-Cdr Jäasalo) with nine VMV boats and the patrol vessel *Vasama* and the 1st and 2nd MTB Flotillas (Lt-Cdr Pirhonen and Lt-Cdr Salo) with four and five motor torpedo boats respectively. The operation fails because of the strong Soviet defence and inadequate co-ordination between Germans and Finns. The island is shelled on 15-16 July by three German torpedo boats which carry out an engagement with Soviet patrol boats.

24-28 June   North Pacific
US TF 94 (Rear-Adm Small), comprising the cruisers *Chester*, *Pensacola* and *Concord* and the destroyers *Picking*, *Wickes*, *Sproston*, *Young*, *W. D. Porter*, *Isherwood*, *Kimberly*, *Luce* and *C. J. Badger*, makes a sortie to the W, protected by a weather front, and shells Paramushiro (Kuriles) on 26 June.

25-26 June   English Channel
To support the attack by VII US Corps on Cherbourg, two Task Forces shell German batteries W and E of the town on 25 June: Group I (Rear-Adm Deyo) with the battleship *Nevada*, the cruisers *Tuscaloosa*, *Quincy*, *Glasgow* (British), *Enterprise* (British) and the destroyers *Ellyson*, *Emmons*, *Rodman*, *Murphy*, *Gherardi* and *Hambleton* in the W shells the batteries near Querqueville; and Group II (Rear-Adm Barbey) with the battleships *Texas* and *Arkansas* and the destroyers *Barton*, *O'Brien*, *Laffey*, *Plunkett* and *Hobson* in the E shells the battery 'Hamburg' which secures 28-cm hits on *Texas* and *O'Brien*. *Glasgow*, *Barton* and *Laffey* are slightly damaged. The German batteries are largely destroyed. On 27 June the US destroyer *Shubrick* shells Querqueville. On 26 June the British battleship *Rodney*, the monitor *Roberts*, the cruisers *Argonaut*, *Belfast* and *Diadem* support attacks by British units in the area of Caen.

26 June-4 Sept   Baltic
Finnish and German submarines are employed in the inner part of the Gulf of Finland because of the critical situation in Karelia. The three large Finnish boats operate from the middle of June S of Koivisto and the two small boats near Tiurinsaari. *Vesihiisi* lays mine barrages near Peninsaari on 4 July

and 7 July; *Vetehinen* lays a mine barrage after two sorties into Koivisto Sound on 2 July and again on 5 July. *Iku-Tursu* operates on the way to Lavansaari (August), but, like *Vesikko* and *Saukko*, has no success. From 26 June the German *U481*, *U748* and *U1193* arrive, from 13 July *U679*, *U475*, *U479*, *U370*, *U242*, *U250* and *U348* and in August *U1001*, *U745* and *U717*. They generally relieve each other every two days in the positions near Koivisto and in Narva Bay. In the Koivisto area *U679* (Lt Breckwoldt) has an engagement on 14 July with torpedo cutters. *U475* (Lt-Cdr Stöffler) damages the patrol cutter *MO-304* on 28 July. *U250* (Lt-Cdr Schmidt) sinks *MO-105* on 30 July, but is then herself sunk by depth charges from *MO-103*. The wreck is later raised. *U370* (Lt Nielsen) damages the *MO-107* on 31 July. In Narva Bay *U481* (Lt Andersen) sinks two motor minesweepers on 30 July and near Seiskari *U242* (Lt Pancke) sinks one survey ship and one lighter on 25 Aug. *U745* (Lt-Cdr v. Trotha) sinks a patrol vessel in Narva Bay on 26 Aug.

28 June-27 Sept North and West Atlantic

U858, *U804* and *U855* operate as weather boats in the North Atlantic from the end of June to the beginning of September. From 24 July US TG 22.6 (Capt Tague), comprising the escort carrier *Wake Island* and the DEs *Douglas L. Howard*, *Fiske*, *Farquhar*, *J. R. Y. Blakely* and *Hill*, is deployed against the weather boats detected in the radio picture. On 2 Aug aircraft find *U804* (Lt H. Meyer) but the boat escapes after she has just missed *Douglas L. Howard* with a T-5 and sunk *Fiske*. As relief, TG 22.2 (Capt Vosseller), comprising the *Bogue* and the DEs *Haverfield*, *Janssen*, *Willis* and *Wilhoite* and a support group of six Canadian frigates, arrives from 4 Aug. On 15 Aug and 18 Aug night aircraft from the *Bogue* sight the approaching schnorkel boat *U802* (Lt-Cdr Schmoeckel). The boat sights the carrier on 16 Aug but does not fire. On 20 Aug six Avengers from the *Bogue* sink *U1229* as she proceeds to Long Island to disembark agents. In the first half of September *U802* and *U541* (Lt-Cdr

Petersen) penetrate into the Gulf of St Lawrence where *U541* sinks a ship of 2140 tons. On 8 Sept and 14 Sept respectively the returning *U541* and *U802* sight TG 22.2 (*Bogue* and seven DEs) which is waiting for the boats S of Cabot Strait. But they obtain no hits with their T-5s fired at the DEs. An attack by *U541* on a convoy on 27 Sept is also unsuccessful. Off the American East Coast the schnorkel boat *U518* (Lt Offermann) torpedoes a Liberty ship of 7176 tons on 12 Sept, which, on the following day, is lost in a hurricane together with the destroyer *Warrington*, the minesweeper *YMS409* and the USCG cutters *Jackson* and *Bedloe*.

1-31 July Pacific

The US submarines which arrive in their operational areas in July make the following sinkings: off Japan, Formosa and the Kuriles *Cobia* (Lt-Cdr Becker) sinks six ships of 11842 tons; *Gabilan* (Lt-Cdr Wheland) the minesweeper *Sokaitei 25*; *Skate* (Lt-Cdr Gruner) three ships of 4394 tons and the destroyer *Usugumo*; *Sunfish* (Lt-Cdr Shelby) two ships of 8861 tons; *Tautog* (Lt-Cdr Baskett) three ships of 2827 tons; *Tinosa* (Lt-Cdr Weiss) two ships of 10687 tons. In the area of the Mandate Islands *Guavina* (Lt-Cdr Teideman) sinks one ship of 3052 tons. In the area of the Malayan Archipelago and the Philippines *Angler* (Cdr Hess) torpedoes one ship; *Apogon* (Lt-Cdr House) sinks one picket boat of 32 tons; *Aspro* (Cdr Stevenson) one ship of 2288 tons; *Bonefish* (Lt-Cdr Edge) three ships of 10293 tons; *Cabrilla* (Lt-Cdr Thompson) one ship of 3145 tons and torpedoes one ship; *Crevalle* (Lt-Cdr Walker) sinks two ships of 20075 tons and torpedoes one ship; *Dace* (Lt-Cdr Claggett) sinks one ship of 1192 tons; *Guardfish* (Lt-Cdr Ward) sinks four ships of 19788 tons; *Lapon* (Lt-Cdr Stone) three ships of 6794 tons; *Mingo* (Lt-Cdr Staley) the destroyer *Tamanami*; *Paddle* (Lt-Cdr Nowell) the destroyer *Hokaze*; *Parche* (Lt-Cdr Ramage) two ships of 14709 tons and torpedoes one ship; *Parche* and *Steelhead* together sink one ship of 8990 tons; *Steelhead* (Lt-Cdr Welchel) two ships of 15364 tons; *Piranha* (Lt-Cdr Ruble) two ships of 12276 tons;

Ray (Lt-Cdr Kinsella) five ships of 25984 tons; and *Sandlance* (Lt-Cdr Garrison) torpedoes one ship.

2 July   South West Pacific
The US VII Amphibious Force (Rear-Adm Fechteler) lands 7100 men of the reinforced 168th Inf Regt on the island of Noemfoor. The landing is preceded by shelling from cruisers of TF 74 and 75 (Commodore Collins RAN, Rear-Adm Berkey) (see 22 Apl) and 14 destroyers.

2 July-31 Aug   Mediterranean/Aegean
In air attacks on German convoys near Rhodes *R38* is sunk on 2 July and the freighter *Agathe* (1259 tons) on 3 July. In July the British submarine *Vox* (Lt Michell) sinks the freighter *Anita* (1165 tons) and misses the KT ship *Pelikan*. *Unruly* (Lt Fyfe) one small ship and misses the KT ship *Pelikan*. *Vivid* (Lt Varley) sinks the freighter *Susanne* (552 tons) and three sailing ships; *Universal* (Lt Gordon) one sailing ship: and *Vigorous* one sailing ship. In August *Vox* sinks three sailing ships and the harbour patrol boat *GK61*; *Unswerving* (Lt Tattersall) sinks one small ship; *Virtue* three sailing ships; *Vigorous* two sailing ships; and *Vox*, again, one sailing ship. The Greek *Pipinos* (Lt-Cdr Loundras) sinks the torpedo boat *TA19* on 9 Aug off Samos and two lighters.

3-30 July   English Channel
British MTB flotillas attack German shipping targets off the Dutch coast, between Boulogne and Le Havre and off Brittany. Among those participating off the Dutch coast are the 58th MTB Flotilla (Lt-Cdr Gemmel) and the Norwegian 54th MTB Flotilla (Lt-Cdr Monssen). In the night 3-4 July the steamer *Weserstein*, escorted by the 20th PB Flotilla (Cdr Puttfarken) consisting of *V2016, V2019, V2022, V1315* and *V1317*, is unsuccessfully attacked by four MTBs. On the following day, when accompanied by the 26th MS Flotilla (Lt-Cdr v. Lüeder), it is attacked by six MTBs, from which *MTB666* is sunk. In the night 8-9 July four MTBs attack a force of the 13th PB Flotilla (Cdr Fischer), comprising *V1313, V1301, V1306* and *V1310*: *MTB434* and *V1306* are sunk. On 17-18 July six MTBs attack the patrol boat *V1313* and three AF ferries and on 19-20 July

the Norwegian *MTB709* and *MTB722* and the British *MTB685, MTB687, MTB729* and *MTB683* attack a German convoy: both sides sustain slight damage. On 21-22 July a force, comprising *V1303* and the 34th MMS Flotilla, is attacked by six MTBs: *M3413* sinks.

Off Fécamp on 1-2 July *MTB632* and *MTB650* from the 55th MTB Flotilla (Lt-Cdr Bradford) attack a force of the 10th MMS Flotilla (Lt-Cdr Nau) and sink *R180*. *MTB632* is put out of action by other minesweepers coming to the scene. In the following night *MTB629, MTB624, MTB621* and *MTB617* from the same flotilla attack a German force near Cap d'Antifer: both sides sustain slight damage. Apart from the 55th MTB Flotilla, the Canadian 29th MTB Flotilla (Lt-Cdr Law), the British 14th MTB Flotilla (Lt-Cdr Shaw), the British 51st MTB Flotilla (Lt-Cdr Lyle) and, later, the 1st MTB Flotilla (Lt Mathias) and the 30th MTB Flotilla (Lt Dixon) are employed in this area, particularly against German motor torpedo boats. The 29th MTB Flotilla, comprising *MTB461, MTB462* and *MTB465*, has engagements on 4-5 July, on 8-9 July and 13-14 July. On 8 July *MTB463* is lost in an attack on German 'Neger' one-man torpedoes.

The Canadian 65th MTB Flotilla (Lt-Cdr Kirkpatrick) is employed off Brittany. On 3-4 July with the *MTB748, MTB743, MTB735* and *MTB734*, it torpedoes the German supply steamer *Minotaure*, sinks the patrol boats *V206* and *V210* and damages *V209* and *M4622*.

On 5 July Allied destroyers begin operation 'Dredger' against German escort vessels at the U-boat meeting points off Brest and to the S of it. In the night 5-6 July the 12th EG, comprising the Canadian destroyers *Qu'Appelle, Saskatchewan, Skeena* and *Restigouche*, attacks three patrol boats off Brest: *V715* is sunk after a courageous defence and the first two destroyers receive many small-calibre hits. The motor torpedo boats *S145* and *S112*, which are proceeding from St Malo to Brest, rescue the survivors of *V715*. In the night 7-8 July the destroyers *Huron* and *Tartar* of the 10th Flotilla attack boats of the 46th MS Flotilla (Lt-Cdr Zimmermann) off the Channel Islands and sink *M4605* and *M4601*. In the night 14-15 July the destroyers *Tartar*, *Haida* and *Blyskawica* make a sortie into the area of Ile de Croix near Lorient and sink the submarine-chasers *UJ1420* and *UJ1421*. On 19-20 July the Canadian 9th EG is attacked off Brest by German aircraft with glider bombs which damage the frigate *Matane* with hits and the frigate *Meon* with near-misses.

In the eastern part of the assault area the battleship *Rodney* supports the land operations on 7 July and 11 July, the Dutch gunboat *Soemba* on 10 July, the monitor *Roberts* and the cruiser *Belfast* on 11 July, the *Roberts* and the cruisers *Mauritius* and *Enterprise* on 17 July and 18 July near Caen and the monitor *Erebus* and the Dutch gunboat *Flores* on 26 July and 29 July.

German motor torpedo boats try often at night to make sorties into the assault area and there are many engagements. In the night 3-4 July the 8th Flotilla (Cdr Zymalkowski) sets out from Le Havre with *S83*, *S127* and *S133*, drops 12 DM-1 mines and proceeds to Dieppe. The 2nd Flotilla (Cdr Opdenhoff) with *S175*, *S176* and *S167* also drops 12 DM-1 mines; but it is driven off and has to return. Then the motor torpedo boats are involved in engagements with the British frigates *Stayner* and *Thornborough* off Cap d'Antifer which are used here as leader ships for the MTB groups.

In the night 4-5 July the 8th Flotilla, in transferring to Le Havre, has an engagement with the frigate *Trollope* and MTBs off Cap d'Antifer and has to return. The 2nd Flotilla with six boats has engagements off Le Havre with destroyers and MTBs, including *MTB 459*, *MTB462* and *MTB464* of the Canadian 29th MTB Flotilla.

In the night 5-6 July the 2nd Flotilla with six boats again has engagements with destroyers off Le Havre: the torpedoes are out-manoeuvred. When coming in, the torpedo repair depot in Le Havre blows up: 41 torpedoes are destroyed and operations are restricted because of torpedo shortages. The 6th Flotilla (Lt-Cdr Matzen) moves some of its boats from Boulogne to Le Havre and suffers heavy fighter bomber attacks in the process.

In the night 7-8 July the 2nd Flotilla sets out from Le Havre in two groups (*S176*, *S177* and *S182*; *S174*, *S181* and *S180*) together with *S167*, *S175* and *S168* from the 9th Flotilla (Cdr v. Mirbach). The boats make several attacks on destroyers and detonations are observed. But the 'Hunt' destroyers *La Combattante* (French) and *Cattistock* and the frigate *Thornborough*, which are involved in the engagements during the night, sustain only slight damage.

In the night 8-9 July the boats setting out from Le Havre (six of the 2nd and three of the 6th Flotillas) have to return because of the weather. The three boats of the 9th Flotilla attack targets off Dieppe without success. Because of bad visibility no further operations are possible before 15 July. The 6th Flotilla with *S132*, *S90* and *S135* has an engagement off Le Havre with the Canadian 29th MTB Flotilla, comprising *MTB459*, *MTB466* and *MTB464*. The 9th Flotilla with *S175*, *S168* and *S167* has an engagement off Dieppe with the boats of the British 64th MTB Flotilla (Lt-Cdr Wilkie) and the 2nd Flotilla with *S180*, *S177*, *S174* and *S182* has an engagement off Le Havre with MGBs and MTBs.

In the night 17-18 July the three boats of the 9th Flotilla set out from Dieppe but return after destroyer engagements and fighter bomber attacks. Three boats of the 6th Flotilla set out from Le Havre and, in engagements, *S135* and *S90* damage the British *MTB361*. Of the boats of the 2nd Flotilla—*S176*, *S177*, *S182*, *S174*, *S180* and *S181*—only the first three come into contact with the enemy. *S91*, *S79* and *S114* move from Ostend to Boulogne to join the 6th Flotilla.

In the night 19-20 July sorties on the convoy routes have no success. In the night 21-22 July the torpedo boat *T28* is transferred with *S132*, *S90* and *S135* from Le Havre to Boulogne and, on the way, has an engagement with the 'Hunt' destroyer *Melbreak*. In the following night the journey is continued from Boulogne to the Hook of Holland with an escort from the 8th MTB Flotilla:

the destroyers *Forester* and *Stayner* with *MTB480* and *MTB484* are outmanoeuvred. The *S190* and *S135*, which have come into Dieppe, are transferred to Boulogne on 25 July with the 4th MMS Flotilla.

In the night 25-26 July an operation by five boats of the 2nd MTB Flotilla against destroyers off Seine Bay is broken off.

In the night 26-27 July the 6th MTB Flotilla makes an attack from Boulogne on a west-bound convoy off Dungeness; the 1st group, comprising *S97*, *S114*, *S90* and *S91*, torpedoes two ships of 14217 tons and escapes from the pursuit made by the destroyers *Obedient*, *Savage* and *Opportune* and the *MTB436*, *MTB432* and *MTB418*, the last two of which suffer slight damage. The 2nd group, comprising *S132*, *S39*, *S135* and *S79*, has engagements with MTB 229, *MTB240* and *MTB354* and Beaufighter bombers. The 9th Flotilla from Boulogne, comprising *S175*, *S168* and *S167*, becomes involved in an engagement with the escort and has to turn back. In a sortie from Le Havre by the 2nd Flotilla, comprising *S176*, *S182*, *S174*, *S181* and *S180*, against destroyers in Seine Bay there is an engagement with the frigate *Retalick* and an MTB group in which *MTB430* sinks as a result of ramming by *S182* and the following *MTB412* sinks on the wreck of the preceding boat. The damaged *S182* has to be blown up.

In the night 27-28 July sorties by the 2nd and 6th Flotillas have to be abandoned because of mist. In the following night *S180* and *S176* of the 2nd Flotilla fire T-5 torpedoes for the first time against destroyers without success. In the night 29-30 July *S97*, *S114* and *S91* (Petty-Officer Waldhausen, Lt Hemmer and Petty-Officer Nelte) of the 6th Flotilla attack an eastbound convoy E of Eastbourne and with six FAT torpedoes sink the British freighter *Samwake* (7219 tons) and hit the *Fort Dearborn* (7160 tons), *Fort Kaskaskia* (7187 tons), *Ocean Volga* (7174 tons) and *Ocean Courier* (7178 tons). They escape from the frigate *Thornborough*.

In the night 30-31 July *S176*, *S180*, *S177*, *S181*, *S174*, *S132*, *S39* and

and *S79* attack destroyer and MTB groups, including the destroyer *Oribi*. *S174*, *S181* and *S132* fire T-5 torpedoes but they detonate prematurely.

In the night 5-6 July 26 *Neger* one-man torpedoes are deployed for the first time against the assault area from Villers-sur-Mer. They sink the minesweepers *Cato* and *Magic*. Nine *Negers* are destroyed. In a second operation on 7-8 July with 21 *Negers*, Senior Ensign Potthast hits the Polish cruiser *Dragon* so severely that she has to be beached as a blockship in 'Gooseberry' harbour. In addition, the minesweeper *Pylades* is sunk. On 20 July *Negers* sink the British destroyer *Isis*. The attackers have heavy losses.

The torpedo boat *T28*, in spite of engagements with the British DE *Melbreak* on 22 July and MTB attacks, is transferred to home waters from 21 July to 27 July.

3 July-27 Aug English Channel

Operations by German schnorkel U-boats in the Channel. From 3 July to 11 July *U309* (Lt Mahrholz) misses a search group; *U953* (Lt Marbach) and *U763* (Lt-Cdr Cordes) each make two attacks on convoys and sink one ship of 1927 tons and 1499 tons respectively. *U390* (Lt Geissler) sinks on 5 July the A/S trawler *Ganilly* from a convoy and torpedoes one tanker of 10584 tons, but is then herself sunk by the destroyer *Wanderer* and the frigate *Tavy*. *U678* (Lt Hyronimus) is sunk when attacking a convoy off Beachy Head on 6 July by the Canadian destroyers *Ottawa* and *Kootenay* and the minesweeper *Statice*. *U243*, coming from Norway, falls victim to aircraft of the Bay Patrol on 8 July and, similarly, *U1222*, returning from Newfoundland. *U415* is lost on a mine on 14 July in Brest harbour. From another group which succeeds in getting into the Channel *U672* has to scuttle herself on 18 July, after being damaged by the DE *Balfour*. *U212* is sunk by the DEs *Curzon* and *Ekins*; and *U741* has to put in to Le Havre. In the last 10 days of July *U309* misses a convoy; *U621* (Lt Struckmann), in four attacks, sinks the landing ship *Prince Leopold* (2938 tons) and torpedoes the troop transport *Ascanius* (10048 tons). *U275* has to put in to Boulogne in a damaged state and

U671, which has set out from there again, is sunk on 4 Aug by the DE *Stayner* and the destroyer *Wensleydale*. The 3rd and 2nd SGs operate with aircraft from the end of July to the middle of August W of the entrance to the Channel against approaching U-boats and those moving from the Brittany ports. In the operation *U214*, *U333*, *U736*, *U608*, *U385*, *U981*, *U270*, *U618*, *U445* and *U107* are sunk. *U180*, which is setting out for East Asia, sinks as a result of bomb hits and a mine. *U667* (Lt Lange), having sunk the Canadian corvette *Regina*, a Liberty ship of 7176 tons and the landing ships *LST921* and *LCI99* on 8 Aug and 14 Aug, is sunk on a mine as she returns off North Cornwall. In the middle of August a new wave arrives in the Channel: of them, *U741* is sunk by the corvette *Orchis* in attacking a convoy, *U621* and *U984* by the destroyers *Ottawa*, *Kootenay* and *Chaudière* of the 11th SG and *U413*, after she has sunk a ship of 2360 tons, by the escort destroyers *Wensleydale*, *Forester* and *Vidette*. *U764* (Lt v. Bremen), in three attacks, sinks a steamer of 638 tons. *U480* (Lt Förster) which is equipped with a rubber skin ('Alberich') against Asdic, sinks in four attacks the Canadian corvette *Alberni*, the minesweeper *Loyalty* and a ship of 5712 tons and torpedoes another ship of 7134 tons. *U989* (Lt-Cdr H. Rodler v. Roithberg) sinks in three attacks a ship of 1791 tons and torpedoes a ship of 7176 tons. Together with *U275* and *U92*, which achieve no successes, the three boats are recalled on 27 Aug to Norway. *U218* lays a mine barrage near Start Point on 20 Aug.

4-21 July   Central Pacific
Preparations for the landings on Guam and Tinian.
TF 58 (Vice-Adm Mitscher) carries out raids on Iwojima and Chichijima on 4 July with TG 58.1 (Rear-Adm Clark) and TG 58.4 (Rear-Adm Davison) and on Guam with TG 58.2 (Rear-Adm Reeves) and TG 58.3 (Rear-Adm Montgomery). Guam is also shelled by the destroyers of TG 58.3. On 5 July carrier aircraft of TGs 58.1 and 58.2 make attacks on Guam (see 11 June for the composition of TF 58).

From 8 July several ships of TG 52.10 (Rear-Adm Ainsworth) (see 14 June) shell Guam until 19 July with 12550 rounds of 6-inch to 16-inch shells and 16214 rounds of 5-inch shells. From 20 June army artillery shells Tinian from Saipan. And from the beginning of June there is regular shelling by ships of TG 52.14. Air support is provided, and carrier attacks on Guam are made by aircraft of the escort carrier group TG 53.7 (Rear-Adm Ragsdale) (see 21 July).

5 July   Air War/Mediterranean
233 B-24s of the USAAF attack the harbour of Toulon. Inter alia *U586* is destroyed, *U471*, *U642*, *U952* and *U969* are badly, and *U466* and *U967* slightly, damaged. Only *U230* remains operational.

8-14 July   North Sea
British bombers sink the German freighters *Miranda* (736 tons) and *Tannhäuser* (1923 tons) and the Swedish steamer *Sif* (1365 tons) on 8 July SW of Heligoland.
Sortie by the British *MTB455*, *MTB457*, *MTB458*, *MTB467*, *MTB468*, *MTB 469* and *MTB470* into the area off Ijmuiden. Here an engagement takes place with three German patrol boats. *V1412* is sunk and three MTBs are damaged.

9-28 July   Arctic
Soviet combined operation (RV-6) against German convoy traffic off the Polar Coast. The submarine *L-15* lays mines off Rolvsöy and reconnoitres. From 13 July *S14*, *S-56*, *Shch-402* and *M-200* take up waiting positions and a torpedo cutter brigade (Capt 1st Class Kuzmin) is alerted. On 10 July and 13 July Soviet torpedo and ground attack aircraft make sorties in groups and do slight damage to some ships. On 13 July a Soviet reconnaissance aircraft reports a German convoy proceeding eastwards in Mageröy Sound. On the evening of 14 July the convoy is reported in Porsangerfjord and early on 15 July *S-56* (Capt 3rd Class Shchedrin) and *M-200* (Lt-Cdr Gladkov) attack unsuccessfully with an hour's interval between them near Cape Harbaken. The torpedo cutters (Capt 2nd Class Alexeev) *TKA-12*, *TKA-13*, *TKA-238*, *TKA-239*, *TKA-240*, *TKA-241*, *TKA-242* and *TKA-243* at first pass by but

are then brought to the scene by two Yak-9 reconnaissance aircraft S of Busse Sound. The escort beats off the attacks and *UJ1211* sinks the *TKA-239*. An attack by ground attack aircraft and fighter bombers of the 14th Mixed Air Div on the incoming ships off Bökfjord causes only slight damage. In further heavy fighter bomber attacks on the area Kirkenes-Vardö on 17 July, 21 July, 22 July and 28 July slight damage is done to the ships. Only *V6307* is sunk.

11-12 July   Mediterranean/Adriatic
British commando troops land on the island of Hvar (Adriatic).

11 July-19 Sept   Mediterranean
Last operations by the German schnorkel U-boats in the Mediterranean. *U596* (Lt-Kolbus) sets out from Pola on 11 July, cruises off Cyrenaica, in the Strait of Otranto, off Malta and Benghazi, but makes no attacks and returns to Salamis on 1 Sept. *U407* (Lt Korndörfer) operates off Derna and Benghazi from 21 Aug to 4 Sept and *U565* (Lt Henning) N of Crete from 26 Aug to 13 Sept. There the boat is relieved from 9 Sept by *U407* (Lt Kolbus), which on 19 Sept falls victim to the British destroyers *Troubridge* and *Terpsichore* and the Polish *Garland*.

14-26 July   South West Pacific
TF 74 (Commodore Collins), comprising the Australian cruisers *Australia* and *Shropshire* and the destroyers *Arunta, Warramunga, Ammen* and *Bache* and from 16 July, *Hutchins* and *Beale*, is employed to shell Japanese troops which try to break through to the W in the area of Aitape.

17 July   Norway
British carrier raid with the carriers *Formidable, Indefatigable* and *Furious* under Rear-Adm McGrigor on the *Tirpitz* lying in Kaafjord. The operation is covered by the battleship *Duke of York* (Adm Moore, new C-in-C Home Fleet) and the cruisers *Kent, Devonshire, Jamaica* and *Bellona*, together with fleet destroyers and the 20th EG. Forty-five Barracuda torpedo bombers and 50 fighters fly off from the carriers, but they are located so early that the target is completely covered in smoke and the AA defence is made fully prepared for operations. The attack is unsuccessful.

19-26 July   Black Sea
The Soviet submarine *Shch-209* (Lt-Cdr N. V. Sukhodolski), which is employed off the Bosphorus against German ships coming from Rumania misses the Turkish steamer *Kanarya* with a torpedo on 19 July and sinks with gunfire the Turkish sailing ship *Semsi-Bahri* on 20 July and another Turkish sailing ship on 26 July. *M-111* operates without success off Constanza. At the end of the month she is relieved by *M-113* and *M117*. *M-113* (Lt-Cdr Volkov) tries to attack a convoy on 28 July inside the flanking mine barrages.
The German U-boats *U9* and *U24* operate off the Caucasus coast at the end of July.

21 July-10 Aug   Central Pacific
US TF 53 (Rear-Adm Connolly) lands the III Amphibious Corps (Maj-Gen Geiger) on Guam on 21 July.
TG 53.1 (Rear-Adm Connolly) lands the 3rd Marine Div (Maj-Gen Turnage) W of Agana with 11 APAs, three AKAs, two LSDs and one hospital ship and sixteen LSTs. Escort: the destroyers *John Rodgers, Stevens, Harrison, McKee, Schroeder, Colahan, Stembel, Haggard, Hailey*, three DMSs and two AMs.
TG 53.2 (Rear-Adm Reifsnider) lands the 1st Marine Brigade and elements of the 77th Inf Div (Brig-Gen Shepherd) near Agat with 12 APAs, three AKAs, one LSD and 14 LSTs. Escort: the destroyers *Farenholt, Sigsbee, Dashiell, Murray, Johnston, Franks, Preston, Anthony, Wadsworth, Wedderburn, Black* and *Ringgold*.
Fire support: TG 53.5 (Rear-Adm Ainsworth) (similar to TG 52.10 at Saipan on 14 June) and, in addition, the battleships *Colorado, Tennessee* and *California*, the cruisers *New Orleans, Indianapolis* and *St Louis*, the destroyers *Fullam, Guest, Monaghan, Dale* and *Aylwin*.
Air support: TG 53.7 (Rear-Adm Ragsdale), consisting of the escort carriers *Sangamon, Suwanee, Chenango, Corregidor* and *Coral Sea*, the destroyers *Erben, Walker, Abbot, Hale, Bullard, Chauncey* and *Kidd*.
54891 troops are landed. They annihilate the bulk of the 19000 Japanese defenders (29th Inf Div, Lt-Gen Takashima†; 6th Expeditionary Battle Group, Maj-Gen

Shigematsu†). The last Japanese island commandant is the Commander of the 31st Army, Lt-Gen Obata†.
US losses: 1290 dead, 145 missing and 5648 wounded. Japanese losses: 10693 dead and 98 prisoners. The rest of the Japanese defenders retire to the jungle and fight on there in small groups, in some cases until the end of the war. (One survivor was rescued only in 1972). TF 58 (Vice-Adm Mitscher) attacks Guam on 21-22 July with TGs 58.1, 58.2 and 58.3. From 23 July the carriers proceed to the W. From 25 July to 28 July TGs 58.2 and 58.3 direct attacks on Palau and TG 58.1 on Yap, Ulithi, Tais, Ngulu and Sorol. After replenishing, TGs 58.1 and 58.3 attack Iwojima and Chichijima under Rear-Adm Clark on 4 Aug and 5 Aug and in the operation the Japanese destroyer *Matsu* is sunk.

22-27 July   Indian Ocean
After the carriers *Victorious* and *Indomitable* arrive in Ceylon on 5 July, the operation 'Crimson' (carrier raid and bombardment of Sabang/Sumatra) is carried out. On 22 July the British Eastern Fleet (Adm Somerville) sets out from Trincomalee. Early on 25 July the carriers *Illustrious* and *Victorious*, escorted by the cruiser *Phoebe* and the destroyers *Roebuck* and *Raider*, fly off 34 Corsairs to attack the airfields round Sabang. Then the battleships, *Queen Elizabeth, Valiant, Renown* and *Richelieu* (French), the cruisers *Cumberland, Nigeria, Kenya, Ceylon* and *Gambia* (New Zealand) and the destroyers *Relentless, Rotherham, Racehorse, Rocket* and *Rapid*, come up to shell Sabang. They fire 294 15-inch, 134 8-inch, 324 6-inch, about 500 5-inch and 123 4-inch shells. After that the Dutch cruiser *Tromp* with the destroyers *Quilliam* (Capt Onslow), *Quality* and *Quickmatch* (Australian) enter the harbour and fire eight torpedoes, 208 6-inch, 717 5-inch and 668 4-inch shells at close range. *Tromp* receives four hits and *Quilliam* and *Quality* one each from the coastal batteries. Thirteen Corsair fighters intercept a Japanese air attack with 10 planes and shoot seven of them down, losing two of their own. The submarines *Templar* and *Tantivy* are employed for air/sea rescue.

In July the following ships are sunk and damaged by British submarines in the Straits of Malacca, off Sumatra and West Thailand: *Stratagem* (Lt Pelly) damages two small ships; *Spiteful* (Lt Sherwood) sinks one sailing ship; *Sturdy* (Lt Andersen) sinks 10 small craft; *Sea Rover* (Lt Angell) sinks three sailing ships; *Porpoise* (Lt-Cdr Turner) sinks one sailing ship; *Spirit* (Lt Langridge) and *Tally Ho* (Cdr Bennington) torpedo a tanker and a steamer respectively; *Stoic* (Lt Marriott) sinks two small ships; *Telemachus* (Cdr King) sinks the Japanese submarine *I-166*; *Sirdar* (Lt Spender) sinks three small ships; and *Storm* (Lt Young) sinks one ship of 554 tons and three small craft.

23-24 July   Air War/Germany
RAF Bomber Command drops 2748 tons of bombs on Kiel. In the harbour *U239, U1164, U2323, Sperrbrecher 25* the U-boat tender *Erwin Wassner*, the passenger ship *General Osorio* (11590 tons) and the freighter *Axel* (1540 tons) are sunk.

24 July-1 Aug   Central Pacific
US TF 52 (Rear-Adm Hill) lands the V Amphibious Corps (Maj-Gen Schmidt) on Tinian with support from army artillery from Saipan. 15614 troops of the 2nd and 4th Marine Divs (Maj-Gen Cates and Maj-Gen Watson) are landed by elements of TG 52.4 (see Saipan 14 June) and by LSTs and smaller landing craft. Fire support is provided by TG 52.17 (Rear-Adm Oldendorf) and TG 52.10 (Rear-Adm Ainsworth) (see 14 June) with the exception of a few ships and air support by TG 52.14 (Rear-Adm Bogan) and TG 52.11 (Rear-Adm Sallada) (see 14 June). The Japanese defenders (elements of the 29th Inf Div, Col Ogata†) and Vice-Adm Kakuta† (1st Air Fleet) lose 6050 dead and 252 prisoners. US losses: 389 dead and 1816 wounded. In the shelling the battleship *Colorado* and the destroyer *Norman Scott* are hit and damaged by a Japanese coastal battery.

26 July-4 Aug   Arctic
Four submarines which are handed over by the Royal Navy to the Soviet Northern Fleet (to compensate for the share of the Italian war booty) proceed from Dundee to Murmansk under the command of Capt 1st Class Tripolski.

The first boat to set out *V-1* (ex-*Sunfish*) (Capt 2nd Class Fisanovich) is sunk in error by a British Liberator bomber on 27 July. The others, *V-2* (Capt Tripolski takes over because the commander is sick), *V-4* (Capt 3rd Class Iosseliani) and *V-3* (Capt 3rd Class Kabo), arrive between 2 Aug and 4 Aug. They are the ex-*Unbroken*, ex-*Ursula* and ex-*Unison*.

27-31 July   South West Pacific
Operation 'Globe Trotter'. The VII Amphibious Force (TF 77, Rear-Adm Fechteler), which sets out on 27 July from Wakde with 11 destroyers, five APDs, eight LSTs, 16 LCIs, three LCI(R)s, four PCs and one ATF, lands the 6th US Div (Maj-Gen Sibert) E of Cape Sansapor off the off-shore islands of Amsterdam and Middelburg on 30 July. The islands are also occupied without opposition. On 31 July one BLT on landing craft with four destroyers and two PTs is landed near Sansapor W of the Cape. The operation is covered by TF 78 (Rear-Adm Berkey) comprising one heavy and two light cruisers and nine destroyers of TF 74 and TF 75. There are no coastal shellings before the landing.

1-31 Aug   Pacific
The following ships are sunk by US submarines arriving in their operational areas in August:
Off Japan, Formosa and the Kuriles *Barbel* (Lt-Cdr Keating) sinks four ships of 5473 tons; *Bowfin* (Lt-Cdr Corbus) three ships of 7196 tons; *Croaker* (Lt-Cdr Lee) three ships of 8418 tons and the light cruiser *Nagara*; *Pintado* (Lt-Cdr Clarey) two ships of 24663 tons; *Pompon* (Lt-Cdr Gimber) one ship of 2159 tons; *Ronquil* (Lt-Cdr Monroe) two ships of 6954 tons; *Sailfish* (Lt-Cdr Ward) one ship of 2110 tons and torpedoes one ship; *Seal* (Lt-Cdr Turner) two ships of 6390 tons and torpedoes the destroyer *Namikaze*; *Sterlet* (Lt-Cdr Robbins) two ships of 347 tons; *Tambor* (Lt-Cdr Germershausen) one ship of 2324 tons; and *Tang* (Cdr O'Kane) three ships of 6021 tons.
In the area of the Mandate Islands *Batfish* (Lt-Cdr Fyfe) sinks the minesweeper *Sokaitei 22* and the destroyer *Samidare*.
In the area of the Malayan Archipelago

and the Philippines *Bluefish* (Lt-Cdr Henderson) sinks one ship of 6500 tons; *Bluefish* and *Puffer* together sink one ship of 5135 tons; *Puffer* (Lt-Cdr Selby) three ships of 10588 tons and torpedoes one ship; *Bluegill* (Lt-Cdr Barr) three ships of 6727 tons and one submarine-chaser; *Cero* (Lt-Cdr Dissette) one ship of 6500 tons; *Cod* (Lt-Cdr Adkins) one ship of 708 tons and Landing Ship *T129*; *Guitarro* (Lt-Cdr Haskins) four ships of 11236 tons and the frigate *Kusagaki* and torpedoes one ship; *Gunnel* (Lt-Cdr O'Neill) one ship of 9929 tons; *Gurnard* (Cdr Gage) one ship of 2500 tons; *Haddo* (Lt-Cdr Nimitz) two ships of 10968 tons, the frigate *Sado* and the destroyer *Asakaze*; *Harder* (Cdr Dealey) the frigates *Matsuwa* and *Chiburi*; *Hardhead* (Lt-Cdr McMaster) the light cruiser *Natori*; *Jack* (Lt-Cdr Krapf) one ship of 5785 tons and the minesweeper *Sokaitei 28*; *Muskallunge* (Lt-Cdr Russillo) one ship of 7163 tons; *Picuda* (Lt-Cdr Donaho) two ships of 3891 tons and the destroyer *Yunagi* and torpedoes one ship; *Rasher* (Lt-Cdr Munson) four ships of 32667 tons and the escort carrier *Taiyo* and torpedoes two ships; *Redfish* (Cdr McGregor) two ships of 15817 tons and torpedoes two ships; and *Spadefish* (Lt-Cdr Underwood) six ships of 31510 tons.

2-21 Aug   English Channel
The British battleship *Rodney* shells the island of Alderney on 12 Aug, the *Warspite* Brest on 25 Aug and the *Malaya* the Ile de Cézembre off St Malo on 1 Sept. The monitor *Erebus* shells Honfleur on 19 Sept.
In the area of the Channel Islands *MTB717*, *MTB716*, *MTB720*, *MTB676* and *MTB677* have engagements on 5-6 Aug with German boats of the 46th MS Flotilla (Lt-Cdr Zimmermann) and the 2nd PB Flotilla (Capt Lensch). On 8-9 Aug in an attempted attack on the boats of the two flotillas by the frigate *Maloy* with the US PT boats *PT503*, *PT500*, *PT507*, *PT508* and *PT509*, the last PT boat is sunk. The frigate *Borum* and *PT500* and *PT502* on 11-12 Aug and the destroyers *Onslaught* and *Saumarez*, the *Borum*, *PT505* and *PT498* and two British MTBs on 13-14 Aug have further engagements with the

L

24th MS Flotilla (Cdr* Breithaupt). In another engagement on 18-19 Aug *M432* is damaged.

In the invasion area German small battle units are again employed. In the night 2-3 Aug 20 *Linsen* (explosive boats) of the Small Battle Unit Flotilla 211 (Lt-Cdr Bastian) attack and sink the destroyer *Quorn*, the A/S trawler *Gairsay* and an LCG and damage the freighters *Fort Lac La Ronge* (7131 tons) and *Samlong* (7219 tons). In the night 8-9 Oct 16 *Linsen* make an unsuccessful attack.

In the nights 15-16 Aug and 16-17 Aug *Negers* are used for the last time. Only the small steamer *Fratton* (757 tons) is lost. In the last night only 16 of 42 *Negers* of Small Battle Unit Flotilla 363 return. The French battleship *Courbet* which has been sunk as a blockship is hit.

In an air attack on Le Havre on 2 Aug *S39*, *S114*, *M4430* and the tender *Planet* and four craft are sunk and *S79* and *S91* are badly damaged. In an engagement with three British MTBs off Le Havre in the following night *S180* and *S181* of the 2nd Flotilla are damaged by gunfire and *S167* and *MTB608* in collisions. The remaining operational boats of the 2nd and 6th Flotillas, *S174*, *S176*, *S177* and *S97*, *S132* and *S135*, undertake operations from Le Havre in the following nights in which the long-range torpedoes T3D *Dackel* are used for the first time. On 4-5 Aug 24, on 5-6 Aug 12, on 6-7 Aug 12, on 8-9 Aug 10, on 9-10 Aug 11 and on 14-15 Aug eight *Dackels* are fired at shipping concentrations in Seine Bay. The freighter *Iddesleigh* (5208 tons) is sunk and the cruiser *Frobisher*, the repair ship *Albatros* and one minesweeper are damaged. Apart from the first night, three boats are used with *Dackels* and two to three as torpedo carriers. In addition, normal torpedo operations are carried out in the nights 11-12 Aug and 13-14 Aug. In these operations of the escort forces and of the 2nd Escort Division (Cdr* v. Blanc) there are many engagements. On 5-6 Aug the motor torpedo boats are attacked off Le Havre by *MTB475*, *MTB476* and *MTB474*; and *S91* is damaged by a torpedo detonation. The 14th MMS Flotillas has an engage-

ment off Cap d'Antifer with the frigates *Thornborough* and *Retalick*. In the night 6-7 Aug the B Group of the 15th PB Flotilla has an engagement off Fécamp with *Thornborough* and the US *PT510*, *PT512* and *PT514*. In the night 7-8 Aug *Retalick* with four PT boats attacks the 14th MMS Flotilla and *PT520* and *PT521* are damaged. In the night 8-9 Aug boats of the 15th PB Flotilla have an engagement with two British SGBs off Fécamp in which *V241* sinks. In the next two nights there are further engagements between the 14th MMS Flotilla and the 15th PB Flotilla and MTB groups.

On 11-12 Aug the 10th MTB Flotilla (Lt-Cdr Müller) with *S183*, *S184*, *S185*, *S186*, *S191* and *S192* is transferred from Ostend to Ijmuiden. It carries out a mining operation off Orfordness in the night 13-14 Aug, in which there is an engagement with the destroyer *Walpole*. In another operation in the night 15-16 Aug the flotilla is driven off. In the night 12-13 Aug the 4th MMS Flotilla in a mining operation off Etaples and the 38th MMS Flotilla N of Cap de la Heve have engagements with MTB groups.

The 8th MTB Flotilla (Cdr Zymalkowski) with *S193*, *S194*, *S195*, *S196*, *S197*, *S198*, *S199* and *S701* is transferred on 14-15 Aug from Rotterdam to Boulogne. In the night 17-18 Aug boats of the flotilla attack a convoy off Dover when there is an engagement with the destroyers *Walpole* and *Opportune* and *MTB433*, *MTB432*, *MTB359*, *MTB353* and *MTB363*. In the night 20-21 Aug the destroyers *Melbreak*, *Watchman* and *Forester* drive the 8th Flotilla away from a convoy off Beachy Head.

In the night 18-19 Aug there are engagements near Le Tréport and Cap d'Antifer between boats of the 36th MS Flotilla and the 14th MMS Flotilla and *Melbreak* and *MTB212*, *MTB208*, *MTB209* and *MTB210*, in which *R218* is torpedoed and sunk.

In the night 19-20 Aug the A group of the 38th MS Flotilla beats off attacks by *MGB321*, *MGB322*, *MTB473*, *MTB479* and *MTB474* off Cap de la Heve and in the following night two motor minesweepers of the 14th MMS Flotilla and one submarine-chaser suffer damage in engagements with *MTB471*, *MTB476* and *MTB477* off Cap d'Antifer.

3-5 Aug Black Sea

With German authorization the small Turkish motor sailing ships *Morina*, *Bulbul* and *Mefkure* set out from Constanza to proceed towards the Bosphorus with 913 (according to other sources 1016) Jewish refugees. They are escorted by two Rumanian KFK submarine-chasers. Near the Rumanian-Bulgarian border, the submarine-chasers turn away and the sailing ships continue their journey alone. In the night 4-5 Aug the Soviet submarine *Shch-215* (Capt 3rd Class A. I. Strizhak), which is employed in the operational area off Burgas against German and Axis shipping to and from the Bosphorus, encounters the *Mefkure* and sinks her in a gun attack. Of the approximately 320 refugees on board, only five and the Turkish crew are rescued by the *Bulbul* on the following morning. The *Morina* arrives in the Bosphorus on the morning of 5 Aug and the *Bulbul* puts into Igneada.

The German U-boat *U18* (Lt Fleige) sinks at the beginning of August a steamer and a motor gunboat off Poti and damages a patrol boat and a steamer.

5 Aug-4 Sept Bay of Biscay/Brittany

After the break-through by the 1st US Army near Avranches on 31 July-1 Aug, Brest, Lorient and St Nazaire are encircled by elements of the 9th US Army from 7 Aug to 13 Aug and Nantes is taken on 13 Aug. British task forces frequently make sorties into the Bay of Biscay. A force, consisting of the cruiser *Bellona* and the destroyers *Tartar*, *Ashanti*, *Haida* and *Iroquois*, sinks the minesweepers *M263* and *M486*, the patrol boat *V414* and the coastal launch *Otto* (217 tons) from a German convoy N of the Ile d'Yeu near St Nazaire. *Haida* is slightly damaged. On 12 Aug the 12th SG, comprising the Canadian destroyers *Assiniboine*, *Qu'-Appelle*, *Skeena* and *Restigouche* and the British destroyer *Albrighton*, sinks a force of three armed trawlers S of Brest and the cruiser *Diadem* with the destroyers *Onslow* and *Piorun* sinks *Sperrbrecher 7* (7078 tons) near La Rochelle. On 14-15 Aug the cruiser *Mauritius*

and the destroyers *Ursa* and *Iroquois* attack a German force consisting of the torpedo boat *T24*, the aircraft repair ship *Richthofen* and *M385*, the last of which is sunk. On 20 Aug the *Diadem* force attacks the Ile d'Yeu and on 22-23 Aug the *Mauritius*, *Ursa* and *Iroquois* sink *V702*, *V717*, *V720*, *V729* and *V730* off Audierne. On 4 Sept the destroyer *Blyskawica* (Polish) lands a commando group on Les Sables d'Olonne.

As a result of Allied air attacks, *M422* is destroyed in St Malo on 4 Aug and *M133*, *M206* and *M343* on 6 Aug; *M271*, *M325* and *V725* in Pauillac on 5 Aug; and *M366*, *M367*, *M428* and *M438* in St Nazaire on 8 Aug. On 12 Aug fighter bombers sink *M370* off Royan.

On 21 Aug 19 Mosquitoes of RAF Coastal Command destroy *M292* in the Gironde Estuary and other aircraft the destroyer *Z23* off La Pallice. *Z24* and the torpedo boat *T24* are destroyed off Le Verdon by British bombers on 24-25 Aug.

When the harbours are evacuated the following ships are scuttled in Nantes on 11 Aug: the passenger steamer *Lindau* (13761 tons), the tankers *Vierlande* (14715 tons), *Monsun* (8038 tons), *Antarktis* (10711 tons) and *Passat* (8998 tons), the freighters *Tenerife II* (6150 tons) and *Olinda* (6068 tons) and many smaller ships. The warships *Sperrbrecher 20*, *V623*, *M384* and the unfinished new torpedo boats *TA1*, *TA2*, *TA3*, *TA5* and *TA6* are blown up. On the Seine, in and near Paris, the motor minesweepers *R182*, *R213*, *R217*, *RA3*, *RA4*, *RA5*, *RA6*, *RA7*, *RA8* are scuttled on 16 Aug. On 25-26 Aug on the Gironde and in Bordeaux 21 merchant ships of 70720 tons, the destroyer *Z37*, the minesweepers *M262*, *M304*, *M363*, *M463*, *Sperrbrecher 14*, *Sperrbrecher 122*, *V404* and *V407* are sunk.

5 Aug-30 Sept Arctic

Operations by German U-boats on the Siberian sea route: after *U957* (Lt Schaar), *U362* (Lt Franz) *U278* (Lt-Cdr Franze), *U711* (Lt-Cdr Lange), *U739* (Lt Mangold) and *U365* (Lt-Cdr Wedemeyer) set out for operations in the Kara Sea. On 12 Aug *U365* attacks the convoy BD.5 (Capt 1st Class

Shmelev), which set out from Archangel for Dikson on 8 Aug, and torpedoes the only steamer *Marina Raskova* (5685 tons). Because the Russians first think that they have hit a mine, the minesweepers halt with the result that *U365* is able to sink the former US minesweepers *T-118* and *T-114* and finish off *Marina Raskova*. Only *T-116* escapes. On 26 Aug *U957* sinks the survey ship *Nord*.

From 1 Sept to 5 Sept *U425* (Lt Bentzien), *U992* (Lt Falke), *U956* (Lt Mohs), *U968* (Lt Westphalen), *U995* (Lt-Cdr Köhntopp) and *U636* (Lt Schendel) form the 'Dachs' group and lay mine barrages in the narrows and channels in the Pechora Sea: of the results nothing is so far known. In those operations *U425* misses a freighter on 2 Sept.

After taking on oil from *U711* and *U957*, which are returning temporarily to refuel, the other three 'Greif' boats continue their operations. In an attempt to attack a Soviet group of steamers escorted by destroyers, minesweepers and trawler patrol ships near the Krakovka Islands on 5 Sept and 6 Sept *U739* misses a destroyer. *U278* does not come up and *U362* is sunk by depth charges from the minesweeper *T-116*. From 21 Sept to 24 Sept the U-boats of the 'Greif' group try to attack the Soviet convoy VD-1 (four transports, one *Groza* patrol ship, two *Fugas* patrol ships, three ex-US minesweepers, one trawler patrol ship and, from 23 Sept, the destroyers *Dostoyny* and *Zhestki*) on the way from the Vilkitski Strait to Dikson. On 21 Sept six successive attacks by *U711* on escort vessels fail as a result of torpedo defects. On 22 Sept *U739* and *U957* each unsuccessfully attack a steamer. On 23 Sept *U957* sinks the patrol ship *SKR-29/ Brilliant* and *U711* again reports defects when attacking three minesweepers and two steamers. On 24 Sept *U739* sinks the minesweeper *T-120*. On 24 Sept the three U-boats land a party on the island of Sterligova, which knocks out the wireless station. The boats return by 4 Oct.

6 Aug   Air War/Mediterranean
US B24 bombers attack Toulon: *U642*, *U952*, *U471* and *U969* are destroyed.

8-24 Aug   Indian Ocean
On 8 Aug the floating dock in Trincomalee collapses and sinks with the battleship *Valiant* which is badly damaged. On the same day the battleship *Howe* joins the Eastern Fleet, whose Commander, Adm Somerville, is succeeded by Adm Fraser on 23 Aug. At the end of August the 8th SM Flotilla with the submarines of the 'S' class is transferred to Fremantle (Australia) and the 2nd SM Flotilla arrives in Ceylon. Operation 'Boomerang': at the end of August the US XX Bomber Command attacks NW Sumatra with B29 Super Fortresses from Trincomalee. The British Eastern Fleet provides air rescue cover on its way. At this point the Eastern Fleet consists of the battleships *Howe, Richelieu, Queen Elizabeth*, battlecruiser *Renown* the carriers *Indomitable, Victorious* and *Illustrious*, 11 cruisers and 32 destroyers. On 24 Aug Rear-Adm Moody makes a carrier raid on Padang (South-West Sumatra) with the carriers *Victorious* and *Indomitable*, escorted by the battleship *Howe*, two cruisers and five destroyers (Operation 'Banquet'). Of the British submarines in the Malacca Straits area *Terrapin* (Lt-Cdr Martin) sinks two small ships; *Trenchant* (Cdr Hezlet) two small ships; *Statesman* (Lt Bulkeley) one ship of 1983 tons; and *Strongbow* three small ships and nine sailing ships.

9-11 Aug   Norway
A British carrier force, comprising the *Indefatigable, Trumpeter* and *Nabob* (Canadian), the cruisers *Kent* and *Devonshire* and the destroyers *Myngs, Vigilant, Verulam, Volage, Virago, Scourge* and the Canadian *Algonquin* and *Sioux*, attacks on 10 Aug the German airfield at Gossen near Kristiansund/North. Six Me 110s are destroyed and three steamers damaged.

9-14 Aug   Mediterranean
Positioning of the landing forces and convoys for the operation 'Dragoon' ('Anvil'). On 9 Aug the convoy SS.1 sets out from Naples; on 10 Aug AM.1 from Oran and TM.1 from Brindisi; on 11 Aug Spec.2 from Oran, SY.1 from Naples and the Delta' Support Force from Taranto; on 12 Aug the convoy TF.1 from Brindisi, the Carrier Force from Malta; the convoys

SM.1 and SF.2 and the 'Sitka' Support Force from Naples; on 13 Aug the 'Alpha' Support Force from Malta, the 'Camel' Support Force from Palermo; and the convoys SF.1 and SM.2 from Naples. Apart from the destroyers and light craft belonging to these forces, the following are additionally deployed to escort the convoys.

The destroyers (US) *Jouett, Benson, Niblack, Hilary P. Jones, Charles F. Hughes, Frankford, Carmick, Doyle, McCook, Baldwin, Harding, Satterlee* and *Thompson*; (French) *Le Fortuné, Forbin, Simoun, Tempête* and *L'Alcyon*; (the British 'Hunt' destroyers) *Aldenham, Beaufort, Belvoir, Whaddon, Blackmore, Eggesford, Lauderdale, Farndale, Atherstone, Brecon, Calpe, Catterick, Cleveland, Haydon, Bicester, Liddesdale, Oakley* and *Zetland*; (Greek) *Pindos* and *Kriti*. DEs (US) *Tatum, Haines, Marsh, Currier, Frederick C. Davis* and *Herbert C. Jones*; (French) *Marocain, Tunisien, Hova, Algérien* and *Somali*. Corvettes (British) *Aubrietia* and *Columbine*. Sloops (French) *Cdt Dominé, La Moqueuse, Cdt Bory, La Gracieuse* and *Cdt Delage*; six PMs and six YMSs.

11 Aug-29 Oct   North Atlantic
The U-boats *U548, U228, U993, U650, U190, U763, U437, U547, U534, U587, U853, U256, U260, U155, U382, U673* and *U267*, which are in the Biscay harbours and not completely operational and most of which are not equipped with schnorkels, are transferred to Norway. In setting out, only *U445* is lost in the Bay of Biscay at the hands of the British DE *Louis*. *U534* shoots down a Wellington bomber of No 172 Sqdn RAF. *U123* and *U129* scuttle themselves in Lorient on 19 Aug; and *U178, U188* and *UIT21* in Bordeaux on 20 Aug. Of the boats which arrive in Bergen *U92, U228, U437* and *U993* are lost in an RAF air attack on 4 Oct.
From 17 Sept to 26 Sept the outward-bounds schnorkel boats *U865* and *U867* and the homeward-bound *U855* are lost in air attacks W of Norway.

15 Aug   Mediterranean
Operation 'Dragoon': Allied forces (7th US Army, Lt-Gen Patch with VI US Corps (Maj-Gen Truscott) and II French Corps (Gen de Lattre de Tassigny)) land on the French Mediterranean coast between Cannes and Toulon. Deployed: the Western Task Force (Vice-Adm Hewitt) with headquarters group (the flagship *Catoctin*, the destroyer *Plunkett* and six minesweepers). Diversionary groups West comprise the destroyer *Endicott*, four MLs, eight PTs, 12 ASRCs and East the gunboats *Aphis* and *Scarab*, four MLs, four PTs and two FDSs.
After constant air attacks by 1300 land-based aircraft, the landings begin at first light: 396 troop transport aircraft land 5000 men of the 1st Airborne Group by parachute. TF 86 ('Sitka', Rear-Adm Davidson) with five LSIs, five APDs, 24 PTs, five AMs, four MLs and one buoy layer lands the 1st Special Force on the island of Levante. Fire support is provided by the battleship *Lorraine* (French), the cruisers *Augusta* (US, flagship), *Omaha, Cincinnati* (US), *Dido* and *Sirius* (British) and the destroyers *Somers, Gleaves* (US) and *Lookout* (British) and *Themistokles* (Greek).
TF 84 ('Alpha', Rear-Adm Lowry on USCG cutter *Duane*) with one LCI, one FDS, two APAs, two APs, three AKAs, 31 LSTs, 45 LCIs, 10 LCTs, 20 LCMs, two LCGs, two LCFs, 13 LCSs, two LCCs, 27 AMs, 10 YMSs, 10 PCs, 12 SCs and 11 tugs and salvage ships lands the 3rd US Div (Maj-Gen Daniels) in the Baie de Cavalaire. Fire support (Rear-Adm Mansfield) is provided by the battleship *Ramillies*, the cruisers *Orion, Aurora, Ajax, Black Prince* (British), *Quincy* (US) *Gloire* (French) and the destroyers *Livermore, Eberle, Kearny, Ericsson* (US) and *Terpsichore* and *Termagant* (British).
TF 85 ('Delta', Rear-Adm Rodgers on the headquarters ship *Biscayne*) with six APs, two AKAs, one LSP, one LSI, one LSG, 23 LSTs, 34 LCIs, 52 LCTS, two LCGs, two LCFs, 12 LCSs, two LCM(R)s, nine LCMs five LCCs, 52 LCVPs, one PC, five SCs, one FT, eight AMs, 10 tugs and salvage ships lands the 45th US Inf Div (Maj-Gen Eagles) in the Baie de Bugnon. Fire support (Rear-Adm Bryant) is provided by the battleships *Texas* and *Nevada* (US), the cruisers *Philadelphia* (US), *Montcalm* and *Georges Leygues* (French), the large

destroyers *Le Fantasque, Le Terrible* and *Le Malin* (French) and the destroyers *Forrest, Ellyson, Rodman, Emmons, Fitch, Hambleton, Macomb* and *Hobson* (US).

TF 87 ('Camel', Rear-Adm Lewis on the headquarters ship *Bayfield*) with two APAs, three APs, three AKAs, one LSI, one LSD, one LSF, 10 LSTs, 32 LCIs, 46 LCTs, 21 LCSs, two LCGs, four LCFs, seven LCCs, 10 LCMs, 32 LCVPs, six MLs, 11 PCs, 17 SCs, 16 AMs, 12 YMSs and 10 tugs and salvage ships lands the 36th US Div (Maj-Gen Dahlquist) both sides of Rade d'Agay. Fire support (Rear-Adm Deyo) is provided by the battleship *Arkansas*, the cruisers *Tuscaloosa, Brooklyn, Marblehead* (US), *Argonaut* (British), *Duguay Trouin* and *Emile Bertin* (French) and the destroyers *Parker, Kendrick, Mackenzie, McLanahan, Nields, Ordronaux, Woolsey, Ludlow, Boyle* and *Champlin* (US).

Air escort in the assault area is provided by Carrier TF 88 (Rear-Adm Troubridge) with TG 88.1, comprising the escort carriers *Khedive, Emperor, Searcher, Pursuer* and *Attacker* (24 fighters each), the cruisers *Royalist* and *Delhi* and the destroyers *Troubridge, Tuscan, Tyrian, Teazer, Tumult, Wheatland* (British) and *Navarinon* (Greek), and TG 88.2 (Rear-Adm Durgin), comprising the escort carriers *Tulagi, Kasaan Bay* (US), *Hunter* and *Stalker,* the cruisers *Colombo* and *Caledon* (British) and the destroyers *Butler, Gherardi, Herndon, Murphy, Jeffers* and *Shubrick* (US). There are also six MLs and a total of 216 fighters.

The landing is successful at all points. The bulk of the divisions are landed on the first day. Losses are slight. *LCI588, LCI590, YMS24, ML563, PT202, PT218* and *BYMS2022* are lost on mines and *LST282* by a glider bomb from a German aircraft.

On the afternoon of 15 Aug Prime Minister Churchill visits the landing fleet on board the destroyer *Kimberley*. By the evening of 17 Aug 86575 troops, 12250 vehicles and 46140 tons of supplies have been landed. By 2 Sept 190565 troops, 41534 vehicles and 219205 tons of supplies have been landed; and by 25 Sept the corresponding figures are 324069 troops, 68419 vehicles and 490237 tons of supplies.

A total of 881 assault vessels with 1370 landing boats on board are deployed.

15 Aug-6 Sept Arctic
Convoy operation JW.59/RA.59A. On 15 Aug JW. 59 sets out with 33 ships, one rescue ship and 11 US SC submarine-chasers for the Soviet Northern Fleet (Lend-Lease). An escort is provided by Vice-Adm Dalrymple-Hamilton on the escort carrier *Vindex* with the *Striker*, the cruiser *Jamaica* and the 20th and 22nd EG with seven destroyers, four sloops, two frigates and five corvettes. The Russian transfer force (Adm Levchenko and Capt 1st Class Fokin), consisting of the battleship *Arkhangelsk* and the destroyers *Zharki, Zhivuchi, Zhyuchi, Zhestki, Derzki, Doblestny, Dostoyny* and *Deyatelny,* which sets out on 17 Aug, proceeds N of the convoy. The Home Fleet (Adm Moore) operates in two groups in order to make raids on the *Tirpitz* lying in Kaafjord: Rear-Adm McGrigor with the carriers *Indefatigable, Formidable* and *Furious,* the battleship *Duke of York,* the cruisers *Devonshire* and *Berwick* and 14 destroyers, including *Myngs, Vigilant, Sioux, Algonquin* (Canadian), *Stord* (Norwegian), *Kempenfelt* and *Zambesi*; in addition, the escort carriers *Trumpeter* and *Nabob* (Canadian) with the 5th EG (Cdr Macintyre) composed of the DEs *Bickerton, Aylmer, Bligh, Garlies, Keats* and *Kempthorne.*

On 20 Aug a Ju 88 of Air Fleet 5 reports a warship force E of Jan Mayen. Early on 21 Aug the convoy reaches the patrol line of the 'Trutz' group (*U344, U668, U394, U363* and *U997*). *U344* (Lt-Cdr Pietsch) unsuccessfully attacks the 22nd EG with two T-5s and then sinks the sloop *Kite* with a FAT salvo. As a result of her report, a patrol line is formed for 22 Aug from the *U703* and *U354,* which have just set out, and the *U365* and *U711* coming from the Kara Sea. The British fleet carriers have had to break off the first attempt to attack *Tirpitz* on 20 Aug because of the weather. On 22 Aug the approach of the Barracuda and Corsair squadrons is detected in time and they are intercepted by the barrage of the heavy guns

and Me 109s of J.G. 5 which shoot down 11 aircraft in all. The ship, which is clouded in smoke, is not hit. On the afternoon of 22 Aug the outward-bound *U354* (Lt Sthamer) encounters the escort carrier group which is preparing to refuel the DEs and torpedoes the *Nabob* with a FAT salvo and the *Bickerton* (Cdr Macintyre) with a T-5. The latter is abandoned. A second attempt to attack the *Nabob* is frustrated by the Avenger bombers which take off from the listing flight deck. The carrier is taken in tow but is not repaired. Near the convoy *U363*, *U668*, *U703*, *U394* and also *U997* (after repelling three Swordfishes and Martlets from the *Vindex* and *Striker* as well as a Soviet Catalina of the 118th Reconnaissance Regt) are compelled to submerge and are driven off. On 23 Aug only *U394*, *U711* and *U365* can occupy the planned patrol line of the 'Trutz' group; the others are too far to the rear. *U394* gets an intermediate wave bearing on the talk of the escorts. *U363* and *U703* are forced underwater near the convoy and the other boats to the rear by the air escort and surface escorts. *U711* (Lt-Cdr Lange) fires a FAT salvo at the *Arkhangelsk* and a T-5 at the *Zharki*, which, however, detonate prematurely. Until 24 Aug the boats try in vain to advance against the air and sea escort. *U668* (Lt v. Eickstädt), *U363* (Lt-Cdr Nees) and *U997* (Lt Lehmann) each miss escorts with two T-5s and *U344* is sunk by the sloops *Mermaid* and *Peacock*, the frigate *Loch Dunvegan* and the leader of the 20th EG, the destroyer *Keppel* (Cdr Tyson). Because the convoy reaches harbour on 25 Aug, the operation is broken off and the 'Trutz' group is moved to the Bear Island Passage to operate against RA. 59A. But the attacks by *U711* on a destroyer group and a Soviet submarine, which turns up, have no success. *U354* is sunk by a Swordfish from *Vindex* with rocket bombs. The fleet carriers make another attack on *Tirpitz* on 24 Aug in which two minor hits are obtained and a fourth and unsuccessful attack on 29 Aug. In all, 247 sorties are flown in these attacks.
RA. 59A sets out on 28 Aug with nine steamers and the escort of JW. 59. But

neither German air reconnaissance nor the U-boats of the 'Trutz' group approach it. On 2 Sept *U394* is damaged by an aircraft from the *Vindex* and is sunk by the destroyers *Keppel* and *Whitehall* and the sloops *Mermaid* and *Peacock*. On 6 Sept the convoy arrives in Loch Ewe.

16-17 Aug Mediterranean
In an attempt to get from Toulon to Marseilles, the two submarine-chasers *UJ6073* and *UJ6081* are found SE of Marseilles by the US destroyer *Endicott*, the gunboats *Aphis* and *Scarab* and a number of smaller units and are sunk. The Allied ships rescue 210 survivors from the German crews.

16-31 Aug Arctic
Soviet combined operation against German convoys on the Polar coast. On 17 Aug there is a heavy Soviet air attack on Kirkenes; in spite of strong fighter defence by J.G. 5 two steamers of 3243 tons are destroyed. On 18 Aug a convoy of six steamers with *M251*, *M252*, *M202*, *M154*, *M35*, *M31*, *K3*, *V6102*, *V6104*, *V6111*, *V6112*, *R160*, *R202*, *UJ1224*, *UJ1219*, *UJ1220*, *UJ1222* and *UJ1211* is located by Soviet reconnaissance aircraft. Of the submarines, *S-15*, *S-51*, *S-103* and *M-201*, which are deployed from their waiting positions, only *M-201* (Lt-Cdr Balin) is able to fire at midnight (when it is light) on 18-19 Aug and sinks *V6112* off Persfjord. Then the torpedo cutters (Capt 1st Class Kuzmin) are deployed.
Three TKAs lay mines S of Busse Sound (Lt Pavlov). An advance detachment of four TKAs (Lt-Cdr Reshetko) supports the attack of the main assault group consisting of five TKAs (Capt 3rd Class Korshunevich) by putting down smoke screens. Two TKAs (Lt-Cdr Efimov) reconnoitre by night as far as Persfjord. In the attack on 19 Aug *V6102* is sunk by two hits and the steamer *Colmar* (3946 tons) by one hit. *M202* and *M31* each sink a TKA, one of which is *TKA-203*. On 23 Aug Soviet air formations make heavy attacks on Vardö and Vadsö. When, in the process, a west-bound convoy is located, the submarines *S-15*, *S-51* and *S-103*, which are in waiting positions, are deployed. The attack by *S-103* (Capt

3rd Class Nechaev) off Makkaur, in which E-torpedoes are used for the first time, fails and goes unnoticed. *S-15* (Lt-Cdr Vasilev) torpedoes the steamer *Dessau* with an E-torpedo off Nordkyn on 24 Aug. The steamer is part of a convoy of five ships with *M251*, *M252*, *M202*, *M154*, *M35*, *M31*, *K3*, *V6110*, *R160*, *R202*, *UJ1219*, *UJ1211*, *UJ1220*, *UJ1224* and *UJ1222*. The *Dessau* (5983 tons) is taken in tow to Mehamn. On 28 Aug *S-103* misses an east-bound convoy escorted by *K3*.

20 Aug   Baltic
The 2nd TF, comprising the heavy cruiser *Prinz Eugen* and the destroyers *Z25*, *Z28*, *Z35*, *Z36* and the torpedo boats *T23* and *T28*, is deployed against Soviet forward troops who have broken through near Tukkum in the Gulf of Riga. With support from naval guns, land communications with Army Group North, which had been cut off, are restored.

20 Aug   Black Sea
Sixty-two bombers, 80 fighters and ground attack planes of the Soviet Black Sea Fleet, after preliminary smoke attacks to eliminate the AA fire, attack the harbour of Constanza and sink the U-boat *U9*, the motor torpedo boats *S42*, *S52* and *S131*, the Rumanian torpedo boat *Naluca* and many smaller craft. The Rumanian destroyers *Regele Ferdinand* and *Marasesti*, the gunboat *Stihi*, the minelayer *Dacia*, the U-boats *U18* and *U24* and other vessels are damaged.

20 Aug-21 Oct   Norway
Intensification of British attacks on German convoy traffic on the Norwegian West Coast. On 20 Aug and 22 Aug the submarine *Satyr* (Lt-Cdr Weston) attacks two German convoys off Skudesnes and Egeröy, but the salvoes explode on the cliffs (a frequent cause of reported false successes in Norway). On 11 Sept and 13 Sept *Venturer* (Lt Launders) attacks two convoys off Lister and with the first torpedo sinks a steamer of 678 tons.
On 11 Sept RAF Beaufighters sink *M246* and *M462* from a force of four minesweepers off south-west Norway.
On 12 Sept a British force, consisting of the carriers *Furious* and *Trumpeter*, the cruiser *Kent* and destroyers, makes a raid on shipping near Stadlandet. Carrier aircraft sink *V5307* and damage *V5309* and *V5105*, which are beached, and the steamer *Ostland* (5374 tons). On 19 Sept Beaufighters sink two small ships in Stavfjord. On 20 Sept the submarine *Sceptre* (Lt-Cdr McIntosh) sinks one ship of 1184 tons and *M132* off Egersund. Between 24 Sept and 26 Sept *UJ1106*, *UJ1715* and two steamers of 11044 tons sink on a mine barrage laid by the French submarine *Rubis* in the Feiestein Channel. On 4 Oct RAF Bomber Command makes a heavy attack on the harbour of Bergen: *U92*, *U228*, *U437*, *U993* and four steamers of 11708 tons are destroyed. On 8 Oct *MTB712*, *MTB722* and *MTB711* of the Norwegian 54th MTB Flotilla attack ships N of Floröy and drive the coaster *Freikoll* (236 tons) on to the beach. On 9 Oct Beaufighters attack a convoy near Egersund and sink *UJ1711* and one ship of 1953 tons; two ships of 4170 tons are damaged as well as the gunboat *K2*. On 14-15 Oct a British force, comprising the cruiser *Euryalus*, the escort carriers *Trumpeter* and *Fencer* and the destroyers *Myngs*, *Volage*, *Serapis*, *Scorpion*, *Algonquin* (RCN) and *Sioux* (RCN), carries out an air-mining operation and air raids on German shipping routes off Norway near Frohavet. On 15 Oct *V1605* is sunk by aircraft and two steamers and *V5716* are damaged and driven on to the beach. On 17 Oct the patrol boat *V6801* falls victim to Beaufighters, on 21 Oct two steamers and on 23 Oct *V5506* off Hjeltefjord. A British force, consisting of the carrier *Implacable*, the cruiser *Bellona* and the destroyers *Venus*, *Scourge*, *Savage*, *Verulam*, *Caprice*, *Zambesi*, *Cassandra* and *Cambrian*, makes carrier attacks on Sörreisa and the airfield at Bardufoss. Reconnaissance aircraft photograph the *Tirpitz* anchored near Tromsö. An attempted attack by the Norwegian *MTB688*, *MTB711* and *MTB653* on a convoy near Stavfjord is frustrated by *V5101* and *V5113*.
The submarine *Viking* (Lt Banner-Martin) sinks on 14 Oct one ship of 1286 tons from a convoy and *Sceptre* on 20 Oct and 21 Oct one steamer of 2207 tons and *UJ1111* from two convoys.

23-30 Aug   Black Sea
Light units of the Soviet Danube Flotilla (Rear-Adm Gorshkov) support on 23-24 Aug the crossing of the Dniester/Liman by elements of the 46th Army and in the following days they enter the Danube Estuary. Of the units of the Black Sea Fleet, the submarines *S-31, S-33, Shch-215, M-62, M-111* and *M-113* are employed on the Rumanian/Bulgarian coast but they only make two unsuccessful attacks. Of the torpedo cutters employed, *TKA-221, TKA-223, TKA-227* and *TKA-233* have a short, indecisive engagement with two submarine-chasers E of Constanza on 22 Aug. Thirty torpedo cutters and six patrol cutters take part in the capture of Constanza on 30 Aug. Minesweepers are also transferred.

23-31 Aug   English Channel
Evacuation of Le Havre. In the night 23-24 Aug the 15th PB Flotilla (Cdr Rall) moves from Le Havre to Dieppe with two trawlers, one submarine-chaser and 16 KFKs and two motor minesweepers with two more in tow. Off Cap d'Antifer and Fécamp the boats are first attacked by the frigate *Thornborough* (Lt Brown), the 'Hunt' destroyer *Talybont* (Lt Holdsworth) and the MTBs (Lt Marshall) *MTB695, MTB694* and *MTB692*, then by the frigate *Retalick* (Lt Brownrigg), the destroyer *Melbreak* (Lt Kirby) and the MTBs (Lt Forster) *MTB212, MTB208* and *MTB205. V716* and *R229* are damaged and *R219* is sunk by fighter bombers as she comes into harbour. In the night 24-25 Aug the 15th PB Flotilla, and the 38th MS Flotilla (Cdr* Palmgren) move from Dieppe to Boulogne with five trawlers, 16 drifters and three MFKs and *R117* and *F840*. The 8th Gun Carrier Flotilla carries out a supply mission to Le Havre with some units. The German ships are successively attacked by the US PT boats (Lt Saltsman) *PT250, PT511* and *PT514*, the frigate *Seymour* (Lt-Cdr Parry) with the MTBs (Lt Shaw) *MTB257, MTB 256, MTB254* and *MTB252*, an MTB group (Lt Yock) consisting of *MTB452, MTB447* and *MTB453* and, also, *Talybont, Retalick* and *MTB205, MTB 209* and *MTB210*. In engagements *S91* from the boats of the 6th MTB Flotilla,

deployed for cover, and *M3857*, sink. *V243* is damaged and *AF103* is lost on a mine. The destroyer *Bleasdale* is the last to intervene in the engagement. The 8th MTB Flotilla, which makes a sortie against a convoy off Beachy Head, is driven off by the SGBs *Grey Wolf* and *Grey Goose*. In the night 25-26 Aug the 8th Gun Carrier Flotilla (Lt Schneider) is attacked near Fécamp by *Thornborough* with an MTB group (Lt Dixon) comprising *MTB450, MTB481* and *MTB482*, the French destroyer *La Combattante* (Cdr Patou) with an MTB group (Lt Shaw) comprising *MTB253, MTB257* and *MTB254* and *Seymour* with a US PT group comprising *PT519, PT513* and *PT516. AF110, AF97, AF105* and *AF111* are lost; *AF101* and *AF109* are brought in, the latter towed by *S174*. In the following night *Retalick* with *MTB208* and *MTB210* and *Middleton* (Lt Cox) with *MTB252, MTB256, PT520, PT511* and *PT514* again attack boats of the 8th Gun Carrier Flotilla and the 14th MMS Flotilla. *AF98* and *AF108* are sunk. In the night 27-28 Aug the 14th MMS Flotilla (Lt-Cdr Nordt) with seven boats sows mines in the Seine Estuary near Le Havre and proceeds with two submarine-chasers to Fécamp. Off Cap d'Antifer there are engagements with *Thornborough, MTB450, MTB447, MTB482* and *La Combattante*, with *MTB693, MTB692* and *MTB695* and *PT519* and *PT512. UJ1433* is sunk and *R231* is towed in damaged.
In the night 29-30 Aug nine motor minesweepers, six AFs, one MFL, one KFK, one submarine-chaser and one tug move from Le Havre to Fécamp. Cover is provided by boats of the 8th MTB Flotilla. Attacks by *Retalick* and the 'Hunt' destroyer *Cattistock* (Lt Keddie†) are beaten off: the latter is damaged. In the two following nights the remaining operational boats of the 2nd Escort Division (Cdr* v. Blanc) are moved from Dieppe, Boulogne and Calais through the Straits of Dover to the E. On 3-4 Sept the last 13 operational motor torpedo boats are moved from the Channel area to Rotterdam and Ijmuiden: in the process *S184* is sunk by the Dover batteries. After shelling by the battleship *Warspite* and the

monitor *Erebus* (the coastal guns secure one hit) on 10 Sept and a heavy air attack by the RAF on 11 Sept, in which 807 tons of bombs are dropped. Le Havre surrenders on 12 Sept.

23 Aug-7 Oct   North Atlantic
Schnorkel U-boats are employed in coastal waters. *U680* and then *U1199* (Lt Nollmann), which remains under water for 50 days, operate off the Scottish East Coast. Each fires a torpedo which misses. *U482, U484, U743, U398, U296, U285, U963, U985, U953, U281* and *U1004* are employed in the Minches, off the Hebrides and in the North Channel for six to twelve days at a time. *U248* and *U309* have to return before they reach the North Channel because of the strong defence. From 27 Aug to 8 Sept *U482* (Lt-Cdr Count v. Matuschka) attacks five convoys and sinks a tanker and the corvette *Hurst Castle* from CU.36, one ship from ONS.251 and two ships from HX.305. totalling 31611 tons. On 9 Sept, while attempting to attack convoys, *U743* is sunk near ONF.252 by the corvette *Portchester Castle* and the frigate *Helsmdale* and *U484* by the Canadian frigates *Dunver* and *Nene* and the corvettes *Hespeler* and *Huntsville* of EG C.5. The other boats return, having achieved no success. On her way into the Bristol Channel *U247* is sunk on 1 Sept by the Canadian frigates *St John* and *Swansea* of the 9th SG. *U758, U262* and *U714* return without success. Off Reykjavik on 22-23 Sept, *U244* and *U979* (Lt-Cdr Meermeier) attack convoys. The latter torpedoes a ship of 5970 tons. *U772* and *U245* are stationed as weather boats in the North Atlantic.

24 Aug-11 Sept   Black Sea
In evacuating the harbour of Constanza on 24 Aug the non-operational warships, including the U-boats *U18* and *U24*, the motor torpedo boats *S28* and *S149* and the KT ship *KT39*, are scuttled. On 29-30 Aug the last warships remaining in the Rumanian-Bulgarian area are scuttled off Varna outside Bulgarian territorial waters. Among the approximately 200 craft there are, inter alia, four motor torpedo boats, 14 motor minesweepers, four large, and about 20 small, submarine-chasers and many ferry barges and some KT ships. Some

of the units in the Danube Estuary, particularly the ferry barges, go up the Danube under the command of Rear-Adm Zieb. The last three German U-boats in the Black Sea, *U19, U20* and *U23*, operate from 25 Aug in the area off Constanza. *U23* (Lt Arendt) fires a salvo into the harbour of Constanza on 1 Sept, when the damaged freighter *Oituz* (2686 tons) is hit (she is not repaired). On 2 Sept *U19* (Lt Ohlenburg) sinks the Soviet minesweeper *T-410/Vrzyv* off Constanza. When their fuel is used up, and an offer to sell them to Turkey has been rejected, the three U-boats are scuttled by their own crews near Erekli on the Turkish coast.

28 Aug-24 Sept   Central Pacific
Carrier TF 38 (Vice-Adm Mitscher) sets out from Eniwetok on 28 Aug to make raids in connection with the Palau-Morotai operation. There take part: TG 38.1 (Rear-Adm McCain), comprising the carriers *Wasp, Hornet, Cowpens* and *Belleau Wood*, the cruisers *Wichita, Boston* and *Canberra* and 11 destroyers; TG 38.2 (Rear-Adm Bogan), comprising the carriers *Bunker Hill, Intrepid, Cabot* and *Independence*, the battleships *Iowa* and *New Jersey* (Adm Halsey, Commander 3rd Fleet), the cruisers *Vincennes, Houston* and *Miami* and 18 destroyers; TG 38.3 (Rear-Adm Sherman), comprising the carriers *Lexington, Essex, Princeton* and *Langley*, the battleships *Washington, Indiana, Massachusetts* and *Alabama*, the cruisers *Santa Fé, Birmingham, Mobile* and *Reno* and 18 destroyers; and TG 38.4 (Rear-Adm Davison), comprising the carriers *Franklin, Enterprise* and *San Jacinto*, the cruisers *New Orleans* and *Biloxi* and 13 destroyers.
On 31 Aug, 1 Sept and 2 Sept TG 38.4 attacks Iwojima and Chichijima and on 1 Sept and 2 Sept the cruisers and destroyers shell the islands.
On 3 Sept TG 12.5 (Rear-Adm Smith) with the cruisers *Chester, Pensacola* and *Salt Lake City* and the destroyers *Dunlap, Fanning* and *Reid*, shells Wake. Air escort is provided by the carrier *Monterey*.
On 6 Sept, 7 Sept and 8 Sept all four TGs attack Palau with 16 carriers. On 9 Sept and 10 Sept the TGs 38.1, 38.2 and 38.3 attack airfields on Mindanao

with 12 carriers against very little resistance. From 12 Sept to 14 Sept the weight of the attacks is therefore shifted to the area of the Visayas (Central Philippines). TG 38.1 attacks Mindanao again on 14 Sept. In 2400 sorties in these three days over 200 aircraft are destroyed. After replenishing, the 12 carriers make attacks on airfields on Luzon on 21 Sept and 22 Sept, particularly in the area of Manila, and again on the Visayas on 24 Sept. In these attacks over 1000 Japanese aircraft, in all, are destroyed. 150 ships of all sizes are sunk and destroyed. The Americans lose 54 aircraft in combat and 18 as a result of accidents. Adm Halsey proposes to cancel the Mindanao landing, planned for 20 Oct, and to land on Leyte on this date.

1 Sept Arctic/Greenland
The US coastguard cutter *Northland* finds the weather observation ship *Kehdingen* when trying to establish a weather station on the ice on the East Coast of Greenland. The escorting U-boat, *U703*, fires torpedoes but they explode in the ice.

1-12 Sept Mediterranean/Adriatic
The Italian Adriatic coast in the area of Rimini is shelled by the British destroyers *Undine*, *Urchin*, *Loyal* and *Kimberley* and the gunboats *Aphis* and *Scarab*.

1-13 Sept Mediterranean/Tyrrhenian Sea
The French Riviera Coast is shelled by the US cruiser *Philadelphia* and the destroyers *Woolsey*, *Edison*, *Ludlow*, *Hilary P. Jones*, *Madison*, the French battleship *Lorraine*, the cruisers *Montcalm*, *Emile Bertin*, *Duguay Trouin* and *Gloire* and the destroyers *Le Malin* and *Forbin*.

1-30 Sept Pacific
US submarines arriving in their operational areas in September sink the following ships: off Japan, Formosa and the Kuriles *Albacore* (Cdr Blanchard) sinks one ship of 880 tons and the submarine-chaser *Kusentai 165*; *Apogon* (Lt-Cdr House) one ship of 1999 tons; *Bang* (Lt-Cdr Gallagher) three ships of 4220 tons; *Finback* (Lt-Cdr Williams) two ships of 1390 tons; *Guardfish* (Lt-Cdr Ward) one ship of 873 tons; *Pipefish* (Lt-Cdr Deragon) one ship of 1018 tons; *Plaice* (Lt-Cdr Stevens) the corvette *Kaibokan 10*; *Queenfish* (Lt-Cdr Loughlin) three ships of 14850 tons and torpedoes one ship; *Sealion* (Lt-Cdr Reich) three ships of 10541 tons and the minelayer *Shirataka*; *Searaven* (Lt-Cdr Dry) torpedoes one ship; *Shad* (Lt-Cdr Julihn) sinks two ships of 498 tons and the gunboat *Ioshima*; *Skate* (Lt-Cdr Lynch) two ships of 3909 tons; *Sunfish* (Lt-Cdr Shelby) two ships of 11154 tons; *Thresher* (Lt-Cdr Middleton) three ships of 9195 tons. In the area of the Malayan Archipelago and the Philippines *Barb* (Lt-Cdr Fluckey) sinks two ships of 15655 tons and the escort carrier *Unyo*; *Bashaw* (Lt-Cdr Nicholas) one ship of 2813 tons; *Bonefish* (Lt-Cdr Edge) two ships of 4632 tons and torpedoes one ship; *Flasher* (Lt-Cdr Whitaker) three ships of 18610 tons; *Growler* (Lt-Cdr Oakley) the destroyer *Shikinami* and the frigate *Hirato*; *Guavina* (Lt-Cdr Teideman) the fast transport *No. 3*; *Haddo* (Lt-Cdr Nimitz) the survey ship *Katsuriki*; *Lapon* (Lt-Cdr Baer) three ships of 14177 tons; *Paddle* (Lt-Cdr Nowell) one ship of 2634 tons and torpedoes one ship; *Pampanito* (Lt-Cdr Summers) two ships of 15544 tons; *Pargo* (Lt-Cdr Bell) one ship of 599 tons and the minelayer *Aotaka* and torpedoes the seaplane tender *Kamoi*.

2-21 Sept Baltic
On 2 Sept the Finnish Prime Minister Hackzell announces the breaking-off of diplomatic relations with Germany and demands the withdrawal of German troops from Finland. On 4 Sept the Finnish armed forces stop fighting on the whole front against the Soviet Union. From 4 Sept to 21 Sept the following are removed by sea from Finnish Baltic harbours: 4049 German troops, 3336 wounded, 332 evacuees, 746 vehicles and 42144 tons of Wehrmacht property. 13064 tons of this is lost because of the defection of Finnish ships in Finnish or Swedish harbours. 110000 tons of Wehrmacht property has to be destroyed on the spot because it is no longer possible to get it away in time. The 3rd TB Flotilla (Cdr Verlohr) makes a reconnaissance sortie with *T18*, *T13* and *T20* to the Aaland Sea as a show of force. On the return *T18* is destroyed by Soviet bombers N of Tallinn (Reval).

On 27 Sept Sweden closes her Baltic ports to German ships.

4 Sept Air War/Mediterranean

US aircraft drop 438 tons of bombs on the harbour installations of Genoa: the torpedo boat *TA28* capsizes in dock, the new *TA33* is sunk and many other ships are damaged, including the hospital ship *Erlangen.*

5-12 Sept North Sea

On the way from Antwerp to Holland the minesweepers *M274* and *M276* are scuttled by their crews in the Scheldt Estuary on 5 Sept.

On 6 Sept 26 Beaufighters attack a German convoy NE of Wangerooge and sink the Swedish freighter *Rosafred* (1348 tons).

On 12 Sept British fighter bombers attack a German convoy anchored in the roads of den Helder. They sink the uncompleted new torpedo boat *T61*, which was to be transferred to Germany for completion.

6-19 Sept Air War/Germany

On 6 Sept RAF Bomber Command drops 580 tons of bombs on Emden.

On 15-16 Sept 490 bombers of RAF Bomber Command drop 1448 tons of bombs on Kiel.

On 18-19 Sept 213 bombers of RAF Bomber Command attack Bremerhaven.

7 Sept-9 Jan Baltic

After the loss of the Finnish harbours the German U-boats (Operations leader Cdr Brandi) operate from Danzig and Gotenhafen off the entrances to the Gulf of Finland. In September and October *U717*, *U958*, *U370*, *U348*, *U475*, *U290*, *U1165* and *U481* take part. On 21 Sept *U242* and *U1001* lay mine barrages near Porkkala, on which the Finnish steamer *Rigel* (1495 tons) sinks. On 8-9 Oct *U370* sinks a motor gunboat and the Finnish tug *No 764*. *U481* (Lt Andersen) sinks three Finnish sailing ships on 15 Oct. *U1165* (Lt Homann) sinks one motor minesweeper and attacks a submarine convoy. *U958* (Lt-Cdr Groth) sinks two Finnish sailing ships. *U1001* (Lt Blaudow) torpedoes a tug on 25 Oct and *U475* (Lt-Cdr Stöffler) sinks a patrol boat. In November until the beginning of December *U475*, *U958*, *U479*, *U481*, *U679* and *U1165* are employed partly in the Gulf of Bothnia and partly in the area

Hangö-Tallinn. *U679* (Lt Aust) sinks a patrol boat and a minesweeper and is lost on 9 Jan as a result of being depth-charged by the patrol boat *MO-124*. *U481* sinks a lighter and probably the Finnish minelayer *Louhi*. *U637* (Lt-Cdr Riekeberg), which sets out at the end of November, sinks a patrol boat. *U479* is lost about 12 Dec on a mine laid by the Russian submarine *Lembit.*

8 Sept Air War/Adriatic

British Beaufighters set the Italian passenger ship *Rex* (51062 tons) on fire in Trieste.

10-28 Sept Arctic

Combined Russian operation against German convoy traffic on the Polar Coast. Deployment of submarines *S-15*, *S-51*, *S-103*, *S-101* and *V-3* (using radar for the first time). On 14 Sept and 15 Sept Russian ground attack and fighter bombers make attacks on Vardö and on Kiberg and Kongsfjord. The naval ferry barge *F223* and *UJ1224* are sunk. On 15 Sept an attack by four Russian torpedo cutters (Lt-Cdr Lozovski) and 15 ground attack aircraft of the type Il-2 on a German Petsamo-Kirkenes convoy is repulsed by the German escort: *TKA-13* is sunk by the 61st PB Flotilla (Cdr Kramer). On 16 Sept in an air attack on Kirkenes the ammunition steamer *Wolsum* (3668 tons) explodes. On 20 Sept in an attack by a torpedo aircraft group off the North Cape the catapult ship *Friesenland* (5434 tons) receives a hit and has to be beached. On 21 Sept Russian aircraft sink their own submarine *Shch-402* in error.

On 24 Sept a convoy located by air reconnaissance is attacked near Nordkyn by the submarine *S-56* (Capt 2nd Class Shchedrin) with a salvo of four torpedoes, but *V6105* out-manoeuvres them. Three submarine-chasers of the 12th SC Flotilla (Cdr Köplin) fight the submarine with depth charges. On 25 Sept two torpedo cutter groups (Capt 2nd Class Alexeev) attack with nine TKAs near Skalneset and Ekkeröy but they are driven off by the escort and one TKA is sunk. In simultaneous attacks by 33 Il-2 ground attack aircraft and 14 Yak-9 and 24 Kittyhawk fighter bombers with cover from 24 fighters, *V6101* is sunk by bomb hits, *V6105* and

F152 are damaged and beached and *V6110* and *R309* are damaged but taken in tow. On 26 Sept *S-56* unsuccessfully attacks the returning minesweepers *M31* and *M251* and is damaged by depth charges.

13-24 Sept   Mediterranean/Aegean
British offensive in the Aegean against German evacuation movements. On 13 Sept the British destroyers *Troubridge* and *Tuscan* sink the small transport *Toni* (638 tons) N of Crete. On 15 Sept the cruiser *Royalist* and the destroyer *Teazer* sink the KT ship *Erpel* and the KT submarine-chaser *UJ2171/Heidelberg* off Cape Spatha. In Salamis German torpedo boat *TA14* sinks in an air attack on 15 Sept and the harbour patrol boat *GD91* and the KT ship *Mannheim* are badly damaged. In attacks by RAF Beaufighters in the Aegean from 20 Sept to 24 Sept the KT ship *Pelikan* is sunk off Paros, the minelayer *Drache* off Samos and the steamer *Orion* (707 tons) off Naxos. Operation 'Odysseus': from 20 Sept to 24 Sept the new torpedo boats *TA39* (Lt-Cdr Lange), *TA37* (Lt Winkelmann) and *TA38* (Sub-Lt Scheller) are transferred into the Aegean from Trieste through the Adriatic, the Strait of Otranto (where there is a short, indecisive engagement with the British destroyers *Belvoir* and *Whaddon*), the Gulf of Patras and the Corinth Canal. In an air attack on Piraeus/Skaramanga the last operational U-boat *U596*, the damaged *U565* and the submarine-chaser *UJ2108* are sunk.

14 Sept   Baltic
German landing operation 'Tanne Ost' on the Finnish island of Suursaari by units of the 3rd and 25th MS Flotillas, the 13th, 21st and 24th Landing Flotillas, the 7th Gun Carrier Flotilla, the 1st MMS Flotilla and the 5th MTB Flotilla. There is strong Finnish resistance. Attacks by Russian aircraft and Finnish torpedo boats compel the assault fleet to withdraw. The troops, which are landed, are compelled to surrender on 15 Sept (1231 prisoners including 175 wounded).

14-24 Sept   Arctic
An attempt by the schnorkel U-boat *U315* (Lt Zoller) to enter the Kola Inlet and to attack the battleship

Arkhangelsk (ex-HMS *Royal Sovereign*) fails because of the net barrages in the inner part of the Inlet. A second attempt with the schnorkel U-boat *U313* (Lt-Cdr Schweiger) fails from 28 Sept to 10 Oct.

15 Sept   Arctic
28 Lancaster bombers of No 9 and No 517 Sqdns RAF, operating from North Russian airfields, attack the German battleship *Tirpitz* in Altafjord with heavy 5.4-ton bombs, but they only hit the smoke-covered ship with one bomb on her bows. The ferry steamer *Kehrwieder* is sunk.

15 Sept   South West Pacific
The VII Amphibious Force (TF 77), which set out from its bases (Aitape, Wakde and Hollandia) on 10 Sept, lands the 31st Inf Div (Maj-Gen Persons) and the 126th RCT (32nd Div) of XI Corps (Lt-Gen Hall) on Morotai on 15 Sept. The force comprises two groups: 'White' (Rear-Adm Barbey in overall command on the headquarters ship *Wasatch*) and 'Red' (Rear-Adm Fechteler on the destroyer *Hughes*). The landing fleet comprises two Australian APAs, five US APDs, 45 LSTs, 24 LCIs, 20 LCTs and one LSD. Support and escort: 24 destroyers, four frigates, 11 LCT(R)s, six PCs, two ATFs and four YMSs. Cover for the operation and pre-landing bombardment is provided by TF 75 (Rear-Adm Berkey) with TG 75.1, comprising the US cruisers *Phoenix Boise* and *Nashville* (Gen MacArthur on board), the destroyers *Hutchins*, *Beale*, *Bache*, *Daly*, *Abner Read* and *Bush*, and TG 75.2 (Commodore Collins), comprising the Australian cruisers *Australia* and *Shropshire*, the destroyers *Arunta*, *Warramunga*, *Mullany* and *Ammen*. Air support is provided by TG 77.1 (Rear-Adm T. L. Sprague), comprising the escort carriers *Sangamon*, *Suwanee*, *Chenango*, *Santee*, *Saginaw Bay*, *Petrof Bay* and eight destroyers. On the first day 19960 troops are landed without resistance. From 16 Sept to 3 Oct a total of 26000 combat troops and 12200 construction and ground personnel are landed.

The 5th USAAF (Lt-Gen Kenney) provides continuous air support from Biak, Noemfoor and Cape Sansapor. On 3 Oct the Japanese submarine *Ro-41*

(Lt-Cdr Shiizuka) attacks a US carrier group consisting of the escort carriers *Fanshaw Bay* and *Midway* E of Morotai and sinks the DE *Shelton*. The other DEs, *Eversole, Richard M. Rowell* and *Edmonds*, take up the search, but they sink in error the US submarine *Seawolf* which is proceeding in the area.

15 Sept-5 Oct Arctic
Convoy operation JW. 60/RA. 60. On 15 Sept JW. 60 sets out from Loch Ewe with 30 ships. Escort (Rear-Adm McGrigor): the escort carriers *Campania* and *Striker*, the cruiser *Diadem*, 12 escorts of the 20th and 8th EG, including the destroyers *Keppel, Bulldog* and *Whitehall*, the sloop *Cygnet* and the corvettes *Allington Castle* and *Bamborough Castle*. Cover is provided by the battleship *Rodney* and the destroyers *Saumarez, Virago, Volage, Venus* and *Verulam*, the Canadian *Algonquin* and *Sioux* and also *Milne, Musketeer, Marne* and *Meteor*. A force, consisting of the cruiser *Jamaica* and the destroyers *Orwell* and *Obedient*, carries out the provisioning of Spitzbergen. The convoy is not located either by German air reconnaissance or by the U-boat group 'Grimm' (*U278, U312, U425, U737, U921, U956* and *U997*) and it arrives in the Kola Inlet on 23 Sept. Some of the ships arrive with a Soviet escort in the White Sea on 25 Sept. RA. 60, which sets out in the night 27-28 Sept with the escort of JW. 60, avoids the 'Grimm' group and the 'Zorn' group (*U293, U310, U315, U363, U365, U387, U636, U668, U965, U968, U992* and *U995*) which has just put out. Only *U310* (Lt Ley), which happens to be overrun, sinks two ships of 14395 tons with FAT salvoes and misses several escorts with T-5s. *U921* is sunk by a Swordfish from the *Campania*. On 5 Oct RA. 60 arrives in Loch Ewe.

15 Sept-23 Oct Central Pacific
Operation 'Stalemate II': landing on Palau by TF 31 (Rear-Adm Wilkinson) with III Amphibious Corps (Maj-Gen Geiger). After the raids by TF 38 from 6 Sept to 8 Sept, there begins on 13 Sept and 14 Sept the shelling of the islands of Peleliu and Angaur, which are to be attacked, by the Fire Support

Group (Rear-Adm Oldendorf), consisting of the battleships *Pennsylvania, Tennessee, Maryland, Mississippi* and *West Virginia*, the cruisers *Louisville, Portland, Indianapolis, Minneapolis, Honolulu* (Rear-Adm Ainsworth), *Denver* (Rear-Adm Hayler), *Columbia* and two others as well as 14 destroyers. Air support is provided by seven to eleven escort carriers (Rear-Adm Ofstie) which alone fly 382 sorties on the day of the landing.

On 15 Sept the 'Northern Attack Force' lands the 1st Marine Div (Maj-Gen Rupertus) on Peleliu. The resistance of the groups of the 2nd Inf Regt of the Japanese 14th Div under Col Nakagawa with 5300 troops, who are deeply entrenched in the mountain ridges, is only overcome with difficulty. A regiment of the 81st Inf Div has to be landed. On 12 Oct the attack phase is ended, but the last 45 defenders are not overwhelmed until 25 Dec.

On 17 Sept the 'Southern Attack Force' lands the 8th Inf Div (Maj-Gen Mueller) on the most southerly island of Angaur, which is defended by one Japanese battalion of 1600 men under Maj Goto. By 23 Oct the resistance is broken. Only 301 Japanese, in all, are taken prisoner on both islands. The bulk of the Japanese 14th Inf Div (Lt-Gen Inoue) remains isolated on the main island of Babelthuap for the rest of the war. Total US losses: 1209 dead and 6585 wounded. From 24 Sept the Kossol passage, mined in March, is again usable.

On 23 Sept an improvised group (Rear-Adm Blandy) lands the 323rd RCT of the 81st Inf Div (Col Watson) on Ulithi Atoll without encountering resistance. It was previously entered on 22 Sept by the Support Group, comprising the cruiser *Denver* and the destroyers *Ross* and *Bryant*. This Atoll is to have great importance as a base for the rest of the war. In March 1945 there are 617 ships in the lagoon.

The Japanese submarine *I-44* (Lt-Cdr Kawaguchi), which makes one unsuccessful attack, and *Ro-47* and *I-177* are deployed against the landing fleet. The latter are lost on 25 Sept and 2 Oct respectively in hedgehog attacks by the US DEs *McCoy Reynolds* and *Samuel S. Miles*.

16-20 Sept   Indian Ocean
Operation 'Light': the British Eastern Fleet, comprising the carriers *Victorious* and *Indomitable*, the battleship *Howe*, two cruisers and seven destroyers, carries out, under Rear-Adm Moody, a carrier raid on Sigli (Northern Sumatra) and photo reconnaissance over the Nicobars.
In September British submarines sink the following ships in the Straits of Malacca and in the western part of the Malayan Archipelago: *Strongbow* eight small ships; *Sirdar* (Lt Spender) three small craft; *Tantivy* one ship of 1799 tons; *Porpoise* (Lt-Cdr Turner) one ship of 3029 tons and two patrol boats with mines; *Tradewind* one ship of 5065 tons and two sailing ships; *Trenchant* (Cdr Hezlet) two sailing ships and *U859*; *Thorough* one small craft. The Dutch submarine *O.19* (Lt-Cdr v. Karnebeek) sinks three small craft.

17-23 Sept   Baltic
Under pressure from the Russian Army advancing towards Estonia the III S.S. Armoured Corps pulls out to the W from the Narva position. After the evacuation of the German garrison from Suur-Tytärsaari by the 5th MTB Flotilla on 17 Sept, the island is occupied by light Soviet forces on 20 Sept. They occupy the evacuated harbours of Kunda and Loksa on 21 Sept and 22 Sept. On the morning of 23 Sept the last German convoy leaves Tallinn with four steamers, one hospital ship and 9000 men, escorted by the torpedo boats *T20*, *T13*, *T17* and *T19*. By then, 50000 troops in all, have been transferred from Tallinn to the Baltic Islands. In addition in August/September 85000 refugees are evacuated.
To block the existing routes in the Gulf of Finland the minelayers *Brummer* and *Linz*, the torpedo boats *T23* and *T28*, the minesweepers *M18* and *M19* and also naval ferry barges, motor torpedo boats and motor minesweepers lay several new mine barrages.

18-19 Sept   English Channel
The German 10th MTB Flotilla (Lt-Cdr Müller) with the transport group, comprising *S185*, *S186*, *S191* and *S192*, brings ammunition and supplies to the encircled fortress of Dunkirk. In the process, the escort group, under the flotilla Commander, comprising *S183*, *S200* and *S702*, runs into a patrol group, consisting of the British frigate *Stayner* (Lt Turner) and the *MTB724* and *MTB728* off Ostend. One of the German boats is crippled by the fire from the MTBs and is sunk by *Stayner*. Then the other two boats collide and are likewise sunk.

20 Sept   Bay of Biscay
The Polish destroyers *Blyskawica* and *Piorun* carry out a landing on Audierne in support of French resistance fighters.

24 Sept-31 Oct   Mediterranean/ Aegean
The 'British Aegean Force' (Rear-Adm Mansfield) is employed to occupy the Aegean Islands and the Greek mainland evacuated by German troops. There take part the escort carriers *Hunter*, *Stalker*, *Emperor*, *Attacker*, *Searcher*, *Pursuer* and *Khedive*, the cruisers *Orion*, *Ajax*, *Royalist* (Rear-Adm Troubridge), *Black Prince*, *Argonaut*, *Aurora* and *Colombo*, the 24th DD Flotilla (Capt Firth), comprising *Troubridge*, *Termagant*, *Terpsichore*, *Teazer*, *Tuscan* and *Tumult*, the Greek *Navarinon* and the Polish *Garland*, the 'Hunt' destroyers *Brecon*, *Calpe*, *Catterick*, *Cleveland*, *Liddesdale* and *Zetland* and the Greek *Themistokles*, *Kriti*, *Pindos*, *Kanaris* and *Miaoulis*. There are many engagements with small German ships, shelling of German positions, airfields and batteries as well as landings.
On 30 Sept to 3 Oct a German convoy proceeds from Piraeus to Salonika consisting of two steamers, escorted by *TA18* and the harbour patrol boats *GD97* and *GK92*. On 2 Oct the French submarine *Curie* (Lt Chailley) sinks the steamer *Zar Ferdinand* (1994 tons) and on 3 Oct the British *Unswerving* (Lt Tattersall) sinks the *Berta* (1810 tons). In addition, of the British submarines, *Virtue* (Lt Cairns) sinks six small craft; *Vampire* (Lt Taylor) the steamer *Peter* (3754 tons); *Vigorous* the steamer *Salomea* (751 tons), two sailing ships and the ferry *SF121*; *Vox* (Lt Michell) one sailing ship. *TA38* and *TA39* carry out a defensive mining operation off Piraeus on 5-6 Oct. On 15 Oct the Greek minesweeper *Kasos* (*YMS74*) and *Kos* (*YMS186*) sink on this mine barrage.

From 6 Oct to 13 Oct the last German ships in the Aegean are transferred from Piraeus to Salonika. In the process the torpedo boat *TA37*, *UJ2101* and the harbour patrol boat *GK32* are sunk on 7 Oct in an engagement SW of Kassandra-Huk with the British destroyers *Termagant* and *Tuscan.* The minelayer *Zeus* escapes. On 9 Oct *TA38* goes aground near Makronisi; she is towed by *TA39* to Volos and sunk there in air attacks from British escort carriers on 12 Oct together with one steamer, two supply ships, one submarine-chaser, one naval ferry barge, one SF, three KFKs, one LS boat and several motor sailing boats. The last operational ships, the steamer *Lola*, *TA39* and three motor minesweepers, are sent to Salonika after Piraeus is evacuated on 12 Oct. On 29 Oct the British destroyer *Kimberley* captures the German hospital ship *Gradisca* (13870 tons) in the Aegean. On 31 Oct, because of the evacuation of Salonika by German troops, the last ships, including *R185*, *R195*, *R210*, *R211* and three auxiliary minesweepers, *Alula*, *Otranto* and *Gallipoli*, are scuttled, *TA39* and *Lola* having sunk on mines on 16 Oct.

26 Sept-13 Nov   North Atlantic
British and Canadian Support Groups operate in the Shetland-Faeroes-Iceland passages against outward-bound German schnorkel U-boats. On 16 Oct *U1006* (Lt Voigt) is found by the Canadian frigates of the 6th SG, *Annan*, *Loch Achanalt* and *Outremont*, and, after surfacing, is sunk by the *Annan* in a sharp gun and torpedo engagement. *U246* has to return on 23 Oct after being pursued with depth charges. On 24 Oct the Canadian destroyer *Skeena* of the 11th SG runs on a shoal off Iceland and is lost in the storm.
Off Reykjavik *U300* (Lt Hein) misses two steamers and sinks on 10 Nov three ships of 7828 tons from a convoy. *U281* has no success in the North Minch. In the North Channel *U1004* twice misses escorts and *U483* (Lt-Cdr v. Morstein) misses two steamers, one monitor and two escorts but torpedoes on 1 Nov the British DE *Whitaker*, which is taken in tow but becomes a total loss. *U1003* is not able to fire.

In the Channel *U978* (Lt-Cdr Pulst) sinks a Liberty ship (7176 tons) and torpedoes a Liberty ship (7177 tons). She also dispatches the wreck of a third Liberty ship which has previously run on a mine. *U773* and *U722* carry out transport missions to St Nazaire.

26 Sept-15 Nov   Atlantic
U245, *U262* and *U518* are stationed as weather boats in the North Atlantic from the end of September to the middle of October. In October they are relieved by *U546* (off Dakar from 24 July to 30 Aug) and *U170* (Lt Hauber) off Freetown from 6 Sept to 5 Oct which return from their distant missions without success. The latter misses escorts of two convoys with T-5s on 28 Oct and 31 Oct. In November *U396* becomes a weather boat. In the North Atlantic at the end of October *U1226* is lost on the way to America as the result of schnorkel trouble.
U1221 (Lt Ackermann) and *U1223* (Lt Kneip) operate from the end of September to the beginning of November off Halifax and in the Gulf of St Lawrence respectively. *U1221* misses a troop transport; *U1223* torpedoes the Canadian frigate *Magog* from the escort of convoy GONS. 33, just misses the the *Toronto* (4 Oct) and torpedoes an independent of 7134 tons on 2 Nov. In spite of the deployment of a U-boat hunting group with the carrier *Core* and MAD aircraft, the boats, which are equipped with the centimetre search receiver 'Naxos' and the 'Kurier' automatic transmitter for radio, are not found.
U1227 (Lt Altmeier) encounters on 4 Oct, on the way to Gibraltar, the convoy ONS.33, escorted by a Canadian escort group. She torpedoes the frigate *Chebogue*, which is brought into the Bristol Channel by the corvettes *Arnprior* and *Chambly,* the frigate *Ribble* and tugs, but she remains a total loss. Off Gibraltar *U1227* misses a naval force on 25 Oct and sinks an unknown tanker on 7 Nov. On the way to Jakarta *U195* and *U219* pass through the Central and South Atlantic in September/October. *U871* is sunk on 26 Sept by a Fortress of No 220 Sqdn RAF from the Azores; *U863* is sunk on 29 Sept by two Liberators of USN-VB.107 from Ascension Island.

The homeward-bound *U1062* falls victim to US TG 22.1 (Capt. Ruhsenberger), operating in the Central Atlantic and comprising the escort carrier *Mission Bay* and the DEs *Douglas L. Howard, J. R. Y. Blakely, Hill, Farquhar* and *Fessenden.*

29 Sept-24 Oct   Baltic
Russian attack on the Baltic Islands. The following landing forces (Rear-Adm Svyatov) are employed: 48-55 torpedo cutters of the TKA Brigade (Capt 1st Class Oleynik), 13 patrol boats, 13 motor minesweepers, 20 harbour defence vessels, 20 tenders of the Tallinn Naval Defence Sector (Capt 1st Class Guskov) and eight armoured cutters. The assault troops consist of units of the 8th Army (Lt-Gen Starikov) with air support from the 13th Air Army (Lt-Gen Rybalchenko). On 29 Sept TKAs and 90 amphibious craft land the first advance troops on Moon Island. The Estonian 247th and 7th Divs are brought into the bridgehead and the German defenders withdraw to Ösel and blow up the bridge. On 2 Oct light forces land advance parties, and, later, the main body of the 109th Rifle Div, on Dagö, which the weak German defences evacuate by 3 Oct. On 5 Oct Soviet forces succeed in landing on Ösel. The German 218th Inf Div is unable to hold up the vastly superior Russian forces and by 20 Oct withdraws to the Sworbe Peninsula. A Russian attack fails in part as a result of coastal shelling by the German Task Force (Vice-Adm Thiele). On 22 Oct *T23* and *T28* shell Sworbe; and on 23-24 Oct the cruiser *Lützow* (Capt Knoke) with the destroyers *Z28* and *Z35* and the torpedo boats *T13, T19* and *T21* shells Russian positions on Sworbe and near Memel. Heavy Russian air attacks, in which a bomb hit is registered on *Z28,* are beaten off.

29 Sept-29 Dec   Baltic
With the help of Finnish minesweepers and pilots, three Russian submarines are brought from the inner part of the Gulf of Finland past the Finnish promontories to Hangö and Abo from 28 Sept to 3 Oct, four from 2 Oct to 9 Oct and three from 5 Oct to 10 Oct. From there during the month of October from 5 Oct onwards *Shch-310* (Capt 3rd Class Bogorad) operates off

Windau, sinking the transport *Ro24* (4499 tons) and one tug, with three misses; and *Shch-407* (Capt 3rd Class Bocharov) off Memel, sinking the training ship *Nordstern* (1127 tons) and registering two misses. They are relieved by *Shch-307* (Lt-Cdr Kalinin) and *D-2* (Lt-Cdr Filov) which have six misses and one miss respectively. Off Brüsterort *Lembit* (Capt 3rd Class Matiyasevich) lays a mine barrage, sinks the minesweeper *M3619* and has two misses; *S-4* (Capt 3rd Class Klyushkin) sinks off Rixhöft the *Taunus, Terra* and *Thalatta,* totalling 4896 tons; *S-13* (Capt 3rd Class Marinesko) sinks the trawler *Siegfried* (563 tons) on the Stolpe Bank; and *L-3* (Capt 3rd Class Konovalov) the Danish steamer *Hilma Lau* (2414 tons) near Bornholm. In addition, the boat lays a mine barrage near Sassnitz on which on 24 Nov the torpedo boat *T34* sinks and the sailing training ship *Albert Leo Schlageter* is damaged. *K-56* has to return. In November/December *Shch-309* (Capt 3rd Class Vetchinkin) operates off Windau and sinks two ships of 5595 tons and has three misses, while *Shch-318* (Capt 3rd Class Loshkarev) has one miss; *Shch-303* (Capt 3rd Class Ignatev) operates off Memel; and, away from the coast on the deep water route, where they try to attack the German convoys, *K-53* (Capt 3rd Class Yaroshevich) and *D-2. Shch-407* penetrates into the Gulf of Danzig and sinks the steamer *Seeburg* (12181 tons). *Lembit* lays a mine barrage W of Rixhöft, on which the steamers *Eichberg* (1923 tons) and *Elie* (1837 tons) are hit but can later be brought into harbour. In the area between Gotland, Stolpe Bank and Bornholm *K-51* (Capt 3rd Class Drozdov) sinks on 24 Nov the Swedish steamer *Hansa* (493 tons) and has two misses; *K-56* (Capt 3rd Class Popov) misses the auxiliary cruiser *Hansa* and sinks the steamer *Baltenland* (3042 tons) and the Swedish *Venersborg* (1044 tons). *S-4* has no success; and *K-52* has to return.

1-2 Oct   Mediterranean/Ligurian Sea
Reconnaissance expedition by the 10th TB Flotilla (Cdr v. Gartzen) with *TA24, TA29* and *TA32* in the western part of the Gulf of Genoa.

M

1-10 Oct   Baltic

To drive the German troops out of Northern Finland, the Finnish III Corps puts pressure on the German units withdrawing to the NW. On 1 Oct the first elements of the Finnish 3rd Div (2900 men of the 11th Inf Regt) are landed from three steamers in Röyottä (northern part of the Gulf of Bothnia), in order to advance to Kemi and Tornio. Strong German counter-attacks at first cause reverses until the remaining parts of the 3rd Div begin to arrive on 2 Oct and the Finnish gunboats *Uusimaa* and *Hämeenmaa* are able to support the assault troops from 6 Oct and to reinforce the AA defence. German air attacks damage several transports.

1-15 Oct   North Sea

The British 11th MTB Flotilla (Lt Bourne), comprising *MTB351, MTB 360, MTB349, MTB347* and *MTB350*, attacks off Ijmuiden in the night 30 Sept-1 Oct the German convoy 1291 (three towing convoys with new constructions and *F6*) on the way from Rotterdam to Borkum. A barrage group of three boats of the 11th MMS Flotilla (Lt-Cdr Rosenow), a mining group of four boats of the 13th MMS Flotilla (Lt-Cdr Eizinger) and the escort (Cdr Fischer), comprising *V1313, V1301, V1310, V1317, V2017, V2019, M3824, M3827, M3838, M3832,* and *MFL675*, beat off all attacks and sink *MTB360* and *MTB347*. The convoy puts into den Helder in the night 2-3 Oct and when it continues on its way there are air attacks off the Dutch North Coast and a new 'Hansa' construction *No 922* (1923 tons) is sunk.
In the night 8-9 Oct the British 4th MTB Flotilla attacks a German patrol boat group repeatedly off the Hook of Holland. Of the boats *V1306, V2004, V2007* and *V1303*, the last is sunk. An attack by the 21st MTB Flotilla near Texel fails. In the night 10-11 Oct *MTB475, MTB473, MTB476, MTB480* and *MTB472* again attack patrol boats off the Hook of Holland and badly damage one boat. In a third attack on 15-16 Oct *V2016* is sunk.

1-31 Oct   Pacific

In the Pacific the US submarines are stationed in groups, partly in connection with the Leyte operation; the boats achieve considerable successes, sometimes jointly, and sometimes individually.
In Japanese waters *Pomfret* (Cdr Acker) sinks on her own one ship of 6962 tons and torpedoes one other ship; *Seal* (Lt-Cdr Turner) sinks two ships of 6639 tons; *Tilefish* (Lt-Cdr Keithley) sinks one ship of 108 tons. Operating in groups in the area of the Volcano and Bonin islands, *Snapper* (Lt-Cdr Walker) sinks one ship of 1990 tons and the minelayer *Ajiro*; *Trepang* (Lt-Cdr Davenport) one ship of 751 tons and one landing ship; *Kingfish* (Lt-Cdr Harper) two ships of 10778 tons and the landing ship *No 138*. SW of Kyushu there cruise *Croaker* (Lt Lee), which sinks three ships of 5839 tons and torpedoes one ship, and *Perch* and *Escolar*. E of Kyushu *Gabilan* (Lt-Cdr Wheland) sinks one ship of 200 tons; *Ronquil* (Lt-Cdr Monroe) torpedoes the corvette *Kaibokan 132*; and *Besugo* has no success. Between Kyushu and Amami-O-shima there are stationed *Sterlet, Skate* and *Sea Dog* (Lt-Cdr Lowrance); the latter sinks two ships of 433 tons. In the Formosa Straits *Tang* (Lt-Cdr O'Kane) sinks six ships of 19250 tons from convoys and torpedoes two more ships but is then a victim of one of her own circling torpedoes. *Salmon, Silversides* and *Trigger* are stationed between Okinawa and Formosa. S of the Formosa Straits *Snook* (Lt-Cdr Browne) and *Sterlet* (Lt-Cdr Robbins) each sink three ships of 16636 tons and 20616 tons respectively, but *Barbero* has no success. *Shark, Blackfish* and *Seadragon* (Lt-Cdr Ashley), which sinks three ships of 13854 tons, operate S of Formosa. NW of Luzon successes are registered by *Sawfish* (Lt-Cdr Bannister) with two ships of 13384 tons; by *Icefish* (Cdr Peterson) with three ships of 14824 tons; by *Drum* (Lt-Cdr Williamson) with three ships of 18497 tons and one ship torpedoed; by *Seahorse* (Lt-Cdr Wilkins) which sinks *Kaibokan 21*; but no success is registered by *Whale*. W of Luzon *Cabrilla* (Lt-Cdr Thompson) sinks four ships 24530 tons and torpedoes one more ship: *Aspro* (Cdr Stevenson) sinks two ships of 10912 tons; *Hoe* (Lt-Cdr McCrea) one ship of

2578 tons and torpedoes *Kaibokan 8*. SW of there *Bonefish*, *Flasher* and *Lapon* have no success, but *Baya* (Lt-Cdr Jarvis), *Hawkbill* (Lt-Cdr Scanland) and *Becuna* (Lt-Cdr Sturr) together sink three ships of 17213 tons. Off Manila *Cod* (Lt-Cdr Adkins) sinks one ship of 6886 tons and torpedoes one ship; and a group, consisting of *Bream* (Lt-Cdr McCallum), *Guitarro* (Lt-Cdr Haskins), *Raton* (Lt-Cdr Shea) and *Ray* (Lt-Cdr Kinsella) sink six ships of 25974 tons and the corvette *Kaibokan 7*. In addition a steamer is torpedoed. *Blackfin* is stationed N of Palawan, *Batfish* in the Sulu Strait and *Cobia* in the north Makassar Strait. A group, comprising *Darter* (Lt-Cdr McClintock) and *Dace* (Lt-Cdr Claggett, which sinks two ships of 12941 tons and damages a ship, and *Rock* and *Bergall* (Lt-Cdr Hyde), which sinks three ships of 24716 tons, operates W of Palawan.

Further to the W, *Angler* (Cdr Hess) sinks one ship of 2407 tons; *Bluegill* (Lt-Cdr Barr) three ships of 19631 tons; *Hammerhead* (Lt-Cdr Martin) five ships of 25178 tons; *Redfin* (Lt-Cdr Austin) torpedoes two ships and *Rock* (Lt-Cdr Flachsenhar) sinks one ship of 834 tons.

By contrast, there is only one Japanese submarine, *I-12* (Cdr Kudo), in the Pacific engaged on distant operations between Hawaii and the American West Coast. She sinks one Liberty ship of 7176 tons and is missing from the end of October.

4 Oct Arctic/Greenland
Crew members of the US ice-breaker *Eastwind* destroy a German weather station on the island of Lille Koldewey (off the North-east Coast of Greenland).

4 Oct-5 Jan Indian Ocean
The first group of East Asian U-boats sets out with raw materials from Jakarta to return to Norway. *U168* is sunk on 6 Oct N of Java by the Dutch submarine *Zvaardfish*; *U181* (Cdr* Freiwald) sets out on 19 Oct, sinks a tanker of 10198 tons in the Central Indian Ocean on 2 Nov but, when S of Africa, has to return because of damage to her screw shaft and puts in again on 5 Jan. *U537* is sunk N of Bali by the US submarine *Flounder* on 9 Nov. *U196* is missing in the Sunda Strait since setting out on

11 Nov. On 28 Nov *U843* sets out and reaches the Atlantic on 28 Dec after having been replenished from *U195* coming from France. *U195* and *U219* arrive in Jakarta from there in December.

When transferring from Singapore to Penang the Japanese submarines *Ro-113* and *Ro-115* are missed by British submarine *Strongbow* on 12 Oct. On 24 Oct *Stygian* misses one of the two boats as they set out for the Bay of Bengal. *Ro-113* (Lt Harada) sinks one ship of 3827 tons on 5 Nov. Neither the shore-based aircraft sent to search nor TF 66 with the escort carriers *Begum* and *Shah* can find the Japanese submarines. The British submarine *Tally Ho* misses one of them as she comes into harbour on 8 Nov. In a second operation *Ro-113* is bombed on 3-4 Dec by a Liberator of No 222 Sqdn RAF, but on 17-18 Dec and 18-19 Dec she attacks two ships off Madras, which just get away, and the boat arrives again off Penang on 28 Dec where the British submarine *Thule* misses her with six torpedoes. *Ro-115* cruises without success off the east coast of Ceylon and is hunted on 22 Dec by the sloop *Flamingo*.

5-6 Oct North Sea
A strong force of *Linsen* (explosive boats) tries to attack British minesweepers off the Belgian coast from the Scheldt. Unfavourable weather conditions and strong defence make the operation a fiasco. 36 *Linsen* are lost or have to be abandoned.

6-17 Oct Central Pacific
Adm Halsey (Commander 3rd Fleet) operates with TF 38 off Formosa and Luzon to eliminate the Japanese air forces. TF 38 (Vice-Adm Mitscher) sets out with three groups from Ultithi on 6 Oct. TG 38.4 joins them on 7 Oct coming from the area W of Palau. On 8 Oct the warships are refuelled from eight fleet tankers. On the same day TG 30.2 (Rear-Adm Smith) shells Marcus Island with the cruisers *Chester*, *Pensacola* and *Salt Lake City* and the destroyers *Dunlap*, *Fanning*, *Case*, *Cummings*, *Cassin* and *Downes*. On 9 Oct TF 38 proceeds to the NW. TG 38.1 (Vice-Adm McCain) comprises the carriers *Wasp*, *Hornet*, *Monterey* and

Cowpens, the cruisers *Wichita, Boston, Canberra* and *Houston*, the destroyers *Izard, Charrette, Conner, Bell, Burns*; *Cogswell, Caperton, Ingersoll, Knapp, Boyd, Cowell*; *McCalla, Grayson, Brown* and *Woodworth*.

TG 38.2 (Rear-Adm Bogan) comprises the carriers *Intrepid, Hancock, Bunker Hill, Cabot* and *Independence*, the battleships *Iowa* and *New Jersey* (Adm Halsey), the cruisers *Vincennes, Miami, San Diego* and *Oakland*, the destroyers *Owen, Miller, The Sullivans, Stephen Potter, Tingey*; *Hickox, Hunt, Lewis Hancock, Marshall*; *Halsey Powell, Cushing, Colahan, Uhlmann, Benham*; *Stockham, Wedderburn, Twining* and *Yarnall*.

TG 38.3 (Rear-Adm Sherman) comprises the carriers *Essex, Lexington, Princeton* and *Langley*, the battleships *Washington* (Vice-Adm Lee), *Massachusetts, South Dakota* and *Alabama*, the cruisers *Santa Fé, Mobile, Birmingham* and *Reno*, the destroyers *Clarence K. Bronson, Cotten, Dortch, Gatling, Healy*; *Porterfield, Callaghan, Cassin Young, Irwin, Preston*; *Laws, Longshaw, Morrison* and *Prichett*.

TG 38.4 (Rear-Adm Davison) comprises the carriers *Franklin, Enterprise, San Jacinto* and *Belleau Wood*, the cruisers *New Orleans* and *Biloxi*, the destroyers *Maury, Gridley, Helm, McCall, Mugford, Bagley, Patterson, Ralph Talbot, Wilkes, Nicholson* and *Swanson*.

Air battle of Formosa: on 10 Oct one group flies off to attack Amami-O-shima, two groups to attack Okinawa and one group to attack Sakishima Gunto. In all, 1396 sorties are flown. The Americans lose 21 planes but the submarine depot ship *Jingei* and five smaller ships and four steamers are destroyed in Okinawa. The 2nd Japanese Air Fleet (Vice-Adm Fukudome), which has 400 aircraft, loses 30 machines in air combat and on the ground. Attempts to attack the carrier groups, which have been located by air reconnaissance, fail because the formations fail to find the targets.

On 11 Oct TGs 38.1 and 38.4 fly 61 sorties against the airfield of Aparri from NE of Luzon: 15 Japanese aircraft are destroyed there. TGs 38.2 and 38.3 refuel to the E from 12 fleet tankers of TG 30.8 (Capt Acuff), comprising 34 tankers, 17 destroyers and 26 DEs, and they take over 61 replacement aircraft in turns from the escort carriers *Altamaha, Barnes, Sitkoh Bay, Cape Esperance, Nassau, Kwajalein, Shipley Bay, Steamer Bay, Nehenta Bay, Sargent Bay* and *Rudyerd Bay*, which are employed as replenishment carriers, during October.

On 12 Oct and 13 Oct all four TGs make continual attacks on airfields and installations on Formosa. On 12 Oct there are 1378 sorties and on 13 Oct 974 sorties. Forty-eight planes are lost, but many Japanese aircraft are destroyed in the air and on the ground. The 2nd Japanese Air Fleet tries to make attacks from Formosa on the two southern TGs, but these are intercepted. 'T' force flies 56 sorties from Kyushu on 12 Oct and 30 sorties on 13 Oct and on both days 52 aircraft fly from Okinawa. The carrier *Franklin* narrowly misses torpedoes; one of the four attacking aircraft crashes in flames on the deck and causes slight damage. When it is getting dark, the *Canberra* is hit by a torpedo and badly damaged.

Early on 14 Oct TG 38.1 makes another attack on Formosa: 246 sorties and 23 aircraft are lost. TG 38.4 attacks Aparri. From bases in China B-29s attack targets in Formosa and Okinawa in 109 sorties. The 2nd Japanese Air Fleet flies a total of 419 sorties from Formosa, Okinawa and Kyushu against the US Fleet: 225 aircraft return without having found their targets. In an attack on TG 38.1 the *Houston* is torpedoed in the evening. The *Canberra* is taken in tow by the *Wichita* and the *Houston* by the *Boston*: TG 30.3 (Rear-Adm Dubose) forms a covering force with the cruisers *Santa Fé* and *Mobile*, the carriers *Cowpens* and *Cabot* and the destroyers *Charrette, Conner, Bell, Burns, Cogswell, Caperton, Ingersoll, Knapp, Boyd, Cowell, Miller, The Sullivans* and *Stephen Potter*. On 15 Oct units of the 2nd Japanese Air Fleet fly 199 sorties against TF 38 as it retires; the *Houston* is again hit by a torpedo. TG 38.4 makes attacks on airfields N of Manila on Luzon, in the course of which there are fierce air battles with 50 fighters of the 1st Japanese Air Fleet (Vice-Adm Teraoka) and attacks by 130 Japanese aircraft on TG 38.4. But the attacks are repelled and 32 machines are shot down. In all, from 12 Oct to 15 Oct, in 881 sorties and with 321 losses to themselves, the Japanese pilots claim to have sunk 11 carriers, two battleships and one cruiser and to have damaged eight carriers, two battleships, one cruiser and 13 other ships. Submarine group A, comprising *I-26*, *I-45*, *I-53*, *I-54* and *I-56*, and the 2nd Striking Force (Vice-Adm Shima), consisting of the cruisers *Nachi*, *Ashigara* and *Abukuma* and the destroyers *Akebono*, *Ushio*, *Kasumi*, *Shiranuhi*, *Wakaba*, *Hatsu-shimo*, *Hatsuharu* and *Suzutsuki* are deployed against the damaged ships. The last-named is torpedoed by the US submarine *Besugo* on 15 Oct. *Skate* reports the force, whereupon TGs 38.2 and 38.3 make a sortie to the N on 16 Oct, followed by TG 38.1 which is, at the time, replenishing. On 16 Oct and 17 Oct the 2nd Japanese Air Fleet flies another 107 sorties against TF 38 without finding targets. Twenty-four aircraft are lost. From Luzon aircraft of the 1st Air Fleet vainly try to find TG 38.4, which after replenishing on 16 Oct, again attacks Central and South Luzon on 17 Oct. On 17 Oct the carrier groups in the N have to return because of the beginning of the Leyte operation. Adm Shima puts into Amami-O-shima, when reconnaissance reports on 16 Oct that there are still 13 carriers, seven battleships and ten cruisers intact.

7-11 Oct Mediterranean
Coastal shelling of the Rivera by the French cruiser *Emile Bertin*, the destroyer *Le Fortuné* and the US destroyers *Eberle*, *Jouett* and *Gleaves*.

7-26 Oct Arctic
The withdrawal of XIX Mountain Corps on the Murmansk front, which is being prepared, coincides with the offensive by the 14th Soviet Army (Col-Gen Shcherbakov) with the 99th, 131st and 31st Rifle Corps and the 126th and 127th Light Rifle Corps (seven rifle divs, one armoured brigade and four rifle brigades) from the southern flank, supported by the air divisions of the 7th Air army. To interrupt the main

supply routes from the N, ships of the Northern Fleet (Adm Golovko) land naval infantry units repeatedly in the rear of the German 6th Mountain Div, which, however, is able with elements of the 2nd Mountain Div to avoid the threatening encirclement. On 10 Oct 2837 men of the 63rd Naval Rifle Brigade (Col Krylov) land in 10 BO, eight MO and 12 TKA cutters (Capt 1st Class Zyuzin) in Maativuono Bay opposite the Fisherman's Peninsula, on 12 Oct 660 men in seven TKA and six MO cutters at the entrance of Petsamo-fjord, on 18 Oct 485 men in six MO cutters near Jakobselv, on 23 Oct 600 men of the 12th Naval Brigade (Col Rassokhin) in six MO and four TKA cutters at Jarfjord, and on 25 Oct 835 men in 15 TKA and four BO cutters and two motor boats at Bökfjord. On the following day they, with units of the 131st Rifle Corps, occupy Kirkenes which, in the meantime, has been evacuated by the Germans.
To cover and support the landings, the air regiments of the Northern Fleet and six destroyers (*Gremyashchi* and *Gromki* for artillery support and four for cover against German attacks) are deployed. Of them, the destroyers *Baku*, *Gremya-shchi*, *Razumny* and *Razyarenny* shell Vardö and Vadsö on 26 Oct.
The submarines *L-20* (mining opera-tion), *S-51*, *V-2*, *S-104*, *M-171* (mining operation), *S-102*, *S-14*, *V-4* and *S-101* are deployed off the Norwegian Polar coast against the expected German evacuation by sea. In 13 attacks the boats claim 18 successes; in fact, only one steamer (1730 tons) and *UJ1220* are lost in an attack by *S-104* (Capt 2nd Class Turaev) on 12 Oct and *UJ 1219* by *V-4* (Capt 3rd Class Iosseliani) on 20 Oct through torpedo fire and one small Norwegian cutter on a mine laid by *M-171*. In two attacks by a total of 10 torpedo cutters only two mine-sweepers—*M303* and *M31*—are lost, instead of the 10 vessels claimed, and *R311* is damaged. Three TKAs are lost. In 14 major air attacks by the 5th Mining and Torpedo Div, the 6th Fighter Div and the 14th Ground Attack Div (all under Maj-Gen Preo-brazhenski), four steamers, one tug, two motor minesweepers, three patro

vessels, one ferry barge and one artillery barge, are lost but the bulk of the German evacuation convoys reach their destinations. Over 40000 tons of supplies are taken away by sea.

6-13 Oct   Baltic
After the Russian break-through to the Baltic between Libau and Memel from 6 Oct to 10 Oct the heavy cruisers *Prinz Eugen* (Capt Reinicke) and *Lützow* (Capt Knoke) and the 6th DD Flotilla (Capt Kothe), comprising *Z25*, *Z35* and *Z36*, shell Soviet assembly positions near Memel. AA defence and submarine defence is provided by the 3rd TB Flotilla, consisting of *T21*, *T13*, *T16* and *T20*. Russian air attacks are beaten off.

15-16 Oct   Arctic/Greenland
The German weather observation ship *WBS 11/Externsteine* in the ice on the Greenland east coast is compelled to surrender by the US Coastguard icebreakers *Eastwind* and *Southwind*.

15-19 Oct   Indian Ocean
Operation 'Millet'. As a diversion for the imminent US landing on Leyte, the British Eastern Fleet sets out from Trincomalee on 15 Oct with TF 63 (Vice-Adm Power) in three groups: TG 63.1 comprising the battlecruiser *Renown* (flagship) and the destroyers (4th Flotilla) *Quilliam*, *Queenborough* and *Quiberon* (RAN); TG 63.2 comprising the cruisers *London*, *Cumberland* and *Suffolk* and the destroyers *Relentless*, *Raider*, *Norman* (RAN) and *Van Galen* (Dutch); and TG 63.3 comprising the carriers *Indomitable* and *Victorious*, the cruiser (fighter direction ship) *Phoebe* and the destroyers *Whelp*, *Wakeful*, *Wessex* and *Wager*. On 17 Oct and 19 Oct the carriers make attacks on the Nicobar Islands. On 17 Oct TG 63.2 shells the islands and in the night *London*, *Norman* and *Van Galen* repeat the shelling. On 18 Oct the *Renown*, *Suffolk*, *Raider*, *Quilliam* and *Queenborough* shell the islands. But the diversion does not succeed because operation 'Sho' has already begun. On 19 Oct, however, the Japanese try to attack with 12 torpedo aircraft. Seven Japanese aircraft are shot down by the fighter cover for a loss of three.
In October in the Straits of Malacca and in the western part of Indonesia *Sea*

Rover (Lt Angel) sinks two small craft; *Tally Ho* (Cdr Bennington) two small craft; *Statesman* (Lt Bulkeley) and *Sturdy* (Lt Andersen) two and 14 small craft respectively; *Strongbow* one ship of 1185 tons and torpedoes one ship; *Stygian* (Lt Clarabut) eight small craft; *Subtle* two small craft; *Tantivy* 22 small craft; *Stoic* (Lt Marriott) five; *Terrapin* (Lt-Cdr Brunner) three small craft; and *Trenchant* (Cdr Hezlet) one ship of 984 tons and one small craft. In addition, the Dutch *Zvaardfish* (Lt-Cdr Goossens) sinks the German U-boat *U168*, the Japanese minelayer *Itsukushima* and three small craft, and torpedoes the minelayer *Wakataka*.

15 Oct-4 Nov   Air War/
Western Europe
RAF Bomber Command drops 2198 tons of bombs on Wilhelmshaven in night attacks on 15-16 Oct and 867 tons of bombs on Bremerhaven on 18-19 Oct. In daylight attacks on 17 Oct 3400 tons of bombs are dropped on encircled Boulogne and on 20 Oct 3365 tons of bombs on Calais.
The 8th USAAF, in daylight attacks, drops 1656 tons of bombs on fuel dumps and oil refineries in Hamburg on 25 Oct and 1030 tons of bombs on the harbour of Hamburg on 4 Nov. In this action the destroyer *Erich Steinbrinck* and the newly-constructed U-boat *U2557* are badly damaged and *Sperrbrecher 30* and the freighters *Hermann Fritzen* (3845 tons) and *Signal* (3176 tons) are sunk. The accommodation ship *Veendam* (15450 tons) is burned out.

17-26 Oct   South West Pacific
Battle for Leyte.
On 16-17 Oct the preparatory air attacks begin: from Morotai long-range P-38 fighters of the 5th USAAF (Lt-Gen Kenney) make fighter sorties and B-24 bombers of the 13th and 5th USAAF from Sansapor and Biak make attacks on airfields on Mindanao. On 16 Oct and 17 Oct the aircraft of the escort carriers of TG 77.4 (Rear-Adm T. L. Sprague) make attacks on Leyte, Cebu and North Mindanao. There take part TU 1 (Rear-Adm T. L. Sprague) consisting of the escort carriers *Sangamon*, *Suwanee*, *Chenango*, *Santee*, *Saginaw Bay* and *Petrof Bay*, the

destroyers *McCord*, *Trathen* and *Hazelwood* and the DEs *Edmonds*, *Richard S. Bull*, *Richard M. Rowell*, *Eversole* and *Coolbaugh*; TU 2 (Rear-Adm Stump), consisting of the escort carriers *Natoma Bay*, *Manila Bay*, *Marcus Island*, *Kadashan Bay*, *Savo Island* and *Ommaney Bay*, the destroyers *Haggard*, *Franks* and *Hailey*, the DEs *Richard W. Suesens*, *Abercrombie*, *Oberrender*, *Le-Ray Wilson* and *Walter C. Wann*; TU 3 (Rear-Adm C. A. F. Sprague) consisting of the escort carriers *Fanshaw Bay*, *St Lo*, *White Plains*, *Kalinin Bay*, *Kitkun Bay*, and *Gambier Bay*, the destroyers *Hoel*, *Heerman* and *Johnston*, the DEs *Dennis*, *John C. Butler*, *Raymond* and *Samuel B. Roberts*. Covering force: TG 77.3 (Rear-Adm Berkey) comprising the cruisers *Phoenix*, *Boise*, *Australia* (RAN) and *Shropshire* (RAN) with the destroyers *Hutchins*, *Bache*, *Beale*, *Daly*, *Killen*, *Arunta* (RAN) and *Warramunga* (RAN). It enters Leyte Gulf early on 17 Oct with the minesweeping and survey force (TG 77.5) and is reported by Japanese coastal guards. Imperial headquarters then puts operation 'Sho-1' into force and the Japanese Fleet movements begin. In the north US TF 38 (Vice-Adm Mitscher) begins with attacks to neutralize the Japanese 1st Air Fleet (Vice-Adm Teraoka) and the 4th Army Air Fleet on Luzon. On 17 Oct TG 38.4 (Rear-Adm Davison) attacks Luzon with the carriers *Franklin*, *Enterprise*, *San Jacinto* and *Belleau Wood*, the battleships *Washington* and *Alabama*, the cruisers *Wichita* and *New Orleans* and 15 destroyers. On 18 Oct, apart from TG 38.4, TG 38.2, comprising the carriers *Intrepid*, *Hancock*, *Bunker Hill* and *Independence*, the battleships *Iowa* and *New Jersey*, the cruisers *Biloxi*, *Vincennes* and *Miami* and 16 destroyers and TG 38.3 (Rear-Adm Sherman), comprising the carriers *Lexington*, *Essex*, *Princeton* and *Langley*, the battleships *Massachusetts* and *Indiana* and the cruisers *Santa Fé*, *Birmingham*, *Mobile* and *Reno* and 12 destroyers, also attacks targets in Luzon. Counter-attacks by 100 Japanese aircraft on TF 38 and by 25 aircraft on TF 77 do not get through. The 5th USAAF and the escort carriers make further attacks on 18 Oct and 19 Oct on Mindanao and the Leyte area respectively. The units of the Japanese 2nd Naval Air Fleet which are still operational are transferred to Luzon where Vice-Adm Onishi assumes command of the 1st Air Fleet.

With massive air escort from aircraft of all carrier groups and the 5th USAAF the 7th US Fleet (Vice-Adm Kinkaid) enters Leyte Gulf with the 6th US Army (Lt-Gen Krueger). The landings begin early on 20 Oct; X Corps (Maj-Gen Sibert) in the N, XXIV Corps (Maj-Gen Hodges) in the S. From N to S, the following forces are landed:
TG 78.2 (Rear-Adm Fechteler) lands the 1st Cavalry Div (Maj-Gen Mudge) on eight APAs, two AKAs, two LSDs, 14 LSTs and nine LSMs.
TG 78.1 (Rear-Adm Barbey) lands the 24th Inf Div (Maj-Gen Irving) on eight APAs, four AKAs, three LSDs, 12 LSTs and smaller craft. Fire support is provided by TF 78, comprising the battleships (Rear-Adm Weyler) *Mississippi*, *Maryland* and *West Virginia* and TG 77.3 (Rear-Adm Berkey) (see above).
In the S TF 79 (Vice-Adm Wilkinson) with TG 79.2 (Rear-Adm Royle) lands the 96th Inf Div (Maj-Gen Bradley) on 14 APAs, four AKAs, four LSDs and 24 LSTs; and TG 79.1 (Rear-Adm Connolly) the 7th Inf Div (Maj-Gen Arnold) on 13 APAs, four AKAs, one LSD and 31 LSTs.
Fire support in the S is provided by Rear-Adm Oldendorf with the battleships *Tennessee*, *California* and *Pennsylvania*, the cruisers *Louisville*, *Portland*, *Minneapolis*, *Honolulu*, *Denver* and *Columbia*. For destroyers see battle of Surigao Strait.
Resistance to the landings is at first slight. The Japanese 16th Inf Div retires to the prepared hill positions to await the arrival of the 30th and 102nd Inf Divs via Ormoc which are to attack with the Air Force and Fleet.
As a result of Japanese air attacks, the cruiser *Honolulu* is torpedoed in the evening of 20 Oct and on 21 Oct a Japanese aircraft crashes on the *Australia*. Both cruisers have to be towed away badly damaged.
On 21 Oct the aircraft of TG 77.4 support the land operations while those

of TGs 38.2 and 38.3 make attacks on the western Vizayan Islands. TGs 38.1 and 38.4 replenish. On 22 Oct the escort carriers stand by E of Leyte Gulf. TGs 38.2 and 38.3 go for replenishment. TG 38.4, which is proceeding with 'Cripdiv' (see 6 Oct) to Ulithi, is recalled on 22 Oct. TG 38.1 (with the carrier *Hancock*) goes on to Ulithi.

After receiving reports of the US landings, the C-in-C Combined Fleet (Adm Toyoda) orders the Japanese Task Forces to set out. On 22 Oct the Centre Force (Vice-Adm Kurita) puts to sea from Brunei (Borneo) with the battleships *Yamato*, *Musashi*, *Nagato*, *Kongo* and *Haruna*, the cruisers, *Atago*, *Takao*, *Chokai*, *Maya*, *Myoko*, *Haguro*, *Kumano*, *Suzuya*, *Chikuma* and *Tone*, the destroyer leaders—the cruisers *Noshiro* and *Yahagi*, and the destroyers *Shimakaze*, *Hayashimo*, *Akishimo*, *Kishinami*, *Okinami*, *Naganami*, *Asashimo*, *Hamanami*, *Fujinami*; *Nowake*, *Kiyoshimo*, *Urakaze*, *Yukikaze*, *Hamakaze* and *Isokaze*. It is followed by the Southern Force (Vice-Adm Nishimura) with the battleships *Fuso* and *Yamashiro*, the cruiser *Mogami* and the destroyers *Michishio*, *Asagumo*, *Yamagumo* and *Shigure*. The 2nd Striking Force (Vice-Adm Shima), comprising the cruisers *Nachi*, *Ashigara* and *Abukuma* and the destroyers *Akebono*, *Ushio*, *Kasumi*, *Shiranuhi*, *Wakaba*, *Hatsushimo* and *Hatsuharu*, is to join it in the Sulu Sea. A transport unit (Vice-Adm Sakonju) composed of the cruisers *Aoba* and *Kinu*, the destroyer *Uranami* and four fast transports, which is to bring troop reinforcements from Manila to Ormoc, is attacked on 23 Oct W of Manila Bay by the US submarine *Bream* (Lt-Cdr McCallum) which torpedoes the *Aoba*. From the N Vice-Adm Ozawa advances with a diversionary force which is to draw TF 38 onto itself. It consists of the carriers *Zuikaku*, *Zuiho*, *Chiyoda* and *Chitose*, the carrier/battleships (Rear-Adm Matsuda) *Ise* and *Hyuga*, the cruisers *Isuzu*, *Tama* and *Oyodo*, the destroyers *Hatsutsuki*, *Akitsuki*, *Wakatsuki* and *Shimotsuki* and the escort destroyers *Maki*, *Kiri*, *Kuwa* and *Sugi* and a supply force comprising two tankers, the destroyer *Akikaze* and the corvettes *Kaibokan 22*, *Kaibokan 29*,

Kaibokan 31, *Kaibokan 33*, *Kaibokan 43* and *Kaibokan 132*.

Shortly after midnight on 23 Oct the US submarines *Dace* (Lt-Cdr Claggett) and *Darter* (Lt-Cdr McClintock) locate Kurita's force N of Salawan and report it. In a torpedo attack *Dace* sinks the *Maya* and *Darter* the *Atago*. *Darter* also torpedoes the *Takao* which has to return with two destroyers. A second attempt by *Darter* to attack fails; the boat runs on a reef and is lost. As a result of the submarines' reports, Adm Halsey comes up with TG 38.3 (Rear-Adm Sherman), comprising *Lexington* (Vice-Adm Mitscher), *Essex*, *Princeton* and *Langley* E of Luzon, TG 38.2 (Rear-Adm Bogan and Adm Halsey), comprising *Intrepid*, *Cabot* and *Independence* E of the San Bernardino Strait and TG 38.4 (Rear-Adm Davison) comprising *Franklin*, *Enterprise*, *San Jacinto* and *Belleau Wood* E of Samar. Early on 24 Oct Japanese aircraft from Luzon attack TG 38.1, but are intercepted. Only one machine gets through and hits the *Princeton* which is burned out and has to be abandoned. In attempts to save the ship, the cruiser *Birmingham* is badly damaged by explosions on the *Princeton*.

Battle in the Sibuyan Sea. On 24 Oct four waves of American carrier aircraft attack the Japanese Centre Force. The first wave, consisting of 21 fighters, 12 dive bombers and 12 torpedo aircraft from the *Intrepid* and *Cabot*, obtains one torpedo hit on the *Myoko*, which is damaged and has to return, and one bomb and one torpedo hit on the *Musashi* (Rear-Adm Inoguchi†). The second wave of 19 fighters, 12 bombers and 11 torpedo aircraft from the same carriers obtains four more bomb and torpedo hits on the *Musashi*. The third wave of 16 fighters, 20 bombers and 32 torpedo aircraft from the *Essex* and *Lexington* obtains another four bomb and two torpedo hits on the *Musashi* and two bomb hits with little effect on the *Yamato*. The almost simultaneously attacking waves from the *Franklin* and *Enterprise* and the *Intrepid* and *Cabot* with 42 fighters, 33 dive-bombers and 21 torpedo aircraft cause the *Musashi* to sink after some ten bomb and six torpedo hits. The other battleships

Above: June 1944: On the morning of June 6 the Allied invasion of Normandy commences. Many types of special landing craft were built. They were designed to destroy or nullify the many ingenious anti-invasion devices planted by Rommel's forces on the beaches. Here a landing craft-rocket has just discharged her load in an attempt to destroy barbed wire and anti-shipping traps on the shore. [*IWM*

Below: German surface vessels cannot penetrate the covering forces and attack the landing forces. In the west the 10th destroyer flotilla intercepts four German destroyers, sinks *ZH1* and drives *Z32* ashore (photo). In the east German torpedoboats attack the covering forces, sink the destroyer *Svenner*, but are themselves destroyed by air raids on Le Havre. [*IWM*

Above: At 'Sword' beach the battleship *Warspite* opens fire on Villerville and the mouth of the river Seine with her 15-inch guns. *[IWM*

Below: June 10 1944: Off Omaha beach many ships of different types are busy unloading troops and supplies. A DUKW rolls up to the beach, while a ferry barge (left) returns to the LCTs and LCVs in the background for further supplies. The land-

ing ships are covered by barrage balloons. *[Official USN*

Foot: June 25, 1944: A joint American-British task force bombards German positions near Cherbourg, under attack by the American Army advancing from the south. German coastal batteries reply to the Allied bombardment and the British cruiser *Glasgow* (photo) received a direct hit at one point. *[IWM*

Above: Mar 1944: In one of the longest U-boat hunts of the war a Canadian escort group with the destroyers *Gatineau*, *Chaudière*, the corvettes *Fennel*, *St Catherine's*, *Chilliwack* and the British destroyer *Icarus* and the corvette *Kenilworth* *Castle* force *U744* to surface after almost 30 hours on Mar 5/6. 291 depth charges were dropped and when the submarine surfaced boarding parties rescued code books from below before the U-boat was sunk by torpedo from the *Icarus*.

Above: Many U-boats fell victim to the Allied air forces, especially to those of 19 Group RAF Coastal Command, as was this Type VII U-boat in the Bay of Biscay.
Below: The most effective weapon the U-boats have to combat the hunting groups is the 'Gnat' acoustic torpedo. Many Allied escorts are hit in the stern and many have close escapes when the torpedoes explode in the wake of the vessel. Here the Canadian frigate *Magog* is hit in the stern off Newfoundland on Oct 14, 1944 by *U1223*.

Above: In nightly penetrations aircraft of RAF Bomber Command sow extensive minefields off the German North Sea and Baltic ports. Here the mine destructor vessel *Sperrbrecher 10*, the former freighter *Belgrano*, is sunk off Borkum. Ships sunk in shallow waters, such as this vessel, were often refloated and repaired. *[BFZ*

Below: 12 Aug 1944: Off Royan, in the Gironde estuary, British Beaufort and Beaufighter aircraft attack a German convoy and sink the minesweeper *M370* and the patrol trawler *V410*. *[IWM*

Top: Apl 7, 1945: The Japanese make a last desperate bid with their remaining serviceable warships and using the last of their oil supplies, to throw the Americans off the island of Okinawa. The bid fails when the battleship *Yamato* (photo), cruiser *Yahagi* and a number of destroyers are sunk before getting anywhere near Okinawa.   *[IWM*

Above: The last offensive operations by the Japanese Navy are the few patrols of the large U-cruisers to launch Kaiten one man suicide torpedoes against American naval bases. Here *I-47* departs for Ulithi with a deckload of Kaiten.   *[BFZ/Fukui*

Above: The Kaiten and midget submarines formed the last defence of the Japanese coasts. Here the launch of a Kaiten on a suicide mission. The Kaiten scored only a few minor successes.   [*IWM*

Below: On Aug 27, 1945 the American Third Fleet entered Sagami Bay off Tokyo. Seen here from the flagship *Missouri* is Mount Fujiyama and the battleship *King George V*, flanked by the cruiser *Gambia* and *Newfoundland* and the American cruisers of the *Cleveland* class. [*Official USN*

Above: During strikes by the British Pacific Fleet at Sakishima Gunto (forming part of the Okinawa operations) the carriers are frequently attacked by Kamikazes. Here HMS *Illustrious* is hit forward, but owing to her armoured flight deck is able to continue flying operations.   [IWM

Below: In May 1945 the carrier *Formidable* became the target for a number of Kamikaze attacks suffering hits on May 4 and May 9 (shown here) when a Kamikaze crashed on the after flight deck among parked aircraft which had just returned from a bombing raid on Miyako.   [IWM

Above: The island of Okinawa required a long preparatory phase of softening up before any landings were attempted, for being close to Japan it was looked upon by the Japanese as part of the homeland. Here the battleship *Idaho* carries out a shoot as the landing forces go in.   *[IWM*
Below: Here part of the American 1st Marine Div unloading supplies at Beach Yellow 3 on Okinawa.   *[Official USCG*

receive hits which do not affect their fighting capacity. In all, 30 US aircraft are lost. From the N, a Japanese reconnaissance plane locates TG 38.3 and Ozawa flies off the 76 operational aircraft from his four carriers but they do not find their targets and fly on to Luzon. Only 25 aircraft remain on the carriers. Adm Halsey orders the Task Groups of TF 38 to concentrate and recalls TG 38.1 which is on the way to Ulithi in order to attack the Japanese carriers located in the afternoon in the N.

Battle of Surigao Strait. In the S the advancing Japanese forces of Nishimura and Shima are located by US air reconnaissance on 24 Oct and the *Wakaba* is sunk. Rear-Adm Oldendorf forms 13 groups each of three PT boats in the southern approaches to Surigao Strait. The attacks are largely beaten off or out-manoeuvred; only *PT137* (Lt Kovar) is able to torpedo the *Abukuma*. In the southern approach to Surigao Strait the Nishimura force is repeatedly attacked by US destroyer groups. *Remey*, *McGowan* and *Melvin* obtain a hit on *Fuso* from the E and *Monssen* and *McDermut* several hits from the W on the destroyer *Yamagumo* which sinks, the *Michishio* which is brought to a standstill and *Asagumo* which returns with her bows blown off. A hit is also obtained on *Yamashiro*. This is followed by attacks from *Hutchins*, *Daly* and *Bache* which sink the *Michishio* and hit the *Fuso* so that she later sinks. Shortly after, *Arunta* (RAN), *Killen* and *Beale* attack with guns and torpedoes. There follow attacks by *Robinson*, *Halford* and *Bryant* from the NE, by *Edwards*, *Leutze* and *Bennion* from the NW and by *Newcomb*, *Leary* and *Albert W. Grant* which is damaged by the fire from the heavy US ships. From the NW the cruisers *Boise*, *Phoenix* and *Shropshire* (RAN) open fire, from the NE the cruisers *Columbia*, *Denver*, *Minneapolis*, *Portland* and *Louisville* and, finally, the battleships *West Virginia*, *California*, *Tennessee*, *Maryland* and *Mississippi*. The *Pennsylvania* is unable to fire because other American ships obstruct her. The *Yamashiro* sinks; the *Shigure* escapes undamaged; and the *Mogami* turns away heavily damaged

but collides with the approaching *Nachi*. Shima returns and on the way the destroyer *Asagumo* sinks and, on the morning of 25 Oct, the *Mogami* has to be abandoned following air attacks.

Battle of Samar.
The Japanese Kurita force passes through the San Bernardino Strait after dark on 24 Oct, unobserved by US air reconnaissance, and by dawn of 25 Oct is E of Samar where it encounters TG 77.4.3 (Rear-Adm C. A. F. Sprague) (see above) mistaken for fleet carriers. Making skilful use of rain squalls, the force flies off its aircraft and tries, with cover from torpedo attacks from the destroyers and DEs and from smoke screens, to escape towards Leyte Gulf. One of the torpedo salvoes from *Hoel* and *Johnston* hits the *Kumano* which is brought to a standstill; the *Suzuya* tries to give help. The Japanese ships are repeatedly forced to take evasive action in the face of further torpedo attacks and air attacks by aircraft from TG 77.4.2 (Rear-Adm Stump) until finally the *Tone* and *Chikuma*, followed by *Haguro* and *Chokai*, are able to come up the weather side and bring the carriers under effective fire in which the *Yamato* and *Nagato* join from the N. *Hoel*, *Johnston*, *Samuel B. Roberts* and the *Gambier Bay* sink. While the *Haruna* and *Kongo* try to attack TG 77.4.2, which has in the meantime been sighted, its aircraft hit the *Chikuma* and *Chokai* so heavily that they sink. The *Tone* and *Haguro* have already approached to within less than 10000 metres from the remaining escort carriers, but Adm Kurita breaks off the attack under the weight of the air attacks, to which *Suzuya* also falls victim, and turns away to the San Bernardino Strait. At that moment, six Japanese Kamikaze aircraft (Sub-Lt Saki) attack TG 77.4.3 and sink the *St Lo* and damage the *Kalinin Bay*, *Kitkun Bay* and *White Plains*; only the *Fanshaw Bay* remains undamaged. From Mindanao a Kamikaze formation of five aircraft attacks TG 77.4.1 and damages the *Sangamon*, *Suwanee* and *Santee*: the latter is a little later torpedoed by the Japanese submarine *I-56* (Cdr Morinaga). *I-54*, in trying to attack this Task Group, is sunk by the

DE *Richard M. Rowell.* TG 38.1 (Vice-Adm McCain), which has been recalled from Ulithi and which comprises the carriers *Wasp, Hornet, Hancock, Monterey* and *Cowpens,* the cruisers *Chester, Pensacola, Salt Lake City, Boston, San Diego* and *Oakland* and 20 destroyers, flies off early on 25 Oct two waves of 147 aircraft in all against Kurita's withdrawing force. They cause damage.

Battle off Cape Engaño. In the meantime the three other groups of TF 38 have advanced in the night 24-25 Oct at high speed to the N to find the Ozawa force. At dawn TF 34 (Vice-Adm Lee) is formed from the battleships *Iowa, New Jersey* (Adm Halsey), *Washington, Alabama, Massachusetts* and *Indiana,* the cruisers *Santa Fé, Mobile, New Orleans* and *Wichita* and ten destroyers, to engage the Japanese ships with gunfire. In the course of the day, the US carriers fly off their aircraft in six waves (in all, 326 dive bombers and torpedo aircraft and 201 fighters) to attack. The destroyer *Akitsuki,* the carriers *Chitose, Zuikaku, Zuiho* and *Chiyoda* fall victim to them in turn. The *Hyuga* escapes in spite of 34 near-misses. In addition, the *Ise* escapes from an attack by the US submarine *Halibut,* which, with *Tuna, Haddock, Pintado, Atule* and *Jallao,* forms a patrol line on the withdrawal route of Ozawa's force. *Jallao* (Lt-Cdr Icenhower) is able to sink the damaged *Tama.* The four cruisers of TF 34 under Rear-Adm Du Bose, deployed for the pursuit, sink the disabled destroyer *Hatsutsuki.* As a result of Rear-Adm Sprague's reports, Adm Halsey has been speeding to the S since mid-day with the six battleships, the cruisers *Biloxi, Vincennes* and *Miami* and eight destroyers, while TG 38.2 follows as air escort. In order to find the Kurita force before it reaches the San Bernardino Strait, Adm Halsey proceeds towards it in the evening at high speed with the fastest battleships, *Iowa* and *New Jersey,* and eight destroyers. But Kurita has already passed through it; only the destroyer *Nowake,* left behind to rescue survivors, is sunk.

On 26 Oct the TGs 38.1 and 38.2, which have arrived E of the San Bernardino Strait, again attack the Kurita force as it returns through the Sibuyan Sea and they sink, partly in co-operation with B-24s from the 5th USAAF from Biak and Morotai, the cruisers *Kinu* and *Noshiro* and the destroyers *Uranami* and *Hayashimo* which, in part, belong to the transport unit. On the South Coast of Panay B-24s of the 13th USAAF sink the disabled cruiser *Abukuma.* A new Japanese Kamikaze attack with five aircraft from Cebu on TG 77.1 damages the *Suwanee.*

20 Oct-10 Nov   Arctic
Convoy operation JW.61/RA.61. On 20 Oct JW.61, consisting of 29 steamers and six Lend-Lease submarine-chasers for the Soviet Northern Fleet, sets out from Loch Ewe. Escort (Vice-Adm Dalrymple-Hamilton):   the escort carriers *Vindex, Nairana* and *Tracker,* the cruiser *Dido,* the 17th DD Flotilla, consisting of *Onslow, Opportune, Orwell, Offa, Obedient* and *Oribi,* the DEs of the 21st EG *Conn, Byron, Fitzroy, Deane, Redmill* and *Rupert* and of the 24th EG *Louis, Inglis, Lawson, Loring, Narborough* and *Mounsey,* as well as the destroyer *Walker,* the sloops *Lark* and *Lapwing* and the corvettes *Camellia, Oxlip* and *Rhododendron* of the 8th and 20th EGs. The convoy passes through the concentration of the 'Panther' U-boat group (*U293, U295, U310, U315, U363, U365, U387, U425, U636, U668, U737, U771, U956, U965, U968, U992, U995, U997* and *U1163*). On 26-27 Oct *U1163* (Lt Balduhn), *U956* (Lt Mohs), *U365* (Lt-Cdr Wedemeyer), *U995* (Lt Hess) and *U295* (Lt Wieboldt) vainly attack escort vessels with T-5s—sometimes repeatedly. On 28 Oct the convoy, met by Russian destroyers, minesweepers and submarine-chasers, arrives off the Kola Inlet. Russian escorts bring some of the steamers into the White Sea on 30 Oct. From 29 Oct to 6 Nov the special convoy JW.61A, consisting of two large transports with 11000 liberated Russian prisoners of war, proceeds from Britain to Murmansk. Escort: the escort carrier *Campania,* the cruiser *Berwick,* the destroyers *Saumarez, Cassandra, Scourge, Serapis, Cambrian* and *Caprice* and the 3rd EG with the DEs *Duckworth, Berry, Cooke, Domett, Essington* and *Rowley.*

Soviet destroyers and minesweepers bring the feeder convoy DB.10 from the White Sea to the Kola Inlet from 30 Oct to 1 Nov. There *U310* (Lt Ley) and *U295* try in vain to attack the escorts with T-5s. On 2 Nov RA.61 with 33 ships and the escort of JW.61, together with the 3rd EG sets out. Off the Kola Inlet *U295* hits the DE *Mounsey* with a T-5. The boats of the 'Panther' group are unable to get to the convoy against the strong escort. But bad radar conditions frustrate the attacks against the U-boats near the convoy. It reaches Loch Ewe without loss on 9 Nov. From 5 Nov to 8 Nov further attacks by the German U-boats *U997* (Lt Lehmann), *U956* and *U771* (Lt Block) on Soviet escort vessels have no success.

20 Oct–29 Nov   Arctic
Soviet convoy operation AB.15: the ice-breakers *Josif Stalin* and *Severny Veter* return from the eastern part of the Siberian sea route through the West Siberian and Kara Sea, escorted by a destroyer, five ex-US minesweepers and five ex-US submarine-chasers. The convoy is under the orders of Rear-Adm Bogolepov and under the overall command of the Commander White Sea Flotilla, Vice-Adm Panteleev. In the Kara Sea 10 U-boat attacks are claimed; but, in fact, there has been no U-boat in the Kara Sea since 2 Oct. After passing through the Kara Strait, the escort is reinforced with seven destroyers. The Gorlo Strait is reached in Force 9 winds.
The U-boat attacks and engagements claimed near Kanin Nos on 24 Oct with the convoy DB.9 and the minesweeper *T-116*, the patrol ship *SKR-20*, the submarine-chaser *MO-251* and the destroyer *Doblestny* and on 1 Nov with the convoy DB.10 and the minesweepers *T-111* and *T-113* and the destroyer *Derzki* must also be based on faulty observation, since all German U-boats were deployed with the 'Panther' group in the operation against the convoys JW.61 and RA.61.

24–28 Oct   Norway
On 24 Oct a British force, comprising the cruiser *Devonshire*, the escort carriers *Trumpeter* and *Campania* and the destroyers *Saumarez, Serapis, Scorpion, Savage, Zambesi* and *Zephyr*, makes a raid and lays air mines in area of Aalesund. Two small Norwegian ships are set on fire and driven ashore. From 26 Oct to 28 Oct another force, consisting of the carrier *Implacable*, the cruiser *Mauritius* and the destroyers *Myngs, Venus, Verulam, Volage, Algonquin* (RCN) and *Sioux* (RCN), makes attacks on Bodö/Sandnessjoen, in which the naval ferry barges *F235* and *F236* are damaged, on Rörvik, in which *V5722* and the aircraft depot ship *Karl Meyer* are destroyed, and on Lodingen and Kristiansund/North, in which *M433, Minenräumschiff 26* and two steamers are destroyed and *U1060* is damaged.

27 Oct–27 Nov   South West Pacific
TF 38 (Vice-Adm Mitscher) continues to support the Leyte fighting. On 27 Oct Gen MacArthur calls for support for Leyte from TF 38 because the USAAF can only employ inadequate forces on Tacloban. TG 38.3 (Rear-Adm Sherman) with the carriers *Essex, Lexington* and *Langley* flies fighter protection for Leyte. An attack by *Essex* hits a small Japanese supply convoy and the destroyers *Fujinami* and *Shiranuhi* are sunk. On 28 Oct TG 38.4 (Rear-Adm Davison) with *Franklin, Enterprise, San Jacinto* and *Belleau Wood* and TG 38.2 (Rear-Adm Bogan) with *Intrepid, Hancock, Cabot* and *Independence* take over the support role. TG 38.4 wards off a Japanese air attack by 44 aircraft; 13 planes are shot down at a cost of four American. The Japanese submarine *I-46* (Lt-Cdr Kawaguchi) tries to attack the group but is located and sunk by the destroyers *Helm* and *Gridley*. *I-26* (Lt-Cdr Nishiuchi) must also have been lost about this time. In the night 28–29 Oct *I-45* (Lt-Cdr Kawashima) sinks the DE *Eversole*, which is proceeding to an escort carrier group, but the submarine is herself sunk by the DE *Whitehurst* belonging to a tanker group in the vicinity. In addition, *I-53, I-56* (which makes several unsuccessful attacks and torpedoes the *LST695*), *I-38* and *I-41* operate E of Leyte and *Ro-43, Ro-46, Ro-109* and *Ro-112* E of Luzon. On 29 Oct TG 38.2 attacks airfields in the area of Manila; while losing 11 of its own aircraft, it shoots down 71 Japanese and destroys 13 on the ground. Only one

Japanese Kamikaze pilot out of 13 lightly hits the *Intrepid*. On 30 Oct TG 38.4 covers Leyte and is attacked by six Japanese Kamikazes, which severely damage the *Franklin* and *Belleau Wood*. TF 38 proceeds to Ulithi: TG 38.1 arrives on 29 Oct, TG 38.3 on 30 Oct and TGs 38.2 and 38.4 on 2 Nov. Vice-Adm Mitscher hands over command to Vice-Adm McCain. Rear-Adm Montgomery takes over TG 38.1.

In Leyte Gulf Japanese aircraft and Kamikaze pilots direct attacks against ships used to support the 6th Army. On 27 Nov the battleship *California* is damaged by aircraft fire. On 28 Nov 12 Kamikazes from Luzon and three from Cebu attack, and one damages the cruiser *Denver*. On 1 Nov seven Kamikazes attack in Leyte Gulf and sink the destroyer *Abner Read* and damage the destroyers *Anderson*, *Claxton* and *Ammen*; *Killen* and *Bush* receive bomb hits. On 2 Nov Japanese bombers attack the airfield at Tacloban and sink the escort vessel *PCER848* and damage a transport. On Leyte the Japanese defenders (the 16th Inf Div, Lt-Gen Makino†) are reinforced by units of the 35th Army (Lt-Gen Suzuki), elements of the 102nd and 1st Inf Divs as well as smaller contingents which are landed in Ormoc. TF 38 has to intervene again. To support the ships in Leyte Gulf, TG 34.5 is sent on 1 Nov with the battleships *New Jersey* and *Iowa*, the cruisers *Biloxi*, *Vincennes* and *Miami* and six destroyers and TG 38.2. But it is recalled on 2 Nov to attack Luzon with TF 38 (three groups but not 38.4). On the way the cruiser *Reno* is torpedoed on 3 Nov by the Japanese submarine *I-41* (Lt-Cdr Kondo); she is detached to Ulithi with four destroyers.

On 5 Nov and 6 Nov TG 38.1 with *Wasp*, *Hornet*, *Monterey* and *Cowpens*, TG 38.2 with *Intrepid*, *Hancock*, *Cabot* and *Independence* and TG 38.3 with *Lexington*, *Langley* and the new *Ticonderoga* attack Luzon. The Americans lose 25 aircraft. But over 400 Japanese aircraft are destroyed. In addition, the cruiser *Nachi* is sunk in Manila Bay and on the West Coast of Luzon the cruiser *Kumano* is hit by no less than nine torpedoes out of 23 fired by a submarine group (Cdr Chapple), consisting

of *Guitarro*, *Bream*, *Raton* and *Ray*. The cruiser can, however, be beached. Twelve Japanese Kamikaze aircraft attack TG 38.3 and badly damage the *Lexington*. Five more Kamikazes are no longer able to find the retiring TF 38 on 7 Nov.

In spite of frequent air attacks by the 5th USAAF Japanese convoys bring troops and supplies to Ormoc at the beginning of November. On 9 Nov a convoy with 2000 troops of the 26th Inf Div is attacked by 30 B-25s but is able to land most of the troops. On the next day a minesweeper and two steamers of the returning convoy are sunk. TF 38 (Rear-Adm Sherman) makes heavy attacks on the reinforcement transports on 11 Nov (347 sorties) with TG 38.1 (*Hornet*, *Monterey* and *Cowpens*), TG 38.3 (*Essex*, *Ticonderoga* and *Langley*) and TG 38.4 (*Enterprise* and *San Jacinto*). Eleven American aircraft are lost; but the Japanese destroyers *Hamanami*, *Naganami*, *Shimakaze* and *Wakatsuki*, the minesweeper *Sokai T-T 10* and five transports are sunk. Of the 10000 troops embarked on the ships, only a fraction reach the shore. A Japanese attempt to find TF 38 with 11 Kamikazes fails. On the same day a Task Force (Rear-Adm Smith), comprising the cruisers *Chester*, *Pensacola* and *Salt Lake City* and destroyers shells Iwojima.

After replenishing on 12 Nov the three Task Groups of TF 38 make new attacks on 13 Nov and 14 Nov on the Luzon area, particularly on ships in Manila Bay. From 14 Nov the *Wasp*, which has returned from Guam with a new Air Group, is again there with Vice-Adm McCain. The Japanese cruiser *Kiso*, the destroyers *Akebono*, *Akishimo*, *Hatsuharu* and *Okinami* and 10 steamers are sunk and the destroyer *Ushio* and five steamers damaged. Kamikaze attacks with four aircraft each are intercepted. After further replenishment on 16 Nov and the relief of TG 38.3 by 38.2 (*Intrepid*, *Hancock*, *Cabot* and *Independence*) the carriers again attack Luzon and ships in Manila Bay on 19 Nov. The cruiser *Isuzu* is damaged and two steamers and one submarine-chaser sunk. Four Kamikaze aircraft are intercepted. When she tries to approach TG

38.2 the Japanese submarine *I-41* is found by a submarine-hunter group with the escort carrier *Anzio* and sunk. The 'Kikusui' group, which set out from Japan on 8 Nov, tries on 20 Nov to use *Kaiten* one-man torpedoes for the first time. But in approaching the Kossol passage (Palau) *I-37* is sunk on 19 Nov by the DEs *McCoy Reynolds* and *Conklin*. *I-36* (Lt-Cdr Teramoto) and *I-47* (Lt-Cdr Orita) launch one and four *Kaiten* respectively off Ulithi on 20 Nov. One of them (Sub-Lt Nishida) destroys the tanker *Mississinewa* (11316 tons); two others, in trying to attack the cruisers *Mobile* and *Biloxi*, are destroyed by gunfire close to the ships, one by the destroyer *Case* and one by a USMC aircraft. Their success is greatly exaggerated in Japan.

After two replenishments on 20 Nov and 23 Nov TGs 38.2 (Rear-Adm Bogan) and 38.3 (Rear-Adm Sherman) again attack Luzon on 25 Nov. There take part four fleet carriers, three light carriers, six battleships, five light cruisers and destroyers. The cruiser *Kumano*, the former Chinese small cruiser *Yashojima*, three landing ships and three steamers are sunk. A Japanese submarine group, consisting of *Ro-41*, *Ro-43*, *Ro-49*, *Ro-50*, *Ro-109* and *Ro-112*, tries to approach the carriers but only *Ro-50* (Lt-Cdr Kimura) fires a salvo which misses. Twenty-five Kamikaze aircraft have, however, more success: the *Intrepid* and *Cabot* are severely, and the *Hancock* and *Essex* slightly, damaged. TF 38 proceeds to Ulithi, TG 4 arriving on 23 Nov, TG 1 on 25 Nov and TGs 2 and 3 on 27 Nov.

In the meantime, frequent air and Kamikaze attacks are made on the ships in Leyte Gulf. On 12 Nov two repair ships and on 17 Nov and again on 23 Nov a troop transport are hit.

28 Oct-12 Nov   Norway
In the night 28-29 Oct 51 Lancasters of RAF Bomber Command drop 200 tons of bombs on harbour installations in Bergen.
On 29 Oct there is an unsuccessful attack by 32 Lancaster bombers of No 9 and No 617 Sqdns from Lossiemouth (Scotland) on the *Tirpitz* at her new anchorage near Tromsö.
On 12 Nov 21 Lancasters of No 9 and

No 617 Sqdns RAF attack the German battleship *Tirpitz* (Capt Weber†) as she lies off Tromsö with 5.4 ton bombs and, as a result of several hits, the ship capsizes. Twenty-eight officers and 874 men of the crew perish on *Tirpitz*; 880 are rescued.

1 Nov   North Sea
Operation 'Infatuate': landing by the 152nd Brigade of the 52nd British Inf Div (Maj-Gen Hakewell-Smith), the 4th Commandos, the 10th Inter-Allied Commandos and the 4th Special Service Brigade (RM Commandos 41, 47 and 48) on the island of Walcheren in the Scheldt Estuary. The island, which is defended by the German 70th Inf Div, (Lt-Gen Daser), bars the approach to Antwerp with its coastal batteries. The island is shelled by the battleship *Warspite* and the monitors *Erebus* and *Roberts*. In the operation, which ends with the surrender of the German garrison on 8 Nov, the following landing craft are lost: the *LCTs 789, 839, 1133* and *7011*, the *LCGs 1, 2, 101* and *102*, *LCFs 37* and *38*, 10 LCAs, one LCI, two LCPs and three LCSs.

1-20 Nov   Mediterranean/Adriatic
The British escort destroyers *Wheatland* and *Avon Vale* sink the German torpedo boat *TA20* and the corvettes *UJ202* and *UJ208* S of Lussino on 1 Nov.
On 3 Nov the minelayer *Kiebitz*, escorted by the torpedo boats *TA40*, *TA44* and *TA45*, carries out a mining operation in the Northern Adriatic. Fighter bomber attacks are held off. In a US air attack on Fiume the torpedo boat *TA21*, the *Kiebitz* and the escort vessel *G104* are sunk.
On 20 Nov a group of boats from the 3rd MTB Flotilla sinks two motor sailing ships off Ancona.

1-27 Nov   Norway
Attacks on German shipping.
On 1 Nov the Norwegian *MTB712* and *MTB709* sink the German patrol boats *V5525* and *V5531* in Sognefjord.
In the night 12-13 Nov a British naval force, consisting of the heavy cruiser *Kent*, the light cruiser *Bellona* and the destroyers *Myngs*, *Verulam*, *Zambesi* and *Algonquin* (Canadian) attacks the German convoy KS.357 off Listerfjord (SE of Egersund). Of the four freighters of the convoy, *Greif* (996 tons) and

Cornouailles (3324 tons) sink and of the six escort vessels the minesweepers *M427* and *M416* and the submarine-chasers *UJ1221*, *UJ1223* and *UJ1713*. In the rescue operations on the morning of 13 Nov the motor minesweeper *R32* is lost in air attacks.

On 13 Nov the Norwegian *MTB688* and *MTB627* attack a German convoy in the southern exit of Krakhelle Sound (Sognefjord). Four torpedoes are out-manoeuvred by the two steamers. The escorting *UJ1430*, which is slightly damaged, *UJ1432* and *V1512* drive the boats off.

In a raid by aircraft from the escort carrier *Pursuer*, escorted by the cruiser *Euryalus* and the destroyers *Caesar*, *Nubian*, *Venus* and *Zephyr*, on 14 Nov off Trondheim, *V6413* is sunk.

On 27 Nov aircraft of the British carrier *Implacable* attack a south-bound German convoy off Mosjöen (N of Namsos) and destroy the Norwegian freighters *Rigel* (3828 tons)—of 2721 men, including 2248 Russian prisoners, only 415 are rescued—and *Korsnes* (1795 tons), as well as the German freighter *Spree* (2867 tons) which is lying at anchor. The carrier is escorted by the light cruiser *Dido* and the destroyers *Myngs, Scourge, Zephyr, Scorpion, Sioux* (Canadian) and *Algonquin* (Canadian).

On 27-28 Nov the Norwegian *MTB715* and *MTB623* unsuccessfully attack off Sognefjord a patrol boat force consisting of *V5514, V5527* and *RA203*. A second group, comprising *MTB717* and *MTB 627*, attacks a German convoy and torpedoes the steamer *Welheim* (5455 tons) which has to be beached. The escort vessels *V5303, V5312* and *R312* obtain hits on the MTBs.

1-30 Nov   Pacific
The following ships are sunk by US submarines which arrive in their operational areas in November: off Japan, Formosa and the Kuriles *Archerfish* (Lt-Cdr Enright) sinks the carrier *Shinano*; *Atule* (Lt-Cdr Maurer) two ships of 23241 tons and the minesweeper *Sokaitei 38* and the fast transport *No 38*; *Bang* (Lt-Cdr Gallaher) two ships of 5223 tons; *Barb* (Cdr Fluckey) two ships of 15261 tons; *Burrfish* (Lt-Cdr Perkins) one picket boat; *Peto* (Lt-Cdr Caldwell) three ships of 12173 tons and

torpedoes one ship; *Picuda* (Lt-Cdr Shepard) three ships of 21659 tons; *Pomfret* (Lt-Cdr Hess) three ships of 14001 tons; *Queenfish* (Lt-Cdr Loughlin) five ships of 14415 tons and torpedoes one ship; *Redfish* (Cdr McGregor) one ship of 2345 tons and the carrier *Unryu* and torpedoes the carrier *Junyo*; *Saury* (Lt-Cdr Waugh) one picket boat; *Scabbardfish* (Lt-Cdr Gunn) two ships of 1282 tons and the submarine *I-365* and torpedoes the frigate *Oki*; *Sealion* (Lt-Cdr Reich) the battleship *Kongo* and the destroyer *Urakaze*; *Spadefish* (Lt-Cdr Underwood) two ships of 9321 tons and the escort carrier *Shinyo* (ex-Lloyd ship *Scharnhorst*); *Sterlet* (Lt-Cdr Robbins) one picket boat; *Sunfish* (Lt-Cdr Shelby) three ships of 16179 tons; and *Tambor* (Lt-Cdr Germershausen) one picket boat.

In the area of the Malayan Archipelago and the Philippines *Barbel* (Lt-Cdr Keating) sinks two ships of 8801 tons; *Barbero* (Lt-Cdr Hartman) two ships of 4949 tons; *Besugo* (Lt-Cdr Wogan) the landing ship *T151*; *Blackfin* (Lt-Cdr Laird) two ships of 3065 tons; *Flounder* (Cdr Stevens) one ship of 5698 tons and the U-boat *U537*; *Guavina* (Lt-Cdr Teideman) one ship of 1916 tons with *Gunnel*; *Gunnel* (Lt-Cdr O'Neill) one ship of 5623 tons and the torpedo boats *Sagi* and *Hiyodori*; *Gurnard* (Cdr Gage) one ship of 6600 tons; *Haddo* (Lt-Cdr Lynch) one ship of 865 tons and torpedoes the destroyer *Hatsutsuki* and the frigate *Shimushu*; *Hake* (Lt-Cdr Hayler) torpedoes the cruiser *Isuzu*; *Hardhead* (Cdr Greenup) one ship of 5266 tons and the corvette *Kaibokan 38*; *Jack* (Lt-Cdr Fuhrmann) two ships of 12255 tons; *Mingo* (Lt-Cdr Staley) one ship of 9486 tons; *Pampanito* (Lt-Cdr Fenno) one ship of 1200 tons; *Parche* (Lt-Cdr Ramage) one ship of 5226 tons; *Pargo* (Lt-Cdr Bell) one ship of 5226 tons; and *Pintado* (Lt-Cdr Clarey) the destroyer *Akikaze*.

2-16 Nov   North Sea
German motor torpedo boats sink the British tanker *Rio Bravo* (1141 tons) off Ostend on 2 Nov. In the same night there is an engagement between British MTBs and German patrol boats in which *V2016* sinks as a result of two torpedo hits.

On 15-16 Nov British MTBs and the frigates *Retalick* and *Thornborough* locate six German motor torpedo boats in the Scheldt Estuary which have come out on a mining operation and, in an engagement, compel them to return.

15 Nov   South West Pacific
The British fast minelayer *Ariadne* with the US destroyers *Shaw* and *Caldwell*, the DE *Willmarth* and 20 landing craft, transports a regiment of the 31st US Inf Div from Morotai to Pegun Island in the Mapia Group for the purpose of erecting a weather station and a Loran Station. The 200 Japanese on the island are overwhelmed by the US troops who land after a shelling by the destroyers.

15 Nov-9 Jan   North Atlantic and English Channel
Operations by German schnorkel U-boats. On the way out to the North Atlantic *U322* is bombed on 24 Nov W of the Shetlands by a Norwegian Sunderland of No 330 Sqdn and sunk on 25 Nov by the frigate *Ascension* of the 5th SG. *U650* is lost from unknown causes in the 'Northern Transit Area' at the beginning of December.
In the area of Reykjavik *U979* (Lt-Cdr Meermeier) from 23 Nov to 1 Dec misses one trawler, one convoy and one frigate. N of Scotland *U296* and *U775* (Lt Taschenmacher) operate from the end of November until the middle of December. The latter sinks the DE *Bullen* with a T-5 on 6 Dec. *U1009* has to return owing to schnorkel trouble. The boats *U1020*, *U297* and *U312* are employed round Scapa Flow against British carrier groups: on 6 Dec *U297* is sunk by the frigate *Loch Insh* and the DE *Goodall*. *U312* is damaged on 28 Dec when she goes aground in Hoxa Sound and *U1020* (Lt Eberlein) torpedoes the destroyer *Zephyr* on 31 Dec. *U482* cruises in the North Channel and *U1202* (Lt-Cdr Thomsen) sinks a Liberty ship (7176 tons) in a convoy in the Bristol Channel. *U400* is sunk on 17 Dec by the frigate *Nyasaland* SW of Ireland when she tries to attack a convoy.
In the Channel *U991* (Lt-Cdr Balke), in addition to three unsuccessful attacks, reports the sinking of a Liberty ship on 15 Dec. On the same day, *U680* misses a trawler. *U772* (Lt-Cdr Rademacher),

after a miss, sinks three ships of 10970 tons from two convoys and torpedoes two ships of 14367 tons on 29 Dec from the convoy TBC.1, one of which becomes a total loss. On 30 Dec the boat is sunk by a Leigh Light Wellington of No 407 Sqdn RCAF. *U486* (Lt G. Meyer) sinks one ship of 6142 tons on 18 Dec, misses a destroyer on 21 Dec and sinks on 24 Dec the troop transport *Leopoldville* (11509 tons) which is escorted by the destroyers *Anthony*, *Brilliant* and three other escorts. 819 men drown. On 26 Dec the DE *Capel* is sunk and the DE *Affleck* damaged in a T-5 attack on the 1st SG. *U1209* runs on rocks off South-west Ireland and is lost. *U485*, the last boat to enter the Channel in 1944, misses a destroyer. The transport U-boats *U773* and *U722* return from St Nazaire. On the way out in the North Atlantic *U877* meets the convoy HX.327 (EG C.3) on 27 Nov and is sunk by the Canadian corvettes *St Thomas* and *Edmundston*. During the preparation of the Ardennes offensive the boats *U1053*, *U870*, *U1232* and *U1009* are used as weather boats in the North Atlantic. As she departs for Gibraltar *U870* (Cdr Hechler) meets a convoy on 20 Dec and from it sinks the *LST359* and torpedoes the *Fogg*, one of four US DEs. When the weather boats are located by DF, a hunter group, equipped with the new DAQ HF/DF equipment and consisting of the US DEs *Otter*, *Hubbard* and *Varian*, is deployed against them, but, at first, it has no success.
Off Cabot Strait *U1228* (Lt Marienfeld) sinks the corvette *Shawinigan* sailing on her own; in the Gulf of St Lawrence *U1230* (Lt-Cdr Hilbig) sinks one ship of 5458 tons; and *U1231* (Capt Lessing) misses two escort vessels and a steamer. *U806* (Lt-Cdr Hornbostel) sinks one ship of 7219 tons from an HX convoy off Halifax and from three convoys forming up, the minesweeper *Clayoquot* on 24 Dec. The corvettes *Fennel* and *Transcona* are narrowly missed by T-5s.

17-23 Nov   Indian Ocean
Operation 'Outflank'. A Task Force of the British Eastern Fleet under Rear-Adm Vian, consisting of the carriers *Indomitable* and *Illustrious*, the cruisers

Newcastle, Argonaut and *Black Prince* and the destroyers *Kempenfelt, Whirlwind, Wrangler, Wessex* and *Wakeful*, sets out from Trincomalee on 17 Nov. After replenishing on 18 Nov from the tanker *Wave King* with the destroyers *Wager* and *Whelp*, 27 Avenger bombers and 28 Corsair and Hellcat fighters are flown off early on 20 Nov to attack Pangkalan Brandan (North-West Sumatra) but, because of the weather, they have to be diverted to the S to the oil installations of Belawan Deli. In the afternoon there is an attack on airfields near Sabang. There are no losses. The force returns on 23 Nov.

18-24 Nov   Baltic
Soviet offensive against the Sworbe Peninsula. On 18 Nov the Soviet 8th Army goes over to the attack with support from strong artillery and air formations and fire support from the gunboats *Volga, Bureja, Zeya* and 11 armoured cutters on the eastern side. On 18 Nov German minesweepers have engagements with Soviet ships on the eastern side of Sworbe: *M328* sinks one armoured cutter. From the W the torpedo boats *T23* and *T28* intervene in the fighting and on 19 Nov they, too, proceed to the eastern side in spite of heavy air attacks. On 20-21 Nov the Task Force (Vice-Adm Thiele), comprising the cruiser *Prinz Eugen* (Capt Reinicke) and the 3rd TB Flotilla (Cdr Verlohr) with *T21, T13, T16* and *T19*, intervenes from the W. On 22 Nov, 23 Nov and 24 Nov the pocket battleship *Admiral Scheer* (Capt Thienemann) with *Z25* and *Z35* and the 2nd TB Flotilla (Cdr Paul) with *T3, T12, T5, T9, T13* and *T16* relieves the force. Several air attacks are repelled. The *Lützow*, which is approaching as a relief for 24 Nov, has to return because the evacuation is completed in the night 23-24 Nov. 4694 men are transported by naval ferry barges. On the East Coast on 20-21 Nov *M328, M423, V1713* and *V302* have engagements with gunboats, armoured cutters and torpedo cutters.

18 Nov-15 Feb   Australia
The German U-boat *U862* (Cdr Timm) proceeds from Djakarta to the W and S of Australia to the Adelaide area, where on 9 Dec she has to break off an attack on the Greek steamer *Ilissos* when an aircraft approaches. A search by the Australian corvettes *Burnie, Lismore* and *Maryborough* on 10 Dec leads to no result. On 24 Dec *U862* sinks the US freighter *Robert J. Walker* (7180 tons) in three approaches off Sydney. The ships deployed in the search, the US submarine-chaser *PC597*, the Australian destroyer *Quickmatch*, the corvettes *Ballarat, Goulbourn, Kalgoorlie* and *Whyalla*, the trawlers *Kiama* and *Yandra* and, the British destroyers from Melbourne, the *Quilliam, Quadrant* and *Quality*, do not find the U-boat but rescue survivors. Liberator bombers of the RAAF, deployed following DF bearings on a W/T message, do not find the U-boat on 29 Jan, 30 Jan and 31 Jan SW of Fremantle. On 5-6 Feb she sinks the US freighter *Peter Sylvester* (7176 tons) in three approaches 820 nautical miles W of Fremantle. The attack only becomes known when a steamer finds survivors. The ships deployed from Fremantle, the US frigate *Corpus Christi* and the Australian corvette *Dubbo*, find other boats. A planned search from 11 Feb to 20 Feb for two missing boats with aircraft, with the British escort carriers *Slinger* and *Speaker*, which are in the course of being transferred, and with the US frigate *Hutchinson* and the Australian corvettes *Warrnambool* and *Castlemaine* leads to no result. Only on 28 Feb does the passing British escort carrier *Activity* find a boat. On 10 Mar the US submarine *Rock*, returning from a patrol in enemy waters, finds the last boat which has covered 1100 nautical miles in 32 days. All 143 survivors are rescued.

20 Nov   Mediterranean
British MTBs, in an attack on a German convoy off Sestri-Levante (SE of Genoa), sink the submarine-chaser *UJ2207*.

21 Nov   North Pacific
A Task Group under Rear-Adm McCrea with two light cruisers and nine destroyers shells Matsuwa in the Kuriles.

22-23 Nov   Indian Ocean
Reorganization of the British Eastern Fleet: Vice-Adm Power forms the British East Indies Fleet with the battleship *Queen Elizabeth*, the battlecruiser

Renown, five escort carriers, eight cruisers and 24 destroyers. The modern ships form the British Pacific Fleet under Adm Fraser and include the battleships *King George V* (Vice-Adm Rawlings) and *Howe*, the carriers *Indefatigable* (Rear-Adm Vian), *Illustrious*, *Victorious* and *Indomitable*, the cruisers *Swiftsure*, *Argonaut*, *Black Prince*, *Ceylon*, *Newfoundland* and the New Zealand *Gambia* and *Achilles* and three destroyer flotillas (the 4th with 'Q' class, the 25th with 'U' class and the 27th with 'W' class).

In November the following ships are sunk by British submarines in the Malacca Straits and in the western parts of the Malayan Archipelago: *Tantalus* (Lt-Cdr Mackenzie) sinks one ship of 1918 tons and one small craft; *Shalimar* three small craft; *Terrapin* (Lt Brunner) the minesweeper *Sokaitei 5* and one small craft; *Storm* (Lt Young) eleven sailing ships; *Tradewind* five sailing ships; *Spirit* (Lt Langridge) one small tanker and damages one ship; *Thorough* sinks five small craft and damages one vessel; *Tudor* (Lt Porter) one small ship; *Tally Ho* (Cdr Bennington) the small minelayer *No 5* and ten sailing ships; *Stratagem* (Lt Pelly) one ship of 1945 tons; *Spark* (Lt Kent) two sailing ships; *Sturdy* (Lt Andersen) two small steamers and six sailing ships; *Stygian* (Lt Clarabut) five small craft; and the Dutch *O.19* (Lt-Cdr v. Karnebeek) one small steamer.

27 Nov-6 Dec   South West Pacific
Japanese attempt to counter-attack on Leyte. Airborne commando troops are to knock out the US airfields and Kamikazes are to hit the ships in order to weaken support for the US troops. TG 77.2 (Rear-Adm Weyler) is in Leyte Gulf with the battleships *Maryland*, *West Virginia*, *Colorado* and *New Mexico*, the cruisers *Columbia*, *Denver*, *Montpelier* and *St Louis* and 16 destroyers. The air landing on 27 Nov fails; bombers and five Kamikazes damage the *Colorado*, *Montpelier* and *St Louis* and the *Maryland* just avoids an air torpedo. But the latter is hit together with the destroyers *Saufley* and *Aulick*, by Kamikazes on 29 Nov. A second attempt is made on 5-6 Dec: three Kamikazes damage the destroyers *Mugford* and *Drayton*. The air landings,

in which paratroops are used, are to some extent more successful; for two days there is hard fighting for the airfield at Burauen. In the same period US destroyers make sorties into Ormoc Gulf, first with *Waller*, *Saufley*, *Renshaw* and *Pringle* on 27 Nov which sink one Japanese midget submarine; then further sorties are made by *Waller*, *Renshaw*, *Cony* and *Conner* on 29-30 Nov and *Conway*, *Cony*, *Eaton* and *Sigourney* on 1-2 Dec, but they are unsuccessful. On 3 Dec *Allen M. Sumner*, *Moale* and *Cooper* intercept two Japanese escort destroyers with reinforcements for Ormoc. They sink the *Kuwa*, but the *Take* sinks the *Cooper* with a torpedo and escapes.

27 Nov-14 Dec   Arctic
Convoy operation JW.62/RA.62 in the Arctic. JW.62 has 30 merchant ships, escorted by the 8th and 20th EGs including the destroyers *Keppel*, *Beagle*, *Bulldog*, and *Westcott*, the sloops *Cygnet*, *Lapwing* and *Lark* and the corvettes *Allington Castle* and *Bamborough Castle* and the Norwegian corvettes *Tunsberg Castle* and *Eglantine* which are being transferred to Murmansk. Covering force: the cruiser *Bellona*, the 1st Div of the 7th DD Flotilla comprising *Caesar*, *Cassandra*, *Caprice* and *Cambrian* and the 17th DD Flotilla comprising *Onslow*, *Orwell*, *Obedient*, *Offa*, *Onslaught* and *Oribi*. And as Support Groups there are the escort carriers *Campania* and *Nairana* with the frigates *Tavy*, *Tortola*, *Bahamas* and *Somaliland* and the Canadian 9th EG with the frigates *St John*, *Stormont*, *Monnow*, *Loch Alvie*, *Nene* and *Port Colborne*.

On 27 Nov the convoy is located by German air reconnaissance. A fighter from the *Nairana* shoots down the contact-keeper. The U-boat groups 'Stock' (*U313*, *U315*, *U293*, *U363*, *U299*, *U365*, *U286*, *U318*, *U995* and *U992*) and 'Grube' (*U295*, *U1163*, *U387*, *U997*, *U668*, *U310* and *U965*) are deployed W of Bear Island off the Kola Coast. On 1 Dec the 'Stock' group is moved to the Kola Coast because it is assumed that the convoy has passed the Bear Island passage. The convoy makes a diversion whilst the support groups make sorties against the suspected U-

N

boat concentration—without result. On 2 Dec *U995* and *U363* (Lt-Cdr Ness) attack the Soviet coastal convoy PK.20 (Kirkenes-Kola), consisting of three steamers, and four large and two small submarine-chasers. *U363* sinks the steamer *Proletari* (1123 tons). On 3 Dec *U1163* (Lt Balduhn) sinks on the eastern Kola coast the steamer *Revolutsioner* (433 tons) from the Soviet convoy KB.35 (Kola-White Sea), comprising two steamers and two former trawler patrol boats, *T-38* and *SKR-20*. On 4 Dec *U363*, *U992* (Lt Falke) and *U995* (Lt Hess) make unsuccessful attacks on a Soviet coastal convoy off the Kola Inlet escorted by ex-US minesweepers. On 4-5 Dec in attacks on a Soviet coastal convoy in the entrance to the White Sea *U997* (Lt Lehmann) misses steamers and sinks the ex-US submarine-chaser *BO-226* (ex-*SC1485*); *U295* (Lt Wieboldt) misses the destroyers *Deyatelny* and *Zhivuchi* with T-5s near Jokanga and is pursued by them. From 5 Dec to 7 Dec *U293* (Lt-Cdr Klingspor), *U992*, *U995*, *U365* (Lt Todenhagen), *U318* (Lt Will), *U997* and *U1163* (Lt Balduhn) attack, sometimes repeatedly, Soviet A/S groups as well as escorts and ships of the incoming JW.62. But only on 7 Dec is the ex-US submarine-chaser *BO-229* (ex-*SC1477*), belonging to a Soviet anti-submarine group (Capt 3rd Class Gritsyuk), comprising *BO-227*, *BO-228*, *BO-229* and *BO-150*, sunk by *U997*. JW.62 comes into harbour without loss. Before the return convoy RA.62 sets out with 28 ships and the escort of JW.62 on 9 Feb, the Allied support groups and a Soviet destroyer force (Rear-Adm Fokin), composed of *Baku*, *Gremyashchi*, *Razumny*, *Derzki*, *Doblestny* and *Zhivuchi*, try to drive off the U-boats from the entrance to the Kola Inlet. In the process *U997* misses the *Zhivuchi* and *Razumny* with T-5s on 9 Dec. *U387* is sunk by depth charges from the corvette *Bamborough Castle* (according to Soviet claims by ramming from the *Zhivuchi*). Only *U365* is able to establish contact with the convoy and to torpedo the destroyer *Cassandra* on 11 Dec after an unsuccessful attack on a tanker the day before. On 13 Dec the boat, while keeping contact

with great determination, is sunk by an aircraft from the *Campania*. An attempt by German torpedo aircraft of K.G. 26 to attack the convoy SW of Bear Island is unsuccessful and results in the loss of two Ju 88s. The Norwegian corvette *Tunsberg Castle* runs on a mine of the German flanking barrage near Makkaur on 12 Dec and sinks.

28-29 Nov North Sea
The first Allied convoy, consisting of 18 ships, arrives in Antwerp on 28 Nov. On 29 Nov German motor torpedo boats make an unsuccessful attempt to attack an Allied convoy proceeding to Antwerp.

1-31 Dec Pacific
The following ships are sunk by US submarines arriving in their operational areas in December: off Japan, Formosa and the Kuriles *Finback* (Lt-Cdr Williams) sinks one ship of 2111 tons; *Greenling* (Lt-Cdr Gerwick) two ships of 1916 tons and the landing ship *No 46*; *Plaice* (Lt-Cdr Stevens) torpedoes the escort destroyer *Maki*; *Sea Owl* (Lt-Cdr Bennet) torpedoes the destroyer *Shiokaze*; *Tilefish* (Lt-Cdr Kaithley) sinks the torpedo boat *Chidori*. In the area of the Malayan Archipelago and the Philippines *Barbero* (Lt-Cdr Hartman) sinks one ship of 4277 tons and the submarine-chaser *Kusentai 30*; *Bergall* (Lt-Cdr Hyde) torpedoes the cruiser *Myoko*; *Blenny* (Lt-Cdr Hazzard) sinks one ship of 4156 tons and the corvette *Kaibokan 28*; *Cavalla* (Lt-Cdr Kossler) the destroyer *Shimotsuki*; *Dace* (Lt-Cdr Cole), one ship of 6925 tons (on a mine); *Flasher* (Lt-Cdr Grider) four ships of 38668 tons and the destroyer *Kishinami*; *Hammerhead* (Lt-Cdr Martin) one ship of 834 tons and, together with *Paddle* (Lt-Cdr Nowell), one ship of 2854 tons; *Hawkbill* (Lt-Cdr Scanland) the torpedo boat *Momo*; *Pintado* (Lt-Cdr Deragon) the corvette *Kaibokan 64*; *Razorback* (Lt-Cdr Brown), together with *Segundo* (Lt-Cdr Fulp), one ship of 6933 tons and the torpedo boat *Kuretake*; *Sealion* (Lt-Cdr Putnam) one ship of 7000 tons; and *Trepang* (Lt-Cdr Davenport) three ships of 13073 tons.

5-9 Dec Mediterranean/Aegean
The British cruiser *Caledon*, the escort destroyer *Easton* and the corvette *La*

Malouine with the Greek destroyer *Navarinon* and the corvette *Sakhtouris* shell E.L.A.S. positions near Piraeus and Salamis. On 21 Dec the cruiser *Ajax* shells E.L.A.S. positions near Piraeus.

7-15 Dec South West Pacific
Following a sortie by the destroyers *Nicholas, O'Bannon, Fletcher* and *La Valette* in the night 6-7 Dec TG 78.3 (Rear-Adm Struble), with eight APDs, 27 LCIs, 12 LSMs and four LSTs and a minesweeper group, lands the 77th US Inf Div (Maj-Gen Bruce) S of Ormoc early on 7 Dec. Cover and support is provided by the destroyers *Hughes, Barton, Walke, Laffey, O'Brien, Flusser, Lamson, Edwards, Smith, Reid, Conygham* and *Mahan*. After the successful landing which encounters no strong resistance, 21 Japanese Kamikaze pilots attack and sink the destroyer *Mahan*, the APD *Ward* and *LST737*. The destroyer *Lamson* and the APD *Liddle* are badly damaged. A Japanese attempt to land a reinforced regiment near Ormoc with the escort destroyers *Ume* and *Sugi* and the APD *No 11* is frustrated by aircraft from Tacloban: the APD sinks and the destroyers are damaged. On 8 Dec three transports are sunk W of Leyte. On 10 Dec the *Hughes* is damaged in Leyte Gulf by Kamikazes. On 11 Dec the destroyer *Coghlan* of a supply convoy has an engagement with the Japanese destroyers *Uzuki* and *Yuzuki* which are sunk by *PT492* and *PT490* and by aircraft which also badly hit a troop convoy near Palompon. On 8 Dec the Japanese midget submarine *Ha-81* fails to secure a hit off Ormoc.

8 Dec Norway
The Norwegian *MTB717* and *MTB653* attack a German convoy off Korsfjord, consisting of two steamers and the patrol boats *V5113* and *V5114*, and sink the freighter *Ditmar Koel*.

8-14 Dec Norway
During the RA.62 convoy operation a British carrier force, comprising the carriers *Implacable, Trumpeter* and *Premier*, the cruiser *Diadem* and the destroyers *Zambesi, Savage, Vigilant, Zealous, Serapis, Stord* (Norwegian), *Sioux* (RCN) and *Algonquin* (RCN), makes a raid on the Haugesund area

in Western Norway in which two ships are sunk.
On 14 Dec torpedo aircraft of K.G. 26 (Lt-Col Stemmler) unsuccessfully attack off the Norwegian West Coast a British naval force consisting of the escort carriers *Premier* and *Trumpeter*, the heavy cruiser *Devonshire* and the destroyers *Zealous, Serapis, Savage, Zephyr, Algonquin* (RCN) and *Sioux* (RCN).

8 Dec-5 Jan Central Pacific
A US Task Group (Rear-Adm Smith), consisting of the cruisers *Chester, Pensacola* and *Salt Lake City* and destroyers, bombards Iwojima on 8 Dec. On 24 Dec and 27 Dec and on 5 Jan the shelling is repeated. On 5 Jan one of the five destroyers, *David W. Taylor*, is damaged on a mine.

11-12 Dec Baltic
The 6th DD Flotilla (Capt Kothe†) carries out an offensive mining operation in the Gulf of Finland with *Z35, Z36, Z43, T23* and *T28*. In the course of the operation *Z35* and *Z36* run on other German mines and sink.

11-20 Dec Indian Ocean
The newly-formed British TF 64 (Capt Bush), comprising the destroyers *Napier* and *Nepal*, minesweepers, landing boats and the Indian ML flotillas 55 and 56, supports the coastal flank of British XV Corps on the Arakan Front (Burma). Operation 'Robson': Rear-Adm Vian makes a carrier raid on 17 Dec on oil, railway and harbour installations of Belawan-Deli in Northern Sumatra with the carriers *Indomitable* and *Illustrious*, the cruisers *Newcastle, Black Prince* and *Argonaut* and seven destroyers.
In the area of the Malacca Straits and in the western part of the Malayan Archipelago the British submarines *Trenchant* (Cdr Hezlet) and *Terrapin* (Lt Brunner) jointly sink four small steamers and seven sailing ships and damage three small craft. *Sea Rover* (Lt Angell) sinks one small steamer; *Strongbow* one tug and one lighter; *Porpoise* (Lt-Cdr Turner) one sailing ship; *Stoic* (Lt Marriott) one ship of 1986 tons; *Shakespeare* (Lt Ainslie) one ship of 2515 tons and torpedoes one other ship; *Shalimar* 11 small craft; *Subtle* three sailing ships; *Spiteful* (Lt

Sherwood) one small steamer; *Thule* (Lt Mars) 20 sailing ships; *Tudor* (Lt Porter) seven sailing ships; *Statesman* (Lt Bulkeley) five small craft. In addition, *Sea Scout* and *Sirdar* (Lt Spender) damage two and one small steamers respectively.

11-22 Dec Central Pacific

On 11 Dec TF 38 (Vice-Adm McCain) sets out from Ulithi.

TG 38.1 (Rear-Adm Montgomery) comprises the carriers *Yorktown, Wasp, Cowpens* and *Monterey*, the battleships *Massachusetts* and *Alabama*, the cruisers *San Francisco, Baltimore, New Orleans* and *San Diego* and 18 destroyers.

TG 38.2 (Rear-Adm Bogan) comprises the carriers *Lexington, Hancock, Hornet, Independence* and *Cabot*, the battleships *New Jersey, Iowa* and *Wisconsin*, the cruisers *Pasadena, Astoria, Vincennes, Miami* and *San Juan* and 20 destroyers.

TG 38.3 (Rear-Adm Sherman) comprises the carriers *Essex, Ticonderoga, Langley* and *San Jacinto*, the battleships *North Carolina, Washington* and *South Dakota*, the cruisers *Mobile, Biloxi, Santa Fé* and *Oakland* and 18 destroyers. After replenishing from the tanker group (Capt Acuff) on 13 Dec, the carriers make continual air attacks on the airfields of Luzon in support of the Mindoro operation from 14 Dec to 16 Dec. In all, there are 1427 fighter and 244 bomber sorties. Twenty-seven aircraft are lost in combat and 38 by accident. About 170 Japanese aircraft are destroyed, as well as four steamers and one landing ship.

On the way to replenishment TF 38 runs into a typhoon on 18 Dec. The destroyer *Spence* sinks; and the carriers *Cowpens, Monterey* and *Cabot*, the destroyers *Dyson, Hickox, Benham* and *Maddox* are damaged. Of the supply group, the destroyers *Hull* and *Monaghan* sink and the following are damaged: the escort carriers *Altamaha, Nehenta Bay, Cape Esperance* and *Kwajalein*, the destroyers *Aylwin* (Capt Acuff), *Dewey* and *Buchanan*, the DEs *Melvin R. Newman, Tabberer* and *Waterman*, the tanker *Nantahala* and one tug. Owing to the search for survivors the attacks on Luzon planned for 19 Dec to 21 Dec have to be abandoned. TF 38 returns to Ulithi.

14 Dec Baltic

In a Soviet air attack on the harbour of Libau the transports *Erika Schünemann* (1177 tons), *Minna Cords* (951 tons) and the tanker *Inka* (427 tons) are sunk. Several other ships are damaged.

15-24 Dec South West Pacific

TG 78.3 (Rear-Adm Struble), comprising the cruiser *Nashville*, eight APDs, 30 LSTs, 12 LSMs, 31 LCIs, 10 large and seven small minesweepers and 14 small craft, lands the Western Visayas T.F. (Brig-Gen Dunckel)—the 503rd Parachute Regt and the 19th RCT of the 24th Div—on Mindoro. Escort: the destroyers *Barton, Walke, Laffey, O'Brien, Allen M. Sumner, Moale, Ingraham, Dashiell, Paul Hamilton, Bush, Stanly, Lowry* and *Howorth*. Covering force (Rear-Adm Berkey): the cruisers *Phoenix, Boise* and *Shropshire* (RAN) and the destroyers *Fletcher, La Valette, O'Bannon, Hopewell, Radford, Arunta* (RAN) and *Warramunga* (RAN). Distant covering force: TF 77.12 (Rear-Adm Ruddock), comprising the battleships *West Virginia, Colorado* and *New Mexico*, the cruisers *Denver, Columbia* and *Montpelier*, the escort carriers *Natoma Bay, Manila Bay, Marcus Island, Kadashan Bay, Savo Island* and *Ommaney Bay*, the destroyers *Waller, Renshaw, Conway, Cony, Eaton, Robinson, Corner, Sigourney, Bennion, Remey, Mertz, McDermut, Patterson, Haraden, Twiggs, Stembel, Ralph Talbot* and *Braine*. On the way the flagship *Nashville* is badly damaged by a Kamikaze attack on 13 Dec. There are many casualties among the command staff. The destroyer *Haraden* is damaged. Following a successful landing on 15 Dec there are further Kamikaze attacks; *LST738* and *LST472* have to be abandoned after hits and the carrier *Marcus Island* and the destroyers *Paul Hamilton* and *Howorth* are slightly damaged.

On the following days there are further Kamikaze attacks. On 21 Dec the *LST460* and *LST479* are sunk. The destroyers *Charles Ausburne, Converse* and *Foote* rescue most of the troops. On 22 Dec the destroyer *Newcomb* is narrowly missed and *Bryant* is damaged. On 18 Dec the Japanese midget submarine *Ha76* misses with a torpedo.

18-19 Dec   Air War/Germany
RAF Bomber Command drops 824 tons of bombs on Gotenhafen: the training ship *Schleswig-Holstein*, the target ship *Zähringen*, the torpedo boat *T10*, the U-boat depot ship *Waldemar Kophamel* and the freighters *Warthe* (4922 tons), *Leverkusen* (1273 tons), *Theresia L. M. Russ* (1694 tons), *Heinz Horn* (3994 tons) and the tanker *Blexen* (715 tons) are sunk.

21 Dec   Norway
UJ1113, *UJ1116*, *R402* and the steamer *Weichselland* (3654 tons) from a German convoy run on a mine barrage laid by the French submarine *Rubis* (Cdr Rousselot) in the Feiestein Channel (19 Dec) and sink. This is the last operation by the most successful mining submarine of the Second World War; she has sunk 15 ships of 25770 tons and eight small warships.

22-25 Dec   North Sea
On 22-23 Dec a group of five German motor torpedo boats lays a mine barrage N of Dunkirk. In an engagement with British escort forces *S185* is lost. In mining operations by a group of three motor torpedo boats NW of Ostend *S192* is lost in an engagement with the British destroyer *Walpole*, the DEs *Curzon* and *Torrington*, the patrol vessel *Kittiwake* and MTBs.
On 24-25 Dec German motor torpedo boats try to operate on the convoy route to Antwerp but they are frustrated by the British DEs *Ekins* and *Thornborough*, the frigate *Caicos* and the corvette *Shearwater*.

23-26 Dec   Norway
In operations by the Norwegian 54th MTB Flotilla (Lt Herlofsen) *MTB722* and *MTB712* attack a German force in Bömlofjord on the evening of 23 Dec and sink the minesweeper *M489*. Early on 26 Dec the *MTB717* and *MTB627* attack a convoy of two steamers and *V5102* and *V5114* near Fröysjoen and sink the tanker *Buvi*.

26 Dec   South West Pacific
A Japanese force, which set out from Camranh Bay/Indochina on 24 Dec, shells the US bridgehead on Mindoro. It consists of the destroyer *Kasumi*

(Rear-Adm Kimura), the heavy cruiser *Ashigara*, the light cruiser *Oyodo* and the destroyers *Kiyoshimo*, *Asashimo*, *Kaya*, *Sugi* and *Kashi*. The Japanese force turns away and escapes after American air attacks and the sinking of the *Kiyoshimo* by the PT boat *PT223*. This is the last Japanese naval sortie into the area of the Philippines.

26-30 Dec   South West Pacific
Japanese aircraft destroy in Philippine waters the American transports *Hobart Baker* (7176 tons), *John Burke* (7180 tons), *James H. Breasted* (7212 tons) and the tanker *Porcupine* (7218 tons); they damage several other ships.

29-30 Dec   Arctic
After several unsuccessful attacks on Soviet coastal convoys on the Kola Coast *U995* (Lt Hess) sinks one small and so far unidentified steamer. *U956* (Lt Mohs) torpedoes the steamer *Tbilisi* (7176 tons) from the convoy KP.24 off Kola Bay. The steamer is beached.

31 Dec   Air War/Germany
Bombers of the 8th USAAF attack Hamburg. In the harbour *U906*, the minesweeper *M445* and the freighters *Faro* (2621 tons), *Mannheim* (897 tons) and *Rival* (809 tons) are sunk.

30 Dec-21 Jan   Arctic
Convoy operation JW.63/RA.63. On 30 Dec JW.63 sets out from Loch Ewe with 35 ships. Escort: the escort carrier *Vindex* (Vice-Adm Dalrymple-Hamilton), the cruiser *Diadem*, the destroyers *Zambesi*, *Myngs*, *Zebra*, *Algonquin* (RCN), *Sioux* (RCN), *Savage*, *Serapis*, *Scourge*, *Scorpion* and *Stord* (Norwegian) from the Home Fleet, and from the 8th and 20th EGs the destroyers *Keppel*, *Westcott* and *Walker*, the sloops *Cygnet*, *Lapwing* and *Lark*, the corvettes *Alnwick Castle*, *Allington Castle* and *Bamborough Castle*. The German U-boats of the 'Stier' group, *U299*, *U956*, *U995* and *U997* are stationed in Bear Island Passage and *U293*, *U310* and *U636* N of Kola. On 8 Jan the ships of the convoy arrive in the Kola Inlet and the White Sea unobserved. The convoy in the opposite direction, RA.63, sets out from the Kola Inlet on 11 Jan with 30 ships and the same escort as JW.63; it arrives in Loch Ewe on 21 Jan without being found by German air reconnaissance.

30 Dec-25 Jan Central and South West Pacific

Operations by the 3rd Fleet (Adm Halsey) in support of the landings on Luzon. On 30 Dec TF 38 (Vice-Adm McCain) sets out from Ulithi:

TG 38.1 (Rear-Adm Radford) comprises the carriers *Yorktown, Wasp, Cabot* and *Cowpens*, the battleships *South Dakota* (Vice-Adm Lee) and *Massachusetts*, the cruisers *San Francisco, Baltimore, Boston* and *San Diego*, the destroyers (Desron 61) *De Haven, Mansfield, Lyman K. Swenson, Collett, Maddox, Blue, Brush, Taussig, Samuel N. Moore*, (Desron 53) *Cushing, Colahan, Benham, Yarnall, Stockham, Wedderburn, Twining* and *Uhlmann*.

TG 38.2 (Rear-Adm Bogan) comprises the carriers *Lexington, Hancock* and *Hornet*, the battleships *New Jersey* and *Wisconsin*, the cruisers *Pasadena, Astoria, Wilkes-Barre* and *San Juan*, the destroyers (Desron 52) *Owen, Miller, The Sullivans, Stephen Potter, Tingey, Hickox, Hunt, Lewis Hancock, Marshall*, (Desron 62) *Ault, English, Charles S. Sperry, Waldron, Haynsworth, John W. Weeks, Hank*, (Desdiv 102) *Capps, David W. Taylor, Evans* and *John D. Henley*.

TG 38.3 (Rear-Adm Sherman) comprises the carriers *Essex, Ticonderoga, Langley* and *San Jacinto*, the battleships *Washington* and *North Carolina*, the cruisers *Santa Fé, Vincennes, Miami, Biloxi* and *Flint* and the destroyers (Desron 50) *Clarence K. Bronson, Cotten, Dortch, Gatling, Healy, Cogswell, Caperton, Ingersoll, Knapp*, (Desron 55) *Porterfield, Callaghan, Cassin Young, Preston, Laws, Longshaw, Prichett* and *Halsey Powell*.

Night TG 38.5 (Rear-Adm Gardner) comprises the carriers *Enterprise* and *Independence* and the destroyers (Desron 47) *McCord, Trathen, Hazelwood, Haggard, Franks* and *Buchanan*. By day it operates with TG 38.2.

After refuelling on 2 Jan, on 3 Jan and 4 Jan carrier raids are made by TG 38.1 on North Formosa, by TG 38.2 on South Formosa and the Pescadores and by TG 38.3 on Central Formosa and the Southern Ryukyu Islands. The operation is considerably impeded by the weather and in part abandoned. Some 100 Japanese aircraft are destroyed for a loss of 22 American planes. After refuelling on 5 Jan, 757 sorties are made on 6 Jan and 7 Jan by the carrier aircraft against Kamikaze airfields in preparation for the Lingayen landing and to ensure air superiority over Luzon. 75-80 Japanese aircraft are destroyed for the loss of 28 American. After refuelling on 8 Jan a new attack is made on Formosa and the Ryukyu Islands, particularly Okinawa, on 9 Jan. The Americans lose 10 aircraft but the destroyer *Hamakaze*, the corvette *Kaibokan 3*, one submarine-chaser and five tankers and freighters are sunk and the frigates *Yashiro* and *Miyake*, four corvettes, one minesweeper, two submarine-chasers and three merchant ships are damaged. Simultaneously, B-29s attack Formosa from China.

On 10 Jan TF 38 enters the South China Sea and refuels until 11 Jan from the fast supply group (Capt Acuff), consisting of the tankers *Manatee, Monongahela, Patuxent, Neosho, Chikaskia, Niobrara, Pamanset* and *Caliente*, the escort carriers *Nehenta Bay, Rudyerd Bay, Cape Esperance* and *Altamaha* and the destroyers *Dale, Welles, Thatcher, Dyson, Hobby, Farragut, MacDonough, Thorn* and *Weaver*. On 12 Jan TG 38.5 flies off its aircraft at night and early in the day all Task Groups attack the coast and harbours of Indochina with the main assault by TG 38.2 on Camranh Bay where large Japanese warships are thought to be. The sortie towards the coast made by *New Jersey, Wisconsin, Baltimore, Boston, Pasadena, Astoria, Wilkes-Barre* and destroyers has no success. In 1465 air sorties, in which 23 American planes are lost, 29 merchant ships from Japanese convoys totalling 116000 tons, the training cruiser *Kashii*, which is sailing as convoy flagship, the frigate *Chiburi*, the corvettes *Kaibokan 23, Kaibokan 51, Kaibokan 17, Kaibokan 19, Kaibokan 35* and *Kaibokan 43* and the submarine-chasers *Kusentai 31* and *Kusentai 43* and one landing ship are sunk. In addition, more frigates, corvettes, minesweepers, landing ships and submarine-chasers are damaged. In Saigon the French cruiser *Lamotte-Picquet* is destroyed.

After further refuelling on 13 Jan and 14 Jan, impeded by strong monsoon winds, the carrier groups make fighter sorties and attacks on South Formosa, the Pescadores and the Chinese province of Fukien on 15 Jan. The Japanese destroyers *Hatakaze* and *Tsuga*, one landing ship, one transport and one tanker are sunk. Twelve aircraft are lost. On 16 Jan targets are attacked on the South China coast between Hong Kong and Hainan. The Americans lose 27 aircraft but two ships are sunk and five escort vessels damaged. The forces are greatly hindered by bad weather. The refuelling W of Luzon, which began on 17 Jan, has to be interrupted on 18 Jan because of the heavy seas. When it is completed on 19 Jan the force returns through the Luzon Strait on the orders of the C-in-C Pacific.

On 21 Jan there is a new attack on Formosa. In 1164 sorties 104 Japanese aircraft are destroyed and 10 merchant ships sunk. The destroyers *Harukaze*, *Kashi* and *Sugi* and two landing ships are damaged. In Japanese air attacks a single bomber gets a bomb hit on the *Langley* and a single Kamikaze fighter hits the *Ticonderoga*. An attack by seven Kamikazes and six fighters from the S is intercepted by the fighter cover from the *Cowpens*. In a second attack by eight Kamikazes (the 'Niitaka' group) of the 1st Air Fleet and five fighters from the N each gets one hit on the *Ticonderoga* and *Maddox*. A returning American bomber loses a bomb when landing on the *Hancock*, which is damaged. In all, there are 205 dead and 351 injured on the ships. The *Ticonderoga* withdraws, escorted by two cruisers and three destroyers.

On 22 Jan the carrier aircraft make 682 sorties against the Ryukyu Islands with the emphasis on Okinawa.

After refuelling on 23 Jan the Task Force returns to Ulithi, arriving there on 25 Jan. In this operation a total of 300000 tons of shipping are sunk and 615 Japanese aircraft destroyed. The American losses are 201 aircraft and 167 pilots.

1945

1-31 Jan   Pacific
The following ships are sunk by US submarines arriving in their operational areas in January: in Japanese waters between Luzon and the Kuriles *Kingfish* (Lt-Cdr Harper) sinks three ships of 4344 tons; *Puffer* (Lt-Cdr Dwyer) the corvette *Kaibokan 42* and torpedoes *Kaibokan 30*; *Sea Robin* (Lt-Cdr Stimson) one ship of 5135 tons; *Silversides* (Lt-Cdr Nichols) one ship of 4556 tons; *Spadefish* (Lt-Cdr Underwood) three ships of 12523 tons and the frigate *Kume*; *Spot* (Cdr Post) two ships of 1387 tons; *Tautog* (Cdr Baskett) two ships of 1900 tons and the transport *No 15* and torpedoes one ship; *Threadfin* (Lt-Cdr Foote) one ship of 1864 tons; *Barb* (Cdr Fluckey) five ships of 24044 tons; *Picuda* (Lt-Cdr Shepard) one ship of 5497 tons and torpedoes one ship; *Barb*, *Picuda* and *Queenfish* (Cdr Loughlin) jointly sink two ships of 12312 tons and torpedo one ship. In the area of Indonesia and the Philippines *Blackfin* (Cdr Kitch) sinks the destroyer *Shigure*; *Boarfish* (Cdr Gross) two ships of 13858 tons; *Cavalla* (Lt-Cdr Kossler) two ships of 1880 tons; *Cobia* (Lt-Cdr Becker) the minelayer *Yurishima*; *Pargo* (Lt-Cdr Bell) the destroyer *Nokaze* and also torpedoes the frigate *Manju*.

2-4 Jan   Indian Ocean
Operation 'Lightning'. TF 64 (Rear-Adm Martin) sets out on 2 Jan from Chittagong with the Australian destroyers *Napier* and *Nepal*, the British sloop *Shoreham*, two LCIs and several MLs and lands some 1000 men of the British 3rd Commando Brigade (Brig Hardy), embarked on three ships, on the north-west tip of the Akyab Peninsula. Then the Indian 74th Brigade is brought over from the mainland when the Indian sloops *Narbada* and *Jumna* are deployed for support. Because the Japanese have evacuated Akyab TF 61 (Rear-Adm Read), comprising the cruisers *Newcastle*, *Nigeria* and *Phoebe* (Fighter Direction Ship) and destroyers, does not need to intervene.

Operation 'Lentil'. TF 63 (Rear-Adm Vian, 1st Carrier Sqdn), comprising the carriers *Indomitable*, *Victorious* and *Indefatigable*, the cruisers *Suffolk*, *Ceylon*, *Argonaut* and *Black Prince* and the destroyers *Kempenfelt*, *Whelp*, *Wager*, *Grenville*, *Urania*, *Undaunted*, *Undine* and *Ursa*, makes a raid on the oil refineries of Pankalan Brandan (Sumatra) on 4 Jan with Avenger bombers and cover from Hellcat and Corsair fighters. One aircraft is lost.

2-8 Jan   South West Pacific
The US landing fleets proceed from Leyte Gulf through the Surigao Strait, the Sulu Sea and the Mindoro Strait to Lingayen Gulf.
On 2 Jan TG 77.6 (Minesweeping and Survey Group), comprising 68 minesweepers, sets out escorted by the US destroyers (Desdiv 48) *Bush*, *Halford*, *Stanly*, *Stembel*, the Australian sloop *Warrego* and the Australian frigate *Gascoyne*.
On 3 Jan there follows the Fire Support Group, TG 77.2 (Vice-Adm Oldendorf)
—Unit 1 (San Fabian; Rear-Adm Weyler), comprising the battleships *Mississippi*, *West Virginia* and *New Mexico*, the Australian cruisers *Australia* and *Shropshire*, the US cruiser *Minneapolis* and the US destroyers (Desron 60) *Allen M. Sumner*, *Lowry*, *Laffey*, *O'Brien*, *Barton*, *Moale*, *Ingraham* and *Walke*; and Unit 2 (Lingayen; Vice-Adm Oldendorf), comprising the battleships *California*, *Pennsylvania* and *Colorado*, the cruisers *Louisville*, *Portland* and *Columbia* and the US destroyers (Desron 56) *Leutze*, *Heywood L. Edwards*, *Kimberly*, *Newcomb*, *Richard P. Leary*, *William D. Porter*, *Bennion*, *Bryant*, *Izard* and the Australian *Arunta* and *Warramunga*. In addition Escort Carrier Group 77.4 (Rear-Adm Durgin) with Unit 1 (Lingayen; Rear-Adm Durgin), comprising the escort carriers *Makin Island*, *Lunga Point*, *Bismarck Sea*, *Salamaua* and *Hoggatt Bay*, the destroyers (Desron 6) *Maury*, *Gridley*, *Bagley*, *Helm*, *Ralph Talbot*, *Patterson*

479

and *McCall* and the DEs *Edmonds* and *Howard D. Clark*, and Unit 2 (San Fabian; Rear-Adm Stump), comprising the escort carriers *Natoma Bay*, *Manila Bay*, *Wake Island*, *Steamer Bay*, *Savo Island* and *Ommaney Bay* and the destroyers (Desron 51) *Hall*, *Halligan*, *Bell*, *Burns*, *Paul Hamilton*, *Twiggs* and *Abbot* and the Hunter Killer Group (Capt Cronin) with the escort carrier *Tulagi* and the DEs *Stafford*, *William Seiverling*, *Ulvert M. Moore*, *Kendall C. Campbell* and *Goss*. There also follows a group of UDTs (underwater demolition teams) on 10 fast transports (APDs).

On 4 Jan the San Fabian Attack Force, TF 78 (Vice-Adm Barbey), with I Corps (Maj-Gen Swift) and the headquarters ship *Blue Ridge* sets out from Leyte. TG 78.1 (Vice-Adm Barbey) has the 43rd Inf Div (Maj-Gen Wing) on eight APAs, two APs, three AKs, three LSDs, 21 LSTs, 10 LSMs, 13 LCIs, six LCTS and 19 support LCIs; escort: the destroyers (Desron 23) *Charles Ausburne*, *Drayton*, *Shaw*, *Russell*, *Jenkins*, *La Valette*, *Converse*, *Foote*, *Braine* and the DEs *Charles J. Kimmel* and *Thomas F. Nickel*. TG 78.2 (Rear-Adm Fechteler) has the 6th Inf Div (Maj-Gen Patrick) on eight APAs, three APs, one AKA, three AKs, two LSDs, one LSV and 30 LSTs, 10 LSMs, three LCIs, six LCTs and nine support LCIs; escort: (Desron 2) *Morris*, *Lang*, *Stack*, *Sterett*, *Mustin*, *Dashiell*, *Wilson*, the DEs *Day*, *Hodges*, *Peiffer* and *Tinsman*.

Air escort is provided by the escort carriers *Kadashan Bay* and *Marcus Island* with the destroyers *Charette* and *Conner*.

On 5 Jan the Lingayen Attack Force, TF 79 (Vice-Adm Wilkinson), with XIV Corps (Maj-Gen Griswold) and head-quarters ship *Mount Olympus* puts to sea from Leyte. TG 79.1 (Rear-Adm Kiland) has the 37th Inf Div (Maj-Gen Beightler) on nine APAs and three Australian LSIs, one AP, three AKs, one LSD, one LSV and 19 LSTs, 18 LSMs, six LCTs and 22 support LCIs; escort: the destroyers (Desron 22) *Waller*, *Saufley*, *Philip*, *Renshaw*, *Cony*, *Robinson*, the DEs *Abercrombie*, *Le Ray Wilson* and *Gilligan*. TG 79.2 (Rear-

Adm Royal) has the 40th Inf Div (Maj-Gen Brush) on 10 APAs, two APs, three AKAs, three LSDs, one LSV and 19 LSTs, 31 LSMs, six LCTs and 21 Support LCIs; escort: the destroyers (Desdiv 48 and 44) *Bush*, *Halford*, *Conway*, *Eaton*, *Sigourney*, *Stembel*, the DEs *Walter C. Wann*, *Richard W. Suesens*, *Oberrender* and also the destroyers (Desron 49), *Picking*, *Isherwood*, *Luce*, *Sproston*, *Wickes*, *Young* and *Charles J. Badger*.

Air escort (Rear-Adm Ofstie) is provided by the escort carriers *Kitkun Bay* and *Shamrock Bay* with the DEs *John C. Butler* and *O'Flaherty*.

From 3 Jan the movements are partly detected by Japanese coastal guard stations and air reconnaissance and the two-men submarines stationed in Cebu and Kamikaze pilots of the 1st Air Fleet (Vice-Adm Onishi) are deployed against them. On 3 Jan the midget submarine *Ha-84* misses three ships and Kamikazes damage the tanker *Cowanesque*. On 4 Jan the escort carrier *Ommaney Bay* is so badly damaged by Kamikaze pilots from Sarangani W of Panay that she has to be sunk by the destroyer *Burns*. On 5 Jan the midget submarines *Ha-69*, *Ha-81* and *Ha-82* unsuccessfully attack TF 78 in the Sulu Sea. Of the flagship group—TG 77.1 with the headquarters ship *Wasatch* (the Commander 7th Fleet, Adm Kinkaid and the Commander of the 6th Army, Lt-Gen Krueger) the cruiser *Boise* (the C-in-C South-West Pacific, Gen MacArthur) and the destroyers *Smith*, *Frazier*, *Coghlan* and *Edwards*—and the close covering group (Rear-Adm Berkey), comprising the cruisers *Phoenix* *Montpelier* and *Denver* and the destroyers (Desron 21) *Nicholas*, *Fletcher*, *Radford*, *O'Bannon*, *Taylor* and *Hopewell*—the midget submarines narrowly miss the *Boise*. The attacking submarine *Ha-82* is sunk by *Taylor*. Off Manila the *Bennion*, with the *Warrego* and *Gascoyne* from the minesweeping group, encounters the Japanese destroyers *Momi* and *Hinoki* which have set out from Manila Bay. The latter escapes, but *Momi* is damaged by *Bennion* and sunk by aircraft. On 5 Jan three groups of 16, 4 and 15 Kamikazes take off from Mabalacat (Luzon) against TF 77. The cruisers *Louisville* and *Australia*, the escort carrier *Manila Bay*, the DE *Stafford*, the tender *Orca*, the tug *Apache* and *LCI(G)-70* are damaged by hits and the escort carrier *Savo Island* and the destroyers *Arunta* and *Helm* by near-misses. There are 54 dead and 168 injured.

On 6 Jan a total of 29 Kamikaze aircraft with 15 escort fighters take off from various airfields and attack TG 77.2 as it enters Lingayen Gulf to shell the assault area. The minesweeper *Long* is sunk; the battleships *New Mexico* (Capt Fleming†) and the British Lt-Gen Lumsden† as observer) and *California*, the cruisers *Australia*, *Columbia* and *Louisville* (Rear-Adm Chandler†), the destroyers *Walke*, *Allen M. Sumner* and *O'Brien*, the minesweepers *Brooks* and *Southard* are damaged by hits and the cruiser *Minneapolis* and the destroyers *Richard P. Leary*, *Newcomb* and *Barton* by near-misses. There are 156 dead and 452 injured. The US escort carriers fly 126 sorties to provide fighter protection. In the night 6-7 Jan individual Japanese torpedo aircraft attack and sink the minesweeper *Hovey*. There are 22 dead and 24 injured.

On 7 Jan individual bombers attack and hit the minesweeper *Palmer* (28 dead and 38 injured) and just miss the *Boise* in Mindoro Strait. The *LST 912* and the transport *Callaway* are damaged by the seven Kamikazes which take off: 33 dead and 22 injured.

In the night 7-8 Jan, in the last surface engagement of the Pacific war, the destroyers *Charles Ausburne*, *Braine*, *Shaw* and *Russell* sink the Japanese escort destroyer *Hinoki* which has come out again.

On 8 Jan several Kamikazes from Clark Field attack the 7th US Fleet off Lingayen Gulf, in the course of which the escort carriers *Kadashan Bay* and *Kitkun Bay* and the cruiser *Australia* are damaged. There are 17 dead and 36 injured.

4-27 Jan Atlantic
In the area both sides of the Pentland Firth (Orkneys) the German U-boats *U278* and *U313* operate against British carrier groups but are only able to fire on steamers and patrol boats—and that without success. *U905* and *U764*

which set out for the area W of Britain have to return because of schnorkel trouble. In the North Channel *U1009* misses a patrol boat and a destroyer. Off the Clyde *U482* (Lt-Cdr Count Matuschka) attacks a convoy and torpedoes the escort carrier *Thane* (not repaired) and one ship of 7429 tons. But she is then sunk on 16 Jan after a lengthy search by the ships of the 22nd EG, the sloops *Peacock*, *Hart*, *Starling*, *Amethyst* and the frigate *Loch Craggie*. In St George's Channel and in the Irish Sea *U1055* (Lt R. Meyer) sinks from 9 Jan to 15 Jan four ships of 19418 tons, including one from the convoy ON.277. *U285* returns home without success. From 20 Jan *U1172* (Lt Kuhlmann), which sinks two ships of 2751 tons, *U825* (Lt Stoelker) and *U1051* (Lt v. Holleben) operate simultaneously in this area. Apart from the 22nd EG, five other escort groups are deployed against these boats. On 26 Jan the 4th and 5th EGs hunt *U1172*, which, after torpedoing the DE *Manners*, is sunk by the DEs *Aylmer*, *Calder* and *Bentinck*. On 27 Jan the two other boats torpedo two ships of 15360 tons from the convoy HX.322; *U1051* is then sunk by the DEs *Tyler*, *Keats* and *Bligh* of the 5th EG. *U325* operates without success in the Channel. *U1199* (Lt-Cdr Nollmann) torpedoes one ship of 7176 tons from a Thames-Bristol convoy off Wolf Rock on 21 Jan and is sunk by the destroyer *Icarus* and the corvette *Mignonette* of the escort.

U1009, *U248*, *U1230* and *U1231* are stationed in turn as weather boats in the North Atlantic. A US DE-hunter group, consisting of *Hubbard*, *Hayter*, *Otter* (Cdr Bowling) and *Varian*, is deployed against the boats which are located by HF/DF. *U248* falls victim to the group on 16 Jan.

W of Gibraltar *U870* (Cdr Hechler) attacks the convoy GUS.63 on 3 Jan and sinks one ship of 7207 tons. On 7 Jan she attacks an east-bound convoy and on 8 Jan a west-bound convoy, both unsuccessfully. On 9 Jan she sinks the French submarine-chaser *L'Enjoue* and on 10 Jan one ship of 4637 tons from an east-bound convoy.

Off Halifax *U1232* (Capt Dobratz) misses a destroyer and a passenger steamer and sinks five ships of 26804 tons from three convoys (one of them is a Liberty ship which is taken in tow but becomes a total loss).

5 Jan Central Pacific
A US Task Group (Rear-Adm Smith) comprising the cruisers *Chester*, *Pensacola* and *Salt Lake City* and the destroyers *Dunlap*, *Fanning*, *Cummings*, *Ellet*, *Roe*, and *David W. Taylor*, shells Iwojima, Hahajima and Chichijima. *David W. Taylor* is damaged on a mine. At the same time there is an attack by B 29s of the 21st Bomber Command USAAF.

5 Jan North Pacific
A US Task Group (Rear-Adm McCrea), consisting of the cruisers *Raleigh*, *Detroit* and *Richmond* and nine destroyers, shells Suribachi Wan near Paramushiro in the Kuriles.

5-8 Jan Arctic
The German U-boats *U295*, *U716* and *U739* each set out with two '*Biber*' midget submarines attached to their superstructures. The intention is to enter the Kola Inlet and to make attacks with them on the battleship *Arkhangelsk* and Allied escort vessels. The operation has to be abandoned because of trouble with the midget submarines.

6 Jan-10 May Indian Ocean/Atlantic
The last German East Asian U-boats return. *U510* (Lt-Cdr Eick), which sets out from Jakarta on 6 Jan, has, after sinking the steamer *Point Pleasant Park* (7136 tons) on 23 Feb in the Indian Ocean, to put in to St Nazaire on 24 Apl because of fuel shortage. *U532* (Cdr* Junker) sets out on 13 Jan and sinks in March the freighters *Baron Jedburgh* (3656 tons) and the tanker *Oklahoma* (9298 tons) in the Atlantic and puts in to Liverpool on 10 May after the surrender where she is inspected by the C-in-C Western Approaches, Adm Horton. *U843* (Lt-Cdr Herwatz) and *U861* (Cdr Oesten) arrive in Bergen in April. *U195* has to return after developing a defect and replenishing *U532*. The last boat to set out, *U183*, is sunk on 23 Apl by the US submarine *Besugo*.

7 Jan-12 Mar Baltic/Courland
At first from the Gulf of Danzig, and later from the Western Baltic, regular German convoys proceed to Libau and Windau to supply the Army Group Courland. For escort, the minesweepers of the 1st, 3rd and 25th and, later, the 12th and 2nd MS Flotillas are employed out at sea, and off the Lithuanian coast KFKs of the 31st MS Flotilla as submarine-hunters, those of the 14th Defence Flotilla as mining escort and the 1st MMS Flotilla and the 7th Gun Carrier Flotilla as defence against the Soviet torpedo cutters stationed in Polangen.

Soviet submarines are deployed against this traffic. In January *Shch-310* (Capt 3rd Class Bogorad) has one miss and *Shch-307* (Lt-Cdr Kalinin) two misses; in February *Shch-318* (Capt 3rd Class Loshkarev) sinks the tanker *Hiddensee* (643 tons) on 4 Feb and misses the steamer *Ammerland* on 10 Feb. *Shch-407* (Capt 3rd Class Bocharov) is pursued with depth charges from *TS8* on 12 Feb. At the end of February *S-4* (Capt 3rd Class Klyushkin) and *Shch-309* (Capt 3rd Class Vetchinkin) are deployed. Both attack the steamer *Göttingen* (6267 tons) on 23 Feb which sinks. The minesweeper *M801* sinks *S-4* in this action in a depth charge attack. On 9 Mar *Shch-303* (Capt 3rd Class Ignatev) sinks the steamer *Borbek* (6002 tons) which has been damaged by air torpedo and set on fire. The Soviet Air Force makes several attacks on harbours and lays mines, on which, on 29 Jan the *Henry Lütgens* (1141 tons) sinks off Windau and on 12 Mar and 23 Mar respectively *M3137* and *M3138* off Libau. But the evacuation of a total of eight of the 35 divisions of Army Group Courland to East Prussia and Pomerania takes place without substantial loss.

9-17 Jan South West Pacific
Operation 'Mike I'. Landing in Lingayen Gulf.
US TFs 78 and 79, with support from TG 77.2 (fire support) and TG 77.4 (escort carriers), land I US Corps in Lingayen Gulf (for composition see 2 Jan). The landing of about 70000 troops on the first day succeeds against slight resistance because the Japanese defence (14th Army Group, Gen Yamashita) in the Lingayen area has withdrawn the 23rd Inf Div (Lt-Gen Nishiyama) and the 58th Brigade to the

mountains. Only from 11 Jan onwards are there major engagements on shore. For this reason the coastal shelling does not have much effect.

The Japanese react with Kamikaze attacks by the 1st Naval Air Fleet and the 4th Army Air Fleet. On 9 Jan nine Kamikazes set off with seven escorting fighters. The battleship *Mississippi* and the cruisers *Columbia* and *Australia* are damaged by hits and the DE *Hodges* by near-misses. In the night 9-10 Jan some 70 Japanese explosive boats attack from San Juan, but the boats sink only *LCI(M)-974* and *LCI(G)-365* and damage the transport *War Hawk*, *LST 925* and *LST 1028*.

On 11 Jan more explosive boats attack and damage *LST 610*. A bomber attacks the destroyer *Wickes* and Kamikaze pilots the DE *Le Ray Wilson* and the transport *Du Page*. During 9-10 Jan there are 114 dead and 377 injured.

On 11 Jan Amphibious Group 3 (Rear-Adm Conolly), with the headquarters ship *Appalachian*, arrives with the 25th Inf Div (Maj-Gen Mullins), the 158th RCT and the 13th Armoured Group on 13 APDs, 17 APAs, three APs, seven AKAs, eight AKs, 10 Liberty ships and 50 LSTs. Escort: the destroyers (Desron 54) *Remey*, *McNair*, *Norman Scott*, *Melvin*, *Mertz*, *McGowan*, *McDermut*, *Monssen* and the DEs *Greenwood* and *Loeser*. Air escort (Rear-Adm Henderson) is provided by the escort carriers *Saginaw Bay* and *Petrof Bay* and the DEs *Richard S. Bull* and *Richard M. Rowell*.

Of the Japanese submarines *Ro-43*, *Ro-46*, *Ro-50*, *Ro-55*, *Ro-109* and *Ro-49* (Lt Sugayoshi) makes an unsuccessful attack on a battleship and *Ro-46* (Lt-Cdr Suzuki) on transports. Kamikaze pilots attack approaching and departing transports and escort vessels: the APD *Belknap*, the APA *Zeilin* and *LST 700*, as well as the DEs *Gilligan* and *Richard W. Suesens*, are damaged. There are 50 dead and 107 injured. Four Liberty ships and one LST from a supply convoy are damaged by six Kamikazes in the area of Bataan: 129 dead and 23 injured. On 13 Jan, in a final Kamikaze attack on the landing fleets, a hit is obtained on the escort carrier *Salamaua*: 15 dead and 88 injured. Because of the loss of all operational aircraft and the withdrawal of the remaining units of the 1st Naval Air Fleet, there is an end to the planned attacks. From 14 Jan to 27 Jan four more supply convoys arrive for the US invasion forces. From 17 Jan the units of the 6th US Army are no longer dependent on naval support and the last formations are withdrawn. The escort carriers have flown a total of 6152 sorties from 6 Jan to 17 Jan, including 1416 for close support. They lose only two of their aircraft.

10 Jan Mediterranean/Ligurian Sea
German explosive boats (*Linsen*) unsuccessfully attack the French destroyer *Le Fortuné* off San Remo.

11-12 Jan Norway
A British cruiser squadron, consisting of the *Norfolk* (Rear-Adm McGrigor) and *Bellona* and the destroyers *Onslow*, *Orwell* and *Onslaught*, attacks a German convoy off Egersund. Shell hits are obtained on some freighters, including the *Bahia Camarones* and *Charlotte*, which are badly damaged and have to be abandoned. In an engagement with the convoy escort the minesweeper *M273* is sunk. An unsuccessful attempt to attack is made by *U427*. The squadron withdraws under fighter cover from the escort carriers *Trumpeter* and *Premier* which frustrate an attack by Ju 88 torpedo aircraft of K.G. 26.

11-21 Jan Central Pacific
Japanese submarine cruisers try to attack American naval bases with *Kaiten* torpedoes (Operation 'Kongo'). *I-36* (Lt-Cdr Teramoto) launches four *Kaiten* off Ulithi. One detonates a few metres from the side of the ammunition ship *Mazama* and another possibly sinks the landing craft *LCI 600*. *I-47* (Lt-Cdr Orita) launches four *Kaiten* in the roads of Hollandia: there are two detonations in the vicinity of the transport *Pontus H. Ross* (7247 tons) and an unexploded one. Attempted attacks by *I-53* on the Kossol Passage in Palau, by *I-56* on Manus in the Admiralty Islands and by *I-58* on Apra Harbour on Guam have no success. Also unsuccessful is an attempted attack by *I-48* on Ulithi on 20 Jan: this boat is sunk on 21 Jan by the US DEs *Conklin*, *Corbesier* and *Raby*.

11 Jan-19 Mar Baltic
Last operations by German U-boats in the Baltic off the Gulf of Finland. On 11 Jan *U745* (Lt-Cdr v. Trotha) sinks a patrol boat off Revalstein and on 16 Jan *U290* (Lt Herglotz) misses a vessel off Baltischport (Paldiski). *U242, U348* and *U1001* return at the end of January from reconnaissance operations into the southern part of the Gulf of Bothnia and the central Gulf of Finland and are then sent to the W.
At the beginning of February *U745, U475, U370* and *U676* are still operating, but *U745* is probably lost on a mine on 4 Feb and *U676* on 19 Feb. *U475* is the last boat to return to Danzig on 17 Mar. On 19 Mar all German U-boats are withdrawn for operations in the W.

12 Jan Indian Ocean
British TF 64 (Rear-Adm Martin) with several transports and landing craft and the Australian destroyer *Napier* and the Indian sloops *Narbada* and *Jumna* lands units of the 3rd British Commando Brigade near Myebon between Akyab and Ramree (Burma). The cruiser *Phoebe* acts as fighter direction ship.

13 Jan Norway
The light cruiser *Nürnberg* (Capt Giessler) and the minelayer *Linz* (Cdr* Abel) carry out defensive mining operations in the Skagerrak. Several British air attacks are repelled.

13-15 Jan North Sea
S176, S210, S174 and *S209* of the 2nd MTB Flotilla lay mines off Cromer. A British FN convoy loses two ships of 8871 tons on these mines. Two other ships are damaged. *S221, S180, S181* and *S177* have to return owing to engine trouble. *S180* sinks on a German mine of Texel. *S127, S48, S92* and *S85* of the 5th MTB Flotilla also lay mines off the British East Coast. *S98* and *S67* have to return because of engine trouble. On the night 14-15 Jan six German MTB Flotillas operate off the British East Coast and the Scheldt Estuary. The 2nd Flotilla (Cdr Opdenhoff) with *S221, S174, S209* and *S181* and the 5th Flotilla (Lt-Cdr Holzapfel) with *S98, S67, S92* and *S48* penetrate as far as the swept channels off the Humber. The 5th Flotilla is engaged by the British destroyer *Farndale*.

The 9th Flotilla (Cdr v. Mirbach) with *S206, S168, S130* and *S175* operates in the Scheldt Estuary and is engaged by the British DE *Seymour* and coastal forces. The 6th Flotilla (Lt-Cdr Matzen) with *S221, S222, S705, S211* and *S223* attacks a convoy W of the Scheldt and fires six torpedoes. *S222* and *S705* report hits with FAT torpedoes. The flotilla is driven off by the British DE *Curzon* and the destroyer *Cotswold* off Westkapelle. The 4th Flotilla (Cdr Fimmen) with *S205, S204* and *S219* operates off Margate and is engaged by the sloop *Guillemot*. The 8th Flotilla (Cdr Zymalkowski) with *S194, S196, S197, S199* and *S701* proceeds to within four miles of Tongue Sand Fort and attacks a convoy of landing ships with eight FAT and LUT torpedoes. *LST 415* is hit by a LUT torpedo. Gunfire from the fort drives off the motor torpedo boats.

15 Jan Mediterranean
The Italian squadron, consisting of the light cruiser *Attilio Regolo*, the destroyers *Carabiniere, Fuciliere* and *Mitragliere*, the torpedo boat *Orsa* and the naval ferry barges *Mz785, Mz780* and *Mz800*, which has been lying at anchor in Port Mahon (Balearics) and interned by Spain since 8 Sept 1943, sets out for Malta.

15 Jan Mediterranean/Ligurian Sea
The French cruisers *Montcalm* (Rear-Adm Jaujard) and *Georges Leygues* shell German positions near San Remo (Riviera).

15-24 Jan Arctic
The German U-boats *U293, U295, U636, U956, U968* and *U997* operate against Soviet coastal traffic off the Kola Coast. On 16 Jan the Soviet convoy KB.1 with six Allied freighters and four tankers proceeds from the Kola Inlet to the White Sea. The escort (Capt 1st Class Rumyantsev) consists of the flotilla leader *Baku* and the destroyers *Deyatelny* (Lt-Cdr Kravchenko), *Derzki, Doblestny, Zhivuchi, Dostoiny* and three others as a covering group and six Pe-3 bombers as air escort. *U997* (Lt Lehmann) comes up and sinks the *Deyatelny* with a T-5.
On 20 Jan a convoy of two steamers, the destroyer *Uritski*, two minesweepers, nine BO submarine-chasers, four TKAs

and a Norwegian group with the corvette *Eglantine* and the trawlers *Karmöy*, *Tromöy* and *Jelöy*, together with the Soviet destroyers *Razumny* and *Razyarenny* as a covering force, sets out from Kola for Liinahamari. *U293* (Lt-Cdr Klingspor) torpedoes the *Razyarenny* which is with difficulty taken in tow by the minesweeper *T-117*.

On 21 Jan and 24 Jan the destroyers *Derzki*, *Zhivuchi*, *Doblestny* and *Dostoiny* look for U-boats located between Jokanga and Kola. *U636* misses a search group on 23 Jan and is hunted by six BO and two MO submarine-chasers and two TKAs. On 26 Jan the Soviet submarines *V-2* and *V-3* are deployed in the U-boat hunt.

15 Jan–24 Feb   Baltic
Soviet attack on East Prussia. On 15 Jan the Soviet 2nd White Russian Front goes over to the attack from the Narew bridgehead near Pultusk with support from the 4th Air Army. Forward troops of the 5th Guards Armoured Army pass Elbing and reach the Frisches Haff coast near Tolkemit on 27 Jan; they sever contact between the 4th Army in East Prussia and the 2nd Army in West Prussia. On 16 Jan the 3rd White Russian front, with support from the 1st Air Army, attacks to the N of Gumbinnen in the direction of Königsberg; the 43rd Army of the Soviet 1st Baltic Front attacks from Tilsit and passes N of Königsberg along the Kurisches Haff. In order to assemble forces to build up a defensive position on Samland, XXVIII German Corps is transferred over the ice from the Memel bridgehead to the Kurische Nehrung (24-28 Jan) and refugees and wounded are evacuated in ships, including the ferry ship *Deutschland* (2972 tons). The Soviet 1st Baltic Front which from 26 Jan pursues them is not able to hold up the evacuation. The Soviet 39th and 43rd Armies have advanced in the meantime into the western Samland between Königsberg and Cranz and have severed land communications between Pillau and Königsberg. In support of the XXVIII Corps attack from the Cranz bridgehead to the SW in an attempt to restore contact, the German TF 2 (Vice-Adm Thiele), comprising the cruiser *Prinz Eugen*

(Capt Reinicke), the destroyers *Z25* (Cdr* Gohrbandt) and *Paul Jacobi* (Cdr Bülter) and the torpedo boats *T23* (Lt-Cdr Weinlig) and *T33* (Lt-Cdr Priebe), shells land targets near the German advance on 29 Jan and 30 Jan. Gun carriers, including *Polaris* and *Joost*, shell forward Soviet armour from the Königsberg Sea Canal. In support of the counter attack by the rest of the German 3rd Army from the Fischhausen area, which is designed to secure a continuous front in W Samland, *Z25*, *T28* (Lt-Cdr Temming) and *T33* repeatedly intervene in the fighting from 2 Feb to 5 Feb. The pocket battleship *Admiral Scheer* (Capt Thienemann) stands by at sea with the torpedo boats *T23*, *T35* (Lt-Cdr Buch) and *T36* (Lt-Cdr Hering). An attempted attack on *T36* by the Soviet submarine *L-3* (Capt 3rd Class Konovalov), which has previously laid mines near Brüsterort, fails on 4 Feb. The SAT *Polaris* is lost by a bomb hit on 5 Feb.

In support of the German 4th Army near Frauenburg against the advancing Soviet 48th and 3rd Armies, the cruiser *Lützow* (Capt Knoke) and *T8* (Lt-Cdr Strömer), *T28* and *T33* are employed on 8 Feb and the *Admiral Scheer* with *Z34* (Cdr Hetz), *T23*, *T28* and *T36* on 9 Feb and 10 Feb.

After bringing up the 93rd Inf Div by sea from Courland from 11 Feb to 13 Feb, the reinforced Samland army detachment makes an attack from 18 Feb to 24 Feb to restore land communications between Pillau/Fischhausen and Königsberg. In support of the attack *Admiral Scheer*, *Z38* (Cdr Frhr v. Lyncker), *Z43*, *T28* and *T35* shell concentrations of the Soviet 39th Army near Peyse and Gross-Heydekrug on the South Coast of Samland on 18 Feb and 19 Feb. On 20 Feb the torpedo boats go into the Sea Canal and continue the shelling from there. On 23 Feb *Z43* (Capt Wenninger) *Z38* and *T28* again intervene in the land fighting which restores the land access to Königsberg.

16 Jan–4 Feb   Indian Ocean
Operation 'Matador'. TF 64 (Rear-Adm Martin on the destroyer *Napier*) with four personnel carriers, two LSIs, two APs, one AK, 55 LCs and 20 MLs lands the British 4th and the Indian 71st

Brigades in the northern part of Ramree Island (off Arakan/Burma). A bombardment force, consisting of the battleship *Queen Elizabeth* (Rear-Adm Walker), the cruiser *Phoebe* (FDS), the destroyers *Rapid*, *Pathfinder* and *Raider* and the sloops *Flamingo*, *Kistna* (RIN) and *Redpole*, supports the operation with preparatory fire on the assault areas. Air escort is provided by the escort carrier *Ameer* with the destroyer *Norman* (RAN). An attack by 18 Japanese aircraft is beaten off.

Operation 'Sankey'. A Task Force, which sets out from Akyab on 24 Jan, comprising the destroyers *Norman* and *Raider* and the frigates *Spey* and *Teviot*, and TF 65 (Rear-Adm Read), consisting of the cruisers *Newcastle*, *Nigeria* and *Kenya* and the destroyers *Paladin* and *Rapid*, lands on 26 Jan 500 marines transported on the cruisers on Cheduba Island S of Ramree. The C-in-C Eastern Fleet, Adm Power, observes the operation on the destroyer *Nepal* (RAN) Air escort is provided by the escort carrier *Ameer* and the FDS cruiser *Phoebe*. Before the landing takes place, the assault area is shelled by *Norman*, *Raider*, *Paladin* and *Rapid*. The Indian 36th Brigade follows on the next day.

Operation 'Crocodile'. The destroyers *Norman* and *Raider* with four LCs put 120 men ashore on the island of Sagu S of Ramree on 30 Jan. The operations are supported by the destroyers *Nepal* and *Pathfinder* until 4 Feb.

Operation 'Meridian'. The British Pacific Fleet, as TF 63, sails from Trincomalee for transfer to the Pacific on 16 Jan. It comprises the battleship *King George V* (Vice-Adm Rawlings), the carriers (Rear-Adm Vian) *Indomitable* (Capt Eccles), *Illustrious* (Capt Lambe), *Victorious* (Capt Denny) and *Indefatigable* (Capt Graham), the cruisers *Argonaut*, *Black Prince* and *Euryalus* and the destroyers *Grenville*, *Undine*, *Ursa*, *Undaunted*, *Kempenfelt*, *Wakeful*, *Whirlwind*, *Wager* and *Whelp*. Later it is joined by the cruiser *Ceylon* and the destroyer *Wessex*. On 20 Jan these ships meet TF 69, comprising the tankers *Echodale*, *Wave King* and *Empire Salvage* and the destroyer *Urchin*, which set out on 13 Jan, and the tanker *Arn-*

dale, which set out from Fremantle on 15 Jan, for refuelling. On 21-22 Jan and 22-23 Jan the weather off Sumatra prevents the carrier aircraft being flown off. On 24 Jan 43 Avenger bombers, 12 Firefly fighter bombers with rockets and 50 Hellcat, Corsair and Seafire fighters fly off from the four carriers SW of Sumatra to make a successful attack on the oil refinery at Pladjoe N of Palembang. The defence is taken by surprise. Only about 20 fighters of the Japanese Army Air Force take off and 14 of them are shot down. Thirty-eight are destroyed on the ground. The British lose 7 aircraft due to enemy action and 25 as a result of crash landings.

After replenishing on 26-27 Jan TF 63 returns on 28-29 Jan and early on 29 Jan flies off 48 Avengers, 10 Fireflies, 24 Corsairs and 16 Hellcats which make a raid on the oil refineries at Soengi-Gerong near Palembang. In air engagements 30 Japanese aircraft are shot down and 38 destroyed on the ground. Sixteen Allied aircraft do not return but some of the crews are rescued. An attempted Japanese attack on TF 63 with 12 bombers is intercepted by the fighter cover and all the bombers are shot down by the fighters or by the AA fire.

After again refuelling from the tankers on 30 Jan TF 63 proceeds to Fremantle where it arrives on 4 Feb.

16 Jan-9 Feb   Norway
In operations off Norway the Norwegian submarine *Utsira* (Lt-Cdr Valvatne) sinks the patrol boat *V6408* off Trondheim on 16 Jan. The British *Venturer* (Lt Launders) sinks the small steamer *Stockholm* (618 tons) on 22 Jan off Stavanger and *U864* on 9 Feb.

22-23 Jan   North Sea
Three boats of the German 9th MTB Flotilla attack an Allied convoy N of Dunkirk. *S168* and *S175* sink the British freighter *Halo* (2365 tons) and are damaged in action with two British MTB groups. Five boats of the 6th Flotilla and four boats of the 4th Flotilla are intercepted N and NE of Ostend and are driven off by MTB groups. The 8th Flotilla (Cdr Zymalkowski) with *S194*, *S196*, *S197*, *S199* and *S701* reaches the Thames NE of North Foreland and is engaged by the

British escort vessels *Seymour* and *Guillemot* and MTBs. The German boats fire two T-5 torpedoes and eight other torpedoes which miss. *S199* is damaged by fire from the Tongue Sand Fort and sinks. The British *MTB 495* collides with *S701*. Both boats are brought in, but *S701* is a total loss.

23-30 Jan   North Sea
Mining operations by German motor torpedo boat flotillas. On the night 23-24 Jan *S98*, *S48* and *S85* of the 5th Flotilla lay mines off East Dudgeon. *S127*, *S92* and *S67* are attacked by aircraft and have to return. In the night 24-25 Jan *S221*, *S181* and *S177* of the 2nd, *S206*, *S175* and *S703* of the 4th and 9th and *S211*, *S222*, *S704* and *S223* of the 6th Flotilla lay mines on coastal routes off Orfordness. In the night 29-30 Jan *S221*, *S174*, *S209*, *S181* and *S177* of the 2nd Flotilla lay mines off the Humber. The 5th Flotilla has to return owing to bad weather.

24 Jan-13 Feb   Central Pacific
Preparatory bombardments of Iwojima. On 24 Jan, 29 Jan and 12 Feb B 29s of the 20th USAAF and, each day from 31 Jan to 13 Feb, B 24s of the 7th USAAF attack Iwojima and drop approximately 6800 tons of bombs. On 25 Jan a US Task Force (Rear-Adm Badger), comprising the battleship *Indiana*, the 5th Cruiser Div (Rear-Adm Smith) with *Chester*, *Pensacola* and *Salt Lake City* and eight destroyers, shells Iwojima with 203 16-inch shells and 1354 8-inch shells.

24 Jan-17 Feb   South-West Pacific
Landings in West Luzon. On 27 Jan the 32nd Inf Div and the 1st Cavalry Div are landed in Lingayen Gulf as reinforcements for the 6th US Army on Luzon. On the way the Japanese midget submarines *Ha-76*, *Ha-81* and *Ha-84* try, unsuccessfully, to attack the convoys in the Mindoro Sea on 24-25 Jan. Operation 'Mike VII': Amphibious Group 9 (Rear-Adm Struble) lands the 38th Inf Div (Maj-Gen Hall) and the 134th RCT of XI Corps (Maj-Gen Siebert) near Zambales N of Subic Bay on 29 Jan. About 30000 troops are landed in one day from 22 transports and 35 LSTs. Air support is provided by the 5th USAAF (Lt-Gen Kenney). Escort: 14 destroyers (Desron 49) and

DEs, 11 minesweepers and 19 YMSs. Fire support is provided by TG 74.2 (Rear-Adm Riggs), comprising the cruiser *Denver* and two destroyers. On 30 Jan four APDs and the LSV *Monitor* land one BLT of the 38th Inf Div on Gamble Island in Subic Bay. Distant cover for both operations: TG 74.3 (Rear-Adm Berkey,) comprising the cruisers *Boise*, *Phoenix* and *Shropshire* (RAN) and four destroyers. Japanese counter-measures: the submarine *Ro-46* (Lt-Cdr Tokunaga) torpedoes the APA *Cavalier* (7800 tons).
Operation 'Mike VI': Amphibious Group 8 (Rear-Adm Fechteler) lands the 11th Airborne Div (Maj-Gen Swing) on four APDs, 35 LCIs and eight LSMs near Nasugbu SW of Manila Bay on 31 Jan. It is escorted by six destroyers (Desron 5) and three DEs. Fire support is provided by TG 74.2 (Rear-Adm Riggs), comprising the cruiser *Denver* and the destroyers *Claxton* and *Dyson*. On 31 Jan the Japanese submarine *Ro-115* is sunk by the US destroyers *O'Bannon*, *Jenkins* and *Bell* and the DE *Ulvert M. Moore* in the vicinity of the distant covering force, TG 74.3. In an explosive boat attack the US submarine-chaser *PC1129* is sunk. The destroyer *Claxton* and the DE *Lough* beat off further attacks. *Lough* and the destroyer *Conyngham* sink the two US motor torpedo boats, *PT77* and *PT79*, in error on 1 Feb.
W of Luzon the Japanese submarine *Ro-55* is severely damaged by the DE *Thomason* on 7 Feb and is probably sunk on the return by the US submarine *Batfish* on 11 Feb.
The submarine *Ro-50* (Lt-Cdr Kimura), which is deployed SW of Leyte, after missing a target on 1 Feb, sinks the US *LST 577* from a supply convoy on 7 Feb. On 13 Feb the midget submarine *Ha-69* has two misses W of Mindanao.
On 13 Feb US motor torpedo boats enter Manila Bay for the first time since 1942. On the same day minesweepers begin clearing operations in the entrance to Manila Bay. TG 74.3 (Rear-Adm Berkey), comprising the cruisers *Boise* and *Phoenix* and the destroyers *Fletcher*, *Hopewell*, *La Valette* and *Radford* (Desron 21), shells the assault area on the southern tip of Bataan and

o

Corregidor. In the process *La Valette* and *Radford* are damaged by mines. On 14 Feb the shelling is repeated. Reinforcements from the reserve force (Commodore Farncomb, RAN) arrive, consisting of the cruisers *Shropshire* (RAN), *Minneapolis* and *Portland* and six destroyers. Amphibious Group 9 (Rear-Adm Struble) lands the 151st RCT and the 34th RCT from the 38th Inf Div, totalling 5300 troops, from 62 landing craft at the southern tip of Bataan on 15 Feb. On 16 Feb the 503rd Parachute RCT is dropped on Corregidor. Landing boats land one battalion of the 34th RCT on Corregidor. Support is provided by the destroyers of Desron 49, including *Picking, Young* and *Wickes*. Since 22 Jan American aircraft of the 5th USAAF have dropped 3200 tons of bombs on the rock island.
An attack by the Japanese submarine *Ro-109* (Lt Masuzawa) on 17 Feb on a convoy and its escort is not successful.

25-26 Jan   South West Pacific
American aircraft drop mines off Singapore, Saigon and in Camranh Bay. Among other ships, the battleship *Ise* is damaged on these mines on 5 Feb and the frigate *Nomi* on 11 Feb.

25 Jan-10 Mar   Baltic
With the Soviet attack threatening East Prussia and Danzig there begins the greatest evacuation operation in history. Overall responsibility for the operations is with the German Naval High Command East (Adm Kummetz); in the area of the Gulf of Danzig—Courland the 9th Escort Div (Cdr* v. Blanc), in the area W of Rixhöft as far as the Danish Islands the 10th Escort Div (Rear-Adm Bütow and from February Cdr* Heydel). The shipping is directed by the Wehrmacht Naval Transport Commander (Rear-Adm Engelhardt). It is chiefly the large passenger ships which are employed and which, until then, have been used as accommodation ships in Pillau, Gotenhafen and Danzig e.g. *Cap Arkona* (27561 tons), *Robert Ley* (27288 tons), *Wilhelm Gustloff* (25484 tons), *Hamburg* (22117 tons), *Hansa* (21131 tons), *Deutschland* (21046 tons), *Potsdam* (17528 tons), *Pretoria* (16662 tons), *Berlin* (15286 tons), *General Steuben* (14660 tons), *Monte Rosa* (13882 tons), *Antonio Delfino* (13589 tons), *Winrich v. Kniprode* (10123 tons) and *Ubena* (9554 tons); also the freighters *Moltkefels* (7862 tons), *Wangoni* (7848 tons), *Neidenfels* (7838 tons), *Lappland* (7650 tons), *Vega* (7287 tons), *Volta* (7258 tons), *Göttingen* (6267 tons), *Sachsenwald* (6261 tons), *Kanonier* (6257 tons), *Duala* (6133 tons), *Vale* (5950 tons), *Wiegand* (5869 tons), *Urundi* (5791 tons), *Tübingen* (5493 tons), *Albert Jensen* (5446 tons), *Brake* (5347 tons), *Tanga* (5346 tons), *Mathias Stinnes* (5337 tons), *Goya* (5230 tons), *Mendoza* (5193 tons), *Cometa* (5125 tons), *Eberhard Essberger* (5064 tons) and many other ships of less than 5000 tons. Auxiliary warships and escort vessels are also used chiefly to evacuate refugees. To protect the convoys the 1st, 3rd and 25th MS Flotillas (Cdr Pinkepank, Cdr Dr Kieffer and Lt-Cdr Vogeler and, from February, Lt-Cdr v. Haxthausen) of the 9th Escort Div are employed in the area Gulf of Danzig/Courland, each with some six operational boats: also the 1st and 17th MMS Flotillas (Lt-Cdr Hoff, Cdr Zaage and, from March, Lt-Cdr Voss), each with 7-10 motor minesweepers, the 3rd and 17th PB Flotillas (Cdr Böttger and Cdr Dittmer) with 6-8 converted trawlers, the 3rd and 14th Defence Flotillas (Cdr Leonhardt, from March, Cdr* Palmgren and Cdr Petersen) with many small fishery vessels and KFKs, the 31st MS Flotilla (Lt-Cdr Prater) with four KFK groups, the 3rd SC Flotilla (Lt-Cdr Dr Teichmann) with many small fishery vessels, the 13th and 24th Landing Flotillas (Cdr Wassmuth and Cdr* Brauneis) with naval ferry barges and the 3rd and 16th Gun Carrier Flotillas (Cdr Dr Schröder and Cdr Dr Sonnemann) with SATs, LATs and AFs. In the area between the Gulf of Danzig and the Pomeranian Bay the newly-formed 12th and 2nd MS Flotillas (Lt-Cdr Ostertag and Lt-Cdr Rosenow) with the modern Type 43 minesweepers of the 10th Escort Div are employed: also the 15th MMS Flotillas (Lt-Cdr Mergelmeyer) with the new motor minesweepers, the 2nd Defence Flotilla (Lt-Cdr Dr Reimann) with many small fishery vessels and KFKs, the 36th MS Flotilla (Cdr

Reinhold) with converted drifters, the KFK Training Flotilla and the newly-formed 6th SC Flotilla (from March, Lt-Cdr Bittkow), as well as the 11th Landing Flotilla (Cdr Wiegand) with naval ferry barges for transport purposes. In the Western Baltic the 1st Defence Flotilla from Kiel is used for mine defence (Capt G. Schulz).

On 25 Jan the *Robert Ley*, *Pretoria*, *Ubena* and others set out as the first ships from Pillau with a total of 7100 refugees. At the end of January more ships follow until by 28 Jan 62000 refugees have been taken by ship. The cruiser *Emden* brings refugees and the sarcophagus of the Reich President Hindenburg to Pillau. The main obstacle to the evacuation is the British air mining offensive by the RAF in the Western Baltic and as far as the Pomeranian Coast. This causes frequent blockages of the compulsory routes within the 20 mile line and considerable delays while the 1st and 2nd Defence Flotillas search for mines. In the month of January 668 mines are dropped in 159 sorties and on them a total of 18 ships of 42673 tons sink and eight ships of 9177 tons are damaged. In February 1354 mines are dropped in 291 sorties and 23 ships of 25642 tons sink and 13 ships of 13490 tons are damaged. In March 1198 mines are dropped in 270 sorties and 26 ships of 69449 tons sink and 11 ships of 48557 tons are damaged. Mines are concentrated in the area off Swinemünde where on 29 Jan the escort vessel *F5* sinks, on 30 Jan the U-boat tender *Memel* (1057 tons) and on 31 Jan the hospital ship *Berlin* (15286 tons), from 12 Feb to 17 Feb the transports *Ditmar Koel* (670 tons), *Dieter H. Stinnes* (2545 tons), *Consul Cords* (951 tons) and the *Minenräumschiff 11* (5095 tons) and the minesweeper *M421* sink and the transport *Drechtdijk* (9338 tons) is damaged. Off Warnemünde between 24 Feb and 5 Mar the transports *Ellen Larsen* (1938 tons), *Erika Fritzen* (4169 tons), *Rixhöft* (5378 tons), *R177* and the *Hansa* (21131 tons) are lost and the tanker *Jaspis* (6049 tons) and the freighter *Irene Oldendorf* (1923 tons) are damaged. On 6-7 Mar off Sassnitz the *Hamburg* (22117 tons) and the destroyer *Z28* run on to mines. Soviet aircraft attack *UJ1119* and the hospital ship *Robert Möhring* at the scene of the accident and sink them. For the rest, the danger from the air at this period is still slight because the Soviet Air Force is largely involved in land operations. As a result, considerable feats of evacuation can be recorded at this time. Each of the large passenger ships takes between 5000 and 9000 persons at a time and the freighters anything up to 5000, according to their size.

Initially, the defence against Soviet submarines operating in the Baltic is completely inadequate because no effective A/S vessels are available until the second half of February when the 11th and 12th SC Flotillas are moved to the area. In this period the Soviet submarines concentrate their activities on the route to Courland; individual large boats operate in the area between Bornholm and Rixhöft. On 28 Jan *K-51* (Capt 2nd Class Drozdov) sinks the Danish steamer *Viborg* (2028 tons) near Bornholm. On 30 Jan *S-13* (Capt 3rd Class Marinesko), which is stationed in the area of the Stolpe Bank, attacks 28 nautical miles NNE of Leba the passenger ship *Wilhelm Gustloff* (25484 tons) sailing without escort. The submarine fires a salvo of four and three torpedoes hit. Of more than 6000 persons on board, 564 are rescued by *T36*, 252 by *Löwe*, 37 by *M341*, 15 by *TS2*, seven by *TF19*, one by *V1703* and 28 by *Göttingen*, which are in the area and answer the distress signal. The cruiser *Admiral Hipper*, which at first also comes up, is unable to participate in the rescue operations because of the submarine danger and has to withdraw to the W with her 1500 wounded on board. About 5200-5400 persons perish in this catastrophe. Two attempts by *L-3* (Capt 3rd Class Konovalov) to attack the fully-laden *Cap Arkona* fail on the following day. *S-13*, which is still cruising in the area of the Stolpe Bank, sights on 10 Feb the passenger ship *General Steuben* (14660 tons), escorted by *T196* and *TF10*, and sinks her with one hit. Because of the low temperature of the water, the escort vessels are only able to rescue some 300 out of more than 3000 on board. From the end of February to the beginning of March K-52 (Capt 3rd Class Travkin) operates in the area of the Stolpe Bank. In six attacks she claims to have sunk one torpedo boat and five ships but, in fact, no losses have been established.

26 Jan-11 Mar   British Coastal Waters/ Atlantic

In operations by German U-boats in the North Sea U245 (Cdr Schumann-Hindenberg) sinks one ship of 7240 tons and torpedoes one ship of 2628 tons from convoys in the Thames Estuary. In the first operations by the new Type XXIII boats on the British East Coast U2324 (Lt Hass) misses one ship and U2322 (Lt Heckel) sinks one ship of 1317 tons. In the area of Moray Firth U309, in attempting to attack convoy WN.74, is found by the Canadian 9th EG and sunk by the frigate St John. On 3 Feb U1279, on 14 Feb U989 and on 17 Feb U1278 fall victim to the 10th EG (Cdr Burnett), employed N of the Shetlands and comprising the DEs Bayntun and Braithwaite and the frigates Loch Eck and Loch Dunvegan which are supporting EN and WN convoys. The 9th EG is summoned to the scene but does not need to intervene. In the area off the North Minch U1104 attacks several steamers and convoys without success. U1014, which has penetrated into the North Channel, is sunk on 4 Feb by the 23rd EG, comprising the frigates Loch Scavaig, Loch Shin, Nyasaland and Papua. U1064 (Cdr Schneidewind) sinks one ship of 1564 tons from a convoy. U483 (Lt-Cdr v. Morstein), after missing a corvette, is badly damaged by depth charges, but gets away. U1019 (Lt Rinck) is attacked W of the North Channel by a Liberator with the help of Sonobuoys and 'Fido' homing torpedoes, but escapes. U963, U1058 and U1276 operate without success in the Irish Sea. U1208 (Cdr Hagene) attacks the convoy HX.337 on 20 Feb and sinks the Canadian corvette Vervain but is herself sunk by the sloop Amethyst of the 22nd EG. U1302 (Lt-Cdr W. Herwatz) sinks four ships of 10312 tons, including two ships from the convoy SC.167, and torpedoes one ship of 6991 tons, but is sunk after a long search by the Canadian frigates La Hulloise, Strathadam and Thetford

Mines of the 25th EG. U775 cruises in the same area but gets away.

In the English Channel U1017 (Lt Riecken) makes several unsuccessful attacks on escorts off Cherbourg and sinks two ships of 10604 tons, including one ship from the convoy TBC.60 on 6 Feb. U244 (Lt Fischer) reports a torpedoing near the Channel Islands. On 22 Feb U1004 (Lt Hinz) sinks the Canadian corvette Trentonian and one ship of 1313 tons from the convoy BTC.76 and U480 (Lt Förster) sinks one ship of 1644 tons from BTC.78 on 24 Feb. U1203 (Lt Seeger) sinks one ship of 580 tons and misses several escorts and convoys. U1018 (Lt-Cdr Burmeister) sinks one ship of 1317 tons from BTC.81 on 27 Feb but is hunted by the 2nd EG and sunk by the frigate Loch Fada. Directed by the report from a Liberator of USN-VPB.112, the 2nd EG, consisting of the frigates Labuan and Loch Fada and the sloop Wild Goose, also sinks U327 on the same day. On 24 Feb U927 is sunk on her way to the Channel by a Wellington of No 179 Sqdn RAF.

U868 and U275 are employed on supply missions to St Nazaire.

Off Gibraltar U300 (Lt Hein) torpedoes two ships of 16727 tons (one total loss) from a convoy on 17 Feb but, after a T-5 miss, is sunk on 22 Feb by the minesweepers Recruit, Invade (US) and Pincher (British). U869 (Lt-Cdr Neuerburg) tries to attack the convoy GUS.74 on 28 Feb but is located and sunk by the US frigate Knoxville, the DEs Fowler and Francis M. Robinson and the French A/S vessels L'Indiscret and Le Résolu. U1233 (Cdr Kuhn), which makes a sortie into the Gulf of Maine (via Bermuda), misses several targets.

U907 has no success off Reykjavik. U1022 (Lt-Cdr Ernst) sinks one ship of 1349 tons from UR.155 on 28 Feb and one tug of 328 tons on 3 Mar.

28 Jan   Norway

When the 4th DD Flotilla (Capt v. Wangenheim), comprising Z31, Z34 and Z38, tries to move from Norwegian waters into the Baltic, it is intercepted off Bergen by the British cruisers Diadem (Vice-Adm Dalrymple-Hamilton) and Mauritius. In an engagement Z31 is damaged. The Flotilla returns to Bergen, from where *Z34* and *Z38* put to sea again the next evening and, in spite of British air attacks, reach Kiel on 1 Feb, after putting in to Stavanger.

30 Jan Norway
Raid on the Stadlandet area by the British escort carriers *Campania* and *Nairana* with the heavy cruiser *Berwick* and destroyers.

1-28 Feb Pacific
The following ships are sunk by US submarines arriving in their operational areas in February: in Japanese waters between Luzon and the Kuriles *Bang* (Lt-Cdr Gallaher) sinks one ship of 2036 tons; *Batfish* (Lt-Cdr Fyfe) the submarines *Ro-112*, *Ro-113* and *Ro-55*; *Bowfin* (Cdr Tyree) one picket of 136 tons and the corvette *Kaibokan 56*; *Flasher* (Cdr Grider) one ship of 850 tons; *Gato* (Lt-Cdr Farrell) one ship of 2325 tons and the corvette *Kaibokan 9*; *Haddock* (Cdr Brockman) damages one picket; *Lagarto* (Cdr Latta) sinks the submarine *I-371*; *Pampanito* (Lt-Cdr Summers) two ships of 10488 tons; *Piper* (Cdr MacMahon) one picket of 111 tons; *Scabbardfish* (Lt-Cdr Gunn) one picket of 137 tons; *Sennet* (Cdr Porter) two pickets of 185 tons and the minelayer *Nariu*; *Sterlet* (Cdr Lewis) one ship of 1148 tons; *Trepang* (Lt-Cdr Faust) two ships of 2261 tons. In the area of Indonesia and the Philippines *Becuna* (Lt-Cdr Sturr) sinks one ship of 1945 tons; *Blenny* (Lt-Cdr Hazzard) one ship of 10238 tons; *Guavina* (Cdr Lockwood) one ship of 6892 tons and torpedoes one ship; *Hammerhead* (Lt-Cdr Smith) the frigate *Yaku*; *Hardhead* (Cdr Greenup) one ship of 834 tons; *Hawkbill* (Lt-Cdr Scanland) the submarine-chaser *Kusen-Tokumu-Tei 114* and torpedoes one ship; *Hoe* (Lt-Cdr Refo) sinks the frigate *Shonan*.

3-13 Feb Arctic
Convoy operation JW.64 to Murmansk with 26 ships, escorted by the escort carriers *Campania* (Rear-Adm Mc-Grigor) and *Nairana*, the cruiser *Bellona* and 17 escort vessels including the destroyers *Onslow*, *Orwell*, *Onslaught*, *Sioux*, *Serapis* and *Zealous* and vessels of the 8th and 20th EGs. On 6 Feb the convoy is located by weather aircraft and reported. The 'Rasmus' U-boat group (*U286*, *U307*, *U425*, *U636*,

U711, *U716*, *U739* and *U968*) is deployed in the Bear Island Passage and the boats *U293*, *U318*, *U992* and *U995* off the Kola Inlet. On 7 Feb K.G. 26 with 48 Ju 88s tries to attack but misses the convoy; seven aircraft are lost. On 8-9 Feb temporary contact is established by reconnaissance aircraft. On 10 Feb an attack by K.G. 26 with some 30 Ju 88s fails to get through the fighter and AA defence. The U-boats are unable to attack in face of the escort and are moved to the area off the Kola Inlet. When the convoy enters the Kola Inlet *U992* (Lt Falke) torpedoes the corvette *Denbigh Castle* on 13 Feb; the corvette is taken in tow by the Soviet salvage ship *Burevestnik* but has to be written off as a total loss. *U995* misses the Norwegian steamer *Idefjord* in the harbour of Kirkenes on 9 Feb.

10 Feb-4 Mar Central Pacific
First major carrier raid on Tokyo and support for the landing on Iwojima by TF 58 (Vice-Adm Mitscher). On the approach route the submarines *Sterlet*, *Pomfret*, *Piper*, *Trepang*, *Bowfin* and *Sennet*, *Lagarto* and *Haddock* are deployed to sink Japanese patrol boats. On 10 Feb TF 58 sets out from Ulithi: TG 58.1 (Rear-Adm Clark) consists of the carriers *Hornet*, *Wasp*, *Bennington* and *Belleau Wood*, the battleships *Massachusetts* and *Indiana*, the cruisers *Vincennes*, *Miami* and *San Juan* and 15 destroyers of Desrons 61 and 25. TG 58.2 (Rear-Adm Davison) consists of the carriers *Lexington*, *Hancock* and *San Jacinto*, the battleships *Wisconsin* and *Missouri*, the cruisers *San Francisco* and *Boston* and 19 destroyers of Desrons 62 and 52 and Desdiv 92. TG 58.3 (Rear-Adm Sherman) consists of the carriers *Essex*, *Bunker Hill* and *Cowpens*, the battleships *South Dakota* and *New Jersey*, the battlecruiser *Alaska*, the cruisers *Indianapolis* (Adm Spruance, 5th Fleet), *Pasadena*, *Wilkes Barre* and *Astoria* and 14 destroyers of Desrons 55 and 50. TG 58.4 (Rear-Adm Radford) consists of the carriers *Yorktown*, *Randolph*, *Langley* and *Cabot*, the battleships *Washington* and *North Carolina*, the cruisers *Santa Fé*, *Biloxi* and *San Diego* and 17 destroyers of Desrons 47 and 48.

TG 58.5 (Night Group, Rear-Adm Gardner) consists of the carriers *Enterprise* and *Saratoga*, the cruisers *Baltimore* and *Flint* and 12 destroyers of Desron 54 and Desdiv 53. By day it operates mostly with TG 58.2

Four patrol boats having been sunk by the submarines, six more are sunk by a patrol line of destroyers advancing in front of the Task Force and consisting of *Haynsworth, Barton, Ingraham, Moale Dortch* and *Waldron*. The approach thus succeeds. On 16 Feb, 125 nautical miles SE of Tokyo, the carriers fly off, first, fighters, to eliminate the enemy fighter defence in the air and on the ground, then bombers which are to attack, in particular, aircraft factories in the Tokyo area. The attacks are greatly impeded by the weather. On 17 Feb there are further attacks also on shipping targets in the area of Yokohama, when the transport *Yamashio Maru* (10602 tons) is sunk and the frigate *Amakusa* and the corvette *Kaibokan 47* are damaged. Including fighter protection, 2761 sorties are flown in all; 60 aircraft are lost in combat and 28 due to accident. On 18 Feb the destroyers are replenished and TG 58.4 makes raids to neutralize Hahajima and Chichijima. TGs 58.1 and 58.5 are detached for replenishment. TGs 58.2 and 58.3 from 19 Feb to 22 Feb and TGs 58.1, 58.4 and 58.5 20 Feb support the landing on Iwojima from the W. On 23 Feb TF 58 assembles and until 24 Feb replenishes from the tanker group (Rear-Adm Beary). On 25 Feb and 26 Feb further carrier raids on the Tokyo area are badly impeded by the weather and are, in part, broken off prematurely. On 27 Feb there is an operation partly in support of Iwojima, on 28 Feb replenishment and on 1 Mar a carrier raid on Okinawa in which the Japanese torpedo boat *Manazuru* and the minesweeper *Tsubame* are destroyed. The ships return on 2 Mar and arrive in Ulithi on 4 Mar.

TU 58.1.22 (Rear-Adm Whiting), consisting of the cruisers *Vicksburgh, Miami Vincennes* and *San Diego* and 15 destroyers, shells Okino-Daito Jima (Ryukyu Islands) on 2 Mar.

14-28 Feb   Arctic
Convoy operation RA.64. The U-boats *U286, U310, U318, U425, U636,* *U711, U739, U968, U992* and *U995* are stationed N of the Kola coast. On 14 Feb *U968* (Lt Westphalen), *U711* (Lt-Cdr Lange) and *U992* attack the Soviet convoy BK.3 coming from the White Sea off the Kola Inlet. The convoy is escorted by a strong group of Soviet destroyers. The U-boats sink the tanker *Norfjell* (8129 tons) and the freighter *Horace Gray* (7200 tons) from the convoy. On 16 Feb *U286* (Lt Dietrich) unsuccessfully attacks another coastal convoy further to the E.

From 14 Feb to 16 Feb the destroyers *Sioux, Zambesi* and *Zest* evacuate the Norwegian inhabitants of the island of Söröy who are distributed among the convoy RA.64.

On 16 Feb groups of Soviet destroyers, minesweepers, submarine-chasers, torpedo cutters and aircraft and a part of the British escort force (Rear-Adm McGrigor), comprising the escort carriers *Nairana* and *Campania*, the cruiser *Bellona* and 16 escort vessels, including the destroyers *Onslow, Orwell, Onslaught, Serapis* and *Zealous* and the destroyer *Whitehall*, the sloop *Lark* and the corvettes *Alnwick Castle, Bluebell,* etc., from the 8th and 20th EGs, all try to drive the German U-boats away from the entrance to the Kola Inlet. The sloop *Lark* and the corvette *Alnwick Castle* sink *U425*. The outward-bound convoy of 34 ships is attacked by *U968* and *U711*: the first torpedoes the sloop *Lark* and the freighter *Thomas Scott* (7176 tons). The Soviet submarine-chaser *MO-434* rescues part of the crew of the *Lark*, which is beached, and the Soviet destroyer *Zhestki* takes the freighter in tow, but she becomes a total loss. *U711* sinks the corvette *Bluebell*. Contact is lost on 18 Feb. *U286, U711, U716, U307, U968* and *U992* are moved to the Bear Island Passage but are unable to establish contact. On 20 Feb the convoy is again located by German air reconnaissance. K.G. 26 (Lt-Col Stemmler) is deployed against the convoy with 40 Ju 88 torpedo aircraft. Six aircraft are shot down by the fighter cover and no successes are achieved. The pilots believe they have sunk two cruisers, two destroyers and at least eight freighters. *U307, U716* and *U286,* which are directed to the supposedly disabled ships, find no targets. The British air escort drives off the U-boats. In a second attack K.G. 26 sinks the straggler *Henry Bacon* (7177 tons) on 23 Feb; this is the last ship to be sunk by German aircraft in the Second World War.

16-18 Feb   North Pacific
A US Task Group, comprising Crudiv 1 and nine destroyers, shells Kurabu Zaki and Paramushiro in the Kuriles on 16 Feb and 18 Feb.

16-19 Feb   Central Pacific
Preparation for the landing on Iwojima. On 16 Feb US TF 54 (Rear-Adm Rodgers), comprising the battleships *Tennessee, Idaho, Nevada, Texas, New York* and *Arkansas*, the cruisers *Chester, Salt Lake City, Pensacola, Tuscaloosa* and *Vicksburgh* and 16 destroyers of Desron 51 and Desdivs 91 and 112, arrives and begins shelling the designated areas in preparation for the assault. TF 52 (Support Force, Rear-Adm Blandy) with the Minesweeper Group 52.3, the Frogman Group 52.4 and the LCI Support Group 52.5 and the escort carrier group 52.2 (Rear-Adm Durgin), comprising the escort carriers *Sargent Bay, Natoma Bay, Wake Island, Petrof Bay, Steamer Bay* and *Makin Island, Lunga Point, Bismark Sea, Saginaw Bay* and *Rudyerd Bay* with their destroyer and DE escort, provide air cover and fly 158 attack sorties. The effect of the shelling is slight because of inadequate observation in poor weather. A repetition on 17 Feb in better weather is more successful. Japanese coastal batteries obtain one hit on the *Tennessee* and six on the *Pensacola*. The UDTs (underwater demolition teams), after being disembarked by the APDs *Bull, Bates, Barr* and *Blessman*, begin the work of removing underwater obstacles. All 12 LCIs used for support are hit by the Japanese coastal batteries and nine are put out of action. The escort carriers fly 226 sorties, some with napalm bombs. Forty-two B 24s of the 7th USAAF make attacks. On 18 Feb the shelling is continued as are the air attacks (28 sorties). Including the air escort, the escort carrier aircraft fly 612 sorties in all and lose three of their number.

17 Feb   Mediterranean/Adriatic
British air attack on the harbour of Trieste: the damaged Italian battleship *Conte di Cavour* and the unfinished *Impero* are sunk and the German destroyer *TA44* is destroyed.

17 Feb-2 Mar   North Sea
Operations by German motor torpedo boat flotillas. In the night 17-18 Feb the 2nd and 5th Flotillas lay mines off the Humber. On these mines the French destroyer *La Combattante* and the trawler *Aquarius* (187 tons) are sunk and two ships are damaged. The 9th Flotilla lays a mine barrage off the South-East Coast of Britain.
An operation off the Scheldt in the night 20-21 Feb has no success.
In the night 21-22 Feb six flotillas are dispatched to the British East Coast with 22 boats in all. NE of Great James the 5th Flotilla and the 2nd Flotilla attack the British convoy FS.1734 and report seven and four torpedo hits respectively The British freighters *Goodwood* (2780 tons) and *Blacktoft* (1109 tons) are sunk. The freighter *Skjold* (1345 tons) is damaged by gunfire from the 2nd Flotilla. The 8th Flotilla attacks a landing ship convoy in the Thames Estuary and sinks the *LCP 707*. *S193* is sunk by the escorts. The 4th, 6th and 9th Flotillas have no success. On the return journey *S167* of the 9th Flotilla sinks in a collision.
In the next two nights the flotillas lay mines on the Thames-Scheldt convoy route. On these mine barrages the freighters *Auretta* (4571 tons), *Sampa* (7219 tons), *Robert L. Vann* (7176 tons) and one trawler sink.
In the night 1-2 Mar *S220* of the 4th Flotilla is sunk in an 'engagement with the British DE *Seymour*.

19 Feb-16 Mar   Central Pacific
Operation 'Detachment': landing on Iwojima. US TF 51 (Vice-Adm Turner) lands the V Amphibious Corps (Lt-Gen H. M. Smith). TF 51 consists of TF 52, 53, 54 and 56—495 ships. On 19 Feb TF 54 (for composition see 16 Feb), reinforced by the battleships *North Carolina* and *Washington*, the cruisers *Indianapolis* (Adm Spruance, Commander 5th Fleet), *Santa Fé* and *Biloxi* and 10 destroyers from two Desdivs of TF 58, carries out a heavy preparatory

bombardment of the assault areas. This is interspersed with air attacks from the carrier planes of TGs 58.2 and 58.3 (see 10 Feb) and extended further inland and speeded up with the assault.

The landing is made by TF 53 (Rear-Adm Hill): in the N the 4th Marine Div (Maj-Gen Cates) by TG 53.2 (Commodore Flanagan) on 15 APAs, six AKAs, two LSDs, 19 LSTs and 12 LSMs; in the S the 5th Marine Div (Maj-Gen Rockey) by TG 53.1 (Commodore McGovern) on 15 APAs, six AKAs, one LSD, 19 LSTs and 16 LSMs. One destroyer squadron is available for each as an escort. A further transport squadron has the 3rd Marine Div ready for combat on board as a reserve. Part of it has to be used on the first day. Some 30000 men are landed on the first day. There is strong resistance from the well-prepared Japanese defenders (Commander: Lt-Gen Kuribayashi, GOC 109th Inf Div) with flanking fire from entrenched positions on Mount Suribachi (taken on 23 Feb) and the northern mountain terrain on the assault area. Carrier aircraft fly 606 sorties on the first day with 274 tons of bombs, 2254 rockets and over 100 napalm bombs.

The only Japanese counter-action from outside comes from a Kamikaze attack with 32 aircraft on 21 Feb, when the escort carrier *Bismarck Sea* is sunk and the fleet carrier *Saratoga*, the escort carrier *Lunga Point*, the transport *Keokuk* and *LST 477* and *LST 809* are damaged. There are 242 dead and 191 injured. Apart from the submarine *Ro-43*, the *Kaiten*-carrying submarines *I-368*, *I-370* and *I-44* are deployed as the 'Chihaya' group and, later, *I-36* and *I-58* as the 'Kamitake' group. Of the carrier/DE groups, *Tulagi* and *Anzio*, used as hunter-killer groups, the latter sinks on 25-26 Feb *Ro-43* and *I-368* and the DE *Finnegan* of a convoy escort sinks *I-370*. Only *Ro-43* (Lt Tsukigata) makes an attack on an escort and torpedoes the destroyer *Renshaw* on 21 Feb.

By 16 Mar Japanese defenders on Iwojima are overcome. They lose 20703 dead and 216 prisoners. The US Marine Corps loses 5931 dead and missing and there are 17272 wounded.

19 Feb-7 Apl   South-West Pacific

Control is gained of the passage through the San Bernardino Strait between Samar and Luzon (Philippines). On 19-20 Feb groups of LCMs, with support from Marine Corps aircraft from Leyte, land company and battalion battle groups of the 182nd RCT on the NW tip of Samar and the offshore islands of Dalupiri, Capul and Biri. The landing on Biri is at first repulsed by the Japanese defenders, but then succeeds on the far side of the island. On 21 Feb the midget submarine *Ha-84* has a miss.

On 3 Mar elements of the 132nd RCT of the Americal Div are landed with LCMs on the islands of Ticao and Burias W of the San Bernardino Strait.

On 1 Apl a US assault group (Capt McGee), consisting of three APDs, five LSTs, four LSMs, nine LCIs and six support LCIs and SCs, lands the 158th RCT (Brig-Gen MacNider) near Legaspi (south Luzon). Fire cover is provided by the destroyers *Bailey* and *Bancroft* and the DEs *Day* and *Holt*.

On 3 Apl elements of the 108th RCT of the 40th Inf Div are landed in the capital of the island of Masbate, which has been occupied by Philippine guerillas since 29 Mar.

22 Feb-4 Mar   Indian Ocean

On 22 Feb and 23 Feb light assault craft, supported by the Indian sloops *Narbada* and *Jumna*, land 6635 men of the 3rd Commando Brigade and other British and Indian Army units on the banks of the Myebon River near Kangaw.

Operation 'Stacey': from 24 Feb to 4 Mar the escort carriers *Empress* and *Ameer* with the cruiser *Kenya* (Vice-Adm Walker), the destroyers *Virago*, *Vigilant*, and *Volage* and the frigates *Spey*, *Swale*, *Plym* and *Trent* carry out air photo reconnaissance of the Kra Peninsula, the NE coast of Sumatra, of Penang and the Simalur and Banjak Islands. They also make raids on Japanese shipping in the Andaman Sea. On 24-25 Feb the destroyers shell the Andaman Islands and again on 3 Mar. In a sortie towards the coast near Tavoy coastal craft are sunk on 1-2 Mar and a Japanese air attack is beaten off on 1 Mar.

24 Feb-5 Mar   South-West Pacific/China

In sorties made by B 29s of the 20th USAAF from India, Singapore is attacked on 24 Feb, the Johore Straits (Singapore) are mined in the night 27-28 Feb and the River Yangtse in China is mined on 4-5 Mar.

26 Feb-18 Mar   Baltic

Soviet attack on Eastern Pomerania. On 26 Feb the armies of the Soviet 1st White Russian Front start an attack from the area E of Stargard in the direction of the Stettiner Haff and Kolberg. From the area of Friedland part of the 2nd White Russian Front advances in the direction of Köslin which is taken by the 3rd Guards Cavalry Corps on 5 Mar. In the W the 2nd Guards Armoured Army reaches the Stettiner Haff on 3 Mar, the 1st Guards Armoured Army and the Polish 1st Army the area near Kolberg and the 3rd Assault Army the crossing to Wollin near Dievenov. To cover the bridgehead opposite Wollin, TF 2, comprising the pocket battleship *Admiral Scheer*, the destroyers *Z38*, *Z31* (Cdr Paul), *Paul Jacobi* and the torpedo boat *T36*, is employed. From 11 Mar to 18 Mar *Z43*, *Z34* and *T33* support the approximately 2500-3000 defenders of Kolberg, which has been encircled since 7 Mar, so as to make possible the evacuation of about 75000 isolated refugees with the help of naval ferry barges of the 11th Landing Flotilla and support from the 5th Gun Carrier Flotilla. In the roads some of them are embarked on the transports *Westpreussen* (2870 tons) and *Winrich von Kniprode* (10123 tons) and warships. In the night 17-18 Mar the evacuation of some 75000 refugees, soldiers and wounded is completed.

28 Feb   South West Pacific

Operation 'Victor III'.

US Amphibious Group 8 (Rear-Adm Fechteler, TG 78.2), with the headquarters ship US Coastguard cutter *Spencer*, lands 8000 men of the reinforced 186th RCT (41st Inf Div, Brig-Gen Haney) on Palawan (Philippines). The asault group consists of four APDs, the LSD *Rushmore*, 19 LSTs, 20 LSMs, 10 LSIs and 14 Support LCIs, one PC and three SCs. Escort: the destroyers (Desron 5) *Flusser*, *Conyng-*ham, *Smith*, *Drayton* and *Shaw*. A minesweeper group comprises four YMSs. The preparatory bombardment and support is provided by TG 74.2 (Rear-Adm Riggs), comprising the cruisers *Denver*, *Montpelier* and *Cleveland*, the destroyers (Desron 21) *Fletcher*, *O'Bannon*, *Jenkins* and *Abbot*. Air escort and support is provided by the 5th USAAF (Maj-Gen Whitehead) and the 13th USAAF (Brig-Gen Wurtsmith).

On 1 Mar the first supply convoy arrives with 19 LSTs and an escort consisting of the destroyers *Waller*, *Sigourney* and *McCalla*. A base for PT squadrons 20 and 23 is set up by the motor torpedo boat depot ship *Willoughby*.

1-31 Mar   Pacific

The following ships are sunk by Allied submarines arriving in their operational areas in March: in Japanese waters between Formosa and the Kuriles the US boat *Balao* (Cdr Worthington) sinks three ships of 12502 tons and torpedoes one ship; *Kete* (Lt-Cdr Ackermann) sinks three ships of 7601 tons; *Segundo* (Lt-Cdr Fulp) one ship of 3087 tons; *Spadefish* (Cdr Germershausen) three ships of 4343 tons; *Springer* (Cdr Kefauver) the fast transport *No 18*; *Sterlet* (Lt-Cdr Lewis) one ship of 1148 tons; *Threadfin* (Lt-Cdr Foote) the frigate *Mikura*; *Tilefish* (Lt-Cdr Schlech) the minesweeper *Sokaitei 15*; *Tirante* (Cdr Street) four ships of 10921 tons, the frigate *Nomi* and the corvette *Kaibokan 31* and damages *Kaibokan 102*; *Trigger* (Cdr Connole) sinks one ship of 1012 tons and the repair ship *Odate*.

In the area between the Malacca Straits and the Philippines the British submarines *Trenchant* (Cdr Hezlet) and *Terrapin* (Lt-Cdr Brunner) sink the submarine-chaser *Kusentai 8*; *Stygian* the auxiliary minesweeper *No 104* and damages the minelayer *Wakataka* and one submarine-chaser; and *Selene* sinks one small craft.

The US boat *Bashaw* (Cdr Simpson) sinks two ships of 15397 tons; *Baya* (Lt-Cdr Jarvis) two ships of 5760 tons; *Blenny* (Lt-Cdr Hazzard) three ships of 2373 tons; *Burrfish* (Lt-Cdr Clementson) the corvettes *Kaibokan 18* and *Kaibokan 130*; *Bluegill* (Lt-Cdr Barr) one ship of

5518 tons; *Hammerhead* (Lt-Cdr Smith) the corvette *Kaibokan 84*; *Sealion* (Lt-Cdr Putnam) torpedoes one ship and *Sea Robin* (Cdr Stimson) sinks four ships of 6122 tons.

3 Mar-6 Apl   British Coastal Waters/ Atlantic

On the Scottish East Coast *U714* (Lt-Cdr Schwebke) sinks in March the Norwegian minesweeping trawler *Nordhav* and one ship of 1226 tons, but is then sunk by the new South African frigate *Natal*. Off St Abb's the new type XXIII Boat *U2321* (Lt Barschkies) sinks one ship of 1406 tons. *U778* off the Moray Firth, *U978* off the Pentland Firth, *U1105* off Cape Wrath and *U1108* off the North Minch have no success. The last has to return when she goes aground. As a result of air patrols with Liberators of Nos 86, 120 and 224 Sqdns RAF *U905*, *U296*, *U1106* and *U1276* are sunk between the Shetland/ Faeroes Passage and the North Channel in the last third of March and the beginning of April and *U249* is bombed and forced to return.

In the area of the Hebrides and the North Minch *U722* (Lt Reimers) sinks on 16 Mar one ship of 2190 tons from the convoy RU.156 and *U965* misses one ship. On 21 Mar *U1003* collides under water with the frigate *New Glasgow* of the Canadian 26th EG which, with *Beacon Hill*, *Jonquière*, *Ribble* and *Sussexvale*, is looking for U-boats. The Canadian frigates *Strathadam*, *La Hulloise* and *Thetford Mines* of the 25th EG, are brought up take part in the search: the last-named finds the survivors of the U-boat which has in the meantime been scuttled. The 21st EG, with the DEs *Conn*, *Rupert* and *Deane* in the N and *Fitzroy*, *Redmill* and *Bryon* in the S, has meanwhile been deployed against the U-boats in the area of the Minches and to it *U965* and *U722* fall victim on 27 Mar and *U1021* on 30 Mar.

In the southern part of the Irish Sea *U1019* operates without success in March and *U260* and *U1169* are lost on British mine barrages. *U681*, having missed a patrol vessel, is bombed by a US aircraft and is beached on the Irish Coast. A Polish aircraft sinks *U321* W of the Channel.

Of the transport boats returning from St Nazaire, *U868* goes to Norway and *U275* (Lt Wehrkamp) into the Channel, where she sinks one ship of 4934 tons from the convoy ONA.289 but is lost on a submarine mine barrage off Beachy Head. On the way to St Nazaire *U878* (Lt-Cdr Rodig) sinks the Canadian minesweeper *Guysborough* (17 Mar). *U683* falls victim to the 2nd EG comprising the frigate *Loch Ruthven* and the sloop *Wild Goose*, W of the Channel on 12 Mar.

SW of Ireland and in the Channel *U1202* (Lt-Cdr Thomsen) attacks an escort carrier group and two convoys. *U399* (Lt Buhse) sinks two ships of 7546 tons from convoys; *U315* (Lt Zoller) one ship of 6996 tons from the convoy TBC.103; and *U1195* (Lt-Cdr Cordes) one ship of 7176 tons from a convoy on 21 Mar (torpedoed but a total loss). *U1002* and *U953* operate without success in, and W of, the Channel. Support groups are deployed against these U-boats: the 3rd EG with its leader, the DE *Duckworth*, sinks *U399* and *U246* (Lt-Cdr Raabe), after the latter has torpedoed the frigate *Teme* from a Canadian search group which is with convoy BTC.111. On 6 Apl *U1195* attacks the convoy VWP.16 in the Channel and sinks the troop transport *Cuba* (11420 tons) but is herself sunk by the escorting destroyer *Watchman*.

Off Iceland *U773* cruises without success. *U1064* is temporarily employed as a weather boat.

On the Canadian Atlantic coast *U866* (Lt Rogowski) repeatedly attacks convoys. Directed to the HF/DF bearings of the boat, the US DEs *Lowe*, *Pride*, *Menges* and *Mosley* sink her. The Canadian 16th EG does not come up in time.

7 Mar-15 Apl   Baltic

On 7 Mar the Soviet 2nd White Russian Front launches an attack from the Köslin-Vistula line near Marienwerder on the area Gotenhafen-Danzig. The German 2nd Army is thrown back to the line Rixhöft-Neustadt-Karthaus, where it is temporarily able to stabilize the front with support from naval guns and so gain valuable time to evacuate refugees. From 10 Mar the cruiser *Prinz*

Eugen (Capt Reinicke) takes part in the operation and from 15 Mar the old battleship *Schlesien* (Capt H.-E. Busch) and the SATs *Soemba*, *Joost* and *Ostsee* and the gunnery training vessel *Drache*. On 21 Mar the *Schlesien* has to withdraw because of lack of ammunition. But her place is taken on 23 Mar by the cruiser *Lützow* (Capt Knoke) with *Z31* and *Z34*. From 25 Mar the cruiser *Leipzig* (Cdr Bach), which has had orders to be made seaworthy, also takes part in the shelling of land targets.

The Soviet naval air force, in particular the 9th Ground Attack Div (Lt-Col Slepenko) and the 8th Mining and Torpedo Div (Col Kurochkin), flies 2023 sorties against embarkation operations in Danzig, Gotenhafen and off Hela. Destroyers, torpedo boats, minesweepers and small auxiliary warships form an AA barrage to protect the transports but on 12 Mar the transport *Gerrit Fritzen* (1761 tons), *M3137* and *UJ303* are sunk and on 18 Mar the transport *Orion* (1722 tons) near Scholpin; the *Ellen* (565 tons) is damaged, as is the *Lisa Essberger* (1172 tons) in the roads of Gotenhafen on 19 Mar. On 22 Mar the *Frankfurt* (1186 tons) sinks and on 26 Mar the *Bille* (665 tons) and *Weser* (999 tons). But before the fall of Gotenhafen on 28 Mar and of Danzig on 30 Mar several large transports and numerous smaller ships are still able to proceed to the W crowded with refugees. For instance, on 23 Mar the *Deutschland* has 11145 persons on board and on 28 Mar 11295 and the *Potsdam* over 9000. Losses are caused by a mine barrage laid off Hela on 8 Mar by the Soviet submarine *L-21* (Capt 3rd Class Mogilevski with the Div Cdr (Capt 1st Class Orel, on board). On 14 Mar the torpedo boats *T3* (Lt-Cdr v. Diest†) and *T5* (Lt Wätjen) sink on this and, later, probably *U367*; on 9 Apl *Z43* is damaged. But mine barrages laid by *Lembit* and *L-3* apparently have no success. In the area of the Stolpe Bank the Soviet submarine *K-53* (Capt 3rd Class Yaroshevich) sinks the freighter *Margarethe Cords* (1912 tons) on 17 Mar. *L-21* sinks the patrol boat *V2022* on 22 Mar and the tug *Erni*; after unsuccessful attacks, she is hunted off Kolberg in the next few days by *F8*, *TS4* and *TS3*.

In Gotenhafen on 27 Mar, before the evacuation, the non-operational wreck of the battleship *Gneisenau* is sunk as a block ship. In the night 4-5 Apl the rest of the VII Armoured Corps, comprising 8000 troops, and about 30000 refugees from the Oxhöfter Kämpe bridgehead is brought to Hela in 25 KFKs, 27 MFPs, five SATs and five other ships in the operation 'Walpurgisnacht'. The operations and the embarkations off Hela are covered in the following days by the cruiser *Lützow*, the destroyers *Z38*, *Z31* and *Paul Jacobi*, the torpedo boat *T36* and the SATs *Ostsee*, *Soemba* and *Robert Müller 6* etc. Among the transports proceeding to the W are the *Pretoria* (7000 refugees), *Deutschland* (10000), *Cap Arkona* (9000) and *Eberhart Essberger* (4750). By 10 Apl 157270 wounded have been evacuated from Hela alone since 21 Mar, while from the still-unoccupied ports in the Gulf of Danzig, Pillau, Kahlberg, Schiewenhorst and Oxhöft, 264887 people are evacuated to Hela in small craft and naval ferry barges in April.

From 7 Apl to 13 Apl a sharp increase in Soviet air operations against the embarkations is apparent. In the process the transport *Flensburg* (5450 tons), the supply ship *Franken* (10850 tons), which, together with her sister ship *Dithmarschen*, has replenished the units of the fleet, the aircraft repair ship *Hans Albrecht Wedel*, *UJ301*, the transports *Albert Jensen* (5446 tons), *Moltkefels* (7862 tons), *Wiegand* (5869 tons), *Karlsruhe* (897 tons), the hospital ship *Posen* (1069 tons) and the minesweeper *TS10*, *UJ1102* and *R69* are lost.

From 9 Apl Soviet torpedo cutters are transferred to Neufahrwasser and from 10 Apl are reported to have made 10 sorties. On 10 Apl the freighter *Neuwerk* (804 tons) is sunk.

The embarkations off Hela continue under the AA cover of the warships but on 8 Apl, because of lack of fuel and ammunition, the cruiser *Lützow* with *Z38* and *Z31* (damaged by bomb hits) are withdrawn; and on 10 Apl *Z39* and *T33* have to bring *Z43*, damaged by mines and bombs, to the west. For AA defence *Z34*, *Paul Jacobi*, *T33*, *M37*, *M391*, *M203* and the SATs *Soemba*, *Ostsee*, *Nienburg*, *Robert Müller 6* and

AF21 remain behind. On 15 Apl the destroyers *Z34, Paul Jacobi, Z39,* the torpedo boats *T23, T28, T33, T36* and minesweepers withdraw with a convoy that consists of the steamers *Matthias Stinnes, Eberhart Essberger, Pretoria* and *Askari* with about 20000 refugees. *Z34* (Cdr Hetz), which returns, is torpedoed by two Soviet TKAs under Lt Korotkevich and Lt-Cdr Solodovnikov: *T36* and *M204* bring the ship to Swinemünde.

8-9 Mar   English Channel
Four minesweepers of the 24th MS Flotilla (Lt-Cdr Mohr) carry out a raid on the harbour of Granville with three gun carriers and six smaller vessels from the Channel Islands. The US patrol boat *PC564* is overwhelmed. Assault troops are landed: they blow up harbour installations and four freighters of 3612 tons, liberate 67 German prisoners and capture a small collier. *M412* runs aground in shallow water and has to be blown up.

10 Mar   South West Pacific
Operation 'Victor IV': US Amphibious Group (Rear-Adm Royal, TG 78.1), with the headquarters ship *Rocky Mount,* lands the bulk of the 41st Inf Div (Maj-Gen Doe) near Zamboanga (south-west tip of Mindanao, the Philippines). The transport group comprises four APDs, one LSD, 23 LSTs, 21 LSMs, 32 LCIs and 17 support LCIs, two PCs and two SCs. The minesweeping group comprises 11 YMSs with the Australian sloop *Warrego.* Escort: the destroyers (Desron 22) *Waller, Saufley, Philip, Sigourney, Robinson, McCalla, Bancroft* and *Bailey,* the DEs *Rudderow* and *Chaffee.* Preparatory bombardment and fire support is provided by TG 74.3 (Rear-Adm Berkey), comprising the cruisers *Phoenix* and *Boise,* the destroyers (Desron 21) *Fletcher, Nicholas, Taylor, Jenkins* and *Abbot.* Air support is provided by elements of the 5th USAAF (Maj-Gen Whitehead) and the 13th USAAF (Brig-Gen Wurtsmith).
Elements of these units land on the Basilan Islands on 16 Mar, on Tawi-Tawi on 2 Apl and on Jolo on 9 Apl. The midget submarines *Ha-79, 84* and *78* miss with their torpedoes.

11-12 Mar   Air War/Germany
B 24s of the 8th USAAF drop 709 tons of bombs on Kiel on 11 Mar. In the harbour the minesweepers *M266, M804* and *M805* and a small tanker are sunk. B 17s of the same formation drop 861 tons of bombs on Bremen.
In Hamburg American bombers sink *U2515, U2530* and six merchant ships totalling 17201 tons.
B 17s and B 24s of the 8th USAAF drop 1435 tons of bombs on Swinemünde on 12 Mar. In the harbour and in the Burmeister yards the (in some cases uncompleted) motor minesweepers *R243, R272, R273, R274, R275* and *R276,* 20 KFKs (*KFK 677, 679, 680, 683-699*), the passenger ship *Cordillera* (12655 tons), the patrol boat *V2003,* four freighters and one tug are destroyed.

11-21 Mar   Arctic
Operation against convoy JW.65 in the Arctic.
On 11 Mar the convoy sets out from the Clyde with 24 merchant ships. Escort: the escort carriers *Campania* (Vice-Adm Dalrymple - Hamilton) and *Trumpeter,* the cruiser *Diadem* and 19 destroyers, sloops, frigates and corvettes. On 13 Mar the 'B' Service learns of its departure. *U307, U312, U363, U968, U716* and *U997* are stationed in the Bear Island Passage as the 'Hagen' group and *U995* off the Kola Inlet. Later, *U711* joins 'Hagen' and *U313* and *U992* proceed to the Kola Inlet. Air reconnaissance from 14 Mar to 17 Mar produces no results. From 17 Mar all the U-boats are moved to the entrance to the Kola Inlet and are stationed in two lines of six and seven boats. At 0900 hrs on 20 Mar the convoy passes through the first line in a snowstorm. *U995* (Lt Hess) (having sunk the Soviet submarine-chaser *BO-223* on 3 Mar) torpedoes the steamer *Horace Bushnell* (7176 tons)—a total loss. When the second line is passed at mid-day, *U716* (Lt Thimme) sinks the sloop *Lapwing* and in attacks by *U313* (Lt-Cdr Schweiger) and *U968* (Lt Westphalen) the latter sinks the steamer *Thomas Donaldson* (7217 tons). An attempt, after the convoy has come in, to operate with the U-boats against the carriers, suspected to be in the Barents Sea, fails.

14-23 Mar   Central Pacific
US TF 58 (Vice-Adm Mitscher) makes

a raid on Japan. On 14 Mar TF 58 sets out from Ulithi (on 11 Mar the carrier *Randolph* was damaged by a Kamikaze in Ulithi).

TG 58.1 (Rear-Adm Clark) comprises the carriers *Hornet, Wasp, Bennington, Belleau Wood* and *San Jacinto*, the battleships *Massachusetts* and *Indiana*, the cruisers *Baltimore, Pittsburgh, Vincennes, Miami, Vicksburgh* and *San Juan* and the destroyers (Desron 61) *De Haven, Mansfield, Lyman K. Swenson, Collett, Maddox, Blue, Brush, Taussig, Samuel N. Moore*, (Desdiv 106) *Wedderburn, Twining, Stockham* (Desron 25) *John Rodgers, Harrison, McKee, Murray, Sigsbee, Ringgold, Schroeder* and *Dashiell*.

TG 58.2 (Rear-Adm Davison) comprises the carriers *Enterprise* and *Franklin*, the cruiser *Santa Fé*, the destroyers (Desron 52) *Owen, Miller, Stephen Potter, Tingey, Hickox, Hunt, Lewis Hancock* and *Marshall*.

TG 58.3 (Rear-Adm Sherman) comprises the carriers *Essex, Bunker Hill, Hancock, Cabot* and *Bataan*, the battleships *Washington, North Carolina* and *South Dakota* (Vice-Adm Lee), the cruisers *Indianapolis* (Adm Spruance, 5th Fleet), *Pasadena, Springfield, Astoria* and *Wilkes-Barre*, the destroyers (Desron 62) *Ault, English, Charles S. Sperry, Waldron, Haynsworth, Wallace L. Lind, John W. Weeks, Hank, Borie,* (Desron 48) *Erben, Walker, Hale, Stembel, Black, Bullard, Kidd* and *Chauncey*.

TG 58.4 (Rear-Adm Radford) comprises the carriers *Yorktown, Intrepid, Langley* and *Independence*, the battleships *Wisconsin, Missouri* and *New Jersey*, the battlecruisers *Alaska* and *Guam*, the cruisers *St Louis, Flint, Oakland* and *San Diego*, the destroyers (Desron 54) *Remey, Norman Scott, Mertz, Monssen, McGowan, McNair, Melvin,* (Desron 47) *McCord, Trathen, Hazelwood, Heerman, Haggard, Franks, Hailey,* (Desdiv 105) *Cushing, Colahan, Uhlmann* and *Benham*.

After refuelling on 16 Mar a strong attack is made early on 18 Mar by the carrier groups on Kyushu, largely concentrating on airfields. Under the command of the Japanese 5th Air Fleet (Vice-Adm Ugaki) 48 Kamikaze aircraft set off for the US carrier groups. Eighteen do not find their targets and return. The main attack is directed against TG 58.4. The *Intrepid* is set on fire by a Kamikaze which crashes near the ship, but she is able to extinguish the fire. The *Yorktown* and *Enterprise* are slightly damaged but all three continue the operations.

On 19 Mar the carrier attacks are concentrated on the Japanese bases in the Inland Sea, especially Kure. There the Japanese carriers *Amagi, Katsuragi, Ryuho, Hosho* and *Kaiyo* and the new *Ikoma*, the battleships *Yamato, Hyuga* and *Haruna*, the cruisers *Tone* and *Oyodo* and the new submarines *I-400, I-205* and *Ro-67* are damaged. A Japanese bomber formation of the 5th Air Fleet obtains a hit on the *Wasp*, which is set on fire, and has 101 dead and 269 injured but which gets the fire under control after 15 minutes, and two hits on the *Franklin*, which is set on fire and suffers heavy damage as the result of bomb and ammunition explosions and has 724 dead and 265 injured. 1700 survivors are rescued by the cruisers *Santa Fé* and *Pittsburgh*. Capt Gehres is able to get the very badly damaged ship under control again and, later, to bring her into the dockyard under her own steam. Thirty-nine Kamikaze pilots (of whom 20 return) achieve lesser damage on the *Enterprise*. The *Essex* is damaged by her own AA fire. On 20 Mar the destroyers are replenished. During this there is an attack by 20 Japanese Kamikaze bombers, one of which just misses the *Hancock* and hits the destroyer *Halsey Powell*. Another damages the lifeguard submarine *Devilfish*. On 21 Mar Japanese reconnaissance aircraft maintain contact with TF 58: 18 twin-engine bombers with 'Oka' bombs (manned rocket bombs, called 'Baka' by the Americans) and 55 Kamikazes (45 of which return) with 15 escort fighters (three of which return) set off. The bomber force is located and intercepted by 150 fighters which shoot all of them down with the exception of one aircraft.

On 22 Mar TF 58 proceeds to the tanker group and is refuelled. In the process, the Task Groups, as a result of the losses, are distributed in three new groups:

TG 58.1 comprises the *Hornet, Bennington, Belleau Wood, San Jacinto, Massachusetts, Indiana, Vincennes, Miami, Vicksburgh* and *San Juan.*

TG 58.3 comprises the *Essex, Bunker Hill, Hancock* (later *Shangri La*), *Bataan, South Dakota, New Jersey, Pasadena, Springfield, Astoria* and *Wilkes-Barre.*

TG 58.4 comprises the *Yorktown, Intrepid, Enterprise, Langley, Wisconsin, Missouri, Alaska, Guam,* and *San Diego.*

The damaged *Wasp* and *Franklin* are accompanied to Ulithi by the *Independence, Washington, North Carolina, Baltimore, Pittsburgh, Santa Fé, Flint* and *Oakland.*

15 Mar   North Pacific
A US Task Group (Rear-Adm McCrea), consisting of Crudiv 1 and seven destroyers, shells Matsuwa (Kuriles).

17-26 Mar   North Sea
German motor torpedo boat flotillas operate off the British East Coast and the Scheldt. In the night 17-18 Mar the 2nd Flotilla carries out a mining operation off Smith's Knoll. A torpedo operation by the 6th and 9th Flotillas off Margate has to be broken off owing to fog.

In the night 18-19 Mar the 6th Flotilla (Lt-Cdr Matzen) lays mines on the East Coast and attacks the British convoy FS.1759 off Lowestoft. The motor torpedo boats report seven hits and sink the freighters *Crichtoun* (1097 tons) and *Rogate* (2871 tons). The 2nd, 4th, 6th and 9th Flotillas operate with mines and torpedoes on the Thames-Scheldt route. The mining operation is successful. *LST 80,* the freighters *Samselbu* (7253 tons), *Empire Blessing* (7062 tons) and one trawler sink; and the Liberty ship *Hadley F. Brown* (7176 tons) is damaged. The 8th Flotilla is temporarily out of action following an air attack on its base at Ijmuiden on 14 Mar.

On 21-22 Mar the 2nd and 5th Flotillas make a sortie against traffic between the Thames and the Scheldt. Engine trouble on *S210* necessitates the breaking-off of the operation. On the return *S181* is sunk NW of Texel by British Mosquito bombers and the 2nd Flotilla commander, Cdr Opdenhoff†, perishes. Seven boats are damaged.

On 22-23 Mar the 6th and 4th Flotillas lay mines on the Thames-Scheldt traffic route. On 25-26 Mar the operation is repeated by the 4th, 9th and 6th Flotillas, but only the 9th Flotilla lays its mines. The 4th and 6th Flotillas are driven off by the destroyers *Arendal* (Norwegian), *Krakowiak* (Polish) and the DE *Riou.* During these operations the following are lost on the mines: the freighters *Eleftheria* (7247 tons), *Charles D. McIver* (7176 tons), one trawler and two small warships, *ML 466* and *LCP 840.*

The 5th and 8th Flotillas are transferred to the Baltic and Norway.

18 Mar   Mediterranean/Ligurian Sea
The 10th TB Flotilla (Cdr Burkart) carries out an offensive mining operation in the Ligurian Sea with *TA 24, TA 29* and *TA 32.* NW of Corsica there is an engagement with the British destroyers *Meteor* and *Lookout. TA 24* and *TA 29* are sunk. The British destroyers rescue 108 survivors, including the flotilla commander.

18-29 Mar   South West Pacific
Operation 'Victor I': US Amphibious Group 9 (Rear-Adm Struble, TG 74.3), with the headquarters ship US Coastguard cutter *Ingham,* lands 14000 men of the 40th Inf Div (Maj-Gen Brush) by 22 Mar on the south coast of Panay. The transport group consists of 16 LSTs, 20 LSMs, 13 LCIs and eight support LCIs. The minesweeping group comprises YMSs with the Australian sloop *Warrego.* Escort: the destroyers (Desron 23) *Charles Ausburne, Thatcher, Claxton, Converse* and *Dyson.* Fire support is provided by TG 74.2 (Rear-Adm Riggs) with the cruiser *Cleveland* and the destroyers (Desdiv 44) *Conway, Stevens* and *Eaton.*

On 29 Mar forces of the 185th RCT, which have been standing by, land on the north-west coast of Negros. On 8 Apl the 503rd Parachute RCT follows.

18 Mar-1 May   Baltic/Courland
On 18 Mar the Soviet armies begin their sixth major offensive against the Army Group Courland. This, like the previous ones, has to be broken off after about 10 days.

On 26-27 Mar Soviet torpedo bombers attack a convoy off Libau and sink the small tanker *Sassnitz*, as well as *R145* and *R260*. Eight fighters of the German J.G.54 then drive off the aircraft, allowing the remaining motor minesweepers to retire. On the scene of the accident, three motor torpedo boats of the German 5th MTB Flotilla (Lt-Cdr Holzapfel) surprise a group of nine Soviet torpedo cutters in the following night and in fierce engagements *TKA-166*, *TKA-181* and *TKA-199* are destroyed and 15 prisoners are taken including the Commander of the Russian 2nd TKA Div.

In April the Russian submarine *Shch-310* (Capt 3rd Class Bogorad) is among those to operate off Libau: on 10 Apl she sinks the freighter *Ilmenau* (1201 tons) and on 16 Apl, probably, the *Cap Guir* (1536 tons). *L-3* (Capt 3rd Class Konovalov) claims to have sunk one ship on 1 May (unclarified). The German freighter *Huelva* (1923 tons) is lost on 24 Apl as a result of air attack.

19-26 Mar   Indian Ocean
Destroyer raids by the British Eastern Fleet in the area of the Andamans. In a coastal shelling on 19 Mar the destroyer *Rapid* is hit by a Japanese battery.

On 26 Mar a destroyer division of four ships attacks a Japanese convoy comprising two steamers and the submarine-chasers *Ch 63* and *Ch 34*. The first salvo of ten torpedoes misses. Then a Liberator bomber sinks one of the steamers and in a second approach the destroyers sink the second submarine-chaser with 16 torpedoes, one of which hits, and the two remaining ships with gunfire.

19-29 Mar   East Prussia
From 19 Mar to 25 Mar the Soviet 3rd White Russian front compresses the pocket of the German 4th Army S of Königsberg on the Frisches Haff. These troops have been supplied by ferry barges across the Haff since January. Now 11365 wounded, 324 troops and 14520 refugees from among them are evacuated to Pillau; and, in the last night, on 25 Mar, as many as 5830 troops and 2830 wounded are evacuated.

Because of the situation near Danzig/ Gotenhafen the embarkations at Pillau are considerably interrupted from 8 Mar to 28 Mar and in air attacks individual ships are lost, for example, the *Meteor* (3717 tons) on 9 Mar and the *Jersbek* (2804 tons) on 30 Mar.

19 Mar-12 Apl   Norway
In Allied submarine operations off Norway the British *Venturer* (Lt Launders) sinks the freighter *Sirius* (998 tons) off Namsos on 19 Mar, the Norwegian *Utsira* (Lt-Cdr Valvatne) the freighter *Torridal* (1501 tons) off Follafjord on 5 Apl and the British *Tapir* (Lt-Cdr Roxburgh) the outward-bound *U486* on 12 Apl.

20 Mar   Air War/Germany
B 17s of the 8th USAAF drop 777 tons of bombs on Hamburg.

In an attack on Bremen on 21 Mar the destroyer *Z51*, which is being fitted out, sinks.

23-31 Mar   Central Pacific
Preparatory phase of the landing on Okinawa.

On 23 Mar TF 58 (for composition see 14 Mar) increases the air attacks with all three Task Groups in preparation for the landings. The attacks are continued on 24 Mar and 25 Mar.

On 24 Mar TG 58.1, in 112 sorties, makes an attack on a convoy sighted S of Kyushu, all of whose eight ships are destroyed. The battleships *New Jersey*, *Wisconsin* and *Missouri* (Rear-Adm Denfeld) with five destroyers and the *Massachusetts* and *Indiana* (Vice-Adm Lee) with six destroyers shell Okinawa on 24 Mar.

On 27-28 Mar TF 58 replenishes, in the course of which the destroyer *Murray* is damaged by a single Japanese aircraft. On 29 Mar TG 58.4 again attacks Okinawa and TGs 58.3 and 58.1 attack the northern Ryukyu islands and Kyushu. On 30-31 Mar TG 58.1 replenishes, while TGs 58.3 and 58.4 make further attacks on the Okinawa area and to the N of it.

The British Pacific Fleet (Vice-Adm Rawlings), which sets out from Ulithi on 23 Mar, replenishes on 25 Mar and, as TF 57 (Vice-Adm Vian), attacks on 26 Mar and 27 Mar the Sakishima-Gunto group of islands of the southern Ryukyus in order to neutralize the airfields there. The British Task Force consists of the carriers *Indomitable, Victorious, Illustrious* and *Indefatigable,* the battleships *King George V* and *Howe,* the cruisers *Swiftsure, Gambia* (RNZN), *Black Prince, Argonaut* and *Euryalus,* the destroyers *Grenville, Ulster, Undine, Urania, Undaunted, Quickmatch, Quiberon, Queenborough, Kempenfelt, Whirlwind* and *Wager.* From 28 Mar to 30 Mar TF 57 replenishes from a supply group consisting of the escort carriers *Striker* and *Speaker,* the sloops *Crane* and *Pheasant,* the frigate *Findhorn,* three tankers and the destroyers *Quality* and *Whelp* which relieve the *Kempenfelt* and *Whirlwind.* On 31 Mar the attacks to neutralize Sakishima-Gunto are resumed.

From 24-25 Mar the units of TF 52 (Rear-Adm Blandy) and of TF 54 (Rear-Adm Deyo) arrive off Okinawa. Three escort carrier groups (TG 52.1 Rear-Adm Durgin) support the air attacks made by TFs 58 and 57 and take over their roles when they are being replenished. There take part:

Group 1 (Rear-Adm Durgin), comprising the escort carriers *Makin Island, Fanshaw Bay, Lunga Point, Sangamon, Natoma Bay, Savo Island* and *Anzio,* the destroyers (Desdiv 120) *Ingraham, Hart, Boyd, Bradford, Patterson* and *Bagley* and the DEs *Lawrence C. Taylor, Melvin R. Newman, Oliver Mitchell, Robert F. Keller, Tabberer, Richard M. Rowell, Richard S. Bull, Dennis, Sederstrom, Fleming* and *O'Flaherty.*

Group 2 (Rear-Adm Stump), comprising the escort carriers *Saginaw Bay, Sargent Bay, Marcus Island, Petrof Bay, Tulagi* and *Wake Island,* the destroyers (Desdiv 91) *Capps, Lowry, Evans* and *John D. Henley* and the DEs *William Seiverling, Ulvert M. Moore, Kendall C. Campbell, Goss, Tisdale* and *Eisele.*

Group 3 (Rear-Adm Sample), comprising the escort carriers *Suwanee, Chenango, Santee* and *Steamer Bay,* the destroyers (Desron 58) *Metcalf, Drexler, Fullam, Guest* and *Helm* and the DEs *Edmonds* and *John C. Butler.*

On 24 Mar the minesweeping group (TG 52.2, Rear-Adm Sharp on the minelayer *Terror*) begins the work of sweeping with three groups of fast minesweepers, consisting of *Forrest,*

Hobson, Macomb, Dorsey, Hopkins; Ellyson, Hambleton, Rodman, Emmons; Butler, Gherardi, Jeffers, Harding; seven groups of 36 fleet minesweepers and four groups each of six YMSs. Each has one fast minelayer allocated for temporary support from the following: *Gwin, Lindsey, Aaron Ward, Adams, Tolman, Henry A. Wiley, Shea, Tracy, J. William Ditter, Robert H. Smith, Shannon, Thomas E. Fraser, Henry F. Bauer* and *Breese.*

On 25 Mar the UDTs arrive on 10 APDs and begin clearing the assault beaches of underwater obstacles. The cruisers *San Francisco* and *Minneapolis* and three destroyers shell the assault areas on Kerama Retto on 25 Mar and, supported by the battleship *Arkansas,* before the assault on 26 Mar. On 26 Mar the 'Western Islands Attack Group' (TG 51.1, Rear-Adm Kiland), with headquarters ship *Mount McKinley,* lands the 77th Inf Div (Maj-Gen Bruce) on Kerama Retto against slight resistance. The transport squadron consists of 13 APAs, six AKAs, 28 LSTs, 11 LSMs and eight support vessels. Escort (Capt Moosbrugger): the headquarters ship *Biscayne,* the destroyers (Desron 49) *Picking, Sproston, Wickes, William D. Porter, Isherwood, Kimberly, Luce, Charles J. Badger* and the DEs *Scribner, Kinzer, Richard W. Suesens, Abercrombie, Oberrender, Riddle, Swearer* and *Stern.*

On 26 Mar the 'Fire Support Group' (TF 54, Rear-Adm Deyo) begins the shelling of Okinawa. Group 1 comprises the battleships *Texas* and *Maryland,* the cruiser *Tuscaloosa* and the destroyers (Desdiv 110) *Laws, Longshaw, Morrison* and *Prichett*; Group 2 comprises the battleships *Arkansas* and *Colorado,* the cruisers *San Francisco* and *Minneapolis,* the destroyers (Desdiv 51) *Hall, Halligan, Paul Hamilton, Laffey* and *Twiggs*; Group 3 comprises the battleships *Tennessee* and *Nevada,* the cruisers *Wichita* and *Birmingham,* the destroyers (Desron 60) *Mannert L. Abele, Zellars, Bryant, Barton* and *O'Brien*; Group 4 comprises the battleships *Idaho* and *West Virginia,* the cruisers *Pensacola, Portland* and *Biloxi,* the destroyers (Desron 55) *Porterfield, Callaghan, Irwin, Cassin Young* and

Preston; Group 5 comprises the battleships *New Mexico* and *New York*, the cruisers *Indianapolis* (Adm Spruance, 5th Fleet) and *Salt Lake City*, the destroyers (Desron 56) *Newcomb, Heywood L. Edwards, Leutze, Richard P. Leary* and *Bennion*; and Group 6 comprises the DEs *Samuel S. Miles, Wesson, Foreman, Whitehurst, England, Witter, Bowers* and *Willmarth*. There are also 53 support landing craft with rocket-throwers.

Japanese counter action: once the enemy's intention to attack Okinawa is recognized, the submarines *I-8, Ro-41, Ro-49* and *Ro-56* are deployed to attack with torpedoes. *Ro-41* encounters TG 58.4 on 22 Mar and is sunk by the destroyer *Haggard* on 23 Mar. *Ro-49* (Lt-Cdr Go) misses the cruisers *Wichita* and *St Louis* on 25 Mar and *Ro-56* the *Pensacola* on 27 Mar. *I-8* is detected by aircraft on 30 Mar and sunk by the destroyers *Morrison* and *Stockton*. On 25 Mar the operation 'Tengo' (the defence of Okinawa and South Japan) is put into force by Japanese Imperial Headquarters. The air formations of the 3rd and 10th Naval Air Fleets are put under the operational command of the 5th Air Fleet (Vice-Adm Ugaki) which operates from Kyushu. The remains of the 1st Air Fleet operate from Formosa. At dawn on 25 Mar the first Kamikaze attack is made with 25 aircraft (three return): the destroyer *Kimberly*, the minelayer *Robert H. Smith*, the fast transports *Gilmer* and *Knudsen* (bomb hits) are damaged. On the evening of 26 Mar eleven Kamikazes attack. Hits are obtained on the battleship *Nevada*, the cruiser *Biloxi*, the destroyers *O'Brien, Porterfield* and *Callaghan*, the DE *Foreman* and the minesweeper *Skirmish*. The destroyer *Halligan* is beached after hitting a mine. With TG 58.1 the destroyer *Murray* is hit with bombs from dive-bombers. On 27 Mar TF 54 continues the shelling. There is an attack by 15 Kamikazes: the minelayer *Adams* and the minesweeper *Southard* are damaged. On 27 Mar there is an unsuccessful attempt by explosive boats to approach TF 51 off Kerama Retto. On 28 Mar there is renewed shelling: the minesweeper *Skylark* is

sunk while searching for mines. The AKA *Wyandot* is damaged by bomb hits. In the night 28-29 Mar there are individual attacks by aircraft from Okinawa: *LSM(R) 188* is badly hit. As a result, airfields are shelled on 29 Mar and TF 52 makes attacks on airfields and bases for explosive boats and midget submarines. On 30 Mar, after further shelling of Okinawa, there is an attack by four Kamikazes in the evening: the flagship of the 5th Fleet, *Indianapolis*, is hit. Adm Spruance transfers to the battleship *New Mexico*. On 31 Mar there are Kamikaze attacks in which the minelayer *Adams*, the APA *Hinsdale* and *LST 724* and *LST 884* are hit.

23-31 Mar   Arctic
Operation against convoy RA.65 in the Arctic.

On 23 Mar the convoy of 25 merchant ships, with the escort of JW.65, sets out from the Kola Inlet. Some of the U-boats have only just again concentrated off the Inlet. *U313* and *U968* respectively hear and sight the convoy and the escort carriers but are not able to attack. An attempt to put a patrol line in front of the convoy with the U-boats *U307, U310, U313, U363, U668, U711, U716, U968* and *U992* produces no results on 25 Mar. Attempts by the Luftwaffe up to 27 Mar to establish contact with the convoy so as to be able to launch an air torpedo attack fail and the operation is abandoned. The convoy arrives on 31 Mar in Scapa Flow.

On 22 Mar and 31 Mar *U711* (Lt-Cdr Lange) and *U312* (Lt v. Gaza) each torpedo one armed trawler on the Kola Coast.

26 Mar-26 Apl   South West Pacific
Operation 'Victor II': US Amphibious Group 8 (Capt A. T. Sprague, TG 78.2), with headquarters ship US Coastguard cutter *Spencer*, lands 14000 men of the Americal Div (Maj-Gen Arnold) near Cebu (Philippines). The transport group consists of four APDs, 20 LSTs, 11 LSMs, 15 LCIs, nine support LCIs and two PCs. The mine-sweeping group comprises eight YMSs. Escort: the destroyers (Desron 5) *Flusser, Shaw, Conyngham, Smith* and *Drayton*. Fire support is provided by

P

TG 74.3 (Rear-Adm Berkey) comprising the cruisers *Phoenix*, *Boise* and *Hobart* (Australian) and the destroyers (Desron 21) *Fletcher*, *Nicholas*, *Taylor*, *Jenkins* and *Abbot*. Air support is provided by the 13th USAAF (Maj-Gen Wurtsmith).
Elements of these forces land a battalion of the 164th Regt on Bohol on 11 Apl and the 164th RCT near Sibulan in SE Negros on 26 Apl.
On 1 Apl another transport division of VII Amphibious Force (Capt McGee), consisting of the destroyers *Bailey* and *Bancroft*, the DEs *Day* and *Holt*, three APDs, nine LCIs, five LSTs and four LSMs, lands the US 158th RCT on Legaspi (South Luzon). On 2 Apl one BLT of the 163rd RCT is landed on the Sulu Archipelago by another group of VII Amphibious Force (Capt Murphy).

27-28 Mar   Japan
B 29s of the 21st Bomber Command begin mining Japanese home waters.

30 Mar   Air War/Germany
B 24s of the 8th USAAF drop 916 tons of bombs on the harbour installations of Wilhelmshaven: the cruiser *Köln*, the U-boats *U96*, *U429* and *U3508*, the escort vessel *F6*, the motor torpedo boat *S186*, the minesweepers *M329* and *M3430*, the U-boat tender *Weichsel*, two tugs and four freighters totalling 11259 tons are sunk.
B 17s of the 8th USAAF drop 1103 tons of bombs on Hamburg and 830 tons on Bremen. In Hamburg *U350*, *U348*, *U1167* and *U2340* are sunk and in Bremen *U72*, *U329*, *U430*, *U870*, *U884*, *U886* and *U3045*.

1-5 Apl   Central Pacific
Operation 'Iceberg': TF 51 (Vice-Adm Turner) with a total of 1213 ships, including 603 landing craft, lands the 10th US Army (Lt-Gen Buckner) on Okinawa. 451866 men, including three reserve divisions, are embarked. The assault areas are previously shelled intensively by TF 54 (see 23 Mar) and continually bombarded by TF 58 (see 14 Mar) and TF 52 (see 23 Mar).
The Northern Attack Force (TF 53, Rear-Adm Reifsnider), with the headquarters ship *Panamint*, lands the III Amphibious Corps (Maj-Gen Geiger) of which TF 53.1 (Commodore Knowles) brings the 6th Marine Div (Maj-Gen

Shepherd) on 16 APAs, six AKAs, one LSD and the LSV *Catskill* and TG 53.2 (Commodore Moyer) the 1st Marine Div (Maj-Gen del Valle) on 15 APAs, six AKAs, two LSDs and the LSV *Monitor*. Also divided among both divisions are 46 LSTs, five LSMs and 16 LCTs, as well as 18 leader vessels (PCSs, PCs and SCs). Escort: TG 53.6 with the destroyers (Desdiv 4) *Morris*, *Mustin*, *Lang*, *Stack*, *Sterett*, (Desdiv 90) *Pringle*, *Hutchins*, *Massey*, *Russell*, *Wilson*, *Stanly*, *Howorth*, *Hugh W. Hadley* and the DEs *Gendreau*, *Fieberling*, *William C. Cole*, *Paul G. Baker*, *Bebas*, two APDs, two PCEs and one SC.
The Southern Attack Force (TF 55, Rear-Adm Hall), with the headquarters ship *Teton*, lands XXIV Corps (Maj-Gen Hodge), of which TG 55.1 (Commodore Carlson) brings the 7th Inf Div (Maj-Gen Arnold) on 16 APAs, seven AKAs, one LSD and the LSV *Ozark* and, in addition, 30 LSTs, 22 LSMs and two LCIs, and TG 55.2 (Commodore Richardson) the 96th Inf Div (Maj-Gen Bradley) on 16 APAs, six AKAs, two LSDs, 23 LSTs, five LSMs, one LCI and six support LCSs. Nineteen leader vessels and 17 more support landing craft are allocated. Escort; TG 55.6 with the destroyers (Desdiv 48) *Anthony*, *Bache*, *Bush*, (Desron 45) *Bennett*, *Hudson*, *Hyman*, *Purdy*, *Beale*, *Wadsworth*, *Ammen*, (Desron 66) *Putnam* and *Rooks* and the DEs *Crouter*, *Carlson*, *Damon M. Cummings*, *Vammen*, *O'Neill*, *Walter C. Wann*, one APD, one PCE and two SCs.
The landing goes according to plan against, initially, slight resistance, because the Japanese 32nd Army (Lt-Gen Ushijima) is firmly entrenched in the southern mountain terrain and has made preparations for long-drawn-out fighting. The troops on shore are daily supported by battleships, cruisers and destroyers of TF 54, by aircraft of the escort carriers of TF 52 (564 aircraft to begin with) and on TF 58 from which two groups are continually in the operational area while the third is being replenished.
British TF 57 carries out daily neutralization raids on the Sakishima-Gunto

island group from 31 Mar to 2 Apl. While it is being replenished on 3 Apl, 4 Apl and 5 Apl, it is relieved by the Escort Carrier Group of Rear-Adm Sample (see 23 Mar).

On the evening of 1 Jan there are Kamikaze and Oka bomb attacks on the landing fleet and the support force. The battleship *West Virginia* and the transports *Alpine, Achernar* and *Tyrrell* are hit; and the destroyer *Prichett*, the minesweeper *Skirmish* and the transport *Elmore* are damaged by bombs from dive bombers and high-level bombers and the DE *Vammen* on a mine. The British carrier *Indomitable* and the destroyer *Ulster* are hit in Kamikaze attacks by the Japanese 1st Air Fleet. The latter is towed to Leyte by the cruiser *Gambia*.

On the evening of 2 Apl there is a Kamikaze attack (14 machines) on the transports with the re-embarked 77th Inf Div; the APAs *Chilton, Henrico, Goodhue* and *Telfair* are badly hit. The APD *Dickerson* is seriously damaged and has to be scuttled on 4 Apl. Bombers hit the destroyer *Prichett* and the DE *Foreman*. Early on 3 Apl *LST 599* is damaged by Kamikaze and in the dusk the escort carrier *Wake Island*, the minesweeper *Hambleton*, the DE *Foreman* and *LCT 876*. The destroyer *Sproston* is damaged in a dive-bombing attack.

On 4 Apl there are no Kamikaze sorties because of heavy storms. Many LSTs are damaged on the beaches. On 5 Apl the battleship *Nevada* receives five hits from a Japanese coastal battery when shelling targets on shore.

1-30 Apl   Pacific
The following ships are sunk by Allied submarines arriving in their operational areas in April: in Japanese waters between Formosa and the Kuriles the US submarine *Cero* (Lt-Cdr Berthrong) sinks four ships of 2090 tons and with *Bream* (Lt-Cdr McCallum) one ship of 1230 tons; *Cod* (Lt-Cdr Adkins) the minesweeper *Sokaitei 41*; *Parche* (Lt-Cdr McCrory) the minesweeper *Sokaitei 3*; *Queenfish* (Cdr Loughlin) two ships of 11341 tons; *Sea Devil* (Lt-Cdr Styles) three ships of 10017 tons; *Sea Dog* (Cdr Hydeman) one ship of 530 tons; *Sea Owl* (Cdr Bennet) the sub-

marine *Ro-46*; *Sennet* (Cdr Porter) one ship of 1901 tons, the repair ship *Hashima* and the auxiliary submarine-chaser *Cha 97*; *Silversides* (Lt-Cdr Nichols) damages one picket boat; *Springer* (Cdr Kefauver) sinks the submarine-chaser *Kusentai 17*, the frigate *Ojika* and the corvette *Kaibokan 25*; *Sunfish* (Cdr Reed) three ships of 4661 tons and the corvette *Kaibokan 73*; *Trepang* (Lt-Cdr Faust) one ship of 4667 tons, *LST 146* and *Sokaitei 20*; *Trutta* (Cdr Smith) damages one picket. In the waters between Malacca and the Philippines the British submarine *Sleuth* together with *Solent* sinks the auxiliary minesweeper *No 3*; *Tradewind* one ship of 1116 tons (on a mine); *Statesman* (Lt Bulkeley) 20 small craft. The US *Besugo* (Cdr Miller) sinks the minesweeper *Sokaitei 12* and the U-boat *U183*; *Gabilan* (Cdr Parham) one ship of 762 tons and, together with *Charr* (Cdr Boyle), the cruiser *Isuzu*; and *Hardhead* (Cdr Greenup) one ship of 6886 tons.

3-4 Apl   Air War/Germany
About 700 aircraft of the 8th USAAF drop 2200 tons of bombs on the harbour installations of Kiel: the mine-layer *Brummer*, the U-boats *U1221, U2542, U3505, U237, U749, U3003*, the minesweeper *M802*, the mine transport *Irben*, the motor mine-sweepers *R59, R119* and *R261*, the passenger ships *New York* (22337 tons) and *Monte Olivia* (13750 tons) and the tanker *Mexphalte* (2578 tons) are sunk.

5 Apl-4 May   British Coastal Waters
In U-boat operations on the British E Coast *U2324* (Lt-Cdr v. Rappard) sinks one ship of 1150 tons off the Thames; *U245* (Cdr Schumann-Hindenberg) two ships of 9847 tons from the convoy TAM.142; *U2329* (Lt Schlott) torpedoes one ship of 7209 tons off Lowestoft and Orfordness; *U2326* (Lt Jobst) misses one ship; and *U2322* (Lt Heckel) reports the sinking of an unknown ship. *U975* (Lt-Cdr Brauel) and *U637* (Lt-Cdr Riekeberg) lay mines off Hartlepool and Newcastle respectively. Off the Firth of Forth *U1274* (Lt Fitting) sinks one ship of 8966 tons from the convoy FS.1784 but is herself sunk by the destroyer *Viceroy* of the

escort on 16 Apl. *U1206* has to be abandoned because of a diving defect and *U398* is missing on the Scottish east Coast. *U287* cruises E of the Orkneys without success.

On the way to the operational areas W of Britain *U396* and *U1017* are lost in attacks by Liberators of Nos 186 and 120 Sqdns RAF on 23 Apl and 29 Apl. In the area of the Hebrides and the North Channel *U218* (Lt-Cdr Stock) lays a mine barrage in the Clyde. *U636* is sunk by the DEs *Bazely*, *Drury* and *Bentinck* of the 4th EG; *U293* (Lt-Cdr Klingspor) or *U956* (Lt-Cdr Mohs) sinks one ship of 878 tons. *U1105* (Lt Schwartz) torpedoes the DE *Redmill* and avoids sonar detection by her pursuers thanks to her 'Alberich' skin. *U1305* has no success.

In the Irish Sea *U1024* (Lt-Cdr Gutteck) unsuccessfully attacks a corvette on 5 Apl and sinks one ship on 7 Apl and one ship on 12 Apl from convoys which together total 14376 tons but she is then forced to surface by a 'Squid' from the frigate *Loch Glendhu* of the 8th EG. The abandoned boat is boarded by the frigate *Loch More* and taken in tow but she sinks. Valuable documents are captured. *U825* has no success nor has *U1052*. *U242* is discovered on 30 Apl by a Sunderland flying boat of No 201 Sqdn RAF as she uses her schnorkel. The aircraft summons the 14th EG, whose destroyers *Hesperus* and *Havelock* sink the U-boat. On 8 Apl, SW of Ireland, *U1001* is sunk by the DEs of the 21st EG, *Fitzroy* and *Byron* and *U774* by the DEs of the 4th EG, *Calder* and *Bentinck*. On 10 Apl the transport boat *U878*, which is returning from St Nazaire, tries to attack an outward-bound convoy and, in doing so, is sunk by the destroyer *Vanquisher* and the corvette *Tintagel Castle*. On 15 Apl *U285* falls victim to the DEs *Grindall* and *Keats* of the 5th EG and *U326* is regarded as missing in this area.

In the Channel *U1063*, in attacking a convoy escorted by the 17th EG, is sunk by the frigate *Loch Killin*. *U1107* (Lt-Cdr Parduhn) which is equipped with an 'Alberich' skin, sinks two ships of 15209 tons from the convoy HX.348 and escapes from the escort. But on 25 Apl she is sunk by a Liberator of USN-VPB.103 with a 'Fido' homing torpedo. *U1055* is located near Ouessant on 30 Apl by a Catalina of USN-VP.63 using MAD and is sunk with a 'Retrobomb'. *U776* and *U249* have no success near Ouessant and off the Scillies respectively. *U255* (Cdr Piening) from St Nazaire lays a mine barrage off Les Sables d'Olonne.

5 Apl-5 May   North and West Atlantic
U1009 is employed as a weather boat in the North Atlantic. *U979* (Lt-Cdr Meermeier) operates off Reykjavik and sinks at the beginning of May a trawler of 348 tons and torpedoes a tanker of 6386 tons. *U541* is sent to Gibraltar as is *U485* from St Nazaire.

The type IX-C boats operate off the American and Canadian east coasts. *U857* (Lt-Cdr Premauer) torpedoes a tanker of 8537 tons in the Gulf of Maine on 5 Apl and is found on 7 Apl and destroyed by a search group consisting of the US frigates *Knoxville* and *Eugene* and the DEs *Gustafson* and *Micka*. *U879* (Lt-Cdr Manchen) sinks a ship of 6959 tons off Cape Hatteras and, five days later, on 19 Apl, is sunk by a search group, TG 22.10, comprising the DEs *Buckley*, *Reuben James*, *Scroggins* and *Jack W. Wilke*. *U190* (Lt Reith) sinks the Canadian minesweeper *Esquimalt*, off Halifax on 16 Apl and escapes. *U548* (Lt Krempl) sinks one tanker of 8300 tons in the Gulf of Maine and torpedoes one ship of 6825 tons. In trying to attack the convoy KN.382 she is located by the frigate *Natchez* on 29 Apl and sunk by her and the DEs of TG 02.10 *Coffman*, *Bostwick* and *Thomas*.

With the U-boats *U805*, *U518*, *U880*, *U858*, *U1235* and *U546*, which set out more or less simultaneously in the middle of March, the Commander U-boats forms a 'Seewolf' group in the North Atlantic on 14 Apl. The intention is to comb the Great Circle route for convoys in a westward direction. The movements are detected by the Allies and the operation 'Teardrop' is organized to deal with it; two carrier groups form search lines N of the Azores on what is known to be the U-boat course to counter what is, at first, thought to be a German attempt to operate V2 rockets from towed launching containers. In the N TG 22.2 (Capt Ruhseeberger), comprising the escort carrier *Mission Bay* and the DEs *Douglas L. Howard, J. R. Y. Blakely, Hill, Fessenden, Farquhar, Pride, Menges* and *Mosley*; in the S TG 22.5 (Capt Craig), comprising the escort carrier *Croatan* and the DEs *Frost, Huse, Inch, Stanton, Swasey, Carter, Neal A. Scott, Muir* and *Sutton*. In spite of bad weather, *U1235* and *U880* are located with sonar on 15 Apl and 16 Apl by TG 22.5 and sunk by the DEs with 'hedgehog'. *U805* is sighted by an aircraft from the Azores, but she twice escapes lengthy searches. On 22 Apl the group also sinks *U518* before two other carrier groups relieve the first two: in the N TG 22.4 (Capt Purvis), comprising the escort carrier *Core* and the DEs *Moore, Sloat, Tomich* and *J. Richard Ward*; in the S TG 22.3 (Capt Dufec), comprising the escort carrier *Bogue* and the DEs *Haverfield, Willis, Wilhoite* and *Swenning*; and, in front, a search line (TG 22.7), consisting of the DEs *Pillsbury, Keith, Otterstetter, Pope, Flaherty, Chatelain, Frederick C. Davis, Neunzer, Hubbard, Varian, Otter, Hayter, Janssen* and *Cockrill*. On 24 Apl an aircraft from the *Bogue* sights *U546*. Hunted by nine DEs, Lt-Cdr Just is able first to sink the *Frederick C. Davis* with a T-5, in spite of 'Foxers' being put out. After almost six hours, *U546* is forced to surface, just misses the *Flaherty* with another T-5 and then sinks. Only *U858* and *U805* get to the American coast, as well as *U853* and *U530*, sailing on their own, and *U889* and *U881* behind them. The last, in trying to attack the carrier group *Mission Bay*, which has again set out, is sunk on 6 May by the *Farquhar*. *U853* (Lt Frömsdorf) probably sinks the submarine-chaser *Eagle 58* on 23 Apl and is, after sinking a collier of 5353 tons, sunk on 5 May by the frigate *Moberly*, the destroyer *Ericsson* and the DEs *Atherton* and *Amick*.

6-8 Apl   North Sea
The German 2nd MTB Flotilla (Lt-Cdr Wendler) carries out a mining operation in the Humber Estuary on 6-7 Apl with *S174, S176, S177, S209, S210* and *S221*. As it withdraws, there is an en-gagement with British MTBs. *S176* sinks *MTB 494* by ramming and has to be abandoned. *S177* sinks after being rammed by *MTB 5001* which is also lost. This is the last operation by the 2nd MTB Flotilla.
In the following night, 7-8 Apl, the 4th and 6th MTB Flotillas (Cdr Fimmen and Lt-Cdr Matzen) with *S205, S204, S219, S202, S703, S304* and *S222, S705, S211, S223, S704, S212* and *S706* lay mines in the Thames-Scheldt convoy route. In engagements with British MTBs the 4th MTB Flotilla loses *S202* and *S703* after a collision. *S223* of the 6th MTB Flotilla sinks off Ostend after hitting a mine. The 9th MTB Flotilla (Cdr v. Mirbach) with *S206, S168, S130, S175, S207* and *S214* has to break off an operation, in which small battle units with *Linsen* are to be transported to the Scheldt, because of bad weather.

6-10 Apl   Central Pacific
Big Japanese attack on the US landing fleet off Okinawa.
On 6-7 Apl the Kamikaze attack 'Kikusui 1' takes place concentrating on the landing fleet round Okinawa and the radar picket destroyers stationed at 16 points round the island. There are weaker attacks on TGs 58.1 and 58.3 NE of Okinawa and on TF 57 S of Okinawa. The escort carriers of TF 52 E of Okinawa are not attacked. On 6 Apl 198 Kamikaze pilots set off from Kyushu, 41 of which return. Fifty-five are shot down by the fighter cover and 35 by the AA defence. Twenty-seven ships are hit, some of them more than once. The picket destroyers *Bush* and *Colhoun*, the destroyer-minesweeper *Emmons*, *LST 447* and the ammunition transports *Hobbs Victory* and *Logan Victory* (each 7607 tons) sink. The destroyers *Leutze, Newcomb,* and *Morris* and the DE *Witter* are damaged beyond repair; the minesweepers *Rodman* and *Defense* and the destroyer *Mullany* suffer severe damage which keeps them out of action for the rest of the war. Medium damage is inflicted on the destroyers *Howorth, Hyman* and *Haynsworth* (TF 58) and the DE *Fieberling*. The carriers *Illustrious* (TF 57) and *San Jacinto* (TF 58), the destroyers *Bennett, Hutchins* and *Har-*

rison (TF 58), the minesweepers *Facility, Ransom, Devastator, YMS 311* and *YMS 321* are slightly damaged. On 7 Apl 54 Kamikaze pilots of the 5th Naval Air Fleet set out from Kyushu, and, in addition, some 125 army Kamikaze pilots are employed on 6-7 Apl. Of the 54 naval Kamikazes 24 return and some 30 Kamikazes are shot down on 7 May by the fighter cover and AA defence. The battleship *Maryland* and the picket destroyer *Bennett* receive serious hits; the carrier *Hancock* (TF 58) and the DE *Wesson* sustain medium damage; and the destroyer *Longshaw* and the minesweeper *YMS 81* minor damage. The motor gunboat *PGM 18* and the minesweeper *YMS 103* are lost on mines.

On 6 Apl a Japanese Task Force (Vice-Adm Ito†) sets out from Tokuyama in the Inland Sea. It consists of the super battleship *Yamato* (Rear-Adm Ariaga†), the cruiser *Yahagi* (Capt Hara with the Commander of the 2nd DD Flotilla, Rear-Adm Komura, on board) and the 17th, 21st and 41st DD Divs comprising *Isokaze, Hamakaze, Yukikaze; Asashimo, Kasumi, Hatsushimo; Fuyutsuki* and *Suzutsuki*. But, shortly after, it is reported by a B 29 and, after passing through the Bungo Channel, by the US submarine *Threadfin* and, a little later, by *Hackleback*.

Early on 7 Apl flying-boats from Kerama Retto and reconnaissance aircraft from TGs 58.1 and 58.3, assembled S of Amami-O-shima, establish contact SW of Kyushu. TG 58.4, which provides the fighter cover over Okinawa, tries to close in at high speed. At 1000 hrs the main attack force of 280 aircraft sets off from TGs 58.1 and 58.3. The *Hamakaze* and *Yahagi* are sunk and the *Yamato* receives two bomb and one torpedo hits. In the second attack with approximately 100 aircraft from 1400 hrs the destroyers *Isokaze, Asashimo* and *Kasumi* sink first, then, after nine more torpedo and three bomb hits, the *Yamato* and with her perish 2498 sailors. The remaining destroyers return, some of them badly damaged. In all, the Japanese Navy loses 3665 dead. Of the 386 US aircraft deployed, only 10 fail to return.

On 8 Apl and 9 Apl there follow only individual Kamikaze attacks in which the picket destroyers *Gregory* and *Sterett* and the minesweeper *YMS 92* are damaged. On 8-9 Apl explosive boats attempt attacks from Okinawa in the course of which the destroyer *Charles J. Badger* and the transport *Starr* are damaged. As a result of Kamikaze attacks, the US Fleet loses 466 dead and has 579 injured in the period 6 Apl to 10 Apl.

The Japanese submarines *Ro-49* and *Ro-56* are lost on 4 Apl and 9 Apl respectively to depth charges from the destroyer *Hudson* and the destroyers *Monssen* and *Mertz*.

6-25 Apl Baltic/East Prussia
On 6 Apl the attack by the Soviet 3rd White Russian Front, supported by strong air forces, begins against Königsberg, whose defenders are overwhelmed on 9 Apl and have to surrender on the following day. In the harbour the hull of the cruiser *Seydlitz* is blown up. The Soviet armies continue the attack towards the W and on 15 Apl break through the front in Samland. Some 70000 refugees are trapped in Pillau; some of them are brought across to the Frische Nehrung and others are evacuated by sea. In the process the freighters *Mendoza* (5193 tons), *Vale* (5950 tons) and *Weserstein* (1923 tons) are lost as a result of air attacks between 8 Apl and 11 Apl. On 16 Apl the SATs of the 7th Gun Carrier Flotilla (Lt-Cdr Eggers), *Soemba, Nienburg, Ostsee, Robert Müller 6, Kemphan* and the gunnery training vessel *Drache* arrive to support the defensive battle near Fischhausen. On 18 Apl the *Drache* is sunk in an air attack and *Robert Müller 6* is damaged and then sunk by the submarine *L-3* (Capt 3rd Class Konovalov) which is summoned to the scene.

In the last night, 24-25 Apl, the naval ferry barges bring another 19200 refugees and troops across. In all, 141000 wounded and 451000 refugees are evacuated through Pillau from 25 Jan.

7-12 Apl Mediterranean/Ligurian Sea
Allied warships shell German bases and traffic routes along the Riviera. There participate: the French cruisers *Gloire* and *Duguay-Trouin*, the destroyers *Tigre, Tempête* and *Trombe*, the British

destroyers *Meteor* and *Musketeer* and the US destroyer *Mackenzie*.

8-10 Apl Air War/Germany

In the night 8-9 Apl RAF Bomber Command drops 1491 tons of bombs on the harbour installations of Hamburg: *U677*, *U747*, *U982*, *U2509*, *U2514* and *U2516* are sunk.

In the night 9-10 Apl RAF Bomber Command drops 2634 tons of bombs on the harbour installations of Kiel: the pocket battleship *Admiral Scheer* capsizes; the *Admiral Hipper* and the light cruiser *Emden* are badly damaged; and the torpedo boat *T1*, the U-boats *U1131* and *U1227*, the minesweeper *M504* and three merchant ships of 2787 tons are destroyed.

On 8 Apl and 9 Apl Mosquito bombers of RAF Coastal Command sink *U804*, *U843* and *U1065* in the Kattegat.

8-14 Apl Central Pacific

On 8 Apl TF 58 (Vice-Adm Mitscher) resumes support for the Okinawa operations. After the return of TG 58.2, TF 58 is composed as follows:

TG 58.1 (Rear-Adm Clark) comprises the carriers *Hornet*, *Bennington*, *Belleau Wood* and *San Jacinto*, the battleships *Massachusetts* and *Indiana*, the cruisers *Vincennes*, *Miami*, *Vicksburgh* and *San Juan* and destroyers of Desrons 25 and 61.

TG 58.2 (Rear-Adm Bogan) comprises the carriers *Randolph*, *Enterprise* and *Independence*, the battleships *Washington* and *North Carolina*, the cruisers *Baltimore*, *Pittsburgh*, *Flint* and *Oakland* and destroyers of Desrons 52 and 53.

TG 58.2 (Rear-Adm Sherman) comprises the carriers *Essex*, *Bunker Hill* and *Bataan*, the battleships *New Jersey* and *South Dakota*, the cruisers *Pasadena*, *Springfield*, *Astoria* and *Wilkes-Barre* and destroyers of Desrons 45, 62 and 48.

TG 58.4 (Rear-Adm Radford) comprises the carriers *Yorktown*, *Intrepid* and *Langley*, the battleships *Wisconsin* and *Missouri*, the battlecruisers *Alaska* and *Guam*, the cruiser *San Diego* and the destroyers of Desrons 47 and 54. At least two Task Groups are daily in the operational area with one group replenishing and another either coming up or withdrawing.

While the British TF 57 is replenishing on 8 Apl and 9 Apl, the escort carrier group of Rear-Adm Sample, comprising *Suwanee*, *Chenango*, *Santee* and *Rudyerd Bay*, takes over the neutralization of the Sakishima-Gunto Islands. From 11 Apl to 13 Apl TF 57, reinforced by the cruisers *Uganda* and *Gambia* and the destroyers *Ursa*, *Urchin* and *Whirlwind*, daily attacks airfields and installations on North Formosa. On 14 Apl and 15 Apl the force replenishes again when the carrier *Formidable* relieves the *Illustrious* and the destroyers *Kempenfelt*, *Wessex*, *Urania* and *Quality*. In this period TG 52.1 (Rear-Adm Sample) continues the operations against Sakishima-Gunto.

On 11 Apl 64 Kamikazes (34 of which return) fly off to attack TF 58. The battleship *Missouri*, the carrier *Enterprise*, the destroyers *Kidd* and *Bullard* and off Okinawa, also the DE *Samuel S. Miles* are hit.

On 12 Apl 83 naval and about 60 army Kamikaze pilots set off in operation 'Kikusui 2' with strong fighter cover to attack the landing fleet with nine Oka bombers. The picket destroyer *Mannert L. Abele* is sunk and *Stanly* damaged by Oka bombs. The picket boat *LCS(L) 33* is sunk and *LCS(L) 57* damaged by Kamikazes. Also damaged are the picket destroyers *Purdy*, *Cassin Young* and *Jeffers* (DMS) and, in the area between Okinawa and Kerama Retto, the battleships *Tennessee* and *Idaho*, the destroyer *Zellars*, the minesweepers *Lindsey* and *LSM 189* (the last three ships are out of action until the end of the war) and the DEs *Rall*, *Whitehurst*, *Riddle* and *Walter C. Wann* and the minesweeper *Gladiator*. In lighter attacks on 13 Apl the DE *Connolly* is damaged.

On 14 Apl 35 of 76 Kamikazes which set off and seven Oka bombers attack again. The first damage the battleship *New York* and the destroyers *Dashiell*, *Hunt* and *Sigsbee*. The last-named is out of action until the end of the war.

Of the 'Tatara' group of submarines which sets out with *Kaiten* torpedoes, *I-47* and *I-58* return without success. *I-44* is sunk on 10 Apl by the DE *Fieberling* and *I-56* is sunk on 17 Apl by the destroyers *Heerman*, *McCord*,

Collett, Mertz and *Uhlmann* and aircraft of the carrier *Bataan*, when she tries to attack TF 58.

8-18 Apl Indian Ocean
Operation 'Sunfish'. Sortie by a part of the British Eastern Fleet (Vice-Adm Walker), consisting of the battleships *Queen Elizabeth* and *Richelieu* (French), the heavy cruisers *London* and *Cumberland* and the destroyers *Saumarez, Vigilant, Verulam, Virago* and *Venus*, towards the north coast of Sumatra. On 11 Apl Sabang is shelled. The escort carriers *Emperor* and *Khedive* provide air escort and on 11 Apl attack Port Blair and Emmahaven when the submarine-chaser *Ch 7* and one small freighter are sunk. On 14-15 Apl the carrier aircraft carry out photographic reconnaissance over Penang, Port Swettenham and Port Dickson. On 16 Apl they again attack Emmahaven and Padang.

10 Apl Baltic
British aircraft sink the torpedo boat *T13* and damage *T16* in the Kattegat.

12 Apl General Situation
Death of President Roosevelt.

12 Apl Mediterranean/Ligurian Sea
The British cruiser *Orion* shells San Remo.

12-13 Apl North Sea/English Channel
Twelve German motor torpedo boats of the 4th, 6th and 9th Flotillas lay mines in the area Nore-Flushing-Channel. In doing so, they are engaged by the British DE *Ekins* and the escort destroyer *Hambledon* and British MTBs. The motor torpedo boats are attacked by aircraft of RAF Coastal Command on their return. On these mines the tanker *Gold Shell* (8208 tons) sinks and the freighters *Conakrian* (4876 tons), *Benjamin H. Bristow* and *Horace Binney* (7191 tons each) are damaged.

13-14 Apl Air War/Germany
RAF Bomber Command drops 1905 tons of bombs on the harbour installations of Kiel.

14-20 Apl Bay of Biscay
From 14 Apl to 16 Apl aircraft of the 8th USAAF in three attacks on Royan and other German bases in the Gironde Estuary drop 2962 tons, 2551 tons and 1290 tons respectively. From 15 Apl to 20 Apl, following the heavy air attacks, there takes place the final battle for the

German fortress 'Gironde-Nord' (Royan). Operation 'Vénérable': after shelling by a French naval force (Vice-Adm Rue), comprising the battleship *Lorraine*, the cruiser *Duquesne*, the destroyers *Basque, Le Fortuné* and *L'Alcyon*, the DE *Hova*, the frigates *L'Aventure, La Découverte* and *La Surprise* and the sloop *Amiral Mouchez*, a land attack is made by the 10th French Div (Maj-Gen de Larminat) and the 66th US Div (Maj-Gen Kramer). On 20 Apl the last pockets of German resistance capitulate.

15-26 Apl Central Pacific
US TF 58 continues the operations off Okinawa with four groups. On 15-16 Apl one group provides fighter protection over Okinawa, two groups make fighter sorties against Kyushu and the fourth replenishes. The British TF 57 makes attacks on Sakishima-Gunto on 16-17 Apl. The US Escort Carrier Groups TG 52.1.1, 2, 3 relieve each other in overlapping operations off Okinawa. The battleships, cruisers and destroyers of TF 54 continue to support the land fighting from off Okinawa.

After weaker attacks by 10 Kamikazes (eight of which return) on 15 Apl, when the destroyer *Wilson* and the tanker *Taluga* are slightly damaged, the Japanese 5th Air Fleet begins the mass attack 'Kikusui 3' with 126 Kamikazes (42 of which return) and six Oka bombers on 16 Apl. On 17 Apl 49 are employed, of which 30 return. In attacks on TF 58 the carrier *Intrepid* is badly damaged and the battleship *Missouri* and the destroyer *Benham* (17 Apl) less seriously damaged. After the *Intrepid* drops out, TG 58.2 is broken up and its ships are distributed among TG 58.1, 3 and 4.

The attacks are concentrated on the landing fleet, particularly the picket destroyers. *Laffey* (Cdr Becton) is attacked by 22 aircraft: seven are shot down by fighters and nine by AA defence. There are six Kamikaze hits and four bomb hits resulting in 31 dead and 72 wounded; nevertheless, it is possible to bring the badly damaged ship into harbour. *Pringle* sinks, *Bryant* and the minelayer *Harding* are damaged beyond repair and the minesweeper *Hobson* is so badly damaged that she is out of action for the rest of the war.

The DE *Bowers* and the picket boats *LCS(L) 116* and *LCS 51* sustain lesser damage.

On 16 Apl an Amphibious Group (Rear-Adm Reifsnider) lands the 77th Inf Div on the small offshore island of Ie Shima which is taken by 21 Apl after offering strong resistance. Later, the 77th Inf Div is brought to Okinawa as a reserve. On 18-19 Apl two groups of TF 58 and two escort carrier groups make strong attacks in 650 sorties on the positions of the Japanese 62nd and 63rd Divs in the first Shuri line. After heavy artillery preparatory fire from the 27th Army Artillery Battery and TF 54, comprising the battleships *Texas, Arkansas, Colorado, Idaho, New Mexico* and *New York*, six cruisers and eight destroyers, as well as the battleships *North Carolina* and *South Dakota* and the destroyers of Desron 48 from TF 58, XXIV Corps attacks with the 27th, 96th and 7th Inf Divs early on 19 Apl. But the attack brings little result. After heavy fighting and strong support from TF 54 and carrier aircraft, the Japanese finally pull out from the first line on 23 Apl and withdraw to the second Shuri position. On 22 Apl 35 Kamikaze aircraft (three of which return) attack TF 58, when the destroyers *Hudson* and *Wadsworth* are damaged, and the landing fleet. The minesweeper *Swallow* and picket boat *LCS 15* are sunk; and the destroyer *Isherwood*, the minelayer *Shea* and the minesweepers *Ransom* and *Gladiator* are damaged.

After replenishment on 18-19 Apl the British TF 57 makes another attack on Sakishima-Gunto on 20 Apl and then returns to Leyte. From 21 Apl the escort carrier group TG 52.1.3, comprising *Suwanee, Sangamon, Chenango* and *Santee*, takes over the task of neutralizing the Ryukyu Islands and North Formosa. An escort carrier group carries out a raid on 25 Apl on the Okino-Daito-Shima group of islands E of Okinawa.

16-25 Apl Arctic

Convoy operation JW.66. On 16 Apl JW.66 sets out from the Clyde with 22 merchant ships. Escort (Rear-Adm Cunningham-Graham): the escort carriers *Vindex* and *Premier*, the cruiser *Diadem* the Home Fleet destroyers *Zephyr, Zest, Zealous, Zodiac, Stord* (Norwegian), *Offa, Haida* (RCN), *Huron* (RCN), *Iroquois* (RCN), the 8th EG, consisting of the sloop *Cygnet*, the corvettes *Alnwick Castle, Bamborough Castle, Farnham Castle, Honeysuckle, Rhododendron, Oxlip* and *Lotus* and, as support group, the 19th EG, consisting of the frigates *Loch Insh, Loch Shin* and *Anguilla* and the DEs *Cotton* and *Goodall*. The German 'B' Service learns of the convoy's departure. *U286, U295, U307, U313, U363* and *U481* are stationed W of Bear Island as the 'Faust' group. Air reconnaissance is unable to locate the convoy up to 21 Apl. The U-boats are therefore moved to positions off the Kola Estuary. In addition, *U318, U427, U711, U992, U278, U294, U312, U716, U968* and *U997* set out for the operational area. Some boats come into contact on 21 Apl and 22 Apl with the Soviet coastal convoy PK.9 from Petsamo to Kola: this consists of two steamers and is escorted by the destroyers *Karl Libknecht* (Capt 1st Class Rumyantsev), *Derzki, Zhestki* and *Dostoiny*, two minesweepers, six BO submarine-chasers, including *BO-131, BO-225* and *BO-228*, four TKAs and a Norwegian group comprising the corvette *Eglantine* and the trawlers *Karmöy, Jelöy* and *Tromöy. U997* (Lt Lehmann) sinks the Soviet steamer *Onega* (1603 tons) and torpedoes the Norwegian steamer *Idefjord* (4287 tons) which is taken in tow. Further attacks by *U997, U481* and *U294* are frustrated by the escort vessels which avoid several T-5s. *U481* (Lt-Cdr Andersen) also claims to have sunk a trawler on 19 Apl. Only *U711* (Lt-Cdr Lange), which has penetrated furthest into the Kola Inlet, is able to fire, unsuccessfully, at JW.66 which reaches harbour on 25 Apl. She also claims to have sunk a small steamer on 19 Apl.

On 22 Apl, with Russian permission, the British minelayer *Apollo* and the destroyers *Obedient, Opportune* and *Orwell* lay a deep minefield (276 mines) as a protection against German U-boats from Syet Navolok to Kildin.

During the convoy operation a British force, comprising the escort carriers *Queen* and *Searcher* and escort forces, carries out operations off the Norwegian coast. On 20 Apl mines are laid; on 26 Apl an air attack on a convoy fails because it is beaten off by Me 109 fighters and on 28 Apl a fighter sortie is made.

16 Apl-4 May Baltic

Continuation of the evacuation from the embarkation points in the Lower Vistula to Hela and from there to the W. On 16 Apl a convoy with eight ships and escort vessels leaves Hela where the aircraft repair ship *Boelcke* sinks in an air attack. In the night the convoy is attacked off Rixhöft by the Soviet submarine *L-3* (Capt 3rd Class Konovalov); she sinks the transport *Goya* (5230 tons). Only 165 of the 6385 persons on board can be rescued.

In air attacks on 19 Apl and 20 Apl the steamer *Altengamme* (5897 tons) is lost off Sassnitz and *Vs 215* and *Königsberg* (180 tons) off Hela. On 25 Apl the *Emily Sauber* (2435 tons) falls victim to one of the attacks made by Soviet torpedo cutters from Neufahrwasser. Attacks by the submarine *K-52* (Capt 3rd Class Travkin) from 21 Apl to 27 Apl and then by *K-53* (Capt 3rd Class Yaroshevich) on the Stolpe Bank do not, as far as is known, have any success.

On 20 Apl the *Eberhard Essberger* sets out from Hela with 6200 persons and the *Lappland* leaves for the W on 21 Apl with 7700 persons. On 21 Apl a total of 28000 refugees are embarked and on 28 Apl seven steamers evacuate 24000 individuals. The total for April is 387000. In the area of the Pomeranian Bay Lancaster bombers of the RAF attack the *Lützow*, which is lying in the Kaiserfahrt, S of Swinemünde, with 5.6-ton bombs. As a result of near-misses she goes aground.

On 25 Apl the uncompleted aircraft carrier *Graf Zeppelin* and four steamers and small craft are blown up in Stettin before the Soviet 2nd Assault Army advances across the Lower Oder via Anklam towards Stralsund. The latter is reached on 1 May and the 19th Army crosses to Wollin near Dievenow and advances on Swinemünde. The old battleship *Schlesien*, which is sent on 2 May into the Greifswalder Bodden to protect the Wolgast Bridge to Usedom, runs on a British air ground mine near Greifswalder Oie and is towed back to

Swinemünde where she is beached. On 4 May the wreck, together with the *Lützow*, is blown up. So, too, are other ships, left behind in the harbour. The Commander Destroyers (Vice-Adm Kreisch) with five steamers, the destroyers *Z38*, *Z39*, *Z34*, *Z43*, *T33*, *T36*, the tender *Jagd*, the auxiliary cruiser *Orion* and the AA ship *Hummel* with 35000 persons on board, sets out for Copenhagen. Off Swinemünde, on 3-4 May, *M14* is lost on a mine, *Orion/ Hektor* and *T36* are lost as a result of mines and bomb hits and *Hummel* from bomb hits.

17 Apl Mediterranean/Ligurian Sea

German motor torpedo boats have an engagement with Allied destroyers off San Remo. The French destroyer *Trombe* is torpedoed.

17-22 Apl South West Pacific

Operation 'Victor V': US Amphibious Group 8 (Rear-Adm Noble) with the headquarters ship *Wasatch* lands X Corps (Maj-Gen Siebert) with the 24th Inf Div (Maj-Gen Woodruff) and the 31st Inf Div (Maj-Gen Martin) on the coast of Moro Gulf, West Mindanao (Philippines). The transport group 'Green' comprises three APDs, 51 LSTs, 13 LSMs, seven LCTs, 22 LCIs, eight Liberty ships and 16 support LCIs and two PCs. The minesweeper group comprises five YMSs. Escort: the destroyers (Desron 23) *Charles Ausburne*, *Braine*, *Robinson*, *Aulick*, (from Desron 5) *Flusser*, *Conyngham*, the DEs *Jobb* and *Albert T. Harris*. The transport group 'Red' (Capt Zurmuehlen) with the US Coastguard cutter *Spencer* comprises 20 LSTs, three LSMs, two APDs, five LCIs and seven support LCIs, as well as two SCs and two YMSs. Escort: the destroyers *Dyson* and *McCalla*. Fire support is provided by TG 74.2 (Rear-Adm Riggs), comprising the cruisers *Montpelier*, *Denver* and *Cleveland* and the destroyers (Desron 22) *Conway*, *Eaton*, *Stevens*, *Young*, *Cony* and *Sigourney*.

18 Apl Air War/Germany

RAF Bomber Command drops 4994 tons of bombs on the island of Heligoland.

19 Apl Mediterranean/Ligurian Sea

Italian 'Small Battle Units', transported by the destroyer *Grecale* and the motor torpedo boat *Ms 72*, sink in Genoa the almost completed aircraft carrier *Aquila* (23350 tons) to prevent her being used as a block ship.

22 Apl   Air War/Germany
RAF Bomber Command drops 969 tons of bombs on Bremen.

23-24 Apl   Kattegat
RAF Coastal Command attacks German shipping in the Kattegat: the freighters *Tübingen* (5543 tons) and *Ingerseks* (4969 tons) are sunk and three ships are damaged.

23-25 Apl   Mediterranean/Ligurian Sea
The French cruisers *Montcalm* and *Duguay Trouin* and the British destroyer *Lookout* shell German bases on the Italian Riviera.

Before Genoa is abandoned on 24-25 Apl, German troops sink in the harbour and blow up in the yards: the destroyers *Alpino, Ghibli, F.R.24, F.R.37, TA31* and *TA32*, the corvettes *UJ2221, UJ2224, UJ2225, UJ2226, UJ2227, UJ2228, UJ6086, F.R.51,* 21 motor minesweepers (five type R, nine type RA and seven type RD) and five auxiliary ships and many merchant ships.

25 Apl   Air War/Germany
RAF Bomber Command drops 2176 tons of bombs on the coastal fortifications of Wangerooge.

27 Apl   Germany
Bremen is taken by British troops.

27 Apl-1 May   South-West Pacific
Operation 'Oboe I': landing on Tarakan (Borneo). On 27 Apl US TG 74.3 (Rear-Adm Berkey), comprising the cruisers *Phoenix, Boise* and the Australian *Hobart*, as well as the US destroyers (Desron 21) *Taylor, Nicholas, O'Bannon, Fletcher, Jenkins* and the Australian *Warramunga*, begins with the preparatory shelling of the assault area in the S of Tarakan. It is continued on 28 Apl and 29 Apl. On 30 Apl a battalion lands on the small offshore island of Sadan. On 1 May Amphibious Group 6 (Rear-Adm Royal), with the headquarters ship *Rocky Mount*, lands 18000 men of the reinforced 26th Australian Brigade (Brig Whitehead) on Tarakan. The transport group comprises two Australian LSIs, one US AKA, one LSD and 45 LSTs. Escort: the destroyers *Waller* (Desron 22), *Philip; Bailey, Bancroft, Caldwell; Dray-*ton, *Smith*, the DEs *Formoe, Charles E. Brannon*, the Australian frigates *Burdekin, Barcoo* and *Hawkesbury* and 21 PTs. The destroyer *Jenkins* is damaged by Japanese mines on 30 Apl; the minesweeper *YMS 481* sinks as a result of coastal shelling on 2 May; and *YMS 334*, and *YMS 364* are damaged by shelling and *YMS 363* on a mine.

27 Apl-2 May   Central Pacific
TGs 58.3 and 58.4 continue to relieve each other in overlapping operations off Okinawa. TG 58.1 goes to Ulithi from 28 Apl to 8 May. Off Sakishima-Gunto TG 52.1.3 is relieved on 28 Apl by TG 52.1.1 comprising the escort carriers *Makin Island, Fanshaw Bay, Lunga Point* and *Salamaua*.

From 27 Apl to 30 Apl, with the main effort on 28 Apl, approximately 65 Japanese naval and 60 army aircraft from Kyushu carry out the Kamikaze operation 'Kikusui 4'. In the process the destroyer *Ralph Talbot* is damaged on 27 Apl; *Wadsworth, Daly, Twiggs* and *Bennion* on 28 Apl; *Hazelwood* and *Haggard* on 29 Apl; and *Bennion* again on 30 Apl; the DE *England* and the APD *Rathburne* on 27 Apl; the minesweeper *Butler*, the hospital ship *Comfort* and the casualty transport *Pinkney* on 28 Apl; and the minelayers *Shannon* and *Harry F. Bauer* on 29 Apl; and *Terror* on 30 Apl. *Haggard, Rathburne* and *Pinkney* are out of action for the rest of the war.

Of the Japanese submarines, *Ro-109* is sunk on 25 Apl by the DE *Horace A. Bass*; the *Kaiten* Group 'Amatake' makes unsuccessful attacks—on 29 Apl *I-36* (Cdr Sugamasa) on the destroyer *Ringgold* and on 1 May, 2 May and 6 May *I-47* (Cdr Orita) on convoys.

27 Apl-7 May   Indian Ocean
Operation 'Dracula': landing near Rangoon. From 27 Apl to 30 Apl British Assault Force W' (Rear-Adm B. C. S. Martin) with the headquarters ship *Largs* sets out in six convoys from Akyab and Kyaukpyu. The 26th Indian Div is embarked on two LSHs, *Waveney, Nith*, four LSIs, one LSE, 45 LSTs and 110 small landing craft. Escort for the landing group is provided by the Indian sloops *Cauvery, Narbada, Godavari, Kistna, Sutlej* and *Hindustan*. There are also 22 minesweepers from

the 7th and 37th MS Flotillas. The landing force is covered by the 21st Carrier Sqdn, consisting of the cruisers *Phoebe* and *Royalist* (Commodore Oliver), the escort carriers *Hunter*, *Stalker*, *Emperor* and *Khedive*, the destroyers *Saumarez*, *Venus*, *Virago* and *Vigilant*, eight frigates and two sloops. On 1 May the landing is made without resistance. Rangoon, which has been evacuated by the Japanese, is occupied on 3 May.

Operation 'Bishop': a covering group (Vice-Adm Walker)—TF 63—comprising the battleships *Queen Elizabeth* and *Richelieu*, the escort carriers *Shah* and *Empress*, the cruisers *Cumberland*, *Suffolk*, *Ceylon* and *Tromp* and six destroyers, makes air attacks and shells Car Nicobar and Port Blair. TF 62, comprising the destroyers *Roebuck*, *Racehorse* and *Redoubt*, shells Martaban on 30 Apl and Car Nicobar on 1 May. In the process a convoy of nine ships is destroyed on 30 Apl. On 5 May and 6 May the 21st Carrier Sqdn with the destroyers *Virago*, *Tartar* and *Nubian*, makes raids on Japanese bases between Mergui and Victoria Point. On 6 May TF 63 shells Port Blair on the Andaman Islands with battleships, cruisers and the destroyers *Rotherham*, *Saumarez*, *Venus*, *Vigilant* and *Verulam*. On 9 May the forces return to Trincomalee.

29 Apl-1 May   Bay of Biscay
Operation 'Jupiter': French troops land on the island of Oleron in the Gironde Estuary with support from a French naval force (Vice-Adm Rue), comprising the cruiser *Duquesne*, the destroyers *Le Fortuné*, *L'Alcyon* and *Basque* and light forces. On 1 May the last German troops surrender.

29 Apl-2 May   Mediterranean/Adriatic
On 29 Apl the British 56th Inf Div takes Venice. On 30 Apl Tito partisans force their way into Trieste. On 1 May New Zealand and Yugoslav troops meet near Monfalcone NW of Trieste.
On 1 May the remaining German ships in Trieste are scuttled. They include the torpedo boat *TA43* and the old and and no-longer operational *TA22* and *TA35*. On 2 May New Zealand army units occupy Trieste.

29 Apl-2 May   Arctic
Last convoy battle of the 2nd World War Against the convoy RA.66, comprising 24 merchant ships and the escort of JW.66 (see 16-25 Apl). It arrives in the Clyde on 8 May.
On 29 Apl, before the departure of the convoy, the Allied escort vessels, supported by Soviet submarine-chasers and minesweepers, are sent to the area off the Kola Inlet to drive off the German U-boats stationed there: *U278*, *U286*, *U307*, *U312*, *U313*, *U318*, *U363*, *U427*, *U481*, *U711*, *U716*, *U968*, *U992* and *U997*. *U307* (Lt Krüger) and *U286* (Lt Dietrich) are sunk by the frigates *Loch Insh*, *Loch Shin*, *Anguilla* and *Cotton* of the 19th EG. *U968* (Lt Westphalen) just misses the corvette *Alnwick Castle* and sinks the frigate *Goodall*. *U427* (Lt Gudenus) just misses the Canadian destroyers *Haida* and *Iroquois* and has to endure a long and severe pursuit during which 678 depth charge explosions are counted. *U313* (Lt-Cdr Schweiger) gets involved in an engagement with Soviet submarine-chasers. But both boats get away. As a result of these actions, the U-boats are driven off and do not approach the convoy. Air reconnaissance is unable to keep contact with the convoy and the operation has to be broken off.

29 Apl-4 May   South West Pacific
US Amphibious Group 9 (TG 78.3, Rear-Adm Struble) lands the US 185th RCT (Maj-Gen Brush) near Padan Point on Los Negros on 29 Apl in LSMs with cover from destroyers.
On 3-4 May TG 78.2 (Rear-Adm Noble) lands a battle group of 1000 men near Santa Cruz in the Gulf of Davao after preparatory fire from the cruiser *Denver*.

1 May   Mediterranean/Aegean
Raid on Rhodes by the destroyers *Kimberley* (British), *Catterick* (British) and *Kriti* (Greek).

1-31 May   Pacific
The following ships are sunk by Allied submarines arriving in their operational areas in May: in Japanese waters the US submarine *Billfish* (Lt-Cdr Farley) sinks two ships of 3211 tons; *Bowfin* (Cdr Tyree) two ships of 3599 tons; *Raton* (Lt-Cdr Shea) three ships of 6759 tons; *Ray* (Lt-Cdr Kinsella) one ship of 144 tons; *Sandlance* one ship of

220 tons; *Sea Poacher* (Lt-Cdr Gambarcorta) two ships of 122 tons; *Shad* (Lt-Cdr Mehlhop) three ships of 5686 tons; *Sterlet* (Lt-Cdr Lewis) two ships of 4155 tons; *Tench* (Lt-Cdr Baskett) six ships of 5921 tons. In the SE Asian area the British submarine *Truant* (Cdr Hazlet) sinks one auxiliary minesweeper and *Thorough* (one ship of 728 tons). The US submarine *Baya* (Lt-Cdr Jarvis) sinks one ship of 2594 tons; *Blenny* (Lt-Cdr Hazzard) one ship of 520 tons; *Chub* (Cdr Rhymes) the minesweeper *Sokaitei 34*; *Hammerhead* (Cdr Smith) two ships of 6845 tons; and *Hawkbill* (Lt-Cdr Scanland) the minelayer *Hatsutaka*.

2 May   Germany
End of the fighting for Berlin. The 6th British Airborne Div meets units of the 70th Soviet Army near Wismar.

2-3 May   Air War/Germany
Last attack by RAF Bomber Command on Kiel. 174 tons of bombs are dropped.

2-3 May   German harbours
On 2 May 39 German U-boats are scuttled: 11 in Bremerhaven, 22 in Wilhelmshaven, one in Vegesack, one in Nordenham, one in Lübeck; and three in Warnemünde.
On 3 May 79 German U-boats are scuttled: 36 in the Bay of Lübeck, 39 in Kieler Förde, two in Eckernförde, one in the Kaiser-Wilhelm Canal and one in Bornholm.

2-6 May   Baltic/North Sea
Mass RAF attacks on shipping concentrations in the Western Baltic and on U-boats (approximately 60) proceeding to Norway.
2 May: Typhoons of the 2nd Tactical Air Force sink off Lübeck Bay the steamer *Florida* (5542 tons) and *U1007*. Mosquitoes of No 18 Group Coastal Command sink *M293* and *U2359* in the Kattegat.
3 May: Typhoons of Nos 83 and 84 Groups of the 2nd TAF sink off Lübeck Bay the steamer *Cap Arkona* (27561 tons) and *Thielbek* (2815 tons), full of concentration camp detainees (some 5000), as well as the steamers *Deutschland* (21046 tons), *Dwarssee* (552 tons) and *Erna Gaulke* (400 tons); off the Bay of Kiel the steamers *Inster* (4713 tons), *Irmtraud Cords* (2814

tons) and *Wolgast* (164 tons); and south of the Belt entrances the escort boat *F3* and the U-boats *U1210*, *U746*, *U904*, *U3030*, *U3032* and *U2540*. In the area of the Belts Beaufighters of No 16 Group of Coastal Command sink the steamer *Pallas* (627 tons) and the U-boat *U2524*. Mosquitoes of No 18 Group sink the minesweeper *M301* in the Kattegat.
4 May: Typhoons of the 2nd TAF sink in the Southern Baltic the steamer *Ostwind*, the motor torpedo boat *S103* and the U-boats *U579*, *U733* and *U876*. Beaufighters of No 16 Group sink in the Belts the minesweeper *M36* and the U-boats *U236*, *U2338*, *U2503* and *U393* and Mosquitoes of No 18 Group sink in the Kattegat the motor ships *Else Hugo Stinnes* (3291 tons) and *Ernst Hugo Stinnes* (3295 tons) and the gunboat *K1*.
5-6 May: Liberators of No 18 Group of Coastal Command sink in the Kattegat the U-boats *U534*, *U3523*, *U2521*, *U2365*, *U3503*, *U2534* and *U1008*.

3 May   Germany
British XII Corps occupies Hamburg. Fifty-nine medium and larger ships, 19 floating docks and about 600 small craft are sunk or scuttled in the harbour.

3-9 May   Baltic
Last evacuations from Hela to the west. From 1 May to 8 May small craft and naval ferry barges of the 13th Landing Flotilla (Cdr Wassmuth) bring approximately 150000 refugees and troops from the landing stages of the Lower Vistula to Hela.
On 3 May the transports *Sachsenwald* and *Weserstrom* proceed to the W with 8550 refugees and the torpedo boats *T36* and *T108* each with 150.
The freighters *Linz*, *Ceuta*, *Pompeji*, the auxiliary cruiser *Hansa*, which after the coming into force of the surrender in NW Germany and Denmark are outside territorial waters, proceed to Hela on 5 May with the destroyers *Hans Lody* (Cdr* Haun), *Friedrich Ihn* (Cdr Richter-Oldekop), *Theodor Riedel* (Cdr Blöse), *Z25* (Cdr Gohrbandt) and the torpedo boat *T17* (Lt-Cdr Liermann), *T19* (Lt-Cdr Frhr v. Luttitz), *T23* (Lt-Cdr Weinlig), *T28* (Lt-Cdr Temming) nad *T35* (Lt-Cdr Buch). There, to-

gether with *V2002*, *M453*, *V303* and the training vessel *Nautik*, they embark 45000 refugees. After beating off Soviet torpedo cutter attacks from Kolberg, the ships arrive off Copenhagen on 6 May, where the fast warships are unloaded in the roads in order to set out again. Together with the destroyers *Z38* (Cdr Frhr v. Lyncker), *Z39* (Cdr Loerke) and the torpedo boat *T33* (Lt-Cdr Priebe) coming from Swinemünde, *Karl Galster*, *Friedrich Ihn*, *Hans Lody*, *Theodor Riedel*, *Z25*, *T17*, *T19*, *T23* and *T28* put in to Hela again on 7 May and, until early on 8 May before the beginning of the Armistice, take on board 20000 soldiers and refugees who are disembarked in Glücksburg on 9 May. In the same night the freighters *Weserberg* and *Paloma* set out with 5730 refugees. The small sea resort steamer *Rugard* with 1500 refugees wards off an attempt by three Soviet torpedo cutters to capture her on 8 May. In all, some 1420000 refugees are evacuated by sea from the area of the Gulf of Danzig and Pomerania between 25 Jan and 8 May. In this figure the short distance evacuations within the Gulf of Danzig are not taken into account: they can be reckoned to have included 600000 refugees.

3-29 May   Central Pacific
Continuation of the Okinawa operations.
From 3 May to 9 May TG 58.3 with the carriers *Essex*, *Bunker Hill*, *Shangri La* and *Bataan* and TG 58.4 with *Yorktown*, *Intrepid*, *Enterprise* and *Langley* operate off Okinawa on an overlapping basis. Constant replenishment is provided by the supply group of the 5th Fleet under Rear-Adm Beary on the cruiser *Detroit*. The supply units consist of tankers, ammunition ships, freighters and spare parts transports, as well as the escort carriers *Attu*, *Admiralty Islands*, *Bougainville* and *Windham Bay*, employed as aircraft transports. Escort: the escort carriers *Shamrock Bay* and *Makassar Strait*, 11 destroyers and 24 DEs.
On 10 Apl TG 58.1 with the carriers *Hornet*, *Bennington*, *Randolph*, *Belleau Wood* and *San Jacinto* relieves TG 58.4 which goes to Ulithi. The night operating carrier *Enterprise* remains with TF 58. On 11 May *Bunker Hill*

(Capt Seitz) is badly damaged by Kamikaze hits: 392 dead and 264 injured. Vice-Adm Mitscher transfers to the *Enterprise* and attacks on 12-13 May Kyushu and the Kamikaze airfields there with TGs 58.1 and 58.3. Early on 14 May, when returning, the *Enterprise* is also badly hit. Vice-Adm Mitscher transfers yet again to the *Randolph*.
The British TF 57 (Vice-Adm Rawlings/Vice-Adm Vian) sets out again from Leyte. It comprises the carriers *Indomitable*, *Victorious*, *Formidable* and *Indefatigable*, the battleships *King George V* and *Howe*, the cruisers *Swiftsure*, *Uganda* (RCN), *Gambia* (RNZN), *Euryalus* and *Black Prince* and the destroyers *Grenville*, *Ursa*, *Urchin*, *Undine*, *Urania*, *Undaunted*; *Quilliam*, *Queenborough*, *Quiberon*, *Quickmatch*, *Quality*; *Kempenfelt*, *Whirlwind* and *Wessex*. After replenishing on 3 May and 4 May, it makes a carrier raid on the Sakishima-Gunto group. The battleships, cruisers, and the first seven destroyers shell the islands and airfields. In the operation *Formidable* is hit by a Kamikaze and *Indomitable* sustains slight damage. After repairs in the night new attacks are made on 5 May. On 6-7 May there is further replenishment. A British supply group consists of tankers, ammunition ships, the transport-escort carriers *Ruler*, *Striker*, *Chaser* and *Speaker* and an escort of the destroyers *Napier*, *Nepal*, *Norman* and *Nizam*, the sloops *Crane*, *Whimbrel*, *Pheasant* and *Woodcock*, the frigates *Avon*, *Parret* and *Findhorn*, the Australian minesweeper corvettes *Whyalla*, *Ballarat*, *Bendigo*, etc. While TF 57 replenishes on 3 May, 6-7 May, 10-11 May, 14-15 May, 18-19 May and 22-23 May, attacks on Sakishima-Gunto are made by US air escort carriers of TG 52.1.3 (*Sangamon*, *Suwanee*, *Chenango* and *Santee*). On 3 May *Sangamon* is damaged beyond repair by Kamikaze pilots. On 9 May, 12-13 May, 16-17 May, 20-21 May and 24-25 May British TF 57 makes attacks. On 9 May damage is inflicted on the *Victorious* and *Formidable* by Kamikaze hits. The destroyers *Napier*, *Nepal*, *Troubridge*, *Tenacious* and *Termagant* operate temporarily with TF 57 as relief for other destroyers. The *Quilliam* is severely

damaged in a collision on 20 May. The New Zealand cruiser *Achilles* joins TF 57 on 23 May. The *Formidable* is detached before the last attacks.

Japanese Kamikaze attacks as part of 'Kikusui 5' on 3 May and 4 May with 75 naval and 50 army aircraft sink the destroyers *Little, Luce* and *Morrison* on picket stations and the boats *LSM(R)-195, LSM(R)-190* and *LSM(R)-194*. The destroyer *Aaron Ward* is damaged beyond repair; and the destroyer *Ingraham* and, after an Oka bomb hit, the minelayer *Shea*, are put out of action until the end of the war. Lesser damage is sustained by the destroyers and destroyer/minesweepers, *Macomb, Bache, Lowry, Massey, Gwin* and *Cowell* and *LCS(L)-25*. With the support group off Okinawa the cruiser *Birmingham* (Rear-Adm Deyo) is damaged on 3 May, the minesweepers *Gayety, Hopkins, YMS 327* and *YMS 331* on 4 May, the tenders *St George* and *Pathfinder* on 5 May. On 9 May the DEs *Oberrender* and *England* are damaged beyond repair. In all, there are 605 dead and 806 injured.

On 10 May new mass attacks ('Kikusui 6') begin with 70 naval and 80 army Kamikaze aircraft. On the picket stations from 10 May to 13 May the destroyers *Evans* and *Hugh W. Hadley* are damaged beyond repair and the *Bache* and the DE *Bright* are put out of action until the end of the war. Off Okinawa the battleship *New Mexico* is badly hit on 12 May but remains in action until 28 May.

On 17 May the destroyer *Douglas H. Fox* is put out of action until the end of the war by a Kamikaze hit. On 18 May the APD *Sims* is damaged; and on 20 May *LST 808* is sunk and the destroyer *Thatcher* and the APD *Chase* are damaged beyond repair and the DE *John C. Butler* slightly damaged. In all, there are 227 dead and 370 injured.

A further wave (Kikusui 7') with 65 naval and 100 Army Kamikazes aircraft attacks on 24-25 May. On the picket stations the destroyer *Stormes* is severely, and *LCS(L)-121* slightly, damaged; but the mass of the aircraft fly round the radar pickets and attack the ships off Okinawa, in the course of which the APDs *Barry* and *Bates* and

LSM 135 are sunk, the APD *Roper* and the minesweepers *Butler* and *Spectacle* are damaged beyond repair and the DE *O'Neill* is severely, and the DE *William C. Cole* and the APD *Sims* and one Liberty ship are slightly, damaged. On 26 May individual Kamikazes damage the destroyer/minesweeper *Forrest*, the submarine-chaser *PC 1603* and the tender *Dutton*.

On 27-28 May there follows the Kamikaze attack 'Kikusui 8' with 60 naval and 50 army aircraft. On the picket stations the destroyer *Drexler* sinks, the *Braine* is severely, and the *Anthony* slightly, damaged. Also slightly damaged are *LCS(L)-52* and *LCS(L)-119*. Off Okinawa the minesweeper *Southard*, the APDs *Loy, Rednour* and the transport *Sandoval* receive hits. On 29 May the destroyer *Shubrick* and the APD *Tatum* are damaged.

Repair ships restore a large part of the damaged ships in the roads of Kerama Retto.

In the second half of May TF 58 continues its sorties against Okinawa. On 24 May two Task Groups make another raid on the Kamikaze airfields on Kyushu, particularly Kanoya, where a group of Oka bombers, which is ready to take off, is surprised on the ground and destroyed.

On 27-28 May Adm Spruance's command is transferred to Adm Halsey; the 5th Fleet becomes the 3rd Fleet; Vice-Adm McCain relieves Vice-Adm Mitscher; and TF 58 becomes TF 38.

4 May   Germany
Signing of the surrender of German troops in NW Germany, Denmark and Holland.

4 May   Norway
Operation 'Judgement': raid by a British Task Force (Vice-Adm McGrigor), comprising the escort carriers *Searcher, Queen* and *Trumpeter*, the cruisers *Norfolk* and *Diadem* and the destroyers *Carysfort, Opportune, Savage, Scourge* and *Zambesi*, and the *Obedient* and *Orwell*, which are returning from Murmansk, on German shipping W of Narvik and on the base at Kilbotn near Narvik: *U711*, the depot ship *Black Watch* and one trawler are sunk.

4-5 May Baltic

The U-boats in Flensburger Förde scuttle themselves after the announcement of the imminent capitulation in the NW German area, in accordance with the order 'Regenbogen' issued earlier, but contrary to the terms of the surrender which forbid the sinking or damaging of ships.

In the inner Flensburger Förde the following boats are scuttled: *U29, U30, U46, U267, U290, U351, U397, U717, U750, U827, U1025, U1132, U1161, U1168, U1234, U1304, U1306, U2333, U2352, U2551, U3033, U3524, U3526, U3529, U4701, U4702, U4703* and *U4704*; in Gelting Bay: *U349, U370, U721,* the Walter boat *U794, U999, U1056, U1101, U1162, U1204, U1207, U1303, U2339, U2343, U2346, U2347, U2349, U2357, U2358, U2360, U2362, U2364, U2366, U2368, U2369, U2507, U2517, U2522, U2525, U2541, U3015, U3022, U3034, U3044, U3510, U4707* and *U4710.*

In Cuxhaven the Walter U-boats *U1406* and *U1407* are scuttled and in Eckernförde *U1405.*

4-5 May Atlantic/British Coastal Waters

When the U-boat war ends, the following German U-boats are in their operational areas:

In the Arctic: *U278, U313, U318, U968, U992* and *U1165.*

In the North Sea: *U2336* and *U287.*

W of the North Channel: *U293, U1105,* and *U1305.*

In the Irish Sea: *U825, U956* and *U1023.*

In the English Channel and its western entrance: *U249* and *U776.*

Off Reykjavik: *U979.*

In the North Atlantic (as weather boat): *U1009.*

On the Canadian coast: *U190, U805* and *U889.*

On the US East Coast: *U530, U853, U858* and *U881.*

On a supply mission to St. Nazaire in the Bay of Biscay: *U516.*

Outward-bound:

To the North Sea: *U2324* and *U2326.*

To the area W of Britain: *U244, U764, U901, U977, U320, U1010, U1057, U1058, U1109, U1272* and *U2511* (4 May: mock attack on British cruiser).

To Gibraltar: *U485* and *U541.*

To the US coast: *U802, U1228* and *U1231.*

To the Caribbean: *U873.*

In addition, *U963* is on her way to a mining operation off Portland.

To East Asia: *U234.*

Homeward-bound:

From the North Sea: *U2322.*

From the North Atlantic: *U826.*

From a mining operation in the Clyde: *U218.*

From East Asia: *U532.*

5-6 May North Atlantic

U853 (Lt Frömsdorf†) sinks off Block Island (R.I.) the US freighter *Black Point* (5353 tons)—the last U-boat success off America—and is then destroyed by the US DE *Atherton* and the frigate *Moberley.*

6 May-7 June Germany/Denmark/ Norway/Arctic

Occupation of the ports in the Northern area.

On 6 May a British force (Capt Williams), comprising the cruisers *Birmingham* and *Dido* and the destroyers *Zealous, Zephyr, Zest* and *Zodiac,* puts to sea, passes through the German mine barrages off the Skagerrak and reaches Copenhagen on 9 May where the German cruisers *Prinz Eugen* and *Nürnberg* are surrendered. The Flag Officer Denmark, Vice-Adm Vesey-Holt, takes over the command. The operation is covered by Vice-Adm McGrigor's Task Force, comprising the escort carriers *Searcher* and *Trumpeter,* the cruiser *Norfolk* and the destroyers *Carysfort, Zambesi, Obedient, Opportune* and *Orwell.*

On 12 May the future Flag Officer Norway (Rear-Adm Ritchie) puts to sea with the cruiser *Devonshire,* the fast minelayers *Apollo* (Crown Prince Olaf of Norway on board) and *Ariadne* and the destroyers *Iroquois* (RCN), *Savage, Scourge* and *Arendal* (Norwegian) and enters Oslo on 13 May. On 15 May the corvette *Buttercup* follows with parts of the Norwegian naval staff.

On 14 May the destroyers *Valorous* and *Venomous,* accompanied by six minesweepers, enter Kristiansand/South and the destroyers *Wolsey* and *Wolfhound* Stavanger. On 15 May the destroyers *Woolston* and *Vivacious,* the Norwegian corvette *Acanthus* and British and Norwegian minesweepers enter Bergen. And on 16 May the destroyers *Mackay* and *Viceroy* with nine minesweepers (Capt Ruck-Keene) enter Trondheim.

On 13 May the Norwegian destroyer *Stord* (with Rear-Adm Danielsen, as Sector Commander Northern Norway on board) and the British destroyer *Broadway* set out from Rosyth. On 16 May they meet the German Arctic U-boats which are being transferred to Trondheim off Vestfjord and hand them over to the escort of convoy JW.67, the 9th EG (see 12-31 May) which is ordered up. The two destroyers arrive in Tromsö on the evening of 16 May. From there *Stord* lands a Norwegian weather station on Bear Island on 25-26 May. On 26 May the Norwegian Brigade in Scotland arrives in Tromsö from Britain on board the transport *Largs Bay*.

The destroyers *Zealous* and *Zodiac* are transferred from Copenhagen to Kiel. In Copenhagen the *Birmingham*, *Zest* and *Zephyr* are relieved from 13 May by the cruiser *Devonshire* and the destroyers *Iroquois* and *Savage* which, together with the *Dido*, take the German cruisers *Prinz Eugen* and *Nürnberg* to Wilhelmshaven from 24 May to 26 May. Vice-Adm McGrigor arrives in Bergen with the cruiser *Norfolk* and the 30th EG and the cruiser *Berwick* with the destroyers *Haida* (RCN) and *Huron* (RCN) and the 5th EG arrive in Trondheim to take over and transfer the U-boats (29-31 May).

The British Flag Officer Wilhelmshaven (Rear-Adm Muirhead) embarks a company of Scots Guards on boats of the German 7th MS Flotilla on 11 May and occupies Heligoland.

On 13 May Rear-Adm Brüning, who has arrived from Holland in a motor torpedo boat, signs in Felixstowe the surrender of the naval forces stationed in Holland.

On 14 May the German minesweeper *M607* arrives in the Firth of Forth with documents on the German mine barrages in the Skagerrak and Kattegat. The first British warships to arrive in Wilhelmshaven are the destroyers *Southdown* and *Brocklesby* and in Cuxhaven the fast minelayer *Adventure*.

On 8 May the destroyers *Beagle* and *Bulldog* proceed to St. Peter Port in Guernsey to receive the surrender of the Channel Islands. The destroyer *Faulknor* and the frigate (DE) *Narborough* escort six minesweepers and two patrol boats to Britain on 17 May.

7 May Norway
A Catalina flying boat of No 210 Sqdn RAF sinks *U320* (Lt Emmrich) off Bergen. This is the last U-boat sunk in the fighting.

7 May General Situation
Signing of the unconditional surrender of the German Wehrmacht in Gen Eisenhower's headquarters in Rheims. It comes into force early on 8 May.

7 May North Sea
Last success by German U-boats in the Second World War. *U2336* (Lt Klusmeyer) sinks the freighters *Avondale Park* (2878 tons) and *Sneland* (1791 tons) off the Firth of Forth.

7 May Germany
Canadian, Polish and British troops occupy Emden, Wilhelmshaven and Cuxhaven.

8 May Baltic
Sixty-five small craft of the German Navy set out from Libau for the W in four convoys with approximately 14400 persons; and 61 craft from Windau in two convoys with approximately 11300 troops. Only some of the slowest units with about 300 men on board are captured by the Soviets on 9 May.

8-9 May Mediterranean
Surrender of the German garrisons in Crete, Milos, Rhodes, Leros, Coo and some smaller islands in the Dodecanese.

9 May Bay of Biscay
Surrender of the German bases at Lorient, La Rochelle and St. Nazaire, as well as the Channel Islands still occupied by German troops.

9-17 May Atlantic/Britain
German U-boats at sea put in to Allied harbours in accordance with instructions:
9 May: *U249* Portland (Channel).
10 May: *U1105*, *U1009* and *U1305* Loch Eriboll; *U1058* Lough Foyle; *U825* Portland; *U1023* Weymouth; and *U532* Liverpool.
11 May: *U826* Loch Eriboll; and *U293* Loch Ailsh.
12 May: *U1109* and *U802* Loch

Eriboll; and *U889* St John's (Newfoundland).

13 May: *U956* Loch Eriboll; *U1228* Portsmouth (USA); and *U858* the Delaware Estuary.

14 May: *U764* and *U1010* Loch Eriboll; *U244*, *U516* and *U1231* Lough Foyle; *U485* and *U541* Gibraltar; *U2326* Dundee; and *U805* and *U234* Portsmouth (USA).

16 May: *U255* Lough Foyle; *U776* Portland; and *U190* St John's.

17 May: *U873* Portsmouth (USA).

Of these boats *U1058* and *U1305* become Soviet war booty, *U1105*, *U805*, *U1228*, *U858*, *U873* and *U234* US war booty and *U190* British war booty. In addition, *U2326* is handed over to France.

The remaining boats are sunk in operation 'Deadlight'.

9-23 May South West Pacific
In support of the 6th Australian Div (Maj-Gen Stevens), which is advancing from Aitape (New Guinea) along the coast eastwards to the centre of Japanese resistance put up by the remains of the 18th Army in Wewak, the 'Wewak Support Force' operates off the coast with the Australian sloop *Swan* and the minesweeper corvettes *Colac*, *Dubbo* and *Deloraine*. On 9-10 May the cruisers *Newfoundland* and *Hobart* (RAN, Commodore Farncomb) and the Australian destroyers *Arunta* and *Warramunga* arrive for support and shell Wewak. On 11 May 623 men of a BLT are landed by one LCM, nine LCIs and two support LCIs in Dove Bay E of Wewak. They capture the Wewak Peninsula and by 23 May the Japanese pockets of resistance in the Wewak area have been overcome.

10 May South West Pacific
A part of Amphibious Group 9 (Rear-Adm Struble, TG 78.3) lands the 108th RCT of the 40th Inf Div in Macalajar Bay in North Mindanao on 10 May.

10-16 May Indian Ocean
On 10 May the Japanese cruiser *Haguro* and the destroyer *Kamikaze* set out from Singapore to evacuate Japanese troops from the Nicobars and Andamans. The ships are reported in the Malacca Straits by the British submarines *Statesman* and *Subtle*. Thereupon TF 61 (Vice-Adm Walker), comprising the battleships *Queen Elizabeth* and *Richelieu*, the cruisers *Cumberland* and *Tromp* (Dutch), the 21st Carrier Sqdn (Commodore Oliver) with the cruiser *Royalist* and the escort carriers *Hunter*, *Khedive*, *Shah* and *Emperor* and eight destroyers sets out from Trincomalee to intercept the Japanese force in the Eleven Degrees Channel. On 11 May the escort carriers make a fighter attack with Hellcat fighters on Car Nicobar and are sighted by a Japanese reconnaissance aircraft. *Haguro* and *Kamikaze* return.

While TF 61 proceeds to the area NW of Sumatra TF 62, comprising the cruiser *Nigeria* and the destroyers *Roebuck*, *Racehorse* and *Redoubt*, sets out from Trincomalee on 13 May. On 14 May Adm Walker detaches the *Cumberland* with the 21st Carrier Sqdn and the 26th DD Flotilla (Capt Power), consisting of *Saumarez*, *Verulam*, *Vigilant*, *Venus* and *Virago*, into the area W of the Six Degrees Channel. On 15 May a reconnaissance aircraft flown off from the *Shah* sights the Japanese ships, which have set out again, NE of Sabang, but they return at once. After the breakdown of the catapult on *Shah*, only three Avenger bombers are able to fly off from the crowded flight deck of the *Emperor* and they have no success. In the night 15-16 May Capt Power with the 26th DD Flotilla approaches the two Japanese ships in the Malacca Straits SW of Penang, and deploys his five destroyers in a classical night pincer attack. *Saumarez* receives three heavy hits in an engagement; then the *Haguro*, after strenuous out-manoeuvring, is hit by the torpedo salvoes and sinks. The *Kamikaze* escapes with only slight damage. Then the *Hunter* and *Khedive* make attacks on the Andaman Islands.

11 May English Channel
Surrender of the German garrison in Dunkirk.

12-31 May Arctic
Last convoy pair JW.67/RA.67 from the Clyde to the Kola Inlet and back, each with 23 ships. The escort includes the escort carrier *Queen*, the destroyers *Onslow*, *Obdurate* and others. In addition, there is the 4th EG with the DEs *Bentinck*, *Drury*, *Bazely*, *Pasley* and *Byard* and the Canadian 9th EG with the frigates *Loch Alvie*, *Monnow*,

Nene, St Pierre and *Matane*. JW.67 arrives in the Kola Inlet on 20 May and RA.67 sets out on 23 May.

On the way out the 9th EG is detached on 16 May in order to halt the Arctic U-boats proceeding from Vestfjord to Trondheim and to accompany them to Loch Eriboll on 19 May. The U-boats include *U278, U294, U295, U312, U313, U318, U363, U427, U481, U668, U968, U992, U997* and *U1165*. The last boat, *U716*, follows later. All boats are sunk in operation ' Deadlight'.

16 May-15 June   Indian Ocean
The Indian sloops *Cauvery, Narbada, Godavari, Kistna, Sutlej* and *Hindustan*, supported at first by the cruiser *Phoebe* and later by the *Ceylon*, patrol between the Mergui Archipelago and Port Blair in the Andaman Sea to prevent the evacuation of Japanese troops and their supply.

On 5 June the 10th DD Flotilla, comprising the British destroyers *Tartar, Eskimo, Nubian, Penn* and *Paladin*, sets out from Trincomalee to intercept shipping between the Nicobars and Sabang. Following a report by the submarine *Trident*, the first three destroyers are directed on 12 June to a convoy and sink the submarine-chaser *Ch 57* and the freighter *Kuroshio Maru*. *Penn* and *Paladin* sink a landing boat off SW Sumatra.

17 May   Central Pacific
US TU 12.5.3 (Rear-Adm C. A. F. Sprague), comprising the carrier *Ticonderoga* and the destroyers *Rowe, Smalley, Stoddart* and *Reid*, makes a raid on the Japanese-occupied Marshall Islands, Taroa and Maloelap.

19 May   North Pacific
US Desdiv 114 shells Paramushiro (Kuriles).

27 May-28 June   Pacific
The Japanese 'Todoroki' submarine group with *Kaiten* torpedoes is used in the open sea against shipping coming from Leyte, Guam, Saipan and other bases to Okinawa. On 27-28 May *I-367* (Lt Taketomi) attacks a convoy with two *Kaiten*, one of which damages the US DE *Gilligan*. On 30 May an aircraft of the 'Hunter-killer' escort carrier *Anzio* sinks *I-361*. *I-36* (Cdr Sugamasa) attacks on 22 June a convoy

E of the Marianas with torpedoes and damages the LST repair ship *Endymion*. On 27-28 June she misses a tanker with one *Kaiten* and just misses the transport *Antares* with two. On 28 June *I-165* is sunk by an aircraft in a search in the area of the Marianas. *I-53* and *I-363* return without success.

29-31 May   Norway
German U-boats in Norwegian harbours are sent to British assembly areas. From Trondheim on 29 May: *U483, U773, U775, U953, U978, U994, U1019, U1064, U1203* (Type VII C) and *U861* (Type IX D). From Bergen on 29 May: *U907, U991, U1052* and *U298*. On 30 May *U245, U328, U928, U930, U1002, U1004, U1005, U1022, U1057, U1104, U1271, U1272, U1301, U1307* (Type VII C), *U218* (Type VII D), *U1061* (Type VII F), *U539, U868* (Type IX C), *U875* (Type IX D), *U2506, U2511, U3514* (Type XXI), *U2328* (Type XXIII), *UD5* (ex-Dutch); and on 31 May *U778* (Type VII C). From Stavanger on 29 May: *U637, U901, U1171* (Type VII C). On 31 May: *U3035* (Type XXI), *U2322, U2324, U2329, U2345, U2348* (Type XXIII). From Kristiansand/South on 29 May: *U281, U299, U369, U712, U1163* (Type VII C), *U2529* (Type XXI), *U2321, U2325, U2334, U2335, U2337, U2350, U2353, U2354, U2361, U2363* (Type XXIII). From Horten on 29 May: *U1108* (Type VII C), *U170* (Type IX C), *U874* (Type IX D), *U2502, U2513, U2518, U3017, U3041, U3515* (Type XXI). Of these U-boats *U1057, U1064, U2529, U3035, U3041, U3515* and *U2353* become Soviet war booty; *U2513* US war booty; *U712, U953, U1108, U1171, U3017* and *U2334* British war booty. In addition, *U2518* and *U2348* are handed over to France. The other boats are sunk by British forces W of the Hebrides in the period 25 Nov-7 Jan as part of operation 'Deadlight'.

For the time being, the following U-boats remain in Norway: *U926* and *U1202* (Bergen) and *U995* (Trondheim)—Type VII C; *U4706* (Kristiansand)—Type XXIII. These are later allotted to Norway as booty. In addition, *U324* and *U1275* (Bergen); *U310* and *U315* (Trondheim); *U975* (Horten)—all Type VII C, which are later scrapped.

29 May–13 June   **Central Pacific**

The US Fast Carrier Task Force continues the operations E of Okinawa as TF 38 under Adm Halsey on the battleship *Missouri* and Vice-Adm McCain on the carrier *Shangri La*. TG 38.2 (Rear-Adm Sherman) goes to Leyte on 29 May. TG 38.1 (Rear-Adm Clark) and TG 38.4 (Rear-Adm Radford) alternate in providing fighter cover for Okinawa. On 2 June and 3 June TG 38.1 remains off Okinawa, while TG 38.4 makes a fighter raid on Kamikaze airfields on Kyushu from the carriers *Shangri La*, *Ticonderoga*, *Yorktown*, *Langley* and *Independence*. On 4 June replenishment from the Logistic Support Force (Rear-Adm Beary) is interrupted because of an approaching typhoon. On 5 June TG 38.1 runs into the centre of the whirlwind and almost all ships, the carriers *Hornet*, *Bennington*, *Belleau Wood* and *San Jacinto*, the battleships *Massachusetts*, *Indiana* and *Alabama*, the cruisers *Pittsburgh* (35 m of her bows torn off), *Baltimore*, *Quincy*, *Atlanta*, *Duluth* and *San Juan* and the destroyers (Desron 61) *De Haven*, *Maddox*, *Blue*, *Brush*, *Taussig*, *Samuel N. Moore* (Desron 25) *John Rodgers*, *McKee*, *Schroeder*, *Dashiell* and *Stockham* of Desdiv 106 are more or less badly damaged. TG 38.4 is able to retire to the N. only the fleet flagship *Missouri* is slightly damaged. Of the supply group, the flagship, the cruiser *Detroit*, the escort carriers *Windham Bay*, *Salamaua*, *Bougainville* and *Attu*, the DEs *Donaldson*, *Conklin* and *Hilbert*, the tankers *Lackawanna* and *Millicoma* and the ammunition transport *Shasta* are damaged. Most of the ships continue their operations. On 6 June refuelling takes place. With TG 38.1 the new carrier *Bonhomme Richard* relieves the *Bennington* and, in place of the *Pittsburgh* and *Baltimore*, come *Topeka* and *Oklahoma City*. On 7 June and 8 June TG 38.1 make sorties over Okinawa. On 9 June it makes experimental sorties with napalm bombs on Okino-Daito-Shima which is also shelled by the

battlecruisers *Alaska* and *Guam* and five destroyers under Rear-Adm Low. TG 38.4 makes another raid on Kanoya (Kyushu) on 8 June. On 10 June the battleships (Rear-Adm Shafroth) *Massachusetts*, *Alabama* and *Indiana* and five destroyers shell Minami-O-shima. Then TF 38 returns to Leyte where it arrives on 13 June. Thus ends three months of uninterrupted operations by the carrier fleet.

1–30 June   **Pacific**

The following ships are sunk by Allied submarines arriving in their operational areas in June: in Japanese waters the US submarine *Apogon* (Lt-Cdr House) sinks the submarine-chasers *Kusentai 58* and *Kusen T-T 65* and one ship of 2614 tons; *Cabezon* (Cdr Lautrup) one ship of 1631 tons; *Dace* (Lt-Cdr Cole) one ship of 1391 tons; *Dentuda* (Cdr McCain) one ship of 88 tons and torpedoes one ship; *Parche* (Lt-Cdr McCrory) two ships of 3668 tons; *Piranha* (Cdr Irvine) sinks one trawler and torpedoes one steamer and the corvette *Kaibokan 196*; *Seadragon* (Lt-Cdr Ashley) one ship of 887 tons; *Sea Owl* (Cdr Bennet) the corvette *Kaibokan 41*; *Segundo* (Lt-Cdr Fulp) one ship of 1591 tons; *Tirante* (Cdr Street) two ships of 3265 tons. In the Sea of Japan, after breaking through the mine barrages in the Tsushima Strait, the US boats *Bonefish* (Cdr Edge) sinks two ships of 12380 tons; *Bowfin* (Cdr Tyree) two ships of 2785 tons and one sailing ship; *Crevalle* (Cdr Steinmetz) three ships of 6643 tons and two small craft and damages the frigate *Kasedo*; *Flying Fish* (Cdr Risser) two ships of 4113 tons and 12 small craft; *Sea Dog* (Cdr Hydeman) seven ships of 7924 tons; *Skate* (Cdr Lynch) three ships of 5256 tons, the submarine *I-122* and one small craft; *Spadefish* (Cdr W. J. Germershausen) six ships of 8647 tons and four small craft; *Tinosa* (Cdr Latham) four ships of 6697 tons; *Tunny* (Cdr Pierce) has an engagement with two escort vessels. In the South East Asia area the US boats *Tiptoe* sinks one ship of 982 tons; *Blueback* (Lt-Cdr Clementson) the submarine-chaser *Kusentai 2*; *Cobia* (Lt-Cdr Becker) the supply ship *Hakusa* and torpedoes one ship; *Hardhead* (Cdr Greenup) the submarine-chaser *Kusentai 42* and *Kusen T-T 113* and damages the landing boat *No 833*; *Tambor* (Lt-Cdr W. T. Germershausen) sinks one ship of 1248 tons.

3-8 June   Indonesia
The Japanese cruiser *Ashigara* (Vice-Adm Hashimoto) sets out from Singapore with the destroyer *Kamikaze* for Batavia, where she takes 1200 Japanese troops on board. When she sails on 7 June she is reported by a US submarine. The British submarine *Trenchant* (Cdr Hezlet), which is deployed, attacks the ships with eight torpedoes in the Bangka Strait. They narrowly miss the *Kamikaze* but sink the *Ashigara* with five hits.

3-22 June   Central Pacific
Last phase in the fighting for Okinawa. On 3 June elements of TF 53 (Rear-Adm Reifsnider) land marines on the island of Ineya Shima and on 9 June on Aguni Shima.
From 3 June to 7 June 20 Japanese naval and 30 army aircraft carry out the Kamikaze operation 'Kikusui 9'. In this action off Okinawa the battleship *Mississippi*, the cruiser *Louisville*, the escort carrier *Natoma Bay*, the destroyer *Anthony* and the destroyer/mine-layers *Harry F. Bauer* and *J. William Ditter* and the picket boat *LCI(L)-90* receive hits. The last two are damaged beyond repair.
A single Kamikaze aircraft sinks on 10 June the destroyer *William D. Porter*. On 11 June the picket boat *LCS(L)-122* is damaged and on 16 June a single torpedo aircraft sinks the destroyer *Twiggs*.
In the final fighting in the S of Okinawa the Commander of the 10th US Army, Lt-Gen Buckner, is killed on 18 June. Maj-Gen Geiger takes over the command temporarily.
From 21 June to 22 June 30 naval and 15 army aircraft make the last co-ordinated Japanese Kamikaze attack, 'Kikusui 10', off Okinawa and Kerama Retto. In this attack the DE *Halloran*, the aircraft tenders *Curtiss* and *Kenneth Whiting*, the minesweeper *Ellyson*, *LST 534* and the picket boats *LSM-59* and *LSM-213* are damaged.

7-20 June   South West Pacific
Operation 'Oboe VI': landing in Brunei Bay (Borneo). On 7 June five fleet minesweepers and 12 YMSs begin to search for mines: in the process the minesweeper *Salute* is sunk on 8 June. By 12 June 102 mines are cleared. Cover for the minesweepers and shelling of the assault areas are undertaken by TG 74.3 (Rear-Adm Berkey), comprising the cruisers *Phoenix*, *Nashville*, *Boise* (Gen MacArthur on board) and the Australian *Hobart*, the destroyers *Killen*, *Albert W. Grant*, *Connor*, *Charette*, *Bell*, *Burns* and the Australian *Arunta*. On 8-9 June the shelling is continued. On 10 June Amphibious Group 6 (Rear-Adm Royal, TG 78.1), with the headquarters ships *Rocky Mount* and the US Coastguard cutter *Spencer*, lands 29361 men of the Australian 9th Inf Div (Maj-Gen Wootten) in Brunei Bay. The transport group comprises three Australian LSIs, one US LSD, two AKAs, nine APDs, 35 LSTs, 21 LSMs and 55 LCIs. Escort: the destroyers *Robinson* (Desron 22), *Saufley*, *Waller*, *Philip*; *Frazier* (Desron 14), *Bancroft*, *Bailey*, *Edwards*, *Caldwell*, *McCalla*; the DEs *Douglas A. Munro*, *Charles E. Brannon*, *Albert T. Harris*, *Dufilho*, *Jobb*, *Day* and the Australian frigates *Hawkesbury*, *Barcoo* and *Lachlan*.
On 20 June elements of these forces land one BLT near Luton (Sarawak/Borneo) which occupies the oilfield of Miri by 25 June.

10-11 June   North Pacific
A US Task Group (Rear-Adm Brown) bombards Matsuwa (Kuriles) with the cruisers *Richmond* and *Concord* and five destroyers.

12-17 June   Central Pacific
Operation 'Inmate': the British TG 111.2 (Rear-Adm Brind) makes a carrier raid on Truk. On 12 June the carrier *Implacable*, the escort carrier *Ruler*, the cruisers *Swiftsure*, *Newfoundland*, *Uganda* and *Achilles* and the destroyers *Troubridge*, *Tenacious*, *Termagant*, *Terpsichore* and *Teazer*, set out from Manus. Early on 14 June the *Implacable* makes an attack with 21 Avengers, 11 Fireflies and 48 Seafires (partly CAP). In the night 14-15 June *Uganda*, *Achilles* and *Tenacious* shell the island of Dublon, the *Newfoundland* and *Troubridge* Uman and *Swiftsure* and *Teazer* Moen. On 15 June aircraft from

the *Implacable* make further attacks. In all, there are 113 attacks and 103 CAP sorties. On 17 June the force returns to Manus.

15 June-9 July   South West Pacific
Operation 'Oboe II': landing in Balikpapan (Borneo). On 15 June three fleet minesweepers and 38 YMSs begin mine clearance on the extensive Japanese minefields in the waters round Balikpapan which were also sown with air mines by the USAAF. Eighteen US air magnetic mines and nine Japanese anchor mines are cleared. *YMS 50* is lost on 18 June, *YMS 39* and *YMS 365* on 26 June and *YMS 84* on 9 July. *YMS 368*, *YMS 47* and *YMS 314* are damaged. *YMS 335*, *YMS 10*, *YMS 364* and *YMS 49* and the destroyer *Smith* are damaged by Japanese coastal guns. Cover and gun support for the minesweepers is provided by elements of TG 74.2 (Rear-Adm Riggs) with the cruisers *Denver* and *Montpelier* and four destroyers. On 24 June the UDTs begin their work. On 25 June there is an unsuccessful Japanese air torpedo attack. It leads to a request for escort carriers.
The shelling of the assault areas is continued from 25 June to 30 June by TG 74.2, comprising the cruisers *Denver*, *Montpelier*, *Columbia*, *Cleveland* and *Tromp* (Dutch), the destroyers *Conway* (Desron 44), *Eaton*, *Cony*, *Stevens*, *Albert W. Grant*, *Killen* and *Arunta* (RAN); in addition, by TG 74.3 (Rear-Adm Berkey), comprising the cruisers *Nashville* and *Phoenix* and the destroyers *Charette* (Desdiv 102), *Bell*, *Conner* and *Burns*, and by TG 74.1 (Commodore Farncomb, RAN), comprising the cruisers *Shropshire* and *Hobart* (RAN) and the US destroyers *Hart* and *Metcalfe*. Gen MacArthur is on board the *Cleveland* and Vice-Adm Barbey (Commander of the Amphibious Forces of the 7th Fleet) on the *Phoenix*. After renewed heavy shelling (in all, 38052 rounds of 3-inch to 8-inch shells from 15 June), 33446 troops of the reinforced Australian 7th Inf Div (Maj-Gen Milford) of I Corps are landed in Balikpapan on 1 July. The landing is effected by TG 78.2 (Rear-Adm Noble) with the three Australian LSIs, *Manoora*, *Kanimbla* and *Westralia*, the head-

quarters ship *Wasatch*, one US AKA, one LSD, five APDs, 35 LSTs, 22 LSMs and 50 LCIs. Escort: the US destroyers *Flusser* (Desron 5), *Drayton*, *Conyngham*, *Smith*; *Frazier* (Desron 14), *Bailey*; *Robinson* (Desron 22), *Saufley*, *Waller*, *Philip*; and the DEs *Chaffee*, *Edwin A. Howard*, *Key*, *Leland E. Thomas* and *Rutherford*. Air support is provided by the 5th USAAF and the 13th USAAF and, from 1 July to 3 July, by an escort carrier group (Rear-Adm Sample), comprising the *Suwanee*, *Gilbert Islands* and *Block Island*, the destroyer *Helm* and the DEs *Cloues*, *Mitchell*, *Kyne*, *Lamons* and *Donaldson*. By 3 July the airfield at Sepinggan is taken and on 4 July the oilfields. On 5 July one battalion of the Australian 9th Inf Brigade is brought across Balikpapan Bay to the W bank near Penadjam; part of it is landed on 9 July further to the N near Djinabora. Small Dutch units land on 7 July N of the Sumbir river near Kariango and Teloktebang.

20 June   Indian Ocean
Operation 'Balsam'.
Aircraft from the escort carriers *Stalker*, *Khedive* and *Ameer* of the British East Indies Fleet attack airfields in Northern Sumatra and Japanese shipping in the Malacca Straits. Escort: the cruisers *Suffolk* and *Royalist* and five destroyers.

20 June   Central Pacific
US TG 12.4 (Rear-Adm Jennings), comprising the carriers *Hancock*, *Lexington* and *Cowpens* and five destroyers, makes a carrier raid on the island of Wake on the way to join TF 38.

21 June   Pacific
End of the ground fighting on Okinawa. Suicide of the Commander of the Japanese defending forces, Lt-Gen Ushijima (Commander of the 32nd Army), and his Chief of Staff, Maj-Gen Cho.
Japanese losses: approximately 130000 dead and 42000 civilians. 10755 Japanese are taken prisoner. The US Army loses 7613 dead and missing and has 31807 wounded; the Navy 4907 dead and missing and 4824 injured. Thirty-six American ships are sunk and 368 damaged. According to American reports, the Japanese lose 7830 aircraft to the Americans' 763.

21-30 June Germany
The U-boats which are still in the North German and Denmark area and are operational are transferred from Wilhelmshaven to Britain.
On 21 June: *U155*, *U883*, *U1230*, *U1233* (Type IX C), *U3008* (Type XXI), *U2336*, *U2341*, *U2351* and *U2356* (Type XXIII).
On 22 June: *U806* (Type IX C).
On 23 June: *U368*, *U1103*, *U1110* and *U1194* (Type VII C).
On 24 June: *U291*, *U680*, *U720*, *U779* and *U1198* (Type VII C).
On 30 June: *U143*, *U145*, *U149*, *U150* (Type II D) and *U739* (Type VII C).
These boats are sunk in operation 'Deadlight', with the exception of *U3008* which becomes US war booty.

25 June-7 July North Pacific
Operations by US TF 92 (Rear-Adm Brown) from Attu: from 25 July to 22 July it makes a sortie with the cruisers *Richmond* and *Concord* and the destroyers *Bearss* (Desdiv 114), *John Hood*, *Jarvis* and *Porter* into the sea of Okhotsk. On 26 June they encounter a Japanese convoy SW of Paramushiro and sink one ship. Others are damaged. The cruiser *Trenton* and the destroyers *Anderson* and *Hughes* operate E of the Kuriles.
From 3 July to 7 July five of the above-named ships make a new raid into the Sea of Okhotsk and shell Shitsuka on South Sakhalin on 5 July.

27 June South West Pacific
End of organized Japanese resistance on Luzon. Individual pockets of resistance hold out until the end of the war.

1-18 July Central Pacific
Attack by TF 38 (Adm Halsey, Vice-Adm McCain) on Japan. On 1 July TF 38 sets out from Leyte.
TG 38.1 (Rear-Adm T. L. Sprague) comprises the carriers *Bennington*, *Lexington*, *Hancock*, *Belleau Wood* and *San Jacinto*, the battleships *Indiana*, *Massachusetts* and *Alabama*, the cruisers *Topeka*, *Duluth*, *Dayton*, *Atlanta* *San Diego*, the destroyers (Desron 61) *De Haven*, *Mansfield*, *Lyman K. Swenson*, *Collett*, *Maddox*, *Blue*, *Brush*, *Taussig*, (Desron 25) *John Rodgers*, *Harrison*, *McKee*, *Murray*, *Ringgold*, *Schroeder*, *Dashiell*, (Desdiv 100) *Caperton*, *Cogswell*, *Ingersoll* and *Knapp*.

TG 38.3 (Rear-Adm Bogan) comprises the carriers *Ticonderoga*, *Randolph*, *Essex*, *Monterey* and *Bataan*, the battleships *South Dakota* and *North Carolina*, the cruisers *Pasadena*, *Springfield*, *Wilkes-Barre*, *Astoria* and *Oakland*, the destroyers (Desron 48) *Erben*, *Walker*, *Hale*, *Abbot*, *Stembel*, *Bullard*, *Black*, *Chauncey*, *Heerman*, (Desron 62) *English*, *Charles S. Sperry*, *Ault*, *Waldron*, *John W. Weeks*, *Hank*, *Wallace L. Lind* and *Borie*.
TG 38.4 (Rear-Adm Radford) comprises the carriers *Yorktown*, *Shangri La* (Vice-Adm McCain), *Bonhomme Richard*, *Independence* and *Cowpens*, the battleships *Iowa*, *Missouri* (Adm Halsey) and *Wisconsin*, the cruisers *Quincy*, *Chicago*, *Boston*, *St Paul* and *San Juan*, the destroyers (Desron 53) *Cushing*, *Colahan*, *Uhlmann*, *Benham*, *Stockham*, *Wedderburn*, (Desron 54) *Remey*, *Norman Scott*, *Mertz*, *Monssen*, *McGowan*, *McNair*, *Melvin* (Desdiv 113) *Rowe*, *Smalley*, *Stoddard*, *Watts*, *Wren* and the radar picket destroyer *Frank Knox*.
After replenishing on 7 July and 8 July the carriers attack the Tokyo area on 10 July with 1022 aircraft, concentrating on air bases. Then the three Task Groups proceed to the N and replenish on 12 July E of the Tsugaru Strait. The attack on 13 July is postponed because of the weather. On 14 July 1391 aircraft set off for targets in North Honshu and South Hokkaido and ferry traffic in the Tsugaru Strait. The attacks are repeated on 15 July. In the operations the escort destroyer *Tachibana*, the corvettes *Kaibokan 65*, *72*, *219*, the minesweeper *Sokaitei 24* and the submarine-chaser *Kusentai 28* are sunk in addition to 37 ferry ships, transports and patrol craft totalling 48717 tons. The escort destroyer *Yanagi*, the frigates *Iwo*, *Fukue* and *Kasado*, the corvettes *Kaibokan 215*, *205*, *55*, *47*, *221*, the submarine-chasers *Kusen T-T 72*, *81*, and *47* and 28 ferry ships, transports and patrol ships totalling 49965 tons are damaged. On 14 July TG 34.8 (Rear-Adm Shafroth) with the battleships *South Dakota*, *Indiana* and *Massachusetts*, the cruisers *Quincy* and *Chicago* and nine destroyers of Desron 48 shells, for the first time, targets on the

Japanese main islands, the steel and iron works at Kamaishi. In all, 802 rounds of 16-inch, 728 rounds of 8-inch and 825 rounds of 5-inch shells are fired. On 14 July and 15 July TG 35.1 (Rear-Adm Jones) with the cruisers *Pasadena, Springfield, Wilkes-Barre* and *Astoria* and six destroyers of Desron 53 carries out a raid on shipping off the east coast of North Honshu but finds no targets. On 15 July TG 34.1 (Rear-Adm Badger) with the battleships *Iowa, Missouri* and *Wisconsin*, the cruisers *Dayton* and *Atlanta* and seven destroyers of Desron 54 and the *Frank Knox* shells the iron and steel works at Muroran (860 rounds of 16-inch shells). On 16 July the destroyers are refuelled and British TF 37 (Vice-Adm Rawlings and Vice-Adm Vian) joins the force with the carriers *Formidable, Victorious* and *Implacable*, the battleship *King George V*, the cruisers *Newfoundland, Achilles* (RNZN), *Uganda* (RCN), *Euryalus, Gambia* (RNZN) and *Black Prince* and the destroyers *Quiberon, Quickmatch, Quality, Quadrant; Troubridge, Tenacious, Termagant, Teazer, Terpsichore; Grenville, Undaunted, Undine, Urania, Urchin* and *Ulysses*.

On 17-18 July the US and British carriers make heavy raids on the Tokyo-Yokohama area. After eliminating the fighter and AA defence, aircraft of the *Yorktown* put the Japanese battleship *Nagato* out of action. In addition, the escort destroyer *Yaezakura*, the submarine *I-372*, the submarine-chaser *Kusen T-T 225* and the motor torpedo boat *PT 28* are sunk; the training cruiser *Kasuga* is badly hit; and the destroyer *Yakaze*, one landing ship, one submarine-chaser and one motor torpedo boat are damaged. In the night 17-18 July TG 34.1 (Rear-Adm Badger) with the battleships *Iowa, Missouri, Wisconsin, North Carolina* and *Alabama*, the cruisers *Dayton* and *Atlanta* and eight destroyers and the British battleship *King George V* and the destroyers *Quality* and *Quiberon*, shells industrial targets in the Hitachi area NE of Tokyo. The US battleships fire 1238 rounds of 16-inch shells, the cruisers 292 rounds of 6-inch and the *King George V* 267 rounds of 14-inch. In the night 18-19

July, after an uneventful sortie against shipping targets, TG 35.2 (Rear-Adm Holden) with the cruisers *Topeka, Duluth, Atlanta* and *Dayton* and eight destroyers of Desron 62 and TG 35.3 (Rear-Adm Jones) with the cruisers *Pasadena, Springfield, Astoria, Wilkes-Barre* and six destroyers shell targets near Cape Nojima SE of Tokyo. Because of a threatening typhoon, the groups withdraw on 19 July to replenish on the following day. The carrier *Indefatigable* with the destroyers *Barfleur, Wrangler* and *Wakeful* joins TF 37 on 20 July.

1-31 July   Pacific
The following ships are sunk by Allied submarines arriving in their operational areas in July:
In Japanese waters the US submarine *Barb* (Cdr Fluckey) sinks one ship of 2820 tons and the corvette *Kaibokan 112; Haddo* (Lt-Cdr Lynch) two ships of 5326 tons and the corvette *Kaibokan 72; Moray* (Cdr Barrows) one ship of 384 tons; *Pogy* (Lt-Cdr Bowers) two ships of 4668 tons; *Runner* (Lt-Cdr Bass) the minesweeper *Sokaitei 27; Sea Poacher* (Lt-Cdr Gambacorta) two ships of 318 tons; *Sea Robin* (Lt-Cdr Stimson) one ship of 1224 tons and the submarine-chaser *Kusen T-T 85; Sennet* (Lt-Cdr Clark) four ships of 13105 tons; *Threadfin* (Lt-Cdr Foote) the minesweeper *Sokaitei 39;* and *Trepang* (Lt-Cdr Faust) one ship of 606 tons.
In the South East Asia area the British submarine *Stubborn* (Lt Gowan) sinks one ship of 1270 tons. The US submarine *Baya* (Lt-Cdr Jarvis) sinks the torpedo boat *Kari; Bluefish* (Lt-Cdr Forbes) the submarine *I-351* and the submarine-chaser *Kusentai 50; Bumper* (Cdr Williams) two ships of 1227 tons; *Hammerhead* (Lt-Cdr Smith) two ships of 1734 tons; *Hardhead* (Lt-Cdr Haines) the submarine-chaser *Kusen T-T 117;* and *Lizardfish* (Cdr Butler) the submarine-chaser *Kusentai 37.*

2 July   North Pacific
The US submarine *Barb* (Cdr Fluckey) shells with rockets Japanese installations on Kaihyo Island on the east coast of Karafuto (Kuriles). This is the first rocket operation by submarines.

5-10 July   Indian Ocean
Operation 'Collie'. Preparatory to the

planned landing on the Malayan North-West Coast (Operation 'Zipper') near Port Swettenham and Port Dickson, British mine-sweepers of the 6th, 7th and 37th Flotillas clear 167 mines off the coast and in the area of the Nicobars. The operation is covered by the cruiser *Nigeria* and the destroyers *Roebuck*, *Eskimo* and *Vigilant* which also shell Nancowry. Air escort is provided by the escort carriers *Ameer* and *Emperor*, which also make carrier raids on North Sumatran airfields with the escort carriers *Stalker* and *Empress*.

12 July North Pacific
A US Task Group, comprising the cruisers *Richmond* and *Concord* and five destroyers, shells Suribachi Point in the Kuriles.

12 July South West Pacific
Allied landing near Andus, Borneo. Australian troops take Maradi in West Borneo.

16 July-12 Aug Central Pacific
US TF 95 (Vice-Adm Oldendorf) operates from Okinawa to support troops on the island and to provide air warning (radar picket stations). It also makes sorties against shipping in the East China Sea. TG 95.1 (Vice-Adm Oldendorf) comprises the battleships *Tennessee* and *Pennsylvania*. It frequently operates together with TG 95.3. TG 95.2 (Rear-Adm Low) comprises the battlecruisers *Alaska* and *Guam* and the cruisers *Cleveland*, *Columbia*, *Denver* and *Montpelier*.
TG 95.3 comprises T.U.1—the escort carriers *Lunga Point*, *Makin Island* and *Cape Gloucester*—and T.U.2—the battleships *California* and *Nevada* and the cruisers *Salt Lake City*, *Chester*, *Wichita* and *St Louis*. There are also 18 destroyers.
TG 95.7 comprises the battleships *Arkansas* and *Texas* and the cruisers *Portland*, *Mobile* and *Vicksburgh* (the two last join TF 38 after the Wake Raid).
In addition, the destroyers of Desrons 23, 45, 49 and 55 are employed as part of TF 95 and are sometimes allocated to the TGs or the radar picket stations. They include from Desron 23 *Charles Ausburne*, *Claxton*, *Dyson*, *Converse* and *Thatcher*, from 49 *Picking*, *Wickes* and *Harridan*, from 55 *Porterfield*,

Callaghan, *Cassin Young*, *Irwin*, *Preston* and *Laws*, and from Desdiv 92 *Boyd*, *Bradford*, *Brown* and *Cowell* and from Desron 24 *Ammen*, *Beale*, *Daly*, etc. Drawing on these forces, TG 95.2 (Rear-Adm Low) makes a raid with two battleships, four light cruisers and eight destroyers on shipping in the East China Sea and in the Yellow Sea from 16 July to 23 July. But it has only small success. From 26 July to 28 July TF 95 (Vice-Adm Oldendorf), comprising the battlecruisers *Alaska* and *Guam*, the battleships *Nevada*, *Tennessee* and *California*, the cruisers *Cleveland*, *Columbia*, *Denver* and *Montpelier*, the escort carriers *Makin Island*, *Lunga Point* and *Cape Gloucester* and 18 destroyers, makes a raid into the area of the Yangtse Estuary off Shanghai with little effect. In this period minesweeping operations in the area SE of Okinawa and in the East China Sea are also covered.
In radar picket operations the destroyer *Callaghan* is sunk on 28 July by Kamikaze pilots and the destroyer *Cassin Young* is damaged on 29 July. From 1 Aug to 7 Aug TF 95 carries out three 'anti-shipping strikes' in the East China Sea. On 5-6 Aug Rear-Adm Litch makes a raid on the area Tinghai/China with the escort carriers *Cape Gloucester*, *Fanshaw Bay*, *Lunga Point* and *Makin Island*. Cover is provided by four battleships, four cruisers, seven destroyers and three DEs.
On 12 Aug the battleship *Pennsylvania* receives an air torpedo hit off Okinawa.
16 July-13 Aug Central Pacific
Last Japanese submarine operation with *Kaiten* torpedoes. From the 'Tamon' group which sets out on 16 July, *I-47* (Lt-Cdr Suzuki) attacks a convoy with torpedoes in the Philippine Sea on 21 July and damages the transport *Marathon* (7607 tons). *I-53* (Lt-Cdr Oba) launches on 24 July two *Kaiten* on a convoy, one of which sinks the US DE *Underhill*. A second attack with two *Kaiten* on 4 Aug E of Formosa does not achieve anything. *I-58* (Cdr Hashimoto) launches a *Kaiten* on 27-28 July against a force on the Guam-Leyte route and probably damages the destroyer *Lowry*. On 29-30 July she sinks with two hits from a salvo of six the unescorted heavy cruiser *Indianapolis* (Capt McVay) E of

Luzon. The cruiser had brought parts of the atomic bombs from San Francisco to Tinian and was proceeding to Leyte. Of the cruiser's crew of 1199 only 316 are rescued by American flying boats and destroyers between 2 Aug and 8 Aug. On 10 Aug *I-58* launches two *Kaiten* on a convoy. The DE *Johnnie Hutchins* avoids them but a search with two hunter-killer groups, comprising the DEs *Kendall C. Campbell, Douglas A. Munro, Rolf, William Seiverling* and *George A. Johnson, Connolly, Metiver* and *Witter* fails to find *I-58*. On 12 Aug the submarine launches two more *Kaiten* against the LSD *Oakhill* and the DE *Thomas F. Nickel* which graze the target but detonate after being deflected.

I-366 (Lt Tokioka) reports on the evening of 11 Aug an attack with three *Kaiten* on a convoy 500 nautical miles N of Palau. *I-367* returns without success. *I-373* is sunk on the way out by the US submarine *Spikefish*.

In the middle of July the 1st SM Div (Capt Ariizumi) sets out from Japan for Truk with the 'aircraft carrier submarine cruisers' *I-400* (Cdr Kusaka), *I-401* (Lt-Cdr Nambu), *I-14* (Cdr Shimizu) and *I-13* (Cdr Ohashi). The last is sunk on 16 July by the hunter-killer group, comprising the escort carrier *Anzio* and five DEs, by an aircraft and the DEs *Lawrence C. Taylor* and *Robert F. Keller*. The others put to sea from Truk in the middle of August with their eight aircraft on board to make a Kamikaze aircraft attack on Ulithi. But the attack is broken off because of the cease-fire and on their return to Japan the submarines are captured between 27 Aug and 29 Aug.

18 July-9 Aug   Central Pacific
Raids by US Task Groups on Wake, chiefly with units which, after being repaired on the US West Coast, are proceeding via Pearl Harbour to join TF 38. Taking part in the carrier raid on 18 July are the carrier *Wasp*, the cruisers *Oklahoma City, Amsterdam, Tuscon* and *Flint* and probably the destroyers *Samuel N. Moore, Twining, Wadleigh* and *Franks* and the new radar picket destroyers *Highbee, Southerland* and *Benner* which join TF 38 on 21-22 July. On 1 Aug the carrier *Cabot* and on 6

Aug the carrier *Intrepid* make a carrier raid. With them sail respectively the destroyers *Walke, O'Brien, Lowry, Allen M. Sumner, Moale* and *R. K. Huntington* from Desron 60 and the cruisers *Mobile* and *Vicksburgh* and the destroyers *Clarence K. Bronson, Cotten, Dortch, Gatling* and *Healy* from Desron 50. They join TF 38 just before and just after the August raids. On 1 Aug TG 95.1 also shells the island with the battleships *Tennessee* and *Pennsylvania*: the latter is hit by coastal guns. On 9 Aug a Task Group, comprising, inter alia, the battleship *Pennsylvania*, cruisers and destroyers, carries out another shelling of Wake.

In the area of the Marianas the escort carrier *Vella Gulf* makes raids on 24 July and 26 July on the islands of Pagan and Rota.

21-22 July   Central Pacific
The greatest supply action of the war at sea. US TG 30.8 (Rear-Adm Beary), comprising the command cruiser *Detroit*, the escort carriers *Chenango, Thetis Bay, Hollandia, Roi, Munda* and *Gilbert Islands*, 15 tankers, five ammunition transports and four freighters for supplies, replenishes TF 38 and elements of British TF 37 with about 60000 tons of oil, 6369 tons of ammunition, 1635 tons of supplies, 99 aircraft and 412 reserve personnel.

21 July-13 Aug   North Pacific
Sorties by US TF 92 (Rear-Adm Brown) from Attu against the North Kuriles from 21 July to 23 July and from 11 Aug to 13 Aug. On 22 July the cruisers *Pensacola, Richmond* and *Concord* and the destroyers (Desdiv 114) *Bearss, John Hood, Jarvis, Porter Anderson, Hughes* and *McDermut* shell Suribachi on Paramushiro. On 12 Aug the same force shells Matsuwa and Paramushiro. *McDermut* is hit by a coastal battery.

24-26 July   Indian Ocean
British minesweepers clear the minefields off Phuket Island on the west coast of the Kra Isthmus; in the operation the minesweeper *Squirrel* is sunk. The operation is covered by Vice-Adm Walker with the battleship *Nelson*, the cruiser *Sussex*, the escort carriers *Ameer* and *Empress* and four destroyers. The carriers make raids on the Kra Isthmus

and the ships shell shore installations. On 26 July there is the first Kamikaze attack on the British East Indies Fleet, when the carrier *Ameer* is damaged and the minesweeper *Vestal* is sunk.

24-30 July   Central Pacific

US TF 38 continues its attacks on Japan with three Task Groups (see 1.7) and the British TF 37.

On 24 July the carrier aircraft make 1747 sorties against harbours and bases in the Inland Sea, particularly Kure and Kobe. The Japanese carrier *Amagi* and the cruiser *Oyodo* are sunk. The battleships *Ise*, *Hyuga* and *Haruna*, the training cruiser *Iwate* and the heavy cruiser *Aoba* are so badly damaged that they sink on the bottom. Also damaged are the carriers *Katsuragi*, *Ryuho* and *Hosho*, the escort carrier *Kaiyo*, the cruiser *Kitakami*, the destroyer *Yoitsuki*, the escort destroyers *Hagi*, *Kaba* and *Tsubaki*, the target ship *Settsu*, the corvettes *Kaibokan 190* and *Kaibokan 4* and one landing ship. Fifteen merchant ships and auxiliary warships totalling 22326 tons are sunk. In the night 24-25 July TG 35.3 (Rear-Adm Jones), comprising the cruisers *Pasadena*, *Springfield*, *Wilkes-Barre* and *Astoria* and six destroyers from Desron 53, shells the seaplane station off Kushimoto and the airfield near Shionomisaki in South Honshu. After replenishing from TG 30.8, the aircraft of TF 38 and TF 37 again attack the harbours of the Inland Sea on 28 July. In addition to the ships already hit and partly destroyed on 24 July, the cruiser *Tone*, the training cruiser *Izumo* and the escort destroyer *Nashi* are destroyed and the unfinished large submarine *I-404* wrecked. The frigate *Habushi*, the torpedo boat *Asagao*, the corvettes *Kaibokan 44*, *Kaibokan 45* and *Kaibokan 190*, the submarine *I-205*, the submarine-chaser *Kusentai 14* and the submarine depot ship *Komahashi* are badly damaged. Eight auxiliary ships and transports totalling 6059 tons sink.

After the destroyers have refuelled, the carrier groups attack the harbours of Kobe, Nagoya and Maizuru on 30 July. There the frigate *Okinawa*, the corvette *Kaibokan 2*, the minelayer *Tojima*, the submarine-chaser *Kusentai 26* and seven ships of 10834 tons are sunk; and the destroyer *Yukikaze*, the frigate *Takane*, the submarines *I-202* and *I-153*, the submarine depot ship *Chogei*, the submarine-chaser *Kusen T-T 182* and two ships of 7516 tons are badly damaged.

TG 34.8 (Rear-Adm Shafroth), comprising the battleships *South Dakota*, *Indiana* and *Massachusetts*, the cruisers *Quincy*, *Chicago*, *St Paul* and *Boston*, the nine destroyers of Desron 48 and the radar picket destroyer *Southerland*, as well as a British group comprising the battleship *King George V* and the destroyers *Undine*, *Ulysses* and *Urania*, shells in the night 29-30 July works and aircraft factories near Hamamatsu (South Honshu). The seven destroyers of Desron 25 under Capt Ludewig make a sortie in the night 30-31 July into Suruga Bay S of Tokyo and shell Shimizu. Then TFs 38 and 37 (the cruiser *Argonaut* relieves the *Uganda* on 27 July) withdraw to the SE to replenish (1-8 Aug).

30 July   Indian Ocean

The midget submarine *XE 3* (Lt Fraser) and *XE 1* (Lt Smart), which are towed by the British submarines *Stygian* and *Spark* into the entrance to Singapore Harbour, damage the Japanese cruiser *Takao* with fixed explosive charges so badly that she sinks to the bottom. The *Myoko* is undamaged.

1-31 Aug   Pacific

The following ships are sunk by US submarines arriving in their operational areas in August: in Japanese waters *Atule* (Lt-Cdr Maurer) sinks the corvette *Kaibokan 6* and torpedoes *Kaibokan 16*; *Billfish* (Lt-Cdr Farley) sinks one ship of 1091 tons; *Jallao* (Cdr Icenhower) one ship of 5794 tons; *Pargo* (Lt-Cdr Bell) one ship of 5462 tons; *Torsk* (Lt-Cdr Lewellen) one ship of 873 tons and the corvettes *Kaibokan 13* and *Kaibokan 47*.

6-9 Aug   Japan

On 6 Aug a B 29 long-range bomber 'Enola Gay' (Col Tibbets) of the 509th Composite Group (20th USAAF) drops the first atomic bomb on Hiroshima. 80% of the city is destroyed. There are at least 92167 dead and 37425 injured among the city's population.

On 9 Aug a B 29 (Maj Sweeney) drops

the second atomic bomb on Nagasaki. There are at least 40000 dead and 60000 injured among the civilian population.

9-12 Aug   Pacific

The Soviet Union declares war on Japan. The Soviet Pacific Fleet (Adm Yumashev) consists of two modern cruisers, the *Kalinin* and the *Kaganovich*; one flotilla leader, the *Tbilisi*; 10 modern destroyers the *Rastoropny*, *Razyashchi*, *Rezvy*, *Ryany*, *Revnostny*, *Redki*, *Rekordny*, *Rezki*, *Retivy* and *Vnushitelny*; two old destroyers, the *Stalin* and *Voikov*; eight patrol ships and torpedo boats of Soviet construction and 11 US Lend-Lease frigates; 10 Soviet minelayers; eight Soviet and 18 ex-US deep-sea minesweepers; 18 ex-US coastal minesweepers; 49 submarine-chasers including 20 ex-US type SC; 204 torpedo cutters including 45 ex-US PT boats; and 78 submarines of Soviet construction. It employs almost exclusively old and ex-US Lend-Lease ships in supports of the land operations and landings.

On 9 Aug MBR-2 flying boats and Il-4 Bombers attack Unegi and Najin. After dawn Yak-9 fighters and Il-2 ground-attack aircraft of the 2nd Mining and Torpedo Air Div, the 10th Dive Bomber Div and the 12th Ground Attack Div (Lt-Gen Lemeshko) attack the harbours again and also Chongjin. On 10 Aug the attacks are repeated. In 552 air sorties and attacks by TKAs of the 1st Torpedo Cutter Brigade (Capt 2nd Class Kukht) the frigate *Yashiro*, the corvettes *Kaibokan 87* and *Kaibokan 82* and 16 merchant ships of 57325 tons are sunk or damaged. On 15 Aug Soviet naval pilots sink the frigate *Kanju* off Wonsan.

To cover the coast of the Amur-Province the submarines *L-14*, *L-17*, *Sh-122*, *Sh-123*, *Sh-102*, *Sh-104*, *Sh-126*, *Sh-127*, *Sh-134* and *Sh-135* take up positions in the Japan Sea. *Sh-119* and *Sh-117* are stationed off West Sakhalin.

9-15 Aug   Central Pacific

After replenishing on 2-3 Aug, TF 38 moves N with the British TF 37. Passing typhoons prevent further attacks on targets in Japan for several days. After the destroyers have refuelled, TGs 38.1, 38.3 and 38.4 and TF 37 make sorties against North Honshu and Hokkaido on 9 Aug. The following reinforcements have arrived and/or alterations have been made in the composition of the Task Groups since 1 July (see that entry):

TG 38.1: the cruisers *Oklahoma City* and *Amsterdam*, the destroyer *Samuel N. Moore*, the radar picket destroyer *Highbee* and the carrier *Cabot*.

TG 38.3: the carrier *Wasp*, the cruisers *Tuscon* and *Flint*, the destroyers of Desron 60, the radar picket destroyers *Benner* and *Southerland*.

TG 38.4: the destroyers *Wadleigh*, *Franks* and *Twining*.

TF 37 (Vice-Adm Rawlings and Vice-Adm Vian) consists of the carriers *Victorious*, *Indefatigable*, *Formidable* and *Implacable*, the battleships *Duke of York* (Adm Fraser, C-in-C British Pacific Fleet) and *King George V*, the cruisers *Achilles* (RNZN), *Gambia* (RNZN), *Newfoundland*, *Uganda* (RCN), *Black Prince* and *Euryalus*, the destroyers *Quickmatch*, *Quadrant*, *Quiberon*, *Quality* (all four RAN), *Grenville*, *Urania*, *Undine*, *Undaunted*, *Urchin*, *Troubridge*, *Tenacious*, *Termagant*, *Ulysses*, *Teazer*, *Barfleur*, *Wrangler* and *Wakeful*.

On 9 Aug the four carrier groups make attacks on airfields and shipping targets in North Honshu and Hokkaido. 251 aircraft are destroyed. A lone Japanese aircraft damages the destroyer *Borie*. TG 34.8 (Rear-Adm Shafroth) with the battleships *Alabama*, *Indiana* and *Massachusetts*, the cruisers *Quincy*, *Boston*, *St Paul* and *Chicago* and seven US destroyers of Desron 48, together with a British group, comprising the cruisers *Gambia* and *Newfoundland* and the destroyers *Terpsichore*, *Termagant* and *Tenacious*, shells Kamaishi on Honshu. Aircraft from the battleships *South Dakota* and *Indiana* serve as artillery spotters.

On 10 Aug there is another carrier raid on shipping targets, airfields and railways in North Honshu. On 9-10 Aug the frigates *Amakusa* and *Inagi*, the minesweepers *Sokaitei 1*, *Sokaitei 33* and nine ships of 6425 tons are sunk and the minelayer *Tokiwa* and the escort destroyer *Yanagi* are badly damaged, as are five ships of 14178 tons.

On 11 Aug and 12 Aug the ships are replenished by TG 30.8 (Rear-Adm Beary). The British TF 37 returns with most of its ships to Manus. The *Indefatigable*, *King George V*, *Gambia*, *Newfoundland* and the destroyers *Barfleur*, *Napier* (RAN), *Nizam* (RAN), *Wakeful*, *Wrangler*, *Troubridge*, *Termagant*, *Tenacious* and *Teazer* form TG 38.5.

On 13 Aug the five groups make new attacks on the Tokyo area. 254 Japanese aircraft are destroyed on the ground. The fighter cover shoots down 18 aircraft.

On 14 Aug the destroyers are refuelled. Early on 15 Aug a new wave of attacks from the carriers begins on Tokyo before orders from the C-in-C Pacific, Adm of the Fleet Nimitz, are received to stop hostilities. Fierce air engagements develop because the order does not reach all the attacking formations in the air. The last Japanese Kamikaze pilots, including the Commander of the 5th Air Fleet, Vice-Adm Ugaki†, fly off from Tokyo.

11-12 Aug   North Pacific
US TF 92 (Rear-Adm Brown), comprising the cruisers *Richmond* and *Concord* and 12 destroyers, shells Japanese installations in the Kuriles.

12-21 Aug   Pacific
Soviet landing operations on the east coast of Korea in support of the advance by the 25th Army.

On 12 Aug a force (Rear-Adm Ivanovski), comprising the frigates *EK-7* and *EK-9*, the minesweeper *T-271*, two patrol boats and eight torpedo cutters, including *TKA-567* and *TKA-578*, lands 879 men of the reinforced 75th Naval Inf Bn in Unggi (Yuki) in NE Korea, which has, in the meantime, been evacuated by the Japanese and reached shortly before by the Soviet 303rd Rifle Div by the land route. On the same day, patrol and torpedo cutters land an advance party of 163 men in Najin (Rashin), which remains in the harbour area until the arrival of the landing force (Capt 1st Class Poltavski) with the reinforced 358th Naval Inf Bn (617 men) and it is possible on 15 Aug to establish contact with the forward troops of the 25th Army. Taking part are the headquarters ship, flotilla leader

Tbilisi, out at sea, the landing force, comprising the frigate *EK-5*, the minesweepers *T-279* and *T-281*, the patrol boats *BO-303*, *BO-305*, *MO-8*, *MO-16*, four coastal patrol boats and two torpedo cutters. On 14-15 Aug *T-279*, one TKA, the transports *Suchan*, *Kamchatneft* and the tanker *No 1* are lost or badly damaged on air mines laid beforehand by US Army aircraft.

On 13 Aug the frigate *EK-2* and the minesweeper *T-278* land an advance party of 260 men near Chongjin (Seishin) which is only able to hold out with difficulty and with losses, as a result of Japanese counter-attacks, until the landing force (Adm Yumashev) arrives on 15 Aug. This force consists of the old destroyer *Voikov*, the frigates *EK-1*, *EK-3*, *EK-8*, *EK-9*, *EK-7*, the minesweepers *T-275*, *T-280*, *T-272*, *T-273*, *T-274*, *T-276*, 18 torpedo cutters, the patrol ships *Metel*, *Vyuga*, the patrol cutters *BO-304*, *BO-306*, *BO-307*, *BO-317*, two MO cutters, the LCI landing boats *DS-31*, *DS-32*, *DS-33*, *DS-38*, *DS-39*, *DS-40*, *DS-41*, *DS-42*, *DS-44*, *DS-45*, the LCT *TDS-01* and seven transports and 5000 men of the 13th Naval Inf Brigade embarked on them.

On 16 Aug the transports *Nogin*, *Navastroy* and *Dalstroy* run on to mines.

On 19 Aug the reinforced 77th Naval Inf Bn with 650 men is landed near Cape Odaejin (Odentsin) by a force (Capt 1st Class Studenichnikov) comprising the patrol ship *Metel* and six TKAs.

On 21 Aug a force (Rear-Adm Frolov), consisting of the destroyer *Voikov*, the frigate *EK-3*, the minesweepers *T-277*, *T-282* and six TKAs, lands a battle group of 2000 men in Wonsan, whose garrison offers no resistance and surrenders on 22 Aug.

16-25 Aug   Pacific
The Soviet North Pacific Flotilla (Vice-Adm Andreev), which comprises nine submarines, one patrol ship, six (and later six more) minesweepers and 24 torpedo cutters, carries out landings on S Sakhalin.

On 16 Aug a force, consisting of the patrol ship *Zarnitsa*, the minelayer *Okean*, the patrol cutters *MO-27*, *MO-29*, *MO-33*, *MO-34*, 14 torpedo cutters, the minesweepers *T-522*, *T-524*,

T-590, T-591, two lighters, the patrol cutters BO-310, BO-314 and five more torpedo cutters, lands 1554 men of a naval landing unit against slight resistance near Toro behind the 88th Japanese Div.

On 20 Aug a force under Capt 1st Class Leonov, comprising Zarnitsa, Okean, the patrol-cutters BO-302, BO-314, MO-25, MO-31, MO-32, MO-35, MO-63, the minesweepers T-588, T-583, T-591, T-522, three transports and two auxiliary ships, as well as the TKA-631, TKA-641, TKA-645, TKA-646 and the submarine Shch-118, lands the 113th Rifle Brigade near Maoka.

On 25 Aug Okean, T-522, T-524, T-599, T-600, T-601, T-602, T-603, T-604, four BO patrol cutters and six TKAs, coming from Maoka, put a landing party ashore in Chonto and Otomari.

18-25 Aug   North Pacific

Forces of the Naval Defence Sector Petropavlovsk (Capt 1st Class Ponomarev) carry out landings on the Northern Kurile islands.

On 18 Aug a force, consisting of the minelayer Okhotsk, the patrol ships Kirov and Dzerzhinski, nine MO patrol cutters, the minesweepers Vekha, T-155, T-156, T-525, the motor minesweepers T-334, and one other, the survey ships Polyarny and Lebed, 14 transports and 15 landing vessels, lands two rifle regiments and a reinforced artillery regiment on Shimushu, the most northerly of the Kurile islands. After strong initial resistance by the elements of the Japanese 91st Div stationed on Shimushu, the Japanese capitulate, on 19 Aug and 20 Aug. In the operations T-152 is lost.

On 23 Aug Soviet units, without encountering resistance, are landed on Paramushiro and on 25 Aug on Onekotan, Harumukotan and Sjasikotan.

19 Aug-20 Sept   China

Japanese surrender in China.

On 19 Aug the Chinese Generalissimo Chiang Kai-shek orders all Red Chinese troops to remain in their positions in North China and the Japanese Expeditionary Army to surrender only to the Nationalist troops. On the instructions of Mao Tse-tung the order is ignored by the Red Chinese troops. After the evacuation of Kalgan (NW of Peking) by the Japanese, Red Chinese troops occupy the city on 20 Aug. On 24 Aug troops of the Red Chinese 18th Army Group (Gen Chu-Teh) occupy the harbours of Chefoo and Wei Hai wei. Then the Japanese troops are ordered to remain in their positions until the arrival of the Nationalist Chinese troops and to defend themselves against Red Chinese attacks.

On 25 Aug the new Nationalist Chinese 6th Army occupies Nanking and there on 9 Sept the Commander of the Japanese China Area Army, Gen Okamura, signs the capitulation of Japanese forces in China in the presence of representatives of Marshal Chiang Kai-shek.

On 10 Sept the Nationalist Chinese 94th Army occupies Shanghai and the US TF 95 and a British carrier group (see 27 Aug-16 Sept) operate off the Yangtse Estuary. A few days later the Nationalist Chinese 3rd Army reaches Hankow.

On 9 Sept the Nationalist Chinese General Li establishes an advance headquarters for Marshal Chiang Kai-shek in Peking, which is held by Japanese troops and where on 17 Sept the first Nationalist Chinese units arrive by air in US transport planes.

On 24 Sept Marshal Chiang Kai-shek requests the USA to land troops in Shanghai, Nanking, Peking and Tientsin. On 21 Sept US and British warships (see above) arrive in Shanghai.

22 Aug   Central Pacific

The garrison of the Atoll Mili (Marshall Islands) is the first Japanese garrison in the Pacific to capitulate: it does so on board the DE Levy.

25-31 Aug   Japan

From 25 Aug carrier aircraft of TF 38 carry out daily patrol flights over Japan to control shipping, rail and road movements and to locate prisoner-of-war camps.

On 28 Aug the first advance parties land to secure Atsugi airfield near Tokyo.

On 30 Aug the airborne landing of the 11th US Airborne Div (Maj-Gen Swing) begins at Atsugi. The 187th Parachute RCT occupies and secures the airport and the 188th Parachute RCT the harbour of Yokohama. On 31 Aug the 511th Airborne RCT follows. On the afternoon of 30 Aug the Commander of the 8th US Army, Lt-Gen Eichelberger, and the Supreme Allied Commander, Gen of the Army Douglas MacArthur, land at Atsugi. On 29-30 Aug the 4th RCT of the 6th Marine Div lands in Yokosuka, whose naval base is surrendered to the 3rd US Fleet on board the cruiser San Diego.

26 Aug-3 Sept   North Pacific
Soviet units occupy the Kurile islands. On 26 Aug units land on Matsuwa, on 27 Aug on Shinshiru, on 28 Aug on Urup and Etorofu. From 1 Sept to 3 Sept units of the North Pacific Fleet occupy the southern Kurile islands of Kunajiri, Shikotan and Taraku.

27 Aug   South West Pacific
The Japanese forces on Morotai and Halmahera under Lt-Gen Ishii surrender to the US 93rd Inf Div.

27 Aug   Japan
The 3rd US Fleet (Adm Halsey) arrives in Sagami Bay. Taking part is TF 38 (Vice-Adm McCain) comprising:
TF 38.1 (Rear-Adm T. L. Sprague): the carriers Bennington, Lexington, Hancock and Belleau Wood, the battleships Alabama and Indiana, the cruisers Topeka, Duluth, Atlanta, Dayton and San Juan; the destroyers (Desron 61) De Haven, Mansfield, Lyman K. Swenson, Collett, Maddox, Blue, Brush, Taussig, Samuel N. Moore, (Desron 48) Erben, Hale, Black, Bullard, Chauncey and Heerman, the radar picket destroyers Highbee, Perkins and Frank Knox.
TG 38.2 (Rear-Adm Ballentine): the carriers Randolph, Intrepid, Antietam, and Cabot, the battleship Wisconsin, the cruisers Oklahoma City, Amsterdam, Mobile, Vicksburgh and Tucson, the destroyers (Desron 60) Walke, O'Brien, Lowry, Allen M. Sumner, Moale, R. K. Huntington, Bristol, (Desron 57) Rowe, Smalley, Stoddard, Watts, Wren, Wadleigh, Norman Scott, Franks, Barton, the radar picket destroyers Rogers and Duncan.
TG 38.3 (Rear-Adm C. A. F. Sprague): the carriers Ticonderoga, Wasp, Monterey and Bataan, the battleships South Dakota and North Carolina, the cruisers

Pasadena, Springfield, Wilkes-Barre and Oakland, the destroyers (Desron 62) English, Charles S. Sperry, Ault, Waldron, John W. Weeks, Hank, Wallace L. Lind, Borie, (Desron 25) John Rodgers, Harrison, McKee, Murray, Kimberly, Ringgold, Schroeder, Dashiell and the radar picket destroyers Benner and Southerland.
TG 38.4 (Rear-Adm Radford): the carriers Yorktown, Shangri La, Bonhomme Richard, Independence and Cowpens, the battleships Iowa and Missouri. the cruisers Quincy, Boston, St Paul, Chicago, San Diego and Flint, the destroyers (Desron 50) Clarence K. Bronson, Cotten, Dortch, Gatling, Healy, Cogswell, Caperton, Ingersoll, Knapp, (Desron 53) Cushing, Colahan, Halsey Powell, Uhlmann, Benham, Yarnall, Twining, Stockham, Wedderburn and the radar picket destroyers Chevalier, Myles C. Fox and Hawkins.
British TG 38.5 (Vice-Adm Rawlings): the carrier Indefatigable, the battleships Duke of York (Adm Fraser) and King George V, the cruisers Newfoundland and Gambia (RNZN), the destroyers Barfleur, Teazer, Tenacious, Termagant, Terpsichore, Napier (RAN) and Nizam (RAN).
The Commonwealth ships are joined on 31 Aug by the Australian TG 70.9, coming from Leyte and comprising the cruisers Shropshire and Hobart and the destroyers Bataan and Warramunga, as well as the minesweepers Ipswich, Ballarat and Cessnock.
In addition, US TG 32.9: the old battleships New Mexico, Mississippi, Idaho, Colorado and West Virginia, the destroyers (Desron 21) Nicholas, O'Bannon, Taylor, Terry, Ross and Hopewell.
Supply fleet: TG 30.8 comprising the cruiser Detroit, the escort carriers Thetis Bay, Hollandia, Roi, Munda and Gilbert Islands, the destroyers Wilkes, Nicholson, Woodworth, Buchanan, Lansdowne, Lardner, Gillespie, Kalk, Stevenson, Stockton and Thorn, the DEs Griswold, Carlson, Reynolds, Mitchell, Donaldson, William C. Miller, Cabana, Dionne, Canfield, Deede, Elden, Lake, Lyman, Crowley, Le Ray Wilson, Joseph E. Connolly, Willmarth, Bangust, Waterman, Weaver, Hilbert, Lamons, Kyne and McClelland.

Of the Pacific submarines, *Archerfish*, *Cavalla*, *Gato*, *Haddo*, *Hake*, *Muskallunge*, *Pilotfish*, *Razorback*, *Runner*, *Segundo*, *Seacat* and *Tigrone* arrive with the depot ship *Proteus*.

There also take part a large number of minesweeping vessels and supply ships. The Japanese destroyer *Hatsuzakura* brings Japanese representatives to the *Missouri* where they receive instructions for the surrender ceremony. Pilots bring the ships to their anchorages. On 29 Aug the C-in-C Pacific, Fleet Adm Nimitz, arrives and embarks on the battleship *South Dakota*.

27 Aug-12 Sept   Indian Ocean
On 27 Aug a British Task Group (Vice-Adm Walker), comprising the battleship *Nelson*, the cruiser *Ceylon*, the escort carriers *Hunter* and *Attacker*, three destroyers and two LSIs, sets out from Rangoon for Penang where it arrives on 28 Aug. Commodore Poland with the cruiser *London* and a destroyer anchors off Sabang. Japanese delegations bring documents concerning mine barrages and give assurances of their peaceful intentions. On 29 Aug the C-in-C East Indies Fleet, Adm Power, arrives with the cruiser *Cleopatra* off Sabang and on 1 Sept off Penang. On 31 Aug Vice-Adm Hirose surrenders on behalf of the forces on Sumatra on board the *London* and on 2 Sept Vice-Adm Uzumi for the Penang area on board the *Nelson*. After minesweepers have cleared the approaches, marines are landed on 2 Sept and 3 Sept in Sabang and on the island of Penang. Spitfire fighters are flown into Penang. The 6th, 7th and 37th MS Flotillas clear the Straits of Malacca. On 2 Sept Adm Power goes with the *Cleopatra* and the Indian sloop *Bengal*, behind the 6th MS Flotilla, to Singapore where he arrives on 2 Sept. On 4 Sept the cruiser *Sussex* follows with the 7th MS Flotilla, one destroyer and a convoy with the headquarters ship *Kedah* from Bombay with the 5th Indian Div, XV Corps HQ and the British 3rd Commando Brigade on board. After Lt-Gen Itagaki and Vice-Adm Fukudome have surrendered on board the *Sussex* on behalf of the Japanese forces in the Singapore and Johore area on 4 Sept, British-Indian forces land. The 3rd Commando Brigade

remains embarked and proceeds to Hong Kong (see below). On 9 Sept the planned operation 'Zipper' begins with the landing of the 25th Indian Div (Maj-Gen Wood) near Morib, 18 nautical miles S of Port Swettenham and the 23rd Indian Div (Maj-Gen Hawthorn) near Sepang, eight nautical miles N of Port Dickson. Over 100000 troops are landed in three days. Covering force: the battleships *Neison* and *Richelieu*, the cruisers *Nigeria*, *Ceylon*, and *Cleopatra*, 15 destroyers and the 21st Carrier Sqdn comprising the cruiser *Royalist*, the escort carriers *Hunter*, *Stalker*, *Archer*, *Khedive*, *Emperor* and *Pursuer* and, as a Spitfire transport, the *Trumpeter*.

On 12 Sept Lt-Gen Itagaki and Vice-Adm Fukudome, representing the indisposed Japanese C-in-C South East Asia, Field-Marshal Terauchi, sign the surrender of all Japanese forces in South-East Asia in the presence of the Allied C-in-C South East Asia, Adm Lord Mountbatten.

27 Aug-16 Sept   South China Sea
On 27 Aug British TG 111.2 (Rear-Adm Harcourt) sets out from Subic Bay to occupy Hong Kong. The force consists of the carriers *Indomitable* and *Venerable*, the cruisers *Swiftsure*, *Euryalus* and *Black Prince*, the destroyers *Kempenfelt*, *Ursa*, *Quadrant* and *Whirlwind*, the Canadian auxiliary cruiser *Prince Robert*, the 8th SM Flotilla with the depot ship *Maidstone* and eight submarines and the Australian minesweepers *Mildura*, *Castlemaine*, *Bathurst*, *Broome*, *Fremantle*, *Strahan* and *Wagga*. On 29 Aug it meets there a Task Group (Rear-Adm Daniel) originally earmarked for Singapore and consisting of the battleship *Anson* and the carrier *Vengeance* and two destroyers. On 29 Aug the minesweepers begin the clearance work. On 30 Aug *Kempenfelt*, *Swiftsure* (with Rear-Adm Harcourt), *Ursa*, *Euryalus*, *Prince Robert*, *Mildura* and *Bathurst* come in. As they do so, three Japanese explosive boats are seen to be setting out from the small battle unit base. Aircraft of the *Indomitable* and *Venerable* then attack the anchorage in Lamma Bay and destroy the boats.

On 11 Sept the convoy with the 3rd

Commando Brigade and the escort carrier *Smiter* with an RAF contingent arrive from Singapore. On 14 Sept the C-in-C British Pacific Fleet, Adm Fraser, arrives with the battleship *Duke of York*. On 16 Sept the Japanese Maj-Gen Okada and Vice-Adm Fujita surrender on behalf of the Japanese forces in the Hong Kong area in the presence of Rear-Adm Harcourt.
On 27 Aug a British Task Group (Rear-Adm Servaes) is formed from the carrier *Colossus*, the cruisers *Bermuda*, and *Argonaut* and the destroyers *Tyrian*, *Tumult*, *Tuscan* and *Quiberon*, in order to occupy the Shanghai area with elements from US TF 95 (see above).

28 Aug-1 Oct   Japan
Mine clearance in Japanese waters.
Under the orders of the Commander Minesweeping Craft Pacific, Rear-Adm Struble, minesweeping forces begin on 28 Aug with the work of clearing the important sea lanes for the occupation of Japan.
From 28 Aug to 4 Sept 23 DMSs and AMs clear the approaches and anchorages of Yokohama, Yokosuka and Tokyo Bay. Seventy-four Japanese and three US mines are cleared. The same force then clears Japanese barrages off Sendai and Chosi (Hondo).
From 1 Sept to 8 Sept a minesweeping force clears the approaches to Kagoshima (Kyushu), then on 9 Sept those to Sasebo and on 10 Sept those to Nagasaki. The force loses five YMSs in the typhoon 'Louisa' on 16 Sept.
On 8 Sept US minesweepers begin clearance work in the Tsugaru Strait.
On 11 Sept 27 minesweepers begin to clear a passage through the Kii Channel to the Inland Sea and the entrances to Kobe and Osaka. In the course of the work some Japanese minesweepers are also used for the first time.
From 22 Sept 32 US and 33 Japanese minesweepers begin to create a passage through the Bungo Channel to Kure and Hiroshima. For the first time mine destructor ships are used against pressure mines: inter alia, *LST 553*, *LST 768* and three US and four Japanese transports, as well as two old Japanese destroyers which are lost.
From 28 Sept a passage is cleared through the Ise Channel to Nagoya.

30 Aug   Central Pacific
Surrender of the Japanese garrison of Marcus Island on board the destroyer *Bagley*.

30 Aug   North Pacific
US TF 92 (Rear-Adm Brown), comprising the cruisers *Richmond* and *Concord*, the headquarters ship *Panamint* and the destroyers *Bearss, John Hood, Jarvis, Anderson, Hughes, Porter* and *Izard* and the DEs *Sellstrom, Ramsden, Mills, Rhodes, Richey* and *Savage*, and the escort carrier group (Rear-Adm Martin), comprising *Hoggatt Bay, Kitkun Bay, Nehenta Bay, Fanshaw Bay, Manila Bay* and *Savo Island*, and the destroyers *Guest, Hudson, Halford, Fullam, Stanly, Wainwright, Bennion, Killen* and *Albert W. Grant*, arrive off Ominato (Northern tip of Honshu) and accepts the surrender of the Japanese bases.

2 Sept   Japan
Signing of the overall Japanese surrender on board the American battleship *Missouri* in Sagami Bay. The Foreign Minister Shigemitsu and the Chief of the Army General Staff, Gen Umezu, sign for Japan. Gen MacArthur accepts the surrender on behalf of the Allies. Fleet Admiral Nimitz signs for the USA; Gen Hsu Yung-chang for China; Adm Sir Bruce Fraser for Great Britain; Lt-Gen Derevyanko for the Soviet Union; Gen Sir Thomas Blamey for Australia; Col Moore-Cosgrove for Canada; Gen Leclerc for France; Adm Helferich for Holland; and Air-Vice-Marshal Isitt for New Zealand.

2 Sept-1 Oct   Pacific
The following surrender to US forces in the Central Pacific are:
On 2 Sept, the US Commandant of Peleliu, Brig-Gen Rogers, accepts the surrender of the Japanese forces on Pagan (Palau Islands) under Lt-Gen Inoue. On the same day the garrison of the Mariana island of Rota surrenders.
On 3 Sept the Japanese C-in-C on the Philippines, Gen Yamashita, accompanied by Vice-Adm Okochi, signs in Baguio the surrender of the Japanese forces on the Philippines in the presence of the Commander of the US Army Force West Pacific (Gen Styler) and the Commander of the 32nd Div (Maj-Gen Gill).

R

On board the *Portland* Vice-Adm Murray accepts the surrender of the Japanese island fortress of Truk and the islands in the area of the Central Carolines.

On board the destroyer *Dunlap* off Chichijima Commodore Magruder accepts the surrender of the Bonin Islands by Lt-Gen Tachibana. Brig-Gen Sanderson on board the DE *Levy* accepts the surrender of the island garrison of Wake.

On 4 Sept the islands of Jaluit (Carolines) and Aguijan (Marianas) surrender and on 5 Sept those of Yap and Ulithi.

On 7 Sept the Kusaie island group (Carolines) is surrendered. In Okinawa the commander of the 10th US Army, Gen Stilwell, accepts the surrender of the remaining forces on the Ryukyu Islands.

On 9 Sept the island of Formosa is surrendered.

On 10 Sept the Marshall Islands of Wotje and Maloelap, and on 11 Sept Ponape, are surrendered.

On 14 Sept Brig-Gen Stevenson on board the Australian frigate *Diamantine* accepts the surrender of the garrison of Nauru (Capt Saeda) and on 1 Oct the surrender of Ocean Island (Cdr Suzuki). On 19 Sept the last major garrison, that of Woleai (Carolines) surrenders.

2 Sept–22 Oct Japan
Operation 'Blacklist': the occupation of Japan.

The occupation of Japan is carried out in the area to the N, and inclusive of, Tokyo by the 3rd Amphibious Force (Vice-Adm Wilkinson with the headquarters ship *Mount Olympus*) and the US 8th Army (Lt-Gen Eichelberger) and, to the S, by the 5th Amphibious Force (Vice-Adm Hill with the headquarters ship *Auburn*) and the US 6th Army (Gen Krueger).

In the area of the 8th Army XI Corps (Lt-Gen Hall) occupies the Tokyo area, XIV Corps (Maj-Gen Griswold) the area of North Honshu (with the exception of Ominato) and IX Corps (Maj-Gen Ryder) the area of the Tsugaru Strait and Hokkaido.

In XI Corps's zone TF 33 lands on 2 Sept the 1st Cavalry Div (Maj-Gen Chase) in Yokohama and on 3 Sept

the 112th Cav RCT is landed in Tateyama to secure Tokyo Bay. On 5 Sept the first reconnaissance of Tokyo is made and on 8 Sept the 1st Cav Div marches in. The flags are raised in the presence of Gen MacArthur, the Allied Supreme Commander in Japan. After the completion of the airlift of the 11th Airborne Div (Maj-Gen Swing) on 6 Sept, the 27th Inf Div (Maj-Gen Griner) is flown to Atsugi from Okinawa from 7 Sept to 14 Sept. From 8 Sept to 10 Sept TF 35 lands the Americal Div in Yokohama. On 14 Sept the 43rd Inf Div (Maj-Gen Wing) follows but is withdrawn to return to the USA on 27 Sept.

XIV Corps begins the occupation of North Honshu in Sendai on 15 Sept. It is allocated the 11th Airborne Div which comes to Sendai by land and the 27th Inf Div which comes to Niigata. As relief, the 97th Inf Div (Maj-Gen Kramer) arrives in the Tokyo area on 20 Sept.

IX Corps zone: on 6 Sept the North Pacific Force (Vice-Adm Fletcher, relieved by Rear-Adm Denebrinck in the middle of September) lands advance detachments of the Marine Corps in Ominato (Northern tip of Honshu). On 8 Sept minesweeping forces begin clearing the Tsugaru Strait. From 25 Sept to 27 Sept an Amphibious Group lands the 81st Inf Div (Maj-Gen Mueller) in Aomori in the Tsushima Strait and on 4 Oct the 306th RCT is landed in Otaru on Hokkaido. The bulk of 77th Inf Div (Maj-Gen Bruce) follows on 15 Oct to Otaru and from there to Sapporo. From 7 Oct IX Corps establishes its HQ in Sapporo.

In the area of the 6th Army V Amphibious Corps (Lt-Gen H. Schmidt) occupies Kyushu, X Corps (Maj-Gen Siebert) Shikoku and South Honshu and I Corps (Maj-Gen Swift) Honshu from the Kii Channel as far as the line Shizuoka-Takaoka.

In the zone of V Amphibious Corps the 127th RCT of the 32nd Inf Div (Maj-Gen Gill) is brought by air on 4 Sept to Kanoya (southern tip of Kyushu). Amphibious Group 4 (Rear-Adm Reifsnider) lands the 5th Marine Div (Maj-Gen Bourke) in Sasebo on 22 Oct. On 22 Sept the 2nd Marine Div (Maj-Gen Hunt) follows to Nagasaki. On 15 Oct the rest of the 32nd Inf Div is landed in Shimonoseki and proceeds to Saga in Central Kyushu. The operations are covered by a group under Rear-Adm Deyo.

In the zone of I Corps Amphibious Group 8 (Rear-Adm Noble) lands the 33rd Inf Div (Maj-Gen Clarkson) in Kobe on 25 Sept; the 98th Inf Div (Maj-Gen Harper) in Wakayama on 27 Sept; and the 25th Inf Div (Maj-Gen Mullins) in Nagoya on 2 Oct. The HQ of 6th Army is established in Kyoto and that of I Corps in Osaka.

In the zone of X corps (HQ Kure) the 24th Inf Div (Maj-Gen Woodruff) is landed by an amphibious group (Commodore Ryan) in Matsuyama (Shikoku) on 7 Oct and the 41st Inf Div (Maj-Gen Doe) by Amphibious Group 11 (Rear-Adm Rogers) in Kure on 22 Sept.

5 Sept-17 Oct   Korea
The occupation of Korea is carried out by the 7th Fleet (Adm Kinkaid) and XXIV Corps (Lt-Gen Hodge).

On 5 Sept an amphibious group (Commodore Brittain), comprising 18 APAs, one AKA, several APDs, a minesweeping group and a covering group, sets out from Okinawa with the US 7th Inf Div (Maj-Gen Arnold). Overall command: the 7th Amphibious Force (Vice-Adm Barbey on the headquarters ship *Catoctin*). On 8 Sept there is a landing at Inchon and from there the capital of Seoul is occupied after moving by land.

On 9 Sept the Japanese Governor-General Abe, the Commander of the 17th Area Army, Lt-Gen Kotsuki, and Vice-Adm Yamaguchi sign in the governmental palace in Seoul, and in the presence of Gen Hodge and Adm Kinkaid, the surrender of the Japanese forces in Korea S of the 38th Parallel.

The plan to bring a BLT on 20 Sept by sea to Pusan cannot be carried out because of the mining of the harbour. On 22 Sept an amphibious group (Commodore Palmer) lands the 40th Inf Div (Brig-Gen Meyers) at Inchon and on 23 Sept a BLT of this Div is brought by land to Pusan. On 17 Oct the 6th Inf Div (Maj-Gen Hurdis) follows to Inchon with the same amphibious group (Commodore Palmer).

Air escort for this operation and that of

VII Amphibious Force off North China (see 26 Sept-31 Oct) is provided by TF 72, comprising the carriers *Antietam*, *Intrepid* (relieved by *Boxer* from 11 Oct) and *Cabot*, cruisers and destroyers.

6-13 Sept   South West Pacific
Acts of surrender in the area of the Bismarck Archipelago and New Guinea. On 6 Sept a British force, comprising the carrier *Glory*, the Australian destroyer *Vendetta*, the sloops *Hart* and *Amethyst* and the Australian minesweeper corvettes *Kiama*, *Dubbo*, *Lithgow*, *Townsville*, tug *Reserve* and two MLs, arrives off Rabaul. On board the *Glory* the Commander of the Japanese 8th Area Army, Gen Imamura, and the Commander of the South East Area Fleet, Vice-Adm Kusaka, sign in the presence of the Commander of the Australian 1st Army, Lt-Gen Sturdee, the surrender of the Japanese forces in the area of the Bismarck Islands, New Guinea and the Solomons (a total of 139000 men). On 8 Sept the Commander of the Japanese 17th Army, Lt-Gen Kanda, and Vice-Adm Samejima sign on board the Australian frigate *Diamantina* off Cape Torokina the surrender of the forces on Bougainville. On 10 Sept on board *ML 805* the Japanese Rear-Adm Sato signs, in the presence of the Commander of the Australian 6th Div, Maj-Gen Robertson, the surrender of the Wewak offshore islands. On 13 Sept the surrender of the Japanese 18th Army is signed by Lt-Gen Adachi in the presence of Gen Robertson on the airfield of Wom near Wewak. On 19 Sept Lt-Gen Ito and Rear-Adm Tamura surrender the forces on New Ireland in the presence of Maj-Gen Eather on board the Australian sloop *Swan* in Nabuto Bay.

6-9 Sept   Central Pacific/Japan
US troops begin to return to the USA. On 6 Sept TF 11 (Vice-Adm Sherman), comprising the battleships *New Mexico*, *Idaho*, *Mississippi* and *North Carolina*, the carriers *Monterey* and *Bataan* and a Desron, sets out from Tokyo for the USA via Okinawa with 'high priority returns'. On 9 Sept the operation 'Magic Carpet' begins with the formation of TF 16.12 (Rear-Adm Kendall), consisting initially of eight escort

carriers. The force expands to 369 warships by December, including six battleships, 18 cruisers, 11 fleet carriers, 46 escort carriers and 12 hospital ships. In some cases they make several trips. By March 1946 1307859 personnel are brought back. The highest single quota is taken by the carrier *Saratoga* with 29204. In the same period transports carry 1815535 personnel.

8-21 Sept Dutch East Indies
Acts of surrender by the Japanese forces in the area of Eastern Indonesia. On 8 Sept the Japanese Vice-Adm Kamada signs on board the Australian frigate *Burdekin*, in the presence of the Commander of the 7th Australian Div, Maj-Gen Milford, the surrender of the Japanese forces in the area of Balik-papan. On 9 Sept the Japanese Maj-Gen Yamamura signs on board the Australian minesweeper *Kapunda*, in the presence of Brig-Gen Eastick, the surrender of the Japanese forces in the area of Kuching/Brunei in North-West Borneo. On the same day the Commander of the Japanese 2nd Army, Lt-Gen Teshima, signs in Morotai, in the presence of the Commander of the Australian Army, Gen Blamey, the surrender of the Japanese forces in the Dutch East Indies. On 10 Sept the Australian minesweeper *Glenelg* arrives with three ships off Ambon and the minesweeper *Latrobe* off Ceram. On 14 Sept Menado (Celebes) is surrendered to the minesweeper *Glenelg*. On 15 Sept the Australian frigates *Burdekin* and *Gascoyne* arrive in Bandjermasin. On 21 Sept the Australian frigate *Barcoo* is the first to occupy Makassar (Celebes) with four ships.

9-10 Sept Central Pacific
On 9-10 Sept the typhoon 'Louisa', whose centre passes 15 nautical miles E of Okinawa and which brings wind speeds of 100 knots and, in gusts, up to 120 knots, causes great damage to US ships off Okinawa. Twelve ships sink, 222 ships and craft are driven aground and 32 more are damaged. By 19 Nov 79 units are salvaged and made seaworthy, 132 are in the course of being repaired and 53 are abandoned as unserviceable.

11 Sept-3 Oct Indonesia
On 11 Sept the Australian survey ship *Moresby* arrives off Koepang/Timor with the minesweepers *Horsham, Benalla, Parkes, Katoomba, Warrnambool* and *Gladstone* and the Dutch minesweeper *Abraham Crijnssen*: it is surrendered by the Japanese Colonel Kaida to Brig-Gen Dyke. On 27 Sept the Portuguese sloops *Bartolomeo Dias* and *Gonçalves Zarco* and, two days later, the transport *Angola*, arrive in Dili to re-occupy the Portuguese port of the island. On 3 Oct the commander of the Japanese 48th Div, Lt-Gen Yamada, surrenders all Japanese forces on Timor in the presence of Brig-Gen Dyke.

15 Sept-1 Nov Indonesia
On 15 Sept the British cruiser *Cumberland* (Rear-Adm Patterson) arrives off Jakarta with one frigate and four Australian minesweepers. On 16 Sept there follow another frigate, two minesweepers and four landing craft and the Dutch cruiser *Tromp*. Because of the disturbances on shore between Indonesian Nationalists and the Japanese, a British battalion is not landed in Batavia before 29 Sept. On 3 Oct a Brigade Group is landed. On 6 Oct advance detachments of the 23rd Indian Div and the HQ of XV Corps arrive and on 10 Oct the 23rd Div. On 10 Oct elements of the 26th Indian Div land on Sumatra. On 19 Oct the troop transport *Glenroy* brings a BLT to Semarang to crush an uprising. On 25 Oct the transport *Waveney* lands the 49th Indian Brigade in Soerabaya. On 1 Nov the Indian 5th Div follows with a convoy under the command of the headquarters ship *Bulolo*. A covering force is provided by the British cruiser *Sussex* with the destroyers *Caesar, Carron* and *Cavalier*.

26 Sept Indian Ocean
The Indian sloop *Narbada* arrives in Port Blair (Andamans) and accepts the surrender of the local Japanese garrison under Vice-Adm Hara.

26 Sept-31 Oct China
US VII Amphibious Force (Vice-Adm Barbey) receives orders to land the III Amphibious Corps (Maj-Gen Rockey) in the area Tientsin/Chinwangtao and on the Shantung Peninsula.

On 26 Sept an amphibious force (Commodore Brittain) sets out from Okinawa with the 1st Marine Div (Maj-Gen Peck). On 30 Sept the troops are disembarked in the Peiho Estuary: a BLT occupies the Taku forts and the remainder are transported by LCI, LCM and LCT to Tientsin. The 1st RCT and the 11th RCT remain there; the 5th RCT goes to Peking and a BLT of the 7th RCT goes later to Chinwangtao. On 6 Oct the approximately 50000 Japanese troops in this area under Gen Uchida surrender to Maj-Gen Rockey in Tientsin. The US Marines protect traffic communications and the coal mines against attacks by Red Chinese units and prepare the repatriation of the Japanese.

On 4 Oct the Amphibious Group (Commodore Short) arrives off Chefoo (Shantung) from Guam with the 6th Marine Div (Maj-Gen Shepherd). Red Chinese troops are in occupation of Chefoo and deny a landing to the Commander of the covering group, Rear-Adm Settle, on the cruiser *Louisville* on 4 Oct and Vice-Adm Barbey who has in the meantime arrived in his flagship *Catoctin* on 7 Oct. The convoy is then re-routed to Tsingtao which the Japanese Maj-Gen Nagano still holds with 10000 troops. On 10 Oct the 6th Marine Div is landed here and Gen Nagano surrenders to Gen Shepherd.

In all, some 53000 US Marines are landed in North China.

Subsequently, the VII Amphibious Force receives orders to transport the Nationalist Chinese 13th Army from Kowloon to Hulutao in Manchuria and then the 52nd Army (each of 30000 troops) from Haiphong (Indochina) to Yingkow in Manchuria. Although Marshal Malinovski has agreed with the Nationalist Chinese commander, Gen Tu Li-ming, to allow the landing in Soviet-occupied harbours, the Soviet troops evacuate the harbours when the landing fleets arrive and hand them over to Red Chinese troops who prevent a landing. The Nationalist Chinese have therefore to be disembarked further S in Chinwangtao which in the meantime has been occupied by a BLT of the 1st Marine Div.

3-20 Oct   Indochina

On 3 Oct the first French troops under Gen Leclerc arrive in Saigon on board the troop transports *Queen Emma* and *Queen Beatrix*. They are escorted, inter alia, by the battleship *Richelieu* and the large destroyer *Le Triomphant*.

From 15 Oct to 20 Oct more French ships arrive, including the carrier *Béarn*, the cruisers *Gloire* and *Suffren*, the destroyers *Le Fantasque*, the DEs *Somali* and *Sénégalais*, the sloops *Annamite* and *Gazelle* and the transport *Quercy*.

INDEX

ORDER OF INDEX

WARSHIPS	542
MERCHANT SHIPS	604
NAVAL FORCES	612
Armies	618
AIR FORCES	622
PERSONALITIES	625
MISCELLANEOUS LISTINGS	
Aircraft	644
Convoys	645
Mine Barrages	648
Operations	649

NOTES ON USE OF THE INDEX

At the request of the authors I have expanded the index to include a number of new sections. By cross-reference and the combined use of the various indices it is now possible to trace the activities of individual ships, persons and forces etc. throughout the war, and will greatly ease the task of analysis of a particular type of craft, navy, etc. When using the index it should be noted that where a person or vessel is listed on a particular page, that name may occur more than once, possibly under a separate date heading. A hyphen in the page index denotes that the name occurs consecutively throughout those pages. The changeover page between Volume I and Volume II is 288, Volume II commencing on page 289. This has not, however, been indicated within the index.

Further notes concerning use of the index and abbreviations used will be found under the respective index headings. The only abbreviations standard throughout the index are those for the countries, which are listed below:

Aus	Australian	Ger	German	Per	Persian
Bel	Belgian	Gr	Greek	Pol	Polish
Bra	Brazilian	Hun	Hungarian	Por	Portuguese
Bul	Bulgarian	Ind	Indian	Ru	Rumanian
Can	Canadian	It	Italian	Sp	Spanish
Chi	Chinese	Jap	Japanese	Swe	Swedish
Colum	Columbian	Lat	Latvian	Thai	Thailand/Siam
Da	Danish	Lit	Lithuanian	Tur	Turkish
Du	Dutch	Mex	Mexican	UK	British
Est	Estonian	Nor	Norwegian	US	American
Fin	Finnish	NZ	New Zealand	USSR	Russian
Fr	French	Pan	Panamanian	Yu	Yugoslavian

Anthony J. Watts 1973

Warships

A number of the vessels listed in this section were originally classified as merchant ships. These were taken over by the various navies concerned and put to use as auxiliaries and transports of various types.

The following points should be noted concerning the various headings under which small warships of the Japanese Navy appear:

Fusetsu-Tokume-Tei	Aux ML	
Gyorai-Tei	MTB	
Ishokaitei	APD	see under P (These were old DD)
Itto-Yuso-Kan	APD	see under P
Kaibokan	Frigate	
Kaiten	Midget SM	
Kusentai	SC	see under Ch
Kusen-Tokumu-Tei	Aux SC	see under Cha
Nito-Yuso-Kan	LST	see under T
Sokaitei	MS	see under W
Sokai-Tokumu-Tei	Aux MS	see under Wa

Russian warships have been given an additional abbreviation which denotes the area where the vessel served during the war. ie

(B)-Baltic, (BS)-Black Sea, (N)-Arctic, (P)-Pacific.

The abbreviations noted below are in addition to abbreviations which will be found on pp vii to x.

AGC	Amphibious Force Flagship	CL	Light cruiser	ML	Minelayer
AR	Repair ship	CV	Fleet carrier	NL	Netlayer
Aux	Auxiliary	CVE	Escort carrier	Q ship	AS vessel disguised as a merchant ship
BC	Battlecruiser	CVL	Light carrier		
CA	Heavy cruiser	DM	Destroyer (mine-layer)	SGB	Steam gunboat
CG				Sperr-	
Cutter	Coastguard Cutter	DMS	Destroyer (mine-sweeper)	brecher	Mine destructor/ Anti-aircraft ship

A . . . : USSR/SM
A-2 (BS): 216
A-3 (BS): 218, 330, 361
A-4 (BS): 216
A-5 (BS): 218, 404, 408, 411

A . . . : UK/Lighters
A2: 141
A7: 141
A18: 141

AF . . . : Ger/Gun Ferry
AF21: 431, 498
AF32: 428
AF39: 426
AF66: 429
AF97: 447
AF98: 447
AF101: 447
AF103: 447
AF105: 447
AF108: 447
AF109: 447
AF110: 447
AF111: 447
Aaron Ward US/DD: 226, 239, 249, 254, 264, 269, 271, 275-276, 316
Aaron Ward (II) US/DM. 502, 517
Abba It/TB: 42, 273
Abbot US/DD. 388, 409, 437, 480, 495, 498, 504, 525
Abdiel UK/ML: 91, 94, 97, 102-103, 126, 134, 143, 148, 293, 300, 313, 350
Abelia UK/Corvette: 297, 310
Abercrombie UK/Monitor: 334, 339, 340, 347, 350-351
Abercrombie US/DE: 461, 480, 502
Abingdon UK/MS: 207
Abner Read US/DD: 323, 337, 409, 418, 451, 466
Abraham Crijnssen Du/MS: 538
Abukuma Jap/CL: 156, 179, 184, 190, 194, 204, 221, 235, 312, 337, 459, 462, 464
Acacia US/Coastal Guard Ship: 192
Acanthus Nor/Corvette: 171, 211, 246, 262, 299, 304, 374, 389, 395, 421, 519
Acasta UK/DD: 33
Acciaio It/SM: 202, 227, 273, 299, 340
Achates UK/DD: 100, 120, 219, 256, 287-288
Achernar US/AKA: 505
Achéron Fr/SM: 36, 280
Achille Fr/SM: 6, 13, 21, 27, 38
Achilles UK/CL: 7, 10, 13-14, 169, 173, 185, 189, 199 (NZ), 290, 471, 517, 523, 526, 530
Aconit (Ex-Aconite) Fr/Corvette: 172, 211, 217, 293, 307, 389, 420
Actéon Fr/SM 36, 274
Active UK/DD 38, 41, 46, 100, 197, 199, 202, 211, 262, 315
Activity UK/CVE: 389, 401, 408, 424, 470
Adams US/DM: 502-503

Adelaide Aus/CL: 25, 54, 167, 280, 298
Admiral Graf Spee Ger/Pocket BB: 1, 6-7, 9, 11-12, 14-15, 19
Admiral Hipper Ger/CA: 19, 21-22, 24-25, 33, 35, 39, 45, 56, 68, 71, 78-79, 86, 201, 230-231, 258, 272, 288, 489, 509
Admiral Lazarev USSR/Icebreaker (N): 334
Admiral Scheer Ger/Pocket BB: 4, 44, 61, 64, 70, 76, 80, 88, 133, 139, 192, 216, 219, 230-231, 244-245, 470, 485, 495, 509
Admiralty Islands US/CVE: 516
Adolf Luderitz Ger/MTB Depot: 294
Adonis UK/AP Trawler: 318
Adopt US/MS: see T-522
Adrias (ex-Border) Gr/DD: 339, 360
Adriatico It/Aux ML: 34, see merchant ship
Adua It/SM: 34, 86, 101, 134, 140
Adventure UK/ML: 4, 120-121, 127, 134, 317, 519
Advocate US/MS: see T-111
Aeger Nor/DD: 24
Affleck UK/DE: 394, 397, 424, 469
Afridi UK/DD: 23-25, 28
Agano Jap/CL: 290, 361, 364-365, 392
Agassiz Can/Corvette: 211, 217, 238, 246
Agent US/MS: see T-112
Agosta Fr/SM: 5-6, 17, 38
Ahrens US/DE: 403, 416
Aigle Fr/DD: 20, 37, 280, 372
Aigli Gr/TB: 94
Aikoku Maru Jap/Aux CL: 222, 279, 392
Airedale UK/DD: 227-228
Airone It/TB: 34-35, 58
Ajax Fr/SM: 50, 56
Ajax UK/CL: 3, 7, 10, 13-14, 58, 62-63, 65, 67, 70, 74, 89, 92, 94, 97-98, 102-103, 106-107, 155-157, 289, 410, 421, 443, 453, 473
Ajiro Jap/ML: 456
Akademik Shokalski USSR/Survey ship (N): 343
Akagi Jap/CV: 156, 179, 184, 190, 194, 197, 204, 220, 223-224
Akashi Jap/Repair ship: 401
Akatsuki Jap/DD: 178, 181, 190, 221, 235, 252, 268-269, 275-276
Akebono Jap/DD: 156, 161, 181, 184, 186, 191, 194, 196, 214, 220, 235, 244, 459, 462, 466
Akebono Maru Jap/Oiler: 223
Akigumo Jap/DD: 156, 179, 190, 204, 220, 235, 248, 254, 264, 268, 270, 290, 337, 356, 361, 403, 415
Akikaze Jap/DD: 252, 462, 468
Akishimo Jap/DD: 415, 430, 462 466
Akitsushima Jap/Seaplane Depot ship: 252

Akizuki Jap/DD: 248, 263, 268, 290, 361, 415, 430, 462, 464
Alabama US/BB: 333, 338, 387, 392, 406, 427, 448, 458, 461, 464, 474, 522, 525-526, 530, 533
Alabastro It/SM: 258
Alagi It/SM: 34, 45, 63, 65, 67, 118, 120, 122, 128, 134, 144, 146, 156, 171, 175, 227, 234 242-243, 247, 273, 283, 340
Alane (Ex-Warwickshire) UK/AS Trawler: see NKi09 (ex-V6114)
Alarm US/MS: see T-113
Alaska US/BC: 491, 499-400, 509, 522, 527
Alaunia UK/Aux CL: 59, 382
Albacore US/SM: 284, 296, 365, 379, 429-430, 449
Albatross UK/Seaplane Depot ship: 38, 255, 440
Albatros Fr/DD: 37, 274
Albatros Ger/TB: 3, 22
Albatros It/TB: 43, 136
Alberico da Barbiano It/CL: see Da Barbiano
Alberni Can/Corvette: 131, 421, 436
Albert Leo Schlageter Ger/Sail training ship: 455
Albert T. Harris US/DE: 512, 523
Albert W. Grant US/DD: 427, 463, 523-524, 535
Alberto di Giussano It/CL: see Di Giussano
Albona It/ML: 34
Albrighton UK/DD: 229, 247, 265, 321, 441
Albury UK/MS: 31
Alcantara UK/Aux CL: 46
Alchemy US/MS: see T-114
Alchiba US/AKA: 264, 271, 277
Alcione It/TB: 34, 41, 52, 57, 67, 159
Aldebaran It/TB: 34, 47, 77, 82, 141
Alden US/DD: 169, 173, 194-195, 402
Aldenham UK/DD: 206, 227, 322, 338, 356 367, 443
Aldersdale UK/Oiler: 231
Alessandro Malaspina It/SM: see Malaspina
Alexander Hamilton US/CG Cutter: 185
Alexander von Humboldt Ger/Hospital Ship: 124
Alfieri It/DD: 42-43, 67, 73, 89
Alfredo Oriani It/DD: see Oriani
Alger US/DE: 417
Algérie Fr/CA: 20, 37, 64, 280
Algérien Fr/DE: 443
Algerine UK/MS: 273
Algoma Can/Corvette: 193, 216, 267
Algonquin (ex-Valentine) Can/DD: 410, 421, 442, 444, 446, 452, 465, 467-468, 473, 475
Algonquin US/CG Cutter: 248
Alhena US/AKA: 244. 258
Alisma UK/Corvette: 315
Alkioni Gr/TB: 94
Allen US/DD: 199

Allen M. Sumner US/DD: 471, 474, 479, 481, 528, 533
Allentown US/Frigate: see EK-8
Allington Castle UK/Corvette: 452, 471, 475
Almaack US/AKA: 277
Alnwick Castle UK/Corvette: 475, 492, 511, 514
Alpine US/APA: 505
Alpino It/DD: 42, 67, 89 98, 101, 118, 120, 149, 154, 157, 166, 175, 183, 189, 193, 202, 228, 239, 300, 513
Alpino Bagnolini It/SM: see Bagnolini
Alresford UK/MS: 247
Alsedo Sp/DD: 327
Alstertor Ger/Supply: 106
Altair It/TB: 35, 41, 52, 61, 73, 141
Altamaha US/CVE: 458, 474, 476
Altmark Ger/Oiler: 1, 7, 9, 19, see Uckermark
Aludra US/AK: 334
Alula It-Ger/Aux MS: 454
Alvise da Mosto It/DD: see Da Mosto
Alynbank UK/AA ship: 219-220, 256
Alysse (ex-Alyssum) Fr/Corvette: 103, 142, 172, 177, 187
Amagi Jap/CV: 499, 529
Amagiri Jap/DD: 159, 163, 166, 173, 178, 181, 187, 194, 200, 204-205, 221, 235, 249-250, 252, 271, 275-276, 335, 341, 372, 383
Amakusa Jap/Frigate: 492, 530
Amatsukaze Jap/DD: 160, 169, 177, 181, 183-184, 191, 194-195, 197, 221, 235, 249, 254, 264, 268, 275, 290, 361
Amazon UK/DD: 96, 143, 212-213, 277
Amazone Fr/SM: 21, 23, 274
Amberjack US/SM: 257, 296
Ambra It/SM: 57, 69, 73, 81, 84, 99, 285, 340
Ameer UK/CVE: 486, 494, 524, 527, 529
Amesbury US/DE: 420
Amethyst UK/Sloop: 402, 481, 490, 537
Ametist (ex-Sulev) USSR/Patrol ship (B): 129
Ametista It/SM: 34, 40, 45, 57, 68, 115, 159, 200, 258
Amgun USSR/GB (B): 129-130
Amherst Can/Corvette: 251, 266-267, 295
Amick US/DE: 507
Amiens Fr/Sloop: 31
Amiral Charner Fr/Sloop: 54, 76
Amiral Mouchez Fr/Sloop: 31, 510
Amiral Murgescu Ru/ML: 142, 232, 304, 368
Amiral Sénès Fr/Sloop: see SG16
Ammen US/DD: 323, 337, 376, 380, 387, 395, 399, 409, 418, 437, 451, 466, 504, 527
Ammerland (I) Ger/Speerbrecher: 345

Ammiraglio Cagni It/SM: see Cagni
Ammiraglio Caracciolo It/SM: see Caracciolo
Ammiraglio Millo It/SM: see Millo
Ammiraglio Saint Bon It/SM: see Saint Bon
Amphitrite Fr/SM: 274
Amsterdam US/CL: 528, 530, 533
Amur USSR/ML (B): 130
Anchusa UK/Corvette: 211
Ancon US/AGC: 339, 350, 420
Ancylus UK/Aux CVE: 412
Andania UK/Aux CL: 37
Anderson US/DD: 92, 190, 199, 214, 221, 224, 226, 254, 258, 269-270, 275, 337, 370, 388, 409, 466, 525, 528, 535
Andrea Doria It/BB: 69, 79, 165-166, 175, 349
Andromeda It/TB: 34, 41, 61, 73
Anemone UK/Corvette: 73, 211, 309
Anfitrite It/SM: 34, 40, 45, 60, 84
Angelo Bassini It/TB: see Bassini
Angle UK/AS trawler: 59, 96
Angler US/SM: 379, 410, 432, 457
Anguilla (ex-PF 72) UK/Frigate: 511, 514
Animoso It/TB: 292-293, 300
Anking Aus/Depot ship: 196
Annamite Fr/Sloop: 256, 539
Annan Can/Frigate: 454
Anson UK/BB: 256, 287, 294, 338, 359, 366, 393, 401, 408, 410, 534
Antares It/TB: 47, 61, 71, 129, 175, 223, 237, 300, 312, 328
Antares US/AKS: 521
Antelope UK/DD: 18, 37, 61, 100, 127, 215, 225, 227, 242
Anthony UK/DD: 31-32, 100, 120, 127, 197, 199, 202, 212, 218, 287, 469
Anthony US/DD: 363, 391, 426, 427, 437, 504, 517, 523
Antietam US/CV: 533, 537
Antietam US/CG: Cutter 247, see Bedloe
Antigua UK/Frigate: 395
Antilope It/Corvette: 293, 300
Antiope Fr/SM: 21, 23, 29, 274
Anton Schmitt Ger/DD: 17, 22, 24
Antonio da Noli It/DD: see Da Noli
Antonio Mosto It/TB: see Mosto
Antonio Pigafetta It/DD: see Pigafetta
Antonio Sciesa It/SM: see Sciesa
Antonio Usodimare It/DD: see Usodimare
Anzio (ex-Coral Sea) US/CVE: 467, 494, 502, 521, 528
Aoba Jap/CA: 163, 168, 179, 199, 214, 235, 241, 249, 263, 383, 418, 462, 529

Aotaka Jap/ML: 177, 181, 449
Apache US/Tug: 481
Apex US/MS: see T-115
Aphis UK/GB: 69,76,92,328, 347, 443, 445, 449
Apogon US/SM: 372, 392, 432, 449, 522
Apollo UK/ML: 408, 425, 511, 518
Apollo UK/AS Trawler: 51
Appalachian US/AGC: 483
Aquila (ex-Roma) It/CV: 513
Aquileja It/Hospital ship: 58
Aquilone It/DD: 34, 37, 54
Arabis (I) UK/Corvette: 59, 109, see Saucy
Aradam It/SM: 34, 39, 45, 63, 65, 67, 74, 90, 128, 134, 140, 144, 150, 156, 171, 175, 202, 208, 227, 273
Ararat Aus/Corvette: 406
Arare Jap/DD: 156, 179, 190, 204, 221, 233
Arashi Jap/DD: 159, 163, 166, 173, 178, 181, 190, 194, 196, 220, 223, 235, 250, 254, 264, 268-269, 283, 290, 341
Arashio Jap/DD: 159, 163, 167, 173, 178, 184, 186, 191, 221, 224, 271, 275, 306
Arawa UK/Aux CL: 74
Arbutus UK/Corvette: 84, 137, 184
Arcade US/MS: see T-116
Arch US/MS: see T-117
Archer UK/CVE: 326, 332, 534
Archerfish US/SM 401, 419, 429, 468, 534
Archimède Fr/SM: 36, 65
Archimede It/SM: 36, 55, 69, 83, 145, 260, 301
Arctic Ranger UK/AS trawler: 34
Arcturus US/AKA: 115
Ardea It/Corvette: see UJ 2225
Ardent UK/DD: 33
Ardente It/TB: 280, 286, 293
Ardimentoso It/TB: 312
Ardito It/TB: 284, 286, 293, 300, see TA 26
Arendal (ex-Badsworth) Nor/DD: 500, 518
Arethusa UK/CL: 23, 26-27, 31-32, 38, 41, 43, 46, 100, 120, 122, 171, 227, 279, 421
Aréthuse Fr/SM: 352
Aretusa It/TB: 34, 41, 52, 61, 175, 200, 255, 313
Argento It/SM: 258, 273, 283, 344
Argo It/SM: 42, 46, 56, 66, 85, 87, 103, 210, 258, 271, 273, 340
Argonaut UK/CL: 265, 274, 282-283, 421, 431, 444, 453, 470-471, 473, 479, 486, 502, 529, 535
Argonaut US/SM: 158, 247, 289
Argonauta It/SM: 34, 40
Argonaute Fr/SM: 274
Argus UK/CV: 29, 45-46, 65, 71, 90 94, 127, 150, 197, 199, 201-202, 218, 227, 274, 277
Argyllshire UK/AS trawler: 33

Aridane UK/ML: 377, 469, 518
Ariake Jap/DD: 194, 214, 221, 235, 252, 283, 286, 341
Ariane Fr/SM: 36, 274
Ariel It/TB: 34-35, 52, 57
Arizona US/BB: 161
Arkansas US/BB: 5, 108, 115, 132, 376, 420, 431, 444 493, 502, 511, 527
Arkhangelsk (ex-Royal Sovereign) USSR/BB (N): 444-445, 451, 482,
Ark Royal UK/CV: 1, 3, 6-7, 9, 12, 14, 18-19, 27, 30, 32-33, 37-38, 40-43, 45-46, 49-50, 52, 54-56, 63, 65, 67, 70-71, 73, 77-79, 87, 90-91, 94, 97, 100-101, 103, 105-107, 113, 120, 122, 128, 133-134, 140, 144, 149-150, 155
Arkona (ex-M115) Ger/MS: 1, 5 22
Armada US/MS: see T-118
Armando Diaz It/CL: see Diaz
Armeria UK/Corvette: 421
Armidale Aus/MS: 280-281
Arndale UK/Oiler: 486
Arno It/Hospital ship: 158, 254
Arnprior (ex-Rising Castle) Can/Corvette: 454
Arras Fr/Sloop: 31
Arrow UK/DD: 33, 180, 183, 189, 204, 338
Arrowhead Can/Corvette: 248
Arseni Rasskin USSR/MS (BS): see T-412
Artem USSR/DD (B): 110, 123, 127, 130
Artemide It/Corvette: 293, 300, see UJ 2226
Artigliere It/DD: 42-43, 58
Artigliere (ex-Camicia Nera) It/DD: 349
Arturo It/TB: see TA 24
Arunta Aus/DD: 250, 268, 293, 310, 334, 367, 372, 375-376, 380, 396, 409, 418, 437, 451, 461, 463, 474, 479, 481, 520, 523-524
Arvida Can/Corvette: 211, 216, 251, 266, 268, 318
Asagao Jap/TB: 529
Asagiri Jap/DD: 159, 163, 166, 173, 178, 181, 187, 194, 200, 204-205, 221, 235, 249
Asagumo Jap/DD: 162, 170 177 194-195, 221, 235, 248, 254, 263, 271, 275-277, 306, 337 361, 415, 418, 430, 462-463
Asahi Jap/Repair Ship: 222
Asaka Maru Jap/Aux CL: 221, see merchant ship
Asakaze Jap/DD: 162, 173, 194, 196, 205, 439
Asanagi Jap/DD: 168, 179, 199, 214, 235, 237, 248, 410
Asashimo Jap/DD: 414, 430, 462, 475, 508
Asashio Jap/DD: 159, 163, 167, 173, 178, 186, 191, 221, 224, 271, 275, 306
Ascari It/DD: 42-43, 67, 75, 82, 89, 95, 103, 118, 139, 166, 175

183, 189, 193, 200, 202, 227, 243, 261, 267, 273, 282, 292, 300
Ascension (ex-PF 74) UK/ Frigate: 469
Ascianghi It/SM: 39, 42, 47, 60, 84, 95, 138, 152, 165, 227, 242 247, 373, 306, 340
Ashanti UK/DD: 32, 60, 171, 198, 219-220, 242-243, 256, 374, 398, 401, 405, 421-422, 427, 441
Asheville US/GB: 196
Ashigara Jap/CA: 162, 190, 194, 196, 459, 462, 475, 523
Ashizuri Jap/Oiler: 415
Ashland US/LSD: 346
Asphodel UK/Corvette: 211, 395
Aspire US/MS: see T-119
Aspro US/SM: 392, 410, 432, 456
Aspromonte It/Aux ML: 126
Assail US/MS: see T-120
Assiniboine Can/DD: 20, 211, 217, 240, 440
Assault Boat German: see Pi.
Asteria It/SM: 218, 234, 242, 247, 271, 273, 283, 299
Asterion US/Q ship: 202
Astoria US/CL: 161, 168, 190, 199, 214, 221, 224, 226, 238, 241
Astoria (II) US/CL: 474, 476, 491, 499-500, 509, 525-526, 529
Asturias UK/Aux CL: 76, 349
Atago Jap/CA: 159, 163, 167, 170, 178, 181, 190, 194, 196, 221, 235, 248, 254, 263, 268, 275-277, 361, 364, 414, 430, 462
Athabaskan Can/DD: 332, 346, 374, 405-406
Atheling UK/CVE: 400, 425
Atherstone UK/DD: 206, 339 351, 443
Atherton US/DE: 507, 518
Atik US/Q ship: 202
Atlanta US/CL: 221, 224, 226, 238, 249, 269, 271, 275-276
Atlanta (II) US/CL: 522, 525-526, 533
Atlantis Ger/Aux CL: see Schiff 16
Atropo It/SM: 38, 44, 48, 62, 65, 98, 115, 124, 143, 151, 227, 229, 236, 271, 360
Attacker UK/CVE: 351, 444, 453 534
Attendolo It/CL: 35, 42, 69, 94, 96-97, 105, 114, 116, 128, 140, 157, 165, 175, 183, 243, 283
Attilio Regolo It/CL: 273, 349, 484
Attu US/CVE: 516, 522
Atule US/SM: 464, 468, 529
Aubrietia UK/Corvette: 96, 443
Auburn US/AGC: 536
Auckland UK/Sloop: 26-27, 46, 61, 95, 102, 108
Audace It/TB: see TA 20
Audacity (ex-Hannover) UK/ CVE: 137, 167-168
Augury US/MS: see T-524

Augusta US/CA: 125, 273, 338, 420, 443
Augusto Riboty It/DD: see Riboty
August Wriedt Ger/Weather Observation ship: 99, 105
Aulick US/DD: 471, 512
Ault US/DD: 476, 499, 525, 533
Aura II Fin/AS yacht: 15
Aurania UK/Aux CL: 146
Auricula UK/Corvette: 96, 211
Auriga It/TB: see TA 27
Aurora UK/CL: 3, 6-7, 9, 11, 24-25, 27, 30, 32, 100, 104-105, 121, 127, 144, 149, 155, 157, 165-166, 202, 270, 274, 282, 293, 328, 333-334, 339, 350-351, 360, 443, 453
Aurora It/GB: 350
Aurore Fr/SM: 280,
Austin US/DD: 275
Australia Aus/CA: 17, 28, 43, 49, 51, 54-56, 75, 80, 169, 173, 185, 189, 199, 214, 226, 238, 241, 249-250, 298, 310, 334, 340, 367, 375-376, 380, 409, 418, 437, 451, 461, 479, 481, 483
Avanturine UK/MS trawler: 372
Avenger UK/CVE: 256, 274, 277
Aviere It/DD: 42-43, 58, 98, 139, 143, 153, 157, 166, 175, 183, 189, 193, 200, 202, 228, 243, 284
Avon UK/Frigate: 516
Avon Vale UK/DD: 120, 132, 152, 189, 201-202, 421, 467
Avorio It/SM: 242, 247, 273, 289, 299
Awaji Jap/Frigate: 410
Axum It/SM: 34, 42, 46, 63, 67, 74, 119, 134, 140, 146, 171, 175, 227, 236, 242, 271, 273
Ayanami Jap/DD: 159, 163, 166, 173, 178, 181, 187, 192, 200, 204-205, 221, 235, 252, 264, 271, 275-277
Aylmer UK/DE: 400, 424, 444, 481
Aylwin US/DD: 161, 168, 182, 185, 199, 214, 221, 224, 323, 336-337, 370, 388, 392, 437, 474
Ayrshire UK/AS trawler: 230-231
Azalea UK/Corvette: 398, 405, 421
Azimut USSR/NL (B): 153
Azio It/ML: 34

BKA . . . : USSR/Armoured Cutter
BKA-111 (BS): 117
BKA-114 (BS): 116
BKA-132 (BS): 365
BKA-134 (BS): 117
BO . . . : USSR/Large SC
BO-78 (N): 272
BO-131 (N): 511
BO-150 (N): 472
BO-201 (ex-SC 719) (N): 366, 409
BO-204 (ex-SC 1073) (N): 366, 409
BO-205 (ex-SC 1074) (N): 366
BO-206 (ex-SC 1075) (N): 366, 409

BO-207 (ex-SC 1076) (N): 409
BO-208 (ex-SC 1283) (N): 366
BO-209 (ex-SC 1284) (N): 366. 409
BO-210 (ex-SC 1295) (N): 366
BO-211 (ex-SC 1286) (N): 366, 409
BO-212 (ex-SC 1287) (N): 366, 409
BO-223 (ex-SC ......) (N): 498
BO-225 (ex-SC ......) (N): 511
BO-226 (ex-SC 1485) (N): 472
BO-227 (ex-SC ......) (N): 472
BO-228 (ex-SC ......) (N): 472, 511
BO-229 (ex-SC 1470) (N): 472
BO-302 (ex-SC ......) (P): 532
BO-303 (ex-SC ......) (P): 531
BO-304 (ex-SC ......) (P): 531
BO-305 (ex-SC ......) (P): 531
BO-306 (ex-SC ......) (P): 531
BO-307 (ex-SC ......) (P): 531
BO-310 (ex-SC ......) (P): 532
BO-314 (ex-SC ......) (P): 532
BO-317 (ex-SC ......) (P): 531

BTSC . . . : USSR/M Type
Fugas: See T-
BYMS . . . : US/MS
BYMS 2022: 444
Babbitt US/DD: 5, 297, 305, 309
Babr Per/GB: 129
Bache US/DD: 336-337, 376, 380, 395-396, 409, 418, 437, 451, 461, 463, 504, 517
Baddeck Can/Corvette: 142, 421, 423
Badger US/DD: 136, 278, 337, 371-372
Badsworth UK/DD: 212, 227-228, 242, 245, see Arendal
Bagley US/DD: 15, 161, 182, 185, 199, 226, 238, 241, 250, 298, 310, 334, 375-376, 427, 458, 479, 502, 535
Bagnolini It/SM: 34, 36, 44, 50, 59, 70, 118-119, 180, 260, 301, see UIT 22
Bahamas (ex-PF 75) UK/Frigate: 471
Bailey US/DD: 312, 370, 388, 494, 498, 504, 513, 523-524
Bainbridge US/DD: 61, 83, 119, 132, 136, 227, 329, 337
Baionetta It/Corvette: 350
Baker US/DE: 416
Baku (ex-Ordzonikidze)USSR/DD (P/N): 236, 279-280, 294, 310, 334, 361, 459, 472, 484
Balao US/SM: 379, 390, 495
Balch US/DD: 161, 168, 183, 190, 207, 221, 224, 226, 238, 249, 323
Baldwin US/DD: 420, 422, 443
Baleno It/DD: 42, 82, 93
Balfour UK/DE: 394, 424, 435
Balilla It/SM: 34, 47
Baliste Fr/TB: 280
Ballard US/APD: 258
Ballarat Aus/MS: 167, 187, 197, 285, 470, 516, 533
Balsam UK/Corvette: 329, 421
Baltimore US/CA: 370, 373, 388,

392, 406, 415, 426, 474, 476, 492, 499, 500, 509, 522
Bamborough Castle UK/ Corvette: 452, 471-472, 475, 511
Banckert Du/DD: 185, 188
Bancroft US/DD: See St. Francis
Bancroft (II) US/DD: 295, 304, 323, 337, 353, 359, 370, 388, 399, 494, 498, 504, 513, 523
Bande Nere It/CL: 42, 44, 69, 78, 82, 94, 97-98, 105, 116, 193, 202, 206
Bandiera It/SM: 39, 60, 63, 70, 74, 106, 120, 122, 128, 140, 144, 150
Banff (ex-Saranac) UK/Cutter: 339, 417
Bang US/SM: 402, 419, 429, 449, 468, 491
Bangust US/DE: 533
Bann UK/Frigate: 339
Baracca It/SM: 50, 59, 64-65, 77, 92, 113, 127
Barb US/SM: 272, 396, 409, 449, 468, 479, 526
Barbarigo It/SM: 34, 40, 42, 46, 59, 61, 77, 81-83, 99-100, 118-119, 147, 180, 260, 301, 326, 332
Barbel US/SM: 439, 468
Barber US/DE: 403, 416
Barbero US/SM: 456, 468, 472
Barcoo Aus/Frigate: 406, 513, 523, 538
Barfleur UK/DD: 526, 530-531, 533
Barham UK/BB: 14-15, 32, 49, 51, 55-56, 62-63, 66, 69, 73-74, 89, 93, 97, 102-103, 155
Barker US/DD: 185, 188, 337
Barletta It/Aux ML: 34, 282, 322, 341
Barnes US/CVE: 370, 458
Barney US/DD: 93, 404
Barr US/DE: 403, 416, (APD 39), 493
Barrier US/MS: see T-525
Barry US/DD: 4, 337, 357, (APD 29), 517
Bartolomeo Colleoni It/CL: see Colleoni
Bartolomeo Diaz Por/Sloop: 538
Barton US/DD: 254, 258, 269, 275-276
Barton (II) US/DD: 420, 431, 473-474, 479, 481, 492, 502, 533
Bashaw US/SM: 401, 419, 429, 449, 495
Basilisk UK/DD: 31-32
Basque Fr/DD: 43, 510, 514
Bassini It/TB: 68, 206, 261, 313, 328
Bataan US/CVL: 406, 426, 430, 499, 500, 509-510, 516, 525, 533, 537
Bates US/APD: 420, 493, 517
Batfish US/SM: 379, 419, 439, 457, 487, 491
Bath (ex-Hopewell) Nor/DD: 125
Bathurst Aus/MS: 534
Battisti It/DD: 45, 49, 52, 55, 90
Battleford Can/Corvette: 286-287, 421

Battler UK/CVE: 350, 382, 400
Batiray Tur/SM: see UA
Bausan It/SM 34, 39, 44
Baya US/SM: 457, 495, 515, 526
Bayfield US/AGC: 420, 444
Bayley US/DD: 427
Bayntun UK/DE: 376, 381, 490
Bayonet UK/NL: 10
Bazely UK/DE: 360, 371, 424, 506, 520
Bditelny USSR/DD (BS): 112, 147, 197, 199, 204, 206, 209-210, 212, 215-216, 218, 225-226, 233
Beacon Hill Can/Frigate: 496
Beagle UK/DD: 33, 212, 226, 286, 374, 401, 408, 421-422, 471, 519
Beale US/DD: 337, 376, 380, 395-396, 399, 409, 418, 437, 451, 461, 463, 504, 527
Béarn Fr/CV: 7, 218, 336, 539
Bearss US/DD: 525, 528, 535
Beatty US/DD: 339-340, 367
Beaufort UK/DD: 189, 201-202, 227, 339, 350, 359, 367, 386, 443
Bebas US/DE: 504
Becuna US/SM: 457, 491
Bedale UK/DD: see Slazak
Bedloe (ex-Antietam) US/CG Cutter: 432
Bedouin UK/DD: 23, 25-26, 32, 84, 113, 155, 171, 198, 227-228
Begum UK/CVE: 400, 417, 457
Beilul It/SM: 34, 42-43, 55, 73, . . 79, 84, 99, 149, 155, 175, 218, 225, 340
Belchen Ger/Oiler: 99, 104-105
Belfast UK/CL: 3, 7-8, 11, 302, 374-375, 383, 401, 421, 431, 434
Belfast US/Frigate: see EK-3
Belfort Fr/Sloop: 31
Belknap US/DD: 307, 311, 320, 326, 338, 357, (APD 34), 483
Bell US/DD: 377, 387, 406, 426, 458, 480, 487, 523-524
Bellatrix US/AKA: 253, 264
Belleau Wood US/CVL: 346, 353, 359, 370, 373, 387, 392, 399-400, 406, 426, 430, 448, 458, 461-462, 465-466, 491, 499-500, 509, 516, 522, 525, 533
Bellona Da/SM: 346
Bellona UK/CL: 398, 420, 437, 441, 446-467, 471, 483, 491-492
Belmont (ex-Satterlee) UK/DD: 182, 185
Belvoir UK/DD: 339, 350, 359-360, 367, 421, 443, 451
Benalla Aus/MS: 406, 538
Bendigo Aus/MS: 164, 187, 197, 406, 516
Bengal Ind/MS: 279
Bengal Ind/Sloop: 534
Benham US/DD: 4, 15, 161, 168, 207, 221, 224, 226, 238, 249, 269, 271, 275-277
Benham (II) US/DD: 428, 458, 474, 476, 499, 510, 525, 533
Benner US/DD: 528, 530, 533
Bennett US/DD: 363, 391, 427-428, 504, 507-508
Bennington US/CV: 491, 499-

500, 509, 516, 522, 525, 533
Bennion US/DD: 428, 463, 474, 479-480, 503, 513, 535
Benson US/DD: 83, 115, 119, 132, 136, 339, 350, 369, 413, 415, 443
Bentinck UK/DE: 360, 371, 424, 481, 506, 520
Bentley UK/DE: 424
Beograd Yu/DD: 91, see Sebenico, see TA 43
Bergall US/SM: 457, 472
Bergamot UK/Corvette: 302, 318
Berillo It/SM: 44, 50, 57
Berkeley UK/DD: 247-248
Berkshire UK/AS Trawler: 51
Bermuda UK/CL: 274, 294, 332, 346, 366, 535
Bernadou US/DD: 83, 115, 119, 136, 193, 339, 350, 413
Bernd von Arnim Ger/DD: 1, 3, 7, 10-11, 22, 24
Berry UK/DE: 360, 371, 394, 424, 464
Bersagliere It/DD: 42, 67, 89, 98, 101, 119-120, 149, 157, 166, 175, 183, 189, 199-200, 202, 228, 245, 292
Berwick UK/CA: 5, 7, 20, 23-24, 32, 63, 65-67, 71, 193, 198, 393, 410, 444, 464, 491, 519
Besposhchadny USSR/DD (BS): 109, 112-113, 116, 126-128, 132, 136, 138, 147, 150, 152, 267, 281, 283, 287, 297, 301, 319, 327, 353, 359
Besugo US/SM: 456, 459, 468, 482, 505
Betelgeuse US/AKA: 275
Beverley (ex-Branch) UK/DD: 212, 296-297, 309, 316
Bévéziers Fr/SM: 6, 56, 212
Bezuprechny USSR/DD (BS): 109-110, 116, 126-128, 136, 138, 147, 171, 173, 175, 180, 183-185, 197, 215, 218, 222, 225
Bianchi It/SM: 48, 62, 69, 77, 81-83, 99, 113
Bibb US/CG Cutter: 297, 305, 329
Biber Ger/Midget SM: 482
Bicester UK/DD: 242, 299, 443
Bickerton UK/DE: 400 424, 444-445
Biddle US/DD: 404
Bideford UK/Sloop: 31-33, 103 138
Billfish US/SM: 410, 514, 529
Biloxi US/CL: 388, 392, 399, 406, 426, 448, 458, 461, 464, 466-467, 474, 476, 491, 493, 502-503
Birdlip UK/AS Trawler: 416
Birka Ger/Hospital ship: 139
Birmingham UK/CL: 21, 25, 27, 29, 32, 98, 100, 227-228, 255, 369, 502, 518-519
Birmingham US/CL: 334, 339-340 353, 359, 364, 426-427, 448, 458, 461-462, 517
Biscayne US/AGC: 339, 350, 385, 443, 502
Bismarck Ger/BB: 99-101, 103

Bismarck Sea US/CVE: 479, 493-494
Bison Fr/DD: 26-28
Bison (II) (ex-Le Flibustier) Fr/DD: 280
Biter UK/CVE: 274, 318, 324-325, 400
Bittern UK/Sloop: 26-28
Bittersweet Can/Corvette: 216
Björnungen Nor/Cutter: 142
Black US/DD: 388, 409, 437, 499, 525, 533
Blackfin US/SM: 457, 468, 479
Blackfish US/SM: 272, 292, 379, 401, 456
Blackfly UK/AS Trawler: 59, 203, 208, 415
Blackmore UK/DD: 350, 385, 443
Black Prince UK/CL: 392-393, 405, 420, 443, 453, 470-471, 473, 479, 486, 502, 516, 526, 530, 534
Black Ranger UK/Oiler: 121, 171
Black Swan UK/Sloop: 26-27, 314, 402
Black Watch Ger/SM Depot: 517
Blackwood UK/DE: 371, 424
Blakeley US/DD: 93, 216, 404
Blanche UK/DD: 10
Blankney UK/DD: 167-168, 197, 199, 202, 227-228, 237, 339-340, 350, 397, 410
Blean UK/DD: 283
Bleasdale UK/DD: 247, 421, 447
Blencathra UK/DD: 313, 338, 367, 397
Blenny US/SM: 472, 491, 495, 515
Blessman (ex-DE 69) US/APD: 420, 493
Bligh UK/DE: 400, 424, 444, 481
Block Island US/CVE: 357, 378, 387, 394, 403, 416, 524
Blücher Ger/CA: 22, 24
Blue US/DD: 161, 168, 183, 190, 226, 238, 241, 244
Blue (II) US/DD: 476, 499, 522, 525, 533
Blue Ridge US/AGC: 480
Blueback US/SM: 522
Bluebell UK/Corvette: 59, 85, 160, 339, 421, 492
Bluefish US/SM: 347, 365, 372, 396, 419, 429, 439, 526
Bluegill US/SM: 402, 439, 457, 495
Blyskawica Pol/DD: 1, 23, 26-27, 30-31, 240, 313, 322, 393, 410-411, 421-422, 434, 441, 453
Boadicea UK/DD: 212, 286, 302, 408, 421, 424
Boarfish US/SM: 479
Bodry USSR/DD (BS): 113, 116, 118, 126-128, 136, 141, 143-144, 147, 162, 170-171, 173, 178, 236
Boelcke Ger/Aircraft Repair Ship: 512
Bogota Ger/Supply Ship: 373
Bogue US/CVE: 307, 311, 320, 326, 329, 337, 371-372, 387, 395, 403, 416, 432, 507
Boiki USSR/DD (BS): 109, 116,

126, 132-133, 136, 138, 141, 147, 152, 158, 171, 173, 175-176, 180, 182, 193, 197, 199, 202, 204, 206, 209, 212, 218, 260, 267, 281, 286, 297, 319, 327, 353
Boise US/CL: 182, 255, 263, 334, 339-340, 346, 350-351, 387, 409, 418, 451, 461, 463, 474, 480-481, 487, 498, 504, 513, 523
Bolebroke UK/DD: see Pindos
Bolzano It/CA: 35-36, 42-43, 57-58, 67, 69, 79, 86, 89, 95, 103, 118, 128, 243, 349, 430
Bombarde Fr/TB: 284, See F.R. 41, See TA 9
Bombardiere It/DD: 280, 292
Bonaventure UK/CL: 71, 73-74, 84
Bonefish US/SM: 347, 365, 390, 402, 415, 432, 449, 457, 522
Bonhomme Richard US/CV: 522, 525, 533
Bordelais Fr/DD: 280
Border UK/DD: see Adrias
Boreas UK/DD: 54, 132
Borie US/DD: 5, 300, 322, 337-338, 357
Borie (II) US/DD: 499, 525, 530, 533
Borum US/DE: 420, 439
Boston UK/MS: 227
Boston US/CA: 388, 406, 415, 426, 448, 458, 464, 476, 491, 525, 529, 530, 533
Bostwick US/DE: 387, 394,16, 4 506
Bouclier Fr/TB: 31, 41
Bougainville Fr/Sloop: 44, 49, 64
Bougainville Fr/Aux CL: 212
Bougainville US/CVE: 516, 522
Boulonnais Fr/DD: 27 274
Bourrasque Fr/DD: 31-32
Bowen Aus/MS: 406
Bowers US/APD: 503, 511
Bowfin US/SM: 347, 365, 379, 396, 410, 439, 491, 514, 522
Boxer UK/LST: 350, 386
Boxer US/CV: 537
Boyd US/DD: 346, 359, 370, 373, 406, 426, 458, 502, 527
Boyle US/DD: 339, 386, 444
Bradford US/DD: 346, 353, 359, 370, 373, 377, 387, 392, 406, 426, 502, 527
Bradman UK/AS Trawler: 27, see Friese, see V6112
Bragadino It/SM: 39, 62, 156, 236, 271
Braid UK/Frigate: see L'Aventure
Braine US/DD: 359, 363, 391, 426, 428, 474, 480-481, 512, 517
Braithwaite UK/DE: 490
Brake Ger/Oiler: 349, 382
Bramble UK/MS: 212, 220, 287-288
Brambleaf UK/Oiler: 74
Bramham UK/DD: 242-243, see Themistockles
Branch US/DD: see Beverley
Brandenburg/SG 7 (ex-Kita) Ger/ ML: 312, 322, 336, 341, 352

Brandon Can/Corvette: 211, 295
Branlebas Fr/TB: 31, 41
Brazen UK/DD: 25, 44
Bream US/SM: 419, 457, 462, 466, 505
Breckinridge US/DD: 247, 404
Brecon UK/DD: 339, 350-351, 386, 397, 443, 453
Bredon UK/AS Trawler: 295
Breeman US/DE: 386, 394, 416
Breese (ex-DD 122) US/DM: 161, 324, 334, 364, 502
Bremse Ger/Gunnery School ship: 22, 121, 127
Brennan US/DE: 314
Brestois Fr/DD: 27, 274
Bretagne Fr/BB: 20, 41
Bridgewater UK/Sloop: 52, 55
Bright US/DE: 517
Brighton (ex-Cowell) UK/DD: see Zharki
Brilliant UK/DD: 105, 406, 469
Brilliant USSR/Patrol ship: see SKR-27
Brin It/SM: 34, 39, 42, 44, 62, 69, 85, 87, 103-104, 199, 210, 223, 242, 271, 273
Brioni It/Aux ML: 34
Brisk US/Corvette: 331
Brissenden UK/DD: 339-340, 388, 398, 421
Bristol US/DD: 339, 350, 353
Bristol (II) US/DD: 533
Britomart UK/MS: 230, 334
Briz/SKR- . . . USSR/Partol ship (N): 151
Broadwater (ex-Mason) UK/DD: 142-143
Broadway (ex-Hunt) UK/DD: 96, 211, 324-325, 519
Brocklesby UK/DD: 206, 247-248, 265, 339, 350, 519
Broke UK/DD: 240, 274
Brommy (ex-M50) Ger/R Boat Depot ship: 427
Bronstein US/DE: 387, 394, 416
Bronzo It/SM: 227, 236, 242-243, 247, 273, 283, 340
Brooke UK/DD: 29
Brooklyn US/CL: 92, 108, 115, 132, 273-274, 333-334, 339-340, 350, 385-386, 444
Brooks (ex-DD 232) US/APD: 334, 348, 355, 376, 395-396, 481
Broome Aus/MS: 285, 406, 534
Broome US/DD: 5, 68, 83
Brown US/DD: 370, 373, 377, 387, 406, 413, 426, 458, 527
Brown Ranger UK/Oiler: 140, 227 242
Brownson US/DD: 337, 376
Bruiser UK/LST: 350, 386
Brummer Ger/Gunnery school ship: 23
Brummer (ex-Olav Tryggvason) Ger/ML: 47, 77, 109, 112, 115, 129, 134, 191, 198, 204, 298, 331, 345, 373, 397, 453, 505
Bruno Heinemann Ger/DD: 1, 3, 14, 17-18, 22

Brush US/DD: 476, 499, 522, 525, 533
Bryant US/DD: 428, 452, 463, 474, 479, 502, 510
Bryony UK/Corvette: 318, 339
Buccari It/ML: 35, 41, 322
Buchanan US/DD: See Campbelltown
Buchanan (II) US/DD: 226, 238, 249, 254, 263, 275-276, 334-335, 364, 391, 474, 476, 533
Buck US/DD: 92, 115, 136, 339, 344, 353
Buckley US/DE: 403, 506
Buctouche Can/Corvette: 211, 217
Buffoluto It/Aux ML: 34, 322, 341
Bug USSR/K Boat (BS): see SKR-113
Bugel USSR/MS (B): see T-214
Bulgaria Ger/ML: 322, 341, 356
Bull (ex-DE 693) US/APD: 493
Bullard US/DD: 359, 365, 370, 373, 388, 409, 428, 437, 499, 509, 525, 533
Bulldog UK/DD: 29, 96, 143, 212, 287, 412, 421, 452, 471, 519
Bullen UK/DE: 469
Bulmer US/DD: 185, 188, 337
Bulolo UK/AGC: 274, 338, 386, 420, 538
Bumper US/SM: 526
Bunbury Aus/MS: 406
Bundaberg Aus/MS: 406
Bunker Hill US/CV: 364, 370, 373, 377, 387, 392, 400-401, 406, 426, 430, 448, 458, 461, 491, 499-500, 509, 516
Burak Reis Tur/SM: See P614
Burdekin Aus/Frigate: 513, 538
Burdock UK/Corvette: 421
Bureja USSR/GB (B): 470
Burevestnik USSR/Salvage Ship (N): 491
Burnie Aus/MS: 164, 197, 470
Burns US/DD: 359, 370, 373, 387, 392, 406, 426, 458, 480, 523-524
Burrfish US/SM: 392, 410, 468, 495
Burwell (Ex-Laub) UK/DD: 123
Burya USSR/Patrol Ship (B): 130
Burza Pol/DD: 1, 23, 26, 31, 281-282, 301-302, 304, 307, 358, 362, 389
Bush US/DD: 337, 376, 380, 387, 395, 409, 416, 451, 466, 474, 479-480, 504, 507
Buster UK/LST: 386
Butler US/DD: 339-340, (DMS 29) 420, 444, 502, 513, 517
Buttercup UK/Corvette: 309, 358, 421, 518
Buttermere (ex-Kos XXV) UK/AS Trawler: 131
Buy USSR/MS (B): see T-202
Byard UK/DE: 360, 371, 424, 520
Byron UK/DE: 464, 496, 506
Bystry USSR/DD (BS): 111

CB . . . : It/Midget SM
CB2: 216
CB3: 225
CB4: 330

Ch . . . : Fr/SC
Ch6: 60
Ch7: 60, 510
Ch19: see RA3
Ch20: see RA4
Ch21: see RA5
Ch44: see RA6
Ch45: see RA7
Ch46: see RA8

Ch . . . : Jap/SC (Kusentai)
Ch1: 177, 181, 184
Ch2: 181, 184, 522
Ch3: 177, 181
Ch4: 194
Ch5: 194, 345
Ch7: 167, 181, 187
Ch8: 181, 187, 205, 495
Ch9: 181, 187
Ch10: 177, 182
Ch11: 177, 182
Ch12: 177, 182, 345
Ch14: 529
Ch16: 194, 221
Ch17: 194, 221, 505
Ch18: 194, 221
Ch22: 250
Ch24: 250
Ch25: 233
Ch26: 529
Ch27: 233
Ch28: 525
Ch30: 472
Ch31: 476
Ch34: 501
Ch37: 526
Ch42: 523
Ch43: 476
Ch50: 526
Ch54: 396
Ch57: 521
Ch58: 522
Ch63: 501
Ch165: 449

Cha . . . : Jap/Aux SC (Kusen-Tokumu-Tei)
Cha47: 525
Cha65: 522
Cha72: 525
Cha81- 525
Cha85: 526
Cha97: 505
Cha113: 523
Cha114: 491
Cha117: 526
Cha182: 529
Cha225: 526
CS13 Cu/SC: 314
Cabana US/DE: 533
Cabezon US/SM: 522
Cabilan US/SM: 505
Cabot US/CVL: 387, 392, 400, 406, 426, 448, 458, 462, 465-467, 474, 476, 491, 499, 528, 530, 533, 537
Cabrilla US/SM: 347, 372, 410, 432, 456

CachalotUK/SM:46-47, 58, 111, 122, 236
Cachalot US/SM: 161, 222
Cache US/Oiler: 381
Cadorna It/CL: 35, 42, 94, 97-98, 153, 158, 341, 349
Caesar UK/DD: 468, 471, 538
Cagni It/SM: 143, 151, 156, 272, 349
Caicos (ex-PF77) UK/Frigate: 475
Caïman Fr/SM: 36, 106-107, 274, 280
Caio Duilio It/BB: 57, 63, 79, 157, 165, 175-176, 183, 189, 193, 349
Cairndale UK/Oiler: 103
Cairns Aus/MS: 339, 344
Cairo UK/CL: 4, 25-26, 29-32, 101, 210, 225, 227-228, 236-237, 242
Calais Fr/Sloop: 56
Calatafimi It/TB: 37, 61, 141, see TA19
Calcutta UK/CL: 27, 31, 49-51, 54, 58, 62, 74, 84, 93-94, 97, 102-103
Caldas Colum/DD: 387
Calder UK/DE: 424, 481, 506
Caldwell US/DD: 295, 304, 323, 337, 353, 359, 388, 421, 469, 513, 523
Caledon UK/CL: 3, 11, 36, 40, 46, 86, 204, 413, 444, 472
Calendula UK/Corvette: 53
Calgary Can/Corvette: 346, 369, 378, 421
Caliente US/Oiler: 476
California US/BB: 161, 427, 437, 461, 463, 466, 479, 481, 527
California It/Hospital ship: 125
Calipso It/TB: 35
Callaghan US/DD: 428, 458, 476, 502-503, 527
Callaway US/APA: 481
Calliope It/TB: 34, 104, 141, 145, 237, 245, 292-293, 300, 321
Calpe UK/DD: 247-248, 339, 351, 369, 443, 453
Calvi It/SM: 41, 56, 69, 95, 119, 126-127, 159, 204
Calvin Castle UK/Aux CL: 68
Calypso Fr/SM: 21, 284, 322
Calypso UK/CL: 3, 11, 29, 34, 36
Cambrian UK/DD: 446, 464, 471
Camellia UK/Corvette: 84, 339, 464
Camicia Nera It/DD: 42-43, 58, 80, 82, 98, 103, 139, 143, 157, 166, 175, 183, 189, 193, 228, 243, 282, 284, 292, 300, see Artigliere (II)
Camito UK/Boarding vessel: 96
Camorin Bra/Corvette: 379
Camoscio It/Corvette: see UJ6081
Campania UK/CVE: 452, 464-465, 471-472, 491-492, 498
Campanula UK/Corvette: 287, 296-297, 421
Campbell UK/DD: 189, 363, 427
Campbell US/CG cutter: 136, 211 216-217, 253, 266, 296, 301-302, 329, 413

Campbelltown (ex-Buchanan) UK/DD: 96, 206
Campion UK/Corvette: 306, 402
Camrose Can/Corvette: 211, 376, 378, 381, 421, 423
Canarias Sp/Cruiser: 101
Canberra Aus/CA: 17, 28, 80-81, 169, 173, 186, 226, 238, 241
Canberra US/CA: 406, 415, 426, 448, 458
Candytuft UK/Corvette: see Tenacity
Canfield US/DE: 533
Canton UK/Aux CL: 112, 116
Cantore It/TB: 61, 79, 214, 245
Cap d'Antifer UK/MS Trawler: 391
Cape Breton Can/Frigate: 394, 408, 424
Cape Esperance US/CVE: 458, 474, 476
Cape Gloucester US/CVE: 527
Capel UK/DE: 394, 424, 469
Capelin US/SM: 365
Caperton US/DD: 387, 426, 458, 476, 525, 533
Capetown UK/CL: 40, 45, 79-80, 90, 421
Capitano Cecchi It/Escort ship: 61
Capitano Tarantini It/SM: see Tarantini
Cappellini It/SM: 34, 56, 73, 91, 96, 126-127, 255-256, 301, 326, see Uit 24
Capponi It/SM: 39, 42, 50, 63, 87
Capps US/DD: 476, 502
Caprice UK/DD: 446, 464, 471
Carabiniere It/DD: 42-43, 67, 75, 89, 95, 118, 139, 154, 157, 166, 175, 183, 189-190, 292, 349, 484
Caracciolo It/SM: 156
Caradoc UK/CL: 9, 68
Caralis It/Aux ML: 34
Caravelas Bra/Corvette: 300
Card US/CVE: 329, 337-338, 357, 375, 416
Cardiff UK/CL: 3, 11
Carducci It/DD: 42-43, 67, 73, 89
Carioca Bra/Corvette: 300
Carinthia UK/Aux CL: 32
Carlisle UK/CL: 26-29, 46, 84, 94, 97, 102, 165, 180, 183, 189, 201-202, 338, 356
Carlo Mirabello It/DD: see Mirabello
Carl Peters Ger/MTB Tender: 22
Carlson US/DE: 504, 533
Carmick US/DD: 420, 443
Carnarvon Castle UK/Aux CL: 68, 147
Carron UK/DD: 538
Carter US/DE: 507
Carter Hall US/LSD: 375-376
Carthage UK/Aux CL: 147
Carysfort UK/DD: 517-518
Casabianca Fr/SM: 6, 13, 21, 27, 352, 358, 414
Cascino It/TB: 34, 80, 293, 300, 349
Casco US/Seaplane tender: 251

Case US/DD: 161, 226, 335, 388, 427, 457, 467
Casque Fr/DD: 280
Cassandra UK/DD: 446, 464, 471-472
Cassard Fr/DD: 37, 280
Cassin US/DD: 161, 457
Cassin Young US/DD: 406, 428, 458, 476, 502, 509, 527
Cassiopea It/TB: 47, 97, 155, 300, 312-313
Castelfidardo It/TB: 61, 87, 206, 272, see TA 16
Castlemaine Aus/Corvette: 280, 406, 470, 534
Castor Fr/ML: 284
Castore It/TB: 95, 175, 183, 200, 208, 245, 251, 293, 300, 328
Cato (ex -BAM 10) UK/MS: 435
Catoctin US/AGC: 443, 537, 539
Catskill US/LSV: 504
Cattaro (ex-Dalmacija) It/GB: see Niobe
Catterick UK/DD: 443, 453, 514
Cattistock UK/DD: 421, 434, 447
Cauvery Ind/Sloop: 513, 521
Cavalier UK/DD: 538
Cavalier US/APA: 487
Cavalla US/SM: 429-430, 472, 479, 534
Cavour It/BB: see Conte di Cavour
Cayuga US/CG cutter: see Totland
Cecilia UK/Corvette: 85
Celandine UK/Corvette: 108, 251, 266-268, 295, 421
Centaur Aus/Hospital Ship: 311
Centauro It/TB: 73, 80, 97, 118, 133, 267
Centurion UK/Dummy battleship 227
Ceres UK/CL: 11, 46, 78-79, 421
Cérès Fr/SM: 274
Cero US/SM: 410, 439, 505
Cervo It/Corvette: see UJ 6086
Cesare It/BB: see Giulio Cesare
Cesare Battisti It/DD: see Battisti
Cessnock Aus/MS: 280, 339, 344, 533
Ceylon UK/CL: 382, 399-400, 407, 412, 438, 471, 479, 486, 514, 521, 534
Chabaaz Ir/GB: 129
Chacal Fr/DD: 31
Chaffee US/DE: 498, 524
Chakdina UK/Aux CL: 46, 86, 107, see merchant ship
Chakla UK/Boarding vessel: 45
Chambly Can/Corvette: 131, 211, 217, 325, 354-355, 454
Chamois Fr/Sloop: 372, see SG 21
Champlain US/CG cutter: see Senenn
Champlin US/DD: 308, 339, 386, 444
Chantala UK/Aux CL: 46, 86, see merchant Ship
Chanticleer UK/Sloop: 339, 368
Chapaev USSR/Patrol Ship (B): 129

Charles Ausburne US/DD: 355, 363, 372, 391, 427, 474, 480-481, 500, 512, 527
Charles E. Brannon US/DE: 513, 523
Charles F. Hughes US/DD: 83, 115, 119, 132, 136, 303, 443
Charles J. Badger US/DD: 431, 480, 502, 508
Charles J. Kimmel US/DE: 480
Charles S. Sperry US/DD: 476, 499, 525, 533
Charlotte Schliemann Ger/Oiler: 82, 114, 315, 373, 382
Charlottesville US/Frigate: see EK1
Charlottetown Can/Corvette: 248
Charr US/SM: 505
Charrette US/DD: 370, 373, 377, 387, 392, 406, 426, 458, 480, 523-524
Charybdis UK/CL: 210, 215, 218, 223, 225, 227, 236-237, 242-243, 247, 270, 274, 350-351, 362
Chase US/DE: 408, (APD 54), 517
Chaser UK/CVE: 393, 516
Chatelain US/DE: 381, 387, 416, 507
Chaudière (ex-Hero) Can/DD: 395, 424, 429, 436
Chauncey US/DD: 359, 365, 370, 373, 388, 409, 428, 437, 499, 525, 533
Chebogue Can/Frigate: 454
Chelan US/CG cutter: see Lulworth
Chelmer UK/Frigate: 421
Chelsea (ex-Crowninshield) UK/DD: see Derzki
Chenango US/CVE: 273, 291, 335, 370, 388, 392, 409, 437, 451, 460, 502, 509, 511, 516, 528
Chernomorets USSR/Survey Ship (BS): 143
Cherusker (ex-Jardine) Ger/Vp boat: see V6117
Chervona Ukraina USSR/CL (BS): 109, 128, 132, 136, 141, 143, 147, 150
Cheshire UK/Aux CL: 58, 247
Chester US/CA: 161, 168, 183, 214, 226, 264, 370, 388, 431, 448, 457, 464, 466, 473, 482, 487, 493, 527
Chevalier US/DD: 291, 324, 335, 345, 356
Chevalier (II) US/DD: 533
Chevalier-Paul Fr/DD: 10, 26-27, 29, 37, 107
Chevreuil Fr/Sloop: 10
Chiburi Jap/Frigate: 439, 476
Chicago US/CA: 161, 168, 185, 189, 199, 214-215, 226, 238, 241, 291
Chicago (II) US/CA: 525, 529-530, 533
Chiddingfold UK/DD: 171
Chidori Jap/TB: 162, 169, 472
Chikaskia US/Oiler: 476
Chikuma Jap/CA: 156, 168, 179, 184, 190, 194, 196, 204, 220,

223, 235, 248, 254, 264, 268-270, 361, 364, 371, 383, 414, 462-463
Chilliwack Can/Corvette: 184, 240, 286-287, 296, 301-302, 395
Chilton US/APA: 505
Chinotto It/TB: 34, 87
Chitral UK/Aux CL: 382
Chitose Jap/Seaplane Carrier: 160, 169, 171, 177, 181, 184, 186, 221, 235, 248-249, 263, 415, 430, 462, 464
Chiyoda Jap/Seaplane Carrier: 194-195, 221, 235, 415, 430, 462, 464
Chogei Jap/SM tender: 529
Chokai Jap/CA: 159-160, 163, 166, 178, 187, 192, 200-201, 204-205, 221, 235, 237, 241, 249, 264, 275-276, 361, 364, 371, 414, 430, 462-463
Cholbury Thai/TB: 76
Chub US/SM: 515
Churchill (ex-Herndon) UK/DD: 211, 246, 295, 320,328, 356, see Deyatelny
Chuyo Jap/CVE: 372
Cicala UK/GB: 170
Ciclone It/TB: 293, 300
Cicogna It/Corvette: 300, 313
Cigno It/TB: 47, 97, 127, 158, 200, 273, 293, 300, 312-313
Cimarron US/Oiler: 150, 207, 221, 239, 359
Cimeterre (ex-PC 1250) Fr/SC: 413
Cincinnati US/CL: 108, 379, 443
Circé Fr/SM: 21, 29, 284, 322
Circe It/TB: 34, 36, 74, 104, 119, 186, 193
Ciro Menotti It/SM: see Menotti
Cisco US/SM: 347
Città di Trapani It/Hospital Ship: 280
Clare UK/DD: 338
Clarence K. Bronson US/DD: 387, 426, 458, 476, 528, 533
Clark US/DD: 182, 185, 199, 275
Clarkia UK/Corvette: 247
Claus von Bevern (ex-T 190) Ger/Experimental vessel: 22
Claxton US/DD: 5, 335, 355, 364, 372, 466, 487, 500, 527
Clayoquot Can/MS: 248, 469
Clematis UK/Corvette: 211, 287, 325, 421
Clemson US/DD: 329, 337, 371-372
Cleopatra UK/CL: 187, 200-202, 227, 292, 333, 339, 340, 534
Cleveland UK/DD: 206, 339, 351, 443, 453
Cleveland US/CL: 273, 291, 307, 334, 363, 376, 399, 426-427, 495, 500, 512, 524, 527
Climene It/TB: 98, 245, 251, 293, 313
Clio It/TB: 34, 36, 70, 73, 104, 129, 255, 282, 293, 300, 312-313
Clive Ind/Sloop: 107
Cloves US/DE: 524
Clyde UK/SM: 10, 23, 37, 39, 104, 111, 247, 271, 278

Cobalto It/SM: 236, 242
Cobia US/SM: 432, 457, 479, 522
Cobra Ger/ML: 3, 47-48, 51, 109, 124, 136, 204
Cockchafer UK/GB: 93, 129
Cockrill US/DE: 507
Cod US/SM: 390, 410, 439, 457, 505
Codrington UK/DD: 23-24, 27, 31, 44
Coffman US/DE: 506
Coghlan US/DD: 295, 304, 312, 323, 337, 353, 359, 388, 427, 473, 480
Cogswell US/DD: 387, 426, 458, 476, 525, 533
Colac Aus/MS: 311, 406, 520
Colahan US/DD: 388, 437, 458, 476, 499, 525, 533
Colbert Fr/CA: 37, 280
Cole US/DD: 83, 119, 136, 339, 350
Colhoun US/APD: 246, 249-250
Colhoun (II) US/DD: 507
Colleoni It/CL: 42, 44
Collett US/DD: 476, 499, 510, 525, 533
Collingwood Can/Corvette: 211, 217, 295, 356
Colombia Du/SM Tender: 299
Colombo It/CL: 11, 78, 147, 338, 367, 402, 444, 453
Colonna It/SM: 57, 76, 106
Colorado US/BB: 222, 226, 335, 370, 388, 392, 427, 437-438, 471, 474, 479, 502, 511, 533
Colossus UK/CVL: 535
Coltsfoot UK/Corvette: 227
Colubrina It/Corvette: see UK205
Columbia (ex-Haraden) Can/DD: 142, 267
Columbia US/CL: 290-291, 334, 355, 363, 376, 391, 399, 452, 461, 463, 471, 474, 479, 481, 483, 524, 527
Columbine UK/Corvette: 443
Comanche US/CG cutter: 296
Comfort US/Hospital ship: 513
Commandant Bory Fr/Sloop: 443
Commandant Delage Fr/Sloop: 329, 443
Commandant Dominé Fr/Sloop: 56, 58, 64, 351, 443
Commandant Duboc Fr/Sloop: 55-56, 58-59, 138
Commandant Estienne D'Orves Fr/Sloop: 421
Commandant Rivière Fr/Sloop: 50, 56, 284
Commandant Teste Fr/Seaplane tender: 41, 280
Commandante Cappellini It/SM: see Cappellini
Commandante Faa' di Bruno It/SM: see Faa' di Bruno
Concord US/CL: 185, 431, 523, 525, 527-528, 531, 535
Confienza It/TB: 61, 69
Conklin US/DE: 467, 483, 522
Conn UK/DE: 464, 496
Conner US/DD: 359, 370, 373, 377, 387, 406, 426, 458, 471, 480, 523-524

Connolly US/DE: 509, 528
Console Generale Liuzzi It/SM: see Liuzzi
Conte di Cavour It/BB: 42, 57, 63, 493
Converse US/DD: 335, 364, 372, 391, 406, 427, 474, 480, 500, 527
Convolvulus UK/Corvette: 124, 167-168, 226, 339, 344
Conway US/DD: 291, 307, 335, 345, 363, 391, 399, 471, 474, 480, 500, 512, 524
Cony US/DD: 307, 345, 355, 363, 428, 471, 474, 480, 512, 524
Conyngham US/DD: 161, 221, 224, 269, 271, 310, 348, 355, 375-376, 380, 427, 473, 487, 495, 503, 512, 524
Cooke UK/DE: 394, 424, 464
Coolbaugh US/DE: 461
Cooper US/DD: 471
Coral Sea US/CVE: 370, 388, 399, 409, 428, 437, see Anzio
Corallo It/SM: 50, 54, 63, 76, 78, 90, 98, 101, 107, 115, 149, 154, 200, 211 223, 227, 271, 273, 283
Corazziere It/DD: 35, 42-43, 82, 89, 103, 118, 139, 154, 157, 166, 228, 239, 273, 282, 292, 349
Corbesier US/DE: 483
Core US/CVE: 337-338, 357, 454, 507
Coreopsis UK/Corvette: 59, 103
Corinthian UK/Boarding vessel: 137, 255
Corner US/DD: 474
Cornwall UK/CA: 7, 9, 52, 54, 98, 186, 197, 204-205
Coronel Ger/Vp boat: see V5909
Corpus Christi US/Frigate: 470
Corregidor US/CVE: 370, 388, 399, 409, 428, 437
Corridoni It/SM: 39, 45, 62, 73, 115, 124, 229, 236, 360
Corry US/DD: 387, 394, 420, 424
Corsaro It/DD: 243, 293
Corsaro (II) (ex-Squadrista) It/DD: see TA33
Corvina US/SM: 370
Cosenz It/TB: 55, 313
Cossack UK/DD: 19, 23, 25, 60, 101, 120, 122, 140, 145
Cotswold UK/DD: 421, 484
Cotten US/DD: 370, 387, 426, 458, 476, 528, 533
Cottesmore UK/DD: 265, 421
Cotton UK/DE: 511, 514
Courage (ex-Heartsease) US/Corvette: 247, 300, 322
Courageous UK/CV: 3
Courbet Fr/BB: 38, 41, 440
Coventry UK/CL: 30, 31, 33, 49-51, 54, 58, 62-63, 66-67, 69, 84, 93-94, 97, 103, 106, 227, 257
Cowanesque US/Oiler: 480
Cowell (I) US/DD: see Brighton, see Zharki
Cowell (II) US/DD: 370, 373, 377, 387, 406, 426, 458, 517, 527
Cowie US/DD: 339-340
Cowpens US/CVL: 359, 370, 373, 387, 392, 400, 406, 427, 448,

458, 464, 466, 474, 476-477, 491, 524-525, 533
Cowra Aus/MS: 406
Crane UK/Sloop: 339, 368-369, 400, 502, 516
Craven US/DD: 161, 168, 190, 335, 341, 388
Crescent City US/AP: 274
Crevalle US/SM: 365, 379, 402, 432, 522
Cricket UK/GB: 117
Crispi It/DD: 34, 83, 88, see TA15
Croaker US/SM: 439, 456
Croatan US/CVE: 338, 403, 412, 416, 507
Crocus UK/Corvette: 260
Cromarty UK/MS: 212
Cromer UK/MS: 212
Croome UK/DD: 127, 167, 197, 199, 202, 227, 238, 385
Crosby US/APD: 334-335, 376
Crotone It/ML: 34
Crouter US/DE: 504
Crowley US/DE: 533
Crowninshield US/DD: see Chelsea, see Derzki
Cubitt UK/DE: 421
Cuckmere Can/Frigate: 369
Culver (ex-Mendota) UK/Sloop: 185
Cumberland UK/CA: 7, 10, 13-14, 28, 52, 54-56, 68, 230, 287, 302, 400, 438, 460, 510, 514, 520, 538
Cummings US/DD: 161, 335, 388, 400, 407, 412, 457, 482
Curaçao UK/CL: 26-27, 261
Curie (ex-Vox I) Fr/SM: 413, 431, 453
Curlew UK/CL: 31
Currier US/DE: 443
Curtatone It/TB: 61
Curtiss US/Flying Boat tender: 161, 523
Curzon UK/DE: 435, 475, 484
Cushing US/DD: 269, 275-276
Cushing (II) US/DD: 458, 476, 499, 525, 533
Cuttlefish US/SM: 188, 222, 248, 370
Cyclamen UK/Corvette: 212
Cyclone Fr/DD: 30-32, 38
Cygnet UK/Sloop: 328, 339, 400, 452, 471, 475, 511
Czajka Pol/MS: 5

D-... : USSR/SM
D-2 (B): 257, 259, 273, 455
D-3 (A): 109, 115, 139, 154, 198, 213, 230
D-4 (BS): 216, 330, 368
D-5 (BS), 216, 284
DS-... USSR/LCI (ex-US LCI(L))
DS-31 (P): 531
DS-32 (P): 531
DS-33 (P): 531
DS-38 (P): 531
DS-39 (P): 531
DS-40 (P): 531
DS-41 (P): 531
DS-42 (P): 531

DS-44 (P): 531
DS-45 (P): 531
D'Encrecasteaux Fr/Sloop: 50, 56, 212
D'Iberville Fr/Sloop: 50, 56, 147, 212
Da Barbiano It/CL: 35, 42, 47, 158
Da Mosto It/DD: 94, 96-97, 105, 114, 116, 126, 157, 206
Da Noli It/DD: 42, 58, 63, 74, 97, 126, 135, 154, 165, 175, 183, 193, 199-200, 265, 267, 272-273, 282, 292, 300, 349
Da Procida It/SM: 39, 48, 68, 71, 106
Da Recco It/DD: 42, 68, 70, 89, 94, 96-98, 105, 114, 116, 127, 135, 145, 165, 175, 245, 251, 282-283, 349
Da Verazzano It/DD: 94, 96-97, 105, 114, 116, 126, 143, 157, 255, 261, 265, 267
Da Vinci It/SM: 56, 73, 91, 113, 127, 132, 137, 197, 270, 315
Dace US/SM: 329, 392, 432, 457, 462, 472, 522
Dacia Ru/ML: 142, 232, 446
Daga It/TB: see TA 39
Dagabur It/SM: 48, 71, 81, 84, 115, 133, 144, 155, 165, 236, 242
Dahlia UK/Corvette: 211, 371
Dainty UK/DD: 39-40, 43, 45, 50, 62, 74, 82, 108
Dakins UK (ex-US)/Frigate: 421
Dale US/DD: 161, 168, 182, 185, 199, 226, 238, 249, 253, 312, 323, 337, 359, 370, 388, 392, 418, 437, 476
Dallas US/DD: 83, 119, 136, 339, 350, 413
Dalmacija Yu/CA: 91, see Cattaro, see Niobe
Daly US/DD: 337, 376, 395-396, 399, 409, 418, 451, 461, 463, 513, 527
Damon M. Cummings US/DE: 504
Danae UK/CL: 21, 164, 180, 186, 194-196, 382, 421
Danaé Fr/SM: 36
Danaide It/Corvette: 407
Dandolo It/SM: 34, 40, 42, 46, 59, 61, 77, 92, 140, 148, 156, 175, 201, 237, 242, 263, 273, 283, 289, 340
Daneman UK/AS Trawler: 96
Daniele Manin It/DD: see Manin
Daphne Da/SM: 346
Dardo It/DD: 42, 67, 87, 98, 127
Daring UK/DD: 19
Darkdale UK/Oiler: 143
Dart UK/Frigate: 339
Darter US/SM: 392, 396, 419, 457, 462
Dasher UK/CVE: 274, 302, 312
Dashiell US/DD: 347, 353, 359, 370, 437, 474, 480, 499, 509, 522, 525, 533
Dauntless UK/CL: 21
Dauphin Can/Corvette: 184, 253, 296, 301

S

Dauphin Fr/SM: 284
David W. Taylor US/DD: 473, 476, 482
Davis US/DD: 4, 108, 379, 420
Davison US/DD: 339
Day US/DE: 480, 494, 504, 523
Dayton US/CL: 525-526, 533
De Haven US/DD: 290-291
De Haven II US/DD: 476, 499, 522, 525, 533
De Lutti It/GB: 116
De Ruyter Du/CL: 185-186, 188, 191, 195
Deane UK/DE: 464, 496
Decatur US/DD: 4, 136, 142, 184, 375, 402
Decker US/DE: 413
Decoy UK/DD: 26, 39-40, 43, 51, 63, 83, 95, 102-103, 107-108, 165, 189, 204
Deede US/DE: 533
Defender UK/DD: 26, 43, 45, 63, 66, 74, 95, 102, 108, 117
Defense US/MS: 507
Deffenu It/Aux ML: 34
Deimos US/AK: 334
Delfino It/SM: 34, 39, 44, 47, 55, 62, 65, 73, 122, 140, 144, 149, 154, 156
Delfinul Ru/SM: 125-126
Delhi UK/CL: 8, 11, 43, 46, 50, 54-55, 64, 274, 338, 350, 386, 404, 410, 444
Delight UK/DD: 32-33, 44
Deloraine Aus/MS: 178, 406, 520
Delphinium UK/Corvette: 227, 339
Denbigh Castle UK/Corvette: 491
Denbydale UK/Oiler: 137
Dennis US/DE: 461, 502
Dent (Ex-DD 116) US/APD: 334-335, 345, 376
Dentuda US/SM: 522
Denver US/CL: 307, 334, 363-365, 452, 461, 463, 466, 471, 474, 480, 487, 495, 512, 514, 524, 527
Deptford UK/Sloop: 124, 132, 137, 167-168, 402
Derby UK/MS: 61
Derwent UK/DD: 242, 298, 306
Derwentdale UK/Oiler: 242
Derzki (ex-Chelsea) USSR/DD (A): 444, 465, 472, 484-485, 511
Derzky Bul/TB: 142
Des Geneys It/SM: 48
Despatch UK/CL: 13, 20, 65, 67, 126, 421
Dessiè It/SM: 47, 62, 67, 70, 76, 101, 120, 175, 218, 227, 236, 242
Detroit US/CL: 161, 319, 323, 337, 391, 482, 516, 522, 528, 533
Deutschland Ger/Pocket BB: 1, 6-9, 11 See Lützow
Devastator US/MS: 508
Deveron UK/Frigate: 389, 395, 421
Devilfish US/SM: 499
Devonshire UK/CA: 11, 23-25, 28-29, 32-33, 49, 51, 54-56, 58, 64, 74, 121, 127, 147, 154, 212, 298, 437, 442, 444, 465, 473, 518-519
Dewey US/DD: 161, 168, 182,

185, 199, 214, 221, 226, 238, 323, 337, 370, 392, 399, 474
Deyatelny (Ex-Churchill) USSR/DD(N): 444, 472, 484
Dezhnev USSR/Patrol vessel (A) See SKR-19
Dezza It/TB: 127, 293, 313
Dhonburi Thai/Coast Defence Vessel: 76
Di Giussano It/CL: 42, 47, 105, 116, 158
Diadem UK/CL: 401, 408, 421, 431, 441, 452, 473, 475, 490, 498, 511, 517
Diamant Fr/SM: 280
Diamante It/SM: 34
Diamantina Aus/Frigate: 536-537
Diamond UK/DD: 45, 49-50, 74, 95
Diana It/Sloop: 121, 232
Diana UK/DD: 27, 32
Diane Fr/SM: 36, 274
Dianella UK/Corvette: 211, 229, 302, 339, 374
Dianthus UK/Corvette: 96, 211, 217, 240, 296, 301-302, 305, 318, 421
Diaspro It/SM: 42, 46, 63, 65, 67, 76, 101, 106, 115, 118, 120, 122, 128, 140, 144, 146, 273, 283, 340, 344
Diaz It/CL: 42, 69, 82
Dickerson US/DD: 329, (APD 21), 505
Dido UK/CL: 64, 94, 97-98, 102-103, 107, 171, 176, 180, 183, 189, 200-201, 227, 279, 293, 339-340, 350, 386, 443, 464, 468, 518-519
Diether von Roeder Ger/DD: 3, 7-8, 22, 24-25
Diomede UK/CL: 3, 11, 68
Dionne US/DE: 533
Disdain US/MS: See T-277
Dithmarschen Ger/Oiler: 216, 219, 497
Dnestr USSR/GB (BS): See SKR-114
Dobler US/DE: 413
Doblestny (Ex-Roxborough) USSR/DD (A): 444, 465, 472, 484-485
Doggerbank (ex-Speybank) Ger/ Aux ML: See Schiff 53
Dolfijn (ex-P47) Du/SM: 300, 336, 398
Dolphin US/SM: 161, 170, 183, 222
Domenico Millelire It/SM: see Millelire
Domett UK/DE: 394, 424, 464
Dominica UK/Frigate: 424
Don USSR/GB (BS): See SKR-112
Donaldson US/DE: 522, 524, 533
Donnell US/DE: 400
Donner (ex-Sneland) Ger/Vp Boat: See V5102
Doran US/DD: 15
Doran (II) US/DD: 339
Doria It/BB: see Andrea Doria
Doris Fr/SM: 21, 29
Doris Gr/TB: 94

Doroteya USSR/MS (BS): see T-39
Dorsetshire UK/CA: 7, 9, 14, 19, 38, 44, 70, 101, 151, 158-159, 204-205
Dorsey (ex-DD117) US/DMS: 502
Dortch US/DD: 387, 426, 458, 476, 492, 528, 533
Dostoiny (ex-St Albans) USSR/ DD (A): 442, 444, 484-485, 511
Douglas UK/DD: 38, 43, 131, 339
Douglas A. Munro US/DE: 523, 528
Douglas H. Fox US/DD: 517
Douglas L. Howard US/DE: 416, 432, 455, 507
Downes US/DD: 161, 457
Doyle US/DD: 329, 420, 443
Drache Ger/MS: 5, 497, 508
Drache (ex-Zmaj) Ger/ML: 323, 341, 356, 360, 398, 451
Dragon UK/CL: 3, 50, 70, 164, 180, 186, 194-196, 204, (Pol) 421, 435
Dragone It/TB: See TA 30
Draug Nor/TB: 141
Drayton US/DD: 161, 168, 182, 185, 199, 282, 290, 310, 348, 355, 375-376, 380, 395-396, 471, 480, 495, 503, 513, 524
Drexler US/DD: 502, 517
Driade It/Corvette: 313
Drum US/SM: 209, 222, 239, 259, 384, 314, 347, 365, 456
Drumheller Can/Corvette: 211, 325, 354, 421
Drury UK/DE: 360, 371, 424, 506, 520
Dryaden Da/SM: 346
Du Page US/APA: 483
Du Pont US/DD: 329, 371-372
Duane US/CG Cutter: 318, 329, 408, 443
Dubbo Aus/MS: 470, 520, 537
Dubrovnik Yu/DD: 91, See Premuda, See TA 32.
Duca d'Aosta It/CL: 35, 42, 57, 69, 94, 96-97, 105, 114, 116, 143, 157, 165, 175, 183, 189, 228, 284, 342, 349, 379
Duca degli Abruzzi It/CL: 36, 57, 69, 80, 89, 97-98, 101, 128, 140, 153-154, 284, 349, 379
Duchess UK/DD: 14
Duckworth UK/DE: 389, 394, 424, 464, 496
Duff UK/DE: 423
Dufilho US/DD: 523
Duguay-Trouin Fr/CL: 8, 36, 39, 43, 444, 449, 508, 513
Duilio It/BB: see Caio Duilio
Duke of Wellington UK/LSI: 247
Duke of York UK/BB: 198, 203, 208, 213, 230, 256, 274, 338, 359, 374-375, 401, 437, 444, 530, 533, 535
Duluth US/CL: 522, 525-526, 533
Dulverton UK/DD: 189, 201-202, 227, 322, 339, 350, 367
Dumitrescu Ru/GB: 142, 210, 232, 368

Dumont d'Urville Fr/Sloop: 54, 76, 256
Duncan UK/DD: 63, 65, 67, 78, 120, 140, 197, 202, 212, 320, 326, 360, 362, 389
Duncan US/DD: 263
Duncan (II) US/DD: 533
Dundalk UK/MS: 31
Dundee UK/Sloop: 53
Dunedin UK/CL: 3, 11, 20, 71, 105, 114, 120, 154
Dunkerque Fr/BB: 7-8, 11, 41-42, 106, 280
Dunlap US/DD: 161, 168, 183, 190, 335, 341, 388, 400, 407, 412, 448, 457, 482, 536
Dunvegan Can/Corvette: 211
Dunvegan Castle UK/Aux CL: 47
Dunver Can/Corvette: 448
Dupleix Fr/CA: 7-8, 10, 37, 64, 280
Dupont US/DD: 83
Duquesne Fr/CA: 36, 43, 510, 514
Durazzo It/ML: 34, 323, 336
Durban UK/CL: 21, 164, 180, 186-187
Durbo It/SM: 34, 42, 45, 50, 60
Durmitor Yu/MTB: 91
Dutton US/Survey vessel: 517
Dyson US/DD: 335, 355, 363, 372, 391, 427, 474, 476, 487, 500, 512, 527
Dzerzhinski USSR/DD (BS): 110, 126, 128, 133, 136, 141, 147, 190, 199, 216
Dzerzhinski USSR/Patrol Ship: (P): 532
Dzik (ex-P 52) Pol/SM: 334, 352

E. . . . : (ex-US Frigates) USSR/Frigate
EK-1 (ex-Charlottesville) (P): 531
EK-2 (ex-Long Beach (P): 531
EK-3 (ex-Belfast) (P): 531
EK-5 (ex-San Pedro) (P): 531
EK-7 (ex-Ogden) (P): 531
EK-8 (ex-Allentown) (P): 531
EK-9 (ex-Machias) (P): 531

Eagle UK/CV: 7, 9, 17, 36, 40, 42-43, 45, 48-51, 58, 62, 66, 69, 74, 90, 99, 101, 105, 197, 199, 202, 215, 218, 223, 225, 227, 236-237, 242
Eagle US/Q ship: 202
Eagle 58 US/SC: 507
Earle US/DD: 339
Easton UK/DD: 299, 339, 344, 472
Eastwind US/Icebreaker: 457, 460
Eaton US/DD: 335, 345, 355, 391, 399, 471, 474, 480, 500, 512, 524
Eberle US/DD: 92, 136, 308, 443, 459
Echo UK/DD: 12, 30, 49, 51, 55, 100, 121, 198, 210, 215, 286, 339-340, 349, 351, 367, (see Navarinon)
Echodale UK/Oiler: 486
Eclipse UK/DD: 12, 23, 49, 51,

55, 121, 198, 203, 208, 230, 286, 302, 315, 318, 326, 339-340, 351, 360
Edinburgh UK/CL: 3, 6-8, 11, 84, 98, 100, 120, 140, 203, 208, 212-213
Edison US/DD: 136, 193, 339, 350, 369, 385, 449
Edmonds US/DE: 452, 461, 480, 502
Edmundston Can/Corvette: 346, 369, 378, 469
Edsall US/DD: 169, 173, 178, 196
Edward Rutledge US/AP: 277
Edwards US/DD: 185, 291, 323, 337, 364-365, 370, 391, 399, 463, 473, 480, 523
Edwin A. Howard US/DE: 524
Effingham UK/CL: 3, 7, 26-27, 30
Egeria It/Corvette: see UJ 201
Egerland Ger/Supply ship: 95, 105
Eggesford UK/DD: 338, 351, 443
Eglantine Nor/Corvette: 171, 211, 246, 262, 278, 281-282, 299, 304, 389, 395, 421, 471, 485, 511
Eglinton UK/DD: 363, 394, 421
Egret UK/Sloop: 281, 346
Eidsvold Nor/Coast Defence vessel: 24
Eisele US/DE: 502
Ekins UK/DE: 421, 435, 475, 510
El Djezair Fr/Aux CL: 26, 28, 38
El Kantara Fr/Aux CL: 26, 28, 38
El Mansour Fr/Aux CL: 26, 28, 38
Elan Fr/Sloop: 18, 53, 106
Elden US/DE: 533
Electra US/AKA: 277
Electra UK/DD: 2, 23-24, 37, 100, 146, 163, 165, 180, 186-187, 194-195
Ellett US/DD: 4, 161, 168, 207, 221, 224, 226, 238, 249, 346, 388, 392, 409, 427, 482
Elliot US/DD: 226
Ellis US/DD: 83, 115, 119, 136, 413
Ellyson US/DD: 203, 415, 421, 431, 444, 502, (DMS 19) 523
Elmore US/APA: 505
Elsass (ex-Cote d'Azur) Ger/ML: 373
Emanuele Filiberto Duca d'Aosta It/CL: see Duca d'Aosta
Emanuele Pessagno It/DD: see Pessagno
Emerald UK/CL: 3, 80, 93, 204, 382, 421
Emden Ger/CL: 2-3, 22, 134, 139, 489, 509
Emile Bertin Fr/CL: 23-24, 26, 218, 336, 444, 449, 459
Emmons US/DD: 245, 415, 420, 431, 444, 502, (DMS 22) 507
Emo It/SM: 40, 42, 50, 69, 84-85, 87, 103, 156, 227, 236, 242, 271, 273
Emperor UK/CVE: 401, 408, 410-411, 444, 453, 510, 514, 520, 527, 534

Empress UK/CVE: 494, 514, 527-528
Enchantress UK/Sloop: 283
Encounter UK/DD: 27, 45-46, 63, 67, 78, 132, 146, 164, 180, 186, 194-196
Endicott US/DD: 443, 445
Endymion US/Repair Ship: 521
Engels USSR/DD (B): 110, 117, 129
England US/DE: 417, 503, 513, 517
English US/DD: 476, 499, 525, 533
Enrico Cosenz It/TB: see Cosenz
Enrico Tazzoli It/SM: see Tazzoli
Enrico Toti It/SM: see Toti
Enterprise UK/CL: 17, 26, 27, 29-30, 32, 38, 41, 43, 45-46, 68, 80, 93, 197, 204-205, 377, 420, 431, 434
Enterprise US/CV: 161-162, 168, 183, 187, 190, 207, 221, 224, 226, 238, 241, 249, 269, 275-276, 291, 370, 373, 387, 392, 399-400, 406, 426, 448, 458, 461-462, 465-466, 476, 492, 499-500, 509, 516
Epée Fr/DD: 56, 64
Epervier Fr/DD: 26, 38, 274
Erben US/DD: 370, 373, 388, 409, 437, 499, 525, 533
Erebus UK/Monitor: 338, 340, 347, 420, 434, 439, 448, 467
Erevan USSR/DD (BS): 126
Erica UK/Corvette: 227-228
Erich Giese Ger/DD: 3, 11, 13, 22
Erich Koellner Ger/DD: 17-19, 22
Erich Steinbrinck Ger/DD: 1, 3, 7, 10, 14, 17, 33, 39, 51, 57, 60, 230, 348, 460
Ericsson US/DD: 92, 136, 443, 507
Eridano It/TB: see TA 29
Eridge UK/DD: 120, 189, 201-202, 218, 227
Erie US/GB: 265
Eritrea It/Colonial Sloop: 81, 327, 349
Erlangen Ger/Hospital Ship: 414, 450
Ermak USSR/Icebreaker (B): 13, 158
Ermland Ger/Supply Ship: 106
Erne UK/Sloop: 238, 339
Erpel (ex-KT 26) Ger/GB: 451
Erwin Wassner Ger/SM Depot: 438
Escabana US/CG Cutter: 296
Escapade UK/DD: 23-24, 26, 38, 45-46, 49, 51, 55, 58, 121, 227, 307, 326, 354
Escolar US/SM: 456
Escort UK/DD: 2, 20, 26-27, 38, 40-41, 43
Esk UK/DD: 4, 15, 21, 23, 29, 31, 51
Eskdale Nor/DD: 265, 318
Eskimo UK/DD: 23-25, 32, 84, 100, 171, 198, 242-243, 256, 334, 338, 340, 421-422, 424, 429, 521, 527

Espadon Fr/SM: 36, 284
Esperance Bay UK/Aux CL: 105
Espero It/DD: 40
Esquimalt Can/MS: 506
Essex US/CV: 347, 359, 364,
  370, 373, 387, 392, 415, 427,
  448, 458, 461-462, 465-467,
  474, 476, 491, 499-500, 509,
  516, 525
Essington UK/DE: 369, 394, 424,
  464
Esso Hamburg Ger/Oiler: 99,
  105
Etourdi Fr/Sloop: 38
Etamin US/AK: 376
Ettore Fieramosca It/SM: see
  Fieramosca
Eugene US/Frigate: 506
Eugene E. Elmore US/DE: 403,
  416
Eugenio di Savoia It/CL: 35, 42,
  57, 69-70, 94-97, 105, 143,
  200, 206, 227, 243, 283, 342,
  349
Euro It/DD: 34, 42, 95, 97, 101,
  127, 129, 149, 356
Euryalus UK/CL: 140, 155-156,
  163, 165, 176, 180, 183, 189,
  200-202, 227, 279, 292, 328,
  333, 339, 350-351, 446. 468,
  486, 502, 516, 526, 530, 534,
Eurydice Fr/SM: 36, 280
Euterpe It/Corvette: 313, See
  UJ 2228
Evangelista Torricelli It/SM: see
  Torricelli
Evans US/DD: 14, See
  Mansfield
Evans (II) US/DD: 476, 502, 517
Evarts US/DE: 413
Eversole US/DE: 452, 461, 465
Evertsen Du/DD: 164, 195-196
Eyebright Can/Corvette: 211
Exe UK/Frigate: 277, 346, 368
Exeter UK/CA: 7, 10, 13-14, 19,
  101, 186-188, 194-196
Exmoor UK/DD: 82
Exmoor (II) (ex-Burton) UK/DD:
  167, 199, 202, 227, 339-340,
  350, 367, 397
Exmouth UK/DE: 12, 18
Express UK/DD: 4, 15, 29,
  31-32, 51, 146, 163, 165, 180,
  197, 255, See Gatineau
Externsteine (WBS/11) Ger/
  Weather Observation Ship:
  460

F . . . Ger/Sloops
F3 (ex-Hai): 515
F5: 489
F6 (ex-Konigin Luise): 22, 456,
  504
F7: 1
F8: 1, 497
F9: 1, 13
F10: 1
F . . . Ger/Naval Ferry Barge
F 124: 399
F 152: 451
F 194: 431
F 223: 450
F 235: 465

F 236: 465
F 237: 431
F 258: 431
F 259: 431
F 305: 365
F 306: 365
F 308: 304
F 332: 304
F 334: 239
F 338: 360
F 341: 365
F 360: 365
F 367: 304
F 369: 365
F 380: 365
F 406: 408
F 419: 365
F 474: 359
F 498: 431
F 565: 404
F 566: 368
F 569: 404
F 571: 365
F 572: 404
F 573: 365
F 574: 365
F 580: 368
F 592: 368
F 594: 365
F 770 (ex-It/Mz 770): 390
F 811: 431
F 840: 447
Fl. J. 23 Ger/AA Escort: 305
Fl. J. 26 Ger/AA Escort: 431
FM 06 Ger/Harbour Patrol
  Boat: 430
F.R. 24 (ex-Valmy) It/DD: 513
F.R. 37 (ex-Le Hardi) It/DD: 513
F.R. 42 (ex-La Pomone) It/TB:
  see TA 10
F.R. 51 (ex-La Batailleuse)
  It/Corvette: 513
F.R. 52 (ex-Commandant
  Rivière) It/Corvette: 328
Faa' di Bruno It/SM: 34, 44, 50,
  59, 64
Fabrizi It/TB: 61, 63
Facility US/MS: 508
Fairfax US/DD: see
  Richmond, see Zhivuchi
Falgout US/DE: 408
Falke Ger/TB: 3, 39, 47-48, 51-
  52, 57-58, 60-61, 68, 71, 189,
  200, 217, 281, 313, 330, 332,
  413, 422, 427
Falkland Ger/Vp Boat: See
  V 5901
Falmouth UK/Sloop: 21, 36,
  93, 129
Fame UK/DD: 3, 27, 31-33, 262,
  281, 299, 304, 360, 362, 389,
  395, 424
Fancy US/MS: See T-271
Fanning US/DD: 161, 168, 207,
  335, 388, 400, 407, 412, 448,
  457, 482,
Fanshaw Bay US/CVE: 428,
  452, 461, 463, 502, 513, 527,
  535
Farenholt US/DD: 226, 239,
  249, 254, 263, 334, 364, 391, 437
Farndale UK/DD: 120, 140, 157,
  187, 339, 351, 443, 484

Farnham Castle UK/Corvette:
  511
Farquhar US/DE: 416, 432, 455,
  507
Farragut US/DD: 161, 214, 226,
  238, 249, 255, 323, 337, 370,
  388, 392, 476
Fasana It/ML: 34, 323
Faulkner UK/DD: 3, 5, 11, 14,
  20, 26-27, 32, 38, 41, 43,
  45-46, 49, 52, 55, 58, 63, 65,
  67, 73, 85, 90-91, 94, 97. 100,
  103, 106, 120, 132, 185, 190,
  198, 256, 286, 302, 318, 339,
  347, 349, 351, 356, 359, 367,
  421, 519
Fearless UK/DD: 5, 21, 25, 32,
  38, 41, 43, 46, 78, 90-91, 97,
  106, 120
Fechteler US/DE: 408, 410
Fedor Litke USSR/Icebreaker:
  (A): See SKR-18
Fencer UK/CVE: 358, 362, 389,
  401, 408-409, 446
Fennel Can/Corvette: 395, 469
Fernie UK/DD: 200, 247-248,
  265
Ferraris It/SM: 36, 48-49, 52, 61,
  65, 68, 71, 83, 145
Fessenden US/DE: 408, 455,
  507
Fidelity UK/Q ship: 287
Fieberling US/DE: 504, 507,
  509
Fieramosca It/SM: 34, 39
Fiji UK/CL: 49, 51, 88, 91, 94,
  97, 102
Filippo Corridoni It/SM: see
  Corridoni
Finback US/SM: 222, 233, 259,
  289, 306, 322, 336, 379, 429,
  449, 472
Findhorn UK (ex-US)/Frigate:
  389, 417, 502, 516
Finnegan US/DE: 494
Finzi It/SM: 34, 59, 64-65, 82,
  124, 126, 159, 192, 285, 312,
  see UIT 21
Fiona UK/Boarding Vessel: 45
Firedrake UK/DD: 3, 20, 31-33,
  49, 60, 62-63, 65, 67, 73, 78,
  120, 211, 278, 286
Fisalia It/SM: 34, 86, 94-95, 101,
  138
Fishguard UK/Cutter: 339
Fiske US/DE: 408, 416, 432
Fitch US/DD: 420, 444
Fitzroy UK/DE: 464, 496, 506
Fiume It/CA: 36, 42, 57, 67, 69,
  89
Flaherty US/DE: 381, 387, 416,
  507
Flamingo UK/Sloop: 26-27, 95,
  102, 108, 117, 156, 161, 457,
  486
Flandern Ger/Vp Boat: See
  V 5716
Flasher US/SM: 379, 402, 419,
  449, 457, 472, 491
Fleetwood UK/Sloop: 27, 29
Fleming US/DE: 502
Fletcher US/DD: 246, 269, 271,
  275-276, 282, 290-291, 295,

307, 324, 370, 373, 388, 418, 473-474, 480, 487, 495, 498, 504, 513
Fleur de Lys (ex-La Dieppoise) UK/Corvette: 103, 140, 141
Fleuret Fr/DD: 56,64
Flier US/SM: 419, 429
Flint US/CL: 476, 492, 499-500, 509, 528, 530, 533
Flora Dan/SM: 346
Flores Du/GB: 339, 350, 386, 421, 434
Flounder US/SM: 419, 457, 468
Flusser US/DD: 161, 185, 310, 348, 355, 375-376, 380, 395-396, 473, 495, 503, 512, 524
Flutto It/SM: 340
Flying Fish US/SM: 222, 296, 314, 336, 358, 372, 396, 410, 429, 522
Foca It/SM: 48, 60
Foch Fr/CA: 7, 10, 37, 64, 280
Fogg US/DE: 469
Föhn (ex-Hadaröy) Ger/Vp Boat: See V 5108
Foley UK/DE: 369
Folgore It/DD: 42, 75, 87, 95, 101, 145, 189, 228, 282
Folkestone UK/Sloop: 66, 303
Fomalhaut US/AK: 244, 271
Foote US/DD: see Roxborough, see Doblestny
Foote (II) US/DD: 355, 364, 474, 480
Forbin Fr/DD: 43, 443, 449
Ford US/DD: 191
Førel USSR/MS (BS): see T-891, see T-32
Foreman US/DE: 503, 505
Foresight UK/DD: 38, 41, 43, 45-46, 49, 52, 55-56, 58, 78, 90-91, 97, 100, 106, 120, 140, 212-213, 217, 242
Forester UK/DD: 3, 5, 25, 32, 38, 41, 43, 45-46, 49, 52, 55, 62-63, 65, 67, 73, 85, 97, 100, 103, 106, 120, 140, 212-213, 217, 287, 395, 435-436, 440
Forfar UK/Aux CL: 66
Formidable UK/CV: 70, 78, 80-81, 89, 93, 97, 102, 204, 239, 274, 333, 339, 351, 437, 444, 509, 516-517, 526, 530
Formoe US/DE: 513
Forrest US/DD: 381, 387, 420, 444 (DMS 24), 502, 517
Forster US/DE: 404
Fortunale It/TB: 284, 293, 300, 312, 407
Fortune UK/DD: 5, 20, 26, 32, 49, 52, 55-56, 62-63, 65, 73, 90, 97-98, 187, 189, 204, 227, 255, See Saskatchewan
Foudroyant Fr/DD: 27, 31-32
Fougueux Fr/DD: 30-31, 38, 56, 274
Fowey UK/Sloop: 18, 59
Fowler US/DE: 490
Foxhound UK/DD: 3, 25, 27, 32, 38, 41, 43, 46, 65, 78, 100, 106, 120, 167, 176, 180, 204, see Qu'Appelle
Foyle Bank UK/Aux AA: 42

Francesco Crispi It/DD: see Crispi
Francesco Morosini It/ML: see Morosini
Francesco Nullo It/DD: see Nullo
Francesco Stocco It/TB: see Stocco
Francis M. Robinson US/DE: 403, 416, 490
Francol UK/Oiler: 197
Frank Knox US/DD: 525-526, 533
Franke (ex-Larwood) Ger/Vp. Boat: see V 6111
Franken Ger/Supply Ship: 497
Frankford US/DD: 420, 422, 433
Franklin US/CV: 448, 458, 461-462, 465-466, 499-500
Franks US/DD: 370, 388, 392, 437, 461, 476, 499, 528, 530, 533
Fraser Can/DD: 5, 14
Fratelli Baniera It/SM: see Bandiera
Frazier US/DD: 291, 323, 328, 337, 370, 388, 391, 480, 523-524
Freccia It/DD: 42-43, 67, 78, 81, 103, 127, 175, 228
Frederick C. Davis US/DE: 386, 443, 507
Freese Ger/Weather Observation ship: 99
Freesia UK/Corvette: 212, 315
Fremantle Aus/MS: 534
Fresnel Fr/SM: 36, 274, 280
Friedrich Breme Ger/Oiler: 99, 105
Friedrich Eckoldt Ger/DD: 1, 3, 7-8, 10, 17-19, 22, 24, 57, 100, 117, 120, 124, 230, 265, 272, 288
Friedrich Ihn Ger/DD: 1, 3, 7, 14, 17, 57, 60, 189, 192, 198, 230, 515, 516
Friese (ex-Bradman) Ger/Vp. Boat: See V 6112
Friesenland Ger/Catapult Ship: 450
Friso Du/GB: 402
Fritillary UK/Corvette: 212
Frobisher UK/CL: 382, 421, 440
Frondeur Fr/DD: 10, 30-31, 38, 56, 274
Frost US/DE: 403, 416, 507
Frunze USSR/DD (BS): 126, 128, 136, 138
Frunze USSR/CA (BS): 126
Fubuki Jap/DD: 159, 163, 167, 173, 178, 181, 187, 194, 196, 200, 204-205, 221, 235, 249-250, 252, 263
Fuchs (ex-M130) Ger/MS: 5
Fuciliere It/DD: 42 67, 89, 98, 118, 120, 149, 154, 157, 166, 175, 183, 189, 199, 202, 243, 300, 349, 484
Fugas USSR/MS (B): see T-204
Fujinami Jap/DD: 361, 364, 414, 430, 462, 465

Fukue Jap/Frigate: 525
Fullam US/DD: 363, 388, 391, 427-428, 437, 502, 535
Fuller US/APA: 115, 253, 271
Fulmine It/DD: 42, 73, 75, 95, 97, 101, 145, 149, 189
Fumitsuki Jap/DD: 162, 169, 173, 194, 356, 377, 392
Furious UK/CV: 7, 11, 14, 24-25, 30, 32, 52, 71, 101, 106, 113, 121, 134, 242, 247, 270, 274, 338, 393, 401, 408, 410-411, 457, 444, 446
Fury UK/DD: 32, 49, 52, 55, 58, 63, 65, 67, 73, 78, 90-91, 97, 100, 103, 106, 120, 140, 198, 203, 208, 229, 242-243, 256, 286, 302, 315, 318, 326, 339, 349, 351, 356, 359, 367, 421, 424
Furutaka Jap/CA: 163, 168, 179, 199, 214, 235, 241, 249, 263
Fusetsu-Tokumu-Tei 5 Jap/Aux ML: 471
Fuso Jap/BB: 221, 235, 414, 418, 462-463
Fuyo Jap/TB: 372
Fuyutsuki Jap/DD: 508

G 1 Ger/Escort Vessel: 342
G 104 Ger/Escort Vessel: 467

G . . . It/ML barge
G 53: 323
G 56: 323
G 58: 323
GA 45 Ger/Q ship: 359-360
GD 91 Ger/Harbour Patrol Boat: 451
GD 97 Ger/Harbour Patrol Boat: 453
GK 32 Ger/Harbour Patrol Boat: 454
GK 61 Ger/Harbour Patrol Boat: 433
GK 92 Ger/Harbour Patrol Boat: 453
GR 02 Ger/Patrol Vessel: 398
GR 94 Ger/Patrol Vessel: 398
Gabbiano It/Corvette: 293, 300, 313
Gabilan US/SM: 432, 456, 505
Gafel USSR/MS (B): see T-205
Gairsay US/AS Trawler: 440
Gak USSR/MS(B): see T-210
Galatea: It/SM 34, 73, 83, 96, 99, 165, 175, 200, 202, 218, 225, 227, 283
Galatea UK/CL: 18, 23-24, 26-27, 30, 32, 100, 155, 163, 165
Galatée Fr/SM: 280
Galicia Sp/CL: 327
Galilei It/SM: 36, see P 711
Galileo Ferraris It/SM: see Ferraris
Galileo Galilei It/SM: see Galilei
Gallant UK/DD: 31-32, 45-47, 60, 62-63, 66, 74, 207
Gallipoli Ger/Aux MS: 454
Galt Can/Corvette: 211
Galvani It/SM: 36

Gambia NZ/CL: 255, 298, 374, 377, 382, 399, 407, 412, 438, 471, 502, 505, 509, 516, 526, 530-531, 533
Gambier Bay US/CVE: 428, 461, 463
Gamble US/DMS: 161, 250, 324, 334, 364
Gandy US/DE: 386
Ganilly UK/AS Trawler: 435
Gannet US/Flying Boat Depot Ship: 5, 222
Gansevoort US/DD: 323, 337, 370, 391
Gar US/SM: 198, 266, 284, 290, 322, 343, 379, 401, 429
Gardenia UK/Corvette: 138, 167, 226
Garibaldi It/CL: 36, 57, 69, 89, 97-98, 101, 119-120, 153-154, 157, 165, 175, 200, 228, 284, 342, 349
Garland UK/DD: 40, (Pol) 50, 140, 219-220, 293, 307, 358, 362, 437, 453
Garlies UK/DE: 394, 424, 444
Garpun USSR/MS (BS): see T-409
Garth UK/DD: 247, 304, 394, 421
Gascoyne Aus/Frigate: 406, 479, 480, 538
Gasperi It/Aux ML: 341
Gatineau (ex-Express) Can/DD: 354, 395, 424, 429,
Gatling US/DD: 387, 426, 458, 476, 528, 533
Gato US/SM: 222, 289, 365, 372, 392, 491, 534
Gawler Aus/MS: 339, 344
Gayety US/MS: 517
Gayret Tur/DD: see Ithuriel
Gdansk Pol/Aux Vessel: 2
Gdynie Pol/Aux Vessel: 2
Gedania Ger/Oiler: 105
Gazelle Fr/Sloop: 50, 56, 539
Geier (ex-Timan) Ger/Patrol Boat: see V 5904
Geelong Aus/Corvette: 406
Gemma It/SM: 34, 40, 47, 57
Gendreau US/DE: 504
General Haller Pol/GB: 2
General William A. Mann US/AP: 416
Generale Achille Papa It/TB: see Papa
Generale Antonino Cantore It/TB: see Cantore
General Antonino Cascino It/TB: see Cascino
Generale Antonio Chinotto It/TB: see Chinotto
Generale Carlo Montanari It/TB: see Montanari
Generale Marcello Prestinari It/TB: see Prestinari
Geniere It/DD: 42-43, 58, 98, 118, 157, 175, 183, 189, 193, 200, 202, 228, 243
Gentian UK/Corvette: 66, 211, 287, 412, 421
Genista UK/Corvette: 212

Georgetown (ex-Maddox) UK/DD: 143, 215, see Zhestki
Georg Thiele Ger/DD: 1, 3, 22, 25
George US/DE: 417
George A. Johnson US/DE: 528
George E. Badger US/DD: 65, 311, 326, 329, 337, 371, 372
George F. Elliott US/AP: 241
Georges Leygues Fr/CL: 7, 8, 11, 53, 56, 318, 379, 420, 443, 484
Geraldton Aus/MS: 339, 344
Geranium UK/Corvette: 363
Gerfaut Fr/DD: 280, 397
Gherardi US/DD: 339, 342, 420, 431, 444, 502
Ghibli It/TB: 349, 513
Ghigulescu Ru/GB: 142, 232, 260, 330, 407
Giacomo Medici It/TB: see Medici
Giada It/SM: 227-228, 242, 283, 289
Gilbert Islands US/CVE: 524, 528, 533
Gillespie US/DD: 295, 304, 396, 409, 533
Gilligan US/DE: 480, 483, 521
Gilmer US/APD: 334, 348, 376, 503
Gioberti It/DD: 42-43, 67, 73, 89, 95, 105, 118, 127, 135, 145, 166, 175, 227-228, 243, 245, 267, 292, 300, 336
Giosue Carducci It/DD: see Carducci
Giovanni Bausan It/SM: see Bausan
Giovanni Berta It/Aux MS: 36
Giovanni da Procida It/SM: see Da Procida
Giovanni da Verazzano It/DD: see Da Verazzano
Giovanni delle Bande Nere It/CL: see Bande Nere
Giuliani It/SM: 34, 44, 50, 66, 87, 326
Giulio Cesare It/BB: 42-43, 57, 67, 69, 75, 79, 166, 175, 349, 381
Giuseppe Cesare Abba It/TB: see Abba
Giuseppe Dezza It/SM: see Dezza
Giuseppe Finzi It/SM: see Finzi
Giuseppe Garibaldi It/CL: see Garibaldi
Giuseppe La Farina It/TB: see Farina
Giuseppe Miraglia It/Seaplane depot: see Miraglia
Giuseppe Missori It/TB: see Missori
Giuseppe Sirtori It/TB: see Sirtori
Gladiator US/MS: 509, 511
Gladio It/TB: see TA 37
Gladiolus UK/Corvette: 38, 91, 108, 131, 142
Gladstone Aus/Corvette: 406, 538

Glaisdale Nor/DD: 265, 277, 318, 336, 421, 423
Glasgow UK/CL: 3, 6, 7, 11, 23-25, 27, 32, 63, 65, 67-68, 80, 86, 294, 314, 332, 374, 377, 420, 431
Glauco It/SM: 39, 42, 56, 73, 76
Glavkos Gr/SM: 111, 149, 207
Gleaner UK/MS: 19, 374
Gleaves US/DD: 83, 115, 119, 132, 136, 339, 350, 385, 415, 443, 459
Glenearn UK/Assault Ship: 95, 381
Glenelg Aus/Corvette: 406, 538
Glengyle UK/Assault Ship: 95, 247
Glennon US/DD: 339-340, 420, 424
Gloire Fr/CL: 7-8, 53-54, 256, 379, 443, 449, 508, 539
Glorious UK/CV: 9, 27, 30-33
Glory UK/CVL: 537
Gloucester UK/CL: 9, 36, 40, 43, 50-51, 57-58, 63, 65, 67, 70, 74, 89, 92-94, 96-97, 102
Glowworm UK/DD: 21,23
Gloxinia UK/Corvette: 67, 74, 97
Gnat UK/GB: 69, 92, 142
Gneisenau Ger/BB: 4, 7, 11, 19, 22, 24-25, 33, 35, 37, 39, 45, 71, 76, 78-79, 81, 85-87, 89, 91-92, 121, 188-189, 197, 497
Gnevny USSR/DD (B): 14, 110
Goathland UK/DD: 262, 321, 421
Godavari Ind/Sloop: 417, 513, 521
Godetia (ex-Dart) UK/Corvette: 291-292, 309, 344, 358, 421
Goff US/DD: 4, 247, 337, 357
Goffredo Mameli It/SM: see Mameli
Goldsborough US/DD: 357
Gonçalves Zarco Por/Sloop: 538
Gondar It/SM: 34, 39, 47, 57
Gonzenheim (II) Ger/Supply Ship: 98, 105
Goodall UK/DE: 469, 511, 514
Goodhue US/APA. 505
Goodson UK/DE: 400, 424
Gordy USSR/DD (B): 110, 117, 128, 130, 132, 138, 151
Gore UK/DE: 394, 424
Gorgo It/SM: 317
Gorizia It/CA: 36, 42, 57, 67, 69, 128, 140, 153, 165-166, 175, 189, 193, 202, 228, 243, 284, 317
Gorleston (ex-Itasca) UK/Sloop: 138
Goss US/DE: 480, 502
Gossamer UK/MS: 31, 203, 213, 220, 232
Gote (ex-Cape Siretoko) Ger/Vp Boat: see V 6113
Göteborg Swe/DD: 136
Gotland Swe/CA: 100
Gouden Leeuw Du/ML: 184, 195
Goulbourn Aus/MS: 164, 197, 406, 470

Gould UK/DE: 394
Gradisca It-Ger/Hospital: 89, 454
Grafton UK/DD: 30-32
Graf Zeppelin Ger/CV: 512
Grampus UK/SM: 35
Grampus US/SM: 198, 264, 266, 289, 307
Granatiere It/DD: 42, 67, 89, 101, 119, 149, 154, 157, 166. 280, 292, 300
Granito It/SM: 242-243
Graph (ex-U 570) UK/SM: 123, 288
Grayback US/SM: 198, 266, 289, 306-307, 322, 358, 372, 390
Grayling US/SM: 222, 290, 314, 322, 343
Grayson US/DD: 92, 119, 132, 207, 226, 238, 249, 255, 355, 364, 409, 458
Grecale It/DD: 42, 47, 98, 116, 127, 149, 202, 239, 243, 282, 349, 430, 512
Greene US/DD: 320, 326, 329, 357
Greenhalgh Bra/DD: 416-417
Greenling US/SM: 209, 222, 237, 239, 259, 284, 289, 329, 372, 472
Greenwood US/DE: 483
Greer US/DD: 15, 83, 119, 130-131, 134, 136, 143, 305, 329
Gregory US/APD: 246, 253
Gregory (II) US/DD: 508
Greif Ger/TB: 3, 22-23, 39, 51-52, 57-58, 60-61, 68, 71, 330, 332, 358, 398, 404-406 413
Gremyashchi USSR/DD (N): 117, 134, 155, 203, 231, 256, 334, 384-385, 401, 409, 459, 472
Grenade UK/DD: 23, 26, 28, 31-32
Grenadier US/SM: 198, 209, 222, 266, 314, 322
Grenville UK/DD: 17
Grenville (II) UK/DD: 346, 362, 421, 479, 486, 502, 516, 526, 530
Grey Goose UK/SGB: 423, 447
Grey Owl UK/SGB: 413
Grey Ranger UK/Oiler: 171, 257
Grey Wolf UK/SGB: 413, 423, 447
Greyhound UK/DD: 21, 23, 31-32, 45-46, 49, 52, 55, 62-63, 66, 74-75, 84, 89, 97, 102
Gridley US/DD: 161, 168, 226, 335, 370, 388, 458, 465, 479
Griffin UK/DD: 23-24, 28, 60, 62-63, 66, 74, 89, 92, 95, 97, 102, 107, 163, 180, 183, 189, 204, 227, see Ottawa (II)
Grille Ger/ML: 108
Grimsby UK/Sloop: 95
Grindall UK/DE: 506
Griswold US/DE: 533

Grom Pol/DD: 1, 23, 26-27, 29
Gromki USSR/DD (N): 117, 134, 155, 310, 334, 361, 409, 459
Groppo It/TB: 284, 293, 300, 312, 321, 328
Grou Can/Frigate: 394, 408, 424
Grouper US/SM: 222, 232, 248, 284, 419
Grove UK/DD: 206, 225
Growler US/SM: 222, 233, 248, 289, 329, 419, 429, 449
Groza USSR/TB (N): 12, 114, 116-117
Grozyashchi USSR/DD (B): 14, 112, 115, 117, 132, 138, 207, 384
Grozny USSR/DD (N): 12, 109, 121, 134, 220, 231, 310, 334, 361, 384-385, 409
Grunion US/SM: 233
Gruz USSR/MS (BS): see T-403
Gryf Pol/ML: 1-2
Guadalcanal US/CVE: 381, 387, 416
Guadeloupe US/Oiler: 190, 347, 353
Guam US/BC: 499-500, 509, 522, 527
Guardfish US/SM: 248, 259, 289, 329 358, 388, 432, 449
Guavina US/SM: 402, 432, 449, 468, 491
Gudgeon US/SM: 161, 164, 176, 198, 222, 237, 266, 306, 314, 347, 365
Guépard Fr/DD: 12, 37, 106-107, 280
Guest US/DD: 363, 388, 391, 427-428, 437, 502, 535
Guglielmo Marconi It/SM: see Marconi
Guglielmotti It/SM: 36, 45, 49 52, 55, 61, 83, 200
Guillemot UK/Sloop: 31, 484, 487
Guitarro US/SM: 410, 439, 457, 466
Gunnel US/SM: 272, 328, 372, 439, 468
Gurkha UK/DD: 18, 23-24
Gurkha (II) (ex-Larne) UK/DD: 140, 167, 171, 176-177, 180
Gurnard US/SM: 272, 358, 372, 407, 410, 415, 439, 468
Gustafson US/DE: 403, 417, 506
Gustav Nachtigal Ger/MTB Depot: 428
Guysborough Can/MS: 496
Gwin US/DD: 92, 132, 207, 221, 224, 226, 238, 263, 275-277, 334-336
Gwin (II) US/DD: 502, 517
Gyller Nor/TB: see Lowe
Gympie Aus/MS: 406
Gyorai-Tei 28 Jap/MTB: 526
Gypsy UK/DD: 10

H . . . : UK/SM
  H.31: 44, 87, 169

H.32: 87
H.33: 87
H.44: 87
H.49: 5, 56, 60
H.50: 87
H . . . : It/SM
  H.1: 34, 39
  H.4: 34, 39
  H.6: 34
  H.8: 34. 39
Ha . . . : Jap/Midget SM
  Ha.10: 277
  Ha.69: 480, 487
  Ha.76: 475, 487
  Ha.78: 498
  Ha.79: 498
  Ha.81: 473, 480, 487
  Ha.82: 480
  Ha.84: 480, 487, 494, 498
Habushi Jap/Frigate: 529
Hackleback US/SM: 508
Haddo US/SM: 402, 429, 439, 449, 468, 526, 534
Haddock US/SM: 248, 273, 314, 347, 379, 402, 464, 491
Haggard US/DD: 388, 392, 437, 461, 476, 499, 503, 513
Hagi Jap/DD: 529
Hagikaze Jap/DD: 159, 163, 166, 173, 178, 181, 190, 220, 223, 235 244, 290, 341
Haguro Jap/CA: 160, 169, 177, 181, 184, 186, 191, 194-196, 214, 221, 235, 248, 254, 361, 364, 314, 418, 430, 462-463, 520
Hai Ger/Escort Vessel: see F3
Haida Can/DD: 374, 405-406, 421-422, 424, 434, 441, 511, 514, 519
Hailey US/DD: 388, 392, 437, 461, 499
Haines US/DE: 443
Hajen Dan/TB: 347
Hakaze Jap/DD: 252, 289
Hake US/SM: 379, 396, 415, 418, 429, 468, 534
Hakusa (ex-Fu Sing) Jap/Supply Ship: 522
Halcyon UK/MS: 31, 171, 230, 302
Haldon UK/DD: see La Combattante
Hale US/DD: 370, 373, 388, 409, 437, 499, 525, 533
Halford US/DD: 347, 359, 391, 427-428, 463, 479, 480, 535
Halibut US/SM: 284, 296, 347, 361, 365, 402, 464
Halifax Can/Corvette: 250
Hall US/DD: 388, 480, 502
Halligan US/DD: 388, 480, 502-503
Halloran US/DE: 523
Halsey Powell US/DD: 427, 458, 476, 499, 533
Halsted UK/DE: 421, 423
Hamakaze Jap/DD: 156, 179, 190, 194, 197, 204, 220, 223, 235, 244, 250, 264, 268, 290-291, 335, 345, 361, 415, 430, 462, 476, 508

Hamanami Jap/DD: 414, 462, 466
Hambledon UK/DD: 339, 350, 397, 510
Hambleton US/DD-DMS: 277, 415, 421-422, 431, 444, 502, 504
Hämeenmaa Fin/GB: 157, 228, 233, 456
Hamilton (ex-Kalk) Can/DD: 238
Hamilton US/CG Cutter: 136
Hamilton US/DMS: 4, 329, 395
Hammann US/DD: 92, 132, 190, 199, 214, 221, 224
Hammerhead US/SM: 457, 472, 491, 496, 515, 526
Hammond UK/AS Trawler: 27, see Salier, see V 6115
Hamul US/AP: 115
Hancock US/CV: 458, 461-462, 464-467, 474, 476-477, 491, 499-500, 508, 524-525, 533
Hank/US/DD: 476, 499, 525, 533
Hans Albrecht Wedel Ger/ Aircraft Repair Ship: 497
Hans Lody Ger/DD: 3, 10, 13, 33, 39, 57, 60, 66, 68, 100, 116, 124, 230, 348, 373, 515-516
Hans Lüdemann Ger/DD: 3, 8, 10, 22, 24
Hansa/Schiff 5 (ex-Meersburg, ex-Glengarry) Ger/Aux CL: 455, 515
Hansestadt Danzig Ger/ML: 22, 77, 109, 116
Haraden US/DD: see Columbia
Haraden (I) US/DD: 388, 474
Harder US/SM: 328, 347, 401-402, 415, 429, 439
Harder US/DMS: 365
Hardhead US/SM: 439, 468, 491, 505, 522, 526
Harding US/DD: 420, 443, 502, 510
Hardy UK/DD: 9, 10, 14, 21, 23-24
Hardy (II) UK/DD: 383-384
Harridan US/DD: 527
Harrier UK/MS: 171, 203, 213, 220, 366
Harrison US/DD: 347, 353, 359, 370, 388, 437, 499, 507-508, 525, 533
Harry F. Bauer US/DM: 513, 523
Harstad (ex-Kos XVII) Nor/MS Trawler: 305
Hart UK/Sloop: 421, 481, 537
Hart US/DD: 502, 524
Hartland (ex-Pontchartrain) UK/Sloop: 274
Harukaze Jap/DD: 162, 169-170, 173, 194-196, 205, 477
Haruna Jap/BB: 159, 163, 167, 170, 178, 181, 190, 194, 204, 220, 223, 235, 254, 263-264, 268, 275, 361, 414, 430, 462-463, 499, 529
Harusame Jap/DD: 162, 170, 177, 182, 194, 221, 235, 248,

252, 268, 271, 275, 289, 361, 414-415, 418
Harveson US/DE: 395
Harvester (ex-Handy, ex-Jurua) UK/DD: 31-32, 61, 97, 211, 307
Hashidate Jap/GB: 410
Hashima Jap/Repair Ship: 505
Hasty UK/DD: 9-10, 14, 18, 39, 43-44, 57, 63, 73, 89, 92, 95, 97, 102, 107, 165, 170, 180, 183, 189, 200-201, 227-228
Hatakaze Jap/DD: 162, 170, 173, 194, 196, 205, 477
Hatherleigh UK/DD: see Kanaris
Hatsuharu Jap/DD: 181, 221, 235, 459, 462, 466
Hatsukari Jap TB: 162, 169
Hatsukaze Jap/DD: 160, 169, 177, 181, 184, 191, 194-195, 197, 221, 235, 248, 254, 264, 268, 290, 361, 364, 419
Hatsushimo Jap/DD: 181, 186, 191, 221, 235, 312, 337, 415, 430, 459, 462, 508
Hatsushio Jap/DD: 181, 184
Hatsutaka Jap/ML: 159, 205, 515
Hatsutsuki Jap/DD: 361, 415, 430, 462, 464, 468
Hatsuyuki Jap/DD: 159, 163, 166-167, 173, 178, 181, 187, 194, 196, 200, 204-205, 221, 235, 249-250, 252-253, 263, 271, 275-277, 335, 341
Hatsuzakura Jap/DD: 534
Havant (ex-Javary) UK/DD: 31-32
Havel Ger/Patrol Boat: see M 136
Havelock (ex-Jutahy) UK/DD: 30-33, 64, 97, 245, 291-292, 309, 317, 332, 358, 424, 506
Haverfield US/DE: 387, 395, 304, 416, 432, 507
Havfruen Dan/SM: 346
Havhesten Dan/SM: 346
Havkalen Dan/SM: 346
Havkatten Dan/TB: 347
Havmanden Dan/SM: 346
Havock UK/DD: 21, 23-24, 27, 44, 57, 63, 89, 95, 97, 102, 107, 165-166, 176, 180, 189, 200-202, 208
Havörnen Dan/TB: 347
Hawkbill US/SM: 457, 472, 491, 515
Hawkesbury Aus/Frigate: 513, 523
Hawkins UK/CL: 78-80, 382-383, 420
Hawkins US/DD: 533
Hayanami Jap/DD: 361, 415, 429
Hayashimo Jap/DD: 415, 430, 462, 464
Hayashio Jap/DD: 160, 169, 177, 181, 184, 186, 191, 194, 221, 235, 248, 254, 263-264, 268, 271, 275, 277

Hayate Jap/DD: 164
Haydon UK/DD: 295, 339, 351, 443
Haynsworth US/DD: 476, 492, 499, 507
Hayo Maru Jap/Aux ML: 170
Hayter US/DE: 481, 507
Hazard UK/MS: 169, 219
Hazelwood US/DD: 353, 359, 370, 388, 392, 461, 476, 499, 513
Healy US/DD: 387, 426, 458, 476, 528, 533
Heartsease UK/Corvette: 53, 59, see Courage
Heather UK/Corvette: 287, 325, 421
Hebe UK/MS: 31-32, 227-228, 243, 369
Hecla UK/SM Depot: 210, 277
Hector UK/Aux CL: 205
Heemskerck Du/CL: see Jacob van Heemskerck
Heerman US/DD: 370, 392, 461, 499, 509, 525, 533
Heian Maru Jap/SM Depot:392
Heide Ger/Tanker: 99
Heidelberg (ex-KT 29) Ger/KT Ship: see UJ 2171
Hektor (ex-Schiff 36/Orion, ex-Kurmark) Ger/Gunnery school ship: 512
Helena US/CL: 161, 263, 269, 271, 275-276, 290, 295, 324, 335
Heliotrope UK/Corvette: 59
Helli Gr/CL: 48
Helm US/DD: 161, 168, 226, 238, 241, 244, 250, 298, 310, 334, 367, 372, 376, 380, 458, 465, 479, 480, 502, 524
Helmsdale UK/Frigate: 448
Henley US/DD: 161, 168, 226, 238, 244, 250, 298, 310, 334, 355
Henri Poincaré Fr/SM: 280
Henrico US/APA: 505
Henrik Gerner Dan/SM Depot Ship: 346
Henry A. Wiley US/DM: 502
Henry F. Bauer US/DM: 502
Herbert US/DD: 329
Herbert C. Jones US/DE: 386, 443
Hercules US/AK: 346
Hereward UK/DD: 9-10 14, 30, 43, 63, 66, 69, 73-74, 83, 89, 95, 97, 102-103
Hermann Künne Ger/DD: 3, 8, 10, 14, 22
Hermann Schoemann Ger/DD: 3, 19, 33, 39, 116, 120, 189, 192, 198, 213
Hermes UK/CV: 3, 7, 10, 29, 38, 43-44, 70, 79-80, 93, 204-205
Hermes Fr/ : 322
Hermes (ex-Vasilefs Georgios) Gr/DD: 279, 313, 321
Hermione UK/CL: 100, 105-106, 113, 120, 122, 128, 133, 140,

144, 150, 197, 199, 202-203, 212, 227-228
Hermitage US/AP: 344
Herndon US/DD: see Churchill, see Deyatelny
Herndon (II) US/DD: 339, 420, 444
Hero UK/DD: 21, 25, 27, 43-44, 63, 73, 95, 97, 102, 143, 180, 200-201, 218, 227, 298, see Chaudière
Herring US/SM: 272, 372, 410
Herzog US/DE: 403
Hespeler (ex-Guildford Castle) Can/Corvette: 448
Hesperus (ex-Hearty, ex-Juruena) UK/DD: 29, 32, 97, 100, 178, 211, 287, 318, 325, 389, 424, 506
Heythrop UK/DD: 140, 189, 201
Heywood US/AP. 115, 271
Heywood L. Edwards US/DD: 428, 479, 503
Hibiki Jap/DD: 178, 181, 190, 221, 337, 415, 430
Hibiscus UK/Corvette: 59
Hickox US/DD: 387, 426, 458, 474, 476, 499
Hiei Jap/BB: 156, 179, 184, 190, 194, 196-197, 204, 221, 235, 248, 254, 263, 268, 275-276
Highbee US/DD: 528, 530, 533
Highlander (ex-Jaguaribe) UK/DD: 32, 61, 91, 143, 211, 309-310, 316-317
Hijirigawa Maru Jap/Seaplane Depot: 179
Hilary UK/AGC 338, 350, 420
Hilary P. Jones US/DD: 83, 115, 119, 132, 136, 303, 415 443, 449
Hilbert US/DE: 522, 533
Hill US/DE: 416, 432, 455, 507
Hindustan Ind/Sloop: 199, 513, 521
Hinoki Jap/DD: 480-481
Hinrich Freese Ger/Weather Observation ship: 105
Hinsdale US/APA: 503
Hirashima Jap/ML: 336
Hirato Jap/Frigate, 449
Hiryu Jap/CV: 156, 168, 178, 181, 190, 194, 197, 204, 220, 223-224
Hissem US/DE: 404
Hiyo Jap/CV: 235, 259, 263, 268, 275, 277, 316, 361, 415, 430
Hiyodori Jap/TB: 468
Hobart Aus/CA: 9, 17, 46, 126, 161, 172, 186-188, 194-196, 214, 226, 238, 241, 249-250, 310, 334, 340-341, 504, 513, 520, 523-524, 533
Hobby US/DD: 308, 396, 409, 476
Hobson US/DD-DMS: 387, 395, 420, 431, 444, 502, 510
Hodges US/DE: 480, 483
Hoe US/SM: 390, 410, 456, 491

Hoel US/DD: 370, 392, 461, 463
Hoggatt Bay US/CVE: 535
Hokoku Maru Jap/AuxCL: 223, 279
Holcombe UK/DD: 339, 351, 369
Holder US/DE: 404
Holderness UK/DD: 421
Hollandia US/CVE: 528, 553
Hollyhock UK/Corvette: 96, 197, 205
Holmes UK/DE: 421
Holt US/DE: 494, 504
Honeysuckle UK/Corvette: 219, 286, 339, 374, 421, 511
Honolulu US/CL: 161, 199, 221, 226, 282, 290, 324, 335-336, 391, 427, 452, 461
Hood UK/BC: 1, 3, 6-7, 9, 12, 29, 32, 38, 41, 43, 46, 54, 64, 68, 100,
Hopewell US/DD: see Bath
Hopewell (II) US/DD: 388, 409, 474, 480, 487, 533
Hopkins US/DMS: 5, 502, 517
Horace A. Bass US/DE: 513
Horatio UK/AS Trawler: 289
Hornet US/CV: 207, 221, 224, 226, 253-254, 258, 263, 269-270
Hornet (II) US/CV: 400-401, 406, 426, 430. 448, 457, 464, 466, 474, 476, 491, 499-500, 509, 516, 522
Hosho Jap/CVL: 221, 499, 529
Horsham Aus/MS: 538
Hostile UK/DD: 9, 10, 14, 21, 23-24, 27, 43, 47
Hotspur UK/DD: 21, 23-24, 45-46, 53, 60, 67, 89, 95, 97, 102-103, 106-107, 155. 163, 170, 180, 204, 227, 255, 356
Houston US/CA: 169, 173, 185, 190, 194-196
Houston (II) US/CL: 427, 448, 458
Hova Fr/DE: 443, 510
Hovey US/DMS: 263, 276, 481
Howard D. Clark US/DE: 480
Howe UK/BB: 294, 333, 339, 340, 348, 350, 442, 453, 471, 502, 516
Howortn US/DD: 409, 474, 504, 507
Hrabi Yu/SM: 91
Hubbard US/DE: 469, 481, 507
Hudson US/DD: 363, 391, 427 504, 508, 511, 535
Hugh L. Scott US/AP: 277
Hugh W. Hadley US/DD: 504, 517
Hughes US/DD: 92, 108, 132, 183, 190, 199, 221, 224, 226, 254, 258, 269, 275, 290, 323, 336, 370, 388 392, 409, 451, 473, 525, 528, 535
Hull US/DD: 161, 168, 182, 185, 199, 226 238, 323, 337, 359, 370, 392, 399, 474
Hummel (ex-M 7022, ex-Auguste Denise) Ger/AA Ship: 512

Hummer Ger/Escort Vessel: 352
Humphreys US/APD: 334, 348, 375-376, 395-396
Hunt US/DD: see Broadway
Hunt (II) US/DD: 387, 426, 458, 476, 499, 509
Hunter UK/DD: 21, 23-24
Hunter (II) UK/CVE: 351, 444, 453, 514, 520, 534
Huntley UK/MS: 61
Huntsville (ex-Wolvesay Castle) Can/Corvette: 448
Huron Can/DD: 374, 405, 421-422, 429, 433, 511, 519
Hurricane (ex-Japarua) UK/DD: 81, 211, 332, 371, 375
Hursley UK/DD: 292, 294, 322, 339, 359, see Kriti
Hurst Castle UK/Corvette: 448
Hurworth UK/DD: 189, 201-202, 218, 227, 339, 360
Huse US/DE: 386, 403, 416, 507
Hussar UK/MS: 203, 213, 220
Hutchins US/DD: 337, 376, 380, 395-396, 399, 409, 418, 437, 451, 461. 463, 504, 507
Hutchinson US/Frigate: 470
Hvalrossen Dan/TB: 346
Hyacinth UK/Corvette: 67, 74, 95, 138, 339
Hyderabad Ind/Corvette: 219, 287, 339
Hydra Ger/Supply Ship: 429
Hydra Gr/DD: 94
Hydrangea UK/Corvette: 85, 122
Hyman US/DD: 504, 507
Hyperion US/DD: 15, 21, 43-44, 58, 63, 69-70
Hythe UK/MS: 227, 243, 344, 353
Hyuga Jap/BB: 221, 462, 464, 499, 529

I . . .:Jap/SM
I-1: 152, 163, 177, 193, 229, 290
I-2: 152, 177, 193, 204, 206, 229, 263, 284, 328
I-3: 152, 177, 193, 204, 206, 229, 284
I-4: 152, 163, 177, 193, 204, 229, 258, 284
I-5: 152, 177, 204, 206, 258, 284, 328, 426
I-6: 152, 163, 177, 204, 206, 229, 284, 328, 346, 426
I-7: 152, 163, 177, 193, 204, 206, 229, 258, 264, 275, 328
I-8: 152, 181, 207, 258, 295, 316, 338, 347, 350, 383, 417 503
I-9: 152, 162, 183, 187, 219, 249, 253, 264, 275, 328
I-10: 152, 162, 223, 295, 316, 349, 426
I-11: 249, 234-235, 253, 341, 381
I-12: 457
I-13: 528
I-14: 528
I-15: 152, 183, 187, 249, 254, 264, 270
I-16: 152, 177, 223, 271, 277, 346, 417

I-17: 152, 162, 183, 187, 249, 276, 306, 311, 341
I-18: 152, 177, 223, 289, 295
I-19: 156, 162, 183, 187, 219, 249, 254 311, 341, 370
I-20: 152, 177, 223, 271, 277, 346
I-21: 156, 162, 207, 215, 264, 270, 275, 295, 328, 346, 370
I-22: 152, 177, 207, 215, 258
I-23: 156, 162, 183, 187
I-24: 152, 177, 207, 215, 264, 271, 328
I-25: 152, 162, 183, 192, 219, 251, 311, 346
I-26: 152, 162, 183, 187, 219, 249, 276, 306, 311, 346, 373 459, 465
I-27: 207, 215, 246, 265, 280, 299, 315, 349, 350, 382, 383
I-28: 207, 209, 215
I-29: 207, 215, 246, 280, 315-316, 373, 403, 417
I-30: 222-223, 250
I-31: 249, 253, 275, 323
I-32: 311, 346, 382
I-34: 350
I-35: 323, 328, 370
I-36: 370, 467, 483, 494, 513 521
I-37: 316, 350, 383, 400, 467
I-38: 356, 426, 465
I-39: 346, 370
I-40: 370
I-41: 426, 465-467
I-42: 401
I-43: 392
I-44: 417, 426, 452, 494, 509
I-45: 459, 465
I-46: 465
I-47: 467, 483, 509, 513, 527
I-48: 483
I-52: 416-417
I-53: 417, 426, 459, 465, 483, 521, 527
I-54: 459, 463
I-56: 459, 463, 465, 483, 509
I-58: 483, 494, 509, 527-528
I-53 to I-75
  Renumbered after May 1942
  to I-153 to 1-175
I-121: 159, 164, 170, 178, 193, 222, 239, 249,
I-122: 159, 164, 170, 178, 193, 222 239, 275, 522
I-123: 164, 170, 178, 193, 222, 239, 249-250
I-124: 164, 170, 178
I-153: 160, 164, 193, 529
I-154: 160, 164, 193
I-155: 160, 166, 176, 186-187, 328
I-156: 166, 176, 186-187, 222
I-157: 160, 166, 176, 222, 328
I-158: 160, 163, 166, 176, 193, 222
I-159: 177-178, 181, 193, 222
I-160: 177-178, 181
I-162: 160, 167, 177-178, 181, 200, 222, 246, 258, 350, 373, 383
I-64: 160, 167, 177-178, 181, 200, 222

I-165: 163, 167, 177, 181, 188, 222, 246, 258, 285, 350, 383, 417, 521
I-166: 160, 167, 177, 181, 188, 222. 246, 258, 280, 285, 350, 383, 417, 438
I-168: 152, 162, 207, 222, 224, 328
I-169: 152, 162, 181, 207, 222, 235, 328, 370
I-170: 152, 162
I-171: 152, 181, 183, 207, 222, 235, 328, 346
I-172: 152, 162, 181, 183, 207, 275
I-173: 152, 181
I-174: 152, 181, 207, 222, 234, 249, 264, 311 406
I-175: 152, 162, 181, 207, 222, 235, 249, 264, 275, 370, 382
I-176: 258, 264, 355, 370
I-177: 311, 355, 372, 380, 452
I-178: 311
I-180: 311
I-181: 346
I-182: 346
I-183: 402
I-184: 426
I-185: 426
I-202: 529
I-205: 499, 529
I-351: 526
I-361: 521
I-363: 521
I-365: 468
I-366: 528
I-367: 521, 528
I-368: 494
I-370: 494
I-371: 491
I-372: 526
I-373: 528
I-400: 499, 528
I-401: 528
I-404: 529
I-8: USSR/GB: 130
Ibis UK/Sloop: 274
Icarus US/CG Cutter: 213
Icarus UK/DD: 12, 21, 23, 25, 31-32, 100, 121, 127, 198, 227, 242-243, 287, 311, 315, 318, 354, 421, 395, 481
Icefish US/SM: 456
Idaho US/BB: 92, 108, 132, 149 226, 323, 337, 370, 388, 399, 427, 493, 502, 509, 511, 533, 537
Ikazuchi Jap/DD: 159, 163, 167, 173, 177, 181, 184, 186, 191, 221, 235, 252, 268, 275, 312, 337, 402
Iki Jap/Frigate: 410
Ikoma Jap/CV: 499
Iku-Turso Fin/SM: 13, 110, 112, 116-117, 261, 432
Ilex UK/DD: 21, 40, 43-44, 49, 51, 63-70, 74, 89, 97, 102, 107, 328, 339-340, 351
Illern Swe/SM: 344
Illustrious UK/CV: 49-51, 54, 57-58, 63, 67, 70, 73-74 76-78, 81, 203, 212, 239, 255, 338, 345, 351, 378, 382, 399,

407, 412, 425, 438, 442, 469, 471, 473, 486, 502, 507, 509
Ilmarinen Fin/Coast Defence Vessel: 134
Iltis Ger/TB: 3, 10-12, 18, 48, 51-52, 62, 68, 77, 83-84, 87, 189, 200, 217
Imizu Maru Jap/Aux ML: 176, 182
Imogen UK/DD: 20-21, 32
Impavido It/TB: see TA 23
Imperial UK/DD: 28, 50, 58, 97, 102-103
Imperialist UK/AS Trawler: 103
Impero It/BB: 493
Impetuoso It/TB: 349
Implacable UK/CV: 446, 465, 468, 473, 523-524, 526, 530
Impulsive UK/DD: 21, 31-32, 256, 287, 302, 320, 374, 393, 421
Inagi Jap/Frigate: 530
Inazuma Jap/DD: 159, 163, 167, 173, 177, 181, 194, 196, 221, 235, 252, 263, 268, 275-276, 312, 337, 402
Inch US/DE: 403, 416, 507
Inconstant (ex-Muavenet) UK/ DD: 212, 227, 255, 338, 340, 358, 362, 408, 424
Indefatigable UK/CV: 437, 442, 444, 471, 479, 486, 502, 516, 526, 530-531, 533
Independence US/CVL: 347, 359, 364, 370, 448, 458, 461-462, 465-466, 474, 476, 499-500, 509, 522, 525, 533
Indiana US/BB: 291, 335, 347, 370, 373, 387, 406, 427, 430, 448, 461, 464, 487, 491, 499-501, 509, 522, 525, 529-530, 533
Indianapolis US/CA: 168, 182, 185, 199, 221, 226, 295, 304, 337, 370, 388, 392, 426-427, 437, 442, 491, 493, 499, 503, 527
Indicative US/MS: see T-279
Indomitable UK/CV: 149, 179, 204, 212, 242, 333, 339-340, 438, 442, 453, 460, 469, 471, 473, 479, 486, 502, 505, 516, 534
Indomito It/TB: 407
Indus Ind/Sloop: 61, 107
Ingersoll US/DD: 387, 426, 458, 476, 525, 533
Ingham US/CG Cutter: 136, 211, 216-217, 268, 286, 296-297, 305, 310, 329, 500
Inglefield UK/DD: 20-21, 32, 49, 51, 55-56, 100, 121, 210, 286, 302, 315, 339, 351, 386
Inglis UK/DE: 464
Ingraham US/DD: 474, 479, 492, 502, 517
Insidioso It/TB: see TA 21
Intrepid UK/DD: 15, 29, 31-32, 100, 121, 155, 185, 190, 198, 215, 242-243, 256, 265, 302, 339, 349, 351, 356
Intrepid US/CV: 387, 392, 448, 458, 461-462, 465-467, 499-500,

509-510, 516, 528, 533, 537
Intrepido It/TB: see TA 25
Invade US/MS: 490
Inver UK/Frigate: 417
Invicta UK/LS: 247
Ioshima (ex-Ning Hai) Jap/GB: 449
Iowa US/BB: 387, 392, 399, 406, 426-427, 448, 458, 461, 464, 466, 474, 525-526, 533
Ipswich UK/MS: 339, 344, 383, 533
Irben Ger/Mine Transport: 505
Iride It/SM: 37, 39, 42, 49
Iris Fr/SM: 36
Iron Duke UK/Training Ship: 8
Iroquois Can/DD: 332, 339, 374, 441, 511, 514, 518-519
Irwin US/DD: 428, 458, 502, 527
Isaac Sweers Du/DD: 140, 150, 158, 165, 180, 183, 204, 273
Isabel US/GB: 197
Ise Jap /BB: 221, 462, 464, 488, 529
Isherwood US/DD: 396, 431, 480, 502, 511
Ishigaki Jap/Frigate: 410
Ishokaitei . . .: Jap/APD: see P . . . :
Isis UK/DD: 21, 32, 78, 95, 97, 102, 106-107, 294, 298, 328, 339, 421-422, 423, 435
Iskatel USSR/MS (BS): see T-406
Islay UK/AS Trawler: 238
Isokaze Jap/DD: 156, 179, 190, 194, 197, 204, 220, 223, 235, 244, 249-250, 264, 268-269, 290-291, 345, 356, 361, 415, 430, 462, 508
Isonami Jap/DD: 159, 163, 166, 173, 178, 181, 187, 194, 200, 205, 221, 235, 252, 263, 268, 314
Isuzu Jap/CL: 263-264, 268, 271, 275-276, 290-291, 370-371, 373, 462, 466, 468, 505
Italia (ex-Littorio) It/BB: 349
Itasca US/CG Cutter: see Gorleston
Itchen UK/Frigate: 319, 326, 354-355
Ithuriel (ex-Gayret) UK/DD: 210, 215, 218, 223, 225, 227-228, 242
Itsukushima Jap/ML: 160, 176, 182, 418, 460
Itto-Yuso-Kan . . .: Jap/APD: see P . . . :
Ivanhoe UK/DD: 15, 21, 23, 29, 31, 33, 51
Iwate Jap/School Cruiser: 529
Iwo Jap/Frigate: 525
Izard US/DD: 370, 373, 387, 392, 406, 426, 458, 479, 535
Izumo Jap/Armoured Cruiser: 163 529

J. R. Y. Blakeley US/DE: 416, 432, 455, 507
J. Richard Ward US/DE: 507
J. William Ditter US/DM: 502, 523
Jack US/SM: 329, 390, 402, 407, 419, 429, 439, 468

Jack W. Wilke US/DE: 506
Jackal UK/DD: 32, 94, 96, 98, 102-103, 106-107, 155, 163, 216
Jackson US/CG Cutter: 432
Jacob Jones US/DD: 188
Jacob van Heemskerck Du/CL: 204, 255, 280, 298, 408
Jagd (ex-M82) Ger/Tender: 512
Jaguar Fr/DD: 31
Jaguar Ger/TB: 14, 39, 47-48, 51-52, 58, 61-62, 68, 83-84, 87, 189, 200, 332, 398, 413, 422-423, 427
Jaguar UK/DD: 31-32, 67, 73, 94, 97, 107, 165, 176, 180, 183, 189, 200
Jaguaribe Braz/DD: see Highlander
Jalea It/SM: 34, 40, 47, 65, 68, 71, 76, 91
Jallao US/SM: 464, 529
Jamaica UK/CL: 256, 274, 287, 366, 374-375, 401, 437, 444, 452
Jan van Brakel Du/ML: 250
Janssen US/DE: 387, 395, 403, 416, 432, 507
Jantina It/SM: 34, 48, 62, 68, 115
Janus UK/DD: 23, 29, 43, 50, 63, 70, 74, 89, 93-94, 97, 102, 106, 386
Japarua Braz/DD: see Hurricane
Jarvis US/DD: 161, 168, 181, 226, 238, 241
Jarvis (II) US/DD: 525, 528, 535
Jaskolko Pol/MS: 5
Jasmine UK/Corvette: 212
Jason UK/MS: 59, 302, 334
Jasper UK/AS Trawler: 282
Jastrzab/P 551 (ex-S 25) Pol/SM: 213
Java Du/CL: 164, 186-188, 191, 195
Javari Braz/SC: 417
Javary Braz/DD: see Havant
Javelin UK/DD: 23, 29, 31-32, 68, 163, 212, 227, 292, 421, 422
Jean Bart Fr/BB: 38, 274
Jean de Vienne Fr/CL: 34, 280, 372
Jeanne d'Arc Fr/CL: 20, 218, 336, 352
Jed UK/Frigate: 321, 326, 331, 346
Jeffers US/DD: 339-340, 342, 420, 444 (DMS), 502, 509
Jelöy Nor/AS Trawler: 485, 511
Jenkins US/DD: 324, 334-335, 340, 370, 373, 409, 418, 480, 487, 495, 498, 504, 513
Jenks US/DE: 416
Jersey UK/DD: 13, 32, 78, 94, 96
Jervis UK/DD: 32, 50, 62-63, 70, 74, 89, 93-94, 97, 102, 107, 155, 163, 165-166, 189, 200-201, 216, 227, 292, 322, 328, 334, 339, 360, 386, 421
Jervis Bay UK/Aux CL: 53, 64
Jingei Jap/SM Depot: 179, 458
Jintsu Jap/CL: 160, 169, 171, 177,

184, 191, 194-195, 221, 235, 244, 249, 335
Jobb US/DE: 512, 523
Johan Maurits van Nassau Du/ Frigate: 402, see Ribble
John C. Butler US/DE: 461, 480, 502, 517
John D. Edwards US/DD: 188, 191, 195, 402
John D. Ford US/DD: see Ford: 182, 194-195
John D. Henley US/DD: 476, 502
John Hood US/DD: 525. 528, 535
John Rodgers US/DD: 347, 353, 359, 370, 388, 437, 499, 522, 525, 533
John W. Weeks US/DD: 476, 499, 525, 533
Johnnie Hutchins US/DE: 528
Johnston US/DD: 388, 392, 437, 461, 463
Jonquière Can/Frigate: 496
Jonquil UK/Corvette: 404
Joost Ger/Gun Carrier: 485, 497
Joseph E. Campbell US/DE: 408, 410
Joseph E. Connolly US/DE: 533
Joseph Hewes US/AP: 277
Joseph T. Dickman US/AP: 150
Josif Stalin USSR/Icebreaker (N): 361, 465
Jouett US/DD: 4, 15 108, 322, 379, 420, 443, 459
Joyce US/DE: 386, 395
Jules Verne Fr/SM Depot: 21
Jumna Ind/Sloop: 180, 187, 197, 339, 383, 479, 484, 494
Juneau US/CL: 254, 258, 269, 275-276
Juniper UK/AS Trawler: 33
Juno UK/DD: 43, 49-50, 62-63 70, 74, 94, 97, 102
Junon Fr/SM: 41, 169, 265
Junyo Jap/CV: 220, 223, 235, 263, 268-269, 275, 277, 316, 361, 365, 415, 430, 468
Jupiter UK/DD: 23-24, 26, 32, 78, 146, 165, 178, 180, 186-187, 194-195
Jura UK/AS Trawler: 289
Jurua Braz/DD: see Harvester
Juruena Braz/DD: see Hesperus
Jutahy Braz/DD: see Havelock

K . . . : Ger/GB (ex-Dutch)
K 1: 385, 393, 414, 515
K 2: 446
K 3: 445-446

K . . . : Du/SM
K IX: 197
K X: 194
K XI: 159, 187
K XII: 159, 166, 187, 191, 197
K XIII: 159, 187
K XIV: 159, 182, 187, 194, 382, 425
K XV: 159, 194, 197
K XVI: 159, 167
K XVII: 159, 166
K XVIII: 182, 197

K . . . : USSR/SM
K-1 (N): 109, 133, 144, 345
K-2 (N): 124, 133, 213
K-3 (B/N): 116, 139, 154, 298, 310
K-21 (B/N): 124, 148, 192, 198, 203-204, 208, 230-231, 240, 302, 310, 331, 375, 393
K-22 (B/N): 124, 148, 154, 180, 203-204, 213, 230, 298, 310
K-23 (B/N): 124, 148, 154, 176, 180, 198, 213
K-51 (B): 170, 455, 489
K-52 (B): 455, 490, 512
K-53 (B): 455, 497, 512
K-56 (B): 455

KFK . . . : Ger/Armed Trawlers, drifters, etc.
KFK 677: 498
KFK 679: 498
KFK 680: 498
KFK 683-699: 498

KT- . . . Ger/Naval Transport
KT 4: see Mannheim
KT 5: 321
KT 9: 321
KT 13: 313
KT 17: see UJ 104
KT 18: 407
KT 20: 381
KT 21: 321
KT 22: 322
KT 23: see UJ 106
KT 25: 407
KT 26: 407
KT 29: see Heidelberg
KT 31: 390
KT 37: see UJ 103
KT 39: 448
KT 40: see UJ 102

KT- . . . (also KATSC . . .): USSR/MMS
KT-173 (BS): 365
KT 411 (BS): 365
KT 509 (BS): 365

Kaba Jap/DD: 529
Kadashan Bay US/CVE: 461, 474, 480-481
Kaga Jap/CV: 156, 179, 184, 190, 194, 197, 220, 223-224
Kaganovic USSR/CA (P): 530
Kagero Jap/DD: 156, 179, 190, 204, 221, 235, 244, 249-250, 254, 263-264, 268, 271, 275, 277, 282-283, 286, 290, 324
Kaibokan . . . : Jap/Corvette
2: 529
3: 476
4: 529
6: 529
7: 457
8: 457
9: 491
10: 419, 449
13: 529
15: 410
16: 529
17: 476
18: 495
19: 476

21: 456
22: 462
23: 476
24: 419
25: 505
28: 472
29: 462
30: 479
31: 462, 495
33: 462
35: 476
38: 468
41: 522
42: 479
43: 462, 476
44: 529
45: 529
47: 492, 525, 529
51: 476
55: 525
56: 491
64: 472
65: 525
72: 525-526
73: 505
82: 530
84: 496
87: 530
102:: 495
112: 526
130: 495
132: 456, 462
190: 529
196: 522
205: 525
215: 525
219: 525
221: 525
Kaiser Ger/ML: 3, 109, 124, 133, 136, 149, 212, 216, 219, 229, 312, 331, 345
Kaiten Jap/Midget SM: 467, 483, 494, 509, 513, 521, 527-528
Kaiyo Jap/CVL: 499, 529
Kajmakčalan Yu/MTB: 91
Kako Jap/Ca: 163, 168, 179, 199, 214, 235, 241
Kalev Est-USSR/SM (B): 110, 116, 130, 133
Kalgoorlie Aus/Corvette: 256, 470
Kalinin USSR/CA (P): 530
Kalinin USSR/DD (B): 130
Kalinin Bay US/CVE: 428, 461, 463
Kalk US/DD: see Hamilton
Kalk (II) US/DD: 396, 409, 533
Kama USSR/GB (B): 233, 428
Kamikawa Maru Jap/Seaplane Tender: 167, 194-195, 221, 235
Kamikaze Jap/DD: 520, 523
Kamikaze Maru Jap/MTB Depot Ship: 235
Kamloops Can/Corvette: 354
Kamoi Jap/Seaplane Depot ship: 379, 449
Kamome Jap/ML: 402
Kanaris Gr/DD (ex-Hatherleigh): 322, 339-340, 453
Kanawha US/Oiler: 239, 316
Kandahar UK/DD: 34, 46, 79, 86, 88, 95, 97, 102, 106-107, 165-166

Kanimbla Aus/Aux CL: 129, (LSI): 524
Kanin USSR/ML (N): 121
Kanju Jap/Frigate: 530
Kapitan Voronin USSR/Patrol vessel: see SKR 70
Kapunda Aus/MS: 406, 535
Karanja UK/LS: 274
Kari Jap/TB: 526
Karkass Iran/GB: 129
Karl Galster Ger/DD: 3, 7-8, 10-11, 17, 19, 33, 39, 51, 57, 60, 66, 68, 116, 120, 230, 348, 516
Karl Libknecht USSR/DD (N): 12, 511
Karl Marx USSR/DD (B): 14, 110, 123
Karl Meyer Ger/Aircraft Depot ship: 465
Karlsruhe Ger/CL: 22-23
Karmöy Nor/AS Trawler: 485, 511
Karukaya Jap/TB: 410
Kasado Jap/Frigate: 522, 525
Kasaan Bay US/CVE: 444
Kasasagi Jap/TB: 347
Kasatka USSR/Patrol ship (B): 129
Kashi Jap/DD: 475, 477
Kashii Jap/Training CL: 159-160, 166, 173, 187, 200-201, 205, 347, 476
Kashima Jap/CL: 235
Kashino Jap/Naval Transport: 248
Kashmir UK/DD: 12, 23, 32, 94, 97-98, 102
Kaskaskia US/Oiler: 239, 359
Kasos (ex-YMS 74) Gr/MS: 453
Kasuga Jap/Training Cruiser: 526
Kasumi Jap/DD: 156, 179, 190, 194, 204, 221, 233, 459, 462, 475, 508
Katoomba Aus/MS: 178, 406, 538
Katori Jap/CL: 183, 235, 392
Katsonis Gr/SM: 71, 111, 323, 351
Katsuragi Jap/CV: 499, 529
Katsuriki Jap/Survey ship: 449
Kawakaze Jap/DD: 160, 170, 182, 186, 191, 194-196, 221, 235, 244, 249-250, 258, 263, 268, 271, 275, 277, 282-283, 286, 290-291, 341
Kaya Jap/DD: 475
Kazegumo Jap /DD: 220, 223, 235, 248, 254, 264, 268, 271, 275, 290, 337, 356, 361, 415, 418
Kearny US/DD: 92, 136, 142-143, 443
Keats UK/DE: 400, 424, 444, 481, 506
Kedah UK/Aux A/S ship: 187, 534
Kehdingen Ger/Weather Observation ship: 449
Keith UK/DD: 31-32
Keith US/DE: 507
Kelly UK/DD: 28-29, 32, 94, 96, 98, 102
Kelvin UK/DD: 23, 32, 67, 94, 96, 98, 102-103, 180, 183, 189,

200-201, 227, 292, 421, 423

Kempenfelt UK/DD: 386, 421, 444, 470, 479, 486, 502, 509, 516, 534

Kemphan Ger/Gun Carrier: 508

Kempthorne UK/DE: 400, 424, 444

Kendall C. Campbell US/DE: 480, 502, 528

Kendrick US/DD: 339, 444

Kenilworth Castle UK/Corvette: 395

Kenneth Whiting US/Seaplane Tender: 523

Kenogami Can/Corvette: 131, 286

Kent UK/CA: 9, 17, 26, 48, 50-51, 54, 158, 169, 208, 217, 219, 294, 366, 383, 393, 437, 442, 446, 467

Kenya UK/CL: 71, 100, 104-105, 139, 141, 155, 171-172, 198, 212, 227, 242-243, 382, 438, 486, 494

Keokuk US/AKN: 494

Keppel UK/DD: 38, 41, 43, 229, 242, 326, 354, 393, 401, 408, 445, 452, 471, 475

Keren UK/AGC: 338

Kersaint Fr/DD: 41, 280

Kete US/DE: 495

Key US/DE: 594

Khabri Bul/TB: 142

Kharkov USSR/DD: (BS): 109, 112-113, 118, 128, 133, 147, 162, 170-171, 184-185, 197, 204, 206, 209, 212, 215-216, 218, 222, 225, 239, 252, 254, 267, 281, 286, 297, 301, 327, 359

Khartoum UK/DD: 36.

Khedive UK/CVL: 444, 453, 510, 514, 520, 524, 534

Khenkin USSR/Aux MS (BS): see T-41

Kiama Aus/MS: 406, 470, 537

Kiautschou (ex-Hval XX) Ger/Vp boat: see V6106

Kidd US/DD: 359, 365, 370, 373, 388, 409, 428, 437, 499, 509

Kiebitz (ex-Ramb III) Ger/ML: 399, 408, 467

Kiev USSR/DD (BS): 126

Kikutzuki Jap/DD: 163, 168, 179, 214

Kilkis Gr/BB: 94

Killen US/DD: 461, 463, 466, 523-524, 535

Kilmarnock UK/Sloop (ex-PCE 837): 415

Kilty (ex-DD 137) US/APD: 335, 345, 376

Kimberley UK/DD: 19, 23, 25, 46, 61, 95, 97, 102-103, 106-107, 156-157, 165, 177, 370, 421, 444, 449, 454, 514

Kimberley US/DD: 396, 431, 479, 502-503, 533

Kingcup UK/Corvette: 211, 299, 304, 389, 395

King George V UK/BB: 68, 86, 100-101, 149, 193, 198, 208, 212-213, 294, 303, 333, 339-340,

348-350, 471, 486, 502, 516, 526, 529-531, 533

Kingfish US/SM: 259, 284, 306, 358, 379, 456, 479

Kingfisher UK/Sloop: 31, 33

Kingston UK/DD: 12, 36, 95, 97, 102, 107, 156-157, 165, 176, 183, 200-202, 207

Kingston Agathe UK/AS Trawler: 123

Kingston Sapphire UK/AS Trawler: 56

Kinu Jap/CL: 163, 166-167, 178, 194, 196, 383, 418, 462, 464

Kinugasa Jap/CA: 163, 168, 179, 199, 214, 235, 241, 249, 263-264, 275-276

Kinzer US/DE: 502

Kios Gr/TB: 94

Kipling UK/DD: 32, 86, 94, 97-98, 102, 165, 170, 176, 183, 189, 200-201, 216

Kiri Jap/DD: 462

Kirishima Jap/BB: 156, 179, 184, 190, 194, 196-197, 204, 220, 223, 235, 248, 254, 263, 268-269, 275-277

Kirkpatrick US/DE: 395

Kirov USSR/CA (B): 12, 108, 112, 114, 128, 130, 132-133, 138, 207-208, 384

Kirov USSR/Aux MS (B): see T-41

Kirov USSR/Patrol ship (P): 532

Kisaragi Jap/DD: 164

Kishinami Jap/DD: 414, 430, 462, 472

Kiso Jap/CL: 221, 235, 337, 466

Kistna Ind/Sloop: 486, 513, 521

Kitakami Jap/CL: 221, 235, 382, 529

Kitchener Can/Corvette: 326, 421

Kite UK/Sloop: 328, 332, 362, 371, 389, 421, 444

Kitkun Bay US/CVE: 428, 461, 463, 480-481, 535

Kittiwake UK/Corvette: 2, 304, 475

Kiwi NZ/AS Trawler: 290

Kiyokawa Maru Jap/Seaplane Tender: 199

Kiyonami Jap/DD: 335, 341

Kiyoshimo Jap/DD: 462, 475

Kiyosumi Maru Jap/Aux CL: 392

Klas Horn Swe/DD: 136

Klas Uggla Swe/DD: 136

Klyuz USSR/MS (B): 153

Knapp US/DD: 387, 426, 458, 476, 525, 533

Knecht USSR/MS (B): see T-209

Knight US/DD: 342, 350

Knoxsville US/DE: 490, 506

Knudson (ex-DE 591) US/APD: 503

Kobac Yu/ML: 91

Kolac Aus/Corvette: 285

Köln Ger/CL: 1-2, 7, 11-12, 14, 22, 139, 142-143, 504

Kolyvan USSR/Patrol ship (B): 129

Komahashi Jap/SM Depot: 529

Komet Ger/Aux CL: see Schiff 45

Komintern USSR/CL (BS): 110, 118, 124, 132-133, 136, 142, 175, 183, 190, 199, 233, 236

Kondor Ger/TB: 3, 22, 39, 47-48, 52, 57-58, 60-61, 68, 74, 189, 200, 217, 281, 313, 317, 330, 332, 348, 358, 398, 404-405, 413

Kondouriotis Gr/DD: 351

Kongo Jap/BB: 159, 163, 167, 170, 178, 181, 190, 194, 204, 221, 235, 254, 263-264, 268, 275, 361, 414, 430, 462-463, 468

Kongo Maru Jap/Aux GB: 179

Königin Luise Ger/ML: 77, 109, 124, 136

Königin Luise Ger/TB: see F6

Königsberg Ger/CL: 2, 10, 22, 24

Kootenay Can/DD (ex-Decoy): 424, 435-436

Korall USSR/Patrol ship (B): 153

Kormoran Ger/Aux CL: see Schiff 41

Kortenaer Du/DD: 188, 191, 195

Kos (ex-YMS 186) Gr/MS: 453

Kota Pinang Ger/Supply ship: 99, 106, 141

Koutoubia Fr/Aux CL: 10

Krab T-... USSR/Aux MS (B): 130

Krait Aus/Drifter: 348

Krakowiak (ex-Silverton) Pol/DD: 171, 226, 265, 306, 339, 351, 367, 421, 423, 500

Krambol USSR/MS (B): see T-213

Krasnaya Abkhaziya USSR/GB (BS): 124, 297

Krasnaya Armeniya USSR/GB (BS): 118, 124, 126, 128, 138

Krasnaya Gorka USSR/GB (B): 14

Krasnaya Gruziya USSR/GB (BS): 118, 124, 126, 138, 172, 297-298

Krasnoe Znamya USSR/GB (B): 133, 279

Krasny Adzharistan USSR/GB: (BS): 124, 126, 141, 172, 179, 297

Krasny Kavkaz USSR/CA (BS): 109, 128, 134, 138, 141, 143, 146-147, 152, 156, 158, 162, 170-173, 175, 267, 297

Krasny Krym USSR/CL (BS): 128, 136, 138, 141, 147, 150, 152, 158, 162, 170-173, 175, 179, 183, 190, 193, 197, 199, 212, 216, 218, 222, 241-242, 245, 247, 254, 267, 283, 297

Krassin USSR/Icebreaker (N): 244, 334

Krebs Ger/Vp boat: see NN 04

Kreta Ger/Night Fighter Direction ship: 352

Krisyanis Valdemars USSR/ Icebreaker (B): 130

Kriti (ex-Hursley) Gr/DD: 386, 443, 453, 514

Kronstadt USSR/GB (B): 14

Kuban USSR/Patrol vessel: see
SKR-101
Kuibyshev USSR/CA: (BS) 126
Kuibyshev USSR/DD (N): 12,
114, 117, 213, 220, 256, 280,
334, 361, 401, 409
Kujawiak (ex-Oakley) Pol/DD:
171, 227-228
Kuma Jap/CL: 162, 382
Kumano Jap/CA: 159, 163, 167,
170, 173, 178, 181, 187, 194,
200-201, 204-205, 221, 235, 248,
254, 263, 268, 341, 361, 364,
377, 414, 462-463, 466-467
Kume Jap/Frigate: 479
Kunajiri Jap/Frigate: 337
Kuretake Jap/TB: 472
Kuroshio Jap/DD: 160, 169, 177,
181, 184, 186, 191, 221, 235,
248, 254, 263-264, 268, 282-283,
286, 290-291, 324
Kuru Aus/Aux Vessel: 280
Kusagaki Jap/Frigate: 439
Kusentai . . . Jap/SC: see Ch. . . .:
Kusen-Tokumu-Tei . . . Jap/Aux
SC: see Cha . . .:
Kuwa Jap/DD: 462, 471
Kwajalein US/CVE: 458, 474
Kyne US/DE: 524, 533

L . . . : UK/SM
L 23: 5, 11
L 26: 5, 87
L 27: 5, 60, 87

L . . . : USSR/SM
L-2 (B): 133
L-3 (B): 110-111, 116, 139, 146,
243, 246, 253, 259, 261, 273,
455, 485, 489, 497, 501, 508,
512
L-4 (BS): 135, 216, 254, 304,
330, 408, 411
L-5 (BS): 125, 135, 216, 254
L-6 (BS): 368, 380, 402, 404,
408
L-14 (P): 530
L-15 (P/N): 251, 259, 331, 345,
366, 375, 436
L-16 (P): 251, 259
L-17 (P): 530
L-20 (B/N): 139, 279, 289, 295,
298, 310, 319, 345, 366, 375,
393, 425, 459
L-21 (B): 497
L-22 (B/N): 139, 279, 289, 310,
319, 331, 345, 375, 385
L-23 (BS): 126, 216, 279, 380
L-24 (BS): 126, 216
L-25 (BS): 126

LCF . . . : Landing Craft (Flak)
LCF 37 UK: 467
LCF 38 UK: 467

LCG . . . : Landing Craft
(Gunfire Support)
LCG 1 UK: 467
LCG 2 UK: 467
LCG 14 UK: 397
LCG 19 UK: 397
LCG 20 UK: 397
LCG 101 UK: 467
LCG 102 UK: 467

LCI . . . : Landing Craft
(Infantry)
LCI 20 US: 386
LCI 32 US: 386
LCI (G) 70 US: 481
LCI (L) 90 US: 523
LCI 99 : 436
LCI 105 UK: 422
LCI 339 US: 348
LCI (G) 365 US: 483
LCI 588 US: 444
LCI 590 US: 444
LCI 600 US: 483
LCI (M) 974 US: 483

LCP . . . : Landing Craft
(Personnel)
LCP 707 UK: 493
LCP 840: 500

LCS . . . : Landing Craft
(Support)
LCS 15 US: 511
LCS (L) 25 US: 517
LCS (L) 33 US: 509
LCS 51 US: 511
LCS (L) 52 US: 517
LCS (L) 57 US: 509
LCS (L) 116 US: 511
LCS (L) 119 US: 517
LCS (L) 121 US: 517
LCS (L) 122 US: 523

LCT . . .: Landing Craft (Tank)
LCT 35 UK: 386
LCT 150 UK: 229
LCT 381 UK: 305
LCT 789 UK: 467
LCT 839 UK: 467
LCT 875 UK: 422
LCT 876 US: 505
LCT 1133 UK: 467
LCT 7011 UK: 467

LSM . . . : Landing Ship
(Medium)
LSM 59 US: 523
LSM 135 US: 517
LSM (R) 188 US: 503
LSM 189 US: 509
LSM (R) 190 US: 517
LSM (R) 194 US: 517
LSM (R) 195 US: 517
LSM 213 US: 523

LST . . . : Landing Ship Tank
LST 66 US: 376
LST 79: 352
LST 80: 500
LST 202 US: 376
LST 280 UK: 424
LST 282 US: 444
LST 289 UK: 405
LST 305 UK: 386
LST 314 US: 376
LST 333 US: 340
LST 336: 386
LST 340 US: 333
LST 342 US: 341
LST 348 US: 386
LST 359 US: 469
LST 362 UK: 395
LST 376 US: 422
LST 387 US: 340
LST 415 UK: 484

LST 418 UK: 386
LST 422 UK: 386
LST 447 US: 507
LST 460 US: 474
LST 469 US: 311
LST 471 US: 348
LST 472 US: 474
LST 473 US: 348
LST 477 US: 494
LST 479 US: 474
LST 496 UK: 423
LST 507 US: 405
LST 531 US: 405
LST 534 US: 523
LST 538 UK: 538
LST 553 US: 535
LST 577 US: 487
LST 599 US: 505
LST 610 US: 483
LST 695 US: 465
LST 700 US: 483
LST 715 UK: 422
LST 724 US: 503
LST 737 US: 473
LST 738 US: 474
LST 768 US: 535
LST 808 US: 517
LST 809 US: 494
LST 884 US: 503
LST 921 US: 436, 481
LST 925 US: 483
LST 1028 US: 483
L'Adroit (ex-L'Epée) Fr/DD: 31,
280
L'Agile Fr/TB: see TA 2
L'Alcyon Fr/DD: 352, 410, 443,
510, 514
L'Alsacien Fr/TB: see TA 3
L'Audacieux Fr/DD: 8, 53, 56,
284, 322
L'Aventure (ex-Braid) Fr/Frigate:
420, 510
L'Enjoue (ex-PC) Fr/SC: 481-482
L'Escarmouche Fr/Frigate: 420
L'Espoir Fr/SM: 60, 70, 280
L'Impassible Fr/Target Ship: 41
L'Impétueuse Fr/Sloop: 372
L'Incomprise Fr/TB: 31, 41
L'Indiscret (ex-PC 474) Fr/SC:
490
L'Indomptable Fr/DD: 8, 12, 27,
280, 396-397
L'Iphigénie Fr/TB: 284
La Batailleuse Fr/Sloop: 284
La Bayonnaise Fr/TB: 280
La Cherbourgoise Fr/Corvette:
see PA1
La Combattante (ex-Haldon)
Fr/DD: 405-406, 412, 421, 434,
447, 493
La Cordillière Fr/TB: 41
La Curieuse Fr/Sloop: 34
La Découverte (ex-Windrush)
Fr/Frigate: 389, 420, 510
La Dieppoise Fr/Corvette: see
Fleur de Lys
La Flore Fr/TB: 31, 41
La Galissonnière Fr/CL: 64, 280
La Gracieuse Fr/Sloop: 57, 329,
443
La Hulloise Can/Frigate: 490,
496

La Lorientaise Fr/Corvette: see PA 2
La Malouine Fr-UK/Corvette: 53, 229-231, 472-473
La Melpomène Fr/TB: 41
La Moqueuse Fr/Sloop: 351, 443
La Paimpolaise Fr/Corvette: see Nasturtium
La Palme Fr/DD: 280
La Pomone Fr/TB: 285
La Poursuivante Fr/TB: 280
La Psyché Fr/SM: 274
La Sibylle Fr/SM: 29, 274
La Sultane Fr/SM: 413
La Surprise Fr/Sloop: 56, 274
La Surprise Fr/Frigate: 420, 510
La Tour d'Auvergne (ex-Pluton) Fr/ML: 5
La Valette US/DD: 291, 347, 356, 370, 373, 388, 409, 418, 473-474, 480, 487-488
Labuan UK/Frigate: 490
Lachlan Aus/Frigate: 523
Lackawanna US/Oiler: 522
Laconia UK/Aux CL: 66, see merchant ship
Lachplesis USSR/Icebreaker (B): 121
Ladybird UK/GB: 49, 69, 76, 83, 92-93
Lady Elsa UK/AS Trawler: 59
Lady Madelaine UK/AS Trawler: 219, 286
Lady Shirley UK/AS Trawler: 138-139, 160
Laertes UK/AS Trawler: 236
Laffey US/DD: 226, 239, 254, 263, 275-276
Laffey (II) US/DD: 420, 423, 431, 473-474, 479, 502, 510
Lafolé It/SM: 34, 42, 60
Laforey UK/DD: 140, 150, 197, 199, 202, 212, 242, 313, 322, 328, 338, 340, 350-351, 386, 397
Lagan UK/Frigate: 325, 354
Lagarto US/SM: 491
Lago Tana It/Escort vessel: 61
Lago Zuai It/Escort vessel: 61
Laine USSR/GB (B): 155, 157
Lake US/DE: 533
Lamerton UK/DD: 145, 171, 299, 322, 339
Lamons US/DE: 523, 533
Lamotte-Picquet Fr/CL: 76, 476
Lampo It/DD: 42, 93, 255, 286, 293, 300, 312, 321
Lamson US/DD: 161, 189, 199, 282, 290, 310, 334, 348, 355 375-376, 380, 473
Lance UK/DD: 100, 106, 140, 144, 149, 155, 165-166, 176, 180, 183, 189, 207
Lanciere It/DD: 35, 42-43, 67, 103, 118, 139, 202
Landguard (ex-Shoshone) UK/Sloop: 346
Lang US/DD: 15, 92, 203, 210, 215, 226, 239, 249, 335, 341, 373, 392, 427, 480, 504
Langley US/Aircraft Depot ship: 196
Langley US/CV: 338, 400, 406, 427, 448, 458, 461-462, 465-466,

474, 476-477, 491, 499-500, 509, 516, 522
Laning US/DE: 408, 410
Lansdale US/DD: 83, 115, 119, 132, 136, 404, 408
Lansdowne US/DD: 232, 254, 269, 271, 303, 364, 391, 409, 427, 533
Lansquenet Fr/DD: 64, 280
Lanzerotte Malocello It/DD: see Malocello
Laomédon UK/Aux CL: 46
Lapon US/SM: 358, 396, 410, 432, 449, 457
Lapwing UK/Sloop: 421, 464, 471, 475, 498,
Lapwing US/Seaplane Tender: 5, 93
Lardner US/DD: 254, 264, 269, 271-272, 275, 282, 364, 391, 409, 427, 533
Largs UK/AGC: 274, 328, 338, 420, 422, 513
Lark US/Sloop: 421, 464, 471, 475, 492
Larwood UK/AS Trawler: 27, see Franke
Latona UK/ML: 126, 134, 143
Latrobe Aus/MS: 538
Laub US/DD: see Burwell
Laub (II) US/DD: 339-340
Lauderdale UK/DD: 322, 339, 443
Lauenburg (WBS-2) Ger/Weather Observation ship: 99, 113
Launceston UK/MS: 383
Laurana It/ML: 34, 341
Laurentic UK/Aux CL: 61
Lavender UK/Corvette: 309, 358, 421
Lawford (ex-US DE) UK/Frigate: 421
Lawrence Ind/Sloop: 93
Lawrence, C. Taylor US/DE: 502, 528
Laws US/DD: 428, 458, 476, 502, 527
Lawson UK/DE: 464
Lazaga Sp/DD: 327
Le Centaure Fr/SM: 36
Le Conquérant Fr/SM: 274
Le Corse Fr/TB: see TA 6
Le Fantasque Fr/DD: 8, 53, 56, 351-352, 376-377, 379, 396, 399, 410, 428, 444, 539
Le Farouche Fr/TB: see TA 5
Le Fier Fr/TB: see TA 1
Le Fortuné Fr/DD: 43, 352, 443, 459, 483, 510, 514
Le Foudroyant (II) (ex-Fleuret) Fr/DD: 280, see FR 36
Le Gladiateur Fr/NL: 390
Le Glorieux Fr/SM: 42, 44, 147, 212
Le Hardi Fr/DD: 38, 56, 64, 280, 381
Le Héros Fr/SM: 42, 44, 147, 212
Le Malin Fr/DD: 8, 12, 27, 53, 56, 329, 377, 379, 394, 410, 444, 449
Le Mars Fr/DD: 280
Le Ray Wilson US/DE: 461, 480, 483, 533

Le Résolu (ex-PC 475) Fr/SC: 490
Le Siroco (II) (ex-Le Corsaire) Fr/DD: 280
Le Terrible Fr/DD: 8, 41, 349, 351-352, 394, 396, 399, 428, 444
Le Tonnant Fr/SM: 36, 274
Le Triomphant Fr/DD: 8, 12, 27, 169, 298, 539
Lea US/DD: 83, 115, 119, 136, 193, 250, 320
Leamington (ex-Twiggs) UK/DD: 131, 206, 229, 309
Leander NZ/CL: 17, 28, 61, 80-81, 93, 106-107, 169, 185, 189, 199, 255, 335
Leary US/DD: 4, 136, 184, 217, 268, 375, 463
Lebed USSR/Survey Ship (P): 532
Leberecht Maass Ger/DD: 1-3, 19-20
Leda UK/MS: 31, 257
Ledbury UK/DD: 229, 242-243, 339, 350, 385
Leeds UK/DD: 421
Leedstown US/AP: 274
Legion UK/DD: 84, 106, 140, 150, 158, 165, 180, 183, 189, 202
Legionario It/DD: 228, 243, 280, 292, 300, 311, 349, 352
Legnano It/ML: 356
Leipzig Ger/CL: 1-2, 10-14, 135, 139, 497
Leith UK/Sloop: 59
Leland E. Thomas US/DE: 524
Lemaire US/CG Cutter: 246
Lembit Est-USSR/SM (B): 110, 139, 146, 243, 246, 450, 455, 497
Lenin USSR/DD (B): 111
Lenin USSR/Icebreaker (N): 244
Leningrad USSR/DD (B): 110, 128, 130, 132, 150, 384
Leningradsovet USSR/School ship (B): 130
Leonardo da Vinci It/SM: see Da Vinci
Leonard Wood US/AP: 150
Leone It/DD: 52, 55, 61, 68, 78, 90
Leone Pancaldo It/DD: see Pancaldo
Leopard Fr/DD: 41, 158, 234
Léopard Ger/TB: 3, 10-12, 22, 28
Leopold US/DE: 395
Lero It/Aux: 34
Lethbridge Can/Corvette: 211
Leutze US/DD: 463, 479, 503, 507
Levis Can/Covette: 135
Levy US/DE: 532, 536
Lewis Hancock US/DD: 387, 426, 458, 476, 499
Lexington US/CV: 161, 168, 182, 185, 199, 214
Lexington (II) US/CV: 353, 359, 370, 373, 399-401, 406, 426, 448, 458, 461-462, 465-466, 474, 476, 491, 523, 525, 533
Libeccio It/DD: 42, 47, 63, 149
Libra It/TB: 34, 136, 293, 300, 313, 349, 407

Libra US/AKA: 275
Liddle (ex-DE 206) US/APD: 473
Liddesdale UK/DD: 339, 351, 407, 443, 453
Lightning UK/DD: 120, 140, 197, 199, 212, 242, 293, 300
Limbourne UK/DD: 362
Lince It/TB: 34, 83, 245, 255, 273, 336
Lincoln UK/DD: 421
Lindsay Can/Corvette: 421
Lindsey US/DM: 502, 509
Linsen Ger/Explosive boats: 440, 457, 483, 507
Linz Ger/ML: 397, 453, 484
Lion Fr/DD: 37, 280
Lira It/TB: 34, 293, 349
Liscombe Bay US/CVE: 370
Lismore Aus/MS: 339, 344, 470
Litchfield US/DD: 161
Lithgow Aus/MS: 178, 285, 406, 537
Little (ex-DD 79) US/APD: 246, 249, 253
Little (II) US/DD: 517
Littorio It/BB: 50, 57, 63, 128, 140, 165-166, 175-176, 202, 228, 283
Liuzzi It/SM: 39-40
Lively UK/DD: 140, 144, 149, 155, 157, 165-166, 176, 180, 183, 186, 189-190, 200-202, 216
Livermoore US/DD: 92, 136, 142, 203, 443
Liverpool UK/CL: 26, 36, 40, 43, 45, 50-51, 57-58, 208, 217, 219, 227-228
Lizardfish US/SM: 526
Ljubljana Yu/DD: 91
Lobélia Fr/Corvette: 211, 293, 297, 326, 354-355
Loch Achanalt UK/Frigate: 454
Loch Alvie UK/Frigate: 471, 520
Loch Craggie UK/Frigate: 481
Loch Dunvegan UK/Frigate: 445, 490
Loch Ecke UK/Frigate: 490
Loch Fada UK/Frigate: 424, 490
Loch Glendhu UK/Frigate: 506
Loch Insh UK/Frigate: 469, 511, 514
Loch Killin UK/Frigate: 424, 506
Loch More UK/Frigate: 506
Loch Ruthven UK/Frigate: 496
Loch Scavaig UK/Frigate: 490
Loch Shin UK/Frigate: 490, 511, 514
Lochy UK/Frigate: 424
Locust UK/GB: 31, 247
Loeser US/DE: 483
Lola Ger/SC: see Schiff 19, see UJ 117
London UK/CA: 101, 105-106, 139-140, 212, 230, 256, 279, 399, 407, 412, 460, 510, 534
Long US/DMS: 181, 395, 481
Long Beach US/Frigate: see EK-2
Long Island US/CVE: 132, 244

Longshaw US/DD: 428, 458, 476, 502, 508
Lookout UK/DD: 198, 212, 242, 328, 334, 338, 350-351, 443, 500, 513
Loosestrife UK/Corvette: 211, 315, 320-321, 326, 360
Lord Austin UK/AS Trawler: 230, 302
Lord Hailsham UK/AS: Trawler: 305
Lord Middleton UK/AS Trawler: 230, 302
Lord Stonehaven UK/AS Trawler: 260
Loring UK/DE: 464
Lorraine Fr/BB: 39, 43, 443, 449, 510
Lossie UK (ex-US)/Frigate: 389, 417
Lot Fr/Oiler: 68, 329
Lothringen Ger/Oiler: 95, 99, 105
Lotus (ex-Phlox) UK/Corvette: 229, 231, 339, 408, 511
Lough US/DE: 487
Louhi Fin/ML: 15, 397, 450
Louis UK/DE: 443, 464
Louisburg Can/Corvette: 184, 299, 421, 423
Louisville US/CA: 183, 190, 199, 221, 226, 290-291, 323, 336, 388, 392, 406, 427, 452, 461, 463, 479, 481, 523, 539
Lowe US/DE: 408, 496
Löwe (ex-Gyller) Ger/TB: 489
Lowestoft UK/Sloop: 51, 53, 358
Lowry US/DD: 474, 479, 502, 517, 527-528, 533
Loy (ex-DE 160) US/APD: 517
Loyal UK/DD: 293, 322, 328, 338, 347, 350-351, 386, 449
Loyalty (ex-Rattler) UK/MS: 436
Lubiana (ex-Lubljana) It/DD: 300, 312-313
Luca Tarigo It/DD: see Tarigo
Luce US/DD: 396, 431, 480, 502, 517
Luchs Ger/TB: 3, 19, 22, 40, 45
Luciano Manara It/SM: see Manara
Ludlow US/DD: 136, 339, 350, 369, 385, 415, 444, 449
Luigi Cadorna It/CL: see Cadorna
Luigi di Savoia Duca degli Abruzzi It/CL: see Duca degli Abruzzi
Luigi Settembrini It/SM: see Settembrini
Luigi Torelli It/SM: see Torelli
Lukomski USSR/ML (BS): 124, 143
Lulworth (ex-Chelan) UK/Sloop: 383
Lunenburg Can/Corvette: 378, 421
Lunga Point US/CVE: 479, 493-494, 502, 513, 527
Lupo It/TB: 83, 102, 155, 251
Lützow Ger/CA: see Petropavlovsk, see Tallin

Lützow (ex-Deutschland) Ger/Pocket BB: 11-12, 22-23, 44, 104, 107, 218-219, 230, 285, 288, 303, 343, 355, 455, 460, 470, 485, 497, 512
Lydd UK/MS: 31
Lyman US/DE: 533
Lyman K. Swenson US/DD: 476, 499 525, 533
Lynx Fr/DD: 41, 280

M . . .: Ger/MS
M 1: 1, 22
M 2: 22
M 3: 1, 5, 397, 431
M 4: 1, 5-6, 22
M 5: 1
M 6: 24
M 7: 1, 17
M 8: 1, 327
M 9: 22, 336
M 10: 336
M 12: 336
M 13: 22
M 14: 431, 512
M 15: 431
M 16: 358
M 18: 233, 358, 390, 431, 453
M 19: 431, 453
M 20: 22, 431
M 22: 148, 431
M 23: 116
M 28: see Pelikan
M 29: 390, 428, 431
M 30: 358, 431
M 31: 115, 426, 445-446, 451, 459
M 35: 426, 445-446
M 36: 515
M 37: 233, 397, 497
M 50: see Brommy
M 61: 22, 29
M 81: see Nautilus
M 82: see Jagd
M 84: 22, 336, 413
M 85: 4
M 89: 22, 29
M 102: 22
M 103: 428
M 104: see M 504
M 107: see von der Gröben
M 109: see Sundevall
M 110: 22
M 111: 1, 6, 22
M 115: see Arkona
M 129: see Otto Braun
M 130: see Fuchs
M 131: 425
M 132: 1, 6
M 132 (II): 446
M 133: 428, 441
M 134: 22, see Jungingen
M 135: 336
M 136 (ex-Havel): 22, 29
M 138: see Nettelbeck
M 143: 431
M 146: see von der Lippe
M 154: 208, 426, 445-446
M 156: 388
M 157: 22, see M 557
M 201: 112
M 202: 426, 445-446
M 203: 497

M 204: 498
M 206: 388, 441
M 246: 446
M 251: 208, 445-446, 451
M 252: 426, 445-446
M 262: 441
M 263: 441
M 264: 425
M 266: 498
M 271: 441
M 273: 385, 483
M 274: 450
M 276: 450
M 278: see TS 4
M 292: 441
M 293: 515
M 301: 515
M 303: 294, 459
M 304: 441
M 307: 425
M 322: 294, 310
M 325: 441
M 328: 470
M 329: 504
M 341: 489
M 343: 319, 427, 441
M 346: 331
M 347: 425
M 348: 425
M 361: 319
M 363: 441
M 366: 441
M 367: 441
M 370: 441
M 372: see TS 3
M 375: see TS 8
M 376: see TS 10
M 383: 305
M 384: 441
M 385: 441
M 387: see TS 2
M 391: 497
M 402: 423, 427
M 412: 427, 498
M 416: 468
M 421: 489
M 422: 427, 441
M 423: 470
M 427: 468
M 428: 441
M 432: 427, 440
M 433: 465
M 438: 441
M 442: 427
M 433: 431
M 445: 316, 475
M 452: 427
M 453: 431, 516
M 459: 358
M 460: 358, 431
M 462: 446
M 463: 441
M 468: 330
M 486: 441
M 489: 475
M 504 (ex-M 104): 509
M 607: 519
M 801: 482
M 802: 505
M 804: 498
M 805: 498

M . . .: Ger/Aux MS (Various types of fishing vessels)
M 1101: 24
M 1101 (II): 141
M 1201: 17, 22
M 1202: 22
M 1203: 22
M 1204: 17, 22
M 1205: 22
M 1206: 22
M 1207: 17, 22
M 1208: 22, 188,
M 1302: 24
M 1503: 191
M 1504: 198
M 1505: 203
M 1506: 203
M 1508: 203
M 1701: 23
M 1702: 23
M 1703: 24
M 1706: 110
M 3109: 431
M 3112: 431
M 3114: 431
M 3128: 431
M 3131: 121
M 3134: 110, 115
M 3137: 431, 482, 497
M 3138: 482
M 3411: 391
M 3413: 433
M 3430: 504
M 3619: 455
M 3630: 398
M 3801: 427
M 3802: 427
M 3815: 427
M 3822: 427
M 3824: 456
M 3827: 456
M 3832: 456
M 3838: 456
M 3855: 427
M 3857: 447
M 3873: 427
M 3874: 427
M 4041: 316
M 4242: 292
M 4430: 440
M 4601: 434
M 4605: 434
M 4611: 429
M 4615: 427
M 4618: 395
M 4620: 308, 429
M 4622: 433
M 4627: 427

M . . . . USSR/SM
M-31 (BS): 216, 330
M-32 (BS): 216, 260
M-33 (BS): 112, 125, 216, 232, 240
M-34 (BS): 112, 135, 158
M-35 (BS): 145, 254, 260, 304, 330, 361, 380, 408, 411
M-36 (BS): 240
M-51 (BS): 172
M-52 (BS): 216
M-54 (BS): 158

M-58 (BS): 158
M-59 (BS): 158
M-60 (BS): 216, 232
M-62 (BS): 239-240, 402, 408, 411, 447
M-71 (B): 111
M-77 (B): 110, 115, 134
M-78 (B): 110-111
M-79 (B): 110-111, 115
M-80 (B): 111
M-81 (B). 110-111, 115
M-83 (B): 110-111
M-89 (B): 111
M-90 (B): 111, 116
M-94 (B): 111, 116
M-95 (B): 111, 130, 139, 228-229
M-96 (B): 111, 243, 246, 273
M-97 (B): 111, 129, 134, 222, 243
M-98 (B): 111, 116, 130, 134, 139
M-99 (B): 111, 116, 134
M-101 (B): 111
M-102 (B): 111, 130, 134, 257, 259
M-103 (B): 152
M-104 (N): 310, 319, 345, 393
M-105 (N): 319, 331, 375, 385, 393, 404
M-106 (N): 319, 331
M-107 (N): 345
M-111 (BS): 240, 254, 260, 304, 330, 368, 408, 437, 447
M-112 (BS): 216, 304, 330, 361, 380, 408
M-113 (BS: 353, 437, 447
M-117 (BS): 216, 304, 330, 368, 402, 437
M-118 (BS): 216, 240, 260
M-119 (N): 302, 366, 385, 393-394
M-122 (N): 302, 319
M-171 (ex-M-87): (N) 133, 139, 152, 154, 180, 191, 198, 204, 209, 295, 302, 310, 319 459
M-172 (ex-M-88) (N): 115, 124, 133, 144, 148, 152, 169, 209, 294-295, 302, 319, 345
M-173 (ex-M-91) (N): 109, 124, 133, 198, 209, 240
M-174 (ex-M-92) (N): 115, 133, 139, 144, 154, 169, 310, 345
M-175 (ex-M-93) (N): 109, 124, 139, 178
M-176 (ex-M-100) (N): 109, 133, 139, 154, 209, 230
M-200 (N): 366, 425-426, 436
M-201 (N): 375, 385, 393, 414, 425-426, 445

MAS . . .: It/MTB
MAS 204: 90
MAS 206: 90
MAS 210: 90
MAS 213: 90
MAS 216: 90
MAS 451: 121

T

MAS 452: 121
MAS 501: 317
MAS 503: 317
MAS 532: 120
MAS 533: 120
MAS 536: 51
MAS 537: 51
MAS 552: 243, 321
MAS 553: 243
MAS 554: 243
MAS 556: 243
MAS 557: 243
MAS 564: 243
MAS 568: 239
MAS 571: 216
MAS 573: 225, 239

MFL . . .: Ger/Minesweeper
MFL 675: 456

MGB . . .: UK/MGB
MGB 6: 246
MGB 10: 246
MGB 17: 307, 423
MGB 20: 307
MGB 21: 307
MGB 38: 318
MGB 39: 318
MGB 40: 399
MGB 41: 366
MGB 42: 366
MGB 74: 318
MGB 75: 318
MGB 77: 305
MGB 79: 305
MGB 81: 305
MGB 82: 255
MGB 84: 255
MGB 87: 201
MGB 88: 201, 318
MGB 91: 201, 255, 318
MGB 108: 328, 356
MGB 110: 328
MGB 111: 305, 318
MGB 112: 318
MGB 116: 328
MGB 117: 356
MGB 118: 328, 356
MGB 214: 405
MGB 314: 206
MGB 315: 363
MGB 321: 313, 412, 440
MGB 322: 440
MGB 327: 363
MGB 330: 246, 247
MGB 331: 246
MGB 333: 313
MGB 603: 363
MGB 605: 322
MGB 606: 322
MGB 607: 363
MGB 608: 318
MGB 609: 246, 363
MGB 610: 322, 363
MGB 611: 399
MGB 612: 322
MGB 613: 399
MGB 614: 399
MGB 615: 318, 399
MGB 617: 396, 405
MGB 624: 396
MGB 629: 396
MGB 634: 397
MGB 658: 414

MGB 659: 397
MGB 660: 397
MGB 662: 397
MGB 668: 396

ML . . .: UK/ML
ML 105: 355
ML 109: 86
ML 141: 366
ML 230: 366
ML 250: 363
ML 293: 366
ML 306: see RA9
ML 339: 261
ML 352: 257
ML 353: 257
ML 464: 366
ML 466: 500
ML 517: 363
ML 563: 444
ML 805: 537
ML 903: 422

MMS . . .: UK/MMS
MMS 1: 352
MMS 51 (Aus): 196
MMS 116: 352
MMS 203: see T-109
MMS 212: see T-110
MMS 227: 413

MO . . .: USSR/SC
MO-8 (ex-US) (P) 531
MO-16 (ex-US) (P): 531
MO-25 (ex-US) (P): 532
MO-27 (ex-US) (P): 531
MO-29 (ex-US) (P): 531
MO-31 (ex-US) (P): 532
MO-32 (ex-US) (P): 532
MO-33 (ex-US) (P): 531
MO-34 (ex-US) (P): 531
MO-35 (ex-US) (P): 532
MO-63 (ex-US) (P): 532
MO-103 (B): 432
MO-105 (B): 432
MO-106 (B): 158
MO-107 (B): 432
MO-112 (B): 130
MO-121 (N): 114
MO-123 (N): 114
MO-124 (B): 450
MO-131 (N): 116
MO-131 (B): 130
MO-132 (N): 116
MO-133 (B): 130
MO-133 (N): 116
MO-142 (B): 130
MO-202 (B): 130
MO-207 (B): 130
MO-210 (B): 158
MO-211 (B). 273
MO-212 (B): 130, 273
MO-213 (B): 130
MO-218 (B): 110
MO-225 (B): 273
MO-238 (B): 110
MO-251 (N): 465
MO-301 (B): 151
MO-304 (B): 432
MO-307 (B): 158
MO-308 (B): 273
MO-405 (B): 157
MO-406 (B): 157

MO-407 (B): 158
MO-434 (ex-RPC 1) (N): 492
MO-510 (B): 130

Ms . . .: It/MTB
Ms 16: 243
Ms 22: 243
Ms 23: 243
Ms 25: 243, 321
Ms 26: 243
Ms 31: 243
Ms 41: 399
Ms 72: 513
Ms 74: 430
Ms 75: 399

MTB . . .: Allied/MTB
MTB 7: 170
MTB 8: 170
MTB 9: 170
MTB 10: 170
MTB 11: 170
MTB 12: 170
MTB 24: 308
MTB 26: 170
MTB 27: 170
MTB 35: 308
MTB 38: 308
MTB 49: 265
MTB 55: 265
MTB 56: 141, 165
MTB 61: 300
MTB 67: 102
MTB 74: 206
MTB 77: 300
MTB 82: 300
MTB 84: 265
MTB 88: 308
MTB 90: 413
MTB 91 (Fr): 412
MTB 92 (Fr): 412
MTB 93: 308
MTB 94 (Fr): 308
MTB 95: 265
MTB 96 (Fr): 308, 412
MTB 202 (Du): 336, 356, 398
MTB 203: 265
MTB 204 (Du): 356, 399
MTB 205: 447
MTB 206: 398
MTB 208: 440, 447
MTB 209: 430, 447
MTB 210: 440, 447
MTB 212: 398, 440, 447
MTB 213: 102
MTB 214: 102
MTB 216: 102
MTB 217: 102
MTB 219: 328
MTB 220: 217
MTB 221: 328
MTB 225: 396
MTB 226: 376
MTB 227 (Fr): 412
MTB 228: 376
MTB 229: 265, 435
MTB 230: 255
MTB 231 (Du): 356
MTB 232: 327
MTB 233: 318
MTB 234: 255, 318, 327, 396
MTB 235: 336, 405
MTB 236: 265

MTB 237 (Fr): 412
MTB 239 (Fr): 412
MTB 240: 336, 435
MTB 241: 318, 327, 396, 399
MTB 244: 327, 396, 399
MTB 245: 399
MTB 246: 405, 412
MTB 252: 447
MTB 253: 447
MTB 254: 437
MTB 256: 447
MTB 257: 447
MTB 259: 227
MTB 260: 292
MTB 266: 313
MTB 305: 340
MTB 308: 257
MTB 310: 257
MTB 311: 340
MTB 312: 257
MTB 314: 257
MTB 315: 313
MTB 321: 440
MTB 322: 440
MTB 339: 234
MTB 342: 234
MTB 347: 456
MTB 349: 456
MTB 350: 399, 456
MTB 351: 456
MTB 353: 440
MTB 354: 435
MTB 359: 398, 405, 440
MTB 360: 456
MTB 361: 434
MTB 363: 440
MTB 412: 435
MTB 415: 395
MTB 417: 398
MTB 418: 435
MTB 430: 435
MTB 431: 395
MTB 432: 435, 440
MTB 433: 440
MTB 434: 433
MTB 436: 435
MTB 439: 363, 391
MTB 441: 391
MTB 442: 363
MTB 443: 391
MTB 444: 391
MTB 447: 447
MTB 448: 422-423
MTB 450: 447
MTB 452: 447
MTB 453: 447
MTB 455: 391, 436
MTB 457: 436
MTB 458: 436
MTB 459: 434
MTB 461: 423, 433
MTB 462: 433-434
MTB 463: 423, 433
MTB 464: 423, 434
MTB 465: 433
MTB 466: 434
MTB 467: 436
MTB 468: 436
MTB 469: 436
MTB 470: 436
MTB 471: 441
MTB 472: 456
MTB 473: 440, 456

MTB 474: 440
MTB 475: 440, 456
MTB 476: 440-441, 456
MTB 477: 441
MTB 478: 422
MTB 479: 440
MTB 480: 435, 456
MTB 481: 447
MTB 482: 447
MTB 484: 435
MTB 494: 507
MTB 495: 487
MTB 607: 328
MTB 608: 440
MTB 609: 394
MTB 610: 394
MTB 617: 308, 433
MTB 618 (Nor): 295, 404, 425
MTB 619 (Nor): 295, 308
MTB 620: 295, 330
MTB 621: 433
MTB 622: 308
MTB 623 (Nor): 295, 404, 425, 468
MTB 624: 308, 322, 422, 433
MTB 625: 295
MTB 626: 295, 330
MTB 627 (Nor): 295, 384, 391, 412, 468, 475
MTB 628: 328
MTB 629: 328, 433
MTB 630: 295, 322
MTB 631 (Nor): 308
MTB 632: 322, 328, 433
MTB 633: 313, 414
MTB 637: 313
MTB 639: 313
MTB 640: 414
MTB 650: 433
MTB 653 (Nor): 384, 391, 404, 412, 446, 473
MTB 655: 414
MTB 666: 425, 433
MTB 671: 405
MTB 676: 439
MTB 677: 439
MTB 681: 425
MTB 682: 422
MTB 683: 425, 433
MTB 684: 425
MTB 685: 433
MTB 687: 425, 433
MTB 688 (Nor): 412, 425, 446, 468
MTB 692: 447
MTB 693: 447
MTB 694: 447
MTB 695: 447
MTB 709 (Nor): 433, 467
MTB 711: 446
MTB 712 (Nor): 425, 446, 467, 475
MTB 715 (Nor): 404, 412, 425, 468
MTB 716: 439
MTB 717: 439, 468, 473, 475
MTB 720: 439
MTB 722 (Nor): 433, 446, 475
MTB 723: 425
MTB 724: 453
MTB 726: 428
MTB 727: 428-429
MTB 728: 453:

MTB 729: 433
MTB 734: 433
MTB 735: 433
MTB 743: 429, 433
MTB 745: 428-429
MTB 748: 428-429, 433
MTB 5001: 507

Mz . . .: It/Landing boat
Mz 780: 484
Mz 785: 484
Mz 800: 484

Macallé It/SM: 36
Macalpine UK/Aux CVE: 354
MacDonough US/DD: 161, 168, 182, 185, 199, 226, 238, 249, 255, 323, 370, 388, 399, 476
Machias US/Frigate: see EK-9
Mackay UK/DD: 31-32, 307, 363, 380, 421, 519
MacKendrick UK/Aux CVE: 412
Mackenzie US/DD: 299, 339, 444, 509
MacLeish US/DD: 68, 83,132, 329, 337
Macomb US/DD: 415, 444, 502, 517
Maddox US/DD: see Georgetown, see Zhestki.
Maddox (II) US/DD: 339-340
Maddox (III) US/DD: 474, 476-477, 499, 522, 525, 533
Madison US/DD: 83, 119, 132, 136, 203, 210, 303, 415, 449
Maestrale It/DD: 42, 47, 98, 116, 127, 149, 166, 175, 193, 243, 245, 282, 293, 349
Maggiore Baracca It/SM: see Baracca
Magic UK/MS: 435
Magog Can/Frigate: 454
Magpie UK/Sloop: 362, 371, 389, 400-401, 421
Mahan US/DD: 161, 183, 269-270, 310, 348, 355, 375-376, 380, 395, 373
Mahratta UK/DD: 393
Maiali It/Midget SM: 49, 57, 62, 121
Maidstone UK/SM Depot: 534
Maikaze Jap/DD: 159, 163, 166, 178, 181, 190, 220, 223, 235, 244, 248, 254, 264, 268, 290-291, 361, 392
Maillé-Brézé Fr/DD: 20, 23-24, 26
Makassar Strait US/CVE: 516
Maki Jap/DD: 462, 472
Makigumo Jap/DD: 220, 223, 235, 248, 254, 264, 268, 270-271, 275, 290-291
Makin Island US/CVE: 479, 493, 502, 513, 527
Makinami Jap/DD: 263, 268, 271, 275, 277, 282-283, 286, 290-291, 361, 372
Makrelen Dan/TB: 346
Maksim Gorki USSR/CA (B): 110, 132-133, 135, 138, 207, 384

Malachite It/SM: 39, 70, 79, 84, 87, 93, 101, 115, 138, 223, 227, 236, 283, 289, 300
Malaspina It/SM: 46, 59, 61, 75, 91, 99, 113, 118, 132, 137
Malaya UK/BB: 9, 36, 43, 45, 48, 50-51, 58, 62-63, 66, 69-70, 73, 77-79, 85-86, 94, 150, 197, 199, 202-203, 227, 338, 439
Malcolm UK/DD: 31-33, 109, 242, 256, 274
Malinska Yu/MS: 91
Mallard UK/Sloop: 391
Mallow UK/Corvette: 145, 306
Malocello It/DD: 58, 63, 74, 97, 118, 143, 165, 175, 183, 193, 209-210, 227, 242, 245, 292, 300
Maloja UK/Aux CL: 20
Maloy US/Frigate: 439
Malygin USSR/Icebreaker (N): 294
Mameli It/SM: 45, 57, 63, 94
Mameluk Fr/DD: 38, 64, 280
Manadzuru Jap/TB: 162, 169, 492
Manara It/SM: 39, 42, 46, 78, 94, 106, 120, 122
Manatee US/Oiler: 476
Manchester UK/CL: 19, 23-25, 27, 32, 67, 98, 100, 120, 230, 242-243
Manila Bay US/CVE: 388, 399, 409, 461, 474, 480-481, 535
Manin It/DD: 49, 52, 55, 68, 90
Manistee UK/Ocean Boarding Vessel: 77
Manju Jap/Frigate: 479
Manley US/APD: 4, 253, 271
Manners UK/DE: 481
Mannert L. Abele US/DD: 502, 509
Mannheim (ex-KT 4) Ger/KT ship: 451, see UJ 2172
Manoora Aus/Aux CL: 86, 197, 524
Manor UK/ Trawler: 234
Mansfield (ex-Evans) Nor/DD: 92, 302, 309
Mansfield US/DD: 476, 499, 525, 533
Manxman UK/ML: 120, 122, 128, 281, 283
Maori UK/DD: 27-28, 60, 101, 120, 122, 158, 165, 180, 183, 189
Marangone It/Corvette: see UJ 2223
Marasesti Ru/DD: 210, 232, 330, 366, 407, 446
Marat USSR/BB (B): 15, 132-133, 135, 138, 384. See Petropavlovsk
Marathon US/APA: 527
Marblehead US/CL: 182, 185, 379, 444
Marcantonio Bragadino It/SM: see Bragadino
Marcantonio Colonna It/SM: see Colonna
Marcello It/SM: 34, 39, 47, 62, 75, 77, 81
Marcilio Dias Bra/DD: 416
Marconi It/SM: 40, 42-43, 50, 59, 64-65, 76, 103, 124, 126, 145

Marcus Island US/CVE: 461, 474, 480, 502
Maresti Ru/DD: 210, 330, 407
Marigold UK/Corvette: 96, 137, 149, 167-168, 226
Marion US/CG Cutter: 247
Mariz e Barros Bra/DD: 416-417
Marne UK/DD: 208, 219, 227-228, 237, 245, 256, 277, 408, 452
Marne Fr/Sloop: 76
Marocain Fr/DE: 443
Marsdale UK/Ocean Boarding Vessel: 105-106
Marseillaise Fr/CL: 64, 280, 396
Marsh US/DE: 443
Marshall US/DD: 426, 458, 476, 499
Marsouin Fr/SM: 274
Marsouinul Ru/SM: 411
Marti USSR/ML (B): 110, 113, 131, 139, 147, 207
Martin UK/DD: 219-220, 237, 245, 256, 273
Martynov USSR/Monitor (BS): 112, 117
Marvel US/MS: see T-272
Maryborough Aus/MS: 164, 197, 339, 344, 470
Maryland US/BB: 161, 222, 226, 335, 370, 388, 427, 452, 461, 463, 471, 502, 508
Mashona UK/DD: 23-25, 27, 32, 100-101
Mason US/DD see Broadwater
Massachusetts US/BB 273-274, 335, 370, 373, 387, 392, 406, 448, 458, 461, 464, 474, 476, 491, 499-501, 509, 522, 525, 529-530
Massey US/DD: 504, 517
Matabele UK/DD: 23-25, 27, 30, 32, 180
Matane Can/Frigate: 424, 434, 521
Matchless UK/DD: 212, 217, 227-228, 242, 245, 287, 326, 374-475, 408
Matrozos (ex-Perla) Gr/SM: 390
Matsu Jap/DD: 438
Matsukaze Jap/DD: 162, 173, 194, 205, 335, 356
Matsuwa Jap/Frigate: 410, 439
Matteucci It/GB: 103
Mauritius UK/CL: 298, 333, 338, 340, 347, 350-351, 377, 386, 421, 434, 441, 465, 490
Maury US/DD: 161, 168, 183, 190, 221, 224, 226, 238, 249, 269 282, 335, 341, 370, 388, 458, 479
Max Schultz Ger/DD: 7, 18-19
Maya Jap/CA: 162, 170-173, 178, 181, 190, 194, 196, 220, 235, 248, 254, 263-264, 268, 275-276, 312, 361, 364, 414, 430, 462
Mayflower Can/Corvette: 211, 217
Mayo US/DD: 83, 115, 119, 136, 350, 385-386
Mayrant US/DD: 92, 108, 132, 151, 308, 339, 342
Mazama US/AE: 483
Mazara It/ML: 323
Mazur Pol/TB: 2

McCall US/DD: 161, 168, 183, 226, 335, 388, 458, 480
McCalla US/DD: see Stanley
McCalla (II) US/DD: 263, 269, 275-276, 334, 355, 427, 458, 495, 498, 512, 523
McCawley US/APA: 263, 274, 335
McClelland US/DE: 553
McCook US/DD: see St Croix
McCook (II) US/DD: 420, 443
McCord US/DD: 392, 461, 476, 499, 509
McCormick US/DD: 83, 119, 136
McCowan US/DD: 427, 463, 483, 499, 525
McCoy Reynolds US/DE: 452, 467
McDermut US/DD: 427, 463, 474, 483, 528
McDougal US/DD: 151
McKean (ex-DD 90) US/APD: 246, 253, 271, 335, 345
McKee US/DD: 347, 353, 359, 365, 370, 388, 437, 499, 522, 525, 533
McLanahan US/DD: 339, 444
McNair US/DD: 427, 483, 499, 525
Meade US/DD: 291, 323, 337, 370, 388, 391, 399
Measure US/MS: see T-273
Medici It/TB: 61
Medusa It/SM: 34, 39, 46, 63, 91, 184
Méduse Fr/SM: 274
Medway UK/SM Depot: 229
Melbreak UK/DD: 336, 398, 420, 434-435, 440, 447
Melpomene It/Corvette: see UJ 202
Melvin US/DD: 427, 463, 483, 499, 525
Melvin R. Newman US/DE: 474, 502
Memel Ger/SM Depot: 489
Memphis US/CL: 108, 379
Mendez-Nuñez Sp/CL: 327
Mendip UK/DD: 296, 339, 350
Mendota US/CG Cutter: see Culver
Menges US/DE: 408, 410, 496, 507
Menotti It/SM: 39, 42, 62, 75, 81, 156, 360
Menzhinski USSR/Aux MS (B): see T-35
Meon Can/Frigate: 424, 434
Meredith (II) US/DD: 92, 132, 207, 264
Meredith (III) US/DD: 420, 424
Meridian USSR/Survey ship (N): 120
Mermaid UK/Sloop: 445
Mertz US/DD: 427, 474, 483, 499, 508, 510, 525
Mervine US/DD: 339
Metcalfe US/DD: 502, 524
Metel USSR/Patrol ship (P): 531
Meteor UK/DD: 256, 287, 374, 384, 408, 452, 500, 509
Method US/MS: see T-274

Metivier US/DE: 528
Meynell UK/DD: 302, 394, 421
Miami US/CL: 427, 448, 458, 461, 464, 466, 474, 476, 491-492, 499-500, 509
Miaoulis (ex-Modbury) Fr/DD: 339, 359, 453
Micca It/SM: 34, 47, 81, 227, 229, 236, 271, 340
Michel Ger/Aux CL: see Schiff 28
Michele Bianchi It/SM: see Bianchi
Michishio Jap/DD: 159, 163, 167, 173, 178, 184, 186, 191, 271, 275-276, 324, 361, 415, 430, 462-463
Micka US/DE: 506
Middleton UK/DD: 227-228, 237, 302, 405, 421, 447
Midway US/CVE: 428, 452
Mignonette UK/Corvette: 211, 287, 296-297, 329, 421, 481
Miguel de Cervantes Sp/CL: 327
Mikatsuki Jap/DD: 221, 335, 341
Mikoyan USSR/Icebreaker (BS/N): 126, 128, 155, 236, 265, 334
Mikuma Jap/CA: 159, 163, 166-167, 178, 181, 187, 194, 196, 200-201, 204-205, 221, 224
Mikura Jap/Frigate: 495
Milan Fr/DD: 26-27, 29, 38, 274
Mildura Aus/MS: 534
Milford UK/Sloop: 44, 52, 55, 64
Millelire It/SM: 48, 65, 76
Miller US/DD: 387, 406, 426, 458, 476, 499
Millicoma US/Oiler: 522
Millo It/SM: 151, 156, 200
Mills US/DE: 402, 535
Milne UK/DD: 256, 287, 302, 326, 366, 374, 383-384, 393, 408, 452
Milwaukee US/CL: 108, 379, 401, 409, see Murmansk
Mimico Can/Corvette: 421
Mimose Fr/Corvette: 131, 142, 172, 211, 217
Mina USSR/MS (BS): see T-407
Minatsuki Jap/DD: 162, 169, 173, 194, 415, 429
Minegumo Jap/DD: 162, 170, 177, 182, 186, 194-195, 221, 235, 254, 258, 307
Minekaze Jap/DD: 390
Minenräumschiff 11 Ger/ML: 115-116, 118, 489
Minenräumschiff 26 Ger/ML: 465
Minerve Fr/SM: 41, 78, 94, 99-100, 126, 230
Mingo US/SM: 432, 468
Minneapolis US/CA: 161, 168, 182, 185, 199, 214, 221, 224, 226, 238, 249, 255, 282, 359, 370, 373, 388, 392, 406, 427, 452, 461, 463, 479, 481, 488, 502
Minrep USSR/MS: see T-402
Minsk USSR/DD (B): 14, 119, 128, 130, 132, 138

Mirabello It/DD: 34, 61, 103
Miraglia It/Aircraft depot ship: 349
Mirth US/MS: see T-275
Mission Bay US/CVE: 455, 507
Mississinewa US/Oiler: 467
Mississippi US/BB: 92, 108, 132, 149, 226, 337, 370, 388, 399, 452, 461, 463, 479, 483, 523, 533, 537
Missori It/TB: 79-80, 92
Missouri US/BB: 491, 499-501, 509-510, 522, 525-526, 533-535
Mistral Fr/DD: 31-32, 41, 424
Mitchell US/DE: 524, 533
Mitragliere It/DD: 228, 245, 261, 273, 282, 292, 312, 349, 484
Miyake Jap/Frigate: 476
Mizuho Jap/Seaplane carrier: 160, 177, 181, 184, 186, 191, 194, 209, 221
Moa NZ/AS Trawler: 290, 316
Moale US/DD: 471, 474, 479, 492, 528, 533
Moberly US/Frigate: 507, 518
Mobile US/CL: 347, 353, 359, 364, 370, 373, 388, 392, 399, 406, 426, 448, 458, 461, 464, 467, 474, 527·528, 533
Mocenigo It/SM: 34, 39, 45, 67, 84-85, 87, 103, 156, 200-201, 218, 263, 273, 283, 289
Mochitzuki Jap/DD: 164, 168, 179, 199, 214, 235, 271, 275-276, 335
Modbury UK/DD: see Miaoulis
Moffett US/DD: 108, 151, 322, 379
Mogador Fr/DD: 8, 11, 41, 280
Mogami Jap/CA: 159, 163, 166-167, 178, 181, 187, 194, 196, 200-201, 204-205, 221, 224, 361, 364, 414, 430, 462-463
Mohawk UK/DD: 8, 23-24, 40, 43, 51, 63, 74, 89, 93
Mohawk US/CG Cutter: 248
Mojave US/CG Cutter: 248
Molotov USSR/CA (BS): 147, 150, 173, 175-176, 182, 197, 199, 225, 239
Momi Jap/DD: 480
Momo Jap/TB: 472
Monaghan US/DD: 161, 214, 221, 224, 312, 323, 328, 336-337, 370, 388, 392, 437, 474
Monge Fr/SM: 36, 60, 70, 212
Monitor US/LSV: 487, 504
Monkshood UK/Corvette: 211
Monnow Can/Frigate: 471, 520
Monongahela US/Oiler: 476
Monrovia US/AGC: 339
Monsambano It/TB: 61
Monsone It/TB: 293, 300
Monssen US/DD: 92, 132, 207, 221, 226, 238, 249, 255, 275-276
Monssen (II) US/DD: 427, 463, 483, 499, 508, 525
Monsun Ger/Tug: 22

Montanari It/TB: 34, 81, 92, 245, 251, 293, 349
Montbretia UK/Corvette: 246, 262, 278
Montcalm Fr/CL: 7-8, 11, 28, 53, 56, 352, 379, 420, 443, 449, 484, 513
Montcalm USSR/Icebreaker (N): 334
Montclare UK/Aux CL: 59
Montecuccoli It/CL: 35, 42, 69-70, 94, 119, 128, 143, 157, 165, 175, 183, 189, 200, 227, 243, 283, 342, 349
Monte Gargano It/SM Depot: 49
Monterey US/CVL: 370, 373, 377, 387, 392, 400, 406, 426, 448, 457, 464, 466, 474. 525, 533, 537
Montgomery (ex-DD 121) US/DM: 161, 291
Montgomery (ex-Wickes) UK/DD: 81, 281
Montpelier US/CL: 291, 307, 334, 363-364, 376, 391, 399, 426-427, 471, 474, 480, 495, 512, 524, 527
Montrose UK/DD: 31-32, 304, 421
Monzambano It/TB: 141, 407
Moonstone UK/AS Trawler: 36
Moore US/DE: 507
Moosejaw Can/Corvette: 131, 267, 421
Moray US/SM: 526
Moresby Aus/Survey ship: 538
Morden Can/Corvette: 211, 325, 354-355
Morosini It/SM: 34, 44, 62, 77, 99, 113, 118, 132, 137, 192, 341
Morosini (Francesco) It/ML: 323
Morris US/DD: 92, 108, 132, 214, 221, 224, 226, 254, 258, 269, 275, 323, 336, 370, 388, 392, 409, 480, 504, 507
Morrison US/DD: 428, 458, 502-503, 517
Morse Fr/SM: 36, 106-107
Moskva USSR/DD (BS): 113
Moskva USSR/GB (B): 129-130
Mosley US/DE: 408, 496, 507
Mosquito UK/GB: 31-32
Mosto It/TB: see Da Mosto
Moth UK/GB: 170
Mounsey UK/DE: 464-465
Mount McKinley US/AGC: 502
Mount Olympus US/AGC: 480, 536
Mount Vernon US/AP: 150-151, 197
Mourne UK/Frigate: 424
Möwe Ger/TB: 3, 22, 28, 330, 332, 348, 398, 404-406, 413, 422-423, 427
Moyola UK/Frigate: 339
Muavenet Tu/DD: see Inconstant
Mugford US/DD: 161, 168, 199,

226, 238, 241, 310, 334, 348, 355, 375-376, 427-428, 458, 471
Muir US/DE: 507
Mull UK/AS Trawler: 397
Mullany US/DD: 337, 376, 380, 387, 395, 399, 409, 418, 451, 507
München (WBS-6) Ger/Weather Observation ship: 98-99, 105
Munda US/CVE: 528, 533
Murakumo Jap/DD: 159, 163, 167, 178, 187, 194, 200, 204-205, 221, 235, 249-250, 252-253, 263
Murasame Jap/DD: 162, 170, 177, 182, 194-195, 221, 235, 248, 252, 258, 268, 271, 275, 307
Murman USSR/ML (N): 18, 230, 343, 361
Murmansk (ex-Milwaukee) USSR/CL (N): 409
Murphy US/DD: 339, 342, 420, 431, 444
Murray US/DD: 359, 365, 370, 388, 437, 499, 501, 503, 525, 533
Musashi Jap/BB: 235, 361, 401, 414, 418, 430, 462
Muskallunge US/SM: 429, 439, 534
Mueskegat US/Weather Observation ship: 253
Musketeer UK/DD: 357, 374-375, 393, 408, 452, 509
Musson USSR/Patrol vessel: 116
Mustin US/DD: 92, 132, 226, 254, 258, 269-270, 323, 336, 370, 388, 392, 409, 418, 480, 504
Mutsu Jap/BB: 221, 235, 248, 331
Mutsuki Jap/DD: 164, 168, 179, 199, 214, 235, 249
Muzio Attendolo It/CL: see Attendolo
Myles C. Fox US/DD: 533
Myngs UK/DD: 442, 444, 446, 465, 467-468, 475
Myoko Jap/CA: 160, 169, 177, 194, 196, 214, 221, 235, 248, 254, 263-264, 268, 361, 364, 414, 418, 430, 462, 472, 529
Myriel UK/Water Tanker: 160
Myrmidon UK/DD: see Orkan

NKi 08 Ger/Vp boat: 426
NKi 09/Alane (ex-V 6114, ex-Warwickshire) Ger/Vp boat: 331
NKi 11 Ger/Vp boat: 385
NKi 12 Ger/Vp boat: 426
NM 01/Vandale Ger/Vp boat: 192
NN 04/Krebs Ger/Vp boat: 84
NT 05/Togo (ex-Otra) Ger/Hs boat: 134
Nabob UK/CVE: 442, 444-445
Nachi Jap/CA: 160, 169, 177, 181, 184, 186, 191, 194-196, 221, 235, 347, 459, 462-463, 466

Nadder UK/Frigate: 404
Naganami Jap/DD: 263-264, 268, 271, 275, 277, 282-283, 286, 290, 337, 361, 364-365, 414, 430, 462, 466
Nagara Jap/CL: 160, 170, 177, 181, 186, 191, 220, 223, 235, 248, 254, 264, 268, 275-277, 370-371, 373, 439
Nagato Jap/BB: 221, 235, 414, 430, 462-463, 526
Nagatsuki Jap/DD: 162, 169, 173, 194, 335
Naiad UK/CL: 64, 71, 75-76, 97, 102, 107, 155-156, 163, 165, 176, 180, 183, 189, 200
Naiade Fr/SM: 280
Naiade It/SM: 34, 47, 69
Nairana UK/CVE: 389, 464, 471, 491-492
Najade Ger/Coastal Defence boat: 368
Naka Jap/CL: 162, 170, 177, 182, 194-195, 206, 370, 392
Nalim USSR/SM (N): see T-31
Naluca Ru/TB: 142, 446
Namikaze Jap/DD: 439
Nani It/SM: 34, 39, 44, 56, 73
Nantahala US/Oiler: 474
Napanee Can/Corvette: 286-287
Napier Aus/DD: 102-103, 126, 173, 179, 204, 227, 255, 400, 407, 411, 473, 479, 484-485, 516, 531, 533
Narbada Ind/Sloop: 479, 484, 494, 513, 521, 538
Narborough UK/DE: 464, 519
Narcissus UK/Corvette: 211, 293, 307, 326, 354, 389, 421
Narhvalen Da/TB: 346
Nariu Jap/ML: 491
Narval Fr/SM: 36, 73
Narvalo It/SM: 45, 55, 62, 65, 69, 75, 140, 144, 150, 165, 202, 236, 271, 292
Narwhal UK/SM: 13, 20, 23-24, 28, 30, 37, 41
Narwhal US/SM: 161, 198, 222, 237, 323, 336, 347, 372, 427
Nashi Jap/DD: 529
Nashville US/CL: 92, 108, 115, 207, 221, 226, 290, 324, 347, 359, 376, 380, 395-396, 409, 418, 451, 474, 523-524
Nassau US/CVE: 323, 370, 388, 458
Nasturtium UK/Corvette: 96, 108, 211, 217, 240, 356, 421
Natal (ex-Loch Cree) S. Afr/Frigate: 496
Natchez US/Frigate: 506
Natoma Bay US/CVE: 388, 399, 409, 461, 474, 480, 493, 502, 523
Natori Jap/CL: 162, 169, 173, 194, 196, 439
Natsugumo Jap/DD: 162, 170, 177, 182, 186, 194-195, 221, 235, 248, 254, 263
Natsushio Jap/DD: 160, 169, 177, 186
Nautik Ger/Training vessel: 516

Nautilus Fr/SM: 36, 284, 322
Nautilus (ex-M 81) Ger/MS: 1, 5, 22
Nautilus US/SM: 222, 247, 259, 323, 396
Navajo US/Tug: 346
Navarinon (ex-Echo) Gr/DD: 444, 453, 473
Nazario Sauro It/DD: see Sauro
Neal A. Scott US/DE: 507
Nebojša Yu/SM: 91
Neches US/Oiler: 168, 181, 183
Neger Ger/One-man torpedo: 408, 433, 435, 440
Neghelli It/SM: 34, 37, 46, 69, 75
Nehenta Bay US/CVE: 458, 474, 476, 535
Nelson UK/BB: 1, 3, 6-9, 11, 13, 32, 54, 64, 68, 76, 86, 99, 101, 105, 120, 122, 128, 134, 140, 242, 274, 333, 339, 347, 351, 357, 420, 528, 534
Nelson US/DD: 339, 342, 420, 423
Nembo It/DD: 34, 37, 45
Nene UK/Frigate: 332, 346, 369, 378, 394, 421, 448, 471, 521
Nenohi Jap/DD: 181, 186, 191, 221, 233
Neosho US/Oiler: 168, 214
Neosho (II) US/Oiler: 476
Nepal (ex-Norseman) Aus/DD: 255, 400, 407, 411, 473, 479, 486, 516
Neptun USSR/Patrol ship (B): 130
Neptune UK/CL: 7, 9-10, 12, 14, 36, 39-40, 43, 45, 70, 105, 155-157, 165-166
Nereide It/SM: 34, 66, 84, 94-95, 101, 218, 234, 258, 340
Nereus Gr/SM: 81, 111, 123, 239, 255, 390
Nerissa UK/DD: see Piorun
Ness UK/Frigate: 303, 315
Nestor Aus/DD: 98, 100. 120, 132, 167, 171, 173, 179, 204, 227-228, 255
Nettelbeck (ex-M 138) Ger/MS: 5-6, 233, 428
Netravati Ind/Trawler: 86
Neunzer US/DE: 507
Neva USSR/Aux MS (N): see T-44
Nevada US/BB: 161, 323, 420, 431, 443, 493, 502-503, 505, 527, 533
Neville US/APA: 271
Newcastle UK/CL: 6-7, 11, 32-33, 65-68, 121, 227-228, 382, 407, 411, 470, 473, 479, 486
Newcomb US/DD: 428, 463, 474, 479, 481, 503, 507
Newell US/DE: 408
Newfoundland UK/CL: 328, 333, 338, 340, 471, 520, 523, 526, 530-531
Newfoundland UK/Hospital ship: 351
New Glasgow Can/Frigate: 496
New Jersey US/BB: 387, 392,

399, 406, 427, 448, 458, 461, 464, 466, 474, 476, 491, 499-501, 509
Newmarket (ex-Robinson) UK/DD: 96
New Mexico US/BB: 92, 108, 132, 226, 337, 370, 388, 399, 427, 471, 474, 479, 481, 503, 511, 517, 533, 537
New Orleans US/CA: 161, 199, 214, 221, 224, 226, 238, 249, 282, 359, 370, 373, 388, 392, 406, 427, 437, 448, 458, 461, 464, 474
New York US/BB: 5, 115, 132, 493, 503, 509, 511
Nezamozhnik USSR/DD (BS): 124, 126, 132, 136, 141, 144, 147, 150, 162, 170-173, 176, 199, 209, 216, 218, 222, 241-242, 245, 247, 260, 265, 267, 283, 286, 297, 361
Niagara (ex-Thatcher) Can/DD: 123
Niblack US/DD: 83, 92, 115, 119, 132, 136, 339, 350, 369, 385, 415, 443
Nichelio It/SM: 258, 271, 273, 283, 340
Nicholas US/DD: 263-264, 290-291, 307, 335, 340, 345, 370, 373, 409, 473, 480, 498, 504, 513, 533
Nicholson US/DD: 136, 193, 339, 396, 409, 458, 533
Nicola Frabrizi It/TB: see Fabrizi
Nicolo Zeno It/DD: see Zeno
Nicoloso da Recco It/DD: see Da Recco
Niedersachsen (ex-Acqui) Ger/ML: 376, 390
Nields US/DD: 317, 339, 386, 415, 444
Niels Juel Da/Coast Defence ship: 347
Nienburg Ger/Gun Ferry: 497, 508
Nigella UK/Corvette: 96, 212, 299
Niger UK/MS: 31, 213, 220, 231
Nigeria UK/CL: 71, 84, 87-88, 113, 121, 127, 180, 185, 190, 203, 208, 212, 217, 219, 230, 242-243, 407, 411, 438, 479, 486, 520, 527, 534
Niitsuki Jap/DD: 335
Nikkai Maru Jap/Aux GB: 179
Ning Hai Ch/CL: see Ioshima
Niobe (ex-Cattaro, ex- Dalmacija) Ger/CL: 368, 376
Niobe (ex-Gelderland) Ger/CL: 430
Niobrara US/Oiler: 476
Noio Gr/Customs Sloop: 360
Nippon Maru Jap/Oiler: 337
Nisshin Jap/Seaplane carrier: 235, 252, 263, 341
Nith UK/LS: 573
Nito-Yuso-Kan . . . Jap/LST: see T . . . :
Nivŏse Fr/Oiler: 367

Nizam Aus/DD: 97, 102, 107, 126, 155, 165, 173, 179, 197, 227, 255, 407, 516, 531, 533
Noa (ex-DD 343) US/APD: 376
Noble UK/DD: see Van Galen
Nokaze Jap/DD: 221, 235, 432, 479
Nomi Jap/Frigate: 488, 495
Nonpareil UK/DD: see Tjerk Hiddes
Nord USSR/Survey ship (N): 442
Nordhav II Nor/MS Trawler: 496
Nordkaperen Da/TB: 346
Nordkyn Ger/Vp boat: see V 6110
Nordmark Ger/Supply ship: 65, 82-83, 95
Nordpol Ger/Vp boat: see V 6109
Nordstern Ger/Training ship: 455
Nordwind Ger/Patrol ship: 148
Norfolk UK/CA: 6, 11-12, 21, 32, 49, 70, 74, 100-101, 208, 217, 219, 230, 256, 374-375, 383, 393, 483, 517-519
Norge Nor/Coast Defence ship: 24
Norman Aus/DD: 204, 227, 255, 400, 460. 486, 516
Norman Scott US/DD: 427, 438, 483, 486, 499, 525, 533
North Carolina US/BB: 226, 238, 254, 291, 335, 370, 373, 387, 392, 406, 427, 474, 476, 491, 493, 499-500, 509, 511, 525-526, 533, 537
Northampton US/CA: 161, 168, 183, 190, 207, 221, 224, 226, 254, 258, 269, 275, 282
Northern Chief UK/AS Trawler: 123
Northern Foam UK/AS Trawler: 354
Northern Gem UK/AS Trawler: 230, 320
Northern Pride UK/AS Trawler: 70
Northern Spray UK/AS Trawler: 219-220, 320, 389
Northern Whale UK/AS Trawler: 286
Northland US/CG Cutter: 449
Northwind US/Icebreaker: see Severny Veter
Norwich City S. Afr/AS Trawler: 299
Noshiro Jap/CL: 361, 364, 377, 414, 418, 430, 462, 464
Notoro Jap/Seaplane mother ship: 290, 347
Nowake Jap/DD: 159, 163, 166, 178, 181, 190, 194, 196, 220, 223, 235, 248, 254, 264, 283, 290, 369, 392, 415, 418, 430, 462, 464
Nubian UK/DD: 25, 28, 40, 43, 51, 63, 74, 89, 93-95, 97, 102, 292, 321-322, 328, 334, 338, 350-351, 468, 514, 521
Nucleus US/MS: see T-276
Numakaze Jap/DD: 372

Nürnberg Ger/CL: 1-2, 10, 13-14, 45, 139, 484, 518-519
Nullo It/TB: 45, 49, 61
Nyasaland UK/Frigate: 469, 490

O . . .: Du/SM
O 9: 87
O 10: 87
O 13: 37
O 14: 126
O 15: 375
O 16: 159, 166
O 19: 159, 178, 194, 453, 471
O 20: 166
O 21: 56, 59, 67, 75, 78, 111, 123, 133, 136, 140-141, 153-154
O 22: 48, 53, 58, 62
O 23: 48, 53, 58, 62, 70, 75, 78, 111, 238, 266, 382
O 24: 56, 61, 65, 87, 104, 111, 123, 133
O 25: see UD 3
O 27: see UD 5
O'Bannon US/DD: 246, 275-276, 290, 295, 307, 324, 335, 340, 345, 356, 409, 473-474, 480, 487, 495, 513, 533
O'Brien US/DD: 108, 119, 132, 226, 254
O'Brien (II) US/DD: 420, 431, 473-474, 479, 481, 502-503, 528, 533
O'Flaherty US/DE: 480, 502
O'Neill US/DE: 504, 517
Oak Hill US/LSD: 528
Oakland US/CL: 370, 387, 392, 399, 426, 458, 464, 474, 499-500, 509, 525, 533
Oakley UK/DD: 339, 443, see Kujawiak
Oakville Can/Corvette: 250
Obdurate UK/DD: 265, 287-288, 302, 318, 383, 520
Obedient UK/DD: 287-288, 302, 311, 411, 421, 435, 452, 464, 471, 511, 517-518
Oberon UK/SM: 5
Oberrender US/DE: 461, 480, 502, 517
Oboro Jap/DD: 235
Ocean Gem UK/AS Trawler: 287
Ochakov USSR/DD (BS): 126
Odate Jap/Repair ship: 495
Odin UK/SM: 35
Offa UK/DD: 171, 229, 256, 311, 319-321, 339, 347, 351, 421, 423, 464, 471, 511
Ogden US/DE: see EK-7
Oglala US/ML: 161
Ognevoi USSR/DD (BS): 126
Oi Jap/CL: 221, 235, 383, 419
Oite Jap/DD: 164, 168, 179, 199, 214, 235, 248, 347, 392
Ojika Jap/Frigate: 505
Oka USSR/GB (B): 131, 384, 428
Oka USSR/ML (B): see Marti
Okean USSR/ML (P): 531-532
Okhotsk USSR/ML (P): 532
Oki Jap/Frigate: 468
Okikaze Jap/DD: 289

Okinami Jap/DD: 414, 418, 430, 462, 466
Okinawa Jap/Frigate: 529
Okinoshima Jap/ML: 163, 179, 214-215
Oklahoma US/BB: 161
Oklahoma City US/CL: 522, 528, 530, 533
Oktyabr USSR/Icebreaker (B): 126, 129, 157
Oktyabr USSR/GB (BS): 252
Oktyabrskaya Revolutsia USSR/BB (B): 15, 132-133, 138, 207, 384, 428
Olav Tryggvason Nor/ML: see Brummer
Oldenburg (ex-Garigliano) Ger/ML: 397
Oliver Mitchell US/DE: 502
Olterra It/SM Depot: 344
Olympus UK/SM: 35, 43, 120, 149, 214
Omaha US/CL: 108, 149, 379, 443
Ommaney Bay US/CVE: 461, 474, 480
Onami Jap/DD: 361, 372
Ondina It/SM: 40, 54, 84, 94-95, 225, 234
Ondine Fr/SM: 41
Onega USSR/NL (B): 130
Onice It/SM: 65, 71, 84, 90, 99, 150, 175, 200-201, 227
Onslaught UK/DD: 245, 256, 294, 311, 374, 393, 421, 423, 439, 471, 483, 491-492
Onslow UK/DD: 171, 198, 219, 227, 256, 287-288, 374, 405, 411, 421, 423, 441, 464, 471, 483, 491-492, 520
Ootori Jap/TB: 427
Opashny USSR/DD (BS): 126
Opytny USSR/DD (B): 131, 384
Opportune UK/DD: 256, 287, 302, 318, 374-375, 421, 435, 440, 464, 511, 517-518
Orage Fr/DD: 31
Orao Yu/ML: 91
Orca US/AVP: 481
Orchis UK/Corvette: 293, 307, 326, 354, 389, 436
Ordronaux US/DD: 339, 386, 444
Orzhonikidze USSR/CA (BS): 126
Oréade Fr/SM: 274
Orfasay UK/AS Trawler: 361
Oriani It/DD: 42-43, 67, 89, 118, 127, 129, 149, 166, 175, 183, 193, 200, 202, 227, 243, 267, 349, 352
Oribi UK/DD: 140, 171, 203, 208, 219, 287, 311, 319-321, 357, 421, 423, 435, 464, 471
Orillia Can/Corvette: 131, 240, 266, 356
Orion Fr/SM: 41
Orion (ex-Kurmark) Ger/Aux CL: see Schiff 36
Orion UK/CL: 9, 15, 36, 39-40, 43, 45, 50-51, 57-58, 62-63, 65, 67, 70, 74, 89, 92, 94,

97-98, 102-103, 328, 333, 338, 340, 347, 350-351, 386, 421, 443, 453, 510
Orione It/TB: 42, 95, 97, 160, 245, 284, 292-293, 300, 312, 349
Orizaba US/AP: 115, 150
Orkan (ex-Myrmidon) Pol/DD: 302, 332, 357
Orlando It/Aux ML: 34
Orphée Fr/SM: 21, 29, 274, 358
Orpheus UK/SM: 35-36
Orsa It/TB: 40, 42, 79, 90, 97, 103, 118, 129, 175, 183, 237, 349, 484
Orsini It/TB: 90
Orwell UK/DD: 287, 302, 311, 357, 374, 421, 452, 464, 471, 483, 491-492, 511, 517-518
Orzel Pol/SM: 1, 4-6, 23, 30
Oshio Jap/DD: 159, 163, 167, 173, 178, 186, 191, 296
Osiris UK/SM: 35, 48, 55
Osmond-Ingram US/DD: 307, 320, 326, 329, 337, 371-372
Ost Ger/Gun Carrier: 342
Ostia It/ML: 34
Ostmark (ex-Cote d'Argent) Ger/Catapult ship: 52
Ostmark Ger/ML: 331, 345, 373
Ostro It/DD: 40, 45
Ostrovsky USSR/Aux ML (BS): 110
Ostsee Ger/Gun Carrier: 497, 508
Osvetnik Yu/SM: 91
Oswald UK/SM: 35, 46
Otaria It/SM: 56, 59, 61, 77, 99, 156, 218, 227, 236, 242, 292
Otra Nor/MS: 134, see NT.05/Togo
Otranto It-Ger/Aux MS: 454
Ottawa Can/DD: 14, 211, 251-252
Ottawa (II) (ex-Griffin) Can/DD: 328, 394, 424, 435-436
Otter US/DE: 469, 481, 507
Otter Ger/Mine transport: 428
Ottersetter US/DE: 507
Otto Braun Ger/MS (ex-M 129): 1, 4-5, 22
Otus UK/SM: 111, 247
Ouessant Fr/SM: 5-6, 14, 38
Ouragan Fr/DD: 41
Outremont Can/Frigate: 394, 408, 424, 454
Overton US/DD: 61, 83, 132, 329, 337
Owen US/DD: 387, 406, 426, 458, 476, 499
Owl US/MS: 4
Owensound Can/Corvette: 395
Oxley UK/SM: 3
Oxlip UK/Corvette: 286, 339, 374, 421, 464, 511
Oyashio Jap/DD: 160, 169, 177, 181, 184, 186, 191, 221, 235, 248, 254, 263-264, 268, 271, 275, 277, 282-283, 286, 290, 324
Oyodo Jap/CL: 377, 401, 462, 475, 499, 529
Ozark US/LSV: 504

Ozornoi USSR/DD (BS): 126

P . . .: Jap/APD (Ishokaitei and Itto-Yuso-Kan)
P1: 177, 181, 191, 221, 244, 249-250, 289
P2: 177, 181, 191, 221, 244, 249
P31: 401
P32: 164, 168
P33: 164, 168
P34: 177, 181, 184, 191, 221, 244, 249-250
P35: 221, 244, 249
P36: 177, 182
P37: 177, 182
P38: 177, 182, 468
P39: 177, 184

P . . .: UK/SM
P31: see Uproar
P32: 111, 127,
P33: 111, 118
P34: see Ultimatum
P35: see Umbra
P36: 190, 202, 207
P37: see Unbending
P38: 186, 193
P41: see Uredd
P42: see Unbroken, see V.2
P43: see Unison
P44: see United
P45: see Unrivalled
P46: see Unruffled
P47: see Dolfijn
P48: 278, 286
P51: see Unseen
P52: see Dzik
P54: see Unshaken
P211: see Safari
P212: see Sahib
P213: see Saracen
P217: see Sibyl
P219: see Seraph
P221: see Shakespeare
P222: 278, 284
P228: see Splendid
P311: 291
P551 (ex-S 25): see Jastrzab
P614 (ex-Burak Reis): 230
P615 (ex-Uluc Ali Reis): 230, 314

P . . .: USSR/SM
P-1 (B): 133
P-2 (B): 138
PA 1 (ex-Cherbourgoise) Ger/Escort vessel: 427
PA 2 (ex-Lorientaise) Ger/Escort vessel: 427
Pi 229 Ger/Assault boat: 359
PC . . .: US/SC
PC 431: 247
PC 458: 232
PC 460: 247
PC 469: 387
PC 471: 295
PC 474: 295, see L'Indiscret
PC 475: 246, see Le Resolute
PC 482: 247, see L'Enjoue
PC 487: 328
PC 492: 247
PC 505: 246
PC 558: 414

PC 564: 498
PC 565: 328
PC 575: 300
PC 592: 300, 322
PC 597: 470
PC 619: 400
PC 624: 340
PC 1129: 487
PC 1250: see Cimeterre
PC 1603: 517
PCE 837: see Kilmarnock
PCER 848: 466

PGM . . .: US/MGB
PGM 18: 508
PT . . .: US/MTB
PT 36: 283, 290-291
PT 37: 271, 283, 290-291
PT 38: 264, 290
PT 39: 271, 290-291
PT 40: 283, 290
PT 43: 283, 290
PT 44: 283
PT 45: 290
PT 46: 264, 290
PT 47: 290-291
PT 48: 264, 283, 290-291
PT 59: 283, 284, 290-291
PT 60: 264
PT 61: 271
PT 66: 306
PT 67: 306
PT 68: 306
PT 71: 425
PT 77: 487
PT 79: 487
PT 85: 304
PT 87: 304
PT 109: 283, 290-291, 341
PT 111: 291
PT 112: 290
PT 115: 290-291
PT 121: 306
PT 123: 290-291
PT 124: 291
PT 128: 306
PT 137: 463
PT 143: 306
PT 150: 306
PT 165: 311
PT 173: 311
PT 202: 397, 414, 444
PT 207: (Yu) 414
PT 208: (Yu) 397
PT 212: 397
PT 213: 397, 414 (Yu)
PT 214: 397
PT 218: 397, 414, 444
PT 223: 475
PT 250: 446
PT 304: 414
PT 306: 414
PT 307: 414
PT 490: 473
PT 492: 473
PT 498: 439
PT 500: 439
PT 502: 439
PT 503: 439
PT 505: 439
PT 507: 439
PT 508: 439
PT 509: 439

PT 510: 440
PT 511: 447
PT 512: 440, 447
PT 513: 447
PT 514: 440, 447
PT 516: 447
PT 519: 447
PT 520: 440, 447
PT 521: 440
PT 552: 414 (USSR)
PT 558: 414
PT 559: 414
PY 20 US/SC: 247
Paddle US/SM: 343, 403, 429,
    432, 449, 472
Pakenham UK/DD: 212, 227,
    292, 298, 300, 313
Paladin UK/DD: 204, 212, 227,
    294, 300, 313, 321-322, 328,
    339, 382-383, 486, 521
Palang Iran/GB: 129
Palestro It/TB: 55
Palisade US/MS: see T-278
Pallade It/TB: 34, 73, 105, 193,
    200, 208, 293, 300, 313
Pallas Fr/SM: 36, 274
Palmer (ex-DD 161) US/DMS:
    481
Palomares UK/AA Ship: 230-231,
    338, 350, 386
Pamanset US/Oiler: 476
Pampanito US/SM: 449, 468,
    491
Panamint US/AGC: 504, 535
Pancaldo It/DD: 42-43, 63, 98,
    300, 313, 321
Pandora UK/SM: 36, 41, 48, 55,
    73, 111, 207
Pangbourne UK/MS: 31
Pantera It/DD: 34, 49, 55, 61,
    78, 90
Panther UK/DD: 204, 212, 319-
    320, 339, 356
Panthère Fr/DD: 280, see FR 22
Papa It/TB: 34, 48, 85, 122, 381,
    see SG 20
Papanicolis Gr/SM: 71, 81, 111,
    228, 280, 294, 306, 323
Papua UK (ex-US PF 84)/
    Frigate: 490
Parche US/SM: 432, 468, 505, 522
Pargo US/SM: 347, 372, 410, 419,
    449, 468, 479, 529
Paris Fr/BB: 41
Paris Ger/MS: 192
Parizhskaya Kommuna USSR/BB
    (BS): 146, 152, 156, 173, 176,
    178, 180, 197, 202
Parker US/DD: 339, 444
Parkes Aus/MS: 538
Parktown S. Afr/MS Trawler: 229
Parramatta Aus/Sloop: 46, 55,
    108, 152
Parret UK (ex-US)/Frigate: 417,
    516
Parrott US/DD: 182, 188, 191,
    197, 338
Partenope It/TB: 73, 127, 255, 280
    291, 293
Partenope It/Aux ML: 34
Parthian UK/SM: 34, 36, 51,
    73, 86, 104, 107, 111, 236, 271,
    278, 323

Partridge UK/DD: 210, 215, 218,
    225, 227-228, 283
Partridge US/Tug: 423
Parvati Ind/Trawler: 86
Pasadena US/CL: 474, 476, 491,
    499-500, 509, 525-526, 529, 533
Pascal Fr/SM: 36, 280
Pasley UK/DE: 520
Passat (ex-Storstad) Ger/Aux ML:
    64
Passat Ger/Tug: 22
Passat/SKR . . . USSR/Patrol
    Ship: 117
Pasteur Fr/SM: 6, 13, 21, 38
Pathan Ind/Sloop: 36
Pathfinder UK/DD: 242-244, 318,
    325, 339, 352, 360, 382, 400,
    417, 421, 486
Pathfinder US/Survey vessel: 517
Patroclus UK/Aux CL: 61
Patron USSR/MS (B): see T-203
Patterson US/DD: 161, 168, 182,
    185, 199, 226, 238, 241, 250,
    310, 346, 355, 427-428, 458, 474,
    479, 502
Patuxent US/Oiler: 476
Paul G. Baker US/DE: 504
Paul Hamilton US/DD: 474, 480,
    502
Paul Jacobi Ger/DD: 7, 19, 22,
    51, 57, 189, 218, 485, 495,
    497-498
Paul Jones US/DD: 182, 194-195,
    338
Paynter UK/AS: Trawler 203,
    208
Peacock UK/Sloop: 445, 481
Peary US/DD: 190
Pecos US/Oiler: 196
Peder Skram Du/Coast Defence
    Ship: 346
Pégase Fr/SM: 36, 60, 70
Pegaso It/TB: 42, 97, 103, 118,
    127, 129, 141, 165, 210, 239,
    300, 349
Peiffer US/DE: 480
Pelagosa It/ML: 34, 311
Pelican UK/Sloop: 234, 321, 331,
    400
Pelikan (ex-M 28) Ger/MS: 1, 5,
    22
Pelikan (ex-KT 18) Ger/KT ship:
    432, 451
Pelton UK/AS Trawler: 71
Penelope UK/CL: 23-24, 32,
    144, 149, 155, 157, 165-166,
    180, 183, 189, 202, 207, 293,
    328, 333, 339, 350-351, 356, 377,
    385-386
Penetrate US/MS: see T-280
Penguin US/MS: 163
Penn UK/DD: 242-243, 319-320,
    339, 360, 367, 382, 407, 411,
    521
Pennsylvania US/BB: 161, 226,
    323, 337, 370, 388, 392, 427,
    452, 461, 463, 479, 527-528
Pennywort UK/Corvette: 211,
    309, 421
Pensacola US/CA: 169, 173, 182,
    185, 199, 221, 224, 226, 254,
    258, 269, 275, 282, 370, 388,
    431, 448, 457, 464, 466, 473,

482, 487, 493, 502-503, 528
Pentstemon UK/Corvette: 137,
167-168, 292, 339
Penylan UK/DD: 283
Penzance UK/Sloop: 48-49
Peony UK/Corvette: 67, 74, see
Sachtouris
Perch US/SM: 164, 194, 197
Perch (II) US/SM: 456
Perekop USSR/DD (BS): 126
Peril US/MS: see T-281
Periwinkle UK/Corvette: 51, 81,
104, 137
Perkins US/DD: 185, 189, 199,
214, 282, 310, 348, 355
Perkins (II) US/DD: 533
Perla It/SM: 36, 83, 202, 234,
352, see P 712, see Matrozos
Permit US/SM: 164, 184, 222,
306, 322, 336, 388
Perlé Fr/SM: 36
Perry US/DMS: 161, 337, 355
Persée Fr/SM: 5, 56
Persefone It/Corvette: 293, 300,
see UJ 2227
Perseo It/TB: 92, 97, 104, 154,
208, 232, 280, 286, 292-293, 313,
321
Perseus UK/SM: 21, 133, 141, 159
Perth Aus/CL: 7, 14, 74, 76, 89,
92, 97-98, 102-103, 107, 169,
173, 194-196
Pessagno It/DD: 42, 68, 70, 89,
94, 96, 98, 114, 116, 126, 135,
165, 193, 218
Petard UK/DD: 298, 321-322,
328, 339, 347, 351, 367, 382-
383, 407
Peterel UK/GB: 163
Peterson US/DE: 386, 395
Peto US/SM: 358, 372, 396, 468
Petrash USSR/GB: see SKR-102
Petrof Bay US/CVE: 451, 460,
483, 493, 502
Petropavlovsk (ex-Marat) USSR/
BB (B): 384
Petropavlovsk (ex-Lützow) USSR/
CA (B): 132, 135, 207, 384,
see Tallin
Petunia UK/Corvette: 260, 270
Pheasant UK/Sloop: 339, 368,
421, 502, 516
Phelps US/DD: 161, 168, 182,
185, 199, 214, 221, 224, 226,
238, 249, 255, 323, 337, 370,
388, 399, 428
Philadelphia US/CL: 92, 108, 132,
273, 333-334, 339-340, 342,
346, 350-351, 386, 443, 449
Philip US/DD: 15
Philip (II) US/DD: 334, 345, 391,
428, 480, 498, 513, 523-524
Phoebe UK/CL: 64, 75, 93-94,
97-98, 102-103, 106, 115, 242,
266, 359, 386, 438, 460, 479,
484, 486, 514, 521
Phoenix UK/SM: 36, 43
Phoenix US/CL: 161, 197, 250,
310, 376, 380, 387, 395-396,
409, 418, 451, 461, 463, 474,
480, 487, 498, 504, 513, 523-524
Phoque Fr/SM: 36, 284

Pickerel US/SM: 178, 182, 210,
215, 296, 314
Picking US/DD: 396, 431, 480,
488, 502, 527
Picotee UK/Corvette: 123
Pictou Can/Corvette: 143, 184
Picuda: 396, 410, 439, 468, 479
Pier Capponi It/SM: see Capponi
Piet Hein Du/DD: 185, 188, 191
Pietro Micca It/SM: see Micca
Pietro Calvi It/SM: see Calvi
Pigafetta It/DD: 42, 47, 68, 70,
94, 96-97, 105, 114, 116, 126,
143, 175, 183, 193, 199, 200,
228, 265, 267, 272-273, 282,
292, 300, 313, see TA 44
Pike US/SM: 164, 191, 222, 314,
343
Pikker USSR/Tender (B): 130
Pillsbury US/DD: 188, 191, 196
Pillsbury (II) US/DE: 381, 387,
416, 507
Pilo It/TB: 42, 80
Pilotfish US/SM: 429, 534
Pimpernel UK/Corvette: 247,
291-292, 309
Pincher UK/MS: 490
Pindos (ex-Bolebroke) Gr/DD:
339, 344, 344, 350, 356, 367,
443, 453
Pine UK/AS Trawler: 388
Ping Hai/Chi: see Yashojima
Pink UK/Corvette: 315, 320-321,
326, 360, 425
Pinkney US/Casualty Transport:
513
Pintado US/SM: 419, 429, 439,
464, 468, 472
Pioneer US/MS: 329
Piorun (ex-Nerissa) Pol/DD: 101,
140, 211, 339, 347, 351, 410-
411, 421-422, 427, 441, 453
Pipefish US/SM: 429, 449
Piper US/SM: 491
Pipinos (ex-Veldt) Gr/SM: 390,
398, 433
Piranha US/SM: 432, 522
Pirmunas/T- . . . USSR/MS (B):
see T-51
Pisani It/SM: 39, 44, 175
Pittsburgh US/CA: 499-500, 509,
522
Plaice US/SM: 419, 429, 449,
472
Planet Ger/NL: 440
Platino It/SM: 201, 218, 227,
237, 273, 289, 299, 340
Platte US/Oiler: 183, 185, 221,
239
Pleiadi It/TB: 47, 99
Plover UK/ML: 4, 408
Plumleaf UK/Oiler: 207
Plunger US/SM: 161, 164, 176,
222, 232, 322, 336, 343, 390,
429
Plunkett US/DD: 83, 115, 119,
136, 142-143, 203, 339, 350,
385, 386, 420, 431, 443
Plym UK/Frigate: 339, 494
Plymouth US/GB: 338
Pogy US/SM: 322, 347, 372, 390,
402, 526

Pola It/CA: 35-36, 42, 57, 67,
69-70, 89
Polarfront Ger/Vp boat: see
V 5903
Polaris Ger/Gun Carrier: 485
Polarkreis Ger/Vp boat: see
V 6107, see V 5913
Polarmeer Ger/Vp boat: see
V 6108, see V 5914
Polarsonne Ger/Vp boat: see
V 5902
Polarstern Ger/Vp boat: see
V 5912
Polyarny USSR/Survey vessel:
532
Pollack US/SM: 161, 164, 176,
198, 209, 222, 322, 343, 396, 410
Polluce It/TB: 35-36, 99, 105, 133,
186, 245, 251
Pollux Fr/Supply Ship: 41
Polyanthus UK/Corvette: 211,
354
Pomfret US/SM: 456, 468, 491
Pommern (ex-Belain d'Esnambuc)
Ger/ML: 312, 323, 341, 352,
397
Pompano US/SM: 161, 170, 209,
222, 336, 347
Pompeo Magno It/CL: 349
Pompon US/SM: 410, 439
Poncelet Fr/SM: 5, 50, 64
Pontchartrain US/CG Cutter:
see Hartland
Poole UK/MS: 212
Poole US/DE: 395
Pope US/DD: 182, 196, 387, 416,
507
Poppy UK/Corvette: 229, 231,
302, 339, 374
Pope US/DE: 191, 381
Porcupine UK/DD: 283
Porfido It/SM: 247, 271, 273, 280,
283
Porpoise UK/SM: 23, 27, 37,
158, 175, 227, 236, 245, 261,
278, 289, 438, 453, 473
Porpoise US/SM: 182, 222, 314
Port Arthur Can/Corvette: 421
Port Colborne Can/Frigate: 424,
471
Portchester Castle UK/Frigate:
448
Portent US/MS: 329, 386
Porter US/DD: 161, 269-270
Porter (II) US/DD: 525, 528, 535
Porterfield US/DD: 388, 428,
458, 476, 502-503, 527
Portland US/CA: 161, 168, 214,
221, 224, 226, 238, 249, 269,
275-276, 336-337, 370, 373, 388,
392, 406, 452, 461, 463, 479,
488, 502, 527, 536
Posen Ger/Hospital Ship: 497
Potentilla Nor/Corvette: 211, 246,
262-263, 278, 281-282, 304, 360,
421
Pozarica UK/AA Ship: 230-231,
289
Preble (ex-DD 345) US/DM: 161,
291, 324, 334
Premier UK/CVL: 473, 483, 511
Premuda (ex-Dubrovnik) It/DD:

186, 193, 228, 292, 300, see TA 32
Prescott Can/Corvette: 211, 421
President Adams US/APA: 274
President Jackson US/APA: 274, 364
Prestinari It/TB: 61, 68, 293
Preston US/DD: 269, 275-277
Preston (II) US/DD: 437, 458, 476, 503, 527
Pretoria Castle UK/Aux CL: 70, 108, 126
Preussen Ger/ML: 28, 108, 116
Price US/DE: 404
Prichett US/DD: 406, 428, 458, 476, 502, 505
Pride US/DE: 408, 410, 496, 507
Priliv/SKR . . . USSR/Patrol Ship: 117
Primauguet Fr/CL: 44, 50, 54, 274
Primrose UK/Corvette: 96, 240, 398, 421
Primula UK/Corvette: 227-228, 339
Prince Albert UK/LSI: 171
Prince Charles UK/LSI: 171, 247
Prince Henry Can/Aux CL: 90
Prince Leopold UK/LSI: 171, 247, 435
Prince of Wales UK/BB: 100, 125, 139, 146, 159, 163-164
Prince Robert Can/Aux CL: 56, (AA Ship) 369, 534
Prince Rupert Can/Frigate: 395
Princess Astrid UK/LSI: 247
Princess Beatrix UK/LSI: 84, 247, 539
Princess Charlotte Bel/LSI: 171
Princess Victoria UK/ML: 29
Princeton US/CV: 346, 353, 364, 370, 388, 400, 406, 426, 448, 458, 461-462
Pringle US/DD: 334, 345, 391, 399, 471, 504, 510
Prins Albert UK/LSI: 247
Prinz Eugen Ger/CA: 40, 99-100, 188, 192. 193, 218, 293, 446, 460, 470, 485, 496-497, 518-519
Procellaria It/Corvette: 293
Procione It/TB: 40, 42, 80, 95, 97, 103, 118, 127, 129, 157, 175, 200, 282-283, 349
Protector UK/NL: 102
Protée Fr/SM: 36,43
Proteus Gr/SM: 71
Proteus UK/SM: 36, 41, 48, 149, 173, 175, 186, 206, 214, 218, 227, 239, 278
Proteus US/SM Depot Ship: 534
Provana It/SM: 34
Provence Fr/BB: 41, 64, 280
Pruitt US/DM: 161
Prunella UK/Q ship: 33
Puckeridge UK/DD: 339, 344
Puffer US/SM: 358, 372, 390, 410, 415, 439, 479
Puffin UK/Sloop: 421
Pugnale It/TB: see TA 40
Punjabi UK/DD: 23, 25, 32, 46, 100, 121, 198, 208, 213
Purdy US/DD: 504, 509
Pursuer UK/CVE: 389, 401, 409, 444, 453, 468, 534

Pursuit US/MS: 370
Pushkin USSR/ML (N): 18
Putnam US/DD: 504
Pylades UK/MS (ex-BAM 21): 435
Pytchley UK/DD: 302, 363, 421
Python Ger/Supply Ship: 143, 154, 159

Qu'appelle (ex-Foxhound) Can/DD: 424, 433, 441
Quadrant UK/DD: 382, 407, 412, 470, 526, 530, 534
Quail UK/DD: 339, 347, 351, 369
Quality UK/DD: 382, 400, 438, 470, 502, 509, 516, 526, 530
Quantock UK/DD: 339, 350-351
Queen UK/CVE: 511, 517, 520
Queen Elizabeth UK/BB: 97-98, 102, 155-156, 166, 378, 382, 399, 407, 411, 438, 442, 470, 486, 510, 514, 520
Queen Emma UK/LSI: 84, 247, 539
Queenborough UK/DD: 339, 347, 351, 382, 400, 407, 412, 460, 502, 516
Queenfish US/SM: 449, 468, 479, 505
Quentin UK/DD: 242, 244, 282-283
Quiberon Aus/DD: 282, 292, 299, 382, 400, 407, 411, 460, 502, 516, 526, 530, 535
Quick US/DD: 277, 339
Quickmatch Aus/DD: 281, 382, 411, 438, 470, 502, 516, 526, 530
Quilliam UK/DD: 339, 347, 351, 382, 400, 407, 412, 438, 460, 470, 516
Quincy US/CA: 5, 92, 119, 132, 151, 226, 238, 241
Quincy (II) US/CA: 420, 431, 443, 522, 525, 529-530, 533
Quintino Sella It/DD: see Sella
Quorn UK/DD: 265, 412, 440

R. . .: Ger/R boat
R 4: 428
R 6: 22
R 7: 22
R 8: 428
R 14: 428
R 15: 428
R 17: 22
R 18: 22
R 19: 22
R 20: 22
R 21: 22
R 22: 22
R 23: 22
R 24: 22
R 25: 22
R 26: 22
R 27: 22
R 28: 22
R 29: 22
R 30: 22
R 31: 22
R 32: 22, 468

R 33: 1, 22
R 34: 1, 22
R 35: 1, 22, 408
R 36: 1, 22
R 37: 22, 408
R 38: 1, 22, 433
R 39: 1, 22, 390
R 40: 1, 22
R 49: 422
R 53: 112, 121
R 58: 133
R 59: 505
R 60: 135
R 61: 135
R 62: 135
R 63: 112, 121
R 67: 431
R 68: 431
R 69: 497
R 76: 431
R 77: 261
R 78: 261
R 81: 427
R 82: 261
R 86: 261
R 92: 427
R 93: 427
R 96: 427
R 97: 423
R 99: 423
R 100: 427
R 106: 243
R 117: 427, 447
R 119: 428, 505
R 120: 428
R 125: 427
R 129: 427
R 130: 427
R 131: 394
R 145: 501
R 159: 426
R 160: 426, 445-446
R 161: 381, 397
R 163: 408
R 164: 408
R 165: 368, 408
R 166: 408
R 169: 121
R 173: 426
R 177: 489
R 180: 433
R 182: 427, 441
R 184: 247
R 185: 408, 454
R 188: 394, 399
R 190: 394, 399
R 191: 394, 399
R 195: 454
R 196: 408
R 197: 368, 408
R 199: 381
R 200: 390
R 201: 381
R 202: 112, 426, 445-446
R 203: 112, 408
R 204: 404
R 205: 112, 368, 404, 408
R 206: 408
R 207: 408
R 209: 368
R 210: 454
R 211: 418, 454
R 213: 441

R 216: 408
R 217: 441
R 218: 440
R 219: 447
R 223: 426
R 229: 447
R 231: 447
R 232: 427
R 243: 498
R 249: 431
R 260: 501
R 261: 505
R 272: 498
R 273: 498
R 274: 498
R 275: 498
R 276: 498
R 306: 374
R 309: 451
R 311: 459
R 312: 468
R 402: 475

R 101 USSR/R-boat: 125

RA . . .: Ger/R-boat (ex-Fr.,
    UK, Du, & It)
RA 3 (ex-Ch 19): 441
RA 4 (ex-Ch 20): 441
RA 5 (ex-Ch 21): 441
RA 6 (ex-Ch 44): 441
RA 7 (ex-Ch 45): 441
RA 8 (ex-Ch 46): 441
RA 54 (ex-Mv VII): 408
RA 203: 468
RA 256 (ex-VAS 303): 397

R.D. . . . : It/MS
R.D. 31: 292
R.D. 36: 292
R.D. 37: 292
R.D. 39: 292

Ro . . .: Jap/SM:
Ro 33: 176, 193, 210, 239, 250
Ro 34: 176, 186, 193, 210, 239,
    249, 275
Ro 35: 346
Ro 36: 346, 426
Ro 37: 381
Ro 38: 370
Ro 39: 381
Ro 40: 381
Ro 41: 451, 467, 503
Ro 42: 381
Ro 43: 465, 467, 483, 494
Ro 44: 381-382, 426
Ro 45: 402
Ro 46: 465, 483, 487, 505
Ro 47: 452
Ro 48: 426
Ro 49: 467, 483, 503, 508
Ro 50: 467, 483, 487
Ro 55: 483, 487, 491
Ro 56: 503, 508
Ro 60: 164
Ro 61: 164, 179, 251
Ro 62: 179, 251
Ro 63: 179, 251
Ro 64: 179, 251
Ro 65: 179, 251
Ro 67: 179, 251, 499
Ro 68: 179, 251

Ro 100: 295, 346, 355
Ro 101: 284, 295, 335
Ro 102: 284, 295
Ro 103: 284, 295, 334, 341
Ro 104: 346, 355, 417
Ro 105: 346, 355, 417-418
Ro 106: 341, 355, 381, 417
Ro 107: 335
Ro 108: 355, 417
Ro 109: 346, 355, 381, 417,
    426, 465, 467, 483, 488, 513
Ro 110: 373, 383
Ro 111: 373, 417
Ro 112: 417, 426, 465, 467,
    491
Ro 113: 417, 426, 457, 491
Ro 114: 426
Ro 115: 426, 457, 487
Ro 116: 417
Ro 117: 417, 426
Ro 501 (ex U-1224): 403
RT-32 USSR/Trawler (N): 117
RT 44/Neva USSR/Trawler: 129
RT-67 Molotov USSR/Trawler
    (N): 117
Raby US/DE: 417, 483
Raccoon Can/AS Yacht: 248
Racehorse UK/DD: 382, 407,
    411, 417, 438, 514, 520
Radford US/DD: 290-291, 307,
    324, 334-335, 340, 355, 370,
    373, 409, 418, 474, 480, 487-488
Rageot de la Touche Fr/Sloop:
    see SG 15
Raider UK/DD: 339, 349, 351,
    382, 417, 438, 460, 486
Raikomvod USSR/Aux MS
    (BS): see T-38
Raimondo Montecuccoli It/CL:
    see Montecucolli
Rainbow UK/SM: 21, 60
Rajputana UK/Aux CL: 91
Raleigh US/CL: 161, 304, 323,
    337, 391, 482
Rall US/DE: 509
Ralph Talbot US/DD: 161, 168,
    183, 190, 226, 238, 241, 310,
    334-335, 355-356, 367, 372,
    376, 380, 428, 458, 474, 479,
    513
Ramb I It/Aux CL: 80
Ramb II It/Aux CL: 81
Ramb III It/Aux CL: 40, 61, 63,
    84, 104, see Merchant Ship
Ramillies UK/BB: 1, 9, 17, 25-26,
    40, 48, 58, 62-63, 66-67, 75,
    79, 100, 204, 212, 223, 382,
    421-422, 443
Rampart US/MS: see T-282
Ramsay US/DMS: 161
Ramsden US/DE: 402, 535
Ramsey UK/DD: 421
Randolph US/CV: 491, 499, 509,
    516, 525, 533
Ranger US/CV: 5, 92, 132,
    150-151, 216, 236, 273-274,
    295, 305, 318, 359
Ranpura UK/Aux CL: 96
Ransom US/MS: 508, 511
Ranunculus UK/Corvette: see
    Renoncule
Rapid UK/DD: 382, 438, 486,
    501

Rasher US/SM: 358, 379, 390,
    410, 439
Rastoropny USSR/DD (P): 530
Rathburne (ex-DD 113) US/
    APD: 513
Raton US/SM: 365, 372, 410,
    457, 466, 514
Rau 7 Ger/Whaler: 22
Rau 8 Ger/Whaler: 22
Rawalpindi UK/Aux CL: 11
Ray US/SM: 365, 372, 390, 410,
    433, 457, 466, 514
Raymond US/DE: 461
Razyarenny USSR/DD (P/N):
    236, 361, 384-385, 401, 409,
    459, 485
Razyashchi USSR/DD (P): 530
Razorback US/SM: 472, 534
Razumny USSR/DD (P/N): 236,
    280, 294, 361, 384-385, 401,
    459, 472, 485
Razvedchik USSR/Patrol Ship:
    130
Recruit US/MS: 490
Redfin US/SM: 403, 419, 429,
    457
Redfish US/SM: 439, 468
Red Gauntlet UK/MS Trawler:
    344
Redki USSR/DD (P): 530
Redmill UK/DE: 464, 496,
    506
Rednour (ex-DE 592) US/APD:
    517
Redoubt US/DD: 281, 382, 514,
    520
Redoutable Fr/SM: 36, 280
Redpole UK/Sloop: 486
Redstart UK/ML: 170
Regele Carol I Ru/ML: 135, 142
Regele Ferdinand I Ru/DD: 158,
    232, 279, 353, 407, 446
Regent UK/SM: 55, 58, 73, 81,
    93, 111, 236, 313
Reggio It/Aux ML: 126
Regina Can/Corvette: 299, 421,
    436
Reginaldo Giuliani It/SM: see
    Giuliani
Regina Maria Ru/DD: 210, 232,
    279, 304, 407
Regolo It/CL: see Attilio Regolo
Regulus UK/SM: 69
Reid US/DD: 161, 226, 251, 348,
    355, 375-376, 395-396, 409, 418,
    448, 473, 521
Rekordny USSR/DD (P): 530
Relentless UK/DD: 299, 382,
    438, 460
Remey US/DD: 388, 427, 463,
    474, 483, 499, 525
Remo It/SM: 340
Reno US/CL: 415, 426, 448,
    458, 461, 466
Renoncule (ex-Ranunculus)
    Fr/Corvette: 211, 307, 326,
    354-355, 389, 420
Renown UK/BC: 3, 6-7, 9-10,
    12, 14, 18, 19, 21, 23-25, 32-33,
    37, 49-50, 57, 62, 64-65, 67,
    70-71, 73, 77-79, 87, 90-91, 94,
    97, 100-101, 105-107, 113, 120,
    122, 198, 203, 210, 215, 274,

345, 368, 378, 382, 399, 407, 411, 425, 438, 442, 460, 471
Renshaw US/DD: 334, 345, 363-364, 391, 399, 428, 471 474, 480, 494
Repulse UK/BC: 1, 3, 7, 11, 14, 23, 26, 32-33, 64, 68, 71, 76, 97, 100, 146, 159, 163-164
Requin Fr/SM: 284
Requinul Ru/SM: 411
Requisite US/MS: 370
Reserve Aus/MS: 537
Resolution UK/BB: 14, 30, 32, 38, 41, 43, 52, 55-56, 204, 298
Restigouche Can/DD: 14, 29, 217, 265, 267, 268, 295, 424, 433, 441
Retalick UK/DE: 421-422, 435, 440, 447, 469
Retivy USSR/DD (P): 530
Retriever UK/AS Trawler: 219
Reuben James US/DD: 4, 83, 119, 132, 136, 147
Reuben James (II) US/DE: 506
Revenge UK/BB: 100, 204, 298
Revnostny USSR/DD (P): 236, 530
Reynolds US/DE: 533
Rezki USSR/DD (P): 530
Rezvy USSR/DD (P): 530
Rhind US/DD: 92, 108, 132, 151, 308, 339, 350
Rhodes US/DE: 402, 535
Rhodedendron UK/Corvette: 64, 167, 287, 339, 464, 511
Ribble (ex-Johan Maurits van Nassau) Can/Frigate: 454, 496
Riboty It/DD: 34, 61, 68, 70, 300, 312, 349
Rich US/DE: 430, 424
Richard Beitzen Ger/DD: 1, 3, 14, 17, 19, 66, 68, 77, 117, 120, 125, 188, 230, 253, 258, 265, 272, 288
Richard M. Rowell US/DE: 452, 461, 464, 483, 502
Richard P. Leary US/DD: 479, 481, 503
Richard S. Bull US/DE: 461, 483, 502
Richard W. Suesens US/DE: 461, 480, 483, 502
Richelieu Fr/BB: 38, 44, 56-57, 393, 400, 407, 411, 425, 438, 442, 510, 514, 420, 534, 539
Rickey US/DE: 535
Richmond (ex-Fairfax) UK/DD: 143
Richmond US/CL: 295, 312, 319, 323, 337, 396, 482, 523, 525, 527-528, 531, 535
Richthofen Ger/Aircraft Repair Ship: 441
Rigault de Genouilly Fr/Sloop: 9, 41
Riddle US/DE: 502, 509
Rigel It/TB: see TA 28
Riilahti Fin/ML: 112-114, 124, 151, 228, 233, 324, 342
Rimouski Can/Corvette: 421
Ringgold US/DD: 347, 353, 359, 370, 388, 437, 499, 513, 525, 533
Rio Branco Bra/Survey Vessel: 300
Rio de Janeiro Maru Jap/SM Depot ship: 392
Riou UK/DE: 500
Robert F. Keller US/DE: 502, 528
Robert H. Smith US/DM: 502, 503
Robert I. Paine US/DE: 416
Robert K. Huntingdon US/DD: 528, 533
Robert Möhring Ger/Hospital Ship: 489
Robert Müller 6 Ger/Gun Carrier: 497, 508
Roberts UK/Monitor: 274, 338, 347, 350-351, 421, 431, 434, 467
Robin UK/GB: 170
Robinson US/DD: see Newmarket
Robinson (II) US/DD: 427, 463, 474, 480, 498, 512, 523-524
Rochester UK/Sloop: 96, 145, 186, 238, 329, 421
Rock US/SM: 457, 470
Rocket UK/DD: 362, 382, 438
Rockhampton Aus/MS: 406
Rockingham (ex-Swasey) UK/DD: 211
Rockrose UK/Corvette: 315
Rockwood UK/DD: 339, 356, 367
Rocky Mount US/AGC: 498, 513, 523
Rodman US/DD: 245, 415, 421, 431, 444, 502, 507
Rodney UK/BB: 1, 3, 6-7, 9, 11, 23-25, 32-33, 37, 54, 64, 68, 76, 86, 100-101, 139, 144, 242, 274, 333, 339, 347, 351, 421, 431, 434, 439, 452
Roe US/DD: 9?, 119, 339, 409, 482
Roebuck UK/DD: 382, 438, 514, 520, 527
Rogers US/DD: 533
Roi US/CVE: 528, 533
Roland Ger/ML: 3, 47-48, 51, 129, 212, 216, 219, 312, 331, 345, 397
Roland Morillot Fr/SM: 38
Rolf US/DE: 528
Roma It/BB: 283, 349
Romania Ger/ML: 304, 411
Romney UK/MS: 212, 344
Ronquil US/SM: 456
Ronis Lat-USSR/SM (B): 111
Ronquil US/SM: 439
Roper US/DD: 209, 517
Rorqual UK/SM: 36, 43, 48, 77, 87, 98, 111, 129, 141, 145, 153, 236, 247, 251, 284, 293, 300, 313, 336, 360, 398
Rosabelle UK/AS Yacht: 160
Rose Nor/Corvette: 211, 278, 281-282, 360, 389, 395, 421
Roselys Fr/Corvette: 211, 219, 293, 307, 326, 354, 389
Rosita Ger/Patrol boat: see UJ 115
Rosolino Pilo It/TB: see Pilo
Ross US/DD: 428, 452, 533
Ross UK/MS: 31
Rosthern Can/Corvette: 211, 217, 253, 296, 301-302, 305
Rostovtsev USSR/Monitor (BS): 110, 112, 117
Rostov Don/SKR ... USSR/GB (BS): 252
Rota Dan/SM: 346
Rother UK/Frigate: 346, 389
Rotheram UK/DD: 382, 407, 411, 438, 514
Rover UK/SM: 80, 111
Rovigo It/ML: 34
Rowan US/DD: 108, 132, 151, 230, 308, 339, 350-351
Rowe US/DD: 521, 525, 533
Rowley UK/DE: 394, 405, 424, 464
Roxborough (ex-Foote) UK/DD: see Doblestny
Royalist UK/CL: 401, 411, 444, 451, 453, 514, 520, 524, 534
Royal Oak UK/BB: 1, 8
Royal Sovereign UK/BB: 1, 40, 43, 45, 48, 197, 204, 451, see Arkhangelsk
Rubin USSR/Patrol Ship (N): 213
Rubino It/SM: 39-40
Rubis Fr/SM: 21, 28, 30, 37, 41, 53, 58, 62, 67, 126, 265, 446, 475
Ruby UK/AS Trawler: 246
Rudderow US/DE: 498
Rudyerd Bay US/CVE: 458, 476, 493, 509
Ruggiero Settimo It/SM: see Settimo
Ruler UK/CVE: 516, 523
Runner US/SM: 319, 329
Runner (II) US/SM: 526, 534
Ruotsinsalmi Fin/ML: 112-114, 124, 151, 228, 233, 312, 324, 397
Rupert UK/DE: 464, 496
Rushmore US/LSD: 495
Russell US/DD: 92, 108, 183, 190, 199, 214, 221, 224, 226, 254, 258, 269, 275, 370, 388, 409, 418, 480-481, 504
Rutherford US/DE: 524
Ryany USSR/DD (P): 530
Rybitwa Pol/MS: 5
Rye UK/MS: 227, 243, 344
Rym USSR/MS (B): see T-211
Rys Pol/SM: 1, 4, 6
Ryuho (ex-Taigei) Jap/CVL: 284, 361, 372, 415, 430, 499, 529
Ryujo Jap/CV: 160, 169, 171, 178, 181, 187-188, 194-196, 201, 204-205, 220, 223, 235, 249

S ... US/SM
S 25: see P 551, see Jastrzab
S 28: 358
S 29: 329

S 30: 329
S 31: 259
S 35: 336
S 36: 164
S 37: 164, 186, 194, 232
S 38: 164, 170, 194-195, 214, 239, 241
S 39: 160, 164, 194, 197, 214, 239
S 40: 164, 170, 182, 214
S 41: 164, 214, 239, 322
S 42: 214-215
S 43: 214, 239
S 44: 214-215, 222, 239, 241, 347
S 45: 214
S 46: 214, 239, 347
S 47: 214

S . . . Ger/MTB
S 7: 22
S 8: 22
S 10: 1
S 11: 1
S 12: 1
S 13: 1
S 17: 22
S 18: 1, 52, 60
S 19: 1, 22, 39, 40, 42, 45
S 20: 42, 45, 47
S 21: 22, 31, 47, 52
S 22: 22, 52
S 23: 22, 31-32
S 24: 22, 32, 60
S 25: 47
S 26: 32, 39, 42, 71, 84, 87, 95, 116-117, 311, 327
S 27: 45, 47, 60, 84, 95, 110, 117, 225, 252
S 28: 71, 81, 83-85, 116-117, 225, 242, 251-252, 311, 319, 359, 447
S 29: 71, 84, 87, 95, 308, 313
S 30: 22, 32, 78, 82, 243
S 31: 22, 29, 84, 112, 169
S 32: 22
S 33: 22, 53
S 34: 31, 33, 71, 112, 169
S 35: 110, 112, 169, 336
S 36: 40, 53, 229, 243
S 39, 84, 87, 116, 318, 344, 429, 435, 440
S 40: 116-117, 225
S 41: 93, 143, 153
S 42: 93, 359, 446
S 43, 93, 112
S 44: 110
S 45: 359
S 46: 261, 278
S 47: 118, 143, 311, 319
S 48: 127, 133, 234, 278, 285, 318, 366, 484, 487
S 49: 125, 133, 327
S 50: 133, 136, 155, 234
S 51: 136, 155, 157, 319, 327, 359
S 52: 133, 136, 155, 157, 359, 446
S 53: 143, 201
S 54: 52, 78, 112, 118, 121, 228-229, 350
S 55: 87, 93, 95, 121-122, 169, 228-229, 300, 367

S 56: 71, 228-229
S 57: 84, 118, 121
S 58: 70-71, 78, 118, 121-122, 126, 228-229, 289
S 59: 71, 78, 84, 109, 112, 228-229, 243
S 60: 84, 109-110, 121, 228
S 61: 84, 112, 169, 350, 366
S 62: 143, 261, 327, 359, 391, 398
S 63: 234, 261, 285, 318, 327, 363
S 64: 157, 391, 394, 398, 405, 412
S 65: 260, 305, 318, 327, 391, 394, 398
S 66: 278
S 67: 234, 327, 391, 394, 398, 405, 412, 484, 487
S 68: 280, 305, 342, 391
S 69: 265
S 70: 200, 234, 278, 306
S 71: 265, 304
S 72: 225, 252, 311, 319, 327
S 73: 278
S 74: 265, 344, 363, 366
S 75: 265, 306
S 76: 308. 327, 429
S 77: 260, 280, 342
S 79: 261, 327, 434, 435, 440
S 80: 261, 278, 285, 344, 391, 394, 398
S 81: 282-283, 305, 318, 327, 342
S 82: 270, 280, 283, 318, 327
S 83: 278, 318, 327, 344, 359, 391, 398, 405, 412-413, 422, 428-429, 434
S 84: 380, 385, 394, 398, 422-423, 427
S 85: 305, 391, 394, 398, 405, 484, 487
S 86: 308, 318, 344, 391, 394, 398
S 87: 318, 385, 405, 412-413
S 88: 318, 342, 363
S 89: 308, 318, 327, 344, 391
S 90: 318, 327, 429, 434-435
S 91: 318, 327, 429, 434-435, 440, 447
S 92: 308, 318, 391, 394, 398, 484, 487
S 93: 359, 391, 394, 398
S 94: 318, 327, 344, 394
S 96: 355
S 97: 429, 435, 440
S 98: 327, 391, 484, 487
S 99: 385, 391, 394, 398
S 100: 366, 380, 385, 398, 405-406, 412-413, 422-423, 427
S 101: 81, 84, 87, 116-117, 261, 278
S 102: 81, 84, 87, 225, 242, 251-252, 311, 319, 332
S 103: 515
S 104: 93, 143, 153, 201, 234, 278
S 105: 143, 153, 261
S 106: 112
S 107: 133
S 108: 261
S 109: 155, 234
S 110: 155, 285, 318, 327, 342, 344
S 111: 201

S 112: 260, 280, 318, 327, 366, 394, 405, 412-413, 423, 433
S 113: 278
S 114: 307, 318, 327, 366, 429, 434-435, 440
S 115: 280, 283
S 116: 280, 283, 318, 327, 366
S 117: 261, 285, 327, 344, 385, 391, 394, 398, 412, 422
S 119: 307
S 120: 318
S 121: 318, 327, 344
S 122: 318, 327
S 127: 359, 391, 394, 405, 412, 422, 428-429, 434, 484, 487
S 128: 394
S 129: 391, 394, 398
S 130: 385, 394, 405, 412-413 422-423, 428-429, 484, 507
S 131: 446
S 132: 429, 434-435, 440
S 133: 391, 398, 405, 412, 422, 428-429, 434
S 135: 394, 429, 434-435, 440
S 136: 342, 366, 376, 380. 385, 394, 405, 412-413, 422-423
S 137: 385
S 138: 366, 376, 380, 385, 398, 405-406, 413, 422-423, 427
S 139: 366, 376, 394, 398, 422
S 140: 366, 376, 398, 405, 412-413, 422
S 141: 366, 376, 380, 385, 398, 405, 412
S 142: 360, 372, 376, 380, 385, 394, 405, 412-413, 422-423, 427
S 143: 366, 376, 380, 385, 394, 398, 405-506, 423, 427
S 144: 394, 398, 405, 413, 422-423, 427
S 145: 394, 398, 405, 412-413, 422, 428-429, 433
S 146: 366, 394, 398, 405, 412-413, 422-423, 427
S 147: 398, 405
S 149: 448
S 150: 385, 398, 405, 412-413, 422, 423, 427
S 159: 398
S 167: 398, 405, 422, 423, 429, 434-435, 440, 493
S 168: 413, 422, 428-429, 434-435, 484, 486, 507
S 169: 413, 422, 423, 427
S 171: 398, 413, 422-423, 427
S 172: 413, 422-423, 427
S 173: 422-423, 427
S 174: 422, 428-429, 434-435, 440, 447, 484, 487, 507
S 175: 413, 422-423, 428-429, 434-435, 484, 486, 487, 507
S 176: 434-435, 440, 484, 507
S 177: 412, 422-423, 428-429, 434-435, 440, 484, 487, 507
S 178: 412, 422-423
S 179: 412, 422-423
S 180: 412, 422, 428-429, 434-435, 440, 484
S 181: 422-423, 428-429, 434-435, 440, 484, 487, 500
S 182: 434-435
S 183: 440, 453

S 184: 440, 447
S 185: 440, 453, 475
S 186: 440, 453, 504
S 187: 398, 413, 422-423, 427
S 188: 413, 422-423, 427
S 189: 412, 422-423
S 190: 412, 423, 428-429, 435
S 191: 440, 453
S 192: 440, 453, 475
S 193: 440, 493
S 194: 440, 484, 486
S 195: 440
S 196: 440, 484, 486
S 197: 440, 484, 486
S 198: 440
S 199: 484, 486, 487
S 200: 453
S 202: 507
S 204: 484, 507
S 205: 484, 507
S 206: 484, 487, 507
S 207: 507
S 209: 484, 487, 507
S 210: 484, 500, 507
S 211: 484, 487, 507
S 212: 507
S 214: 507
S 219: 484, 507
S 220: 493
S 221: 484, 487, 507
S 222: 484, 487, 507
S 223: 484, 487, 507
S 304: 407
S 701: 440, 484, 486, 487
S 702: 453
S 703: 487, 507
S 704: 487, 507
S 705: 484, 507
S 706: 507

S . . . : USSR/SM
S-1 (B): 13, 111
    S-2 (B): 15
    S-3 (B): 110
    S-4 (B): 111, 116, 130, 139, 146,
        228-229, 238, 455, 482
    S-5 (B): 111, 130
    S-6 (B): 111, 130
    S-7 (B): 111, 116, 137,
        146-147, 229, 233, 241,
        259, 271
    S-8 (B): 111, 116, 146,
    S-9 (B): 110, 116, 147, 152,
        257, 259, 343
    S-10 (B): 111-112
    S-11 (B): 116
    S-12 (B): 257, 259, 273, 343
    S-13 (B): 246, 253, 261, 455,
        489
    S-14 (N): 385, 425-426, 436,
        459
    S-15 (N): 375, 385, 414,
        445-446, 450
    S-31 (BS): 216, 254, 330, 368,
        402, 404, 447
    S-32 (BS): 216
    S-33 (BS): 304, 330, 353, 368,
        411, 447
    S-34 (BS): 149
    S-35 (BS): 126
    S-36 (BS): 126
    S-37 (BS): 126
    S-38 (BS): 126

S-51 (P/N): 259, 319, 331,
    345, 445, 450, 459
S-54 (P/N): 259, 319, 331, 345,
    404
S-55 (P/N): 259, 310, 319, 331,
    345
S-56 (P/N): 259, 310, 319, 331,
    385, 393, 414, 436, 450-451
S-101 (B/N): 111, 139, 169,
    191, 208, 219, 310, 319, 331,
    343, 450, 459
S-102 (B/N): 111, 117, 139,
    148, 169, 176, 198, 310, 319,
    345, 375, 385, 459
S-103 (N): 375, 385, 414,
    445-446, 450
S-104 (N): 385, 404, 425-426,
    459
SAT 27/Ostee Ger/Aux. GB: 233
SC . . . : US/SC
    SC 497: 247
    SC 405: 247
    SC 514: 247
    SC 530: 247
    SC 1042: 344
    SC 1045: 344

Sh . . . : USSR/SM
    Sh-102: 530
    Sh-104: 530
    Sh-117: 530
    Sh-119: 530
    Sh-122: 530
    Sh-123: 530
    Sh-126: 530
    Sh-127: 530
    Sh-134: 530
    Sh-135: 530
SF . . . : Ger/Siebel Ferry
    SF 121: 453
    SF 270: 399
    SF 273: 399
    SF 274: 399
    SF 284: 419
SG . . . : Ger/Patrol Vessels
    SG 7: see Brandenburg
    SG 11 (ex-Alice Robert): 414
    SG 15 (ex-Rageot de la
        Touche): 390, 414
    SG 16 (ex-Amiral Sénès): 390
    SG 20 (ex-Generale Achille
        Papa): 381
SGB . . . : UK/Steam Gunboat
    SGB 5: 247
    SGB 6: 229, 318
    SGB 7: 229
    SGB 8: 229

Shch . . . : USSR/SM
    Shch-118 (P): 532
    Shch 201 (BS): 172, 330, 361,
        368, 408, 411
    Shch-202 (BS): 402, 408, 411
    Shch-203: (BS) 330, 361
    Shch-204 (BS): 112
    Shch-205 (BS): 112, 158,
        216, 218, 240, 380, 411
    Shch-206 (BS): 112, 135
    Shch-207 (BS): 260, 330
    Shch-208 (BS): 216
    Shch-209 (BS): 112, 216, 304,
        380, 437
    Shch-210 (BS): 125

Shch-211 (BS): 125, 135, 149
Shch-212 (BS): 145, 216
Shch-213 (BS): 193, 216
Shch-214 (BS): 149, 173, 216,
    218
Shch-215 (BS): 149, 330, 404,
    441, 447
Shch-216 (BS): 125, 260, 330,
    368, 380
Shch-301 (B): 130
Shch-302 (B): 138, 261
Shch-303 (B): 6, 139, 229,
    233, 241, 259, 261, 273, 324,
    455, 482
Shch-304 (B): 228-229, 233,
    261
Shch-305 (B): 259, 261
Shch-306 (B): 138, 259, 261
Shch-307 (B): 121, 129, 257,
    259, 273, 455, 482
Shch-308 (B): 129, 246, 253,
    257
Shch-309 (B): 15, 111, 152,
    243, 246, 455, 482
Shch-310 (B): 111, 257, 259,
    455, 482, 501
Shch-311 (B): 15, 111, 116,
    139, 261
Shch-317 (B): 13, 135, 137,
    228-229, 233
Shch-318 (B): 455, 482
Shch-319 (B): 13, 137
Shch-320 (B): 139, 228-229,
    238, 261
Shch-322 (B): 13, 111, 130
Shch-323 (B): 13, 111, 142,
    253
Shch-323 (B): 312
Shch-324 (B): 15, 111, 147
Shch-401 (N): 109, 115, 124,
    144, 176, 208
Shch-402 (N): 12, 115, 124,
    144, 191-192, 230, 240, 294,
    319, 345, 436, 450
Shch-403 (N): 109, 152, 169,
    191, 218, 230, 240, 295, 319,
    331, 345
Shch-404 (N): 12, 109, 169,
    176, 203-204, 294, 345
Shch-405 (B): 243
Shch-406 (B): 229, 232, 241,
    259, 261, 271, 324
Shch-407 (B): 243, 246, 257,
    455, 482
Shch-408 (B): 324
Shch-421 (N): 109, 124, 148,
    180, 203-204
Shch-422 (N): 115, 133, 180,
    198, 240, 302, 319, 331
Shch-423 (N/P): 47

SKA-. . . : USSR/Patrol Boats
(SC type MO IV based in BS)
    SKA-025: 352
    SKA-032: 352
    SKA-041: 327
    SKA-051: 297
    SKA-063: 173
    SKA-065: 311
    SKA-084: 352
    SKA-0105: 365
    SKA-0111: 176
    SKA-0114: 365

SKA-0135: 365
SKA-0141: 297
SKA-0158: 365
SKA-0178: 365
SKA-0192: 365
SKA-01012: 366
SKR. . .: USSR/Patrol vessels (ex-trawler etc)
SKR-12/Tuman (N): 125
SKR-18/Fedor Litke (N): 245, 334, 361
SKR-19/Dezhnev (N): 244, 361
SKR-20/ . . (N): 465, 471
SKR-23/Musson (N): 119, 245
SKR-27/Brilliant (N): 116
SKR-28/Rubin (N): 334
SKR-29/Zhemchug (N): 442
SKR-30/Sapfir (N): 334
SKR-70/Voronin (N): 116
SKR-101/Kuban (BS): 144
SKR-102/Petrash (BS): 144
SKR-112/Don (BS): 172
SKR-113/Bug (BS): 141, 144
SKR-114/Dnestr (BS): 141, 144, 172
Sabine US/Oiler: 183, 190, 207, 239
Sabre UK/DD: 31-33
Sachsenwald Ger/Weather Observation Ship: 101
Sackville Can/Corvette: 211, 238, 354
Sado Jap/Frigate: 410, 439
Saelen Dan/TB: 346
Saetta It/DD: 42-43, 67, 78, 81, 90, 95, 165, 189, 228, 245, 280, 292-293
Safari/P 211 UK/SM: 227, 234, 245, 261, 267, 278, 286, 293, 313, 323, 336, 339
Sagara Maru Jap/Seaplane Depot Ship: 166
Sagi Jap/TB: 468
Saginaw US/CVE Bay: 451, 460, 483, 493, 502
Sagiri Jap/DD: 159-160, 163, 167
Sagittario It/TB: 47,67, 74, 102, 186, 245, 267, 300, 312-313, 349
Saguenay Can/DD: 5, 9, 66, 211, 238
Sahib P 212 UK/SM: 230, 255, 278, 284, 293, 300, 313
Sailfish US/SM: 164, 194, 197, 232, 329, 372, 439
St Albans (ex-Thomas) UK/DD: 122, 212-213
St Apollo UK/AS Trawler: 96
Saint Bon It/SM: 143, 151, 156, 175
St Catherines Can/Frigate: 395
St Croix (ex-McCook) Can/DD: 211, 217, 234, 251, 265, 354
St David UK/Hospital Ship: 386
St Elstan UK/AS Trawler: 219
St Francis (ex-Bancroft) Can/DD: 211, 354
St George US/Seaplane Tender: 517
St John Can/Frigate: 424, 448, 471, 490

St Laurent Can/DD: 5, 14, 29, 66, 286-287, 326 395, 424
St Lo (ex-Midway) US/CVE: 461, 463
St Louis US/CL: 161, 183, 221, 226, 290, 324, 335-336, 391, 427, 437, 471, 499, 503, 527
St Paul US/CA: 525, 529-530, 533
St Pierre Can/Frigate: 521
St Thomas (ex-Sandgate Castle) Can/Corvette: 469
Sakhtouris (ex-Peony) Gr/ Corvette: 339, 473
Saladin UK/DD: 31-32, 131, 405, 421
Salamander UK/MS: 31, 230
Salamaua US/CVE: 479, 483, 513, 522
Salamonie US/Oiler: 115
Salier (ex-Hammond) Ger/Patrol boat: 27, see V6115
Salinas US/Oiler: 146
Salisbury UK/DD: 215
Salmon UK/SM: 5, 13, 41
Salmon US/SM: 170, 185, 222, 279, 343, 347, 358, 456
Salopian UK/Aux CL: 99
Salpa It/SM: 34, 40, 71, 76, 91, 99, 111
Salt Lake City US/CA: 161, 168, 183, 190, 207, 226, 239, 249, 254, 263, 312, 337, 370, 388, 448, 457, 464, 466, 473, 482, 487, 493, 503, 527
Saltash UK/MS: 31
Salute US/MS: 523
Salvia UK/Corvette: 67, 74, 95, 170
Samidare Jap/DD: 162, 170, 177, 182, 194-195, 221, 235, 248, 252, 264, 268, 271, 275-277, 337, 356, 361, 364, 414, 418, 430, 439
Samphire UK/Corvette: 167-168, 289, 292
Sampson US/DD: 592, 119, 418
Samuel B. Roberts US/DE: 461, 463
Samuel Chase US/APA: 339, 350
Samuel N. Moore US/DD: 476, 499, 522, 528, 530, 533
Samuel S. Miles US/DE: 452, 503, 509
San Diego US/CL: 226, 254, 258, 269, 275, 335, 364, 370, 373, 387, 392, 415, 426, 458, 464, 474, 476, 491-492, 499-500, 509 525, 533
San Franciso US/CA: 5, 161, 168, 182, 185, 199, 226, 239, 249, 254, 263, 269, 271, 275-276, 323, 336-337, 359, 370, 373, 388, 392, 406, 427, 474, 476, 491, 502
Sangamon US/CVE: 273, 335, 388, 392, 409, 437, 451, 460, 463, 502, 511, 516
San Giorgio It/CA: 36, 76
S. Giusto It/Aux MS: 34
San Jacinto US/CVL: 415, 426, 448, 458, 461-462, 465-466, 474,

476, 491, 499-500, 507, 509, 516, 522, 525
San Juan US/CL: 226, 238, 241, 249, 254, 269, 335, 364, 370, 373, 388, 426, 474, 476, 491, 499-500, 509, 522, 525, 533
San Martino It/TB: 292
San Pedro US/Frigate: see EK-5
Sanae Jap/TB: 365
Sandlance US/SM: 410, 433, 514
Sandoval US/APA: 517
Sands (ex-DD 243) US/APD: 334, 348, 375-376, 395, 396
Sandwich UK/Sloop: 238
Santa Fe US/CL: 319, 323, 336-337, 353, 359, 364, 370, 373, 388, 392, 399, 406, 426, 448, 458, 461, 464, 474, 476, 491, 493, 499-500
Santarosa It/SM: 39, 42, 60, 74, 78, 90, 94, 98, 107, 146, 165, 202, 236, 292
Santee US/CVE: 273, 329, 337, 409, 451, 460, 463, 502, 509, 511, 516
Santorre Santarosa It/SM: see Santarosa
Sanuki Maru Jap/Seaplane Depot Ship: 162, 177, 182
Sanyo Maru Jap/Seaplane Depot Ship: 162, 177, 182, 186, 194
Sapfir USSR/Patrol Vessel: see SKR-30
Saphir Fr/SM: 36, 284
Saracen/P 213 UK/SM: 240, 278, 293, 300, 313, 336,
Saranac US/CG Cutter: see Banff
Saratoga US/CV: 163, 168, 177, 222, 226, 238, 241, 249, 253, 290-291, 335, 364, 370, 388, 400, 407, 412, 492, 494, 538
Sardonyx UK/DD: 85, 421
Sargent Bay US/CVE: 458, 493, 502
Sargo US/SM: 164, 166, 184, 257, 329, 365, 390, 402
Saskatchewan (ex-Fortune) Can/DD: 424, 433
Satsuki Jap/DD: 162, 169, 173, 194, 335
Satterlee II US/DD: 420, 443
Saturn USSR/Patrol Ship (B): 129-130
Satyr UK/SM: 384, 396, 419, 446
Saucy (ex-Arabis) US/Corvette: 322
Saufley US/DD: 334, 345-346, 355, 391, 399, 471, 480, 498, 523-524
Saukko Fin/SM: 13, 115, 432
Saumarez UK/DD: 374-375, 421-422, 439, 452, 464-465, 510, 514, 520
Sauro It/DD: 49, 52, 61, 68, 90
Saury US/SM: 164, 170, 182, 192, 194, 238, 322, 468
Savage UK/DD: 374-375, 410, 435, 446, 465, 473, 475, 517-519, 535
Savage US/DE: 402
Savannah US/CL: 92, 108, 132,

273, 308, 334, 339-340, 342, 350-351
Savo Island US/CVE: 461, 474, 480-481, 502, 535
Savorgnan de Brazza Fr/Sloop: 55, 58, 64
Sawfish US/SM: 296, 322, 336, 372, 417, 456
Saxifrage UK/Corvette: 291, 309, 344
Sazanami Jap/DD: 194-195, 214, 220, 235, 244, 345, 379
Sborul Ru/TB: 142
Scabbardfish US/SM: 468, 491
Scamp US/SM: 306, 322, 347, 365, 379
Scarab UK/GB: 347, 443, 445, 449
Scarborough UK/Sloop: 51, 59, 88, 421
Sceptre UK/SM: 355, 396, 446
Scharnhorst Ger/BB: 4, 11, 19, 22, 24-25, 33, 37, 39-40, 71, 76, 78-79, 81, 85-87, 89, 91, 121, 188-189, 293, 303, 348, 355, 374,375
Schenck US/DD: 268, 297, 375
Schiff 5: see Hansa
Schiff 9 (ex-Koblenz) Ger/Aux: 22
Schiff 10/Thor Ger/Aux CL: 36, 41, 46, 57, 68, 91, 94, 202, 229, 236, 292
Schiff 11 (ex-Hanonia) Ger/ML: 20
Schiff 14/Coronel Ger/Aux CL: 301
Schiff 16/Atlantis Ger/Aux CL: 21, 28-29, 36, 52, 54, 77, 80, 83, 93, 99, 106, 143, 154, 159
Schiff 18/Meteor Ger/Q ship: 22, 279
Schiff 19/Lola Ger/SC: 145, 330, 360, 361, 380
Schiff 21/Widder Ger/Aux CL: 37, 47
Schiff 23/Stier Ger/Aux CL: 217, 224, 241, 259
Schiff 28/Michel Ger/Aux CL: 200, 210, 214, 236, 246, 291, 332, 344
Schiff 33/Pinguin Ger/Aux CL: 37, 39-40, 50, 65, 76, 98
Schiff 36/Orion Ger/Aux CL: 22, 37, 48, 52, 67-68, 128, 158
Schiff 41/Kormoran Ger/Aux CL: 68, 74, 82, 112, 153
Schiff 45/Komet Ger/Aux CL: 41, 67-68, 71, 126, 128, 152, 158, 261, 264
Schiff 53/Doggerbank (ex-Speybank) Ger/ML: 200, 210, 303
Schlesien Ger/BB: 6, 22, 497, 512
Schleswig-Holstein Ger/BB: 1, 4-6, 22, 475
Schley (ex-DD 103) US/APD: 161, 334-335
Schroeder US/DD: 347, 353, 359, 370, 388, 437, 499, 522, 525, 533
Schwabenland Ger/Catapult Ship: 396

Sciesa It/SM: 34, 42, 47, 69, 236, 271
Scilla It/Aux ML: 35, 41, 47
Scimitar UK/DD: 31-32, 53, 85, 109
Scipione Africano It/CL: 340-341, 350
Scirè It/SM: 37, 42, 46, 57, 62, 137, 166, 238
Scirocco It/DD: 42, 47, 98, 105, 116, 127, 175, 183, 193, 200, 202
Scorpion UK/DD: 374-375, 421, 423, 446, 465, 468, 475
Scorpion US/SM: 314, 319, 336, 365
Scotstoun UK/Aux CL: 8, 35
Scott UK/Aux Ship: 171
Scourge UK/DD: 374, 421, 423, 442, 446, 464, 468, 475, 517-518
Scout UK/DD: 165, 194-196, 204
Scribner US/DE: 502
Scrivia It/Aux ML: 261
Scroggins US/DE: 506
Sculpin US/SM: 164, 178, 257, 329, 343, 365
Scylla UK/CL: 256, 274, 289, 302, 332, 350-351, 420
Seabelle UK/AS Trawler: 93
Sea Cat US/SM: 534
Sea Devil US/SM: 329, 505
Seadog UK/SM: 288, 375, 384
Seadog US/SM: 456, 505, 522
Seadragon US/SM: 183-184, 232, 257, 284, 306, 379, 402, 456, 522
Seagull UK/MS: 213, 220, 286, 374
Seaham UK/MS: 227
Seahorse UK/SM: 5, 17
Seahorse US/SM: 379, 402, 419, 429, 456
Seal UK/SM: 13, 23, 28
Seal US/SM: 164, 170, 194, 197, 222, 238, 279, 322, 388, 392, 439, 456
Sealion UK/SM: 5, 23, 37, 40, 78, 85, 87, 152, 154, 171
Sealion US/SM: 419, 449, 468, 472, 496
Seanymph UK/SM: 355
Sea Owl US/SM: 472, 505, 522
Sea Poacher US/SM: 515, 526
Searaven US/SM: 164, 257, 279, 289, 365, 388, 392, 449
Searcher UK/CVE: 401, 408, 410, 444, 453, 511, 517-518
Sea Robin US/SM: 479, 496, 526
Sea Rover UK/SM: 382, 400, 412, 438, 460, 473
Seascout UK/SM: 474
Seawolf UK/SM: 5, 23, 29, 48, 58, 152, 198, 230
Seawolf US/SM: 162, 164, 184, 191, 197, 206, 222, 238, 266, 314, 329, 343, 358, 379, 429, 452
Sebago US/CG Cutter: see Walney
Sebenico (ex-Beograd) It/DD: 145, 206, see TA 43

Sederstrom US/DE: 502
Seeadler Ger/TB: 3, 10-12, 14, 19, 22, 57-58, 60-61, 68, 71, 77, 189, 200, 217
Seerobbe Ger/Vp boat: see V 5309
Seeteufel Ger/Vp boat: see V 5505
Segundo US/SM: 472, 495, 522, 534
Selene UK/SM: 495
Selfridge US/DD: 161, 168, 226, 238, 249-250, 310, 335, 356, 427-428
Sella It/DD: 34, 83, 88, 136, 307, 350
Sellstrom US/DE: 402, 535
Seminole US/Tug: 269
Sendai Jap/CL: 159-160, 163, 166, 173, 178, 181, 187, 194, 196, 201, 205, 221, 253, 252-253, 271, 275-277, 364
Senegalais Fr/DE: 410, 539
Sennen UK/Sloop (ex-Champlain): 321, 326
Sennet US/SM: 491, 505, 526
Sentinel US/SM: 340
Sep Pol/SM: 1, 4, 6
Seraph/P 219 UK/SM: 278, 280, 339
Serapis UK/DD: 421, 446, 464-465, 473, 475, 491-492
Serdity (ex-Lichoi) USSR/DD (B): 112, 115, 117-118
Serp-I-Molot USSR/Repair Ship (B): 130
Serpente It/SM: 57, 70, 75, 84, 122, 128, 134, 140, 144
Sesia It/Aux ML: 261
Sestroretsk USSR/GB (B): 14, 131, 384
Settembrini It/SM: 42, 47, 62, 70, 94-95, 115, 134, 144, 149, 154-155
Settimo It/SM: 34, 42, 54, 74, 76, 81, 94, 98, 120, 122, 156, 292
Settsu Jap/Target Ship: 529
Severn UK/SM: 23, 27-28, 37, 111, 360
Severny Veter (ex-Northwind) USSR/Icebreaker (N): 465
Seydlitz Ger/CA: 508
Seymour UK/DE: 447, 484, 487, 493
Sfax Fr/SM: 6, 13, 21, 27, 68
Sgarallino It/Aux ML: 34
Shad US/SM: 272, 292, 314, 358, 449, 515
Shah UK/CVE: 400, 417, 457, 514, 520
Shakespeare/P 221 UK/SM: 278, 323, 336, 339, 350, 473
Shalimar UK/SM: 471, 473
Shamrock Bay US/CVE: 480, 516
Shannon US/DM: 502, 513
Shangri La (exHancock): US/CVE: 500, 516, 522, 525, 533
Shark UK/SM: 5, 23, 29, 41
Shark UK/DD: see Svenner
Shark US/SM: 164, 183

Shark (II) US/SM: 419, 456
Sharpshooter UK/MS: 31, 203
Shasta US/AE: 522
Shaumyan USSR/DD (BS): 112,
   118, 124, 126, 132, 141-143,
   147, 150, 172-173, 175, 179,
   183, 190, 197, 199, 206
Shaw US/DD: 161
Shaw II US/DD: 271, 275-276,
   375-376, 428, 469, 480-481,
   495, 503
Shawinigan Can/Corvette: 469
Shchit USSR/MS (BS): see
   T-404
Shea US/DM: 502, 511, 517
Shearwater UK/Corvette: 391,
   475
Shediac Can/Corvette: 184,
   216, 286
Sheffield UK/CL: 3, 6-8, 11, 23-25,
   27, 32, 49-50, 63, 65, 67, 70-71,
   73, 77-79, 87, 90-91, 94, 97,
   100-101, 105, 140, 198, 274,
   287-288, 302, 374, 401, 411
Sheldrake UK/Corvette: 306,
   412
Shelton US/DE: 452
Shepparton Aus/MS: 406
Sherbrooke Can/Corvette: 251,
   295, 310
Shigure Jap/DD: 214, 221, 235,
   252, 271, 275, 341, 345, 356,
   361, 364, 414, 418, 430,
   462-463, 479
Shikari UK/DD: 31, 53
Shikinami Jap/DD: 159, 163,
   166, 173, 178, 181, 187, 194,
   196, 205, 221, 235, 248, 252,
   271, 275-277, 306, 383, 418,
   449
Shimakaze Jap/DD: 337, 361,
   415, 418, 430, 462, 466
Shimotsuki Jap/DD: 415, 430,
   462, 472
Shimushu Jap/Frigate: 159-160,
   166, 173, 187, 468
Shinano Jap/CV: 468
Shinonome Jap/DD: 159, 163,
   167
Shinyo (ex-Scharnhorst) Jap/
   CVL: 468
Shiokaze Jap/DD: 160, 169-170,
   235, 472
Shipley Bay US/CVE: 458
Shirakumo Jap/DD: 159, 163,
   167, 178, 187, 194, 196, 200,
   204-205, 221, 235, 249
Shiranui Jap/DD: 156, 179, 190,
   194, 204, 221, 233, 290-291,
   459, 462, 465
Shirataka Jap/ML: 169, 194, 196,
   235, 449
Shiratsuyu Jap/DD: 214, 221,
   235, 252, 268, 271, 275, 361,
   364, 414, 418, 430
Shkiv USSR/MS (B): see T-208
Shirayuki Jap/DD: 159, 163, 166,
   173, 178, 181, 187, 194, 196,
   204-205, 221, 235, 263, 271,
   275-277, 306
Shkval USSR Patrol Ship (BS):
   148, 225, 265, 267, 286, 327,
   330

Shoho Jap/CVL: 214
Shokaku Jap/CV: 156, 179, 184,
   204, 214, 235, 248-249, 254,
   263, 268-269, 361, 415, 430
Shonan Jap/Frigate: 491
Shoreham UK/Sloop: 26, 36, 46,
   88, 129, 339, 344, 479
Shoshone US/CG Cutter: see
   Landguard
Shpil USSR/MS (B): see T-207
Shropshire UK/CA: 7, 9, 12-14,
   28, 78-80, (Aus), 367, 375-376,
   380, 396, 409, 418, 437, 451,
   461, 463, 474, 479, 487-488,
   524, 533
Shtag USSR/MS (B): see T-212
Shtorm USSR/Patrol Ship (BS):
   148, 172, 252, 254, 260, 267,
   319, 327, 330
Shubrick US/DD: 339-340, 342,
   420, 431, 444, 517
Sibiryakov USSR/Ice Breaker (N)
   244
Sibyl/P 217 UK/SM: 278, 280,
   300, 313, 352
Sibylle Fr/SM: 21, 23
Sicard (ex-DD 346) US/DM:
   161, 364
Sickle UK/SM: 313, 317, 323,
   336, 358
Sidi-Ferruch Fr/SM: 6, 49, 274
Sigourney US/DD: 363, 391,
   399, 471, 474, 480, 495, 498,
   512
Sigsbee US/DD: 347, 359, 370,
   388, 437, 499, 509
Sikh UK/DD: 23-25, 27, 29, 60,
   101, 120, 150, 158, 165, 176,
   180, 189 200-201, 227, 238,
   257
Silach USSR/Icebreaker (B): 111
Silja Nor/MS Whaler: 203
Silny USSR/DD (B): 112, 115,
   117, 132, 138, 207, 384
Silversides US/SM: 209, 237, 289,
   329, 358, 372, 402, 410, 456,
   479, 505
Silverton UK/DD: see
   Krakowiak
Simoon UK/SM: 336, 358
Simoun Fr/DD: 443
Simpson US/DD: 68, 83, 132,
   136, 184
Sims US/DD: 92, 108, 132, 183,
   190, 199, 214
Sims (II) US/APD (ex-DE 154):
   517
Sioux (ex-Vixen) Can/DD: 421,
   423, 442, 444, 446, 452, 465,
   468, 473, 475, 491-492
Sirdar UK/DD: 400, 438, 453,
   474
Sirena It/SM: 39-40, 50, 66, 79,
   96, 101, 225, 227
Sirène Fr/SM: 280
Sirio It/TB: 67, 133, 293, 300
Sirius UK/CL: 242, 274, 282,
   293, 339-340, 350, 356, 360,
   421, 443
Sirocco Fr/DD: 10, 30-32
Sirtori It/TB: 127
Sisu Fin/Icebreaker: 358
Sitkoh Bay US/CVE: 458

Skagerrak Ger/ML: 108, 294,
   384
Skagerrak Ger/Vp boat: see
   V 6408
Skate UK/DD: 53, 131, 421
Skate US/SM: 377, 392, 410,
   432, 449, 456, 459, 522
Skeena Can/DD: 5, 29, 51, 131,
   211, 238, 259, 318, 326, 424,
   433, 441, 454
Skill US/MS: 353
Skipjack UK/SM: 31-32
Skipjack US/SM: 164, 215,
   238, 388, 392
Skirmish US/MS: 503, 505
Skory USSR/DD (B): 130
Skylark US/MS: 503
Slavny USSR/DD (B): 130, 132,
   147, 157
Slazak (ex-Bedale) Pol/DD: 247,
   339, 351, 421
Sleuth UK/SM: 505
Slinger UK/CVE: 470
Sloat US/DE: 402, 507
Smalley US/DD: 521, 525, 533
Smartt US/DE: 413
Smeli Bul/TB: 142
Smeli Yu/SM: 91
Smely (ex-Letuchy) USSR/DD
   (B): 110, 121
Smeraldo It/SM: 34, 42, 70, 75,
   84, 87, 101
Smerch (S-8) USSR/Patrol Ship:
   114, 117
Smetlivy USSR/DD (B): 112,
   115, 130, 132, 148
Smeul Ru/TB: 142, 210, 232,
   285
Smiter UK/CVE: 535
Smith US/DD: 269, 310, 348,
   355, 375-376, 380, 395-396,
   473, 480, 495, 503, 513, 524
Smolny USSR/SM Depot ship
   (B): 138
Smyshleny USSR/DD (BS):
   112-113, 128, 143-144, 148,
   152, 156, 171, 173, 175-176,
   180, 182, 197, 215
Snapdragon UK/Corvette: 129,
   227
Snapper UK/SM: 5, 23, 29, 40,
   48, 58, 78,
Snapper US/SM: 164, 296, 347,
   365, 456
Sneg USSR/TB (B): 117, 130
Snook US/SM: 319, 336, 347,
   365, 379, 456
Snowberry Can/Corvette: 250,
   346, 369, 378
Snowden US/DE: 403, 416
Snowflake UK/Corvette: 213,
   315, 320-321, 326
Söbjörnen Dan/MS: 346
Soemba Ger/Gun Carrier: 497,
   508
Soemba Du/GB: 339, 420, 434
Soerabaja Du/Coast Defence
   Ship: 167, 191
Söhesten Dan/MS: 347
Söhunden Dan/MS: 346
Sokaitei . . . : Jap/MS: see W. . . :
Sokai-Tokumu-Tei . . . :
   Jap/Aux MS: see W . . . :

Sokol (ex-Urchin) Pol/SM: 87, 140, 153, 334, 358, 360
Sokol Yu/ML: 91
Sokrushitelny USSR/DD (N): 109, 121, 134, 203, 213, 220, 256, 279-280
Solent UK/SM: 505
Solferino It/TB: 61
Solomons US/CVE: 403, 416-417
Sölöven Dan/MS: 347
Somali Fr/DD: 443, 539,
Somali UK/DD: 23-25, 27, 32, 84, 98, 100-101, 171, 212, 217, 230, 243, 256-257
Somaliland (ex-PF 90) UK/ Frigate: 471
Somers US/DD: 108, 331, 379, 420, 423, 443
Somersetshire UK/Hospital Ship: 206
Sondra S. Afr/AS Trawler: 299
Songkhla Thai/TB: 76
Soobrazitelny USSR/DD (BS): 113, 128, 132, 136, 138, 147-148, 152, 155, 173, 175, 179, 183, 206, 209-210, 212, 216, 222, 226, 252, 254, 260, 267, 281, 285, 287, 297, 301
Söridderen Dan/MS: 347
Soryu Jap/CV: 156, 168, 178, 181, 190, 194, 196-197, 204, 220, 223-224
Souffleur Fr/SM: 36, 106-107
Söulven Dan/MS: 346
South Dakota US/BB: 269-270, 275-277, 333, 338, 370, 373, 387, 392, 406, 427, 430, 458, 474. 476, 491, 499-500, 509, 511, 525, 529-530, 533-534
Southampton UK/CL: 3, 6-8, 11, 23-25, 27, 31-33, 67, 74, 274
Southard (ex-DD 207) US/DMS: 263, 275-276, 481, 503, 517
Southdown UK/DD: 306, 394, 519
Southerland US/DD: 528-530, 533
Southwind US/Icebreaker: 460
Southwold UK/DD: 189, 201-202
Sovershenny USSR/DD (BS): 150
Sovetskaya Ukraina USSR/BB (BS): 126
Soya Maru Jap/Aircraft Depot ship: 200
Spada It/TB: see TA 38
Spadefish US/SM: 439, 468, 479, 495, 522
Spark UK/SM: 471, 529
Spartan UK/CL: 386
Speaker UK/CVE: 470, 502, 516
Spearfish UK/SM: 5, 6, 23, 37 41, 46
Spearfish US/SM: 164, 182, 210, 232, 379, 419
Spectacle US/MS: 517
Speed US/MS: 402, 408
Speedwell UK/MS: 109, 171, 203, 208
Speedy UK/MS: 169, 227, 243
Spence US/DD: 346, 355, 364, 372, 391, 427, 474

Spencer US/CG Cutter: 136, 253, 296, 301-302, 305, 318-319, 329, 495, 503, 512, 523
Speri It/SM: 45, 60, 75, 79
Sperrbrecher . . .: Ger/Mine destructor vessel
6 (ex-Magdeburg): 115
7 (ex-Sauerland): 441
11 (ex-Petropolis): 115
13 (ex-Minerva): 100
14 (ex-Richard Bornhofen): 441
20 (ex-Kolente): 441
21 (ex-Nestor): 316, 376
25 (ex-Ingrid Horn): 438
30 (ex-Eilbek): 460
31 (ex-Saturn): 100
122 (ex-Cap Hadid): 441
181 (ex-Atlas): 411
191 (ex-Motor I): 233
Spey UK/Frigate: 226, 234, 321, 326, 389, 390, 486, 494
Spica It/TB: see TA 45
Spichern Ger/Supply Ship: 99, 106
Spidola Lat-USSR/SM (B): 111
Spikefish US/SM: 528
Spikenard Can/Corvette: 184
Spingarda It/Corvette: see UJ 208
Spirit UK/SM: 438, 471
Spiteful UK/SM: 400, 425, 438, 473
Splendid/P 228 UK/SM: 280, 284, 293, 300, 313
Sportsman UK/SM: 323, 336, 358, 390, 398
Sposobny USSR/DD: (BS): 128, 133, 136, 148, 155, 173, 175-176, 209, 353, 359
Spot US/SM: 479
Springer US/SM: 495, 505
Springeren Dan/TB: 347
Springfield US/CL: 499-500, 509, 525-526, 529, 533
Sproston US/DD: 396, 431, 480, 502, 505
Spry (ex-Hibiscus) US/Corvette: 247
Squalo It/SM: 34, 39, 45, 55, 101, 119, 128, 140, 144, 150, 154, 156, 165
Squirrel US/MS: 528
Sri Ayuthia Thai/GB: 76
Stack US/DD: 92, 108, 132, 226, 239, 249, 335, 341, 364-365, 370, 373, 387, 480, 504
Stafford US/DE: 480-481
Stalin USSR/DD (P): 530
Stalker US/CVE: 351, 444, 453, 513, 524, 527, 534
Stanley (ex-McCalla) UK/DD: 167-168
Stanly US/DD: 335, 364, 391, 427, 474, 479, 504, 509, 535
Stanton US/DE: 404, 507
Starfish UK/SM: 5, 17
Starling UK/Sloop: 328, 332, 362, 371, 389-390, 395, 400-401, 424, 481
Starr US/APA: 508

Starwort UK/Corvette: 219, 339, 421
Statesman UK/SM: 442, 460, 474, 505, 520
Statice UK/Corvette: 435
Statny USSR/DD (B): 123, 126
Stawell Aus/MS: 406
Stayner UK/DE: 412, 421-423, 434-436, 453
Steady US/MS: 413
Steamer Bay US/CVE: 458, 480, 493, 502
Steelhead US/SM: 358, 379, 432
Stella Dorado UK/AS Trawler: 33
Stella Polare It/TB: see TA 36
Stembel US/DD: 392, 409, 437, 474, 479-480, 525
Stephen Potter US/DD: 387, 406, 426, 458, 476, 499
Steregushchi USSR/DD (B): 110, 117-118, 125, 132, 138
Sterett US/DD: 92, 108, 132, 203, 215, 226, 239, 249, 263, 271, 275-276, 335, 341, 364, 370, 373, 387, 392, 427, 480, 504, 508
Sterlet UK/SM: 5, 24
Sterlet US/SM: 439, 456, 468, 491, 495, 515
Stern US/DE: 502
Stettin Ger/Icebreaker: 22
Stevens US/DD: 347, 353, 388, 437, 500, 512, 524
Stevenstone UK/DD: 362, 405, 421, 423
Stevenson US/DD: 395-396, 409, 533
Stewart US/DD: 185, 188, 191, 197
Stier Ger/Aux CL: see Schiff 23
Stihi Ru/GB: 232, 330, 368, 407, 446
Stingray US/SM: 164, 170, 173, 178, 232, 279, 319, 396, 429
Stocco It/TB: 61
Stockdale US/DE: 404
Stockham US/DD: 427, 458, 476, 499, 522, 525, 533
Stockton US/DD: 395, 409, 503, 533
Stoddard US/DD: 521, 525, 533
Stoic UK/SM: 382, 400, 425, 438, 460. 473
Stoiki USSR/DD (B): 112, 115, 117, 132, 147, 150, 157
Stonecrop UK/Corvette: 314
Stonehenge UK/SM: 382
Stord (ex-Success) Nor/DD: 374-375, 384, 421-423, 429, 444, 473, 475, 511, 519
Stork UK/Sloop: 29, 31, 33, 167-168, 210, 226, 273
Storm UK/SM: 400, 417, 438, 471
Stormes US/DD: 517
Stormont Can/Frigate: 424, 471
Storozhevoi USSR/DD (B): 112, 132
Strahan Aus/MS: 406, 534
Strale It/DD: 35, 42, 87, 95, 101, 165, 193, 198, 200, 206, 239

Strasbourg Fr/BB: 7, 12, 41, 64, 280
Strashny USSR/DD (B): 112, 115, 132, 384
Strategem UK/SM: 400, 417, 438, 471
Strathadam Can/Frigate: 490, 496
Straub US/DE: 403, 417
Stremitelny USSR/DD (N): 117, 119
Strickland US/DE: 404
Striker UK/CVE: 375, 389, 408, 410-411, 444-445, 452, 502, 516
Stringham US/DD: 290, 345, 376, 388
Strogi USSR/DD (B): 131, 384
Stroiny USSR/DD (B): 131, 384
Strolaga It/Corvette: see UJ 2224
Strong US/DD: 307, 324, 335
Strongbow UK/SM: 442, 453, 457, 460, 473
Stronghold UK/DD: 21, 164, 180, 187, 196
Stronsay UK/AS Trawler: 299
Stuart Aus/DD: 9, 39, 43, 45, 49, 57, 74, 76, 89, 93-94, 102, 106, 108, 268
Stubborn UK/SM: 355, 384, 526
Sturdy UK/DD: 59
Sturdy UK/SM: 438, 460, 471
Sturgeon UK/SM: 3, 5, 11, 29, 48, 62, 85, 87, 230, 240, 257
Sturgeon US/SM: 164, 182-183, 206, 232, 379, 410, 419
Sturtevant US/DD: 61, 83, 119, 136
Stygian UK/SM: 457, 460, 471, 495, 529
Subtle UK/SM: 460, 473, 520
Success UK/DD: see Stord
Sudwind Ger/MS: see V 5907
Suffren Fr/CA: 9, 17, 25-26, 36, 39, 43, 379, 539
Suffolk UK/CA: 11, 26, 32, 100, 121, 127, 140, 256, 279, 382, 412, 460, 479, 514, 524
Sugi Jap/DD: 462, 473, 475, 477
Sulla Nor/MS Whaler: 203
Sumba Nor/MS Whaler: 203
Summerside Can/Corvette: 421
Sundewall (ex-M 109) Ger/MS: 1, 5
Sunfish UK/SM: 5, 23, 48, 58, 67, 85, 87, 439
Sunfish US/SM: 306, 343, 388, 392, 432, 449, 468, 505
Sunflower UK/Corvette: 320-321, 326, 360, 362, 421
Surcouf Fr/SM: 41, 172, 192
Surf UK/SM: 358, 400
Surovy USSR/DD (B): 123, 127, 129, 132, 148, 151
Surprise Fr/Sloop: 50
Sussex UK/CA: 7, 9-10, 12, 32-33, 55, 303, 382, 528, 534, 538
Sussexvale Can/Frigate: 496
Sustain US/MS: 408, 410, 413

Sutlej Ind/Sloop: 186, 339, 351, 417, 513, 521
Sutsuki Jap/APD: 361
Sutton UK/MS: 31
Sutton US/DE: 507
Suur-Töel USSR/Icebreaker (B): 130
Suwanee US/CVE: 273, 291, 335, 370, 388, 392, 409, 437, 451, 460, 463-464, 502, 509, 511, 516, 524
Suzukaze Jap/DD: 160, 170, 182, 186, 221, 235, 244, 249-250, 263, 268, 271, 275, 277, 282-283, 286, 290, 335, 361, 388
Suzunami Jap/DD: 361, 365
Suzutsuki Jap/DD: 459, 508
Suzuya Jap/CA: 159, 163, 167, 173, 178, 181, 187, 194, 200-201, 204-205, 221, 235, 248, 254, 263, 268-269, 275-276, 361, 364, 371, 377, 414, 462-463
Svenner (ex-Shark) Nor/DD: 421-422
Svir USSR/Training Ship (B): 207
Svirepy USSR/DD (B): 132, 158, 384
Svobodny USSR/DD (BS): 126, 199, 204, 206, 209, 218, 222, 225
Swale UK/Frigate: 293, 309, 325, 400, 494
Swallow US/MS: 511
Swan Aus/Sloop: 190, 250, 520, 537
Swansea Can/Frigate: 395, 400, 424, 448
Swanson US/DD: 136, 277, 314, 339, 396, 409, 458
Swasey US/DD: see Rockingham
Swasey (II) US/DE: 404, 416, 507
Swearer US/DE: 502
Sweetbriar UK/Corvette: 211, 287, 325
Swenning US/DE: 387, 395, 507
Swift UK/DD: 393, 421, 424
Swift US/MS: 400
Swiftsure UK/CL: 471, 502, 516, 523, 534
Swordfish UK/SM: 3, 5, 23, 40, 45, 48, 62
Swordfish US/SM: 164, 166, 181, 184, 215, 222, 289, 343, 379, 419, 429
Sydney Aus/CA: 17, 25, 36, 39-40, 43-45, 50-51, 57-58, 62-63, 65, 67, 70, 74, 152-153
Syöksy Fin/MTB: 133, 139, 279
Syrtis UK/SM: 355, 396
Syzran USSR/ML: (BS): 142-143

T . . .: Ger/TB
T 1: 52, 64, 509
T 2: 47, 52, 134, 139, 143, 189, 313, 317, 324
T 3: 52, 470, 497
T 4: 64, 189, 236, 265
T 5: 48, 51-54, 77, 134, 139, 143, 189, 216, 313, 317, 324, 332, 470, 497

T 6: 51-54, 64
T 7: 47, 48, 51-54, 64, 135, 139, 143, 216, 219, 230
T 8: 51-54, 64, 134-135, 139, 143, 431, 485
T 9: 64, 77, 313, 470
T 10: 64, 236, 239, 265, 431, 475
T 11: 134-135, 139, 189, 218
T 12: 77, 189, 218, 313, 470
T 13: 189, 236, 239, 449, 453, 455, 460, 470, 510
T 14: 236, 239, 265
T 15: 189, 201, 218, 230, 374
T 16: 189, 201, 460, 470, 510
T 17· 189, 201, 453, 515-516
T 18: 313, 324, 449
T 19: 265, 313, 332, 348, 358, 453, 455, 470, 515-516
T 20: 449, 453, 460
T 21: 455, 460, 470
T 22: 281, 317, 324, 330, 332, 347, 358, 362, 376-377, 431
T 23: 281, 313, 317, 324, 358, 362, 376-377, 431, 446, 453, 455, 470, 473, 485, 498, 515-516
T 24: 332, 336, 347, 376-377, 405-406, 413, 422, 441
T 25: 332, 336, 347-348, 358, 362, 376-377
T 26: 358, 362, 376-377
T 27: 348, 358, 362, 376-377, 398, 404-406
T 28: 385, 422-423, 434-435, 446, 453, 455, 470, 473, 485, 498, 515-516
T 29: 385, 388, 398, 404-405
T 30: 428, 431
T 31: 428
T 32: 431
T 33: 485, 495, 497, 498, 512, 516
T 34: 455
T 35: 455, 515
T 36: 485, 489, 495, 497-498, 512, 515
T 61: 450
T 108: 515
T 196: 1, 4, 489

T . . .: Jap/Landing Craft
T 3: 449
T 11: 473
T 15: 479
T 18: 495
T 46: 472
T 127: 418
T 129: 439
T 138: 456
T 146: 505
T 151: 468
T 833: 523

T . . . & TShch . . .: USSR/ MS (old MS & Trawlers); identical numbers used in different fleets) TShch in Black Sea
T-31 (ex-T-890, ex-Nalim) (N): 343
T-32/Zhemlyak (BS): 142

T-32 (ex-T-891, ex-Forel) (N):
see T-891
T-35/Menzhinski (B): 153
T-38/Raikomvod (BS): 141
T-38/ .... (N): 472
T-39/Doroteya (BS): 141, 144
T-41/Kirov (B): 139
T-41/Khenkin (BS): 141
T-42/ .... (B): 153
T-42/ .... (N): 343
T-48/ .... (B): 273
T-51/Pirmunas (B): 126
T-58/ .... (B): 153, 238
T-58/ .... (N): 341
T-63/ .... (N): 343
T-68/ .... (N): 180

T . . . & TSch . . .: USSR/MS
(Lend-Lease ships, &
BTSHCH, Type Fugas
(Number 2 . . ., and 4 . . .)
T-109 (ex-MMS 203) (N): 341
T-110 (ex-MMS 212) (N): 341
T-111 (ex-Advocate) (N): 366,
465
T-112 (ex-Agent) (N): 361, 366,
409
T-113 (ex-Alarm) (N): 361,
366, 465
T-114 (ex-Alchemy) (N): 361,
366, 409, 442
T-115 (ex-Apex) (N): 361,
366
T-116 (ex Arcade) (N): 366,
442, 465
T-117 (ex-Arch) (N): 366, 485
T-118 (ex-Armada) (N): 442
T-119 (ex-Aspire) (N): 409
T-120 (ex-Assail) (N): 442
T-152 (ex-YMS 144) (P): 532
T-155 (ex-YMS 145) (P): 532
T-156 (ex-YMS 59) (P): 532
T-201/Zaryad (B): 125, 150
T-202 /Buy (B): 126
T-203/Patron (B): 146
T-204/Fugas (B): 110-111, 130,
273
T-205/Gafel (B): 130, 148, 153,
157-158
T-206/Verp (B): 130, 148, 151
T-207/Shpil (B): 130, 147-148,
151, 157-158
T-208/Shkiv (B): 112
T-209/Knecht (B). 129
T-210/Gak (B): 130, 147, 157
T-211/Rym (B): 148, 150-151,
157-158
T-212/Shtag (B): 129
T-213/Krambol (B): 129
T-214/Bugel (B): 130
T-215 (B): 130, 147, 150-151,
157-158
T-216 (B): 130
T-217 (B): 130, 147, 150, 153,
157
T-218 (B): 130, 150, 153, 157
T-271 (ex-Fancy) (P): 531
T-272 (ex-Marvel) (P): 531
T-273 (ex-Measure) (P): 531
T-274 (ex-Method) (P): 531
T-275 (ex-Mirth) (P): 531
T-276 (ex-Nucleus) (P): 531
T-277 (ex-Disdain) (P): 531

T-278 (ex-Palisade) (P): 531
T-279 (ex-Indicative) (P): 531
T-280 (ex-Penetrate) (P): 531
T-281 (ex-Peril) (P): 531
T-282 (ex-Rampart) (P): 531
T-297/Virsaitis (B): 153, 157
T-334 (P): 532
T-401/Tral (BS): 175
T-402/Minrep (BS): 173
T-403/Gruz (BS): 297-298
T-404/Shchit (BS): 144, 297
T-405/Vrzyvatel (BS): 144, 176
T-406/Iskatel (BS): 144, 285,
287
T-407/Mina (BS): 285, 287,
297, 327
T-408/Yakor (BS): 144, 176,
285, 287
T-409/Garpun (BS): 327
T-410/Vrzyv (BS): 448
T-411/Zashchitnik (BS): 297,
411
T-412/Arseni Rasskin (BS):
183, 285, 287 297
T-413/No. 27 (BS): 112, 225
T-522 (ex-Adopt) (P): 531-532
T-524 (ex-Augury) (P): 531-532
T-525 (ex-Barrier) (P): 532
T-583 (ex-YMS 75) (P): 532
T-588 (ex-YMS 237) (P): 532
T-590 (ex-YMS 272) (P): 532
T-591 (ex-YMS 273) (P): 532
T-599 (P): 532
T-600 (P): 532
T-601 (P): 532
T-602 (P): 532
T-603 (P): 532
T-604 (P): 532
T-890 (ex-Nalim) (N): 116
T-891 (ex-Forel) (N): 116

TA . . . : Ger/TB (ex-French)
TA 1 (ex-Le Fier): 441
TA 2 (ex-L'Agile441):
TA 3 (ex-L'Alsacien): 441
TA 5 (ex-Le Faouche): 441
TA 6 (ex-Le Corse): 441
TA 10 (ex-FR 42, ex-La
Pomone): 351

TA . . . : Ger/TB (ex-It)

TA 14 (ex-Turbine): 367, 390,
418, 451
TA 15 (ex-Francesco Crispi):
367, 390
TA 16 (ex-Castelfidardo): 367,
418
TA 17 (ex-San Martino):
367, 398, 418
TA 18 (ex-Solferino): 453
TA 19 (ex-Calatafimi): 367,
390, 398, 418, 433
TA 20 (ex-Audace): 399, 467
TA 21 (ex-Insidioso): 368, 399,
467
TA 22 (ex-Giuseppe Missori):
514
TA 23 (ex-Impavido): 376, 390,
397
TA 24 (ex-Arturo): 376, 390,
414, 431, 455, 500
TA 25 (ex-Intrepido): 390, 430

TA 26 (ex-Ardito): 390, 397,
414
TA 27 (ex-Auriga): 390, 397,
414
TA 28 (ex-Rigel): 390, 397,
431, 450
TA 29: (ex-Eridano): 397, 414,
430, 431, 455, 500
TA 30 (ex-Dragone): 414
TA 31 (ex-Dardo): 513
TA 32 (ex-Premuda, ex-
Dubrovnik): 455, 500, 513
TA 33 (ex-Corsaro II, ex-
Squadrista): 450
TA 35 (ex-Giuseppe Dezza):
514
TA 36 (ex-Stella Polare): 394,
399
TA 37 (ex-Gladio): 394, 451,
454
TA 38 (ex-Spada): 451, 453-454
TA 39 (ex-Daga): 451, 453-454
TA 40 (ex-Pugnale): 467
TA 43 (ex-Sebenico, ex-
Beograd): 514
TA 44 (ex-Antonio Pigafetta):
467. 493
TA 45 (ex-Spica): 467
TDS-01 (ex-LCT . . .) USSR/LS
(P): 531

TF . . . : Ger/Torpedo Recovery
Vessel
TF 10: 489
TF 19: 489

TKA . . . : USSR/Torpedo
cutters
TKA-11 (N): 134
TKA-12 (N): 134, 142, 436
TKA-13 (N): 135, 345, 404,
436, 450
TKA-14 (BS): 404
TKA-14 (N): 142
TKA-15 (N): 135, 142, 345
TKA-17 (B): 111
TKA-21 (N): 345
TKA-27 (B): 111
TKA-31 (B): 233
TKA-37 (B): 111
TKA-47 (B): 111
TKA-52 (B): see Vasama
TKA-57 (B): 111
TKA-67 (B): 111
TKA-71 (B): 120
TKA-72 (B): 233
TKA-73 (B): 130
TKA-74 (B): 130
TKA-83 (B): 233
TKA-85 (BS): 404
TKA-86 (BS): 404
TKA-94 (B): 130, 404
TKA-101 (BS): 366
TKA-101 (B): 233
TKA-103 (B): 130
TKA-104 (BS): 404
TKA-113 (B): 130, 233
TKA-115 (BS): 327
TKA-122 (B): 122
TKA-123 (B): 233
TKA-124 (BS): 352
TKA-125 (BS): 327, 352
TKA-141 (B): see Vihuri

U

TKA-166 (ex-PT . . . .) (B): 501
TKA-181 (ex-PT . . . .) (B): 501
TKA-199 (ex-PT . . . .) (B): 501
TKA-203 (ex-PT . . . .) (N): 404, 445
TKA-212 (ex-PT . . . .) (N): 404
TKA-221 (ex-PT . . . .) (BS): 447
TKA-223 (ex-PT . . . .) (BS): 447
TKA-227 (ex-PT . . . .) (BS): 447
TKA-233 (ex-PT . . . .)(BS): 447
TKA-238 (ex-PT . . . .) (N): 436
TKA-239 (ex-PT . . . .) (N): 436-437
TKA-240 (ex-PT. . . .) (N): 436
TKA-241 (ex-PT. . . .) (N): 436
TKA-242 (ex-PT. . . .) (N): 436
TKA-243 (ex-PT. . . .) (N): 436
TKA-567 (ex-PT. . . .) (P): 531
TKA-578 (ex-PT. . . .) (P): 531
TKA-631 (ex-PT. . . .) (P): 532
TKA-641 (ex-PT. . . .) (P): 532
TKA-645 (ex-PT. . . .) (P): 532
TKA-646 (ex-PT. . . .) (P): 532

TS . . . : Ger/MS
TS-2 (ex-M 387): 489
TS-3 (ex-M 372): 497
TS 4 (ex-M 278): 497
TS 8 (ex-M 375): 482
TS 10 (ex-M 376): 497

Tabberer US/DE: 474, 502
Tachibana Jap/DD: 525
Tachikaze Jap/DD: 252, 392
Tactician UK/SM: 323, 407
Tahure Fr/GB: 76
Taiho Jap/CV: 415, 430
Taiyo Jap/CVE: 235, 244, 259, 347, 439
Taifun (S-2) USSR/Patrol Ship (B): 138
Takanami Jap/DD: 263, 264, 268, 271, 275, 282
Takane Jap/Frigate: 529
Takao Jap/CA: 159, 163, 167, 170 178, 181, 190, 194, 196, 220, 235, 248, 254, 263, 268, 275-277, 361, 364, 414, 430, 462, 529
Takasaki Jap/Oiler: 415
Take Jap/DD: 471
Taku UK/SM: 27-28, 37, 48, 62, 87, 98, 105, 111, 227, 255, 267, 284, 384
Talbot (ex-DD 114) US/APD: 334-335, 345, 388
Taluga US/Oiler: 510
Talisman UK/SM: 46, 141, 144, 158-159, 165, 255
Tallin (ex-Petropavlovsk) USSR/CA: 384
Tally Ho UK/SM: 365, 382, 438, 457, 460, 471
Talybont UK/DD: 362, 388, 420, 447
Tama Jap/CL: 221, 235, 312, 337, 462, 464
Tamanami Jap/DD: 361, 414, 430, 432
Tamarisk UK/Corvette: 186
Tambor US/SM: 158, 198, 209, 222, 224, 237, 266, 284, 322,

379, 410, 439, 468, 523
Tampa US/CG Cutter: 296
Tanatside UK/DD: 388, 420
Taney US/CG Cutter: 408, 410
Tang US/SM: 392, 401, 406, 419, 439, 456
Tangier US/Aircraft Depot Ship: 168
Tanikaze Jap/DD: 156, 168, 178, 181, 190, 194, 197, 204, 220, 223-224, 235, 248, 250, 265, 268, 283, 286, 290, 335, 361, 415, 429
Tannenberg Ger/ML: 48, 51, 77, 109, 116
Tannenfels Ger/Supply Ship: 79-80
Tantalus UK/SM: 382, 412, 417, 425, 471
Tantivy UK/SM: 382, 438, 453, 460
Tapir UK/SM: 501
Tarantini It/SM: 34, 41, 50, 66
Taranto It/CL: 34, 349
Tarbell US/DD: 83, 119. 136
Tarigo It/DD: 58, 74, 78, 93
Tarmo Fin/Icebreaker: 18, 134
Tarn Fr/Oiler: 50, 54, 148
Tarpon UK/SM: 23-24
Tarpon US/SM: 164, 222, 296, 344
Tartar UK/DD: 23, 27, 29, 32, 46, 84, 100-101, 113, 121, 198, 242, 256, 313, 322, 328, 338, 347, 350-351, 398, 421-422, 433-434, 441, 514, 521
Tartu Fr/DD: 23-24, 26-27, 29, 37, 280
Tashkent USSR/DD (BS): 116, 127-128, 147-148, 155, 171, 173, 175-176, 184, 197, 202, 206, 212, 216, 218, 222, 225-226, 233
Tasker H. Bliss US/AP: 277
Tatekawa Maru Jap/Oiler: 415
Tatsumiya Maru Jap/Aux ML: 160
Tatsuta Jap /CL: 164, 168, 179, 199, 214, 235, 237, 245, 250, 258
Tattnall US/DD: 247
Tatum (ex-DE 789) US/APD: 443, 517
Taurus UK/SM: 300, 313, 323, 350, 382, 400, 412
Taussig US/DD: 476, 499, 522, 525, 533
Tautog US/SM: 161, 209, 215, 238, 266, 284, 290, 314, 329, 365, 379, 396, 410, 432, 479
Tavy UK/Frigate: 435, 471
Tay UK/Frigate: 315, 320, 326, 417
Taylor US/DD: 291, 307, 324, 335, 345, 355-356, 370, 373, 409, 480, 498, 504, 513, 533
Tazzoli It/SM: 39, 56, 70, 95, 159, 192, 234, 285, 326
Tbilisi USSR/DD (P): 530-531
Teazer UK/DD: 385, 444, 451, 453, 523, 526, 530-531, 533
Teiyo Maru Jap/Oiler: 220
Telemachus UK/SM: 417, 438

Telfair US/APA: 505
Tembien It/SM: 47, 57, 67, 73, 78, 122
Teme UK/Frigate: 424, 496
Tempest UK/SM: 186
Tempête Fr/DD: 352, 443, 508
Templar UK/SM: 382, 412, 417, 438
Tenacious UK/DD: 385-386, 407, 516, 523, 526, 530-531, 533
Tenacity (ex-Candytuft) US/Corvette: 300, 322
Tench US/SM: 515
Tenedos UK/DD: 21, 163-164, 194-196, 205
Tennessee US/BB: 161, 226, 337, 370, 388, 392, 399, 427, 437, 452, 461, 463, 493, 502, 509, 527-528
Tenryu Jap/CL: 164, 168, 179, 199, 214, 235, 237, 241, 250, 258, 271, 275, 284
Tenyo Maru Jap/Aux ML: 179
Termagent UK/DD: 407, 443, 453-454, 516, 523, 526, 530-531, 533
Tern UK/GB: 170
Terpsichore UK/DD: 437, 443, 453, 523, 526, 530, 533
Terrapin UK/SM: 396, 442, 460, 471, 473, 495
Terre Neuve Fr/Aux: 42
Terror UK/Monitor: 63, 69, 73, 76, 81
Terror US/ML: 502, 513
Terry US/DD: 363, 391, 426, 428, 533
Terutzuki Jap/DD: 264, 268, 270, 275-277, 283
Tervani UK/AS Trawler: 299
Test UK/Frigate: 339
Tetcott UK/DD: 227, 238, 339, 350, 386
Teton US/AGC: 504
Tetrarch UK/SM: 23, 31, 37, 48, 58, 62, 92, 99, 111, 129, 136, 141
Teviot UK/Frigate: 339, 486
Teviot Bank UK/ML: 21
Texas US/BB: 5, 108, 132, 273, 420, 431, 443, 493, 502, 511, 527
Thames UK/SM: 5, 41
Thane UK/CVE: 481
Thanet UK/DD: 165, 181
Thatcher US/DD: see Niagara
Thatcher (II) US/DD: 347, 364, 406, 427, 476, 500, 517, 527
Themistokles (ex-Bramham) Gr/DD: 339, 356, 386, 443, 453
Theodor Riedel Ger/DD: 3, 22, 57, 230, 288, 298, 348, 373, 515-516
Theresia Wallner Ger/Escort Ship: 135, 146
The Sullivans US/DD: 387, 406, 426, 458, 476
Thetford Mines Can/Frigate: 490, 496
Thetis US/CG Cutter: 223
Thétis Fr/SM: 21, 29, 280

Thetis Bay US/CVE: 528, 533
Thistle UK/SM: 5, 11, 23
Thomas US/DD: see St Albans, see Dostoiny
Thomas (II) US/DE: 387, 394, 416, 506
Thomas E. Fraser US/DM: 502
Thomas F. Nickel US/DE: 480, 528
Thomas Stone US/AP: 273
Thomason US/DE: 487
Thompson US/DD: 420, 443
Thor Ger/Aux CL: see Schiff 10
Thorn UK/SM: 173, 184, 227, 239
Thorn US/DD: 396, 409, 476 533
Thornborough UK/DE: 421, 434-435, 440, 447, 469, 475
Thorough UK/SM: 435, 471, 515
Thracian UK/DD: 170
Thrasher UK/SM: 122, 145, 153, 175, 208, 218, 227, 232, 237, 251, 255, 263, 271, 278, 355
Threadfin US/SM: 479, 495, 508, 526
Threat US/MS: 329
Thresher US/SM: 161, 209, 232, 266, 284, 296, 365, 379, 449
Thrush US/Seaplane Tender: 5
Thruster UK/LST: 350
Thule UK/SM: 457, 474
Thunderbolt UK/SM: 66, 133, 141, 175, 184, 291, 294, 300
Thyella Gr/TB: 94
Thyme UK/MS: 212
Ticonderoga US/CV: 466, 474, 476-477, 521-522, 525, 533
Tifone It/TB: 300, 312-313, 321
Tigre Fr/DD: 41, 280, 508
Tigre It/DD: 49, 52, 68, 78, 90
Tigris UK/SM: 46, 52, 62, 78, 90, 113, 124, 133, 144, 280, 283, 294, 300
Tigrone US/SM: 534
Tilefish US/SM: 456, 472, 495
Tillman US/DD: 339-340
Tingey US/DD: 406, 426, 458, 476, 499
Tinosa US/SM: 358, 365, 379, 410, 432, 522
Tinsman US/DE: 480
Tintagel Castle UK/Corvette: 506
Tippecanoe US/Oiler: 214
Tiptoe US/SM: 522
Tirante US/SM: 495, 522
Tirpitz Ger/BB: 44, 139, 149, 151, 198, 206, 214, 230-231, 303, 348, 355, 391, 401, 409-411, 437, 444-446, 451, 467
Tirso It/Aux ML: 261
Tisdale US/DE: 502
Tito Speri It/SM: see Speri
Tjerk Hiddes (ex-Nonpareil) Du/DD: 255, 281, 298, 382, 400
Togo (ex-Otra) Ger/Vp boat: see NT 05
Tojima Jap/ML: 529
Tokitsukaze Jap/DD: 160, 170,

177, 181, 184, 191, 194-195, 221, 235, 249, 254, 264, 268, 290, 306
Tokiwa Jap/ML: 163, 183, 235, 530
Tolman US/DM: 502
Tomich US/DE: 402, 507
Tomodzuru Jap/TB: 162, 169
Tone Jap/CA: 156, 168, 178, 181, 190, 194, 196, 204-205, 220, 223, 235, 249, 264, 268-269, 275, 361, 364, 383, 414, 462-463, 499, 529
Toowoomba Aus/MS: 187, 197, 280
Topazio It/SM: 34, 40, 60, 63, 79, 84, 93, 101, 128, 133, 144, 165, 271, 273
Topeka US/CL: 522, 525-526, 533
Torbay UK/SM: 87, 104, 111, 115, 144, 198, 208, 300, 313, 336, 358-359
Torelli It/SM: 50, 75, 91, 96, 113, 118, 132, 137, 159, 192, 300, 327
Tornade Fr/DD: 274
Tornado (ex-Lianen) Ger/Vp boat: see V 5105
Toronto Can/Frigate: 454
Torricelli It/SM: 36
Torrington UK/DE: 475
Torsk US/SM: 529
Tortola (ex-PF 91) UK/Frigate: 471
Toti It/SM: 39, 44, 60, 236
Totland (ex-Cayuga) UK/Sloop: 303
Tourville Fr/CA: 36, 43
Townsville Aus/MS: 406, 537
Towy UK/Frigate: 326, 354, 381, 389
Tracker UK/CVE: 362, 400-401, 424, 464
Tracy (ex-DD 214) US/DM: 161, 291, 502
Tradewind UK/SM: 453, 471, 505
Tral USSR/MS (BS): see T-401
Tramontane Fr/DD: 274
Transcona Can/MS: 469
Transylvania UK/Aux CL: 8, 20, 46
Trat Thai/TB: 76
Thrathen US/DD: 359, 392, 416, 418, 461, 476, 499
Traveller UK/SM: 251, 271, 278
Trenchant UK/SM: 417, 442, 453, 460, 473, 495, 523
Trent UK/Frigate: 339, 494
Trento It/CA: 35-36, 42, 57-58, 63, 67, 69, 79, 86, 89, 128, 140, 149, 153, 166, 175, 189, 193, 202, 228
Trenton US/CL: 185, 344, 525
Trentonian Can/Corvette: 421, 490
Trepang US/SM: 456, 472, 491, 505, 526
Trespasser UK/SM: 288, 382
Trever (ex-DD) 339 US/DMS: 161, 268
Triad UK/SM: 5, 11, 23, 29, 60

Tribune UK/SM: 46, 230, 293, 313
Tricheco It/SM: 34, 39, 42, 47, 57, 62, 101, 128, 138, 154, 156 175, 200
Trident UK/SM: 5, 21, 23, 27-28, 37, 58, 124, 129, 139, 148, 193, 210, 230, 313, 323, 347, 521
Trieste It/CA: 57-58, 67, 69, 79, 86, 89, 95, 103, 118, 128, 140, 149, 153, 228, 243, 284, 317
Trigger US/SM: 222, 259, 284, 289, 306, 329, 347, 365, 379, 402, 456, 495
Trillium Can/Corvette: 253, 296, 301-302, 305, 356
Trinidad UK/CL: 203, 217
Tripoli US/CVE: 403
Trippe US/DD: 92, 151, 308, 339, 342, 350, 369, 385
Triton Gr/SM: 87, 111, 228, 279
Triton UK/SM: 3, 5, 19, 23, 27, 54, 58, 69
Triton US/SM: 158, 186, 209, 222, 233, 284, 306
Tritone It/SM: 289
Triumph UK/SM: 5, 48, 58, 80, 84, 98, 104, 111, 116, 128, 136, 145, 153, 175
Trollope UK/Frigate: 434
Trombe Fr/DD: 280, 508, 512
Tromöy (ex-Pol IV) Nor/AS Trawler: 485, 511
Tromp Du/CL: 185-186, 188, 191, 298, 382, 400, 407, 411, 438, 514, 420, 524, 538
Trooper UK/SM: 291, 294, 300, 340, 359
Troubridge UK/DD: 328, 339, 347, 351, 385, 394, 437, 444, 451, 453, 516, 523, 526, 530-531
Trout US/SM: 158, 161, 184, 186, 209, 222, 259, 290, 322, 346-347, 390
Truant UK/SM: 5, 23, 31, 37, 52, 54, 69, 77-78, 86, 93, 98, 111, 145, 159, 191, 206, 515
Trucluent UK/SM: 355, 382, 400, 425
Trumpeter UK/CVE: 442, 444, 446, 465, 473, 483, 498, 517-518, 534
Trumpeter US/DE: 403, 417
Trusty UK/SM: 140, 159, 222, 232, 279
Trutta US/SM: 505
Truxtun US/DD: 5, 83, 132
Trygg Nor/TB: 27
Tsiklon USSR/Patrol Ship: 130
Tsingtau Ger/SM Depot ship: 1, 22
Tsenit USSR/Survey Ship (BS): 143
Tsubaki Jap/DD: 529
Tsubame Jap/MS: 492
Tsuga Jap/TB: 415, 430, 477
Tsugaru Jap/ML: 163, 179, 199, 214, 235, 237, 252-253, 286, 418-419
Tsurmi Jap/Oiler: 197

Tucha USSR/TB: 117
Tucker US/DD: 161
Tudor UK/SM: 471, 473
Tuffeto It/Corvette: see UJ 2222
Tui NZ/AS Whaler: 340
Tulagi US/CVE: 444, 480, 494, 502
Tullibee US/SM: 343, 358, 379, 401
Tulsa US/GB: 197
Tuman USSR/Patrol Ship: 116
Tumult UK/DD: 339, 351, 385, 394, 397, 444, 453, 535
Tuna UK/SM: 52, 87, 171
Tuna US/SM: 198, 209, 222, 306, 372, 410, 464
Tunguska USSR/Aux GB (B): 111
Tunisien Fr/DE: 413, 443
Tunny US/SM: 296, 306, 329, 401, 410, 429, 522
Tunsberg Castle (ex-Shrewsbury Castle) Nor/Corvette: 471-472
Turbine It/DD: 34, 36-37, 79, 81, 90, 95, 101, 154, 165, 214 239
Turbulent UK/SM: 208, 218, 232, 239, 245, 261, 278, 286, 293, 300
Turchese It/SM: 34, 42, 46, 73, 78, 81, 90, 94-95, 140, 144, 150, 171, 202, 271, 273
Turquoise Fr/SM: 36, 284, 322
Turunmaa Fin/GB: 233
Tuscaloosa US/CA: 5, 15, 92, 132, 149, 203, 212, 230, 245, 273-274, 338, 348, 359, 366, 420, 431, 444, 493, 502
Tuscan UK/DD: 444, 451, 453-454, 535
Tuscon US/CL: 528, 530, 533
Tutch USSR/TB: (B) 6
Tutuila US/GB: 122
Tweed UK/Frigate: 346, 369, 378
Twiggs US/DD: 14, see Leamington, see Zhyuchi
Twiggs (II) US/DD: 474, 480, 502. 513, 523
Twining US/DD: 427, 458, 476, 499, 528, 530, 533
Tyler US/DE: 481
Tynedale UK/DD: 206, 265, 339, 369
Typhon Fr/DD: 274
Tyrian UK/DD: 339, 347, 351, 444, 535
Tyrrell US/APA: 505

U . . . : Ger/SM
U1: 21-23
U2: 21, 23
U3: 5, 21, 23
U4: 5, 21-24
U5: 1, 23
U6: 1, 5, 23
U7: 1, 5, 21, 23, 29
U8: 31
U9: 3, 18-19, 21-22, 26, 29-30, 301, 319, 343, 360, 368, 411, 437, 446
U10: 19, 23
U12: 3, 6

U13: 3, 9, 13, 18, 23, 30
U14: 1, 18-20, 22
U15: 3, 10, 18
U16: 3, 6, 8
U17: 3, 18, 20
U18: 1, 10, 18, 327, 332, 343, 353, 360, 368, 380, 402, 411, 441, 446, 448
U19: 3, 8, 10, 17-18, 21, 23, 301, 310, 319, 332, 343, 368, 380, 411, 448
U20: 3, 10, 13, 17-18, 20-21, 332, 353, 368, 380, 411, 448
U21: 8, 11-13, 18
U22: 1, 10, 13, 18
U23: 8, 13, 17-19, 21, 27, 332, 343, 360, 402, 411, 448
U24: 8, 17-18, 21, 301, 310-311, 332, 343, 360, 380, 411, 437, 446, 448
U25: 9, 18, 22, 24-25, 35, 47
U26: 2, 9, 18-19, 26, 38
U27: 1-2, 5
U28: 1-2, 10, 20, 35, 48-49, 51, 53, 59, 61
U29: 1-3, 10, 20, 29, 32, 53, 55, 61, 64-65, 518
U30: 1-3, 15, 20, 22, 35, 38, 47, 518
U31: 1-2, 5, 8, 12-13, 18, 20, 55, 58, 61
U32: 1-2, 15, 20, 35, 48-49, 51, 53, 55, 61
U33: 1-2, 8, 12, 19
U34: 1-2, 9, 18, 22, 25-26, 38, 41, 45-46
U35: 1-2, 12, 35
U36: 5, 13
U37: 1-2, 7-8, 18-19, 22-23, 25, 30, 47-49, 55, 68, 79, 84-85
U38: 1-2, 13, 20, 25-26, 47-48, 55, 59, 70, 73, 95, 123, 130, 146, 148
U39: 1-3
U40: 1-2, 6-7
U41: 1-2, 10, 18
U42: 7-8
U43: 10, 20, 29, 32, 53, 55, 65-66, 100, 104, 108, 122-123, 130-131, 151, 178, 234, 238, 261, 295, 303, 308, 332, 337
U44: 18, 20
U45: 1-2, 7-8
U46: 1-2, 7-8, 15, 20, 22, 26, 29, 32, 38, 47, 53, 55, 59-60, 82, 87-88, 99-100, 104, 122, 518
U47: 1-2, 8, 12-13, 20, 22, 25-26, 35, 51, 53, 59-60, 64, 66, 82-84
U48: 1-2, 8, 12-13, 18-19, 22, 25, 29, 32, 47-48, 53, 55, 59-60, 77, 81, 87-88, 100, 104, 110
U49: 10, 20, 22, 25, 327
U50: 18-19, 22
U51: 18, 20, 22, 24, 26, 35, 46-47
U52: 1-2, 20, 22, 38, 45-46, 66, 69, 75, 77, 91-92
U53: 2, 9-10, 18-19
U54: 19

U55: 18
U56: 3, 9, 12, 15, 18, 21-22, 31, 44, 46, 48-49, 51
U57: 1, 10, 14, 18-19, 21, 23, 44, 46, 48-49
U58: 3, 12, 15, 18, 23, 31, 44-46, 53, 58
U59: 3, 9, 12, 14, 18, 21, 23, 46-49, 53, 58
U60: 13, 18, 22, 30, 47-49, 55
U61: 12-13, 18-19, 37-38, 44, 53, 55-56
U62: 22, 30, 32, 37-38, 44
U63: 19-20
U64: 22, 25
U65: 22, 25-26, 38, 47, 51, 53, 65, 91-92
U66: 99-100, 104, 114, 117, 119, 138-139, 147, 178, 209, 234, 295, 303, 308, 328, 337, 387, 403
U67: 138, 167-168, 192, 223, 260, 264, 308, 312, 331, 337
U58: 118-119, 138-139, 143, 154, 159, 197, 224, 250, 261, 301, 332, 357, 361, 387
U69: 81-82, 87-88, 95, 114, 132, 135, 148, 151, 156, 188, 216, 253, 289, 296, 299
U70: 83-84
U71: 108, 122-123, 128, 132, 141, 145, 168, 178, 201, 226, 234, 238-239, 266-268, 289, 295, 297, 316
U72: 504
U73: 81-83, 88, 91, 100, 104, 123, 132, 142, 145, 185, 202, 242-243, 273, 289, 340 344, 353, 369
U74: 83, 85, 87-88, 99-101, 118-119, 122, 135, 145-146, 148, 160, 167, 170, 211
U75: 92, 104, 108, 122, 125, 128, 136, 141, 170
U76: 88
U77: 104, 108, 114, 122-123, 132, 142, 145, 147, 151, 160, 167, 170, 177, 225, 227, 229, 238, 273, 299, 310
U79: 104, 108, 114, 119, 124, 136, 142, 155-156, 170
U81: 116, 119, 130-131, 149-150, 156, 188, 209, 218, 225, 227. 273, 294, 306, 340, 344, 353, 369, 381
U82: 123, 130-131, 146, 148, 182, 185-186
U83: 122, 125, 128, 132, 141, 145, 160, 170, 188, 200, 218, 225, 247, 289, 299
U84: 123, 130-131, 146, 148, 177, 203, 208-209, 226, 232, 262, 266-268, 278, 304-305, 308-309, 311, 316-317, 338
U85: 130-131, 146, 148, 151, 182, 187, 208
U86: 177, 185, 209, 234, 240, 277, 283, 307, 309, 311, 333, 369, 371
U87: 177, 184, 226, 251, 260, 295, 303
U88: 213, 230-231, 256
U89: 226, 229, 237, 266-268,

296, 304-305, 308, 322, 324-325
U90: 234
U91: 251-252, 258, 277-278, 301, 305, 308-309, 311, 325, 327, 357, 360, 362, 389, 394
U92: 251, 252, 272, 277-278, 283, 301-302, 320, 325-326, 329, 373-374, 376, 395, 400, 436, 443, 446
U93: 59, 64-65, 75, 99-100, 104-105, 117-118, 124, 146, 148, 178
U94: 66, 75, 88, 96, 99-100, 117-119, 124, 132, 135, 188, 193, 203, 216-217, 239, 250
U95: 66, 70, 82-83, 91-92, 96, 114, 118, 128, 132, 153-154
U96: 69, 75, 77, 81-82, 91-92, 96, 99, 108, 114, 122-123, 132, 147-148, 151, 155, 188, 216-217, 251-252, 258, 293, 504
U97: 81-83, 87-88, 96, 99-100, 114, 118-119, 136, 141, 210, 225, 229
U98: 87-88, 99-100, 114, 118, 132, 147-148, 151, 182, 213, 240, 272, 277
U99: 38, 45, 51, 53, 55, 59-61, 66, 83-85
U100: 47-48, 53, 55, 59-60, 64-65, 69, 85
U101: 29, 32, 48-49, 51, 55, 59-60, 66, 75, 77, 88, 91, 104, 108, 123, 128, 142-143, 145
U102: 38
U103: 55, 64-66, 77, 95, 113-114, 138-139, 147-148, 182, 215, 270, 277, 283, 303, 308, 324, 357, 361
U104: 64-65
U105: 75, 82, 85-86, 95, 123, 130-131, 151, 185, 201, 285, 290-291, 314
U106: 75, 82, 86, 95, 125, 145, 148, 182, 215, 260, 283, 308, 332
U107: 77, 81, 95, 138-139, 147-148, 167-168, 182, 215, 250-251, 260, 297, 303, 320, 324, 338, 371, 375, 416, 436
U108: 82-83, 91-92, 104, 108, 114, 125, 131, 138, 167-168, 182, 211, 236-237, 277, 295, 317-318, 320
U109: 99, 117, 124, 142, 144, 178, 208, 241, 285, 290, 299, 308
U110: 85, 87-88, 91-92, 96, 105
U111: 99, 104-105, 108, 114, 131, 138
U116: 217, 234, 236, 259. 262
U117: 287, 299, 314, 337-338
U118: 259-260, 262, 278, 295-296, 329
U119: 304, 328, 332
U122: 38
U123: 55, 59-60, 64-65, 77 82, 91-92, 96, 114, 117, 124, 146, 148, 178, 201-202, 286-287, 293, 312, 314, 352, 387, 443
U124: 48-49, 51, 59, 61, 70, 73,

82, 85, 117-118, 124, 137, 143, 154, 159, 198, 216-217, 285, 290, 314
U125: 131, 138-139, 168, 178, 211, 241, 291, 295, 320-321
U126: 118-119, 124, 139, 143, 154, 216, 219, 236, 266, 279, 314, 332
U127: 167
U128: 182, 216, 219, 260, 272, 322
U129: 123, 141, 143, 154, 159, 192, 223, 265, 314, 338, 357, 371, 403, 443
U130: 164, 178, 209, 277, 283, 307-308
U131: 167
U132: 140, 185, 226, 229, 233, 237, 266-268
U133: 147-148, 151, 161, 170, 177, 180, 200
U134: 164, 172, 175, 180, 198, 226, 232, 270, 279, 291-292, 309, 311, 315, 317, 331, 338
U135: 177, 184, 213, 222, 246, 253, 281, 285, 296-297, 304, 329
U136: 184, 208, 234
U137: 55, 58, 64-65, 109
U138: 53, 58-59, 64, 99, 106
U140: 66, 111, 116
U141: 96, 104, 119, 128
U142: 111
U143: 96, 114, 128, 525
U144: 110-111, 121
U145: 111, 525
U146: 109
U147: 82, 91-92, 96, 104
U149: 111, 525
U150: 525
U153: 232
U154: 84, 207, 232, 265, 322, 361, 387, 416
U155: 188, 193, 216, 237, 277-278, 283, 301, 332, 357, 361, 403, 443, 525
U156: 192, 216, 250, 255-256, 260, 301
U157: 223
U158: 188, 193, 219
U159: 219, 224, 261, 272, 308, 312, 331
U160: 201, 234, 264, 265, 299, 337
U161: 192, 216, 219, 266, 279, 314, 338, 352
U162: 211, 244, 247
U163: 243, 247, 265
U164: 238-239, 250, 286
U165: 248, 298
U166: 234
U167: 289, 308, 312
U168: 311, 315, 317, 320, 349, 382, 457, 460
U169: 311
U170: 329, 332, 352, 386, 454, 521
U171: 234
U172: 224, 250, 262, 273, 308, 312, 330, 372
U173: 234, 277
U174: 240, 246, 272, 314
U175: 253, 286, 318-319

U176: 240, 246, 253, 259, 279, 314
U177: 272, 315, 387
U178: 272, 315, 373, 382, 443
U179: 261
U180: 315, 436
U181: 272, 291, 312, 315, 403, 417, 457
U182: 291, 299
U183: 260-261, 267, 297, 301, 349, 382, 417, 482, 505
U184: 278
U185: 277, 283, 301, 330-332, 338
U186: 293, 296, 299, 301-302, 319, 324-325
U187: 295-297
U188: 311, 316, 349, 382, 443
U189: 318
U190: 305, 307, 309, 328, 403, 443, 506, 518, 520
U191: 315, 317-318
U192: 320-321
U193: 329, 357, 371
U195: 315, 454, 457, 482
U196: 315, 403, 417, 457
U197: 315, 337
U198: 315, 403, 417
U199: 330
U201: 91-92, 96, 99, 104, 108, 114, 125, 137, 147-148, 151, 156, 208, 234, 236, 259-260, 289, 296, 299
U202: 108, 114, 123, 130-131, 146, 148, 161, 201, 203, 227, 236, 259-260, 295, 303, 308, 325, 327-328
U203: 108, 118-119, 137, 146, 148, 177, 201, 203, 232, 270, 285-287, 317-318, 320
U204: 104, 122, 125, 141, 145
U205: 122, 128, 137, 149-150, 156, 177, 202, 206, 218, 225, 227-228, 250, 273, 294
U206: 123, 132, 141, 145, 160
U207: 123, 130-131
U208: 142, 144-145, 160
U209: 203, 208, 245, 318, 320, 325-326
U210: 238-240
U211: 251-252, 258, 281, 285-286, 298, 329, 363, 368-369
U212: 265, 341, 362, 368, 381, 389, 394, 424, 435
U213: 184, 213, 222, 238
U214: 247, 250-251, 285, 290, 299, 314, 352, 387, 425, 436
U215: 229, 233
U216: 253, 257-259, 262, 266
U217: 238-239, 285, 290, 329
U218: 251-252, 277-278, 295, 303, 325-326, 332, 361, 387, 425, 436, 506, 518, 521
U219: 265, 372, 454, 457
U220: 352, 357,
U221: 253-254, 257, 262, 281-282, 307, 309, 324-326, 329
U223: 296, 299, 301-302, 319-320, 324-325, 353, 369, 386, 397
U224: 266, 272, 278, 298

U225: 286-287, 301
U226: 289, 296, 299-300, 304, 318-320, 362
U228: 305, 307, 309, 326, 329, 363, 368, 371, 424, 443, 446
U229: 299, 305, 307, 309, 315, 253-354
U230: 305, 322, 324-325, 386, 414, 436
U231: 320, 324, 326, 360, 362, 378, 381, 389-390
U232: 329
U233: 415-416
U234: 518, 520
U235: 327
U236: 327, 515
U237: 327, 501
U238: 353, 355, 369, 371, 381, 389
U239: 438
U240: 362, 415
U241: 415
U242: 419, 432, 450, 484, 506
U243: 435
U244: 448, 490, 518, 520
U245: 448, 454, 490, 505, 521
U246: 454, 496
U247: 412, 415, 448
U248: 448, 481
U249: 496, 506, 518-519
U250: 432
U251: 213, 230-231, 244, 257
U252: 210
U253: 260
U254: 237, 240, 260, 262, 281-282
U255: 230-231, 244-245, 257, 294, 302-303, 343, 295, 400, 424, 506, 520
U256: 240, 246, 357, 389-390, 394-395, 424, 443
U257: 260, 289, 295, 311, 316-317, 333, 389, 394
U258: 253-254, 257, 259, 262-263, 266, 295, 303, 317, 320, 325-326
U259: 253, 273
U260: 258, 260, 262, 266, 286-287, 311, 315, 317, 320, 353-357, 376, 381, 389, 424, 443, 496
U262: 278, 280, 295-297, 318-319, 338, 363, 368, 371, 394-395, 400, 424, 448, 454
U263: 277-278
U264: 278, 295, 303, 318-321, 325-327, 357, 390
U265: 295-296
U266: 293, 296, 319-321, 325
U267: 295-297, 312, 316-317, 321, 324, 332, 360, 362, 395, 400, 443, 518
U268: 293, 296, 298, 332
U269: 344, 373, 412, 424
U270: 315, 317, 320, 353-355, 375, 377-378, 424, 436
U271: 331, 357, 361, 381
U273: 325
U274: 362, 368
U275: 353, 356-357, 375, 377-378, 424, 435-436, 490, 496

U276: 419
U277: 344, 361, 366, 374, 401-402, 409
U278: 383-384, 393, 401, 409, 441-442, 452, 481, 511, 514, 518, 521
U279: 356-357
U280: 362, 368
U281: 360, 362, 381, 389-390, 394, 424, 448, 454, 521
U282: 362, 368
U283: 381, 389
U284: 374
U285: 448, 481, 506
U286: 419, 471, 491-492, 511, 514
U287: 506, 518
U288: 393, 401
U290: 419, 450, 484, 518
U291: 525
U292: 415
U293: 452, 464, 471-472, 475, 484-485, 491, 506, 518-519
U294: 419, 511, 521
U295: 417, 464-465, 471-472, 482, 484, 511
U296: 448, 469, 496
U297: 469
U298: 521
U299: 419, 471, 475, 521
U300: 454, 490
U301: 262, 266
U302: 343, 374, 376, 381, 395, 400
U303: 293, 296, 299, 301, 317, 323
U304: 293, 325-328
U305: 309, 311, 326, 353-354, 356-357, 375, 377-378, 381
U306: 311, 317-318, 333, 363
U307: 344, 361, 366, 393, 409, 491-492, 498, 503, 511, 514
U309: 357, 360, 362, 376, 380-381, 435, 448, 490
U310: 452, 464-465, 471, 475, 492, 503, 522
U311: 374, 376, 381, 395, 400
U312: 384, 393, 401, 452, 469, 498, 503, 411, 514, 521
U313: 384, 393, 401-402, 409, 451, 471, 481, 498, 503, 511, 514, 518, 521
U314: 374, 383-384
U315: 393, 401, 409, 451-452, 464, 471, 496, 522
U317: 419
U318: 471-472, 491-492, 511, 514, 518, 521
U319: 419
U320: 518-519
U321: 496
U322: 469
U324: 522
U325: 481
U326: 506
U327: 490
U328: 521
U329: 504
U331: 118-119, 124, 136, 141, 155-156, 209, 225, 242, 250, 273
U332: 151, 198, 227, 260, 264,

297, 299, 301, 304-305, 322
U333: 177, 213, 247, 251, 260, 289, 295, 298, 307, 309-311, 333, 363, 368, 394, 424, 436
U334: 230-231, 331
U336: 284, 287, 307, 309, 311, 326, 329, 356-357
U337: 293
U338: 298, 309, 353-354
U340: 325, 333
U341: 331, 353-354
U342: 400
U343: 368-369, 380, 387, 397
U344: 444-445
U347: 402, 419
U348: 432, 450, 484, 504
U349: 518
U350: 504
U351: 518
U352: 184, 213
U353: 262
U354: 272, 288-289, 343, 361, 366, 374, 393, 401, 409, 444-445
U355: 230-231, 344, 401
U356: 253, 257-259, 262, 266, 285-287
U357: 287
U358: 296, 299, 301-302, 318, 320-321, 333, 363, 368, 371, 394
U359: 304-305, 307, 324-325, 331, 337
U360: 344, 361, 366, 383, 401
U361: 393, 401-402, 419
U362: 393, 402, 441-442
U363: 444-445, 452, 464, 471-472, 498, 503, 511, 514, 521
U364: 374, 376, 380
U365: 441-442, 444-445, 452, 464, 471-472
U366: 307, 393
U367: 497
U368: 525
U369: 521
U370: 432, 450, 484, 518
U371: 108, 119, 124, 136-137, 142, 166, 170, 200, 250, 289, 299, 317, 340, 344, 353, 386, 397, 410
U372: 118, 122, 131, 135, 151, 160, 211, 229, 238
U373: 131, 135, 147-148, 151, 201, 226, 246, 253, 259, 284-285, 287, 307, 309, 311, 337, 362, 424
U374: 142, 144, 148, 160, 170, 175
U375: 160, 185, 229, 234, 250, 283, 310, 317, 333, 340
U376: 203, 208, 230-231, 298, 304
U377: 198, 208, 265, 301, 304, 319-320, 324, 353-355, 377-378, 381
U378: 203, 320, 325-327, 353, 356-357
U379: 234, 239-240, 362,
U380: 251-252, 258, 273, 310, 344, 353, 369, 380, 387, 397
U381: 266-268, 291-292, 295,

317, 320, 325-326
U382: 260, 262, 303, 318-319, 333, 337, 375, 377-378, 381, 424, 443
U383: 266, 272, 278, 293, 296, 299, 304, 319-320, 324-325, 332
U384: 287, 289, 295, 309-310
U385: 400, 412, 436
U386: 320, 353-354, 376, 381, 389-390
U387: 344, 361, 366, 374, 409, 452, 464, 471-472
U388: 331
U389: 356-357
U390: 376, 380-381, 435
U391: 368, 371
U392: 374, 376, 381, 397
U393: 515
U394: 444-445
U395: 342
U396: 419, 454, 506
U397: 419, 518
U398: 448, 506
U399: 496
U400: 469
U401: 118-119, 122
U402: 151, 156, 180, 208, 229, 266-267, 295-297, 320, 324-325, 153-357
U403: 198, 208, 257, 289, 296, 299-300, 324-325, 333, 337
U404: 188, 222, 251-252, 258, 289, 295, 312, 316-318, 332
U405: 213, 256, 304-305, 307, 357, 362
U406: 216-217, 247, 250-251, 286-287, 307, 309, 322, 331, 337, 381, 389-390
U407: 251-252, 258, 273, 299, 317, 340, 369, 381, 404, 437
U408: 230, 257
U409: 251, 270, 285, 287, 304-305, 340
U410: 253, 258-259, 262, 266, 285, 303, 317, 344, 353, 386, 397
U411: 251-252, 277
U413: 277-278, 293, 296-297, 317-318, 320, 325-327, 360, 362, 389-390, 394, 424, 436
U414: 289, 296, 317
U415: 299, 311, 317, 331, 373, 375, 395, 424, 435
U418: 299, 325, 327
U419: 356-357
U420: 331, 335, 362
U421: 373-374, 396, 377, 397, 402, 404
U422: 353, 355, 357
U423: 419
U424: 368, 371, 389
U425: 383-384, 393, 442, 452, 464, 491-492
U426: 360, 362
U427: 483, 511, 514, 521
U429: 504
U430: 320, 504
U431: 118-119, 122, 135, 151, 154, 160, 185, 202, 206, 218, 225, 227, 258, 273, 294, 310, 340, 344, 353, 358
U432: 130-131, 142, 145, 160,

188, 213, 222, 246, 253-254, 283, 304-305, 307
U433: 130-131, 149
U434: 151, 167
U435: 203, 208, 244, 257, 281, 284, 287, 305, 308-309, 329
U436: 203, 213, 220, 266, 272, 291, 295, 322, 324-325
U437: 226, 232, 260, 262, 266-267, 299, 303, 360, 362, 389-399, 394-395, 424, 443, 446
U438: 240, 246, 266-268, 293, 296-297, 299, 317, 320-321
U439: 281, 285, 305, 307, 309, 322
U440: 257, 270, 286-287, 299, 307, 309, 311
U441: 262, 266, 287, 289, 299, 307, 309-311, 326, 332, 363, 389, 394, 412, 424
U442: 260, 262, 266-268, 291-292, 295
U443: 262, 266, 283, 299
U444: 289, 295, 307
U445: 280, 284-285, 303, 333, 389, 424, 436, 443
U447: 305, 307, 317, 322
U448: 304-305, 307, 319, 324, 356-357, 360, 394, 400
U449: 332
U450: 360, 397, 402
U451: 123, 129, 161
U452: 123
U453: 160, 206, 221, 227, 289, 317, 333, 340, 344, 369, 381, 406
U454: 172, 180, 203, 234, 238-240, 262, 266-268, 278, 280, 295-297, 301, 324, 332
U455: 184, 213, 222, 253, 281-282, 284, 287, 314, 357, 387
U456: 203, 208, 213, 230-231, 244, 295-297, 322, 324-325
U457: 230-231, 256
U458: 229, 232, 237, 273, 299, 344
U459: 211, 261, 299, 332
U460: 251, 299, 304, 314, 322, 354, 357
U461: 234, 258, 303, 332
U462: 246, 253, 279, 305, 317, 332, 337
U463: 244, 262, 266, 295, 299, 309, 315, 317
U465: 281, 295-297, 299
U466: 296, 319, 324, 331, 337, 363, 397, 436
U468: 301-302, 305, 308, 324, 326, 333
U469: 311
U470: 360
U471: 374, 376, 381, 404, 436, 442
U472: 384, 393
U473: 400
U474: 342
U475: 432, 450, 484
U476: 415
U477: 419
U478: 419
U479: 432, 450

U480: 436, 490
U481: 432, 450, 511, 514, 521
U482: 448, 469, 481
U483: 454, 490, 521
U484: 354, 448
U485: 469, 506, 518, 520
U486: 469, 501
U487: 337
U488: 329, 357, 403
U490: 416
U501: 123, 130-131
U502: 142, 145, 147, 192, 216
U503: 198
U504: 188, 219, 250, 261, 303, 308, 320, 324-325, 332
U505: 197, 232, 265, 403, 416
U506: 201, 211, 241, 255, 299, 332, 337
U507: 201, 211, 255, 286
U508: 245, 265, 298, 333, 338
U509: 234, 270, 277, 299, 337
U510: 238, 270, 277-278, 300, 331, 382, 482
U511: 238-239, 250, 277, 291-292, 295, 303, 315
U512: 253
U513: 248, 308, 312, 330
U514: 253, 291, 295, 318, 320, 324, 332, 337
U515: 253, 277-278, 283, 308, 312, 314, 368, 371, 387
U516: 253, 264, 299, 361, 381, 416, 518, 520
U517: 248
U518: 261, 267, 300, 332, 352, 386, 432, 454, 506-507
U519: 277, 283, 297-298
U520: 267
U521: 267-268, 278, 295, 303, 308, 328
U522: 267-268, 278, 280, 291-292, 303
U523: 299, 305, 309-311
U524: 281, 284-285, 308
U525: 287, 289, 296, 298-300, 319, 324, 338
U526: 305, 309, 311, 316
U527: 305, 309-311, 337
U528: 320
U529: 301
U530: 305, 307, 309, 311, 315, 317, 329, 357, 371, 416, 507, 518
U531: 320-321
U532: 315, 317, 320, 349, 382, 482, 518-519
U533: 320-321, 349
U534: 412, 443, 515
U535: 329, 332
U536: 329, 332, 352, 369
U537: 403, 417, 457, 468
U538: 368-369
U539: 356-357, 381, 386, 416, 521
U540: 360
U541: 343, 375, 377, 403, 432, 506, 518, 520
U542: 368, 371
U543: 373, 377, 403, 416
U544: 373-374, 381
U545: 376, 381, 389
U546: 376, 389, 394, 454, 506-507

U547: 376, 381, 389, 416, 443
U548: 400, 403, 443, 506
U549: 389, 394, 416
U550: 386, 394
U551: 87
U552: 81-83, 91-92, 104, 125, 131, 135, 147, 151, 177, 201, 226, 234, 238, 260, 279, 295, 317, 320, 326-327, 362, 368, 394
U553: 104, 108, 114, 123, 132, 142-143, 177, 184, 213, 222, 238, 243, 247, 281-282, 295
U556: 96, 99-101, 108, 185
U557: 99-100, 104-105, 108, 114, 128, 132, 154-155, 160, 165
U558: 104, 108, 122, 128, 132, 142, 155, 188, 193, 215, 239, 250, 257, 295, 303, 308, 326, 329-330, 332
U559: 104, 108, 114, 122, 124, 136, 141, 152, 155-156, 170, 188, 200, 225, 227
U561: 114, 118-119, 128, 132, 152, 185, 209, 229, 234, 258, 273, 310, 317, 340
U562: 108, 114, 118-119, 132, 135, 154-155, 170, 209, 229, 234, 283, 294
U563: 123, 132, 141, 145, 262, 266, 272, 286, 289-299, 315, 317
U564: 108, 114, 118-119, 125, 135, 141, 145, 182, 213, 236, 244, 247, 272, 277, 283, 311, 315, 331-332
U565: 118-119, 122, 132, 149, 156, 200, 211, 218, 238, 273, 283, 299, 317, 353, 381, 406, 437, 451
U566: 123, 129, 182, 213, 222, 247, 250, 272, 277-278, 304-305, 307, 338
U567: 123, 132, 147, 151, 168
U568: 123, 132, 142, 145, 147, 160, 170, 200, 218
U569: 123, 130-131, 146, 148, 160, 184, 216-217, 246, 253, 259, 281, 284, 303-304, 324, 326, 329
U570: 123, 288
U571: 129, 147-148, 151, 178, 201, 226, 232, 262, 266-268, 291-292, 295, 312, 316-317, 333, 377, 381
U572: 131, 135, 147-148, 151 180, 201, 234, 236, 270, 277, 289, 295, 297, 311, 315, 329-331
U573: 142, 144, 160, 170, 211
U574: 151, 167-168
U575: 131, 135, 151, 182, 185, 208, 226, 232, 262, 266, 291-292, 295, 320, 324, 326-327, 362, 368, 395
U576: 140, 182, 208, 229, 236
U577: 147-148, 151, 161, 170, 177
U578: 151, 188, 222
U579: 515
U581: 180

U582: 177 209, 234, 236, 258, 260
U584: 172, 178, 180, 198, 227, 251-252, 258, 289, 295, 297, 315, 317, 320-321, 324, 353-354, 356-357
U585: 203
U586: 220, 265, 272, 303, 341, 362, 368-369, 371, 387, 436
U587: 188, 193, 206, 443
U588: 179, 193, 213, 238,
U589: 203, 213, 245, 256
U590: 216-217, 247, 251, 260, 307, 309, 311, 331
U591: 184, 220, 245. 284-285, 287, 299 304-305, 311, 330, 337
U592: 257, 265, 311, 315, 331, 362, 368, 381, 389
U593: 184, 201, 213, 239-240, 273, 306, 323, 340, 353, 369
U594: 247, 251-252, 293, 296, 299, 315
U595: 240, 253, 258-259, 273
U596: 246, 253, 273, 299, 310, 317, 344, 353, 369, 381, 406, 437, 451
U597: 234, 238-240, 260, 262
U598: 243, 246, 293, 309, 311, 317, 337
U599: 253, 259 262, 266
U600: 243, 246, 281, 285, 301-302, 305, 308-309, 322, 324, 332-333, 368, 371
U601: 237, 244, 280, 341, 343, 374, 383-384, 393
U602: 260, 262, 266, 283, 299, 317
U603: 301-302, 305, 308-309, 325-326, 329, 356-357, 389, 394
U604: 251, 270, 281, 284, 302-303, 330, 337
U605: 237, 240, 246, 273, 305
U606: 266, 272, 278, 289, 296, 299, 301
U607: 234, 238-240, 253, 258-259, 262, 289, 296, 299, 304, 322, 324-326, 332
U608: 251-252, 272, 296-297, 304, 307, 309-310, 329, 360, 362, 369, 389, 394, 424, 436
U609: 237, 251, 266, 281, 285-286, 295-297
U610: 260, 262, 266, 281-283, 285, 309, 311, 317-318, 357
U611: 278, 280-282
U613: 272, 277-278, 293, 296, 316-317, 337
U614: 295-297, 318-320, 332
U615: 253, 257, 259, 262, 266, 281-282, 284-285, 287, 305, 308-309, 311, 316, 331
U616: 305, 309, 317, 344, 353, 369, 380, 386, 413, 415
U617: 253-254, 257-259, 273, 283, 293-294, 317, 340, 344
U618: 257, 259, 262, 266, 283, 305, 307, 309, 311, 333, 369, 271, 375, 389, 397, 436
U619: 258, 260

U620: 260, 262, 266, 391-393, 395, 320
U621: 262, 266, 285-286, 297, 299, 301-302, 305, 308, 320, 324, 326-327, 394, 424, 435-436
U622: 294, 302
U623: 280-282, 285, 301
U624: 266, 272, 278, 293, 296-297
U625: 280, 294, 341, 343, 373-374, 376, 395
U626: 286
U628: 282, 284, 287, 297, 301-302, 318-320, 324-325, 332
U629: 341, 343, 373-374, 377 424
U630: 315, 317, 320
U631: 289, 295, 309-311, 317 356-357, 360
U632: 289, 295, 311, 315
U633: 307, 329
U634: 304-305, 319-320, 324, 331
U635: 315
U636: 325, 327, 341, 343, 361, 366, 374, 402, 409, 442, 454, 464, 475, 484-485, 491-492, 506
U637: 450, 505, 521
U638: 305, 308, 320-321
U639: 341, 343
U640: 325
U641: 305, 307, 309, 311, 329, 353-354, 356-357, 375, 377-378, 381
U642: 305, 307, 309-311, 326, 329, 380, 387, 436, 442
U643: 356-357
U645: 325-327, 353-354, 356-357, 375
U646: 325
U648: 299, 318, 320, 337, 362, 368-369, 371
U650: 320, 324, 326-327, 332, 381, 389-390, 424, 443, 469
U651: 108-109
U652: 116, 119, 123, 130-131, 152, 156, 170, 188, 200-201, 218
U653: 184, 188, 213, 222, 247, 277, 283, 297, 301-302, 305, 308-309, 331, 373-374, 376, 395
U654: 177, 187, 208, 236, 244
U655: 203
U656: 188
U657: 230, 303, 325
U658: 243, 245, 247, 266-267
U659: 251-252, 270, 286, 304-305, 307, 322
U660: 240, 246, 273
U661: 262
U662: 262, 266, 286-287, 293, 299, 312, 316, 320, 331, 337
U663: 280, 284, 299, 311
U664: 285-287, 304-305, 308-309, 325, 328, 338
U665: 305, 307, 309
U666: 299, 309-311, 326, 329,

353, 355-357, 376, 381, 389
U667: 331, 373, 375, 395, 400, 436
U668: 360, 444-445, 452, 464, 471, 503, 521
U669: 331
U671: 415, 424-425, 436
U672: 373-374, 376, 395, 400, 435
U673: 393, 412, 443
U674: 393, 401, 409
U675: 415
U676: 484
U677: 419, 509
U678: 435
U679: 432, 450
U681: 496
U683: 496
U701: 177, 184, 226-227
U703: 213, 220, 230-231, 257, 341, 343, 393, 402, 444-445, 449
U704: 234, 238-240, 263, 265-267, 293, 296
U705: 240, 246
U706: 260, 262, 266, 289, 293, 311, 315, 317, 320, 332
U707: 296, 299, 302, 320-321, 325-326, 363
U709: 304-305, 319, 324, 362, 368-369, 389, 394
U710: 318
U711: 343, 401-402, 409, 441-442, 444-445, 491-492, 498, 503, 511, 514, 517
U712: 521
U713: 344, 366, 384, 393
U714: 362, 368, 371, 389, 424, 448, 496
U715: 419
U716: 374, 383, 401-402, 482, 491-492, 498, 503, 511, 514, 521
U717: 432, 450, 518
U719: 412, 415
U720: 525
U721: 518
U722: 454, 469, 496
U729: 393
U731: 325, 327, 353-357, 376, 380-381, 389, 415
U732: 317-318, 320, 331
U733: 515
U734: 373, 389
U736: 400, 412, 436
U737: 344, 383-384, 452, 464
U739: 383, 401, 409, 441-442, 482, 491-492, 525
U740: 400, 424
U741: 374, 376, 380, 395, 400, 435-436
U742: 419
U743: 448
U744: 374, 376, 394
U745: 419, 432, 484
U746: 389, 515
U747: 509
U748: 432
U749: 505
U750: 518
U751: 104, 108, 122-123, 128, 132, 145, 168, 182, 215
U752: 129, 151, 184, 208, 234,

236, 277, 293, 296, 324, 326
U753: 184, 201, 215, 260, 262, 266, 272, 278, 297, 301, 304, 324-325
U754: 177, 201, 229, 232, 237
U755: 246, 253-254, 259, 260, 273, 299, 310, 317
U756: 251
U757: 260, 262, 266, 307, 333, 376, 381
U758: 281-282, 304-305, 308-309, 329, 353, 355-357, 377-378, 424, 448
U759: 304, 331
U760: 325, 338
U761: 373, 387
U762: 357, 360, 362, 376, 380-381, 389
U763: 381, 424, 435, 443
U764: 368, 371, 389-390, 394, 412, 424, 436, 481, 518, 520
U765: 400
U766: 400, 424
U767: 415, 424
U771: 419, 464-465
U772: 448, 469
U773: 454, 469, 496, 521
U774: 506
U775: 469, 490, 521
U776: 506, 518, 520
U778: 496, 521
U779: 525
U781: 376
U792: 369
U794: 369, 518
U801: 373, 375, 377, 387
U802: 386, 432, 518-519
U804: 419, 432, 509
U805: 506-507, 518, 520
U806: 469, 525
U821: 400, 424
U825: 481, 506, 518-519
U826: 518-519
U827: 518
U841: 360
U842: 360, 362
U843: 362, 368, 371, 403, 417, 457, 482, 509
U844: 360
U845: 386, 395
U846: 381, 389
U847: 338
U848: 361
U849: 371
U850: 372
U851: 387
U852: 383
U853: 412, 445, 507, 518
U855: 432, 443
U856: 386
U857: 412, 506
U858: 432, 506-507, 518, 520
U859: 403, 417, 453
U860: 416
U861: 416-417, 482, 521
U862: 415, 417, 470
U863: 454
U864: 486
U865: 419, 443
U866: 496
U867: 443
U868: 490, 496, 520
U869: 490

U870: 469, 481, 504
U871: 454
U873: 518, 520
U874: 521
U875: 521
U876: 515
U877: 469
U878: 496, 506
U879: 506
U880: 506-507
U881: 507, 518
U883: 525
U884: 504
U886: 504
U889: 507, 518, 520
U901: 518, 521
U904: 515
U905: 481, 496
U906: 475
U907: 490, 521
U921: 452
U926: 521
U927: 490
U928: 521
U930: 521
U951: 329
U952: 325-326, 353-355, 380, 386, 436, 442
U953: 329, 363, 378, 412, 424, 435, 448, 496, 521
U954: 317-318, 320-321, 325-326
U955: 412, 424
U956: 344, 384, 393, 401, 442, 452, 464-465, 475, 484, 506, 518, 520
U957: 374-375, 383-384, 411, 441-442
U958: 415, 419, 450
U959: 393, 409
U960: 343, 374, 376, 381, 415
U961: 401
U962: 373, 375, 394-395, 400
U963: 362, 368, 389-390, 394, 424, 448, 490, 518
U964: 360
U965: 383-384, 452, 464, 471, 496
U967: 362, 368-369, 387, 410, 413, 436
U968: 401, 442, 452, 465, 484, 491-492, 498, 503, 511, 514, 518, 521
U969: 362, 368-369, 371, 387, 402, 404, 408, 436, 442
U970: 400, 424
U971: 424
U972: 374, 376, 380
U973: 384, 393
U974: 396
U975: 419, 505, 522
U976: 374, 376, 381
U977: 518
U978: 454, 496, 521
U979: 448, 469, 506, 518
U980: 419
U981: 374, 376, 380, 424, 436
U982: 419, 509
U984: 381, 389, 412, 424-425, 436
U986: 381, 389, 394, 424, 448
U986: 395, 400
U987: 415, 419

U988: 415, 424
U989: 381, 389, 394, 424, 436, 490
U990: 384, 393, 401-402, 415
U991: 469, 521
U992: 442, 452, 464, 471-472, 491-492, 498, 503, 511, 514, 518, 521
U993: 400, 424, 443, 446
U994: 419, 521
U995: 442, 452, 464, 471-472, 475, 491-492, 498, 521
U996: 342
U997: 444-445, 452, 464-465, 471-472, 475, 484, 498, 511, 514, 521
U998: 419
U999: 419, 518
U1000: 419
U1001: 419, 432, 450, 484, 506
U1002: 496, 521
U1003: 454, 496
U1004: 448, 454, 490, 521
U1005: 521
U1006: 454
U1007: 419, 515
U1008: 515
U1009: 469, 481, 506, 518-519
U1010: 518, 520
U1011: 342
U1014: 490
U1017: 490, 506
U1018: 490
U1019: 490, 496, 521
U1020: 469
U1021: 496
U1022: 490, 521
U1023: 518-519
U1024: 506
U1025: 518
U1051: 481
U1052: 506, 521
U1053: 469
U1055: 481, 506
U1056: 518
U1057: 518, 521
U1058: 490, 518-520
U1059: 387
U1060: 465
U1061: 521
U1062: 382, 417, 455
U1063: 506
U1064: 490, 496, 521
U1065: 509
U1101: 518
U1102: 342
U1103: 525
U1104: 490, 521
U1105: 496, 506, 518-520
U1106: 496
U1107: 506
U1108: 496, 521
U1109: 518-519
U1110: 525
U1131: 509
U1132: 518
U1156: 419
U1161: 518
U1162: 518
U1163: 419, 464, 471-472, 521
U1164: 438
U1165: 450, 518, 521
U1167: 504

U1168: 518
U1169: 496
U1171: 521
U1172: 481
U1191: 415, 424
U1192: 419
U1193: 432
U1194: 525
U1195: 496
U1198: 525
U1199: 448, 481
U1202: 469, 496, 521
U1203: 490, 521
U1204: 518
U1206: 505
U1207: 518
U1208: 490
U1209: 469
U1210: 515
U1221: 454, 505
U1222: 416, 435
U1223: 454
U1225: 419
U1226: 454
U1227: 454, 509
U1228: 469, 518, 520
U1229: 432
U1230: 469, 481, 525
U1231: 469, 481, 518, 520
U1232: 469, 481
U1233: 490, 525
U1234: 518
U1235: 506-507
U1271: 521
U1272: 518, 521
U1274: 505
U1275: 522
U1276: 490, 496
U1278: 490
U1279: 490
U1301: 521
U1302: 490
U1303: 518
U1304: 518
U1305: 506, 518-520
U1306: 518
U1307: 521
U1405: 518
U1406: 518
U1407: 518
U2321: 496, 521
U2322: 490, 505, 518, 521
U2323: 438
U2324: 490, 505. 518, 521
U2325: 521
U2326: 505, 518, 520
U2328: 521
U2329: 505, 521
U2333: 518
U2334: 521
U2335: 521
U2336: 518-519, 525
U2337: 521
U2338: 515
U2339: 518
U2340: 504
U2341: 525
U2343: 518
U2345: 521
U2346: 518
U2347: 518
U2348: 521
U2349: 518

U2350: 521
U2351: 525
U2352: 518
U2353: 521
U2354: 521
U2356: 525
U2357: 518
U2358: 518
U2359: 515
U2360: 518
U2361: 521
U2362: 518
U2363: 521
U2364: 518
U2365: 515
U2366: 518
U2368: 518
U2369: 518
U2502: 521
U2503: 515
U2506: 521
U2507: 518
U2509: 509
U2511: 518, 521
U2513: 521
U2514: 509
U2515: 498
U2516: 509
U2517: 518
U2518: 521
U2521: 515
U2522: 518
U2524: 515
U2525: 518
U2529: 521
U2530: 498
U2534: 515
U2540: 515
U2541: 518
U2542: 505
U2551: 518
U2557: 460
U3003: 505
U3008: 525
U3015: 518
U3017: 521
U3022: 518
U3030: 515
U3032: 515
U3033: 519
U3034: 518
U3035: 521
U3041: 521
U3044: 510
U3045: 504
U3503: 515
U3505: 505
U3508: 504
U3510: 518
U3514: 521
U3515: 521
U3523: 515
U3524: 518
U3526: 518
U3529: 518
U4701: 518
U4702: 518
U4703: 518
U4704: 518
U4706: 521
U4707: 518
U4710: 518

UA (ex-Batiray) Ger/SM: 37, 84, 95, 114, 143, 154, 159, 203
UD . . .: Ger (ex-Du)/SM:
UD 3 (ex-O 25): 279
UD 5 (ex-O 27): 260, 521
UIT . . .: Ger (ex-It)/SM
UIT 21 (ex-Finzi): 443
UIT 22 (ex-Bagnolini): 382, 387
UIT 23 (ex-Guilini): 382
UIT 24 (ex-Cappellini): 382
UJ . . .: Ger/SC (ex-fishing vessels & It corvettes)
UJ-B (ex-Treff V): 24
UJ-D (ex-Treff VIII): 30
UJ 102 (ex-KT 40): 368
UJ 103 (ex-KT 37): 368, 380, 407-408
UJ 104 (ex-KT 17): 407-408
UJ 106 (ex-KT 23): 407
UJ 113 (ex-Westfalen): 110, 116
UJ 115 (ex-Rosita): 407
UJ 116 (ex-Gronland): 60
UJ 116 (II) (ex-Xanten): 330, 407
UJ 117 (ex-Gustav Korner): 12
UJ 117 (II) (ex-Schiff 19, ex-Lola): see Schiff 19
UJ 118 (ex-Elbe): 60
UJ 125 (ex-Johannes Klatte): 24
UJ 126 (ex-Steiermark): 24, 44
UJ 128 (ex-Franken): 24
UJ 172 (ex-Freiherr von Stein): 22
UJ 177 (ex-Nordmeer): 62, 115
UJ 178 (ex-Faroer): 115
UJ 201 (ex-Egeria): 394
UJ 202 (ex-Melpomene): 467
UJ 205 (ex-Colubrina): 394, 339
UJ 206 (ex-Bombarda): 399
UJ 207 (ex-Cerabina): 399
UJ 208 (ex-Spingarda): 467
UJ 301 (ex-KFK 87): 407, 497
UJ 302 (ex-KFK 88): 407
UJ 303 (ex-KFK 89): 380, 407
UJ 303 (II) (ex-KFK 547): 497
UJ 304 (ex-KFK 91): 407
UJ 305 (ex-KFK 90): 407
UJ 306 (ex-KFK . . . .): 380, 407
UJ 307 (ex-KFK . . . .): 407
UJ 310 (ex-KFK 194): 407, 411
UJ 312 (ex-KFK . . . .): 380
UJ 313 (ex-KFK 317): 407
UJ 314 (ex-KFK . . . .): 407
UJ 315 (ex-KFK . . . .): 407
UJ 316 (ex-KFK . . . .): 380, 407
UJ 317 (ex-KFK . . . .): 407
UJ 318 (ex-KFK . . . .): 407
UJ 1101 (ex-UJ 111, ex-Alemania): 208, 213, 240, 295, 298
UJ 1102 (ex-UJ 113, ex-Westfalen): 192, 219, 310, 497
UJ 1104 (ex-UJ 114, ex-

Oldenburg): 62, 209, 240, 294
UJ 1105 (ex-UJ 115, ex-Wilhelm Loh): 192, 219, 294
UJ 1106 (ex-UJ 116, ex-Gronland): 310, 446
UJ 1108 (ex-UJ118, ex-Elbe): 209, 219, 240, 295, 298
UJ 1109 (ex-UJ 119, ex-St Georg): 198, 213, 219
UJ 1110 (ex-F.D. 6): 154, 208, 213
UJ 111 (ex-F.D. 36): 310, 446
UJ 1112 (ex-Star XXIII): 240
UJ 1113 (ex-KUJ 7): 475
UJ 1116 (ex-KUJ 16): 475
UJ 1119 (ex-Julius Pickenpack): 489
UJ 1201 (ex-UJ 126, ex-F.D. 33): 139
UJ 1202 (ex-UJ 123, ex-Franz Dankworth): 345
UJ 1204 (ex-UJ 152 (II), ex-Bohmen): 261
UJ 1205 (ex-UJ 129, ex-F.D. 81): 176, 191
UJ 1206 (ex-UJ 130, ex-F.D. 5): 319, 331, 385
UJ 1208 (ex-Gotland): 385
UJ 1209 (ex-KUJ 8): 345, 385, 414, 426
UJ 1210 (II) (ex-Zeebrugge): 414
UJ 1211 (ex-UJ-B (II), ex-Rau X): 241
UJ 1211 (II) (ex-Narvik): 426, 437, 445-446
UJ 1212 (ex-UJ-D (II) ex-Rau IX): 385, 414
UJ 1213 (ex-UJ-E (II), ex-Rau IV): 149
UJ 1214 (ex-UJ-F, ex-Rau V): 169, 191
UJ 1216 (ex-Star XXI): 243
UJ 1217 (ex-Star XXII): 331, 345
UJ 1219 (ex-KUJ 1): 414, 426, 445-446, 459
UJ 1220 (ex-KUJ 5): 426, 445-446, 459
UJ 1221 (ex-KUJ 15): 468
UJ 1222 (ex-KUJ 23): 426, 445-446
UJ 1223 (ex-KUJ 25): 468
UJ 1224 (ex-KUJ 10): 445-446, 450
UJ 1402 (ex-UJ 122, ex-Berlin): 321
UJ 1403 (ex-UJ 127, ex-Mecklenburg): 154, 176
UJ 1404 (ex-UJ 128, ex-Franken): 247
UJ 1416 (ex-UJ-C), ex-Treff VII): 154
UJ 1420 (ex-Eylau): 434
UJ 1421 (ex-Deltra II): 434
UJ 1430 (ex-KUJ 2): 468
UJ 1432 (ex-KUJ 4): 468
UJ 1433 (ex-KUJ 9): 447
UJ 1702 (ex-F.D. 62): 384
UJ 1703 (ex-KUJ 21): 396
UJ 1704 (ex-KUJ 22): 396

UJ 1708 (ex-UJ 178), ex-Faroer): 154
UJ 1711 (ex-M 1308, ex-Otto N. Anderson): 446
UJ 1713 (ex-KUJ 14): 468
UJ 1715 (ex-M 5207, ex-M 1101, ex-Lesum): 446
UJ 2101 (ex-Strimon): 351, 418 454
UJ 2102 (ex -Birgitta): 279
UJ 2104 (ex-Darvik): 351
UJ 2105 (ex-Ertha): 418
UJ 2106 (ex-Tenedos): 419
UJ 2108 (ex-Avra): 451
UJ 2109 (ex-Widnes): 359
UJ 2111 (ex-   ): 356
UJ 2124 (ex-Elaki): 390
UJ 2127 (ex-Theodoros): 398
UJ 2141 (ex Tassia Christa): 398
UJ 2171 (ex-Heidelberg): 451
UJ 2201 (ex-Bois Rose): 313
UJ 2202 (ex-Jutland): 313
UJ 2203 (ex-Austral): 313
UJ 2204 (ex-Boreal): 313
UJ 2205 (ex-Jacques Coeur): 313
UJ 2207 (ex-Cap Nord): 313, 470
UJ 2208 (ex-Alfredo): 313
UJ 2209 (ex-Minerva): 300, 397
UJ 2210 (ex-Marcella): 300, 313, 414
UJ 2211 (ex-Hardi): 430-431
UJ 2213 (ex-Heureux): 323
UJ 2220 (ex-Lago Zvai): 300
UJ 2221 (ex-Vespa): 513
UJ 2222 (ex-Tuffeto): 414
UJ 2223 (ex-Marangone): 414
UJ 2224 (ex-Strolaga): 513
UJ 2225 (ex-Ardea): 513
UJ 2226 (ex-Artemide): 513
UJ 2227 (ex-Persefone): 513
UJ 2228 (ex-Euterpe): 513
UJ 2301 (ex-KFK 81): 368, 380
UJ 2302 (ex-KFK 82): 407
UJ 2304 (ex-KFK 84): 408
UJ 2305 (ex-KFK 85): 407
UJ 2307 (ex-KFK 92): 407
UJ 2309 (ex-KFK . . . .): 368
UJ 2312 (ex-KFK . . . .): 407
UJ 2313 (ex-KFK . . . .): 407, 411
UJ 2314 (ex-KFK 202): 411
UJ 2318 (ex-KFK . . . .): 407
UJ 6073 (ex-Nihmed Allah): 445
UJ 6075 (ex-Clairvoyant): 397
UJ 6076 (ex-Volontaire): 358
UJ 6078 (ex-La Havraise): 414
UJ 6081 (ex-Camoscio): 445
UJ 6086 (ex-Cervo): 513
Uarsciek It/SM: 34, 54, 78, 84, 101, 119, 144, 200, 227-228, 242
Ubier (ex-Rutlandshire) Ger/Vp boat: see V 6116
Uckermark (ex-Altmark) Ger/ Oiler: 80, 282

Udarnik USSR/MS (B): 153, 157, 273
Udarny USSR/Monttor (BS): 112, 137
Uebi Scebeli It/SM: 34, 40
Uganda UK/CL: 333, 338, 340, 350-351, 509, 516, 523, 526, 529-530
Ugolino Vivaldi It/DD: see Vivaldi
Uhlmann US/DD: 458, 476, 499, 510, 525, 533
Uisko Fin/Escort Vessel: 342
Ula (ex-Varne) Nor/SM: 366, 384, 396
Ullswater (ex-Kos XXIX) UK/AS Trawler: 280
Ulm Ger/ML: 204, 245
Ulpio Traiano It/CL: 291
Ulster UK/DD: 421, 502, 505
Ulster Monarch UK/LS: 27, 33, 340
Ulster Prince UK/LS: 27
Ulster Queen UK/AA ship: 212, 256, 350, 386
Ultimatum/P 34 UK/SM: 176, 184, 200, 227, 358, 398, 431
Ultor UK/SM: 313, 323, 334, 336, 352, 358, 386, 390, 398, 413-414, 430
Uluc Ali Reis Tur/SM: see P 615
Ulvert M. Moore US/DE: 480, 487, 502
Ulysses UK/DD: 408, 421, 526, 529-530
Umbra/P 35 UK/SM: 171, 175, 184, 208, 227-228, 251, 255, 267, 278, 280, 284, 292
Ume Jap/DD: 473
Umikaze Jap/DD: 160, 170, 182, 186, 191, 194-195, 221, 235, 244, 249-250, 258, 263, 268, 271, 275, 290, 361, 365, 388
Una UK/SM: 186, 200, 206, 227, 255, 278, 280, 300
Unbeaten UK/SM: 77, 111, 118, 129, 135, 140, 165, 175, 198, 200, 237
Unbending/P 37 UK/SM: 261, 267, 278, 293, 300
Unbroken/P 42 UK/SM: 227, 243, 267, 286, 292, 313, 323, 334, 439
Undaunted UK/SM: 85, 87, 99
Undaunted UK/DD: 421, 479, 486, 502, 516, 526, 530
Underhill US/DE: 527
Undine UK/SM: 5, 17
Undine UK/DD: 421, 449, 479, 486, 502, 516, 526, 529-530
Unicorn UK/CVE: 338, 351, 378, 382
Union UK/SM: 111, 119
Unique UK/SM: 77, 80-81, 85, 104, 111, 127, 176
Unison/P 43 UK/SM: 227, 261, 278, 300, 313, 323, 338, 439
United/P 44 UK/SM: 245, 255, 273, 278, 280, 292, 323, 334, 340
Unity UK/SM: 5, 23
Universal UK/SM: 336, 358, 414, 430-431, 433
Unrivalled/P 45 UK/SM: 230,

278, 280, 286, 292, 300, 313, 323, 336, 338
Unruffled/P 46 UK/SM: 227, 255, 263, 273, 278, 284, 292, 300, 323, 338
Unruly UK/SM: 288, 313, 323, 334, 340, 356, 359, 433
Unryu Jap/CV: 468
Unseen/P 51 UK/SM: 278, 292, 300, 313, 336, 338, 352
Unshaken/P 54 UK/SM: 230-231, 240, 278, 313, 323, 334, 336, 396
Unsparing UK/SM: 336, 360, 419
Unswerving UK/SM: 433, 453
Untiring UK/SM: 358, 397, 414
Unyo Jap/CVE: 235, 379, 449
Upholder UK/SM: 77-78, 80, 92, 95, 101, 103, 111, 115, 119, 127-128, 135, 140, 149, 175, 186, 198, 200, 210
Upright UK/SM: 73, 81-82, 111, 119, 135-136, 140, 165, 214
Uproar/P 31 UK/SM: 99-100, 175, 198, 227, 334, 336, 352, 358, 385, 390
Upshur US/DD: 15, 83, 115, 119, 136, 309, 329
Upstart UK/SM: 390, 413 431
Uragano It/TB: 293
Urakaze Jap/DD: 156, 168, 178, 181, 190, 194, 197, 204, 220, 223, 235, 244, 250, 264, 268, 283, 286, 290, 361, 365, 415, 429, 462, 468
Ural USSR/ML (B): 110, 150-151
Ural USSR/Patrol ship (B): 129
Uranami Jap/DD: 159, 163, 166, 178, 181, 187, 194, 200, 205, 221, 235, 248, 252, 271, 275-277, 306, 383, 418, 462, 464
Urania It/Corvette: 407
Urania UK/DD: 421, 479, 502, 509, 516, 526, 529-530
Urchin UK/SM: 85
Urchin UK/DD: 386, 421, 449, 486, 509, 516, 526, 530
Uredd (ex-P 41) Nor/SM: 265, 294
Urge UK/SM: 90, 101, 103, 111, 115, 129, 140, 145, 165, 206
Uritski USSR/DD (N): 114, 256, 280, 302, 334, 484
Ursa UK/DD: 411, 421, 423, 441, 479, 486, 509, 516, 534
Ursula UK/SM: 5, 13, 21, 23, 73, 81, 111, 135, 140, 145, 230, 278, 280, 286, 439
Ushio Jap/DD: 156, 161, 194-195, 214, 220, 235, 244, 459, 462, 466
Usk/SM: 62, 97
Usodimare It/DD: 42, 98, 105, 135, 145, 165-166, 175, 193
Usugumo Jap/DD: 159, 163, 167, 178, 235, 432
Usurper UK/SM: 336
Utah US/Target ship: 161
Utmost UK/SM: 78, 80, 85, 87, 111, 119, 140, 145, 147, 153, 165, 263, 278, 280
Utsira (ex-Variance) Nor/SM: 486, 501
Uusimaa Fin/GB: 157, 228, 233, 456

Uzuki Jap/DD: 163, 168, 179, 214, 235, 237, 249, 372, 415, 430 473

V . . . : Ger/Vp boat (ex-fishing vessels cutters etc.)
V 102 (ex Cressida): 22
V 103 (ex-Sylvia): 22
V 203 (ex-Carl Rover): 427
V 205 (ex Franz Westerman): 413
V 206 (ex Otto Bröhan): 433
V 207 (ex-Heinrich Bueren): 427
V 208 (ex-Walter Darre): 413
V 209 (ex-Gauleiter Telschow): 11, 433
V 210 (ex-Heinrich Hey): 413, 433
V 211 (ex-Seydlitz): 413
V 213 (ex-Claus Bolten): 429
V 241 (ex-KFK 346): 440
V 243 (ex-KFK 348): 447
V 301 (ex-Weser): 12
V 302 (ex-Bremen): 470
V 303 (ex-Tannenberg): 516
V 403 (ex-Deutschland) : 24
V 404 (ex-Baden): 441
V 407 (ex-Dorum): 441
V 408 (ex-Haltenbank): 292
V 414 (ex-Sachsenwald): 441
V 623 (ex-Jupiter): 441
V 701 (ex-Este): 12
V 702 (ex-Memel): 27, 441
V 704 (ex-Claus Wisch) : 12
V 709 (ex-Guido Mohring): 27
V 715 (ex-Alfred I) 433
V 716 (ex-Alfred II): 447
V 717 (ex-Alfred III): 441
V 720 (ex- . . . 307): 441
V 725 (ex-Petit Poilu): 441
V 729 (ex-Marie Simone): 441
V 730 (ex-Michel-Francois): 441
V 1232 (ex-Elise): 404
V 1236 (ex-KFK 457): 404
V 1237 (ex-Loctse 22): 404
V 1241 (ex-Strangenwalde): 322
V 1301 (ex-Uranus): 433, 456
V 1302 (ex-John Mahn): 189
V 1303 (ex-Freiburg): 433, 456
V 1304 (ex-Eisenach): 305
V 1305 (ex-Wuppertal): 305
V 1306 (ex-Otto Krogmann): 433, 456
V 1309 (ex-Kapitan Stemmer): 305
V 1310 (ex-Gotland): 433, 456
V 1311 (ex-Döse): 412
V 1313 (ex-Nordstern): 305, 433, 456
V 1314 (ex-M 1301, ex-Gustav Hugo Deiters): 305, 425
V 1315 (ex-M . . ., ex-Karlsburg): 433
V 1317 (ex-M . . ., ex-Wilhelm Michaelson): 433, 456
V 1318 (ex-M 1305), ex-Julius Pickenpack): 305
V 1409 (ex-Limburgia): 318
V 1412 (ex-Witte Zee): 436
V 1501 (ex-Wiking VII): 356
V 1505 (ex-Wal VIII): 427
V 1506 (ex-Wal IX): 427
V 1507 (ex-Rau VI): 23

V 1509 (ex-Rau III): 422
V 1511 (ex-Unitas VII): 427
V 1512 (ex-Unitas VIII): 468
V 1537 (ex-KFK 288): 427
V 1540 (ex-KFK 295): 427
V 1541 (ex-KFK 296): 427
V 1605 (ex-M 1903, ex-Mosel): 446
V 1606 (ex-M 1904, ex-Julius Fock): 366
V 1703 (ex-Unitas IV): 489
V 1705 (ex-Rau IX): 431
V 1707 (ex-Wiking IV): 431
V 1713 (?): 470
V 1805 (ex-Senateur Louis Brindenau): 427
V 1814 (ex-V 1513, ex-Linz): 427
V 1815 (ex-V 1526, ex-Lootse A6): 427
V 2002 (ex-V 1313, ex-Nordstern): 516
V 2003 (ex-V 1315, ex-Karlsburg): 498
V 2004 (ex-V . . ., ex- . . .): 456
V 2007 (ex-Hannover): 456
V 2016 (ex-V . . ., ex- . . .): 433, 456, 468
V 2017 (ex- . . .): 456
V 2019 (ex-V. . ., ex-Adolf Hitler): 433, 456
V 2020 (ex-V . . .): 425
V 2021 (ex-M 1705, ex-Nurnberg): 425
V 2022 (ex-M 1303, ex-Emil Colzmann): 433, 497
V 5101/. . . (ex-Beitz): 446
V 5102/Donner (ex-Sneland): 172, 475
V 5105/Tornado (ex-Lianen): 446
V 5108/Föhn (ex-Hadaröy): 171
V 5113/Donar: 473
V 5114/Seebär: 473, 475
V 5303/. . . (ex-Balder): 468
V 5307 (ex-V 5506, ex-Felix Scheder): 384, 446
V 5309/Seerobbe: 446
V 5312/. . . (ex-Brachvogel): 468
V 5505/Seeteufel: 141
V 5506 /Ziek: 446
V 5513 (ex-Libelle): 446
V 5514 (ex-Sperber): 468
V 5525 (ex-KFK 331): 467
V 5527 (ex-KFK 218): 468
V 5531 (ex-KFK 190): 467
V 5716/Flandern: 446
V 5722/Hornack: 465
V 5901 /ex-Falkland): 415
V 5902/Polarsonne: 310
V 5903/Polarfront: 176
V 5904/Geier (ex-Timan): 171
V 5906/Nordpol: 295
V 5907/Sudwind: 310
V 5909/Coronel: 289, 295
V 5912/Polarstern: 385
V 5913 (ex-V 1607/Polarkreis): 385
V 5914 (ex-V 6108/Polarmeer): 385
V 5916 (ex-M 1903, ex-Vardo): 385

V 6101 (ex-V 5911, ex-M 1902, ex-Gauleiter Bohle): 450
V 6102 (ex-M 1901, ex-Koln): 426, 445
V 6104 (ex-M 1502, ex-Wien): 445
V 6105 (ex-M 1503, ex-Holstein): 240, 450
V 6106/Kiautschau (ex-Hval XX): 213
V 6106 (II) (ex-M 1504, ex-Tirol): 375
V 6107/Polarkreis (ex-V 5913) 213, 426
V 1607 (II) (ex-V 5915, ex-M 1905, ex-Wilhelm Solle): 426
V 6108/Polarmeer (ex-V 5914): 213
V 6109/Nordwind: 310, 394
V 6110/Nordkyn: 426, 446, 451
V 6111 (ex-Franke): 27
V 6111 (II) (ex-M 1505, ex-Masuren): 385, 426, 445
V 6112/Friese (ex-Bradman): 27, 445
V 6113/Gote (ex-Cape Siretoko) 414
V 6114 (ex-Warwickshire): see Nki 09
V 6115/Salier (ex-Hamkond): 295
V 6116/Ubier (ex-Rutlandshire): 279
V 6117/Cherusker (ex-Jardine): 279
V 6307 (ex-Schiff 31, ex-Jupiter): 437
V 6408/Skagerrak: 486
V 6413/Fro: 468
V 6722 (ex-KFK 224): 426
V 6725 (ex-KFK 514): 426
V 6801/Wikinger (ex-Torild): 446

V . . . USSR (ex-UK)/SM
V-1 (ex-Sunfish) (N): 439
V-2 (ex-Unbroken) (N): 439, 485
V-3 (ex-Unison) (N): 439, 450, 485
V-4 (ex-Ursula) (N): 439, 459

VAS . . . : It/R boat
VAS 303: see RA 256

VMV . . . : Fin/Patrol boats
VMV-1: 134
VMV-8: 233
VMV-9: 233
VMV-10: 233
VMV-12: 233
VMV-13: 261
VMV-14: 134
VMV-15: 134, 261
VMV-16: 134
VMV-17: 233

Vs 215 Ger/Experimental MTB: 512
Väinämöinen Fin/Coast Defence vessel: 134
Vaindlo USSR MS (B): 130
Valentine UK/DD: 30
Valentine (II) UK/DD: see Algonquin

Valerian Kuibyshev USSR/DD (N): see Kuibyshev
Valiant UK/BB: 23-25, 32-33, 38, 41, 43, 46, 49-51, 54, 57-58, 63, 67, 70, 73-74, 89, 93-94, 97 102, 155, 166, 333, 339, 347, 349, 351, 378, 382, 399, 407, 411, 438, 442
Vallelunga It/ML: 323, 341
Valleyfield Can/Frigate: 403
Valmy Fr/DD: 12, 18, 37, 106-107, 280, 381
Valoroso It/GB: 105
Valorous UK/DD: 518
Vammen US/DE: 504-505
Vampire Aus/DD: 9, 40, 43, 45, 62, 69, 76, 94, 108, 163, 165, 180-181, 197 204-205, 419, 430
Vampire UK/SM: 453
Vandale (ex- . . .) Ger/Vp boat: see NM 01
Van Dyck UK/Auxiliary ship: 36
Vanessa UK/DD: 267-268, 287, 296
Van Galen Du/DD: 29
Van Galen (II) (ex-Noble) Du/DD: 255, 382, 400, 407, 411, 460
Van Ghent Du/DD: 185, 188
Van Kinsbergen Du/GB: 68, 104
Van Nes Du/DD: 191
Vanoc UK/DD: 85, 258, 397
Vanquisher UK/DD: 31, 168, 360, 389, 413, 421, 506
Vansittart UK/DD: 242
Varian US/DE: 469, 481, 507
Variance UK/SM: see Utsira
Varne UK/SM: see Ula
Vasama (ex-TKA-52) Fin/TB: 233, 431
Vascama UK/AS Trawler: 123
Vasilefs Georgios Gr/DD: see Hermes
Vasilissa Olga Gr/DD: 292, 298, 328, 339, 349, 351, 356
Vauban Fr/DD: 20, 37, 280
Vautour Fr/DD: 37, 280
Vauquelin Fr/DD: 107, 280
Vega It/TB: 70, 74
Vekha USSR/MS (P): 532
Veldt UK/SM: see Veldt
Velella It/SM: 34, 48, 67, 83, 85, 103-104, 210, 227, 236, 273, 336
Velite It/DD: 280, 349
Vella Gulf US/CVE: 528
Velox UK/DD: 97
Vendetta Aus/DD: 9, 45, 63, 69, 89, 94, 102, 108, 117, 406, 537
Venerable UK/CVL: 534
Venetia UK/DD: 31
Vengeance UK/CVL: 534
Vengeur Fr/SM: 36, 60, 70, 280
Veniero It/SM: 34, 37, 41, 56, 69, 84-85, 87, 103-104, 124, 156, 165, 200, 210
Venomous UK/DD: 31, 33, 212, 242, 338, 518
Venturer UK/SM: 396, 446, 486, 501
Venus UK/DD: 384, 421, 429, 446, 452, 465, 468, 510, 514, 520

Vénus Fr/SM: 36, 280
Verdun Fr/DD: 12, 37, 280
Verity UK/DD: 31
Veronica UK/Corvette: 143
Verp USSR/SM (B): see T-206
Versailles Ger/ML: 108
Versatile UK/DD: 421
Verulam UK/DD: 408, 421, 442, 446, 452, 465, 467, 510, 514, 520
Vervain UK/Corvette: 211, 278, 281-282, 299, 304, 389, 395, 490
Vesihiisi Fin/SM: 15, 110, 112, 116, 123, 261, 431
Vesikko Fin/SM: 15, 115, 432
Vespa It/Corvette: see UJ 2221
Vesper UK/DD: 389, 420
Vestal US/AR: 161, 529
Vetehinen Fin/SM: 13, 110, 114-116, 261, 432
Vetch UK/Corvette: 167-168, 210, 317, 339
Veteran UK/DD: 33, 131, 258
Vettor Pisani It/SM: see Pisani
Viceroy UK/DD: 338, 505. 519
Vicksburgh US/CL: 492-493, 499-500, 509, 527-528, 533
Victorious UK/CV: 100, 105, 107, 121, 127, 142, 149, 193, 198, 203, 208, 212, 230, 242, 274, 335, 401, 408, 410-411, 438, 442, 453, 460, 471, 479, 486, 502, 516, 526, 530
Vidette UK/DD: 34, 41, 215, 218, 227, 315, 320-321, 326, 360, 362, 420, 436
Vieste It/ML: 34, 38, 323, 341
Viforul Ru/MTB: 126, 144
Vigilant UK/DD: 421, 442, 444, 473, 494, 510, 514, 520, 527
Vigorous UK/SM: 433, 453
Vihuri (ex-TKA-141) Fin/MTB: 279
Vijelia Ru/MTB: 126, 144
Viking UK/SM: 446
Ville d'Oran Fr/Aux CL: 38
Vimiera UK/DD: 31
Vimy UK/DD: 30-31, 33, 137, 244, 296-297. 310, 316, 421
Vincennes US/CA: 5, 14, 92, 119, 132, 151, 207, 221, 224, 226, 238, 241
Vincennes (II) US/CL: 427, 448 458, 461, 464, 466, 474, 476, 491-492, 499-500, 509
Vincenzo Gioberti It/DD: see Gioberti
Vincenzo Giordano Orsini It/ TB: see Orsini
Vindex UK/CVE: 395, 400, 424, 444-445, 464, 475, 511
Vindictive UK/Training CL: 27, 33
Vinha Fin/MTB: 139, 279
Violet UK/Corvette: 109, 381
Virago UK/DD: 374-375, 408, 421-422, 442, 452, 494, 510, 514, 520
Vironia USSR/Staff ship: 130
Virsaitis USSR/MS: (B): see T-297
Virtue UK/SM: 433, 453
Viscolul Ru/MTB: 126

Viscount UK/DD: 66, 211, 246, 262, 299, 358
Vita UK/Hospital ship: 47
Vittorio Alfieri It/DD: see Alfieri
Vittorio Veneto It/BB: 50, 57, 67, 69, 75, 79, 88-89, 128, 140, 165, 228, 283, 349
Vivacious UK/DD: 31, 33, 189, 421, 518
Vivaldi It/DD: 42-43, 46, 58, 63, 74, 97, 127, 143, 154, 165, 175, 183, 193, 199, 209-210, 214, 228, 311, 323, 341, 349
Viviana S. Afr/AS Trawler: 299
Vivid UK/SM: 419, 433
Vivien UK/DD: 394
Vixen UK/DD: see Sioux
Vizalma UK/AS Trawler: 87, 287
Vnushitelny USSR/DD (P): 530
Voikov USSR/DD (P): 530-531
Volage UK/DD: 442, 446, 452, 465, 494
Volframio It/SM: 242, 283
Volga USSR/GB (B): 132, 157, 384 428, 470
Volodarski USSR/DD (B): 14, 130
Volta Fr/DD: 8, 12, 41, 280
Voltaire UK/Aux CL: 91
Volturno It/Aux CL: 323
Volunteer UK/DD: 85, 206, 219, 309, 358, 405, 421
Von der Gröben (ex-M 107) Ger/R boat Depot ship: 1, 4, 22. 413, 427
Von der Lippe (ex-M 146) Ger/R boat Depot ship: 427
Voroshilov USSR/CA (BS): 113 136, 148, 209, 216, 222, 281
Vortigern UK/DD: 38, 40-41. 43, 201
Vox UK/SM: see Curie
Vox (II) UK/SM: 433, 453
Voyager Aus/DD: 9, 40, 43, 62, 69, 76, 93-94, 97, 102, 108, 256
Vrzyv USSR/MS (BS): see T-410
Vrzyvatel USSR/MS (BS): see T-405
Vyatka USSR/NL (B): 130
Vyuga (S-10) USSR/Patrol ship (P): 531

W . . . : Jap/MS (Sokaitei)
W1: 159, 181, 187, 194, 530
W2: 159-160, 166, 181, 187, 194, 196
W3: 159-160, 167, 181, 187, 194
W4: 159, 166, 181, 187, 194
W5: 159, 181, 187, 471
W6: 159, 167
W7: 177, 181, 184, 186, 191, 400
W8: 177, 181, 184, 186, 191
W9: 177, 181, 184
W10: 162
W11: 177, 181, 184
W12: 177, 181, 184, 505
W13: 177
W14: 177
W15: 177, 182, 186, 194, 495
W16: 177, 182, 186, 194
W17: 177, 182, 186
W18: 177, 182, 186

W19: 162
W20: 505
W21: 377
W22: 377, 439
W24: 525
W25: 432
W27: 526
W28: 439
W33: 530
W34: 515
W38: 468
W39: 526
W41: 505

Wa . . .: Jap/Aux MS (Sokaitei-T)
Wa 3: 505
Wa 10: 466
Wa 104 (ex-Djember): 495

W. D. Porter US/DD: 396, 431
Wadleigh US/DD: 427, 528, 530, 533
Wadsworth US/DD: 363, 391, 426-427, 437, 504, 511, 513
Wager UK/DD: 460, 470, 479, 486, 502
Wagga Aus/MS: 406. 534
Wahoo US/SM: 284, 289, 306 347
Wainwright US/DD: 92, 151, 203, 230, 308, 339, 350, 369, 535
Wakaba Jap/DD: 181, 186, 191, 221, 235, 312, 337, 459, 462-463
Wakamiya Jap/Frigate: 365
Wakataka Jap/ML: 177, 182, 194, 460, 495
Wakatake Jap/TB: 401
Wakatsuki Jap/DD: 361, 364, 415, 430, 462, 466
Wake US/GB: 163
Wake Island US/CVE: 416, 432, 480, 493, 502, 505
Wakeful UK/DD: 31-32
Wakeful (II) UK/DD: 410-411, 460, 470, 486, 526, 530-531
Waldemar Kophamel Ger/SM Depot ship: 475
Waldron US/DD: 476, 492, 499, 533
Walke US/DD: 108, 119. 183, 190, 199, 214, 226, 275-277
Walke (II) US/DD: 420, 473-474, 479, 481, 528, 533
Walker UK/DD: 27, 31, 85, 119, 267, 408, 464
Walker US/DD: 331, 388, 409, 421, 437, 475, 499, 525
Wallace UK/DD: 338
Wallace L. Lind US/DD: 499, 525, 533
Wallasea UK/Trawler: 380
Waller US/DD: 291, 307, 334, 345, 355, 391, 471, 474, 480, 495, 498, 513, 523-524
Wallflower UK/Corvette: 421
Walney (ex-Sebago) UK/Sloop: 275
Walpole UK/DD: 189, 200, 421, 440, 475

Walter C. Wann US/DE: 461, 480, 504, 509
Walter S. Scott US/DE: 413
Wanderer UK/DD: 27, 29, 104, 122, 338, 381, 421, 435
War Hawk US/AP: 483
War Mehtar UK/Oiler: 153
Ward US/DD: 152, 345, 376, 473
Warambool Aus/Corvette: 256, 470, 538
Warramunga Aus/DD: 310, 334, 367, 372, 375-376, 380, 395-396, 409, 418, 437, 451, 461, 474, 479, 513, 520, 533
Warrego Aus/Sloop: 190, 479, 480, 498, 500
Warrington US/DD: 432
Warspite UK/BB: 11, 24-27, 36, 43, 45, 48, 50-51, 57, 58, 63, 67, 70, 73-74, 89, 93, 97, 102, 204, 239, 255, 298, 333, 339-340, 347, 349, 351, 421-422, 439, 447, 467
Warwick UK/DD: 29, 358, 390
Wasatch US/AGC: 451, 480, 512, 524
Washington US/BB: 203, 212, 230, 263, 269-270, 275-277, 291, 370, 373, 387, 427, 448, 458, 461, 464, 474, 476, 491, 493, 499-500, 509
Waskesiu Can/Frigate: 394, 408, 424
Wasmuth US/DMS: 161
Wasp US/CV: 91, 119, 132, 203, 210, 215, 226, 239, 241, 249,254
Wasp (II) US/CV: 415, 426, 448, 457, 464, 466, 474, 476, 491, 499-500, 528, 530, 533
Wastwater UK/Trawler: 123
Waters (ex-DD 115) US/APD: 334-335, 345, 388
Watchman UK/DD: 38, 43, 369, 440, 496
Waterhen Aus/DD: 9, 49, 62, 69, 93-94, 97, 102, 108
Waterman US/DE: 474, 533
Watts US/DD: 525, 533
Wave King UK/Oiler: 470, 486
Waveney UK/LS: 513
Wear UK/Frigate. 326
Weaver US/DE: 476, 533
Wedderburn US/DD: 437, 458, 476, 499, 525, 533
Weichsel Ger/SM Depot ship: 504
Weissenburg Ger/Oiler: 99
Welles US/DD: 395, 409, 476
Welshman UK/ML: 215, 227-228, 236, 271, 293-294
Wensleydale UK/DD: 336, 362, 388, 421, 436
Wessex UK/DD: 31
Wessex (II) UK/DD: 460, 470, 486, 509, 516
Wesson US/DE: 503, 508
West Ger/Gun Carrier: 342
West Virginia US/BB: 161, 452, 461, 463, 471, 474, 479 502, 505, 533
Westcott UK/DD: 27, 29, 32, 51, 96, 180, 215, 218, 223, 225, 227, 242, 374, 408, 421, 471, 475
Westerwald Ger/Oiler: 1

Westminster UK/DD: 318
West Point US/APA: 150
Westralia Aus/Aux CL: 199, (LSI), 375-376, 524
Wetaskiwin Can/Corvette: 131, 142, 211, 238, 318
Weyburn Can/Corvette: 248, 296
Whaddon UK/DD: 328, 339, 443 451
Whale US/SM: 289, 306, 322, 343 379, 402, 419, 456
Wheatland UK/DD: 171, 299, 339, 444, 467
Whelp UK/DD: 460, 470, 479, 486, 502
Whimbrel UK/Sloop: 339, 400-401, 516
Whipple US, D D: 169, 173, 197, 402
Whirlwind UK/DD: 31, 38
Whirlwind (II) UK/DD: 470, 486, 502, 509, 516, 534
Whitaker UK/DE: 454
Whitehall UK/DD: 31, 33, 59, 197, 199, 202, 325, 358, 363, 374, 384, 408, 445, 452, 492
Whitehaven UK/MS: 344
White Plains US/CVE: 428, 461, 463
Whitehurst US/DE: 465, 503, 509
Whitshed UK/DD: 18, 31, 189, 366, 405, 421
Whyalla Aus/MS: 285, 406, 470, 516
Wicher Pol/DD: 1-2
Wichita US/CA: 92, 132, 149, 203, 212, 230, 273, 291, 323, 336-337, 387, 392, 406, 427, 448, 458, 461, 464, 502-503, 527
Wickes US/DD: see Montgomery
Wickes (II) US/DD: 396, 431, 480, 483, 488, 502, 527
Widgeon UK/Corvette: 318
Widnes UK/MS: see UJ 2109
Wild Goose UK/Sloop: 328, 332, 362, 371, 389, 395, 400-401, 424, 490, 496
Wild Swan UK/DD: 31, 132, 226
Wilhelm Heidkamp Ger/DD: 7-8, 10, 17, 19, 22, 24
Wilhoite US/DE: 403, 413, 416, 432, 507
Wilk Pol/SM: 1-2, 4-6, 37
Wilkes US/DD: 339, 396, 409, 458, 491, 533
Wilkes-Barre US/CL: 476, 499-500, 509, 525-526, 529, 533
Willem van Ewijck Du/MS: 4
William B. Preston US/Seaplane Tender: 190
William C. Cole US/DE: 504, 517
William C. Miller US/DE: 533
William D. Porter US/DD: 396, 431, 479, 502, 523
William P. Biddle US/AP: 115
William Seiverling US/DE: 480, 502, 528
Willis US/DE: 387, 395, 403, 416, 432 507
Willmarth US/DE: 469, 503, 533
Willoughby US/MTB Depot Ship: 495

Wilson US/DD: 92, 203, 226, 238, 241, 335, 364-365, 370, 373, 387, 427, 480, 504, 510
Wilton UK/DD: 229, 242, 322, 339, 386
Winchelsea UK/DD: 31, 211, 369
Winchester UK/DD: 30
Windermere (ex-Kos XXVII) UK/Trawler: 123
Windham Bay US/CVE: 516, 522
Windrush UK/Frigate: see La Decouverte
Windsor UK/DD: 30-31, 296, 306, 313, 421
Winooski US/Oiler: 277
Winslow US/DD: 92, 108, 151, 379
Wisconsin US/BB: 474, 476, 491, 499-501, 509, 525-526, 533
Wishart UK/DD: 38, 43, 65, 67, 197, 199, 202, 211, 215, 218, 223, 225, 227, 242, 338, 387
Witch UK/DD: 29, 168
Witherington UK/DD: 302
Witte de With Du/DD: 195
Witter US/DE: 503, 507, 528
Wivern UK/DD: 296
Wizard UK/DD: 410
Wolf Ger/TB: 3, 10-12, 22, 58, 60-61, 74
Wolfgang Zenker Ger/DD: 1, 17-19, 22
Wolfhound UK/DD: 31-32, 518
Wollongong Aus/MS: 187, 197, 339, 344
Wolverine UK/DD: 29, 84, 88, 242
Wolsey UK/DD: 31, 518
Woodcock UK/Sloop: 362, 516
Woodpecker UK/Sloop: 328, 332, 389, 390
Woodstock Can/Corvette: 356, 421
Woodworth US/DD: 334-335, 364, 391, 458, 533
Woolsey US/DD: 277, 339, 350 369, 385, 415, 444, 449
Woolston UK/DD: 338, 518
Worcester UK/DD: 31-32, 189, 363
Worcestershire UK/Aux CL: 88
Worden US/DD: 161, 168, 214, 221, 224, 226, 238, 249, 255, 293
Wrangler UK/DD: 470, 526, 530-531
Wren UK/DD: 44
Wren UK/Sloop: 328, 332, 400-401, 424
Wren US/DD: 525, 533
Wrestler UK/DD: 38, 41, 46, 60, 97, 103, 211, 215, 218, 223, 225, 227, 242, 277, 338, 358, 374, 408, 421, 424
Wryneck UK/DD: 95
Wyandot US/AKA: 503
Wyffels US/DE: 413
Wyoming US/BB: 5

X . . . : UK/Midget SM
X5: 355
X6: 355
X7: 355

X8: 355
X9· 355
X10: 355
X24: 396
XE1: 529
XE 3: 529
Xanten Ger/SC: 330, see UJ116

YMS . . . : US/Coastal MS
YMS 10: 524
YMS 24: 444
YMS 30: 386
YMS 39: 524
YMS 47: 524
YMS 49: 524
YMS 50: 246, 524
YMS 59: see T-156
YMS 75: see T-583
YMS 81: 508
YMS 84: 524
YMS 92: 508
YMS 103: 508
YMS 144: see T-152
YMS 145: see T-155
YMS 186: see KOS
YMS 237: see T-588
YMS 272: see T-590
YMS 273: see T-591
YMS 311: 508
YMS 314: 524
YMS 321: 508
YMS 327: 517
YMS 331: 517
YMS 334: 513
YMS 335: 524
YMS 363: 513
YMS 364: 513, 524
YMS 365: 524
YMS 368: 524
YMS 409: 432
YMS 481: 513

YO 159 US/Harbour tanker: 381
YP 284 US/Harbour craft: 269
YP 389 US/Harbour defence
    boat: 227
Yääkarhu Fin/Icebreaker: 134
Yaezakura Jap/DD: 526
Yahagi Jap/CL: 415, 430, 462,
    508
Yaeyama Jap/ML: 160
Yakaze Jap/DD: 526
Yakor USSR/MS (BS): see T-408
Yakov Sverdov USSR/DD (B):
    130
Yaku Jap/Frigate: 491
Yamagumo Jap/DD: 162, 169,
    248, 263, 361, 377, 415, 418,
    430, 462-463
Yamakaze Jap/DD: 160, 170,
    182, 191, 194-196, 221
Yamashiro Jap/BB: 221, 235, 462-
    463
Yamato Jap/BB: 221, 235, 244,
    361, 377, 414, 418, 430,
    462-463, 499, 508
Yanagi Jap/DD: 525, 530
Yandra Aus/Trawler: 470
Yarnall US/DD: 427, 476, 533
Yarra Aus/Sloop: 55, 61, 93,
    129, 161, 180, 186, 196
Yashiro Jap/Frigate: 476, 530

Yashojima (ex-Ping Hai) Jap/
    CL: 467
Yayoi Jap/DD: 164, 168, 179,
    199, 214, 235, 249-250
Yoitsuki Jap/DD: 529
York UK/CA: 5, 7, 19, 23-25,
    27-28, 32, 57-58, 63, 65, 67,
    74, 88
Yorktown US/CV: 92, 132, 183,
    190, 199, 214-215, 220-221,
    224
Yorktown (II) US/CV: 347, 359,
    369, 373, 387, 392, 400, 406,
    426, 430, 474, 476, 491,
    499-500, 509, 516, 522,
    525-526, 533
Young US/DD: 396, 431, 480,
    488, 512
Yubari Jap/CL: 164, 168, 179,
    199, 214, 235, 241, 248, 335,
    365
Yudachi Jap/DD: 162, 170, 177,
    182, 194-195, 221, 235, 250,
    252-253, 268, 271, 275-276
Yugiri Jap/DD: 159, 163, 166,
    173, 178, 181, 187, 194, 200,
    204-205, 221, 235, 249, 372
Yugumo Jap/DD: 220, 235, 248,
    254, 264, 268, 271, 275, 290,
    337, 356
Yugure Jap/DD: 194, 214, 221,
    235, 252, 271, 275, 283, 286,
    322, 335, 341
Yukaze Jap/DD: 221
Yukikaze Jap/DD: 160, 170,
    177, 181, 184, 191, 194-195,
    221, 235, 248-249, 254, 264,
    268, 275, 290, 306, 335, 361,
    415, 430, 462, 508, 529
Yunagi Jap/DD: 168, 179, 199,
    235, 237, 241, 245, 248, 335,
    356, 415, 430, 439
Yura Jap/CL: 163, 167, 178,
    181, 187, 194, 196, 200-201,
    204-205, 221, 235, 248, 252,
    258, 264, 266, 268-269
Yurishima Jap/ML: 479
Yuzuki Jap/DD; 163, 168, 179,
    214, 235, 237, 245, 248, 473

Z . . .: Ger/DD
Z 23: 100, 169, 179, 314, 317,
    332, 377, 441
Z 24: 169, 179, 201, 203, 213,
    230, 314, 317, 332, 376-377,
    422, 441
Z 25: 139, 169, 179, 189, 192,
    198, 203, 213, 218, 397, 446,
    460, 470, 485, 515-516
Z 26: 139, 201, 203
Z 27: 139, 169, 230, 265, 272,
    348, 377
Z 28: 230, 258, 397, 446, 455,
    489
Z 29: 188, 230, 253, 258, 288,
    348, 374
Z 30: 201, 230, 253, 258, 265,
    272, 288, 348, 374
Z 31: 288, 298, 348, 373, 490,
    495, 497
Z 32: 314, 317, 332, 376-377,
    422

Z 33: 348, 374
Z 34: 374, 485, 490-491, 495,
    497-498, 512
Z 35: 397, 446, 455, 460, 470,
    473
Z 36: 446, 460, 473
Z 37: 314, 376 441
Z 38: 374, 485, 490-491, 495,
    497, 512, 516
Z 39: 397, 431, 498, 512, 516
Z 43: 473, 485, 495, 497, 512
Z 51: 501
ZH 1: 376-377, 422
Zaffiro It/SM: 34, 40, 45, 57, 62,
    68, 71, 122, 128, 144, 155, 175,
    227
Zagreb Yu/DD: 91
Zähringen Ger/Target ship: 475
Zambesi UK/DD: 444, 446, 465,
    467, 473, 475, 492, 517-518
Zane (ex-DD 337) US/DMS:
    161, 268. 334
Zara It/CA: 36, 42, 57, 69, 89
Zarnitsa USSR/Patrol ship:
    531-532
Zaryad USSR/MS (B): see T-201
Zashchitnik USSR/MS (BS): see
    T-411
Zbik Pol/SM: 1, 4, 6
Zealous UK/DD: 473, 491-492,
    511, 518-519
Zebra UK/DD: 475
Zeffiro It/DD: 40, 42
Zeilin US/APA: 263, 275, 483
Zellars US/DD: 502, 509
Zeno It/DD: 42, 47, 94, 96, 126
    165, 193, 228, 265, 272-273,
    282, 292, 300, 349
Zephyr UK/DD: 465, 468-469,
    473, 511, 518-519
Zest UK/DD: 492, 511, 518-519
Zetland UK/DD: 242, 322, 443,
    453
Zeus (ex-Francesco Morosini)
    Ger/ML: 454
Zeya USSR/GB (B): 131, 384,
    428, 470
Zharki (ex-Brighton) USSR/DD
    (N): 444-445
Zheleznyakov USSR/DD (BS):
    147, 152, 156, 158, 172-173,
    178, 180, 197, 202, 212, 218,
    254, 297, 301, 319
Zheleznyakov USSR/Monitor
    (BS): 110, 112
Zhemchug USSR/Patrol Boat
    (N): 123
Zhemchuzhin USSR/Monitor
    (BS): 110, 112, 117
Zhemlyak USSR/Aux MS
    (BS): see T-32
Zhestki (ex-Georgtown) USSR/
    DD (N): 442, 444, 492, 511
Zhivuchi (ex-Richmond, ex-
    Fairfax) USSR/DD (N): 444,
    472, 484-485
Zhyuchi (ex-Leamington)
    USSR/DD (N): 444
Zinnia UK/Corvette: 125
Zmaj Yu/Aircraft depot ship: 91,
    see Drache
Zodiac UK/DD: 511, 518-519

Zoea It/SM: 39, 41, 60, 71, 81,
    98, 115, 124, 227, 229, 236,
    271, 360
Zoemba Du/GB: 386
Zuiho Jap/CVL: 221, 235, 254,
    263, 268-269, 316, 361, 415,
    430, 462, 464
Zuikaku Jap/CV: 156, 179, 184,
    204, 214, 235, 248-249, 254,
    263-264, 268-269, 316, 415,
    430, 462, 464
Zulu UK/DD: 23, 27, 29, 46,
    101, 140, 180, 183, 186, 189,
    200-201, 227, 238, 257
Zvaardfish (ex-Talent) Du/SM:
    457, 460

W

Merchant Ships

I have placed the different types of merchant ship in this section under broad categories, not distinguishing between the various types of propulsion used nor between the different categories of vessel of a particular type. Thus all cargo carrying vessels, irrespective of type or size, have been listed as freighters, while all passenger carrying vessels (except ferrys which are listed as such) have been placed under the broad category of liner. The only category which might cause some confusion is CRS, which were small cross-channel type passenger vessels. These were fitted out with sick bays, dormitories and a medical staff not normally found on warships sailing with the close escort of convoys, nor on merchant ships. They were found mainly on the Arctic Convoys where they were used for the express purpose of staying behind to rescue seamen from damaged and sinking ships.

CRS   Convoy Rescue
        ship
F   Freighter
F (C)   Freighter fitted
        with catapult for
        flying off aircraft
FV   Fishing Vessel
L   Liner
SV   Sailing Vessel
T   Tanker
WFS   Whale Factory
        Ship
Y   Yacht

A. Andreev USSR/F: 343
Aagtekerk Du/F: 227-228
Abkhaziya USSR/F: 136, 141, 143, 175, 199, 225
Abosso UK/L: 266
Accrington UK/CRS: 295
Acrity UK/F: 33
Adana Ger/F: 80, 93
Aden Maru Jap/F: 407
Adolf Leonhardt Ger/F: 13
Adolf Woermann Ger/F: 9
Adriatico It/Ferry: 157
Aegina Ger/F: 80, 93
Afric Star UK/L: 74
Africander Pan/F: 256
Africa Shell UK/T: 9
Agathe Ger/F: 433
Agnete Dan/F: 308
Ajax Ger/F: 310
Ajax UK/L: 139, 180, 189, 227
Akbar UK/L: 46
Akka Ger/F: 279
Alamar US/F: 220
Alba Julia Ru/F: 407-408
Albert Jensen Ger/L: 488, 497
Albert Leborgue Fr/F: 28
Albert L. Ellsworth Nor/F: 291
Alberte le Borgne Fr/F: 28
Albuera UK/T: 40
Alcoa Cadet US/F: 223
Alcoa Ranger US/F: 231
Alev USSR (ex-Est)/L: 130
Algarve UK/F: 81
Alicante Ger/F: 79
Almeda Star UK/L: 75
Almeria Lykes US/F: 243
Almora Ger (ex-Nor)/F: 410
Alsterufer Ger/F: 377
Altenfels Ger/F: 330
Altengamme Ger/F: 512
Altkirch Ger/F: 154
Ambrose Fleming UK/F: 95
Amienois Fr/F: 27
Ammerland (II) Ger/F: 482
Andes UK/L: 28
Andrei Zhdanov USSR/L: 150
Andrew G. Curtin US/F: 383
Anglo Indian UK/L: 187
Anhalt Ger/F: 172
Anita Ger/F: 433
Anita L.M. Russ Ger/F: 171
Ankara Ger/F: 79, 165, 280, 284, 293
Ankara Ger/Tug: 240
Anneliese Essberger Ger/F: 134
Antarktis Ger/F: 441
Antje Fritzen Ger/F: 345
Antonio Delfino Ger/L: 488
Antonio Locatelli It/F: 63
Antwerp UK/CRS: 227
Aquarius Fr/FV: 493
Aquitania UK/L: 14, 28, 173, 298
Arabistan UK/F: 246
Arandora Star UK/L: 33, 35
Arauca Ger/F: 14-15
Arcturus Ger/F: 79
Ardeal Ru/F: 210, 218, 330, 407-408
Argun USSR/F: 140
Argull UK/F: 42
Ariguani UK/F(C): 145
Arizona Maru Jap/L: 277

Arkadia Ger/F: 210
Arkhangelsk USSR/F: 343
Armeniya USSR/F: 141-143
Arta Ger/F: 93
Aruba UK/F: 153
Arucas Ger/C: 19
Asaka Maru Jap/F: 312
Ascanius UK/L: 435
Ashanti UK/F: 423
Askari Ger/F: 80, 498
Asperity UK/T: 157
Assiria It/F: 292
Astral US/T: 151
Atheltemplar UK/T: 256
Athenia UK/L: 2
Atho II Fr/L: 17
Atis Kronvalds USSR (ex-Lat)/F: 130
Atlanta Ger/F: 106
Atlas Gr/T: 52
Aude Fr/F: 372
Ausma USSR (ex-Lat)/F: 130
Auretta UK/F: 493
Avanesov: see Variaam Avanesov
Avelona Star UK/F: 32
Aviemore UK/C: 5
Avondale Park UK/F: 519
Awatea UK/F: 273-274
Ayatosan Maru Jap/F: 237
Axel Ger/F: 438
Azerbaidzhan USSR/T: 230-231
Azov USSR/F: 173
Azumasan Maru Jap/F: 264

Babitonga Ger/F: 106
Bahia Ger/F: 152
Bahia Camarones Ger/F: 483
Bahia Laura Ger/F: 124
Balkhash USSR/F: 130
Balilla It/F: 147
Baltenland (ex-Tautmila) Ger (ex-Lit)/F: 142
Baltenland (II) (ex-Valdona) Ger (ex-Lit)/F: 455
Bankok Fr/F: 89, 147
Barbara It/F: 129
Barcelona Ger/F: 127
Barn Hill UK/F: 21
Baron Jedburgh UK/F: 482
Bateau Pan/F: 203
Batory Pol/L: 25, 33
Beacon Grange UK/F: 49
Beatrice C. It/F: 105
Behar UK/F: 383
Bellingham US/F: 231, 257
Belluno It/F: 321
Belostok USSR/F: 141, 175
Bengt Sture Swe/F: 259
Benjamin Harrison US/F: 231
Benjamin H. Bristow UK/F: 510
Berlin Ger/F: 488-489
Bernhard Schulte Ger/F: 84
Berta Ger/F: 453
Berto Nor/F: 285
Bertrand Rickmers Ger/F: 88
Bessheim Ger (ex-Nor)/F: 148
Bhima UK/F: 55
Bhutan UK/F: 227-228
Bianca Ger/F: 8
Bille Ger/F: 497
Birchbank UK/F: 367
Biskaya Ger/F: 8
Bitterfeld Ger/F: 21

Bizon Fr/F: 412
Blackheath UK/F: 33
Black Point US/F: 518
Blacktoft UK/F: 493
Blairnevis UK/F: 155
Blankenese Ger/F: 209
Blexen Ger/T: 475
Boj Feddersen Ger/F: 330
Bolheim Ger/F: 13
Bolshevik USSR/F: 141, 143
Bolton Castle UK/F: 231
Borbek Ger/F: 482
Borgny Nor/T: 141
Botavon UK/F: 213
Boulderpool UK/F: 84
Brackenfield UK/F: 423
Brake Ger/F: 488
Brarena It/T: 120
Braunfels Ger/F: 308
Breconshore UK/F: 74, 93-94, 97, 139, 161, 165–166, 176, 183, 189, 201-202
Bremen Ger/L: 1, 3, 11, 13
Brestois Fr/F: 27
Brighton Queen UK/Ferry: 32
Brisbane Maru Jap/F: 277
Brisbane Star UK/F: 243
Britannic UK/L: 100
British Advocate UK/T: 80
British Chivalry UK/T: 383
British Dominion UK/T: 292
British Loyalty UK/T: 223
British Vigilance UK/T: 291
Britsum Du/F: 42
Bronte It/T: 129
Browning UK/F: 273
Bruges Bel/F: 35
Brüsterort Ger/Tug: 135, 146
Buccaneer Nor/F: 207
Budapest Hun/F: 210, 407
Bulbul Tur/F: 441
Bulkoil UK/F: 227
Burdwan UK/F: 227-228
Burgenland Ger/F: 164, 379
Bury UK/CRS: 261, 266
Buvi Ger/T: 475

Caboto It/F: 129
Caleb Sprague UK/F: 388
California UK/L: 339
Calitea It/F: 42, 78, 158
Cambridge UK/F: 64
Cameronia UK/L: 283
Campinas Ger/F: 22
Campobasso It/F: 321
Canadian Cruiser UK/F: 80
Canberra Maru Jap/L: 276
Cap Arkona Ger/L: 488-489, 497, 515
Cap Blanc Fr/F: 27
Cap des Palmes Fr/F: 50
Cap Guir Ger (ex-Fr)/F: 501
Cap Norte Ger/L: 7, see Empire Trooper
Cap Padaran Fr/L: 50, 147
Cap Touraine Fr/L: 147
Cape Corso UK/F: 213
Cape York UK/F: 50
Capo Faro It/F: 157
Capo Orsam It/F: 165
Capo Vado It/F: 63
Carl Fritzen Ger/F: 3
Carlier UK/F: 367

Carlo del Greco It/F: 165
Carlton UK/F: 220, 231
Casamaoce Fr/F: 64
Carpati Ru/F: 210, 260
Cassel Ger/F: 21
Castillo Oropesa Sp/F: 148
Catalani It/F: 63
Cathay UK/L: 273-274
Cavarna Ru/F: 144
Cedarbank UK/F: 26
Celeno It/T: 330, 333
Ceramic UK/L: 283
Cesteriane Ger (ex-Pan)/T: 390
Ceuta Ger/F: 515
C. F. Liljevalch Swe/F: 246
Chakdina UK/L: 156
Champagne Fr/T: 352
Champlain Fr/L: 38
Chant US/F: 227-228
Chapaev USSR/F: 143
Chantala UK/L: 156
Chantilly UK/L: 73
Charlotte Ger/F: 483
Charles D. McIver UK/F: 500
Château Pavie Fr/F: 27
Château Yquem Fr/F: 107
Chatham US/L: 248
Chekov USSR/F: 142
Chemnitz Ger/F: 5
Chenonceaux Fr/L: 28
Cherokee US/Tug: 115
Chevington UK/F: 143
Chieti It/F: 390
Christopher Newport US/F: 230
Chrobry Pol/L: 25, 29
Chulmleigh UK/F: 272
Città di Messina It/F: 73
City of Calcutta UK/F: 139, 180, 189, 227
City of Edinburgh UK/F: 227
City of Flint US/F: 2, 7, 295
City of Joliet US/F: 220
City of Lincoln UK/F: 139, 227
City of Nagpur UK/L: 92
City of Pretoria UK/F: 120, 227
Clan Campbell UK/F: 97, 189, 201-202
Clan Chattan UK/F: 97, 189
Clan Cumming UK/F: 73, 75
Clan Ferguson UK/F: 139, 180, 189, 243
Clan Forbes UK/F: 67
Clan Fraser UK/F: 67, 91
Clan Lamont UK/F: 97
Clan MacAuley UK/F: 74
Clan MacDonald UK/F: 73, 139
Clement UK/F: 6
Cliona UK/T: 292
Coburg Ger/F: 80-81, 428
Colmar Ger/F: 445
Colombie Fr/L: 28
Colombo It/L: 90
Columbus Ger/L: 14-15
Cometa Ger (ex-Nor)/F: 488
Commandant Dorise Fr/F: 147
Commissaire Ramel Fr/L: 36, 55
Compiègne Fr/L: 147
Conakrian UK/F: 510
Conch UK/T: 33, 66
Consul Cords Ger/F: 489
Consul Horn Ger/F: 17
Conte di Misurata It/T: 149

Conte Rosso It/L: 78, 82, 86, 90, 103
Copeland UK/CRS: 256, 325
Corbrook UK/F: 52
Cordelia Ger/F: 144
Cordillera Ger/L: 498
Cordoba Ger/F: 22
Cormarsh UK/F: 157
Cornouailles Ger (ex-Fr)/F: 468
Cornwall UK/F: 50
Cortellazzo It/F: 281
Costa Rica UK/L: 95
Cotswold UK/F: 33
Crichtoun UK/F: 500
Cromarty Firth UK/F: 33
Cuba UK/L: 496
Cuma It/F: 198
Curityba Ger/F: 209
Czenstochowa Pol/F: 127

D'Annunzio It/F: 292
Dalstroy USSR/F: 531
Dalhousie UK/F: 242
Dallas City UK/F: 42
Daniel Morgan US/F: 231
Daniel Webster US/F: 380
Danubius Ru/F: 210, 407, 411
Daphne II Fr/F: 87
Daugava USSR-Lit/F: 129
Dekabrist USSR/F: 272
Delius UK/F: 369
Dempo Du/L: 397
Derrymore UK/F: 187
Desirade Fr/F: 108
Dessau Ger/F: 446
Deucalion UK/F: 42
Deucalion (II) UK/F: 120, 242
Deutschland Ger/L: 488, 497, 515
Deutschland Ger/Ferry: 485
Devonshire UK/L: 172
Dieter Hugo Stinnes Ger/F: 489
Dikson USSR/F: 343
Ditmar Koel Ger/F: 473, 489
Dixie Ger (ex-Nor)/F: 426
Djenné Fr/L: 27
Dmitrov USSR/F: 173
Dnepr USSR/Barge: 111
Dnepr USSR/F: 136, 141
Domala UK/L: 20
Dona Isabel Ger/F: 366
Donau Ger/F: 124
Donbass USSR/T: 231, 272
Donizetti It/F: 351
Dorchester US/F: 296
Doric Star UK/F: 12
Dorset UK/F: 243
Drachenfels Ger/F: 308
Drava Yu/F: 36
Drechtdijk Ger (ex-Du)/F: 489
Drossel Ger/Tug: 135, 146
Duala Ger/F: 488
Duatape Tur/F: 218
Duchess of Atholl UK/L: 272
Duchess of Bedford UK/L: 14
Duchess of York UK/L: 33, 339
Duilio It/L: 206
Duisburg Ger/F: 149
Dunarea Ru/Lighter: 330
Dunedin Star UK/F: 139
Dunera UK/L: 17, 25, 44
Dungrance UK/F: 423
Duquesa UK/F: 70
Durazzo Ger/F: 30

Durham UK/F: 120, 137
Durostor Ru/F: 407, 411
Düsseldorf Ger/F: 13
Dwarssee Ger/F: 515

Earlston UK/F: 231
Eberhart Essberger Ger/F: 488, 497-498, 512
Edda It/F: 292
Edith Hasseldiek Ger/F: 15
Edmund Hugo Stinnes 4 Ger/F: 21
Edward Bates US/F: 387
Effingham UK/F: 203
Egeo It/F: 94
Egurtsa USSR/F: 141
Ehrenfels Ger/F: 308
Eichberg Ger/F: 455
Eilenau Ger/F: 84
Eismeer Ger/T: 171
El Argentino UK/F: 342
El Biar Fr/F: 408
El Capitan Pan/F: 231
El Grillo UK/T: 391
El Occidente Pan/F: 208
Elbe 5 Ger/Lighter: 411
Elbe Ger/F: 105
Eleftheria UK/F: 500
Elie Ger/F: 455
Elihu Yale US/F: 386
Elizabeth Bakke Nor/F: 76, 227
Ella USSR-Est/F: 130
Ellen Ger/F: 497
Ellen Larsen Ger/F: 489
Elmcrest UK/F: 42
Else Hugo Stinnes Ger/F: 515
Emba USSR/T: 343
Emerald UK/F: 388
Emily Sauber Ger/F: 512
Emma It/F: 293
Emmy Friedrich Ger/T: 8
Empire Baffin UK/F: 220
Empire Beaumont UK/F: 256
Empire Blessing UK/F: 500
Empire Byron UK/F: 231
Empire Centaur UK/F: 285
Empire Cowper UK/F: 208
Empire Defender UK/F: 151
Empire Gilbert UK/F: 272
Empire Haven UK/F: 255, 344
Empire Hope UK/F: 242-243
Empire Housman UK/F: 376
Empire Howard UK/F: 208
Empire Impala UK/F: 305
Empire Lawrence UK/F(C): 220
Empire Lytton UK/F: 292
Empire March UK/T: 291
Empire Moon UK/F(C): 226
Empire Morn UK/F(C): 212, 219, 256
Empire Newcomen UK/F: 157
Empire Pelican UK/F: 151-152
Empire Purcell UK/F: 220
Empire Ranger UK/F: 203
Empire Salvage UK/T: 486
Empire Sky UK/F: 272
Empire Song UK/F: 73, 97
Empire Star UK/F: 187, 266
Empire Starlight UK/F: 207, 223
Empire Stevenson UK/F: 256
Empire Tide UK/F: 232
Empire Tourist UK/F: 393

Empire Trooper (ex-Cap Norte) UK/L: 71
Empire Wave UK/F(C): 135
Empress of Australia UK/L: 14, 25
Empress of Britain UK/L: 14, 28, 61
Empress of Canada UK/L: 17, 28, 127, 315
Empress of Japan UK/L: 17, 28, 65, see Empress of Scotland
Empress of Scotland UK/L: 239
Emshörn Ger/F: 169
Emsland Ger/F: 384
Enseigne Maurice Préchal Fr/F: 28
Ergonautis USSR-Lat/F: 130
Erika Fritzen Ger/F: 489
Erika Schünemann Ger/F: 474
Erlangen Ger/F: 121
Ermioni It/T: 45
Erna Gaulke Ger/F: 515
Ernani It/F: 114
Erni Ger/Tug: 497
Ernst Hugo Stinnes Ger/F: 515
Esperia It/L: 40, 42, 78, 82, 90, 103, 113, 127
Essen Ger/F: 21
Essex UK/F: 73
Estonia Est/F: 109
Ethiopia UK/L: 172
Ettrick UK/L: 25, 277
Ettore Ger/F: 390
Eurosee Ger/T: 311
Eurostadt Ger/T: 319
Everita USSR-Lat/F: 130
Executive US/F: 303

Fabio Filzi It/F: 165
Fabritsius USSR/F: 173
Fairfield City US/F: 231
Faro Ger/F: 475
Fauna It/F: 321
Fechenheim Ger/F: 298
Felix Neumann Ger/F: 84
Fenris Swe/F: 15
Ferncastle Nor/T: 332
Firmin UK/F: 27
Firuz Ger/T: 330, see Friederike
Flandre Fr/L: 27
Flensburg Ger/F: 497
Florianopolis Ger/F: 426
Florida Ger/F: 411, 515
Flottbek Ger/F: 148
Foam Queen UK/F: 366
Fort Bellingham UK/F: 383
Fort Dearborn UK/F: 435
Fort Kaskaskia: 435
Fort Lac La Ronge UK/F: 440
Fort Lamy Fr/F: 64
Fort Stikine UK/F: 407
Francesco Barbero It/F: 42
Francis W. Pettygrove US/F: 344
Franco Martelli It/T: 90
Franconia UK/L: 33, 358
Franctireur Fr/FV: 355
Franken Ger/F: 21
Frankfurt Ger/F: 497
Frans Hals Du/F: 270
Fratton UK/F: 440
Freikoll Ger/F: 446

Friederike (ex-Firuz) Ger/T: 411
Fulham V UK/F: 52

Gaisma Lat/F: 109
Gambia UK/F: 42
Gamma USSR/F: 130
Garlinge UK/F: 273
Gedania Ger/T: 62
Geiserich Ger/F: 407, 411
Gemstone UK/F: 224
Generaal v.d. Heyden Du/F: 407
Generaal van Swieten Du/F: 407
General Artigas Ger/L: 342
General Osorio Ger/L: 438
General Steuben Ger/L: 488-489
Georgic UK/L: 33, 117
Gerrit Fritzen Ger/F: 497
Gertrud Ger/F: 418
Giuliana It/T: 428
Giulio Cesare It/L: 206
Glenfinlas UK/F: 274
Glengyle UK/L: 93, 106, 183
Glenorchy UK/L: 243
Glenroy UK/L: 155, 538
Gloria Ger/F: 8
Gloria Stella It/F: 54
Gneisenau Ger/L: 321
Gold Shell UK/T: 510
Gonzenheim Ger/F: 8
Goodwood UK/F: 493
Gorgon UK/F: 187
Göttingen Ger/F: 482, 488, 489
Goya Ger/F: 488, 512
Greif Ger/F: 467
Greylock UK/F: 294
Grigorios CII Gr/F: 80
Groenlo Du/F: 155
Gruzit USSR/F: 143
Gruziya USSR/L: 136, 144, 225
Gudrun Maersk Da/F: 171
Guilia It/F: 292
Gumbinnen Ger/F: 84
Gurpinar Tur/F: 330

Haakon Jarl Nor/F: 124
Hadley F. Brown US/F: 500
Hainburg Ger/Lighter: 330
Halle Ger/F: 8
Halizones UK/F: 342
Halo UK/F: 486
Hamburg Ger/F: 84
Hamburg Ger/L: 488-489
Hanau Ger/F: 115
Hanne UK/F: 152
Hannover Ger/F: 20, see Audacity
Hans Ger/F: 124
Hans Leonhardt Ger/F: 411
Hans Rickmers Ger/F: 279
Hansa Ger/L: 488-489
Hansa Swe/F: 455
Harald Da/F: 42
Harmatris UK/F: 180
Harmattan UK/F: 33, 285
Harpalion UK/F: 208
Harrison Gray Otis US/F: 344
Hartlebury UK/F: 231
Hauxley UK/F: 60
Havsten Nor/T: 234
Heddernheim Ger/F: 21
Heffron US/F: 231
Heidelberg Ger/F: 20
Heinrich Jensen UK/F: 199
Heinz Horn Ger/F: 475

Helga Ger/F: 407, 411
Helgoland Ger/F: 61
Henrietta Schulte Ger/F: 385
Henry Nor/F: 391
Henry Bacon US/F: 493
Henry Lütgens Ger/F: 482
Herborg Nor/T: 229
Hermann Fritzen Ger/F: 460
Hermes Ger/F: 116
Hermonthis Ger/F: 90
Herta Ger/F: 426
Herta Engeline Fritzen Ger/F: 414
Hiddensee Ger/T: 482
Hidlefjord Nor/T: 90
Hilda It/F: 129
Hilma Lau Da/F: 455
Himalaya It/F: 81, 313, 316
Hirokawa Maru Jap/F: 277
Hobart Baker US/F: 475
Hobbs Victory US/F: 507
Höegh Hood Nor/T: 120
Hoegh Silverdawn Nor/F: 332
Hohenfels Ger/F: 129
Hohenfriedberg (ex-Herborg) Ger/T (B): 303
Hohenhörn Ger/F: 146
Holland Ger/F: 137
Honomu US/F: 231
Hoosier US/F: 231
Horace Binney US/F: 510
Horace Bushnel US/F· 498
Horace Gray US/F: 492
Horai Maru Jap/L: 198
Hororata UK/L: 283
Hudayi Bahri Tur/SV: 330
Huelva Ger/F: 501
Hybert US/F: 231

Idarwald Ger/F: 65, 68
Iddesleigh UK/F: 440
Idefjord Nor/F: 491, 511
Ile de France Fr/L: 298
Ilissos Ger/F: 470
Ilmenau Ger/F: 501
Ilona Siemers Ger/F: 295
Imperial Star UK/L: 139-140
Inabasan Maru Jap/F: 188
India It/F: 88
Indian Prince UK/F: 367
Induna UK/F: 203
Indus UK/F: 236
Indus Nor/T: 344
Ingar Nielsen Nor/F: 154
Ingeborg Ger/F: 360
Ingerseks Nor/F: 513
Ingöy Nor/F: 169
Inka Ger/T: 474
Inster Ger/F: 515
Internatsional USSR/F: 327
Irene (ex-Silvaplana) Ger/F: 314, 317
Irene Oldendorf Ger/F: 489
Iridio Mantovani It/T: 157
Irma Nor/F: 391
Irmtraud Cords Ger/F: 515
Ironclad US/F: 231
Iseo It/F: 157, 165
Iserlohn Ger/F: 93
Island Nor/F: 154
Itape Bra/F: 68
Ivan Papanin USSR/F: 130
Izhora USSR/F: 198

James H. Breasted US/F: 475
James Stove Nor/T: 36
Jamestown US/F: 264
Jared Ingersoll US/F: 402
Jaspis Ger/T: 489
Jaunty UK/Tug: 171
Jean Laborde Fr/F: 50
Jean Nicolet US/F: 383, 417
Jersbek Ger/F: 501
Jeypore UK/F: 268
Johannisberger Ger/F: 310
John Bakke Nor/F: 76
John Burke US/F: 475
John Randolph US/F: 231
John Witherspoon US/F: 231
Joseph Swan UK/F: 52
Josif Stalin USSR/L: 157-158
Junak Ger/Tug: 408
Jupiter UK/CRS: 225
Jutland UK/F: 213
Jungingen Ger/F: 356

Kalinin USSR/F: 141-143, 173, 175
Kalpaks USSR-Lat/F: 130
Kamchatneft USSR/F: 531
Kanarya Tur/F: 437
Kanonier Ger/F: 488
Kapitän Diederichsen (ex-Sebastiano Venier) Ger/F: 394
Karaltepe Tur/SV: 149
Kari Ger/F: 359
Karin Ger/F: 308
Karlsruhe Ger/F: 497
Karsik Du/F: 285
Kassa Hun/F: 210, 407
Kassari Est/F: 13
Kaynakdere Tur/SV: 173
Kazakhstan USSR/F: 130
Kehrwieder Ger/Ferry: 451
Kentucky US/F: 256
Kentucky US/T: 227-228
Kerov USSR/FV: 232
Kertosono Du/F: 41
Ketty Brovig Nor/T: 80-81
Khedive Ismail UK/F: 383
Khipka Bul/F: 135
Kiev USSR/F: 208
Killoran Fin/SV: 47
Kinryu Maru Jap/F: 244, 249
Kinagawa Maru Jap/F: 277
Knute Nelson Nor/F: 2
Kjölborg Nor/T: 296
Koçiboglu Tur/SV: 284
Kolga Est/F: 42
Kolozsvar Ru/M: 210
Komsomolets USSR/Tug: 245
Kong Harald Nor/F: 171
Kong Ring Nor/F: 154
Königsberg Ger/F: 512
Konsul Schulte Ger/F: 180
Korsnes Nor/F: 468
Kosmos Nor/WFS: 57
Kosmos II Nor/WFS: 266
Kotoku Maru Jap/F: 237
Kotovski USSR/F: 141, 143
Krasnogvardeets USSR/F: 173, 175
Krasny Partizan USSR/F: 289
Krasny Profintern USSR/F: 173, 301
Kreml USSR/T: 319
Krestyanin USSR/F: 237

Krossfonn Nor/T: 37
Kuban USSR/F: 173, 175
Kumari USSR/F: 130
Kuretake Maru Jap/F: 182
Kuroshio Maru Jap/F: 521
Kursk USSR/F: 143, 173
Kuttabul Aus/Accomodation ship: 215
Kybfels Ger/F: 80, 103
Kuru Aus/F: 256
Kyushu Maru Jap/F: 264

L. D. Dreyfus Fr/F: 20
L. M. Russ Ger/F: see Theresia L. M. Russ
Labor It/T: 86
Laconia UK/L: 255, 260
La Coruna Ger/F: 20
Lafayette (ex-Normandie) US/L: 187
Lake Lucerne USSR-Est/F: 130
Lalande UK/F: 273
Lancashire UK/L: 172
Lancastria UK/L: 33, 37
Lappland Ger/F: 488, 512
Largs Bay UK/F: 519
Le Progrès Ger (ex-Fr)/T: 210, 260
Lech Ger/F: 82, 105
Leda Ger/F: 390
Lehigh US/F: 139
Leinster UK/L: 120, 122
Leningrad USSR/F: 332
Leopardi It/F: 350
Leopoldville Bel/L: 469
Leuthen (ex-Madron) Ger/T: 282
Levante Ger/F: 124
Leverkusen Ger/F: 475
Libau Ger/F: 390
Lichtenfels Ger/F: 88
Lidaza USSR-Est/F: 112
Lindau Ger/F: 441
Lindenfels Ger/F: 21
Linz US/F: 515
Lisa Ger/F: 390
Lisa Essberger Ger/T: 497
Lisbon Maru Jap/F: 248
Llandovery Castle UK/L: 66
Llangibby Castle UK/L: 180
Llanishen UK/F: 49
Lofoten Ger-Nor/L: 133
Logan Victory US/F: 507
Lola Ger/F: 454
Lorentz W. Hansen Nor/F: 7
Lowther Castle UK/F: 220
Lübeck Ger/F: 124
Luga USSR/F: 110, 130
Lunacharski USSR/F: 129
Lüneburg Ger/F: 398
Lvov USSR/L: 199

Macbeth US/F: 256
Madali Ger/F: 356
Madrono Nor/T: 229, see Leuthen
Maimoa UK/F: 65
Majaba UK/F: 271
Makalla UK/F: 49
Malines UK/CRS: 227
Manfredo Campiero It/F: 251
Mannheim Ger/F: 475
Manor UK/FV: 234
Manvantara UK/T: 187
Manzoni It/F: 42

Maplin UK/F(C): 122
Marburg Ger/F: 103
Marco Foscarini It/F: 42, 292
Marco Polo It/L: 78, 82, 86, 90, 103, 118, 127
Marga Cords Ger/F: 426
Margarethe Cords Ger/F: 497
Margot UK/F: 29
Marguerite Ger (ex-Fr)/F: 359
Maria It/F: 149
Maria Eugenia It/F: 54
Maria Toft Da/F: 388
Marienburg Ger/F: 358
Marienfels Ger/F: 129
Marigola It/F: 147
Marina Raskova USSR/F: 442
Mariposa US/L: 239
Maritza Ger/F: 155
Mariya Ulyanova USSR/F: 129
Marnix van St. Aldegonde Bel/L: 367
Marocchino It/F: 292
Maron UK/F: 273
Marsa UK/F: 369
Mary Luckenbach US/F: 256
Massmar US/F: 231
Master Slanfast UK/F: 366
Mathias Stinnes Ger/F: 488, 498
Matina UK/F: 61
Mauritania UK/L: 28
Maya (No. 539) USSR/F: 157
Meero USSR-Est/F: 133
Mefkure Tur/SV: 441
Meiyo Maru Jap/F: 241
Meknes Fr/F: 45
Melbourne Star UK/F: 120, 243
Melrose Abbey UK/CRS: 305
Mendoza Ger/F: 488, 508
Mendoza Fr/L: 76
Menelaus UK/F: 214
Merula UK/T: 187
Metallist USSR/T: 6
Meteor Ger/F: 501
Meteor USSR/CRS: 130
Mexique Fr/L: 28
Mexphalte Ger (ex-Fr)/T: 505
Michael Ger/T: 203
Mimi Horn Ger/F: 20
Mimona Nor/F: 191
Minatitlan It/T: 149
Minister Wedel Nor/T: 292
Minna (No. 548) USSR/F: 153
Minna Cords Ger/F: 474
Minorca UK/F: 83
Minotaure Ger/F: 433
Mira Ger (ex-Nor)/F: 84
Miranda Ger (ex-Nor)/F: 436
Mittnattsol Nor/F: 135
Modavia UK/F: 305
Moltkefels Ger/F: 488, 497
Monarch of Bermuda UK/L: 14, 25, 28, 33
Moncalieri It/F: 80
Monginevro It/F: 165
Moni Rickmers Ger/F: 21
Monsun Ger/T: 441
Monte Olivia Ger/L: 505
Monte Pasqual Ger/L: 390
Monte Rosa Ger/L: 488
Monte Sarmiento Ger/L: 197
Montello It/F: 105
Monviso It/F: 239
Moravia UK/F: 308

Morea Ger/F: 18
Morina Tur/SV: 441
Mormacsul US/F: 220
Mormacsun US/F: 17
Moskva USSR/T: 141-142
Mossovet USSR/F: 113, 343
Muansa Ger/F: 289
München Ger/F: 90
Münsterland Ger/F: 362, 385
Myrland Nor/FV: 84

N. C. Monberg Dan/F: 70
Nagara Maru Jap/F: 276
Naissaar USSR/F: 130
Nako Maru Jap/F: 277
Napoli It/F: 165
Narkunda UK/L: 273
Naumburg Ger/F: 21
Navarino UK/F: 230
Navastroy USSR/F: 531
Navemar Sp/F: 180
Nea Hellas Gr/L: 260
Neidenfels Ger/F: 488
Neptun USSR/CRS: 158
Neptunia It/L: 118, 127, 135
Nerissa Ger/F: 426
Neuralia UK/L: 25
Neuwerk Ger/F: 497
Nevada Fr/F: 64
Nevasa UK/L: 25
New Lambton UK/F: 52
New Westminster City UK/F: 207
New York Ger/L: 505
New Zealand Star UK/F: 67, 98
Newton Nor/T: 207
Niagara UK/L: 37
Nicoline Maersk Ger/F: 376
Nieuw Amsterdam Du/L: 298
Nieuw Zeeland Du/L: 273
Nieuwland Du/F: 52
Ninfea It/F: 116
Nino Bixio It/F: 245
Nita It/F: 123
Nogin USSR/F: 173, 531
Nord USSR/Tug: 245
Nordeflinge UK/F: 418
Norderney Ger/F: 126
Nordfels Ger/F: 292
Nordland Nor/F: 171
Nordmark Ger/F: 21
Nordmeer Ger/T: 14
Nord Norge Nor/F: 29
Norfjell Nor/T: 499
Norma Ger/F: 171
Normandie Fr/L: 187, see
    Lafayette
Northern Prince UK/F: 90
Norvik Pan/T: 292

Ocean Courier UK/F: 435
Ocean Freedom UK/F: 231
Ocean Hunter UK/F: 380
Ocean Vanquisher UK/F: 285
Ocean Voice UK/F: 220, 357
Ocean Volga UK/F: 435
Oceania It/L: 118, 127, 135
Odenwald Ger/F: 149
Oder Ger-It/F: 88
Ohio UK/T: 242-243
Oil Pioneer UK/T: 33
Oituz Ru/F: 158, 210, 285, 407,
    448.
Oituz Ru/Tug: 260, 404

Oklahoma US/T: 482
Ole Wegger Nor/WFS: 76
Oligarch UK/T: 33
Olinda Ger/F: 3
Olinda (II) Ger/F: 441
Oliver Ellsworth US/F: 256
Olivia Du/T: 229
Olopana US/F: 231
Oltenia II UK (ex-Ru)/T: 292
Olympos Ger (ex-Gr)/F: 356
Ondina Du/T: 279
Onega USSR/F: 511
OP-8 USSR/Tug: 138
Orama It/F: 165
Orari UK/F: 227-228, 242, 245
Orcades UK/L: 17
Oregonian US/F: 256
Orford UK/L: 17, 33
Orion Ger/F: 451
Orion Ger (ex-Du)/F: 497
Orion UK/L: 17
Orizaba Ger/F: 19
Orkanger Nor/T: 34
Ormonde UK/L: 33
Oronsay UK/L: 33, 260
Oropesa UK/L: 75
Oscar Midling Fin/F: 67
Oslofjord Nor/L: 68
Osorno Ger/F: 375-376
Ossag Ger/T: 279, 407-408
Ostland Ger/F: 446
Ostpreussen Ger/F: 124
Ostwind Ger/F: 515
Otaio UK/F: 128
Othmarschen Ger/F: 295
Otranto UK/L: 17
Ottar Jarl Nor/F: 133
Otto Ger/Launch: 441

P-IV USSR/Lighter: 245
Pallas Ger/F: 515
Paloma Ger/F: 516
Pampas UK/F: 201-202
Pan Atlantic US/F: 231
Pan Kraft US/F: 231
Panuco It/T: 118
Pasajes Ger/F: 84
Passat Ger/F: 441
Pasteur Fr/L: 239
Patagonia Ger/F: 414
Paula It/F: 351
Paul Hamilton US/F: 408
Paulus Potter Du/F: 231
Pelagos Nor/WFS: 76
Peles Ru/L: 125
Peleus Gr/F: 383
Penelope Barker US/F: 383
Pennland UK/L: 56, 95
Pensilvania It/T: 80
Peredovik USSR/T: 199
Pericles Nor/T: 88
Pernambuco Ger/F: 414
Perth UK/CRS: 278, 281
Pescagel Fr/Tug: 53
Pessacus US/Tug: 268
Pestel USSR/F: 175, 411
Peter Ger/F: 390, 453
Peter Kerr US/F: 231
Peter Sylvester US/F: 470
Petrella Ger/F: 390
Petrovski USSR/F: 343
Philipp M. UK/F: 394
Phrygia Ger/F: 65

Piave It/F: 88
Pietro Orseolo It/F: 314
Pilsudski Pol/L: 10
Plumleaf UK/F: 50
Pluto It/F: 351
Point Pleasant Park Can/F: 482
Polifemo It/Tug: 273
Polperro UK/F: 380
Pomella UK/T: 234
Pompeji Ger/F: 515
Pontus H. Ross US/F: 483
Porcupine US/T: 475
Port Chalmers UK/F: 120, 243
Port Fairy UK/F: 339
Portland Ger/F: 158, 318
Poseidon Ger/F: 8
Posidonia Ger/T: 23
Potaro UK/F: 227-228
Poti Bra/F: 379
Potsdam Ger/L: 488, 497
Premuda It/F: 63
President Doumer Fr/L: 27, 270
President Harrison US/F: 163
Pretoria Ger/L: 488-489, 497-498
Preussen Ger/F: 120
Procida It/F: 155
Prodromos Ger (ex-Gr)/T: 407,
    411
Proletari USSR/F: 472
Puerto Rican US/F: 303

Queen Elizabeth UK/L: 239
Queen Mary UK/L: 28, 239, 261,
    298, 345
Queen of Bermuda UK/L: 298
Quercy Fr/L: 539

RO-24 Ger/F: 455
Raceland UK/F: 203
Rajula UK/L: 172
Ramb III It/F: 368
Ramses Ger/F: 280
Rangitane UK/L: 67-68
Rangitata UK/L: 17
Ranja Nor/T: 76
Rantaupandjang Du/F: 80
Rasma Lat/F: 116
Rathlin UK/CRS: 231, 257,
    354-355
Rauenfels Ger/F: 24
Ravens Point UK/F: 257
Regensburg Ger/F: 106, 113, 257,
    314
Reimar Edzard Fritzen Ger/F:
    171
Reina del Pacifico UK/L: 25
Rekum Ger/T: 398
Rembrandt UK/F: 227
Remuera UK/F: 50
Rendsburg Ger/F: 21
Renöy Nor/F: 133
Revolutsioner USSR/F: 244, 472
Rex It/L: 450
Rhakotis Ger/T: 289
Rhein Ger/T: 65
Rheingold Ger/F: 8
Rheinland Ger/F: 21
Richard Bland US/F: 303
Richard Hovey US/F: 383
Richard With Ger/F: 133
Rigel Fin/F: 450
Rigel Nor/F: 468
Rigmor Nor/T: 207

Rina Corrado It/F: 149
Rio Bravo UK/T: 468
Rio de Janeiro Ger/F: 23
Rio Grande Ger/F: 141, 149, 379
Rival Ger/F: 475
River Afton UK/F: 231
Rixhöft Ger/F: 489
Robert J. Walker US/F: 470
Robert Ley Ger/L: 488-489
Robert L. Vann UK/F: 493
Robin Moor US/F: 95
Rochester Castle UK/L: 243
Rodina USSR/F: 231
Rogate UK/F: 500
Rohna UK/F: 372
Roode Zee Du/Tug: 405
Rosafred Swe/F: 450
Roseburn UK/F: 39
Rosolino Pilo It/F: 245
Rostock Ger/F: 18
Rovereto It/F: 316
Rowallan Castle UK/F: 139, 183, 189
Roy Nor/F: 143
Royal Star UK/F: 408
Royal Ulsterman UK/F: 33
Rüdesheimer Ger/F: 345
Rugard Ger/L: 22, 516
Ruhno Est/F: 110
Ruhr Ger/F: 80
Ryfylke Nor/F: 78

SP-12 USSR/Tug: 111
SP-14 USSR/Tug: 138, 141, 176
Saarburg Ger/T: 410
Sabaudia It/F: 93
Sabine Ger/F: 418
Sachsenwald Ger/F: 488, 515
Sado Maru Jap/F: 276
Safak Tur/F: 218
Sagadahoc US/F: 154
Sagitta It/F: 149
Sagona Nor/T: 166
St. Clair Fr/F: 28
St. Didier Fr/F: 107
Sakhalin USSR/T: 155
Sakito Maru Jap/F: 312
Sakura Maru Jap/F: 196
Salomea Ger (ex-Gr)/F: 453
Salzburg Ger/F: 210, 260
Samite UK/F: 408
Samland Ger/T: 37
Samlong UK/F: 440
Sampa UK/F: 493
Samselbu US/F: 500
Samuel Chase US/F: 231
Samuel Huntingdon US/F: 386
Samwake UK/F: 435
San Casimiro UK/T: 87
San Conrado UK/T: 90
San Demetrio UK/T: 64
San Diego Ger/F: 316
San Florentino UK/T: 135
San Marco It/F: 149
Sangro It/F: 96
Sant' Antonio It/F: 321
Santa Elena US/F: 367
Santa Elisa US/F: 243
Santa Fé Ger/F: 8, 324, 353, 368
Sardegna It/L: 71
Sarpedon UK/L: 173
Sasago Maru Jap/F: 191, 264
Sassnitz Ger/T: 501

Saturnia It/L: 206
Saule USSR-Lat/F: 130
Saumar Fr/F: 27
Scharnhorst Ger/L: see Shinyo
Scotia UK/F: 32
Seattle Ger/F: 20
Sebastiano Venier It/F: 157-158, 394
Seeburg Ger/L: 455
Seirstad UK/T: 187
Semsi-Bahri Tur/SV: 437
Sereno It/F: 45
Sergei Kirov USSR/F: 343
Sergo USSR/T: 141-142, 199
Serov USSR/F: 173, 212, 216
Serpa Pinto Por/L: 403
Sesostris Ger/F: 30
Shakhter USSR/F: 173
Shchors USSR/F: 265
Shinanogawa Maru Jap/F: 277
Shkval USSR/CRS: 341
Sibir USSR/F: 126
Siegfried Ger/FV: 455
Sif Swe/F: 436
Sifnos Ger (ex-Gr)/F: 390
Signal Ger/F: 460
Silvaplana Nor/F: see Irene
Silver Sword UK/F: 231, 257
Sinfra Ger (ex-Fr)/F: 360
Sir Russell UK/F: 125
Sirius Ger/F: 501
Skjold Nor/F: 493
Skrunda USSR/F: 130
Skytteren Nor/WFS: 207
Slamat UK/L: 95
Slavol UK/T: 200
Sneland Nor/F: 519
Sobieski Pol/L: 17
Solglimt Nor/WFS: 76
Solviken Ger/F: 414
Solstad Swe/F: 380
Soneck Ger/F: 21
Sophie Rickmers Ger/F: 21
Soudan UK/F: 210
Somalia It/F: 80
Southern Cross Swe/Y: 2
Southern Empress UK/WFS: 262
Southern Princess UK/WFS: 309
Sovietskaya Neft USSR/T: 311
Speybank UK/F: 80
Spree Ger/F: 468
Springbank UK/F: 137
Stad Almaer Du/F: 53
Stad Maastricht Du/F: 71
Staffordshire UK/L: 88
Stalingrad USSR/F: 256
Stanlake UK/F: 318
Stanvac Calcutta Pan/T: 224
Stari Bolshevik USSR/F: 220
Stassfurt Ger/F: 21
Statendam Du/L: 29
Steel Worker UK/F: 223
Steinbek Ger/F: 164
Stensaas Nor/F: 208
Stephen Austin US/F: 408
Stephen Hopkins US/F: 259
Stockholm Ger/F: 486
Stockport UK/CRS: 246, 267-268 302
Stonegate UK/F: 6
Stör Ger/F: 404
Storaa UK/F: 366
Storsten Nor/T: 207

Strathaird UK/L: 17, 25, 77
Strathallan UK/L: 283
Strathnaver UK/L: 17
Stromboli It/F: 292
Streonshalh UK/F: 12
Struma Bul-Pan/F: 193
Sturmfels Ger/F: 129
Sturzsee Ger/F: 319
Subadar UK/F: 187
Suchan USSR/F: 531
Suceava Ru/F: 210, 304
Sukhona USSR/F: 256
Sulina Ru/F: 210, 218
Sumanoura Maru Jap/F: 182
Superga It/T: 135
Susanne Ger/F: 433
Svend Foyn Nor/WFS: 142
Sydney Star UK/F: 120
Syros UK/F: 220

Tacoma Da/F: 42
Taijima Maru Jap/F: 407
Tairoa UK/F: 12
Tai Shan Nor/F: 76
Takoradian UK/F: 42
Talabot Nor/F: 201-202
Tampico It/T: 135
Tanais Ger (ex-Gr)/F: 418
Taney US/F: 408
Tanga Ger/F: 488
Tanimbar Du/F: 227-228
Tanker No. 1 USSR/T: 531
Tanker No. 2 USSR/T: 130
Tannenfels Ger/F: 259
Tannhäuser Ger/F: 436
Tashkent USSR/F: 173
Tatekawa Maru Jap/F: 204
Tatsukami Maru Jap/F: 182
Taunus Ger/T: 455
Taurus Nor/F: 76
Tayyari Tur/F: 330
Tbilisi (I) USSR/F: 343
Tbilisi (II) USSR/F: 475
Teddington UK/F: 136
Teja Ger/F: 407, 411
Tenerife II Ger/F: 441
Tenryu Maru Jap/F: 199
Tenshizan Maru Jap/F: 407
Terje Viken Nor/WFS: 84
Terney USSR/F: 236
Terra Ger/T: 455
Tevere It/F: 292
Thalatta Ger/T: 455
Theoderich Ger/F: 368
Theresia L.M. Russ Ger/F: 426, 475
Thermopylae UK/F: 180
Theseus UK/F: 33
Thetis Gr/F: 403
Thielbek Ger/F: 515
Thisbé Ger/F: 330
Thode Fagelund Nor/F: 147
Thomas Donaldson US/F: 498
Thomas Scott US/F: 492
Thorn Ger/T: 90
Thorshövdi Nor/T: 344
Tinombo Du/F: 407
Tirranna Nor/F: 52
Tisza Hung/F: 210, 407
Tjisalak Du/F: 383
Tobol USSR/F: 130
Todaro It/F: 106
Tonan Maru Jap/WFS: 257

Tonan Maru No. 2 Jap/WFS: 232
Toni Ger/F: 451
Torcello It/T: 149
Torridal Nor/F: 501
Totila Ger/F: 407, 411
Touareg Fr/F: 50
Toward UK/CRS: 193, 286, 297
Trapani It/F: 360
Trautenfels Ger/F: 127
Trevethoe UK/F: 85
Trifels Ger/F: 10
Troilus UK/F: 77, 227, 242, 245
Troja Ger/F: 20
Tropic Sea UK/F: 52
Troubadour Nor/F: 256
Tsiolkovski USSR/F: 213
Tsukushi Maru Jap/F: 177, 181
Tsuruga Maru Jap/F: 182
Tuapse USSR/T: 155
Tübingen Ger/F: 488, 513
Türkheim Ger/F: 176
Tyra No. 5 Ger/Lighter: 361

Ubena Ger/T: 488-489
Ufa USSR/F: 294
Uhenfels Ger/F: 9
Ukraina USSR/F: 143
Ulrich Da/F: 42
Ulster Prince UK/F: 33, 95
Uncas US/Tug: 268
Underwood UK/F: 380
Ungvar Hun/F: 144
Unicoi US/F: 236
Ural USSR/F: 151
Uralets USSR/F: 141
Uruguay Ger/F: 20
Urundi Ger/F: 488
Ussukuma Ger/F: 13

Vale Ger/F: 488, 508
Valencia Ger/F: 384
Vancouver Island (ex-Weser)
  UK/F: 142
Van Dyck Du/L: 33
Vanja Nor/T: 292
Variaam Avanesov USSR/T:
  155-156
Varna Bul/F: 330
Varsova UK/F: 172
Vaterland Ger/L: 342
Veendam Du/L: 29, 460
Vega Ger (ex-Nor)/F: 488
Venersborg Swe/F: 455
Verviske Tur/F: 330
Vesco Nor/T: 152
Vesteraalen Nor/F: 144
Vestfold Nor/WFS: 293
Vettor Pisani It/L: 42, 165, 237

Viborg Dan/F: 489
Viborg USSR/F: 115
Viceroy of India UK/L: 273
Victoria It/L: 40, 82, 86, 90, 97,
  103, 183
Vierlande Ger/T: 441
Vigilant Aus/F: 256
Ville d'Alger Fr/L: 27-28
Ville de Bruges Bel/L: 30
Ville d'Oran Fr/F: 26
Ville de Rouen Fr/F: 120
Ville de Tamatave Fr/F: 114
Ville du Havre Fr/F: 272
Viminale It/F: 291
Vingaland Swe/F: 64
Vireo US/Tug: 264
Virgilia UK/T: 155
Viril Swe/F: 390
Vital de Oliveira Bra/F: 416
Vogtland Ger/F: 21
Volga USSR/F: 141
Volo UK/F: 50
Volta Ger/F: 488
Volturno It/T: 157, see Aux ML
Voroshilov USSR/F: 332
Vostok USSR/F: 143
Vtoraya Pyatiletka USSR/F: 130
Vulcain Fr/F: 28
Vulcania It/L: 135, 206
Vulkan Ger/F: 426
Vyacheslav Molotov USSR/F: 125

Wachtfels Ger/F: 239
Wacosta US/F: 256
Wahehe Ger/F: 18
Waimarama UK/F: 243
Wairangi UK/F: 243
Wakama Ger/F: 19
Wakefield US/L: 151
Waldinge UK/F: 153
Walmer Castle UK/CRS: 137
Wangoni Ger/F: 19, 488
Warthe Ger/F: 475
Wartheland Ger/F: 319
Warwick Castle UK/L: 277
Wasgenwald Ger/F: 21
Washington UK/F: 231
Watussi Ger/F: 10
Waveney UK/F: 538
Waziristan UK/F: 175
Weichselland Ger/F: 475
Weissenfels Ger/F: 129
Welheim Ger/F: 468
Wellington Star UK/F: 32
Werdenfels Ger/F: 21
Weser Ger/F: 56, see Vancouver
  Island

Weser (II) Ger/F: 139, 497
Weserberg Ger/F: 516
Weserland Ger/F: 379
Weserstein Ger/F: 433, 508
Weserstrom Ger/F: 515
Westernland UK/L: 56, 58
Westpreussen Ger/F: 495
Westsee Ger/F: 279
Wiegand Ger/F: 488, 497
Wildenfels Ger/F: 129
Wilhelm Gustloff Ger/L: 488-489
Wilhelmsburg Ger/F: 398
William Clark US/F: 272
William F. Humphrey US/F: 236
William H. Berg US/T: 187
William Hooper US/F: 230
William S. Thayer US/F: 409
William Stephen UK/FV: 363
Wilpas Finn/F: 15
Windsor Castle UK/L: 62, 310
Winnepeg Fr/F: 104
Winrich von Kniprode Ger/L:
  488, 495
Winston Salem US/F: 232
Wisconsin US/F: 20
Wolfsburg Ger/F: 20
Wolga-Don Ger/T: 368
Wolgast Ger/F: 515
Wolsum Ger/F: 450
Wuppertal Ger/F: 21
Wyoming UK/FV: 413

Yaka US/F: 218
Yamashio Maru Jap/F: 492
Yana USSR/F: 130
Yärvamaa USSR/F: 130
Yenice Tur/F: 149
Yilmaz Tur/F: 330
Yokohama Maru Jap/F: 199
Yoshida Maru Jap/F: 407
Yamatsuki Maru Jap/F: 277
Yamamura Maru Jap/F: 277

Zaafaran UK/CRS: 231
Zamalek UK/CRS: 231, 257,
  309
Zamzam Egypt/L: 93
Zar Ferdinand Bul/F: 210, 285,
  453
Zealandic UK/L: 75
Zhan Tomp USSR/F: 251
Zhan Zhores USSR/F: 141, 143,
  173
Zheleznodorozhnik USSR/F: 110,
  129
Zyryanin USSR/F: 173

Naval Forces

These have been listed under their various countries. It should be noted that the British and American forces in particular often contained warships of other nationalities within their context, and in one or two cases personalities from different countries. Abbreviations used in the text will be found after the main headings for the different types of forces. Regarding the U-boat patrol groups: in one or two cases the same name has been given to different groups operated at different times during the war. No differentiation has been made between these in the index, but the distinction is obvious from the wide spacing of the page numbers. Composite squadrons formed for operations of short duration, such as those groups used to track the Graf Spee in 1939, have not been listed.

American
Fleets and Forces
Asiatic Fleet: 164, 169-170
Atlantic Fleet: 119, 132
Cactus Striking Force: 290-291,
    307
Central Atlantic Neutrality Patrol:
    108
Dixie Patrol: 422-423
Pacific Fleet: 29, 92, 169, 222,
    226, 239
Support Force Atlantic: 83
Neutrality Patrol 0 to 9: 4
White Patrol: 132
III Amphibious Force: 363, 391,
    536
V Amphibious Force: 536
VII Amphibious Force: 334, 347,
    355, 376, 379, 418, 433, 439,
    451, 504, 537-539
3 Fleet: 448, 457, 476, 517, 533
5 Fleet: 388, 416, 491, 493, 499,
    503, 516-517, see 3 Fleet
7 Fleet: 310, 395, 409, 429, 461,
    480-481, 524, 537
10 Fleet: 327
Task Forces (TF)
Fast Carrier: 373, 522
1: 119, 226
3: 108
5: 169, 182
8: 161, 168, 183, 187, 190, 221,
    226, 293
11: 161, 168, 182, 185, 190, 199,
    214, 226, 233, 537
14: 168, 177, 359
15: 347, 353
16: 207, 220-221, 226, 233,
    275-276, 323
17: 183, 185, 190, 199, 214,
    220-221, 226, 254, 258, 263,
    269, 429
18: 226, 233, 253-254, 291
19: 115
31: 334-335, 363, 391, 452
33: 536
34: 464
35: 536
38: 364, 391, 448, 452, 457-459,
    461-467, 474, 476, 517, 522,
    524-525, 527-530, 532-533
39: 203, 363-365, 391
41: 379
42: 239
44: 214, 226, 250, 310
50: 367, 369
51: 323, 493, 503-504
52: 367, 370, 388, 427-428, 438
    493, 502-504, 507
53: 367, 370, 388, 437, 493-494,
    504, 523
54: 493, 502-504, 510-511
55: 504
56: 493
58: 387-389, 392, 400-401, 406,
    426-427, 430, 436, 438, 491-493,
    498-499, 501-502, 504, 507-511,
    516-517, see TF 38
60: 413
61: 238, 249, 269
62: 238, 337
63: 239, 269
64: 263-264, 269, 275-276, 402

65: 254, 404
66: 329, 408, 410
67: 282, 290
68: 307, 324
72: 537
74: 310, 334, 340-341, 345, 367,
    375, 395-396, 409, 416, 418, 433,
    437, 439
75: 409, 416, 418, 433, 439, 451
76: 310, 334, 347, 355, 375-376,
    379, 433
77: 409, 418, 439, 451, 461, 480
78: 439, 461, 480, 482
79: 461, 480, 482
80: 339, 350
81: 339, 350, 385
84: 443
85: 339, 350, 443
86: 339, 443
87: 444
88: 342
92: 525, 528, 531, 535
94: 431
95: 527, 532, 535

Task Groups (TG)
1.5: 132
02.10: 506
7.3: 92
8.1: 183
8.3: 183
8.5: 183
8.6: 295, 304, 319
12.4: 524
12.5: 448
14.4: 150
16.6: 323, 337
16.12: 537
16.17: 337
16.21: 336
16.22: 337
21.5: 395
21.11: 387, 395, 403
21.12: 381, 387
21.15: 403
21.16: 387, 394
22.1: 416, 455
22.2: 403, 416, 423, 507
22.3: 416, 507
22.4: 416, 507
22.5: 416, 507
22.6: 432
22.7: 507
22.10: 416, 506
30.2: 457
30.3: 458
30.8: 458, 527, 529, 531, 533
32.9: 533
34.1: 526
34.5: 466
34.8: 525, 529-530
35.1: 526
35.2: 526
35.3: 526, 529
36.1: 335
36.2: 334-335
36.3: 335
36.4: 335
36.5: 335
38.1: 448-449, 457-459, 462-464,
    466-467, 474, 476, 522, 530, 533
38.2: 448, 458-459, 461-462,
    464-467, 474, 476, 533

38.3: 448, 458-459, 461-463,
    465-467, 474, 476, 525, 530,
    533
38.4: 448, 457-459, 461-462,
    465-467, 522, 525, 530, 533
38.5: 476
41.6: 416-417
44.3: 298
50.1: 367, 369, 373
50.2: 370, 377
50.3: 364-365, 367, 370, 373
50.4: 367, 370
50.8: 373
50.9: 392
50.10: 399
50.15: 388
51.1: 323, 502
51.2: 388
51.11: 391
52.1: 502, 509
52.2: 370, 493, 502
52.3: 370, 428, 493
52.4: 428, 438, 493
52.5: 493
52.8: 388
52.9: 388
52.10: 427, 436, 438
52.11: 428, 438
52.14: 428, 436, 438
52.17: 427, 438
53.1: 437, 494, 504
53.2: 437, 494, 504
53.5: 388, 437
53.6: 370, 388, 504
53.7: 436-437
53.10: 437
55.1: 504
55.2: 504
55.6: 504
58.1: 387-388, 392, 400-401, 406,
    426-427, 436, 438, 491-492,
    499-501, 503, 507-510, 513, 516
58.2: 387, 392, 400-401, 406, 415,
    426-427, 436, 438, 491-492,
    494, 499, 509-510
58.3: 387, 392, 400-401, 406,
    426-427, 436, 438, 491-492,
    494, 499-501, 507-510
    513, 516
58.4: 387, 392, 427, 436, 491-492,
    499-501, 503, 508-510, 513, 516
58.5: 400, 492
58.7: 427
61.1: 238, 249
61.2: 238, 249
61.3: 238, 249
62.1: 238
62.2: 238
62.3: 238
62.4: 238, 271, 275
62.5: 238
67.1: 274
67.4: 271, 275-276
74.1: 376, 524
74.2: 372, 376, 387, 395, 487,
    495, 500, 512, 524
74.3: 487, 498, 500, 504, 513,
    523-524
74.5: 399
75.1: 451
75.2: 451
76.1: 396
76.2: 395

76.3: 395
77.1: 409, 451, 464, 480
77.2: 409, 418, 471, 479, 481-482
77.3: 409, 418, 461
77.4: 460-461, 479, 482
77.5: 461
77.6: 479
77.12: 474
78.1: 409, 461, 480, 498, 523
78.2: 409, 461, 480, 495, 503, 513, 524
78.3: 473-474, 513, 520
79.1: 461, 480
79.2: 461, 480
95.1: 527-528
95.2: 527
95.3: 527
95.7: 527
Support group 6: 307

Task Units (TU)
1: 460, 527
2: 461, 480, 527
3: 461
4.1.1: 136
12.5.3: 521
52.1.1: 510, 513
52.1.2: 510
52.1.3: 510-511, 513, 516
58.1.22: 492
77.4.1: 463
77.4.2: 463
77.4.3: 463

Battle Divisions (BatDiv)
3: 92

Cruiser Divisions (Crudiv)
1: 493, 500
2: 108
5: 487
7: 108
8: 92, 108
12: 363

Destroyer Squadrons (Desron)
1: 168, 182, 185, 199, 221, 226
2: 108, 132, 221, 226, 254, 480
4: 168, 226, 238, 310
5: 269, 310, 487, 495, 503, 512, 524
6: 168, 190, 207, 226, 479
7: 83, 115, 119, 132
8: 132, 203, 342
11: 92, 119
12: 254, 335, 391
14: 523-524
17: 420
18: 420
21: 335, 480, 487, 495, 498, 504, 513, 533
22: 391, 399, 480, 498, 512-513, 523-524
23: 363, 372, 391, 512, 480, 500, 527
24: 527
25: 491, 499, 509, 522, 525, 529, 533
30: 83, 119
31: 83
33: 420
44: 524
45: 363, 391, 504, 509, 527

47: 476, 491, 499, 509
48: 491, 499, 509, 511, 525, 529, 530, 533
49: 480, 487-488, 502, 527
50: 476, 491, 528, 533
51: 479, 493
52: 476, 491, 499, 509
53: 476, 492, 509, 525-526, 529, 533
54: 483, 492, 499, 509, 525-526
55: 476, 491, 502, 527
56: 479, 503
57: 533
58: 502
60: 420, 479, 502, 528, 530, 533
61: 476, 491, 499, 509, 522, 525, 533
62: 476, 491, 499, 509, 525-526, 533
66: 504
91: 493
102: 476
112: 493

Destroyer Divisions (Desdiv)
1: 168
2: 168
4: 504
7: 168
8: 168
11: 168
12: 168, 207
15: 226
18: 420
20: 420
22: 132, 207
23: 226
32: 386
34: 420
42: 418
44: 480, 500
47: 418
48: 418, 479-480, 504
51: 502
60: 115
62: 119
90: 504
91: 502
92: 491, 527
100: 525
102: 524
105: 499
106: 499, 522
110: 502
113: 525
114: 521, 525, 528
120: 502

MTB Squadron
15: 342

British Commonwealth and Allied Forces under British Command
Fleets and Forces
Aegean Force: 453
China Force: 180
Eastern Fleet: 204, 212, 223, 239, 382, 399, 407, 438, 442, 453, 460, 469-470, 486, 510
East Indies Fleet: 470, 524, 529, 534
Force H: 38, 40-41, 43, 45-46, 49-50, 52-53, 55, 57, 62-65,

70-71, 73-74, 77-79, 85, 87, 90-91, 94, 97-98, 100-101, 103, 105-107, 113, 115, 118, 120, 122, 128, 140, 144, 149-150, 167, 171, 197, 199, 201-203, 218, 223, 225, 235, 237, 247, 270, 274, 333, 348, 351
Force K: 93-94, 96, 105, 121, 144, 149, 154-157, 165-166, 180, 183, 189, 292, 322
Force Q: 293, 300, 322
Home Fleet: 1, 3, 5-7, 9-11, 18, 21, 23-25, 32-33, 37, 64, 68, 76, 86, 100, 120, 142, 149, 180, 193, 198, 203, 217, 219, 226, 286, 303, 338, 358, 374, 401, 437, 444, 475, 511
Humber Force: 3, 7
Inshore Squadron: 294
Malaya Force: 21
Mediterranean Fleet: 35-36, 43, 45, 50, 57-58, 62-63, 66, 70, 74, 78, 81, 86-87, 92-94 97-98, 102, 120, 143, 154-155, 161
Northern Patrol: 3, 7-8, 11, 18-19, 37
Pacific Fleet: 471, 486, 501, 530, 535
South American Squadron: 14
1st Composite Squadron: 256

Task Forces (TF)
27: 405
37: 526, 528-531
57: 501-502, 504, 507, 509-511, 516-517
61: 479, 520
62: 514, 520
63: 460, 479, 486, 514
64: 473, 479, 484-485
65: 411, 486
66: 411-412, 457
67: 412
69: 407, 486
70: 407
88: 350, 444

Task Groups (TG)
38.5: 531, 533
63.1: 460
63.2: 460
63.3: 460
70.9 (Aus): 533
88.1: 444
88.2: 444
111.2: 523, 534

Escort (EG) and Support Groups (SG)
A.3 (EG): 211, 217, 246, 253, 257, 261-262, 266, 296, 301, 305, 318
B.1 (EG): 211, 311, 317, 332, 363, 371, 375, 389
B.2 (EG): 211, 266, 281, 287, 289, 296, 308, 311, 317-318, 325, 389
B.3 (EG): 211, 262, 284, 293, 307, 316-317, 326, 354, 378, 381, 389
B.4 (EG): 211, 260, 281, 308-309, 317
B.5 (EG): 291, 309, 317, 325, 332, 358, 400
B.6 (EG): 211, 234, 246 262, 278, 281, 293, 299, 304, 311,

316, 360, 362, 389, 395
B.7 (EG): 211, 285, 315, 320,
   326, 360, 362, 389
C.1 (EG): 211, 217, 240, 257,
   272, 286, 293, 304, 316, 319,
   326, 362, 389, 395
C.2 (EG): 211, 234, 251, 257,
   266, 289, 293, 324, 354, 395
C.3 (EG): 211, 238, 259, 261,
   285-286, 301, 326, 469
C.4 (EG): 211, 251, 260, 263,
   265, 267, 289, 295, 320, 328,
   356, 381
C.5 (EG): 328, 394, 448
1 SG: 321, 326, 331, 346, 394,
   424, 469
2 EG: 131
2 SG: 328, 332, 362, 371, 389,
   395, 400, 424, 436, 490, 496
3 EG: 96, 212
3 SG: 311, 319-320, 357, 389,
   394, 424-425, 436, 464-465, 496
4 EG: 360, 369, 371, 381, 424,
   481, 506, 520
4 SG: 315, 318, 326
5 EG: 85, 119, 125, 332, 346,
   369, 378, 381, 481, 506
5 SG: 318, 324-325, 400-401, 424,
   444, 469, 519
6 SG: 311, 320, 326, 329, 377,
   389, 394, 408, 424, 454
7 EG: 96, 122
7 SG: 368, 400
8 EG: 408
8 SG: 358, 362, 452, 464, 471,
   475, 491-492, 506, 511
9 SG (Can): 354, 400, 424, 434,
   448, 471, 490, 519-521
10 SG: 389, 490
11 SG (Can): 424, 436, 454
12 SG (Can): 424, 433, 441
14 SG: 424, 506
16 EG (Can): 496
17 EG: 506
19 EG: 511, 514
20 EG: 437, 444-445, 452, 464,
   471, 475, 491-492
21 EG: 464, 496, 506
22 EG: 444, 481, 490
23 EG: 490
24 EG (Can): 131, 464
25 EG (Can): 490, 496
26 EG (Can): 496
30 EG: 519
36 EG: 167, 210, 226
37 EG: 314, 402
39 EG: 329, 389
40 EG: 320, 332, 346, 368

Battle Squadrons
1 Battle Sqdn: 89, 155, 378, 382
2 Battle Sqdn: 8, 32
2 Sqdn Mediterranean Fleet: 62
Battlecruiser Sqdn: 32, 100

Carrier Squadrons
1: 479
21: 514, 520, 534

Cruiser Squadrons
1: 32, 54, 100
2: 5-6, 32, 100
3: 50, 54, 58, 63, 67

4: 227, 239, 382
7: 3, 5, 8, 36, 40, 50, 63, 67, 70,
   97
10: 139-140
12: 3, 350
15: 64, 106, 227, 279
18: 32, 100, 140

Destroyer Flotillas
2: 21, 24, 48, 50, 57, 63, 89, 227
3: 32, 408
4: 6, 101, 140, 333, 351, 382, 460,
   471
5: 32, 94, 96, 98, 201, 227, 257
6: 1, 5, 14, 32
7: 6, 173, 227, 255, 471
8: 1, 5-6, 11, 14, 32, 38, 46, 49,
   63, 94, 97-98, 333, 351, 421
9: 32
10: 48, 50, 108, 421-422, 433-434,
   521
11: 382
12: 227
13: 38, 140
14: 48, 50, 57, 63, 89, 94, 201,
   227
16: 189, 382
17: 421, 464, 471
19: 4, 140, 350
20: 51
21: 189, 350
22: 201, 227
23: 421
24: 333, 351, 385, 453
25: 421, 471
26: 520
27: 421 471

Submarine Flotillas
1: 73, 80, 86, 98, 111, 120, 278
2: 5, 23, 442
3: 5, 23
4: 382
6: 5, 23
8: 104, 111, 278, 400, 442, 534
9: 75, 78, 85, 126, 293, 302, 366,
   375
10: 73, 77, 80, 111, 207, 278

MTB Flotillas
1: 433
3: 467
4: 456
9: 408
10: 102
11: 456
13: 408
14: 408, 429, 433
21: 408, 456
29 (Can): 422-423, 433-434
30 (Nor): 295, 433
31: 322
35: 423, 429
51: 433
53: 396
55: 422-423, 433
54 (Nor): 425, 433, 446, 475
58: 425, 433
64: 408, 422, 434
65 (Can): 428-429, 433

MGB Flotilla
17: 322

ML Flotillas
10: 408
50: 328, 408
51: 408
52: 328, 408
55 (Ind): 473
56 (Ind): 473

Minesweeping Flotillas
6: 203, 527, 534
7: 514, 527, 534
14: 212
21 (Aus): 197
37: 514, 527, 534

Dutch
East Indies Fleet: 159

Finnish
Armoured Ship Div: 134
2 Patrol Flotilla: 431
1 MTB Flotilla: 431
2 MTB Flotilla: 431

French
Force X: 43
2 Battleship Division: 41
3 Squadron: 37
1 Cruiser Division: 37
2 Cruiser Division: 37
8 Destroyer Division: 27
2 Submarine Division: 21
10 Submarine Flotilla: 21, 23

German
*Commands, Forces and Composite
Flotillas*
Baltic Experimental Force: 117
Baltic Fleet: 139
Danube Flotilla: 144, 146, 210,
   232
Experimental Barrage Command:
   1
Naval Group Command East: 1,
   22
Net Defence Force: 397
Nörd Minelaying Group: 77, 204
Ostland Coast Defence Flotilla:
   212
Task Force: 2: 446, 485, 495
Training Flotilla: 22

Destroyer Flotillas
1: 3, 17-19
2: 3, 19
4: 3, 10, 17-18, 348, 374, 490
5: 3, 10, 51, 188, 272, 288, 348
6: 116, 120, 122, 124, 348, 397,
   460, 473
8: 169, 179, 203, 208, 314, 375,
   377, 422

Torpedo Boat Flotillas
1: 52, 64
2: 44, 51-54, 64, 78, 189, 324,
   431, 470
3: 189, 236, 239, 265, 449, 460,
   470
4: 358, 362, 376-377, 398-399,
   405
5: 3, 44, 47-48, 51-52, 57-58, 60,
   68, 71, 189, 200, 206, 217, 330,

348, 358, 398-399, 404-406,
    422, 427
6: 3, 10-12, 431
9: 367, 398, 418
10: 390, 397, 414, 431, 455, 500

Submarine Flotillas
2: 2
6: 2
7: 2

Patrol Boat Flotillas
2: 316, 412, 439
3: 134, 157-158, 211, 342-343, 488
4: 316
6: 316
7: 27, 316
12: 322
13: 22, 308, 328, 433
14: 328
15: 356, 440, 447
17: 488
18: 398
20: 433
61: 331, 450

MTB Flotillas
1: 1, 29, 45, 47, 52, 71, 81, 83-84,
    87, 95, 109, 115-117, 124-125,
    133-134, 225, 252, 267, 286,
    298, 311, 319, 332, 353, 359,
    366, 404, 408
2: 78, 93, 109, 111-112, 115, 122,
    125, 134, 143, 153, 189, 200,
    234, 261, 278, 296, 303, 306,
    313, 318, 327, 344, 355, 359,
    362, 366, 391, 394, 398-399,
    412-413, 422-423, 428-429,
    434-435, 440, 484, 487, 493,
    500, 507
3: 84, 109-112, 115, 118, 120-121,
    129, 134, 169, 179, 201, 209-210,
    214-215, 228-229, 272, 289, 313,
    318, 351
4: 125, 127, 133, 136, 155, 157,
    189, 261, 285, 296, 303, 306,
    318, 327, 344, 355, 359, 362-363,
    366, 385, 398-399, 404-405, 413,
    422-423, 427, 484, 486-487, 493,
    500, 507, 510
5: 109, 112, 133, 260, 280, 283,
    305, 318, 324, 327, 344, 366,
    372, 376, 380, 385, 388, 391,
    394, 398, 404-406, 412-413,
    422-423, 427, 451, 453, 484,
    487, 493, 500-501
6: 189, 265, 296, 303, 306, 318,
    327, 344, 355, 359, 362-363,
    366, 429, 434-435, 440, 447,
    484, 486-487, 493, 500, 507, 510
7: 340, 373
8: 355, 359, 362, 366, 391, 394,
    398-399, 404-405, 412-413,
    422-423, 429, 434, 440, 447,
    484, 486, 493, 500
9: 391, 394, 398, 404-406, 412-413,
    422-423, 427, 429, 434-435, 484,
    486-487, 493, 500, 507, 510
10: 440, 453

Minesweeping Flotillas (M/S)
1: 1, 4, 17, 122, 143, 188, 327,
    482, 488

2: 22, 143, 188, 316, 336, 482,
    488
3: 211, 219, 342, 380, 428, 431,
    451, 482, 488
4: 22, 188
5: 100, 115, 125, 143, 188, 426
6: 108, 316, 413
7: 327, 519
8: 316
10: 316, 398
11: 425
12: 22, 188, 482, 488
17: 211
18: 211
21: 308
24: 316, 440, 498
25: 342, 451, 482, 488
26: 316, 433
28: 316
31: 115, 211, 324, 343, 482, 488
34: 211, 391, 396
36: 398, 440, 488
38: 440, 447
40: 316
42: 316
46: 434, 439
56: 279

*Motor Minesweeper Flotillas
(MMS)*
1: 22, 211, 428, 431, 451, 482, 488
2: 22, 117, 121, 143, 188, 261,
    356
3: 1, 22, 188, 252, 285, 319, 353,
    359, 365, 407
4: 188, 413, 422, 435, 440
5: 109, 115, 117, 124, 131, 134
6: 257
7: 426
8: 301
9: 327
10: 246, 433
11: 369, 397, 456
12: 367
13: 456
14: 440, 447
15: 488
17: 488
21: 426
30: 359
34: 433
38: 440

Submarine Chaser Flotillas (SC)
1: 368, 380, 404, 407
3: 380, 407, 488
6: 489
11: 489
12: 211, 331, 450, 489
14: 316
21: 356, 367, 418
22: 300
23: 359-360, 368, 380, 407

Escort Divisions
2: 440, 447
3: 316
4: 316
9: 488
10: 380, 403, 407, 488

Defence Flotillas
1: 489

2: 488-489
3: 488
14: 482, 488

Mine Detonating Flotillas
2: 316
6: 316

Small Unit Battle Flotillas
211: 440
363: 440

Landing Flotillas
1: 252, 329, 353, 403, 407
2: 300
3: 304, 329, 353, 407
5: 304, 329, 353
7: 353, 407
11: 489, 495
13: 451, 488, 515
21: 451
24: 312, 324, 343, 397, 428, 431,
    451, 488
27: 211, 219

Gun Carrier Flotillas
3: 488
5: 495
6: 429
7: 451, 482, 488, 508
8: 447
KFK Training Flotilla: 489

U-Boat Patrol Groups
Adler: 316
Amrum: 374, 376
Amsel: 319-320, 324
Arnauld: 149
Benecke: 151
Blitz: 401
Blücher: 247
Boreas: 393
Borkum: 375, 377-378, 381
Bosemüller: 132
Brandenburg: 135
Breslau: 141, 145
Büffel: 284
Burggraf: 305
Coronel: 371, 373, 375
Dachs: 343, 442
Delphin: 291, 295
Donau: 325-327
Donner: 402, 409
Drachen: 280
Dragoner: 412
Draufgänger: 281
Dränger: 309
Drossel: 322, 324
Eisbär: 250, 261
Eisenbart: 361, 366, 368, 374
Eisteufel: 230
Elbe: 324
Endrass: 226
Falke: 289, 293, 295-296
Faust: 511
Fink: 320
Föhr: 374, 376
Geier: 329
Gödecke: 151
Greif: 442
Grimm: 452
Grube: 471
Habicht: 293

Hagen: 498
Hai: 234, 236, 390
Hammer: 401
Hartherz: 297
Hartmut: 393
Haudegen: 296, 299
Hecht: 216
Hinein: 381
Igel: 389
Iller: 325
Iltis: 250
Inn: 325
Isar: 325
Isegrim: 383
Jaguar: 293
Jahn: 362
Keil: 402, 409
Knappen: 301
Körner: 362
Kreuzotter: 272, 278
Kurfürst: 104, 132
Landwirt: 400, 412, 424
Laudsknecht: 295
Lech: 325
Leopard: 262
Lerche: 317
Letzte Ritter: 156
Leuthen: 353-354
Lohs: 246, 253
Löwenherz: 315
Luchs: 260
Markgraf: 130
Meise: 317-318
Mitte: 412, 419
Monsun: 337, 343, 349, 382
Mordbrenner: 144, 146
Mosel: 326-327
Nahe: 325
Natter: 272
Neptun: 304
Neuland: 305, 307
Nordsturm: 296
Oder: 326
Ostmark: 305, 307
Panther: 262, 265-266, 281, 464-465
Pfadfinder: 219, 222
Pfeil: 253, 257-258, 296
Pirat: 238
Preussen: 394-395
Prien: 35
Puma: 266
Rasmus: 491
Raubgraf: 308-309
Raubritter: 146, 148
Raufbold: 285
Reissewolf: 144-145
Rhein: 324
Ritter: 301
Robbe: 303
Rochen: 295, 303
Rösing: 29, 32
Rossbach: 356-357
Rügen: 376, 380
Schill: 363, 368-369, 371
Schlagetot: 146, 277
Schlei: 179
Schlieffen: 360
Seehund: 299
Seeräuber: 167, 312
Seeteufel: 311
Seewolf: 132, 311, 506
Seydlitz: 178

Siegfried: 362
Specht: 320
Spitz: 286-287
Star: 320
Steinbrinck: 239
Steuben: 151
Stier: 251, 475
Stock: 471
Störtebecker: 148, 151
Stosstrupp: 145, 147
Streitaxt: 270
Sturmbock: 304
Stürmer: 309, 381
Sylt: 374, 376
Taifun: 299-300
Thor: 401
Tiger: 259
Tirpitz: 362
Trutz: 329, 444-445
Tümmler: 303, 308
Ulan: 172, 180
Ungestüm: 284-285, 287
Unverzagt: 308
Veilchen: 266-267
Vorwärts: 251, 253, 258
Weddigen: 371, 373
Werwolf: 384, 393
West: 99-100, 104, 108
Westmark: 305
Westwall: 277, 283
Wiking: 343
Wildfang: 305
Wohlgemut: 308
Wolf: 234, 238
Wotan: 262-263, 266
Ziethen: 177
Zorn: 452

Italian
2 Squadron: 40, 42, 67, 69

Battleship Divisions
5: 42, 57, 69, 349
9: 57, 128, 228, 283, 349

Cruiser Divisions
1: 36, 42, 57, 67, 69, 89
2: 42
3: 36, 42, 57-58, 67, 69, 89, 128, 153-154, 166, 228, 284
4: 42, 69, 105, 116, 158
7: 40, 42, 57, 69, 94, 96, 105, 114, 116, 157, 165, 227-228, 349
8: 36, 42, 57, 69, 89, 128, 153, 228, 284, 349

Destroyer Flotillas/Divisions
1: 37
7: 42-43, 67, 228
8: 42
9: 37, 43, 67, 73
10: 42
11: 36, 42-43, 58, 228
12: 36, 42-43, 67, 139, 349
13: 40, 67, 149, 228
14: 42-43, 58, 63, 349
15: 42, 68, 265
16: 37, 42

Torpedo Boat Flotillas/Divisions
1: 58
4: 42
10: 67

12: 61
13: 104
14: 73

MTB/MAS Flotillas
4: 311, 319
10: 121
13: 37, 61

Japanese
Fleets and Forces
Malaya Force: 163, 166, 204
North Philippine Force: 162
South East Area Fleet: 537
Southern Expeditionary Fleet: 159-160
1 Southern Expeditionary Fleet: 200-201
South Philippine Force: 160
South West Area Fleet: 209
Striking Force: 156, 161, 268
Combined Fleet: 134, 220, 235, 243, 248, 263, 268, 361, 462
1 Mobile Fleet: 414
1 Fleet: 235
2 Fleet: 235, 244, 254-255, 263-264, 275, 277, 361, 364, 400, 414
3 Fleet: 162, 194, 235, 244, 254-255, 263-264, 361, 364, 415
4 Fleet: 163, 199, 235
5 Fleet: 235, 323
6 Fleet: 235
8 Fleet: 235, 237, 241, 244, 271, 275, 286, 364
Base Force 1: 170, 177, 181, 186
Base Force 2: 169, 176, 194
Base Force 4: 235
Base Force 5: 163, 235
Base Force 6: 235
Base Force 7: 235
Base Force 8: 235
Base Force 9: 194
Special Base Force 9: 201
Special Base Force 12: 201
1 Carrier Fleet: 204-205, 207, 400
2 Carrier Force: 220

Carrier Squadrons
1: 156, 179, 190, 194, 204, 220, 235, 263, 361, 414-415
2: 156, 178, 190, 194, 204, 220, 224, 235, 263, 268, 275, 361, 414-415
3: 414-415
4: 160, 178, 194, 204, 220
5: 156, 179, 204
11: 160, 177, 181, 186, 221, 235
22: 194
24: 194

Battle Squadrons
1: 221, 235, 361, 414
2: 221, 235
3: 156, 159, 178-179, 190, 194, 204, 220-221, 235, 263, 275, 361, 414
11: 235, 263, 275

Cruiser Squadrons
4: 159, 178, 190, 194, 220-221, 235, 263, 361, 364, 414
5: 160, 169, 191, 194, 221, 235,

263, 361, 364, 414
6: 163, 168, 179, 199, 235, 263
7: 159, 166-167, 173, 178, 194,
    204, 221, 235, 263, 361, 364,
    383, 414
8: 156, 179, 190, 194, 204, 220,
    235, 264, 361, 364
9: 221, 235
16: 194
18: 164, 179, 199, 235, 237
21: 221

Destroyer Flotillas
1: 156, 179, 190, 194, 204, 235
2: 160, 169, 177, 194, 196, 221,
    235, 244, 249, 254, 263, 268,
    271, 275-276, 283, 286, 290,
    361, 364, 414, 508
3: 159, 166, 178, 192, 194, 205,
    221, 235, 252-254, 258, 264,
    271, 275
4: 177, 192, 194, 196, 221, 235,
    252-254, 258, 263-264, 268, 271,
    275, 290
5: 173, 192, 294
6: 164, 199
10: 220, 235, 254, 264, 268, 275,
    361, 364, 415

Destroyer Divisions
2: 162, 177, 194, 221, 235, 252,
    268, 275
4: 159, 162, 166, 173, 178, 190,
    194, 220, 235, 244, 264, 361, 415
5: 173, 194, 205
6: 159, 178, 190, 221, 235, 252,
    275
7: 194, 220, 235
8: 159, 173, 178, 184, 186, 191,
    221, 275
9: 177, 186, 194, 221, 235, 254
10: 220, 235, 264, 271, 275, 361,
    415
11: 159, 178, 194, 204-205, 221,
    235, 252, 275
12: 159-160, 167, 178, 194, 221
15: 160, 169, 171, 177, 181, 184,
    186, 191, 221, 235, 254, 263, 275
16: 160, 169-170, 177, 181, 184,
    191, 194, 221, 235, 264, 275,
    361
17: 190, 194, 204, 221, 235, 244,
    264, 361, 415, 508
18: 190, 194, 204, 221

19: 159-160, 166, 178, 194, 205,
    235, 252, 275
20: 159-160, 166, 173, 178, 194,
    196, 204, 221, 235, 249, 252
21: 181, 186, 191, 220, 235, 508
22: 160, 173, 194, 196
23: 168, 179
24: 170, 186, 191, 194, 221, 235,
    263, 275, 361
27: 221, 235, 252, 275-276
29: 164, 168, 179, 235, 361, 414
30: 164, 168, 179, 235
31: 263, 275, 361, 414
32: 361, 414
34: 252
41: 508
61: 361, 415

Submarine Flotillas
1: 152, 162, 204, 219, 235, 249,
    253-254, 264, 528
2: 152, 162, 177, 229, 235
3: 152, 162, 177, 181, 207, 234-
    235, 249, 253
4: 176, 186-187
5: 177-178
6: 164, 170, 178, 235
7: 179, 235, 239, 284, 381
8: 215, 222, 235

Minelaying Divisions
17: 160
19: 163, 179

Minesweeping Divisions
1: 181, 192, 194
15: 163
17: 177
21: 177
30: 177

Submarine Chaser Divisions
11: 166
59: 163
60: 163

Gunboat Divisions
7: 163

Anti-Submarine Divisions
11: 181

Escort Squadrons
2: 235

Midget Submarine Attack Groups
Amatake: 513
Chihaya: 494
Kamitake: 494
Kikusui: 467
Taman: 527
Tatara: 509
Todoroki: 521

Russian
Fleets, Flotillas and Defence Sectors
Baltic Fleet: 12, 15, 109, 129, 131,
    133, 136, 138-139, 147, 207,
    384, 431
Black Sea Fleet: 109, 111, 128,
    133, 140, 143, 146, 152, 197,
    216, 225, 403-404, 446-447
Northern Fleet: 12, 109, 113, 123,
    134, 180, 203, 220, 236, 259,
    366, 385, 393, 401, 438, 444,
    459, 464
Pacific Fleet: 259, 530
Azov Flotilla: 172, 252, 353, 365
Danube Flotilla: 112, 116, 118,
    124-125, 447
North Pacific Flotilla: 531, 533
White Sea Flotilla: 334, 465
Petropavlovsk Naval Defence
    Sector: 532
Tallin Naval Defence Sector: 455

Smaller Naval Forces
Cruiser Brigade (BS): 138, 239
1 DD Division (N): 134
2 DD Division (BS): 116, 127
Submarine Brigade: 298
1 SM Brigade (B): 13, 110-111
1 SM Brigade (BS): 112
1 SM Division (N): 133, 154,
    298
2 SM Brigade (B): 13, 111
2 SM Brigade (BS): 112
2 SM Division (N): 139, 154
3 SM Division (N): 209
17 SM Division (B): 15
5 MS Division: 124
1 Torpedo Cutter Brigade: 407,
    530
2 Torpedo Cutter Brigade: 124,
    380, 404, 407, 501
1 Patrol Cutter Division: 297

Armies

American
Armies
1: 420, 425, 441
5: 350
6: 461, 466, 480, 483, 487, 536-
    537
7: 338, 340, 342, 443
8: 533, 536
9: 441
10: 504, 523, 536

Corps
I: 291, 409, 480, 482, 536-537
II: 339
III Amphibious: 437, 452, 504,
    538
V: 420
V Amphibious: 427, 438, 493,
    536
VI: 350, 385, 443
VII: 420, 431
IX: 536
X: 461, 512, 536-537
XI: 451, 487, 536
XIV: 345, 480, 536
XXIV: 461, 504, 511, 537

Brigades
1 Marine: 115, 132, 437

Infantry Divisions
1: 274, 333, 339, 420
2: 425
3: 273, 333, 339, 385, 443
4: 420
6: 439, 480, 537
7: 323, 388, 461, 504, 511, 537
8: 452
9: 273-274, 333, 425
24: 409, 461, 474, 512, 537
25: 345, 483, 537
27: 370, 388, 392, 511, 536

29: 420
31: 451, 469, 512
32: 380, 451, 487, 535, 537
33: 537
34: 274
36: 350, 444
37: 335, 345, 364-365, 399, 480
38: 487-488
40: 480, 494, 500, 520, 537
41: 409, 418, 495, 498, 537
43: 304, 334, 345-346, 480, 536
45: 333, 339, 350, 443
66: 510
77: 437, 473, 502, 504, 511, 536
81: 452, 536
90: 425
93: 533
96: 461, 504, 511
97: 536
98: 537
Americal: 199, 494, 503, 536

Marine Divisions
1: 241, 244, 271, 376, 452, 504, 539
2: 271, 370, 428, 438, 536
3: 363, 437, 494
4: 388, 399, 428, 438, 494
5: 494, 536
6: 504, 533, 539
21: 365

Airborne Divisions
11: 487, 532, 536
82: 339, 420
101: 420

Armoured Divisions
1: 274
2: 273, 333, 339, 425

Cavalry Divisions
1: 461, 487, 536

Regiments
5 Cavalry: 395
7 Marine Corps: 254
8 Marine: 271
17: 323
106: 392
112 Cavalry: 334, 375, 536
147: 271
158: 334
164: 263, 504
168: 433
182: 275
503 Parachute: 474

Battalions
2 Raider: 247
2 Marine Airdrome: 346
2 Marine Parachute: 363
4 Marine Raider: 334
7 Marine Defence: 346

Regimental Combat Teams (RCT)
1: 539
4: 533
5: 539
7: 539
11: 539
18: 339
19: 474

30: 342
34: 488
35: 345
103: 304
108: 494, 520
126: 380, 451
127: 536
132: 494
134: 487
151: 488
158: 483, 494, 504
163: 409, 415, 504
164: 504
169: 304
172: 346
182: 494
185: 500, 514
186: 495
187 Parachute: 532
188 Parachute: 533
306: 536
323: 452
503 Parachute: 488, 500
511 Airborne: 533
1 Airborne Group: 443
13 Armoured Group: 483
3 Ranger Battalion Landing Team: 350

British and Commonwealth
Armies and Forces
BEF: 4, 31, 33
Western Desert Force: 69
21 Army Group: 419
1 Army (Aus): 537
2 Army: 420, 425
8 Army: 92, 152, 161, 294, 338, 340, 351
Gull Force (Aus): 167
Maurice Force: 28
Norman Force: 37
Scissor Force: 29
Sickle Force: 27
Sparrow Force (Aus): 167

Corps
I: 420
I (Aus): 524
X: 350
XII: 515
XIII: 338, 347
XV: 473, 534, 538
XXX: 338, 420

Divisions
1: 328, 386
1 Airborne: 338, 350
1 (Can): 14, 37, 333, 338
2 (Can): 247
3: 420
3 (Can): 420
3 (NZ): 391
5: 203, 333, 338
5 (Ind): 534, 538
6 Airborne: 420, 515
6 (Aus): 76, 520, 537
7 Armoured: 350, 425
7 (Aus): 524, 538
9 (Aus): 298, 347, 523
23 (Ind): 534, 538
25 (Ind): 534
26 (Ind): 513, 538
46: 350

49: 425
50: 333, 338, 420
51: 35, 334, 338, 425
52: 37, 467
56: 350, 514
78: 274

Brigades
1 Armoured (Can): 333
4: 485
4 Armoured: 333
4 (Can): 247
6 (Can): 247
8 (NZ): 363
9 (Aus): 524
15: 27
20 (Aus): 347, 355
23 Armoured: 334
24 Guards: 25
24 (Aus): 348
26 (Aus): 348, 513
29: 255
36 (Ind): 486
49 (Ind): 538
71 (Ind): 485-486
73 AA: 333
74 (Ind): 479
146: 25
148: 26
152: 467
231 Independent: 333, 338
Guards: 29
Scots Guards: 519

Commandos
3: 247, 333, 338, 479, 484, 494, 534-535
4: 247, 467
4 Special Service: 467
10 Inter Allied: 467
40: 333
41: 333, 467
47: 467
48: 467
268: 206
353: 208

Chinese
Armies
18 Group: 532
3: 532
6: 532
13: 539
52: 539
94: 532

Estonian
7 Inf Div: 455
247 Inf Div: 455

Finnish
III Corps: 456
IV Corps: 428
3 Inf Div: 456
18 Inf Div: 204
11 Inf Regt: 456
Group P: 204

French
Foreign Legion: 30-31
II Corps: 443
9 Colonial Div: 429
10 Div: 510

5 Chasseurs Alpins Demi-Bde: 26
27 Chasseurs Alpins Demi-Bde: 27
Foreign Legion Demi-Bde: 28

German
Armies and Groups
Group Courland: 482, 500
Group North: 208, 446
1 Panzer Army: 152
2 Army: 485, 496
3 Army: 485
4 Army: 485, 501
6 Army: 402
11 Army: 152, 172, 180, 216, 225
17 Army: 330, 352, 402, 407, 411
18 Army: 33, 133

Corps
Afrika: 79-80, 83-86, 90, 92-94, 95, 229
Kaupisch: 5
VII Armoured: 497
XIX Mountain: 114, 134, 459
II SS Armoured: 280, 453
V: 252, 319, 403
XXVII: 485
XLII: 172

Divisions
5 Armoured: 38
7 Armoured: 38
2 Mountain: 114, 116-117, 459
3 Mountain: 114, 116
6 Mountain: 127, 459
9 Inf: 252
22 Inf: 367
46 Inf: 172, 252
50 Inf: 403
61 Inf: 134
70 Inf: 467
71 Inf: 368
73 Inf: 252
93 Inf: 485
111 Inf: 402
125 Inf: 252
218 Inf: 455
291 Inf: 111
302 Inf: 247

Regiments and Battle Groups
Battle Group Müller: 367
Naval Assault Detachment Bigler: 111
349 Grenadier: 348
136 Mountain: 114, 123
42 Inf: 172
71 Inf: 247
72 Inf: 172

Italian
Expeditionary Corps: 54
10 Army: 55

Japanese
Armies
China Area Army: 532
Expeditionary Army: 532
8 Area Army: 537
17 Area Army: 537
14 Army Group: 482
2 Army: 538

14: 162, 170
16: 192
17: 250, 258, 268, 291, 537
18: 380, 520, 537
25: 166, 173, 186-187
31: 438
32: 504, 524
35: 466

Special Landing Forces etc.
South Sea Detachment: 163, 179, 199, 214, 237, 245
South Philippines Force: 169, 171
Yokosuka Naval Air Landing Force: 177
Kashima Naval Landing Force: 179
Kure Naval Landing Force: 184
Maizuru Naval Landing Force: 179
2 Kure Special Landing Force: 177
3 Kure Special Landing Force: 214, 250
5 Kure Special Landing Force: 250
2 Maizuru Special Landing Force: 168
1 Sasebo Special Landing Force: 177, 181, 186
5 Sasebo Special Landing Force: 250
2 Yokosuka Special Landing Force: 166-167
5 Yokosuka Special Landing Force: 244
6 Expeditionary Battle Group: 437
Ichiki Detachment: 244
Kawaguchi Detachment: 249-250, 253-254
Nankai Detachment: 245

Infantry Divisions
Guards: 173, 186
1: 466
2: 192, 258, 263-264
5: 159, 166, 186
6: 399
14: 452
16: 160, 166, 170, 173, 178, 461, 466
18: 159, 173, 180, 186, 201, 205
23: 482
26: 466
29: 437-438
30: 461
33: 199
38: 165, 170, 187, 192, 264, 271, 275
43: 428
48: 170, 191-192, 538
51: 306
55: 159
56: 201
62: 511
63: 511
88: 532
91: 532
102: 461, 466
109: 494

Infantry Regiments
2: 452
56: 159
143: 159
144: 179
228: 191, 271
229: 187
230: 187, 192, 271
56 Regimental Combat Group: 177, 182, 192
56 Independent Mixed Brigade: 169, 171
58 Infantry Brigade: 482

Polish
1 Army: 495

Rumanian
3 Army: 402
3 Inf Div: 252
10 Inf Div: 403
13 Inf Div: 137
15 Inf Div: 137
Cavalry Div: 252
5 Cavalry Div: 252
6 Cavalry Div: 252

Russian
Armies and Fronts
1 Baltic Front: 485
Leningrad Front: 384
3 Ukrainian Front: 402
4 Ukrainian Front: 402
1 White Russian Front: 495
2 White Russian Front: 485, 495-496
3 White Russian Front: 485, 501, 508
2 Assault Army: 384, 512
3 Assault Army: 495
Coastal Army: 403, 411
2 Guards Army: 403, 410
1 Guards Armoured Army: 495
2 Guards Armoured Army: 495
5 Guards Armoured Army: 485
3 Army: 485
8 Army: 133, 455, 470
9 Army: 152
14 Army: 12, 134, 459
18 Army: 365, 428
19 Army: 512
21 Army: 428
25 Army: 531
37 Army: 152
39 Army: 485
42 Army: 131
43 Army: 485
44 Army: 172, 175, 197, 216
46 Army: 447
47 Army: 216, 252
48 Army: 485
51 Army: 140, 146, 150, 172, 216, 403, 411
55 Army: 131
56 Army: 365
59 Army: 428
70 Army: 515

Corps
3 Guards Cavalry: 495
126 Light Rifle: 459
127 Light Rifle: 459
X Rifle: 129

XIV Rifle: 118
31 Rifle: 459
99 Rifle: 459
131 Rifle: 459

Divisions
224 A/A: 175
2 Cavalry: 144
32 Guards Rifle: 245
9 Mountain Rifle: 283
14 Rifle: 114, 116
25 Rifle: 112
52 Rifle: 114, 116
63 Rifle: 173
67 Rifle: 110
77 Rifle: 252
95 Rifle: 144
104 Rifle: 12
109 Rifle: 455
157 Rifle: 135, 137, 141, 173
244 Rifle: 172
302 Rifle: 172
303 Rifle: 531
345 Rifle: 171

386 Rifle: 175
388 Rifle: 162
408 Rifle: 260
421 Rifle: 137, 144

Brigades
8 Guards Rifle: 267
9 Guards Rifle: 267
10 Guards Rifle: 267
2 Naval Inf: 252
3 Naval Inf: 252
7 Naval Inf: 146
8 Naval Inf: 146
9 Naval Inf: 222
12 Naval Inf: 459
13 Naval Inf: 531
14 Naval Inf: 252
79 Naval Inf: 170
83 Naval Inf: 172, 252, 297
142 Naval Inf: 252
255 Naval Inf: 297, 352
63 Rifle: 459
113 Rifle: 532
122 Rifle: 172

138 Rifle: 225
143 Rifle: 172
165 Rifle: 297

Regiments
3 Marine Rifle: 138
226 Mountain: 176, 179
1 Naval Rifle: 126
3 Naval Rifle: 137
137 Rifle: 254
145 Rifle: 254
325 Rifle: 117, 123
544 Rifle: 183

Infantry Battalions
16 Naval: 146
17 Naval: 146
18 Naval: 146
19 Naval: 146
75 Naval: 531
77 Naval: 531
358 Naval: 531
386 Naval: 365

Air Forces

For explanation concerning the various types of squadron operated by the various countries please see Abbreviations and Glossary on page vii. The only non-standard abbreviations used in this section are:- FAA Fleet Air Arm, OTU Operational Training Unit, and RCAF Royal Canadian Air Force. In the section on the German Air Force the relevant Staffel belonging to a particular Group is indicated by suffixing the Group Number with a Roman numeral relevant to the Staffel number, ie, K.Fl.Gr. 506/III.

American

Army Air Forces
Far East Air Force: 162
South Pacific Air Force: 335
9 Air Fleet: 283
5 USAAF: 344-345, 359, 364,
    375, 406, 451, 460-461, 464,
    466, 487-488, 495, 498, 524
7 USAAF: 353, 487
8 USAAF: 294, 296, 306, 311,
    319, 322, 327, 334, 342, 359,
    366, 372, 374, 380, 390, 460,
    475, 498, 501, 504-505, 510
13 USAAF: 460, 464, 495, 498,
    504, 524
14 USAAF: 372
15 USAAF: 460
20 USAAF: 487, 495, 529
1 Air Division: 392
11 Bomber Group: 353
20 Bomber Command: 442
21 Bomber Command: 482, 504
509 Composite Group: 529
343 Bombardment Squadron: 255
1 Composite Air Squadron: 255
339 Fighter Squadron: 316
A/S Squadron 1: 298, 329, 332
A/S Squadron 2: 297-298, 329
A/S Squadron 4: 332
A/S Squadron 19: 332

Naval Air Forces
Patrol Wing 7: 115

Patrol Squadrons (VP)
32: 331
33: 5
51: 5, 93
52: 5
53: 5, 301
54: 4
63: 332, 387, 397, 415, 506
72: 322
73: 119, 143, 251
74: 119, 143, 330, 352
83: 286, 301
84: 262, 282, 317, 321, 325, 334
94: 331
125: 314

Patrol Bomber Squadrons (VPB)
103: 506
112: 490

Bomber Squadrons (VB)
107: 330, 372, 379, 454
127: 330
128: 357
129: 330

**British Commonwealth and Allied
units under RAF Command**
Commands and Groups
Bomber Command: 2, 4, 6, 20-21,
    25, 44, 85, 91-94, 98, 105,
    133-135, 137, 140, 143, 146-147,
    197, 206, 245, 293-294, 306,
    311, 314, 316, 321, 342, 380,
    408, 427, 438, 446, 450, 460,
    467, 475, 509-510, 512-513, 515
Coastal Command: 25, 50, 107,
    293, 298, 332, 376, 381, 415,

419, 424, 428, 441, 509-510,
    513, 515
Fighter Command: 301, 331
2 Tactical Air Force: 515
1 Group: 408
2 Group: 133
3 Group: 408
4 Group: 206, 408
5 Group: 25, 408
6 Group: 408
10 Group: 331
15 Group: 381, 389
16 Group: 515
18 Group: 415, 419, 515
19 Group: 298, 332, 346, 376,
    381, 424
83 Group: 515
84 Group: 515
247 Group: 358

Squadrons
4 OTU: 415
5 (RCAF): 320
8: 383
9: 4, 15, 451, 467
10 (RAAF): 38, 281, 298, 332
10 (RCAF): 267, 354-355, 362
10 OTU: 331-332
22: 9
35: 85
36: 415
37: 15
38: 13, 228
42: 107, 218
44: 25
45: 61
46: 31
49: 25
50: 25
53: 332, 369
58: 298, 332
59: 298, 332, 360, 415
61: 25
69: 149
86: 298, 315, 325, 332, 357, 360,
    368, 419, 496
99: 14
107: 4
110: 4
115: 13
120: 131, 240, 262, 266, 268, 301,
    305, 309, 325-326, 354, 357,
    360, 496, 506
139: 4
143: 423
144: 6, 25
145 (RCAF): 267
149: 4, 13, 15
162 (RCAF): 419
172: 298, 332, 378, 395, 443
179: 329, 368, 371, 490
186: 506
200: 333
201: 310, 376, 506
202: 60, 62
206: 293, 311, 318, 395, 419
209: 101, 123
210: 231, 260, 298, 318, 331, 393,
    415, 419, 519
217: 228
220: 282, 296-297, 307, 363, 371,
    378, 454

222: 457
224: 7, 298, 332, 337, 362, 424,
    496
226: 332
228: 298, 331-332
230: 40, 57
233: 211, 312
236: 423
248: 331
263: 30
265: 417
269: 123, 282, 325, 356-357
304 (Pol): 298, 332, 424
311 (Czech): 298, 332, 377
330 (Nor): 415, 469
333 (Nor): 419
407 (RCAF): 298, 389, 395, 469
422 (RCAF): 369, 376, 395
423 (RCAF): 325, 357, 360
426 (RCAF): 332
461 (RAAF): 298, 322, 332, 376
502: 160, 298, 332
517: 451
612: 389
617: 467
621: 383
701 (FAA): 30
800 (FAA): 24
803 (FAA): 24
810 (FAA): 63, 101
812 (FAA): 155
813 (FAA): 43, 63
815 (FAA): 63, 107
818 (FAA): 63, 101
819 (FAA): 63
820 (FAA): 63
824 (FAA): 43, 49, 63
825 (FAA): 189
828 (FAA): 101
829 (FAA): 107
832 (FAA): 355

French
4 Naval Air Group: 107

German
Air Fleets
1: 208 312
2: 2, see X Fl.Div, 373
3: 189
4: 94
5: 444

*Air Divisions (later renamed Air
    Corps) (Fl.Div or Fl.K)*
I: 207-208, 327
II: 202, 207, 380, 387, 404, 418
IV: 110, 150
VIII: 95, 102, 225
IX: 26, 28, 47, 49, 52, 54, 57, 60
X: 2, 15, 17, 21, 69, 76, 86, 88,
    90, 367
XI: 102

Wings
Long Range Recce Wing (F.A.Gr)
5: 368, 378, 381, 389
22/I: 401
124/I: 491

Coastal Air Wing (K.Fl.Gr.)
106: 226

106/III: 13
406: 272
406/I: 8, 294
406/II: 203
506: 48-50
506/III: 2, 13
706: 294
706/III: 2
806: 110, 118, 123, 130
906/I: 230
906/III: 13, 65

Flying Boat Recce Wing (S.A.Gr)
127: 324
129/I(F): 363, 368, 371
130/I: 401

Groups
Bomber Group (K.G.)
1: 207
1/II: 101
2: 102, 323
4: 29, 121-123, 207
4/II: 77-78, 81, 83, 91, 111
4/III: 24
26: 7, 20-21, 24, 256, 289, 310,
    344, 367, 472-473, 483, 491-493
26/I: 6, 213, 217, 220, 230, 256,
    367, 413
26/II: 19, 233
26/III: 220, 256, 367, 408, 413
27: 90
30: 21, 24, 31, 220, 230-231, 256,
    272
30/I: 6-8, 272, 302-303, 306
30/II: 26, 30, 231, 272
30/III: 102, 203, 208, 217, 220
30/V: 119
40: 64, 77, 83, 339
40/I: 62, 64-65, 75, 77, 81, 83,
    87-88, 91, 93, 96, 99, 114, 118-
    119, 122, 124-125, 132, 137,
    141, 145, 148, 167, 226, 391
40/II: 61, 79, 346, 369, 372, 389
40/III: 363, 369, 401
41/I: 109
51: 148
51/II: 356
54/I: 227
54/II: 101
77/I: 101
77/II: 4, 130
77/III: 408
100: 29, 101
100/I: 233
100/II: 346, 351, 367
100/III: 349, 351
100/V: 367

Air Trainer Group (L.G.)
1: 7, 89, 103, 117, 228, 356
1/I: 102, 216
1/II: 102, 107, 216, 313
1/IV: 1-2, 45, 114
2/I: 102

Dive Bomber Group (St.G)
1: 207
1/I: 28, 30, 74
1/II: 45
1/III: 207
2: 42, 102
2/I: 102, 138, 207
2/II: 74, 98, 102, 207
2/III: 102-103, 138
3: 143, 228, 242, 289
3/I: 81-82
3/II: 356, 367
3/III: 257
5/I: 218, 223, 232, 302
77: 138, 147, 175, 359
77/I: 150

Fighter Group (J.G.)
1: 189
1/III: 218
2: 189
2/X: 248
5: 331, 345, 393, 445
5/VI: 121
26: 189
26/X: 248
53: 289
54: 207, 501
77/III: 102

Heavy Fighter Group (Z.G.)
1/I: 331

Carrier Groups
Tragergruppe 186/IV: 2
Bord Fl.Gr. 196/I: 28

Italian
4 Air Fleet: 202
274 Long Range Bomber
    Squadron: 258
13 Fighter Bomber Group: 257

Japanese
Air Fleets
1: 168, 477, 505
1 Naval: 156, 459, 461, 480, 483,
    503
1 Carrier: 179, 184, 190, 194, 220,
    438
2 Naval: 458-459, 461
3 Naval: 503
4 Army: 461, 483
5 Naval: 499, 503, 508, 510, 531
10 Naval: 503
11 Naval: 162, 269, 275-276,
    316, 364

Air Divisions
3: 186
5 Army: 162, 170

Air Flotillas
21 Naval: 162, 169-170, 177, 196
22 Naval: 164

23 Naval: 162, 170-171, 177, 181-
    182, 185, 196
24 Naval: 199
25 Naval: 185, 245
Genzan Air Corps: 187

Russian
Air Armies
1: 485
4: 411, 485
7: 459
8: 411
13: 455

Air Brigades
62: 111
63: 111, 113

Air Regiments
2: 111
4: 111

Fighter Wing
151: 127

Fighter Division
6: 459

Fighter Regiments
9: 404
11: 404
25: 404
40: 404
95: 319

Dive Bomber Division
10: 530

Ground Attack Division
9: 497
11: 404
12: 530
14: 459

Ground Attack Regiments
23: 404
46: 404, 426

Mining and Torpedo Air Division
2: 530
2 Guards: 404
5: 331, 345, 459
8: 497

Mining and Torpedo Air Regiment
9 Guards: 414
24: 319

Mixed Air Division
14: 437

Reconnaissance Regiment
30: 404
118: 445
Abe Jap/RA-VA: 168, 204, 220,
    235, 263, 268-269, 275-276

Personalities

For explanation concerning the following ranks—Cdr*, C1, C2 and C3—please see Translator's Note on page v and abbreviations on page vii. Where identical surnames appear in the index they are differentiated by giving the initial of the first name, but this has not necessarily been given for identical surnames of different nationalities.

Please note that the ranks of many personalities have been designated thus: L-Cdr. This denotes the original and final rank attained by that officer as applicable to the references in this translation. These may not necessarily be the final rank attained by that officer. It should also be noted that some intermediate ranks attained will not have been noted in the text, unless the name has appeared.

A	Admiral	FltL	Flight Lieutenant	Ma	Marshal
AM	Air Marshal	FltS	Flight Sergeant	PO	Petty Officer
ACM	Air Chief Marshal	FMa	Field Marshal	RA	Rear Admiral
AVM	Air Vice Marshal	FO	Flying Officer	SA	Squadron Admiral
B	Brigadier	G	General		(Italian Navy only)
C	Captain	GA	General Admiral	Sgt	Sergeant
Cdr	Commander		(German Navy	SL	Sub-Lieutenant
Col	Colonel		only)	SqL	Squadron Leader
CPO	Chief Petty Officer	L	Lieutenant	VA	Vice Admiral
Cre	Commodore	LCpl	Lance Corporal	WCdr	Wing Commander
DA	Divisional Admiral	M	Major		
	(Italian Navy only)				

It should be noted that not all abbreviations used in this section have been listed. Any not listed above will be combinations of rank made up from the above abbreviations.

Abe Jap/G: 537
Abel (H.) Ger/Cdr*: 484
Abel (U.) Ger/SL: 191
Abele US/LCdr: 233
Abel-Smith UK/C: 318
Abramov USSR/RA: 112, 172
Abrosimov USSR/C3: 116, 229, 238
Achilles Ger/LCdr: 192, 219, 266, 279, 314, 352
Acker US/Cdr: 456
Ackermann US/LCdr: 495
Ackermann (P.) Ger/L: 454
Acuff US/C: 458, 474, 476
Adams UK/C: 129
Adachi Jap/LG: 380, 537
Adkins US/LCdr: 439, 457, 505
Afanasev USSR/C3: 229, 246
Afonin USSR/C3: 289
Agar UK/C: 158, 205
Agnew UK/C-Cre: 144, 149, 155, 165-166, 350
Agostini It/Cdr: 67
Ainslie UK/L: 323, 336, 473
Ainsworth US/C-RA: 132, 290, 324, 335, 376, 391, 427, 436-438, 452
Aittola Fin/LCdr: 115, 261
Akada Jap/C: 224
Akiyama Jap/RA: 335, 388
Albanese It/Cdr: 54, 321
Alberts Ger/Cdr: 288
Albrecht Ger/A: 1
Alexander (H) UK/G: 199, 338
Alexander UK/L: 400, 425
Alexeev USSR/C2: 436, 450
Alexeyev USSR/C3: 304, 404, 411
Allen UK/Cdr: 59, 397
Allen US/MG: 339
v. Allwörden Ger/C: 149, 379
Alston US/LCdr: 296, 314
Altmeier Ger/L: 454
Ambrosius Ger/LCdr: 10, 32, 55
Ambruster US/LCdr: 266, 284, 322
Anchor UK/C: 213
Andersen UK/L: 438, 460, 471
Andersen (K.) Ger/L-LCdr: 432, 450, 511
Anderson US/RA: 221-222
Anderson US/LCdr: 209
Andreani It/Cdr: 211, 223
Andreev USSR/LG: 385
Andreev (V. A.) USSR/Cl-VA: 147, 172, 179, 183, 531
Andrew UK/L: 323
Andrews US/LCdr: 358, 372, 410
Angell UK/L: 400, 412, 438, 460, 473
Angerstein Ger/MG: 207
Anhalt Ger/LCdr: 422
Ankyu Jap/Cdr*: 193
dell'Anno It/Cdr: 157
Antonov USSR/C2: 129
Aoki Jap/C: 224
Apostolov USSR/LCdr: 149
Arendt Ger/L: 411, 448
d'Argenlieu Fr/Cdr*: 64
Arho Fin/LCdr: 124
Ariaga Jap/RA: 508

Ariizumi Jap/Cdr-C: 383, 417, 528
Arillo It/LCdr: 84, 285
Arita Jap/C: 249
Arnold US/MG: 425, 461, 503-504, 537
Ashburn (Lord) UK/C: 338
Ashley US/LCdr: 284, 379, 402, 456, 522
Askim Nor/Cdr*: 24
Aslanoglu Gr/Cdr: 149
Ata Jap/L: 426
Atkins US/LCdr: 306
Atkinson UK/L: 320
Auconi It/LCdr: 148
Auffermann Ger/LCdr: 253, 291, 295
Aust Ger/L: 450
Austin US/LCdr: 403, 419, 429, 457
Avgustinovich USSR/C3: 133, 144
Azer US/LCdr: 289

Babbel Ger/L: 40
Baberg Ger/L-LCdr: 262, 266, 333, 369
Baccarini It/Cdr: 321
Bach Ger/Cdr: 497
Bachmann Ger/Cdr: 288
Back UK/C: 103
Bacon US/LCdr: 178, 210, 215
Badger US/RA: 487, 526
Badoglio It/Ma: 342, 357, 360
Baer US/LCdr: 449
Bahl Ger/C: 134
Bahr Ger/LCdr: 309, 311, 326, 354, 378
Baker UK/LCdr: 428
Baker US/C-RA: 83, 337, 390, 396
Baker-Creswell UK/Cdr: 96
Balbo It/Ma: 40
Balduhn Ger/L: 464, 472
Balin USSR/LCdr: 385, 393, 414, 426, 445
Balke Ger/LCdr: 469
Ballentine US/RA: 533
Balme UK/C: 96
Baltz Ger/L: 325
Bandini It/Cdr: 60
Banfi It/Cdr: 58
Banks UK/Cdr: 131
Banner-Martin UK/L: 446
Bannister US/LCdr: 372, 417, 456
Barber Ger/L: 352
Barbey US/RA-VA: 334, 347, 355, 375-376, 379, 409, 431, 451, 461, 480, 524, 537-539
Bargsten Ger/L-LCdr: 145, 267, 278, 295, 308, 328
Barker UK/LCdr: 33
Barlow UK/L: 323
Baroni It/LCdr: 34
Baroni It/Cdr*: 40
Barr US/LCdr: 439, 457, 495
Barrois Fr/C: 41
Barrows US/Cdr: 526
Barry UK/C: 166
Barschkies Ger/L: 496
Bartel Ger/LCol: 247
Barthel Ger/Cdr: 116
Bartels Ger/L-LCdr: 119, 152, 209, 315

Bartke Ger/L: 329, 357
Barthes Fr/C: 27
Barton US/MG: 420
Basisty USSR/C2-RA: 150, 172, 222, 239, 297
Bashchenko USSR/C3: 343
Baskett US/LCdr-Cdr: 410, 432, 479, 515
Bass US/LCdr: 336, 343, 390, 526
Basse Ger/LCdr: 383
Bassenge Ger/Cdr: 19
Bastian Ger/LCdr: 440
Bätge Ger/LCdr: 133, 155, 189, 285
Batstone UK/LCdr: 159
Bauer (E.) Ger/LCdr: 119, 124, 139, 143, 154, 219, 236, 279
Bauer (M.H.) Ger/LCdr: 18
Baumann Ger/Cdr: 167
Baur Ger/L: 240
Bayendor Ir/RA: 129
Bayldon UK/Cdr: 371
Bear US/LCdr: 322
Beary US/RA: 492, 516, 522, 528, 531
Beattie UK/LCdr: 206
Beaverbrook (Lord) UK/Minister: 139
v. Bechtolsheim Ger/C: 422
Becker US/LCdr: 432, 479, 522
Becker (A) Ger/Cdr: 312
Becker (K) Ger/LCdr: 383, 401
Becker (R) Ger/LCdr: 252, 326
Beckley UK/L: 382
Becton US/Cdr: 510
Bedeschi It/C: 282
Beduhn Ger/LCdr: 27, 35
Behrens Ger/LCdr: 20
Beightler US/MG: 480
Belben UK/C: 328
Belkov USSR/C3: 153
Bell UK/C: 14
Bell US/LCdr: 449, 468, 479, 529
Bellet Fr/L: 358, 414
Belorukov USSR/C3: 368
Belousov USSR/C1: 15
Beltrami It/LCdr: 299
Benker Ger/L-LCdr: 272, 280, 294, 343
Benn UK/C: 8
Bennett US/LCdr: 314
Bennett US/LCdr-Cdr: 472, 505, 522
Bennington UK/Cdr: 245, 261, 278, 365, 382, 438, 460, 471
Bennion US/C: 161
Benson US/LCdr: 284, 289, 306, 329
Bentlage Ger/C: 51, 108
Bentzien Ger/L: 383, 442
Beranger Fr/C: 76
Berdine US/C: 402
Berengan It/Cdr: 63, 133
Bergamini It/SA-A: 165, 175, 183, 189, 349
Berger (F) Ger/Cdr*-C: 17-18, 51, 188
Berger (J) Ger/LCdr: 177, 226, 260
Berger (W) Ger/Cdr: 22
v. Berger Ger/Cdr: 203

Berkey US/RA: 376, 380, 387, 395, 409, 416, 418, 433, 439, 451, 461, 474, 480, 487, 498, 504, 513, 523-524
Bernabo It/Cdr: 41, 60
Bertarelli It/Cdr: 50
Bertelsmann Ger/L: 301, 309
Berthrong US/LCdr: 505
Betzendahl Ger/Cdr: 20
Beucke Ger/Cdr*: 234
Bevan UK/C: 80
Bey Ger/Cdr*-RA: 3, 10, 18, 57, 60, 66, 68, 188, 374
Bianchi It/SM: 166
Bibeev USSR/LCdr-C3: 154, 198
Bickford UK/LCdr: 13
Biet Ger/LCdr: 245
Bielfeld Ger/LCdr: 220, 230, 257 416
Bigalk Ger/LCdr: 104, 168, 182, 215
Bigler Ger/LCdr: 111
Binney UK/C: 76, 536
Birch UK/Cdr: 369
Birnbacher Ger/LCdr: 45, 47, 52, 84, 124, 225
Birnie UK/Cre: 305
Bisset UK/RA: 351, 401
Bittkow Ger/LCdr: 489
Blackburn UK/C: 91
Blackman UK/Cre: 100
Blagrove UK/RA: 8
Blakely US/LCdr: 419
v. Blanc Ger/Cdr-Cdr*: 440, 447, 488
Blanchard US/LCdr-Cdr: 379, 430, 449
Blamey (Sir Thomas) Aus/G: 535, 538
Blandy US/RA: 452, 493, 502
Blaudow Ger/L: 450
Blauert Ger/L: 389
Bleichrodt Ger/LCdr: 53, 59, 110, 178, 208, 241, 285
Blischke Ger/L: 376, 394
Block Ger/L: 465
Bloedorn Ger/M: 231, 256
Blömker Ger/PO: 350
Blöse Ger/LCdr-Cdr: 362, 515
Blyth UK/C: 214
Bobrovnikov USSR/LCdr: 222
Bocharov USSR/C3: 455, 482
Bockett-Pugh UK/Cdr: 96
v. Boddien Ger/LCol: 176
Bode US/C: 161
Boehm Ger/A: 7
Boehmer Ger/L: 395
van Boetzelaer Du/LCdr: 197
Bogan US/RA: 428, 438, 448, 458, 462, 465, 467, 474, 476, 509, 525
Bogdanov USSR/C2: 129
Bogolepov USSR/RA: 465
Bogorad USSR/C3: 455, 482, 501
Bohm Ger/Cdr: 124, 219, 149
Bohmann Ger/LCdr: 230, 256
Böhmer Ger/C-RA: 48, 211, 312
Bohusz Pol/G: 28
Boisson Fr/Governor: 56
Boit Ger/Cdr: 398
Bole US/LCdr: 257
Boltunov USSR/C1-RA: 112, 407

Bondarevich USSR/LCdr: 209
Bone UK/LCdr-Cdr: 52. 62, 78, 113, 124, 133
Bonesteel US/MG: 132
Bonezzi It/LCdr: 80
Bonham-Carter UK/RA-VA: 208, 212, 256
Bonte Ger/C-Cre: 3, 10, 14, 17, 19, 22, 24
de Booy Du/LCdr: 104, 123, 133
Bopst Ger/LCdr: 262
Borcherdt Ger/LCdr: 182, 188, 193, 206, 222
Borchers Ger/LCdr: 300, 319
Borghese It/Cdr-Cdr*: 57, 62, 137, 166
Boris It/LCdr-Cdr: 34, 46
Bork Ger/L: 375, 378, 424
Borm Ger/Cdr: 265
Borsini It/Cdr: 61
Bosse Ger/SL: 155
Botta It/Cdr: 34
Böttger Ger/Cdr: 488
Bouan Fr/C: 28
Bourke US/MG: 536
Bourland US/LCdr: 329
Bourne UK/L: 456
Bourrague Fr/RA: 53
Bouxin Fr/RA: 41
Bovell UK/C: 46, 100
Bowers US/LCdr: 526
Bowes-Lyon UK/C: 317
Bowling UK/Cdr: 481
Boyd (D. W.) UK/C-RA: 63, 77, 89, 204, 212
Boyd UK/L: 358, 397, 414
Boyle UK/Cdr: 291, 309, 317, 505
Bradford UK/LCdr: 422, 433
Bradley (J. L.) US/MG: 461, 504
Bradley (O.) US/LG: 339, 420, 425
Brandenburg Ger/Cdr: 230, 256
Brandi Ger/LCdr-Cdr: 254, 257, 259, 283, 293-294, 344, 410, 450
Brandt Ger/Cdr: 367, 418
Brasack Ger/LCdr: 383
Bratishko USSR/C3: 331
v. Brauchitsch Ger/C: 45
Brauel Ger/LCdr: 505
Brauneis Ger/Cdr*: 488
Brauns Ger/L: 243
Breckwoldt Ger/L: 432
Breithaupt Ger/Cdr*: 440
v. Bremen Ger/L: 371, 390, 424, 436
Breuning Ger/C: 316
Brewer UK/C: 321
Bridge UK/C: 45
Bridgeman Can/LCdr: 319, 354
Briggs UK/FO: 101
Brill Ger/Cdr: 47, 109, 124, 298
Brind UK/RA: 523
Brindupke US/Cdr: 343, 358, 379, 401
Brinker US/LCdr: 343
Brinkmann Ger/C-VA: 99, 188, 218, 407
Briscoe US/C: 290, 307
Bristol Jr. US/RA: 83, 136
Bristowe UK/LCdr: 44
Brittain US/Cre: 537-538
Brivonesi It/DA: 42, 69

Broach US/LCdr: 379, 396
Brockman US/LCdr-Cdr: 259, 491
Brocksien Ger/C: 265
Brodda Ger/LCdr: 203, 245, 326
Bromage UK/L: 255, 278, 284, 293, 300, 313
Bromet UK/AVM: 298, 358
Brook UK/C: 320
Broome UK/Cdr: 229
Brosin Ger/LCdr: 331
v. Brosy-Steinberg Ger/Cdr: 127
Brown UK/L: 447
Brown (A. E.) US/MG: 323
Brown (J. H.) US/RA: 523, 525, 528, 531, 535
Brown (W.) US/RA: 168, 182, 185, 199
Brown US/LCdr: 472
Browne UK/LCdr: 58, 73, 81, 93
Browne US/LCdr: 456
Brownrigg UK/LCdr: 422, 447
Bruce US/MG: 473, 502
Brücker Ger/C: 102
Brüller Ger/L-LCdr: 252, 273, 340, 369
Brüning Ger/LCdr-RA: 305, 519
Brünner Ger/L: 341, 343, 393, 402
Brunner UK/L-Cdr: 460, 471, 473, 495
Bruns Ger/LCdr: 253, 286, 319
Brush US/MG: 480, 500, 514
Bruton US/LCdr: 209, 237, 259 284
Bruun Nor/LCdr: 262
Bryant UK/LCdr-Cdr: 23, 40, 78, 234, 245, 261, 267, 278, 286, 293, 313, 323
Bryant (C. F.) US/RA: 420, 443
Buch Ger/LCdr: 485, 515
Buchholz Ger/LCdr: 3, 315
Buchel Ger/Cdr: 2
Büchel Ger/Cdr*: 416
Büchler Ger/LCdr: 409
Büchting Ger/LCdr-Cdr: 252, 408
Buck US/C: 259
Buckmaster US/C: 224
Bucknall UK/LG: 420
Buckner US/LG: 504, 523
Bugs Ger/L: 341, 343, 377
Buhse Ger/L: 496
Buldrini It/LCdr: 243
Bulkeley UK/L: 442, 460, 474, 505
v. Bülow Ger/LCdr: 188, 222, 252, 258, 312, 316, 318
Bülter Ger/Cdr: 485
Bunkley US/C: 161
Burch UK/Cdr: 24, 28, 30, 37
Bürgel Ger/L: 225, 229, 294
Burkart Ger/Cdr: 500
Burke US/Cdr-C: 341, 363, 372, 391
Burlingame US/LCdr: 209, 237, 289, 329
Burmeister Ger/LCdr: 490
Burnashev USSR/LCdr: 145
Burnett Aus/C: 152
Burnett (R. L.) UK/RA-VA: 256-257, 287, 302, 374
Burnett Can/Cdr: 354
Burnett UK/Cdr: 490

Burnyak USSR/LCdr: 222
Burrough UK/RA: 155, 171, 180, 212, 217, 219, 242, 274
Burrows US/LCdr: 306, 322, 343, 379
Burton US/LCdr: 289
Busch Ger/C: 497
Bush UK/C: 473
Buslaev USSR/C2: 176
Bussemaker Du/LCdr: 166
Butler US/Cdr: 526
Bütow Ger/RA: 488
van der Byl UK/LCdr: 28, 62, 98, 105

Cabanier Fr/Cdr: 28, 30, 37, 62
Cadart Fr/RA: 26, 28
Cafiero It/SL: 243
Cairns UK/L: 453
Calcagno It/L: 243
Calda It/Cdr: 113
Caldwell US/LCdr: 468
Callaghan US/RA: 271, 275-276
Calvani It/LCdr: 243
Cailey UK/L: 291
Camicia It/C: 323
Cameron UK/L: 355
Caminati Fr/LCdr: 36
Campbell UK/C: 302, 366, 374, 383, 393
Campbell UK/LCdr: 111
Campioni It/SA: 42-43, 67, 69
Capponi It/C: 149
Caputi It/Cdr: 74
Caridi It/Cdr: 69
Carls Ger/A: 22
Carlsen Ger/L: 317, 331
Carlson US/Cre: 504
Carmick US/LCdr: 329
Carpender US/A: 310
Carr US/LCdr: 322
Carter US/C: 345, 380. 395-396
Casardi It/DA: 42, 44, 69, 94, 96, 105, 114, 116
Caslon UK/C: 84
Cassedy US/L: 290
Cassedy US/LCdr: 257, 279
Cates US/MG: 438, 494
Cattaneo It/DA: 42, 69, 89
Causemann Ger/LCdr: 366
Cavaye UK/LCdr: 21
Cavagnari It/A: 69
Cavanagh-Mainwaring UK/LCdr: 52
Cayley UK/L-LCdr: 78, 80, 85, 87, 111, 119, 145, 147, 153
Ceccacci It/Cdr: 313
Chailley Fr/L: 431, 453
Chapman UK/L: 390, 413, 431
Chandler US/C-RA: 149, 355, 481
Chapilin USSR/L: 135
Chappell US/L-LCdr: 164, 170, 178, 257, 329, 343
Chapple US/L-Cdr: 222, 306, 322, 336, 419, 466
Charr US/LCdr: 266
Chase US/BG-MG: 395, 536
Chesterman UK/LCdr: 320
Chevasse Can/C: 324
Chialamberto It/Cdr: 40, 43, 50, 64-65, 118
Chiang-Kai Shek Chi/G: 368, 532

Cho Jap/MG: 524
Christiansen Ger/L-Cdr: 31-32, 52, 60, 252, 267, 298, 311, 332
Christie US/C-RA: 239, 429
Christophersen Ger/L: 309
Churchill UK/Minister-PM: 17, 56, 125, 155, 294, 344-345, 368, 444
Chu-Teh Chi/G: 532
Cigala It/Cdr*: 102
Ciliax Ger/VA: 139, 188, 198
Claggett US/LCdr: 432, 457, 462
Clarabut UK/L: 460, 471
Clarey US/LCdr: 419, 439, 468
Clark (M. W.) US/LG: 350
Clark (J. J.) US/RA: 406, 426-427, 430, 436, 438, 491, 499, 509, 522
Clark US/LCdr: 322, 347, 390, 526
Clarke UK/C: 288, 377
Clarkson US/MG: 537
Clausen (H-E) Ger/LCdr: 208, 300, 325
Clausen (N.) Ger/LCdr: 68, 79, 85, 159, 192, 299
Clay US/G: 278
Clemenson US/LCdr: 347, 365
Clementson US/LCdr: 495, 522
Clutterbuck UK/L: 300, 313, 336, 358
Cocchia It/C: 282
Coe US/LCdr: 197, 215, 228
Coeler Ger/MG: 1
Cohausz Ger/LCdr-Cdr: 37, 203
Cohen US/C: 83, 119
Cole US/LCdr: 379, 390, 472, 522
Collett UK/L: 85, 104
Collett UK/LCdr: 323
Collinet Fr/C-A: 41, 256
Collins (J.) Aus/C: 44
Collins Aus/Cre: 180, 433, 437, 451
Collins US/LG: 420
Coltart UK/L: 56
Colthurst UK/Cdr: 277
Colvin UK/L-LCdr: 123, 152, 154, 294
Connole US/Cdr: 495
Conolly US/RA: 339, 350, 388, 437, 461, 483
Converse US/C: 415
Coode UK/LCdr: 101
Cook US/RA: 92, 150
Cooke (C. M.) US/C: 161
Cooke (G. C.) UK/C: 155
Cooke (W. D.) US/C: 355
Coombe UK/L: 263
Corbus US/LCdr: 439
Cordes Ger/LCdr: 424, 435, 496
Cork (Lord) UK/A: 25, 27, 30-31, 33
Corlett US/MG: 388
Corsi It/C: 89
Corvetti It/Cdr*: 39
Coumou Du/LCdr: 166
de Courten It/DA: 157, 165, 183, 200, 228
Cowell UK/L-LCdr: 40, 122
Cowen UK/LCdr: 423
Cox UK/L: 447

Coye US/LCdr: 358, 372, 402, 410
Crace US/RA: 185, 189, 199, 214
Craig US/LCdr: 266, 289
Craig (K.) US/C: 507
Crawford UK/L: 292, 300, 313, 336, 352
Creighton UK/RA: 137
Cremer Ger/LCdr: 177, 247, 260, 298, 363, 368
Crepas It/LCdr: 66
Crist US/C: 403, 416
de Cristofaro It/Cdr*: 93
Croiset Fr/C: 38
Crocker UK/LG: 420
Crombie UK/C: 212
Cronin US/C: 480
Crouch UK/L-Cdr: 66, 133, 141, 175, 184, 291
Crowley US/LCdr: 419
Crutchley UK/C-VA: 25, 102, 226, 238, 249-250, 334, 376, 380, 396, 409, 416, 418
Cunningham (A. B.) UK/A: 36, 43, 50-51, 57-58, 62-63, 66-67, 70, 73-74, 89, 93, 97, 155, 338, 345, 350
Cunningham (J. H. D.) UK/VA: 23, 28, 49, 51, 53, 55
Cunningham UK/G: 152
Cunningham US/BG: 375
Cunningham-Graham UK/RA: 511
Curio Ger/L: 321, 354, 386
Currie UK/Cdr: 360, 362, 389
Curteis UK/RA-VA: 100, 139-140, 198, 203, 213, 227
Cutter US/LCdr: 402, 419, 429
Czygan Ger/Cdr: 260, 296

Dahlhaus Ger/L: 304
Dahlquist US/MG: 444
Dalrymple-Hamilton UK/C-VA: 101, 401, 421, 444, 464, 475, 490, 498
Dangschat Ger/LCdr: 278
Daniel UK/RA: 534
Daniell UK/Cre: 210, 215, 300, 313, 323
Daniels US/MG: 443
Danielsen Nor/RA: 519
Danielson Nor/SL: 141
Dankleff Ger/L: 424
Dannenberg Ger/Cdr*: 22
Darlan Fr/A: 38, 274, 286
Daser Ger/L: 467
Dau (H.) Ger/C: 1, 19
Dau (R.) Ger/LCdr: 7
Dauter Ger/L: 400
Davenport US/LCdr: 314, 347, 402, 456, 472
David US/L: 416
v. Davidson (H.) Ger/Cdr: 77, 142, 288
Davidson (L. A.) US/RA: 342, 350, 443
Davidson US/LCdr: 292, 379
Davis Can/LCdr: 395
Davis US/LCdr: 365, 372, 410
Davis (G. B.) US/C-RA: 277, 335, 387
Davis (R. O.) US/C: 291
Davison US/RA: 388, 409, 436,

448, 458, 461-462, 465, 491, 499
Dawley US/MG: 350
Day UK/Cdr: 309, 317
Dealy US/LCdr-Cdr: 328, 347, 365, 402, 415, 429, 439
Deckert Ger/L: 273, 289, 340, 353, 369
Dedaev USSR/MG: 110
Dechaineaux Fr/C: 395
Deecke Ger/LCdr: 178, 227, 251, 317, 321, 354
Deetz Ger/LCdr: 307, 333
Degen Ger/LCdr: 177, 184, 226
Del Cima It/Cdr*: 52
Dempsey UK/LG: 338, 420
Dempsey US/L: 186
Dempsey US/LCdr: 210, 232, 390, 410
Denebrinck US/RA: 536
Denfeld US/RA: 501
Denny UK/C: 486
Densch Ger/VA: 1, 2, 10-12
Dentz Fr/G: 107
Deragon US/LCdr: 449, 472
Derevyanko USSR/LG: 535
di Derio It/LCdr: 138
Derrien Fr/RA: 23, 26, 28, 37
Detlefsen Ger/L: 32
Detmers Ger/Cdr-Cdr*: 68, 74, 153
Devereux US/M: 164
Devyatko USSR/LCdr: 125, 135
Dewhurst UK/LCdr: 43, 48, 77, 87, 98
Deyo US/C-RA: 92, 136, 420, 431, 444, 502, 517, 537
Dierkson Ger/LCdr: 240, 246, 279, 314
v. Diest Ger/LCdr: 497
Dieterichs Ger/L: 217, 247, 287
Dietl Ger/MG-G: 26, 114
Dietrich Ger/L: 318, 492, 514
Diggins Ger/LCdr: 232, 237
Dinort Ger/M-LCol: 42, 102, 138
Dissette US/LCdr: 439
Dittmer Ger/Cdr: 488
Dixon UK/L: 433, 447
Dobbert Ger/L: 387
Dobberstein Ger/LCdr: 124
Dobberstein (W.) Ger/L: 424
Dobratz Ger/C: 481
Dobson Can/LCdr: 251, 354
Dodge US/LCdr: 322
Doe US/BG-MG: 409, 415, 498, 537
Doench Ger/C: 8
Döhler Ger/L: 266, 301
Doi Jap/LCdr: 383
Dominik Ger/Cdr*: 398, 418
Dommes Ger/LCdr-Cdr: 135, 218, 225, 258, 273. 315
Donaho US/LCdr: 296, 314, 347, 358, 439
Dönitz Ger/RA-GA: 22, 52, 296, 328
Doolittle US/LC: 207
Doorman Du/RA: 185-186, 188, 190-191, 194-195
Doran UK/FltL: 4
Dornin US/LCdr: 365
Dornis US/LCdr: 379
Dotta It/LCdr: 120

Douglas-Pennant UK/Cre: 420
Dowding UK/C: 127
Dowding UK/Cre: 229, 231-232
Drayson UK/SL: 265
v. Dresky Ger/LCdr: 2, 8, 12, 19
Drewitz Ger/LCdr: 300
Driver Ger/LCdr: 108, 119, 142, 166, 170
Dropp US/LCdr: 322
Drodz USSR/RA-VA: 12, 112, 115, 117, 147, 157
Drozdov USSR/C2: 455, 489
Drummond UK/L: 313, 323, 336, 358
Dry US/LCdr: 365, 449
Du Bose US/RA: 364, 458, 464
Dufec US/C: 507
Duff UK/L: 384
Duke US/LCdr: 232
van Dulm Du/LCdr: 123, 133, 136, 141, 153-154
Dunbar Nasmith UK/A: 18
Dunckel US/BG: 474
Dunkelberg Ger/L: 374, 383
Dunn US/C: 337, 372, 387, 395
Duplat Fr/VA: 37
Dupont Fr/LCdr: 358
Durand de la Penne It/LCdr: 166
Durgin (C. T.) US/RA: 444, 479, 493, 502
Durgin (E. R.) US/LCdr: 92
Durnford-Slater UK/C: 368
Dus USSR/LCdr: 153
Duvall US/C: 408, 410
Dwyer US/LCdr: 479
Dyakov USSR/LCdr: 222
Dyke DU/BG: 538
Dykers US/LCdr: 329, 390, 402
Dymott UK/LCdr: 120

Eagles US/MG: 443
Earle US/LCdr: 279, 363
Earle (R.) US/C: 391
Eastick Aus/BG: 538
Eather Aus/MG: 537
Ebato Jap/L: 373, 383
Eberlein Ger/L: 469
Ebert US/LCdr: 306, 322, 347, 365, 379
Eccles UK/C: 486
Eck Ger/LCdr: 383
Eckhardt Ger/LCdr: 307
Eckelmann Ger/L: 315
Eckermann Ger/Cdr: 84, 159
Eddy US/LCdr: 347, 372, 410, 419
Edelsten UK/C: 79
Eden UK/Foreign Sec: 158
Edgar UK/Cre: 421
Edge US/LCdr-Cdr: 402, 432, 449, 522
Edmonds UK/L: 190
Edward-Collins UK/VA: 23, 26-27
van Erkel Du/LCdr: 111
Efet USSR/C3: 151
Efimov USSR/LCdr: 445
Egerton UK/VA: 286
Eggers Ger/LCdr: 508
Egipko USSR/C1: 111
Egorov (N. E.) USSR/LCdr: 139, 169

Egorov (P. I.) USSR/C2: 331, 343
Egorov (V. A.) USSR/C3: 233
Egusa Jap/LCdr: 205
Eichelberger US/LG-MG: 291, 409, 533, 536
v. Eichhain Ger/LCdr: 139, 169
Eick Ger/L-LCdr: 331, 382, 482
Eicke Ger/C: 230
v. Eickstädt Ger/L: 445
Eisenhower US/G: 328, 338, 348, 357, 419, 425, 519
Eizinger Ger/LCdr: 456
Eliseev USSR/LCdr: 158
Ellis UK/C: 100
Emi Jap/Cdr*: 181
Emmermann Ger/LCdr: 224, 261, 272, 308, 312, 330
Emmrich Ger/L: 519
Endo Jap/Cdr*: 222, 250
Endrass Ger/L-LCdr: 32, 47, 55, 59, 82, 88, 104, 147, 168
Engel Ger/LCdr: 355
Engelhardt Ger/RA: 488
Engelmann Ger/Cdr: 247, 265
England UK/RA: 227
Ennecerus Ger/M: 74, 102
Enright US/LCdr: 468
Erdmann (G.) Ger/L: 118
Erdmann (H.) Ger/Cdr: 189, 324
Erdmenger Ger/C: 314, 375-377
Eremenko USSR/G: 411
Erler It/LCdr: 273
Ermachenko USSR/BrigCdr: 12
Ermachenkov USSR/LG: 403
Ernst Ger/LCdr: 490
Eroshenko USSR/C3: 222, 225
Erskine UK/MG: 350
v. Esch Ger/LCdr: 272, 303, 341
Esmonde UK/Cdr: 189
Esposito It/C: 228
Evans UK/Cdr: 326, 354, 381, 389
Evenou Fr/Cdr*: 158
Ewerth Ger/LCdr: 2, 9
Ey Ger/L-LCdr: 131, 149
Eyssen Ger/C-RA: 41, 67, 68, 71, 126
Ezaki Jap/Col: 396

Fadeev USSR/RA: 285, 287
Faggioni It/LCdr: 88
Fahr Ger/LCdr: 132
Falke Ger/L: 442, 472, 491
Farell US/LCdr: 491
Farley US/LCdr: 514, 529
Farncomb Aus/C-Cre: 81, 488, 520, 524
Fartushny USSR/C3: 279, 380
Faulknor UK/C: 213
Faust US/LCdr: 491, 505, 526
Fechner Ger/Cdr: 239, 250, 286
Fetcheler US/RA: 395, 409, 418, 433, 439, 451, 461, 480, 487, 495
Fecia di Cossato It/Cdr-Cdr*: 95, 159, 192, 234, 285
Fegen UK/C: 64
Feiler Ger/LCdr: 188, 213, 222, 247, 302, 308-309
Fein Ger/C: 78, 85-86, 188
Feldt Ger/L-Cdr: 78, 82, 93, 143,

189, 234, 278, 313, 318, 327, 344, 366, 391, 394
Fenno US/LCdr: 188, 209, 468
Fenski Ger/L: 303, 344, 353, 386, 410
Ferracuti It/LCdr: 69, 75
Ferrall US/LCdr: 183, 232, 257
Ferrieri-Caputi It/Cdr*: 321
Ferrini It/LCdr: 242
Ferro Ger/LCdr: 354, 357
Feurstein Ger/LG: 29
Fick US/C: 329, 337
Fiedler Ger/L: 311
Fiehn Ger/L: 317
Filipov USSR/C2: 173
Filov USSR/LCdr: 455
Fimmen Ger/L-Cdr: 32, 39, 385, 398, 413, 422, 484, 507
Fioravanzo It/DA: 228
Firth UK/C: 453
Fisanovich USSR/LCdr-C2: 124, 133, 209, 295, 439
v. Fischel Ger/L 144, 148, 160
Fischer (H-G) Ger/Cdr: 99
Fischer (H) Ger/M: 368
Fischer (R.) Ger/L: 490
Fischer Ger/Cdr: 433, 456
Fischer (W.) Ger/LCdr: 22
Fitch US/RA-VA: 168, 214, 222, 226, 269, 335
Fitting Ger/L: 505
Fitzgerald UK/LCdr: 246
Fitzmaurice UK/Cre: 167
Flachsenberg Ger/LCdr: 145, 201
Flachsenhar US/LCdr: 457
Flanagan US/Cre: 494
Fleige Ger/L: 332, 343, 353, 360, 368, 380, 402, 441
Fleming US/C: 481
Fleischer Fr/BG: 27
Fletcher US/RA-VA: 168, 183, 190, 199, 214, 221, 224, 226, 238, 241, 249, 536
Fliegel Ger/C: 79
Flores It/LCdr: 145
Fluckey US/LCdr-Cdr: 409, 449, 468, 479, 526
Fokin USSR/C1-RA: 444, 472
Foley US/LCdr-Cdr: 289, 365, 372, 392
Folkers Ger/LCdr: 178, 211, 241, 320
Fontana It/Cdr: 74
Foote US/LCdr: 479, 495, 526
Forbes (C.) UK/A: 1, 3, 6, 9, 11, 23-24, 37, 68
Forbes (J. H.) UK/LCdr: 526
Forbes US/LCdr: 23
Förschner Ger/Cdr*: 22
Förste Ger/C: 11
Forster (H.-J.) Ger/L: 436, 490
Förster (H.) Ger/L: 324
Förster (Helmuth) Ger/G: 207
Forster (Hugo) Ger/Cdr: 131
Forster (L.) Ger/L: 177, 187, 208, 236, 244
Forster UK/L: 447
Forstmann Ger/LCdr: 22
v. Forstner (S.) Ger/LCdr-Cdr: 180, 208, 267, 297, 325, 354
v. Forstner (W.-F.) Ger/L: 384, 393
Forsythe UK/C: 326

Fraatz Ger/L-LCdr: 116, 130, 156, 200-201
Frahm Ger/LCdr: 10, 18
Francke Ger/LCpl: 6
Franco Sp/G: 61, 80
Franke (H.) Ger/L: 278, 280, 297, 318, 363, 371
Franken (W.) Ger/LCdr: 211, 238, 283, 299, 317
Franz (J.) Ger/LCdr: 2
Franz (L.) Ger/L: 393, 402, 441
Franze Ger/L-LCdr: 383, 393, 401, 409, 441
Franzius Ger/LCdr: 240, 246, 267
Fraser (Sir Bruce) UK/VA-A: 256, 287, 294, 338, 374, 401, 442, 471, 530, 533, 535
Fraser UK/L: 529
Fraternale It/LCdr: 113, 192
Frauenheim Ger/LCdr: 8, 11-13, 32 49, 59
Fredendall US/MG: 273
Freeman-Attwood UK/MG: 350
Freiwald Ger/Cdr*: 403, 417, 457
v.Freyberg-Eisenberg-Allmendigen Ger/LCdr: 260, 266, 285-286, 311
Freytag Ger/LCdr: 369, 397
Friedrich Ger/L: 331
Friedrichs (A.) Ger/LCdr: 260
Fröhlich Ger/LCdr: 5, 13
Frolov USSR/RA: 172, 386, 531
Frömsdorf Ger/L: 507, 518
Frost UK/LCdr: 130
Fuchida Jap/Cdr*: 161
Fuhrmann US/LCdr: 468
Fujii Jap/Cdr*: 162, 187, 219
Fujita Jap/CPO: 372
Fujita (R.) Jap/RA-VA: 177, 184, 186, 221, 535
Fukudome Jap/VA: 458, 534
Fukumura Jap/LCdr: 299, 315, 349-350, 382
Fuller US/MG. 409, 418
Fulp US/LCdr: 472, 495, 522
Fumon Jap/LCdr: 426
Fyfe UK/L: 313 323, 356, 359, 433
Fyfe US/LCdr: 419, 439, 491

Gage US/Cdr: 439, 468
Gadzhiev USSR/C2: 133, 154, 180, 213
Galantin US/LCdr: 347, 365, 402
Galati It/C: 58
Gale UK/C: 220
Gallaher US/LCdr: 402, 419, 449, 468, 491
Gallery US/C: 381, 387, 416
Galloway UK/L: 111
Gambacorta US/LCdr: 515, 526
Gampert Ger/Cdr: 407
Gardner US/RA: 476, 492
Garnett US/LCdr: 365, 390, 402
Garrison US/LCdr: 410, 433
v. Gartzen Ger/Cdr: 377, 390, 397, 455
Gasparini It/C: 90
Gasparri It/RA: 273
Gatch US/C: 277

Gatehouse UK/L: 323, 336, 358, 390, 398
Gaude Ger/L: 301, 310
de Gaulle Fr/G: 53-54, 56, 59, 286
Gause Ger/MG: 284
v. Gaza Ger/L: 503
Gazzana-Priaroggi It/LCdr: 270, 315
Gehres US/C: 499
Geiger US/MG: 437, 452, 504, 523
Geiger Ger/SL-L: 70, 126, 229
Geisler Ger/LG: 2
Geissler Ger/L: 435
Gelhaar Ger/LCdr: 7
Gelhaus Ger/L-LCdr: 128, 168, 182, 215, 251, 260, 303, 320
Gemmel UK/LCdr: 433
Gengelbach Ger/L: 168
Gensoul Fr/VA-A: 8, 11, 41
George VI UK/King: 334
Gericke Ger/LCdr: 198
Gerlach (H.) Ger/Cdr*-C: 217, 224, 241, 259
Gerlach (P.) Ger/L: 386, 397
Germershausen (W. T.) US/LCdr-Cdr: 439, 468, 495, 522-523
v. Gernet Ger/L: 84
Gerow US/LG: 420
Gervais de Lafond Fr/C: 106
Gerwick US/LCdr: 472
Getting Aus/C: 241
Ghilieri It/Cdr: 46
Ghormley US/VA: 239, 264
de Giacomo It/Cdr: 113, 118, 159, 192
Giele Ger/LCdr: 252, 353, 403, 407
Giessler (H.-H.) Ger/LCdr: 213, 253
Giessler (H.) Ger/C: 484
Giffen US/RA: 132, 149, 203, 212, 291 323, 336, 388
Gigli It/LCdr: 273
Gikhorovtsev USSR/C3: 130
Gilardone Ger/LCdr: 237, 282
Giliberto It/Cdr: 60
Gill US/MG: 535-536
Gillan US/C: 355
Gillerman USSR/L: 110
Gilmore US/LCdr: 233, 248, 289
Gimber US/LCdr: 410, 439
Ginder US/RA: 387, 400
Ginocchio It/Cdr*: 47
Giorgis It/C: 89
Giovannini It/Cdr: 77
Giovanola It/DA: 105, 116, 157
Giraud Fr/G: 278
Giudice It/Cdr: 159, 192
Gladilin USSR/LCdr: 259
Gladkov USSR/LCdr: 426, 436
Glasford UK/Cdr: 33
Glassford US/RA: 182
Glattes Ger/LCdr: 3
Glenn US/L: 347
Glennie UK/RA-VA: 102, 392
Go Jap/LCdr: 503
Göbel Ger/L: 257
Godfroy Fr/VA: 36, 43
Godwin US/C: 161
Gohrbandt Ger/Cdr*: 485, 515
Göing Ger/LCdr: 253, 310

Göllnitz Ger/L-LCdr: 230, 325
Golovko USSR/VA-A: 109, 385, 459
Good US/RA: 269
Goossens Du/LCdr: 460
Göransson Fin/Cdr*: 134
Gorbachev USSR/C3: 150
Gordon UK/L: 336, 358, 414, 430, 433
Gordon (O. L.) UK/C: 196
Gorodnichi USSR/C3: 176
Gorshenin USSR/C3: 359, 385
Gorshkov USSR/C1-RA: 138, 172, 252, 353, 365, 447
v. Gossler Ger/LCdr: 10
Goto (A.) Jap/RA: 163, 168, 179, 214, 235, 263
Goto (U.) Jap/M: 452
Gouton Fr/RA: 106
Govorov USSR/G of the Army: 384
Gowan UK/L: 526
Grady US/LCdr: 402, 419
Graef Ger/L: 286, 304, 338
Gräf Ger/L-LCdr: 216, 253, 299
Grafen Ger/L: 380. 411
Graham UK/MG: 350
Graham UK/C: 486
Gramitzky Ger/L: 99, 106
Grant US/LCdr: 329, 372
Grant Can/C: 377
Grantham UK/C: 200
Grattenauer Ger/C: 353
Grau (P.) Ger/Cdr: 1
Grau (P.-O.) Ger/LCdr: 237, 244, 280, 341, 343
Greenman US/C: 241
Greenup US/Cdr: 468, 491, 505, 522
Greenway UK/LCdr: 92, 99, 129, 136, 141
Grenfell US/LCdr: 176, 198
Greer US/C: 337
Greger Ger/L: 131, 182, 208
Gregory UK/L: 11, 48, 62
Gregory US/LCdr: 257
Gremyako USSR/LCdr: 330, 368, 380, 404
Gren USSR/RA-VA: 131, 384
Greshilov USSR/LCdr-C3: 145, 260, 330, 404
Gretschel Ger/L: 302, 321
Gretton UK/LCdr-Cdr: 242, 315, 320, 326, 360, 362, 389
Grider US/LCdr: 472, 491
Griffin US/RA: 337, 370, 399
Griffith US/LCdr: 365, 379, 396, 410
Grimer US/MG: 536
Grishchenko USSR/C3-C2: 111, 146, 246, 259
Griswold US/MG: 480, 536
Gritsyuk USSR/C3: 472
Gross US/LCdr-Cdr: 284, 314, 329, 343, 358, 379, 479
Grosse (H.) Ger/Cdr: 18-19
Grosse (W.) Ger/Cdr: 398
Grossi It/Cdr: 260
Groth Ger/LCdr: 450
Grudzinski Pol/LCdr: 5, 23
Grund Ger/L-LCdr: 52, 405
Gruner US/LCdr-Cdr: 392, 410, 432

Gudenus Ger/L: 514
Guggenberger Ger/L-LCdr: 131, 149-150, 209, 273. 330
Gumanenko USSR/L: 117
Gumprich Ger/C: 202, 229, 236, 282, 332, 344
Gunn US/LCdr: 468, 491
Günther Ger/SL: 125
Gushchin USSR/C2: 156
Guskov USSR/C1: 455
Gutteck Ger/LCdr: 506
Gysae Ger/LCdr: 88, 99, 114, 132, 182, 272, 315

Haag Ger/SL: 112
Habekost Ger/LCdr: 2, 8, 12-13, 18, 20
Hackländer Ger/LCdr: 180
Hackzell Finn/Prime Minister: 449
Hagberg US/LCdr: 365
Hagen (Walter) Ger/LCol: 207
Hagen (Wilfred) Ger/C: 316
Hagene Ger/Cdr: 490
Haggard UK/LCdr: 31, 52, 55, 69, 78, 86, 93, 98, 145, 159, 206
Haines US/LCdr: 526
Hakewell-Smith UK/MG: 467
Håkon VII Nor/King: 27, 33
Hale UK/LCdr: 63
Halifax (Lord) UK/Minister: 44
Hall UK/LCdr: 422
Hall (C. P.) US/MG-LG: 451, 487, 536
Hall (J. L.) US/RA: 339, 350, 420, 504
Halliday UK/L: 261
Hallifax UK/RA: 107
Halsey US/RA-A: 161, 168, 183, 190, 207, 264, 276, 282, 448-449, 457-458, 462-464, 476, 517, 522, 525, 533
Hamilton UK/RA: 171, 230
Hamm Ger/L: 135, 155, 209, 234, 283
Hammond US/LCdr: 347, 372
Hampton UK/C: 102
Hanabusa Jap/Cdr*: 215
Hänert Ger/LCdr: 386
Haney US/BG: 495
Hansen Ger/L: 374, 383
Hansmann Ger/LCdr: 167
Hanson US/RA: 387
Happe Ger/L: 320
Hara (K.) Jap/RA: 162, 169, 192, 194, 264
Hara (Tadaichi) Jap/RA: 204, 214, 235, 249
Hara (Tameichi) Jap/C: 508
Hara Jap/VA: 538
Harada (H.) Jap/LCdr: 177, 188, 311, 341
Harada (K.) Jap/L: 457
Harcourt UK/RA: 274, 282, 328, 338, 350, 534-535
Hardegen Ger/LCdr: 82, 92, 114, 117, 146, 178, 201-202
Harden US/L: 256
Harder Ger/C: 114
Hardin US/LCdr: 372
Hardy (C. C.) UK/C: 227
Hardy (H. W. M.) UK/C: 68
Hardy UK/B: 479

Harlfinger US/LCdr: 402
Harlinghausen Ger/Col: 92, 101
Harms (E.) Ger/L: 343, 395
Harms (O.) Ger/L: 44, 46, 49, 51
Harney Ger/LCdr: 251
v. Harpe Ger/L: 371, 403
Harper US/LCdr: 456, 479
Harper US/MG: 537
Harrel US/LCdr: 365, 372, 390, 410
Harrill US/RA: 427
Harriman US: 139
Harris UK/AVM: 293
Harrison UK/L: 184, 200
Hart UK/L: 320
Hart US/A: 170, 185, 190
Hartenstein Ger/LCdr-Cdr: 83, 192, 216, 250, 255, 301
Hartman US/L-LCdr: 322, 468, 472
v. Hartmann Ger/LCdr: 286, 299, 315, 317
Hartmann (H.) Ger/Cdr*-C: 3, 10, 272, 288
Hartmann (K.) Ger/LCdr: 287, 289, 310, 424
Hartmann (O.) Ger/LCdr: 273, 299, 310
Hartmann (W.) Ger/Cdr-C: 7, 18-19, 25, 315
Hartwig Ger/LCdr: 248
Harwood UK/Cre: 10, 14
Harvey UK/LCdr: 48, 55
Haselden UK/Col: 257
Hasenschar Ger/L-LCdr: 282, 287, 302, 319-320, 325
Hashimoto (M.) Jap/Cdr: 527
Hashimoto (S.) Jap/RA-VA: 167, 187, 192, 194, 221, 235, 252, 271, 275-276, 416, 523
Haskins US/LCdr: 410, 439, 457
Hass Ger/L: 490
Hauber Ger/L: 454
Haun Ger/Cdr*: 515
Haupt Ger/L: 309
Hause Ger/LCdr: 252, 258, 286
de Hautecloque Fr/C: 49, see Leclerc
Haward UK/L: 23
Hawes UK/Pilot Officer: 228
Hawthorn UK/MG: 534
v. Haxthausen Ger/LCdr: 488
Hayakawa Jap/RA: 414
Hayler (F. E.) US/LCdr: 468
Hayler (R. W.) US/RA: 452
Hazikostantis Gr/LCdr: 71
Hazzard US/LCdr: 472, 491, 495, 515
Headden US/Cdr: 404
Heathcote UK/Cdr: 262, 281, 299, 304
Henchler Ger/Cdr: 469, 481
Heckel Ger/L: 490, 505
Hegewald Ger/LCdr: 425
Heidberg Ger/C: 303
Heidel Ger/L-LCdr: 5, 18
Heidtmann Ger/L-LCdr: 125, 141, 152, 170, 225
Heilmann Ger/LCdr: 82, 88, 99, 141
Hein Ger/L: 454, 490
Heine Ger/LCdr: 301

Heinemann US/Cdr: 217, 253, 296, 301, 305, 318
Heinicke (E.-G.) Ger/LCdr: 2, 9-10
Heinicke (H.-D.) Ger/LCdr: 182, 208, 236
Heinrich Ger/L: 343, 381, 415
Heinsohn Ger/LCdr: 160, 317
Heise Ger/C· 233
Helbig Ger/C: 216
Helfrich Du/VA: 190, 194, 535
Hellmann Ger/C: 376
Hellriegel Ger/L-LCdr: 116, 217, 251, 258, 378, 416
Hemingway UK/L: 186
Hemmer Ger/L: 435
Henderson US/LCdr: 396, 419, 439
Henderson (G. R.) US/RA: 483
Henke Ger/LCdr: 253, 277, 283, 314, 368, 371
Henne Ger/Cdr: 47-48, 51-52, 57-58, 60, 68, 223
Henning (F.) Ger/L: 381, 437
Henning (H.) Ger/LCdr: 349
Hensel US/LCdr: 379
Hepp Ger/L: 354, 369, 371
Herbschleb Ger/LCdr: 272, 288-289, 343
Herglotz Ger/L: 484
Herlofsen Nor/L: 475
Hering Ger/LCdr: 485
Hermann Ger/Cdr: 287
d'Herminier Fr/Cdr*: 352, 358
Herrick UK/L: 352, 390
Herrle Ger/L: 409
Herrman Ger/C: 231
Herwatz Ger/LCdr. 371, 403, 482, 490
Hesemann Ger/LCdr: 293, 302
Hess (H.-G.) Ger/L: 389, 464, 472, 475, 498
Hess (F. G.) US/Cdr: 432, 457
Hess (J. H.) US/LCdr: 468
Hesse (H.-J.) Ger/Cdr: 260, 267, 292, 295
Hesse (H.) Ger/LCdr: 177, 180
Hessler Ger/LCdr-Cdr: 77, 95, 138
Hester US/MG: 304, 334
Hetz Ger/Cdr: 485, 498
Hewitt US/RA-VA: 273, 338-339, 350, 443
Heyda Ger/LCdr: 167
Heydel Ger/Cdr-Cdr*: 336, 488
Heydemann (E.) Ger/L: 293
Heydemann (G.) Ger/LCdr: 135, 182, 208, 226, 232, 266, 292, 295
Heye Ger/C: 19, 22, 33, 45
Heyke Ger/Cdr: 3
Heyse Ger/LCdr: 182, 216, 219, 272
Hezlet UK/LCdr-Cdr: 127, 135, 145, 442, 453, 460, 473, 495, 515, 523
Hibbard Can/Cdr: 131
Hichiji Jap/Cdr*: 235, 253
Hickling UK/C: 86
Hicks US/LCdr: 202
Hilbig Ger/LCdr: 469
Hildebrand Ger/LCdr: 341, 343, 361

Hill US/RA-VA: 335, 370, 388, 391, 438, 494, 536
Hindenburg Ger/President: 489
Hinsch Ger/L-LCdr: 66, 148, 184, 216
Hintze Ger/C: 374
Hinz Ger/L: 490
v. Hippel Ger/L: 88
Hirose Jap/RA-VA: 162, 169, 176, 186, 534
Hirsacker Ger/LCdr: 201, 234, 236
Hitler Ger/Führer: 26, 41, 44, 46, 50, 52, 54, 61, 75, 78, 104, 179, 231, 296, 411
Hitschhold Ger/C: 102
Hodge US/LG: 537
Hodges US/MG: 425, 461, 504
Hoeckner Ger/LCdr: 233
v. Hoff (Carl) Ger/Cdr: 322
Hoff (Carl) Ger/LCdr: 488
Hoffmann (C.) Ger/C: 102
Hoffmann (E.) Ger/Cdr: 248
Hoffmann (Eberhardt) Ger/LCdr: 123
Hoffmann (H.) Ger/Cdr: 398, 422
Hoffmann (K.) Ger/C: 11, 19, 22, 33, 78, 85-86, 188
Hogan US/LCdr: 347, 365, 390
Holden US/RA: 526
Holdsworth UK/L: 447
Holland UK/VA: 67, 100
v. Holleben Ger/L: 481
Holt UK/Cre: 358
Holtorf Ger/LCdr: 246
Höltring Ger/LCdr: 111, 251, 270, 281, 301
Holzapfel Ger/LCdr: 484, 501
Hölzerkopf Ger/Cdr: 252
Homann Ger/L: 450
Homma Jap/LG: 170
v. Hooff Du/LCdr: 425
Hopmann Ger/Cdr: 256, 304-305, 357
Hoppe Ger/L: 92
Horii Jap/MG: 214
Horn Ger/LCdr: 246
Hornbostel Ger/LCdr: 469
Hornkohl Ger/LCdr: 338
Horrer Ger/LCdr: 203, 245, 256
Horstmann Ger/C: 22
Horton (Sir Max) UK/VA-A: 23, 318, 389, 482
Hosogaya Jap/VA: 221, 235, 312
Hossfeld Ger/L: 352
Hottel US/LCdr: 188, 248
House US/LCdr: 432, 449, 522
Howden UK/C: 195
Hozzel Ger/C: 28, 45, 74
Hryniewiecki Pol/Cdr: 357
Hsu Yung-chang Chi/G: 535
Huber Fr/LCdr: 107
Huddart UK/LCdr: 213
Huebner US/MG: 420
Hüffmeier Ger/C: 139, 143, 348
Hughes US/C: 387, 403, 416
Hull US/Secretary of State: 155
Hull US/LCdr: 259, 289, 306, 365
Hummerjohann Ger/L: 360
Hunger Ger/LCdr: 287, 307

Hunt UK/L: 313, 323, 336, 352, 358, 390, 398, 414, 430
Hunt US/MG: 536
Hurd US/LCdr: 164, 170, 222, 238, 279
Hurdis US/MG: 537
Hustvedt US/RA: 338, 387
Hutchins US/LCdr: 357
Hutchinson UK/LCdr: 23, 198
Hutchinson US/LCdr: 358
Huth (J.) Ger/Col: 247
Huth (W.) Ger/L: 317
Hüttemann Ger/L: 301
Hutton UK/C: 313
Huy Ger/L: 102
Hyakutake Jap/LG: 250, 258, 268, 399
Hyde US/LCdr: 457, 472
Hydemann US/Cdr: 505, 522
v. Hymmen Ger/LCdr: 230
Hyronimus Ger/L: 435

Iachino It/SA-A: 67, 69, 79, 88, 128, 140, 165-166, 175, 202, 228
Iaschi It/Cdr: 41
Iatrides Gr/L: 71, 81
Ibel Ger/Col: 247
Ibbeken Ger/C: 272
Icenhower US/LCdr-Cdr: 464, 529
Ichimura Jap/L: 334
Ichioka Jap/RA: 229
Ignatev USSR/C3: 455, 482
Ihlefeld Ger/C: 102
Ijuin Jap/RA: 345, 355-356, 364
Ikezawa Jap/Cdr*: 181
Imamura Jap/G: 537
Inaba Jap/Cdr*: 163, 177, 206
Inada Jap/Cdr*: 193, 206
Inada Jap/Cdr: 346
Ingham UK/C: 46
Ingram (D. C.) UK/LCdr-Cdr: 37, 39, 104
Ingram UK/LCdr: 320
Ingram US/RA: 108
Inoguchi Jap/RA: 462
Inoue Jap/Cdr*: 181
Inoue Jap/Cdr*: 162
Inoue (S.) Jap/LG: 452, 535
Inouye Jap/VA: 163, 199, 214, 235
Ionides UK/C: 382
Irvin US/Cdr: 396
Irvine US/Cdr: 522
Irving US/MG: 409, 461
Isaev USSR/LCdr: 193
Isbell US/C: 329, 337, 357, 375
Ishikawa Jap/Cdr*: 187, 270
Ishizaki Jap/RA: 222
Ishii Jap/LG: 533
Isitt NZ/AVM: 535
Isobe Jap/Cdr*: 181
Itagaki Jap/LG: 534
Ites Ger/L-LCdr: 109, 135, 188, 203, 217, 250
Ito (S.) Jap/VA: 508
Ito (Y.) Jap/RA: 418
Ito Jap/LG: 537
Ivanov (A. P.) USSR/LCdr: 172
Ivanov (M. G.) USSR/C1: 132, 384

Ivanov (V. A.) USSR/C2: 203, 294
Ivanovski USSR/RA: 531
Ivantsov USSR/L-C3: 13, 142
Iwagami Jap/C: 370
Izaki Jap/RA: 335
Izawa Jap/C: 214
Izu Jap/Cdr*: 215, 246, 280, 315-316
Izu Jap/Cdr: 381

Jäasalo Fin/LCdr: 431
Jacobs Ger/C: 289
Jacobsen Ger/LCdr: 77, 83, 217
Jaenecke Ger/G-ColG: 352, 407
Jahn Ger/LCdr: 246, 253, 299, 310, 344
v. Jakobs Ger/LCdr: 278
Janssen Ger/L: 270, 283
Jarman Du/LCdr: 167
Jarvis US/LCdr: 457, 495, 515, 526
Jaujard Fr/RA: 484
Jay UK/Cdr-C: 203, 366
Jebsen Ger/L-LCdr: 200, 403, 417
Jenisch (H.) Ger/L: 15, 20, 49, 51, 53, 55, 61
Jenisch (K. H.) Ger/LCdr: 10, 13, 18, 35
Jenkins US/C: 276
Jennings US/RA: 524
Jensen US/LCdr: 358
Jephson UK/C: 307
Jeppener-Haltenhoff Ger/LCdr: 8
v. Jessen Ger/LCdr: 321
Jobst Ger/L: 505
Jodl Ger/G: 26
Johannesson Ger/C: 279, 348, 374
Johannsen Ger/LCdr: 423, 427
Johnson US/LCdr: 272, 372
Johnson (G. W.) US/Cdr: 130
Jones UK/C: 422
Jones US/RA: 526, 529
Jones US/BG: 293
Jope Ger/L: 61
Josephi Ger/Cdr: 398
Joshima Jap/RA: 263, 415, 430
Josseliani USSR/LCdr-C3: 240, 330, 368, 439, 459
Jukes US/LCdr: 379
Juli Ger/LCdr: 260, 262, 303
Julihn US/LCdr: 449
Junker Ger/Cdr*: 349, 382, 482
Jupp UK/L: 396
Jürst Ger/L-LCdr: 9, 12, 14, 18, 65
Just Ger/LCdr: 507

Kabanov USSR/LG: 157
Kabo USSR/C3: 246, 439
Kacharev USSR/C: 244
Kaden Ger/LCdr: 60
Kagawa Jap/C: 372
Kahl Ger/C: 231
Kähler Ger/C: 36, 41, 46, 68, 91, 94
Kaida Jap/Col: 538
Kaiser Ger/Cdr*: 288
Kaithley US/LCdr: 472
Kajatsalo Fin/L: 279

Kajioka Jap/RA: 164, 168, 179, 214
Kaku Jap/C: 224
Kakuta Jap/RA-VA: 178, 194, 204, 220, 223, 235, 263, 268, 275, 438
Kalinin USSR/LCdr: 455, 482
Kals Ger/Cdr: 164, 178, 209, 277
Kamada Jap/VA: 538
v. Kameke Ger/Cdr: 328
v. Kamptz Ger/Cdr: 22
Kanda Jap/LG: 537
Kandler Ger/L: 320, 376
Kapitzky Ger/LCdr: 262, 266, 316, 331
Karbovski USSR/C3: 260, 330, 380
v. Karnebeek Du/LCdr: 453, 471
Karnicki Pol/Cdr: 153, 358, 360
Karpf Ger/LCdr: 289, 295, 315
Karpov USSR/C2: 150
Kassbaum Ger/Cdr: 431
Katunin USSR/C: 404
Kautski USSR/C3: 294
Kawaguchi Jap/LCdr: 452, 465
Kawasaki Jap/Cdr: 181, 258
Kawashima Jap/LCdr: 465
Kayahara Jap/Cdr*: 152, 162, 223
Keating US/LCdr: 439, 468
Keddie UK/L: 447
Kefauver US/LCdr-Cdr: 379, 410, 495, 505
de Kehror Fr/LCdr: 49
Keithley US/LCdr: 456
Kelbling Ger/LCdr: 213, 239, 306, 340, 353, 369
Kell Ger/LCdr: 104, 122, 125, 141, 145
v. Keller Ger/L: 376
Keller (P.) Ger/L: 248
Keller (S.) Ger/L: 307-308
Kellner Ger/LCdr: 287
Kemnade Ger/LCdr: 84, 121, 169, 179, 201, 209-210, 215, 229, 272, 289
Kendall US/RA: 537
Kennedy UK/C: 11
Kennedy (J. F.) US/L: 341
Kennedy (M. G.) US/LCdr: 284
Kenner US/C: 395
Kenney US/LG: 306, 406, 451, 460, 487
Kent UK/L: 471
Kentrat Ger/LCdr: 84, 88, 122, 135, 145, 148, 315, 403, 417
Kern Yu/C: 91
Kerr UK/C: 100
Kershaw US/L: 198, 336
Kesaev USSR/LCdr: 368
Kessler (H.) Ger/LCdr: 234, 239, 265, 389
Kessler (U.) Ger/LG: 363, 369
Kett UK/L: 358, 398
Kettner Ger/LCdr: 240
Keyes UK/LCol: 144
Khakhanov USSR/L: 361

Kholostyakov USSR/RA: 252, 352, 365
Khomyakov USSR/C3: 191, 408
Khotiashvili USSR/Cdr: 111
Khrulev USSR/LCdr: 331, 393-394
Khryukin USSR/LG: 411
Kidd US/RA: 161
Kiderlen Ger/C: 304
Kieffer Ger/Cdr: 431, 488
Kieseritzky Ger/VA: 353
Kietz Ger/L: 314
Kijanen Fin/LCdr: 110, 116, 123
Kiland US/RA: 480, 502
Kimmel US/A: 169
Kimura (M.) Jap/RA: 337, 475
Kimura (M.) Jap/LCdr: 467, 487
Kimura (S.) Jap/RA: 220, 235, 264, 275, 277, 306, 415
Kinashi Jap/LCdr-Cdr: 178, 200, 311, 341, 373, 403
King (E. L. S.) UK/RA-VA: 95, 102-103, 106
King (W. D.) UK/L-Cdr: 23, 40, 222, 232, 279, 417, 438
King US/A: 327, 425
Kingman US/RA: 323, 337, 370
Kinkaid US/C-A: 151, 214, 221, 238, 249, 269, 275-276, 293, 323, 395, 409, 461, 480, 537
Kinsella US/LCdr: 433, 457, 514
Kinzel Ger/LCdr: 298, 309, 354
Kirby UK/L: 447
Kirk (A. G.) US/RA: 339, 420, 425
Kirk (O. G.) US/L: 215
Kirkpatrick Can/LCdr: 428, 433
Kirkpatrick US/LCdr: 209, 222, 233, 284
Kirtland US/C: 136
Kishi Jap/RA: 221
Kishigami Jap/Cdr: 164
Kitamura Jap/LCdr-Cdr: 163, 176, 193, 265
Kitch US/Cdr: 479
Kitts US/C: 282
Kivilinna Fin/SL: 124
Klakring US/LCdr: 248, 259, 289
Klapdor Ger/L: 360
Klassmann Ger/LCdr: 285, 365, 407
Kleikamp Ger/C: 1, 6, 22
Kleiner Ger/L: 279
Kleinschmidt Ger/LCdr: 99, 131
Klevenski USSR/C1: 110-111
Klingspor Ger/LCdr: 472, 485, 506
Klocke Ger/L: 283, 318
Klose Ger/L: 200
v. Klot-Heydenfeldt Ger/LCdr: 5, 18, 20, 38
Klövekorn Ger/LCdr: 376
Klüber Ger/C: 13
Klug Ger/L-Cdr: 45, 52, 71, 83, 85, 280, 283, 318, 327, 366, 385, 398, 404, 413, 422
Klümper Ger/M: 256, 344, 367
Klünder Ger/Cdr: 426
Klusmeyer Ger/L: 519
Kluth Ger/L: 354
Klyushkin USSR/C3: 455, 482

Knackfuss Ger/L: 424
Knapp UK/Cdr: 51, 53
Kneip Ger/L: 454
Knight UK/L: 123
Knoke Ger/C: 455, 460, 485, 497
Knoops Du/LCdr: 178
Knorr Ger/LCdr: 18, 24, 26, 35, 47
Knowles US/C-Cre: 428, 504
Knuth Ger/Cdr*: 219
Kobayashi Jap/Cdr: 193
Kobayashi Jap/RA: 160
Koch Ger/L: 326
Kofanov USSR/LCdr: 345
Koga Jap/A: 316, 361, 400
Kögl Ger/C: 1
Kohlauf Ger/LCdr-Cdr: 77, 358, 362, 376, 398, 405
Köhler Ger/LCdr: 265
Köhntopp Ger/LCdr: 442
Koitschka Ger/L: 305, 309, 353, 386, 415
Koivisto Fin/Cdr*: 134
Koizumi Jap/Cdr-Cdr*: 193, 206, 229
Kojima Jap/C: 187
Kolbus Ger/L: 377, 437
Kolchin USSR/C1: 294, 334, 401
Kölle Ger/Cdr: 184, 207, 232
Kollewe Ger/C: 102, 107, 216
Kolosov USSR/LCdr: 394
Kolyshkin USSR/C2: 124, 139, 154, 180, 204
Komarov USSR/LCdr: 240
Komatsu Jap/VA: 235
Komura Jap/RA: 508
Kondo (F.) Jap/LCdr: 460
Kondo (N.) Jap/VA: 159, 163, 167, 170, 178, 190, 194, 196, 221, 223, 235, 244, 248, 254, 263, 268, 270, 275-277
Könenkamp Ger/LCdr: 229, 234, 250, 283, 340
Konishi Jap/C: 156
Kono Jap/RA: 164, 234
Konovalov USSR/C3: 455, 485, 489, 501, 508, 512
Konstantinov USSR/LCdr: 139
Konyaev USSR/LCdr: 15
Köplin Ger/Cdr: 450
Koppe Ger/Cdr: 47
Köppe Ger/LCdr: 272, 316
Koppenhagen Ger/Cdr: 330, 348, 431
Koreeda Jap/L: 426
Korndörfer Ger/L: 381, 404, 437
Korotkevich USSR/L: 498
Korshunevich USSR/LCdr-C3: 142, 445
Korth Ger/LCdr: 10, 14, 18-19, 21, 59, 75, 99
Kosbadt Ger/L: 266, 278
Kosmin USSR/C1: 13
Kossler US/LCdr: 430, 472, 479
Kostylev USSR/C3: 246
Kotelnikov USSR/C3-C2: 154, 180, 298
Kothe Ger/C: 348, 397, 460, 473
Kotsuki Jap/LG: 537
Kottmann Ger/L: 270
Kovalenko USSR/LCdr: 169, 191

Kovar US/L: 463
Koyanagi Jap/RA: 290-291
Krage Ger/C: 379
Kramer Ger/Cdr: 450
Kramer US/MG: 510, 536
Krancke Ger/C: 61, 64, 70, 76, 80, 88
Krankenhagen Ger/LCdr: 416
Krapf US/LCdr: 419, 439
Kratzenberg Ger/C: 22
Kraus Ger/L-LCdr: 141, 145, 200, 225, 247, 330
Kravchenko (F. I.) USSR/C1: 156
Kravchenko (K. A.) USSR/LCdr: 484
Krech Ger/LCdr: 128, 142, 188, 193, 215, 239, 250, 257, 303
Kreisch Ger/C-VA: 107, 512
Kreiser USSR/LG: 411
Krempl Ger/L: 506
Krestovski USSR/C1: 380
Kretschmer Ger/LCdr: 8, 13, 17-19, 38, 45, 51, 53, 60-61, 66, 84-85
Krieg Ger/L: 294, 306, 340, 369
Kröning Ger/LCdr: 188
Krüder Ger/C: 40, 50, 98
Krüer Ger/L: 331
Krueger US/LG-G: 461, 480, 536
Krüger (E.) Ger/L: 514
Krüger (J.) Ger/L: 309
Krulak US/LCol: 363
Kruschka Ger/L: 286, 302, 308
Krylov USSR/Col: 459
Kubo Jap/RA: 160, 170, 177, 181, 186, 191
Kucherenko USSR/C2: 331, 345
Kucherov USSR/RA: 334, 361
Kudo Jap/Cdr: 457
Kühl Ger/C: 77, 91
Kuhlmann (H.-G.) Ger/L: 234
Kuhlmann (J.) Ger/L: 481
Kuhn Ger/Cdr: 490
Kuhnke Ger/LCdr: 2, 10, 20, 35, 49, 51, 53, 61
Kukht USSR/C2: 530
Kukuy USSR/L: 218
Kulbakin USSR/C3: 298
Kuleshov USSR/RA: 126
Kummetat Ger/L: 329-330
Kummetz Ger/RA-GA: 22, 230, 272, 288, 348, 488
Kunets USSR/LCdr: 133
Kunkel Ger/C: 331
Künzel Ger/LCdr: 242, 251-252
Kuppig Ger/LCdr: 407.
Kuppisch Ger/LCdr: 12, 15, 18, 31, 66, 75, 88, 96, 99
Kuribayashi Jap/LG: 494
Kurita Jap/RA-VA: 159, 163, 167, 178, 194, 204-205, 221, 235, 263-264, 275, 361, 364, 414, 430, 462-464
Kuriyama Jap/Cdr: 239
Kurochkin USSR/Col: 497
Kusaka Jap/VA: 269, 276, 537
Kusaka Jap/Cdr: 311, 373, 383, 528
Kusch Ger/L: 322
Küster Ger/LCdr: 22

Kutschmann Ger/LCdr: 19
v. Kutzleben Ger/Cdr*-C: 47, 219
Kuznetsov (K. M.) USSR/C1: 13
Kuznetsov (N. G.) USSR/A: 108
Kuzmin (A.V.) USSR/CI: 436, 445
Kuzmin (P. S.) USSR/LCdr: 324
Kuzume Jap/Col: 418

La Baume Ger/LCdr: 230, 401
de Laborde Fr/RA-A: 38, 280
Lacrois Fr/RA: 41
Lacomblé Du/Cdr: 195
de Lafond Fr/RA: 274
Laird US/LCdr: 468
Lake US/LCdr: 284, 296
Lakin UK/L: 280, 286, 323, 336
Lamb US/LCdr: 232
Lambe UK/C: 486
Lambert UK/L: 358
Lamby Ger/LCdr: 260
Lancelot Fr/LCdr-C: 56, 394
Landriau Fr/RA: 56
Landrum US/MG: 323
Landt-Hayen Ger/L: 411
Lange (H.-G.) Ger/L-LCdr: 343, 401, 409, 441, 445, 492, 503, 511
Lange (K.-H.) Ger/L: 436
Lange (K.) Ger/LCdr: 305, 315, 371
Lange (Werner) Ger/LCdr: 451
Lange (Werner) Ger/C-RA: 22, 351
Langenburg Ger/L: 393
Langfeld Ger/L: 307
Langobardo It/Cdr*: 75
Langridge UK/L: 438, 471
Langsdorff Ger/C: 1, 9, 12, 15
Larcom UK/C: 100
de Larminat Fr/MG: 49, 510
Larson US/C: 355
Laskos Gr/LCdr: 323, 351
Lassen Ger/L-LCdr: 201, 234, 264, 299
Latham US/Cdr: 522
Latta US/LCdr-Cdr: 347, 372, 491
de Lattre de Tassigny Fr/G: 443
Laughon US/LCdr: 379, 390, 410
Launders UK/L: 396, 446, 486, 501
Laurin Fr/Cdr*: 274
Lautenschlager Ger/C: 316
auterbach-Emden Ger/LCdr:L 416
Lautrup US/LCdr-Cdr: 343, 379, 522
Lauzemis Ger/L: 301
Laval Fr/Minister: 39
Law Can/LCdr: 422, 433
Layard UK/LCdr: 240
Layton UK/VA: 23-24, 27, 33
Leach UK/C: 100, 164
Leatham UK/VA: 9, 79-80, 93
Leary US/VA: 185
Leclerc Fr/Col-G: 49, 64, 535, 539
Leclerc Fr/VA: 274
Lee US/LCdr: 290, 314, 322, 439, 456

Lee (W. A.) US/RA-VA: 263-264, 269-270, 275-277, 291, 346, 373, 387, 399, 406, 427, 458, 464, 476, 499, 501
Leese UK/C: 103
Leese UK/LG: 338
Legassick UK/Cdr: 368
Legnani It/DA: 42, 69, 89
Lehmann Ger/L: 445, 465, 472, 484, 511
Lehmann-Willenbrock Ger/LCdr-Cdr: 69, 75, 77, 92, 99, 114, 147, 188
Leimkuhler Ger/L: 287
Leino Fin/LCdr: 261
Leissner Ger/C: 22
Lemaire Fr/C: 41
Lemcke Ger/LCdr: 238, 240
Lemeshko USSR/LG: 530
Lemp Ger/L-LCdr: 2, 15, 35, 38, 47, 85, 88, 92, 96, 99
Lensch Ger/C: 439
Lent US/LCdr: 188, 209
Leonardi It/RA: 340
Leonhardt Ger/Cdr: 488
Leoni It/Cdr: 46, 59
Leonov USSR/C1: 532
Leonov (M. V) USSR/LCdr: 411
Leopold Bel/King: 31
Lerchen Ger/LCdr: 210
Leslie US/LCdr: 224
Lessing Ger/C: 469
Levasseur Fr/LCdr: 307
Levchenko USSR/VA-A: 140, 384, 409, 444
Lewis (H. G. A.) UK/Cdr: 302
Lewis (H. H.) US/LCdr: 491, 495, 515
Lewis (J. H.) US/LCdr: 286, 289
Lewis US/Cdr: 266
Lewis US/RA: 444
Ley Ger/L: 452, 465
Li Chi/G: 532
Liannazza It/Cdr-Cdr*: 50, 272
Liebe (H.) Ger/LCdr: 2, 13, 20, 25-26, 35, 47, 55, 70, 95
Liebe (J.) Ger/LCdr: 198, 227 260, 264
v. Liebenstein Ger/C: 345, 352
Liermann Ger/LCdr: 515
Likholetov USSR/C3: 146
v. Lilienfeld Ger/L: 262
Li-Ming Chi/G: 539
Lindemann Ger/C: 99
Lindenberg USSR/C2: 259
Linder Ger/LCdr: 130, 148, 201, 227, 236
Lindsey US/LCdr: 224
Linke Ger/M: 227
Linton UK/LCdr-Cdr: 55, 73, 208, 218, 232, 239, 245, 261, 278 286, 293, 300
Lisin USSR/C3: 137, 229, 261
List Ger/FMa: 94
Litch US/RA: 527
Litterscheid Ger/L: 252
Llewellen US/LCdr: 322, 343, 396, 410, 529
Lockwood (C. A.) US/RA-VA: 222, 429
Lockwood (R. H.) US/Cdr: 491
Loehr Ger/C: 149

Loerke Ger/Cdr: 516
Loerzer Ger/G: 207
Loeser Ger/L-LCdr: 201, 226, 284
Loewe (A.) Ger/LCdr: 197, 232
Loewe (O.) Ger/LCdr: 246, 260, 262, 317
Lohmann Ger/LCdr: 237, 268, 322
Lohmeyer Ger/LCdr: 108
Lohse Ger/LCdr: 203
Lombardi It/DA: 153
Long UK/LCdr: 189
Longanesi-Cattani It/Cdr: 104, 197
Longhi It/LCdr: 283
Longley-Cook UK/C: 420-421
Lonsdale UK/LCdr: 28
Looff Ger/LCdr: 38
Looks Ger/L-LCdr: 278, 303, 321, 357
Loomis (D. W.) US/C: 428
Loomis (S. C.) US/LCdr: 396
Lorentz Ger/L: 19-20
Loshkarev USSR/C3: 455, 482
Lott Ger/LCdr: 2, 12
Loughlin US/LCdr-Cdr: 449, 468, 479, 505
Loundras Gr/LCdr: 433
Loveitt UK/FS: 107
Low US/RA: 522, 527
Lowrance US/LCdr: 259, 284, 306, 456
Lowry US/RA: 385, 443
Lozovski USSR/LCdr: 450
Lübsen Ger/L: 401
Lucas US/MG: 385
Luce UK/Cdr: 46-47
Lüdden Ger/LCdr-C: 316, 349, 382
Lüders Ger/SL: 112
Ludewig US/C: 529
v. Lüeder Ger/LCdr: 433
Lueders Ger/LCdr: 159
Lührs Ger/L: 381, 406
Luis Ger/L: 325
Lukyanov USSR/LCdr: 310, 345
Lumby UK/L: 240, 278, 293, 300, 313, 336
Lumsden UK/LG: 481
Lunin USSR/LCdr-C2: 148, 180, 192, 231, 302
Lüth Ger/L-Cdr: 18-19, 26, 29-30, 53, 58, 66, 104, 131, 151, 178, 272, 315
Luther Ger/L: 329
Lutjens Ger/RA-A: 1-2, 8, 22, 71, 79, 85, 99
v. Luttitz Ger/LCdr: 515
Lützow Ger/LCdr: 318, 327, 359, 363
Lvov USSR/LG: 172
Lyle UK/LCdr: 433
Lynch (F. C.) US/LCdr: 449, 468, 526
Lynch (R. B.) US/Cdr: 522
v. Lyncker Ger/Cdr: 485, 516
Lyon (d'Oly) UK/VA: 9, 12, 14, 38
Lyon US/C: 338
Lyster UK/RA: 54, 63, 242, 274

MacArthur US/G: 193, 395, 409, 451, 465, 480, 523-524, 533, 535-536
MacGregor US/LCdr: 292, 314
Mack UK/C: 89, 93-94, 102, 163
Mackendrick UK/Cdr: 137, 167
Mackenzie (H. S.) UK/L-LCdr: 145, 153, 175, 208, 218, 232, 251, 263, 412, 425, 471
Mackenzie UK/Cre: 131
Macintyre (D.) UK/Cdr: 85, 119, 287, 318, 325, 389, 400, 424, 444-445
Macintyre (I. A. P.) UK/C: 302
MacKintosh UK/C: 242
MacMahon US/LCdr-Cdr: 365, 491
MacNider US/BG: 494
Mäder Ger/LCdr: 357
Magee UK/Cre: 301
Magrin-Verneret Fr/Col: 28
Magruder US/Cre: 536
Mahn Ger/Cdr*: 260
Mahrholz Ger/L: 435
Maiorana It/Cdr: 45
Makarenkov USSR/LCdr: 345
Makeig-Jones UK/C: 13
Makino Jap/LG: 466
Makowski Ger/L: 258, 260
Malanchenko USSR/LCdr: 246
Mallmann Ger/LCdr: 367
Malofyev USSR/C3: 154, 298, 310
Malyshev USSR/LCdr: 133, 180, 240, 408
Mamontov USSR/C2: 157
Manca It/Cdr: 62
Manchen Ger/LCdr: 506
Mangold Ger/L: 393, 401, 441
Manke Ger/LCdr: 296, 321, 394
Manners UK/RA: 136
Mannesmann Ger/LCdr: 376
v. Mannstein Ger/LCdr: 215, 278, 301, 325
Manseck Ger/LCdr: 282, 309, 329, 355, 357, 378
Mansfield UK/RA-VA: 386, 443, 453
v. Manstein Ger/Col-G: 172, 216, 225
Manuti It/Cdr: 243
Manwaring UK/C: 98, 205
Mao Tse-Tung Chi: 532
Marabotto It/C: 158
Marbach Ger/L: 378, 424, 435
Marceglia It/C: 166
Marcellariu Ru/RA: 407
Marenco di Moriondo It/DA: 35, 42, 47, 69
Margottini It/C: 58
Marguth Ger/C: 22
Marienfeld Ger/L: 469
Marinesko USSR/LCdr-C3: 246, 455, 489
Marino It/SgtM: 166
Marks Ger/LCdr: 203, 230
Markov USSR/C1: 148, 222
Markworth Ger/LCdr: 234, 295, 303, 328, 361
Marotta It/Cdr: 321
Marriott UK/L: 425, 438, 460, 473

Y

Mars UK/L: 243, 267, 286, 292, 313, 474
Marschall Ger/VA-A: 11, 19, 33
Marshall UK/L: 447
Marshall US/LCdr: 365
Marshall US/G: 425
Marston US/BG: 115
Martellotta It/C: 166
Martin UK/LCdr: 396, 442
Martin (B. C. S.) UK/C-RA: 101, 479, 484-485, 513, 535
Martin (C. A.) US/BG-MG: 380, 512
Martin (J. C.) US/L-Cdr: 457, 472
Martinoli It/C: 313
Marumo Jap/RA: 214
Marzin Fr/C: 38
Masara Yu/LCdr: 91
Masberg Ger/C: 219
Maslov USSR/C2: 148
v. Mässenhausen Ger/LCdr: 262, 320
Massey US/LCdr: 224
Massmann Ger/L: 270, 305
Masuzawa Jap/L: 488
Mathes Ger/LCdr: 18, 20
Mathias UK/L: 433
Matiyasevich USSR/L-C3: 146, 246, 455
Matschulat Ger/L: 412
Matsuda Jap/RA: 462
Matsui Jap/LG: 159
Matsumura Jap/Cdr*: 162, 215, 270, 275, 295
Matsunaga Jap/RA: 164
Matsuyama Jap/RA: 179, 235, 250
Matsuyama Jap/LG: 258
v. Matuschka Ger/LCdr: 448, 481
Matveev USSR/LCdr: 404, 408, 411
Matteucci It/DA: 42, 67
Matz Ger/LCdr: 46-47, 49, 58, 84
Matzen Ger/LCdr: 434, 484, 500, 507
Maugeri It/C: 44
Maund UK/C: 100, 150
Maurer US/LCdr: 468, 529
Maus Ger/LCdr: 283, 301, 330
Mayall US/Cre: 309
Maydon UK/L-Cdr: 175, 184, 208, 228, 251, 255, 267, 280, 284, 292
Mayuzumi Jap/C: 383
Mazzola It/C: 82
McBeath UK/Cdr: 208
McCain (J. S.) US/RA-VA: 239, 448, 457, 464, 466, 474, 476, 517, 522, 525, 533
McCain (J. S. Jr) US/LCdr-Cdr: 328, 372, 522
McCallum US/Cdr: 457, 462, 505
McCarthy UK/C: 58, 97, 156
McClintock US/LCdr: 457, 462
McClure US/MG: 345
McClusky US/LCdr: 224
McCowen UK/LCdr: 429
McCoy UK/C: 311, 319-320, 374-375

McCrea (J. L.) US/RA: 470, 482, 500
McCrea (V. B.) US/LCdr: 390, 410, 456
McCreery UK/LG: 350
McCrory US/LCdr: 505, 522
McDougal Le Breton US/RA: 115
McFall US/RA: 335
McGee US/C: 494, 504
McGeoch UK/LCdr: 280, 284, 293, 300
McGivern US/LCdr: 329
McGovern US/Cre: 494
McGrath UK/Cdr: 362
McGregor (D.) US/LCdr: 198, 266, 284
McGregor (L. D.) US/LCdr-Cdr: 314, 343, 439, 468
McGregor (R. R.) US/LCdr: 248, 284
McGrigor UK/C-RA: 100, 328, 338, 408, 437, 444, 452, 483, 491-492, 517-519
McInerney US/Cdr-C: 307, 335
McIntosh UK/LCdr: 396, 446
McKenzie US/LCdr: 306
McKinney US/LCdr-Cdr: 185-186, 222, 279, 377
McKnight US/LCdr: 289
McMahon US/LCdr: 284, 314, 329, 347, 365, 491
McMaster US/LCdr: 439
McMillan US/LCdr: 379
McMorris US/RA: 295, 304, 312, 319, 323
McVay US/C: 527
Meckel Ger/LCdr: 8
Meendsen-Bohlken Ger/C: 139, 231, 244
Meermeier Ger/LCdr: 448, 469, 506
Mehl Ger/LCdr: 289, 299, 317, 340, 344, 353, 386, 397
Mehler Ger/Cdr: 304, 353
Mehlhop US/LCdr: 515
Meisel Ger/C-RA: 3, 56, 68, 71, 78-79, 86, 201, 231, 258
Melnikov USSR/C3-C2: 222, 252
Melodia It/C: 139
Melson US/Cdr: 386
Melsom Nor/LCdr: 125
Mengersen Ger/L-LCdr: 10, 18, 66, 77, 104, 143, 234, 238, 240, 262, 296, 322, 325
Meneghini It/Cdr*: 34
Menzies UK/C: 328
Mercier Fr/C: 274
Mergelmeyer Ger/LCdr: 488
Merten Ger/Cdr: 138, 143, 159, 197, 224, 261
Merrill (A. S.) US/RA: 307, 334-335, 363, 391
Merrill (W. R.) US/LCdr: 379
Meshcherski USSR/C1: 113, 147, 150
Metcalf US/LCdr: 372, 390, 402
Metz Ger/L: 337
Metzler Ger/LCdr: 82, 88, 95, 116
Mewhinney US/LCdr: 238
Meyer (G.) Ger/L: 469

Meyer (F.) Ger/L: 131
Meyer (Hans) Ger/C: 348, 401
Meyer (H.-J.) Ger/L: 157
Meyer (Herbert) Ger/L: 432
Meyer (R.) Ger/L: 481
Meyer (W.) Ger/L: 393, 401
Meyers US/BG: 537
Mezzadra It/L: 243
Michalowski Ger/L: 30, 32, 37, 44
Michelier Fr/VA: 274
Michell UK/L: 433, 453
Micklewait UK/C: 257
Middleton US/LCdr: 449
Middleton US/MG: 339, 350
Miers UK/LCdr-Cdr: 104, 115, 198, 208
Mikawa Jap/VA: 156, 204, 221, 235, 237, 241, 264, 271, 275-276
Milford Aus/MG: 524, 538
Milner UK/L: 336, 358
Miller UK/Cdr: 505
Millican US/LCdr: 232, 266, 284, 296
Mills UK/Cdr: 389
Mills (R. G.) UK/LCdr: 31, 37, 62
Mimbelli It/Cdr*: 102, 155, 225
Del Minio It/C: 272, 282
v. Mirbach Ger/L-LCdr: 31, 95, 127, 303, 398, 405, 413, 422-423, 434, 484, 507
Mirow Ger/C: 134-135, 139
Mitchell US/M: 316
Mitscher US/RA-VA: 226, 341, 387, 392, 400, 406, 426, 430, 436, 438, 448, 457, 461-462, 465-466, 491, 498, 509, 516-517
v. Mittelstaedt Ger/LCdr: 111
Miwa Jap/RA: 152, 181
Moehle Ger/LCdr: 10, 13, 17, 55, 65, 77, 92
Mogilevski USSR/C3: 497
Möglich Ger/LCdr: 305
Möhlmann Ger/LCdr: 129, 201, 232, 292, 316
Mohr (C.-F.) Ger/LCdr: 498
Mohr (J.) Ger/LCdr: 137, 154, 159, 198, 216, 285, 290, 314
Mohs Ger/L-LCdr: 384, 393, 442, 464, 475, 506
Moiseev USSR/LCdr-C3: 115, 208
Mokhov USSR/LCdr: 229
Möller Ger/L: 360
Molumphy US/LCdr: 388
Momot USSR/C3: 259
Monechi It/LCdr: 200
Monroe US/L-LCdr: 336, 439, 456
Mons Ger/M: 369, 372
Monssen Nor/LCdr: 262, 278, 425, 433
Montgomery US/RA: 359, 364, 370, 373, 387, 392, 400, 406, 415, 426, 436, 466, 474
Montgomery UK/G: 338, 419
Montross US/LCdr: 419
Moody UK/RA: 351, 382, 407, 411-412, 442, 453
Moon US/RA: 420, 425
Moore (H. R.) UK/VA-A: 366,

401, 408, 410-411, 437, 444
Moore (J. A.) US/LCdr: 358, 372, 390
Moore (J. R.) US/L-LCdr: 215, 222, 241, 329
Moore (R. J.) US/LCdr: 173, 178
Moore (S. N.) US/C: 241
Moore UK/FO: 424
Moore-Gosgrove Can/Col: 535
Moosbrugger US/Cdr-C: 341, 502
Moran US/C: 269
Morgan (F. E.) UK/LG: 340
Morgan UK/C: 102, 166
Mori Jap/RA: 312
Morin Fr/Cdr*: 49, 64
Morinaga Jap/Cdr: 239, 463
Morone It/LCdr: 36
Morosov USSR/C3: 209
de Morsier Fr/LCdr: 297
v. Morstein Ger/LCdr: 454, 490
Morton US/LCdr-Cdr: 289, 306, 347
Mosely US/LCdr: 176, 198, 209
Moskalenko USSR/RA: 132, 150
Mott UK/L: 336
Mountbatten (Lord) UK/C-A: 28, 94, 96, 98, 534
Moyer US/Cre: 504
Mudge US/MG: 461
Mueller US/MG: 452, 536
Mugler Ger/L-LCdr: 2, 10, 18
Muhs Ger/L: 401
Muirhead UK/RA: 519
Müller (A.) Ger/L-LCdr: 71, 109, 112, 440, 453
Müller (F.-W.) Ger/LG: 367
Müller (H.-E.) Ger/LCdr: 312
Müller (K.) Ger/L-LCdr: 155, 157, 260, 318, 380
Müller-Arnecke Ger/LCdr: 10
Müller Edzards Ger/LCdr: 217
Müller-Stöckheim Ger/LCdr: 138, 168, 192, 223, 260, 264
Mullins US/MG: 483, 537
Mullinix US/RA: 370
Mumm Ger/L: 252
Münnich Ger/LCdr: 296
Munroe US/RA: 132
Munson US/LCdr: 241, 365, 379, 439
Murakami Jap/C: 249
Muraoka Jap/Cdr: 295
Murdaugh US/Cdr: 193
Murray US/RA-VA: 136, 253-254, 258, 263, 269, 536
Murphy (C. L.) US/LCdr: 379, 410, 419
Murphy (J. W.) US/LCdr: 198, 210
Murphy US/C: 504
Murzi It/Cdr: 119
Muselier Fr/VA: 172
Musenberg Ger/Cdr: 315
Muser Ger/LCdr: 301
Mussolini It/Statesman: 80, 342
Mützelburg Ger/LCdr: 118-119, 137, 148, 177, 201, 203, 232
Mylnikov USSR/LCdr-C3: 134, 259, 343

Nagano Jap/MG: 539
Nagel Ger/L: 325

Nagumo Jap/VA: 156, 179, 184, 190, 194, 196-197, 204-205, 207, 220, 223-224, 235, 244, 248, 254, 263, 268-269, 428
Nakagawa (H.) Jap/LCdr: 311, 383
Nakagawa (K.) Jap/Cdr*: 163, 193
Nakagawa (K.) Jap/Col: 452
Nakajima Jap/LCdr: 186-187
Nakamura (M.) Jap/L: 341
Nakamura (N.) Jap/LCdr: 373
Nakamura (S.) Jap/Cdr: 193
Nakano Jap/LG: 306
Nakashima Jap/Cdr: 176
Nambu Jap/LCdr: 528
Nanbu Jap/LCdr: 311
Napier UK/L-LCdr: 129, 141, 145, 153, 251, 284, 313, 336, 398
Napp It/LCdr: 83
Narahara Jap/Cdr*: 162, 219, 249, 254
Nardi It/Cdr: 36
Narykov USSR/C2: 148, 151
Nau Ger/LCdr: 433
Nechaev USSR/C3: 414, 446
Neckel Ger/LCdr: 321
Nees Ger/LCdr: 445, 472
Negoda USSR/C3-C2: 173, 359
Neide Ger/LCdr: 317, 375
Neitzel Ger/Cdr: 238, 270, 300
Nelson US/LCdr: 358, 372
Nelte Ger/PO: 435
Nesvitski USSR/Flag 2: 15
Netzbandt Ger/C: 19, 22, 33
Neuerburg Ger/LCdr: 490
Neumann (H.-W.) Ger/Cdr: 314
Neumann (H.-J.) Ger/LCdr: 122, 131, 229
Neuss Ger/LCdr: 71
Newman UK/LCol: 206
Newstead UK/L: 313, 323
Newton US/RA: 161
Nicholas US/LCdr: 343, 347, 358, 449
Nicholl UK/C: 149, 166, 183
Nichols US/LCdr: 401, 419, 479, 505
Nicolay Ger/LCdr: 393, 401
Nicolay UK/LCdr: 133, 141
Nicolson UK/C: 89
Niculescu Ru/Cdr: 142
Nielson Ger/L: 432
Niemeyer Ger/L: 416
Nimitz US/A: 169, 531, 534-535
Nimitz (C. W. Jr) US/LCdr: 232, 402, 439, 449
Nishida Jap/SL: 467
Nishida Jap/MG: 392
Nishimura Jap/RA-VA: 162, 170, 177, 182, 192, 194, 221, 235, 263-264, 275-276, 341, 462-463
Nishino Jap/Cdr*: 162, 187, 249
Nishiuchi Jap/LCdr: 465
Nishiyama Jap/LG: 482
Nissen Ger/L-LCdr: 285, 290-291, 314
Noble US/C-RA: 409, 415, 512, 514, 524, 537
Nocken Ger/C: 256
Nölke Ger/LCdr: 278
Nollmann Ger/L-LCdr: 448, 481

Nomura Jap/VA: 315
Nonn Ger/L: 353, 369, 381, 406
Nordheimer Ger/LCdr: 384, 393, 401
Nordt Ger/LCdr: 447
Norfolk UK/LCdr: 173, 184, 239
Norita Jap/LCdr: 403
Norman UK/L: 82, 186, 200, 206, 300
Notari It/Cdr: 344
Novaro It/C: 44
Novikov USSR/RA: 113,
Nowell US/LCdr: 403, 432, 449, 472
Noyes US/RA: 226, 238, 249, 254

Oakley US/LCdr: 449
Oba Jap/LCdr: 527
Obata Jap/LG: 438
Obayashi Jap/RA: 415
Obermaier Ger/L-Cdr: 33, 189, 303, 327, 344, 366
O'Connor UK/C: 166
Oddie UK/Cdr: 23
Oehrn Ger/LCdr: 30, 47, 49, 55
Oelrich Ger/L-LCdr: 252, 272, 278, 301, 326
Oesten Ger/LCdr-Cdr: 12-13, 18-19, 37, 44, 75, 86, 95, 416-417, 482
Oesterlin Ger/L: 102
Oestermann Ger/LCdr: 177, 201, 232, 237
Offermann Ger/L: 386-387, 432
Ofstie US/RA: 452, 480
Ogata Jap/Col: 438
Ogawa Jap/Cdr: 178, 200
O'Hare US/L: 185
Ohashi Jap/Cdr: 176, 186-187, 528
Ohlenburg Ger/L: 380, 411, 448
Ohling Ger/L: 383
Ohno Jap/C: 221
O'Kane US/LCdr: 392, 419, 439, 456
Okada Jap/MG: 535
Okamura Jap/G: 532
Okochi Jap/VA: 535
Oktyabrski USSR/VA: 109, 133, 146, 225
Okunevich USSR/L: 117
Olaf Nor/Crown Prince: 518
Oldendorf US/RA-VA: 388, 392, 406, 427, 438, 452, 461, 463, 479, 527
Oldorp Ger/LCdr: 234
Oleynik USSR/C1: 455
Oliva It/DA: 349
Oliver (G. N.) UK/Cre: 350, 420, 514, 520
Oliver (R. D.) UK/C: 154, 212
Olivieri It/Cdr: 159, 204
Olsen US/LCdr: 379, 410
Omori Jap/RA: 156, 204, 221, 235, 263-264, 364
O'Neill US/LCdr: 439, 468
Onishi Jap/RA-VA: 179, 461, 480
Onslow (R. F. J.) UK/C: 43, 205
Onslow (R. G.) UK/Cdr: 219
Onslow UK/C: 382, 438
v. Oostrom-Soede Du/LCdr: 300, 336, 398

Opdenhoff Ger/L-Cdr: 29, 110, 398, 412, 422, 429, 434, 484, 500
Opitz Ger/L-LCdr: 23, 141, 145
Orel USSR/C2-C1: 15, 111, 497
Orita (T.) Jap/C: 335
Orita (Z.) Jap/LCdr-Cdr: 467, 483, 513
Ormsby UK/Cdr: 389
Orthofer Ger/C: 150
Osipov (E. Ja.) USSR/C3-C2: 229, 259, 324, 428
Osipov (S. A.) USSR/L: 111
Ostertag Ger/LCdr: 488
Osugi Jap/RA: 364
Ota Jap/LCdr: 186
Otani Jap/Cdr: 223, 316, 350
Otsuka Jap/LCdr: 346
Otto Ger/LCdr: 354, 378
Outerbridge UK/LCdr: 152
Ouvery UK/LCdr: 11
Ovaskainen Fin/CPO: 139
Oxborrow UK/L: 240
D'Oyly-Hughes UK/C: 33
Ozawa Jap/VA: 159, 163, 166, 178, 187-188, 192, 200-201, 204-205, 414-415, 430, 462-464

Paget UK/MG: 26
Pakholchuk USSR/C1: 229
Pakkala Fin/LCdr: 110, 116, 261
Paladini (A.) It/C: 281
Paladini It/DA-SA: 35, 42
Palles Gr/LCdr: 398
Palliser UK/VA: 366, 383, 393
Palmas It/Cdr: 186
Palmer US/Cre: 537
Palmgren Ger/Cdr*: 447, 488
Panaglotes Gr/LCdr: 390
Pancke Ger/L: 432
Panteleev USSR/RA-VA: 130, 465
Paolucci It/CPO: 36
Paramor UK/Cdr: 360, 371
Paramoshkin USSR/C3: 408, 411
Parduhn Ger/LCdr: 506
Parham US/Cdr: 505
Parker US/LCdr: 343, 347
Parkhomenko USSR/C3: 359
Parks US/LCdr: 209
Parmigiano It/C: 149
Parona It/DA: 52, 153, 166, 189, 201, 228
Parry UK/C-RA: 14, 421
Parry UK/LCdr: 447
Patch US/LG: 443
Patou Fr/Cdr: 412, 447
Patrelli-Campagnone It/LCdr: 289
Patrick US/MG: 480
Patterson UK/C-RA: 100, 421, 538
Patton US/MG-LG: 273, 338-339
Pauckstadt Ger/Cdr: 371
Paul Ger/Cdr: 470, 495
Paulshen Ger/L-LCdr: 104, 128, 155, 165
Pavesi It/RA: 328
Pavlov USSR/L: 445
Peck US/MG: 539
Pekkanen Fin/LCdr: 110, 116-117
Pelly UK/L: 375, 384, 438, 471
Pelosi It/Cdr: 36

Pendleton US/LCdr: 417
Penney UK/MG: 386
Percival UK/LG: 186
Perkins US/LCdr: 410, 468
Persons US/MG: 451
Pervukhin USSR/MG: 172
Perzo Fr/C: 352
Pétain Fr/Ma: 39, 41, 80
Peters (B.) Ger/L: 74
Peters (H.) Ger/Cdr*: 213
Peters (R.) Ger/C: 383
Petersen (C.) Ger/Cdr: 488
Petersen (K.) Ger/LCdr: 310, 332, 343, 360, 411 ↗
Petersen (Kurt) Ger/LCdr: 377, 403, 432
Petersen Ger/M: 77
Petersen US/C: 391, 399
Peterson US/LCdr-Cdr: 306, 343, 456
Petroni It/Cdr: 69, 87, 103
Petrov USSR/LCdr: 121
Petrov USSR/Col-G: 353
Petzel Ger/Cdr: 144, 146
Peuranheimo Fin/LCdr: 134
Pfeffer Ger/LCdr: 234, 352
Phillips (A. J. L.) UK/C: 100
Phillips UK/LCdr: 13
Phillips UK/A: 146, 163-164
Phipps UK/Cdr: 304
Piaczetkowski Pol/LCdr: 257
Piatek Ger/C: 377
Pich Ger/LCdr: 317, 349, 382
Pierce US/Cdr: 522
Piening Ger/LCdr-Cdr: 188, 193, 216, 237, 277, 283, 301, 361, 506
Piers Can/LCdr: 267, 295
Pietsch Ger/LCdr: 310, 444
Pinkepank Ger/Cdr: 488
Piomarta It/Cdr: 48, 83
Piper UK/L: 336, 360, 419
Pierhonen Fin/LCdr: 431
Pisa It/C: 89
Pitt UK/L: 384
Pitułko Pol/Cdr: 301
Le Pivain Fr/C: 41
Pizey (C. T. M.) UK/C: 189
Pizey (E. F.) UK/LCdr-Cdr: 23, 158, 175
Plaice UK/L: 355
Platonov USSR/C1: 116-117
Plomer UK/Cdr: 320
Poel Ger/L-LCdr: 277, 293, 297, 390
Pohle Ger/C: 8
Pokhmelnov USSR/C3: 343
Polacchini It/C: 61
Poland UK/C-Cre: 216, 534
Polizzi It/Cdr: 56
Pollina It/LCdr: 103, 124
Poltavski USSR/C1: 531
Polyakov (A. J.) USSR/SL: 135
Polyakov (E. P.) USSR/C3: 135, 254, 411
Pönitz Ger/C: 169, 179, 203
Ponomarev USSR/C1: 532
Popov USSR/C3: 455
Popp (K.) Ger/LCdr: 279
Popp (P.) Ger/L: 53, 153
Port US/LCdr: 306, 314, 365
Portal UK/C: 58
Porter UK/L: 471, 474

Porter US/LCdr-Cdr: 365, 372, 491, 505
Poser Ger/L-LCdr: 259, 303, 328
Post US/LCdr-Cdr: 347, 479
Poske Ger/Cdr: 188, 219, 261
Potapov USSR/C3: 148, 154, 176, 180, 213
Potthast Ger/Senior Ensign: 435
Pound (Sir Dudley) UK/A: 230, 345
Power (A. J.) UK/RA-A: 279, 348, 350, 382, 407, 411, 425, 460, 470, 486, 534
Power (M. L.) UK/C: 520
Powlett UK/C: 102
Pownall US/RA: 347, 353, 369, 373
Praetorius Ger/LCdr: 177, 213, 222, 246
Prater Ger/LCdr: 488
Prellberg Ger/LCdr: 55, 61
Premauer Ger/LCdr: 506
Preobrazhenski USSR/MG: 459
Preuss Ger/L-LCdr: 19, 123, 142, 170, 218
Pridham-Wippell UK/VA: 43, 63, 70, 74, 89, 94, 97, 102, 155
Priebe Ger/LCdr: 485, 516
Prien Ger/LCdr-Cdr: 2, 8, 12-13, 20, 25-26, 35, 51, 53, 60, 66, 82, 84
Priggione It/LCdr: 299
Prini It/LCdr: 113
Prokofev USSR/LCdr: 361, 408, 411
Protsenko USSR/C2: 352, 380
Proudfoot UK/LCdr: 296
Ptokhov USSR/C1: 12
Puccini It/LCdr: 234, 242
Pullen Can/Cdr: 394
Pulst Ger/LCdr: 454
Pumphrey UK/Cdr: 189
Purkhold Ger/LCdr: 260, 287, 354
Putnam US/LCdr: 472, 496
Puttfarken Ger/Cdr: 433
v. Puttkamer Ger/L: 266, 283
Purvis US/C: 507
v. Pückler und Limburg Ger/LCdr: 267, 291, 326
Pye US/VA: 161, 226

Quaet-Faslem Ger/LCdr: 240, 273
Queck Ger/LCdr: 294
Quedenfeldt Ger/LCdr: 377
Querville Fr/L: 265
Quick US/LCdr: 290, 322
de Quièvrecourt Fr/Cdr: 54

Raccanelli It/Cdr: 56, 70
Raabe Ger/LCdr: 496
Rademacher Ger/LCdr: 469
Radford US/RA: 370, 476, 491, 499, 509, 522, 525, 533
Raeder Ger/GrandA: 296
Ragsdale US/RA: 370, 388, 392, 409, 436-437
Rahe Ger/LCdr: 260
Rahmlow Ger/L: 123
Rahola Fin/C-RA: 134, 312
Raikes UK/L: 152, 198
Rall Ger/Cdr: 447

Rall USSR/RA-VA: 130, 384
Ramage US/LCdr: 259, 290, 432, 468
Ramishvili USSR/C1: 12
Ramsay UK/A: 338, 420, 425
Ramsey (De Witt) US/RA: 291, 335
Ramsey (L. C.) US/C: 378, 394
v. Rappard Ger/LCdr: 505
Rasch Ger/L-LCdr: 145, 182, 215, 261
Rashid El-Gailani Iraq/Minister: 93, 96
Rassokin USSR/Col: 459
Rath Ger/Col: 207
Rathke Ger/LCdr: 213
Raw UK/C: 73
Rawlings US/RA-VA: 69, 74, 88, 102, 155, 471, 486, 501, 516, 526, 530, 533
Rayborn US/LCdr: 396, 410
Rayner UK/LCdr: 270
Read UK/RA: 382, 479, 486
Reche Ger/LCdr: 230, 244, 257, 294, 303
Rechel Ger/Cdr*: 288, 313, 321
Reed US/Cdr: 505
Reeder Ger/LCdr: 247, 250, 285
Rees UK/Cre: 208
Reeves US/RA: 387, 392, 400, 406, 426, 436
Refo US/LCdr: 49
Regensburg Ger/L: 153
Rehwinkel Ger/Cdr: 188, 222
Reich (C.) Ger/LCdr: 360
Reich US/LCdr: 419, 449, 468
v. Reiche Ger/LCdr: 3
Reichenbach-Klinke Ger/L: 239, 285, 290
Reichmann Ger/Cdr: 232
Reid US/RA: 379, 407
Reifsneider US/Cre-RA: 399, 437, 504, 511, 523, 536
Reimann Ger/LCdr: 488
Reimers Ger/L: 496
Reinhold Ger/Cdr: 488-489
Reinicke Ger/C: 460, 470, 485, 497
Reischauer Ger/LCdr: 257
Reith Ger/L: 506
Remus Ger/L: 247, 250, 272
Rendtel Ger/L: 354
v. Rennenkampff Ger/Cdr: 52, 64
Renouf UK/RA: 74
Reordan US/C: 161
Reschke Ger/LCdr: 149-150, 228, 273
Reshetko USSR/LCdr: 445
Revedin It/LCdr: 255
Rhymes US/Cdr: 515
Rice US/LCdr: 209, 259, 343
Riccardi It/A: 69
Richardson US/C: 256
Richardson US/Cre: 504
Richmond UK/Cdr: 212
Richter-Oldekop Ger/Cdr: 515
v. Richthofen Ger/G-ColG: 102, 225
Ridgeway UK/L: 412
Riecken Ger/L: 490
Rieckhoff Ger/Col: 102

Riede Ger/Cdr: 51-53, 64, 288, 367
Riefkohl US/C: 238, 241
Riekberg Ger/LCdr: 450, 505
Rieger Ger/L: 98
Rieve Ger/C: 22
Rigele Ger/Cdr*: 279
Riggs US/RA: 487, 495, 500, 512, 524
Rigoli It/LCdr: 273, 301
Rimington UK/LCdr-Cdr: 34, 73, 86, 104, 107
Rinck Ger/L: 490
Ringelmann Ger/LCdr: 92, 104, 122, 141, 170
Rioult Fr/VA: 274
Risser US/LCdr-Cdr: 372, 396, 410, 429, 522
Ritchie UK/VA: 518
Rivett-Carcac UK/RA: 351
Roach US/Cdr: 379
Robbins US/LCdr: 439, 456, 468
Robert (G.) Fr/A: 336
Roberts Can/MG: 247
Roberts UK/Cdr: 23
Robertson Aus/MG: 537
Robinson US/C: 185
Robson UK/C: 383
Rochefort US/Cdr: 220
Rockey US/MG: 494, 538-539
Rockwell US/RA: 323
Rodig Ger/LCdr: 496
Roeder Ger/L: 201
Rodgers US/RA: 443, 493
Rodluff Ger/LCdr: 297
Rodocannacchi It/C: 158
Roether Ger/LCdr: 344
Rogers US/BG: 535
Rogers US/RA: 537
Rogge Ger/C: 21, 29, 36, 54, 77, 83, 93, 99, 143, 154
Rogowsky Ger/L: 496
v. Roithberg Ger/L-LCdr: 234, 436
Rollmann Ger/LCdr-Cdr: 2, 9, 18, 25, 38, 45, 131, 146, 182, 185, 361
Romanov USSR/C2-C1: 113, 173, 225
Romanowski Pol/Cdr: 352
Romei It/LCdr-Cdr: 39, 63
Rommel Ger/G: 144
Ronarch Fr/C: 38
Roope UK/LCdr: 21
Rooks US/C: 196
Roosevelt US/President: 29, 44, 85, 125, 134, 155, 193, 294, 344, 368, 510
Rören Nor/L: 265, 294
Rosenbaum Ger/LCdr: 82, 88, 242
Rosenberg (G.) Ger/L: 259-260, 299
v. Rosenberg-Gruszczynski Ger/L: 289, 309
Roselli-Lorenzini It/LCdr-Cdr: 87, 103, 349
Rosenow Ger/LCdr: 456, 488
v. Rosenstiel Ger/LCdr: 142, 192, 216
Rosica It/L: 122
Rösing Ger/Cdr: 32, 47, 110

Roskill UK/C: 335
Ross US/LCdr: 296
Rossetto It/LCdr: 312
Rostin Ger/LCdr: 188, 193, 219
Rotas Gr/LCdr: 81, 123
Röther Ger/LCdr: 252, 258, 273, 310
Rouselle It/C: 149, 153
Roussen Gr/LCdr: 306, 323
Rousselot Fr/LCdr-Cdr: 126, 265, 475
Row NZ/BG: 363
Rowland UK/Cdr: 84, 88
Rowley UK/C: 102
Roxburgh UK/L-LCdr: 245, 255, 292, 501
Royal US/RA: 461, 481, 498, 513, 523
Ruble US/LCdr: 432
Ruck-Keene UK/C: 519
v. Ruckteschell Ger/Cdr-C: 37, 200, 210, 214, 236, 291
Ruddock US/RA: 474
Rudel Ger/L: 138
Rudloff Ger/L: 237, 251, 266, 285
Rue Fr/VA: 510, 514
Ruge Ger/C-VA: 1, 5, 22, 316
Ruge Nor/MG: 27, 35
Ruggieri It/Cdr*: 37
Rüggeberg Ger/Cdr: 248
Ruhfus Ger/C: 22
Ruhsenberger US/C: 455, 507
Rumyantsev USSR/C1: 484, 511
Ruppelt Ger/L: 286-287
Rupertus US/MG: 376, 452
Russell UK/LCdr: 59
Russillo US/LCdr: 439
Rutherford Can/LCdr: 252
Rutter US/LCdr: 306, 379
Ryan US/C-Cre: 335, 345, 537
Rybalchenko USSR/LG: 455
Ryder US/MG: 274, 536
Rysegrave UK/LCdr: 362

Saalwächter Ger/A: 22
Saccardo It/LCdr: 260
Safonov USSR/LCol: 220
Saito Jap/LG: 428
Sakharov USSR/ColG: 411
Saki Jap/SL: 463
Sakiyama Jap/C: 205, 224
Sakonju Jap/RA-VA: 383, 418, 462
de Salis UK/C: 132
Sallada US/RA: 428, 438
Salman Ger/LCdr: 38, 46, 66, 77, 92
Salo Fin/LCdr: 431
Salter UK/Cdr: 213
Saltsman US/L: 447
Saltzwedel Ger/Cdr: 213
Salvatori It/Cdr: 83
Samejima Jap/VA: 364, 537
Samokhin USSR/LG: 431
Sample US/RA: 502, 505, 509, 524
Sanderson US/BG: 536
Sands US/LCdr: 296, 322, 336
Sano Jap/LG: 275
Sansonetti It/DA: 35, 40, 42, 67, 69, 89
Sars Nor/L: 384-385, 396

Sasaki (K.) Jap/C: 215
Sasaki (N.) Jap/MG: 355
Sato Jap/RA: 152, 224, 537
Sato Jap/C: 244, 271
Sauer Ger/L: 393
Saunders (L. S.) UK/C: 217
Saunders US/C: 422
Saunders (W. A.) US/LCdr: 198
de Saussine Fr/Cdr: 5, 64
Sautot Fr/Governor: 54
Savin USSR/LCdr: 240, 260
Scanland US/LCdr: 457, 472, 491, 515
Scartchard UK/LCdr: 304
Schaar Ger/L: 383
Schacht Ger/Cdr: 201, 211, 255, 286
Schade US/LCdr: 329, 419
Schäfer Ger/Cdr: 261, 301, 349
Schamong Ger/L: 308, 326
Scheibe Ger/LCdr: 314
Scheller Ger/SL: 451
Schemmel Ger/C: 272, 288
Schendel (E.) Ger/L: 442
Schendel (R.) Ger/LCdr: 164, 175, 270, 279, 318
Schepke Ger/LCdr: 5, 17-18, 21, 47, 53, 60, 65, 69, 85
Schergat It/LCpl: 166
Scheringer Ger/LCdr: 13, 18, 26, 38
Schetelig Ger/L: 305, 315, 354
Schewe Ger/LCdr: 13, 30, 75, 85-86, 95, 131
Schiller Ger/C: 47
Schlech US/LCdr: 495
Schlieper Ger/L: 145
v. Schlippenbach Ger/LCdr: 160, 206, 289, 340, 369
Schlott Ger/L: 505
Schmetz Ger/L: 349
Schmid (H.) Ger/LCdr: 280, 284
Schmidt (H.) US/MG-LG: 428, 438, 536
Schmidt (K.) Ger/SL: 28
Schmidt (K.-D.) Ger/L: 350
Schmidt (M.) Ger/Cdr*: 189, 200, 217
Schmidt (W.-K.) Ger/LCdr: 432
v. Schmidt (W.) Ger/LCdr-Cdr: 7, 217, 234
Schmidt-Weichert Ger/L: 319
Schmoeckel Ger/LCdr: 386, 432
Schmundt Ger/RA: 1, 22, 45
Schnee Ger/L: 47, 49, 55, 96, 99, 125, 137, 208, 234, 236
Schneewind Ger/LCdr: 292, 315, 382, 417
Schneider (H.) Ger/LCdr: 267, 278, 292, 303
Schneider (W.) Ger/L: 252
Schneider Ger/L: 447
Schneider (W. E.) Ger/LCdr: 431
Schneidewind (H.) Ger/Cdr: 490
Schneidewind (P.) Ger/LCdr-C: 200, 210, 303
Schniewind Ger/GA: 230
Schnoor Ger/LCdr: 251, 357
Schoeni US/LCdr: 372
Schöler Ger/L: 353
Scholtz Ger/LCdr-Cdr: 82, 91-92, 104, 114, 167, 182, 211, 236-237

Schomburg (H.) Ger/L: 229, 234, 258
Schomburg (O.) Ger/Cdr*: 1
Schonder Ger/L-LCdr: 44, 46, 58, 104, 167, 177, 225, 238
Schöneboom Ger/L: 294, 310
v. Schönermark Ger/Cdr*-C: 48, 77, 109, 116, 204
Schreiber Ger/LCdr: 66, 70, 82, 92, 118, 154
Schrewe Ger/LCdr: 403, 417
Schröder Ger/Cdr: 488
Schroeder (W.) Ger/Cdr: 22, 116
Schroeter (K.-E.) Ger/L-LCdr: 129, 151, 208, 234, 236, 326
v. Schroeter (H.) Ger/L: 287, 314
Schröter Ger/L: 248
Schuch Ger/Cdr: 123, 185, 201, 265
Schug Ger/LCdr: 177, 209, 240
Schuhart Ger/LCdr: 2-3, 10, 20, 32, 55
Schüler Ger/L-LCdr: 104, 119, 128, 283
Schulte (M.) Ger/L-LCdr: 18, 30
Schulte (W.) Ger/LCdr: 177, 209, 234, 236, 258, 260
Schultz (G.) Ger/Cdr: 377
Schultz (K.-O.) Ger/LCdr: 257-258
Schultze (H.-O.) Ger/L-LCdr: 131, 142, 145, 188, 213, 254, 283
Schultze (H.) Ger/LCdr: 2, 8, 12-13, 18, 25, 77, 88, 104, 110
Schultze (W.) Ger/LCdr: 253
Schulz (G.) Ger/C: 489
Schulz (W.) Ger/LCdr: 49, 59, 70, 82, 85
Schulze (G.) Ger/LCdr: 27
Schulze (W.) Ger/Cdr: 240
Schulze-Hinrichs Ger/C: 116, 213
Schümann Ger/L: 376
Schumann-Hindenberg Ger/Cdr: 490, 505
Schünemann Ger/LCdr: 266
Schütz Ger/C: 164, 379
Schütze (H.-V.) Ger/LCdr: 237, 246
Schütze (V.) Ger/Cdr: 9, 18, 24, 55, 65, 77, 95, 114
Schwaff Ger/L: 504
Schwankte Ger/L: 261, 303
Schwarz Ger/L: 506
Schwebke Ger/LCdr: 496
Schweichel Ger/L: 277
Schweiger Ger/L-LCdr: 384, 401, 451, 498, 514
Scott (J. A.) US/LCdr: 296, 306, 401, 410
Scott (N.) US/RA: 238, 249, 254, 263, 269, 271, 275-276
Scott-Moncrieff UK/C: 302, 326
Seale UK/LCdr: 21, 23, 28
Sears Nor/L: 366
Seeger Ger/L: 490
Seehausen Ger/L: 387
Seibicke Ger/LCdr-Cdr: 203, 213, 266, 291, 325
Seidel Ger/LCdr: 402
Seifert Ger/Cdr: 425

Seitz US/C: 516
Selby US/LCdr: 372, 390, 410, 439
Sellars US/L: 259
Senkel Ger/LCdr: 245, 247
Servaes UK/RA: 535
Settle US/RA: 539
Shafroth US/RA: 522, 525, 529-530
Shapalin USSR/SL-L: 134, 142, 345
Sharp US/RA: 502
Shaw UK/L-LCdr: 429, 433, 447
Shchedrin USSR/C3-C2: 319, 331, 385, 436, 450
Shcherbakov USSR/ColG: 459
Shea US/LCdr: 457, 514
Shean UK/L: 396
Shelby (E. E.) US/LCdr: 392, 432, 449, 468
Shelby (W. H.) UK/Cdr: 294
Shepard US/LCdr: 468, 479
Shepherd US/MG: 437, 504, 539
Sherbrooke UK/C: 287-288
Sherman US/C-RA: 214, 290, 364, 370, 377, 387, 392, 448, 458, 461-462, 465-467, 474, 476, 491, 499, 509, 522, 537
Sherwood UK/L: 425, 438, 473-474
Sherwood (R. E.) UK/LCdr: 320
Shestakov USSR/SL: 125
Shevchenko USSR/LCdr-C2: 222, 359
Shevtsov USSR/LCdr: 157
Shibasaki Jap/RA: 370
Shibata Jap/Cdr*: 162
Shigematsu Jap/MG: 437-438
Shigemitsu Jap/Foreign Minister: 535
Shiizuka Jap/LCdr: 452
Shima Jap/RA-VA: 179, 214, 459, 462-463
Shimai Jap/C: 336
Shimizu Jap/LCdr-Cdr: 383, 528
Shimose Jap/Cdr: 258
Shmelov USSR/C1: 442
Shock US/C: 183
Short US/C-Cre: 307, 311, 320, 326, 329, 539
Shuyski USSR/C3: 240, 295, 331
Sibert US/MG: 439, 461, 536
Sibille It/SL: 330
Sickel Ger/LCdr: 343, 400
Siebert US/MG: 487, 512
Sieder Ger/L: 424
Sieglaff US/LCdr: 290, 314, 329, 365, 379, 396
Siegmann Ger/LCdr: 305, 325, 386, 414
Siemon Ger/L: 230
Siegel Ger/LCol. 143, 228
Simeon UK/C: 24
Simmermacher Ger/L-LCdr: 338, 371, 416
Simmonds Can/MG: 338
Simpson UK/Cdr: 73
Simpson US/C: 391
Simpson US/LCdr: 495
Simonov USSR/C2: 114
Sims UK/C: 165
Sislet US/LCdr: 358

Sivenko USSR/L: 311
Sladen UK/Cdr: 124, 139, 148, 193, 210
Slaughter UK/LCdr: 23
Slepenko USSR/LCol: 497
Small US/RA: 427, 431
Smart UK/L: 529
Smedberg US/Cdr: 232
Smith (A. C.) US/Cdr: 505
Smith (A. E.) US/RA: 214, 221, 448, 457, 466, 473, 482, 487
Smith (C. C.) US/Cdr: 164, 181, 215, 222
Smith (F. T.) US/LCdr-Cdr: 491, 496, 515, 526
Smith (H. M.) US/MG-LG: 388, 427, 493
Smith (R.) US/MG: 370
Sobe Ger/Cdr*: 261
Sobottka Ger/L: 318
v. Soden-Frauenhofen Ger/L-LCdr: 266, 278, 296
Sohler Ger/LCdr: 7-8, 15, 26
Söiland Nor/LCdr: 262
Solodovnikov USSR/LCdr: 498
Solovev USSR/C1: 112
Somerville UK/VA-A: 38, 41, 43, 50, 63, 65, 67, 77-78, 91, 94, 97, 100-101, 120, 122, 128, 140, 144, 150, 204-205, 239, 382, 399, 407, 411, 438, 442
Sommer Ger/LCdr: 412
Sonnemann Ger/Cdr: 488
Sonneville Fr/L: 94
Sowell US/Cdr: 413
Spagone It/Cdr: 83
Spahr Ger/LCdr: 373
Spanides Gr/SL: 71
Spano It/Cdr: 36
Sparzani It/C: 88
Spasié Yu/LCdr: 91
Speer Ger/Armaments Minister: 328
Spender UK/L: 438, 453, 474
Sperrle Ger/FMa: 189
v. Sponeck Ger/LG: 172
Sprague (A. T.) US/C: 503
Sprague (C. A. F.) US/RA: 461, 463-464, 521, 533
Sprague (T. L.) US/RA: 451, 460, 525, 533
Sprice UK/L: 280, 286, 313, 323
Spruance US/RA-A: 168, 183, 190, 207, 221, 224, 369, 388, 392, 400, 426, 430, 491, 493, 499, 503, 517
Staats Ger/LCdr: 245, 265, 333
Stahl Ger/L: 362, 369
Staley US/LCdr: 432, 468
Stalin USSR/Ma: 158
Stange Ger/C: 218, 285, 288
Stanley UK/L: 261, 267, 293, 300
Starikov (F. N.) USSR/LG: 455
Starikov (V. G.) USSR/LCdr-C3: 139, 152, 180, 191, 209, 295
Stark US/A: 425
Steen Ger/C: 138
Stein Ger/LCdr: 262, 292
v. Steinaecker Ger/LCdr: 281. 308
Steinert Ger/LCdr: 322
Steinhoff Ger/LCdr: 250

Steinmetz US/Cdr: 522
Stelter Ger/Cdr: 353, 407
Stemmler Ger/LCol: 473, 492
Stengel Ger/L: 310
Stephan US/Cdr: 266, 289, 306, 322
Sternberg Ger/LCdr: 400
Stevens (C. B.) US/LCdr: 419, 449, 472
Stevens (E. B. K.) UK/C: 33, 313
Stevens (J. E.) US/Cdr: 468
Stevens US/LCdr: 419
Stevens (J. S.) UK/L: 255, 263, 273, 284, 292, 300, 323
Stevens Aus/MG: 520
Stevenson Aus/BG: 536
Stevenson (W. A.) US/LCdr-Cdr: 329, 392, 410, 432, 456
Sthamer Ger/L: 401, 445
Stichling Ger/C: 135, 139
Steibler Ger/L: 18, 55
Stiegler Ger/LCdr: 258
Stimson US/LCdr-Cdr: 479, 496, 526
Stilwell US/G: 536
St. John UK/LCdr: 251, 323
Stock (H.) Ger/LCdr: 252, 270
Stock (R.) Ger/LCdr: 387, 506
v. Stockhausen Ger/LCdr: 25-26, 38, 51, 53, 65
Stoelker Ger/L: 481
Stöffler Ger/LCdr: 432, 450
Stoffregen Ger/Cdr: 231
Stohwasser Ger/L: 318
Stokes UK/Cdr-C: 158, 165
Stolbov USSR/LCdr-C3: 115, 144, 192, 240
Stone US/LCdr: 358
Stone (L. T.) US/LCdr: 358, 410, 432
Stonehouse UK/LCdr: 320
Stones US/LCdr: 396
Storp Ger/2L: 6
Stovall US/LCdr: 237, 266, 396, 419
Sträter Ger/LCdr: 297
Strecker Ger/LCdr: 217
Street US/Cdr: 495, 522
Strelow Ger/LCdr: 203, 208, 244, 257, 287, 309
Strempel Ger/Cdr*: 304, 353
Strizhak USSR/C3: 441
Strömer Ger/LCdr: 485
Struble US/RA: 473-474, 487-488, 500, 514, 520, 535
Struckmann Ger/L: 424, 435
Struckmeier Ger/L-LCdr: 252, 272, 310
Studenichnikov USSR/C1: 531
Studholme UK/LCdr: 23
Studt Ger/LCdr: 403
v. Studnitz Ger/C: 139
Stump US/RA: 461, 463, 480, 502
Sturdee Aus/LG: 537
Sturm Ger/Cdr: 258, 262, 308, 312
Sturr US/LCdr: 457, 491
Styler US/G: 535
Styles US/LCdr: 505
Sugamasa Jap/Cdr: 513, 521
Sugayoshi Jap/L: 483
Sugiura Jap/C: 341

Suhren Ger/L-LCdr: 108, 114, 125, 145, 182, 213, 236, 244, 247
Sukhomlinov USSR/LCdr-C3: 158, 218, 240
Sukhodolski USSR/LCdr: 437
Sukhoruchenko USSR/C1: 132
Summers US/LCdr: 449, 491
Suñer Sp/Foreign Minister: 54
Sushkin USSR/LCdr-C3: 310, 319, 345
Suzuki (S.) Jap/LG: 466
Suzuki (S.) Jap/LCdr-Cdr: 483, 527, 536
Suzuki Jap/VA: 414
Svetlov USSR/LCdr: 134
Svyatov USSR/C2-RA: 110, 130, 158, 455
Sweeney US/M: 529
Swenson US/C: 276
Swift US/MG: 480, 536
Swing US/MG: 487, 532, 536
Syfret UK/RA-VA: 120, 197, 199, 202-203, 212, 242, 274

Tabata Jap/LCdr: 370
Tabata Jap/Cdr*:162
Tachibana Jap/LG: 536
Tagami Jap/Cdr*: 192, 219, 251, 311, 341
Tague US/C: 416, 432
Tait UK/Cdr: 293, 307
Takagi Jap/RA-VA: 160, 169, 177, 181, 184, 186, 191, 194-196, 214, 221, 235
Takahashi Jap/VA: 162, 170, 194, 196
Takama Jap/RA: 235, 252, 263-264, 268, 271, 275
Takashima Jap/LG: 437
Takasu Jap/VA: 221, 235, 383
Taketomi Jap/L: 521
Talbot UK/RA: 351, 420
Talbot US/Cdr: 182
Tamman USSR/C3: 289, 295, 345
Tamura Jap/RA: 537
Tanabe Jap/L-LCdr: 224, 264
Tanaka (M.) Jap/Cdr: 259, 280, 346
Tanaka (R.) Jap/RA: 169, 171, 177, 184, 191, 194, 221, 235, 244, 249, 254, 263-264, 271, 275, 277, 282-283, 286, 290
De Tar US/LCdr: 198, 209, 306
Tarchioni It/LCdr: 314
Taschenmacher Ger/L: 469
Tattersall UK/L: 433, 453
Taylor (A. H.) US/LCdr: 248, 273
Taylor (C. W.) UK/LCdr: 28
Taylor UK/L: 419, 430, 453
Techand Ger/L: 355
Tedder UK/ACM: 338, 420
Teichert Ger/LCdr: 203, 213, 230, 245, 295, 297, 325
Teichmann Ger/L-LCdr: 407, 488
Teidemann US/LCdr: 402, 432, 449, 468
Temming Ger/LCdr: 485, 515
Tennant UK/C-RA: 100, 164, 227, 255

Teppati It/Cdr: 75
Teramoto Jap/LCdr: 467, 483
Teraoka Jap/VA: 459, 461
Terauchi Jap/FMa: 534
Terekhin USSR/LCdr: 209
Terra It/LCdr: 103
Terraux Fr/RA: 76
Tesei It/M: 121
Teshima Jap/LG: 538
Thebaud US/C-RA: 136, 142, 388
Theobald US/RA: 221, 226, 293
Thiele Ger/C-RA: 22, 455, 470, 485
Thienemann Ger/C: 301, 470, 485
Thilo Ger/Cdr: 272
Thimme Ger/L: 498
Thoma Ger/Cdr: 22
Thomas UK/Cdr: 40
Thomas (W. M.) US/LCdr: 336, 347
Thompson UK/SqL: 123
Thompson (W. E.) US/LCdr: 410, 432, 456
Thomsen Ger/LCdr: 469, 496
Thurmann Ger/LCdr-Cdr: 104, 142, 177, 213, 238, 247, 288
Tibbets US/Col: 529
v. Tiesenhausen Ger/L: 141, 155, 209
Tillessen Ger/LCdr: 361, 416
Timm Ger/LCdr: 213, 230, 244, 417, 470
Tinschert Ger/LCdr: 321
Tisdale US/RA: 238, 249, 269, 290
Tobias Ger/Cdr-Cdr*: 112, 134, 191
Todaro It/Cdr: 56, 73
Todenhagen Ger/L: 472
Togami Jap/Cdr: 162, 181, 183
Tokioka Jap/L: 528
Tokunaga Jap/LCdr: 487
Tokutomi Jap/LCdr: 251
Tomkinson UK/L-Cdr: 90, 115, 129, 145, 165, 206
Tomonaga Jap/LCdr: 224
Tona It/Cdr*: 245
Töniges Ger/L-LCdr: 39, 42, 81, 87, 225, 242, 251-252
Tonozuka Jap/Cdr*-C: 193, 206, 316, 349
Topp (E.) Ger/L-Cdr: 44, 46, 49, 82, 92, 104, 125, 131, 135, 147, 177, 201, 226, 234, 238
Topp (K.) Ger/C: 139, 198, 231
Torisu Jap/Cdr: 246, 258
Toscano It/DA: 158
Tosoni-Pittoni It/Cdr: 34, 36, 50, 70
Tovey UK/VA-A: 36, 39-40, 43, 68, 76, 100, 149, 193, 198, 212, 230
Toyoda Jap/A: 400, 430, 462
Trampedach Ger/Cdr: 19
Trautloft Ger/M: 207
Travkin USSR/C3: 229, 259, 324, 490
v. Treuberg Ger/L: 314
Tributs USSR/Flag 2-A: 12, 109, 130, 384
Triebel US/LCdr: 336, 347, 365, 379

Tripolski USSR/LCdr-C1: 13, 259, 438-439
Trofimov (E. N.) USSR/LCdr: 343
Trofimov (I. J.) USSR/LCdr: 284, 368
Trojer Ger/L-LCdr: 257, 262, 282, 307, 309, 325
v. Trotha (C.) Ger/LCdr: 317, 333
v. Trotha (W.) Ger/LCdr: 432, 484
Troubridge UK/Cre-RA: 273, 338, 340, 386, 444, 453
Trummer Ger/Cdr: 340, 373
Truscott US/MG: 339, 385, 443
Tsukahara Jap/VA: 162
Tsukigata Jap/L: 494
Tsurikov USSR/LCdr: 218
Tucci It/Cdr: 52
Tucker US/C: 403
Tünemann Ger/C: 158, 318
Turaev USSR/C3-C2: 259, 426, 459
Turcio It/LCdr: 340
Turnage US/MG: 363, 437
Turner (E. J. D.) UK/L: 300, 313, 352
Turner (G. H. B.) UK/LCdr: 438, 453, 473
Turner (H. B.) UK/L: 292, 300, 336
Turner UK/L: 453
Turner (J. H.) US/LCdr: 439, 456
Turner (R. K.) US/RA-VA: 238, 241, 254-255, 263, 274-276, 334, 370, 388, 427, 493, 504
Tyree US/LCdr-Cdr: 322, 336, 379, 491, 514, 522
Tyson UK/Cdr: 393, 445

Uchida Jap/G: 539
Uchino Jap/C: 295, 316, 347
Ueno Jap/Cdr: 164
Ugaki Jap/VA: 316, 414, 418, 499, 503, 511
Uhl Ger/L: 424
Uhlig Ger/LCdr: 305, 310
Ulbricht Ger/M: 90
Ulstrup Nor/Cdr: 92
Umezu Jap/G: 535
Underwood US/LCdr: 439, 468, 479
Unger di Lowenberg It/Cdr: 104
Uno Jap/Cdr: 235, 416
Unrug Pol/RA: 1, 7
Uphoff Ger/L-LCdr: 131, 146, 177, 208, 232, 267, 316
Urquhart UK/B: 338
Urvoy de Porzamparc Fr/C: 31
Ushijama Jap/LG: 504, 524
Ustinov USSR/C3: 151
Utke Ger/C: 6
Utkin USSR/C3: 124, 133
Utsuki Jap/Cdr-Cdr*: 164, 206, 311
Uzumi Jap/VA: 534

Valdambrini It/Cdr*: 282
Valenza It/SL: 90
Valkenburg Du/LCdr: 238, 266
val Valkenburgh US/C: 161

della Valle It/C: 265
del Valle US/MG: 504
Valvatne Nor/LCdr: 486, 501
Vandergrift US/MG: 241
Vanifatev USSR/C1:132
Van Leunen US/LCdr: 396
Vannutelli It/Cdr: 62
Varley UK/L: 419, 433
v. Varendorff Ger/L: 213, 238
Vasilev USSR/LCdr: 414, 446
Vdovichenko USSR/C2-RA: 15, 110, 124
Vedel Da/VA: 346
Vekke USSR/C3: 191, 219
Verbizki USSR/C3: 155
Verlohr Ger/Cdr: 362, 449, 470
Vershinin USSR/LCdr: 15
Vershinin USSR/ColG: 411
Vesey-Holt UK/VA: 518
Vest US/C: 403, 416
Vetchinkin USSR/C3: 455, 482
Viale It/M: 257
Vian UK/C-VA: 19, 28, 60, 101, 121, 127, 157, 163, 165-166, 176, 180, 183, 189, 200-202, 227, 338, 350, 420, 469, 471, 473, 479, 486, 501, 516, 526, 530
Victor Emmanuel III It/King: 342
Vidyaev USSR/LCdr-C3: 204, 240, 319
Vinogradov (A. D.) USSR/C2: 119
Vinogradov (N. I.) USSR/C1-RA: 109, 154, 298
Vishnevski USSR/LCdr-C3: 137, 229
Vivian UK/RA: 28, 31, 33
Vladimirski USSR/RA-VA: 138, 155, 176, 180, 197, 202, 225, 260, 281, 297
Vlasov USSR/LCdr-C3: 149, 173, 218
Vocaturo It/LCdr: 99
Voelcker UK/C: 362
Voge US/LCdr: 197, 232
Vogel Ger/LCdr: 179, 213
Vogeler US/MG: 488
Vogler Ger/LCdr: 341
Vogelsang Ger/LCdr: 140, 185, 233, 237, 268
Voigt Ger/L: 454
Volkov USSR/LCdr: 437
Vollheim Ger/LCdr: 351
Voltersvik Nor/LCdr: 262
Vorkov USSR/C3: 222, 252
Voss Ger/LCdr: 488
Vosseller US/C: 403, 416, 432
Vowe Ger/L: 253, 279
Vuorensaari Fin/L: 279

Wächter Ger/LCdr: 296, 302, 325, 353, 369
Wada Ger/LCdr: 381
Wagner Ger/SL: 121
Wahlen Ger/L: 343, 360, 402, 411
Wainwright US/G: 193, 209
Wake-Walker UK/RA-VA: 32, 100, 120, 127
v. Waldegg Ger/L: 403, 417
Waldhausen Ger/PO: 435
Waldron US/LCdr: 224
Wales US/LCdr: 322, 347

Walker (F. J.) UK/Cdr-C: 167-168, 210, 226, 328, 332, 362, 371-372, 389, 400-401
Walker (F. D.) US/LCdr: 402, 432
Walker (F. R.) US/C: 355
Walker (H. T. C.) UK/VA: 486, 494, 510, 514, 520, 528, 534
Walker (W. W.) US/LCdr: 456
Walker US/MG: 350
Walkerling Ger/LCdr: 252, 309
Waller Aus/C: 89, 196
Walling US/LCdr: 419
Walsh US/LCdr: 250
v. Wangenheim Ger/C: 490
Wanklyn UK/LCdr: 77-78, 95, 103, 115, 119, 127, 135, 149, 175, 186, 198, 200, 210
Warburton-Lee UK/C: 24
Ward (N. G.) US/LCdr: 329, 358, 388, 432, 449
Ward (R. E. M.) US/LCdr: 372, 439
Ward (W. R.) UK/L: 81
Warder US/LCdr: 206, 222, 238, 266
Wards UK/LCdr: 80, 84, 104, 111
Warning Ger/LCdr: 64
Wassmuth Ger/Cdr: 488, 515
Watanabe Jap/Cdr-Cdr*: 181, 235
Waterhouse UK/LCdr: 262
Waterman US/LCdr: 396
Wätjen Ger/L: 497
Watkins (B.) UK/LCdr: 55, 58, 69
Watkins (F. T.) US/C: 336
Watson (B. C.) UK/R-VA: 5, 267
Watson (A. P.) US/Col: 452
Watson (T. E.) US/MG: 428, 438
Wattenberg Ger/Cdr*: 211, 244, 247
Waugh US/LCdr: 468
Waue Ger/Cdr: 3
Wavell UK/G: 93, 175
Webb US/Cdr: 136, 147
Weber (H.) Ger/SL-L: 110, 112, 228-229, 243, 300
Weber (R.) Ger/C: 467
Weber (W.) Ger/Cdr: 386, 395
Wedemeyer Ger/LCdr: 441, 464
Wegener Ger/M: 257
Wehrkamp Ger/L: 496
Weingaertner Ger/LCdr: 35
Weinlig Ger/LCdr: 362, 485, 515
Weiss US/LCdr: 379, 410, 432
Weissenborn Ger/L: 367
Weitz Ger/L: 393, 409
Welchel US/LCdr: 379, 432
Wellborn US/C: 308
van Well Groeneveld Du/LCdr: 167, 182
Wellner Ger/LCdr: 8
Wells UK/VA: 9, 27
Wemyss UK/Cdr: 362
Wendler Ger/L-LCdr: 282, 507
Wendt Ger/C: 317
Wendt (W.) Ger/L: 400
Wennecker Ger/C: 1

Wenninger Ger/C: 485
Weston UK/L-LCdr: 384, 419, 446
Westphalen Ger/L: 401, 442, 492 498, 514
Wetjen Ger/L: 104
Weyher Ger/Cdr*-C: 22, 37, 48, 67, 128, 380, 403, 407
Weyler US/RA: 461, 471, 479
Wheland US/LCdr: 432, 456
Whitaker US/LCdr: 379, 402, 419, 449
White UK/Cre: 309
White UK/LCdr: 137
White US/LCdr: 176, 410
Whitehead Aus/B: 513
Whitehead US/MG: 495, 498
Whiteway-Wilkinson UK/L: 118
Whiting US/RA: 492
Whitton UK/L: 313, 323, 336, 396
Whitworth UK/VA: 12, 21, 23, 25
Wichmann Ger/L: 341, 343
Wickler Ger/L: 315
Wiebe Ger/Cdr: 253, 264, 299
Wieboldt Ger/L: 464, 472
Wiegand Ger/Cdr: 489
v. Wilamowitz-Moellendorf Ger/LCdr: 211, 261, 299
Wilcke (H.) Ger/Cdr: 189, 236, 239, 265
Wilcke (F.-W.) Ger/L: 157
Wilcox US/RA: 203
Wilkes US/A: 425
Wilhelmina Du/Queen: 30
Wilkie UK/LCdr: 422, 434
Wilkins US/LCdr: 198, 237, 456
Wilkinson US/RA-VA: 345, 363, 391, 452, 461, 480, 536
Will Ger/L: 472
William-Powlett UK/C: 377
Williams (H.) UK/C: 518
Williams (J. W.) US/LCdr-Cdr: 379, 419, 526
Williams (R. R.) US/LCdr: 449, 472
Williams UK/WCdr: 218
Williamson (D. F.) US/LCdr: 456
Williamson (K.) UK/LCdr: 63
Willingham US/LCdr: 209, 215, 238, 266, 284, 347
Willis UK/VA: 204, 333, 339, 351
Willmott UK/LCdr: 141, 158-159
Willoch Nor/Cdr*: 24
Wilson UK/LCdr: 279
Wiltse US/RA: 387
Wimberley UK/MG: 338
Windeyer Can/Cdr: 286
Wing US/MG: 480, 536
Wingfield UK/L: 240
Wingfield (M. R. G.) UK/LCdr: 300, 313, 323, 400, 412
Winkelmann Ger/L: 451
Winner UK/LCdr: 362
Winter Ger/LCdr: 138, 182, 215
v. Winterfeldt Ger/M: 102
Wintermeyer Ger/LCdr: 305
de Winton UK/C: 382
Wissmann Ger/L-LCdr: 261, 300
Witt Ger/LCdr-Cdr: 223, 265, 314
de Witt US/RA: 335

Witte (H.) Ger/LCdr: 219, 224, 261, 272, 312
Witte (W.) Ger/L-LCdr: 270, 299
v. Witzendorff Ger/L: 320
Wogan US/LCdr-Cdr: 296, 344, 468
Wohlfahrth Ger/L-LCdr: 18-20, 55, 58, 65, 96, 99, 101, 108
Woldag Ger/C: 22
Wolfbauer Ger/Cdr: 244, 295
Wolff (K.-H.) Ger/Cdr: 234
Wolff (M.-E.) Ger/C: 348
Wolfram Ger/LCdr: 64, 317
Wolters Ger/Cdr: 407
Wood UK/MG: 534
Woodhouse UK/C: 14
Woodruff US/MG: 512, 537
Woods UK/LCdr: 128, 136, 145, 153
Woodward UK/L: 118, 129, 135, 175, 198, 200, 237
Wootten Aus/MG: 523
Worthington US/Cdr: 495
Wraith UK/L: 135-136, 165, 214, 291, 300
Wrampe Ger/L: 344
Wright (C. H.) US/RA: 282
Wright (J. P.) UK/C: 189
Wright (W. H.) US/LCdr: 419
Wright (W. L.) US/LCdr: 183, 206
Wünning Ger/LCdr: 124, 136
Wuppermann Ger/L: 109, 112, 228
Würdemann Ger/LCdr: 211, 241, 255, 299
Wurtsmith US/BG-MG: 495, 498, 504
Wylie US/LCdr: 314, 336, 365

Yamada (K.) Jap/Cdr*: 223
Yamada (T.) Jap/Cdr*: 223
Yamada (T.) Jap/Cdr: 295
Yamada Jap/LG: 538
Yamaguchi (T.) Jap/RA-VA: 178, 181, 204, 220, 224, 537
Yamaguchi Jap/LCdr: 370
Yamamoto Jap/A: 134, 220-221, 224, 235, 244, 316
Yamamura Jap/MG: 538
Yamashiro Jap/C: 335
Yamashita Jap/LG-G: 166, 187, 482, 535
Yamazaki Jap/Col: 323
Yamazaki Jap/RA: 152, 219, 249
Yanagimoto Jap/C: 224
Yanson USSR/C2: 129
Yaroshevich USSR/C3: 259, 455, 497, 512
Yendo Jap/Cdr: 164
Yock UK/L: 447
Yokota Jap/Cdr*: 152, 162, 219, 249, 276, 311
Yoshimatsu Jap/Cdr: 178, 193
Yoshimura Jap/Cdr*: 215, 271
Yoshitome Jap/Cdr: 167, 177, 188
Yoshitome Jap/RA: 176, 239
Young UK/L: 400, 438, 471
Young US/C: 276
Yumashev USSR/A: 530-531
Yunakov USSR/C2: 259

Zaage Ger/Cdr: 488
Zabriskie US/LCdr: 410
Zahn Ger/LCdr: 9, 12, 15, 135, 188
Zaidulin USSR/C3: 47
Zander Ger/LCdr: 395
Zannoni It/C: 154
Zapp Ger/Cdr: 114, 117, 139, 178, 209
da Zara It/DA: 228, 349
Zaruba USSR/C2: 173
v. Zatorski Ger/Cdr: 282
Zech Ger/LCdr: 304
Zeplin Ger/L: 424
Zepos Gr/L: 87

Zetzsche Ger/LCdr: 184, 285, 287, 305
Zhdanov USSR/Party Secretary: 6
Zhdanov (A. S.) USSR/LCdr: 135, 254
Zhukov (A. A.) USSR/C3: 148
Zhukov (G. V.) USSR/RA: 124
Zieb Ger/RA: 448
Zimmermann (E.) Ger/L: 403
Zimmermann (H.) Ger/LCdr: 184, 208, 234
Zimmermann (W.) Ger/L: 32
Zimmermann Ger/LCdr: 434, 439

Zinovev USSR/C1: 150
v. Zitzewitz Ger/LCdr: 262, 315, 317
Zoller Ger/L: 401, 451, 496
Zorn Ger/L: 375, 378
Zschech Ger/LCdr: 265
Zubkov USSR/C2: 222
Zurmuehlen US/C: 512
Zurmühlen Ger/LCdr: 243, 246, 281, 302, 309
Zymalkowski Ger/LCdr-Cdr: 224, 366, 391, 394, 398, 405, 412, 422, 434, 440, 484, 486
Zyuzin USSR/C: 459

Miscellaneous Listings

AIRCRAFT

Abbreviations used.
B   Bomber
BR   Bomber/Reconnaissance
DB   Dive Bomber
F   Fighter
FB   Fighter/Bomber
R   Reconnaissance
S   Seaplane
TB   Torpedo/Bomber

Airacobra US/F: 319, 404, 426
Albacore UK/TB: 78, 80, 107, 121, 144, 198, 218, 385
Ar 196 Ger/S: 324, 418
Avenger US/TB: 224, 326, 337, 359, 401, 412, 416-417, 432, 445, 470, 479, 486, 520, 523
B17 US/B: 133, 162, 223-224, 244, 252, 254, 258, 269, 276, 282, 290, 293, 296-298, 306, 311, 318, 322, 327, 332, 342, 358, 363, 366, 371, 378, 392, 395, 419, 454, 498, 501, 504
B18A US/B: 253
B24 US/B: see Liberator
B25 US/B: 207, 466
B26 US/B: 224
B29 US/B: 442, 458, 476, 482, 487, 495, 504, 508, 529
BV138 Ger/R: 203, 244, 294, 338, 343, 380, 401, 426
BV222 Ger/R: 357, 363, 368, 371, 373, 375
Bachstelze Ger/Helicopter: 315
Baltimore US/B: 418
Barracuda UK/TB: 410-411, 425, 437, 444
Battle UK/FB: 50
Beaufighter UK/TB: 218, 242, 318, 331, 355, 360, 369, 385, 387, 394, 397, 413, 418-419, 423, 428, 435, 446, 450-451, 515
Beaufort UK/TB: 91, 107, 218, 228, 314
Blenheim UK/B: 2, 4, 12, 20, 61,

106, 113, 150, 188, 199, 205, 218
Boston US/B: 331, 358, 414
Buffalo US/FB: 168
CR42 It/F: 51, 97
Canso It/R: 320, 419
Cant It/R: 90
Catalina US/BR: 101, 119, 123, 145, 159, 205, 231, 250-251, 260, 262, 269-270, 282, 286, 298, 301, 315, 317, 320, 325, 331-332, 382, 387, 393, 397, 415, 417, 419, 445, 506, 519
Condor Ger/BR: see FW200
Corsair US/F: 401, 410, 412, 425, 438, 444, 470, 479, 486
Do17 Ger/B: 102
Do18 Ger/R: 13
Do217 Ger/T: 323, 346, 349, 351, 367
DB-3 USSR/B: 111, 319, 331
Dauntless US/FB: 359, 412
Digby US/B: 267
Emily Jap/FB: 185
FW190 Ger/F: 331
FW200 Ger/BR: 61-62, 64-65, 75, 77, 79, 81-83, 87-88, 91, 93, 96, 109, 114, 119, 122, 124-125, 132, 137, 141, 148, 167-168, 198, 226, 339, 363, 369, 373, 375, 389, 391, 393, 401
Firefly UK/BR: 486, 523
Flying Fortress US/B: see B17
Fulmar UK/F: 63, 90, 94, 97, 121, 137, 205
G42 It/B: 242
Gladiator UK/F: 27, 30
He111 Ger/B: 6-7, 19, 21, 24, 29, 77, 86, 91, 101, 207, 220, 222, 230, 242-243, 344, 367
He115 Ger/R: 8, 49-50, 65, 230, 256, 294, 426
He177 Ger/B: 346, 369, 372, 381, 389
Halifax UK/B: 85, 206, 214, 298, 332
Hampden UK/B: 6, 21, 25-26, 245, 331
Hellcat US/F: 401, 412, 470, 479, 486, 520
Hudson US/B: 7, 107, 123, 188, 211, 267, 282, 325, 356-357
Hurricane UK/F: 31, 46, 65, 73,

90, 94, 98, 101, 106-107, 113, 121-122, 127, 134, 150, 179, 188, 205, 219, 220, 226
Il-2 USSR/F: 404, 426, 450, 530
Il-4 USSR/F: 414, 426, 530
Ju87 Ger/DB: 1, 28, 30, 42, 45, 50, 74, 81-82, 97-98, 102, 114, 138, 143, 147, 150, 175, 207, 218, 223, 227-228, 232, 236, 242-243, 257, 289, 302, 327, 356, 359, 367
Ju88 Ger/B: 6-8, 21, 24, 26, 30-32, 50, 89, 101-103, 107, 110, 117-119, 123, 125, 130, 148, 176, 183, 198, 203, 207-208, 216-217, 220, 225, 228, 242-243, 272, 302-303, 313, 331-332, 346, 356, 361, 367, 374, 376, 389, 393, 401, 418, 444, 472, 483, 491-492
Ju290 Ger/B: 368-369, 373, 378, 381, 389, 419
Kate Jap/TB: 392
Kittyhawk US/FB: 404, 426, 450
Le R4 Fin/F: 233
Lancaster UK/B: 214, 427, 451, 467, 512
Liberator US/B: 228, 240, 247, 255, 262, 268, 281-282, 297-298, 301, 303, 305-306, 309, 311, 315, 317, 321, 325-333, 337, 344, 353-355, 357, 360, 362, 364, 368-369, 372, 377, 379, 387, 415, 419, 424, 436, 439, 442, 454, 457, 460, 464, 470, 487, 490, 493, 496, 498, 501, 504, 506, 515
Lightning US/F: 316, 364
London UK/B: 60, 62
MBR-2 USSR/R: 530
Me109 Ger/F: 4, 14, 102, 207, 218, 414, 445, 512
Me110 Ger/F: 97, 442
Manchester UK/B: 83
Marauder US/FB: 398, 418
Mariner US/B: 119, 219, 322, 330-331
Martlet US/F: 137, 168, 326, 338, 393, 401, 409, 445
Maryland US/B: 105, 149, 167
Mitchell US/B: 360
Mosquito UK/FB: 331, 369, 441, 500, 509, 515

Mustang US/F: 418
P38 US/F: 460
P40 US/F: 119, 162, 216, 236
P108 It/B: 258
Pe-2 USSR/F: 414
Pe-3 USSR/F: 484
Potez Fr/BR: 314
Re2001 It/FB: 242
S84 It/B: 242-243
SB-2 USSR/B: 111
S79 It/B: 43, 57, 74, 97, 228,
    242-243
Seafire UK/F: 410, 486, 523
Sea Hurricane UK/F: 256
Skua UK/F: 3, 24, 37, 65, 90
Spitfire UK/F: 201-202, 210, 215,
    218, 223, 225, 236-237, 242,
    247, 271, 306, 418, 534
Stuka Ger/DB: see Ju87
Sunderland UK/BR: 18, 29, 38,
    40, 57-58, 64, 122, 242, 281,
    298-299, 310, 322, 325,331-332,
    357, 360, 362, 369, 376-377,
    395, 415, 469, 506
Super Fortress US/B: see B29
Swordfish UK/TB: 39, 42, 44, 46,
    49-51, 57-58, 63, 87, 89, 101,
    122, 128, 144, 150, 155, 161,
    167, 189, 205, 237, 318, 324-326,
    354, 362, 394-395, 401, 409,
    412-413, 445, 452
Tarpon UK/F: 355
Torbeau UK/TB: 314 (see
    Beaufighter)
Typhoon UK/F: 306, 336, 515
Ventura US/B: 314, 330, 357, 417
Walrus UK/R: 30
Wellington UK/B: 2, 4, 7, 13-15,
    26, 75, 198, 228, 298, 329, 332,
    368, 371, 378, 383, 389, 395,
    415, 424, 443, 469, 490
Whirlwind UK/FB: 301
Whirlibomber: see Whirlwind
Whitley UK/B: 13, 21, 160, 298,
    331
Wildcat US/F: 375, 402, 410
Yak-1 USSR/F: 404
Yak-9 USSR/F: 437, 450, 530

CONVOYS
AB.15: 465
AB.55: 361
AFN.23: 90
AM.1: 442
AN.2: 45
AN.6: 62
AP.47: 349
AS.2: 45
AS.23: 90
Bansin-Geleite: 330
BC.2: 315
BD.5: 441
BK.3: 492
BM.7: 93
BM.9A: 172
BN.7: 61
BP.1: 93
Bromberg: 398
BT.6: 300
BT.14: 322
BT.18: 330
BTC.76: 490

BTC.78: 490
BTC.81: 490
BTC.111: 496
BX:218
CB.21: 315
CD.20: 315
CU.13: 389
CU.16: 395
CU.17: 395
CU.36: 448
CW: 394, 405, 413
CW.8: 45
CW.9: 47
CW.221: 366
CW.243: 388
DB.9: 465
DB.10: 465
Dervish: 127
DN.21: 299
DN.68: 417
EMC.17: 425
EN: 490
EON.18: 236
ET.16: 310
FN: 484
FN.366: 71
FN.889: 285
FN.1160: 362
FN.1170: 366
FP.1: 26
FP.1b: 26
FP.2: 27
FP.3: 28
FS.1: 27
FS.2: 27
FS.3: 28
FS.273: 53
FS.1074: 313
FS.1371: 394
FS.1734: 493
FS.1759: 500
FS.1784: 505
FSM.1: 348
FSM.1X: 348
FSS.1: 348
FSS.2: 348
FSS.2X: 348
FSS.2Y: 348
FSX.3: 348
G.1 to G.13: 420
GA.8: 84
GAT: 265
GAT.49: 301
Gibr.2: 295
GK: 301
GONS.33: 454
GUF.: 291
GUS.7a: 329
GUS.8: 329
GUS.8a: 329
GUS.9: 337
GUS.10: 337
GUS.18: 353, 357
GUS.23: 372
GUS.24: 375
GUS.38: 410
GUS.39: 415
GUS.63: 481
GUS 74: 490
H: 282
HA.11: 369
HA.43: 407
Hagen.1-91: 329

Hecht: 398
HG.1: 6
HG.3: 8
HG.47: 66
HG.53: 78-79
HG.64: 103
HG.66: 113
HG.67: 118
HG.68: 119, 122
HG.69: 117, 124
HG.70: 126
HG.71: 127-128
HG.73: 137
HG.74: 145
HG.75: 148
HG.76: 167
HG.78: 178
HG.84: 226
HN.14: 20
HN.24: 23
HX: 7, 11, 47, 64, 136, 210, 381,
    469
HX.1: 5
HX.2: 5
HX.5A: 9
HX.11: 13
HX.12: 13
HX.48: 35
HX.65: 48
HX.65A: 50
HX.66: 48
HX.72: 53
HX.75: 59
HX.79: 55, 59-60
HX.84: 64
HX.89: 64
HX.90: 66
HX.92: 69
HX.106: 79
HX.109: 82
HX.112: 85, 88
HX.114: 86
HX.115: 86, 88
HX.121: 91
HX.122: 96
HX.123: 96
HX.126: 99-100
HX.127: 100
HX.128: 100
HX.129: 104
HX.133: 108
HX.145: 123
HX.150: 136
HX.151: 136
HX.156: 147
HX.168: 178
HX.175: 184
HX.186: 210
HX.187: 211
HX.188: 211
HX.189: 211
HX.190: 211
HX.191: 211
HX.209: 260, 262
HX.212: 266, 272
HX.213: 267
HX.217: 281, 285
HX.218: 284-285
HX.219: 287
HX.222: 293
HX.223: 296
HX.224: 295-296
HX.225: 299

HX.226: 301, 304
HX.227: 304
HX.228: 307, 309-310
HX.229: 308-310
HX.230: 311, 315
HX.231: 315
HX.232: 316-317
HX.233: 318
HX.234: 317-318
HX.235: 320
HX.237: 322, 324-325
HX.238: 325-326
HX.239: 326
HX.240: 328
HX.258: 356
HX.259: 357
HX.262: 362
HX.263: 362
HX.264: 362, 368
HX.265: 368
HX.268: 373
HX.277: 389
HX.278: 389
HX.280: 395
HX.281: 395
HX.305: 448
HX.322: 481
HX.327: 469
HX.337: 490
HX.348: 506
HXF.1: 5
HXF.11: 13
IR.2F: 34
J.1 to J.13: 420
JC.36: 383
JS.1: 187
JT.39: 417
JW.51: 288
JW.51A: 286
JW.51B: 287
JW.52: 294
JW.53: 302-303
JW.54A: 366
JW.54B: 366
JW.55A: 374
JW.55B: 374-375
JW.56: 383
JW.56A: 383-384
JW.56B: 383-384
JW.57: 392-393
JW.58: 401-402
JW.59: 444-445
JW.60: 452
JW.61: 464-465
JW.61A: 464
JW.62: 471-472
JW.63: 475
JW.64: 491
JW.65: 498, 503
JW.66: 511, 514
JW.67: 519, 520, 521
KB.1: 484
KB.35: 472
KG.123: 301
KJ.3: 7
KJ.4: 8
KJF.1: 5
KJF.3: 7
Kleiner Bär 1-99: 304
KN: 218
KN.382: 506
KMF: 317
KMF.4: 281

KMF.11: 310
KMF.18: 333
KMF.19: 333
KMF.25A: 367
KMF.26: 372
KMS: 295
KMS.8: 299
KMS.10: 303
KMS.15: 330
KMS.18: 338
KMS.18A: 333
KMS.18B: 333, 340
KMS.19: 333
KMS.30: 371
KMS.31: 363, 367
KMS.34: 369, 371
KMS.36: 375, 377
KMS.37: 380
KMS.38: 381
KMS.39: 381
KMS.40: 381
KMS.41: 389
KMS.42: 389
KMS.44: 397
KMS.45: 397
KN.382: 506
KP.24: 475
KRS.2: 278
KS.27: 10
KS.357: 467
LMD.17: 315
M.41: 165
M.42: 165
M.43: 175
MA.3: 40
MB:50
MB.5:57
MB.6: 58
MB.8:63
MC.2: 70
MC.3: 70
MC.4: 73
MC.8: 81
MC.9: 87
ME.3: 63
ME.8: 171
ME.10: 189
MF.2: 176
MF.3: 180
MF.4: 183
MF.5: 189
MKF: 363
MKF.1: 277
MKF.18: 338
MKS: 310
MKS.21: 344
MKS.28: 363
MKS.29A: 363
MKS.30: 368
MKS.31: 371
MKS.33: 375
MKS.34: 377-378
MKS.35: 378
MKS.38: 389
MKS.41: 395
MS.5: 197
MW.3: 62-63
MW.5: 70
MW.5½: 74
MW.8A: 180
MW.8B: 180
MW.9: 189
MW.9A: 189

MW.9B: 189
MW.10: 201-202
MW.11: 227
MW.20: 294
MW.22: 306
MWF.36: 333, 338
MWF.37: 333
MWS.36: 333, 338, 340
MWS.36X: 333
MWS.37: 333
NA: 185
NCF.1: 333, 339
NCF.2: 333
NCS.1: 333
NCS.2: 333
NG: 314, 328
NG.376: 331
NK: 218
NP.1: 25
NSF.1: 348
NSF.1X: 348
O.1: 420
O2A: 420
O.2B: 420
O.3: 420
O.3C: 420
O.4A: 420
O.4B: 420
O.5: 420
O.A: 4
OA.80G: 18
OA.84: 18
OA.178: 42
OA.203: 49
OA.204: 48
OA.210: 53
OB: 4
OB.4: 5
OB.17: 7
OB.202: 48
OB.205: 48
OB.216: 53
OB.227: 59
OB.228: 59
OB.229: 59
OB.244: 64-65
OB.259: 69
OB.279: 77
OB.287: 81
OB.288: 81
OB.289: 82
OB.290: 82-83
OB.292: 83
OB.293: 84
OB.302: 88
OB.318: 96, 99
OB.323: 100
OB.324: 100
OB.325: 101
OB.326: 101
OB.336: 108
OG: 4, 75, 151
OG.7: 10
OG.16: 18
OG.18: 19
OG.47: 67
OG.56: 87
OG.63: 103
OG.66: 114
OG.68: 118
OG.69: 119
OG.71: 125
OG.72: 132

OG.74: 137
OG.75: 141
OG.77: 156
OG.82: 210
ON: 136, 144-145, 210-211, 239, 246, 260
ON.3: 11
ON.14: 135
ON.18: 136
ON.20: 136
ON.24: 142
ON.25: 23
ON.55: 178
ON.67: 193
ON.72: 198
ON.77: 203
ON.111: 234
ON.113: 234, 237
ON.115: 238-239
ON.127: 251
ON.129: 257
ON.131: 259
ON.135: 262
ON.137: 263, 265-267
ON.139: 266
ON.143: 272
ON.145: 261
ON.153: 285
ON.166: 301, 304
ON.168: 304
ON.170: 308-309
ON.176: 316
ON.178: 317
ON.184: 326
ON.202: 353-354
ON.203: 356
ON.204: 357
ON.206: 360
ON.207: 362
ON.208: 362
ON.214: 373
ON.217: 376
ON.220: 381
ON.221: 381
ON.223: 389
ON.224: 389
ON.227: 395
ON.277: 481
ONA.289: 496
ONF.252: 448
ONM.234: 403
ONS: 136, 210-211, 281
ONS.33: 148
ONS.61: 187
ONS.63: 184
ONS.67: 188
ONS.76: 201
ONS.92: 216
ONS.94: 217
ONS.96: 217
ONS.100: 217
ONS.102: 217
ONS.122: 246
ONS.136: 262
ONS.138: 266
ONS.144: 278, 280
ONS.146: 261
ONS.148: 281
ONS.150: 281
ONS.152: 285-286
ONS.154: 286
ONS.158: 289
ONS.159: 289

ONS.160: 289, 293
ONS.165: 299
ONS.167: 304
ONS.169: 308
ONS.251: 448
ONS.1 (Series 2): 311
ONS.2: 316
ONS.4: 317-318, 320
ONS.5: 318, 320, 324
ONS.7: 325
ONS.8: 328
ONS.18: 353-354
ONS.19: 356
ONS.20: 360
ONS.21: 362
ONS.24: 371, 373
ONS.29: 389
ONS.33: 454
OS: 266, 281, 295
OS.1: 119
OS.4: 128
OS.10: 147
OS.11: 148, 151
OS.18: 186
OS.28: 219
OS.33: 234, 236
OS.34: 236
OS.44: 303
OS.45: 314
OS.51: 329
OS.59: 371
OS.60: 371
OS.62: 375, 377
OS.64: 381
OS.65: 381
OS.66: 381
OS.67: 389
OS.68: 389
OW.1: 280
PA.44: 316
Pamphlet: 298
PG.6: 243, 247
PK.9: 511
PK.20: 472
PQ.1: 140
PQ.2: 145
PQ.3: 150
PQ.4: 150
PQ.5: 156
PQ.6: 164, 169
PQ.7A: 173, 175
PQ.7B: 175
PQ.8: 173, 180
PQ.9: 185
PQ.10: 185
PQ.11: 186
PQ.12: 198
PQ.13: 203, 207
PQ.14: 208
PQ.15: 212-213
PQ.16: 219-220
PQ.17: 229-230, 232, 237
PQ.18: 256-257, 265
PW.323: 318
QP.1: 140
QP.2: 149
QP.3: 156
QP.4: 171
QP.5: 179
QP.6: 183
QP.7: 190
QP.8: 198
QP.9: 203

QP.10: 208
QP.11: 212-213
QP.12: 219
QP.13: 229-231
QP.14: 237, 257
QP.15: 279
QS: 233
QS.15: 233
QS.32: 248
QS.33: 248
RA.51: 288
RA.52: 294
RA.53: 302
RA.54A: 366
RA.54B: 366
RA.55A: 374-375
RA.55B: 375
RA.56: 383-384, 389
RA.57: 392-393
RA.58: 401-402
RA.59: 408-409
RA.59A: 444-445
RA.60: 452
RA.61: 464-465
RA.62: 471-473
RA.63: 475
RA.64: 492
RA.65: 503
RA.66: 514
RA.67: 520-521
RB.1: 253, 258-259
RS.3: 312
RU: 320
RU.156: 496
S.1 to S.8: 420
SBF.1: 333, 338
SBF.2: 333
SBF.3: 333
SBM.1: 333, 338
SBS.1: 333, 338
SC: 136, 210, 381
SC.1: 48
SC.2: 49, 51, 53
SC.3: 53
SC.7: 55, 59-60
SC.11: 65
SC.13: 66
SC.19: 75
SC.26: 88
SC.29: 96
SC.30: 99
SC.31: 100
SC.42: 131-132
SC.44: 135
SC.48: 142, 144-145
SC.52: 144, 146, 148
SC.53: 152
SC.67: 184
SC.81: 211
SC.82: 211
SC.83: 211
SC.84: 211
SC.85: 211
SC.94: 240, 246
SC.95: 246
SC.97: 251
SC.99: 257
SC.100: 253-254, 257-259
SC.101: 260
SC.104: 262, 266
SC.107: 267
SC.109: 261
SC.116: 293

SC.117: 293
SC.118: 296
SC.119: 299
SC.121: 305, 307, 308-310
SC.122: 308-310
SC.123: 311
SC.125: 316
SC.126: 317
SC.127: 319-320
SC.128: 320
SC.129: 324-325
SC.130: 325-326
SC.143: 357
SC.145: 362
SC.146: 368
SC.153: 394
SC.154: 395
SC.156: 400
SC.157: 403
SC.167: 490
SF.1: 443
SF.2: 443
SG.6F: 248
SG.6S: 248
SG.19: 296
SJ.1: 187
SL: 5, 71, 132
SL.67: 82, 85, 95
SL.68: 82, 86, 95
SL.73: 99
SL.74: 101
SL.75: 101, 104
SL.76: 95, 114, 117
SL.80: 119
SL.81: 122, 125
SL.87: 138
SL.89: 146
SL.91: 148
SL.93: 185
SL.109: 216, 219
SL.118: 247
SL.119: 250-251
SL.125: 270
SL.126: 312
SL.128: 322
SL.138: 363
SL.139: 368
SL.140: 371
SL.142: 375
SL.143: 377-378
SL.144: 378
SL.147: 389
SL.150: 395
SLS.64: 79
SM.1: 443
SM.2: 443
SNF.17: 397
SQ.36: 248
SS.1: 442
SU.1: 197
SY.1: 442
T.18: 183
TAG.5: 257
TAG.18: 265
TAG.19: 265
TAG.20: 265
TAM.142: 505
TAW.12: 243, 246
TAW.13: 243, 247
TAW.15: 250
TAW(S): 244, 247
TB.1: 285, 290
TBC.1: 469

TBC.60: 490
TBC.103: 496
TC.1: 14
TF.1: 442
TF.2: 331
TJ.1: 331
TJF.1: 333, 339
TJM.1: 333, 339
TJS.1: 333, 339
TM.1: 291, 442
TS.37: 314
TSF.1: 348
TSF.1X: 348
TSM.1: 348
TSS.1: 348
TSS.2: 348
TSS.3: 348
TU.5: 376
TX.1: 294
U.1: 420
U2A: 420
U.2B: 420
U.3: 420
U.3C: 420
U.4: 420
U.5A: 420
U.5B: 420
UC.1: 303
UC.12: 389
UGF.1: 277
UGF.10A: 333
UGF.10B: 333
UGS.4: 295
UGS.6: 308
UGS.7: 317
UGS.8A: 330
UGS.9: 329
UGS.10: 329
UGS.11:337
UGS.12: 337
UGS.13: 337, 344
UGS.14: 338
UGS.15: 338
UGS.17: 353
UGS.19: 357
UGS.20: 357
UGS.24: 371
UGS.30: 387
UGS.36: 402
UGS.37: 404
UGS.38: 408
UGS.40: 413
UGS.42: 418
UR: 237
UR.59: 296
UR.155: 490
US.1: 17
US.2: 25
US.3: 28, 32
US.9: 80
VA.18: 343
VD.1: 442
VWP.16: 496
WAT.13: 243, 245
WAT.15: 250
WN.74: 490
WP: 405
WP.457: 380
WP.492: 398
WP.526: 413
WS: 151
WS.5A: 71
WS.5B: 75, 80

WS.8B: 100, 101
WS.12: 150
WS.17: 206
XK.1: 307
XT.2: 294
XT.3: 294
XT.4: 306
Y: 212
Z: 212
ZK.1: 86
ZK.5: 169, 173
ZK.7: 199
10.RS: 19
20.K: 9
65.KS: 19
8: 304
41: 304
88: 304
89: 304
92: 304
99: 304

MINE BARRAGES

Finnish

F 3-6, 15-22: 110, 114, 117, 120, 123-124
Kipinola: 112
Kulemajärvi: 113
Rukajärvi A to C, R, S, U: 229, 312, 342
Valkjärvi: 114, 120, 131

German

D 1-2, D 10-30: 112, 124
MT 1-9, MT 13-27: 169, 179, 201, 210, 215, 272
N 24: 398
NW 1-2: 44-45
SW 1-3, SW 12: 47-48, 51, 327
Allirahu: 125
Apolda: 109-110, 115
Blitz 25, 38-39: 406, 422
Brücke: 399
Brutmaschine: 312
Bube: 397
Coburg: 109
Corbetha: 109, 115, 148, 151, 157
Eisenach: 109
Erfurt: 109
Gotha: 109
Herz Dame: 397
Hütte: 397
Juminda (also Finnish): 117, 124, 126-127, 129-132, 136, 149, 151
König: 397
Masuren: 239
Mona I: 125
Nashorn 1-10: 216, 233, 312, 397
Notung: 369
Pinnass 1-6: 125
Paul: 265
Rusto: 129
Seeigel I-VIII: 219, 222, 228, 232, 233, 238, 241, 243, 312, 324, 342, 397, 431
Stein: 414
Walross (Submarine net): 312, 397
Wartburg I-III: 108
Weimar: 109
Westwall: 2, 5

Italian
AN.4-7: 47, 58
LK: 35
M.1-4, M.6, M.7: 52, 58, 104, 139, 210
S.2, S.8, S.11-13, S.31-32, S.41-44, S.51-52, S.61, S.71-73, S.91-93, S.96-97: 94, 114, 116, 126, 209, 261, 265, 273, 282
St.1: 245
St.2: 273
T: 96, 166
X2, X3: 74

OPERATIONS
Achse: 348
Aerial: 39
A-GO: 414, 418, **429**
Agreement: 257
Alacrity: 358
Alfred: 62
Angel: 414
Anklet: 171
Anvil: 340, 442
Aphrodite: 397
Appearance: 86
Archery: 171
Attacke: 376
Augsberg: 84
Augsberg A: 83
Auster: 397
Avalanche: 348, 350
B: 143
Balsam: 524
Banquet: 442
Barbarossa: 77
Baritone: 247
Bayleaf: 393
Baytown: 347
Berlin: 76, 87
Bernau: 376-377
Bernhard: 54
Bishop: 514
Blacklist: 536
Blücher: 252
Bowery: 215
Breach: 78
Boomerang: 442
Brosche: 414
Brunhild: 352
Bumerang: 397
Calendar: 210
Cartwheel: 334
Catapult: 41
Catchpole: 391
Cerberus: 188
Chronometer: 107
Claymore: 84
Cleanslate: 304
Coat: 63
Cockpit: 407
Collar: 66
Collie: 526
Composition: 80
Corkscrew: 328
Countenance: 129
Cottage: 337
Crimson: 438
Crocodile: 486
Crusader: 152
Cycle: 39
Deadlight: 520-**521**, **525**
Delphin: 390

Demon: 94
Derange: 299, 346
Dervish: 127
Desecrate: 400
Detachment: 493
Dexterity: 376
Diplomat: 399
Director: 375
Dracula: 513
Dragoon: 442-443
Dredger: 433
Dunlop: 94
Dynamo: 31-33, 39
Eisbär: 356
Eistoss: 207
Enclose I: 298
Enclose II: 298
Excess: 71, 73-74
Felix: 49, 69, 75
Flintlock: 387-388
Forager: 425-427, 430
Galvanic: 367, 369
Gatter: 397
Gemse: 414
Gesellenprüfung: 359
Globe Trotter: 439
Gondola: 298
Gotz von Berlichingen: 207
Hailstone: 392
Haken: 414
Halberd: 139
Hannelore: 53
Harpoon: 227
Hats: 50
Herkules: 215
Hermelin: 408
Hurry: 46
Husky: 333, 338
I: 316
Iceberg: 504
Infatuate: 467
Inmate: 523
Insect: 237
Ironclad: 202-203, 212
Jane: 255
Jaywick: 348
Jubilee: 247
Judgement: 63
Judgement: 517
Juno: 33
Jupiter: 514
K.7: 193
KA: 248
Karo Ass: 397
K.E.: 291
Kikusui
  1: 507
  2: 509
  3: 510
  4: 513
  5: 517
  6: 517
  7: 517
  8: 517
  9: 523
  10: 523
Kobra: 390
Kon: 415, 418
Kongo: 483
Landcrab: 323
Languste: 414
Läufer: 399
Leader: 359

Lehrgang: 345
Lentil: 479
Leopard: 367
Light: 453
Lightning: 479
Lila: 280
Lupo: 206
Lustre: 84
Magic Carpet: 537
Matador: 485
Marianne: 68
Maulwurf: 390
Maurice: 25
Menace: 49, 51, 54-55, 57
Meridian: 486
Merkur: 102
Messer: 430
Mike
  I: 482
  VI: 487
  VII: 487
Millet: 460
Mincemeat: 128
Musketry: 332
Nadel: 414
Neptun: 319
Neptune: 408, 419, **425**
Neuland: 192
Nordmark: 19
Nordwind: 134
Nussknacker: 390
Oboe
  I: 513
  II: 524
  VI: 523
Odysseus: 451
Ose: 397
Oskar: 68
Ostpreussen: 143
Outflank: 469
Overlord: 340, 345, **419**
Paukenschlag: 178
Paul: 245
Pedal: 425
Pedestal: 242
Percussion: 346
Perpetual: 150
Persecution: 409
Peter: 245
Pinpoint: 235
Pommern: 77
Probestück: 355
Quadrant: 344
R.4: 21
Railway: 113
Rappen: 397
Rebhuhn: 348
Reckless: 409
Regenbogen: 287, 518
Renate: 74
Rhein: 236
Rheinübung: 95, 99, **105**
RO: 361
Robson: 473
Rocket: 106
Rösselsprung: 230
Rügen: 78
RV-1: 385
  2: 393
  3: 404
  4: 414
  5: 425
  6: 436

Salpa: 312
Sankey: 485
Schimmel: 397
Schlange: 390
Seaslug: 332
Seelöwe: 44, 48, 50-52, 54-55
Sextant: 368
Shingle: 385
Sho: 460
Sho-1: 461
Sickle: 26
Sirio: 200
Sizilien: 348
Slapstick: 350
Sleuth: 382
Source: 355
Splice: 101
Stab: 239
Stacey: 494
Stachelschwein: 397
Stalemate II: 452
Status: 133
Stein: 236
Steinhäger: 431
Stemmbogen: 327
Stich: 397
Stone Age: 279
Stream: 255

Style: 122, 223
Stonewall: 374, 377
Substance: 120, 122
Sudwind: 134
Sunfish: 510
SW.A: 70
SW.O: 52
TA: 399
Take-Ichi: 407
Talsohle: 358
Tanne Ost: 451
Taube: 348
Teardrop: 506
Tengo: 503
Tiger: 97-98
Tiger: 312
Tor: 414
Torch: 270, 272-273, 278, 283
Tracer: 107
Transom: 411
Trave: 377
Tungsten: 401
Ulan: 373
V.5: 199
Vénérable: 510
Victor
  I: 500
  II: 503

III: 495
IV: 498
V: 512
Vigorous: 227
Walpurgisnacht: 497
Walter: 52
Watchtower: 233, 238-239, 241
Weber: 77
Weide: 414
Werner: 57
Weserubung: 21-22, 35
Westfalen: 143
Westwind: 134
White: 65
Widerhaken: 414
Wiking: 359
Wikinger: 19
Wilfred: 21, 23
Winch: 90
Wunderland: 244
Wunderland II: 343
Zar: 245
Zarin: 258
Zauberflöte: 218
Zipper: 527, 534
Zitronella: 348